A TYPOGRAPHIC JOURNEY
THROUGH THE INLAND PRINTER

1883-1900

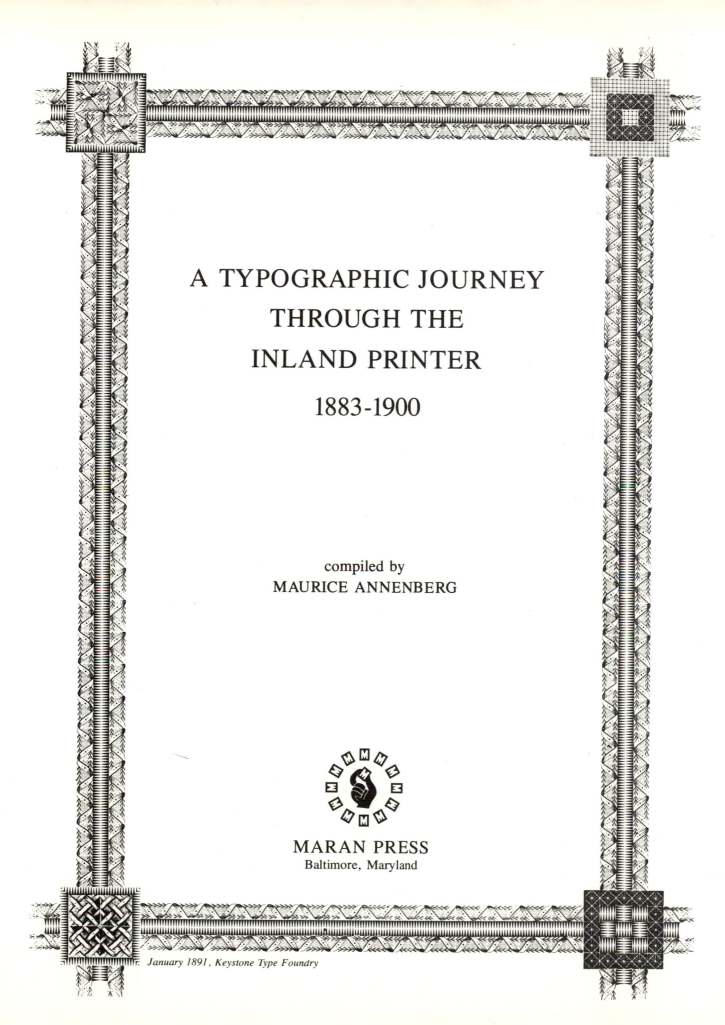

A TYPOGRAPHIC JOURNEY
THROUGH THE
INLAND PRINTER

1883-1900

compiled by
MAURICE ANNENBERG

MARAN PRESS
Baltimore, Maryland

January 1891, Keystone Type Foundry

Library of Congress Catalog Card Number 77-89269
ISBN 0-916526-04-6
COPYRIGHT 1977

A TYPOGRAPHICAL JOURNEY THROUGH THE INLAND PRINTER 1883-1900

MARAN PRESS, BALTIMORE, MARYLAND
Printed in the United States of America

DEDICATED
TO THE MEMORIES OF

GEORGE LABAN HARDING
1893-1976
Master Collector, Printing Historian of Berkeley, California

AND

C. WILLIAM SCHNEIDEREITH
1886-1976
Master Printer of Baltimore, Maryland

I N ITS FIRST FOUR HUNDRED YEARS, PRINTING as other technical trades, was barely able to record its many improvements and inventions except by "word of mouth." Typesetting and paper were important ingredients that limited the volume of printed products, especially in the magazine and periodical field, although a few books existed on most trade subjects.

The eighteenth century American magazine, starting with Andrew Bradford's *American Magazine* and Benjamin Franklin's *General Magazine*, both in 1741, were limited as to content and scope, appearing to be merely an extension of their newspapers. What is a magazine and what is a newspaper? The newspaper should carry news, although advertising appears to take prominence, whereas the majority of items in a magazine should be articles, stories, poems, and probably reviews.

In England, Daniel Defore is credited with starting the first magazine, *The Review*, while in prison in 1704. It was followed by the *Tatler*, the *Spectator*, and a dozen others. In the United States there were the *Pennsylvania Magazine* and the *Columbian Magazine*. But none of these could be considered *trade* magazines. The *Penny Magazine* of 1833, London, New York, and Boston, printed four supplements that described the manufacture of a publication, including typefounding and presswork.

The start of newer methods of manufacturing printing material in the nineteenth century spawned an entirely new field of writers and publishers. Printing methods had not really changed since the invention of John Gutenberg, they were practically dormant. Type was still being made by the hand mold process, paper by single sheets, and the first cylinder press was not manufactured by Frederich Koenig until 1812-1813. Hundreds of printing improvements had never been recorded.

In the United States, the *Genesee Farmer*, an agricultural magazine, was started by Luther Tucker in 1826 and considered the first *trade* magazine. From that beginning it was only a short time period for other trades and magazines to start their individual publications. Entrepreneurs crisscrossed the country, suggesting new trade magazines with beautiful formats, but the printing industry was leading the field in the realm of quality, and because it was written, printed, and circulated within its own trade circles were excellent examples of graphic arts craftsmanship.

Science has awakened America to study and appreciate the nineteenth century industry expansion, and printing has unlocked the doors of ages of untold data. Students of all arts are finding in those years the principal ingredients of modern techniques and a century that was full of inventions.

There are hundreds of printing periodicals on record, and many others unrecorded, that were short-lived and quickly defunct. The owner of a printing plant with some idle time, a flair for writing, and an urge to publish his own work, or merely to produce a notable sample of his plant's quality, would take the short step forward to print his *own* work. The closest and easiest subject was the one with which he was the most familiar and had daily contact—printing. Some of the specimens produced have been unequalled in quality of production.

No other trades or industry had as many representatives. It was in this climate that the INLAND PRINTER was conceived.

The first number of volume one was dated October 1883 and contained twenty-four pages, thirteen of copy and eleven of advertisements. No one has recorded the hours of advance planning or preparation prior to the publication date but it must have been enormous. To arrange the physical requirements for a monthly magazine which expanded to two hundred pages in about seven years must certainly have stretched the mechanical capabilities of any printing plant in the Chicago, Illinois area.

One should attempt to visualize the operations of the hand compositors of the period. It took a battery of typesetters to prepare just one single issue. Although the Linotype had been field-tested and used in the New York *Tribune* in 1886, it was not for several years that it was to be used in the INLAND PRINTER.

The printing industry was commencing to reap the results of the Industrial Revolution. Articles in the INLAND PRINTER claimed the superiority of electricity versus steam to run machinery. It was the era of the invention of typesetting machinery and the magazine dutifully reported and depicted in woodcut engravings all new advances, whether from American or foreign sources. Half-a-dozen machines for mechanical typesetting were on the market or being field-tested but the magazine remained impartial. It was still being composed by a long list of hand compositors.

Nearly every month a new size or new model press was introduced to the public, or shown via the drafting table. The names and advertising or "puff" articles of Scott, Hoe, Prouty, Whitlock, Galley, Babcock, Kidder, Huber, Campbell, Cottrell, and others, started a gold mine of creativity in printing machinery improvements.

The early volumes were saturated with articles about type and printing but the scope quickly changed and expanded to cover a wider range. The style of writing became self-respecting, moralizing, instructive—and extremely controversial. Woe to the compositor who smoked while he worked! All of the early articles were presented to describe conditions as they existed, dirt, fire hazards, and spittoon included, with the hope that the reader or shop owner would be provoked to answer. The articles of several years covered apprentice training, how a type case should be designed, how many letters should be in a new font, and most interesting, a long debate on women's suffrage. Contrary correspondence from around the world was welcomed and exploited, resulting in myriad viewpoints. Each locality gave its individual solution to the question, or offered suggestions for trade improvement.

The small country printer was definitely not a ''research specialist.'' Gossip was paramount, and many of the half-truths eventually appeared as biographical certainties. Hundreds of embryonic authors would be constantly utilizing their evening hours by mailing in articles about work habits and advice to compositors and apprentices, mostly written under aliases or with initials. Probably the most difficult task for the editor was the selection of the article, as there would be a dozen solutions to the question, with an over-emphasis of details and mixtures of prejudices and unproved statements. Why should a woman take a job away from a man? Who was ''Pica Antique,'' ''Agate,'' ''Slug-O,'' or the ''Senator?''

Self-education was still the primary method of education for many of these small-town writers, and despite long hours of labor there were not the diversions of radio, television, travel, and entertainment. He could read and *write*. A good journeyman, depending on location, could earn the princely wage of $15.00 to $25.00 weekly, but he took pride in his trade. He devoured news items and magazines about printing. He admired, but still ridiculed, the ''tramp printer.''

◆ ◆ ◆ ◆

The concept of journalism and publishing has changed with the times—whether for the better is debatable. The printing magazine of the past century was more personal and much more interesting than those of the present era. Each name was *news* and treated accordingly and with reverence. Pages would be allotted for CORRESPONDENCE, NEWS OF THE TRADE, and LOCAL ITEMS. Printers have always loved to see their names in print.

A Trip to the Rockies could spread over pages, and thirteen pages of six point type was used to cover a Typothetae meeting. The problems of the 1880 period parallels the 1980 period: price-cutting, strikes, salaries, labor unions, and jobs. Many of the articles were written by the leading printers and technicians, such as Charles Francis, Gustav Boehm, Thomas MacKellar, William E. Loy, and Henry L. Bullen.

The majority of articles were primarily written for educational purposes, pointed towards both the technical and financial eye. Sometimes a self-glorifying article could be written about an early machine or invention, released by its advertising manager. The point system was explained and expanded; pricing and the methods of installing a cost system was stressed and a continuing feature in the magazine for many years; each of the newer presses and typesetting methods were introduced as they were invented.

But it was the reports of meetings, such as the Typothetae, that would be reported in its deepest detail, even to the last moment that a meeting was adjourned. Every participant's name was put into type, and each word landed up as an historical record, recorded in six and eight point type. Dialogue was important and respectfully reported. When photography and illustrations became the vogue group pictures with each and every name was stressed.

An obituary was not a six-line blurb, but a full history. Complete pages were used to record the life stories of the pioneer printers or affiliates to printing. Present day historians are constantly using the INLAND PRINTER as the ''bible'' of printing history and more footnotes and references cite this magazine than any other source of printing information.

Throughout the pages of the INLAND PRINTER, in both prose and rhyme, are compositions and renderings of hundreds of authors and poets. Some of these have been selected for inclusion in privately printed books, and many others have been reprinted many times. This type of journalism is missed in contemporary printing magazines.

◆ ◆ ◆

The examples of type faces displayed in the INLAND PRINTER is a study by itself of marketing methods and probably should be prepared as a separate volume. The designs would challenge the ingenuity of any of the modern school of type compositors and it is doubtful if anyone alive can match some of the full page advertising, especially those which called for rule bending in all directions and curves. They were released during a period when the type founding industry was in complete disarray and running in circles. No one knew which way the industry was headed. Bankruptcy followed bankruptcy, and those who had run a profitable industry fought among themselves for survival.

At the end of the Civil War there were over two dozen plants making type in the United States and Canada, with about fifty distributors. They sold all kinds of printing machinery as well as type, offering discounts that guaranteed a loss in manufacturing cost.

Although our present legal procedures would protest the action, the type founders attempted to organize an association to establish and stabilize selling prices and discounts. After many organizational meetings, and tumultuous accusations it was proven ineffective and the battle continued at a more vicious pace. It was only through the mediation and efforts of John Marder of the Chicago Type Foundry and Arthur Brower of the Union Type Foundry, also of Chicago, that a "combined" company of twenty-three scattered plants was organized in 1892 to form the American Type Founders Company.

The consolidation of 1892 was not the final answer. The individual plants of the combine continued to compete with each other until convinced by Robert W. Nelson, new general manager of the combined plants, that selling under their individual names, issuing their own catalogs, and releasing their own type designs was contrary to the basic organizational plan. After 1894 they eliminated the plant name in their magazine releases, and in 1895 issued the first type catalogue using the American Type Founders Company name.

During this time period the type founding battle was continuing at a demoralizing rate for the industry. Each foundry believed that the key to success was more and more type designs, one creation worse than the other. Foundries hopefully pirated type faces they believed would be successful, sometimes fed with false information, by purchasing a font of type as soon as released, making a new set of electrotype matrices, changing one or two letters and then releasing the type as their own creation and under a new name. Actually, for a short time they ran out of names, and the same name would be used to describe an entirely different series of type.

A few type foundry plants had refused to join the combine, and other new foundries started operating. For a period it was believed that the type design contest would be abated, but instead it continued at a more rapid rate, with the incentive to reach the market before their competitors. This was exemplified by more and more magazine page presentations, some only showing parts of a series. However, by 1919 all these small foundries realized they were fighting a lost cause against "the type trust" and closed their operations, selling out to the American Type Founders Company. This company dominates the type founding scene in the United States until the present day.

Around the corner, waiting to deliver the death blow to the type foundries were the Linotype, the Monotype, and the Ludlow. These great machines, and a few others that could perform the same operations, made printers independent of type foundries by reducing the market for single body and display type. As early as 1900 the INLAND PRINTER was conducting classes and giving instructions on Machine Composition, had changed from hand to machine type setting, and was actually a laboratory for modern printing methods. In that year practically every newspaper of size had converted to mechanical typesetting machinery and was being printed on either flat-bed or the newer rotary printing presses.

◆ ◆ ◆ ◆

The type faces shown throughout this book could be termed ''The Great American Type Catalogue.'' It is a complete showing of all faces from all foundries, in sequence as they were released, but in several cases the larger and more complete family is shown. Some faces have been eliminated, as the same types were sold under different names by competing foundries who exchanged matrices. Most border showings have also been eliminated.

Some of these type faces never again appeared in any publication or type catalogue. To make a complete series of type is and was an expensive procedure, and the original purpose of some of these showings was a marketing solution of ''testing''—to let the printing public recognize what was available.

The sample pages of type faces were composed at the different foundries, or at a printing plant, and furnished to the magazine in electrotype form. The compositors who worked on these showings were a breed apart from the average compositor, usually the best in the trade, and the examples have not been surpassed. These early compositors were also loaded with humor. They probably created their own copy to make lines fit, and it gave them the opportunity to blast at the local politicians, the butcher, the baker, the candlestick maker, but mostly against the medical fakes and get-rich schemes then flooding the country. They were able to record for posterity against the loan sharks who grabbed interest on loans to printers and printing plants as high as 20%, ''five for four.''

Perhaps it is an error to again breathe life to some of these designs, or as they should be called, monstrosities. A number of these can not be read, and if it can not be read it should not be used. Unfortunately, some of our ''modern'' type designers will change a few letters, and film lettering artists and producers will issue another *new* design, under another name.

◆ ◆ ◆ ◆

The circulation and distribution of the INLAND PRINTER is a success story of the printing magazine field. When the magazine released its first issue in October 1883 there were 200 subscribers on the list, all from the rapidly closing *Chicago Printer*. In three months the subscription list had expanded to 4,500, some from the former magazine, and the balance from printers around the world.

The magazine stressed the point that it would not be possible to publish only for the subscription price of $1.00 a year (although the price quickly rose to $1.50 before the second year) but must have additional income from advertising sources. However, they explained that all advertising would be ''clean and select'' and every item would be heartily recommended. They also provided the reader a list of services and firms ''that can be relied on.''

◆ ◆ ◆ ◆

The INLAND PRINTER has given to American printing historians a gold mine of such wealth and depth that it will never be thoroughly explored, with new veins of discovery constantly being uncovered. It would take ten lifetimes to completely research just *one* volume. In the section of articles for this first compilation of typographical topics the compiler can offer no apologies or reasons.

Choice of articles ran the gamut of the rainbow: *Establishing a Newspaper, Wood Engraving, The Machinist and the Printer, A Study of Proofreading, Cutting of Shapes,* and myriad others. Many of these ran in serial form for many years. We have selected only a sampling of stories and articles that ran as special features, mostly in the typographic field.

It was regretful that it was necessary to eliminate certain stories as they were composed using the ''run-around'' theory. Halftones were in their growing pains era and used profusely throughout a story, most times without any connection with the article. This practice of setting the type a different measure around illustrations, plus starting an article on any section of a page, made selection a difficult project.

There were so many articles that one could practically use every page, and we made hundreds of negatives that were never used. It resulted in a book that could never be issued because of size, and a decision was made to eliminate many duplicate articles, continuations of a theme, controversial subjects, and most of the advertising. The advertisements in the INLAND PRINTER were mostly classical in design and presented with few discordant type faces. It will never be surpassed on the legibility scale and should be a model for generations.

It was during these *Years of Transition* that typesetting started to change from a craft to a technology. In former years style was not stressed, but after 1895 the type of article changed and techniques were discussed. Words such as readability, width of lines, white space, emphasis, and margins started to creep into the columns, mostly in the articles criticizing printer's specimens and advertising.

A volume of twice this size could be prepared of the items that were *not* selected, with still enough fresh and untouched material for a shelf of books. Other compilers could select an entirely different set of articles. The choice is unlimited.

◆ ◆ ◆ ◆

There has been no attempt to record the volume number with the dates on each page as they have been varied in different bound collections. Many collections have two volumes in one book. The earlier volumes were advertised and sold by the magazine for only a few dollars, at one time as low as $1.25 a volume. In later years, and after the INLAND PRINTER stopped issuing bound volumes, a collection was bound to the whim of the owner, and it is extremely difficult to find a collection with only one style of binding.

The magazine continued to advertise the advantages of keeping bound volumes as a source for a complete history of printing. As late as 1892 they were even offering a bound volume as a premium to anyone that would send in the names of eight subscribers at $2.00 each. In one time period they were offering a bound volume with each subscription.

While full collections are still being maintained in large libraries or printing schools, the individual collector could be termed fortunate if he could compile a complete series to the first year's issues, especially in an unmutilated condition. Many volumes that have been examined have been incised or bowdlerized to appropriate a beautiful picture, a drawing, or a type specimen. They will never be replaced.

◆ ◆ ◆ ◆

To answer the physical questions of manufacture: this book has been reproduced by using the photographic and lithographic processes. Many articles were used as they were written, but in a few cases it was necessary to edit or extract redundant sentences or words. Pagination is in sequence to the articles as they appeared, but some pages are combinations of various articles from the same issue.

The manufacture of negatives was extremely difficult due to the curvature of the spine of the book, many of which were over three inches thick. Different shades are due to the letterpress original, from light ink to dark ink, and even on special stock. We have attempted to "touch up" many characters which were broken in early printing, but others have been reproduced exactly as they appeared.

MAURICE ANNENBERG

The Years of Transition

HENRY O. SHEPARD,

Head of the firm of Henry O. Shepard & Co., and president of THE INLAND PRINTER COMPANY, whose portrait is herewith presented, one of Chicago's representative business men, was born in the town of Eaton, Madison County, New York, May 23, 1848. In 1852 his family removed to Norwich, Chenango County, where he resided until he was nineteen years of age. Being of an ambitious turn of mind, and having a natural desire to become a printer, by permission of Mr. James H. Sinclair, of the Chenango *Union*, he was granted the privilege of setting type before and after school hours, with the result that when he went to learn his trade in the office of the Chenango *Telegraph*, he was the equal of any compositor on the paper. Leaving Norwich, he went to the village of Oneida, where he worked a year as a journeyman printer. In September, 1866, he moved to the city of Appleton, Wisconsin. Not being satisfied with the location, however, he shortly after gravitated still farther west, to Des Moines, Iowa, where he engaged in the milling business. Tiring of this, he came to Aurora, Illinois, and there worked for a year in the *Herald* and *Beacon* offices. Returning to Des Moines, he secured employment on the *Register*. While there he engaged in a typesetting contest to settle a controversy as to who was the swiftest compositor, in which he came out victor, beating his competitor by eight hundred ems.

In 1871 he came to Chicago, entering the establishment of Church, Goodman & Donnelley, where he

their endeavors, and business accumulated to such an extent that, in a short time thereafter, they were compelled to seek more commodious quarters, which they secured at 140 and 146 Monroe street, occupying 90 by 90 feet. Here they remained for five years, securing, during that time, a reputation second to that of no printing firm in the United States. Again, however, business demanded increased space and facilities, which, after a prolonged search, were obtained in the premises located at 181 to 187 Monroe street, to which they removed in March, 1887. In September, of the same year, Mr. Shepard purchased the interest of his partner, Mr. William Johnston, since which time the business has been conducted with phenomenal success under the firm name of Henry O. Shepard & Co. This establishment has not only secured a local, but a national reputation, and is at present recognized as one of the most prosperous and best conducted of its kind in the United States. Each department is under the immediate supervision of tried and experienced workmen, and a casual inspection of its various workrooms impresses the visitor with the fact that order is there recognized as nature's first law. There is a place for everything, and everything is kept in its place. It has been the boast of the house that its imprint is a guarantee of good work, no matter what its character; and in corroboration of this statement, we may mention the fact that no solicitors are, or have been, employed in any capacity. The composing room is 60 by 120 feet, and the pressrooms 59 by 60 and 20 by 160 feet, respectively. The force employed varies from eighty to one hundred and twenty-five.

remained between four and five years. It had been the custom of this firm, who were the printers of the Directory of the City of Chicago, to award, for the purpose of expediting its publication, a weekly bonus of $20, $15, $10 and $5, respectively, to the four compositors getting up the longest string, and Mr. Shepard captured the highest premium for three consecutive weeks over eighty competitors. In 1876 he assumed the foremanship of Knight & Leonard's, one of the best known printing houses in Chicago, 105 and 107 Madison street, which position he retained until August, 1880, when he formed a copartnership with Mr. William Johnston, under the firm name of Shepard & Johnston, at 146 South Clark street. Fortune smiled on

Mr. Shepard is in the prime of life; is an active, wide-awake, agreeable man of business; devoting his undivided time and energy to the interests of his large and growing establishment. As a man, he is courteous and affable; as an employer just and considerate, and ready and willing at all times to listen to and remove any grievance; as a friend, genial and whole-souled; as a printer, an honor to his profession; and if present indications may be accepted as a criterion by which the future may be judged, has a bright and prosperous career before him. He is also prominently identified with Masonic interests, is a member of the Illinois and La Salle clubs, and a life member of the Press Club of Chicago.

THE INLAND PRINTER

Registered at the Chicago Postoffice for transmission through the mails as second-class mail matter.

VOL. I.—No. 1.   CHICAGO, OCTOBER, 1883.   TERMS: { $1.00 per year in advance. / Single copies, 10 cents.

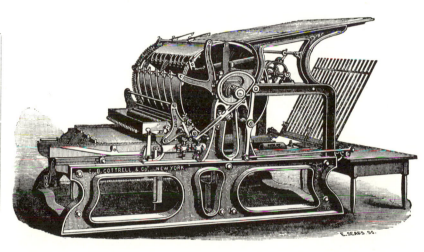

THE INLAND PRINTER,

AN OPERATIVE JOURNAL, CONDUCTED BY WORKMEN.

Published Monthly by

THE INLAND PRINTER COMPANY,

2 TAYLOR BUILDING, MONROE ST., CHICAGO.

J. W. LANGSTON, President.   JOS. PEAKE, Sec'y-Treas.
S. H. TRELOAR, Vice-President.   H. H. HILL, Editor.

PRICE $1.00 PER YEAR.

CHICAGO, OCTOBER, 1883.

THE first number of THE INLAND PRINTER is now before you. We do not deem any excuse necessary. That a medium through which printers and kindred workers may be able to express their ideas and receive encouragement from their brethren engaged in the same calling is necessary there is no doubt. We have often wondered why the business of printing, to which all other lines of industry necessarily resort for the purpose of interchange of sympathy and experience, was not better known through our own art. There is scarcely a line of business so scantily represented as the one that thus represents all others. Is it on the same enterprising principle that the farmer sells all his freshest eggs, yellowest butter and finest apples, and keeps the poorer articles for his own use? Or is it the careless method that some shoemakers have of allowing their own children to go barefoot, and that of some ministers permitting their boys to learn theology on the streets after nightfall? Whatever may be the cause, whether negligence or lack of confidence or enthusiasm for the work, it should not exist.

We know you will be pleased with our project. We hope you will like our first number; if you do, commend the enterprise and give it the encouragement of your subscription and an occasional item of news; if not, be fair and suggest some means of improvement.

As working-men ourselves, we may be pardoned if our proclivities possibly tend toward our peers, although it will be our aim to hold the balance justly, to eradicate class distinctions, to disseminate useful and instructive information, and do aught that lies within the scope and influence of a journal to promote the interests of those we seek to represent.

Our aim is, not only to make THE INLAND PRINTER a successful business enterprise, but to make it so as a result of its value to all who may be pleased to give it substantial support.

WHAT OF THE FUTURE?

A FEW years ago there were those claiming to be well informed on scientific matters who asserted that the field of electricity had been thoroughly searched and that no more useful appliances were likely to be discovered. Scarcely had the words left their mouths before electric lights and telephones began to be talked about, and now we are ready to believe that we have but just entered the border of this wonderland.

If we are to believe information lately received, the art of printing is about to see some very decided improvements which, if the anticipations of their inventors are realized, will work a revolution. A man in Chicago claims to have almost perfected a machine that will entirely dispense with type-setting. The machine is similar in its operation to the type-writer, the steel dies or types making their impressions on strips of papier maché which are to be cut into proper length for adjustment and finally to be stereotyped from sheets composed of these adjusted strips. If it were not for the adjustment, we could see how such a machine could be made practical. Should the invention be perfected, a small article, in appearance and size similar to the smallest cottage organ, might become the companion of the sewing-machine in many houses, and the work of a number of compositors at as many cumbersome cases be superseded by this parlor ornament manipulated by a single pair of skillfully trained hands. Typos, however, need not be alarmed. A score of years may not find the machine what its friends hope to make it.

A new and revolutionary method is promised in newspaper presswork. This new system is based on the lithographic process, using, however, a zinc plate instead of stone. The impression from the types is taken with lithographic transfer ink and transferred to the zinc plate, and from this the printing is done direct. It is claimed that the plates treated in this way will print several thousand impressions, and that for small editions where it is not desired to have stereotype plates this will be a great saving, not only in the wear and tear, but that it will thereby facilitate the rapid handling of the type.

LEAVES FROM A NOTE-BOOK.
SILVER TYPES.

The belief for some time prevailed among book collectors that certain books of uncommon elegance were, by a peculiar dilettanteism of the typographer, printed from silver types. In reality types of silver would not print a book more elegantly than types of the usual composite metal. The absurdity of the idea is also shown by the circumstances under which books are for the most part composed. Some one has asked very pertinently, if a set of thirsty compositors would not have quickly discovered " how many ems long primer would purchase a gallon of beer." It is surmised that the notion took its rise in a mistake of *silver* for *Elzevir* type, such being the term applied early in the last century to types of a small size, similar to those which had been used in the celebrated miniature editions of the Amsterdam printers, the Elzevirs. —*Notes and Queries.*

CONCAVE CONDENSED.

24A	Two-line Nonpareil Concave Condensed.	$2 00

SLUMBER NOT IN THE TENT IN
YOUR COLUMNS THE WORLD IS ADVANCING
44 ADVANCE YOU WITH IT 33

24A	Two-line Brevier Concave Condensed.	$2 45

THE EVIL THAT MEN DO
LIVES AFTER THEM THE GOOD IS
9 BURIED WITH THEIR BONES 9

18A	Two-line Long Primer Concave Condensed.	$2 70

WHAT NATURE DENIES
THE FACE SHE OFTEN GIVES
8 THE UNDERSTANDING 8

16A	Two-line Pica Concave Condensed.	$3 65

EARTH HAS NO
SORROWS THAT HEAVEN
4 CAN NOT HEAL 4

10A	Two-line Columbian Concave Condensed.	$4 00

4 QUOTH THE RAVEN NEVERMORE

8A	Two-line Paragon Concave Condensed.	$5 15

SUFFERING SAD HUMANITY 3

6A	Four-line Pica Concave Condensed.	$5 45

2 LIVE AND LET LIVE

5A	Five-line Pica Concave Condensed.	$6 00

PRAISE IN SONG 5

4A	Six-line Pica Concave Condensed.	$7 45

2 MICROSCOPIC

THE DIFFERENT SIZES OF THIS SERIES JUSTIFY BY SIXTHS OF PICA AND LINE EXACTLY AT THE BOTTOM. SPACES AND QUADS GO WITH EACH FONT.

SOUND PRINTING.

A FEW years ago, when the phonograph first made its appearance, there was no end to speculation as to the possibilities of its future. It was predicted by some that it would supersede printing, to some extent; that the impressions of the needle on the metallic sheet would eventually be perfected so that duplicates of impressed sheets could be produced as readily as sheets of paper; and that by the use of a perfected machine for reproducing the sounds the eyes would, in a great measure, be relieved of the strain of reading poor type. The gate seemed opening to a wonderful field of invention, but the phonograph has never yet proved to be more than a very interesting toy. To some it may seem strange that such a wonderful invention should be made and no practical results follow, but this has been the history of many wonderful discoveries. America had been discovered more than one hundred years before a permanent settlement was made. Probably a majority of the valuable articles used today have been tardy in coming into practical use.

Should this or any other method of recording and preserving the literature of the world ever be perfected by which the ear, instead of the eye, would be brought into requisition, the whole system of education would be revolutionized. Reading, as now practiced, would be transferred to the classical scholar, who now devotes several years of his school life to the study of Greek and Latin for the purpose of making himself acquainted with the literature of the ancients, or to the antiquarian, interested in searching ancient inscriptions and parchments. The voice itself, and not arbitrary characters representing the different sounds of the voice, could thus be preserved; and not only so, but even the tones peculiar to the individual would thereby be heard generations after the tongue had ceased to speak.

DISCREET ADVERTISING.

A DVERTISING pays; there is no doubt of it. But to say that any and all kinds of advertising afford large returns for the outlay, we very much doubt. In the earlier ages of printing, when it was yet a novelty, perhaps any kind of hand-bill, newspaper or printed sign would attract attention; but it is not so now. The novelty is now gone. Everybody has seen thousands of advertisements, and as simple, rough ads. they do not care to see them more. However, even these plain faces do thrust themselves upon our attention and make their impression upon our minds, though it may not be so favorable as it might be. To get the best return for money spent in setting a business before that portion of the public that we wish to interest is a matter that in this age requires a good deal of thought and discretion. There are two kinds of advertisements that attract attention, and they are in some respects exactly opposite in their natures. One is the sensational, which, from its grotesqueness or peculiar statement, illustration or form, attracts the eye as a curiosity. These accomplish their end by making their subject talked

about or wondered about. The other class to which we refer is the more genteel method of the use of very neatly displayed advertisements in such newspapers or other periodicals as are pecularly suited to the kind of goods represented. Advertisements of school books find interested readers in school journals, while persons interested in the breeding of cattle, as a general thing, are not subscribers to other trade journals than the ones representing their own line of business. Then there are the fine catalogues, cards, letter and bill heads which by their appearance denote the respectability of the parties whom they represent. There is no doubt business firms make a great mistake in sending out cards, letters, or any other representations of their enterprises that are of a slouchy or homely nature. In such case the firm and goods, if of high character, are in reality misrepresented. The impression that one gets from such advertisements is the same as when waited on by impudent or slovenly clerks. Like the parade that the circus makes on the streets, which the showman always makes as attractive as, and of a corresponding character to that within the tent, so these little displays are supposed to represent, in a great measure, the store or shop or office. Money expended in discreet advertising brings a large return.

BUSINESS PRINCIPLES NECESSARY.

P RINTING, like any other business, to make it successful, should be attended to in all of its details. It so happens that very many who engage in the business as proprietors of small or large establishments, have spent all their years either at the case or in the pressroom, and about all that they have seen of the financial matters of the establishment has been on pay-day, when they went to draw their salaries. Occasionally one of these men, by industry and economy, finds in his possession a few hundred dollars, and his first laudable ambition is to have an office of his own. He accordingly settles on a location, and probably the first mistake he makes is in selecting a stock unsuited to the locality in which he proposes to work. He soon finds that much of the fine material suitable to the trade in the city, where he has spent most of his time in a large first-class establishment, is dead stock. He also finds that in a small establishment more inventive genius is required to supply small necessities, which in the city were for sale next door. He finds, too, that while he is a good compositor, he has neither the ability to run the press nor even give directions to the hired pressman, whose interest is not quite so great in the work as is that of the proprietor. And then, when it comes to the finances of the establishment, he is all at sea. His business will not afford a bookkeeper, and he has no education in that line, so his accounts are kept in the head, in various memorandum-books, or on slips of paper thrust into drawers or pigeonholes. In his anxiety to please his patrons and get a start, collections are neglected, and much well-earned money lost by failure to ask for it, until the account is forgotten.

JOB COMPOSITORS.

BY ALFRED PYE.

THE observant printer cannot but notice that the average "job" compositor of the present day is away below the standard to which he should attain, and it may not be out of place to devote a little time to a consideration of the fact, and to endeavor to show what a job printer should really be. It is not an unusual thing for a man to apply for a stand in the job department of a printing-office when he knows very little about general jobwork, having, perhaps, put in his time on three or four different kinds of composition outside of book or newspaper work, and feeling thereby qualified to class himself as a "job" printer. There are many foremen who can tell what trouble they have had, and how very difficult it is to get a competent workman upon whom they could rely to do any and every kind of work that is executed in the jobroom. Many compositors are first-class workmen on tables or catalogues who would hardly know how to begin on a fancy circular or business card, or even on a well displayed advertisement. They do not possess the skill and ability necessary to plan and execute the artistic style of printing that is being called for more and more every day. These remarks not only apply to the old school of printers, who were trained up to and have worked the best part of their time on the plain, bold style of printing which was thought good enough a few years ago, but also to the rising generation, who cannot help noticing the great progress that is being made in the art of typography.

A job compositor ought to possess a knowledge of every branch of typography, and should be able to set an elaborate piece of rule-and-border work as easily as he could a plain personal card, or make up a work into pages and lock it up for press as well as set the matter therefor, or set a large poster with as much ease as a dodger—in fact, nothing should come amiss to him, whether large or small, simple or intricate. But how many are there who could do so?

There are many reasons why this is thus. No doubt the need of an apprenticeship system has something to do with it, but a great deal depends upon individual exertion. A man who wishes to be a good printer, and makes up his mind to be one, will be a good printer in spite of all obstacles. He will watch other good workmen and note the manner in which they do their work, and ask questions as to the why and wherefore of this and that, and try to imitate or excel in his own work that which he sees to be good in the labor of others. The want of ambition is one cause why we have so many indifferent workmen in our profession. If every young man who set out to learn printing aimed at being the *best* printer of his time, and strove to make himself so, the skillful workman would not be such a rarity as he is now.

Another reason for the scarcity of good workmen is that very few look upon printing as an *art*, which it undoubtedly is, but consider it merely mechanical labor, of which a certain quantity has to be performed for a certain amount of remuneration. We should not have a very high opinion of the work of an artist who painted pictures for so much per foot, without a thought of the fame which his work should bring to him. There is no doubt that much of the printing of the present day will be preserved for many years—perhaps centuries—and it should be the desire of printers to convey to future generations the idea that they were artists, not mechanics. All work should be studied and a plan decided upon, and the whole work should be perfectly clear to the mind's eye before a line of type is set, just in the same way as an artist sees his picture before him when as yet he has not a stroke of color upon his canvas. Young printers especially should cultivate an artistic taste, as they will find it of great service to them in their work.

Yet another reason for a lack of good job printers is the desire of our young men to earn large wages without giving sufficient time to make themselves proficient in their work. Just as soon as they can set type swiftly and tolerably clean a desire to quit their training-school and work for so much per thousand ems in some book or newspaper office takes possession of them, and so they become mere type-setting machines, and spend their lives without giving a thought to the higher and wider sphere in which the job printer lives and moves and has his being. There are some who, try as they will, can never be good job printers, but they are few and far between, and the writer maintains that if a desire to excel in their work could be implanted in beginners we should have a far better class of workmen than at present exists.

Then the system of exclusiveness practiced in many offices has a great deal to do with the evil of which we are now complaining. When it is discovered that a young man has an aptitude for a particular class of work, he is kept working right along at it, greatly to his own detriment and also to his employer's, who might on occasion more profitably employ him on work of a different character. And so, on account of this system, we have printers who are first-class workmen in some branches, but whose ideas of other branches of the profession are very limited indeed. To remedy this, a plan might be adopted whereby a learner should be placed under the instruction of a capable man, who not only knows how to do things himself, but has the faculty of imparting his knowledge to others. If employers were to give a little more attention to this matter than they usually do, they would reap the fruits of their labor in the certainty of their younger employés being able to perform more remunerative work than could be expected under the present plan, while at the same time preparing fresh material to supply the place of those good workmen who from death or removal or other causes drop out of the ranks of the profession, and whose places they now find it so difficult to fill.

A great deal more might be written upon this subject, but probably sufficient has been said to awaken an interest on the part of all concerned which shall have the effect of awakening a determination to improve the character and ability of job printers, and help to lessen the almost general complaint that it is hard to find a really good job printer when he is needed.

MANUFACTURED BY

MARDER, LUSE & CO., AMERICAN SYSTEM OF INTERCHANGEABLE TYPE BODIES. TYPE FOUNDERS,

139 AND 141 MONROE ST., CHICAGO.

LATIN CONDENSED.

| 24A, 48a | LONG PRIMER LATIN CONDENSED | $3 25 | 18A, 36a | PICA LATIN CONDENSED. | $2 75 |

A HISTORY WHICH TAKES NO ACCOUNT

Of what was said by the press in memorable emergencies

500   Befits an earlier age than ours.   103

THERE ARE MANY VICES WHICH

Do not deprive us of friends there are many virtues

467   which prevent our having any   346

| 18A, 36a | COLUMBIAN LATIN CONDENSED. | $4 00 | 12A, 24a | DOUBLE PICA LATIN CONDENSED. | $4 20 |

A GREAT NOISE IS OFTEN

Made by a small stone the loudest talk is

77   not always the deepest   33

LIFE IS WHAT WE

Make it for Nature has made it a

88   Tragedy long ago.   55

| 8A, 16a | DOUBLE ENGLISH LATIN CONDENSED. | $5 55 |

THO' THE MILLS OF THE GODS GRIND SLOWLY

55   Yet they grind exceeding small   31

| 6A, 12a | DOUBLE COLUMBIAN LATIN CONDENSED. | $5 90 |

FORETELLING now by your Merry Peals 6

| 5A, 10a | CANON LATIN CONDENSED. | $6 65 |

4 Many DAYS of HAPPINESS

| 4A, 8a | FIVE-LINE PICA LATIN CONDENSED. | $9 10 |

JOYS and SORROWS 8

| 4A, 8a | SIX-LINE PICA LATIN CONDENSED. | $10 80 |

2 OH Merry BELLS

WHAT BECOMES OF ALL THE BOOKS.

THE perplexing question "What goes with all the pins?" has agitated the minds of many persons ever since pins began to be made by machinery. Before pin machines came into use and while pins were a luxury some account was kept of them, but since they have become so plenty, everybody knowing their large production wonders where they all go to. Aside from the few swallowed by babies and ruined by bad boys in making lively seats for schoolmasters to sit on, the loss of this useful article seems to be a mystery.

The same remarks apply equally to books. Not many years ago books were comparatively scarce because their production was slow and expensive, and the demand for them was not as great as today. Then a library was as much of a curiosity as of practical value. Now books are produced so fast that hundreds of respectable libraries could be supplied every year, besides giving to every person in the world able to read all the reading matter he could use. It is estimated that for several years there have been published an average of 20,000 books of from 1,000 to 25,000 volumes each, or probably 200,000,000 copies a year. Most of these are printed and read by English, German and French people, and when we take into account that the book producing and reading people of the world are but a fraction of the whole population of the earth, we cannot but wonder "What becomes of all the books?"

A great many books having failed to find purchasers, go to the paper-mill and are ground up and made into paper for new books to be printed upon. Books are now very cheap, and the same care is not taken to preserve them as formerly; this is notable especially in school books.

Many large libraries, the accumulation of years, have been destroyed in an hour in time of war or by accident, or the incendiary match. The great Alexandrian library was destroyed by Cæsar forty-eight years before Christ, and again seven hundred years later by the Saracens. In these two conflagrations nearly 1,000,000 volumes were burned. At Carthage 500,000 were destroyed.

When Mohammed captured Constantinople, he ordered the great libraries of that city thrown into the sea. These are but a few instances of the wholesale destruction of large depositories of the world's learning and literature. To superstition and prejudice can be credited the annihilation of millions of the most valuable works in all ages, and carelessness and vandalism have done their part in the great waste of the product of the author's brain and printer's skill.

WOMEN AS PRINTERS.

WE are frequently asked why women do not engage in the business of printing. Some of them do, and succeed in their work; but that there are but few ladies engaged in type-setting, although it is considered a light employment, and seemingly well adapted to their purpose, is a fact that can scarcely be explained. There are a great many ladies employed in all the large telegraph offices as operators, usually at lower wages than the men, and as teachers their salaries are generally about one half that paid to male teachers; while in most printing establishments the work is done by the piece, and a woman stands the same chance to make money that a man does.

The fact that handling type is not quite so clean as handling the keys of the telegraph instrument or the teacher's ferule may keep some out of the printing-office, though printing is by no means what might be termed dirty work. The compositor's work necessarily compels him to be on his feet all day, and a woman's inability to stand for so long a time is a physical objection to her engaging in this line of work for a long period. The same objection is made to ladies as saleswomen in stores, and was thoroughly discussed in the papers a few years ago; and yet the discussion did not result in providing the female clerks with seats on which they could recline a part of the time as proposed, nor deter them from engaging in that business.

Probably the principal reason that there are so few lady compositors in our printing-houses, is the long time required to perfect anyone in the art. As a general thing, women do not engage in any kind of business, except as a temporary employment, the ultimate object being to preside over a household instead of a school or a store or a printing-office. We do not say that this is a result of correct home teaching, but it is the fact. Several years must necessarily be spent in learning the business of printing, and almost every young woman expects to be married before several years have passed, and she therefore looks at the time spent in educating herself as a first-class printer as lost; and so she turns to teaching, for which she has already been trained in the public or private school, or to clerking in a store, which needs only a few days' preparation, or to telegraphy, which requires only as many months for its acquisition as equals the number of years to become a good printer.

THE PIONEER PRINTER OF RUSSIA.

DURING the present month the Russians will celebrate the three hundredth anniversary of the first printer in that country. Ivan Feodoroff, the first printer in Russia, died December 17, 1583. The establishment was at Moscow, and his first work was the printing of the bible twenty years before his death.

IDEAS.

WE know that among the fraternity there are men of ideas. We mean to say there are those who have ideas of their own — valuable to themselves, and would become so to others could they get possession of them. We should like to give these ideas to all of our readers and will welcome to our columns any practical thought that may be sent us. A simple inquiry or suggestion acted upon by several thousand minds may return to its author after a short period to benefit him and many others who may happen to have read it in the columns of our paper.

ON THE SQUARE.

"WHY cannot the advertising business be conducted on the same principles as other respectable kinds of business?" is a question that we are glad to notice is being discussed. Most merchants now sell their wares at uniform prices, many of them marking their goods in plain figures, so that a customer may know he is paying just as much and no more than others. With many newspapers it is not so. They have an advertised price that they will take from a customer who asks no questions, and a special price for "close buyers." Another method, not less objectionable, is the misrepresentation of circulation. It *may be* business for a publisher to decline to state to a customer the extent of his circulation, but it does not seem to us fair to base the price of an advertisement on a circulation twice or thrice what it actually is, just because he imagines some competitor is practicing the same deception. If a merchant should do a similar thing, and give short weight or short measure, he would be called dishonest, and not only lose custom, but make himself liable to prosecution for fraud. A great many men are engaged in gambling and other kinds of disreputable trade, who make excuse for themselves that, as there are plenty of lambs that will be fleeced by somebody, they might as well realize a profit from fleecing them as anybody. Yet this does not make the business any more respectable. It seems to us a straightforward statement of the actual advantages that a publication possesses as an advertising medium, with a fair price for space occupied, would not only be the most honorable way, but might in the end prove most profitable. A great many advertisers keep an account of inquiries received in which are mentioned the publication, and thus by comparison determine whether the statements of the publisher correspond with the actual returns, and thus in time learn to discriminate between those who deal fairly and those who do not.

TOO CHEAP.

COMPETITION is the life of trade. Probably very few doubt this old saying. It has been standard for a century. We have heard it almost ever since we began to hear, and had not dreamed but that the saying was as infallible as figures, which the mathematicians say never lie. Indeed, we had come to look upon it as an axiom. But to-day a gentleman happened in upon us, and made the startling assertion that competition is the *death* of trade. Now, once the editor was a pedagogue, and remembers to have advised pupils that it was not always necessary to learn rules verbatim, but that if a word were sometimes substituted it would not be counted in their recitation as an error, having in mind, of course, that the sense was to be preserved. Our teaching, while correct in theory, sometimes resulted in ludicrous blunders; and when our visitor repeated the axiom, as above related, we inadvertently scanned his face to see if it were not that of one of our old pupils. Noticing our inquiring look, he repeated, with more emphasis: "Yes, sir, competition is the DEATH of trade," and then closing the door, left us to meditate. For an hour we sat reflecting and trying to test the truth of the modified rule, by the different phases of business as they presented themselves to our mind, and the conclusion is, that out friend was warranted in modifying the proverb. Especially does it seem to apply pretty well to some lines of the printing trade. Printers are complaining that there is but little profit in the business, and that much of the trouble comes from a disreputable method that some customers and some competitors have of cutting respectable and living prices to such an extent the life of the trade is literally choked out of it. Upon inquiry it is found to be a common method of many customers to make the rounds of a number of second or third rate printing establishments for estimates of a particular job, ending up with an office with a reputation for first-class, honest work, and where only first-class material is used, if such is promised. With the lowest of these estimates he confronts the proprietor, and, too often, compels him to drop to the figures that barely pay for the work. He reasons that, as he has in his employ certain persons who would otherwise be idle, it would be better for him to do the work than that he should pay his help for lost time, hoping that a reasonable profit can be realized out of other customers. Of course such transactions have their effect on other good houses, and a general hacking and cutting are the consequence. There are men in every kind of business who never expect to pay for their stock, and they can afford to cut prices, their gains in the business being represented by whatever they can beat their creditors out of, and the printing business is blessed (?) with some of this peculiar class of individuals. Another class of printers are those who will not scruple to use stock inferior in quality or weight to that suitable to the job. In this matter the honorable dealer cannot compete, and so he must simply cut on his own profits to enable him to supply the deficiencies of his dishonorable competitor. Comparatively few people are good judges of printing, and the workman who would prefer to use first-class stock, and who would take pains in every particular to make a nice job, finds himself rewarded with a look of incredulity when he assures his customer that it is a superior article. Then there is a class of printers who never make careful estimates of work, but rather estimate the customer. If he looks, talks and acts as if he knew but little about the matter, and would likely go no further, the printer will make him as high a price as any first-class house; but if his customer is evidently posted, from having been to several other establishments with the same job, he will cut the figures down to a cent within actual cost before he will let him go.

These practices are to be deplored. The effect is to bring the business into disrepute. No increase of business is a result, but, on the contrary, an inferior grade of work is turned out, and a general distrust, leading, in many cases, to embarrassment and failure, is the consequence.

The proper and only honorable way is to take a job at just what it is worth, basing the price on a careful estimate of every detail. Then let the competition be in promptness in getting out the work, in polite treatment of customers, and in a constant improvement in style and quality.

DO THE BEST YOU CAN.

A YOUNG lawyer once complained to a member of the same profession who was a very successful practitioner, that the profession was crowded, and that there was but little chance for a young man like himself; whereupon the old, wise lawyer gave the young man a little advice. He said: "Young man, that the lower stratum of the profession is crowded there is no doubt, and it always will be; but as in all kinds of business, so in ours — there is plenty of room at the top. Get out of the lower ranks and come up higher, and you will not be crowded." While these are not the exact words of the wise doctor, they convey the idea actually expressed, and teach a lesson to every laborer or professional man. Did you never notice in an orchard the finest apples and cherries and peaches are always in the very top of the tree, and that they are not crowded, but have plenty of room to grow, and plenty of air and sunshine and dew and rain to assist in their development? Do you not know that the upper rooms of a building are the healthiest to live in, because of the pure air and sunshine? But you will notice they are almost always unoccupied, because, we suppose, it is too much like work to climb the stairs.

There are some printers who are never idle. They always have employment and get good wages, and it is just because they have climbed the stairs and have thoroughly mastered their business; and not only so, they have mastered themselves, and, in addition to being proficient in the art, they have trained themselves to be gentlemen, and have given some attention to business principles. They are known to be sober, industrious and well qualified. Such men do not have to seek business, but employers have an eye on them, and when they wish to change their locations, positions are open to them. Such men become the foremen and eventually the proprietors.

In the lower stratum, representing three-fourths of the workmen, will be found those who are all the time complaining that their ranks are crowded. They whine that they get no work to do. The trouble is that they have not the ambition to get up into the place where there is room. Do you ask how can I get to the top? Begin with yourself, if you have nothing else, and be a gentleman. Be sober and honest, and when you find some kind of an opening, go right in and do your best. Slight nothing, and present the best work it is in your power to perform, and you have made several steps toward the upper room. Too many of our profession are given to frequenting drinking places.

Spinner Script.

PATENTED.

Job Fonts, 15A, 75a, $8.00.　　　　　PICA SPINNER SCRIPT.　　　　　Card Fonts, 6A, 25a, $3.25.

We take pleasure in introducing to our Friends and Patrons the "Pica Spinner Script." The popularity of this Face has been greatly stimulated by the addition of this, the minimum size of the Series. Printers will notice that its Compactness, Legibility and Freedom from Kerned Letters (enabling it to be set solid), makes it available in places where many other styles of Type would be impracticable. By the

American System of
Interchangeable Type Bodies

The Artistic Printer will be able to work it to advantage with the other sizes, producing effects that will be pleasing and fulfilling the requirements of good taste. The handsome appearance of the Pica Spinner Script speaks more decidedly than any words, but we must state that in addition to its Great Beauty it possesses Wearing Qualities no less desirable and important. 1 2 3 4 5 6 7 8 9 0 $ & ﬂ

Job Fonts, 12A, 60a, $10.00.　　　GREAT PRIMER SPINNER SCRIPT.　　　Card Fonts, 6A, 16a, $4.35.

We offer for the approval of the Craft this the Great Primer Size of our Spinner Script; its style is striking and suggestive of uncommon durability. By the absence of kerned letters, the hair lines are so well protected that they will stand as strong a pressure as any portion of the letter. It combines qualities Printers have long felt the need of in scripts, namely: Novelty, Gracefulness, Legibility and freedom from too much ornamentation, making it one of the most useful Scripts that has yet been designed. Used in connection with the other sizes in Circulars, Letter Heads, etc., very pleasing results may be attained.

1 2 3 4 5 6 7 8 9 0 $ & ﬂ

SWEDISH, GERMAN AND SPANISH ACCENTS ARE CAST WITH ALL SIZES OF THIS SERIES AND ARE FURNISHED UPON APPLICATION.

NONPAREIL TELESCOPIC GOTHIC ITALIC.

PRICE OF SERIES COMPLETE, $4.75.

32A　NONPAREIL TELESCOPIC GOTHIC ITALIC, No. 1.　$1.00.	32A　NONPAREIL TELESCOPIC GOTHIC ITALIC, No. 2.　$1.05.
THE BOOK IS COMPLETED, AND CLOSED LIKE THE DAY, AND THE HAND THAT HAS WRITTEN IT LAYS IT AWAY, DIM GROW ITS FANCIES, FORGOTTEN THEY LIE LIKE COALS IN THE ASHES THEY DARKEN AND DIE　234	SONG SINKS INTO SILENCE, THE STORY IS TOLD, THE WINDOWS DARKENED, THE HEARTH-STONE IS COLD, DARKER AND DARKER THE BLACK SHADOWS FALL SLEEP AND OBLIVION REIGN OVER ALL　567
32A　NONPAREIL TELESCOPIC GOTHIC ITALIC, No. 3.　$1.20.	32A　NONPAREIL TELESCOPIC GOTHIC ITALIC, No. 4.　$1.50.
SOLEMNLY, MOURNFULLY, DEALING ITS DOLE, THE CURFEW BELL IS BEGINNING TO TOLL, COVER THE EMBERS, PUT OUT THE LIGHT TOIL COMES WITH THE MORNING, AND REST WITH THE NIGHT　234	DARK GROW THE WINDOWS AND QUENCHED IS THE FIRE, SOUND FADES INTO SILENCE, ALL FOOTSTEPS RETIRE, THERE IS NO VOICE IN THE CHAMBERS　23

ONE IS PAINED TO FIND THAT THE MOST EXCLUSIVE FOLKS HAVE FREQUENTLY PASSED
THEIR EARLY DAYS IN SELLING TAPE OR WEST INDIA GOODS IN HOMŒOPATHIC QUANTITIES. NOW THIS IS NOT AN
IMMORAL THING IN ITSELF, BUT IT IS CERTAINLY VERY ILLOGICAL OF THESE PEOPLE TO BE SO INTOLERANT OF THOSE LESS
FORTUNATE ONES WHO HAVE NOT YET DISPOSED OF THEIR STOCK
THICK SETTLED HAMLETS CLUSTER ROUND THE SILVERY LAKES AND STREAMS OF LIGHT WHILE THICKLY STUDDED STARS ABOVE DWELL IN THE AZURE SKIES AT NIGHT

MARDER, LUSE & CO., TYPE FOUNDERS, CHICAGO.

CONCAVE.

32A — NONPAREIL CONCAVE. — $1.55

HIGH ON A THRONE OF ROYAL STATE
THAT FAR OUTSHONE THE WEALTH OF ORMUS AND OF
123 * IND SATAN EXALTED SAT * 456

24A — BREVIER CONCAVE. — $1.75

OLIVES ON HER BROW WERE
BLOOMING HER STEP WAS LIGHT AND AIRY
12 * AS THE TRIPPING OF A FAIRY * 34

24A — TWO-LINE PEARL CONCAVE. — $1.90

THE CHRISTIAN'S LANCE
STEADY PIERCED THE MOSLEM RIGHT
34 * THROUGH THE BRAIN * 56

18A — TWO-LINE NONPAREIL CONCAVE. — $2.15

HE WILL STAND ON
THY RIGHT HAND AND KEEP
6 * THE PORTAL * 8

16A — TWO-LINE BREVIER CONCAVE. — $2.90

HARK I HEAR THE FOEMAN'S
CRY, STRIKE ALARUMS, TRUMPET, DRUMS

12A — TWO-LINE LONG PRIMER CONCAVE. — $3.55

THE GODS HAVE TOLD
AUGURS, ALTARS, CIRCLING WING

10A — TWO-LINE PICA CONCAVE. — $4.00

THOUGH LOST TO
SIGHT, IS TO MEMORY DEAR

8A — TWO-LINE ENGLISH CONCAVE. — $4.30

LEARNED ARGUMENTS

6A — TWO-LINE COLUMBIAN CONCAVE. — $4.25

FEAR NOT CURSES

4A — TWO-LINE GREAT PRIMER CONCAVE. — $5.00

DIVINE MILTON

ALL FONTS COMPLETE WITH FIGURES. THE DIFFERENT SIZES OF THIS SERIES JUSTIFY AND LINE AT THE BOTTOM. SPACES AND QUADS WITH ALL SIZES EXCEPT NONPAREIL

A TRADE THE BEST.

FIRST-CLASS mechanics are often spoiled to make third-rate lawyers, doctors and other professional men; and some that would make a comfortable living as mechanics are doomed to a life of drudgery and want as clerks and bookkeepers.

An ordinary clerk bears no comparison with that of the artisan in point of worldly advantage. The latter is not only better paid, but has a degree of independence to which the clerk is a stranger. His clothing and his rental costs less, and, except in times of great depression, there is ten times the demand for his services than there is for that of the clerk. There are hundreds of them idle in large cities where there are not scores of unemployed mechanics. The demand for the clerk does not keep pace with the supply, and parents are, in a measure, the ones to blame for this. They have a vague idea that they are opening the way to social preferment, such as they themselves have never been able to obtain, by sending their sons to a desk or behind a counter, instead of to a trade, after they leave school. In a large number of cases they discover too late that they have doomed their offspring to a life of constant struggle to make ends meet, and that a clerk is much more dependent on the caprices of an employer than is the artisan. The public schools are a draw-farm for the merchant's desk, and boys fresh from pupilage will, at a nominal salary, undertake the duties of the old hand.

Old hands thus thrown out of employment in the larger cities of the country, can be seen every morning closely scanning the first issue of the daily paper under the head of " Help wanted." It must be a sad spectacle —and the reflection must be sadder still—of the hours and days of suspense, waiting, Micawber-like, for the summons that will never come, or if it come, only with the offer of excessive work at starvation wages.

The moral is plain: Bookkeepers and clerks are at a discount. Teach your boys a trade.

Office of MARDER, LUSE & CO.,
Type Founders,
Chicago, March 1, 1884.

(Dictated)

To our Customers:

After Thirty years of careful experiment made with an ever-increasing desire to meet the many wants of our patrons, it gives us pleasure to acknowledge the commendations our type has received from all points of the compass for its Durability, its Absolute Accuracy of Body and Height and the Mathematical Precision with which all the sizes justify with each other. This accuracy extends not only to our Type but to our Metal Furniture, Rules, Borders, Slugs and Leads as all are cast upon our well-known and justly celebrated AMERICAN SYSTEM OF INTERCHANGEABLE TYPE BODIES.

Thanking you for favors already received, we solicit your further orders, referring to the past as an assurance of our future good faith.

Yours Respectfully,

MARDER, LUSE & CO.

ALIGN CALIGRAPH, No. 2.
PRICE:
Long Primer, 15A, 70a, - - $6.55.

20 a 10 A   PICA AMALGAMATED SCRIPT. $3.60

Last December the Russian printers celebrated the three hundredth anniversary of the first printer in that country. Ivan Feodoroff, December 17, 1583.

20 a 8 A   GREAT PRIMER AMALGAMATED SCRIPT. $4.50

Great care should be taken in distributing script and light faces, as most of the wear of such type may be attributed to carelessness.

15 a 8 A   DOUBLE SMALL PICA AMALGAMATED SCRIPT. $5.50

Unnecessary planing of forms causes more wear and breakage of type than most printers would imagine.

15 A   PICA OCTAGON SHADED. $1.80

CHICAGO, NEW YORK & LONDON SUBMARINE RAILWAY
1234567890

12 A   GREAT PRIMER OCTAGON SHADED. $2.50

CHICAGO, BURLINGTON & QUINCY RAIL
1234567890

10 A   DOUBLE PICA OCTAGON SHADED. $3.65

REPUBLICAN CONVENTION 5
1234567890

6 A   DOUBLE GREAT PRIMER OCTAGON SHADED. $4.40

ARTISTIC PRINTING!
2·27·1884

INCONGRUITIES.

THE job compositor of 1884 certainly possesses many marked advantages over his less favored and pretentious predecessor of twenty-five or thirty years ago. The improvements and appliances of the art now in daily use in every branch of the business, as compared with the period to which we refer, are so marked, so many and so varied, that comparisons seem odious, the changes amounting to a positive revolution. But while this is true, it is questionable, very questionable, if the workman himself has kept pace with the march of improvement, or that a change for the better has been effected in his social, financial or intellectual position, his training, his practical knowledge or his tastes. While here and there one may be found whose superiority is conceded, and whose abilities, mechanical or otherwise, raise him above his fellows, we doubt if the great majority of the craft are as qualified, as a class, as they were before the numerous appliances which now facilitate and lighten their labors were in vogue. When the ornamental fonts, corners and combination borders, brass and metal flourishes, and the innumerable designs which are now found in every well stocked printing establishment, were comparatively unknown embellishments, frequently home-made, the result of care and study, were used to the best advantage, and only in cases when their necessity was apparent. Today the situation is entirely changed. The compositor has everything of this character furnished in endless profusion, and, as a consequence, too often fails to use that judgment and discrimination which the public have a right to expect at his hands. In no manner is this lack of judgment more painfully apparent than in the recklessness with which many of these combinations are maltreated. Designs, unmeaning and offensive to good taste, are scattered promiscuously from a poster to a business card, and as the evil is increasing from day to day, we think the present an opportune time to call attention to the fact.

From a number of samples, collected from time to time, the following will suffice to show the nature of our plaint: Here is the billhead of one who follows the æsthetic calling of a night-scavenger, upon which the compositor has evidently exhausted his skill, embellished with what is supposed to be a songster in his cage; while a circular from a coal-dealer exhibits an oriental eagerly scanning a line, perhaps intended to represent a mummy fishing for a fossilized silurian; but really what connection there is between the subject-matter and the surroundings our readers must judge for themselves.

Here, again, is an illustrated catalogue, published by one of our wholesale boot and shoe manufacturers, containing the latest designs in top-boots, brogans and rubber overalls, suggestive of the aroma of the stockyards; yet in a corner of each page we find a fragrant flower, a pansy, japonica, heliotrope, mignonette, etc. Calling the attention of a printer to this travesty on good taste, he replied, "Oh, you see he (the compositor) wanted *something* to fill up the gap,"—the question of harmony or good taste evidently never entering the mind of the author of the outrage or his apologist.

Nor are these incongruities confined to the work of the unpretentious, often appearing in publications intended to illustrate the perfection of typography. In one of these now lying before us is a specimen circular, with the heading, "The Fellowship of Jesus Christ. An Hour for Simultaneous Prayer throughout the World," flanked on each side by a sphynx (a centaur would have been as appropriate) and a couple of Egyptian idols, perhaps a labored attempt to establish an identity between the "known" and "unknown God." A contemporary writer of Nero's court states that it was easier to find a god in Athens than a man, but it appears to have been easier for this designer to find four heathen symbols than one in harmony with the teachings of Christianity. Now what would be thought of an artist producing a picture representing "Nature in Repose" with a sirocco in the background, or a revivalist closing services with a chorus by a minstrel troupe? Yet neither of these inconsistencies would be more out of character with the nature of the subjects than some of the designs to which we have taken exception.

Again: these incongruities are not so much the result of a lack of mechanical skill as a lack of knowledge. *Intelligence pays*. Knowledge is power, and intelligence and skill should go hand in hand, the one being the helpmeet of the other. These can only be acquired by patient study and reflection. The mind as well as the taste requires cultivation. Superficial knowledge cannot successfully cope with *educated skill*. The printer who "cares for none of these things," will undoubtedly be outstripped in the race by the student who spends his leisure hours in improving his mind, acquiring practical knowledge and mastering details. Show us a workman whose ambition is bounded by the walls of the printing-office, who can tell the latest joke (?) in *Peck's Sun*, or the details of the latest crime, but who has no time or inclination to peruse his trade's journal, and we will show you a man who has mistaken his vocation, who, in all probability, will remain, as he deserves to remain, "a hewer of wood and drawer of water." Cause and effect go together. Nor should the ignorance existing be a matter of surprise. In many instances a boy who has been rushed through school at a breakneck speed, and who has obtained a smattering on this or that subject only sufficient to prove that a "little learning is a dangerous thing," is thrust into a printing-office, without desire or qualification, where he is too frequently allowed to think and act for himself, or placed under the tutelage of one whose knowledge is as limited as his own. When devices are attempted in which discrimination is required, he seldom if ever succeeds, *because* his knowledge is not based on intelligence.

It is in this connection that a school of technique becomes a public benefactor, because under its fostering care no such incongruous productions as those to which we have referred would be allowed to see the light of day. The efforts of the apprentice would be intelligently directed; the *why* and *wherefore* pointed out; the absurdity of this or that combination, which now passes unchallenged, explained, and the graduate be enabled to "give a reason for the faith that is in him."

A SLOVENLY PRACTICE.

THE slovenly habit of making the quad-box the depository for bad or broken letters, etc., in fact a veritable hell-box, is one of the most reprehensible in which the compositor can indulge. Pi resembles geometrical progression—it increases at an astounding ratio. There is no reason why the quad-box should not be kept as clean as any other box in the case—and a little care will do so—instead of being turned into a miniature printing-office, as it too often is. We know of no better evidence of a slovenly printer than a pied quad-box, and yet there are many men, who would feel insulted were they ranked as other than first-class compositors, who never think of cleaning it out from one month's end to another. But especially is this practice to be deprecated in the job office, because what is supposed to be everybody's business is nobody's business, and, as a consequence, it is here where this pernicious habit runs riot. It is generally just as convenient, and in the long run far more profitable, to put a stray letter *at once* in the proper case, than to throw it where it has no business—into the quad, hyphen, or colon box. There is an old saying, "If you want to keep the floor clean, when you drop one letter, pick up two." So it is the first wrong move that does the mischief; it is like the bell-wether of a flock—others follow its lead. Keep out the first wrong-font letter or space, and the second will never get in. Perhaps the safest plan is to keep the space and quad boxes of the job cases empty, justifying from the sort cases entirely. It is also a good plan for a compositor to place a hell-box on or near his stand, and have the contents of the same emptied on the dead-stone *every* morning. By adopting this method, all excuses for dirty quad-boxes and the accumulation of pi will be effectually removed, and the culprit or culprits who make a practice of throwing every word or line pied into them will soon be detected.

AN ERA OF FRAUD.

THE number of new corporations—printing and publishing companies contributing their full quota—which are springing up in this state is perfectly marvelous. The reckless manner in which twenty-five thousand to two hundred and fifty thousand dollars are slung around—metaphorically speaking—must astonish the natives. Pseudo-inventors, broken-down tricksters and impecunious adventurers, to whom a fifty-dollar bill would be a bonanza, have the cheek to send to Springfield for a charter incorporating this or that company with an authorized capital equal to a prince's ransom—*on paper*, at least. But why protest, as this fact is accepted as *prima-facie evidence* of returning business prosperity; and when the authorized capital stock is computed at the end of the year Illinois will be many millions of dollars richer than she was last January? That's the rosy way to look at it. The proper way, however, is to regard them as the outgrowth of an era of speculative craze, and to estimate most of them at least at their true value—as the schemes of confidence adventurers. But if gudgeons will bite, gudgeons must suffer.

CONSUMPTION AMONG COMPOSITORS.

THE London Society of Compositors have called the attention of the trade to the excessive mortality prevailing among the members of their craft, which possesses a special interest to the American printer, because the principal causes of this mortality exist as much on this side as on the other side of the Atlantic. In THE PRINTER, statistics are given concerning funeral allowances, which for 1883 amounted to seventy-four. Of this number twenty-two compositors died from consumption and thirteen from bronchitis, etc., giving a total of thirty-five deaths, or nearly fifty per cent, due to diseases of the respiratory organs. The position in which the compositor is required to stand, the irregularity of the hours of labor, the insufficient ventilation of the workrooms, and the general want of cleanliness, are acknowledged to be the chief factors of evil. The first two grievances, we are afraid, will continue to contribute their quota to the death list, though in job offices at least the overtime *system*, to which we took exception in our last issue, could be practically abolished. While there has recently been a great improvement in the construction of our composing-rooms, compared to the dilapidated rookeries of a few years ago, from which light and ventilation were carefully excluded and access to which was only accomplished at risk of life or limb, there is still room for great improvement, in the matter of ventilation at least. The violent and dangerous change of atmosphere admitted by the opening of doors or windows is *not* ventilation; and it is difficult to determine which is the most fruitful source of disease, inhaling week after week a polluted atmosphere, or being constantly subjected to a chilling and sudden draft. As to the last cause, truth compels the admission that the men have nobody but themselves to blame. A correspondent, writing on this subject, says: "I could point to composing-rooms that have not been thoroughly swept for years, the corners and out-of-the-way places of which are receptacles for old boots and other inodorous refuse, but, to a great extent, also, they are attributable to our own irregularities when in health. It was impressed on me by a physician whom I consulted for an attack of colic many years ago, 'Never eat food in the office without previously washing the hands, for, no matter how careful you may be, it is next to impossible to prevent the type-dirt getting into the system.' A hurried stand-up meal is frequently taken in offices where men nearly always work at high pressure, and I have often seen compositors drop their sticks for a minute and hurriedly take a mouthful, and while masticating this resume work, and so on till the food was finished." Cleanliness is next to godliness, and we believe a practical recognition of this fact, with a judicious daily indulgence in physical exercise, will materially diminish the mortality list. We believe also that the establishment of a gymnasium, with bathrooms attached, by the larger typographical unions, would prove a paying investment in more than one sense, and be the means of removing many of the nervous diseases now caused by high pressure, work and foul atmosphere.

Office Barnhart Bros. & Spindler,

Manufacturers Superior Copper-Mixed Type,

Fifth Ave., Chicago, Illinois.

80a 16A $9 75   PICA LAKESIDE No. 2.   40a 8A $5 00

Chicago, Ill., April 18, 1884.

Dear Sirs:—

The very best evidence of the high esteem in which our Superior Copper-Mixed Type is held by the leading printers and publishers in the West is furnished by the numerous orders we are receiving from them. Within the last few months we have supplied the Chicago Tribune, Chicago Times, Chicago Daily News, St. Paul Globe, Kansas City Journal, Minneapolis Tribune, Minneapolis Journal, Western Newspaper Union, and a number of weekly journals throughout the country with handsome new dresses. We have no hesitation in saying that our Superior Copper-Mixed Type stands without a successful rival in this country to-day in wearing qualities, and it has only to be used to substantiate the assertion. We are receiving numerous testimonials from our patrons bearing out the above statement. Don't waste your money on poor material when the best in the market can be had at bottom prices.

Respectfully Yours,

Barnhart Bros. & Spindler.

60a 12A $10 00   GREAT PRIMER LAKESIDE No. 2.   30a 6A $5 25

Barnhart Bros. & Spindler.

Gentlemen:— I take pleasure in stating that during the past twelve years your firm has furnished the Tribune with a New Dress on four different occasions; that the last dress has been in use since the first of January, 1880; that the quality of your manufacture has been highly satisfactory to the Tribune Co.,—the faces clean cut and material of the best quality, hard and durable. The fact that you have furnished us during so long a time is evidence that we consider your type the best in the market, and our experience with your house has been such that we feel that any representation made by you and any agreements can be relied upon fully. Respectfully Yours,

A. Cowles, Sec'y Tribune Co.

THIS SERIES AND THE LAKESIDE SCRIPT WORK NICELY IN COMBINATION AS WILL BE SEEN ABOVE.

25 a 10 A   PICA ELITE. $3 00

UPRIGHT AND HONEST AMERICAN CONGRESSMEN

Biggest And Most Stupendous Humbugs Under the Popular Political System of the United States

25134 MILWAUKEE & PHILADELPHIA 67890

Political Bums of Every Nation From Constituencies Representing Nobody but Themselves

Milwaukee, Philadelphia, Columbus, Oconomowoc

20 a 8 A   GREAT PRIMER ELITE. $3 80

ORGAN GRINDERS & OTHER MUSICIANS

Vessels Plying on The Northern Rivers Frequently Pass Through Uninjured

12345 CRITERION THEATRE 67890

From Parnassus Lofty Heights The Flowery Legend Came

14 a 6 A   DOUBLE PICA ELITE. $4 80

GODS IN AWFUL CONCLAVE MET

Jove Himself Held the Gavel and Called the Meeting to Order

2345 COSWEL & REFERN 6789

Graceful And Delicate Coloring Preserves The Effect

MANUFACTURED BY BARNHART BROS. & SPINDLER.

❧ HANDSOME LATTICE

PATENTED DECEMBER 25, 1883

WESTERN TYPE FDY CHICAGO

---

12 A	PICA LATTICE.	$2 35

❧ CHICAGO LEADS THE WORLD ❧

❧ SLEIGHING PARTIES GOING TO RIVERSIDE FOURTH OF JULY ❧

DETROIT AND BOSTON BASE BALL ASSOCIATIONS

❧ 1234567890 ❧

10 A	GREAT PRIMER LATTICE.	$3 00

❧ PANSY BLOSSOM PLEASURE CLUB ❧

❧ GRAND EXCURSIONS ON THE SOUTHERN RIVERS ❧

BOOK OF THE CHECKERED LIFE

❧ 1234567890 ❧

8 A	DOUBLE PICA LATTICE.	$3 60

LOUISE & GEORGE

❧ THE MICHIGAN CENTRAL DEPOTS ❧

❧ LINGERING SUNBEAMS ❧

1 2 6 7 8 4 5

MANUFACTURED BY BARNHART BROS. & SPINDLER.

VULCAN SERIES.

PATENTED B&S FEBRUARY 19, 1884. WESTERN TYPE F'DRY, CHICAGO.

30 A	LONG PRIMER VULCAN.	$1 95

PINCH CLEAN BABIES

LAMENTATION OF THE ESTHETICS

59 FATHER IS BALD NOW 74

20 A	PICA VULCAN.	$2 15

SNOW AND RAIN

BABCOCK PRINTING PRESS

89 SONGS OF LARKS 76

12 A	GREAT PRIMER VULCAN.	$2 50

UNITED STATES ROUTES

SUPERIOR COPPER-MIXED TYPE METAL

35 HARDBANK FOR BASHFUL 62

10 A	DOUBLE PICA VULCAN.	$3 85

LAUGHING MAIDENS

BEAUTIFUL DAYS OF SUMMER

76 SEEKING FLOWERS 53

6 A	DOUBLE GREAT PRIMER VULCAN.	$4 20

SACRAMENTO

SAINT ALBANY HOTEL

43 THERMOMETER

MANUFACTURED BY BARNHART BROS. & SPINDLER.

PATENTED INCLINED FACES.

---

50 a 30 A   NONPAREIL INCLINED BOLDFACE. $2.35

SHOOTINGSTICK, TWEEZERS & GAUGEPIN,
Practical Delineators of the Art Preservative of all other Branches of
Like Respectable Avocations,
No. 12,345 Stoneproof Alley, State of Wornoutprinterdom

50 a 30 A   BREVIER INCLINED BOLDFACE. $3.15

COMMERCIAL PRODUCTIONS
American Contributions to Food, and Industrial Arts
The Grain Growing
Sections of Illinois, Minnesota and Indiana 83

---

0 a 25 A   LONG PRIMER INCLINED BOLDFACE. $3.15

FROM THE PERIOD OF THE FIRST SAXON WRITINGS
Our Language has suffered a great many Changes in Orthography. The first writers, having no
Other Guide than the Ear, followed each
His own judgment. The natural result was Great Confusion of Style 123

---

30 a 20 A   PICA INCLINED BOLDFACE. $3.60

LIVES OF CELEBRATED FEMALE SOVEREIGNS
Containing the Memoirs of Semiramis, Queen of Assyria; Cleopatra,
Queen of Egypt; Zenobia, Queen of
Palmyra; Mary, Queen of Scots, &c. December 31st, 1882.

---

50 a 30 A   NONPAREIL INCLINED ANTIQUE. $2.75

INTRODUCTION OF NEWSPAPERS IN EUROPE
Nearly sixteen hundred years of our Christian Era elapsed
before a single Newspaper
Had appeared in Europe. Chicago, December 1, 1883.

50 a 30 A   BREVIER INCLINED ANTIQUE. $3.15

THE ART OF TYPE FOUNDING
The Italic Letter was invented by a Roman, by
the name of Aldus
Manutius, in or about the year of 1490

---

40 a 25 A   LONG PRIMER INCLINED ANTIQUE. $3.35

ACCURATE CALCULATIONS IN THE SCIENCE OF ASTRONOMY
The Origin of the Science of Astronomy is involved in Considerable Obscurity
Close Scrutiny of the Unaccountable and
Apparently Erratic Movements of the late Wonderful Comet in 1882

---

30 a 20 A   PICA INCLINED ANTIQUE. $3.50

QUARTERLY AMERICAN LITERARY REVIEWS
American Literature seems to be but little understood abroad; but at
Home its biting Sarcasm and Scintillating
Wit are read with great Pleasure and keen Enjoyment 1883

ILLINOIS TYPE FOUNDING COMPANY, 265 FRANKLIN STREET, CHICAGO.

AMERICAN SYSTEM OF
INTERCHANGEABLE TYPE BODIES.

GOTHIC, No. 3.

32A,64a, $3.10   NONPAREIL   SM. CAPS, 24A, $0.75

THIS RUSTIC SEAT IN THE OLD APPLE TREE WITH

Its o'erhanging golden Canopy of Leaves illuminate with hues

AUTUMNAL SHALL BE OUR PLACE OF REST 45

24A,48a, $3.50   BREVIER   SM. CAPS, 18A, $0.75

BENEATH US LIKE AN ORIOLE'S PENDANT

Nest from which the Laughing Birds have taken Wing,

BY THEE ABANDONED HANGS THY VACANT SWING 77

20A,40a, $3.30   LONG PRIMER   SM. CAPS, 12A, $0.70

DREAM-LIKE THE WATERS OF

The river gleam as a Sailless Vessel drops

ADOWN THE MURKY STREAM

18A,36a, $4.00   PICA   SM. CAPS, 10A $0.80

AND LIKE IT TO SEA AS

Wide and Deep Thou Driftest gently

DOWN THE TIDE OF SLEEP 22

12A,24a, $4.70   GREAT PRIMER   SM. CAPS, 8A, $1.10

STONE WALLS DO

Not Encircle the TOWN LOT

10A,20a, $5.95   PARAGON   SM. CAPS, 8A, $1.70

SUPERFLUOUS

Studied ARGUMENT 88

6A,12a, $6.60   DOUBLE ENGLISH   SM. CAPS, 6A, $1.80

HE DOES IT WITH A BETTER

Grace but I do it MORE NATURAL 66

5A,10a, $8.30   DOUBLE GREAT PRIMER   SM. CAPS, 5A, $2.55

HE CAME TOO NEAR

That came to BE DENIED 88

4A,8a, $9.85   CANON   SM. CAPS, 4A, $2.80

RIDES ON THE

And directs THE STORM

MARDER, LUSE & CO., TYPE FOUNDERS, CHICAGO.

AN APPRENTICESHIP SYSTEM.

BY BELL.

Much has been said and written about the need of some system of instruction which shall make thorough workmen of boys who enter American printing-offices to learn the printing business, and yet the importation of foreign laborers continues, to the disadvantage of native talent, except, perhaps, in the single item of display,—and even that may be accounted for by the tendency of novelty and a progressive taste, both in material and design, as against an extreme utilitarianism and a biased conservatism. That we do not, nay, cannot produce our own printers may be pardonably true; but another truth—that we do not concern ourselves about the boys, so long as we can get our good men from abroad—should spur us on to take active measures for the removal of what looks like a foundation for the taunts which we sometimes hear from foreign craftsmen. The English, Scotch and German apprenticeship systems, with proper modifications, would, with the assistance of the law of the land, secure all that is desired. How to bring the matter under the notice of the several state legislatures is, therefore, the main consideration. It is doubtful if success would crown any initial attempt in this direction, but that should not deter future efforts. If our legislators could be impressed with the necessity as the craft understands it, the road to a better condition of things would be comparatively easy.

But there is one feature about "binding" boys which might require much competent discussion, namely, the length of time requisite to thoroughly teach an apprentice what he ought to know. The short terms of three and four years,—though, perhaps, sufficient to acquaint him with the details of the department of his choice (as, for instance, the composing department),—must of necessity be inadequate to so establish him that he may become inured to his business as a printer in the sense of a devotee. And here is a secret, as well as a difficulty, which in the consideration of an apprenticeship system must not be overlooked. If an apprenticeship is not all the good it is intended to be, it would be worse than waste time to inaugurate it. A boy must become *devoted* to his trade, to the exclusion of other trades, whether there is "more money" in them or not, or else he will be an indifferent workman. On the other hand, the seven years term may, after due deliberation, be deemed too long, because the conditions under which an apprentice begins his trade in countries where indentures of apprenticeship are used are different from those which he would be required to subscribe to in this country. An examination of the following copy of a short form of English indenture will make this fact plain:

The words "lawful commands" (outside of large cities) cover a good deal of ground, and must be construed to mean a progress through the successive stages of the printing business something like this, the figures meaning the "terms":

1. Washing ink-tables, sweeping, sorting pi, delivering, collecting, and doing odd jobs around the office.

2. Sweeping, sorting pi, rolling small forms, delivering, collecting.

3. Straight composition, rolling in general, washing and caring for rollers, delivering, collecting.

4. Composition and coarse presswork, and the taking down, cleaning and setting up of presses; and, in many country offices, apprentices at this stage are expected to understand something about making rollers, as well as binding checkbooks, making tablets, etc.

5. Composition (book and display), fine presswork, and the charge of one or two subordinates.

6 and 7. Competent hand, under finishing instructions.

Opinions differ with regard to the justice of retaining a "competent hand" in servitude; but it is more than probable that, with a "little encouragement" betimes from his employer, the last two years of a boy's apprenticeship are the happiest days of his life, and that it is just this period, of the entire seven years of his novitiate, that fastens him down to his calling and "makes a man of him."

There is something, too, more than appears at first sight, in the age at which it is considered advisable, in Europe, to place a youth at his business by apprenticeship. The reason will not differ greatly on this side of the ocean. At fourteen, notwithstanding the importance which is, as a general thing, taken on, a boy is most impressible; he can be moulded and set to any calling for which he may by education or natural bent be qualified.

In any future disposition of the apprenticeship question, the placing of boys under specified instructors in our large offices should have ample consideration and be well provided for. If there is anything beyond unfitness that can cause a beginner to dislike his vocation, it is that of having "too many bosses." A workman who is competent to train a boy must be chosen; and he must be also the boy's master, to be successful with his pupil, who, in turn, will become a thorough craftsman, for "as the twig is bent the tree is inclined."

The sooner an apprenticeship system is established in America, the sooner will an end come to the influx of poorly-informed "typesetters" who stroll about our cities or hold situations that should be filled by competent workmen. The presentation of positive proof of ability in the form of apprenticeship indentures, together with a working card, or the production of the former as the *sine qua non* to the latter, would in due time result in a beneficial economy.

𝕿𝖍𝖎𝖘 𝕴𝖓𝖉𝖊𝖓𝖙𝖚𝖗𝖊 𝖂𝖎𝖙𝖓𝖊𝖘𝖘𝖊𝖙𝖍 That —— —— of —— in the County of —— an Infant of the age of Fourteen years or thereabouts by and with the consent of his Father —— of —— in the County of —— aforesaid testified by his execution of these presents doth put himself APPRENTICE to —— —— of —— in the County of —— aforesaid PRINTER to learn his Art and with him after the Manner of an Apprentice to serve from the day of the date hereof unto the full End and Term of Seven Years from thence next following to be fully complete and ended DURING which Term the said Apprentice his Master faithfully shall serve his secrets keep his lawful commands everywhere gladly do he shall do no damage to his said Master nor see to be done of others but to his Power shall tell or forthwith give warning to his said Master of the same he shall not waste the Goods of his said Master nor lend them unlawfully to any he shall not commit fornication nor contract Matrimony within the said Term he shall not play at Cards or Dice Tables or any other unlawful Games whereby his said Master may have any loss with his own Goods or others during the said Term without License of his said Master he shall neither buy nor sell he shall not haunt Taverns or Playhouses nor absent himself from his said Master's service day or night unlawfully But in all things as a faithful Apprentice he shall behave himself towards his said Master and all his during the said Term AND the said —— —— Printer his said Apprentice in the Art of Printing which he useth by the best means that he can shall Teach and Instruct or cause to be taught and instructed [*Finding unto the said Apprentice sufficient Meat Drink Lodging and all other Necessaries during the said Term]* paying to his said Apprentice [†*in lieu of Meat Drink Lodging and all other Necessaries during the said Term]* weekly and every week during the First year of his Apprenticeship the sum of —— during the Second year of said Apprenticeship the sum of —— per week during the Third year of said Apprenticeship the sum of —— per week during the Fourth year of said Apprenticeship the sum of —— per week during the Fifth year of said Apprenticeship the sum of —— per week during the Sixth year of said Apprenticeship the sum of —— per week during the Seventh year of said Apprenticeship the sum of —— per week AND for the true performance of all and every the said Covenants and Agreements either of the said Parties bindeth himself unto the other by these Presents 𝕴𝖓 𝖂𝖎𝖙𝖓𝖊𝖘𝖘 whereof the Parties above named to these Indentures interchangeably have put their Hands and Seals the —— day of —— and in the —— Year of the Reign of our Sovereign —— by the Grace of God of the United Kingdom of Great Britain and Ireland —— Defender of the Faith and in the year of our Lord ——

> **STAMP**

—— —— [SEAL]
—— —— [SEAL]
—— —— [SEAL]

Signed sealed and delivered in the presence of }
—— of —— in the County of —— }

N. B. The Indenture Covenant Article or Contract must bear date the day it is executed and what Money or other thing is given or contracted for with the Clerk or Apprentice must be inserted in Words at length otherwise the Indenture will be void the Master forfeit Fifty Pounds and another Penalty and the Apprentice be disabled to follow his trade or be made Free.

* For Indoor Apprentice.   † For Outdoor Apprentice.

SHALL WE HAVE AN APPRENTICESHIP SYSTEM?

AMONG the many social questions affecting the mutual interests of the employer and the employe, few outrank in importance that of securing an equitable and efficient apprenticeship system. The necessity for and the advantages to be derived from its adoption are so numerous and self-evident, so keenly appreciated, and so generally acknowledged, that the great leverage of popular opinion may truthfully be said to be almost a unit in its support. But in considering it from a standpoint of mutual advantage it is well to take into consideration the fact that the curb and rein must be judiciously applied, and the talent of the rising generation developed in consónance with the genius of the age in which we live. We have no sympathy with the idiotic claims on the one hand that the American boy is intelligent enough to learn his trade without the aid of an appenticeship system, or the pessimist view of impracticables that it is contrary to the spirit of our institutions and a curtailment of the rights of the citizen, nor with those who advocate the retention of the seven years' clause, on the other. Each is devoid of reason. The latter feature, to which reference has recently been made in our columns, may have been necessary a century ago, but today society lives, moves and has its being under very different auspices; and the American youth, feeling the vitalizing, quickening power of the times, will not and should not be bound by the iron-clad requirements and one-sided avarice of a feudal age.

It is essential, then, to strike the mean — the *quantum suffcit*— between these extremes. Let us illustrate by a reference to the printing business. The hand-press, with its roller and fly boy, which usually occupied the attention of the apprentice for a couple of years, has given place to the modern printing machine, which, by the application of steam, not only dispenses with the old-time agencies, but turns out more impressions in one hour than the hand-press did in fifty. We live in a progressive, utilitarian age, and the tendencies of these ever-increasing modern inventions is to lessen manual labor and add to the wealth and enjoyment of the human race; and so in other branches of trade. A number of the features which consumed the time of the apprentice, and added to the length of his indentures, have disappeared, yet these very changes demand a higher order of intelligence and a thorough system of education, which can only be secured by years of patient labor and examination. Scarcely a mail or exchange reaches us that does not bring some new development, some discovery dragged from Nature's exhaustless storehouse, some claim to a new process or an improvement on an old one — and the boy who is too indolent, or too indifferent to appreciate these facts, or who has not his ambition whetted by their discovery, is as certain to be the drone of the future as that cause precedes effect. Parents, as well as employers, have a responsibility in the premises which they cannot ignore, and in all efforts to make their offspring thoroughly proficient members of their craft, and establish a higher standard of American workmanship, we have a right to expect their hearty co-operation.

Whether the enactment and enforcement of such a system can be more easily obtained by legislation, or by the fiat of our national organizations, may be an open question. Taking into consideration the fact that no national law on the subject can be secured, and that if enacted by state legislation it would have to run the gauntlet of a veto from every governor who chose to poise as a constitution-stickler, we believe the simplest and most effective method would be secured by concerted action by our international unions, and when made law by custom it will be a comparatively easy matter to confirm the custom by law.

As we consider this subject one of vital importance, we shall refer to it again at greater length.

DON'T SPARE THE SORTS.

IT is a penny-wise and pound-foolish policy which is pursued in too many of our larger printing offices, viz.: to keep workmen continually skirmishing for leads, slugs, metal furniture or, in fact, sorts of any kind which are in general demand, instead of providing a supply sufficient for all ordinary emergencies. Were a strict account kept of the time thus needlessly consumed, and consequently lost, in *one year* it would be found to represent a sum sufficient to supply all legitimate demands. Let us take an every-day example for illustration: Suppose ten men *waste* — for that is the proper name to give it — an hour each day, a by no means extravagant estimate, picking from dead and frequently from live matter. In one month, twenty-seven days, at current wages, this would represent $81 ; in one year, exclusive of holidays, $960. Now let us see how far even $900 would go to furnish the necessary supplies at market prices: $200 of this amount would give 1,666 pounds of six-to-pica leads, $200, 2,000 pounds of slugs, and $500, 2,500 pounds of metal furniture — in the aggregate over three tons of the most useful and often required material to be found in an office. And yet, how many employers, both in this and other cities, would hold up their hands in holy horror were such a proposition made to them; while in twelve months they pay out for lost time more than is represented by this amount, with absolutely nothing to show for the expenditure. The advantages of having a well-stocked office in such material are generally appreciated when an important job, where it is required, is wanted in a hurry, or where competition narrows the margin of profit. When the supply is deficient, three or four compositors are generally sent to hunt sorts to keep half a dozen other compositors busy, thus entailing an extra cost, while in an office where the supply is equal to the demand, the services of the extras can either be profitably employed on other work, or else added to the working force on the hurried job. Now common sense suggests that labor performed under such circumstances must either be turned out at a loss or else an overcharge allowed for extra time. And where business is conducted on business principles, this disadvantage is certain to militate against the competing establishment which is blind to its best interests.

Another and very important objection against the chronic *picking* system is that it handicaps the compositor, because it frequently happens that no allowance is made for labor spent in this manner.

2-Line Pica Lady Text, Price $4.50.

No Job-Room Should be Without this Handsome Series.

$1234567890.

3-Line Pica Medallic, Price $4.60.

ORNAMENTAL CHARACTER

$135. Beautiful Design for Fine Job Work! 1884.

2-Line Pica Medallic, Price $3.95.

ELEGANT, ARTISTIC CONTOUR

£500. ~ Medallic! The Favorite Series with Artistic Printers. ~ 1884.

3-Line Nonpareil Medallic, Price $3.00.

THE BEAUTY OF YOUR WORK ENHANCED

$267. By a Judicious Use of this Impossible-to-get-along-without-it Letter! 1884.

MacKellar, Smiths & Jordan,   Nos. 606–614 Sansom Street, Philadelphia, Pa.

THREE LINE NONPAREIL ROMANIC.

8 a 5 A $4 25

BEYOND THE ROCKIES
Spotted Tail and Other Ring-Tailed Curiosities
$1,234,567,890.

QUADS AND SPACES FURNISHED WITH THIS FONT.

---

a 4 A   Two Line Pica Romanic. $4 25

OUR ROMANY RYE
The Noblest Roman of Them All
1234567

---

36 a 8 A 10 A—$6 50   Great Primer Card Gothic.   Without Small Caps—$5 25

THE PRINTING PRESS, there is a mighty power in the flap of its iron wing:
It finds its way to the Peasant's Bower, and the Palace of the King.

---

25 a 8 A 6 A—$6 75   Two Line Pica Card Gothic.   Without Small Caps—$5 00

FARMER, LITTLE & CO. take pleasure in presenting to their Patrons, and
the Craft in general, this Beautiful Gothic Series.

---

16 a 4 A 5 A—$8 60   Two Line Great Primer Card Gothic.   Without Small Caps—$7 00

Few are the Letters, but how Great is the Variety.
THOUGHTFUL MOMENTS

---

63 & 65 Beekman St., New York.   FARMER, LITTLE & CO.   154 Monroe Street, Chicago.

SIXTEENTH SEASON
CHICAGO COLLEGE OF DESIGNS
JANUARY, 1884.

QUADS AND SPACES FURNISHED WITH THIS FONT.

---

8 A   TWO LINE PICA SOUVENIR. $4 25

PACIFIC COAST
CALIFORNIA NATIONAL BANK
$54860

---

5 A   THREE LINE PICA SOUVENIR. $6 00

MONTANA
MINERS' JOURNAL
1886

QUADS AND SPACES FURNISHED WITH THIS FONT.

---

63 & 65 BEEKMAN ST., NEW YORK.   FARMER, LITTLE & CO.   154 MONROE STREET, CHICAGO.

10A,8A,20a   GREAT PRIMER OLD STYLE, No. 3. $4.90

EVEN THE LIGHT
Harebell Raised its head Elastic
1 2   FROM HER AIRY TREAD   34

10A,20a   GREAT PRIMER OLD STYLE ITALIC, No. 3. $4.45

HE NEVER SAYS
Foolish Thing and Never does
24   a wise one   65

8A,6A,16a   DBL. SM. PICA OLD STYLE, No. 3. $5.65

HAD SIGHED
To many, tho' he Loved
46   BUT ONE   95

8A,16a   DBL. SM. PICA OLD STYLE ITALIC, No. 3. $4.75

AS LIKE AN
Arrow swift he flew shot
4   Bowman strong   5

8A,5A,16a   DBL. PICA OLD STYLE, No. 3. $5.60

SMILES AT
Scars who never felt
24   THE WOUND   62

8A,16a   DBL. PICA OLD STYLE ITALIC, No. 3. $4.30

LATE AT
His Cross and earliest
2   at his grave   6

6A,4A,12a   DBL. COLUMB. OLD STYLE, No. 3. $8.65

OUR MEN
They are as true
2   AS STEEL   4

5A,10a   DBL. COLUMB. OLD STYLE ITALIC, No. 3. $6.75

EARTH
Have Bountiful
2 Hercules 5

3A,6A   CANON OLD STYLE, No. 3. $6.90

MUSIC
Hath Soul 2

3A,6A   CANON OLD STYLE ITALIC, No. 3. $6.95

TEARS
Angel like 2

3A,6A   FIVE-LINE PICA OLD STYLE, No. 3. $10.90
ORIGINAL.

MEN as Children 4

POSTER ROMAN, No. 3.

WITH SMALL CAPS.

28A,18A,165a, $12.48 — PICA POSTER ROMAN, No. 3. — Italic, 12A,24a, $3.10

SECOND GRAND PUBLIC SALE OF HOMESTEADS.

ON FRIDAY, DECEMBER 30th, 1885, at TEN O'CLOCK, will be sold to the highest bidder, all that Parcel or Parcels of Land known as Lots 58, 59, 61, 63 and 78, Block 3, Judson's Subdivision, S. E. ¼ of S. W. ¼. Lots will be sold separately or together with all the Improvements.

TERMS : One-third Cash, Balance Monthly Payments at Seven per

1 2 3 4 5 6 7 8 9 0 ¼ ½ ¾

20A,14A,120a, $12.48 — GREAT PRIMER POSTER ROMAN, No. 3. — Italic, 12A,24a, $4.30

PUBLIC NOTICE.

THE UNDERSIGNED, will sell, on MONDAY, JUNE 2, 1885, on the premises at ELEVEN O'CLOCK, precisely, the following described property, to-wit: The good-will and fixtures of a Sale, Exchange and Boarding

This property MUST BE SOLD as the owner is going out

1 2 3 4 5 6 7 8 9 0 ¼ ½ ¾ ⅓ ⅔

10A,6A,63a, $12.00 — DOUBLE SMALL PICA POSTER ROMAN, No. 3. — Italic, 10A,20a, $5.20

GRAND RALLY !

You are invited to attend a GRAND MASS MEETING to be held at the Wigwam, Tuesday Evening, November 23d, at EIGHT O'CLOCK,

Come Early and bring your Friends.

1 2 3 4 6 6 7 8 9 0 ¼ ½ ¾ ⅓ ⅔

10A,6A,40a, $12.00 — DOUBLE ENGLISH POSTER ROMAN, No. 3. — Italic, 6A,12a, $5.40

PEDIGREE.

HERMET, STALLION was sired by Chippewa Chief, foaled in 1882, is

Bright Sorrel, black points has Trotted

1 2 3 4 5 6 7 8 9 0 ½ ¼ ¾ ⅓ ⅔

13 A.   822.—Great Primer London.   Price $2.00.   10 A.   918.—Double Pica London.   Price $3.00.

SIBERIAN FREIGHT TARIFF ◄1234567890►

CHICAGO-FIJI MAIL ◄1234567890►

8 A.   821.—Double Great Primer London.   Price $4.00.

NEW ORLEANS ◄123456►

Patent Pending.

Daniel Spence,

Jennie U. Robinson,

Married;

Thursday, October 24, 1884,

Ilion, N. Y.

Dbl. Pica Clark Script.

Price $5.00.

11 A, 15 a.   817.—Double Pica Rubens.   Price $4.25.   7 A, 11 a.   919.—Double Great Primer Rubens.   Price $5.00.

WILLIAM & HAIGHT. Newport 123450

LATTIN-GREEN. Oshkosh 497

4 A, 6 a.   924.—5-Line Pica Rubens.   Price, $7 50.

5 A, 7 a.   915.—Canon Rubens.   Price, $6.00.

MEVRO! Nemot 5

LYONS. Silk, Lace 31

THESE FONTS MAY BE HAD OF ALL TYPE FOUNDRIES AND DEALERS IN PRINTING MATERIAL.

Boston Type Foundry,   -   -   -   -   -   -   -   No. 104 Milk Street, Boston, Mass.

NEW AND USEFUL STYLES OF TYPES

DESIGNED AND MADE AT

The COLLINS & M'LEESTER FOUNDRY

ALEX. M'LEESTER. — THOS. A. WILEY.

No. 705 Jayne Street, Philadelphia.

Complete Outfits, of Superior Quality, for Newspaper, Book and Job Offices.

Two-line Nonpareil Dart.   18 A.—$2.00

WONDERFUL ELECTRICAL EXHIBITION
EDISON, BRUSH AND OTHER DAZZLING LIGHTS

Three-line Nonpareil Dart.   14 A.—$2.75

AMERICAN IRON-CLAD LAUNCHED
CAPACITY 7658 TONS

Four-line Nonpareil Dart.   10 A.—$2.75

DELIGHTFUL FRAGRANCE

Six-line Nonpareil Dart.   5 A.—$3.00

STRIKING POINTS

Two-line Nonpareil Gothic, No. 6.   25 A.—$2.25

AUTUMN COSTUMES
COMPRISING 48523 GARMENTS

Four-line Nonpareil Gothic, No. 6.   10 A.—$2.85

PUBLIC GROUND

Five-line Nonpareil Gothic, No. 6.   7 A.—$2.90

OUTLANDISH

Six-line Nonpareil Gothic, No. 6.   5 A.—$4.05

SCREACH

Three-line Nonpareil La Belle.   5 A, 14 a.—$3.85

PRECIOUS STONES
Diamonds $2645 Saphires

Four-line Nonpareil La Belle.   5 A, 10 a.—$.60

MINISTERS
Preaching Earnestly

Six-line Nonpareil La Belle.   4 A, 7 a.—$7.50

LONDON SPECIAL
Dispatched by Atlantic Cable

PATENT PENDING.

THE PRINTING OFFICE.

"THE PROPER PROPORTION OF TYPE AND ARRANGEMENT OF A
PRINTING OFFICE."

THE following essay delivered at the last meeting of the Arkansas Press Association, by Mr. James R. Bettis, of the *Arkansas Democrat,* is replete with valuable suggestions, and will no doubt be read with interest and profit, alike by employer and employé :

Your essayist has been given a subject that pertains entirely to the practical side of our profession. "The Proper Proportion of Type and Arrangement of a Printing Office." Here is a topic upon which every printer — particularly he who has achieved the dignity of foremanship — has his own peculiar theories; theories in which he believes as firmly as in his own existence, and which he will never surrender before the assaults of any man's argument. It is not alone from the printer's standpoint that your essayist today presents his views for your consideration. For some four years he was a member of the great army of commercial travelers, and roamed unfettered the broad West and South in search of confiding printers whom he might inveigle into the purchase of type and paper. He has been a seller of types as well as a buyer, and has had occasion to study the subject from both sides.

In the starting of a newspaper office the very first thing your correspondent has found to be necessary has been money in bank; not indefinite promises of support, but spot cash, subject to draft. Taking the weekly paper as our especial subject, such being largely in the majority, the establisher thereof should have at least $25 for each column which his proposed journal is to contain; $30 would be better. This would give a twenty-eight-column paper (about the average in the state) from $700 to $850 to start upon. If a job department is to be included, add from $300 to $500 more. With this amount of money, judiciously expended, the publisher should find himself prepared to print his paper, and a moderate run of commercial job work, in good style. Better put up with less if the money is not on hand to put down for it. And your essayist will conclude these preliminary remarks with this record from his experience : given, a man attentive to his business and conducting it with a reasonable amount of good sense — starting out square with the type foundry and paper house — the result will be immediate and continued success. On the contrary, if a blanket mortgage is put on to keep things warm about the office, the way will be hard and weary, and the final result doubtful. In a traveling experience of four years, among newspaper men of twelve states, the essayist has never known the first of these conditions to produce failure, and he regards a well established newspaper, efficiently conducted, as quite as sure to yield an income as a government bond, and with this advantage over the bond, the longer it runs the more valuable it gets.

In selecting the body letter for your proposed newspaper, consider, among other things, your location; that is, don't try to run a nonpareil paper in a small pica town. It's ruinous. Determine as nearly as possible how much labor you can afford to expend upon each week's edition, and then select your size of sheet and body letter accordingly, taking care that your paper is one of the standard sizes carried in stock by all the paper dealers. In the opinion of your essayist, a good round face of bourgeois is "the noblest Roman of them all." The auxiliary publisher uses that size, as best adapted to the purpose. Bourgeois is plenty large enough not to tire the eye, and small enough to justify in a narrow column without bad spacing. Long primer with brevier for the advertisements, will do very well, and where the newspaper type is also required to do service in job work, these sizes are more convenient than bourgeois and minion. But stop at long primer! Small pica or pica in anything less than twenty-four ems measure is an abomination. There is neither good sense, good taste, nor economy in using large Roman to fill up a big sheet cheaply; much better cut down the size two or three columns and use suitable material.

For your display type, buy good, strong fonts of standard letter, and, above all things, buy only in series. Select, for instance, an extended, a medium, a condensed and an extra condensed series, and take four or five sizes of each. This will be much more convenient in use, and

present a more uniform and much handsomer appearance than the same number of fonts picked helter-skelter, no two of the same kind. Very large sizes and very heavy faces are neither necessary nor ornamental in a weekly paper. It is not the size of the displayed line that makes it appear prominent, but its comparative size. In a New York *Herald* advertising page, where nothing is allowed larger or heavier than nonpareil roman, a line of these caps, with plenty of white space about it, in a column "ad," catches the eye as quickly, and is quite as efficient in every way as a big heavy line in a page where other equally prominent lines are in use. If the rule of smaller faces of type and more white space in the display of advertisements were adopted, the result would be a greatly improved appearance in our newspapers, with no loss whatever of effectiveness to the advertiser. We suppose it is almost unnecessary to say that, of all things, fancy type is most out of place in a newspaper column. Your essayist always has a feeling of sympathy for a handsome fancy face in such a position. It seems to look up mournfully and say : " Please don't think hard of me, sir! I know I've no business here, but it's not my fault. I couldn't help it. I look very well in my proper place, sir; indeed I do ! "

Let your printing office furniture, racks, stands, etc., be strongly made, and convenient. Money spent in serviceable cabinets, dust-tight, is well invested. After your furniture is all together, stones mounted and cases in racks, a ten-cent pot of stain applied to the woodwork will add greatly to its appearance. And here let me say that neatness and taste in the furnishing and arrangement of an office are about as important elements as convenience, for they are essential to the material being kept in good condition. Employés will feel the influence of such surroundings, and gain a respect for neatness and order, which will exert a restraining power through all their manipulation of material and machinery. On the other hand, let slovenliness once gain a hold, and every quad box will soon be half full of odd sorts, every dark corner conceal a pile of pi, and everything in general be out of place and out of condition for use. Don't expect employés to themselves establish and carry out the rules of economy and order. In this matter more than any other it is "like master, like man," and the spirit you manifest at your desk will permeate and pervade the whole house.

Select a plentiful supply of leads, rules and furniture. These things do not cost much, and the want of them will be certain to cause great inconvenience.

In the selection of a job office you will, of course, be largely governed by the class of work you expect to do. There are, however, a few rules of almost universal application. First, buy your type in full series, and the plain faces, like Celtics, Gothics, etc., in strong fonts. That which is most valuable in the printing-office, and upon which the employer expends the largest amount of money, is time ; and the observance of these two points at the outset will save many an hour which the compositor would otherwise waste in hunting sorts or a line to just fit a place.

In this day of many type foundries, each making its own special patented faces, it is impossible to select a large job office from any one, and so maintain absolute uniformity of body in the various sizes; but this should be insisted upon in all the Romans and the plainer job type. Decide at first what foundry you will patronize, and then stick to it just as far as possible. Buy but little fancy letter, add desirable faces as they appear, and so keep up with the times. When a font of type is out of style and well worn, it is better to get rid of it, even as old metal, than to keep it around to waste the time of pressmen and injure the looks of fresher material. Don't put much money into many charactered and elaborate combination borders. They can only be used occasionally, and few customers are willing to pay for the time they consume. Provide plenty of labor-saving rule, brass leaders and furniture, and quads and spaces of all sizes. They are time-savers. Lastly, in this connection, your essayist would most urgently advise, do not buy second-hand material or presses unless you are buying out an office where the good-will of the business is a consideration. Worn-out type and dilapidated machinery are by themselves a dear purchase at any price.

For the rooms that are to be the abiding-place of a newspaper outfit, the chief essentials of central location, accessibility, plenty of room, and abundance of light, are, of course, first to be considered. These being secured, the arrangement of the office is the next thing our publisher has to consider. The business office and editorial room, which, in nine cases out of ten, will be combined, should be separate entirely from the printing-office proper. From the age of Gutenberg to the present the craft of printing has been somewhat of a mystery to the uninitiated. This mystery begets respect, which we should have a care to foster, not by deception, but by the prevention of unnecessary familiarity. A patron may enter the snug little business office of the publisher, and being impressed with his business-like demeanor and ready ability to answer the demands upon him, go away with a vague idea that there are three web perfecting presses and an army of compositors somewhere in the building, carrying on the inner work of the establishment, while, if he finds our editor at a dilapidated desk in one corner of the room, while the foreman, a girl and the "devil," evidently the whole corps of the concern, are killing time over the case in another corner, he will not go away very deeply impressed with the magnitude and importance of the business. And then there are many pieces of work in a composing-room that ought not to be exposed to the inspection of every chance caller, while the conversation of the editor's visitors will not assist the compositors to concentration of mind upon their work.

Furnish your business office suitably and tastefully, and keep it in order. It will be taken by the public as an index of the management of your whole business; and, if made especially attractive, will be one of the best advertisements you can have.

And in your work room, locate your stands, cabinets, stones, presses, etc., as near together as possible, without crowding. Extra steps in a printing-office consume that time that runs into money so fast. Of course, good light is a chief consideration, and warmth in cold weather.

It would be a pleasant task for your essayist to continue at further length the consideration of these and other topics kindred to the glorious "Art Preservative," but your committee, with due consideration for the time and patience of the association, set a limit to the length of this paper, which has now been reached. So I will say finally, brethren of the press, let these abodes of "the devil" be governed throughout, by the same great principle that rules the higher spheres, let "order be their first law," and with a well-selected office, conveniently arranged, and all paid for, go on to that glorious and enduring success which the conscientious editor, above all others, so abundantly merits.

A WORD WITH THE BOYS.

IT should be the ambition of every father to so train his sons that they will become honored and respected members of society, no matter what the nature of their calling or financial position. It should be the aim of every son to follow the counsels of his parent, so that these aims may be realized; and it is to the boy of today, the adult of the future, we have a word to say. Young man, your future depends in a great measure on your *own* conduct and exertions. Remember, there is no royal road to learning. If you commence life aright, with a laudable desire to learn and excel, to improve your leisure and avail yourself of every advantage offered, the chances are the goal of your ambition, if within the bounds of reason, will be reached. If, on the contrary, you prefer to become the teacher instead of the scholar; think it manly to insult your superiors in years and experience; affect a bravado where docility is requisite; refuse the advice of those who advise for your own benefit, it is safe to infer that you will become a recruit in the grand army which carries "*failure*" on its banners, and as you have sowed to the wind you will assuredly reap to the whirlwind. The great trouble with the rising generation is, that they want to be men before they are well developed boys; know, or rather *think they know*, all that can be taught, and that it is a sheer waste of time to commence at the first round of the ladder.

Let us take two boys, for example, entering the race of life together. One is attentive to business, puts his mind on his work, is anxious to learn, realizes that civility costs nothing, avoids slang, is courteous and obliging to his superiors, and in general makes his presence and companionship a pleasure. The other acts as though it is *smart* to be offensive, affects to know more, or at least, as much as his instructor, "don't care whether school keeps or not," chaffs at restraint, looks with contempt on details, who feels that if his employers are not suited he "can go somewhere else"; and it is safe to affirm that while the former will become master of his profession and an ornament to society, the latter will become a ne'er-do-well, a nuisance to himself and to everybody with whom he is brought in contact. Boys, think of this. You may laugh at our advice today. You certainly will not do so when regrets are too late; when lost opportunities cannot be recalled; and when you realize to your sorrow that what you now term the "good luck" of those more fortunate was the result of following the same line of policy which we have laid down, and which you affected to despise.

WHAT CONSTITUTES GOOD TYPE-SETTERS.

With the increase of typographic literature there has come a wider interest in typography. The eager quest for rarities in printing has attracted a broader, deeper attention toward the class of men trained to set the types that first revolutionized the world and now rule it. Intelligent, thinking readers of books and newspapers, too, have learned that composition is the most exacting work to which a man can be put, requiring, for anything like its proper performance, good eyes, nimble fingers, and a physical organism capable of sustained effort. Standing at case, handling type, is no weakling's effort, and no delicate or impaired physique can stand the strain for any length of time. Besides keenness of vision, steadiness of nerve, and tough muscles, the compositor must possess a general education above the average. Not a knowledge of the dead languages, nor a smattering of the modern ones; but he must be well grounded in the grammar of his own tongue. It is absolutely necessary that he shall be a master of orthography; faulty spelling is an unpardonable ignorance in a compositor, a defect that would disqualify him for his calling almost as completely as loss of eyesight. He must be as perfect in punctuation as in spelling. There are many authors whose names are written high up on the roll of fame, who did not know how to properly construct sentences, who trusted implicitly to the compositor for the proper punctuation of their work. Compositors, like poets, are born, not made; the man who has no natural adaptation for type-setting, will never be competent in the craft. All other requirements being equal, men of sanguine temperament make the best compositors. There is an ancient aphorism which says that red-haired printers are always the fastest. Perhaps this is true, because a sanguine temperament, as a rule, accompanies an inherently healthy physique,

---

NEW TYPE-SETTING MACHINE.

The type for the *Citizen* of Ilion, N. Y., was entirely set up by machinery one week lately and an edition of five thousand printed by the aid of electricity. The machine that set the type was invented by John L. McMilan of Ilion. His machine avoids all complications in mechanism, report says, and produces a method whereby the letters follow direct and uninterrupted courses in all their movements. Two operators are required, one to manipulate the keyboard and one to space out, while the distributer requires about one half the time of an attendant to feed the lines to it. The capacity of the machine is five thousand ems per hour, and no power other than the fingering of the keyboard is required. The distributer is automatic in its distribution of the letters, and has a capacity equal to the setting machine. The face of the type is not touched in its passage through either machine.

10A.
Quads and Spaces. 38c.

THREE-LINE NONPAREIL IDEAL

CUYAHOGA'S SHADY SUMMER GROVE EXCURSIONS

$2.85

7A

DOUBLE PICA IDEAL.

SYLVAN TROUT STREAMS PISCATORIAL

$3.00

5A.

THREE-LINE PICA IDEAL.

MILD & FAIR ROYAL

$4.80

THE H. H. THORP MFG. CO.   22   CLEVELAND TYPE FOUNDRY

Cleveland Type Foundry,
Cleveland, Ohio.

6A, 12a.

TWO-LINE PICA SIGNET SHADE.

DEEP THINKING Artists Enjoy Odd Conceits 1234567890

$5.00

4A, 8a.

THREE-LINE PICA SIGNET SHADE.

RECHERCHE Exquisite and Grand 1234567

$7.30

IN COMBINATION.

Leopard National Bank Received of $

THE H. H. THORP MFG. CO.   23   CLEVELAND TYPE FOUNDRY

IMPROVE THE LEISURE HOURS.

THERE is a great deal of unmeaning twaddle indulged in by a class of ne'er-do-wells concerning the hardships and misfortunes of life; men who seem to forget that it is not the possession, but the proper use of privileges, which avail aught in the struggle for the mastery. The brightest lights of our profession are those who have risen from the humbler walks of society. But they certainly didn't sit moping, as too many of our chronic growlers do, cursing society and bemoaning the fact that they were not born with a silver spoon in their mouths. Difficulties but nerved them to greater exertions and a determination to surmount them. They utilized every leisure hour; availed themselves of every opportunity to study and improve their minds. They watched and waited, and in the meantime qualified themselves for a higher plane, so that when the sought-for opening presented itself they were in a position to accept it, while sobriety, frugality and strict attention to business enabled them to achieve success and eventually reach the top round of the ladder. Of course, misfortune, in spite of all precautions and foresight, will become an occasional visitor; human judgment is fallible at best, yet conceding all that is claimed, it is too often the case that many, very many, of life's failures are the result of carelessness, neglect of business, incapacity or extravagance, of causes within instead of beyond control.

The great trouble is that workingmen, as a class, and printers are no exception to the rule, do not make the most of their opportunities. A few years ago, at the earnest request of several labor organizations, the writer of this article secured the services of two self-made men of national reputation, the announcement of whose names could at any time fill the largest auditorium in Chicago, to deliver, without money and without price, a series of lectures specially devoted to the interests of the producing classes. The admission fee was reduced to a nominal sum, barely sufficient to defray the necessary expenses, and though these entertainments were, through the kind courtesy of the press, gratuitously advertised, and the nature of the subjects announced in the workshops and factories, a beggarly array of empty benches greeted the men who had kindly devoted their time and energies for the benefit of those who had enlisted their sympathies. On the other hand a visit, the first evening referred to, to the dens of iniquity, misnamed "concert rooms," found them crowded with workingmen, for whom the filthy jest of the bedizened harlot had apparently more attractions than words of wisdom from one of the foremost orators in the land. In these rooms, filled with the fumes of poisoned liquors and viler tobacco, were to be found many of the very men who had been the most persistent in their demands for these series of entertainments, *because,* as they claimed, they were unable to pay seventy-five cents or one dollar. These same lectures, repeated by public request, at the usual prices, found standing room at a premium. Comment is unnecessary, though straws show which way the current runs. It is customary to point with pride to Benjamin Franklin, Horace Greeley and others who have graduated from a printing-office, but it is safe to affirm that if they had spent their leisure hours as a number of their fellow craftsmen do, their names would not now be held in the veneration they are.

In the race of life so-called *luck* has less to do with success than most people are willing to concede. Cause and effect go together. The Cunard line of steamships is frequently referred to as a lucky (!) line, but when it is taken into consideration that every timber in these vessels, from the keel upward, is inspected and tested by a special agent of the company, in fact, that everything that enters into their composition, from a bolt to the ponderous engine, is subjected to the closest scrutiny; that only skilled workmen are employed; that the officers are promoted grade by grade, capacity being the only test, after being subjected to a thoroughly practical training under the company's auspices; that the rules controlling the management of the vessel, crew, etc., etc., are iron-clad, and also that every detail is reduced to a science, it will be found that good management has formed an important factor in the *good luck* which has enabled the steamers of this company to plough the waves of the Atlantic for fifty years without the loss of a passenger or a pound of baggage.

There is too much theorizing and misdirected effort in life's struggle. Perseverance in the right channel will be found a far more valuable ally than luck, and a determination to make the most of what we have, a better augury for success than the vaporings of would-be philosophers. There was a fund of common sense in the rebuke of the ferryman on one of the Scottish lochs, who had for passengers, a stalwart clergyman and a dyspeptic, callow youth. A storm arising midway across, the gentleman of the cloth suggested that the dyspeptic help the boatman, while he invoked divine aid. "Nay, nay," replied the canny Scot, "let the little fellow do the praying; *you* can do better service by giving me a hand at the oar."

> "Honor or shame from no condition rise;
> Act well your part; there all the honor lies."

P·E·N·C·I·L·I·N·G·S

PATENT APPLIED FOR.

| 8A,24a | PARAGON PENCILINGS. | $6 65 | 8A,24a | PARAGON PENCILINGS, NO. 2. | $5 85 |

Yes·the·Year·is·growing·Old
And·his·eye·is·pale·and·bleared !
Death,·with·frosty·hand·and·cold,
Plucks·the·old·Man·by·the·Beard !

Through·woods·and·Mountain·Passes
The·winds·like·Anthems·roll;
They·are·chanting·solemn·masses,
Singing·"Pray·for·this·poor·Soul !"

And·the·Hooded·Clouds·like·Friars,
Tell·their·beads·in·drops·of·Rain,
And·patter·their·doleful·Prayers !
But·their·Prayers·are·all·in·vain !

Yes·the·Year·is·growing·Old
And·his·eye·is·pale·and·bleared !
Death·with·frosty·hand·and·cold,
Plucks·the·old·man·by·the·Beard !

And·the·Hooded·Clouds·like·Friars,
Tell·their·beads·in·drops·of·Rain,
And·patter·their·doleful·Prayers !
But·their·Prayers·are·all·in·vain !

There·he·stands·in·the·foul·weather,
The·foolish·fond·Old·Year !
Crowned·with·Flowers·and·with·Heather,
Like·weak·despised·Lear !

LONG PRIMER IN PREPARATION.

Mabel E. Cawthorn.

Daniel R. Knox.

PROVERBS AND THEIR APPLICATION.

IN all ages, from the time of King Solomon, if not for hundreds of years previously, and in all countries, proverbs have found a place in the daily intercourse of private and business life, and though very good things in their way, are liable, like other good things, to be abused or misapplied. Elderly persons are specially fond of instructing the young by means of proverbs, sometimes greatly to their disadvantage. To show how the misapplication of proverbs may mar the future of promising and aspiring young persons, more especially in connection with the printing profession, we propose to quote some of the most familiar ones and give examples of the results effected by their too literal interpretation.

It is well known that printers, as a class, are of a wandering disposition, changing from one situation to another, or from town to town and state to state, and the proverb,

"A ROLLING STONE GATHERS NO MOSS,"

has, no doubt, been often applied to a young man upon leaving his native place and setting out to see a little of the world. He is told that he had far better stay where he is known; that the chances for promotion are much better in a place where he has spent many years of his life than they would be in a strange city, and many other reasons are urged against his becoming a "rolling stone." All these reasons may be very plausible, and in some cases are very true, but there are other reasons why he should not stay in one place and "gather moss," if he feels disposed to roam.

The stone that is continually in motion acquires a polish, and if it possesses any value in itself will soon attract attention; whereas the stone that lies secluded and becomes moss-covered is liable to lose its identity altogether. It is hardly to be expected that a man who spends the whole of his life in a quiet printing-office, in a small town, can ever be such an experienced workman as one who has traveled from place to place, working in different offices, becoming acquainted with various styles of doing work, and gaining practical experience of such value as will fit him to occupy the best position it is possible to obtain. Because such a one is migratory in his habits, it does not follow that he will become the restless, shiftless, penniless tramp his advisers see with their minds' eye when they try to dissuade him from setting forth from his home. The majority of our most skilled workmen, who are occupying positions of responsibility in large printing-offices, are not those who have learned their business and spent the greatest part of their lives in them, but are those who have gathered knowledge, little by little, in various places, and have worked their way up from the lowest rung of the ladder to the highest. They are the stones that have roiled around, getting a rough place polished here, an excrescence knocked off there, a little rubbing against some other stone in another place, and so on until the beauty and brilliancy of their polish makes itself evident to those most capable of appreciating the same, and the future of such is an honored position as the reward of their exertions.

But we would not advise every young man to leave his native place and wander forth on the world's highway. All have not the same will power and determination to push their way in spite of difficulties. All have not the same qualities that go to make up a first-class workman. Two persons may set out at the same time; may both go through the same experiences; both have the same opportunity, and yet one will attain eminence, while the other fails grievously. It is a young man's duty to consider well whether it will be any benefit to himself to become a "rolling stone." He may have the desire to go forth and make acquaintance with other places and other things, and yet circumstances may be favorable to his remaining where he is, and the prospect good if he does so remain. Such a one we would advise to stay at home, and gather diligently such "moss" as is likely to come in his way. Still there are a great number who would be much benefited by a little rolling around, even though they might have to pay for the experience gained by so doing. All stones of any value lose a little in the process of being prepared for the position destined for them to occupy, but their loss eventually becomes their gain, in the increased value placed upon them because of their form or luster. So, though experience may have to be paid for, the gain in most instances greatly affects the outlay.

There can be little doubt that the author of the above proverb had in view the temptations to thriftlessness attaching to continual change of location, and desired to warn those given to change of the almost inevitable result of such action — poverty. At the time when this proverb was written or first spoken the means of locomotion were limited and expensive, and such advice would be apt to carry some weight with it. But in these days, when locomotion is rapid, easy, and comparatively cheap, it is almost counted an absolute necessity that one should travel, be it ever so little. Those who have been trained in small places, where the prospect of advancement is not very promising, naturally gravitate toward the large towns, where they hope to make a better living, if not to make a mark in their profession. They carry their experience with them, and while they are gaining knowledge may be able to impart some, thus benefiting the places they visit in return for the benefit they acquire. How many men whose names are familiar in our mouths as household words might possibly have been unknown to the world if they had not become rolling stones? Not only in literature, but in science, art, politics and other spheres of public life, there are many examples of the good resulting from a little ambition on the part of some to see the world, and do what they could for its advancement and their own. The pioneers in our own profession, that of the "art preservative," either from choice or necessity, were mostly "rolling stones" in one sense of the term, for they carried the knowledge of the art from place to place, and the consequence is that scarce a single corner of the earth is without a printing-press or a printer.

We would therefore say to all those who desire to avoid becoming moss-covered fossils, hidden away in some obscure corner, and who have a longing after better things, do not let the application of this proverb deter you from endeavoring to better your condition.

PRINTING-OFFICE CHARACTERS.

HUMAN nature is, no doubt, much the same the world over, though its gradual unfolding is largely dependent on surroundings and circumstances. Thus the characteristics of printers seem to be more positive and thoroughly developed, than in those in many other walks of life. This, we believe, arises from the nature of their calling, the tendency of which, unless a man is an incorrigible dolt, is to sharpen the faculties and bring to the surface certain traits which, under other auspices, would remain comparatively dormant. That these characteristics, which make or mar the comfort of their associates, are more observable in a printing-office than elsewhere, we think will be conceded by those who have given the matter due consideration. Perhaps among other characters the following may be recognized: First, there is the Professional Growler, who, go where he may, is always sowing the seeds of dissension; he is the Ishmaelite whose hand is against every one, and who always sees the dark side, but never the silver lining of the cloud. He was evidently born a churl, and will die the same; he possesses the unenviable faculty of making a mountain out of a molehill and magnifying every petty difficulty. If a set of rules he discovers are a pica too short, or the *very line* he wants a nonpareil too long, he growls like a bear with a scalded head, and annoys the entire office with his profanity, or the declaration that "life is a vast conspiracy at best"; and if he ever enters the happy hunting grounds, will continue to growl, for the reason there is nothing further to growl about.

Next there is the Cynic, generally as full of conceit and poison as an egg is full of meat, and who seldom, if ever, has a good word to say about anybody. He takes more delight in retailing than refuting a slander; watches the movements of an embarrassed stranger, criticises his job, and makes it his especial business to enlighten those who are willing to listen, as to its merits or defects; he always magnifies the mote in his neighbor's eye, but is blind to his own defects, and displays his *mal* propensities in a hundred different ways, repulsive to a true manhood.

Then there is the Wiseacre, who has evidently mistaken his calling, but is a firm believer in the doctrine that republics are ungrateful. He is a man who can discount the epidermis of a rhinoceros, and the cheek of a government mule; and knows more about business than the manager, more about finance than the owner, more about editing than the editor, more about presswork than the pressman, more about punctuation than the proofreader, who, in fact, knows all about everything except what he is paid to know, and in that direction his ignorance is generally as dense as Egyptian darkness, yet the *sang-froid* with which he dispenses his unsolicited opinions is as exhilarating as a Dakota blizzard.

Following is the Earthworm, the meanest of all created things; the man (!) who regrets that the day does not consist of forty-eight instead of twenty-four hours; who, when asked to contribute to a charity, no matter how worthy, invariably has a note to meet, a payment to make, or a mortgage to raise. He hopes there will not be a holiday on Washington's Birthday or Decoration Day, or, in fact, any day; a groveler who does not know what social or intellectual enjoyment means, and is determined, so far as in his power lies, that no one else shall know. His horizon is bounded by the dingy walls of a printing-office, and he thinks that man's chief end is to drudge three hundred and sixty-five days in the year, and *overtime* whenever the opportunity is presented. He munches his lunch in the workroom, and when the final summons comes, will, no doubt, seriously inquire if he cannot be allowed to make a full week before obeying it.

Nor must we omit the Castle-in-the-Air-Enthusiast, whose balance-wheel is out of gear, and who is always advocating some visionary project, and counting his chickens before they are hatched; whose schemes, like Jonah's gourd, grow up in a night and perish in a day. He *knows* that the man who establishes a paper or job office in such and such a locality will coin money, even though his past experience with similar surroundings have ended in disastrous failure. Nothing disheartened, however, he intends to make another break, which, it is safe to predict, he will succeed in doing, and also in breaking somebody else before he again reaches *terra firma*.

Next we have the Sycophant, the apology for a man, who is afraid to say his soul is his own, and never expresses an opinion until he is sure it is in consonance with the views of the powers that be, and who invariably concurs, in chapel meeting or elsewhere, with the foreman's views, whether he knows what these views are or not. Yet it will be found advantageous to keep an eye on this *genus homo*, because a man who is false to his own best interests, is very apt to be false to the interests of others, and employers are shrewd enough to take such obsequious services at their true value.

Then last, but not least, we have the redeeming feature, the True Man, who has a kind, cheery word and helping hand for everybody, especially the stranger; when asked a courteous question, he invariably gives a courteous reply, no matter who the interrogator may be, and receives all favors with thanks, as he is ever ready to grant one. He is studiously avoided by the scandal-monger, and is never connected with a dirty, unmanly action; always minds his own business, and leaves other people's severely alone. And it is almost needless to add, that as a rule, the manhood and qualifications as a printer, of such a representative, generally correspond.

Reader, the counterparts of some of these characters may be found in every job and newspaper office. Which is the man who commands your esteem, or the one whose traits you prefer to emulate?

GROTESQUE.

AMERICAN SYSTEM OF INTERCHANGEABLE TYPE BODIES.

BREVIER.	18A, 36a, $2.80	18A, 36a	LONG PRIMER.	$3.40

HE SHALL NEVER FIND OUT

Fit mate, but Such as some Misfortune brings Him

Or mistake, or whom he Wishes

Most shall seldom Gain through her Preverseness

62   But shall see her Gained.   47

AS YON SUMMITS SOFT AND FAIR,

Clad in Colors of the Air, which to Those who

Journey near Barren, Brown and Rough

8   Appear, still we Tread   6

12A, 24a	PICA.	$2.55

IF SHE LOVE HIM, HELD BACK BY LOVING PARENTS

Or his Happiest Choice too late Shall meet already Linked and Wedlock   864

10A, 20a	COLUMBIAN.	$4.10

THE COBBLER SANG FOR HIS HEART

Was light as he Watched his Child at Play, but a Shadow   62

10A, 20a	PARAGON.	$5.60

HE WORKS IN MOODY DESPAIR, THE

Sun never Shines and Nobody Smiles in the Glo   2

6A, 12a	DOUBLE ENGLISH.	$6.35

HE NEVER LIFTS HIS HEART

Or eyes, he never Breathes Prayer   3

FANCY GROTESQUE.

PATENT APPLIED FOR.

12A, 24a	PICA.	$2.65	10A, 20a	COLUMBIAN.	$4.15

TIC TACK, THE LONG HOURS

The Hammer drops from his Hardened

2   Hand, as the Tears   5

THE SUMMER NIGHT

His Garret under the Tiles 3

10A, 20a	PARAGON.	$5.70

HE MENDS AND PATCHES ON AND ON

He scarcely Ponders why, or whether the Winter   5

6A, 12a	DOUBLE ENGLISH.	$6.35

IT IS TO FAIR PARADISE

From the Gloom that Fall beneath   4

IN the present issue will be found a communication from a "Type-Founder," presenting the "other side" of the question on the adoption of a standard measurement, and justice compels the admission that he presents some plausible arguments to sustain the position he assumes, that the difficulties in the way of its adoption are almost insurmountable. But while conceding this, there are certainly "two sides" to the question, we think that many of the objections urged would disappear before united and intelligent action. The subject, however, is one worthy of attention, and we shall refer to it at length in our next.

STANDARD MEASUREMENT.

To the Editor :   CHICAGO, January 22, 1885.

In the December issue of THE INLAND PRINTER, an editorial, under the caption of "Standard Measurement," in my opinion, places the type-founders of the United States in a false position. The subject at issue—the adoption of a universal standard—has received long and careful attention from type-founders, not only in Chicago, but throughout the country, and the more its feasibility has been investigated, the more formidable have the difficulties attendant on its adoption appeared, and I verily believe that the *selfishness* of which you complain will, upon investigation, be found to be the same selfishness which would deter ninety-nine business men out of a hundred from making a similar venture.

Let us first look at the expense entailed—a very important item. What right have you to expect that business firms will sink from $75,000 to $100,000, without a guarantee that they will be in some manner recouped for this outlay, merely to *accommodate* their customers? Human nature is not constructed on such a philanthropic principle. What is to be done with the vast amount of material on hand, which would be practically tabooed by the adoption of such a standard? How many establishments are able to afford such a loss in the first place, or are willing to commit *hara kiri* in making the attempt? Will the printers of the United States agree to bear a *pro rata* assessment to help tide over the emergency? No, sir; they will not, and if the change were effected under this hallucination, the type founders would find they had been trusting to a broken reed.

Another question is, whose standard should be adopted, or, what is the likelihood that firms represented would agree to vote for any other than their own? But for the sake of argument, let us concede that this objection is waived, and the standard of a certain foundry adopted. What then? In what position would such action place the non-successful contestants? Would it not give a virtual monopoly of the trade, for the time being, at least, to one firm at the expense of all the others? Would it not mean a boom for one establishment, and ruin to those who were left, or if not ruin, at least disaster? Is it at all likely that the successful firm would be willing to share even a part of its profits with its less fortunate competitors? If asked to do so, would not the reply be, "Gentlemen, upon what is your claim based? The change does *not* affect us. The fact that you have agreed to recognize our standard in future, and shape your actions accordingly, is, to our minds, *prima facie* evidence that you conceded that standard to be the correct one. Why, then, should we be required or expected to pay tribute to anybody, under such circumstances?" What answer would you give, Mr. Editor, to such a statement, that would be likely to prove effective?

There are type-founders doing business today which have at least ten million pounds of material, representing a certain standard, in offices scattered over the length and breadth of the country, a large proportion of which is comparatively new, or at least good for many years' service. Now, is it reasonable to expect that all establishments using the non-standard type would discard it for new material, simply because a new (to them) standard had been adopted? I think not, and if they persisted, as they no doubt would, in ordering all needed sorts to correspond with the material on hand, would such action not necessitate the running of two distinct foundries, the keeping of a double set of books, and the incurring of many other incidental expenses? I insist these are pertinent questions, and are worthy of due consideration.

While I do not claim a patent for the idea, I believe that a great many of the annoyances of which you complain, arising from the present system, or rather lack of system, would be removed, if western printers would patronize western type-founders, and eastern printers order from eastern founders, more largely than they do at present. I have not presumed to cover all the points which have presented themselves to my mind, but I think I have said enough to convince both yourself and readers that there are two sides to this important question.

A TYPE-FOUNDER.

STANDARD MEASUREMENT.

IN our last issue there was published the communication of a "type-founder," in which exception was taken to the editorial on standard measurement, which appeared in the January number of THE INLAND PRINTER. While conceding that the "other side" of the question was presented in a very able and forcible manner, we think many of the difficulties referred to are more imaginary than real, and that the ultimate advantages sure to accrue to all parties interested from its adoption, would more than compensate for any temporary embarrassment or loss incurred in securing it. Summed up, the principal objections urged are the expense such change would entail, the undue advantages the successful contestant would have over the non-successful competitors, and the petty annoyances experienced both by founders and customers during the period of transformation.

First, then, as to the question of *expense*. This would consist principally in the furnishing of new matrices, because the material remaining after the "multiple standard" system had been discarded, could be recast at comparatively little extra cost; and as the change would be a gradual one, when once effected would be for all time, and would change for the better, the relationship existing between type-founder and printer, we again insist that this bugbear of expense would lose half its terrors, and that the end would justify the means.

To the objection that the adoption of a common standard would redound to the benefit of one firm at the expense of all non-successful competitors, we reply that such objection could be modified, if not entirely removed, by a definite understanding arrived at *before* a decision is reached, making the award *conditional* on the acceptance of the terms laid down. Let us assume, for the sake of argument, that an average service of four years could be obtained from the fonts now in use belonging to the discarded standards. What is the proportion of offices which have been supplied exclusively from one foundry to those which have been supplied from half-a-dozen. Not one in six—aye in ten. If this is true, and investigation will prove we are within the limit, is it not rational to suppose, that all but material of the accepted standard would be *gradually* weeded out, and that at the end of three years, every foundry in the United States would be equipped for the change. In the interim, however, all orders sent through the different foundries could be filled at a discount sufficient to enable them to meet part of the expense involved, by which means each establishment would be enabled to retain the patronage of its own customers. Certainly there is nothing chimerical in this proposition; nothing that does not commend itself to a sense of justice. Again, what is to prevent all foundries, after a given date, replenishing the various offices on the same principle that a sewing machine factory accepts its discarded productions in part payment, for the sake of replacing them with the "latest improved?" That sacrifices would have to be made, we admit, but what reform has ever been inaugurated without sacrifice? A few months ago the representatives of the maritime powers assembled in Washington for the specific purpose of agreeing on a common longitude, to be universally recognized and adopted, in place of each power continuing to be a law unto itself; and although such action involved sacrifices both in money and national pride, the world at large is the gainer by the change. A few years ago a number of our connecting western lines were built on the broad gauge, and others on the narrow gauge system, and although the transfer to a uniform gauge entailed expense and labor, the accommodation of the traveling public, from whose patronage their income was derived, amply compensated for the change. The same argument applies to the substitution of the new translation of the Scriptures for the old, and in fact to a score of examples which might be cited.

With regard to its *practicability*, we refer to the fact that the largest type-foundry in the United States has two distinct standards, and one of the best known of our western foundries, has, within the past three years, discarded its old time standard, and adopted one modeled on an entirely different system. This change no doubt cost time, money and anxiety, but *if* one establishment has been able to initiate and successfully carry out such a movement on its own responsibility, what is to prevent a combination of type-founders carrying out a similar programme, where a common standard is recognized?

The concluding suggestion that the true remedy is for the eastern manufacturers to supply the eastern printer, and the western foundries to supply the western printers, bears too close a resemblance to the Chinese-wall-of-exclusion idea. Under our proposed system, the country at large would furnish the market, and the ability to supply it would depend on the ability to compete, and in such a contest we feel satisfied the West would have no cause for alarm.

Having referred to the objections urged from a type-founder's standpoint, let us again briefly look at them from a printer's. It is certainly no exaggeration to claim, that at least seventy-five per cent of all the printing-offices in the United States have drawn their supplies from different type-foundries, and this too, not from choice, but from necessity. And it is equally safe to affirm that each of these foundries represents different standards in such a degree that it is well nigh impossible to utilize the product of one foundry (especially in body type) with the products of another. How often, even in offices where railroad work is a specialty—when fifteen or twenty rate sheets and time tables are kept standing—no matter whether set in long primer, brevier or nonpareil, will cases labled *bastard* be found? Now, what is the significance of this word? It simply means that the type so labled does not line or justify with the fonts in general use in the office; that a "bastard" table must be corrected with "bastard" type, or a botched job is sure to follow; that half-a-dozen tables may require half-a-dozen changes; and no matter how much care is taken, sooner or later fonts used under such circumstances will eventually become mixed. In regard to body type, the evil complained of is still more observable, and pieing more likely to occur.

CHASTE DESIGN.

---

25 a 10 A   PICA CLEMATIS $3 20

GRANDEUR & MAGNITUDE

Good Display of Chromos and Statuary of Great

92 Ancient Masters 48

20 a 8 A   GREAT PRIMER CLEMATIS $4 00

MORRIS & RANSOM

Elegant Pictures of Siege of Paris

43 Slow but Sure 65

General Western Agents for Babcock Air-Spring Presses.

Superior Copper-Mixed Type

BARNHART BROS. AND SPINDLER

Great Western Type Foundry

1115-1117 Fifth Avenue   Chicago,........................188

---

14 a 6 A   DOUBLE PICA CLEMATIS $5 70

NORTH WESTERN AGENTS

The Beautiful Stars   Shine Very Brightly

34 Travelers of Indiana 58

CIRCLET  SERIES.

20 A	NONPAREIL CIRCLET	$2 15	15 A	BREVIER CIRCLET	$2 00
	HISTORY OF GREAT CRIMES			WOOD AND METAL	
	EARLIEST AGES OF THE PRESENT TIME			BEAUTIFUL BATTLE GROUNDS	
	1234567890			1234567980	
	STARLIGHT MOUNTAIN EXCURSION			PHOTOGRAPH GALLERY	

Circular  Gothic.

Caps, 12 A $2 35 L. Case, 20 a $2 00   GREAT PRIMER CIRCULAR GOTHIC   Sm. Caps, 12 A $1 80

THERE WAS A LITTLE GIRL AND SHE HAD

Little Curl Right In The Middle Of Her Forehead And When She

685 WAS GOOD SHE WAS VERY GOOD BUT WHEN 472

Caps, 8 A $2 05 L. Case, 14 a $2 15   DOUBLE PICA CIRCULAR GOTHIC   Sm. Caps, 8 A $1 60

HAPPY WEST POINT CADET

Gymnastic Exercises Carefully Conducted

72 BOULEVARD SPORTS DELIGHT 39

8 A 8 A   DOUBLE PICA GROTESQUE GOTHIC $3 65

BEAUTIFUL SEASIDE SUMMER RESORT

58 ELEGANT BATHING COSTUMES 46

 Myrtle Script.

Office Barnhart Bros. & Spindler,

M'f'rs Celebrated Superior Copper=Mixed Type

115=117 Fifth Avenue.   Chicago, February, 1885.

Dear Sir: Our Superior Copper=Mixed Type has fairly

Miss B. Myrtle Script.

Mr. S. Copper Mixed.

Married
Miss Beautiful Myrtle Script,
to
Mr. Superior Copper Mixed,
Thursday Afternoon, October twenty third,
eighteen hundred and eighty four,
Chicago, Illinois.

no successful rival in market.   We shall continue to main=

tain the high standard of excellence which it has always

enjoyed, relying for support upon the class of customers who

prefer and are willing to pay fair prices for the best material.

Soliciting your further orders, we remain

Yours Respectfully,

Barnhart Bros. & Spindler.

MYRTLE SCRIPT.
Double Pica, 60a 10A $11 25
    "   "   30a   5A   6 00
Great Primer, 80a 12A   9 00
    "   "   40a   6A   5 00

Radial  *Italic.*

40 a 8 A $8 85 GREAT PRIMER RADIAL ITALIC 20 a 4 A $4 50

Bethany, Mo., Dec. 20, 1884.

Barnhart Bros. & Spindler,

 Gentlemen:--After eighteen months use of a Babcock Country Press, I can say I am more than satisfied with it in every respect. I believe it to be the best press made for the money, or sold as a Country Press.

     Yours Respectfully,

       F. H. Ramer.

Artistic  *Script.*

PATENT APPLIED FOR.

Battle Creek, Mich., Nov. 14, 1884.

Barnhart Bros. & Spindler,

 Gentlemen:--The longer we run the Babcock Press purchased of you, the better we like it. It works noiselessly; the Tapeless Delivery and Air Springs work to perfection. Every one admires the ease with which it runs, as also the many Convenient Improvements, such as the Eccentric Throw=off for throwing the Ink Rollers off the forms, the handy Lock=up, Cover to Air Springs, etc. The Press does more than you claim for it.

    Very Truly Yours,

      M. E. Brown.

DBL. PICA ARTISTIC SCRIPT.
 20 a 7 A $7 00

This Script is cut with less slope than any others of same character: the letters overhang comparatively little, consequently will prove more durable.

TWO EXTREMES.

THE furnishing of a printing-office, the judicious selection of material adapted to legitimate requirements of the trade, combining the useful with the beautiful, the beneficial with the indispensable, requires the possession of sound judgment, good taste, and practical experience ; and it is to the lack of this judgment, or rather its exercise, that a number of our business failures may be attributed. There is so much to tempt in the specimen book of today, such a bewildering maze of new designs, etc., that ambition is apt to get the better of discretion and the superfluous secured at the expense of the necessary. Nor yet should it be a matter of surprise that mistakes of this kind occur. The beginner realizes that successful competition can only be obtained by keeping pace with the demands of the times, and that the reputation to be made depends on the efforts put forth. It is to this desire to excel, and the means to gratify it placed within his reach that we are indebted for the wonderful improvements recently made in the art preservative both in the old and new worlds. But here lies the danger of *overdoing*—on the one hand, counterbalanced by the croak of the old fogy on the other, that it is best to leave well enough alone—extremes which should be equally avoided.

In Great Britain, for example, a very gratifying progress has been made in the past five years in the character of the work turned out, and yet in many quarters there is vast room for improvement. A short time since we received the programme and advertising sheet of the Coventry (English) races, set up and printed in a manner which was a standing disgrace to the firm producing it, and which would not have been turned out in an American frontier village. Surrounded by an ancient apology for a border, which had apparently seen its best days when printing was in its infancy; containing the same heavy uninviting Roman faces and old-fashioned battered texts, which have long since been discarded by progressive printers; rules which represented a valley and hill panorama; with body-type dirty, weary and worn, composition slovenly, and presswork to correspond, bearing altogether a remarkable resemblance to a severe attack of small-pox ; every advertiser in its columns had just cause of action for damages against its publisher. Yet we have no doubt this same individual, who disgraces his profession, would have resented a kind suggestion as to the propriety of replenishing his establishment with type and material which had seen the inside of a foundry during the last decade, as impertinence, begotten of extravagance. The example cited may have been an exceptional one, though further investigations in the same quarter do not warrant this conclusion. This conservatism, run to seed, can only be left to the care of an overruling Providence and the operation of Nature's laws, accompanied by the hope that his successor may have imbibed a little of the progress characteristic of the latter part of the nineteenth century.

On the other hand, while it cannot be successfully denied that the average specimens of the typographic art turned out by American type-founders and American printers are far ahead of those of all competitors, too many of them show the absence of " intelligent application of knowledge to use." In fact, some of the more pretentious, issued as artistic designs, are only a travesty on good taste, and a direct insult to every feature of a truly artistic character. Before us lies a professional card from an establishment which prides itself in turning out artistic work, its only special feature being the employment of the grotesque mongrel-shaped specimens to which we have referred, and which should never be allowed to enter a printing-office. Some of them look as though mutual disgust had taken possession of the several characters, and that each one was trying to squirm out of the company it was in, while others seem to be laboring under a violent attack of inflammatory rheumatism. They are not only offensive to the eye, but expensive to the pocket, and for all practical purposes worthless to the office. Their use reminds us of the antics of a Feejee chief arrayed in epaulets and shirt, parading before his taterdemalions, desirous of impressing them with his importance without realizing the proper use of the toggery he exhibits. Of course ideas of beauty vary. Some specimens of the *genus homo* believe that their appearance is improved by the insertion of a ring in their nasal appendage ; others by splitting their ears, the use of ochre or palm oil; others again by tattooing or the disfigurement of their features, though it is safe to affirm that such ideas would not receive an indorsement at the hands of the American people if submitted to a popular vote. And yet not more grotesque or out of keeping with good taste are many of the " designs " now issued by our type-founders, if they can be dignified with that term. Novelty without merit has no claims for popular favor. Idle curiosity may prompt us to look at a five-legged calf or a two-headed colt, but we would be very apt to leave them with the impression that such freaks are *not* an improvement on the ordinary productions of nature, and this argument can be carried to its legitimate conclusions in regard to the " fearfully and wonderfully made " designs with which the trade is now being flooded, much to its detriment.

All this straining after effect in forbidden pastures is without warrant, because there are many standard series which by a judicious embellishment, can be made a thing of beauty and a joy forever—whose ornamentation furnish a limitless field to the true artist—which have heretofore been neglected, whose use and appropriateness would be universally recognized, and whose services would *not* be confined to a job produced once in six months. Between the extremes of an ultra conservatism on the one hand, and an ultra radicalism on the other, it may be difficult to draw the line accurately at the " happy medium " where useful practicability ends and extravagance begins, but when type-founders learn by experience that burned children dread the fire, that printers are no longer carried away by the latest craze, that utility and neatness have superior attractions to useless artistic (?) extravagance—they will be more apt to cut the coat to the cloth ; business will become more profitable and failures of less frequent occurrence, and then the only question will be whether the man who designed them, the founder who cast them, or the printer who invested in them displayed the least common sense.

"STANDARD MEASUREMENT."

THE articles which have recently appeared in THE INLAND PRINTER under the above title have awakened a new interest in a subject near to the heart of every practical, progressive printer, who realizes the truth of the old maxims, that "Time is money," and that "Whatever saves time, lengthens life."

We desire to call particular attention to what has already been accomplished in this line by wide-awake, energetic type-founders, who know what printers need, and endeavor to promptly provide for their wants. The present situation is admirably stated in the following article from the last *Printers' Specimen Sheet*, published at Baltimore, Md., by John G. Mengel & Co., type-founders.

"THE SYSTEM OF JUSTIFIABLE TYPE-BODIES.

It is to the Interest of every Practical Printer to buy his Type cast on the System of Bodies that are Justifiable to Pica.

Ever since the introduction of the "American System of Interchangeable Type-Bodies," inaugurated by the enterprising firm of Marder, Luse & Co., Chicago, Ill., over ten years ago, printers have come to understand and appreciate this beautiful system more and more, until at this time there has been such a demand upon the old foundries that all the leading ones have found it necessary to work toward the ultimate adoption of the same as fast as it is possible to do so. There are now eight foundries casting all their type on this system throughout, and all the foundries in the country are casting their larger type, borders, ornaments, etc., on this system. The system, in brief, is, that beginning with a unit called "American," the twelfth of a pica in thickness, it advances by this unit until pica is reached, when the unit of advance becomes a sixth of a pica, because of the bodies being twice the thickness of those between nonpareil and pica. The nonpareil, brevier and pica are unchanged, and match those bodies as cast in the Johnson Type-Foundry; but the so-called bastard bodies — minion, bourgeois, and small pica — are now made as useful as any others, because they are parts of a common-sense system. The bourgeois is the 9-point body, or three-line excelsior of the Johnson Type-Foundry; the great primer becomes three-line nonpareil; the two-line great primer, three-line pica, or 36-point. Each body has the number of its "points" cast in the side — nonpareil 6, minion 7, brevier, 8, etc. — and

the bodies will work together in the same manner as their numbers will arithmetically: 8 and 6 added equal 14, or English; 14 and 8 added equal 22, or two-line small pica.

The beauty of the system is apparent to any printer who will give it a few moments' thought, because he can see how certain he is to find a body which will justify with two others, and how easily he can find a lead or rule to justify a line of small caps of one body with a cap letter of a larger body. All of our leads, rules, etc., are made up to the same system throughout, and a job that with the old bastard bodies would be almost impossible, is now rendered comparatively easy to execute. Printers who have not already availed themselves of this system will find that it will pay them to become acquainted with and understand the simplicity of the same, and they will use no type but such as are cast on this system."

As the beauty of this scheme becomes apparent on the most casual investigation, the question naturally arises, "Why was not this adopted before?" The expense and difficulty attending a change so radical, have for many years deterred type-founders from carrying the same into effect, who otherwise would gladly have been pioneers in this reform. The Chicago fire, which seemed at first a heavy calamity to Marder, Luse & Co., has really proved to them a blessing in disguise. By reason of the destruction of their molds and matrices in the fire of '71, a new start was rendered necessary, thus enabling them to make this important change with less trouble and expense than it would incur upon other founders, and also decreasing the liability of mixing the old with the new bodies.

It is hardly possible in this day of new designs for fancy and display letter, for any one firm to meet the requirements of the live job printer from type, ornaments, etc., of their own manufacture. But this need not hinder anyone from adopting and easily carrying into effect the "American system of Interchangeable Type-Bodies," while at the same time giving room to the latest novelties in the Art Preservative. By using a little care in the selection of sizes, a printer who has selected his outfit in accordance with the admirable system invented by Marder, Luse & Co., can now add such fancy faces from other foundries as he may desire, and still preserve the harmony unbroken.

MARDER, LUSE & CO.

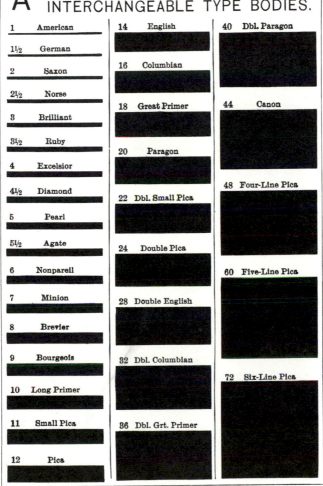

AMERICAN SYSTEM OF INTERCHANGEABLE TYPE BODIES.

1	American
1½	German
2	Saxon
2½	Norse
3	Brilliant
3½	Ruby
4	Excelsior
4½	Diamond
5	Pearl
5½	Agate
6	Nonpareil
7	Minion
8	Brevier
9	Bourgeois
10	Long Primer
11	Small Pica
12	Pica

14	English
16	Columbian
18	Great Primer
20	Paragon
22	Dbl. Small Pica
24	Double Pica
28	Double English
32	Dbl. Columbian
36	Dbl. Grt. Primer

40	Dbl. Paragon
44	Canon
48	Four-Line Pica
60	Five-Line Pica
72	Six-Line Pica

⇒ PROGRAM. ⇐

PATENTED APRIL 11 1882.

32A,64a   NONPAREIL PROGRAM. $3.50

LOOKING • AT • THIS • USEFUL • LETTER, • PROCLAIM

⇒ TO MILLIONS UNBORN, ⇐

The Pen is Mightier than the Sword; its bright scintillations

of wit, humor, geniality, sympathy, pathos

☆ * • ⇒ ⇐ ⇒ 1234567890 ⇐

24A,48a $3.85   BREVIER PROGRAM.   18a $1.00

THE FROST IN ITS BEAUTY LIES OVER

⇒ THE * MEADOWS * GREEN ⇐

⇒ Like Down newly shaken from Winter's Young ⇐

Wings; The Sun is Ascending, and

☆ * * ⇒ ⇐ ⇒ ⇐ * ⇐ ⇒ ⇐

24A,48a $4.75   LONG PRIMER PROGRAM.   18A $1.20

UNSOPHISTICATED CUBS TRANSFORMED INTO MODELS

⇒ GENTILITY * IN * APPAREL * AND * SWAGGER ⇐

Awkward Rehearsals of Slang and Dubious Witticisms till Pupils become Adepts to

1234567390   ☆ * * ⇒ ⇐ ⇒ ⇐ * ⇐ ⇒ ⇐   1234567890

18A,36a $4.00   PICA PROGRAM.   12A $1.15

WASHINGTON PLUMS STUNG IN THE LEGISLATIVE

⇒ SWEET GARDEN AND BITTER FLOWERS ⇐

⇒ Respectfully Dedicated to Elegant Triflers and Daintiful Donothings, are

1234567890   ☆ * ⇒ ⇐ ⇒ ⇐ * ⇒ ⇐ ⇒ ⇐   1234567860

12A,24a $4.55   COLUMBIAN PROGRAM.   8A $1.15

UNBOUNDED CAPACITY EVER FILLING

⇒ WONDERFUL BRAIN BASKET ⇐

Written some Sixteen Thousand Years Ago 23456784567890

☆ * * ⇒ ⇐ ⇒ ⇐ * * ⇒ ⇐ ⇒ ⇐

8A,16a $4.50   GREAT PRIMER PROGRAM.   6A $1.30

⇒ WHORTER * VANDERHUYDEN ⇐

BANKER AND BROKER

⇒ Mount * Washington * Square, * Springfield, * Illinois. ⇐

386 ☆ * ⇒ ⇒ ⇐ ⇒ * Cº 942

6A, 12a $4.60   DOUBLE PICA PROGRAM.   4A $1.30

⇒ TRUSTFULLY * CLINGING ⇐

TO * THE * GREAT * HOPE

Of all Kindred Blessings in the Twilight

93 ⇒ ⇐ ☆ ⇒ ⇒ ⇐ Cº ⇒ ⇐ 27

8A. 16a. DOUBLE SMALL PICA ACADIAN, No. 3. $3.70

ARCADIAN HAPPINESS
The Peaceful Cultivation of Floral Beauties
1234567890

6A. 12a. DOUBLE ENGLISH ACADIAN, No. 3. $4.50

THE QUIET READER
Never Mixes in the Street Brawls
1234567890

4A. 8a. DOUBLE GREAT PRIMER ACADIAN, No. 3. $5.65

TRANQUILITY
The Peace of Contentment
123,456,00

Cleveland Type Foundry,
Cleveland, Ohio.

12A. GREAT PRIMER ACADIAN, No. 4. $2.50

UMBELS OF BLOSSOMS
WITH GARLANDS OF FOLIAGE
GENTLY WAVING

10A. DOUBLE SMALL PICA ACADIAN, No. 4. $2.85

FRUITS & GRAIN
GATHERED OR GLEANED
IN AUTUMN

8A. DOUBLE PICA ACADIAN, No. 4. $3.10

DECORATIONS
SNOW, FROST & CO
GRAINERS

Ladies Hand Script No. 2.

PATENT APPLIED FOR.

Card Fonts, 6A, 16a, $3.75 GREAT PRIMER. Job Fonts, 10A, 75a, $10.75

The Farmers & Drovers National Bank, of Bloomington, Illinois

Capital, $1,600,000.   Surplus, $755,000

Transact a General Banking business   Accounts of Individuals, Corporations and

Banks received.   Collections throughout the United States

National State and County Bonds on hand.   Commission Orders filled

Exchange drawn on England, Scotland, Ireland

Card Fonts, 4A, 12a, $4.50 DOUBLE PICA. Job Fonts, 8A, 50a, $12.55

Buckingham, Struthers, Lyons & Co.

Invite inspection of their Large and Varied stock of Art Goods

Unequalled Assortment of Fine and Curious Pieces

Complete in Every Department

Modern and Antique Cabinet Work, Marbles, Bronzes, Etc.

158 and 160 Yonge Street, San Francisco

Card Fonts, 3A, 8a, $4.75 DOUBLE COLUMBIAN. Job Fonts, 5A, 25a, $10.80

(Incorporated 1835.)

Erie & Ontario Fire and Marine Insurance Co

Accumulated Capital, $800,000.

Hazardous Risks taken at Lowest Premiums

All Fonts complete with Figures.   Spaces and Quads with all Sizes.

A GOOD WORD FOR THE BOYS.

THERE is a class of men to be found in many establishments, printing-offices included, whose actions seem to prove that they deem it a test of manhood to browbeat and insult a boy; who seldom have a kind or encouraging word to say of any beginner, and have evidently forgotten they were once youngsters themselves, or ever tried the patience of their superiors. We have known men who had a chronic habit of placing all the blunders at the door of the apprentice, and making him a scapegoat for their own shortcomings. It is needless to add that the influence of such individuals is *mal*, and that a boy raised under these auspices is almost certain to prove a failure both as a man and a workman. And the reason is obvious; a learner who is continually rebuffed, reminded that he is worthless, is very apt to determine he may as well have the game as the name. Constant belittling destroys ambition and begets indifference. Reproof, which, administered in the right spirit and under certain restrictions, would be productive of beneficial results, becomes monotonous and has a tendency to make him listless and hardened. Boys have pride and feelings, different tempers and temperaments, the same as men, which have just as much right to be studied. A certain mode of treatment, successful in one instance, may prove a failure in another, but it is safe to assume that a kindly remonstrance or a word of encouragement will accomplish more, no matter what the disposition, than constant denunciation. Let doubting Thomases give it a trial and their skepticism will disappear. Kindness is the key which unlocks the door to the human heart, and many boys who have been given up as incorrigibles under the " browbeating" process, have become bright and shining lights under the influence of kindly reasoning.

Many men, and foremen, too, who complain of the listlessness manifested by apprentices and their lack of authority over them, have themselves to thank for the result. *Too much familiarity breeds contempt.* Instead of pursuing a steady, even course, their discipline goes by fits and starts. They will make boon companions of them one day and curse them the next, and, as a result, lose all restraint, as well as respect, because in order to secure it they must first respect themselves. Boys make mistakes. Men, who are but "children of an older growth," do likewise. Some boys, like men, make more mistakes than others, and require to be more frequently corrected. But there is a wrong way of doing a right thing. Besides, many a misdeed is placed at the door of a boy, who, though guiltless, must depend on future developments for acquittal. The following example is one of many which we could cite to sustain our position. A case of new labor-saving rule had been obtained for a particular job, and strict injunctions given against *cutting* it under any circumstances. A few weeks after, it was discovered that several lengths had been destroyed. Inquiry failed to develop the criminal, but one individual was positive that the *boy* was the guilty party, which charge he strenuously denied. A watch was kept, and, in a few days after, it was proven that the man who had falsely charged the apprentice with the crime was the culprit himself. And, if we are not much mistaken, there are several readers of THE INLAND PRINTER who will admit that this is *not* an exceptional case.

Boys have sins enough of their own to account for — sins of omission and sins of commission — without charging them with misdeeds of which they are innocent; and there is no surer method to destroy a boy's usefulness or prospects than to make him the pilgarlic on all occasions, no matter who the offender may be.

Curses and ill treatment, like chickens, too, come home to roost. Some years ago, there was employed in a certain office in this city, an errand boy, part of whose duties it was to sweep out the counting and editorial rooms. One day a cowardly bully, employed on the editorial staff, dropped a sheet of manuscript, and, being too lazy to pick it up, called to the boy to do so, who, being unfortunately defective in his hearing, failed to understand what was required. Beckoning the boy to him, the brute raised his foot and kicked the little fellow insensible. When he had sufficiently recovered, he was taken to his widowed mother's home, where he was confined for several days. The widow was placated by promises which were never fulfilled. Years rolled on. The boy grew to be a stripling, the stripling to be a handsome young man, who had improved his opportunities, and in the course of time secured the responsible position of paying teller in one of our banking institutions. The incident had apparently been forgotten. One morning, however, a gentleman (?) presented a check for payment, and after the money had been counted, he asked the teller if he had not seen him before. "Yes," he replied, "you *have* seen me. I am the same fatherless boy you kicked insensible *seventeen years* ago in the ——- office. *I will remember you till I die*, and if you think you would like to repeat the experiment, I will be very glad to accommodate you." The feelings of the inquirer, under this explanation, may be more easily imagined than described.

In dealing with boys there is but one safe course to pursue. Tell them firmly and kindly what they are expected and required to do, but don't blow hot and cold at the same time. Talk to them in a proper spirit, and always take a fitting opportunity to reprove or admonish. No benefit accrues to either party by needlessly wounding their feelings. If a proper question is asked, don't snap like a coach dog. *Civility costs nothing.* Don't tell them they are lazy hulks, boobies or good-for-nothings. They can be answered properly or shown "how to do it" in less time, and, unless they are ingrates, they will duly appreciate your efforts. Be positive, be kind, be consistent. Secure their *confidence* and *esteem*. Inculcate a manly spirit. Tell them what they *may* become if they improve their opportunities — what they *will* become if they neglect them. Enforce respect for age and responsibility, and in ninety-nine cases out of a hundred such treatment will secure far better results than a system of bullying, bickering or browbeating. Try it.

PROVERBS AND THEIR APPLICATION.

"HONESTY IS THE BEST POLICY,"

YET we should be honest from *principle*, not as the result of policy. It sometimes needs great effort to be strictly honest in these rushing, grasping times, when the sole aim of many appears to be to follow the advice contained in the admonition: "Get money, honestly if you can, but get money." No method by which they can make a few dollars appears to be dishonest or dishonorable, and the result is an amount of sharp practice, and the adoption of schemes or following out of plans which leave the honest business man very little prospect of making headway under the fierce competition which he has to meet. To secure orders, some will even agree to fill them at prices which barely cover the cost of material, leaving nothing for labor or profit; and one instance came under our observation where a large order for printing was booked at a price *less than the actual cost of the stock required.* Can we wonder at the number of failures daily recorded when such a loose manner of transacting business is indulged in? The evil resulting from such a course is not confined to those who eventually have to give way beneath their heavy burden of responsibilities, but is felt by others who are endeavoring to conduct their business on sound principles. A person or firm who gets an order filled under such circumstances as above stated will naturally expect others to fill similar orders at the same price, and when told it cannot be done, will produce invoices to show that it has been done; and if the honest trader would like to get the order, he must make a large reduction in the percentage of profit that should accrue to him in order to secure it. The "cutting" business, about which so much has been written in all trade journals, cannot be cried down too much. It is dishonest in every shape or form, and ends disastrously to all who engage in it. The workman has to suffer, because the employer cannot afford to pay him the full value for his labor; the employer has to suffer because he does not get a legitimate profit on the order, if he gets any at all; the dealer who supplies the material for filling the order often suffers by having to accept a compromise of forty or fifty cents on the dollar (that is, if he is very fortunate); and even the customer, who gets the greatest benefit, suffers, because in the future he will consider he is being cheated when charged a fair price for his work by other parties.

Besides the cutting in prices, other cutting processes are indulged in by those who are making haste to get rich, such as giving short count, poor stock, slovenly workmanship, etc. Though the customer may be considered "green," and expected to take anything that is foisted on to him, he will learn by experience that he is not being fairly dealt with, and the result will be that some other printer gets his work and Mr. Smart gets a bad name. To earn a good reputation is far better than to have a big banking account and be known as a man of sharp practice, and to gain such reputation it is necessary to be strictly honest in all things.

Not only should employers be honest to their cus-tomers, but also to their workmen, by paying a fair price for the labor of all, and to each according to his qualifications. Employes should be looked upon and treated as men, and not as so many pieces of machinery, made use of only because they are the necessary means to the attainment of particular ends. They need to be treated with respect and have confidence placed in them, and employers who so treat their workmen reap much better results from their labor than those who do otherwise. Confidence begets confidence, and when a man knows that his employer is honest toward him, he will do his best to be honest to his employer.

Honesty should be a cardinal principle in the workman. When paid a fair rate for a day's work see that you put in a good, solid ten hours or nine hours as the case may be. Some excellent workmen have the failing of being just a little late in showing up at their work; only a *little*, say five or ten minutes each day, but just calculate how much time it amounts to in a year. "But," they may say, "we are 'docked' for the time we lose." That may be, yet still your lateness is liable to be a source of loss to your employer. A press may be kept idle, or a job delayed because your part of it is not ready on time, and trouble and vexation ensue. Then again, the few minutes spent in private or frivolous conversation with your fellow workman, while the work is standing still on account thereof, is a loss to the employer, just as much as if the few cents represented by those minutes were taken from his pocket. It may appear somewhat harsh to look at the matter in this light, but it is none the less just; and if the position of employer and workman were reversed, he who thinks it no great matter to lose a few minutes would be the first to deprecate the same action on the part of his employé. Others are careful to put in full time, but are careless in handling material, and waste which might be avoided is the natural consequence. Various other matters crop up in the course of a day's work which may be a source of gain or loss to the employer according to the way in which they are treated by the workman. In all things "study to show thyself a workman that needeth not to be ashamed."

A workman should be honest to himself. His labor is the only capital he possesses, and he has the right to get the best value he can for it. If he is content to sell his labor for much less than it is worth he is not honest to himself or to his fellow workman of equal merit, for he is lowering the standard of value which should be placed upon labor. There are times when it is not possible to get a high rate of wages for labor, such as general depression in business or overstocking of the labor market; but when circumstances permit, the very highest rate obtainable should be sought for. In the printing business, for instance, many first-class workmen are laboring in "rat" offices for from ten to twenty-five per cent less wages than they could obtain in "fair" offices. By working for such low wages they are not acting uprightly to themselves or their fellows, whereas if they made a determined stand they could obtain a higher rate of pay, because their employers know it would be a hard matter to get others like them to fill their places.

PATENT PENDING

8a 4A   TWO LINE PICA GEM. $4 00

Messrs. Stitchem and Proudfit

Artistic Gents Furnishers   Correct Wedding Outfits

Direct Importations

1457 Threadneedle Circle, North Side

At Home   New York City   Reception

6a 3A   THREE LINE PICA GEM. $5 50

Annual Masonic Festival

Installation Ceremony   Sumptuous Banquet

Excellent Programme

Musical and Literary Entertainment

To   236th Appearance   Dr.

NEW YORK:
65 BEEKMAN STREET,

FARMER, LITTLE & CO., TYPE FOUNDERS,
NEW YORK AND CHICAGO.

CHICAGO:
154 MONROE STREET,

✳MONUMENTAL✳ORNAMENTED.✳

10 A.   GREAT PRIMER MONUMENTAL ORNAMENTED. $4.50

✳BILL·OF·FARE·✳
✳NEW·YEAR'S·1885·✳

8 A.   TWO LINE PICA MONUMENTAL ORNAMENTED. $6.00

✳ANNOUNCEMENT✳
✳BOYS·A·FISHING.✳

5 A.   THREE LINE PICA MONUMENTAL ORNAMENTED. $6.50

✳B.·&·O.·R.·R.·✳
✳CAR·NO.·81·✳

MG & CO.
PATENTED, Dec. 30, 184.

➤JOHN✳G.✳MENGEL✳&✳Co.✳
✳MONUMENTAL✳TYPE✳FOUNDRY.✳
➤31✳GERMAN✳ST.✳BALTIMORE,✳MD.✳

✳AMERICAN✳BANK✳NOTE.✳

5 A. 10a. DBL. GRT. PRIM. (3 LI. PICA.) AMERICAN BNK. NOTE. $7.50
3 A. 5 a $4.50

EXHIBITION

Lake Michigan Yacht Club.

Chicago, Ilinois.

Office of

Boughton

Type Founders & Dealers.

FOR SALE BY ALL TYPE FOUNDERS AND DEALERS IN PRINTERS' SUPPLIES GENERALLY.

Marder, Luse and Company

Type Founders, 139 and 141 Monroe St., Chicago, Ills., U. S. A.

Parisian Black.

AMERICAN SYSTEM OF INTERCHANGEABLE TYPE BODIES.

10A,30a   NONPAREIL. $3.00

How sleep the Brave, who sink to rest
By all their Country's wishes blest. When Spring,
With dewy fingers cold,
Returns to deck their hallowed mold, she there
Shall dress a sweeter sod than Fancy's
Feet have ever trod.
49   By fairy hands their knell is rung   63

8A,24a,   BREVIER. $3.25

Beneath those rugged Elms,
Yon yew tree's shade, where heaves the Turf
In many a moldering heap, each
In his narrow cell
Forever laid, the rude Forefathers of the
51   Hamlet Sleep   94

8A,24a,   LONG PRIMER. $4.00

The Curfew tolls the knell of parting day; the
Lowing Herd winds slowly o'er the lea; the Plowman homeward plods his
Weary way, and leaves the World to Darkness and to me
Ring out the Grief that saps the Mind
For those that here we see no more; ring out the feud of rich and poor,
18   Ring in Redress for all Mankind   76

6A,16a,   PICA. $3.25

Trust no Future, howe'er Pleasant, let the dead Past
Bury its Dead; act - act in the
Living Present! heart within and God o'erhead. Lives of great men
All remind us we can make our lives Sublime,
5   And, departing, leave behind us Footprints on the   8

5A,12a,   GREAT PRIMER. $4.90

Diligently Revised and Compared
Dealers in Tapestries, Bronzes, Porcelains and Antique
Silver, Marbles, Tall Clocks, Etc. Etc.
8 Great Easter Musical Festival Promenade 7

5A,12a,   DOUBLE SMALL PICA. $5.60

Board of Trade Speculations
The Belvidere Patent Fire Escape Company
Capital, $250,000
Art, Ships, Commerce and Agriculture

GERMAN AND SWEDISH ACCENTS ARE PUT UP WITH THIS SERIES.

LARGE vs. SMALL JOB OFFICES.

THE question is frequently asked, which affords the best opportunities for producing first-class workmen —large or small job offices? Like most questions of a similar character, the answer must be—a great deal depends on surroundings and circumstances. A firm which employs, or rather retains, good men, and prides itself on its reputation and imprint, is very apt to turn out good work, no matter whether ten or fifty printers are employed, while establishments which think more of quantity than quality, or care little about its merits or defects, so long as it is gotten out, are as likely to produce inferior work, irrespective of the number of employés. We believe as a rule, however, all things being equal, that the greater number of our first-class job compositors have been graduates from the smaller offices where fine commercial work is a specialty, rather than from the mammoth establishments, where the sea of heads resembles a cotton-field, because more care and attention have been bestowed on the training of the apprentice.

And yet it should not be forgotten that the position to be occupied by the workman depends more on his own aptitude and exertions than any other agency—no matter how favorable or disadvantageous the surroundings. You can drive a horse to the water, but you cannot make him drink. So it is not the possession, but the proper use of advantageous circumstances which places a workman on the top round of the ladder. A third-class printer may graduate from a first-class office, and *vice versa*. There are boys, and men, too, whose name is legion, now working at the business, who will never become proficient, even if they live to the age of Methuselah, simply because they have mistaken their calling. Years of vexation and mortification would be saved to many if the question was brought directly home, in time: "Am I adapted to, or really in love with my chosen profession?" And if the answer is unsatisfactory, as egregious a blunder is committed by continuing to follow it, as the woman makes who ties herself for life to a man under the belief that she *may* love him *after* the marriage ceremony has been performed. The experiment *may* prove successful, but it is a dangerous one at best. This adaptation can be illustrated in a hundred different ways. Let us take two men, for example: give both the same job, with the requisite instructions, the material furnished, and the facilities being equal. One comprehends its nature at a glance; it is mapped out in his mind's eye, or, if necessary, its main features are penciled, and in due course of time is completed in accordance with the preconceived design. The other stumbles along as best he can. He has formed no definite idea. Line after line is tried and changed; nothing suits him; he meets with a hundred stumbling-blocks, and when the job is finished there is neither judgment, symmetry nor workmanship displayed. And thus the one remains master of the situation, commanding a premium for his labor, while the other, as a makeshift, ekes out a hum-drum existence. We remember a remark made by the wife of one of America's most celebrated landscape painters on a somewhat memorable occasion. After he had finished what he considered his masterpiece, and scores of friends had congratulated him on his triumph, his better half, who was present, was asked if she was not proud of a husband who could turn out such a picture? "I think I would rather examine the merits of a new cooking range," was the reply. Think of the yoking of two such individuals, who evidently had not a sympathy or sentiment in common with each other; and yet, not more incongruous was such an alliance than is the selection of a profession too frequently made by those who have neither the taste, the ability, the patience nor bent of character to successfully master its details.

Our advice then, to those seeking it, is: Don't marry in haste, to repent at leisure. Be thoroughly satisfied, in the first place, you can bring to the discharge of your duties those qualifications necessary to achieve success. If you are satisfied you are moving in the right groove, adopt "Excelsior" as your motto. Adhere to your determination through evil and through good report, and the result will show the wisdom of your resolve. Select, whenever practicable, for your field of labor an office which has an established reputation for turning out first-class work and keeping good material; which employs say from six to a dozen hands, and where the so-called department system does not prevail. By so doing, you will be far more apt to acquire a thorough, practical insight into the various branches of the business, and receive the benefit of the advice of your superiors than by being dependent on the assistance of those retained at one class of work from January to December, and who have not the same opportunities to instruct, even if they had the desire. Avail yourself of every opportunity to learn; improve your leisure hours, but above all things, don't become a bore. Exhaust your own resources before you ask assistance, but when asked, let no false modesty stand in your pathway. *Think* and study. *Study* and think. And as an incentive to this line of conduct, remember, a proficient job printer is, as a rule, master of the situation; that his services are always in demand; that he is in little, if any danger of becoming a tramp, provided his habits correspond with his ability. We have seen first-class wrecks, but their visits are like angels, few and far between. Remember, also, a good workman not only commands respect, but commands good wages. His opinion is not only respected, but solicited, and that the job compositor who has the brains to suggest, the ability to design, and the hands to fashion the evidences of his skill, is the man who will continue to be regarded as the expert representative of his craft, who need fear no innovation, and for whom the automatic typesetter can have no terrors.

CRITIC.

PATENTED JUNE 2, 1885.

16A, PICA. $3.00

THE CHARLES F. ZIMMERMAN BOOT & SHOE M'F'G CO.

THE·CELEBRATED·PHŒNIX·HAND·AND·MACHINE·SEWED·SHOES.

17   HEAD OFFICE : CALUMET B'LD'G, CHICAGO.   46

12A, PARAGON. $4.75

THE·HOHENLEN·WILSON·HODGE·CO.

MANUFACTURERS·OF·YANKEE·NOTIONS,·ETC.

159·PENNSYLVANIA·AVENUE.

CHICAGO,·ILL.

8A, DOUBLE ENGLISH. $5.30

THE·DAY·WAS·WANING

AND I KNEW NOT WHAT THE NIGHT

36 WOULD BRING FORTH. 14

BOUGHT OF MARDER, LUSE AND CO.

TYPE·FOUNDERS,

TELEPHONE NO. 1349.   139 AND 141 MONROE STREET.

SPACES AND QUADS WITH PARAGON AND DOUBLE ENGLISH.

To align the Double English and Paragon sizes of this Series, place a 6-to-pica lead at the bottom of the Paragon and a Nonpareil slug at the top. The Paragon and Pica will align in the same way. To align the Double English and the Pica, place a 3-to-pica lead at the bottom of the Pica and a Pica slug at the top.

PROVERBS AND THEIR APPLICATION.

"ALL THAT GLITTERS IS NOT GOLD."

IN view of the fact, that many tempting offers are held out to persons possessing a small capital which they are desirous of investing to the best advantage, a very strong warning is needed to put such on their guard against being induced to part with their hard-earned savings by the representations of unscrupulous persons, whose only object is to get money without giving an equivalent therefor. In many of the daily papers have lately appeared advertisements somewhat after this style :

"WANTED—A good job printer, to take charge of small office. One with $200 or $300, willing to take an interest in the business, preferred. Address X. Y. Z., etc."

Now here is an opportunity for the ambitious printer who has saved some money to realize his long cherished hopes of becoming a "boss," which he could not otherwise accomplish on account of his limited capital, and he thinks he sees an avenue for increasing it by becoming a working partner in an already established concern. Here is the opportunity for which he has so long been watching and waiting, and the prospect is so enchanting that he is captivated thereby and puts himself in communication with the advertiser, who is perfectly willing to explain the reason why such a small capital can be invested to so great advantage. Trade has been dull, and creditors are pressing for the payment of a few small accounts ; but orders sufficient to keep them employed for some time are on hand and future prospects are good. When the present needs are met nothing is to prevent them making money rapidly, and by working hard and keeping expenses down the foundation of a flourishing business can be laid. Other inducements are held forth, such as only these experienced schemers can advance, and the would-be "boss" gives up a good situation in a responsible firm, and casts in his lot with the man who is going to give him so much for almost nothing.

For two or three weeks everything is lovely. The new partner gets the salary agreed upon, which is paid him out of his own money, and then the senior partner skips out and leaves him in possession of a plant which is heavily mortgaged, and without the means to pay current expenses ; the sheriff steps in and seizes the stock-in-trade to satisfy the claims of creditors, and he, who a short time ago was in possession of what to him was a small fortune, finds himself penniless and without a situation, a very much sadder, yet wiser, man. This picture is not overdrawn. Many printers now working at the case can testify to its reality, and the exposures of such schemes, as sometimes related in the daily papers (which yet continue to advertise the very schemes they denounce) should be sufficient to open the eyes of the unwary. What looked like a nugget of pure gold proves to be the veriest dross, and ofttimes of the most brassy kind. At the present time, when business all around is dull, tempting offers such as the above look as handsome as the gilded fly does to the trout, who snaps at it only to find that it brings sure destruction. The glitter is only on the surface, and takes but a very little time to wear off.

To a far-seeing man who calculates the chances, and goes to the trouble of working out a little profit and loss account, with his small fortune as the basis to work upon, is not liable to be caught in such a trap ; but where we meet one of this kind we can find a dozen of the other who are anxious to snap up whatever comes across their path.

There is another matter which possesses a great deal of glow and glitter for a good many excellent workmen, and that is the ambition to be a foreman. It is a commendable trait in a man's character that he should be anxious to raise himself above his fellows and command instead of being commanded ; and where one possesses the necessary qualifications to fill such a position he would be neglecting his duty if he did not endeavor to secure it if an opportunity presented. But some only think, "What a nice thing it must be to be a foreman, and tell others what to do, and walk around and see that they do it." To them a foreman is a king, or president, with absolute right to do or say what he pleases, whose authority must not be disputed. They do not consider that he has to bear the whole responsibility of the department over which he presides ; that he has to calculate and plan the best means of handling the work that comes to him ; that he has to keep track of all work that is being done, so that he may, whenever called upon to do so, be able to state just how far it is toward completion, or how long a time it will be before it is completed ; that if anything goes wrong it is he who is called to account by the employer for the wrong-doing. They do not think that often when they are enjoying their rest after the day's labor the foreman is wrestling with some unsolved problem that has cropped up in the course of the day's work, and which he has to settle before the following morning. And not only this, but he has to govern his temper with an iron will to keep the peace in his department with all the various characters to be found in every workshop ; he has to be the medium between the employer and the employé, looking to the interests of both, not being the tool of either ; he has to be prepared for any emergency and ready to act when the emergency arises. All the material of his department is under his especial care, and he is accountable for its preservation and proper use ; and a thousand-and-one other matters are attached to and depending upon the position of foreman which go far to take away the glamor which such position may appear to have in the sight of him who is not a foreman, but thinks he would like to be one. To the foreman himself the position does not always seem a golden one, and many a time he would be glad to exchange his lot for that of the workman who envies him.

When all these various matters are rightly thought out and considered, in nine cases out of ten the would-be aspirant will surely exclaim, "Well, I can see that 'All is not gold that glitters.'"

Space forbids the consideration of other matters that might be touched upon in connection with the above proverb, but instances are numerous, and every day something arises to prove its truth.

SEVEN-LINE EXCELSIOR CHAMELEON. $5.80

8A, 16a.
Quads and Spaces, 38c.

Waltz Once More
Ancient House in the Rocks
12 Quickly 80

FIVE-LINE NONPAREIL CHAMELEON. $6.75

6A, 12a.
Quads and Spaces, 45c.

Crow & Robin
American Lard Butter
23 Time 45

SEVEN-LINE NONPAREIL CHAMELEON. $8.50

4A, 8a.
Quads and Spaces, 60c.

Majestically
Beautiful Chromos
5 Flow 8

Cleveland Type Foundry,
Cleveland, Ohio.

CHARACTERS:

1 2 3 4
5 6 7 8

Daisy Border, No. 3.
HALF NONPAREIL, NONPAREIL AND PICA BODY.

$2.20
Per Font.

$1.50 Per Font.

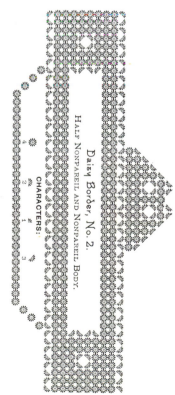

Daisy Border, No. 2.
HALF NONPAREIL AND NONPAREIL BODY.

CHARACTERS:

1 2
3 4

BRANCHES AT ☆
MINNEAPOLIS AND SAN FRANCISCO.

AMERICAN SYSTEM
—OF—
INTERCHANGEABLE
TYPE BODIES.
THE ONLY TRUE STANDARD

TYPE FOUNDERS
MONROE · STREET,
CHICAGO.

MARDER, LUSE & CO.

Skeleton Antique No. 2.

36 A,	BREVIER.	$2.55

(8 Points Standard Measure.)

THE SHADES OF NIGHT WERE FALLING FAST, AS THROUGH A DIRTY
LANE THERE PASSED A MAN WHO BORE, 'MIDST SLEET AND RAIN, A BASKET
12345   AND IT DID CONTAIN FRESH OYSTERS.   67890

24 A,	TWO-LINE PEARL.	$2.00

(10 Points Standard Measure.)

AN OYSTER-KNIFE AND SHEATH, AND LOUDLY, LIKE
AS A CLARION, RUNG THE ACCENTS OF THAT WELL-KNOWN
12345   TONGUE, "FRESH OYSTERS!"   67890

24 A,   TWO-LINE NONPAREIL.   (12 Points Standard Measure.) $2.70

THE PEOPLE THERE ARE ALL IN BED, AND OYSTERS, TOO, THEY NEVER BUY.
HIS ONLY ANSWER WAS THE CRY "FRESH OYSTERS!"   JUST STEP INSIDE AND TAKE A REST, AND
HAVE A GLASS OR TWO OF BEST; A LONGING TWINKLE   1234567890

16 A,   TWO-LINE BOURGEOIS.   (18 Points Standard Measure.) $2.70

DARK AND WIDE, BEWARE THE DITCH ON EITHER SIDE: THIS WAS THE
POLICEMAN'S LAST GOOD-NIGHT; A VOICE WAS HEARD FAR IN THE   1234567890

12 A,   TWO-LINE PICA.   (24 Points Standard Measure.) $3.65

A MAN AT BREAK OF DAY WAS FOUND, AND NOT
FAR FROM HIM IN THE LANE HIS BASKET, THAT   1234567890

8 A,   TWO-LINE COLUMBIAN.   (32 Points Standard Measure.) $4.45

THEY LAID HIM TO REST IN A COLD DAMP
CELL WITH HIS BASKET BESIDE HIM 28

6 A,   CANON.   (44 Points Standard Measure.) $5.55

MARCHING THROUGH GEORGIA 57

THE ABOVE SERIES JUSTIFY BY SIXTHS OF PICA AND LINE AT THE BOTTOM.   SPACES AND QUADS WITH EACH FONT.

A WORD WITH THE TYPEFOUNDERS.

To the Editor: INDIANAPOLIS, July 19, 1885.

As I think it would be to the best interests of all parties concerned if typefounders had occasional instruction from practical printers as to how they should manufacture their wares, I take the liberty of saying a few words to them. I see that some of the suggestions already offered in THE INLAND PRINTER have been followed by a few type-founders, and hence I am encouraged to intrude this article upon your space. What I have to say may have been said before, in which case I shall be only too glad to add to the force of former advice by a further stirring up of the subjects touched upon.

If the founders thoroughly understood the various ways in which type is used, they would perhaps offer us printers fewer of those new meaningless faces, and would go to improving the faces which they have already, in order to make them more useful and labor-saving. But some typefounders (and prominent ones, too) are wofully ignorant of the minutiæ of the compositor's business, and therefore waste their spare energies in devising new styles of type, instead of making their old faces more desirable and handier for the working printer.

I am pleased to see that the American founders have at last awakened to the importance of the universal (or Didot or French) system of type bodies, and that the majority of the prominent ones have adopted, or are working toward the adoption of this excellent system; and I would advise my colleagues not to invest another dollar in any font that is not cast on these multiple of twelve to pica bodies, and that you had best discard as soon as you can all type you have which does not justify with it, and that you insist on being furnished with type cast on this system, no matter what your typefounder may say.

While I rejoice over this important move in regard to bodies, I want to lecture those founders who have adopted the new system, and yet have neglected the *most important part* of it, namely, the casting of each series to a *uniform and systematic line*, so that the different sizes may be used as caps and small caps in combination, and line accurately, without the use of paper and cardboard in justifying. About twenty series have been produced where perfect lining is obtained by the means of six to pica leads. This is an improvement that ought to be insisted on in every face cast on the new bodies, and it is, in fact, the *chief* recommendation for the universal bodies.

However, in investigating this matter with some of the series in my office, I find that a number of the smaller faces (from pearl to long primer) would "kern" or run over too much at the bottom of the body when cast to line with six to pica leads. Therefore I would advise the founder to cast such faces so that we can line them by using twelve to pica leads. In fact I see that in two Johnson foundry series the eight and nine-point faces line with twelve to pica leads. I would rather pay for twelve to pica leads than fill up my office with small caps to all my job fonts, which latter is the alternative that some founders suggest in their opposition to the Didot bodies. The money that extra small caps will cost I would prefer to spend in other series, and thus have a larger variety of faces.

From what little knowledge I have of typefounding, I know it is as much, if not more trouble to cast small caps for job fonts than it would be to adjust the lining plates or standards on their molds so as to cast all sizes to a uniform line, either for twelve or six to pica leads justification. Perhaps it may require more care in founding to institute

this improvement, but I venture to say that the founder who introduces it in all his faces will have the advantage over the founder who does not, and will have *greater sales* on account of the immense superiority of type cast with a "labor-saving line, if I may so call it. Don't "go off half-cocked" in the adoption of the Didot system. If you find the change of bodies a good one to make, don't omit the best feature of it. Let no typefounder hold back because his present matrices are not fitted to line according to this idea. Either refit them for a new line, or invent appliances for your molds by which the proper line may be obtained. Your inventive genius is certainly equal to that. It will be worth your while, if it is your intention to make the best and most salable type.

I notice that one foundry (the Cincinnati) has discarded the double small pica body, and is casting all faces usually cast on that body on the new paragon (20 points). This is a very laudable change. Double long primer is everywhere preferable to double small pica. Small pica being used only on bookwork, why should we have the double of it in bodies in the joboffice? This foundry should have gone a step further, and should have adopted five-line nonpareil and seven-line nonpareil (which are adopted by the Johnson, Cleveland & Collins, and McLeester foundries). These bodies are preferable to double English, double Columbian, and double paragon, in being multiples of nonpareil. We could use slugs instead of quads in long blank lines, and save much labor. I am much pleased with Johnson's new system of bodies, preferring it to the Marder, Luse & Co's. I would, however, add the 4, $4\frac{1}{2}$, 5, $5\frac{1}{2}$, 7, 10, 11, and 20 point sizes, which would be all that are necessary to a most serviceable series of bodies, and I would only cast book faces on the 11-point body, as the job printer doesn't want it nor its double. I am "down" somewhat on 14-point (English) for job faces, and would exclude it, were it practicable. At least I would advise casting such faces either on 12 or 16 point wherever possible.

It makes me feel almost like "cussing" to see that some founders still persist in casting minionette and emerald borders. It seems as if these founders could admit into their business no ideas regarding type-making, except such as they learned when they served their apprentice-ship. I see, also, that some fiend has cast a border (called "Letter Combinations") on a long primer body. He ought to be made to eat every pound of it cast. Will our typemakers ever learn that pica and nonpareil bodies are the only ones on which the printer wants his borders, cuts, and ornaments cast?

While on this point, I feel like kicking those electrotypers who can't trim their cuts to even ems or ens of pica. But since we can't expect them to even trim their electros truly square, how can we hope to have them trim their wares by exact measure? I will arise in all my might and just anger some day, and slay a few of these electrotype chuckleheads. They need an infusion of sense into their business.

Another point I want to give a boost, too, namely: All figures should be cast on a uniform body, and so as to justify with even spaces. How much we tablework compositors would bless you if you would only cast job font figures on either $\frac{1}{2}$, $\frac{1}{3}$, $\frac{2}{3}$, $\frac{1}{4}$, $\frac{3}{4}$, $\frac{2}{5}$, $\frac{3}{5}$, $\frac{4}{5}$, or full em bodies, is scarcely estimable. All the punctuation marks should be cast on one of these fractions of the body; likewise, "justifiers" for use in tabular matter. There is certainly no reason why founders should not favor us in this particular. I have lost enough time in setting tables where no two figures or points were of like thickness, and where they failed to justify with the spaces. And I have wasted many a "d—n it" also.

A WORKING PRINTER.

LAGERMAN'S COMPOSING, DISTRIBUTING AND JUSTIFYING MACHINE.

WE are indebted to the *Printers' Register*, London, for the accompanying description and illustration of this machine, which is the invention of Mr. Alex. Lagerman, of Sweden, and is now on exhibition in England.

We made an inspection of them a few days since, and were much struck with the manner in which they performed their functions, though it would have been better could some of the noise of working been dispensed with. That they are rapid and, so far as the actual setting and distributing are concerned, simple, is certain; while the automatic justifier is at once the most ingenious, the most interesting, and the most intelligent piece of mechanism attached to a composing machine yet brought out. Whether it may always be relied on, or whether some of its parts are liable to become deranged, we have not had an opportunity of judging. This, however, we can say, that we gave no intimation of our visit, that we found all in perfect order, and that there was no hitch while we were present.

The accompanying illustration will show the character of the machine. The types to be set are to be seen in their vertical grooves or slots, the plane being sloped, to assist them in maintaining their places. The faces of the letters are exposed, so that the operator, by running his eye along any line can at once detect the presence of any wrong letter.

The types are placed in the grooves, either direct from the founder's page, or from the grooved store galley B, or they are distributed into them by the distributor, which is seen at the top of the machine, on the left hand. It is one of the features of Mr. Lagerman's invention that composing and distributing may go on simultaneously, the compositor

sitting at the right hand, in front of his copy, and the distributor standing up on a mounted platform on the left.

The serrated iron bar E, the three rings resting on it, the composing-stick — unlettered and indistinctly shown in the cut, but distinguishable as the vertical piece extending almost from the top of the nearest space box to the type grooves above — and the rods and pivots connecting them constitute the whole composing apparatus. The composing-stick is an iron instrument, grooved vertically, and having at its topmost extremity a pair of pincers opening and closing, like a finger and thumb. It and all the other parts connected with it slide with great ease laterally all along the lower ends of the grooves. The notches in E are each for three letters, and any one of the three rings may be depressed into any one of the notches. Assume that a par-

ticular notch is appropriated to the letters A, B, C. The operator, if he desired to set A, would press the first ring into the notch; if he desired B, he would press the middle ring into it, and if C, he would press the outer ring into it. The rings are depressed by one or other of the three first fingers of the right hand, which are placed through them. They move with great freedom up and down the notched plate E, so that at one instant the middle ring, say, may be depressed into the notch at the extreme right, and at the next the outer ring may be depressed into the notch at the extreme left; but, of course, this is an unusual proceeding, for the notches in the middle of the plate are appropriate to the letters most wanted. As the rings are moved, so does the composing-stick, to which they are intimately united by means of the rods. The depression of any of the rings causes the upper end of the composing-stick to be slightly elevated, and the little iron pincers to open and take a type from the bottom of the groove to which they are advanced. When the pressure is removed, and the ring rises out of the notch, the stick descends again, and with it the type, which falls into the vertical groove in the stick, before mentioned, and this operation is repeated until the said groove is full. Then the rings are brought to the extreme right; one is depressed, and the composed line travels up into the justifier. The operator troubles no more about this, but goes on to set another stickful. In the meantime, the composed line is slowly mounting in a vertical direction, its ultimate haven being the galley C. As it goes, a tiny finger every now and then knocks out one of the en quads or spaces and replaces it with a thinner space, of which a store is kept in a horizontal groove hard by. If the line as set in the stick is the precise measure or less than the measure of the galley C, no spaces will be rejected, but if it be slightly longer, as it is generally taken care it shall be, one or more must be removed in order that it may be of the proper width. It would puzzle many a competent engineer to understand how this discrimination is effected by the mechanism, even if described in the most lucid manner, and we will not, therefore, trouble the reader with a technical statement of the combined actions of rods, eccentrics, notched wheels, and pawls which effect the purpose, but will be content with saying that by the time the topmost end of the line has reached the top of the opening in C (it is adjustable according to the measure desired), the justification is complete, and a bar advances laterally and presses the line into the galley, immediately after which the traveling groove which lately held it descends, and awaits the next line to be justified.

Distribution is done very much in the same way as composition, only vice versa. The matter to be distributed is inserted in the galley at the top of the machine, and then, by means of the apparatus at the extreme left, the first line is lifted out and is inserted in the grooved distributing stick O, which is brought under it. Then the operator goes to work with his fingers in the three rings attached to that stick, depressing them as needs be into one or other of the notches in bar D, and as each depression is made, so the letter in the lowest part of the distributing stick is deposited into the groove over which it has stopped. Spring clips inserted into these grooves prevent the types from falling, and give way gradually as type after type is distributed.

The machine occupies a floor space of about six feet six inches by three feet, and its extreme height is rather more than six feet. As regards its rapidity of execution, we may say that we timed the operator, and found that he set and justified 10 lines, consisting of 480 types, in three minutes and a half.

FEMALE LABOR.

THERE is a great deal of unmeaning twaddle indulged in, by a certain class of namby-pamby sentimentalists, about the selfishness of the male sex whenever a protest is raised against the employment of women in vocations for which they are unfitted alike by sex, nature, and association. In a great majority of instances these special pleadings, in which the merits of the case are grossly misrepresented, instead of being the promptings of disinterested philanthropy, are the offspring of *inherent selfishness*. Home is woman's sphere, and man is her natural provider, and no amount of pettifogging can prove the contrary. We admit there are many positions in life in harmony with her character and surroundings, which she can fill with advantage to herself and society, outside the family circle, in which the competition of men would be altogether out of character; but there is a vast difference between occupying *such* positions and virtually compelling her to earn her living by following a trade which requires years of application to master, to which she is altogether unsuited by her tastes and condition, while the tendency of that labor must inevitably lead to the lowering of the standard of workmanship, and this, too, when the demand for a higher standard is the acknowledged desideratum of the hour. We repeat that the tendency to force women — for that is the proper term to use — under such circumstances, into indiscriminate competition with men, must eventually prove disastrous to both, and is calculated to lower her in the social and moral scale, despite all that can be said to the contrary; and those who have had the most extended practical experience in this matter, will bear testimony to the truth of this assertion.

An English engraver, in referring to this matter, gives the following reasons for not employing females.

When a young man comes to me and begins his work, he feels that it is his life's business. He is to cut his fortune out of the little blocks before him. Wife, family, home, happiness, and all are to be carved out by his own hand, and he settles steadily and earnestly to his labor, determined to master it, and with every incitement spurring him on. He cannot marry until he knows his trade. It is exactly the other way with the girl. She may be as poor as the boy, and as wholly dependent upon herself for a living, but she feels that she will probably marry by and by, and then she must give up wood engraving. So she goes on listlessly; she has no ambition to excel; she does not feel that all her happiness depends on it. She will marry, and then her husband's wages will support her. She may not say so, but she thinks so, and it spoils her work.

And this is just as applicable to the girl entering a printing-office as an engraving-office. The don't-expect, or don't-want-to-marry kind are like angels' visits, few and far between; and with their change of circumstances comes an entire change in the current of their lives. With the one sex such employment is but a makeshift; with the other, a permanent investment. On the one hand, where *individual* responsibility ceases, on the other *dual* responsibility commences. We remember, a few years ago, an occurrence that may aptly be referred to in this connection. A young woman, who prided herself on her *independence*, declared her intention to carve her own future, and that she would not marry the best man living, and everybody seemed to take her at her word. But all's well that ends well. Going, shortly after, to a dry goods store, she was waited on by an old deacon, with whom she was personally acquainted, and who had often heard of her determination. Her purchases aroused his suspicion. "Mary," said he, "what does this mean?" "It means, sir, that I'm tired of working for myself; have changed my mind, and am going to get married." "Don't you know," he replied, "what the New Testament says: They that marry, do well; but they that don't, do better?" "Well, I am going to do well, sir, and they can just do better *who can't help it*," was the rejoinder. And there was a good deal of human nature in the reply.

THE HEATHEN CHINEE AS A COMPETITOR.

WE learn from the last number of the *Pacific Printer*, published in San Francisco, that there are three Chinese printing-offices in full blast in that city, fully equipped with type and presses doing commercial work and employing white men. Alluding to the discovery made, it says: "Notwithstanding the beggarly prices ruling the trade here, we venture to say that if he once gets a foothold the heathen Chinee will double discount the worst, and flourish like a burdock." In referring to the remedy it advises that "every printer in business refuse to allow a Chinaman to work in his office, and also refuse to give employment to any white man that has worked in a Chinese office. Form a club. Spot every man who patronizes a pigtail office, and let the entire fraternity withhold their trade from that man, and use their influence with others to the same end. It will make his job printing expensive if he gets it for nothing."

TYPEFOUNDING
By Alfred Pye

THE average printer's knowledge of typefounding is so limited that some description of the process by which type is produced will come as a boon to many who have longed to know something about the manufacture of the material which they daily handle, but have had no means of satisfying their desire in this direction. No idea of the number of hands through which the type has to pass, after it is cast and before it is ready for the printer, can be formed by anyone who has not seen the process or had it described; and the amount of work, both artistic and mechanical, that is necessary *to be* performed *before* a type can be cast is likely to create a feeling almost of wonder in the uninitiated as he is made acquainted with the manufacture of matrices and molds, the two implements which give form to the face and body of the type. A printer should, whenever it is possible to do so (and in large cities where typefoundries are located this should be an easy matter), make a knowledge of typefounding a part of his education. Most artisans and mechanics are intimately acquainted with the quality of the material used by them, and can tell how the tools they handle are constructed, and printers ought not to be behind them in this matter. For their benefit we will describe in as interesting a manner as possible how type is made, from the initial point to the finished type ready for use.

Considerable mystery surrounds the invention of typefounding, from the fact that no authentic record exists of the implements used for the purpose of casting type by Gutenberg, who is generally acknowledged to have been the inventor; but from vague references to "casting letters in brass" (no doubt meaning brass matrices), and the use of a mold in connection therewith, in such records as do exist, it is safe to infer that the principle of typefounding has remained the same during the more than four centuries that have elapsed since its invention. Without the mold and matrix, types cannot be made with that regularity and exactness of body and line of face that is so necessary to produce good printing. The face of the type is formed in the matrix, the body in the mold.

A matrix is an oblong, rectangular piece of copper, with the form of the letter it is intended to produce deeply impressed near one end, in such a manner that when fitted to the mold it will be directly in position for giving a correct face to the metal type that is formed in the mold. The making of matrices is an operation requiring considerable artistic skill and minute attention to details. The form of the letter has first to be cut in steel by an artist called a punchcutter, the steel letter thus cut being called a punch. Really good punchcutters, like good workmen in other businesses, are few and far between. Not only must they be skillful engravers, but must have a profound knowledge of the proportion one letter should bear to another; have correct ideas as to the form of letters, and should be, in fact, first-class artists in every sense of the term.

In the preparation of a set of matrices for a font of Roman letter two sets of punches are actually needed. The sunken portions of letters need to be first cut in relief and driven into the steel that is to be used for the punch. These primary punches are termed counter-punches, and are made to secure uniformity of impression in all the faces of a font of letter, which could scarcely be attained if the sunken portions were gouged out.

The illustration here given represents the counter-punch for a capital H. The white space in the center is cut into the counter, and when driven into the steel to be used for the punch leaves the fine line across the center of the letter in relief, while the dark portions form the hollow spaces in the upper and lower portions of the letter. The other illustration shows the finished punch after the punchcutter has formed the outside of the letter.

The steel used for the punches and counters is of the finest quality obtainable; it is first annealed to render it easily workable, and afterward retempered so as to be able to overcome the resistance developed in driving, either the counter-punches into the steel for making the punches, or the punches into the matrices. Such letters as I, i, l, etc., do not need a counter-punch, as all the cutting is on the outside of the letter; but all other letters in the alphabet have to be counter-punched, or countered, which is the technical term. During the process of punchcutting delicate measuring instruments are constantly used to

PUNCH.

determine the exact depth of sinking, accurate lining, etc. These instruments are so constructed that they will measure the one-thousandth part of an inch, sometimes even less. The necessity for such close measurement will be apparent to anyone who will examine a single line of type, and observe the perfect proportion which one letter bears to another in the size of face and thickness of the lines which give it the right form or shape. The amount of time expended and expense involved in making a set of punches for a font of letter is something enormous, and the printer who carelessly tosses a " busted " type into the hellbox little thinks how much it would cost to produce another letter like it if the matrix in which it was formed were destroyed.

When the punches for a font of letter are all cut the operation of making the matrices begins. A separate slab of copper is required for each character in the font. The surface of the copper is highly burnished, so that when the punch is driven into it, the face of the letter will be a perfectly even surface, without flaw or blur of any kind. The copper slab is firmly fixed in an apparatus called a driving-block, the punch is placed in the right position, and by means of a smart blow is driven into the copper. Sometimes it will happen that the punch gets broken in the process of driving; even the detachment of a small portion of the face of the punch is sufficient to cause trouble, and the process of punchcutting for that character has to be gone over again.

The copper slab as thus prepared is termed a drive. Around the spot where the punch made its impression is a raised surface, or bur, caused by the displacement of the copper in the process of driving. This has to be smoothed away, and the drive made of even surface. This portion of the work is intrusted to another person called a fitter, who has to test the drive in many ways before it becomes a matrix.

ROMAN and Italic body type, small faces of job type, and most of the scripts are cut on steel, and matrices made with the punches. Most of the job type, and the larger faces of Roman letter are made by the electrotype process, which is less costly, and, in fact, more practicable. Some large faces are cut in steel, but it is not usual to do so, as it is a somewhat difficult matter to make a good drive with a large punch.

For the electrotype process the letters are engraved on metal which is a composition of the same ingredients as typemetal, but blended in different proportions. Typemetal is too brittle for engraving purposes, as in cutting fine lines it would break, so a somewhat softer composition is needed for cutting the originals upon. Equal care is necessary in cutting letters on metal as in punchcutting, seeing that both are destined to produce the same result ; namely, the making of a matrix for reproducing the form of the original as often as needed.

The face of the letters so engraved are highly polished, and every line needs to be sharp and clear, or the inaccuracies, if any exist, will appear in the matrix. When the cutter has finished all the characters in a font, he hands them to the electrotyper, who proceeds to convert them into matrices in the following manner:

A small brass plate, varying in thickness according to the size of the type to be made, with a hole punched near one end, is needed for each character, letter, figure or point, and sometimes ornaments, in the font. These plates are laid upon a flat surface, the letters placed in the holes, face down, and fastened in position with quads or spaces, care being taken to get them as square as possible to the head and sides of the plate. Wax is poured over the portions not intended to be exposed to the action of the battery, and a number of these plates are fastened together, side by side, and placed in a battery, being connected with it and a copper plate by means of wires forming a complete circuit. The battery causes the copper to be deposited around the face of the type in the opening in the brass plates, filling up the opening, and becoming virtually a part of the plate. The time necessary for the accomplishment of this process varies according to the size of the letter, some of the larger sizes needing to be immersed twice or three times as long as the smaller. When sufficient copper has been deposited to fill the opening in each plate, they are taken out of the battery, the letters withdrawn, leaving their image deeply imbedded in the copper, the back of the plate filed smooth, and another brass plate firmly riveted thereto, making the whole of sufficient thickness for use as a matrix, and are then handed to the fitter.

All the tools used by a fitter are very delicate and exact, being constructed to measure the slightest difference between one matrix and another, to the one-thousandth part of an inch, or even less. With a fine pointed gauge the depth of the face of the letter is measured, and made exactly parallel to the surface of the matrix. This gauge, when once set, is used for all the matrices in a font, thus insuring regularity in height of the type from shoulder to face. Printers will see the necessity of such accurate measurement when they think of the trouble that would arise in making ready a form if the letters varied in height even the thickness of a tissue paper. The sides of the matrix are then made of equal distance from the face of the letter, so that the face may stand exactly in the center of the body. The matrices vary in width according to the width of the letter, but the space on either side of the face must be the same. For instance, supposing the space on either side of a capital I to be a long primer, the capital M must also have a long primer space on either side, the difference in the width of the matrix being as great as the difference in the width of the I and M. Should the matrix be too wide, the superfluous metal is taken off by the fitting-machine, which has a gauge corresponding line for line with the fitter's measuring gauge. If the space should be too little, the matrix has to be placed in the battery until sufficient copper has been deposited thereon to bring it up to the required size. The head of the matrix has now to be made square to the sides and surface, and the faces of each brought into line.

The punchcutter's and fitter's guides in determining the width and line of letters are the capital letters H and O for the caps, and the lower case m and o for the lower case letters. During the process of fitting, trial types are cast from each matrix for the purpose of measuring and determining their accuracy. These are cast in a hand mold, which will be described and illustrated in a future issue. It will thus be seen that considerable time is expended in fitting a complete set of matrices, on account of the extreme nicety of adjustment necessary for making a font of type proportionate and exact in line. The accompanying illustration shows a matrix in its finished condition. The letters and figures at the bottom are the typefounder's index to the set of which the matrix forms a part. Each set of matrices is kept in a separate drawer, and on account of their great value special care is taken to keep them in a safe place.

MATRIX.

The fitter having finished his part of the work, the matrices are passed to the typecaster, who casts a trial font therefrom. A specimen page is set and proofs taken which are closely examined for faulty letters. Should there be any (and it is seldom that all the letters are perfect on a first trial), the matrices of the faulty letters are corrected, and those letters recast. After changing them in the specimen page, other proofs are taken; and this process is repeated until the font is declared perfect.

The matrices being ready, a mold becomes necessary for forming the body of the type, the matrix creating the face only. A typemold is an ingenious piece of mechanism in two parts, each part being constructed of several pieces of steel screwed and fitted together with mathematical exactness. The steel used in its construction has to be very finely tempered to resist the action of the heat engendered during the operation of casting; and each of the two parts need to be of the same degree of fineness in this respect, or trouble might ensue from the tendency to expansion caused by heat, and the body of the type would become affected.

UNTIL within the last fifty years, all type had to be cast in hand molds, which was a tedious process, and one which would not begin to meet the requirements of printers in these days. The hand mold was constructed of several pieces of steel, scientifically screwed together, in two halves, which were inclosed in a wood box or shield, to protect the hand of the workman from injury. The

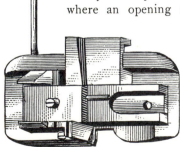

two halves of the mold lock together, fitting closely in all parts except just in the center, where an opening remains of sufficient extent to form the body of the type, into which the molten metal is poured. Each half is a counterpart of the other, except that attached to one half (the lower half shown in the engraving), is a

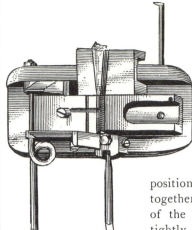

HAND-MOLD.—OPEN.

spring for holding the matrix in position, and in the other half is a ridge for forming the nick in the type.

The operation of casting was as follows: Taking the mold in his left hand, the caster with his right adjusted the two halves, and placed the matrix in position. Drawing the halves together, the clamps or cheeks of the mold held the matrix tightly, and the spring was then adjusted to press the surface of the matrix close to the mold,

TYPECASTING IN 1683.

the point of the spring fitting into a hole at the back immediately beneath the face of the type. Standing beside a furnace or oven, upon which was a kettle of molten metal, the caster took a spoonful of the metal and quickly poured it into the opening in the mold, at the same time giving the mold an upward jerk or throw. This throw was necessary to cause the metal to penetrate the finer lines of the matrix and give a good face to the type; for the metal cooled so rapidly that it otherwise would set before reaching its destination, and an imperfect type would result. The matrix was then removed, the mold opened, and the type pulled out with one of the hooks shown in the engraving. Each half of the mold had a hook attached, as, according to the method of casting, the type would remain sometimes in one half and sometimes in the other. In the lower half of the engraving a type is shown in the position it would occupy on the opening of the mold. A very large jet filled the mouth-piece of the mold (much larger than is produced in machine-casting), being attached to the letter, and the labor of breaking off these jets was very great.

The illustration on page 144, copied from a work entitled "Mechanick Exercises, or the Doctrine of Handy Works applied to the Art of Printing," published in London, England, by Joseph Moxon, 1683, shows the typecaster in the act of carrying the metal from the kettle to the mold.

Mr. David Bruce, Jr., in 1838, patented a typecasting machine which wrought a revolution in the art of type-founding. By the hand-casting process, from two to three thousand letters per day of ordinary body type was considered a good day's work; by the machine-casting process the quantity produced is greatly increased, the method of casting greatly simplified and the labor rendered less arduous. In place of the many motions necessary in hand casting, the simple turning of a crank produces a letter in a marvelously short space of time. The mold has undergone little, if any, change, beyond being adapted to its new position on the machine. The wooden shield is discarded, being of no further use. The following illustrations show the mold as at present used. In Fig. 1 the lower half of the mold is shown, which is attached to the mold block of the machine, and becomes a fixture. This half contains the ridges which form the nicks in the type. It is shown upside down

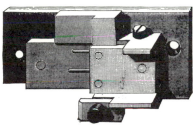

FIG. 1. LOWER HALF OF THE MOLD.

for the purpose of more clearly disclosing all its parts. Fig. 2 shows the upper half of the mold, which is movable, being lifted for the purpose of removing the type every time a letter is cast. This half is adjustable in a lateral direction, to accommodate the mold to the varying width of the matrices. Fig. 3 shows the mold complete, with the matrix removed, disclosing the face of the type in the

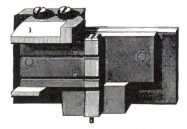

FIG. 2. UPPER HALF OF THE MOLD.

mold. The matrix fits in between the cheeks on either side of the face of the letter, being held close to the mold by a spring as in the hand mold. A separate mold is made for each type body. It would be impossible to attain satisfactory results in uniformity of body if adjustable molds

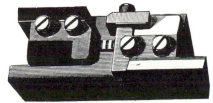

FIG. 3. TYPE MOLD COMPLETE.

could be constructed with the view of using them for more than one body. The adjustment could not be effected with the accuracy which is such an essential feature in type bodies. The number of molds needed in a foundry is therefore considerable, when all the varying bodies of type, from brilliant up to six or eight-line pica, are taken into consideration. It is not necessary to have a mold for every face of type that is made, as the matrices for any number of faces on the same sized body can be used on one mold.

THE type-casting machine is a very compact apparatus, occupying but little space. At the back is a small furnace, above which is a reservoir or metal pot for containing the molten metal. In the metal pot is a well containing a pump, and a tube leads from the well to the front of the metal pot where is a nipple, through which the metal is injected into the mold. The mold is fitted to the

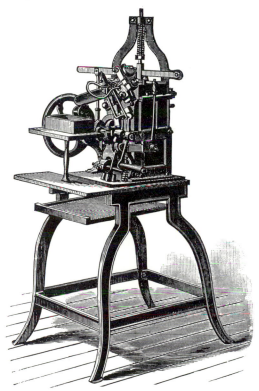

TYPE-CASTING MACHINE.

mold block in front of the machine, the lower half being screwed to the block, becoming a fixture. The upper half is attached to an arm which opens the mold for the purpose of releasing each type as it is cast. The matrix is held firmly in place by a spring in front of the machine. At each revolution of the crank the mouth of the mold is brought close up to the nipple; a cam attached to the shaft turned by the crank presses down a lever which withdraws from the nipple a pin that blocks the passage, called the "joker," thus permitting the metal to flow through, while another cam at the same moment presses down a bar which operates the pump, forcing the fluid metal into the mold. Sufficient metal to fill the mold only is allowed to pass through the nipple, the joker immediately closing it as the mold is removed. As the mold block returns to its original position, the upper half of the mold is raised and the type released, when it falls into the box on the stand in front of the machine. A type is cast at every revolution of the crank, and small sized letters can be made as rapidly as the caster can turn the crank. On large type the caster has to work slowly, holding the machine for a few seconds after filling the mold, in order that the metal may set, for if the type was released from the mold immediately, the metal in the center not being set would burst the type. When practicable a current of cool air is directed by means of a tube on to the mold for the double purpose of keeping it from being overheated and aiding the type to set rapidly.

Job type is cast by means of the hand machine, as, the fonts being small, the matrices need to be changed frequently. When a sufficient quantity of the letter *a*, for instance, has been cast, the matrix is removed and the matrix for the letter *b* takes its place, and so on throughout the font. The upper half of the mold has to be adjusted to the width of each matrix, and the caster is responsible for any inaccuracies that may result from possible negligence. Body type is cast on machines operated by steam power, the matrices not needing to be changed so frequently, and two steam machines can be attended to by one man.

Each foundry makes its own type-molds, for the reason, as printers know, to the great vexation of their souls, that the type bodies of no two foundries in the United States being exactly alike, molds useful in one foundry would be useless in another. The repairing of molds forms a considerable item of expense in a type foundry, for, like all other pieces of mechanism, they will wear out with constant use, or get out of order, and therefore need some careful attention. The expansion caused by heat is one of the troubles that type molds are subject to, and this fault would be fatal to correctness of body if not detected and adjusted.

On account of the great expense that would be involved in changing the size of the type bodies to make them uniform with those of any other foundry (necessitating a complete new set of molds), typefounders are unwilling to agree to that much-desired result which printers are now agitating for, namely, uniformity in size of type bodies throughout the foundries of the United States. That such a result must come, sooner or later, is an admitted point in the argument; but it will depend largely upon the willingness of the majority of typefounders to incur the necessary outlay. Some are working to this end by changing a few of their molds at intervals, thus spreading the expense over a long period of time. No doubt a uniform system would be a boon to both typefounders and printers, because printers would then place some orders with the nearest foundry, which now have to be sent to particular foundries (sometimes hundreds of miles away), because the body must match.

The metal used for type varies in hardness according to the purpose for which it is needed. Most printers know that type metal is a combination of lead, tin and antimony. The average proportions of the respective metals are as follows: lead, 60 per cent; antimony, 33 per cent, and tin 7 per cent, with a small quantity of copper added. For body type and small job type hard metal is used, containing a greater proportion of antimony, as there is more wear on these types than on any other. Larger sizes of job type are cast with a little softer metal, and spaces and quads with softer yet, wear on these being very slight.

The type as it leaves the mold is in a far from finished condition. There is attached to the foot of each letter a piece of metal called a jet, formed by the metal remaining in the mouth of the mold when the letter is cast. This has to be detached, and for this purpose the type, as it leaves the machine, is passed to a boy called a breaker, whose work it is to break off these jets.

Around the shoulder of the type where the matrix and the mold meet is a bur, or roughness, which also has to be removed. This is done by rubbers, usually girls. The operation of rubbing may be thus briefly described: Seated at a table, upon which is laid a file specially made for this purpose, the rubber takes each type separately, and rubs first one side, then the other, upon the file, removing all superfluous metal that may adhere to the sides of the letter. Each letter, as rubbed, is dropped into a tray or drawer, in readiness to be passed to the setter. This is the best and most perfect method of rubbing type, and is practiced in most foundries. There is another mode of rubbing type, called "bunching," where the type is rubbed on a sandstone, several letters being rubbed at one time. This is a quicker way of getting the work done, and is less expensive, but the work is not always so good as when rubbed on the file.

After rubbing, the type is taken in hand by the setter, who sets it up in single lines, about three feet long, on wooden sticks ready for the dresser. The rapidity with which the girls pick up the letters would excite envy in the breast of many a poor comp. who is toiling on a "lean take," and can only scoop up from four to five thousand ems per day. Of course, the setter in a typefoundry has no bad copy to perplex her, and no spacing out to attend to, but the quantity some of them can pick up in an hour is something wonderful.

FROM the setter the type goes to the dresser, who places each stickful of type in a dressing rod, screws it up tightly, turns the type on its face and clamps it tightly in a bench. Then with a plane he cuts a groove in the bottom of the type, giving it feet to stand upon. Unclamping the rod from the bench, he then smooths off the back and front of the letter, and with a powerful magnifying glass carefully examines the face and throws out all bad letters. Sometimes this portion of the work is done by another workman called a picker. The long stickfuls of type are then broken up into shorter lines, made up into pages, and sent to the dividing-room to be made up into fonts. Kerned letters such as *f, j, ff*, and italic letters have to be finished on the kerning machine. This is an apparatus constructed with swiftly revolving knives beneath a flat surface, with an opening for the kern of the letter to be placed in. By means of a treadle the knives are brought close up to each letter, and cut away as much metal as is desired.

In the dividing-room job type is laid out on long tables with galley tops, the letters being arranged in lines proportionate to the size of the fonts intended to be made up. These lines are gathered up into complete fonts on galleys, tied and wrapped up, labeled and passed to the warehouse for sale. Body type is divided into fonts without being laid out on tables. The pages as they come from the foundry are placed on galleys and the proportionate quantities of each letter, figure, space and quad are separated from the bulk and made up into fonts (usually) of 25 lbs., 50 lbs., or 100 lbs., properly wrapped up and labeled, ready for sale. Special orders, of course, have to be made up according to instructions.

In making up fonts of type, carefully prepared schemes are used, which vary somewhat in different foundries. The following figures will give a general idea of the proportion the letters should bear to one another, without going into detail: *Lower case.*—*e*, 6 lbs.; *a*, *n*, *o*, 4¼ lbs. each; *h*, *r*, *s*, *t*, 3½ lbs. each; *m*, *d*, 3 lbs. each; *i*, 2½ lbs.; *u*, 2 lbs., and the other letters varying from 2 lbs. down to 2 oz. each. *Points*, etc., vary from 1¼ lbs. of *commas* down to 1 oz. each for *reference marks*. *Figures* average 5 oz. each, with 1 oz. each for the fractions. *Caps* average 6 oz. each, a greater proportion being allowed for A and E, while J, K, Q, U, etc., are in the minority. The *Small Caps* average about one-third the weight of the Caps, varying from 3 oz. down to ½ oz. *Braces, Dashes* and *Leaders* are put in small quantities, as they are seldom drawn upon for use, except on special work. About 18 lbs. of *Spaces* and *Quads* are needed in a 100-lb.-font, ranging from 5½ lbs. of "3-em" spaces down to 3 oz of "hair" spaces.

Any printer who cares to think for a few moments about the matter will see that it needs some nice calculation to so proportion a font of type that it will work out evenly in setting. There may be in some cases errors made in the dividing-room, which will give a greater or less quantity of some letter than ought to be, or sometimes omit a letter altogether, but such instances are not frequent, and printers can easily determine, by careful examination of a font of type upon opening the packages and before laying the type in case, whether he has a complete font, rightly proportioned, for *then* is the proper time to have mistakes rectified.

In job fonts the letters are proportioned by number to the letter "a," and the size of the font is designated as 12 A, 24 a, etc., a similar scheme being followed, as described above, in relation to Roman type.

A few words with regard to ordering sorts may not be out of place. Most printers, having purchased a font of body type, lay it in case, and straightway forget the number of the face, and sometimes, when they buy from two or three foundries, will forget from which foundry it was bought. Some sorts are needed, and one or two letters, it does not much matter which, are sent as a sample of the type to the foundry, with an order for a pound or two of certain letters. We have seen a colon sent as a sample, and on another occasion, a comma and a period. Such samples as this are not much of a guide to the typefounder in determining to which font they belong. A lower case "m" or a cap "H" of the letter needed should be sent as a sample. Another guide in ordering sorts, for quantities, is, that in an ordinary news or book case the large square boxes, for letters *a*, *c*, *d*, *m*, etc., hold about two pounds of type; the half-size boxes, for letters *b*, *f*, *g*, etc., hold about fourteen ounces, while the quarter-size boxes hold about six ounces each.

Leads, slugs, metal furniture and brass rule are necessary adjuncts to a printing-office, the manufacture of which forms part of the operations of a typefoundry. Leads and slugs are cast sometimes in hand molds, sometimes in machine molds, the number cast at one time varying from one to a dozen. On one end, where the metal enters the mold, is a clump, similar to the jet on type. This is cut away, and the leads are shaved singly, on both sides, by a hand planer, making them of even thickness throughout their entire length. Various kinds of power machines have been tried for the purpose of superseding the hand process, but none have yet been found to answer so satisfactorily.

Leads are cast in thicknesses of 12, 10, 8, 6, 4, and sometimes 3-to-pica. Above 3-to-pica thick they are called slugs, and are made in thicknesses of nonpareil, pica, great primer and double pica. These are shaved by a power machine, the slugs being forced between two sharp-edged knives, set apart exactly the distance the slug should be shaved down to.

Metal furniture is cast in hand molds in lengths of about fourteen inches, being cored to lessen its weight. It is shaved in the same manner as slugs, and is afterward sawed up into lengths of from four to fifty picas. The ends are smoothly planed off, making the lengths of accurate measurement. Metal furniture varies in width from two to ten picas. Another kind of metal furniture is made which is not cored, but cast similar to a section of railroad iron, and is called "railroad furniture." This is of greater strength than the ordinary furniture, there being no danger of its giving way at any point.

Brass rule is received from the brass manufacturers in strips of varying thickness from 12-to-pica up to great primer, and a little more than type high. The face is cut with a planer, the strip of rule being clamped tightly in a bench while it is being cut. Wave and fancy rules are made with special tools cut for the purpose of producing the various patterns. The rule is dressed and gauged to the height of the type made in the foundry, and is sold to the printer in strips of twenty-four inches length, or cut to measure as needed.

From the foregoing remarks printers can easily see that though a type may seem an insignificant piece of metal, which might be produced in a moment, the amount of skill and number of hands necessary to produce it and give it the necessary qualifications for serving its purpose are very great.

JUDICIOUS ADVERTISING.

"WE advertise by circular exclusively" is the argument frequently used by some of our business (?) men, who believe, or rather who affect to believe, that this method of advertising is preferable to and more effective than using the columns of a trade journal. Yet never was a greater fallacy indulged in. It is safe to affirm that in nine cases out of ten the wastebasket is the destination of the average productions of the circular advertiser, who evidently labors under the hallucination that his special pleadings will take precedence over those of his competitors, who are exactly in the same box with himself. "If customers don't need or want to buy, you can't make them, no matter how much advertising you do," is the self-satisfied explanation generally given by this class of Solons. Certainly you can't, and no sensible business man ever claimed to the contrary; but, friends, let us put a flea in your ear. *If* your circular was the *only* circular of the kind issued there might be some force in your argument. The mail which carries your missive, however, probably carries half-a-dozen others, couched in almost the same language, claiming the same advantages, seeking the same patronage and offering the same inducements. The merits of your goods or machines as claimed, are duplicated by your business rivals, so a cursory glance, a pooh! pooh! and they have accomplished their mission. No memorandum is made, your name, aye, and even your special pleadings are forgotten. They may help to swell the janitor's perquisites, but their claims are valued accordingly.

Not so with the trade journal, at least the independent journal which deserves the name of such. The information which each number contains is alone worth the price of subscription, and cannot be obtained at twice the cost outside its own columns. It is *not* thrown aside as waste paper. It compels every tub to stand on its own bottom, and makes true merit and practical experience, instead of gush, the test of success. It advocates no special crotchets, and gives all a fair field, without fear or favor. Such a medium for reaching purchasers and obtaining for the advertiser — sooner or later — substantial returns, is worth more than all the circulars which have been issued since the art of printing has been discovered. And the reason is obvious. It is recognized as an authority and book of reference. *When* an order is required, the purchaser has a broad field to select from; the names and addresses of a score of advertisers are available. He can use his judgment to the best advantage, intelligently select the machine or material best suited to his needs, on the most favorable terms, or obtain the information desired before investing. And in doing so he will no doubt have been assisted in coming to a correct conclusion by the testimony and experience of disinterested parties he has gleaned from its pages.

The circular method of advertising may occasionally hit the nail on the head, but as a permanent, reliable, available medium between buyer and seller, the trade journal, without a reasonable doubt, has precedence over all other channels.

$3.60. Two-line Nonpareil Ornamented, No. 1,077. 15 A
3 lb. 2 oz.

LE PLUS ANCIENNE GRAVURE CONNUE AVEC UNE DATE 1418
BARON DE F. A. REIFFENBERG, BRUXELLES, 1845.

$5.00. Two-line Bourgeois Ornamented, No. 1,077. 12 A
5 lb.

VERZAMELING VAN WOORDEN. 2 PARTS.
C. SCHOOK, GORINCHEM, 1860.

$7.10. Two-line Pica Ornamented, No. 1,077. 10 A
7 lb. 14 oz

L'ART DE PEINDRE LA PAROLE.
E. PIERAGGI, PARIS, 1874.

$10.65. Two-line Great-primer Ornamented, No. 1,077. 8 A
13 lb.

MANUEL DU GRAVURE.
PERROT, PARIS, 1830.

GEORGE BRUCE'S SON & CO., Type-Founders, No. 13 Chambers-Street, NEW-YORK.

$2.45. TWO-LINE NONPAREIL ORNA'D, No. 1,078. 15 A 2 lb. 2 oz.

DISCORSO INTORNO L'ARTE DELLA STAMPA.

J. BAPT. NATOLINI, UDINE, 1606.

$3.00. TWO-LINE BOURGEOIS ORNA'D, No. 1,078. 12 A 3 lb.

POLYTYPEN DER HOLZSCHNITTE.

W. PFNORR, DARMSTADT, 1833.

$4.15. TWO-LINE PICA ORNAMENTED, No. 1,078. 10 A 4 lb. 10 oz.

AN ESSAY ON THE ILLUSTRATION OF BOOKS. 8VO,

J. PLOWMAN, LONDON, 1824.

$5.95. TWO-LINE GREAT-PRIMER ORNAMENTED, No. 1,078. 8 A 7 lb. 4 oz.

ENCYCLOPAEDIE DER BUCHDRUCKERKUNST

HERMANN NEUBURGER, LEIPZIG, 1844.

$5.70. FOUR-LINE PICA ORNAMENTED, No. 1,078. 5 A 7 lb. 14 oz.

LES ORIGINES DE L'ALPHABET.

M. MARTIN, PARIS, 1859.

GEORGE BRUCE'S SON & CO., TYPE-FOUNDERS, No. 13 CHAMBERS-STREET, NEW-YORK.

$2.30.   TWO-LINE NONPAREIL ORNA'D, No. 1,079.   15 A
                                                   2 lb.

BUCHDRUCKER UND REFORMATOREN, 8VO.

G. RETTIG, BERN, 1879.

$3.00.   TWO-LINE BOURGEOIS ORNA'D, No. 1,079.   12 A
                                                  3 lb.

HISTOIRE DE L'IMPRIMERIE.

P. H. DE MAROUZE, PARIS, 1862.

$4.30.   TWO-LINE PICA ORNAMENTED, No. 1,079.   10 A
                                                          4 lb. 12 oz.

PRESAGI SCIENTIFICI SULL' ARTE DELLA STAMPA.

JOANNES BAPTIST MICHELLETTI, AQUILA, 1814.

$6.05.   TWO-LINE GREAT-PRIMER ORNAMENTED, No. 1,079.   8 A
                                                                  7 lb. 6 oz.

A SHORT TREATISE ON LITHOGRAPHY.

F. SCHENCK, EDINBURGH, 1870.

$5.60.   FOUR-LINE PICA ORNAMENTED, No. 1,079.   5 A
                                                           7 lb. 12 oz.

LES CARTES À JOUER. 8VO.

R. MERLIN, PARIS, 1856.

GEORGE BRUCE'S SON & CO., TYPE-FOUNDERS, No. 13 CHAMBERS-STREET, NEW-YORK.

$2.05. TWO-LINE NONPAREIL ORNA'D, No. 1,080. 15 A / 1 lb. 12 oz.

DER HOLLÄNDISCHE BUCHHANDEL SEIT COSTER.
OTTO MUEHLBRECHT, LEIPZIG, 1867.

$2.75. TWO-LINE BOURGEOIS ORNA'D, No. 1,080. 12 A / 2 lb. 12 oz.

THE PRINTER'S BOOK OF DESIGNS.
C. MACHRIS, DETROIT, MICH., 1877.

$3.95. TWO-LINE PICA ORNAMENTED, No. 1,080. 10 A / 4 lb. 6 oz.

DELLA STAMPERIA DEL SEMINARIO DI PADOVA, MEMORIA.
GAETANO SORGATO, PADOVA, 1843.

$5.65. TWO-LINE GREAT-PRIMER ORNAMENTED, No. 1,080. 8 A / 6 lb. 14 oz.

THE HISTORY OF THE BALLANTYNE PRESS.
SIR WALTER SCOTT, EDINBURGH, 1871.

$5.20. FOUR-LINE PICA ORNAMENTED, No. 1,080. 5 A / 7 lb. 4 oz.

ZEITUNG FÜR LITHOGRAPHEN.
C. SCHMALTZ, LEIPZIG, 1841.

GEORGE BRUCE'S SON & CO., TYPE-FOUNDERS, No. 13 CHAMBERS-STREET, NEW-YORK,

$2.05. Two-line Nonpareil Orna'd, No. 1,081. 15 A 1 lb. 12 oz.

LA LITHOGRAPHIE APPLIQUÉE À L'ENSEIGNEMENT FILS. SELVES, PARIS, 1823.

$2.75. Two-line Bourgeois Orna'd, No. 1,081. 12 A 2 lb. 12 oz.

THE BEST PORTRAITS IN ENGRAVING CHS. SUMNER, NEW-YORK, 1872.

$4.05. Two-line Pica Ornamented, No. 1,081. 10 A 4 lb. 8 oz.

CATALOGUE RAISONNÉ DE L'OEUVRE DE CLAUDE MELLAN. ANATOLE DE MONTAIGLON, ABBEVILLE, 1856.

$5.75. Two-line Great-primer Ornamented, No. 1,081. 8 A 7 lb.

BENJAMIN FRANKLIN, EEN LEVENSBEELD. J. MICHEELS, GAND, 1878.

$5.30. Four-line Pica Ornamented, No. 1,081. 5 A 7 lb. 6 oz.

COLORIS DES LITHOGRAPHIES. A. ROBIN, PARIS, 1837.

GEORGE BRUCE'S SON & CO., Type-Founders, No. 13 Chambers-Street, NEW-YORK.

$3.75.   PICA ORNAMENTED, No. 1,557.   30 a and 15 A / 3 lb. 4 oz.

How to Tell a Caxton, with some Hints where and how the same may be Found.

WILLIAM BLADES, LONDON, 1870.

$4.00.   GREAT-PRIMER ORNAMENTED, No. 1,557.   25 a and 12 A / 4 lb.

Variétés Bibliographiques et Littéraires. R. 8vo.

AUG. DE REUME, BRUXELLES, 1850.

$5.60.   DOUBLE PICA ORNAMENTED, No. 1,557.   20 a and 10 A / 6 lb. 4 oz.

American Encyclopaedia of Printing. Edited by J. Luther Ringwalt. Large 8vo.

J. LUTHER RINGWALT, PHILADELPHIA, 1871.

$7.70.   DOUBLE GREAT-PRIMER ORNAMENTED, No. 1,557.   15 a and 8 A / 9 lb. 6 oz.

Kerkgeschiedenis van Nederland voor de hervorming. 4to.

W. MOLL, ARNHEM, 1864.

$6.50.   CANON ORNAMENTED, No. 1,557.   5 a and 5 A / 9 lb.

Annali tipografici Piemontesi del secolo XV.

GIUSEPPE MANZONI, TORINO, 1856.

GEORGE BRUCE'S SON & CO., TYPE-FOUNDERS, No. 13 CHAMBERS-STREET, NEW-YORK.

$3.75.   PICA ORNAMENTED, No. 1,558.   30 a and 15 A / 3 lb. 4 oz.

ssai Typographique et Bibliographique sur l'Histoire de

la Gravure sur Bois

AMBROISE FIRMIN DIDOT, PARIS, 1863

$4.75.   GREAT-PRIMER ORNA'D, No. 1,558.   25 a and 12 A / 4 lb. 12 oz.

Gutenberg. Geschichte und Erdichtung aus

den Quellen nachgewiesen

M. A. VAN DER LINDE, STUTTGART, 1878.

$7.20.   DOUBLE PICA ORNAMENTED, No. 1,558.   20 a and 10 A / 8 lb.

Verhandeling over de uitvinding der Boekdrukkunst door Koster

JACOBUS KONING, AMSTERDAM, 1794.

$10.05.   DOUBLE GREAT-PRIMER ORNAMENTED, No. 1,558.   15 a and 8 A / 12 lb. 4 oz.

Ueber das Alter der Venetianischen Druckereyen

M. KINDERLING, ZÜRICH, 1790

$7.65.   CANON ORNAMENTED, No. 1,558.   5 a and 5 A / 10 lb. 10 oz.

Shadows of the Old Booksellers

CHAS. KNIGHT, LONDON, 1865.

GEORGE BRUCE'S SON & CO., TYPE-FOUNDERS, No. 13 CHAMBERS-STREET, NEW-YORK.

October 1885   79

$5.00. GREAT-PRIMER CHIROGRAPH, No. 688. 25 a and 8 A
5 lb.

Ambroise Firmin Didot, in 1820, gave up the use of Dog=skin Inking Balls, and did all his presswork from Rollers of Glue and Molasses. His cousin Jules Didot persisted in the use of the old=fashioned Balls, which he, and others, claimed inked the type more evenly by Beating, than could be done by the Rotation of an Inking Roller. All the Working Pressmen of Paris were violently opposed to the introduction of Inking Rollers and Machine Presses.

$6.30. DOUBLE PICA CHIROGRAPH, No. 688. 20 a and 7 A
7 lb.

During the Revolution at Paris in 1830, and even as late as 1848, the journeymen pressmen of Paris mobbed the offices that had Machines and Inking Rollers, and destroyed the offensive materials. They clamored for the restoration of Hand Presses and Inking Balls, saying that the New Inventions were, or would be, their ruin, as well as the ruin of the Printing Business.

$8.80. DOUBLE GREAT-PRIMER CHIROGRAPH, No. 688. 15 a and 6 A
10 lb. 12 oz.

The Inking Roller and the Machine Press have not destroyed but have increased the work of pressmen. Pressmen have more steady employment, with less of hard work and are much better paid. See Didot's Essay on Engraving on Wood, page 288.

GEORGE BRUCE'S SON & CO., TYPE-FOUNDERS, No. 13 CHAMBERS-STREET, NEW-YORK.

IMPERIAL SERIES.
PATENTED.

12A, 24a, PICA. (12 Points Standard Measure.) $2.85.

SOFT WHISPERINGS OF A SMITTEN LOVER.
An unexpressed affection dwelt in every flitting vision; fast beat my
Heart, the Time, I felt, was here for Swift Decision. And She,
She placed her hand in mine, her
12345 grace seemed not unwilling, I thought 67890

10A, 20a, GREAT PRIMER. (18 Points Standard Measure.) $3.80.

THE SENSATION WAS DIVINE
The Situation Thrilling! Oh, wily Art and Soft
Perfume, red lips and waving
12345 Tresses, a smile of bright 67890

6A, 12a, DOUBLE PICA. (24 Points Standard Measure.) $5.25.

HISTORICAL ROMANCES!
Truth compels Fiction to Take a Back
Seat and shed bitter tears
12345 of vexation and 67890

SPACES AND QUADS WITH GREAT PRIMER AND DOUBLE PICA.   DOUBLE GREAT PRIMER IN PREPARATION.

12A, 24a,   PICA. (12 Points Standard Measure.) $2.85.

··»»»THOU·WINTRY·WIND«««··

∘ Thou art not so unkind as Man's ∘

Ingratitude;∘thy∘tooth

12345 ∘ Art Not Seen ∘ 67890

8A, 16a,   GREAT PRIMER. (18 Points Standard Measure.) $3.75.

··»»»FINE ORATION«««··

Fellow·Citizens,∘Do·your

2 duty and Drink 4

MARDER, LUSE & Co

Type·Founders,∘Electrotypers,

··»»»And∘Dealers∘in«««··

Printers' Supplies of all kinds,

··»»»139∘AND∘141∘MONROE∘STREET,«««··

∘ ∘ ∘ Chicago, Ill. ∘ ∘ ∘

6A, 12a.   DOUBLE PICA. (24 Points Standard Measure.) $4.50.

··»»»SWEET∘NIGHTINGALE«««··

Singing∘so∘Cheerfully∘in∘Shady∘Grove∘at

18 Evening Tide. 94

4A, 8a,   DOUBLE GREAT PRIMER. (36 Points Standard Measure.) $6.50.

··»»»GRAND∘PRIZE«««··

4 Every Fourth Tuesday 8

UNIFORM TYPE BODIES.

To the Editor :   CINCINNATI, November 2, 1885.

The time is nearly here when the printer may exclaim, " Eureka " ! and congratulate himself and the trade in general that he no longer has the small, yet the very consequential differences in the type bodies of the various founders to contend with. Nearly all the prominent and influential founders have adopted the bodies of the point system, some taking whole gamut, while others have taken the principle ones only, the latter perhaps with the intention of going into the system gradually. It only remains for the printer now to do his share of the reforming; namely, to root out of his office all type which does not justify with the bodies of the uniform system. The founders are going to great expense in the changing of molds and making of new ones, refitting of matrices, recasting of their old faces, etc., and they are entitled to the hearty coöperation of the users of type in their efforts to bring about uniformity.

It is certainly to the interest of all printers who buy new type, both Roman and jobbing letter, to have it cast according to the point scale of sizes. Every font they buy of the old bodies will tend to keep back the millennium, and aid in keeping up the present confusion and diversity in type bodies. Of course, in buying an entirely new outfit, the intelligent, wide-awake and economical printer will admit no types, borders, rules, leads, furniture, etc., into his office which are not in exact accordance with the uniform standard. The printer now no longer has the excuse he used to have, that the foundry he deals with cannot furnish him with the point or Didot (or interchangeable, or justifiable, or labor-saving, or aliquot, or what-not) bodies. That excuse held good when there was but one foundry using the system ; but now, since the system is nearly universal, he need have no fear his founder cannot supply him. If stringently requested he will make the proper molds, should he not have them, and cast type for you on the point bodies.

If there is any disposition on the part of founders not yet in the new ring, to oppose the system or to ridicule it, it is believed that they can easily be brought into line by the customers' demanding that their purchases of new type be all made on the proper system. A disposition on the part of the printer to insist on proper bodies, will have more effect on the founders than many columns of advice to them in trade journals. Therefore, I direct my advice to the printer and tell him to ask for the point bodies, and positively refuse to take any other. That is the quickest way to settle the matter and bring about the desideratum.

Not only as regards the bodies, but in the matter of the thickness of the letters, of the figures and points especially, so that they be uniform and of some definite proportion to the body, should the purchaser be strenuous in insisting. There is no reason why the figures of a job font should be of ten different thicknesses, as they often are. Roman figures have long been cast on a regular thickness, or set, as I believe the founders call it, which usually is an en, and sometimes $\frac{2}{3}$ or $\frac{3}{5}$ of an em. Why not have the jobbing figures on those or some other regular proportion of the body? It is only because we printers are too timid to insist upon and demand that they be cast as they should be. And why should only Roman points bear a definite relation to the size of the body, generally on an en or 3-to-em body? Only because we don't make the founder furnish us jobbing points in the same or other regular proportions to the body. That's why I say, insist, demand, make the founder toady a little to you, instead of you to him.

If this is done with a vim, some day we can also demand other desirable reforms in the thicknesses of the different letters of the alphabet. There is much room for improvement in that respect, but I shall not now dilate upon that matter. The self-spacing type is coming somewhere near the proper thing, but yet it has its defects, the greatest one being its restriction to certain widths of the column. In addition to uniformity in type bodies and the thickness of points and figures, the thing also to insist on is, that the founder cast type so that we can line one size with another with the use of the common one and two point, 12 to pica or 6 to pica, leads. A few series are cast that way, but not enough of them by a great deal. There are comparatively few series where caps of one are not used as small caps of another size. We do not want to be forever compelled to use cardboard and paper for justification, and that is why we must " kick," and " kick " hard, too. Make the founders realize for once in their lives that they exist to furnish us with what we need in the way of type, and that we are not merely made to act as feeders to them, to whom they can sell whatever they have a mind to unload on us.

While I think of it, the attempt of a certain foundry to introduce what it calls " unit " bodies deserves mention, but not of a laudable kind. It is very little short of idiotic to attempt to introduce such a system when the point or 12-to-pica system is so firmly grounded in the United States, and when so many foundries are already casting type on it. This venturesome foundry divides the pica into eight parts, instead of twelve, and calls each part a unit. Thus nonpareil is 4 units ; a sort of a bastard body between minion and brevier is called 5 units ; 3-line excelsior is called 6 units, and another bastard between long primer and small pica is called 7 units. Then we have 9 units, a sort of bastard English, and 10, 14 and 18 units, all bastards, justifying with nothing either in the old or the new systems.

As there seems to be no reason to be dissatisfied with the point, or 1 to 12 pica system, and as there is nothing commendable in the units, I am totally at a loss why such a venture is made. The foundry can certainly not hope that its system will either be copied or thought of by other foundries. As I am not afraid that the unit bodies will gain favor anywhere, I shall waste no more paper on them. But I would advise that foundry to drop them like a hot poker, and come into the ring with the sensible founders and the only sensible system.

In conclusion, I heartily commend the action of a foundry which lately adopted the uniform standard, namely, that of calling the bodies by the number of points in them instead of by the old names : thus 24-point instead of double pica, 18-point instead of 3-line nonpareil, 12-point for pica, 10-point for long primer. It gives the printer, and especially the apprentice, a better idea of the relative proportions of one size to another, than the old names did. In my devil days I often wondered why a certain type should be called by such an odd name as long primer, another by a still odder one, small pica, a third brevier, etc. It didn't strike me as at all sensible. The new names are as simple as the addition table, will be as easily learnt, and their greater fitness be more appreciable to every one. I make a motion that all founders adopt the new style of nomenclature. It will be the best way to avoid confusion, and distinguish their old and the new system. At present the same body is called by one foundry bourgeois, by another 3-line excelsior, by another nonpareil - and - a - half, and finally by another 9-point, which latter, in my humble opinion, is just exactly the proper name, and the one that all should accept.

Yours, for uniformity,   A JOB COMPOSITOR.

☆ BRANCHES AT ☆
MINNEAPOLIS AND SAN FRANCISCO.

AMERICAN SYSTEM
—OF—
INTERCHANGEABLE
TYPE BODIES.
THE ONLY TRUE STANDARD

MARDER, LUSE & CO.

TYPE FOUNDERS

MONROE·STREET,
CHICAGO.

CLARENDON CONDENSED, No. 2.

12A, 24a,   COLUMBIAN. (16 Points Standard Measure.) $3.00

IT SEEMS TO ME THAT EDITORS GET EVERYTHING THEY NEED

They get the Biggest and the Best of Everything that Grows, and get in Free to Circuses

12345   The biggest bugs will speak to them   67890

12A, 24a,   GREAT PRIMER. (18 Points Standard Measure.) $3.45

SOME FOSSILIZED SPECIMENS OF ANTIQUATED HUMANITY

Properly belonging to the Paleozoic Age obtrude their Carboniferous forms upon the

123   Volatile Society of Modern Times   789

8A, 16a,   DOUBLE PICA. (24 Points Standard Measure.) $4.35

CURIOUS ÆSTHETIC REPRODUCTIONS

4   Inspiration drawn from Sunflower and Lily Contemplation   7

Incomprehensible Designs.

6A, 12a,   DOUBLE COLUMBIAN. (32 Points Standard Measure.) $5.50

LAND OF LIGHT AND FREEDOM

23 Splendid Photographic Views of the Rhine 56

4A, 8a,   FOUR-LINE PICA. (48 Points Standard Measure.) $6.65

16 Honor the HEROES of Peace 89

3A, 6a,   FIVE-LINE PICA. (60 Points Standard Measure.) $7.00

Seek thy RECOMPENSE above 47

4 A. 36-POINT ATLANTA. $6.75

RHINE ✦ WINES

SIX-LINE NONPAREIL OF THE POINT STANDARD.

6 A. 24-POINT ATLANTA. $4.50

✦ MILD · WINTER ✦

FOUR-LINE NONPAREIL OF THE POINT STANDARD.

8 A. 18-POINT ATLANTA. $3.50

ASSEMBLIES
✦ SING · 25 ✦

THREE-LINE NONPAREIL OF THE POINT STANDARD.

12 A. 12-POINT ATLANTA. $3.00

LECTURE ✦ JOURNEY
✦ TOURISTS · 60 ✦

TWO-LINE NONPAREIL OF THE POINT STANDARD.

16 A. 10-POINT ATLANTA. $2.75

ENCHANTED ✦ DREAMER
✦ MOONSHINE ✦

LONG PRIMER OF THE POINT STANDARD.

20 A. 8-POINT ATLANTA. $2.50

BANISH ✦ MADNESS ✦ AND ✦ FAMINE
✦ FAMED · NATIONS ✦

BREVIER OF THE POINT STANDARD.

THE DIFFERENT SIZES OF THE ATLANTA SERIES ARE CUT AND CAST TO LINE WITH EACH OTHER AT THE TOP, THE BOTTOM AND THE CENTRE OF THE FACE.
NEITHER CARDBOARD NOR PAPER REQUIRED IN COMBINING THE SERIES AS CAPS AND SMALL CAPS. USE LEADS AND SLUGS.

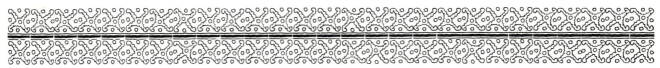

20 a, 6 A, with Ornaments. 18-POINT SANTA CLAUS. $4.00

THREE-LINE NONPAREIL OF THE POINT STANDARD.

The Central Type Foundry, St. Louis, Mo., takes this opportunity to announce that it has lately adopted a new System of Type Bodies, being graded by Points or 12ths of Pica. This System is fully explained in the December issue of THE · PRINTERS · REGISTER a copy of which will be sent to all who apply for it. The indications are that the Point · System · of · Bodies will be adopted by all American Type Founders.

18-POINT SANTA CLAUS BORDER.

We also put up the Santa Claus Ornaments in separate fonts, which contain a larger quantity of them than is put up with the cap and lower case fonts.
Price of Border fonts, $2.00.

24-POINT SANTA CLAUS INITIALS NO. 1.
Per font, $1.50.

CENTRAL

24-POINT SANTA CLAUS INITIALS NO. 2.
Per font, $1.50.

CENTRAL

These Initials Nos. 1 and 2 make a handsome effect when worked in colors. Use No. 1 as a background and print No. 2 over it in a darker ink.

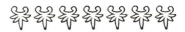

ANNOUNCEMENT.
25% Discount.

TYPE.

FOR some time past it has been well known that various manufacturers of type on irregular bodies—and what may now be termed in printers' parlance as bastard sizes—have been flooding the country with offers to furnish the printing fraternity with their productions at discounts varying from ten to twenty-five per cent from list prices. These offers, by circular and otherwise, while apparently honest, were disingenuous, and were really made because the parties referred to realized that the tide of popular favor was setting in so strongly toward our American system of interchangeable type bodies that they must do something to turn the current into another channel, and therefore took this method to work off their virtually unsalable and undesirable productions.

The beginning of the new year being recognized as a favorable point for new departures and good resolutions, we have determined that, from January 1, 1886, and until further notice, we will allow a discount of twenty-five per cent from our list prices of type and material manufactured on the American system of interchangeable type bodies, to all cash buyers, and to customers who have established with us a line of credit, providing settlement be made between the first and tenth of each month. This discount, it will be noticed, is only offered for cash settlements, and old type and other material offered in exchange to us will be paid for in type and material of our manufacture at list prices. It will also be noticed that our price list contains various articles made by other manufacturers, some of which are patented, and these are not included in our offer of discount, as made above, but will be furnished at the lowest market rates. Our offer is based upon complete fonts and the supply of deficiencies in sorts that may appear therein. Our fonts are schemed with great care, and we have been frequently highly complimented in regard thereto, yet it is possible that the font when used for a special purpose may prove deficient in some respect as to sorts required, and these deficiencies we are always happy to fill within a reasonable time, at the same rate as charged for the regular font; but orders for sorts must hereafter be considered as strictly net since the extra time and expense of filling these orders is such that if our foundry should devote itself entirely to filling orders for sorts the business would be conducted at an absolute loss, as the manufacture and shipment of small items frequently requires as much time and expense as would be needed to fill an order of considerable amount, while the return is simply nominal. It sometimes happens that letters are broken in shipment by careless handling, and in such cases we will cheerfully replace them without charge, on being acquainted with the fact.

In connection with the statement that this discount of twenty-five per cent is made from our list prices, it should be stated that a uniform price per pound is charged by all foundries throughout the United States for Display and Fancy Type, as well as for Roman faces, except as to reduced rates given by us on large fonts. Any apparent discrepancy in the prices as quoted by ourselves and other foundries can be accounted for in one of two ways. The schemes upon which the fonts are made up may differ, so that while the number of a's in both fonts is the same, or nearly the same, the fact will not hold good regarding the other letters and characters of the fonts. Spaces and quads are put up with all the fonts manufactured by the Chicago Type Foundry, except those on Nonpareil and Pica bodies, of which we suppose nearly every printing-office to have a supply in stock. Some foundries do not put up any spaces and quads with their fonts, and

thus their price would be apparently lower. Our customers can rest assured that, taking into account the weight of our fonts, our prices are as low as the lowest, and our customers have the additional advantage of obtaining fonts well schemed and cast upon a standard system of type bodies.

It is a well known fact that type and other printing material can always be bought better from the manufacturers than by forwarding orders through second parties, and if our customers will lend us their aid, we will promptly fill all orders from any section of the country, however remote. To expedite matters cash should accompany the order, except when a line of credit with our house has already been established, as when references are inclosed it requires considerable time to write for the same and obtain replies. Prices are given in our list for all articles furnished by us, so that our customers can readily estimate the cost of their orders, and should any change in your estimate be required it will be our aim to make everything perfectly satisfactory in settlement. We are sometimes requested by those with whom we have no business acquaintance, to forward an order at once, and references are at the same time inclosed. Should we take time to write to these references, from five to ten days' delay would be occasioned and sometimes even longer, while all trouble and annoyance could be obviated by remitting cash in advance, either by Bank Draft, Express or Postoffice Order; and should the amount so remitted be more than the value of the material desired, we will at once return the overplus, if so requested.

We hope, after reading the above announcement, all that contemplate purchasing and who have hitherto felt themselves unable to meet the additional expense incurred at the outset in discarding their outfit of irregular bodies for one symmetrically based on the American System of Interchangeable Type Bodies, will now feel encouraged to make the reformation. Our offer is made in good faith, and should we be led at any future time to withdraw the same, due notice will be given.

ELECTROTYPING.

A varying scale of discount on Electrotyping has been in use for some time past, and much dissatisfaction and annoyance has been created thereby. Recently the Electrotypers of this city met and arranged a new scale of prices, a copy of which we will send on application. We think that this scale will soon become universal throughout other cities. We therefore announce that, in common with other Electrotypers of this city, we will, until further notice, allow a discount of twenty-five per cent from scale prices on all cash orders, as well as to customers who have a line of credit on our books, providing settlements are made between the first and tenth of each month. In connection with this announcement we beg to say that our Electrotype Establishment is one of the largest and most perfect in the country, and our facilities for turning out first-class work are unexcelled. Possessing the most improved machinery the market affords and employing the most skilled workmen, we are prepared to execute with promptness and satisfaction to our patrons all orders committed to our trust.

CASES, STANDS, ETC.

Until further notice a discount of twenty-five per cent from list prices will be allowed on all cash orders for cases, stands, cabinets, chases, galleys, brass rules and dashes, wood and metal furniture and reglet, lead, slugs and ink, as well as to customers who have a line of credit with us, providing settlements are made between the first and tenth of each month. Address

MARDER, LUSE & CO.
TYPE FOUNDERS,
CHICAGO, ILL.

MARDER, LUSE & CO., TYPE FOUNDERS,
CHICAGO, ILL.

AMERICAN SYSTEM OF INTERCHANGEABLE TYPE BODIES.

ROMAN EXTENDED.
IMPROVED SERIES.

AMERICAN SYSTEM OF INTERCHANGEABLE TYPE BODIES.

32A, 64a,   PEARL (ON NONP., 6 Points Standard Measure.) $4.15

RARE BILLS OF FARE EXCELLING

For Utility this Series tells a Beautiful Story Modestly

Agitators of the Public Stomach 234

32A, 64a,   AGATE (ON NONP., 6 Points Standard Measure.) $3.55

SPLENDID LODGING ROOMS TO LET

Elegant and Airy Apartments Rich of Ornamentation

Fancy Tobacco Juice Sketches. 0987

The above are also cast on Pearl and Agate bodies when so desired.

18A, 36a,   NONPAREIL. (6 Points Standard Measure.) $2.65

FINE BOOK AND JOB PRINTERS

Slaves Chained to the Chariot of Triumphal Art

Riders in the Black Maria 567

18A, 36a,   BREVIER. (8 Points Standard Measure.) $3.80

TRUST TO PROVIDENCE

Money to Loan at Twenty Per Cent

Confidence Operator 65

16A, 32a,   BOURGEOIS. (9 Points Standard Measure,) $3.75

NATIONAL GRATITUDE

A Pair of Wooden Legs to Hop with

Graceful Movement 34

12A, 24a,   LONG PRIMER. (10 Points Standard Measure.) $3.15

PERT QUESTIONS

Ghosts do Die Natural Deaths

Climbing Miners 4

12A, 24a,   PICA. (12 Points Standard Measure.) $4.35

UNEXAMPLED GENEROSITY
Home for Friendless Canines and Strayed Felines
Weird Chorus of Gratitude 79

8A, 16a,   GREAT PRIMER. (18 Points Standard Measure.) $5.65

BULLS OF BASHAN
Relation to Our Irish Bovines 58

6A, 12a,   DOUBLE PICA. (24 Points Standard Measure.) $7.40

WATERFALL PATH
Hungry and Thirsty Souls 7

5A, 10a,   DOUBLE ENGLISH. (28 Points Standard Measure.) $7.35

WILD TIGERS
Searching for Oysters 4

4A, 8a,   DOUBLE GREAT PRIMER. (36 Points Standard Measure.) $10.85

SILKEN Thread

SPACES AND QUADS WITH ALL SIZES EXCEPT NONPAREIL AND PICA.

✦ TITLE EXPANDED. ✦
IMPROVED SERIES.

24A, 48a,   AGATE. (5½ Points Standard Measure.) $4.00
SIMPLIFIED DONOTHINGNESS
The Grandest Policy for Statesmen to adopt.
Splendid Array of Native Talent
1234567890

18A, 36a,   NONPAREIL. (6 Points Standard Measure.) $3.15
BRALOUDE & SPREDEAGLE,
Loud Elocutionary Gymnastic Professors
Political Fine Work Demonstrators.
1234567890

18A, 36a,   BREVIER. (8 Points Standard Measure.) $3.70
JOURNALS OF AMERICA
The Pen is Mightier than the Sword.
Slander Circulators 48

12A, 24a,   LONG PRIMER. (10 Points Standard Measure.) $3.20
LONGING GLANCES
Harp of the Thousand Strings
Melody Producer 39

10A, 20a,   PICA. (12 Points Standard Measure.) $3.60
SPLENDID SERIES FOR JOB WORK
Energetic Inducements Offered to those Strong-minded
Advocates of Woman's Rights 4678

6A, 12a,   GREAT PRIMER. (18 Points Standard Measure.) $3.85
CHILDHOOD'S MEMORIES
Depleting Purses, Replenish Stockings 25

6A, 12a,   PARAGON. (20 Points Standard Measure.) $5.75
DETECTIVE OFFICER
Modest and Pretty Maidens 765

4A, 8a,   DOUBLE PICA. (24 Points Standard Measure.) $5.45
FAST RAILWAYS
Lightning Speed Train 5

3A, 6a,   DOUBLE COLUMBIAN. (32 Points Standard Measure.) $6.80
EQUESTRIAN
Brilliant Comet 32

DOUBLE PARAGON AND FOUR-LINE PICA IN PREPARATION.

AGATE CAST ON NONPAREIL BODY WHEN DESIRED.   SPACES AND QUADS WITH ALL SIZES EXCEPT NONPAREIL AND PICA.

9 a, 7 A.　　　　　　　18-POINT OLD STYLE BOLD.　　　　　　　$4.50

Industry Lubricated
MERCHANDIZE EXCHANGE
COMMODITIES
Daily Market Reports $36

THREE-LINE NONPAREIL OF THE POINT STANDARD.

16 a, 12 A.　　12-POINT OLD STYLE BOLD.　　$4.00

Intellectual
EDITORIAL WORK
Reported
MORNING MAIL
Hurried Pens

TWO-LINE NONPAREIL OF THE POINT STANDARD.

18 a, 14 A.　　10-POINT OLD STYLE BOLD.　　$3.50

Novels Printed
ROMANCERS EARNINGS
Emolument
RIGHTS PROTECTED
Literary Product

LONG PRIMER OF THE POINT STANDARD.

22 a, 16 A.　　8-POINT OLD STYLE BOLD.　　$3.50

Neat Garments
BEST HOMESPUN CLOTHES
Economize
COTTON HABILIMENTS
Ancient Modes 25

BREVIER OF THE POINT STANDARD.

22 a, 16 A.　　6-POINT OLD STYLE BOLD.　　$3.00

Civilized Natives
WESTERN CONTINENT PRAISED
Enterprising
INDEPENDENT AMERICAN
Modern Advance 48

NONPAREIL OF THE POINT STANDARD.

THIS SERIES BEING CUT AND CAST ACCORDING TO SYSTEMATIC LINES MAY BE COMBINED EASILY IN THE SEVERAL WAYS HERE SHOWN.

HHHHHHHHHHHHHHHHHHHHHHH

HHHHHHHHHHHHHHHh

HHHHHHHHHHHHHHHHHHHH

ACCURATE JUSTIFICATION SECURED BY USE OF POINT SYSTEM LEADS OR SLUGS AND DISPENSING WITH CARD BOARD OR PAPER.

CAST BY THE CENTRAL TYPE FOUNDRY, ST. LOUIS, MO.

3 A $1.46, 3 a $1.30, figs. 52c.   No. 96, 2-line, 2c.

MINDE
Chair 8

3 A $1.46, 3 a $1.30, figs. 52c.   No. 96, 2½-line, 2c.

HIDE

3 A $1.46, 3 a $1.30, figs. 52c.   No. 96, 3-line, 2c.

Nod 3

MOB

3 A $2.19, 3 a $1.95, figs. 78c.   No. 96, 4-line, 3c.

BID

3 A $2.19, 3 a $1.95, figs. 78c.   No. 96, 5-line, 3c.

DE

3 A $2.92, 3 a $2.60, figs. $1.04.   No. 96, 6-line, 4c.

BI

3 A $3 65, 3 a $3.25, figs. $1.50.   No. 96, 8-line, 5c.

H

3 A $2.19, 3 a $1.95, figs. 78c.   No. 95, 6-line, 3c.

DREGS OF MUD
New Clarendon 5

3 A $2.92, 3 a $2.60, figs. $1.04.   No. 95, 8-line, 4c.

DRUM CORPS

3 A $2.92, 3 a $2.60, figs. $1.04.   No. 95, 10-line, 4c.

MEDICINE

3 A $3.65, 3 a $3.25, figs. $1.50.   No. 95, 12-line, 5c.

HOUNDS

THESE STYLES MADE ANY SIZE DESIRED.   PRICES OF LARGER SIZES GIVEN ON APPLICATION.

THE MIDNIGHT BURGLARY.

A *MELLOW*-DRAMA.

BY ALONZO W. STURGES.

SCENE — *A Printing-Office.* TIME — *Midnight.* DRAMATIS PERSONÆ — *Two Burglars.*

FIRST BURGLAR.

How, now, Bill—where away?
Here is a window raised—assist, I say,
And in I'll go to search for needed spoils;
So lively, boy, and free from watchman's toils,
We'll try our luck and see what we can find,
For bless me if I wouldn't mind
A good, rich haul tonight, something that would
Supply the inner man with drink and food.

SECOND BURGLAR.

Good luck, old boy, 'tis well arranged;
Our quarters may be quickly changed
By this most lucky oversight, and we,
Though vagrants, will in clover be.
Hark! there's no noise; no force is near—
So tumble in, we need not have a fear
Of interruption, for the night is dark,
And scarce a "cop" is out upon a lark.

FIRST BURGLAR (*within*).

Ah! here we are, and darkness reigns;
We'll get our labor for our pains
Unless some ray of light we can bestow
Upon the scene around to let us know
Whether 'tis lawyer's crib or broker's till
From which we may our empty pockets fill.
But then, to think of it, 'twould never do;
Our work would be espied the window through,
And we, exposed with all our freight,
Would sorry 'pearance make before the magistrate.
We'll do this job with darkness as our aid,
And thank our fortune for the friendly shade.
Then steady, now, tread lightly here;
That there is rubbish of some sort 'tis clear,
And racks and benches, quite a motley mixture,
With various other kind of fixture.

SECOND BURGLAR (*within*).

You're right, old doughty, I will lightly tread,
For 'tis a place where one should needs be *lead*,
And then the *case* might not be very clear
Unless some gas jet cast its favors near,
Revealing to his sight a little *plainer*
The obstacle which proves my firm detainer;
It seems as though I'd break my very bones
Over some rude, *imposing-stones*,
Yet, for my part, I can no *form* perceive,
And think we may as well this *rat*-hole leave.

FIRST BURGLAR.

Tut! tut! man—what, give up this *job?*
Yours is the heart of very swab.
Come, *chase* away your girlish fears,
Stick to the *rule* we've had for years,
Of clearing deeds of darkness in the eyes
Of other folks by use of subtle *lyes*.

SECOND BURGLAR.

Go on! go on! I will await you here,
And warn you if there's footsteps coming near.
Proceed, and ransack well each hole and corner,
And to your name and business prove an honor.
The world knows well you're but an outlawed knave,
But better you'd be that than *galley*-slave.

FIRST BURGLAR.

There, silence! Bill—you're sadly *out of sorts*.
Why need you make such rash retorts,
And seek to breed a foul contention
When I your laxity should barely mention;
Your language, so severe, my nature pricks,
And were we not in this blest fix,
I'd dare you to the use of *shooting-sticks*.
But here—what have I now?
Some papers in a till, a pocket-book, I vow!
And that well stuffed with greenbacks, I dare say.
Really, this dark night's job is going to pay.
I'll close the drawer, for I can see no more;
But hark, there is a *rat*-ling at the outer door!
Make way! I'm coming! put your *form* outside,
And I will quickly from the window glide.

SECOND BURGLAR (*outside*).

In open air again; I freer breathe, I'll own;
This work is dang'rous, and should quick be done.
But say, what have you got?—let's seek a light,
And see what spoils we have secured tonight.
I trust the thing will prove well in the sequel,
And we will share the dosh quite equal.

FIRST BURGLAR (*outside*).

So! so! you are not slow to count the booty,
Though you are wont to shirk your duty.
Bill, you're an avaricious cuss, withal,
And hardly fit to tote with decent pal.
But hold—here is a light, and I must see
How good a prize this hasty haul may be.
I long to feast my eyes, which used, of old,
To sate their longings on the shining gold;
But in this reckless age there aint a haper,
And we must now content ourselves with paper.
So here I have it at my own disposal,
And note you well the rich disclosal.
Observe! observe, while I the package ope,
And give full freedom to your wildest hope.
This is a God-send, as I really think,
And bids my palate crave e'n now for drink.
Here, here, come forth, ye charms, and feast my gaze;
But O, what can it be? why this amaze?
What have I here? I am astound, dismayed;
'Tis but a file of printers' bills, and those unpaid!

[*Leave in disgust.*]

BUSINESS COURTESY.

In visiting business offices one meets a great variety of persons. Most are kind, courteous and accommodating; others are fair to medium in these respects; another class—fortunately very small—are in ill-humor nearly all the time, full of gruffness, and cranky, having much of the nature of such unpleasant and fretful animals as bears and porcupines; a fourth class are languid and indifferent in their replies to civil questions, and are apt to be tinctured more or less with a sort of superciliousness and a well-developed self-importance. These persons seem to think that if they would unbend, throw off their awful dignities, and try to be accommodating, they would not be estimated at their true worth and importance. This class is generally composed of young men who have more conceit than good sense, and it requires a good many years for some of them to get cured, the time required for the cure depending upon the vigor of their mental constitution. The newspaper man has met all these characters and "sized them up," and can pigeon-hole them as rapidly as a postal clerk can pigeon-hole letters.

A TRAMP PRINTER, to whom the editor of the Northeast (Md.) *Star* gave a quarter two years ago, acknowledged the kindness recently by an editorial on Maryland hospitality in a prosperous Minnesota paper. The ex-tramp is now its editor and proprietor.

18 POINTS.   THREE-LINE NONPAREIL CRAYON.   Price, $4.05

Oakland Forestry Association

Safety Deposit Company   Eighth National Bank

Sprightly & Nimble, Stenographers

1234567890

24 POINTS.   TWO-LINE PICA CRAYON.   Price, $5.15

Matrimonial Contractors

Youthful Dandy   Artful Maiden

Gretnagreen, Tuesday Evening

36 POINTS.   THREE-LINE PICA CRAYON.   Price, $6.30

Atlantis Steamship Co.

Merchandise   Transporters

ALL COMPLETE WITH FIGURES.

Grasshopper Jumping Contest

Eleventh Spring Meeting

Sunnyside Meadows

Karnac Series

Phelps, Dalton & Co.

Dickinson Type Foundery,

Boston, Mass.

No. 236 Washington Street.

PHELPS, DALTON & CO.,

DICKINSON

TYPE

FOUNDERY

No. 236 WASHINGTON STREET, BOSTON.

We meet Competition with the best material and the best terms, for cash or its equivalent.

AMERICAN SYSTEM OF
INTERCHANGEABLE TYPE BODIES.

AMERICAN SYSTEM OF
INTERCHANGEABLE TYPE BODIES.

IMPERIAL.
PATENTED.

12A, 24a,   PICA. (12 Points Standard Measure.) $2.85

CARBONIZED SUNSHINE

Lay in a Large Stock for use in

Depressed Seasons 25

10A, 20a,   GREAT PRIMER. (18 Points Standard Measure.) $3.80

FAIR IMOGENE

Ardent Lovers Crowd

To meet thee 46

6A, 12a,   DOUBLE PICA. (24 Points Standard Measure.) $5.25

CRUDE IDEAS OF DUDEISM
Transient Flickerings of Intellect 678

4A, 8a.   DOUBLE GREAT PRIMER. (36 Points Standard Measure.) $6.25

SKATING RINKLES
Bright Sparkling River 459

SPACES AND QUADS WITH ALL SIZES EXCEPT PICA.

SKELETON ANTIQUE.
ORIGINAL.

3A (Caps), $5.35   SIX-LINE PICA. (72 Points Standard Measure.)   4a (Low. Case), $4.20

Critical INSPECTION of the 37

3A (Caps), $7.75   EIGHT-LINE PICA. (96 Points Standard Measure.)   4a (Low. Case), $5.65

CHARMING Simplicity 25

SPACES AND QUADS FURNISHED WITH BOTH THE ABOVE SIZES.

935. CANON COPLEY, 3 A, 3 A, $7.25.

BOND & MINER
No. 30 MOTT

908. DOUBLE GREAT PRIMER COPLEY, 4 A, 4 A, $5.00.

GRINSON & MERRY
ROOM No. 618 OPEN

933. DOUBLE PICA COPLEY, 6 A, 6 A, $4.00.

SUPERFINE DECORATOR
CHARGES 5 CENTS A MILE

934. PARAGON COPLEY, 7 A, 7 A, $3.25.

CARTRIDGE, SHOTWELL & RIFLE
No. 47 SHELL STREET, GUNTON

BOSTON TYPE FOUNDRY, JOHN K. ROGERS, AGENT, 104 MILK STREET.

THE REAL CULPRIT.

BEFORE us lies an illustrated catalogue of a New England amateur printers' furnishing establishment which has probably done as much to demoralize legitimate trade and furnish as big a crop of botches as any house in America. The inducements held out are not only specious, but in many instances absolutely false, as the following extracts, culled from its pages, abundantly prove:

BOYS AND YOUNG MEN!

Or young Ladies! Nothing in the world will give you so much pleasure, real enjoyment, and earn many a dollar at the same time as a printing press. On the last page of this book read what others HAVE done; YOU can do as well—perhaps better. What else gives you fun and pocket money both? Any boy can do all his father's printing, and very nicely too, after a little experience. PARENTS, TEACHERS, and all having care of young people, should aid and encourage their proteges in amateur printing, for it gives them a SAFE, BENEFICIAL amusement; they improve in reading, spelling, punctuation, grammar; they love the fun and get a good idea of business from the work. And they do not tire of it, because of its never-ending novelty and variety.

DO YOUR OWN PRINTING!

It pays. Think of it a moment! Whatever your occupation, you can do most of the printing you need at QUARTER printers' prices. The lively competition in EVERYTHING nowadays, compels ALL to use printers' ink freely, or else a more wide-awake rival draws the business. But newspaper advertisements cost high and reach only part of the people, and the printers charge a round price for circulars, etc. But have your own press at hand and a card, circular, hand bill, or the like, can be turned off at any time, at TRIFLING COST. The best known names of this country are those which keep themselves before the public by print. It is pleasant relaxation to do the work, and we with EVERYBODY would read the PROOFS on the last page of this Catalogue.

"It pays," quoth this genius, "to become an amateur printer." No, sir; it does *not* pay. It does *not* pay anybody to debauch public taste, take the bread out of the mouths of honest, qualified workmen, and injure legitimate trade. It does *not* pay to help swell the flood of botches with which the country is already cursed, or encourage boys to make a nuisance of themselves, even if by so doing an unprincipled humbug is enabled to dispose of some worn out or discarded stock of material; and the man who advises to the contrary, shows a moral turpitude which proves that he is unworthy to be recognized either as parent or teacher. Tradesmen who make a habit of doing their own printing under the conditions advocated above, have no reason to complain if they are paid back in their own coin, and the patronage of their customers is transferred to firms which do business on business principles.

But here is another precious *morceau*, which will, no doubt, be news to all of our readers:

IT IS A MISTAKE if any one imagines it is a long job to learn type setting and to do *good printing*. Any one of ordinary intelligence can, by the aid of the very excellent, concise instructions we send, learn the first principles *very quickly*, and then, "practice makes perfect." With hardly an exception buyers take hold instantly, and have a very presentable job done in a few hours after receiving their Press.

Think of this, ye numbskulls, who have devoted the best years of your lives to master the details of your trade, and yet realize from day to day you can learn something you never knew before, that you have been laboring under a fatal mistake. What were you thinking about when you *wasted* (?) four or five years in learning the business, when, according to this Solon, you could have turned out a very "respectable job" *a few hours after you had entered the printing-office!* remembering at the same time the important fact that the term of apprenticeship is decided by the employé, not by the employer. Is there an intelligent man in the United States who believes any such rubbish? Is there an employer, foreman or journeyman, who values his reputation, who will affix his signature to such a statement? *Not one;* and nobody knows this fact better than the party holding out such false inducements. On the contrary, we will guarantee that nineteen out of every twenty of these so-called self-instructed amateurs would be kicked out of any printing establishment claiming to do good work, for incompetency, even as an apprentice! Their handiwork, instead of being "respectable," reminds us of the effort of the amateur artist, which, visited by a wag in his absence, placed beneath it: "This is a hoss." Indignant at such intrusion, the amateur corrected the mistake as follows: "This is neither a hoss nor a muel, it is a jackass."

Boys, take our advice. If you have determined to be a printer, determine to be a *good one;* learn the business in its entirety, under the guidance of a careful and competent foreman, and you will, in after years, respect yourselves and command the respect of your associates. If you have not so determined, get your fun and pocket money in a more honorable manner than filching it from those who depend on an honest day's wages for an honest day's work.

OUR SPECIMEN PAGES.

WE direct the special attention of the trade to the many new and beautiful designs published in our specimen pages in the present issue of THE INLAND PRINTER. It may be proper here to state that we have recently concluded arrangements with the leading typefounders in the United States, by which their latest productions will appear monthly in our pages, and employers who desire to keep up with the times would do well to make a note of this fact.

CHICAGO SCRIPT.

PATENTED FEB. 12. 1884.

Card Font, 6A, 16a, $4.10 GREAT PRIMER. (18 Points Standard Measure.) Job Font, 12A, 48a, $10.20

Gracefulness and Beauty in the execution of Job Printing

Attained by a Judicious Use of the

Novelties Introduced by us, of which This Series of "Chicago Script"

Is one of the Most Attractive 1234567890

Card Font, 4A, 12a, $4.70 DOUBLE PICA. (24 Points Standard Measure.) Job Font, 8A, 36a, $11.75

For Artistic Designs in Spring Dresses

Ladies should Visit the extensive Establishment of

Dame Nature 1234567890

Card Font, 3A, 8a, $6.00 DOUBLE GREAT PRIMER. (36 Points Standard Measure.) Job Font, 5A, 25a, $15.30

Argentine National Bank

Pay to Jeremiah Grabitall the sum

$1,286,743.95

Address all Orders for "Chicago Script" to

Marder, Luse & Co.

139 & 141 Monroe Street,

Chicago, Ill.

SPACES AND QUADS WITH ALL SIZES.

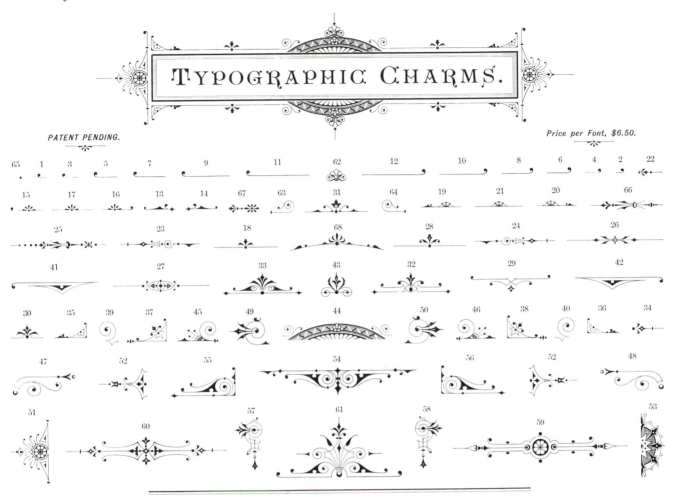

Typographic Charms.

PATENT PENDING.

Price per Font, $6.50.

~Didot~Series.~

16 A.	Pica Didot No. 3.	$2.00

LATEST + AMERICAN + INVENTION + 23

12 A.	Pica Didot No. 1.	$2.00

GOVERNMENT + BUILDING + 5

10 A.	Three-Line Nonpareil Didot No. 1.	$2.75

MARINE + BANK + 3

8 A.	Two-Line Pica Didot.	$3.00

MONUMENT + 5

12 A.	Pica Didot No. 2.	$2.00

SPRING + FASHION + MAGAZINE + 7

10 A.	Three-Line Nonpareil Didot No. 3.	$2.25

IMPORTANT NOTICE 9

10 A.	Three-Line Nonpareil Didot No. 2.	$2.50

FOREST + HOMES + 8

6 A.	Five-Line Nonpareil Didot No. 2.	$3.50

GENERAL + 6

6 A.	Five-Line Nonpareil Didot No. 1.	$4.25

NONPAREIL + JOBBER

All sizes of this Series are cast so as to line perfectly with each other.

PATENT APPLIED FOR.

18 A   TWO LINE NONPAREIL SUPERIOR. [12 Points] $1 75

THIS WORLD WITH ALL ITS BEAUTY, ITS SUNSHINE AND ITS SHOWERS, WAS
MADE FOR HIGHEST DUTY, AND NOT FOR IDLE HOURS; EACH LEAFLET HAS ITS MISSION, EACH
2345 BLADE OF GRASS ITS PLACE 6789

12 A   THREE LINE NONPAREIL SUPERIOR. [18 Points] $2 10

THE AVERAGE WEIGHT OF TWELVE INCHES OF SOLID
MATTER SET IN THIRTEEN EMS PICA MEASURE IS SIX AND THREE
2345 QUARTER POUNDS 6789

10 A   FOUR LINE NONPAREIL SUPERIOR. [24 Points] $2 60

THE HAUGHTY YOUTH WILL NEVER
SPEAK THE TRUTH UNLESS HE FINDS IT PAYS
45 TOMBSTONE AVENUE 68

6 A   SIX LINE NONPAREIL SUPERIOR. [36 Points] $3 05

THE HOUR OF BLISS IS DEAD
AND GONE IN SILENT SADNESS THEY
23 LIVE ALONE 68

UMBRA  SERIES.

PATENT APPLIED FOR.

8 A   THREE LINE NONPAREIL UMBRA. [18 Points] $2 55

PRINTERS' FAVORITE
THE GREAT WESTERN TYPE FOUNDRY
2345 CHICAGO ILLINOIS 6789

6 A   FOUR LINE NONPAREIL UMBRA. [24 Points] $3 25

SALT LAKE CITY
ENGLISH OPERA COMPANIES
43 SHERMAN HOUSE 58

4 A   SIX LINE NONPAREIL UMBRA. [36 Points] $4 95

CHICAGOANS
ELEGANT GARDENS
43 FLOWERS 75

PATENT PENDING FOR THE CENTRAL TYPE FOUNDRY

5a 3A   72-POINT ART GOTHIC. (Twelve-line Nonpareil.) $10.00

Ninety Abstract Books

5a 4A   60-POINT ART GOTHIC. (Ten-Line Nonpareil.) $9.20

Recorder of Property

5a 4A   48-POINT ART GOTHIC. (Eight-line Nonpareil.) $6.50

Explains Theoretical Science
Modern Philosophy

8a 6A   36-POINT ART GOTHIC. (Six-line Nonpareil.) $5.00

Political Schemers   Secret Assemblies
Absolutely Corrupt Methods 80

10a 8A   24-POINT ART GOTHIC. (Four-Line Nonpareil.) $4.00

Transitory Geometrical Colored Forms Portrayed
Revolutions of a Kaleidoscope 462

16a 12A   18-POINT ART GOTHIC. (Three-line Nonp.) $3.00 | 20a 14A   12-POINT ART GOTHIC. (Two-line Nonp.) $3.00

Romantic Experiences of Travelers   Deepest and Strongest Streams of Learning

Extraordinary Incidents 369   Often Moving in Narrow Channels

WE ALSO CAST THE ART GOTHIC SERIES ON OUR OLD SYSTEM OF TYPE BODIES. PRICES OF FONTS ARE THE SAME IN BOTH SYSTEMS.

CAST BY THE CENTRAL TYPE FOUNDRY, ST. LOUIS, MO.

5a 4A   72-POINT ST. LOUIS. (Twelve-line Nonpareil.) $12.50

RANKEST WOODLAND
Grandeur Noted

6a 5A   48-POINT ST. LOUIS. (Eight-line Nonpareil.) $7.50

COLLECTED STATE REVENUE
Heavy Taxes Reported 15

6a 5A   36-POINT ST. LOUIS. (Six-line Nonpareil.) $5.00

MEANDERING LOVERS MUCH DEVOTED
Sweethearts at Sundown 24

10a 6A   24-POINT ST. LOUIS. (Four-line Nonp.) $4.00

SUMMER PICNIC JAUNTS
Rustic Pleasures 48

14a 8A   18-POINT ST. LOUIS. (Three-line Nonp.) $3.25

AUTUMN MOONLIGHT EXCURSIONS
Viewing River Scenes 360

New Lining Face
Uniform Bottom Line

Labor-Saving System

NOTE.—The five sizes of the ST. LOUIS Series line with each other, and can be used in combination as Caps and Small Caps, accurate lining and justification being secured with Nonpareil Slugs and Six-to-Pica Leads—thus avoiding the use of cardboard or paper, an advantage which every practical printer will appreciate. This lining feature will be added to all new faces made by this foundry.

CAST BY THE CENTRAL TYPE FOUNDRY, ST. LOUIS, MO.

BOSTON TYPE FOUNDRY
PATENT PENDING
ACCURACY BEAUTY & DURABILITY.

940. DOUBLE ENGLISH WEIMAR, 6 a, 3 A, $4.00.

The Old Boston Type Foundry
Hard and Tough
No. 104 Milk Street $1886

946. GREAT PRIMER WEIMAR, 10 a, 5 A, $3.25.

Grand Anniversary of the Old Thirteen Guardsmen
Massasoit Hall, September 25
Music by Squeak.   Catering by Fish & Pate

BAYARD SERIES.

947. GREAT PRIMER BAYARD, 20 a, 6 A, $2.75.

Grand World's Exposition at Paris.   Excursions Daily by Air Ships.   Passage Free
Supplies Furnished by the Boston Type Foundry
Continuous Telegraphic, Telephonic Communications en Route to all Countries

950. PICA BAYARD, 24 a, 8 A, $2.50.

Discoveries, Inventions, Improvements, Everything in the Lines of Creation, Manufacture and Importation
Transcendental Literature, Surprising Revelation of Facts, Ethereal Phenomena
Tickets to Celestial Music by Metaphysical Choirs Given Free to Patrons of the House

BOSTON TYPE FOUNDRY. JOHN K. ROGERS, AGENT, 104 MILK STREET.

104   April 1886

POINTS.   NONPAREIL CULDEE.   Price, $2.55.

⊱⊰ Boreal League Autumnal Meeting ⊱⊰
Opening of Cyclone, Hurricane, and Tornado Season
Preventive Measures Discussed
Schemes Directing their Pathway Upward
1234567890

Price, $2.80.   THREE-LINE EXCELSIOR CULDEE.   9 POINTS.

⊱⊰ Retirement from Business ⊱⊰
Future Home, Stone Building in Suburbs
Necessary Change of Occupation
1234567890

12 POINTS.   PICA CULDEE.   Price, $3.25.

⊱⊰ Broadgauge, Romanesque and Company ⊱⊰
Warerooms, 236-954 Commercial Avenue, South Merchantville
Superior ❖ Work, ❖ Economy, ❖ Promptness

CULDEE SHOWN IN COMBINATION.

Sweeping, Dusting and Scrubbing

Artistically Performed by the

Household ❖ Detersive ❖ Company

For Terms, Apply at Sign of the

Bucket, Soapdish and Ashpan

18 POINTS.   THREE-LINE NONPAREIL CULDEE.   Price, $3.80.

⊱⊰ Eighteen ✳ Superb ✳ Volumes ⊱⊰
Forty Dollars Each
Influence of the Grindstone on Civilization

24 POINTS.   TWO-LINE PICA CULDEE.   Price, $4.60.

⊱⊰ OPPORTUNITIES ⊱⊰

Bathing Costume   Wedding Garment
Requisites for Housekeeping

ALL COMPLETE WITH FIGURES.

A CHRONOLOGY OF TYPEFOUNDING.

NO part of the history of the typographical art is hidden in more settled darkness than the early manufacture of the types. Doubtless, considerable secrecy accompanied all the operations of the first printers, and, indeed, was maintained down to a late period. Whether Caxton was acquainted with the manufacture as well as the use of type there is no evidence to decide. The probability is that his first two fonts were cast, by his instruction, at Bruges, the second being brought over by him to Westminster.

The first allusion in any book to English typefounders, appears in Abp. Parker's preface to " Asser's Chronicle of King Alfred (Lond. 1574). The editor says, that as far as he knew, Day was the first to cut types. It is presumed, hence, that John Day was only one typefounder among others, and that therefore the art was by no means a novel one. Day printed from (circ.) 1546-1584.

SEVENTEENTH CENTURY.

About the beginning of this century, typefounding and printing was separated from each other. The former was exercised as a trade by itself and divided into the several branches of cutting, casting and dressing; the workers in which were indiscriminately called letter-founders, though few did or could perform the whole work themselves.

1637.—Decree passed " That there shall be four founders of letters for printing and no more." This shows that typefounding was now a distinct trade in London, and under rigid government protection.

The four founders under this decree were : John Grismand, Thomas Wright, Arthur Nicholas and Alex. Fifield, who cast from matrices obtained from Holland; no attempt having been made, as far as can be ascertained, to recognize original founders. These restraints were taken away, as well as those on printers, by the dissolution of the court of Star Chamber, by 16, Charles I.

1662.—An act more burdensome than the decree of 1637 was passed (13-14 Cat. II.) by which the number of master founders was again reduced to four. This continued, with some slight alterations, till 1693, when it was abolished.

Notwithstanding these restraints, Moxon, writing in 1683, states that the number of founders and printers had grown very many.

1669.—The first dated type specimen issued—" Proves of Several Sorts of Letter cast by Joseph Moxon."

1685.—Appointment of typefounders revived by James II. for seven years. This was not afterward revived.

1690.—Matrices given to Oxford University by Dr. Fell and Junius.

EIGHTEENTH CENTURY.

The eighteenth century witnessed the last of the old school of typefounders, John James (d. 1772), and the rise of the new race, in William Caslon.

Despite the restrictive care of the government during the previous century, the typefounders of Holland and Flanders supplied English printers with better types than native art could produce; and this continued up to the establishment of the first *Caslon* foundry.

Rowe Mores was the historian of early typefounding. His " Dissertation upon English Typographical Foundries" was published in 1778. He was born in 1730, and died 1771; thus not living to see the publication of his work. He was in possession of nearly all the early English matrices and molds. These were sold by auction in 1782; what became of them is not known.

About 1750 a foundry was established by Baskerville at Birmingham. It is doubtful whether any specimen book was issued. The plant was sold to Beaumarchais, removed to Paris, and probably absorbed by one of the large Parisian foundries.

Rowe Mores speaks of the following foundries : John Grover, Thomas Grover, his son; his foundry purchased in 1758 by John James. Part of this foundry is said to have belonged to Wynken de Worde.

Mores also names Goring, Robert Andrews, Silvester Andrews, his son, whose foundry was purchased by James Skinner, Head, Robert Mitchell, Thomas James, who served apprenticeship with R. Andrews,

who began business in 1710, and died 1738, and Jacob Ilife, 1730.

About the middle of the eighteenth century there were working contemporaneously John Baskerville, at Birmingham, the Caslons, at London, and Alex. Wilson, at St. Andrews, Scotland.

1720.—William Caslon (born 1692, died 1766) was an engraver on gunlocks and barrels, brass for bookbinders' blocking-tools, and silver for silversmiths. He was induced to devote attention to cutting punches. After having an opportunity of seeing the general process of typefounding at James' foundry, he applied himself to the pursuit of the art, being supported pecuniarily by several of the leading printers. It has always been understood in the family of the Caslons, and handed down to the present time, that William Caslon cut his first punches as early as 1716.

Ultimately he brought the art to a perfection previously unattained in England, and rendered English printers independent of the Dutch, from whom they had previously obtained all their *best* fonts. We believe *all* his punches are in use to this day.

1736.—John James succeeds his father, who died in 1772. His foundry in Bartholomew-close, bought by auction by Rowe Mores in 1782, and in his possession when he wrote his book. He was called " The last of the old English letter-founders."

The successor to William Caslon the first, was his son, William Caslon the second, who died in 1778, when the property was equally divided between his two sons, and his widow who died in 1795.

He had two sons; first, William Caslon the third, who disposed of his share in 1793 to Mrs. William Caslon the second, and Henry Caslon's widow; second, Henry, who died 1788.

Mrs. W. Caslon bought in 1799 her mother-in-law's share interest, and carried on the business till she took a partner, Nathaniel Catherwood. She died in 1809. Catherwood also in 1809.

Her son Henry then took the business with a partner, John James Catherwood, brother of Nathaniel Catherwood. The partnership was dissolved in 1812.

Henry Caslon carried on business alone till 1822, when he took into partnership Martin W. Livermore. The foundry then went on to Henry W. Caslon, who died in 1874. He was the last of the Caslons in male line; thus the foundey was carried on by father, son and son's sons to the fifth generation.

Rowe Mores also refers to Thomas Cottrell, apprenticed as dresser to Caslon; he began business in 1757. Joseph Jackson was also apprenticed to Caslon. These, he says, with Isaac Moore, of Queen street, Upper Moorfields, " are the present English letter-founders. There are some others of less note, who of late years have exercised the occupation here, but have either quitted it or exercised it occasionally, or left the kingdom—as the Westons, Dummers and Jalleson, George Anderton, John Baine (left England and is now, we think, alive in Scotland), Baskerville or Birmingham, Joseph Fenwick, and McPhail."

THE SCOTCH FOUNDERS.

1742.—John Baine and Alexander Wilson, professor of astronomy in Glasgow University, start, at St. Andrews, the first foundry in Scotland.

1744.—They remove to Glasgow and start the " Glasgow Foundry."

1747.—Baine goes to Dublin to start a branch.

1749.—The partnership dissolved. Wilson remaining at Glasgow, where the types of the celebrated Foulis editions were cast.

Baine goes back to Scotland in 1749.

Baine goes to America and dies there in 1777.

On the death of Wilson, the Glasgow foundry carried on by his sons.

In 1830, it descended to the grandsons of the founder, Alexander A. P. Wilson and Patrick Wilson. In 1845, the plant of this and the London branch (established 1834) was sold to various founders, the greater portion to H. W. Caslon and Dr. James Marr (trading as Marr & Co.). Dr. Marr died 1866; business carried on by widow till 1874, when bought by Marr Typefounding Co. (limited). Wilson's fonts are still in use, and supplied by both Marr & Co. and Caslon & Co., Alex. Wilson himself being with H. W. Caslon from 1851 until his death, which took place in 1873.

1809.—Miller & Richard. Miller, the founder, was employed by Alexander Wilson & Son, at Glasgow, leaving them early in the present century to start a foundry in Edinburgh. The first specimen book issued in 1809.

ORIGIN OF EXISTING ENGLISH FOUNDRIES.

It is worthy of remark that the principal English foundries all sprang from William Caslon or his apprentices or successors.

1764.—Foundry in Type street, Chiswell street, of Fry & Pine (manager, Isaac Moore) prints imitations of Baskerville's. His successors were Joseph Fry & Sons, and afterward Fry & Steele, afterward Edmund Fry, who retired about 1828. He sold the business to W. Thorowgood.

Here we must mention the collateral line. Caslon the first had an apprentice, Thos. Cottrell, who established a foundry which passed to Robert Thorne (died 1820). He was an apprentice of Jackson. His first specimen book was issued 1803; his foundry in Barbican was removed to Fann street, by W. Thorowgood, who united with it Fry's foundry. This foundry has successively passed through the hands of Thorowgood & Co., Thorowgood & Besley, Robert Besley & Co., Reed & Fox, and Sir Charles Reed; being now conducted by the firm of Sir Charles Reed & Sons.

As has already been stated, Wm. Caslon the third sold his share of the fraternal foundry to his mother and sister-in-law.

He bought Jackson's foundry on the death of the latter. He was first typefounder to the king. In 1807, he relinquished business in favor of his son, Wm. Caslon the fourth. In 1819 he disposed of the foundry to Blake, Garnett & Co., of Sheffield, who removed the foundry there. Garnett shortly afterward retired and the firm became Blake & Stephenson. The business has now been conducted for many years by the son of the latter in the name of Stephenson, Blake & Co.

About 1850, J. R. Johnson, a chemist, having invented a typecasting machine, offered to sell it to the typefounders. He met with refusal, and then formed a partnership with John Huffman King, a punchcutter and founder, who had succeeded to the business of his father (the firm being called King & Co.). In 1857, J. Staines Atkinson formed a company, chiefly of Manchester gentlemen, to purchase from King & Co. their patents in the casting machine and patent hard metal. The business was removed to Red Lion square, where it was carried on under the style of "The Patent Typefounding Co. (limited)." The company was subsequently wound up, the business and plant being bought by Mr. P. M. Shanks and Captain H. R. Revell. On Captain Revell dying, Mr. P. M. Shanks became sole proprietor. The foundry is now carried on with much enterprise by Mr. Shanks and his sons.

In the above article, has been given particulars of the work of the most celebrated typefounders. It may be useful to supplement the information with a chronology of

THE PROCESS OF TYPEFOUNDING.

The art itself was invented about 1450. There is a statement current that Schoeffer was the first founder, but that is probably inaccurate, as the man who invented letterpress printing was he who first cast types. Little or no improvement was made until three and a half centuries had passed.

1800.—The Lever, or American mold, invented, "which renders the work of the typefounder somewhat more easy."—(*Jury Reports, 1851, p. 401.*)

1823.—Henri Didot's polymatype, which is still used successfully in France, introduced into England by Pouchée. On the failure of Pouchée to sustain the competition of the Associated Founders, Didot's machine and valuable tools were purchased by them through their agent, Mr. Reed, printer, King street, Covent Garden, and destroyed on the premises of Messrs. Caslon and Livermore.—(*Jury Report, 1851, p. 409.*)

1851.—The hand mold and the ordinary type metal still used by the English founders. In the description of their products shown at the International Exhibition, no reference is made in the official catalogue or in the jury awards to any improved process or superior materials. Indeed, the jury expressly say: "Since the invention of casting types, a process which goes back as far as the origin of printing itself, this art has made little progress" (*Jury Reports, 1851, p. 409*); yet it is believed that about this time the casting machine, invented in Germany and improved in America, was in the possession of at least one British typefounding firm.

1852.—Mr. J. R. Johnson patented hard type made of zinc and its alloys, which was subsequently found to oxidize in damp air, and had to be abandoned.

1853.—Mr. Johnson patented his machine for casting type mechanically without variation of body. This machine has since been worked extensively by the Patent Typefounding Company (limited), 31 Red Lion square; the University Press, Oxford; the Imprimerie Imperiale, of Paris, etc.

1854.—Mr. Johnson patented a process for making hard type by substituting tin for lead entirely, or partially, in the ordinary compounds.

1855.—Mr. Besley patented a mode of making hard type by the use of lead, tin, antimony, zinc, copper and nickel, in certain proportions.

1856.—The circulars issued by the British founders in this year show that two kinds of metal were then sold — the ordinary type and the extra hard, the latter being introduced as a new alloy.

1859.—In December of this year Messrs. Johnson and Atkinson patented their apparatus for rubbing, dressing and setting up type.

1862.—Messrs. Johnson and Atkinson showed at the London International Exposition their machinery for the complete manufacture of type without the aid of manual labor.—*British and Colonial Printer and Stationer.*

FEMALE COMPOSITORS AT HOME AND ABROAD.

Although it may be a familiar fact, that to James Franklin, Rhode Island is indebted for having been the first to open a printing-office within her boundaries (in a room under the town school house at Newport), whence he issued, in 1732, the first newspaper that ever appeared in the colony, it may not be so well known that this remarkable man taught the art of printing to his wife and two daughters, who became correct and rapid compositors, and at his death, in 1735, he left to them his stock of type, and that now famous press. It was no barren bequest, as the business was, for several years, successfully conducted by his widow, who printed for the government in 1744, a stately volume of more than three hundred folio pages, containing "The Acts and Laws of his Majesty's Colony of Rhode Island and Providence Plantations." It is a memorable fact, that this, the first book ever made by woman's hands, in this land and probably in any other, was printed and published in the town of Newport.

At a later period in the last century, we find several other instances of women doing the work of the printing-office in America. Among them were the daughters of Hall, Ben. Franklin's partner in Philadelphia, where, at the same time, were two other women at the press, who could do their week's work with as much fidelity as most of the journeymen. "The Declaration of Independence" was set up in type from the original document, by Mrs. Mary Goddard, a gentlewoman of station. Clementina Byrd edited and printed the *Virginia Gazette*, having Thomas Jefferson for a contributor. In 1771, Penelope Russell, who succeeded her husband in printing *The Censor* at Boston, could work at case without the aid of copy. Margaret Draper, printer of the *Boston News Letter*, was so good a tory, that King George III. gave her a pension. Jane Aitkin, a New Englander, was noted as a thorough printer, as well as an accurate proofreader, and Elizabeth Bushell, of Halifax, who assisted her father, both at case and press, is spoken of by contemporaries as handsome but unfortunate.

An entire volume might be written concerning English and Scotch women as printers, in the last century, but we have only space to add that Foulis, the famous typographer of Glasgow, was aided by his daughter in the production of the immaculate edition of Horace.—*Newport (R. I.) News.*

PANSY  SERIES.

---

8 A 14 a   Two Line Nonpareil Pansy. [12 Points] $2 15

OUR GREAT MIKADO, VIRTUOUS MAN, WHEN HE TO RULE

Our Land Began, Resolved to Try a Very Good Plan Whereby Young Men Might

12345 Reach the Van Yum Yum 67890

6 A 10 a   Three Line Nonpareil Pansy. [18 Points] $2 65

CELEBRATED SUPERIOR COPPER-MIXED

Type Manufactured only by Barnhart Bros. & Spindler

45 Great Western Type Foundry 67

5 A 8 a   Four Line Nonpareil Pansy. [24 Points] $3 90

GREAT THREAT'NING CLOUDS

Have Passed Away and Brightly Shines

34 The Dawning Day 78

4 A 6 a   Six Line Nonpareil Pansy. [36 Points] $5 25

PRINTERS' MACHINERY

General Printers' Supply House

5 Salt Lake City 8

MANUFACTURED BY BARNHART BROS. & SPINDLER, CHICAGO.

12 POINTS.   PICA TINTED.   Price, $2.15.

TOUGHMENOT EXCLUSIVENESS
IMPORTANT PERSONAGE   EGOTISTIC POMPOSITY
1234567890

30 POINTS.   FIVE-LINE NONPAREIL TINTED.   Price, $3.85.

WANDERING AWAY SOBERLY

18 POINTS.   THREE-LINE NONPAREIL TINTED.   Price, $2.65.

CONSERVATOR AWAKENING
ORIENTAL ZAYATS   TAWDRY FANATICS

36 POINTS.   THREE-LINE PICA TINTED.   Price, $4.60.

IMMENSE WATERWAYS

24 POINTS.   TWO-LINE PICA TINTED.   Price, $3.30.

MORNING RAMBLES
CROOKED PATHWAY HOMEWARD

ALL COMPLETE WITH FIGURES.

NATURAL LINING OF SERIES.

HHHHH MMMMMMMM HHHHH

955. DOUBLE GREAT PRIMER KISMET, 6 a, 3 A, $4.50.

THE PURITAN & GENESTA

Grand Ocean Races

Showing Excellent Speed

NEW ORNAMENTS.

1. Double   Paragon.   2. Double   2.   1. Double   Paragon.
                                    Paragon.

10 Cents Each.   10 Cents Each.

3. Long Primer, 15 cents per set.   4. Great Primer, 25 cents per set.   5. Pica, 20 cents per set.

DOWN BY AULD KIRK HOME

Left on the 31st on Foot

Miss Jumbo's Friday Primp

BOSTON TYPE FOUNDRY, JOHN K. ROGERS, AGENT, 104 MILK STREET.

MARDER, LUSE & COMPANY,

TYPE FOUNDERS AND ELECTROTYPERS,

NORTHWESTERN BRANCH:
MINNEAPOLIS, MINN.

CHICAGO, ILL.

PACIFIC TYPE FOUNDRY CO.
SAN FRANCISCO, CAL.

AMERICAN SYSTEM OF INTERCHANGEABLE TYPE BODIES.

NEW TUSCAN.

AMERICAN SYSTEM OF INTERCHANGEABLE TYPE BODIES.

10A, 20a,   PARAGON. (20 Points Standard Measure.) $4.85

HUNTING THE CRAFTY BENGAL TIGER

Relation of Exciting Incidents and Hairbreadth Escapes!
All previous Stories Eclipsed 235

8A, 16a,   DOUBLE PICA. (24 Points Standard Measure.) $5.55

UNDER THE SPREADING MAPLE

Where are you Going, my Pretty Maid? 678

6A, 12a,   DOUBLE COLUMBIAN. (32 Points Standard Measure.) $8.00

PRECONCERTED

Our Nautical Contributor 2

5A, 10a,   DOUBLE PARAGON. (40 Points Standard Measure.) $7.75

ROUND NUMBERS

68 Eloquent Legal Advocate

4A, 8a,   FOUR-LINE PICA. (48 Points Standard Measure.) $10.20

MONASTIC Recluse 4

PICA AND COLUMBIAN IN PREPARATION.   SPACES AND QUADS WITH ALL SIZES.

CONSISTENCY A JEWEL.

THE March number of *The Pacific Printer* contains a scathing article on printing amateur humbugs in general, and one Nelson C. Hawks, a $100 "amateur supplyer," in particular, which we cordially endorse, especially the first portion, because our own arguments and language are employed. The following excerpt from "the Hawks's" business circular, is the object upon which the vials of our esteemed contemporary's wrath is poured:

The attention of druggists, merchants, and business men generally, as well as the amateur printers, is directed to our facilities for furnishing

CHEAP PRINTING OUTFITS

with which amusement, instruction and profit may be considered. We keep a large variety of presses, such as the Army, Novelty, Young America, Excelsior, Prouty, Columbian and Caxton. Also small fonts of type, inks, leads, rules reglet, cuts, dashes, cases, etc. A small press, with type, etc., for cards, envelopes and tags, can be furnished for $50; a complete business outfit costs $100. Call and see us.

So far so good. But, friend Dearing, consistency is a jewel. Judge of our surprise, when after reading your deserved strictures on the above, we found the following startling announcement on the page immediately preceding your editorial:

A COMPLETE PRINTING OFFICE FOR $250.—Embracing a Pearl press, in first-rate order, 6 by 9 inch chase, foot-power; long primer, brevier, and nonpareil Roman type; stands, cases, leads, a large quantity of job type of modern faces; rules, borders, ornaments, etc. It is a big bargain for the money. Send order to Palmer & Rey, 405 Sansome street, San Francisco. Part cash, time on balance.

Can you consistently denounce N. C. Hawks for offering to furnish a "printing outfit" for $100, when the representative printing journal of the Pacific Coast is *Hawk*-ing a "complete job printing office" at $250? To us, the difference between the two offers seems the difference between tweedle-dum and tweedle-dee.

AN EXPLANATION FROM N. C. HAWKS.

To the Editor :   SAN FRANCISCO, May 27, 1886.

Understanding from my friend Loy, managing clerk of the Johnson agency here, that you indorsed an article which appeared in the *Pacific Printer* of recent date, which attacked me viciously, and placed me in a bad light with the craft, I write to say that, like some others, you have been deceived, and to ask the favor of a hearing, in the full belief that when you are in possession of the facts, you will readily right any unintentional wrong done me.

The article in question is so worded as to convey the idea that I have, not long ago, been engaged, individually, in selling small presses and type to amateurs; and the motive is clearly to create a bitter feeling among the regular craft against me, and induce them to withdraw their trade.

To begin with, this is a barefaced falsehood. It is a well-known fact that *for four years past I have not been in the type business at all,* neither individually nor as a member of any firm; and the only amateur business that has come under my notice during that four years was done while I was employed by P. & R., in sight and hearing and with the knowledge and by order of the writer of that libel on me! And, in justice to the firm of which I was a member, and which, in common with nearly every other foundry at the time (eight years ago) sold indiscriminately, I wish to state that we were among the first to discountenance and discourage the amateur business, and as soon as we became convinced that boys were beginning to work for profit, instead of pleasure and instruction, we refused to sell to them.

It is transparently plain to be seen why I am singled out and attacked for that which a business firm did *eight years ago.* And I will simply dismiss the subject by asking you to place truth to displace falsehood, and thus do me the full justice I am sure you will cheerfully accord. The wolf who dirtied the clear waters of the stream, and brazenly accused those farther down the stream of it, is a parallel case to this. And, if I do not mistake the intelligence of the printing craft of our good land, this method of attempting to injure a business rival will react severely, and prove in the end a benefit to the traduced.

Respectfully,   N. C. HAWKS.

THE "GUTENBERG" TYPESETTER.

The last issue of *The Paper and Printing Trades Journal,* of London, contains the following:

"A new composing machine, called the 'Gutenberg Typesetter,' is the invention of a German engineer, Herr Fischer. It is different from other machines in being a kind of case in which the type is, to a certain extent, brought to the worker, so that it is in fact an improved case, with mechanical action. The letters are ranged one over the other in perpendicular pipes, the arrangement being nearly the same as in the ordinary case. The principle of the machine—the rapid and easy bringing of the type before the compositor—may be realized in three different ways. In the first, in each type-rail is a slide horizontally moving backward and forward; the slide has a plate or shield on its foremost end, with an indication of the letters contained in the type-holders, while a driver in the other end causes the lowest type to project one-half of its length out of the column. Every time a type is taken out (by the fingers) this driver returns to its place as the pressure is taken off the shield, and another type is driven into position to be seized by the compositor. An india-rubber strip prevents the letter from being thrown out altogether.

"Another device for feeding the type consists in two rotary levers fastened to each letter-rail, so arranged that when the top of one lever is pressed by seizing the type, the other lever pushes the type forward with its top. A third device is purely mechanical and automatic; the rails have an oscillatory motion, by means of rods and eccentrics on a driving shaft. The drivers push forward all equal type where not already advanced; in the latter case they move to and fro in the empty space between the sole of the type-holder and second lowest letter without any action. As the type has always the nick in the same direction, the compositor has simply to put the type in the composing stick. The new machine, or 'automatic case,' has been constructed more for the purpose of increasing the power of the compositor than for doing away with him. In fact, intellectual work is so intimately connected with typesetting that machine labor must always play a subordinate part.

"The distributing machine is very ingeniously constructed. It works automatically and simultaneously at eight different places. The matter for distribution is taken up by a small apparatus and placed in long metal pipes. The quads are first taken out, and then the pipes are placed on the distributing machine. The under part then begins to rotate. As said before, all of the nicks are in the same direction, and while the empty pipes below are revolving rapidly, movable feeders take rapid hold of the nicks from the end of the distributing pipes. Of these nicks each letter has from two to eight in various order. When two feeders fit into two nicks the right letter is found, and it falls out and drops into the pipe. When the pipe is full the machine gives notice by stopping. This principle is the same as that adopted in the Chubb safe-lock. The letters are passed twice through the machine; the first time all types of the same thickness are sorted together.

"As much as 6,000 ems per hour have been set by the apparatus, but the average is placed at 3,700. These are, however, German figures, and the average work of a German compositor is 1,800 ems. The composing apparatus costs from 600 to 700 marks (£30 to £35); the distributing machine, for three or four type-machines, 3,500 marks. The general opinion seems to be that the construction of the machines is based on sound ideas, and that they will prove of great practical utility."

NEW TYPESETTING AND DISTRIBUTING MACHINE.

It is stated on what we deem reliable authority that Mr. Arthur D. Moe, a former Milwaukee printer, has patented a machine for setting and distributing type, which has every appearance of being a thoroughly practical one. Many of the objections embraced in other inventions of this sort have been overcome, and the result is a simple, compact, durable and inexpensive machine, which will materially lessen the slow and tedious labor of placing the little bits of metal in columns for the press. Only one operator is required. It is calculated that a person can do 75 to 100 per cent more work with the machine than by hand. The machine is designed for both newspaper and bookwork. Mr. Moe thinks it can be made to work effectually in the composing-room of a daily newspaper, which will be the severest test to which it can be put. The machine is designed to use any kind of type, and two different-sized bodies may be used in the same machine, a slight change only being required in the " distributing " apparatus, which can be changed in five minutes. There is also a mechanism to replace the type in the " setting " machine, taking it direct from the column. This is a neat arrangement, and can be worked very rapidly. This arrangement is quite important in itself, the success of the " setting " machine depending upon the rapidity with which the " distributer " can be worked.

THE EIGHT-HOUR MOVEMENT.

THE recent movement for the reduction of the hours of labor from ten to eight, especially in the printing trade, must, we think, have convinced its most sanguine advocates that its adoption, under existing circumstances, is inexpedient if not impracticable. While we sympathize with every legitimate demand for the elevation of labor, we recognize the important fact that all such efforts must be feasible and based on and supported by united action before success can crown their claims. So long as labor's ranks are divided, so long as such demands are coupled with provisos which render these concessions impossible, so long will failure be assured. When a law or demand is made universal in its application, and organized labor speaks as a unit; when no undue advantage is claimed or allowed; when a "fair field and no exemption" is the motto, the eight-hour movement will prove successful, not before. It is the sheerest nonsense to expect that, in this age of excessive competition, one city or state can lessen the hours of productive industry (either by manual or mechanical agencies) twenty per cent, and successfully hold its own with manufacturing centers where ten instead of eight hours' labor is the rule. Common sense and experience alike say no. How, for example, could an employer in Chicago successfully compete in an estimate for presswork, based on the eight-hour system, when St. Louis, Cincinnati, Indianapolis, Kansas City, and even Omaha, employed their machinery and pressmen ten hours, and at a lower rate of wages, too, than prevails in our midst? Business is bloodless; it knows no friendship; it takes no stock in maudlin sentimentality; it deals, and deals remorselessly, with existing facts, and its sympathy is invariably with the lowest reliable estimate, whether the order comes from a " misfit " garment store or the wealthiest corporation in the land. For example, two clipper ships, exact counterparts, await cargoes in the port of Liverpool, the one flying the American, the other the British flag. An American consignor realizes he can land a cargo in New York at lower rates by the vessel which carries the British ensign than by the one representing his country's flag, all things being equal, no matter whether these lower rates are secured by lower wages paid to the seamen, or by lower rates of interest on the capital invested, what is the result? Patriotism is tucked away in his pocketbook; the British vessel, with its cheaper freight rate, secures the cargo, while the American clipper lies idle at her dock. This statement may not be palatable, but it is true, and truth can discount both buncombe and fiction.

There are two special features connected with the eight-hour movement, which seem in a great measure to have been overlooked. The first is, that to secure its universal recognition and enforcement by legal enactment, it must be sanctioned by every state legislature in the country, because the national congress has no jurisdiction over services rendered outside of a national establishment. *State sovereignty* interposes a veto, which declares " thus far shalt thou go, and no farther;" and while the initiative must be taken at our manufacturing centers, other states must follow their example, or the removal of plant employed in manufactures to more favorable locations is simply a question of time. Let us illustrate our position: A murder may be committed within twenty feet of an ideal state boundary. If committed in Wisconsin, a life incarceration at Waupun follows conviction; if in Illinois, death by hanging may be the verdict, though in either case interference by the federal authority is inadmissible, and those who insist that congress should pass a universal eight-hour law should keep this important truth in mind.

Another fact is, that where its enforcement depends on the voluntary action of employés, the same principle must be virtually carried out, and until our international and national organizations put forth the fiat that eight hours shall constitute a day's work, and have the power to enforce it, irrespective of location, all local, straggling efforts in this direction are simply a waste of time. It is true, there are certain employments, such as the building trades, which possess a quasi-independence, but when the operation is applied to manufacturing establishments, the enhancement of whose productions is simply measured by the cost of transportation, it neither requires a prophet nor the son of a prophet to see that competition under such disadvantages is an utter impossibility.

We believe that the hours of labor may be advantageously reduced, under a universally recognized system, but it will not be accomplished by robbing Peter to pay Paul.

MARDER, LUSE & CO.

American System of Interchangeable Type Bodies.

DORIC.
IMPROVED SERIES.

American System of Interchangeable Type Bodies.

24A, 48a,   PEARL ON NONP. (6 Points Standard Measure.) $3.10

TRULY MIND IS THE NOBLEST PART OF MAN

And of Mind, Virtue is the Noblest Distinction: nobility Of Thought and Expansive Ideas 234

24A, 48a,   MINION. (7 Points Standard Measure.) $3.70

MARCH OF THE MIDNIGHT MARAUDERS

Conscious of Their Instability Men Look Around for Something to Stand Upon 346¼

16A, 32a, LONG PRIMER. (10 Points Standard Measure.) $3.90

ARCHITECTS DESIGN

5¾ Handsome Marble Residence

10A, 20a,   PARAGON. (20 Points Standard Measure.) $5.70

TIGER HUNTS

Indian Jungles 4¼

24A, 48a,   NONPAREIL. (6 Points Standard Measure.) $3.20

CHANGEFUL SCENES OF A CENTURY

Large Faces Acquire Prominence on Small Bodies, but Cheek is no Indication of Merit 54½

20A, 40a,   BREVIER. (8 Points Standard Measure.) $4.10

POLITICAL INTRIGUERS

37¾ Ward Strikers' Ambitious Desires

12A, 24a,   PICA. (12 Points Standard Measure.) $3.40

STAUNCH LEADERS

Bold and True Followers 8¼

8A, 16a,   DOUBLE PICA. (24 Points Standard Measure.) $7.25

OLD MAIDS

2½ Beauty Show

4A, 8a   DOUBLE GREAT PRIMER. (36 Points Standard Measure.) $6.25

AVENGING WARFARE

Splendid Official Strategy 4¾

4A, 8a,   DOUBLE PARAGON. (40 Points Standard Measure.) $6.75

FAVORITE FAWN

32½ Beautiful Song Birds

3A, 6a,   CANON. (44 Points Standard Measure.) $8.00

Climb HIGH Poles 6¼

3A, 6a,   FOUR-LINE PICA. (48 Points Standard Measure.) $10.20

1 Her RICH Dad 9

Spaces and Quads with all sizes except Nonpareil and Pica.

964. FIVE LINE PICA TENIERS, 4 A, 4 A, $6.00.

RECITATIONS AND MUSICAL SELECTIONS

HOME MELODY BY CHARMERS

965. CANON TENIERS, 5 A, 5 A, $5.00.

MODERN RIDING SCHOOL ILLUSTRATIONS

OLD NATIONAL DRIVING PARK GROUNDS

ADDRESS HOME 267 COMMERCIAL EXCHANGE

963. DOUBLE GREAT PRIMER TENIERS, 7 A, 7 A, $4.00.

BRIGHTMAN & BURNHOUSE BROKERAGE AND COMMISSION

ADVANCES MADE IN SUMS TO SUIT VALUATION

OFFICE 74 GLOOMY PLACE DARKER TOWN INVISIBLE STATE

BOSTON TYPE FOUNDRY, JOHN K. ROGERS, AGENT, 104 MILK STREET.

Three-Line Nonpareil.   18 POINT ARTISTIC, WITH 24 POINT INITIALS.   18 Point, (without Initials,) Price, $3.65
24 Point Initials, ... 1.50

Boodletumville · Whitewashing · Association

Bribed · Politicians · Vindicated   Assisted · Canadian · Tourists

Tarnished · Reputations · Polished · Successfully

Two-Line Pica.   24 POINT ARTISTIC, WITH 30 POINT INITIALS.   24 Point, (without Initials,) Price, $4.20
30 Point Initials, ... 2.25

Fifteenth · Regiment, · Company · M

Overfilled · Haversacks

Meeting · for · Foraging · Manœuvres · at · Midnight

Five-Line Nonpareil.   30 POINT ARTISTIC, WITH 36 POINT INITIALS.   30 Point, (without Initials,) Price, $5.00
36 Point Initials, ... 3.00

Beautiful · Autumnal · Paintings

Plants · and · Flowers   Insects · and · Birds

ALL COMPLETE WITH FIGURES.

Artistic in Combination.

Twentieth · Annual · Exhibition

American FRUIT Industries

Wednesday · Evening, · September · 26, · 1983

Complete sets of Initial Capitals may be had separately or with the regular fonts.

THE MACKELLAR, SMITHS & JORDAN CO., PHILADELPHIA, PA.   SHNIEDEWEND & LEE CO., AGENTS, CHICAGO, ILLINOIS.

116   *June 1886*

THE BARB SERIES.

Sorrow stings like the Thrust of an Envenomed Barb.

The Decoration Day Parade.

$1234567890.

BARB STEEDS

Running with Speed and Endurance.

GREAT SUMMER TRAVEL.

$1234567890.

Our Prices will meet competitive rates for Cash—all sales on satisfactory terms—while the well-known excellence of Our Manufacture will be scrupulously maintained.

FARMER, LITTLE & CO., NEW YORK AND CHICAGO.

Six-line Nonpareil.   36-Point Victoria.   6A, $6.75

FREAKS · OF · NATURE
✠ MENAGERIES ✠

Four-line Nonpareil.   24-Point Victoria.   8A, $4.50

HIGHER ✠ MOUNTS ✠ CLIMBED
✠ PROCURE · EXERCISE ✠

Three-line Nonpareil.   18-Point Victoria.   10A, $3.50

EXPLAIN · METEOROLOGICAL · REPORTS
SCIENTISTS ✠ 365 ✠ OBSERVING

New English.   14-Point Victoria.   12A, $3.25

MARBLE ✠ TOMBSTONE
✠ CENOTAPH ✠
BURIAL · CUSTOMS

Two-line Nonpareil.   12-Point Victoria.   16A, $3.00

INCINERATION ✠ ADVANCING
✠ PROGRESSIVE ✠
ERECT · CREMATORIES

New Long Primer.   10-Point Victoria.   20A, $2.75

CONCERT ✠ PROGRAMME ✠ PRINTING
✠ PECULIAR FASHIONS ✠
SUPERIOR · WORKMANSHIP · 24

New Brevier.   8-Point Victoria.   28A, $2.50

FORLORN ✠ HABITATION ✠ AND ✠ SIMPLE ✠ HABITS
✠ HUMBLE HERMIT DISTURBED ✠
ENDURANCE · OF · STRICT · SOLITUDE · 180

—— VICTORIA ——

The Victoria Series, being cut systematically, lines in the several ways here shown. Neither cardboard nor paper required in combining the different sizes with each other; use Point Standard Leads and Slugs in justifying.

HHHHHHHHHHHHHHHHHH ✠ NEAT ✠ FACE ✠ HHHHHHHHHHHHHHHH

OLD : STYLE : ATHENIAN : EXTENDED.

PATENT PENDING

15 A 10 A 30 a, Nonpareil O. S. Athenian Extended. $3.05

NAPOLEON'S FALL.
Sequel to that Insane Nightmare
SLIPPERY STAIRS
ILLUSTRATED BY DORAN.
52 Old Politicians 74

15 A 10 A 25 a. Brevier O. S. Athenian Extended. $3.50

LITTLE LADY.
An Ode to a Divine Damsel.
LOVELINESS
VIRTUE'S REWARD.
84 Te Deum. 36

10 A 10 A 30 a, Long Primer O. S. Athenian Extended. $3.35

PROGRAMME
Five Grand Tableaux
BALLETS.
LABOR KNIGHTS
21 Trader 68

8 A 8 A 15 a, Pica O. S. Athenian Extended. $4.00

ATHENIAN
Fine Art Printers
GRECIEN 45
Mound Builder

6 A 6 A 12 a, Great Primer Old Style Athenian Extended. $4.80

MAID OF ATHENS.
Political Economy Lectures.
GREEK RUINS.
Free Silver Coinage. 36

PATENT COLONIAL PENDING

15 A 15 A, Great Primer Colonial. $4.25.

LANDING OF THE PILGRIM FATHERS.
COLONIAL INAUGURATION OF YOUNG AMERICA'S TURKISH THANKSGIVING.
86 MAYFLOWER 25
RECEPTION TO THE WITCHES OF SALEM.

10 A 10 A, Double Pica Colonial. $5.40.

NEW YORK MUSIC TOURNAMENT.
VARIOUS NOTES ON THE LAST DAYS OF HERCULANEUM

JAMES CONNER'S SONS, TYPE FOUNDERS, NEW YORK.

ANGLICAN LIGHT MEDIAEVAL. No. TWO.

Patented   Aug. 9, '81.

10 A 15 A 20 a,   PICA ANGLICAN NO. 2 $4.85

SPANISH CASTLE
The Corsican Brothers of Elbe
93 CARLISTS 42

8 A 12 A 20 a,   GREAT PRIMER ANGLICAN NO. 2 $6.75

FAIRY TALES.
Mother Goose's Fables.
24 CHILDREN. 13

6 A 8 A 12 a,   DOUBLE PICA ANGLICAN NO. 2 $8.50.

JASON'S GOLDEN ARGOSY
Sketches from Late Venecian History
4 THE HERMITAGE 3

CAST FROM LIGHT MEDIAEVAL. ORIGINAL. MATRICES.

PATENTED AUG. 9, 1881.

10 A 20 a,   PICA LIGHT MEDIÆVAL. $3.65

GEORGIA FARMS
Diary of our Wild Adventures
37 Far West 86

10 A 20 a,   GREAT PRIMER LIGHT MEDIÆVAL. $5.50

BROADWAY
Grand Republican Army
27 Politics 48

8 A 12 a,   DOUBLE PICA LIGHT MEDIÆVAL. $6.05

AN AMERICAN SOLDIER
History and Anecdotes of the Late War
7 Musical Festival 5

PICA ANGLICAN NO. 2 AND LIGHT MEDIÆVAL, IN COMBINATION.

CHARGE OF THE LIGHT BRIGADE--NOBLE SIX HUNDRED

GREAT PRIMER ANGLICAN NO. 2 AND LIGHT MEDIÆVAL, IN COMBINATION.

GREAT HOGGARTY DIAMOND FIELD

DOUBLE PICA ANGLICAN NO. 2 AND LIGHT MEDIÆVAL, IN COMBINATION.

WONDROUS ALCON MYTHOLOGY.

JAMES CONNER'S SONS NEW YORK.

25 A 40 a,   BREVIER OLD STYLE EGYPTIAN. $2.90

Expert Milk-Maidens.
CIBARIOUS LACTESCENT COMPOUNDS.
New Cheese.
OLEOMARGARINE, KINE & CO.
Milky Beverages 25

20 A 15 A 30 a,   LONG PRIMER OLD STYLE EGYPTIAN. $3.60

Artistic Garments!
FOREIGN STYLE CLOTHING.
TAILOR-MADE.
FIT TO PERFECTION!
Guaranteed. 78

15 A 10 A 20 a.   PICA OLD STYLE EGYPTIAN. $4.05

Elaborate Gastronomic Collation.
FIRST CONFERENCE OF EPICUREAN DISCIPLES
FRIED BIVALVES!
BILL OF FARE COLLABORATEUR.
42 Empirical Pies. 63

10 A 10 A 15 a,   GREAT PRIMER OLD STYLE EGYPTIAN. $4.80

British Frontier Wars.
LIFE IN THE AUSTRALIAN JUNGLES
Fun with Zulus
DODGING THE FESTIVE BOOMERANG
89 South Wales 67

8 A 6 A 12 a,   DOUBLE PICA OLD STYLE EGYPTIAN. $6.05

Modern Designers.
ARTISTS IN SCENE PAINTING
Decorations.
EXPERT BRUSH WORKERS.

JAMES CONNER'S SONS, TYPE FOUNDERS, NEW YORK.

PATENT PENDING.

15 A 25 a   GREAT PRIMER NUBIAN. $5.00

Our Renowned African Lake Explorers.
Insipid Pinguidinous Southern Maidens of Rich Mahogany Complexion.
75 HAPPY BRIDES 43
Excruciating Agonies of American Wedded Existence.

10 A 20 a,   DOUBLE PICA NUBIAN. $5.40

Dusky Pugilistic Nubian Wariors.
Uncompromising Cannibals, Less Black Than We're Painted.
74 DRAGOMAN 39
Airily Garmented Heathens Striking for Short Clothes!

9 A 15 a.   DOUBLE GREAT PRIMER NUBIAN. $6.70

Panorama of Revolutionary War.

Vivid Pictures Descriptive of That Great Struggle.

35 LAFAYETTE 27

20 A 75 a, $2.15.   BREVIER COSMOPOLITAN.   FONTS OF 25, 50 OR 100 LBS. AT 48C PER POUND.

Pleasant Trips over the Hills and Vales of Pennsylvania.
DWELLING AMONG THE GRAND OLD CRAGS OF THE ALLEGHANY MOUNTAINS.
Soul-Inspiring Views in Natures Domain.
As look'd the Traveller for the World below,
The lively Morning Breeze began to blow,
The Magic Curtain rolled in Mists away,
And a gay Landscape smiled upon the Day.
As light the fleeting Vapours upward glide,
Like sheeted Spectres on the Mountain Side.

[Patent Pending]

JAMES CONNER'S SONS, TYPE FOUNDERS, NEW YORK.

Crusader Series

COMPLETE WITH ORNAMENTS

DICKINSON TYPE FOUNDERY, 236 WASHINGTON STREET, BOSTON.

FOUR-LINE NONPAREIL, $2.50

❧ ANCIENT ∙ RECORDS ∙ ❧
❧ CAREFULLY ∙ 276 ∙ CHRONICLED ❧

SIX-LINE NONPAREIL, $3.50

❧ MASON ∙ 38 ❤ CHARM ❧

THREE-LINE NONPAREIL, No. 1, $2.00

❧ HASTY ∙ RETREAT ❧
❧ STRANGE ∙ 75 ∙ MORTALS ❧

THREE-LINE NONPAREIL, No. 2, $2.25

❧ MERCHANTS ❧
❧ BOUND ∙ 36 ❤ SOUTH ❧

SEVEN-LINE NONPAREIL, $4.50

❧ ROAD ∙ 5 ∙ BEDS ❧

FIVE-LINE NONPAREIL, $3.50

❧ COMPLICATIONS ❧
❧ BOUNDLESS ∙ 24 ❤ EXPANSE ❧

EIGHT-LINE NONPAREIL, $4.90

❧ RICH ∙ 8 ◆ SOAP ❧
HHHHHHHHHHHH

ALL THE SIZES LINE TOGETHER AT THE BOTTOM, AND JUSTIFY WITH EACH OTHER BY NONPAREILS

AMERICAN SYSTEM OF
INTERCHANGEABLE TYPE BODIES.

INTERCHANGEABLE GOTHIC.

Complete Series of 14 Sizes, $35.00.

36 A,   EXCELSIOR ON NONPAREIL (6 Point). $1.15

DOES THE EDITOR SIT IN HIS SANCTUM GRIM?
NOT MUCH, MY SON, NOT ANY FOR HIM.   AMID SYLVAN GROVES AND PASTURES
GREEN, WHERE HILLS RISE UP THE VISTAS BETWEEN
1 2 3 4 5 6 7 8 9 0

36 A,   DIAMOND ON NONPAREIL (6 Point). $1.20

THE EDITOR SITS BENEATH THE SKIES,
DOTH FISH AND WISH DEATH UNTO THE FLIES; TO-MORROW HIS PAPER
WILL SWARM WITH---NOT LIES, BUT FISH STORIES
1 2 3 4 5 6 7 8 9 0

36 A,   NONPAREIL (6 Point). $2.05

FUNNY THINGS ARE SAID ABOUT EDITORS
AND EDITORS WRITE LAUGHABLE ITEMS IN RETURN, BUT
KNIGHTS OF SCISSORS AND PASTE
1 2 3 4 5 6 7 8 9 0

36 A,   PEARL ON NONPAREIL (6 Point). $1.50

A WASP CAME BUZZING TO HIS WORK
AND VARIOUS THINGS DID TACKLE; HE STUNG A BOY AND
THEN A DOG, THEN MADE A ROOSTER CACKLE
1 2 3 4 5 6 7 8 9 0

36 A,   AGATE ON NONPAREIL (6 Point). $1.65

AT LAST UPON AN EDITOR'S CHEEK HE
SETTLED DOWN TO DRILL; HE PRODDED THERE FOR
HALF-AN-HOUR AND THEN HE BROKE HIS BILL
1 2 3 4 5 6 7 8 9 0

The above Series of Five Sizes on Nonpareil body, complete, $7.00.

HHHHHHHH HHHHHHHH
HHHHHHHHHHHHHHHHHHHHHHHHH

24 A   BREVIER (8 Point). $1.90

GLEAMS OF SUNLIGHT
BRIGHTEN THE SHADOWS AND CHASE
246 AWAY THE GLOOM 357

18 A,   TWO-LINE PEARL (10 Point). $1.80

SILVER MOONBEAMS
THEIR SOFTENING INFLUENCE
123 SHED AROUND 456

18 A,   TWO-LINE NONPAREIL (12 Point). $2.10

SILENT STARS
IN CANOPY OF HEAVEN
987 WATCHFUL 543

12 A,   TWO-LINE BREVIER (16 Point). $2.85

BRIGHT ORBS
32 LUSTROUS 58

Spaces and Quads with all sizes except Nonpareil and Two-Line Nonpareil.

ALL THE SIZES IN THIS SERIES LINE EXACTLY AT THE BOTTOM; THE LARGER SIZES, FROM TWO-LINE NONPAREIL UP TO FOUR-LINE PICA, LINE AT BOTH TOP AND BOTTOM

Price, $7.00.　　PICA CIRCULAR SCRIPT.

Hardscrabble, Oct. 3, 1886.

Messrs. Rubhard & Co.

I am troubled with a feeling of Drowsiness, Weakness of the Back, with general Indisposition to Labour. The symptoms commence on Monday morning and last till Saturday evening. If you can help me you will greatly oblige your most miserable friend,

Gregory Lackthrift.

THREE-LINE NONP. CIRCULAR SCRIPT.　　Price, $12.20.

Bustleton, Nov. 2, '86.

Mr. Lackthrift:

Have carefully studied your symptoms, and would recommend Elbow Grease, to be diligently applied.

Rubhard & Co.

TWO-LINE PICA CIRCULAR SCRIPT.　　Price, $18.65.

Notice is hereby given that an Election for Five Hundred Directors of the Soap-bubble Packing Company will take place on Wednesday Evening next, April 1, 2886.

Price, $4.70.　　PICA CHAUCER.

Impressions and Cogitations

10th month, 25, 1682. On land at last, though in a New World. Carried on shore my kit, and under a Chestnut Tree mended shoes for fellow-passengers. Leather, wax-ends and heel-ball are getting scarce. The natives cover their feet with untanned skins.

Obadiah Thinkwell.

THREE-LINE NONPAREIL CHAUCER.　　Price, $5.55.

Notice to our Patrons

Monday, June 6, 1893, opening of a complete Stock of Antique Furniture and rare Bric-a-Brac collected from remote Europe.

Castleman & Co.

TWO-LINE PICA CHAUCER.　　Price, $6.10.

Twelfth Annual Exhibition
Importation of Japanese Crochet Embroideries
Silk Handkerchiefs
Feathery Plumes from Australia

THE MACKELLAR, SMITHS & JORDAN CO.

SANSOM STREET, PHILADELPHIA.

Mikado Series.

THE MFG CO — Patent Pending.

6A, 6A, 12a. TWO-LINE PICA MIKADO. $8.85

We take pleasure in presenting this unique series
To your Notice, believing you will agree with us
In saying it is one of the Most Serviceable
Letters yet Produced for Commercial and Ornamental
Printing. 15 Ornamental Characters

4A, 4A, 8a. THREE-LINE PICA MIKADO. $10.65

Old Time is a droll wag
Who puzzles the World with Rules,
He can give to-day to the wise
But the Morrow is Promised.
$234.58 of Legal Money

3A, 3A, 6a. FOUR-LINE PICA MIKADO. $12.50

Our Greeting to Everyone
Something New Each Day
18 Commercial Job Printers

CLEVELAND TYPE FOUNDRY 147 ST. CLAIR ST.

HAVE WE REACHED THE END?

THE development of the art of printing has been so great, the improvements so rapid, and the inventions pertaining to it so numerous, that those who can remember the old hand-lever, tympan, frisket, one-token-an-hour press have often forced upon them the conviction that the limit has been reached, and that it is a flight of the imagination to suppose of anything beyond.

The doubter says "aye." He stands upon the borders of a veritable wonder-land, and, looking within, fancies he sees, "Thus far shalt thou go and no farther," inscribed upon the desire and ambition of the craft. And he has much to sustain him in his belief. Especially within the last decade, the growth and possibilities of printing have been phenomenal, more so probably than can be claimed for any of the arts whose purpose is the elevation, the enlightenment, the progress of humanity in the broadest and best interpretation.

To trace the onward progress from the slow, crude and tedious labors of even a quarter of a century ago would be a task of almost insurmountable difficulties; nor yet is it necessary. We have the practical results, and they are sufficient. We touch a tiny lever with our finger tips, and blanket sheets fly from the press more swiftly than human tongue can count. The same machinery that prints, cuts, pastes and folds, with unerring precision, counts sheets as well. Human hands are out of competition in the race, and human muscles would fail before it had hardly begun. So perfect, intricate, and apparently self-assured has machinery become that it may almost be said to be endowed with the principles of immortality.

No wonder, then, that the skeptic hesitates to believe in a beyond. Every feature presented seems the embodiment of perfection. He contrasts the old "Albion" or "Washington" of his apprentice days with the "lightning changes" of the press of 1886, and is perplexed. He well remembers the time when, as an ambitious aspirant for fame, he managed to set, correct and distribute his eight thousand ems in ten hours, and stands amazed at the latest record of the champions. He counts upon his thumbs the thousands of impressions produced by a press during working hours in the past, while he cannot upon the fingers of both hands the number of thousands worked off in the twentieth portion of that time in the present. He staggers in the attempt to lift the immense rolls of paper now used, and thinks humorously of the old-fashioned 24 by 38 that came to him in two-ream bundles, and was fed by single sheets. He reflects upon the roller-boy, sees how entirely he is shelved, and how much better his work is done by brass, iron and steel. He whistles dubiously at the banishment of soft blankets, and is loath to admit that better work can be done with hard packing. He looks in vain for the wetting trough, and smiles when told that paper is now used dry. In place of the wooden quoins, shooting-stick and mallet he finds only metal contrivances that have to be locked with a nondescript key. In the "electro" department he finds simplicity has taken the place of mystery, and greyhound swiftness the slow, cumbersome movements of the tortoise.

Nor is this all. He cannot comprehend the cleanliness, the cog-wheel system of today. The dingy, creaking alley stairs no longer lead to a spidered rookery, yclept a printing-office. The change from a "sky parlor" to one lower, well lighted and ventilated has been as perfect as it is pleasant. Health and comfort have been considered in all the arrangements. The floor is no longer a wilderness of ink-begrimed paper, or tobacco juice, and even the hellbox occupies a more dignified position than its old-boot namesake, formerly nailed to the corner of a dilapidated case. The glimmer of the tallow-dip has been superseded by the full blaze of electricity, an agency which will yet doubtless play an important part in the future development of printing.

Practically, there has been no limit to its progress. Discovery has not only kept pace with, but outstripped both needs and desires. So it has been in every branch. The boiling metal has been molded into forms of beauty and utility; in fact, so much has printing trespassed upon the bounds of what was once called "art" that even the graver finds in it a formidable rival. Rule, that but a few years ago was as unbending as a "country squire," now willingly yields to every curve of symmetry and beauty, shaped by the magic touch of the skilled compositor.

And well, also, has the paper-maker done his part. The gloss, the smoothness, the tints, the toughness are all that can reasonably be desired. New fiber has been found and utilized, not alone to satisfy a craze for something new, but for the most realistic of uses — cheapness — a great desideratum, if coupled with merit, for the printer.

In a thousand and one of the littles that go to make up the grand total of success, the good work has been steadily going on. No one article can be named that has not been touched with the magic wand of improvement. Little, if any, that is crude remains to baffle intelligence or annoy the skilled workman. He simply wills, and it is done. So thoroughly has this been accomplished that it would seem as if the bounds of possibility had been reached, as if man had arrived at the limit beyond which only divinity can pass.

Is this true? Have we really come to the end of the journey of improvement as a craft? Must we be content with what has already been done, and make no effort to attain a loftier plane? Has the past been greater than the present can be? Have the mines of invention been so deeply and carefully worked that no golden nuggets remain undiscovered? Has the plummet sounded the uttermost depths and left nothing of use to be yet made known? It would be galling to our pride to acknowledge this, even were it true, but fortunately for civilization it is not. It was, in fact, but as the rude foundation to the magnificent structure of today, as today will be to the years to follow, and he who believes that printing, the most useful of all arts, has reached the *ultima thule* is strangely blind to its destiny and inspiration. There never has been and never will be more than a passing check to its development, because underlying its progress is the interest of all humanity, discovery, enlightenment and civilization.

With every step measuring the notes of the march of human progress must the printer keep time. Every forward move has created the necessity of another and a greater; every meritorious specimen of the typographic art has created a desire and a demand for something still higher in the scale of excellence, something still nearer absolute perfection. To meet this requirement, to keep pace with the demands of the age, calls for incessant vigilance and continued improvement in workmanship, material, machinery, and labor-saving inventions.

"But," questions the chronic doubter—and the question is pertinent—"where shall be found any power to assist in eclipsing the past, a more compact, cheaper motor than steam, a genie more potent than we now possess? Upon what depends these utopian dreams of the future?" The answer is so plain that a printer, of all other callings, should never need enlightenment on the subject. It is whispered to him by telegraph, voiced to him by telephone, and Franklin gave him the "key" to its subtle mystery when he caught the lightning and fettered its wanderings by the chains of a master will. True, much, we deem, is known of it now; but our present knowledge is as nothing to its coming uses, the film it throws over an electroplate is but as the gossamer web to what the fabric yet will be.

Electricity will yet come to the printer as the spiritual inspiration that illuminated the minds of the German fathers of the art, as the solver of mysteries to the student in our own century. Its touch is magical, and its range of use beyond all present human calculation, though each day increases our knowledge, and each new development gives us a clearer insight into future possibilities. Already it has achieved wonders; has given us the most useful of "plates;" perfect and easy communication, be the distance what it may; has lighted our workshops as brightly as the noonday sun, and tuned our bells as with spiritual music. Why can it not do more? When we learn to control its forces, to make it entirely subservient to our wishes, may it not exceed even the most sanguine hopes of the "dreaming enthusiast"? It runs other machines, and why not printing-presses? It produces in stable form the type, and why may it not supersede type itself? It duplicates "cuts," and why may not its delicate touches, mind-guided, engrave the cut itself? In a hundred ways it aids the printer now, and who shall dare to draw the line beyond which it shall pass?

A MARVELOUS MACHINE.

WE have published, from time to time, as our readers know, illustrations and descriptions of various automatic typesetting and distributing machines, the use of which, their inventors claimed, would eventually dispense with the services of the compositor, and have generally done so in a rather skeptical mood. If the statements of Mr. L. McMillan, of Ilion, New York, and his friends can be substantiated, however, we shall be compelled to admit that the problem has to all intents and purposes been solved. Dispensing with the usual explanatory or introductory remarks, about trials and triumphs, etc., suffice it to say that the inventor claims that he has at length *perfected* a piece of mechanism which can set from sixty-five to seventy thousand ems per day, thus reaching the capacity of eight first-class workmen, at a saving of over sixty per cent over the cost of hand composition.

A single machine occupies a space about four feet square, and weighs about one thousand pounds. Its appearance resembles that of a huge type-writer, though the only point of exact similarity is the keyboard, before which the operator sits while he manipulates the buttons. The low cases, which hold a row of individual letters, are arranged parallel above each other in the form of an inverted pyramid, the ends of each reaching forward to a common vertical plane, are supplied with narrow channels and form a confluence with a center main channel. When the operator strikes a key, a finger draws out a letter from its special case, and sends it to the bottom *instantaneously.* All the types thus drawn reach their destination at the same place, and are next pushed forward in a long, curved, horizontal channel to the "spacer," who sits waiting to "justify" them to the required width of the column. The force necessary to operate the "keyboard" is no more than that required to operate a Remington type-writer under the best conditions, and it is further claimed there is no reason why the speed should be any less, allowing the operator to be equally expert, and upon these conditions the capacity of the typesetters would exceed that given above.

The distributing machine is made of one wheel, revolving horizontally within a wide tire or rim of another. Upon the inner wheel, radiating from the center, are cut channels to its outer edge, and in these channels the types are set line by line. From the center of the wheel a spring pushes against the whole line of type in each channel, tending to throw it out of the channel's end; but just at this point are little "feeling-pins," which prevent this until the proper position is reached. These pins are attached to small bars, which are constantly traveling around with the wheel, and by a most ingenious invisible contrivance are constantly moving up and down and assuming various positions.

The types are all specially nicked by a small machine made for the purpose, each class of letters having a uniform though distinct pair of nicks, each letter and sign having a special mark. Now, as the wheel laden with matter to be distributed moves around, the nicks in the type and the pins in the bar correspond at their proper channels, and the letter flies into the case, which is held in the outer wheel before mentioned. When the case is filled it is ready to be inserted into the compositor, for it is the same case used, the type pieces never being handled by men at all. The capacity of this machine is claimed to be equal to that of two "setters," or in other words it will distribute one hundred and forty thousand ems minion per day.

That all these claims will be permanently established we are not prepared to say, but it is evident that in this machine the compositor has a rival which he cannot afford to ignore or underrate.

4 A, 20 a, complete with 3 A Initials, . . $6.80
4 A, 20 a, without Initials, ... 3.50

THREE-LINE NONPAREIL PENCRAFT, No. 2.
With Three-Line Pica Initials.

20 a, extra lower-case, ... $2.00
3 A, Initials, (separately) 3.30

Science of Deceptive Book=Keeping

Mathematical Exactness Developed in Signature Reproduction

Evening Lessons in Imitative Penmanship

1234567890

PICA PENCRAFT.
With Two-Line Pica Initials.

Typography versus Lithography

Valuable Investment for Printing Establishments

Progressive Craftsmen

The series of Pencraft here shown will be found
very convenient in printing=offices for use in diplomas,
circulars, cards, bill=heads, and in many classes of work
where space is limited. Many printers, who take pride
in issuing neat and tasty work from their establishments,
will welcome it as another step in the ladder leading to
the ideal of perfection in typography toward which they
have so long been industriously climbing.

1234567890

8 A, 32 a, with 4 A Initials, ... $5.25
8 A, 32 a, without Initials, ... 3.50

32 a, extra lower-case, ... $2.05
4 A, Initials, (separately) 1.75

4 A, 12 a, complete with 3 A Initials, . . $6.80
4 A, 12 a, without Initials, ... 3.50

THREE-LINE NONPAREIL PENCRAFT.
With Three-Line Pica Initials.

12 a, extra lower-case, ... $2.00
3 A, Initials, (separately) 3.30

Progress in American Typography

Mortised Types, a Novelty Printers will Appreciate

Durability with Comprehensive Usefulness

1234567890

OH! MAY THESE TYPES
Always Tell the Stories of Our
Nation's Grandest Glory
$12,345 Proud 678.90

Mersenville, Zip,————————— 188

To KNIFE & BUTCHER, Dr.

MANUFACTURERS OF

Cutlery and Pipe Razors

Terms:————————   123 Buckenham Place.

MANY A TALE
The Card to Printers
My Mother's Home
$12,345,678.90?
Type & Press Co's.
HHHHHHHHHHH

6 points Nonpareil, 8 points Brevier, 10 points New Long Primer, 12 points Pica, 18 points 3-Line Nonpareil, 24 points Double Pica, 36 points 3-Line Pica.

CLEVELAND TYPE FOUNDRY, CLEVELAND, O.

GREAT PRIMER SCRIBBLE.

To the American Printing Trade

Farmer, Little & Co., 154 Monroe St., Chicago, have much pleasure in drawing your attention to this New Script, which has been named Scribble. The design is to imitate the hurried writing of the present day. This you will perceive has been successfully accomplished.

Circulars that are issued from the Press, no matter how important, are often cast aside unread, or thrown into the waste paper basket. We think it a pardonable ruse, therefore, to imitate handwriting so that the same attention shall be ... ar Type Printing as now accorded ... Lithographic facsimiles.

... orts to increase the ...t your favor... th the and tion

Logos with Fonts — Eight Dollars.

50 a 10 A —

50 a　14 A—$4 50　　　LONG PRIMER FRANKLIN CIRCULAR.

CIRCULAR OF HANDSOME NEW FACES.

Circulars containing a Selection from our New Designs will shortly be issued from the Press in the usual form.

They will be sent by Mail to all our Customer and to the Trade,

These Designs are both Novel and Attractive.

FARMER, LITTLE & CO., TYPE FOUNDERS, CHICAGO & NEW YORK.

A MERICAN SYSTEM OF INTERCHANGEABLE TYPE BODIES.

LIGHTFACE CELTIC.
IMPROVED SERIES.

A MERICAN SYSTEM OF INTERCHANGEABLE TYPE BODIES.

24A, 48a,   NONPAREIL. (6 Points Standard Measure.) $3.00

SHE TURNED ON ME HER EYES OF JET

Fancy I See them Sparkling yet, and Feel the Thrill

246 When our Glances Met 357

24A, 48a,   BREVIER. (8 Points Standard Measure.) $3.80

THE SONG OF A LOVER BOLD

Knight of the Old Romance, with a Doublet

16 And Spurs of Gold 23

18A, 36a, LONG PRIMER. (10 Points Standard Measure.) $3.35

FACE OF GRECIAN MOLD

With Other Historical Charms Untold

8 And Necessary Lance 9

16A, 32a,   PICA. (12 Points Standard Measure.) $3.70

THOSE GLORIOUS DAYS

Such Gallants now Never Come

36 Riding Past 47

8A, 16a,   GREAT PRIMER. (18 Points Standard Measure.) $3.70

FESTIVITIES OF WINTER
Skating, Toboggan Slides, Frozen Ears 36

6A, 12a,   DOUBLE SMALL PICA. (22 Points Standard Measure.) $5.00

FEAST OF LANTERNS
Variegated Chinese Light Repast 52

5A, 10a,   DOUBLE ENGLISH. (28 Points Standard Measure.) $5.50

LOST OR STRAYED
8 Art Treasures, Musical Gem

4A, 8a,   DOUBLE GREAT PRIMER. (36 Points Standard Measure.) $7.95

VANITY FAIR
Brilliant Meteors 7

3A, 6a,   FOUR-LINE PICA. (48 Points Standard Measure.) $10.05

BRAVE Defense

SPACES AND QUADS WITH ALL SIZES EXCEPT NONPAREIL AND PICA.

MEETING OF THE TYPE FOUNDERS OF THE UNITED STATES.

IT has been known for some months past that a rather spirited and lively competition for business has been going on between our various type-founding establishments, a competition which time only seemed to increase in intensity and volume. It was hoped, however, that wiser counsels would ultimately prevail and put an end to a strife which could only result in loss to all concerned. But such has not proven to be the case. The chasm widened; active competition grew into open antipathy, and the rivalry became keener day by day. Prices were cut to the rocks, and the methods resorted to by some houses to secure business were alike injurious and indefensible.

With the view of terminating this state of affairs, and placing the trade upon a more satisfactory basis, a meeting of the type founders of the United States was called, and accordingly held at the Spencer House, Niagara Falls, on the 16th of September last, and, as might have been expected, considerable interest was manifested in the results of its deliberations. Thomas MacKellar, the venerable president of the association, occupied the chair. The representatives of twenty of the largest and best foundries in the United States were present, and never was there a congregation of men more in earnest, and resolved to change the aspect of affairs. To "render unto Cæsar the things that are Cæsar's" was their paramount object. The meeting continued three days, and six executive sessions were held; consequently the grievances of the trade were thoroughly ventilated and discussed, and plans for the future government of business arranged, which will be finally determined upon at a subsequent meeting of the association to be held in New York City some time this month.

As a representative journal of the trade, THE INLAND PRINTER feels deeply interested in the action of the founders, as their welfare and its own is indissolubly linked, while two other branches connected therewith, and largely dependent on their action, also cluster round their protecting wings. It is therefore of the greatest importance that a permanent and satisfactory arrangement should be made, an arrangement that will save capital and

time, husband the strength of some of the very best men in the land, and which will herald the principles and doctrines of our best political economists. Type founding is a grand art, and demands the exercise of the mental capacity in a very high degree; and, in common phrase, "are the men connected therewith not worthy of their hire?" We believe they are, and trust they will get it too; but this result depends more or less upon the unanimity existing between themselves, and their own ability to carry out their plans.

We sincerely trust that such will be the case. The president, Mr. MacKellar, is a fair, just and honorable man, and his example will certainly act as a powerful incentive with the founders themselves to keep rigidly to their engagements, and do what is right. He is indeed the father of the trade, and the principal partner of one of the largest and best type-founding establishments in the world; a man of education and large experience, who has blended with these the accomplishments of the dignified gentleman, cautious and conservative, but true to his word and just in all his business transactions.

THOS. MACKELLAR, PH.D., PHILADELPHIA.

The vice-president is Mr. John Marder, of the firm of Marder, Luse & Co., a man of wide capacity, rare judgment and large experience; the president of an organization that has evinced as much push, enterprise and vigor as any concern throughout the length and breadth of the country. His foundry was consumed by the Chicago fire, when the work of half a lifetime perished in a night; but, like a true representative of the western country, he commenced at once the work of reconstruction, and, with an indomitable will and inflexible purpose, raised his establishment from the ground and placed it on a firmer basis than it had ever occupied, and the Chicago Type Foundry has since kept pace with the growth of the city and the progressive tendencies of the West. His portrait will be found on the page opposite.

These, then, are the men who lead the Type Founders' Association, and under their guidance and ripe experience there should be no insurmountable difficulty in making an arrangement which will be as lasting as it will be honorable and beneficial to everyone connected with the trade. At least, such is the opinion of THE INLAND PRINTER.

Caxton  Black.

THREE-LINE EXCELSIOR CAXTON BLACK.   Price, $5.00

Lectures on the Problems of Human Sustenance

Capabilities of the Crust of the Earth   Methods of Tillage in Various Countries

Machinery as Applied to Husbandry

Illustrated by Agricultural Scenes in all Quarters of the Globe

PICA CAXTON BLACK.   Price, $2.25

Ploughing, Harrowing, Sowing and Planting

Warfare With Destructive Enemies   Vegetable, Animal and Elemental

Gentle Rains and Genial Sunshine

Subduing, Cultivating and Enriching Mother Earth

THREE-LINE NONPAREIL CAXTON BLACK.   Price $2.75

Gathering in the Bounties of Dame Nature

Overflowing Granaries

Generous Recompense for Intelligent Efforts and Patient Industry

Labourers Rejoicing at the Harvest-Home

FIVE-LINE NONPAREIL CAXTON BLACK.   Price, $3.00

Gleaning the Wheatears

Searching Diligently   Trudging Homeward

Merrily Consuming Frumenty

The MacKellar, Smiths & Jordan Co., Philadelphia.   Shniedewend & Lee Co., Agents, Chicago, Ill.

24 POINT ARGENT.

She Hankered for Knowledge of Books

Money Disappeared   Happy and Free

$1234 Wise and Masterly Inactivity 56789

OFFICE OF

The H. H. Thorp Mfg. Co.

PROPRIETORS OF THE

Cleveland Type Foundry

147 ST. CLAIR STREET.

Cleveland, O.,_____1886

36 POINT ARGENT.

A Daniel Come to Judgement

Butler's Hudibras   Thomas Tusser

Marie Stewart, February 18, 1587

Cleveland Type Foundry,   -   -   -   -   -   147 St. Clair Street.

Elberon  Series.

10A, 18a.   12 POINT ELBERON, No. 2. $3.90

HUMAN PASSIONS ARE QUICK TO RISE AND FALL

Many Men of Different Hues but to Keep Feet Warm Wear big Shoes

Often in the Still of Night the Cry of Fire is Heard

12345 Beautiful Shadows of this Grand Old Forest City 67890

8A, 14a.   18 POINT ELBERON, No. 2. $5.25

BETRAYED BY A HAIR ON HIS COAT

A Violet from Mother's Grave Cherished with Care

12345 Their Perpendicular Elevation 67890

6A, 10a.   24 POINT ELBERON, No. 2. $6.70

COMPARISONS ARE ODIOUS

A Paradise of Fools Belongs to Milton

123 Knowledge is Power 678

4A, 6a.   36 POINT ELBERON, No. 2. $8.80

WIT AND WISDOM

A Base Ball Player's Luck

23 Political Frauds 56

12 point Pica, 18 point 3-Line Nonpareil, 24 point Double Pica, 36 point 3-Line Pica.

Cleveland Type Foundry, Cleveland, Ohio.

983. D<small>OUBLE</small> G<small>REAT</small> P<small>RIMER</small> M<small>ONROE</small>, 7 A, 7 A, $3.75.

A BENEVOLENT TREASURY BONDHOLDER
Remember his Kindness

984. D<small>OUBLE</small> P<small>ICA</small> M<small>ONROE</small>, 12 A, 12 A, $3.00.

FOR MEAGER TALKERS AND UNGRACEFUL SAPHEADS
Contrite and Marriageable Maidens

985. G<small>REAT</small> P<small>RIMER</small> M<small>ONROE</small>, 16 A, 16 A, $2.50.

REMARKABLE BOAT CUSHIONS AND SEAMLESS TROUSERS AT BOTTOM PRICES
Exceedingly Desirable for Retired Mustang Riders. 147 Miles

986. P<small>ICA</small> M<small>ONROE</small>, 22 A, 22 A, $2.25.

ADVENTURES OF INDEPENDENT AND ORIGINAL COMPOSERS FROM THE METEOROLOGICAL NATIONS
345 Aproned Professors of the Art Preservative of Arts

987. L<small>ONG</small> P<small>RIMER</small> M<small>ONROE</small>, 30 A, 30 A, $2.00.

THOSE WHO RECOMMEND HONESTY ON THE GROUND OF ITS BEING THE BEST POLICY, IN CASES LEAD MEN INTO DISHONESTY
Valuable Hints to Young Men. Enclose 50 Cents and Stamp

988. D<small>OUBLE</small> P<small>ICA</small> B<small>ANNER</small>, 5 A, 8 A, $3.50.

THE BEAUTIFUL SEASIDE COTTAGE
Good Home Influences, 1886

955. D<small>OUBLE</small> G<small>REAT</small> P<small>RIMER</small> K<small>ISMET</small>, 6 a, 3 A, $4.50.

Popular Musical Entertainments For November, 1886

991. D<small>OUBLE</small> P<small>ICA</small> K<small>ISMET</small>, 9 a, 5 A, $3.50.

Picturesque America, Bound in Splendid Style
12345 Volumes 67890

BOSTON TYPE FOUNDRY, JOHN K. ROGERS, AGENT, 104 MILK STREET.

November 1886 139

REGISTERED, No. 47,495.

Price, $2.70 — THREE-LINE EXCELSIOR CRUIKSHANK.

NEEDED RENOVATION OF MANKIND
MUNICIPAL PROTECTION FOR THE INDUSTRIAL CLASSES
SAFETY FOR THE INNOCENT
FREEDOM FROM THE WILES OF DEPRAVITY
1234567890

PICA CRUIKSHANK. — Price, $3.30

SUPERFLUOUS EXTRADITIONS
CITIZENS RELIEVED FROM ONEROUS BURDENS
PRISONS ABROGATED
IMPROVED CORRECTIVE METHODS
1234567890

THREE-LINE NONPAREIL CRUIKSHANK. — Price, $3.85

PROPOSED NATIONAL REFORMATORIES

FALLEN BROTHERS RESTORED — HONEST LIVING ENCOURAGED

KINDNESS, JUSTICE, PENITENCE, MANHOOD

FIVE-LINE NONPAREIL CRUIKSHANK. — Price, $5.15

PHILANTHROPIC TREATMENT
SOLITARY CONFINEMENT RELINQUISHED

TWO-LINE PICA CRUIKSHANK. — Price, $4.65

REDUCTION OF TAXATION
MORALS ELEVATED, PROPERTY SECURE

THREE-LINE PICA CRUIKSHANK. — Price, $5.80.

RUFFIANISM EXTINCT
HEREDITARY CRIME ANNIHILATED

ALL COMPLETE WITH FIGURES.

THE MACKELLAR, SMITHS & JORDAN CO., PHILADELPHIA, PA.

SHNIEDEWEND & LEE CO., AGENTS, CHICAGO, ILLINOIS.

BIOGRAPHICAL SKETCH OF CARL SCHRAUB-STADTER.

ONE of the best known of American type founders is the president of the Central Type Foundry, St. Louis, Mr. Carl Schraubstadter, whose portrait is herewith presented. Starting at the bottom of the ladder, when the business was still in its infancy, he has, through his energy and ability brought himself to the front, and although forty-five years have elapsed since his apprenticeship was served, is still as enterprising and anxious for improvements as when younger blood coursed through his veins. Mr. Schraubstadter was born in Dresden, Germany, on the 12th of May, 1827, and attended school until his fourteenth year, when he entered the type founding department of Meinhold & Sons' printing establishment. At that time all type was cast in hand-molds with a small ladle; and he often refers to the incredulity with which the reports of a casting machine were received.

After six years of hard apprenticeship he became a journeyman, and as such, visited the principal cities of Germany, Austria, and Hungary, working at his trade — or art, as it was called — and, though frequently offered fine positions, moved to new localities, perfecting himself in all the branches of the business.

CARL SCHRAUBSTADTER.

In November, 1854, he arrived in New York, where a younger brother had preceded him, and at once found employment in the foundry of Jas. Conner's Sons. During a temporary depression of the business he accepted an invitation to work a few weeks in the Boston Type Foundry, though the few weeks lengthened into twenty years. He there became a well-known and popular member of Boston society, and in 1860, married Miss Augusta Stern. Of their eleven children, nine are still living, the three eldest sons being practical type founders like himself. At the time of his arrival, the Boston Type Foundry was a small concern, but by his tireless energy, it soon became widely known, and when it was incorporated he became a prominent stockholder, and assumed the charge of the manufacturing department. As the business increased it was found necessary to open a branch in St. Louis,

Mr. Jas. A. St. John assuming its business management. In the great Boston fire of 1872, the building and stock of the type foundry were completely destroyed, and it was only by his personal efforts, and his encouragement of the few employes whom he had gathered about him, that the matrices and machines were saved from destruction.

Notwithstanding the fatigue of working all night, he immediately procured another building, and two days after the fire the foundry was again started, working night and day, to supply the demands of the burned out printing offices. Foreseeing the rapid growth of the business in the West, in 1874 he severed his connection with the Boston Type Foundry, and associating with him Mr. James A. St. John, the manager of the St. Louis branch of that establishment, started what is now known as the Central Type Foundry. With Mr. Schraubstadter at the head of the factory, and Mr. St. John in the office, the business was bound to prosper, and from a small beginning, it has risen in importance, until it is now one of the best-known type-founding establishments in the world.

Its magnificent building is admirably adapted to its purpose, and completely furnished with the latest and most approved machinery, Mr. Schraubstadter being a firm believer in the firm's motto, "The best is the cheapest,"

and in few factories are the wants and comforts of the employes so well attended to.

In social life he is a great favorite, making friends wherever he goes, and in musical circles his fine baritone voice is well known. A prominent member of the Orpheus Musical Society, of Boston, and the Liederkranz Society of St. Louis, he has sung the principal parts of many operas, oratorios and other works, earning great applause.

The most of olden type founders are rapidly being relegated to the rear, but he has not only tried to keep pace with the times, but endeavored to keep ahead, and many of the recognized and adopted improvements in the business are due to his enterprise.

In spite of his years he is still a young man, and THE INLAND PRINTER wishes him a long and prosperous career.

MECHANICAL PATENT,
FEB. 16, 1886.

SPARTAN.
PATENTED DECEMBER 7. 1886.

AMERICAN SYSTEM OF
INTERCHANGEABLE TYPE BODIES.

6 A, TWO-LINE PICA. (24 Points Standard Measure.) $4.10

POETS INSPIRED SING
MANY ROMANTIC THEMES 25

4 A, TWO-LINE GREAT PRIMER. (36 Points Standard Measure.) $5.85

ENTERPRISE

3 A, FOUR-LINE PICA. (48 Points Standard Measure.) $6.40

NEAR HOME 4

SPACES AND QUADS WITH ALL SIZES.   TWO-LINE BOURGEOIS (18) IN PREPARATION.

THE LARGER SIZES OF THIS SERIES HAVE MORTISED LETTERS.

EXCELSIOR

CHICAGO TYPE FOUNDRY
BEST QUALITY ONLY

AMERICAN SYSTEM OF
INTERCHANGEABLE TYPE BODIES.

MECHANICAL PATENT,
FEB. 16, 1886.

PARTHENIAN.
PATENTED AUGUST 31, 1886.

12A, 24a,   PICA. (12 Points Standard Measure.) $3.40

WONDERFUL FREAKS OF NATURE
The Chough and Crow to Roost Have Gone, the Owl Sits
37 Hooting in the Cold 48

8A, 16a,   GREAT PRIMER. (18 Points Standard Measure.) $5.10

CONSCIENCE FOR SALE
Owner Has No Further Use For It
25 Will sell Cheap 79

6A, 12a,   DOUBLE PICA. (24 Points Standard Measure.) $6.25

HANDSOME SERIES
All Printers Should Get This 5

4A, 8a,   DOUBLE GREAT PRIMER. (36 Points Standard Measure.) $8.00

WATERWAYS
Cheated by a Coon 34

3A, 6a,   FOUR-LINE PICA. (48 Points Standard Measure.) $10.60

HARMONY
Quiet Strains 16

LOGOTYPES WITH ALL THE ABOVE SIZES.   MORTISED LETTERS WITH CAPS OF THE LARGER SIZES.

139-141 MONROE STREET, CHICAGO.

MARDER, LUSE & CO., TYPE FOUNDERS.

14-16 SECOND ST. SOUTH, MINNEAPOLIS.

MECHANICAL PATENT, FEB. 16, 1886.

AMERICAN SYSTEM OF INTERCHANGEABLE TYPE BODIES.

ROUMANIAN.

PATENTED NOVEMBER 30, 1886.

12 A.   TWO-LINE DIAMOND. (9 Points Standard Measure.) $2.75

✠ ROCKED ✠ IN ✠ THE ✠ CRADLE ✠ OF ✠ THE ✠ DEEP ✠
I LAY ME DOWN TO REST! THE LOBSTERS RED UPSET
✠ 23 ✠ MY SLEEP BY SITTING ON MY CHEST ✠ 45 ✠

10 A,   TWO-LINE NONPAREIL. (12 Points Standard Measure.) $3.00

EVERY MAN SHOULD BE THE ARCHITECT
5 ✠ OF HIS OWN FORTUNE ✠ 8

8 A,   TWO-LINE BOURGEOIS. (18 Points Standard Measure.) $4.90

✠ TWO MIGHTY HUNTERS ✠
3 ✠ SHOT A DUCK ✠ 6

6 A,   TWO-LINE PICA. (24 Points Standard Measure.) $5.80

DRIVE AWAY CARE 2

4 A,   TWO-LINE GREAT PRIMER. (36 Points Standard Measure.) $8.25

NOBLE ✠ MAN

3 A,   FOUR-LINE PICA. (48 Points Standard Measure.) $8.50

DELIGHT ✠ 4

NONPAREIL IN PREPARATION.   SPACES AND QUADS WITH ALL SIZES EXCEPT TWO-LINE NONPAREIL.

THE LARGER SIZES OF THIS SERIES HAVE MORTISED LETTERS.

HHHHHH HHHHHH HHHHHHHHHHH

ALL THE SIZES OF THIS SERIES ARE MADE TO LINE AT BOTH TOP AND BOTTOM.

REGISTERED, No. 47,496.
MECHANICAL PATENT, MAR. 31, 1885.

25 a, 5 A, with 3 A Initials, . $6.30	
25 a, 5 A, without Initials, . 5.00	
25 a, Lower-case only, . . . 3.10	
A, Initials, separately, . . 1.30	

THREE-LINE NONPAREIL MASTER SCRIPT.

50 a, 10 A, with 3 A Initials, $11.30	
50 a, 10 A, without Initials, . 10.00	
50 a, Lower-case only, . . 6.15	
3 A, Initials, separately, . . 1.30	

Improved Commercial Printing

Fanciful Productions of Intelligent Typographers

Pleasing Appearance

Comprehensive Usefulness Realized

GOODS SHIPPED IMMEDIATELY ON THE RECEIPT OF ORDER.

Longacoming, July 4, 1886

Mr. Joseph Reliable

Bought of Laborhard & Bros, Limited

No. 97 Elbow Lane

Terms, Cash on Demand

20 a, 5 A, with 3 A Initials, . $8.40	
20 a, 5 A, without Initials, . 6.10	

TWO-LINE PICA MASTER SCRIPT.

20 a, Lower-case only, . . $3.60	
3 A, Initials, separately, . . 2.30	

Artistic Masterpieces

Durable Appliances   Beautiful Printing

Quaintly Harmonizing Letters

ALL COMPLETE WITH FIGURES, SPACES, AND QUADS.

The Initial Capitals are cast on the same body as the Lower-case, and do not require justification. Those of the three larger sizes, wherever practicable, are mortised to allow the insertion of the Lower-case letters a, e, o and u, which have been specially fitted for that purpose.

THE MACKELLAR, SMITHS & JORDAN CO., PHILADELPHIA.

SHNIEDEWEND & LEE CO., AGENTS, CHICAGO, ILL.

December 1886   145

Astral Series.

10A, 18a.   12 Point Astral, No. 2. $4.30
18a Lower Case (extra), $2.15

THE SUN IS SETTING IN THE WESTERN HILLS

There she Stands and Waves her Hand at me in Parting. See?

12345   A Sailor's Wife is She   67890

8A, 14a.   18 Point Astral, No. 2. $5.65
14a Lower Case (extra), 2.75

SLOWLY AND SADLY HE CLIMBED

The Distant Hill and was Soon Lost to Sight

12345   Among the Shades   67890

6A, 10a.   24 Point Astral, No. 2. $6.95
10a Lower Case (extra), 3.45

WHITE WINGS NEVER

Friends are Invited to Attend the

2345   Last Sad Rites   7890

4A, 6a.   36 Point Astral, No. 2. $9.15
6a Lower Case (extra), 3.65

CURSE OF ROME

24 Beautiful Climax 68

12 point Pica, 18 point 3-Line Nonpareil, 24 point Double Pica, 36 point 3-Line Pica.

Cleveland Type Foundry, Cleveland, Ohio.

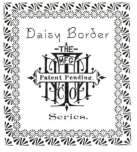

Illyrian Series.

| 10A, 20a. | 10 Point Illyrian | $1.85 |
| | 20a Lower Case, (extra) | 0.95 |

They were Lovers and Pain would Wed and
on his Breast she had Nestled her Head, he Glanced
Down and Painted her Cheeks they had
Colored his only Clean Shirt Bosom Light Red

| 8A, 16a. | 12 Point Illyrian | $2.00 |
| | 16a Lower Case, (extra) | 1.00 |

The Evening Star its Vesper Lamp
Above the West had Lit,
The Dusky Curtains of the Night
Were following over it.

| 6A, 14a. | 18 Point Illyrian. | $2.80 |
| | 14a Lower Case, (extra) | 1.30 |

The Ball and Bat are Put Away, Ceased is the Long Strife,
And now the Festive Umpire May Obtain Insurance on his Life Courier
Peculiarities of Noted People in Years Gone Bye

12 Point Daisy Border.
Cast on 6 and 12 Point Bodies.
$2.70 Per Font.

$3.15
Per Font.

18 Point Daisy Border.
Cast on 9 and 18 Point Bodies.

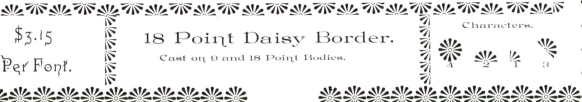

Cleveland Type Foundry,   ~   ~   ~   147 St. Clair Street.

SELF SPACING TYPE.

The common widths of book pages, miscellaneous jobs and newspaper columns are some number of Pica ems, therefore the Pica em is taken as the basis for Self Spacing type. The thinnest space in all fonts is some exact fraction of a Pica, and this fraction of Pica is called the unit of measure. All characters, spaces and quads in the font are made some exact multiple of this unit in width, so that the sizes of all faces will work perfectly together in the regular labor-saving measures. This unit of measure may be one-sixth, one-seventh, one-eighth one-ninth, one-tenth, etc. of a Pica em, as may be desired, to produce condensed, medium or extended faces. The following table gives the sizes of bodies, units of measure, and lengths of alphabets. In the first column will be found the various sizes of bodies; in the second, the number of units contained in one em Pica; and in the third the measurements of a lower case alphabet in ems of each particular body:

Body.	No. Units to Pica em.	Length of Alphabet.
5½ Point (Agate)	13	15⅝
5½ Point (Agate)	12	16⅞
6 Point (Nonpareil)	13	14⅓
6 Point (Nonpareil)	12	15½
6 Point (Nonpareil)	11	16⅞
6 Point (Nonpareil)	10	18⅝
7 Point (Minion)	12	13¼
7 Point (Minion)	11	14½
7 Point (Minion)	10	16
8 Point (Brevier)	10	14
8 Point (Brevier)	9	15½
8 Point (Brevier)	8	17½
9 Point (Bourgeois)	10	12⅜
9 Point (Bourgeois)	9	13¾
9 Point (Bourgeois)	8	15½
10 Point (Long Primer)	9	12⅜
10 Point (Long Primer)	8	14
11 Point (Small Pica)	8	12⅔
11 Point (Small Pica)	7	14½
12 Point (Pica)	8	11⅝
12 Point (Pica)	7	13¼
12 Point (Pica)	6	15½

In the foregoing table will be noticed a Nonpareil with one-twelfth of Pica as unit of measure. This is one-sixth of the body of Nonpareil, or the six-to-em space, which preserves in this particular font the old three-to-em space and the old en and em quads. The same is true of the Brevier on one-ninth of Pica, the Bourgeois on one-eighth of Pica and the Pica on one-sixth of Pica.

The Minion on one-twelfth of Pica will have as its unit a seven-to-em space, or one-seventh of the Minion body, and will set at right angles or work into squares of the body, as will also the Pica on one-seventh of Pica. The Nonpareil on one-tenth of Pica has the old five-to-em space of Nonpareil as its unit, and will work into squares of Nonpareil or Pica.

In a complete font of the old kind of body type there are about 190 widths of bodies. Appended is a table showing the different widths of bodies of Self Spacing Old Style. It will be readily seen that there are but *nine* widths of bodies all told,

and that the four-unit width predominates largely over any other, there being fifty-nine characters of this width. We omit the Italic characters from the table as they all go on the same widths of bodies, and are interchangeable with the Roman:

```
1 unit  —Space...................................................   1
2 units —Space, f i j l , : ; . - ' ! I ɪ J '  |.............  16
3 units —Quad, c e r s t z ? ) ] * † ‡ § ‖ ¶ I J s z - °...  22
4 units —Quad, a b d g h k n o p q u v x y fi fl ff $ £
         1 2 3 4 5 6 7 8 9 0 S Z A B C D E F G L N O
         P Q R T U V X Y & .. - { } ] ⌡ ⌠...............  59
5 units —æ A B C D E F G L N O P Q R T U V Y H
         K M...................................................  21
6 units —Quad, m ct w ffi ffl œ H K X & w Æ Œ ℔ ,
         ₱ @ - ... ¼ ½ ¾ ⅓ ⅔ ⅛ ⅜ ⅝ ⅞ ................  28
7 units —M W................................................   2
8 units —Æ Œ................................................   2
12 units—Quad, ...... —  ☜ ☞ ..........................   5
```
9 sizes.	Roman characters	156
	Italic characters	77
		233

In Roman fonts, except Old Style, there are but eight widths of bodies, the eight unit width being omitted.

Any compositor can see that no combination of units can be made that will not come within a certain number of exact units of filling a line. If a line of matter lacks, it must lack one or more exact units.

Self Spacing type sets line for line with the ordinary Roman, where the lengths of the alphabets are the same.

Repeated experiments with the new type have shown that the average compositor gains about twenty-five per cent. in speed, with no trouble in justification whatever. In the matter of the correction of proofs the gain is enormous. Say there is an "a" for an "e"; as "a" is four units wide and "e" three, "e" and a one-unit space justify the line perfectly. Even this measure of trouble is avoided in many instances. As twenty-six of the most common lower case characters are of the same width, they can be substituted for one another without the change of a space.

Another item worthy of consideration is the greater durability of the type. It is always on its feet, and therefore is not worn by "pounding."

In tabular work there is a great gain in speed and neatness. By the addition of a new character, viz: "|", it is easy to set perpendicular lines of any length, line by line.

Self Spacing type does not require a conscious effort to master its principle—the compositor acquires intuitively and at once all that is necessary for the perfect use of the system. He is relieved of the mental process of spacing and justifying which he now goes through.

This system secures a proper relation between letters, spaces and figures. Under the present lack of system, the three-em space and the en figure are used, no matter whether the face be expanded or compressed; in Self Spacing type every character and space will be increased or decreased in width relatively with the face of the type.

Finally, the changes in the proportions of the letters have made the type more legible and less injurious to the eyes.

The foregoing article is set in Self Spacing Long Primer Old Style No. 24, and Brevier Old Style No. 22.

BENTON, WALDO & CO., SOLE MANUFACTURERS, MILWAUKEE, WIS., ST. PAUL, MINN.

0a 12 A   LONG PRIMER YORK. $4 25 | 24 a 8 A   THREE LINE NONP. YORK. $5 75 | 36 a 10 A   PICA YORK. $4 50

CITY OF YORK

CHICAGO

YORK SERIES

Situate in Yorkshire, England, is

Capital City of the

Has Won the Admiration of

Celebrated for

North West.

All Practical Printers.

Its Ancient Cathedral.

8 a 4 A—PRICE PER FONT, $17 50   NEW FACE.—FIVE LINE PICA HEADING SCRIPT No. 4.—PATENTED.   LOWER CASE ONLY, $8 50

Beautiful Specimens

70 a 12 A   PICA SCRIBBLE. $6 00

Circulars that are issued from the Printing Press, no matter how important their contents may be, are cast aside into the waste paper basket, because they present the appearance of ordinary printed matter. We think it a pardonable ruse, therefore, to imitate handwriting so that the same attention shall be secured for Type Printing as now so generally accorded to Lithographic facsimiles.

Logos with Fonts— th the and tion

ALL PATENT RIGHTS SECURED.

PATENT PENDING.   FOUR LINE PICA INSET.   FONT $4 50

THE GREAT NORTH WESTERN STATES

THIS LINE SHOWS THE INSET IN COMBINATION WITH OUR NEW PICA ABBEY.   LETTER SCHEMES ISSUED WITH EACH INSET FONT.

SMALL PICA OLD STYLE, No. 5.—NEW, COPYRIGHT PENDING.

FARMER, LITTLE & CO.'s Roman and Italic Body Type, Book and News Faces, including all Modern and Modern Old Styles are cast from matrices made from the drive of the steel punch. Wherever matrices of these faces have been ELECTROTYPED from the type so produced, it is without the consent of FARMER, LITTLE & CO., and is a very reprehensible and dishonorable act, and should be condemned by all printers and publishers. It is like appropriating the brains and capital of an author or publisher, who may have written or published a book that becomes very popular. To produce, it has cost not only his time and labor, but a great expense for composition and plates. An unscrupulous person, reproduces the work by photo-engraving, or other process, without the consent of either author or publisher, for a fraction of the original cost.

FARMER, LITTLE & CO.'s Nonpareil and Pica Bodies are the exact standard, and accordingly their multiples agree with the so called point system. Always have been so, never changed.

FARMER, LITTLE & CO., TYPE FOUNDERS.

Baltimore Type Foundry.

Charles J. Cary & Co.,   No. 116 Bank Lane, Baltimore, Md.

10-POINT RHOMBIC.	15 A 40 a $2 15

HANDSOME RIVERSIDE COTTAGE

Meagre Talkers   123   Ungraceful Heads

12-POINT RHOMBIC.	15 A 15 A 25 a $3 10

EXCELLENT TICKETHOLDER

Remember his   234   Money Return

18-POINT RHOMBIC.	12 A 12 A 18 a $4 30

VALUABLE HINTS TO YOUNG MEN AND WOMEN

Recommend Honesty on   235   The Grounds of its Being

24-POINT RHOMBIC.	10 A 10 A 15 a $6 00

THE GOVERNMENT PRINTING OFFICE

Respect Yourself   257   Fair Wages Paid

36-POINT RHOMBIC.	4 A 5 A 8 a $6 00

ANARCHIST IMPORTANCE

The Process   124   Descriptions

18-POINT EASTER.	PATENTED.	8 A 20 a $3 00
		Extra Lower case, $1 50

Opening Day.   Autumn.   September, 29, 1886.

The   Only   Practical   Stereotype   Outfits.

Special Attention Given.   Winter.   Descriptive Circular,

24-POINT EASTER.	6 A 14 a $3 75
	Extra Lower case, $1 75

Sole Agents.   Smith, Jones & Brothers.

Manufacturers,   Jobbers   and   Dealers.

NOTE.—In view of the action of the Type Founders' Convention, held October 26th, recognizing the point system, we wish to call attention to the fact, that we were the first Foundry with an established plant to announce to the printers of the United States, that the point system would be THE SYSTEM of the future, and we went to a very heavy expense in making new moulds and altering matrices to adopt it in our Foundry.

MALTIC  SERIES.

PATENTED.

6 A   THREE LINE PICA MALTIC CONDENSED. $4 50.

GREAT CLEARING SALE

5 A   THREE LINE PICA MALTIC. $5 00.

HIGH PRICES DROP

5 A   SIX LINE PICA MALTIC EXTRA CONDENSED. $8 00.

FUR SEAL BITTER SKINS

6 A   TWO LINE PICA MALTIC. $3 75.

SUCCESS IN TREATING

6 A   FOUR LINE PICA MALTIC CONDENSED. $5 50.

ELEGANT COSTUMES

5 A   FIVE LINE NONPAREIL MALTIC. $4 00.

NUMEROUS SALES

Princess Script.

PATENT APPLIED FOR.

Three Line Nonp. Princess Script (18 Points)   Four Line Nonp. Princess Script (24 Points)

| 40 a 6 A | $ 5 50 |
| 80 a 12 A | 10 00 |

| 30 a 5 A | $ 6 50 |
| 60 a 10 A | 12 00 |

THIS SERIES IS CUT EXTRA STRONG, AND IS ESPECIALLY RECOMMENDED FOR DURABILITY AND BEAUTY.

MANUFACTURED BY BARNHART BROS. & SPINDLER, CHICAGO.

DOTTED  SERIES.

PATENT APPLIED FOR.

20 A   TWO LINE NONPAREIL DOTTED [12 Points] $1 40

THE POET SAID MISCHIEF IS WROUGHT BY WANT OF THOUGHT AS MUCH 345 AS WANT OF HEART AND THE POET KNEW 728

15 A   THREE LINE NONPAREIL DOTTED [18 Points] $2 10

PLETHORIC UNITED STATES TREASURY ATTRACTS 257 AMBITIOUS CORMORANTS 435

10 A   FOUR LINE NONPAREIL DOTTED [24 Points] $2 50

DOUBTING THOMAS IN MISERY STANDS 867 ANXIOUSLY WAITING 543

8 A   FIVE LINE NONPAREIL DOTTED [30 Points] $2 90

BERLIN WINTER OPERA SEASON 75 SWEET MEMORIES 46

6 A   SIX LINE NONPAREIL DOTTED [36 Points] $3 80

MANSION AND DUNGEON 85 STAND ANEAR 23

BARNHART BROS. & SPINDLER,   115-117 FIFTH AVENUE, CHICAGO.

Holly Wood *versus* Wood Type.

A COMPARISON OF PRICES.

HOLLY WOOD TYPE will print as well and will give as good satisfaction as ordinary wood type, and costs less than one-half as much as the latter. A printed guarantee accompanies every font we send out, *and if any letter is defective, or if the face comes off any letter, we will replace them free of charge.*

In Holly Wood Type the face is cut from holly wood and cemented to a hardwood base. There is no danger of this cement giving way as long as the type is not wet. This we *positively guarantee,* and we will replace every font that has faces loosened from the base.

The following table gives comparative prices of all sizes of a few well-known styles. Printers can compare our prices with other manufacturers and see for themselves whether we are stating *facts* or not.

STYLE OF LETTER.

NUMBER OF LINES PICA.	PRICE PER LETTER.		PRICE PER LETTER.		PRICE PER LETTER.		PRICE PER LETTER.		PRICE PER LETTER.		PRICE PER LETTER.		PRICE PER LETTER.	
	Holly Wood.	Wood Type.	Holly Wood.	Wood Type.	Holly Wood.	Wood Type.	Holly Wood.	Wood Type.	Holly Wood.	Wood Type.	Holly Wood.	Wood Type.	Holly Wood.	Wood Type.
4	$0.03	$0.06	$0.03	$0.05	....	$0.06	$0.03	$0.05	$0.02	$0.06	$0.02	$0.05	$0.02	$0.05
5	.03	.06	.03	.05	$0.03	.06	.03	.05	.03	.07	.03	.05	.03	.05
6	.03	.07	.03	.05	.03	.07	.03	.05	.04	.08	.03	.06	.03	.06
8	.04	.09	.04	.07	.04	09	.04	.07	.05	.10	.04	.08	.04	.08
10	.04	.11	.04	.09	.04	.11	.04	.09	.06	.12	.05	.10	.05	.10
12	.05	.13	.05	.10	.05	.13	.05	.10	.07	.14	.05	.12	.05	.12
14	.05	.15	.05	.11	.05	.15	.05	.11	.07	.16	.06	.14	.06	.14
15	.05	.16	.05	.12	.06	.16	.05	.12	.08	.18	.07	.15	.07	.15
16	.06	.17	.06	.13	.06	.17	.06	.13	.08	.20	.07	.16	.07	.16
18	.06	.18	.06	.14	.07	.18	.06	.14	.09	.22	.08	.17	.08	.17
20	.07	.19	.07	.15	.08	.19	.07	.15	.10	.24	.09	.18	.09	.18
24	.08	.22	.08	.17	.10	.22	.08	.17	.13	.28	.12	.21	.12	.21
25	.09	.23	.09	.18	.10	.23	.09	.18	.13	.30	.12	.22	.12	.22
30	.10	.26	.10	.21	.12	.26	.10	.21	.15	.38	.14	.25	.14	.25
36	.12	.28	.12	.23	.15	.28	.12	.23	.18	....	.16	.28	.16	.28
40	.15	.30	.15	.25	.17	.30	.15	.25	.20	....	.18	.30	.18	.30
45	.17	.32	.17	.27	.18	.32	.17	.27	.23	....	.20	.33	.20	.33
50	.18	.35	.18	.30	.18	.35	.18	.30	.25	....	.20	.36	.20	.36
60	.21	.41	.21	.35	.21	.41	.21	.35	....	....	.25	.44	.25	.44
72	.25	.48	.25	.42	.25	.48	.25	.42	....	....	.30	.52	.30	.52
100	.30	.60	.30	.55	....	.60	.30	.55	....	....	....	.65	....	.65

It will be seen from the above table that in many instances Holly Wood Type is at least 75 per cent cheaper than ordinary Wood Type, and in nearly *all* cases it is 50 per cent cheaper. To settle the matter of quality we will send you a sample letter on receipt of two cent stamp.

JAMES A. ST. JOHN.

A SUCCESSFUL REPRESENTATIVE TYPE FOUNDER.

WE are indebted to the *Printer's Review*, of Boston, for the following sketch of the career of a gentleman well and favorably known to the readers of THE INLAND PRINTER:

James A. St. John was born in the town of Harbor Grace, in the Island of Newfoundland, September 23, 1841, and is the youngest son of W. C. St. John, a writer and publisher, and a man well known for his scholarly learning and fondness for scientific study.

The family removed to the United States in 1853, and Mr. St. John's father and elder brothers, in company with J. S. Bartlett, started an English literary paper called the *Anglo-Saxon*. In 1856 James A. graduated from his school and entered the *Anglo-Saxon* office, but the

JAMES A. ST. JOHN.

panic in 1857 put an end to the *Anglo-Saxon*, and the subject of our sketch sought and obtained employment in the Boston Type Foundry, where his mental and physical activity in a few years won for him a responsible position. In 1869 he was elected manager of the concern, which position he retained until 1871, when he resigned this place and the highest salary ever paid a type founder in the United States, and removed to St. Louis, starting a branch of the Boston Type Foundry. The success of the new venture was great, and in a very few years the branch supplied every daily paper in St. Louis, and many of the largest offices in the Southwest. In 1875, with Mr. C. Schraubstadter, Mr. St. John bought out the branch of the Boston Type Foundry, and began manufacturing in St. Louis, changing the name to the Central Type Foundry. This concern has grown under his management to be an immense establishment, having agencies in England, Australia, and every large city on the continent. Many of the styles brought out by the Central Type Foundry are of Mr. St. John's own design, and for which he has received patents. He has also invented many useful appliances for printers' use, all of them having met with great success. Mr. St. John is editor of the *Printer's Register*, and is very fond of literary work; this trait, in fact, is general in the St. John family, his brothers and sisters having all written for the press.

Mr. St. John is the patron of all athletic exercises, and finds much enjoyment in rowing, fishing, cricket, and other field sports. He is either president or vice-president of about every athletic society in or about St. Louis, and has been liberal in the support of various clubs. He is the warm personal friend of Hanlan, Trickett, Ross, and scores of professional oarsmen and athletes, all of whom are delighted to engage his services as referee in their contests. Three years ago he brought out Gaudaur, the oarsman, who, it will be remembered, won

two important races on the Charles river, in Boston, on July 4, 1885, and who is now champion of America.

Whatever Mr. St. John does he does with enthusiasm; the result is success. His life has been full of sunlight, and he often tells his friends: "*Let us have a good time while we live, for we will be a long time dead.*" Mr. St. John is married, and has a son in his sixteenth year, "a chip of the old block." His house is always open to his friends, and the family are never happier than when entertaining a houseful. He intends staying in this world as long as he can.

TYPE FOUNDRY LITERATURE.

To the Editor: TOPEKA, January 5, 1887.

A country foreman writing to a type-foundry journal complains that "in order to get hold of specimen sheets," etc., he has often to "fish them out of the waste-basket or exchange pile." From personal experience, I know such complaints are too often well founded, and are by no means restricted to the "country districts." It sometimes seems the proprietor is afraid the "boys" will see some new face, and possibly ask for its purchase, or else will catch onto some new-fangled idea, and spend a little extra time talking about it or trying to work it out. Of course there are exceptions, but the above fits entirely too many men in the counting room. Type founders expend a good deal of money on specimen pages, sparing no expense in the way of first-class composition, stock and ink, and it is not right that productions representing so much money and skilled labor should find their way into the waste-basket, unread. That is not what they are issued for. The working printer of today will be the employing printer of the near future, and his abilities or inclinations will then be just what his past education accomplished for him. Our trade is making wonderful strides, and to remain apace with it, the workman must keep himself well posted if he has any ambition to stay at the front. To do so, he must first read his trade journals, exchange opinions and experiences with fellow-workmen, and next, mentally devour every type-foundry specimen sheet and price list of printing material that comes within his reach.

Two of our most wide-awake foundries, the "Central" and the "Cleveland," and also the Messrs. Morgans & Wilcox Manufacturing Company, have undertaken to arrest this premature destruction of type foundry literature by mailing their specimen sheets, etc., direct to such actual and worthy journeyman printers whose addresses they can get, thus putting copies thereof where they will certainly be appreciated, and where, I believe, they will ultimately do the most good. New faces or novelties are generally purchased on the suggestion or demand of the foreman or workman, and one order so secured by the foundry would repay postage expended.

I would like to suggest to all foundries and to manufacturers of printing material and inks to revise their mailing list so as to embrace the resident job men in the various towns. Try the experiment, and you will at least have the satisfaction of knowing that you are a potent factor in the production of a happier and technically better educated class of printers.

What say you, Mr. Typefoundryman? T. B. B.

NO EPHS NOR CAYS.

The following, clipt from the *Rocky Mountain Cyclone*, shows how completely the English language is adapted for sudden and unforeseen emergencies:

"We begin the publication of the *Roccay Mountain Cyclone* with some phew diphphiculties. The type phounders phrom whom we bought our outphit phor this printing ophphice phailed to supply us with any ephs or cays, and it will be phour or phive weex bephore we can get any. The mistaque was not phound out till a day or two ago. We have ordered the missing letters, and will have to get along without them till they come. We don't lique the loox ov this variety ov spelling any better than our readers, but mistaques will happen in the best regulated phamilies, and iph the phs and cays and xs and qs hold out, we shall ceep (sound the c hard) the *Cyclone* whirling, aphter a phashion, till the sorts arrive. It is no joque to us—it is a serious aphphair."

Auroral  Series.

10A, 18a.   12 POINT AURORAL, No. 2. $4.55
                                                            18a Lower Case (extra), 2.40

DESPITE ALL HIS IMPERFECTIONS

Nature Might Stand up and say to this Beautiful Universe

$2345   This is an Intelligent Man   67890

8A, 14a.   18 POINT AURORAL, No. 2. $6.05
                                                            14a Lower Case (extra), 3.05

MORE TRUTH THAN POETRY

Our Journalistic Poetry Caught in its Flight

35   The Poetic Muse   78

6A, 10a.   24 POINT AURORAL, No. 2. $7.25
                                                            10a Lower Case (extra), 3.45

MOUNT HOLYOKE MILL

Welcome to Peace and Happiness

24 An Oversight 67

4A, 6a.   36 POINT AURORAL, No. 2. $9.70
                                                            6a Lower Case (extra), 3.95

THE OUT CAST

More Dirt than Bread 3

12 point, Pica; 18 point, 3-Line Nonpariel; 24 point, Double Pica; 36 point, 3-Line Pica.

Cleveland Type Foundry, Cleveland, Ohio.

COME TELL A LUXURIANT STORY OF WEALTH

Where Cabbage are Most Plentiful there take them to Market

Camels wanted Horns and Ears

12345 Silk Thread of Gold 67890

MOPING MOONSTRUCK MADNESS

Nail Your Loose Change for Rainy Days to come

Always Speak Plain

234 Ten Measures of Talk 678

UNIFORM GOVERNMENT BETTER REGULATED

When the Jurors Have Agreed   Conduct them into the Court

235 Love Comes Like a Summer's Dream 789

FORMS OF RECOGNIZANCES

Charged for Admission   Order of Views Taken

123 Great Wavering Thoughts 589

LONELY SERENADERS

Our Congress 87 The Rectory

12 point, Pica; 18 point, 3-Line Nonpareil; 24 point, Double Pica; 36 point, 3-Line Pica; 48 point, 4-Line Pica.

Cleveland Type Foundry,   Cleveland, Ohio.
158   January 1887

HARDWARE SERIES.

ORIGINAL.

10A. Two-Line Pearl. (10 Points Standard Measure.) $2.15

INTERESTING LECTURE ON WHYNESS OF THE WHEREFORE BY INQUIRENDUM 245

10A, Two-Line Nonpareil. (12 Points Standard Measure.) $2.55

OPERA COMIQUE A PIRATE'S MISTAKE 7.30 TO-NIGHT

6A, Two-Line Bourgeois. (18 Points Standard Measure.) $3.00

GRAND DISPLAY OF FIREWORKS 34

6A. Two-Line Pica. (24 Points Standard Measure.) $5.00

RASH FEATS 8 DARING

3A, Two-Line Great Primer. (36 Points Standard Measure.) $5.50

HUMAN 4

ALL THE SIZES IN THE ABOVE SERIES ARE MADE TO LINE EXACTLY WITH EACH OTHER AT THE BOTTOM.

SPACES AND QUADS WITH ALL SIZES EXCEPT TWO-LINE NONPAREIL.

AT THE CASE.

BY PICA ANTIQUE.

ALL old compositors find ample reasons for regret that they were not more cautious in forming bad habits when young. They stick to them through life, and frequently are not only a source of annoyance, of positive discomfort, but sadly detrimental to their swiftness and usefulness.

This, in a measure, comes from want of proper attention on the part of those to whom their training is intrusted, and they should be ashamed of the neglect. Having passed beyond the ordinary probation of setting up " pi," then distributing it, the boy is given a case, and (after learning it) is left to his own sweet will as to the manner in which type should be distributed, picked up from the various boxes, placed in the stick, spaced, justified and emptied.

This is not only unfortunate, but wrong. It is much easier to make errors than to do anything correctly, as is proven every hour and in every business. The old adage that " figures do not lie," is a fallacy in printing. They do falsify, and that most egregiously, by getting into wrong positions, and letters have a most provoking antipathy to being in the right places. So with errors. They intrude themselves in the most preposterous manner, when and where they are not wanted, turn sense into nonsense, and upset the wisdom of the lawmakers and the devotion of the saints.

CARE is the first principle that should be instilled in the youthful mind ambitious for printers' honors. Early taught, it is easily acquired, and becomes a fixed habit. The importance of exactness and perfectness cannot be too strongly enforced ; the opposite is the bane of a printer's life. Our nature is imitative. We are but copies, and in a marked degree, of those older ; and the vast majority, looking upon labor as a curse and not a blessing, are disposed to slip along with just as little trouble as possible. Boys (you can't put old heads on young shoulders try you ever so hard) are full to the brim of animal life, bubbling over with fun, and confinement is irksome. Thus when taken from play, and forced to the stern duties of life, they seek for some way of avoiding its punctilious doing, and become careless as to the method and manner ; but trained into one groove, they will remain in it through life.

FALSE MOTIONS are not only unpleasant to the makers, but ridiculous to the looker-on. Many who have grown old in the service never manage to secure a type without making two or three abortive attempts. By some metallic hocus-pocus, the particular letter they are diving after with their fingers, always appears to manage to get out of the way, and is only secured after a desperate effort. This method of procedure retards progress, and wears out strength. The hand of the faithful compositor travels over an almost incredible amount of space during the hours of labor, and every false motion is unnecessarily tiresome, and should be avoided. There should be a single, certain attempt made in picking up type, and once established, is never departed from.

Another false, or more correctly speaking, tiresome and ungraceful movement, is bending the knees every time the hand is extended. This is particularly to be noticed in old-time printers, in those who learned the trade many years since. For it no good reason has or can be found, and a later generation, we are happy to see, have avoided falling into the error, and may be pardoned for laughing at it. How or why it was inaugurated is too hard a question to be solved upon any principle of physical philosophy, save it may be from some inherent sympathy between the nerves of different portions of the body, a sort of jumping-jack bending together of arms and limbs, when the brain pulls the string. But whatever the cause, it should be strictly avoided ; the old eliminate it if possible, and the young never be permitted to fall into it, for it will be a constant source of regret.

To stand straight, with head erect, firm on his limbs, breast thrown forward, should be among the first lessons taught the apprentice. We were created in His image. Man makes his stature, builds himself, and should look upward. Then all requisite movements can be gracefully and readily executed. Stooping over a case produces weakness of the muscles of the chest, hollows it, cramps the breathing organs, is provocative of coughs, and consumption is inaugurated, even if there is no hereditary predisposition. The habit at the case becomes the habit when away from it. The boy entails the curse upon the man, and printing is charged with being unhealthy when there is no just ground for the statement, and the many gray heads still at the case, and the rosy faces, robust forms, and muscular men seen at unions and typographical festivals, abundantly prove the contrary.

PUTTING TYPE IN THE MOUTH is a pernicious habit. We of the composing and pressrooms know enough of ink and washing forms to warn us against it for prudential reasons of cleanliness, if nothing else. We are not of the number who believe in "lead poisoning" in connection with printing, save in the abstract ; have never seen a well-defined case ; yet there may be organizations so excessively fine as to be injuriously affected by handling type, and certainly to put them into one's mouth is neither sensible nor pleasant.

PURE AIR is desirable in all places, and especially so in a printing office, but we are sorry to say is often and continuously excluded, as if to breathe were death. It is not very long since that an old printer told the writer, that " he could not work until his hands were sweating." How must it have been with the covered portions of his body ! Why compositors are inclined to live in an atmosphere so heated, and often foul with many breaths, with oxygen exhausted by gas lights, is a question very difficult of solution. They, if anyone, should know the rules of health, and to disregard them as many do, is little better than suicide. Stripping, and unreasonably so, necessitates artificial heat, and by the strangest infatuation men go out without even the putting on of a coat, inviting colds, soliciting pneumonia, and deliberately paving the way for rheumatism. Pure air, not drafts, never yet hurt a printer ; the lack of it has, and the wise man is he who will enjoy as much as possible one of the best gifts.

THREE-LINE NONPAREIL RONALDSON. (18 POINT.)   Price, $4.30

SPECIAL SALE
Genuine Raphael Masterpiece
Guaranteed
Discovered in Belgium
1234567890

TWO-LINE PICA RONALDSON. (24 POINT.)   Price, $4.70

SKETCHES
Artistic Mural Painting
Relics of Angelo
12345678

FIVE-LINE NONPAREIL RONALDSON. (30 POINT.)   Price, $5.85

ANCIENT TABLETS
Autobiography of Nabuchodonosor

THREE-LINE PICA RONALDSON. (36 POINT.)   Price, $7.00

EARLY RECORDS
Methods of Egyptian Architecture

FOUR-LINE PICA RONALDSON. (48 POINT.)   Price, $8.00

ENORMOUS
Monster Deinotherium

ALL COMPLETE WITH FIGURES.

HHHHHHHHHH

These fonts may be justified with one another by using leads and quads of our point system.

4A, 18a.
30 POINT HOYT SCRIPT.
$8.85
Card Fonts, 3A, 8a, 4.75

The following is what the Iowa Press Association made of Horace Greeley's note declining the invitation to meet with them the following June:

"I have wondered all along whether any squint had denied the scandal of the President meeting June in the woods on Saturday. I have hominy, carrots, and R. R. ties more than I can mow with right stem. If eels are blighted, dig them early. Any insemination that brick ooze are dangerous to harm give are the honors."

Yours Truly,

Horace Greeley.

Cleveland Type Foundry, Cleveland, Ohio,

8A, 16a. 18 POINT CIRROUS. 16a Lower Case, (extra) 2.00 $4.10

TYPE OF EVOLUTION

Ring-Tailed Roman, Designed to Hold Fast

1234567890

6A, 12a. 24 POINT CIRROUS. 12a Lower Case, (extra) 2.25 $4.95

ADMONITIONS

General Information for Learners

1234567890

4A, 8a. 36 POINT CIRROUS. 8a Lower Case, (extra) 2.65 $6.10

GROTESQUE

And Curiously Graceful

1234567

Cleveland Type Foundry,

147 St. Clair Street, - - Cleveland, Ohio.

Occasional Specimens

OF THE

Cleveland Type Foundry.

147 St. Clair St.,

Cleveland, - - Ohio.

CIRROUS IN COMBINATION.

MODOC.

PATENTED AUG. 12, 1884.

12A, 24a,   PICA. (12 Points Standard Measure. $2.50

EXTENSIVE COLLECTION OF WORKS OF ART FOR SALE

Comprising Many Choice Productions of both the Old Masters and Old Maids

Including the Famous "Horse Fair," by Joe Key

24 TO BE DISPOSED OF WITHOUT RESERVE 76

8A, 16a,   GREAT PRIMER. (18 Points Standard Measure.) $3.40

THE FINE ART STATIONERY Co

Engravers and Printers, Chromo-Lithographers, etc.

Unique Designs in Cards and Envelopes

6A, 12a,   DOUBLE PICA. (24 Points Standard Measure.) $4.60

YE PENSIVE MAIDEN

A Playntive Ballade of ye 16th Centurie

By Poet Softheart Weepington

4A, 8a,   DOUBLE GREAT PRIMER. (36 Points Standard Measure.) $6.30

DANGER AHEAD

Most Thrilling Narrative 8

FIGURES AND ORNAMENTS WITH ALL SIZES.   SPACES AND QUADS WITH ALL SIZES EXCEPT PICA.

WOMAN'S INDUSTRIAL FUTURE.

BY R. MEARS.

IT has become a favorite assertion with modern writers, especially in this country, that the height of the civilization of a nation or race may be gauged by its treatment of woman; that the lower we descend in the scale of cultivation, the more degraded and debased becomes the lot of the female, until she degenerates into the slave or plaything of her lord and master, man. On the other hand, among the most highly cultivated peoples, woman is said to drop her burden of labor to become the shrine of man's worship, the light of his home, and the friend, companion and counselor of her husband.

The position of woman in Europe has been repeatedly described by travelers as being much inferior to that of her sisters in this country, and the boast has been made that America was "woman's paradise." While in Europe the wife not uncommonly waited upon her husband, even to the extent of blacking his boots, and other menial services, doing all the domestic drudgery, building fires, cutting wood, tilling the soil and performing a host of other degrading and laborious duties, her American sister has been shown to be exempt from nearly all these cares, the husband being the one who had to haul fuel, make fires, and often to do the marketing for the family.

While this picture was, to some extent, true years ago, at the present time it is possible that the women of this country perform their full share of work, and are constantly pushing their way into the vocations formerly supposed to belong exclusively to the other sex.

It would be reasonable to suppose that the elevation and emancipation of woman so claimed for this country, partly owing to the greater respect in which she has been held by man, and partly to the introduction into every home of a host of labor-saving appliances, and which have afforded her ampler opportunities for the cultivation of mind and intellect, would have stimulated her efforts in the direction of invention and discovery; but scientists tell us this has not been the case. While man, during the last half century, has made rapid strides toward mastering the forces of nature, utilizing steam and electricity, devising new tools, machinery, and processes, and improving old ones, scarcely anything has been accomplished by woman toward benefiting or improving the race.

From this fact, these scientists argue that man is advancing intellectually more rapidly than woman, and at such a pace, too, as threatens ultimately to reënslave her.

Has not woman, herself, been helping onward her enslavement? Let us see. Some years ago it became the fashion among a few women to clamor loudly for the equality of the sexes—an equality of rights, politically, socially, and industrially. Their arguments would seem to imply that the boast of woman's superiority in this country had no actual foundation. Be that as it may, the clamor continued. Yielding to this demand, colleges, workshops, factories, etc., one by one, were thrown open to women, until now, not only do they entirely monopolize whole industries, but are to be found working side by side with men in almost every department of labor. In our cities they have largely supplanted men as clerks, bookkeepers, cashiers, telegraph and telephone operators, waiters, book peddlers, school teachers, etc., but in factories bid fair soon to completely exclude men, except as foremen or superintendents. They are numerically superior in bookbinderies, clothing, boot and shoe, and paper-box factories; they run most of the sewing machines and other light machinery; have invaded the counting-room and private office, by reason of the type-writer; are in our public buildings at Washington and elsewhere; are displacing a few men as typesetters,—in short, there are few places in which they cannot be found. So far, men seem to have retained a monopoly in the building trades, the army and the police force, but who shall say that, when a generation of labor has hardened the female muscle, women may not be seen laying brick or wielding club and hammer?

In the country, also, the instinct of labor has propelled woman toward the harder forms of toil. The Chicago *Tribune* recently stated that over a thousand farms in Iowa are run by women, a majority of whom are unmarried; while on the Pacific slope, fruit-farming is becoming a favorite occupation of the sex. In Michigan, and elsewhere, the peach, apple and berry crops are gathered by women and children; while in the market gardens, adjacent to large cities, most of the labor of cultivation is performed by female hands.

It is probable that this omnipresence of women in our industries may be accounted for more by reason of the avarice of our capitalists than from any desire to better the condition of the sex. In fact, the universal introduction of female labor has the opposite tendency. As soon as it had been discovered that woman's labor could be obtained cheaper than that of man, every position that could be filled by a woman was opened to her, and her advent in any industry was a signal for the lowering of wages. Bookkeeping. clerking, etc., have gradually fallen in value, until now the remuneration received for such service is of the most meager character. Women, too, who have started enterprises for the employment of their sex, have invariably paid little more than half the price of male service to their female helpers. And so, in every employment where woman's labor could be utilized, wages have steadily fallen, until, having almost excluded men, the capitalist has paid his female help as little as he possibly could, in many cases next to starvation prices.

Already we are being told, by press and social science statisticians, that marriages are decreasing in number; that too many of our young men are unable to support a wife, much less a family; that the women of this country are gravitating toward too widely distinct divisions, the one, comparatively few in number, belonging to the well-to-do class, who are too weak or too indolent to assume the cares and duties of maternity, and the other the army of industrial slaves who are competing with man and each other for a bare subsistence, and to whom maternity will mean financial shipwreck; hence, that the race must ultimately diminish or die out.

In view of the present tendency toward the employment of cheap female labor, the question of the future of "our boys" will soon take the place of our solicitude for "our girls." What is to be the condition and position of man among our industrial masses? All men cannot be bankers, lawyers, doctors, parsons, or saloon-keepers, neither can they all be merchants, office-holders, stock exchange or other gamblers, or capitalists. What are they to do to earn a livelihood? Shall we be compelled to maintain an army to provide bread for the ablebodied, while the others go to the poorhouse, or will they marry and be compelled to subsist upon the meager earnings of their wives?

Is there to come a time when woman will demand and receive a better remuneration for her labor, thus putting the sexes upon a financial equality, or will she go on lowering the wage standard until she becomes the only wage earner, and man be excluded from all our industries? Should the latter condition be only approximately reached, the young man of the future may be brought face to face with the degrading alternatives—starvation, emigration, or marriage under the condition above stated.

ELECTROTYPE MATRICES.

BY CARL SCHRAUBSTADTER, JR.

WHILE almost every treatise on the history of printing mentions or describes the copper matrices struck from a punch; the electrotype matrices—which in this country probably exceed the other kind in a proportion of seven or eight to one—are barely mentioned, and where a few words are spoken of them, it is only to condemn their use.

Though there are many imperfect matrices of this kind, and the comparative ease with which faces can be copied, has tempted a few to open foundries without proper tools or appliances, there is no doubt as to their producing, when well made, as good type as that cast from a copper strike. In the larger sizes, 36, 48 and 60 point, the tendency of the matrix struck from the punch, is toward hollowness of the face—a bad fault which the electrotype does not have. Besides its many other advantages, it has rendered possible the production of the handsome modern faces, with their delicate lines and shadings. Soon after the discovery of electrodeposition, type founders attempted to use it in producing matrices. The first results were crude, and were almost wholly confined to copying faces that had been cut on steel. A type was hung in the battery by a thin copper wire, and the face covered with a sheet of copper. When this was of sufficient thickness, the shank was cut away, and the head of the type, or "eyelet," placed in an oblong iron box, about the shape of the matrix, and held in position with a wire, as in Fig. 1. Melted lead was then poured in the box, and the wire withdrawn or

FIG. 1.

nipped off. The matrix was then taken from the box and a cast taken. The shank of the type thus cast soldered itself to the head of the original type, and drawing it out, left a perfect reverse copy of it. These matrices were then fitted up in line, set and height exactly like the copper strikes. Afterward quads were placed about the type to be copied, in order to give the copper deposition a wider face or bearing, and zinc was substituted for the lead.

Though much cheaper than the copper strikes, these matrices had fatal defects. The lead first used easily bent or wore. The zinc, though harder, was still too soft, and was brittle and porous; besides, the "eyelet" often

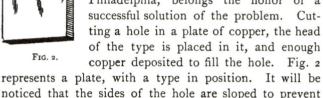

became loose. In such a case, nothing remained but to make a new one. To obviate these faults, a mold of type metal was cast around the type, and the whole matrix deposited therein by the battery. But this was slow and expensive, and it was difficult to obtain a thick, smooth deposit.

FIG. 2.

To an American, Edwin Starr, of Philadelphia, belongs the honor of a successful solution of the problem. Cutting a hole in a plate of copper, the head of the type is placed in it, and enough copper deposited to fill the hole. Fig. 2 represents a plate, with a type in position. It will be noticed that the sides of the hole are sloped to prevent the eyelet from slipping out. When the hole is filled, the type is withdrawn, the surplus copper removed, and this plate riveted to a heavier one. This not only makes the matrix stronger, but prevents the eyelet from becoming loose. Brass plates were afterward substituted for the copper, and this form is the one in use today.

Fig. 3 represents the plates riveted together, and Fig. 4, the matrix as it appears when fitted in line, set, position and height. The minutest perfection or blemish is copied by the deposition, and the type cast from such a matrix is a perfect counterpart of the original.

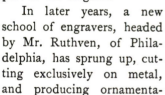

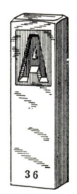

In later years, a new school of engravers, headed by Mr. Ruthven, of Philadelphia, has sprung up, cutting exclusively on metal, and producing ornamentation and finish the punch cutters never dared to attempt.

FIG. 3.   FIG. 4.

In perfection of finish, such faces as the Raphael, Ruskin, Steelplate Gothic, etc., silence all attempts to bring the process into disrepute, and lately Mr. Benton has cut Roman type on metal with his engraving machine, having such a high finish that it is safe to say that even in this field, until this time wholly given up to the punch cutter, the electrotype matrix will also drive out its copper rival.

TYPE-COMPOSING MACHINES.

A PAPER READ BEFORE THE POLYTECHNIC TYPOGRAPHICAL ASSOCIA-
TION BY MR. THOMAS FISHER, NOVEMBER, 1886.

A large number of attempts at supplanting human compositors, and substituting mechanical instead, have been made within recent years, in which inventors have endeavored to make capitalists less dependent on labor, to insure greater rapidity in the execution of work, and to lessen the cost of production. The craze for type-composing machinery followed very closely the introduction of steam printing. Now, the mechanical production of impressions has fairly ousted the original hand process out of the field. Not so with the automatic compositor; in spite of the advance in mechanical science, we are yet far from perfection. This is not due to the want of ingenuity, time or money, for more has been spent upon this than upon any similar industrial enterprise. It is the result of the difficult nature of the task, which requires a machine to be rapid and correct in composing, distributing and justifying, simple in working, perfectly noiseless, and to justify any sized type to various measures. It should not require specially made or specially nicked type; it should be capable of manipulating every sort from a cap A to a hair space; it should not break or unnecessarily wear the type, and it should also admit of being worked by power, foot or hand, with very little supervision.

It is all very well to say that the compositor's work is mechanical, but the inability to replace him by competent machinery gives the lie direct to the assertion. In all other machines the same operations are repeated from time to time, whereas an apparatus for composing may be at work for years, and not once perform exactly similar motions for five minutes together. In short, you want a piece of mechanism which can *think*, and the numerous efforts to secure this phenomenon show us on how sure a foundation the compositor's art is based. Over 400 years have elapsed since the immortal Caxton put together his ponderous, rough black letter, with thumb and finger, and nowadays we pick up the best cut Baskerville's and Elzevirs, the most delicate diamond, and the stoutest great primer in a similar manner, but it cannot be denied that the introduction of machinery for setting up type goes on apace. One or two extensive London book houses have on trial machines by different makers, and several news offices are testing them, one daily journal having as many as six composers and thirteen distributers at work, and each year more and more type is being put together by machinery, which is slowly but surely being improved.

It is curious to note how anxious master printers are for some piece of mechanism which will enable them to be independent of the compositor. It is beyond doubt desirable, that where existence depends upon rapidity of production, and where competition is very keen, that advantage should be taken of anything which promises only a portion of what composing machines claim to do. Accordingly we find large firms ready to encourage all such efforts at whatever expense, and it is stated that a London firm have stowed away in a lumber room on New-street square, a sufficient number of typesetting automata to form a small museum. Although these machines are competing, and sometimes successfully, with the deft fingers and intelligent brain of the compositor, we must not follow the example of the pressmen on the introduction of printing machinery, who held meetings and decided to "put it down," arguing "that it was impossible to produce good work, it was against the Scriptures, and it would increase pauperism and crime." The bitter feeling between master and man on this question seems hardly eradicated by the course of years, and there is not the least doubt that the introduction of machinery was accelerated by unreliable conduct of the men. Johnson even proposed that a tax be levied on all work produced with the aid of machinery. Even now, the same sentiment prevails in some composing rooms; for, a short time ago, in a London establishment, the compositors compelled the clicker to refuse to make up some matter lifted by one of these machines. I believe none of the members of the association would adopt such a short-sighted and bigoted policy, but would be prepared to discuss, and endeavor to understand the various principles involved in their construction, and to become proficient in their manipulation, and thus keep pace with the times. It is with this belief that I have ventured to place a few notes on the subject before you, as such discussion cannot fail to be of interest to all concerned.

The *first patent* for the setting up of type was granted to W. Church, in 1822, and since that time over 120 machines have been introduced. In many cases a large number of patents have been taken during a course of years by the same inventors, in their search after a perfect machine.

A typical machine is the "Hattersley," patented in England, in 1857, which consists of a horizontal top stage, on which is placed a partitioned tray, each partition containing a row of letters. Descending vertically along the front of this tray is a series of wires with pistons, and the pistons are depressed by the keys acting by bell cranks, which are brought back to their first position by india-rubber bands or springs. A propeller, kept in a state of tension by an india-rubber spring, is placed in the rear of each row, and draws them forward to the piston. If we press on a key, it depresses the piston, which pulls down with it a type, and drops it into a tube, which conveys it to the stick. The series of channels converge to a common mouth, through which every type in succession must pass.

In the "Fraser" machine, a later invention, by an Edinburgh printer, the same principle is adopted, and it is claimed for it that from 10,000 to 20,000 can be set in a continuous line per hour; in fact "the only limit to the speed of the machine is the skill of the operator." A distributer is added, and is almost a duplicate of the composer. It separates the different letters by switches, acted on by keys. On the depression of a key, the corresponding switch is opened, and the type guided to its proper compartment in the composing machine reservoir. In working this machine, I have noticed that it makes the hand ache, and the fingers are liable to slip; a wrong letter being very often the result. This may be due more to incompetence than to any defect in the mechanism.

Another machine of a similar class is the "Bracklesberg." In this there are as many grooves as there are characters in the font, and they are so placed by the distributer that they stand on their feet, with their sides toward the operator, and their nicks to the right hand. It is arranged for hand or treadle power.

A machine, which has been in use for some time, turning out a lot of work, is that invented by Dr. Mackie, of Warrington. It is worked like the previous ones, on the piano key principle, but there its similarity ends. The process is very elaborate, and the action purely automatic, being governed by strips of perforated paper. It consists of two parts, the perforator and composer. The perforator is a tiny instrument consisting of fourteen keys, by means of which narrow strips of paper are perforated. The composer consists of three horizontal rings about three feet in diameter, and two inches broad, the end one at the top being at rest. On the top of the ring twenty pockets are inserted, each of which contains compartments for seven different kinds of type, and sufficiently open at the bottom to allow the apparatus to extract the bottom type from any one of the divisions as wanted. The middle or carrying ring, has twenty pickpockets, each carrying seven of what are called the "legs-of-man," and seven fingers. At the place where the operations commence, there is a drum with fourteen perforations across its upper surface, and over this drum the previously perforated paper is made to travel about one-tenth of an inch each movement. Over the top of the drum of paper there are fourteen levers with pegs which are always seeking to enter the perforation in the drum, but are only able to enter those which have corresponding perforations in the paper. Two holes are made in the paper for the "legs-of-man," and from one to seven for the fingers. On the type being extracted, it lies upon the traveling ring till it reaches the delivery channel, when a pusher places it on the traveling belt, a few inches longer, from which it is pushed down a syphon spout, one letter upon another, on to the delivery slab, ready to be justified to lines of the required length. It has been worked at the rate of 12,000 per hour, costing 3½d. per 1,000. The motive power can be supplied by steam or hand.

Another invention, adopting quite a different method to secure the same object, is the "Matrix Compositor," of J. E. Sweet, which was introduced, but did not work very satisfactorily at the Paris Exhibition of 1867. It was designed to form a mold or matrix for stereotype plates, disposing of movable types, and the labor of setting and distributing them. By operating on the keys of the machine, impressions are made in thick, soft, or dry paper, of the letters required. From the mold thus formed, the plates are cast in the usual way.

A somewhat similar attempt but going still further—casting the type—is that of " E. Codignola," one of the last in the field, the patent having only been published last month. On the front of the machine is a key board of eighty-one keys, forty upper and forty-one lower case. To each key there is a separate lever, all being centered in the cross piece, and separately jointed, working in hollow nozzles leading out of the melting pot containing the alloy from which the type is to be cast. When these keys are depressed, the matrices are pushed down by spiral springs, and are inclosed between the two pieces forming the front and back of the mold, and the rods have their holes opposite those of the plates beneath, and at this moment each matrix forms a complete mold. Thus the matrices corresponding with the keys are filled by jets of the molten alloy. The matrices are raised, but the letters which have been cast adhere to the bars, and are supported by their heads on the upper face of such bars. The rods break off first the conical tails, and they next trim the lower ends of the type. During the operation of cleaning the rods by brushes, one of the extensions of the chain slips between the bars forming the front and back of the type mold, and pushes the type into the composing arrangement. The type is gathered up on a stick, which has two lateral files at its mouth, which remove the beard from the letters.

This class of machine may prove an ugly rival in plain reprint, but in defective manuscript it is another question, as the smallest " literal " will necessitate the recasting of the line, and if there should be an " out " or " double," half or even an entire column would have to be recast.

The " Alden " composing and distributing machine is interesting, showing how Herculean a task is the invention of a perfect machine, and for the affecting details of the life of the inventor, who worked twenty years trying to perfect the machine, and spent $40,000 upon it, and then died six months after taking out the patent. Some idea of the complicated nature of the mechanism may be derived from the fact that it contained 14,626 pieces, and weighed more than 1,420 lbs. It is estimated both to set and distribute 8,000 per hour, and on a brief trial it has composed 2,000 ems in ten minutes. The principle is novel. A half-round table incloses a horizontal revolving wheel, about two feet in diameter. Between the outer table and the inner revolving wheel is a vacant space about one-eighth of an inch broad. Between this and the outside of the table are arranged the type cases. In front, where the operator stands, is the matter for distribution. There are 180 alleys radiating from the central carrying wheel holding the 154 different characters (for unlike most machines all sorts are set up). On the revolving wheel are thirty-six hands, made as near as possible like human hands. These are placed alternately, one-half distributing and the other composing. The types are arranged round the wheel, and the fingers of the hand are pushed out by the pressing of the keys, when opposite the required type. Although its distributing arrangements are said to be perfect, each letter or space requires a distinguishing nick, so that ordinary type would be of no use. Since the death of the inventor it has been much improved, the working parts largely diminished, and the composer and distributer altered into two separate machines.

An apparatus best known on the other side of the Atlantic is the " Brown " composing, justifying and distributing machine. The case consists of a series of grooves or channels ranged side by side. In these channels the types stand on their feet, the case being put at such an angle that they slide downward by their own gravity, and rest upon the bar which closes the lower end of the groove. Across the foot a shield is placed provided with openings for the types to pass through, and an index showing the letters which the case contains. Below, and in front of the case, sliding backward and forward, at the will of the operator, is a " stick " (or mechanical hand) which takes the letters from the case. The uppermost end of the " stick " forms an indicator corresponding to the index upon the shield. The key is provided at one end with a tongue or plunger for lifting the type, and the other forms a handle for working it, which does not weigh more than a few ounces, and can be moved with ease and rapidity. The operator holds the handle with finger and thumb, and runs it opposite the letter to be taken. This is so

arranged with a distinguishing gauge that no greater accuracy is required than in playing a piano. As the handle is raised again, the follower pushes the stamp just lifted sufficiently down the channel for the next one to be taken. This operation is repeated till the stick is full, when it is run to one end and the line is slipped into the justifier. The distributer consists of a rotating ring about ten inches in diameter. At regular intervals on the edge of the ring are recesses for holding the type while being carried to their places. Radiating from this ring are the channels into which the types are distributed, and which when full are transferred to the composer, and constitute a part of the case. It takes one line at a time, and lifts it into a channel in which it is fed towards the distributing ring a little below. This ring has an intermittent motion, and each motion brings one of the recesses directly over the line. One after another the types are forced up into this recess. The recess is large enough to receive any sized type, and is formed by cutting a slit in the ring and inserting a set of levers. The ejector, which forces out the letter, when it arrives at its proper place, forms the back of the recess, and the nicks are opposite one of the levers. As the short arms shut against the edge of the type some of them enter the nicks, the long arm taking a corresponding position. This position acting in connection with the keys determines where the type shall be ejected. The keys slide in and out, and the motion of the ring brings each set of levers successively in front of each key. The keys advance a short distance by the ends of the levers, and when the shape of the keys correspond to the position of the levers, the keys advance further, and acting upon the ejector, forces out the letter.

The Americans are noted for their prolific inventions in most industries, and judging from the number of patents granted, they are endeavoring to solve the problem of the automatic compositor; but we have only time for the briefest notice of a few: The " W. H. Mitchell " machine consists of an apparatus for distributing types from the form, and setting them up in rows within grooves, with the face of the type upward. From these grooves the types are removed, each row of a given letter at a time, and placed within conductors which supply them to the apparatus connected with the finger keys. The stroke of any finger key drops one of the types upon a series of belts which are removed by pulleys. The belts conduct the type to a composing wheel in the order in which the keys drop them.

The " F. W. Gilmer." This machine consists of three parts—the case holding the types, the composing stick for withdrawing type from the case, and setting it in line, and the distributing stick for transferring the type from the line to the case.

The schemes of Major Benowiski (1856) deserve notice, as curiosities, not for their practical value. This gentleman proposed to have type marked with the character it represented, on all sides and at the bottom, so that authors could compose the type for their own manuscript " like a child at school with its toy alphabet," and after it was composed it was to be turned face upward to be printed. He also introduced air rollers. His " Authoriton " consisted of a case with type boxes in the shape of long quadrangular prisms, placed in an inclined position in a circular-shaped frame, similar to a chest of drawers. Each drawer is a grooved board, and its front portion protrudes from that immediately above it by one inch or more, according to the size of the fingers of the operator. The inventor suggested the use of tweezers for picking up the type to lessen this space. The remaining space in the size of an ordinary case was used for logotypes, the inventor arguing that the reason other attempts at the use of wood letter had failed was because what was gained in the number of lifts was lost in the distance traversed. In the " Authoriton," 1,600 compartments are included in the space of a pair of ordinary cases. Imagine (if you can) a compositor setting 10,000 per hour from such a maze of divisions.

Another attempt at the acceleration of composition was introduced in 1882, under the title of " Porter's " type-composing machine. The apparatus is simple, and consists of a collection of troughs in which the types to be composed stand upright with the nicks all one way. The composing is done in the ordinary manner. The invention consists of the ready way in which the compositor can get his types into the " stick." When the operator requires a letter, he places his foot on a small lever near the ground, and this action causes the letter required to move slightly forward, ready for the compositor's hand; this letter is taken by him with the finger and thumb as in ordinary composition, with the difference of taking a single letter to his "stick," he can gather up several to make a complete word or words. Another method is that of justifying the matter in a double-sided galley with setting-rule and guide, without taking it to the stick. The distribution is slow, and consists in filling up the troughs with a supply of type. In estimating the cost of production with the aid of this apparatus, ¾d. per thousand is calculated for distribution, but I think there are very few children even, who would place each letter in the respective troughs with their faces upward and the nick one way for such a sum. They have been tried in various provincial news offices.

Dr. Alexander Mackie has introduced an apparatus in order to supply duplicate columns for newspapers, and for the headings of books. It is called "The Manifold Typesetting Machine," and although it only sets at half the speed of ordinary composition, it actually performs about twenty times the work. Upon thin brass rules are placed twenty letters, all alike on the flat. When ready for setting, one brass after another is emptied into a common setting stick, with the following result: Suppose you want to set the words "Polytechnic Typographical Association," you empty one brass of cap P's into the "stick," the narrow way, then one of O's, one of L's, and so on. When the stick is full you will have twenty lines of thirty-five letters each, set by thirty-seven movements of the hand, emptying the same number of brasses. The distributing is done by reversing the operation, and a slicing machine puts each row upon its own brasses.

The "Kastenbein" machine has been made famous by the assistance it rendered in the unique system of late news supply adopted by the *Times*. The compositor is in direct telephonic communication with the reporter at the houses of parliament, who speaks to the compositor, who puts the words into type with the machine, ringing a bell to indicate that he is ready for the next instalment. The machine has been much modified and improved since its introduction soon after the termination of the Franco-German war, until it has now reached a state of great efficiency.

The "Colts" machine has a very novel arrangement, enabling it to distribute while it sets; the work of distribution being more rapid than the composition, the cases are always full. The distributer is regulated in such a way that the instant the lower case "e" box is full the work of distribution stops. Each letter goes to its appropriate case as regularly as a key fits its own lock.

Those who visited the exhibition of 1880 will doubtless remember the stir caused by the working of the "Hooker" machine. This machine has neither keys nor buttons, and a speed of 22,000 per hour is claimed for it. It contains forty-eight letters, points and spaces, the remainder being conveniently placed in a case at the operator's left hand. As in most other machines, the types are contained in a series of troughs, and are abstracted from these receptacles in the order desired, by the opening of a small trap, which allows the stamps to fall upon endless moving tapes, carrying them forward to a collector which builds them into a continuous line to be justified by hand. The discharge of the letters from the troughs is effected by means of an electric current passing through a series of electro-magnets corresponding to the troughs. A wire from the battery brings the electric current to the metal stylus in the hand of the compositor, who touches the contact plates (arranged like an ordinary lower-case) with this stylus and completes the circuit, which sends a current through the electro-magnet corresponding to the letter required. Despite the simplicity of this machine, in one establishment of which I am cognizant it was discarded, as it could not be made to pay, as the types twisted on the tapes, and when the proof came from the reader the compositor had very often to perform that disagreeable and unprofitable operation sometimes known as "making ready for Spike Island." Its

ease in manipulation is one of its especial features and chief recommendations.

A machine introduced very recently to compose, justify and distribute is the "Tagerman." The types are placed in a series of upright tubes. Attached to the composing apparatus is a gripper, by which the types required are taken from these tubes and placed in the composing stick letter by letter. Two thick spaces are inserted between each word as the line is composed, and by a very ingenious contrivance the spacing out of the line is altered as required, and the line is then placed on a galley, and so on; each line is deposited till the column is composed. The compositor, by keeping his first three right-hand fingers in the hollow thimbles attached to the composing apparatus touches a string as it passes under the tube containing the type required, and the gripper then catches the letter from the bottom of the tube and deposits it in the composing stick. The alleged rate of composition is about 5,000 per hour, and the machine can be worked by treadle or power.

In the "Winder" machine the composing and distributing machines are separate and it does not justify, but it works with precision and takes up very little room. In the distributer the types are driven along singly until they reach their own siding, when they are shunted into it out of the way. These, when full, are cleared into other slips and hung on nails or hooks waiting till the composing machine wants them, when they are emptied into the case, and wait there until the operator touches the key that shoots them out to a leather band. The action of this band is not continuous, for it stops when the letters are falling on it, and then carries them to a metal landing place, where they are collected by means of an iron finger and launched on to another band on which they ride safely for a few inches, lying on their flat side. Another contrivance takes every stamp as tenderly as though it loved it, and puts it on its back, nick uppermost. Presently the line reaches a stick which is part of a galley, and the matter is justified as if set by hand.

From these brief and incomplete notes it will be seen that great progress is being made toward a perfect machine, more so, perhaps, for composition than for distribution. We cannot take up a technical magazine without seeing recorded some advance in mechanical ingenuity. In one only issued last Saturday, a machine is announced which not only sets type by electricity, but also (paradoxical as it may seem) corrects all the errors before the type is composed. A tape is prepared which is run through the machine and passed over a steel roller and under a row of ten steel fingers, and by the rows of holes prepared in the tape electro-magnetic communication is set up. The corrections can be made in the tapes. It is remarked that it only needs the appearance of some genius to endow a machine of this kind with brains, and the jobbing compositor and the table hand will have to take a back seat.

Even when the purely automatic compositor is produced shall we have anything to fear? I think not, for as in the case of steam printing, there will always be certain work upon which it cannot be profitably employed, and cheap production will cause more work to be required—*cacoethes scribendi* will increase to an enormous extent; the only difference will be that a greater degree of efficiency will be required of the artisans employed, the "botches" will be deleted, with a consequent raising of the status of the art. When our solid matter is composed like lightning, and our jobbing compositor takes a walk round the office with an automaton for company, the artisans then occupying the positions at present filled by compositors will be required to possess a more perfect, general, technical and artistic education, and great as is the necessity at the present time for such a society as this, greater still will be the scope and usefulness of the then existing descendants of the Polytechnic Typographical Association.

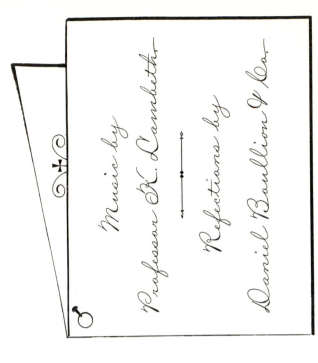

Music by
Professor K. Lambeth

Refections by
Daniel Baullion & Co.

⊷—24 POINT CLEVELAND SCRIPT.—⊶

Miss Anna Canda.

Mr. & Mrs. Ladaund.

30 Point Carpenter Script, $12.50
  Lower Case, (extra) 8.50
21 Point Carpenter Script $8.50
  Lower Case, (extra) 5.40
24 Point Cleveland Script, $8.50
  Lower Case, (extra) 5.50

Mr. & Mrs. N. O. Gripper

Request your presence at the
marriage of their daughter

Irenes

to

Will. S. Shaker,

Monday Eve., June 5th 1896.

Ceremony at 8 o'clock

At Home February 1st 1985.

CARPENTER AND CLEVELAND SCRIPTS IN COMBINATION.

Cleveland Type Foundry, 147 St. Clair St., Cleveland, Ohio.

PATENTED JAN. 29, 1884.

TWO-LINE PICA ARBORET.   Price, $5.00.

TRAILING VINE

TROPICAL SHRUB

TWO SIZES IN COMBINATION

LAZY HABIT

EMANCIPATORS

PLOD & THRIFT

Characters Furnished with the Two-Line Pica Fonts.

Characters Furnished with the Three-Line Pica Fonts.

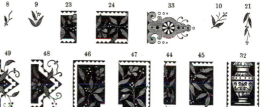

FURNITURE

PRICE LISTS

THREE-LINE PICA ARBORET.   Price, $5.75.

ASSEMBLY

SCHEDULE

ALL COMPLETE WITH FIGURES.

THE MACKELLAR, SMITHS & JORDAN CO., PHILADELPHIA, PA.

NORTHWESTERN BRANCH:
MINNEAPOLIS, MINN.

MARDER, LUSE & CO.

AMERICAN SYSTEM
—OF—
INTERCHANGEABLE
TYPE BODIES.
THE ONLY TRUE STANDARD

* TYPE FOUNDERS *

MONROE·STREET,
CHICAGO.

CRITERION.

COVERED BY PATENT OF   AUGUST 12, 1884.

12A, 24a,	Pica (12 Points Standard Measure).	$2.85

LADIES' SEWING CIRCLE
Meets Tuesdays and Fridays for
Business and Pleasure
24 Scandalous Gossip 58

8A, 16a,	Great Primer (18 Points Standard Measure).	$3.75

MUSICAL VOICES
Those Strains Melodious
3 Night Owls 6

>>> SHARP AND FINDEM, <<<
Fire, Life, and Marine
Insurance Agents
25 High Premium St. 25
ooo
All Claims for Losses Vigorously Contested.

6A, 12a,	Double Pica (24 Points Standard Measure).	$4.50

>>> HOWLING TAX-EATERS <<<
42 Schemes for Depleting Treasuries 38

4A, 8a,	Double Great Primer (36 Points Standard Measure).	$6.50

LAND AND WATER
The Art of making Mud Pies

ORNAMENTS AND FIGURES WITH ALL SIZES.   SPACES AND QUADS WITH ALL SIZES EXCEPT PICA.

STENCIL.

PATENTED DEC. 12, 1882.

12 POINT. PICA STENCIL. Price, $3.30.

JANUARY EVENING EXCURSION
Competitive Bicycle Riding   Juvenile Coasting Exploits
Snow-shoe Contest Between Octogenarians
1234567890

24 POINT. TWO-LINE PICA STENCIL. Price, $5.20.

JUDICIAL DECISION
Legal Process   Musty Ruling
Documentary Evidence

18 POINT. THREE-LINE NONPAREIL STENCIL. Price, $4.20.

NATIONAL CENTENNIAL
Industrial Exhibit   Military Evolution
Congratulatory Oration
1234567890

36 POINT. THREE-LINE PICA STENCIL. Price, $7.90.

FRANKNESS
Earnings   Relieved

ALL COMPLETE WITH FIGURES.

THE MacKELLAR, SMITHS & JORDAN CO., PHILADELPHIA.   SHNIEDEWEND & LEE CO., AGENTS, CHICAGO, ILL.

April 1887

Price List of Monastic Series.

8 Point Monastic, No. 4.	14A, 16A, 16A, 22a.	$3.80
10 Point Monastic, No. 4.	12A, 14A, 14A, 20a.	$3.40
12 Point Monastic, No. 4.	10A, 12A, 12A, 16a.	$4.30
18 Point Monastic, No. 4.	8A, 10A, 10A, 14a.	$4.75
24 Point Monastic, No. 4.	6A, 8A, 8A, 12a.	$6.40
36 Point Monastic, No. 4.	4A, 6A, 6A, 10a.	$9.20
8 Point Monastic, No. 5.	16A, 16A.	$1.80
10 Point Monastic, No. 5.	14A, 14A.	$1.65
12 Point Monastic, No. 5.	12A, 12A.	$2.30
18 Point Monastic, No. 5.	10A, 10A.	$2.45
24 Point Monastic, No. 5.	8A, 8A.	$3.35
36 Point Monastic, No. 5.	8A, 8A.	$5.85
8 Point Monastic, No. 6.	16A.	$1.10
10 Point Monastic, No. 6.	14A.	$1.00
12 Point Monastic, No. 6.	12A.	$1.50
18 Point Monastic, No. 6.	10A.	$1.55
24 Point Monastic, No. 6.	8A.	$2.10
36 Point Monastic, No. 6.	8A,	$3.75

Cleveland Type Foundry,

Cleveland, Ohio.

GREATE CONCERTE.

Ye Good People of Ye Towne of Saffville are Respectfully Invited
to attend a

CONCERTE

— of —

Olde Tyme Songes,

To be given at ye

First Cross Avenue M. E. Meetynge House,

(on ye corner of Longwood Avenue.)

Wednesday Ye 19 Day of Ye Mo. of September,

MDCCCLXXXIV.

By Neighbour Powerfull Thompson, hys Choir.

Admission: One Englifh Shyllinge.

Ye doors shall be open'd at 7 of ye clocke,
Ye syngynge will begin at 7:45 of ye clock.

8A, 16a.
21 Point Chameleon.
$5.80
16a Lower Case (extra), 3.25

Our Likeness, Such as Here You View

The Glass itself were not More True. Chameleon

234 Along the Slippery walk he went 567

6A, 12a.
30 Point Chameleon.
$6.75
12a Lower Case (extra), 3.75

If you can but Remember Dear

My Feelings Have Undergone a Change

35 Girl by Your Heart be Led 89

4A, 8a.
42 Point Chameleon.
$8.50
8a Lower Case (extra), 4.00

The Weekly Advertiser

Expressing the Public Opinion

123 Fancy Dry Goods 579

Cleveland Type Foundry, - - - Cleveland, Ohio.

April 1887 175

MARDER, LUSE & CO., TYPE FOUNDERS.

✦ CONCAVE EXTENDED. ✦
ORIGINAL.

12A, 24a,   BOURGEOIS. (9 Points Standard Measure.) $3.20

✦ NAUTICAL ✦ WONDER ✦

Briny Ocean's Curiosity Shop

3 Coral Factory 5

12A, 24a,   PICA. (12 Points Standard Measure.) $3.90

✦ CATTLE ✦ RANCH ✦

Lively Texan Bronchos

2 Meditation 8

8A, 16a,   GREAT PRIMER. (18 Points Standard Measure.) $5.75

✦ FLOATING ✦ ISLANDERS ✦
Pensive Goat and Sportive Cow!
36 Home Dreams 58

6A, 12a,   DOUBLE PICA. (24 Points Standard Measure.) $7.50

ELEVATED PATH
3 The Rocky Mountain 4

4A, 8a,   DOUBLE GREAT PRIMER. (36 Points Standard Measure.) $10.10

✦ NIMROD ✦
7 Home Rulers 5

3A, 6a,   FOUR-LINE PICA. (48 Points Standard Measure.) $13.50

NICE ✦ Hands

FIGURES AND ORNAMENTS PUT UP WITH ALL SIZES.   NONPAREIL IN PREPARATION.   SPACES AND QUADS WITH ALL SIZES EXCEPT PICA.

THE TWO SMALLER SIZES LINE EXACTLY WITH EACH OTHER AT THE BOTTOM, AND THE FOUR LARGER SIZES LINE EXACTLY WITH EACH OTHER AT THE BOTTOM.   BY PLACING A 6-TO-PICA LEAD
AT THE BOTTOM OF THE TWO SMALLER SIZES THEY WILL LINE EXACTLY WITH THE LARGER.

AMERICAN INTERCHANGEABLE TYPE BODIES.

To the Editor :   CHICAGO, March 29, 1887.

A good deal of your valuable space has, of late, been diverted to *interchangeable type bodies*, and their relative bearing on the present and future aspects of the printing business. I would not, therefore, at this time, have traversed upon your patience, but for the widespread interest this subject has created in the minds of the printing fraternity, and others equally interested on the onward tendencies and progressive paths of the art preservative. The art of printing is probably one of the grandest achievements pertaining to the genius of man, and all improvements tending to facilitate the news, and strengthen, perfect, and perpetuate the glory of the art is watched with that abiding interest which is characteristic of the higher sentiments, and nobler instincts of the American people.

All changes, however, although they denote elements of progress, cannot be taken as proof, on their introduction, that any material benefit has been reached; indeed, they are often subversive of good results, and, in many cases, it would have been decidedly better to have let well enough alone, and that they had never been made. However, the hollowness of this theory, on general principles, will be readily apparent, for if the channels of invention had been stifled in this fashion, the great time and money savers of the present day, and now in prevalent use in every branch of art and mechanical and manufacturing industry, would have been lost to the world. The mere introduction of a new method is but a business link in the inventive chain, and it cannot be until the chain, as a whole, and in its every link, has sustained the crucial test of opposition, in all its practical bearings, and proved beyond the shadow of a doubt its adaptability for the work, in perfect accordance with the demands of the inventor, that it can be justly named an improvement. Has the interchangeable system of type bodies borne this test? The invention has been assailed by able pens, and, indeed, by men of " all sorts," and even members of the craft themselves have joined in the grand crusade against the inventors. Let us see.

Marder, Luse & Co., of Chicago, were the first to promulgate the new departure in letter founding, by announcing their twelve-point system, and that, with its multiples, divides exactly and proportionately into every requisite size of type; its repleteness has often been commented upon, for, " cast it up " as you may, its conclusions are always correct and to the point; and not to this day, although other systems have been forced upon the market, has it been intelligently met. Of course, we do not propose here to advocate the productions and claims of one foundry over those of another, but we intend to speak of the merits and saving capacity of interchangeable type, and to render honor to whom honor is due in connection therewith.

Every printer knows what troublous times were had in matter of justification. Types bore no relative proportion toward each other, but they had to be squeezed in somehow to get off the job, and meet the emergency. Resort to cutting up good stock, and often with blunt scissors, was the only remedy; nor was this sufficient: Leads were often not thin enough to give perfect lining, and cardboard and paper had to be resorted to to give anything like presentable work. The delay entailed in consequence was perplexing, vexatious and annoying, and in the matter of the morning dailies, where speed and time to get in the latest news were imperative in the public interest, it could not con-

tinue. Job offices and book houses, although so seldom rushed, were placed in the same predicament. Time in getting out all kinds of work, in these days of excessive competition, is an important factor in annual balance sheets, and it has to be saved, in order to enhance the value of the profit and loss account, and increase the business assets. And will any one deny that to have type so cast as to forever do away with these perpetual annoyances and detriments to business, that a great advance in typography has not been made? Interchangeable type has, indeed, sapped the foundations of the printing business as it was formerly conducted, and placed it on a basis which will be as permanent and enduring as the calling itself is lofty, ennobling and exalted.

The beauty of the system has always been apparent to all practical men, and as such it has ever been welcomed. Its gain, however, had, of necessity, to be gradual, and indeed could not be otherwise, for printers could not afford to throw out their type until it had served its purpose, and done its work. But after years of patient labor the reward has been fully reached, and we are told there is now none but interchangeable type cast in the Chicago Type Foundry; indeed we believe there is little else cast by any western type foundry.

But now, what are the special advantages of this new system over old methods? Two pearls were always a long primer, as were two nonpareils a pica, but beyond that no types had any relative bearing toward each other. Now, all the characters commencing at twelve-to-pica, and gradually ascending upward, have their significance and place, and the complexities of all kinds of composition are mastered quickly, and with ease, comfort and perfect accuracy.

Each size is a factor. Three nonpareils (6) are a great primer (18); three breviers (8) are a double pica (24); a nonpareil and a brevier (8) are an english (14); a pica (12) and an excelsior (4)—two six-to-pica leads—are columbian (16); a double english (28) and a brevier (8) are a double great primer (36); a long primer (10) and a brevier (8) are a great primer (18); and a long primer (10) and a nonpareil (6) are a columbian (16); so with all the other sizes, making the combination of two or more sizes of type in a word, or line, the simplest thing imaginable in composition. Bourgeois (9) is now a respectable size, being a nonpareil (6) and one-half exactly.

The above includes all that is necessary, and it must be gratifying to the foundry of Marder, Luse & Co. to know that their system of bodies is so highly appreciated, and that the opposition which at one time threatened their carrying them into use, has not only dwindled to a cipher, but actually become an ally with them in carrying out the work. Out of twenty-three of the best type foundries in the country, seven have adopted the interchangeable system entirely; fourteen partially, while only two hold on to old methods. The signs of the times are ominous for the old methods, and everything indicates that at no distant day, interchangeable type only will be cast in the United States.

The pica of Marder, Luse & Co. is the same as that now recognized by the Type Founders' Association, as its regular standard, and it is the same on which all interchangeable type is built. It would have thus been easy to have had the same bodies all through; but whether from business jealousy or from fear of suit from copying Marder, Luse & Co's system, we do not know; but at any rate we are free to say that the bodies substituted are poor compensation for those they have taken away.   A TRUTH SEEKER.

LEAKAGES AND THEIR CAUSES.

BY H. G. BISHOP.

MANY a printer has been puzzled to account for the small amount of net profit shown at the end of a month's or quarter's trading. When he has figured on or charged up a job, he has allowed what he thought a fair margin for profit, and has perhaps been congratulating himself, as the month rolled along, that he would have a good showing in his favor. But, alas, when the balancing up time came he found but little cause for rejoicing.

Now, why was this? Maybe he did not allow enough for profit, over and above the cost of production and general expenses. And yet it is quite possible that he did do so, and that there was every reason to expect good results, and therefore his disappointment must be accounted for in some other way. In a great many cases the reason for this disappointment is that there are too many leakages, through which the profits drop like money through a hole in the pocket, and which are too often forgotten and not allowed for.

Let us try and find out what these leakages are :

1. Picking for sorts may be mentioned as one leakage, through which much precious time slips.

2. Sending out proofs of jobs takes time and causes much unnecessary loss.

3. Sending forms to press, before the matter has been properly corrected or the form properly locked up, causing delay of press and loss of pressman's time.

4. Waiting for stock, either after form is on press or ready to be put on, is another very common leakage, for which the employer or foreman is generally responsible.

5. Work spoiled on press and quietly thrown away, fresh stock being obtained when nobody is looking, may often be the cause of loss which puzzles anyone to account for.

6. Asking questions about quantity, style, type, stock, color of ink, etc., swallows up more time than most people think.

There are perhaps many other such things which deserve the name of leakages, and which are too often lost sight of until attention is called to them.

But now let us see how some of these leakages may be prevented :

First, with regard to picking. This is caused largely through neglecting to distribute regularly in proportion to the amount of composition done. There are two ways of meeting this difficulty. Either let one or more persons be engaged constantly on distribution, or let all turn to at certain periods and distribute all the dead jobs. Any man who works ten hours a day on jobwork can do more work by devoting two hours to distribution and eight hours to composition than he can by working on composition for ten hours, with empty cases, and having to pick for half the type he needs.

Second, with regard to sending out proofs. There are certain classes of work for which it is necessary to send out proofs, and in doing such work the proofs are generally allowed for in figuring. But on small jobs it is better to shut down upon the practice. Some customers get into the bad habit of asking for proofs, as a matter of course,

but if the matter were explained to them or a charge were made, they would soon learn better.

Third, with regard to sending forms to press in an unfinished state. This is a matter that should be dealt with firmly. Let a fine be imposed on the compositor who commits such an offense, or let him be charged with the pressman's lost time, and such carelessness would soon disappear. The loss occasioned may be much greater than the pressman's time. It may delay some other job and upset the most perfectly formed plans for the day's work.

Fourth, with regard to waiting for stock. It may be difficult to prevent this occurring at times, but it ought not to occur often in a well-managed office. Very often, jobs are sent into the composing room without any thought as to the stock, and when the job is ready for press, there is a great hustling to try and find some stock that will do, and perhaps this results in being compelled to use a more expensive kind than was intended, and away goes the profit. It is better to have the stock looked out before the job is sent forward at all, the slight delay caused being more than made up by having it ready when wanted. It sometimes happens that a job gets on the press and is all made ready except setting the guides, before it is discovered that the stock is not in the house. An employer or foreman who is responsible for such delay, ought to feel like kicking himself.

Fifth, with regard to work spoiled on press. Everyone is liable to mistakes and mishaps, and if a pressman or feeder should spoil some paper, and then own up like a man, it would be best to let him off with a caution, at any rate, for the first offense. But, if he should add to this offense that of sneaking round after more paper, and running it off without mentioning the fact, let him be dealt with severely. But as these things do occur, some responsible person should be on the lookout to prevent them. The stock account will run off on one side, and that the losing side, if this state of things is allowed to exist.

Sixth, with regard to asking questions. There is one very simple way of preventing the leakage in this direction, and I am glad to find so many printers adopting it. I refer to the work ticket which should accompany every job, and on the face of which full instructions should be given as to all the various details connected with it from start to finish. This ticket should be carefully filled up by the person who puts the job in hand, nothing being left for questioning. Verbal instructions are often misunderstood, and lead to serious mistakes. By all means, let everything be put in writing that can be, and it is then more easy to fix responsibility if anything goes wrong.

In conclusion, let me say, that where the size of the business will admit of it, well paid, competent men should be placed in charge of the various departments. Such men will often effect more saving of lost time and materials than their salaries amount to. To place a man in a responsible position without giving him fair remuneration, is the poorest kind of economy. Better pay him well, so that he can afford to forget his own concerns and devote himself to yours.

REGISTERED No. 71,445.

18 Point.   Three-Line Nonpareil Pynson.   Price, $4.50

Attention to Business Association
Inordinate Curiosity a Sufficient Cause for Expulsion
Talebearing Positively Prohibited
1234567890

12 Point.   Pica Pynson.   Price, $3.75

Wanted for Positions of Responsibility
Individuals of Integrity
Industrious Habits Indispensable   Perseverance Absolutely Necessary
Permanent Employment and Liberal Compensation

24 Point.   Two-Line Pica Pynson.   Price, $5.65

Mantelpiece Banking Company
Receives Deposits Morning, Noon or Evening
Payments Always on Demand

ALL COMPLETE WITH FIGURES.

Oldest American Type Foundry.

MacKellar, Smiths & Jordan Co.,

Sansom Street, Philadelphia.

The MacKellar, Smiths & Jordan Co., Philadelphia.   Shniedewend & Lee Co., Agents, Chicago, Ill.

June 1887   179

SPECIMENS FROM FARMER, LITTLE & CO., TYPE FOUNDERS.

NEW YORK—63 & 65 Beekman St.
And 62 & 64 Gold Street.

CHICAGO—154 Monroe Street.
Chas. B. Ross, Manager,

PATENT PENDING.
10 a 6 A

THREE LINE NONPAREIL FLIRT.

$2 75

ATTRACTIVE FLIRTS

Doctors Prescribe Exercise and Recreation 26

8 a 5 A

TWO LINE PICA FLIRT.

$3 00

RIVERSIDE TOILERS

Pleasing and Distinct Character 1887

9 a 4 A

THREE LINE PICA FLIRT.

$5 00

FRESH ROSE

Eventful Histories 1887

60 a 36 A

NONPAREIL HALF TITLE No. 2.

$3 40

NOTE—TO PRINTERS.—Our Type is cast from Tin (largely), Antimony, Copper and Lead,
Producing a Hard, Tough, and a Tenacious Metal.
OUR NEWS AND BOOK FONTS are cast from Matrices driven from Steel Punches, not Electrotype Matrices,
or Matrices made from Type, which are apt to swell and
Become rough, and produce a type "out of line" and with imperfect "face."

Also Brevier Half Title, No. 2, with New Lower Case, now ready.

PATENT PENDING.
8 a 5 A

TWO LINE PICA PALM.

$3 00

PALM LEAF FANS

Refresh the Weary in Summer Time 187

16 a 10 A   PICA PALM. $1 90

CALMS THE STORM

Palm Oil Acts like a Charm 1887

12 a 8 A   THREE LINE NONPAREIL PALM. $2 80

DESERT PALMS

Rest Under the Shade 18

6 a 4 A

THREE LINE PICA PALM.

$4 50

PALMISTRY

Welcome Fortune 1887

AMERICAN SYSTEM OF INTERCHANGEABLE TYPE BODIES.   *AMERICAN SYSTEM OF INTERCHANGEABLE TYPE BODIES.*

ROYAL GOTHIC.

18A, 36a,   LONG PRIMER. (10 Points Standard Measure.) $3.55   16A, 32a,   PICA. (12 Points Standard Measure.) $3.65

BURNING THE MIDNIGHT OIL   **CIRCUMLOCUTION OFFICE**

Climbing High on the Ladder of Fame   **Instruction Given in the Art of**

23 Herculean Labor 56   **8 How Not to Do it 9**

10A, 20a,   COLUMBIAN. (16 Points Standard Measure.) $4.20   10A, 20a,   PARAGON. (20 Points Standard Measure.) $6.05

HOMEWARD BOUND   **BORDER LIFE**

From the North Pole 2   **4 Cowboys at Home**

8A, 16a   DOUBLE PICA. (24 Points Standard Measure.) $6.80

BRING UP THE GUNS

3 Open Fire on the Enemy 5

6A, 12a,   DOUBLE ENGLISH. (28 Points Standard Measure). $6.70

Clothed in GOLDEN Raiment 2

5A, 10a,   DOUBLE GREAT PRIMER. (36 Points Standard Measure.) $8.20

Drink WATER Bright

4A, 8a,   FOUR-LINE PICA. (48 Points Standard Measure.) $10.80

Berlin OPERA House

BREVIER IN PREPARATION.

SPACES AND QUADS WITH ALL SIZES EXCEPT PICA.   MORTISED LETTERS WITH CAPS OF THE LARGER SIZES.

SPECIMENS FROM FARMER, LITTLE & CO., TYPE FOUNDERS.

NEW YORK—63 & 65 Beekman St.
And 62 & 64 Gold Street.

CHICAGO—154 Monroe Street.
Chas. B. Ross, Manager,

PATENT PENDING.

10 a 6 A   THREE LINE NONPAREIL VASSAR SHADED. $3 50

VASSAR COMMENCEMENT

Premier College for the Mental Training of Woman

8 a 5 A   TWO LINE PICA VASSAR SHADED. $4 50

STUDIOUS MAIDENS

Report from Vassar College Catering Department

6 a 4 A   THREE LINE PICA VASSAR SHADED. $6 00.

VASSAR RULES

Opportunities allowed for Talking

PATENT PENDING.

10 a 6 A   THREE LINE NONPAREIL VASSAR. $3 50

THE VASSAR GRADUATES

Armed in Head and Heart for War against Mankind

8 a 5 A   TWO LINE PICA VASSAR. $4 50

THE CHURCH FAIR

Audience Requested not to take away the Pews

6 a 4 A   THREE LINE PICA VASSAR. $6 00

VASSAR GIRLS

Active Mind in Beautiful Form

12 POINT.   PICA BIJOU.   12 A, 32 a, $4.55   32 a (extra), 2.75

Waiting · for · Purchasers : One · male · and · eight · female · unicorns ; seven sea · serpents ; three · griffins, · fully · developed ; four · mermaids, · extremely beautiful ; seven · dragons, · descendants · of · the · one · slain · by · St. George ; one · hippogriff, · just · weaned ; four · salamanders, · basking · in · the · glow · of an · anthracite · furnace ; eleven · sphinxes, · very · docile · and · amiable ; three centaurs, · lately · domesticated ; with · many · other · interesting · curiosities.

✳ Open ✳ for ✳ Inspection ✳ on ✳ Monday, ✳ April · 6, ✳ 1894 ✳

18 POINT.   THREE-LINE NONPAREIL BIJOU.   8 A, 20 a, $5.35   20 a (extra), 3.15

Blatherskite's ✳ Concentrated ✳ Palaverite

Highly · Recommended · for · those · Desiring · Invitations, · Gifts, · Legacies

Loans, · Puffs, · Free · Passes · or · other · Favours

Aims ✳ of ✳ this ✳ Society

Evening · Amusement
Social · Intercourse
Health · Improvement
Athletic · Exercise
And · Occasionally
To · let · others · see
What · fools · we · can · be

Programme
Of · the
Entertainment
Given
May · 2, · '87

24 POINT.   TWO-LINE PICA BIJOU.   6 A, 14 a, $5.75   14 a (extra), 3.40

Meeting · to · Report · Progress

Society ✳ for ✳ the ✳ Investigation ✳ of ✳ Perpetual ✳ Motion

ALL COMPLETE WITH FIGURES.

THE MACKELLAR, SMITHS & JORDAN CO., PHILADELPHIA, PA.   SHNIEDEWEND & LEE CO., AGENTS, CHICAGO, ILLINOIS.

BIOGRAPHICAL SKETCH OF JAMES M. CONNER.

IN the death of James M. Conner, which occurred on the 16th day of July, whose likeness is herewith presented, the type founders of the United States have lost one of the most expert and well informed members of

their trade. Born in 1825, at the age of fourteen years he entered the office of the United States Type Foundry established by his father, James Conner, but in a few years was promoted to the charge of the mechanical portion of the business, where the next forty years of his life were spent.

Possessed of a truly mechanical mind, and excellent memory, and a decided leaning for the profession chosen, he was not slow to improve the opportunity presented him for advancing the interest of the foundry, and "Conner's type" soon became known for its excellence in every respect, and as familiar in the printing offices of the United States as "household words."

With the introduction of the world renowned machine for casting type, invented by David Bruce, still living, at the age of eighty-four years, an impetus was given to the manufacture of type, and Mr. Conner may be said to have witnessed not only the revolution in the mode of manufacturing type caused by it, but also the birth and introduction of the sister art of electrotyping.

Upon the death of Mr. James Conner the business was continued by his sons, James M. and William C., and upon the death of the latter, the management of the entire business passed into the hands of the subject of this sketch. We have often thought the additional burden thus placed upon Mr. Conner, of leaving the workshop which had been his constant thought for many years, and where he was most certainly at home, and each tool or machine was an old friend, and removing to the counting room was an error, for his heart was still "up stairs," where he had labored so faithfully and assiduously for many years, which labor was a pleasure; but the lot was cheerfully

accepted by him, and borne with the patient submission to fate which has characterized his entire life.

The foundry was not to die, if its originator had. The business was not to stand still, if the business manager had passed away; but the metals were to be mixed with the same care, the machinery, in all its branches, was to be looked after and improved, if possible; new faces were to be produced; and the work, formerly devolving upon three men, was now to be superintended by a single mind.

If any reader of this article has been placed in a similar position, then, and only then, can he fully realize the strain such a work brings with it.

Friends urged a vacation, but except a day or two of recreation occasionally, none came. Such was the active, non-tiring and patient energy of the man, and his indomitable will and steadiness of purpose.

His improvements in type-casting machines were many, and in a letter addressed to him about a year since, Mr. David Bruce gave public acknowledgment of them.

The first patent for improvement in this machine was granted in 1872, and is thus described:

This improvement was for the purpose of overcoming the expansion and contraction of the various parts of the machine, also to overcome lost motion in several of the working parts, and all tending to insure a more complete type in face and body. This necessitated a newly constructed furnace, dispensing with the side arm used in working the pump, a complete change in cross beam over the pot, alteration in oblique lever that opens and closes the mold, and a novel universal motion attached to the bedplate for the opening and closing of the mold, and also alteration of vibrating beam.

In 1873, a second patent was granted him for means by which a dwell was given to the mold at the nipple, while the metal is being forced into the mold, thus preventing the swelling of the type.

In addition to improvements in this direction, he invented and patented a machine for ornamenting the faces of brass rules; made improvements in the construction of type molds; and in one improvement prepared to force the molten metal in a direct line into the mold with a view to obtaining a closer and more compact form of type, particularly for the large sizes of metal type.

As a designer of new faces his contributions have been numerous and useful, among which may be named his Athenian, Egyptian shaded, Venetian, Amalgamated Script, and Cosmopolitan, while the "Sidographic," introduced by him, although designed by another, became an exceedingly useful letter and one of great value to the printer.

For many years a number of our prominent newspapers have employed the Conner type, and it is said that with but two exceptions every dress for the New York *Herald* since its establishment has been supplied by the Conner foundry.

His death creates a vacancy it will hardly be possible to fill, but to his children he has left a legacy far better than gold or silver, bonds or worldly possessions — the recollection that in the father was found an honest and just man and a firm friend.

SPECIMENS FROM FARMER, LITTLE & CO., TYPE FOUNDERS.

NEW YORK—63 & 65 Beekman St.
And 62 & 64 Gold Street.

CHICAGO—154 Monroe Street.
Chas. B. Ross, Manager,

PATENT PENDING.
70 a   12 A—$12 00.   40a Lower Case Font, $6.00   GREAT PRIMER IDYL SCRIPT.   35 a   6 A—$6.00

The Famous Chawangunk Mountain House

This Popular Hotel is situated on the most Elevated Point of Land in Orange County.

Attractive Views of the Picturesque Delaware and Neversink Valleys.

Spacious Balconies, from every Room! The Cuisine is Unsurpassed in Excellence and Sumptuousness,

and the Parlors Spacious and Handsomely Appointed.

PATENT PENDING.
70 a   8 A—$14.00.   36a Lower Case Font, $5.00   TWO LINE PICA BELLE SCRIPT No. 1.   24 a   4 A—$7 00

The Society for the Encouragement of Grace and Elegance in Penmanship

and the Dissemination of Refined and Standard

Literary Works, will hold its Fourteenth Annual Session in the Rooms of the Historical

Association, Academy of Music, on next Wednesday afternoon.

70 a   8 A—$14.00.   36a Lower Case Font, $5.00   TWO LINE PICA BELLE SCRIPT No. 2.   24 a   4 A—$7.50

We Respectfully Invite your Attention to our Extensive Assortment of

Fashionable and Seasonable Tailor-made Garments and Millinery Goods,

now Displayed for the delectation of our Lady Friends and Customers, in

Various Departments we make an Elegant Display.

FARMER, LITTLE & CO., TYPE FOUNDERS, CHICAGO.

Standard Script Series.

PATENT APPLIED FOR.

9 A 25 a   THREE LINE NONPAREIL STANDARD SCRIPT (18 Points) $6 00

Quincy Obliging Printing and Stationery Company

Chicago Rock Island and Pacific Railroad Yards at Lincoln Nebraska

Saturday Evening July 23d 1887

The Merchants and Traders National Banking Association

7 A 20 a   FOUR LINE NONPAREIL STANDARD SCRIPT (24 Points) $8 00

The Hudson River Steamboat Company

Numbers 138 to 254 West Indiana Avenue Dayton Ohio

Young Ladies Zither Club

Desires the Presence of Miss Edna Julia Lowell

5 A 15 a   SIX LINE NONPAREIL STANDARD SCRIPT (36 Points) $10 00

Bond and Note Dealers

American Trust and Fund Company

Received Saturday October 24th

Eight Line Nonpareil Standard Script will be ready in a short time. Size of font, 4 A 10 a, Price, $12.00

Manufactured by **BARNHART BROS. & SPINDLER.**

PATENT APPLIED FOR.

25 A 40 a   NONPAREIL LIGHTFACE CHALLENGE (6 Points) $3 25

GREAT PORTION OF THE FINANCIAL DISASTERS OF THE WORLD
Grow Out of Speculation and the Effects of the Practice are Quite as Recognizable in Good as Bad Times
No Sooner do the Times Point to an Improvement in Business than a Great Number of
245 People Begin to cast About for a Chance to Make a Fortune 678

20 A 30 a   BOURGEOIS LIGHTFACE CHALLENGE (9 Points) $3 75

BELIEVING AN OLD STYLE ITALIC EXTENDED
Useful we Submit this Improved Face for the Approval of the Fraternity in the
Opinion that it Will be Suitable for Circulars Cards Note Heads
234 And Similar Classes of Job Work 567

15 A 25 a   TWO LINE NONPAREIL LIGHTFACE CHALLENGE (12 Points) $4 25

SPECIAL BUSINESS COMMODITIES
The Merchandise Markets Summarized and Reported
38 Sweet Songsters of Early Morning 42

10 A 15 a   THREE LINE NONPAREIL LIGHTFACE CHALLENGE (18 Points) $4 50

BEAUTIFUL BRILLIANT
Babcock Air-Spring Optimus Presses
734 Gems of the Ocean 256

6 A 10 a   FOUR LINE NONPARIEL LIGHTFACE CHALLENGE (24 Points) $5 75

BRIGHT HEAVENS
Navies of Russia and France
98 Financial World 35

Manufactured by BARNHART BROS. & SPINDLER.

PATENT APPLIED FOR.

20 A   TWO LINE NONPAREIL SPENSER (12 Points) $1 40

◅HANGING ON THE OUTSKIRTS OF POLITE SOCIETY AN IGNOBLE THING▻

◅1234∴FOR∴INTELLIGENT∴AMERICAN∴PEOPLE∴5678▻

15 A   THREE LINE NONPAREIL SPENSER (18 Points) $2 25

◅UMBRELLA∴DAY∴ON∴WEST∴SANGAMO∴STREET▻

345 DRIPPING BEAUTIES IN DISGUISE 789

10 A   FOUR LINE NONPAREIL SPENSER (24 Points) $2 80

◅THIS∴CENTURY∴IS∴GROWING∴OLD▻

24 THE ANCIENT MARINER 37

8 A   FIVE LINE NONPAREIL SPENSER (30 Points) $3 35

◅WALNUT∴STREET∴GUIDES▻

34 MONUMENTAL 85

6 A   SIX LINE NONPAREIL SPENSER (36 Points) $4 00

RUSTY∴HINGES∴OF∴TIME

◅25 FIRST YEAR 36▻

Manufactured by BARNHART BROS. & SPINDLER.

3A, Ornamental Caps, $1.60
8A, (Including Short Letters) $2.95

24 POINT OXFORD.

3A, 8A, Complete, $4.55

Oxford Edition

Lieut. Colonel Woodford

23 Kate Claxton 67

Inland Routes for the West

3A, Ornamental Caps, $3.20
6A, (Including Short Letters) $3.75

36 POINT OXFORD.

3A, 6A, Complete, $6.95

Children at Play

Additional Radiation

34 Chippewa 78

The Old Cross Road

Cleveland Type Foundry,   -   -   147 St. Clair Street.

August 1887   189

NONPAREIL OXONIAN. Price, $2.15.

ORATORICAL EFFORTS OF YOUNG DEMOSTHENES
CUPID'S MEANDERINGS AMONG CONSTANTINOPLE'S BUXOM LASSES
FIGMENTS OF HEATHEN MYTHOLOGY
1234567890

BREVIER OXONIAN. Price, $2.30.

GOBELIN TAPESTRY AND EMBROIDERY
REMINISCENCES OF THE COURTSHIP OF CLEOPATRA
EXPLOITS OF THE CRUSADERS
1234567890

LONG PRIMER OXONIAN. Price, $2.50.

OLDENTIME FESTIVITIES
PANTOMIME AMUSEMENTS OF CHRISTMAS
TWELFTH CENTURY MIMICRIES
1234567890

PICA OXONIAN. Price, $3.05.

UNCOUTH CEREMONIALS
RAMBLE THROUGH HEATHEN LANDS
SUPERSTITIOUS ORIENTALS
1234567890

GREAT PRIMER OXONIAN. Price, $3.70.

CUSTOMS IN ANCIENT PALMYRA
MECHANICAL APPLIANCES USED BY PRIMITIVE BUILDERS
WANDERINGS OF THE SHIPWRECKED

TWO-LINE LONG PRIMER OXONIAN. Price, $3.95.

PICKAXE AND SHOVEL GYMNASTICS
EXCAVATING FOR CURIOSITIES AT HERCULANEUM

TWO-LINE PICA OXONIAN. Price, $4.25.

OLYMPIAN TRAINING SCHOOL
REGIMEN DEVELOPING YOUTHFUL MUSCLES

ALL COMPLETE WITH FIGURES.

THE MACKELLAR, SMITHS & JORDAN CO., PHILADELPHIA. SHNIEDEWEND & LEE CO., AGENTS, CHICAGO, ILL.

FRENCH CLARENDON EXTENDED.

IMPROVED SERIES.

20A, 40a,   Pearl. (5 Points Standard Measure.) $3.40

LOVE'S LYRICS IN LOOSE QUANDARY

Tenderest Sentiments Best Befit Love-Sick Humanity

Now is the Witching Hour of Night 24

18A, 36a,   Nonpareil. (6 Points Standard Measure.) $2.75

MAKE HAY WHEN SUN SHINES

The Press is the Lever that Moves all Worlds

78 Rolling Waves and Billows

18A, 36a,   Brevier. (8 Points Standard Measure.) $3.65

NEVER GO ASTRAY

68 Valleys of Bright Waving Corn

16A, 32a,   Long Primer. (10 Points Standard Measure.) $3.95

VIRTUE'S REWARD

Morn Awakes in Gladness 2

12A, 24a,   Small Pica. (11 Points Standard Measure.) $3.95

GREENBACKS

Lively Mugwumps 35

10A, 20a,   Pica. (12 Points Standard Measure.) $4.25

PENTAGONS

24 Mountain Walk

8A, 16a,   Great Primer. (18 Points Standard Measure.) $5.00

FLOATING

2 Pensive Goats

6A, 12a,   Dbl. Small Pica. (22 Points Standard Measure.) $5.65

ISLAND

Sportive Cow

4A, 8A,   Double English. (28 Points Standard Measure.) $5.70

VALENTINES

The Beautiful Snow

3A, 6a,   Double Columbian. (32 Points Standard Measure.) $7.05

WONDERS

Have not Ceased 4

3A, 5a,   Double Paragon. (40 Points Standard Measure). $10.10

ENRAGE

Driven to Win

ON THE INTERNAL ECONOMY OF PRINTING OFFICES.

To the Editor: CHICAGO, August 1, 1887.

The papers of Messrs. Shepard and McNally, read before the Typothetæ of this city, and published in THE INLAND PRINTER, are deservedly worthy the careful attention of every printer. For years it has seemed impossible to render dynamic the latent knowledge and power existing among the intelligent practical printers of this city, and arouse them from the lethargy which had overtaken them. There seems now to be in our sky a bow of promise, that by the methods of the Typothetæ the whole body of the fraternity will come to learn from the monitions of experience how best they may attain at least some of that measure of success which has crowned the efforts of the wise—a prosperous establishment, a well-conducted printing office. Be this as it may, one can draw many a lesson from the success of the few and the failure of the many.

One cannot but respect the earnest spirit of the advisers, and the ease with which the strong words, *must, ought* and *should,* are used in the papers of the contributors referred to; and at the same time wonder why the necessity should exist at all for the free expression and discussion of the sound principles which ought to govern the business conduct or mechanical operation of the printing office. Why is it that abuses still exist, wrong methods go unrighted, necessary reforms remain untouched, and the failure to overcome obstacles result in disaster to so many?

Reminded of Byron's

> " Men must serve their time to every trade
> Save censure—critics all are ready made,"

and observing the undercurrent of good will and zeal existing in the discussion of these facts, we venture to set down some thoughts upon a subject of so great interest to all.

One obstacle to success among printers is a too great conservatism in methods and practice. A stupid, unreasonable clinging to the ways and means of our fathers and grandfathers is a prime characteristic of too many in the present day. One can call to mind no other trade or art which has not made greater progress in the processes of manufacture and adaptation of means to the end. The arrangement of stands, the layout of cases, the relative position of stones, furniture racks, and the other adjuncts of the printing office, are the same today, in many instances, as obtained fifty years ago. Composing sticks; how utterly useless and inaccurate they are, even when new,—how worthless they become after a few days' use! Quoins, chases, almost all the tools of the printer, are constructed, not with a view to save time, but to waste time in unnecessary labor. It is true many valuable improvements in and interesting attachments to the machinery of the printing office have, in the last few years, been made; and the trade has benefited by the progress in invention among press-builders. But it is that " insatiable whirlpool," the " unprofitable composing room," we are writing about. How well is this unreasoning old fogyism illustrated in the refusal of the average employer to replace the barbaric wooden quoin and shooting-stick with the modern metal quoin and key? The writer recalls two or three cases within his knowledge where employers absolutely would have nothing to do with this improvement. Columns might be filled with instances of refusal to adopt what few improvements occasionally offer for facilitating the work of the composing room. A few weeks ago a newly-appointed foreman suggested what seemed to him some practical improvements in the methods of the office in his charge, and was met by an outburst of objections. It would not do, his employer said, because we have followed a different method for twenty-five years. Thus far the old fogies.

A stupid conservatism manifests itself also in the purchase of material. The young employer is too often guided by the flattering tongue of our friends the type founders and material men, or by the pretty illustrations of the price lists. Because some other man has bought an " economic" (?) cabinet and paid $130 for it, or some other piece of furniture at a price from $50 to $85, he must go and commit the same foolish act. For half the money he could buy plain racks, have them inclosed, and be of just as good service as the high-toned, black walnut absurdities of the price lists. In purchasing type he is inclined to order a lot of ray shades, and some of those recent abominably inartistic faces of the specimen books, rather than obtain a good line of gothics, celtics, antiques, or the standard roman faces. His pigheaded following of the blind prevents him from knowing that ninety-nine out of a hundred of his prospective patrons from the factories and counting rooms will spurn his jim-crack faces and demand their work be set up in good plain type. Why should not that good judgment which prevails in his contracting for the necessaries of life, enter also into his dealings with the type founders? Buy only what you actually need. Have nothing to do with the veneered and gilded spread-eagles of the books. The printing office needs no luxuries of any kind.

This brings one to notice the forcible statement of Mr. McNally, that the " printer pays from fifty to one hundred per cent more for his plant than any other manufacturer." How many ever stop to consider the truth contained in that remark? Presses and machinery of some classes are listed much higher than they should be. Type, leads, brass rule, many kinds of printers' material, are priced out of all proportion to actual worth.

It has been well stated in both papers under notice that one consideration leading to success is the investiture of the foreman (assuming, of course, he is the faithful man he should be), with full authority in his particular department. Go a little further, and give him some insight as to how your business stands; how the volume of the output compares with the cost and expenses of production. Of course it is not advised that the scores of matters and items proper only to the knowledge of the firm should be exposed to him. But just these little confidences in the direction suggested, will prompt him in maintaining a watchful care for your interests. A foreman who is made something more of than a mere automaton for receiving and giving out copy, will, if he has the right qualifications in other directions, stand firmly in the gap of unnecessary expenditure and wasteful misuse of your material. Consult him often, or as occasion may present, and he will consult and confide in you, and be fully alive to every circumstance inuring to your benefit.

One other obstacle to success is the want of appreciation of the dual character of your business. The two-fold nature of the art is seldom considered by some of the printers of today. On the one hand the artistic quality of your work is magnified to the detriment of considerations which ought to be cultivated for the profit of the office. On the other hand, you sacrifice fair and attractive typography for the basest consideration of beating your neighbor in the race for work, or, as some very foolish proprietors claim is a good thing, particularly in dull seasons, make an empty show of noise and clamor, in " keeping things running "—into the ground.

It may appear a mere platitude to say all this. But the whole theory of the internal economy of the printing office is contained in a just regard for the superiority of your business—call it art if you will—above the greater number of other occupations, coupled with a sound and reasonable demand for the full money worth of your wares. A good lawyer, a good physician, can always obtain fair reward. So with the printer—his reward is of right rated higher than the ordinary manufacturer, because his productions demand greater energy, skill, and brain, than the building a house, sewing a coat or pegging a shoe.

At the commencement of this letter the wonder was expressed that a necessity should exist for this discussion. It is almost paradoxical that a body of men so intelligent—in other matters shrewd, painstaking and careful—as are the majority of practical employing printers of today, should need instruction or guidance from their fellow craftsmen in such grave matters as have been presented. " He alone reads history aright who sees in past events a guide to present duties." If this fact can be kept in view, will it not result in this much of good, that before one undertakes the management of a printing office he must admit it demands greater ability than that needed to conduct a mercantile enterprise. The fundamental axioms so ably set out in the papers of the gentlemen above named, must be taken as the guide posts along the road, the guidons of the march toward success. Clearly understood and appreciated, will not these facts prevent at least a part of the ambitious horde from reaching after the unattainable, through their foolish ignorance and misapplied enterprise,—the starting a printing office?   T. D. PARKER.

DAVID BRUCE.

INVENTOR OF THE TYPE-CASTING MACHINE.

A TRUE benefactor to his race, a man to whom every printer and type founder of the present time is immeasurably indebted, is living, at the advanced age of eighty six years, in modest retirement at 182 South Fourth street, Brooklyn, New York. It is with great pleasure that we present to our readers a very satisfactory portrait of the venerable inventor of the type-casting machine, and record our opinion that among all men now living connected with the art preservative, as an art or industry, there is none so worthy of honor as Mr. David Bruce.

A patent for a type-casting machine was issued to David Bruce in 1836, again on March 17, 1838, and for a more perfect machine on November 6, 1846. Although previous to this there had been attempts to cast type by machines. they had been unsuccessful, and type was still made in hand molds, the speed of which was twelve to fifteen a minute. The machine patented in 1834 is now used (with later improvements) by all American and nearly all foreign type founders, and is run by steampower as well as by hand, producing on an average one hundred types per minute. It is not our purpose to describe the machine, as the process of making type is or ought to be familiar to every intelligent printer, but the indisputable fact that but for this invention the type founders of the present day could not produce type in its present

DAVID BRUCE.

perfection should be known and appreciated by all.

Its silent influence on mankind has been marvelous, but on this point we will quote from a letter from the inventor to the late Mr. Jas. M. Connor, of New York:

Of the machine — well, what of it? The mere renown of the invention has only this effect with me, as I trust with other inventors, the consciousness of having contributed something toward the advancement of the world's progress. The term "progress" was at one time as repulsive and unfamiliar to the ear as that of evolution is now, and yet they are both so well recognized by their trails that it would betray childishness to ignore them.

The world is apt to be forgetful of the past, and yet the world is replete with familiarized miracles. It is to be hoped that there are few so obtuse, so dull, so idiotically refined in intellect, as to ask, book in hand, Well, what has all this greasy, plebeian workshop business to do with the enjoyment of life? The pleasure-seeking lady or gentleman in their summer rambles, the millionaire, the traveler, the politician, the statesman, the historian, in short any searcher after education, cannot but be interested in any advance in those arts tending to the spread of knowledge. The reading public is rejoiced at the rapid multiplication of papers, books and periodicals through the agency of the modern printing press; but from whence came their type — these twenty-six

little symbols of our language? At the present day speed in the manufacture of type is as essential as speed in printing.

Mr. Bruce is a thoroughly practical type founder, having been a mold-maker, a justifier of matrices, and letter-cutter. In the latter capacity we owe to him the well-known series of Rimmed Shade, Title Expanded, Roman Extended, Ionic, Title, Secretary, and many others. The following highly interesting communication from the venerable inventor will, we are sure, be regarded by our readers with more interest than any words we can pen, although it is to be regretted that no fuller account of Mr. Bruce's career is at present obtainable:

MR. BRUCE'S LETTER.

BROOKLYN, N. Y., April 19, 1887.

Gentlemen,—I am now in my eighty-sixth year, and as modesty is the chief ornament of youth I must decline your invitation to write a synopsis of my life. In short it might be said my life differs very little from the routine of other inventors and projectors — always poising between inflated hopes and blasting disappointments. But let me confine myself more particularly to the times about and preceding my invention.

In the year 1834 I cut myself loose from the firm of George Bruce & Co., of New York, of whom I had been one of the partners for two years, and retired to reside on my father's farm in New Jersey, on which I continued five years. It was my idea to construct, if possible, a machine capable of producing a more perfect type than was then being offered to the printer. The only *machine* type then being sold to them by Mr. Elihu White, was too *porous* and *light* to be satisfactory, ranging from twenty to twenty-five per cent lighter than hand-cast type, and which was urged as an inducement to the purchaser. (See Mr. White's specimens of those dates, 1834, 1840.)

Let it be fairly understood I was by no means a pioneer in facilitating the casting of type by machinery. Mr. Edwin Starr, of Boston; Mr. George B. Lothian; my father; Messrs. Mann and Sturtevant; Mr. Wm. M. Johnson, and Mr. George F. Peterson, had all preceded me, but with little success.

My uncle, Mr. George Bruce, became purchaser of my No. 1 patent of 1836, and knowing my inventive idiosyncrasy he requested me, as a favor, that I should make him the first offer of purchase of any improvement I might subsequently invent. Hence the present machine was spurred into existence by his encouragement, and I might almost say *for* him. When finished, he was invited over to Brooklyn to give it an examination. Unfortunately he sent over his machinist, who saw it, but to suit his own views totally misrepresented its manifest superiority over all former machines, inasmuch as it had the capability of being driven, as now, by steam or other power, and with greater speed. Hence he rejected it without seeing it.

I assure you, gentlemen, that I was mortified and disappointed; but rallying, took the first opportunity to find for it a purchaser. Hence its first introduction in that very cautious, venerable and tasty type foundry in Boston — the Boston Type and Stereotype Foundry.

It is pleasant to look back upon the past fifty-three years and review my conflict with artists, type metal and type founders, and I may truly say that with one nameless exception my intercourse with these old typos has always been agreeable. Many have manifested their friendship in various kindly ways, and Mr. Lawrence Johnson, type founder, of Philadelphia, in the procurement, without my knowledge, of a costly medal from the Franklin Institute of that place.

Truly yours,   DAVID BRUCE.

Long may our venerable and talented friend live to enjoy his honors is the sincere desire of THE INLAND, PRINTER.

IN THE JOB COMPOSING ROOM.

Artists are proverbially a difficult class of people to manage, with little regard for the commercial aspect of their calling, so long as they attain their artistic ends. All job compositors are, or should be, artists, and that they are no exception to their class the employing printer too often learns, when he finds that a common everyday billhead, which he figured could be set in two hours, has taken the artist who set it (very handsomely, too,) just four hours; or when a very matter-of-fact circular shows up several hours after it was promised, fairly groaning under the *weight* of combination borders, lavished on it by a genius who saw a chance to "spread himself." Of course, the average customer likes (but won't pay extra for) that sort of thing, and the average artist considers himself entitled to an increased stipend in consideration of his efforts to put as much work into the job as it will stand. Many employers, even, appreciate such artistic efforts, and yet wonder why there is no profit in the composing room. There is misdirected talent and energy in a job office where "art" is practiced at the expense of the employer. How would it strike the printer if he had a cylinder press, with brains and artistic longings strong enough to enable it to insist on using $2 ink on a poster, because "it looks better, you know," and "good work pays the best."

The artistic temperament of job comps crops out strongly when the "enterprising" employer buys some new job type. With one impulse, all the compositors strive to be the first to lug it into the work in hand, no matter what it is, regardless of good taste, sometimes, but always regardless of economy.

We have read of a celebrated painter, who, being at one time too poor to buy furniture, painted on the walls of his cottage the finest furniture, upholsteries and draperies he could imagine, and revelled in luxuries (?) while wanting the common necessaries of life. We have found the counterpart to this luxurious cottage in many job printing offices. The artists in them revel in a profusion of fancy type and borders, and when they set up a job their ideas had no difficulty whatever in evolving themselves, but all their inventiveness and energy is required to evolve enough leads, quads, spaces, reglet and furniture to sustain the beautiful lines in their proper positions. The line is set, and then the comp pulls out a dozen cases to find spaces enough to justify it, or has to untie a form to get leads, or throw in a fat job to get quads, until finally the job is nicely set, satisfactorily delivered, and paid for at the price agreed on, and the printer feels that he has done his duty well, and at the end of the month he will tell you there is no money in the printing business, *because* Smith, Jones and Brown are cutting prices, and actually doing work for less than he can buy the paper for! Perhaps they are, but that is no reason why he should oblige his men to waste hours in setting the job he did secure, just because he had spent his money on luxuries, and couldn't afford the necessities.

When an employing printer estimates that a job will consume a certain time, and he knows it can be done in that time, the compositor should be instructed to do it in that time, or quicker, and avoid unnecessary elaboration. If an ornate or particularly nice job is *paid* for, then by all means let the compositor take plenty of time to do it, but the average, ordinary run of work should be done well, quickly, neatly, and without striving after "effect." Do good work always, but do it with some regard to propriety. Don't waste your sweetness on a butcher's card or a simple business announcement. If your compositor cannot discriminate, dictate the type it is to be set in yourself. He will not like it, but you will perhaps be able to soothe his feelings by increasing his pay out of your increased profit.

Material wears out too quickly in the jobroom, especially the more expensive type, and this will always be an evil where every style of type is open to free use by every good, bad and indifferent compositor in

your employ. Our theory is, that scripts, borders, fancy rules, and all delicate letters should be kept in cabinets apart, and only a select few of your men allowed to use them, and then only on such work as will afford a proper *extra* return for such material. This plan would preserve the novelty of new faces in your work, preserve the type, and compel your average work to be executed with good, durable type. Cutting of brass rule should be done only by permission of the foreman, and all dotted and single brass rule, at least, should be labor-saving. It is easier for the compositor to cut what rule he wants from strips, but it does not pay. Leads, slugs, furniture should be abundant, and all labor-saving. These articles are all cheap — cheaper than time, every time, and for fear we are encroaching too much on the time of our readers, who have followed us so far, we end, by hoping that not one of them can honestly convict himself of expecting his men to do good work in quick time without an ample supply of material, or of employing artists of such unrestrained artistic tendencies as will prevent them from remembering that we are all in business to make a dollar.— *H. L. B. in Printers' Review.*

THE AMATEUR WORK NUISANCE.

To the Editor: BALTIMORE, July 23, 1887.

The evils inflicted on the trade by the productions of the amateur have long been appreciated by the craft, and have also been ably pointed out from time to time in the columns of THE INLAND PRINTER. The truth is, however, its efforts have not been seconded as they should have been by the printers, type founders and press manufacturers, and it is doubtful if there are not as many amateurs in business today as there were five years ago. Yet we cannot always see the good that is being accomplished in a quiet way. It is an old saying, "a lean horse for a long chase." Well, THE INLAND PRINTER, we may say, is the "lean horse." It has been exposing the evil referred to for a number of years, and I trust it will before long win the race, succeed in driving these nuisances out of the business, and receive, as it certainly deserves therefor, the thanks not only of the printing fraternity, but of the entire community.

There are business men all over the country who know as much about printing as a number of those engaged in the trade, who can pick out the defects in a job as soon as they put their eyes on it. Well, they sometimes get hold of a miserable piece of work, turned out by a so called amateur; the result is it is held up to ridicule as a sample of the printer's skill, and the innocent have to suffer for the guilty. Now, it is time, I insist, that effective steps be taken to stop this crying evil. Let each convention of employers or society of employers, type founders or press manufacturers, enter a protest against its continuance, and urge the adoption and enforcement of a proper *apprenticeship system*, a system which will require that each apprentice, before being acknowledged as a full-fledged journeymen, shall be compelled to pass an examination which will test his proficiency, and if such examination prove satisfactory, let him be presented with a certificate which will be recognized all over the United States. If the proper steps are taken, there is no reason why the name of every proficient apprentice who has passed such examination cannot be obtained, on the same principle that we can always find out if such a man is a member of such a local union, by reference to the books kept for that especial purpose. I would go further. If a person who passed an examination did not agree to become a member of the union, I would not only withhold his diploma from him, but have him *black-listed*, as also an employer who engaged him, because no employer should hire a man who had not his diploma, as an evidence of competency. Further, if any type founder or press maker refused to indorse a system which has for its object the protection of the trade, and the turning out of good workmen, let them be known from one end of the country to the other. This may seem somewhat harsh, but desperate cases require desperate remedies, and we have got to do something to protect our trade, which it has taken so many of us long years to acquire, from the inroad of botches, who are permitted to turn out work that is a disgrace to the printing art.

I would like to hear from some of the western printers on this subject, through the columns of THE INLAND PRINTER.

Yours truly,   PROGRESS.

New York—63 & 65 Beekman St.
And 62 & 64 Gold Street.

Chicago—154 Monroe Street.
Chas. B. Ross, Manager.

PATENT PENDING.
70 a 12 A—$12 00. 40a Lower Case Font, $6.00   GREAT PRIMER IDYL SCRIPT.   35 a 6 A—$6.00

The Famous Shawangunk Mountain House

This Popular Hotel is situated on the most Elevated Point of Land in Orange County.

Attractive Views of the Picturesque Delaware and Neversink Valleys.

Spacious Balconies, from every Room! The Cuisine is Unsurpassed in Excellence and Sumptuousness,

and the Parlors Spacious and Handsomely Appointed.

PATENT PENDING.
70 a 8 A—$14.00. 36a Lower Case Font, $5.00   TWO LINE PICA BELLE SCRIPT No. 1.   24 a 4 A—$7 00

The Society for the Encouragement of Grace and Elegance in Penmanship

and the Dissemination of Refined and Standard

Literary Works, will hold its Fourteenth Annual Session in the Rooms of the Historical

Association, Academy of Music, on next Wednesday afternoon.

70 a 8 A—$14.00. 36 a Lower Case Font, $5.00   TWO LINE PICA BELLE SCRIPT No. 2.   24 a 4 A—$7.50

We Respectfully Invite your Attention to our Extensive Assortment of

Fashionable and Seasonable Tailor-made Garments and Millinery Goods,

now Displayed for the delectation of our Lady Friends and Customers, in

Various Departments we make an Elegant Display.

FARMER, LITTLE & CO., TYPE FOUNDERS, CHICAGO.

Grolier

MECHANICAL PATENT, MAR. 31, 1885.
REGISTERED, No. 69,178.

24 POINT.   TWO-LINE PICA GROLIER.
With Three-Line Pica (36 Point) Initials.

Seventeenth International Convocation

Association for Encouraging Habits of Industry

Pledge on Initiation of Members

Knowing that the Human Hand, intelligently educated and skilfully employed, has rescued man from Barbarism, and made his position far superior to that of animals not possessing this useful appendage, also believing that it can, by judicious use, still further Elevate humanity and Lighten the Burdens yet weighing heavily on some of its unfortunate sons, I therefore

Hereby Faithfully Covenant

That my hands, as well as those of others placed under my care, shall be carefully instructed in some Handicraft beneficial to the race, and that I will on all occasions endeavour to keep them fully employed in works of use or beauty, and will refrain from uplifting them in any way that may injure my fellows, or mar the fair face of Nature.

May 26, 1987.   Philanthropic Busybody.

Meetings for Nomination

THE MACKELLAR, SMITHS & JORDAN CO., PHILADELPHIA, PA.   SHNIEDEWEND & LEE CO., AGENTS, CHICAGO, ILLINOIS.

TITLE EXPANDED.
IMPROVED SERIES.

24A, 48a,   Agate. (5½ Points Standard Measure.) $4.00

SIMPLIFIED DONOTHINGNESS

The Best Policy for Statesmen to adopt 268

Silver-Tongued Orators

Agate Cast on Nonpareil body when desired: 24A, 48a, $3.70

18A, 36a,   Brevier. (8 Points Standard Measure.) $3.70

JOURNALS OF AMERICA

5 The Pen Mightier than the Sword

Slashing Leader Writer

12A, 24a,   Long Primer. (10 Points Standard Measure.) $3.20

GRECIAN COMFORTS

Harp of Thousand Strings 83

6A, 12a,   Great Primer. (18 Points Standard Measure.) $3.85

MEMORIES

5 Childhood's Days

18A, 36a,   Nonpareil. (6 Points Standard Measure.) $3.15

BRALOUDE & SPREDEAGLE

Loud Elocutionary Gymnastic Professors

143 Political Enthusiasts

18A, 36a,   Bourgeois. (9 Points Standard Measure.) $4.05

SLANDER CIRCULATORS

Conducted within Party Lines 357

Envenomed Utterances

10A, 20a,   Pica. (12 Points Standard Measure.) $3.60

FROZEN OCEAN

64 Arctic Explorationist

6A, 12a,   Paragon. (20 Points Standard Measure.) $5.75

RATIONS

For Artillery 2

4A, 8a,   Double Pica. (24 Points Standard Measure.) $5.45

FAST RAILWAY

Lightning Speed Train

3A, 6a,   Double Columbian. (32 Points Standard Measure.) $6.80

Read NOTE Book

3A, 5a,   Double Paragon. (40 Points Standard Measure.) $10.00

Ten FAT Mice

3A, 5a,   Four Line Pica. (48 Points Standard Measure.) $13.25

HOLD Fast

THREE-LINE NONP. FANCY CELTIC.   Price, $2.90.

ELABORATE DESIGNING
Handkerchief Studies from Rembrandt
1234567890

TWO-LINE PICA FANCY CELTIC.   Price, $3.60.

DIAMOND MINING
Dividend and Stock Distribution
1234567890

THREE-LINE PICA FANCY CELTIC.   Price, $4.80.

MARRIAGE CERTIFICATE
Maternal Depositor for Keeping Hurtful Secrets

PICA STEELPLATE GOTHIC.   Price, $2.15.

SUMMER SUNSHINE
RELIABLE WARM WEATHER
1234567890

REGISTERED No. 9218.

THREE-LINE NONP. STEELPLATE GOTHIC.   Price, $2.45.

DISTURBANCE
EVENING SERENADES
1234567890

TWO-LINE PICA STEELPLATE GOTHIC.   Price, $3.00.

NORTHERN ICEBERG PROVINCE

THREE-LINE PICA STEELPLATE GOTHIC.   Price, $4.10.

ENORMOUS BAROMETERS

ALL COMPLETE WITH FIGURES.

THE MACKELLAR, SMITHS & JORDAN CO., PHILADELPHIA.   SHNIEDEWEND & LEE CO., AGENTS, CHICAGO, ILL.

CLIPPER ⟨monogram⟩ EXTENDED.

20 A — 10-POINT—LONG PRIMER — $4 85

MODERN DESIGNS

PRODUCED BY AMERICAN ARTISTS

43   UNIQUE AND ELEGANT   58

8 A — 18-POINT—THREE-LINE NONPAREIL — $5 50

BOYS IN BLUE

ANNUAL REUNIONS

29 CAMP FIRES 35

20 A — 6-POINT—NONPAREIL — $2 75

OPENING OF SEASON

OYSTERS ON HALF SHELL

98   BLUE POINTS   39

20 A — 8-POINT—BREVIER — $3 70

ANNUAL CRUISE

OUR IRON CLAD SHIP

52 CAPE HORN 62

6 A — 24-POINT—TWO-LINE PICA — $6 00

FORESTERS

MODERN HUNTER

35 LESSON 28

10 A — 12-POINT—PICA — $4 05

CAMP SHERIDAN

INTERNATIONAL SQUADRON

25   CHICAGO   68

ILLINOIS TYPE FOUNDING COMPANY,   -   -   -   No. 202 South Clark Street, CHICAGO.

SKELETON ANTIQUE.
IMPROVED SERIES.

24A, 48a,   Brevier. (8 Points Standard Measure.) $3.80

WORDS STIR UP ANGER AND ANGER BRINGS FORTH BLOWS

Always Take Care Not to Get Mad with a Bigger Fellow than Yourself 23456789

24A, 48a,   Long Primer. (10 Points Standard Measure.) $4.20

WE ALL HAVE TO PAY THE DEBT OF NATURE

348 Each Day Some of our Friends leave us to join the Silent Majority

18A, 36a,   Pica. (12 Points Standard Measure.) $4.40

MAGNIFICENT DISPLAY OF FIREWORKS

269 Fourth of July Celebration, Crackers and Toy Pistols

16A, 32a,   Great Primer. (18 Points Standard Measure.) $5.80

ECSTATIC INFLUENCE OF OPIUM

Simple Economy of John Chinaman's Happiness 8

10A, 20a,   Dbl. Sm. Pica. (22 Points Standard Measure.) $5.40

HE THAT REVENGES knows no rest 23

8A, 16a,   Dbl. English. (28 Points Standard Measure.) $6.80

57 CHANGEFUL Scenes of Life

6A, 12a,   Dbl. Paragon. (40 Points Standard Measure.) $8.60

52 DISTANCE Enchants

6A, 12a,   Four-Line Pica. (48 Points Standard Measure.) $9.30

SOCIAL Intercourse 8

4A, 8a,   Five-Line Pica. (60 Points Standard Measure.) $9.20

25 Educated PONIES Dancing 37

3A, 4a,   Six-Line Pica. (72 Points Standard Measure.) $9.55
ORIGINAL.

8 Rural EXPOSITION Open 9

3A, 4a,   [Eight-Line Pica. (96 Points Standard Measure.) $13.40
ORIGINAL.

4 BRILLIANT Scenes 6

Spaces and Quads with all sizes except Pica.

GEORGIAN.

PATENTED SEPT. 20, 1887.

| 6A, 12a, | Great Primer. (18 Points Standard Measure.) | $4.10 |

UNION REAL ESTATE & LOAN ASSOCIATION
148 Rents Collected and Money Loaned on Merchandise 526
Dealers in Government and other Bonds

| 5A, 10a. | Double Pica. (24 Points Standard Measure.) | $4.95 |

BEAUTIFUL WOODLAND SCENERY
213 Moonlight Excursions on the Hudson 456
New York Yacht Club Regatta

| 4A, 8a, | Double Great Primer. (36 Points Standard Measure.) | $7.70 |

WEATHER INDICATIONS
United States Bureau of Statistics
2 Old Probability 4

| 3A, 6a, | Four-Line Pica. (48 Points Standard Measure.) | $9.10 |

AMERICAN TOURIST
Killing Bears in California

FIGURES, SPACES AND QUADS WITH ALL SIZES IN THIS SERIES.

NEW YORK—63 & 65 Beekman St.
And 62 & 64 Gold Street.

CHICAGO—154 Monroe Street.
Chas. B. Ross, Manager.

PATENT PENDING.

50 a   12 A   LONG PRIMER YORK. $4 25

YORK, A CITY OF ENGLAND IN YORKSHIRE COUNTY.

York is surrounded by Ancient Walls, and Entered by Five principal Gateways and Five smaller ones.

At the head of the Public Buildings is the Cathedral

Which is the Glory of York. The greater part of the Building was erected in the

13th and 14th Centuries.

Now, York, or never, steel thy fearful thoughts,
And change misdoubt to resolution;
Be that thou hop'st to be, or what thou art
Resign to death; it is not worth the enjoying.

Saint Alban's battle, won by famous York,
Shall be eternis'd in all age to come,—
Sound, drums and trumpets!—and to London all;
And more such days as these to us befall!

36 a   10 A   PICA YORK. $4 50

NEW YORK, CHIEF CITY OF THE EMPIRE STATE,

The Harbor is a large Bay, with a circumference of 25 Miles, spreading before the City on the South side; it is deep enough for the largest vessels.

Sweet Duke of York! our prop to lean upon.
Now thou art gone, we have no staff, no stay
O Clifford! boisterous Clifford! thou hast slain
The Flower of Europe for his chivalry;
And treacherously hast thou vanquished him.

Great Lord of Warwick, if we should recount
Our baleful news, and at each word's deliverance
Stab poniards in our flesh till all were told,
The words would add more anguish than the wounds.
O valiant Lord! the Duke of York is slain.

24 a   8 A   THREE LINE NONPAREIL YORK. $5 75

THE WHITE ROSE OF YORK.

Yorktown, Virginia, situated on the South side of the River York, Sixty Miles from Richmond.

Memorable in History as the Scene of the Surrender of Lord Cornwallis and his Army on the 19th October, 1781

Specimens from Farmer, Little & Co., Type Founders.

New York—63 & 65 Beekman St.
And 62 & 64 Gold Street.

Chicago—154 Monroe Street.
Chas. B. Ross, Manager,

PATENTED.

25 a 8 a 6 A—$6 75   Two Line Pica Card Gothic.   Without Small Caps—$5 00

Farmer, Little and Co. have much pleasure in presenting to their patrons,

the American Printing Trade, this

Original and Beautiful Series of Gothics,

Feeling confident that it will meet a favorable reception; its appearance is peculiarly striking,

while there is nothing fragile about it that could mar its usefulness.

36 a 8 a 10 A—$6 50   Great Primer Card Gothic.   Without Small Caps—$5 25

The Introduction of the Printing Art into Great Britain

What glorious Things achieved have been by a Free and Fearless Press

The Introduction to our land,
Between Corsells and Caxton stand;
Most authors have decreed.
Which has a right to lead the van,
The Foreign, or the Kentish man;
The learn'd are not agreed.

It boots us little now to know,
To whom our gratitude we owe,
The blessing we enjoy.
Corsells may claim a rude essay,
Caxton's the merit of our way;
HE brought us this employ.

13 a 8 a 5 A—$8 60   Two Line Great Primer Card Gothic.   Without Small Caps—$7 50

THIS beautiful Series of CARD GOTHICS has justified

its production, being popular with the Craft

Owing to The Originality of Its Design.

6 POINT.   NONPAREIL RONALDSON EXTENDED.   Price, $2.45

WREATHED AND FLOWERED
Bride's Wedding Dress
Meadows Rainbowed with Summer's Verdure
Blossoms Garlanding the Precipice
1234567890

8 POINT.   BREVIER RONALDSON EXTENDED.   Price, $2.70

NEHEMIAH TRUTHFUL
Testimonials for Proprietary Medicines
Calligraphic Munchausenist
1234567890

LONG PRIMER RONALDSON EXTENDED.   Price, $3.00

CLIMBING HIGHER
Placing the Steeple Weathercock
Tempestuous Situation

Made also on 10 Point.

12 POINT.   PICA RONALDSON EXTENDED.   Price, $3.50

REMINISCENCE
Neighbourly Congratulation
Borrowed Flatirons

18 POINT.   THREE-LI. NONPAREIL RONALDSON EXTENDED.   Price, $4.00

WINSOME
Toddling Babyhood

24 POINT.   TWO-LINE PICA RONALDSON EXTENDED.   Price, $4.65

WAYSIDE
Earning Ability

30 POINT.   FIVE-LINE NONPAREIL RONALDSON EXTENDED.   Price, $5.40

STATE HOUSE
Birthplace of Independence

36 POINT.   THREE-LINE PICA RONALDSON EXTENDED.   Price, $6.55

PATRIARCH
Honoured Grandam

48 POINT.   FOUR-LINE PICA RONALDSON EXTENDED.   Price, $8.45

Marginal NOTES

ALL COMPLETE WITH FIGURES.

The Point Bodies may be justified with one another by using leads and quads of our point system.

THE MACKELLAR, SMITHS & JORDAN CO., PHILADELPHIA.

SHNIEDEWEND & LEE CO., AGENTS, CHICAGO, ILL.

HOMELY TALKS ON HOW TO SUCCEED.

BY HERBERT L. BAKER.

NOT so fast, my boy. Before you blame your lack of success so entirely upon your " confounded luck," as you call it, suppose we make a little honest inquiry into the matter. You say there is so much competition that there is no longer living profit in printing; that you have to bid for every job and are never lucky enough to get a decent job even when your figures compare favorably with those of other bidders; that you get only the work you have bid so low for that there is no profit in it; that you have the crankiest lot of customers in town anyhow, who are always "kicking" about their work, or price, or something; that you are completely disgusted with the "biz," and would sell out in a holy minute if you only could.

Do you keep samples of your jobs? Well, let's have a look at them and see whether they will help our inquiry. Here they are all spread out in a confused heap, and now let's first pick out the fine jobs. By the way, my boy, don't you know that to shove such a mess of all sorts of specimens before a customer, and make him paw over a lot of trash to find what he wants, gives him a very poor impression of you in the first place? Just imagine yourself hurriedly coming in here to get some business cards printed. You ask me for samples, and I dump down in front of you a bushel of dodgers, envelopes, programmes, stationery, labels, etc., wrinkled, and soiled, and torn; how disgusted you would feel at being obliged to waste precious time in overhauling the pile, with little hope even then of finding what you wanted. A customer is always pleased to go where he is promptly waited on by some one who seems to understand his business, and who goes about it in a business-like way. It would be very little trouble to get some boxes and keep samples of each kind of work separate. A better way still is to make some books of 100 pound manila, large enough for letterheads say, and paste in samples, one book for each sort of work. This will enable you to wait upon several customers at once, for while you are helping one to pick out a billhead, you can give another a specimen book of cards to make his selection from while waiting for you. It looks business-like, too, and that counts for more than you think. Now get your memorandum book, and let's put down these items as we go along.

ITEM 1. *Keep samples neat and clean, each kind of work by itself, and where the hand can be put on them instantly.*

Do you want me to tell you frankly what strikes me most forcibly in looking over this lot of samples? It is the exceeding monotony and commonplaceness of the whole batch. There is scarcely a variation anywhere from plain, straight work, in black ink, with plain, common styles of type, and such a constant repetition of the same combinations of types and borders as to be positively wearisome to the eye. Yes, the presswork is good, and most of the composition in good taste and well-balanced, but—what a lot of "chestnuts!" Now, this fancy goods card—why didn't you improve the opportunity to sling a little style into it and get up something new? See how prettily these two words would have curved over a big initial there, and how much a little fancy line with an artistic ornament would have improved the whole. That fancy goods man is a crank, is he, and bound to kick anyhow, is he, and wouldn't appreciate such a waste of time, eh? Well, my son, don't be so sure of that! Did you ever get up for him a really fine job, to see how he would appreciate it? I don't blame him for kicking about such a card as that. Double pica black gothic and bold faced roman in a fancy goods card! Why, I would throw such a looking job in your face, if I were in his place, and I don't admit that I am a " crank " or " kicker " either. He always objects to the price, does he, and won't pay enough so you can waste any time on his work? Don't you know it takes very little more time to do a dainty, tasty piece of work than to get up such a coarse, billboard card?—takes more thought and study, of course—more attention to the possibilities of your material, and more observation of what others are doing. But until you try it you will never know the vast amount of satisfaction and substantial reward there is in such work. Just surprise this "kicker" with as nice a job as you can get up next time, and see whether it does not work a marvelous transformation in his habits in regard to fault-finding. I myself think he must be unusually good-natured to remain a customer of yours so long.

It won't do, my boy, to say you have to do work so cheap that you cannot afford to do it well. I tell you, and you might as well write this down as

ITEM 2. *No man can afford to do botch work at any price.*

Don't you suppose that Jones sees the poor work you do for Smith, and sizes you up by it, regardless of the price you got from Smith? On the other hand, if Jones sees some elegant printing you did for Smith, isn't it human nature for him to ask who did it and come to you likewise? Suppose you did not make much on Smith's job, won't it pay in the end to have it a nice one?

Men generally are not nearly so indifferent in this regard as you think. Please one of these " cheap price " men with your work, get his good will and confidence, and nine cases out of ten you can soon ask and get any reasonable price without trouble. Then it is profitable to have fine samples to show customers. When a man comes in to get a price on a job, he will not hesitate about paying a little more, even, if something in your samples strikes his fancy. Men get tired of the old things, and are constantly seeking novelties. A new line of type, a novelty in stock, a new color, or a new way of handling the old things, will always attract.

Now to be frank, what can be found in this lot of samples that is new in any respect? They all have the same stereotyped appearance — just as near alike as the difference in copy will allow. This leads to

ITEM 3. *Don't fall into ruts, but constantly strive for new effects and tastily attractive novelties.*

And then — but say, my boy, I am due at a little tea party at five, and cannot stay longer today, but will come in again soon to finish our little talk. True, we are in some sense competitors here, but there is business enough for us all, and I want to help you if I can.

PATENTED OCT. 20, 1885.   REGISTERED, No. 30,592.
6 POINT.   NONPAREIL CULDEE.   Price, $2.55.

Meeting of Boreal Association
Inauguration of Cyclone, Hurricane and Tornado Season
Preventive Measures Discussed
1234567890

9 POINT.   THREE-LINE EXCELSIOR CULDEE.   Price, $2.80.

Broadgauge & Romanesque
Printers, Stationers and Blank Book Makers
Commercial Avenue, Merchantville

12 POINT.   PICA CULDEE.   Price, $3.25.

Swindler and Company
Residence, Suburban Stone Building

18 POINT.   THREE-LINE NONPAREIL CULDEE.   Price, $3.80.

Eight Dollars
History of the Packsaddle

24 POINT.   TWO-LINE PICA CULDEE.   Price, $4.60.

Washing Machine

PATENTED APRIL 10, 1883.
9 POINT.   THREE-LINE EXCELSIOR KITCAT.   Price, $1.25.

HEDGEHOG and PORCUPINE
Salesmen · of · Quills, · Needles · and · Pointed · Instruments
1234567890

12 POINT.   PICA KITCAT.   Price, $1.55.

INDUSTRY and FRUGALITY
Household · Providers · and · Accumulators

18 POINT.   THREE-LINE NONPAREIL KITCAT.   Price, $2.45.

Weekly · CLERICAL · Meeting

24 POINT.   TWO-LINE PICA KITCAT.   Price, $2.85.

PIONEER · Business

36 POINT.   THREE-LINE PICA KITCAT.   Price, $4.15.

Round · POLE

48 POINT.   FOUR-LINE PICA KITCAT.   Price, $6.00.

BIG · Dog

PATENTED JUNE 21, 1881.
16 POINT.   TWO-LINE BREVIER OBELISK.   Price, $2.50.

SPONTANEOUS COMBUSTION
Interesting Discourses on Volcanic Pyrotechnics
1234567890

24 POINT.   TWO-LINE PICA OBELISK.   Price, $3.20.

EASTERN RAILROAD
Daylight View of Sand-Clad Plain

36 POINT.   THREE-LINE PICA OBELISK.   Price, $5.15.

NEGLECTED Monument

PATENTED JAN. 29, 1884.   REGISTERED, No. 24,025.
18 POINT.   THREE-LINE NONPAREIL MONKISH.   Price, $2.15.

GEOLOGICAL LABYRINTHS
Travels in Pennsylvania Mines and Caverns
1234567890

24 POINT.   TWO-LINE PICA MONKISH.   Price, $2.60.

TOXICOLOGICAL
Vegetable and Mineral Medicines

36 POINT.   THREE-LINE PICA MONKISH.   Price, $3.80.

Silver Mine PRODUCTS

ALL COMPLETE WITH FIGURES.

THE MACKELLAR, SMITHS & JORDAN CO. PHILADELPHIA.

SHNIEDEWEND & LEE CO., AGENTS, CHICAGO, ILL.

TYPESETTING MACHINES.

THE INLAND PRINTER has published from time to time illustrations and descriptions of the several typesetting machines produced both in Europe and America; and while giving their inventors credit for ingenuity and persistency, has, so far, been skeptical about their ability to successfully compete with the intelligent, expert compositor. The complex mechanism of some, the impossibility of correction, and the absolute infallibility of the operator, demanded by others, and the expense connected with the production of each, together with the successive failures to permanently prove their superiority, either from a mechanical or financial standpoint, over the nimble fingers of the human competitor, seemed to amply justify this opinion. But that these difficulties will eventually be surmounted, so far as their availability for straight composition is concerned, we have not the slightest doubt, and hugging the mantle of self-complacency, or presuming that the production of a perfect machine is an impossibility, are tactics with which we have no sympathy. From present indications the typesetting and distributing machines, the invention of Mr. John L. McMillan, of Ilion, New York, illustrated and explained in the present number, and now in operation in several printing establishments, are perhaps the most successful attempts yet made to solve the problem; the former setting fifty thousand and the latter distributing one hundred thousand ems per day, of ten hours, when operated by proficients. While not claiming perfection, it is asserted by experts, whose testimony is worthy of acceptance, that the trifling defects connected with their working are of a character which warrant the statement that "Skepticism must be put aside, and an examination of the McMillan machines made."

But improvement follows improvement in rapid succession. Major E. Fitzgerald Law, of London, England, has recently patented a method of electrically operating and controlling a typesetting machine, or two or more such machines, at different stations, simultaneously. According to specifications furnished, at each of the places where the matter is to be printed, a suitable typesetting machine is placed, provided with levers or keys for releasing and arranging the different letters or other characters, and for operating the printing devices. Each of these machines is comprised within an electric circuit, which also comprises a machine of a similar kind, located at the place from which the news is to be sent. The mechanism and connections are so arranged that when the typesetting machine at the transmitting office is being operated by the printer for the purpose of setting up the type or for printing at the transmitting station, the same characters will be automatically set up or printed at each of the other offices comprised within the same circuit.

And still another. Messrs. Carhart and Goodson, of Minneapolis, a short time since, conceiving the idea that *electricity* might be employed in operating a typesetting or rather a matrix-making machine, submitted their plans to Mr. C. L. Redfield, a mechanical engineer, and editor of *Wood and Iron*, and have, with his aid, succeeded in constructing a machine which, it is claimed, gives two hundred impressions per minute, or five thousand ems per hour. By it the letters are punched in a strip of cardboard, the width of the column, from which a stereotype is made in the same manner as stereotypes are made from pasteboard matrices. Punching the dies in, feeding in the cardboard, and preparing it for the next stroke, is performed by electricity. The operator simply pushes the die to its proper place, and strikes the key. This striking of the key makes an electrical connection, which throws the matrix the proper distance for the letter to be printed, and at the same time throws down a hammer upon the die, which drives it through the hole into the matrix. The sole duty of the operator is to press the key into the proper place, and throw the spaces. When the line is finished a touch upon another key moves the matrix to the beginning of another, when a movement upon a third key returns it either for leaded or solid matter, as may be desired.

What next? Verily, verily, we live in an age of wonders.

ABOUT JOB COMPOSITION.

BY A. V. HAIGHT.

A CAREFUL observer of specimens of printing from various parts of the world cannot fail to notice the characteristics which distinguish the work done in European countries from that produced in the United States. The German style, which prevails to a greater or less degree all over the continent, may always be recognized by the general use of ornamental combination borders in nearly all classes of printing, and in the peculiar management of delicate tints in their color work. It cannot be denied that the descendants of Gutenberg lead Europe, if not the world, in elaborate decorative printing. Their work has not often the freshness and originality to be found in the productions of American printers; but they do not take the risks in striking out so boldly for novel effects. Their work, however, is at least always correct, and tasteful. A piece of German composition may be distinguished almost at a glance. German printers depend more upon the use of their combination borders for effect than on the combination of type and brass rule, while our printers call into requisition every appliance of type, rule, flourishes, ornaments, and, in fact, every possible product of the typefounder and rule-maker, and every conceivable combination of those products. The German style is distinct and well known, being chiefly architectural in its general character.

It has been asked, What is the American style of printing? The wide range taken by our printers, made possible by the innumerable styles of type and its auxiliaries supplied so lavishly by the American typefoundries, would seem to make the question pertinent from one unused to seeing such versatility as is displayed in American work. The foregoing query is generally made with additional emphasis after a critical examination of a piece of overdone ornamental work from the hand of some ambitious aspirant. The superabundance of ornamental type and fanciful designs is often a great temptation to the compositor to use them too freely, and thus go beyond the bounds of good taste.

Many of the novelties from the typefoundries are short-lived, and must be used while new and fresh, else they may become hideous and offensive to the eye before the piece of work on which they are printed has served its purpose.

A great many employing printers and many good workmen offer objections to the use of brass rule for fanciful designs in the ornamental grades of printing. The principal objection is made on the ground of a waste of time in its manipulation. Brass rule is one of those conveniences which may be much abused or its use be carried to extremes in ornamentation. But the same is no less true of combination borders and typographic ornaments of every description. The idea of attempting to imitate the work of the wood engraver or pen artist with the misapplied contortions of brass rule is really absurd, as much better effects may be produced by legitimate engraving, and at less outlay of time and expense. But putting this matter aside, there are many instances where a design may be executed with brass rule in a more effective and economical manner than by any other means.

The first idea of a compositor when about to commence a piece of ornamental work should be the general form or design of the job in hand. Something definite is necessary that will make the whole appearance of the work graceful and harmonious. A sketch of the general outline being first made on paper, may be followed more or less closely, and a saving of time and material thereby effected. In this way some of the most attractive results may be accomplished, superior to any other method, and at less cost. The theory that the working of brass rule is unprofitable will apply to the use of borders and ornaments as well, if one does not know how to use it properly, and attempts too much with it. The clean, sharp impression of brass rule cannot be equaled by the work of the engraver, and in its legitimate field it has no successful rival in respect of beauty, utility and economy. With the combination border, though it may contain so many characters that a specially constructed case be necessary to hold them, the piece of work on which it is used will be judged and known by the border itself, on account of the prominence as an ornament it necessarily occupies. So every piece of work on which it appears must have a " family resemblance." A good compositor, gifted with a little imagination and some artistic ability, will take three or four faces of labor-saving rule, if necessary, and two or three simple characters, and, without cutting a single piece of rule, construct a piece of work in two or three hours that will disclose a more definite idea than may be obtained by as many days' work with an intricate and complicated combination border. Some of the simplest manipulations by one who has a good idea of construction and symmetry will often give superior results. But as good taste in this kind of composition, as well as in typographic display and in color printing, is a matter of natural ability, study and practice, the best work cannot be accomplished by everyone. No arbitrary rules may be laid down that will transform a botch into an artist. The best of materials and appliances in the hands of the former are useless.

I would not be understood as depreciating the use of combination borders altogether. Those containing innumerable small characters are the ones on which time is usually wasted. Many of the recent designs in this line are not only beautiful, but are so made that they may be composed economically, and may be used sparingly with good effect.

My own idea of tasteful composition in type, as well as in that of brass rule and combination borders, is that the styles of type, the variety of rules, and the number of combination border characters, should always be kept at a minimum. A conglomeration of different faces of type, or an assortment of various styles of ornaments and borders, are as offensive to good taste as would be the employment of a number of incongruous styles of architecture in the construction of a building.

A well-defined sense of harmony and proportion should prevail in the selection of type as well as in the general form or design of the piece of work. Not more than two or three different styles of type, as a rule, should be employed in the display of a piece of composition that is intended to exhibit correct taste. When it is impossible to conform to this idea, care should be taken to select such type as will harmonize, and to avoid violent contrast. The juxtaposition of a very light face and a very heavy face are as distasteful as the close proximity to each other of colors that clash severely.

In most cases the light or medium face letters, with plenty of white space between the lines, are the most satisfactory. A sparing use of ornaments is always advisable, and they should never be employed where they are apparently forced in for their own sake, or when they overshadow the text. Ornament should be used only to give grace to the composition proper, and should be unobtrusive, and always subordinate to the text.

Heavy face type and ornamental letters are often useful and effective in advertising, but if crowded together without sufficient white space to give proper relief, the object sought in its use is entirely defeated. In color work, where strong contrasts are desired, the heavy faces are seen at their best. A mass of heavy face type crowded together, and printed in black, though often insisted on by a customer, to give emphasis to an announcement, is always disappointing, and seldom has the desired effect. If it must be used, the effect of light and shade, which is necessary to make any piece of work attractive, must be obtained by the contrast of large and small lines and a proper amount of white space, otherwise the whole appearance of the job becomes confusing to the eye and altogether abominable.

In the more elaborate kinds of composition, curved and serpentine lines may often be introduced with good effect, but oftener they may be met with the same objection that applies to the use of unnecessary and obtrusive ornaments. Straight lines, properly balanced, generally produce a more chaste effect.

A careful study of a piece of work that is pleasing and attractive will often be more valuable as a lesson in correct composition than hours of experiment. To a discerning and an ambitious workman a careful analysis of a tasteful piece of composition will often suggest ideas that will aid an ordinary compositor to become a proficient and superior workman.

ASSYRIAN.

ORIGINAL.

6A, 12a, Great Primer. (18 Points Standard Measure.) $2.75

HOW BEAUTIFUL THE SILENT HOUR WHEN

Morning and Evening thus Sit Together, Hand in Hand Beneath

34 The Starless Sky of Midnight 12

5A, 10a, Double Pica. (24 Points Standard Measure.) $3.60

MERCHANTS PROTECTIVE ASSOCIATION

Fine Accommodations for Burglars and Safe-Blowers

3 Furnished on Short Notice 6

4A, 8a, Double Great Primer, (36 Points Standard Measure.) $5.20

CHICAGO DRIVING CLUB

Longest Drive in The United States

Grand Entertainment

3A, 6a, Four-Line Pica. (48 Points Standard Measure.) $7.15

GRAIN EXCHANGE

Latest Market Quotations

SPACES AND QUADS EXTRA. 1 LB. FONTS 38 CENTS.

UTOPIAN.

PATENTED,
AUGUST 16, 1887.

MECHANICAL PATENT
FEB. 16, 1886.

12A, 16a, Paragon. (20 Points Standard Measure.) $6.25

IDEAL PLEASURE CLUB

Annual Reception at The Chickering Temple of Music

12 Hendricks, Allen and Co. 34

6A, 11a, Double English. (28 Points Standard Measure.) $7.75

BANK OF CHICAGO

Dealers in County and Railroad Bonds

4 Foreign Letters of Credit 6

5A, 8a, Double Great Primer. (36 Points Standard Measure.) $9.00

SEATING

2 Western Cotton Exchange 3

4A, 5a, Four-Line Pica. (48 Points Standard Measure.) $9.50

HOLIDAY

The Chicago Yacht Club

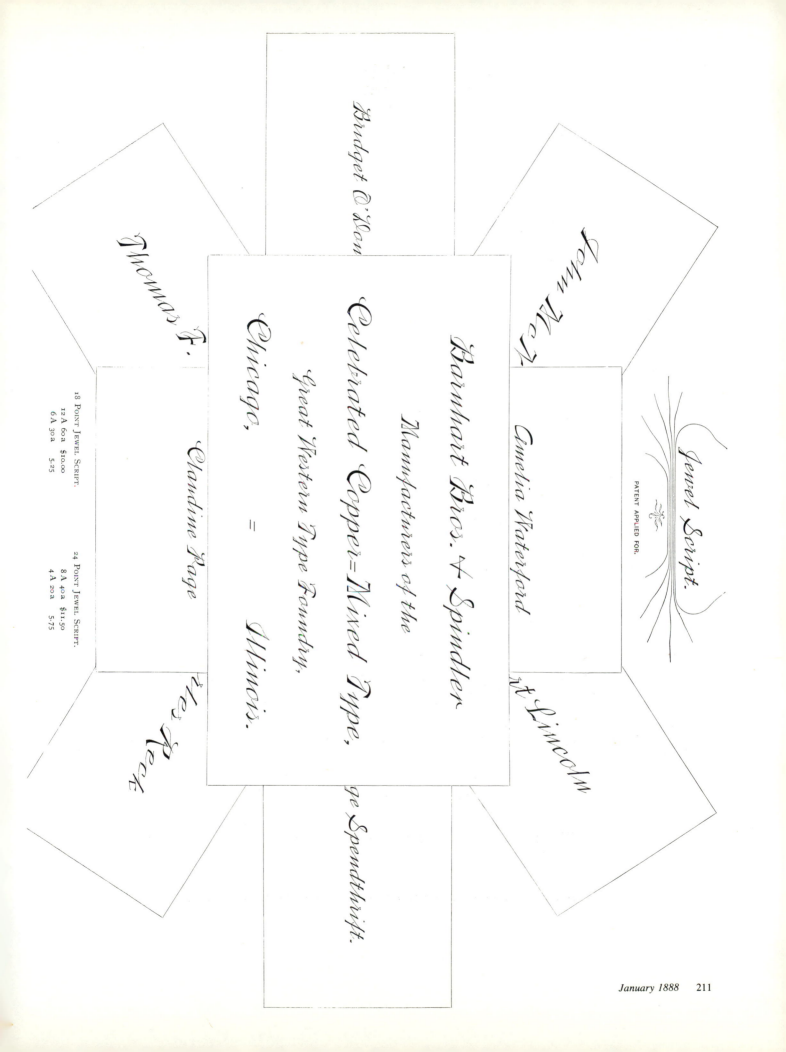

Cadence Specimen.

PATENT APPLIED FOR.

25 a 10 A   12 POINT CADENCE $2 80

GREAT PORTION OF THE FINANCIAL DISASTERS OF THE WORLD

Grow Out of Speculation and the Effects of the Practice are Quite as Apparent in Good as Bad

TIMES NO SOONER DO THE TIMES POINT

345 To an Improvement in Business than a Great Number of People Begin to cast 678

20 a 8 A   18 POINT CADENCE $3 80

MUGWUMPERY IN THE ASCENDENCY THIS YEAR

Rousing Majorities For All Political Organizations in The State of Maine

A GROUND HOG CASE SURELY

34 What is Home in Country Without a Sister or Mother 56

14 a 6 A   24 POINT CADENCE $4 95

THE NATIONAL CONVENTION OF

The Employing Printers was held at Chicago the Eighteenth

DAY OF LAST OCTOBER

32 Eighteen Hundred and Eighty Seven 75

Manufactured by BARNHART BROS. & SPINDLER, Chicago, Ill.

CHALLENGE SPECIMENS.

PATENT APPLIED FOR.

25 A 40 a   6 POINT CHALLENGE $3 25

BELIEVING AN OLD STYLE ITALIC
Extended Useful we Submit This Improved Face
Suitable for all Classes of Fine Job
2345 Printing 6789

20 A 30 a   9 POINT CHALLENGE $3 75

COPPER-MIXED TYPE
From Great Western Type Foundry
115 Fifth Avenue 117

15 A 25 a   12 POINT CHALLENGE $4 25

YOUNG AND OLD
The Chicago Drug Clerk
8 Association 6

10 A 15 a   18 POINT CHALLENGE $4 50

AIR-SPRING
Standard Presses
Optimus 4

8 A 12 a   24 POINT CHALLENGE $5 75

NORTH SIDE CABLE
Supposed to be in Working Order
3 About October 5

6 A 10 a   36 POINT CHALLENGE $7 00

JOB PRINTERS
Diamond Paper Cutter 6

48 POINT CHALLENGE

HUGE DIN
Domes Homes 3

Manufactured by BARNHART BROS. & SPINDLER, Chicago, Ill.

PATENT APPLIED FOR.

20 A   10 POINT CAPRICE $1 60

SWEET MEMORIES
LITTLE ÷ TOM ÷ GREEN ÷ IN ÷ LUCK
34 =BANK CASHIER= 56

15 A   12 POINT CAPRICE $1 65

SWEET MAIDEN
THE CHESTNUT BELLE
23 =BLUE ÷ ROOM= 45

10 A   18 POINT CAPRICE $2 40

STORMS ÷ UPON ÷ THE ÷ OCEANS
314 =KENTUCKY= 156

8 A   24 POINT CAPRICE $3 30

COUNTY ÷ COURT ÷ CLERK
79 =CASES= 28

6 A   30 POINT CAPRICE $4 10

CHESTNUT ÷ BELLS
3 =GREAT= 5

5 A   36 POINT CAPRICE $4 40

COURT ÷ HOUSE 8

4 A   48 POINT CAPRICE $7 30

CHICAGO ÷ 5

THIS SERIES LINES AT TOP AND BOTTOM.

Manufactured by BARNHART BROS. & SPINDLER, Chicago, Ill.

COSMOPOLITAN.

PATENTED BY JAMES CONNER'S SONS, NEW YORK

BREVIER COSMOPOLITAN WILL BE SUPPLIED ON OUR OLD BODY, IF REQUIRED.   OTHER SIZES ON THE POINT SYSTEM ONLY.

---

20 A 75 a,   8 POINT—BREVIER—COSMOPOLITAN. $3.15

Under a Spreading Chestnut Tree the Village Smithy Stands;

The smith, a mighty man is he, with large and sinewy hands; and the muscles of his brawny arms, are

Strong as iron bands. His hair is crisp, and black,

THE OLD VILLAGE BLACKSMITH OF NEW ENGLAND'S HOMESTEAD GROUND.

His brow is wet with honest sweat; he earns whate'er he can,

And looks the whole world in the face, for he owes not any man.

15 A 50 a,   10 POINT COSMOPOLITAN. $3.10

Week in, and out, from Morn till Night, You can hear his

Bellows blow; you can hear him swing his heavy sledge, with measured beat, and slow

Like a sexton ringing the village bell,

WHEN THE SUMMER EVENING SUN IS SINKING LOW

12345 Singing in the old church choir. 67890

15 A 40 a,   12 POINT COSMOPOLITAN. $3.15

Seventh Annual Tuesday Evening Twilight Coterie.

Large Quantities of Refreshments.   Very Entertaining Concert Program

THE FALCON ASSEMBLAGE OF VETERAN SOLDIERS.

Scotch and Irish Field Sports.

10 A 25 a,   18 POINT COSMOPOLITAN. $4.10

National Rowing Club Association.

White Winged Yachts.   Cruise of the Atalanta

TUXEDOR BOULEVARD.

8 A 15 a,   24 POINT COSMOPOLITAN. $4.40

Monmouth Park Horse Races.

Great Steeple Chase. Over High Hedges.

ARION JOCKEY CLUB.

ILLINOIS TYPE FOUNDING CO., 202 S. CLARK STREET, CHICAGO.

THE McMILLAN COMPOSING AND DISTRIBUTING MACHINES.

The illustrations herewith presented are those of the typesetting and distributing machines invented by Mr. John Loudon McMillan, of Ilion, New York, a reference to which has previously appeared in the columns of THE INLAND PRINTER. After years of patient experimenting and labor, its inventor has succeeded in producing a machine which can set on an average of 50,000 ems per day. We are indebted to the *Paper World* for the following detailed description of the same:

Each character used in the setting machine is provided with a number of cases especially adapted to it, and the types stand in these cases side by side. The types are separated into three general classes, thick, medium and thin letters. The cases are held in the machine in a substantially horizontal position, as seen in the upper right part of the cut, in a compact group of superposed tiers, and discharge their types into subordinate races inclined from the perpendicular at an angle of 10 degrees, and the types gravitate with friction only on one narrow side, into a main vertical race in the center of the case frame. At the foot of the main race either a revolving eccentric operated by power, or a reciprocating bunter operated by the key board, feeds the letters forward to the justifier. The letters used more frequently are placed in the cases near the bottom.

The key board has eighty-four keys and looks like the key board of a type-writer. When the operator depresses a key it acts through the medium of a lever and bell crank on an ejecting finger that swings on pivots, and carries the first type of its case through a lateral slot of the case into the race, where it gravitates to the line below where it is bunted forward, moving the whole line toward the justifier. Near the foot of the main race a pendulous gate is suspended, and it acts uniformly on every type that passes it and prevents its rebounding and striking with such force as to upset at the heel, and also keeps it from canting around and entering the line inverted or edgewise.

The set up matter advances toward the justifier with a three em space between the words, an em quad at the end of the sentence, two em quads between the last word of a paragraph and the first word of the following paragraph. The justifier, who is a man, has a rule of suitable length, with an abutment at one end, and cuts the advancing line between the words or syllables, and draws it between two justifying posts that correspond to the sides of a hand compositor's stick, and puts in the various spaces required.

When a line is spaced, he depresses a lever with his foot and the line is pushed on to an ordinary galley. The line that is forming is long enough to permit the cutting of several lines of the required measure by the justifier, so that any irregularity on the part of either workman does not retard the other.

Just in front of the operator a long case containing either small capitals or italics is placed so that he may quickly deposit any letter not in the machine in the line of set up type at his right. Over 99 per cent of the letters used in ordinary composition, however, are held in the machine. The alignment of work done by this machine is just as perfect as that of hand setting.

Mr. McMillan's distributer is likewise a great mechanical achievement. This consists in a revolving horizontal disk, in the upper face of which are a large number of radial channels, each of which is adapted to receiving a line of type. The disk is surrounded by a ring, having a greater number of channels for receiving the distributed type, and forms a support for one end of the cases which make continuations of said channels. Between the channels of the disk, which we shall denominate distributing channels, and the channels of the ring which we shall denominate receiving channels, are two vertically movable feeling pins, a pair for each distributing channel, having arms that extend over the edge of the said distributing channel, and preventing the escape of the type until the position of the feeling pins registers with the nicks of the type or types next to the receiving ring, where a spring, pressing from behind, forces them into their receiving channel. Each distributing channel has a follower, which is pressed toward the periphery of the disk by a spring; the follower has an arm that projects above the channel, so it may be pressed back by the hand of the attendant to admit a line of type. The disk has a circumferential depression of two-hundreths of an inch, and the feeling pins travel in this depression, and thus prevent the type from rubbing against the ring as the disk revolves. The cases used in the machine are those used in the typesetting machines, and are removed when filled and fresh ones supplied without stopping the machine.

Each character separated by the machine has its own peculiar nicks, and all the characters of the same denomination have the same nicks. These nicks exactly correspond to the position of the feeling pins, and the spring pressure from behind forces the types into the receiving channels. The machine requires an attendant to feed the lines to it

MCMILLAN TYPESETTING MACHINE.

and to remove the filled cases, and both operations are done without stopping the machine. The number of receiving channels considerably outnumber the variety of letters and characters used, for the purpose of getting more rapid distribution. It is calculated that one letter passes out from the revolving disk to every eighteen receiving channels passed, and to see the tiny bits of unconscious metal flash from one channel to another seems strange enough. The capacity of the machine is about one hundred thousand ems a day. The machine is automatic and noiseless in its operation, does not wear the type, will handle type that has " caked," is easily accessible, and is not subject to derangement. A nicking machine is also devised for preparing ordinary foundry type for the distributers, and it has a capacity of about one thousand ordinary letters at a single cut, and is capable of an adjustment of one-thousandth of an inch.

McMILLAN TYPE-DISTRIBUTING MACHINE.

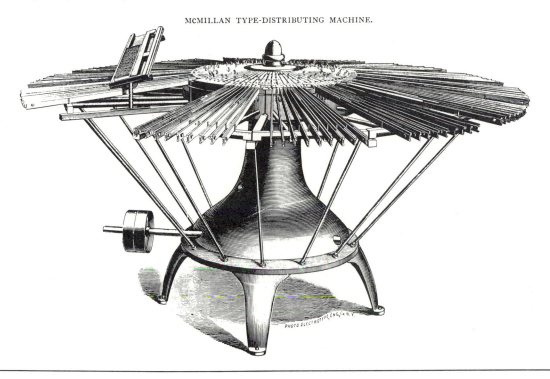

JOHN WATTS, THE FIRST AMERICAN STEREO-TYPER.

Current histories of the introduction of stereotyping in America state that John Watts, the first American stereoper, after making the plates for the larger catechism, abandoned the art. His first attempt is thus described by Dr. John W. Francis: " I well remember the anxious John Watts when he showed me his first undertaking in this branch of labor in New York, just forty years ago. It was a copy of the larger cate-chism, the one I now hold in my hand. Notwithstanding the doubts of many, he felt confident of its ultimate success, yet suffered by hope deferred." Dr. Francis uttered this in 1852, and forty years back was in 1812. The catechism was ready the next year, and at about the same time David Bruce also produced his first work. To learn how to make plates he had made a journey to England, and had been courteously treated by Lord Stanhope, who, however, refused to tell him how to proceed, and Bruce was obliged to pay a sum of money to a workman to acquire the secret. This man, however, knew but very little about it, and in the end Bruce was obliged to reinvent the processes.

Until lately this has been all that was known about Watts. Why he should have abandoned a discovery that seemed to promise so much and why he first turned his attention to it were inscrutable mysteries. Light has come upon this from a German source, and this, an attentive examination of the few facts we already know, gives an explanation as good as we can probably ever reach. John Watts was an Englishman, who first made his appearance in this city in the year 1809. He must have had a little money, for he was located as a printer at 51 Murray street, in the directory of that year, and in 1810 he blossomed forth as " *imprimeur et agent pour mm. les étrangers*" (printer and agent for foreigners). The mm. are thus printed, instead of the customary way with capitals, for Longworth, the proprietor of the directory, had a great aversion to their use. In 1812 we find him making plates, concerning which he had most likely learned something either in England or France. As he understood the French language, it is probable that he

had spent some time there, and the system of Didot being older than that of Stanhope he might have had an opportunity to hear about his processes, or possibly he might have acquired knowledge in both countries. It is clear, however, that this understanding was only theoretical, for a long time elapsed between the beginning of his experi-ments and the completion of a series of plates. In 1815 his stereotype foundry was at 154 Broadway, while his house was in Broome street, near the present Centre Market. Tradition asserts that it was in the latter place his experiments were made.

In 1816 he disappeared from the directory, but it is known that he disposed of his foundry to B. & J. Collins, sons of the worthy Isaac Collins, the Quaker. They carried it on for a dozen years, of course, with the improvements which experience would suggest. The oldest stereotypers, next to the four mentioned, were Lawrence Johnson, Thomas B. Smith and Hammond Wallis, who are said to have been three runaway apprentices from England. They came here in 1819, and all turned out men of mark. The earliest Americans to learn the art were Dill and Chandler.

What became of Watts after this? This question is answered in Meyer's " Handbuch der Stereotypie," printed in Brunswick in 1838. It says that in the year 1819 the Stanhope system, modified in practice by the North Americans, John Watts and his nephew, William Watts, was introduced into the Austrian kingdom by them, and they began a foundry in connection with the University printing office in Vienna. In March, 1822, twenty-eight works had already been stereotyped, and by instruction there received the principal German printers, typefounders and booksellers learned the methods which they subsequently practiced in their own towns. They included Tauchnitz in Leipsic, Brönner in Frankfort, Meisner in Hamburg, and Enschede in Holland. No further information is to be had of him, except that he was aided in his original experiments by Fay, the father of Theodore S. Fay, a well-known man of letters of the last generation, who was once Minister to Switzerland. — *The American Bookmaker.*

A REPRESENTATIVE ESTABLISHMENT.

THE MACKELLAR, SMITHS & JORDAN COMPANY.

THIS well-known typefounding and electrotyping establishment is located at 606 to 614 Sansom street, Philadelphia, the home of the art typographic in the new world. It was here that Benjamin Franklin began that career of usefulness that has rendered his name imperishable, and it is here that the highest achievements in the above line have been recorded. No historical review of the rise and progress of the printing, publishing and typographic interests of this city would be complete without making prominent mention of that great and enterprising corporation, " The MacKellar, Smiths & Jordan Company," whose immense typefoundry is within a few years of its centennial anniversary. This extensive business dates back to 1796, when Messrs. Binny and Ronaldson entered the field in response to the growing demand for printing material, due to the increased activity and spirit of enterprise manifested in the young republic. In 1815 Mr. Binny retired, and Mr. Ronaldson was afterward, in 1833, succeeded by his brother, Mr. Richard Ronaldson, who was soon after succeeded by Messrs. Johnson & Smith. The new firm brought to bear special qualifications, and Mr. Johnson established a stereotype foundry that was the most reliable and popular in the city. This was succeeded by the present electrotype foundry which has grown to large proportions. The business grew apace, and in 1845, on the retirement of Mr. Smith, Mr. Johnson formed a co-partnership with Mr. Thomas MacKellar and Messrs. John F. and Richard Smith (sons of the former partner) under the familiar name of " L. Johnson & Co." The progress made by the house as thus constituted was remarkably rapid and permanent, Mr. MacKellar being a practical young printer, who since 1833 had been the efficient foreman of the stereotype foundry. Mr. Johnson died in 1860, concluding a long and honorable career in the business world. Mr. MacKellar, in conjunction with the Messrs. Smith and Mr. Peter A. Jordan, continued the business under the widely celebrated name and style of MacKellar, Smiths & Jordan, their establishment being given the appropriate title of " The Johnson Typefoundry," in memory of their former associate. Shortly afterward, under the editorship of Mr. MacKellar, the house issued a handsomely gotten-up specimen book, far superior to anything of the kind ever attempted before, and marking an epoch in the typographic art. In 1867 the firm secured possession of the large adjoining building known as the Sansom Street Hall, and refitted every department of the entire establishment with the latest improved machinery and appliances.

In February, 1885, the MacKellar, Smiths & Jordan Company was incorporated under the laws of the state of Pennsylvania. The officers are as follows : President, Mr. Thomas MacKellar ; vice-president, Mr. Richard Smith ; treasurer, Mr. John F. Smith ; secretary, Mr. William B. MacKellar ; and assistant secretary, Mr. G. Frederick Jordan. The executive thus formed has no equal elsewhere as regards resources, facilities and experience at command in the line of typefounding, and the immense establishment stands prominently in the fore-

ground, as regards all standard fonts of type, in addition to new styles of ornamental and fancy type and the best of material generally. The foundry is one of the largest, and the best equipped on the continent. A thorough system of organization pervades every department ; skilled experts are in personal charge of all the processes of manufacture. The most perfect type-casting machines in the world are built on the premises specially for the company's work, while electrotyping is carried on upon the most extensive scale and with results the most satisfactory to the trade. The company carries the largest stock of fonts of all sorts of type, labor-saving rules of all sizes, fixtures and material, etc., to be found in their line, while their vast accumulation of thousands of matrices and molds renders them fully prepared to promptly meet all orders or any special demand that arises. From his earliest connection with this industry Mr. MacKellar at every stage left an impress indicative of his superior talents and force of character. He is a successful author and editor, and his work, " MacKellar's American Printer," has passed its sixteenth edition, and is the standard work of reference. His high scientific attainments have been devoted to the advancement of the typographic art. Mr. MacKellar has ever retained the confidence and esteem of our leading financial circles, and is interested in many leading institutions, being a director of the Guarantee Trust Company, and of the Girard and Reliance Fire Insurance Companies. He has done much for the introduction and elevation of art to the industrial realms of the " art preservative of all arts." Mr. Richard Smith, the company's vice-president, is one of the most prominent members of typefounding circles in the United States. He received a careful practical training not only in this foundry, but in one of the leading European establishments. His lengthy identification with this industry, and his high attainments render him peculiarly well qualified to take the vice-presidential chair and perform the duties incumbent upon him. The company's treasurer, Mr. John F. Smith, has likewise been long and intimately identified with the business, and is universally esteemed. He has been a successful financier independent of his legitimate business, and much of his surplus he has devoted to charitable objects. Mr. Smith is an influential member of financial circles, and among other positions held by him, is that of a director of the Bank of the Republic. Mr. William B. MacKellar, the company's secretary, is unusually well qualified to fill this important executive position, and is a young business man of energy. In addition to the official position occupied by him, he has for several years edited the elegant trade journal of the house, the *Typographic Advertiser*. He is also the treasurer of the Bedford Street Mission, of Philadelphia. Mr. G. Frederick Jordan, the assistant secretary, ably performs the duties incumbent upon him, and is efficient and active. Mr. Jordan also superintends the purchasing of the various metals and material used in the products of the foundry. The control of the establishment is today left largely in the hands of the two latter gentlemen. The company holds an honored position at the head of an industry of worldwide importance, and is in every sense of the word a standing source of credit.

——OFFICE OF——

✠ CENTRAL ✠ TYPE ✠ FOUNDRY ✠

Corner Fourth & Elm Streets,

(DICTATED.)   ST. LOUIS, Mo. February 7th,   188 8

TO PRINTERS AND PUBLISHERS.

Dear Sirs:—

It is now four and a half years since we brought out the style of type known as ''Type-Writer.'' It was originated by the Central Type Foundry, and has had a larger sale than any face ever before produced. It was suggested to us by Mr. J. C. Blair, manufacturing stationer,~~a~~ of Huntingdon, Pa., one of the most progressive men in the country.

After this type came into general use, the founders in different parts of the country began displaying their usual enterprise by copying and imitating the face. Their doing so, however, has had little effect upon the demand for our type, printers preferring the original face, cast with Copper Alloy (guaranteed to be the most durable metal in the world), to the clumsy imitations cast with cheaper and comparatively worthless metal used by ~~the~~ several type founders.

We take much pleasure now in presenting this specimen of our new 12-Point (Standard Pica) Earle Type-Writer face, a correct imitation of the most perfect type-writer work. It is put up in convenient fonts, 108a 20A, at $7.50 per font, and is cast with our Celebrated Copper Alloy Metal. Spaces of the same thickness as the characters go with each font. Address orders to us, or to any type foundry or dealer in printing material in the country.   Respectfully,

CENTRAL TYPE FOUNDRY,

J. A. St. John
Tres. & Mgr.

P. S.——Send for Specimen Sheets of our novelties adapted for artistic printing.

18a 6A, including Quads and Spaces, $9.00   30-POINT OLD STYLE SCRIPT.   Lower Case alone, $4.50 ; Caps alone, $4.50
Five-line Nonpareil.

Masterly Execution by American Engravers
Superior Designers and Workmen, 25

24a 8A, including Quads and Spaces, $6.00   18-POINT OLD STYLE SCRIPT.   Lower case alone, $3.00 ; Caps alone, $3.00
Three-line Nonpareil.

Rudimentary Lessons Given in Architectural and Inventors' Drawing
Specifications and Estimates Made to Order, 278

Greeting to Artistic Job Printers:—

Sirs: Since the popularity of Old Style effects in news, book and jobbing type designs is by no means on the wane, we felt encouraged to carry out the idea in a Script face, which has resulted in the presentation of this Novelty for the favorable consideration of the craft.—

We have no doubt that our friends will be delighted at once with its many excellent qualities, which we now allow to speak for themselves, and that they will give it the same generous welcome as that which they have so kindly extended to our other original and patented designs in types for artistic printing.— Its unique character and its great durability are features especially noteworthy. Yours truly,

Central Type Foundry.—

NOTE.— Quads and Spaces go with the Lower Case fonts ; Figures and Points with the Cap fonts.

NEW YORK—63 & 65 Beekman St.
And 62 & 64 Gold Street.

CHICAGO—154 Monroe Street,
Chas. B. Ross, Manager.

10 A   PICA SPREAD - 12 POINT. $1 75

SIT BENEATH
❋ THE ❖ SPREADING ❖ BRANCHES ❋
OF THE OAK 678

18 A   BREVIER SPREAD——OR ON 8 POINT. $2 00

SPREAD THE NEWS
❋ WHILE ❖ THOUGHTS ❖ DRIFT ❋
A SHIP SPREADING SAILS
EXTENDED 678

14 A   LONG PRIMER SPREAD——OR ON 10 POINT. $1 85

ALL THE WORLD
SPREAD ❖ BEFORE ❖ YOU
DRIVE IN AND WIN
ALL HANDS 78

8 A   TWO LINE BREVIER SPREAD——OR ON 16 POINT. $2 25

THE SPREAD TYPE
❋ GAZE ❖ WITH ❖ ADMIRATION ❋
MERIT 678

6 A   TWO LINE PICA SPREAD—21 POINT. $3 75

THE WORLD
SPREADING ❖ FAME
TRUE 678

5 A   TWO LINE ENGLISH SPREAD——OR ON 28 POINT. $5 00

GOLDEN ❖ HARBOR
ANGEL 678

4 A   THREE LINE PICA SPREAD—36 POINT. $6 00

Cabinet ◎ Series.

PATENT APPLIED FOR.

10 A 20 a   12 POINT CABINET $3 20

FINE ART PRINTERS

Will Appreciate this Handsome Series

2345 ◎ 6789

6 A 14 a   18 POINT CABINET $3 75

THE ADAMS

Fire Insurance Companies

345 ◎ 678

◎ ◎ Western Agents for Babcock Air-Spring Presses. ◎ ◎

Barnhart Bros. & Spindler,

Superior ◎ Copper-Mixed ◎ Type,

Great Western Type Foundry,

115 Fifth Ave.

Chicago, Ill.

5 A 10 a   24 POINT CABINET $4 50

BOARD ◎ OF ◎ TRADE

American Banks   Trust Corporations

345 ◎ Speculators ◎ 678

20 A   6-POINT—NONPAREIL $2 75   20 A   8-POINT—BREVIER $3 70

OPENING OF SEASON   ANNUAL CRUISE

OYSTERS ON HALF SHELL   OUR IRON CLAD SHIP

98   BLUE POINTS   39   52   CAPE HORN   62

20 A   10-POINT—LONG PRIMER $4 85

MODERN DESIGNS

PRODUCED BY AMERICAN ARTISTS

43   UNIQUE AND ELEGANT   58

4 A   36 POINT—THREE-LINE PICA $6 75

2 SPECIMEN 3

10 A   12-POINT—PICA $4 05

CAMP SHERIDAN

INTERNATIONAL SQUADRON

25   CHICAGO   68

8 A $5 00   18-POINT—THREE-LINE NONPAREIL   .5 A 8 a No. 2—$5 50

ANNUAL REUNIONS

65   Pork and Beans   65

4 A   48-POINT—FOUR-LINE PICA $10 00

8 BANKED 6

6 A   24-POINT—TWO-LINE PICA $5 65

MODERN HUNTER
35   LESSON   28

ILLINOIS TYPE FOUNDING CO., 202 S. CLARK STREET, CHICAGO.

THE FRASER COMPOSING AND DISTRIBUTING MACHINES.

These machines, correct illustrations of which are herewith presented, have been thoroughly tested, and have been for several years in constant use on all kinds of work, in the well-known printing establishment of Neill & Co., Edinburgh, government book printers for Scotland. They have also been tried in several offices throughout Great Britain

THE FRASER TYPE COMPOSING MACHINE.

and her colonies. They are so constructed as to set and distribute ordinary fonts of body type — no special nicking or adaptation of the

THE FRASER DISTRIBUTING MACHINE.

same being required. Either machine occupies very little floor space, and both can be put down without delay in any position, and no power or gearing is required for their working. Like other semi-automatic machines, the limit of speed is governed by the rate at which the keys can be pressed. Each machine is made to set or distribute two or four sizes of type — small pica to minion. The letters most in use are arranged within a few inches of each other, and the types are released with the greatest rapidity, a fairly expert operator having no difficulty in attaining a rate of ten or twelve thousand or more types per hour. The matter set is at once spaced out and finished in the machine, or it may be set in continuous line by one operator, while another spaces it out into lines of the required width. The mechanism is simple and ingenious, and it is claimed can only be put out of order by purposed ill treatment.

The distributing machine is the counterpart of the composing machine, and with it the types are distributed direct from the page or column as printed.

PRINTERS' EYESIGHT.

BY S. K. PARKER.

I DO not remember ever having seen anything in print regarding printers' eyesight; but I think this would be a fruitful and profitable topic for discussion and relation of experience by the craft. No one can deny that the most important "tool" (if the term is applicable) the printer works with is his optical apparatus. Probably no other trade or occupation uses artificial light, or a poor supply of daylight, to a greater extent than the printer, and to no other is light of greater importance. The effect upon the eyes of the craft at large must necessarily be of great consequence and interest. My observation is that the use of spectacles by printers is on the increase.

The poor gaslight, so common in printing offices, is usually owing to the building not being supplied with sufficiently large pipes. Most offices are located in buildings that were never designed for that use, and a large number of burners are tacked on to a pipe intended to supply but a few; and as business increases the evil multiplies itself. It is a false economy to have poor light, whatever the source may be, as time cannot be so well utilized. Good daylight is the cheapest to the employer, and the most satisfactory to the employé, both as to conserving his precious eyesight and facility of working.

Color blindness is a condition which railroad men consider a fatal defect in those of their employés who are in any way connected with their motive power. It is reasonable to presume that this condition exists to a greater or less extent among printers. A great many abortions of color work may perhaps thus be accounted for.

I believe that what may be termed "size blindness" also exists among us. Many compositors seem unable to distinguish between four and five em spaces, and sling them in indiscriminately. I know of a young man, who was an apprentice several years ago, who could not (and he acknowledged the fact) discern the difference between a four and a five em piece of metal furniture without actual measurement. The last I heard of this young man he was running a barber shop successfully.

In addition to the experiences of the craft which this communication may draw out, I would respectfully offer the suggestion that THE INLAND PRINTER employ a competent person to go over the ground, from the scientific and professional point of view, and publish the results.

RUNIC CONDENSED.
IMPROVED SERIES.

18A, 36a,　　Long Primer.　(10 Points Standard Measure.)　　$1.95

INTERNAL WITH REGARD TO A COUNTRY
Pertaining to the Intermediate State, between Death
And every Spirit's Folded Bloom 234

12A, 24a,　　　Pica.　(12 Points Standard Measure.)　　$1.80

RESUMPTION OF TRAVEL IN EUROPE
Airless Dungeon, nor Strong Links of Iron
Retentive to the Strength 567

10A, 20a,　　English.　(14 Points Standard Measure.)　　$2.05

SEE THE MORNING MEADOWS
Why didst thou promise such a day

8A, 16a,　　Great Primer.　(18 Points Standard Measure.)　　$2.60

NO EVIL ENTERS HERE
Inscriptions on a Monument

6A, 12a,　　　　Double Small Pica.　(22 Points Standard Measure.)　　$2.80

BE BOWED IN MEEKNESS
6 Deep Contentment in his Calm Eyes Shone 4

5A, 10a,　　　　Double English.　(28 Points Standard Measure.)　　$3.40

MUSIC AROUND ME STEALING
Learn the New and Holy Song of Peace

4A, 8a,　　　　Double Paragon.　(40 Points Standard Measure.)　　$4.60

Popular WATERING Places

3A, 6a,　　　　Four-Line Pica.　(48 Points Standard Measure.)　　$6.10

2 From STORMY North 7

3A, 5a,　　　　Five-Line Pica.　(60 Point Standard Measure.)　　$8.25

Fresh BROOK Trout

SPACES AND QUADS EXTRA.　I LB. FONTS AT ROMAN RATES.

PUNCH-CUTTING.

BY JOHN WEST.

MUCH has been said and written in regard to punch-cutting matrices from punches and electrotype matrices, and so many have exhausted their ideas, that little remains for the writer to discuss in relation thereto. Some years ago punch-cutting was done in a manner that left very heavy bevels on each side, which frequently gave the type-rubbers an opportunity to give vent to their surcharged feelings in language far from choice, on account of the heavy shoulders that had to be rubbed off. At the present time there are a few cutters who use the counter in place of the graver, and it is therefore an impossibility to have every one standing perpendicular with the square body of the steel, a result which gives the matrix-fitter an extra amount of labor to make it straight. I mention these points to show where the improvement in punch cutting of the present day comes in, and to which I propose to refer to at length in the present article.

I will take up first the well-worn subject of electrotype matrices. Those who cannot procure any others are always loud in their praise, and ofttimes give them more credit than electrotype matrices deserve. I do not mean by this to condemn them, by any means; because in large jobwork they answer very well, as they are less trouble to fit, and there is not such a wear and tear on them as on book or body type in general; but who can say that an electrotype body-letter matrix can compare with the hard copper punch matrix that can be produced today. And when it comes to the production of these matrices the question arises, which is the cheapest? I answer, the punch matrix. Take, for example, the cost of an original electrotype matrix, embracing the cutting of the type on metal, routing out the brass, putting up the forms, brass, attention to the form while in the battery, etc., and it figures up quite a little sum; and when the metal-cut type is taken from the battery, the chances are almost even that the original is lost forever. The hard metal at present used by the typefounders soon plays havoc with an electrotype matrix. I feel certain that no typefounder dare contradict me in saying that he does not use extremely hard metal when an electrotype matrix is employed. In fact one of the main disadvantages of an electrotype matrix is that, as a rule, it will give out in the midst of a hurried order, and when such is the case it takes four or more days before another one can be reproduced, whereas, if a steel punch is at hand, a new matrix on the old system can be furnished in less than an hour, and on the new system in less than fifteen minutes.

But some will say that the cost of fitting punch drives is more expensive than that of fitting electrotype matrices. Well, if they refer to the old system, their statement is correct, but if to the new system, the tables are turned entirely, and the reason is easily given. Under the old system, in order to cut a punch, a piece of steel, about two inches long, was used, and the letter was drawn and cut on the face of this piece of steel irrespective of its position, its alignment being left to the fitter. When this punch was finished and ready for driving it was placed in a half

square clamp, held by a screw, and then driven home. If a large punch, it would distort the copper very much, which gave the fitter considerable work. The new system introduced by my father, James West, and by myself, prevents this distortion of the copper, while the risk of breaking the punch is lessened seventy-five per cent, even when using the hardest copper. To make our new system plain to all, our steel punches are cut as if they came from a type-casting machine, being made of steel in place of metal. The alignment is perfect all through, both in height and width, and perfectly straight on the sides, so that the type cast from the matrices made from these punches are non-rubbing. When the punches are finished they are hardened by a new system which prevents any shrinkage or throwing the punch out of alignment, which is a very important feature.

Now, the steel punch is placed in a specially constructed machine; the copper, as hard as can be procured, is put in a steel box, and is sawed straight on the sides and end. The punch is then placed in position, and in order that the line will be correct and true to one side, a gauge regulates the depth. When the first punch is adjusted it answers for the entire font of punches. What is the result? The matrix only requires turning on one side, and a few rubs on the face, and it is finished, as there is no bend to the copper. So far the only typefounding establishments which have availed themselves of the advantage of this new system are the Union Typefoundry, with which the writer is now connected, and, by special arrangement, Barnhart Bros. & Spindler.

The question may be asked, "Do these punches cost much in excess of the old system?" The answer is, the extra cost is only a matter of a few cents, while the copper used is so hard that the matrices will stand the roughest usage for years. I believe no fair minded typefounder will object to the claim that such a matrix is far in advance of any electrotype matrix, both in matter of cost and rapidity of production.

THE UNION TYPE FOUNDRY OF OMAHA.

A VALUABLE ACQUISITION.

The Union Type Foundry of Omaha, with its customary enterprise and push, has just concluded a deal whereby Mr. H. P. Hallock, for the past three years Marder, Luse & Co's representative in the West, and prior to that connected with Messrs. Golding & Co., Boston, Massachusetts, has purchased an interest in its business, and will hereafter take an active part in the management of the Pioneer Printers' Supply Warehouse west of Chicago.

We have known Mr. Hallock personally ever since his advent in the West, and have always found him to be an energetic gentleman; and we feel satisfied success will attend him in his new field of labor.

We understand it is the intention of this establishment to carry a full line of Marder, Luse & Co's type, which will certainly prove beneficial to the printers of the West, and proves that it is alive to their interests, and is determined to place itself in such a position that all orders intrusted to it will receive prompt attention. Controlled by young, wide-awake, pushing, reliable men, there is no reason why it cannot score a magnificent success.

P. S.—Since the above was written the name has been changed from the "Union" to the "Omaha" Type Foundry.

MacKellar, Smiths & Jordan Co.

Nos. 606=614 Sansom Street,

Philadelphia,   May 3,   1888.

To the Trade.

Through courtesy of the manufacturers of the Remington Standard Type-Writer, we are permitted to present in type (from ~~a~~ fac-simile impressions furnished by them) ~~and~~ an exact counterpart of the type-writing of their No. 2 machine.

As the above Type-Writer has the approval of business people in general, and as the number in use far exceeds ~~the~~ those of any other make, the printing craft will doubtless avail itself of the style of type herewith presented as being the latest and correct imitation of the type-writing of ~~the~~ that popular machine.

The characters are of ~~a~~ uniform thickness, and but one space is required for justifying. We have designated this face as ~~the~~ Pica "STANDARD TYPE-WRITER." The founts are made up as follows:

        20 A, 100 a, complete, _ _ Price, $7.45

        100 a, separately, _ _ _ _   "   5.95

This, as well as all of our type productions, is made from the highest known grade of type-metal.

The MacKellar, Smiths & Jordan Co.

                Type Founders and Electrotypers.

FINE TYPE.

PATENTED MAY 18 '87 — ILL. WESTERN TYPE FDRY CHICAGO

30a 20A   6 POINT EMERALD No. 3 $2 20

BOOKS OF KNOWLEDGE
Very Entrancing Musical Gems by Beethoven
78 On the Mountain Far and Wide 67

25a 15 A $2 25   8 POINT EMERALD No. 3   15 A $0 85

LOT OF STEEL PENS
That Were Sold at Wholesale Bought
25 At Fabulous Prices 38

18a 12 A $2 30   10 POINT EMERALD No. 3   12 A $0 95

TYPE FOUNDRY
Running Through Tunnels
8 Recent Discovery 3

15a 10 A $2 90   12 POINT EMERALD No. 3   10 A $1 15

CRUISERS
Printers Association
4 Comical Sign 5

10a 8 A $3 60   18 POINT EMERALD No. 3   8 A $1 50

HORSES
Gentle Maiden
4 Sea Road 3

Superior Copper-Mixed Type,   *Barnhart Bros. & Spindler.*

OLD STYLE COND. NO. 2.

25 A 40 a   12 POINT OLD STYLE COND. No. 2 $2 90

PEOPLE OF SOCIAL STANDING
27 The Poems in This Little Volume Are Light

15 A 25 a   18 POINT OLD STYLE COND. No. 2 $3 30

HIS WERE EYES LIKE
Earth Stones And Broken Branch 3

10 A 15 a   24 POINT OLD STYLE COND. No. 2 $4 20

STAR OF NIGHT
8 Great Cæsar by Bacchus

6 A 10 a   30 POINT OLD STYLE COND. No. 2 $4 75

WILD BELLS
Comedy of Errors 7

4 A 6 a   36 POINT OLD STYLE COND. No. 2 $4 05

EASTERN
8 Pope And Swift

Superior Copper-Mixed Type,   *Barnhart Bros. & Spindler.*

BISQUE SERIES.

20 A 10 POINT BISQUE (Long Primer) $1 20
SEVEN BABY ELEPHANTS AND
THE CELEBRATED BLACKVILLE TWINS 435

15 A 12 POINT BISQUE (2 line Nonp.) $1 20
TOUGHEST IN MARKET
67 SUPERIOR COPPER-MIXED TYPE

15 A 18 POINT BISQUE (3 line Nonp.) $2 05
THE UNITED STATES
TARIFF REFORM LEAGUE 13

12 A 20 POINT BISQUE (2 line Lg. Primer) $2 25
FLORIDA ORANGE
FINE FRUIT BASKETS 5

10 A 24 POINT BISQUE (4 line Nonp.) $2 75
MANY PEOPLE
3 THE CIGAR STAND

Superior Copper-Mixed Type,   Barnhart Bros. & Spindler.

---

20 A 10 POINT LINING GOTHIC (Long Primer) $1 65
GENERAL WESTERN AGENTS
2 PAPER CUTTERS 8

20 A 12 POINT LINING GOTHIC (2 line Nonp.) $2 10
NATIONAL CONVENTION
3 DEMOCRATIC 5

12 A 18 POINT LINING GOTHIC (3 line Nonp.) $2 70
6 CASE STANDS

8 A 24 POINT LINING GOTHIC (4 line Nonp.) $3 10
PRINTERS 3

6 A 30 POINT LINING GOTHIC (5 line Nonp.) $3 50
4 TRAINS

4 A 36 POINT LINING GOTHIC (6 line Nonp.) $3 35
MUSIC 8

HHHHHHHHHHHHHHH

The six larger sizes line at both top and bottom.

Superior Copper-Mixed Type,   Barnhart Bros. & Spindler.

REGISTERED, No. 96,696.
MECHANICAL PATENT, MAR. 31, 1885.

12 POINT.

PICA KOSTER.
With Two-Line Pica (24 Point) Initials.

14 A, 22 a, with 6 A Initials, $5.30
14 A, 22 a, without Initials, 2.55
6 A, Initials, separately, . 2.75

SOMNOLENT, HIBERNATE & CO.

Carefully Distribute

Rocking-Chairs and Lounges   Mattresses and Night-Caps

Hammocks and Soothing-Sirups

Corner of Morphia Street   Near the Haven of Rest

Builders of Air-Castles and Day-Dreams

1 2 3 4 5 6 7 8 9 0

18 POINT.

THREE-LINE NONPAREIL KOSTER.
With Three-Line Pica (36 Point) Initials.

10 A, 15 a, with 4 A Initials, $7.45
10 A, 15 a, without Initials, 3.55
4 A, Initials, separately, . 3.90

DILIGENT & QUICKSTEP

Retail Dealers

Water-Pails, Coal-Shovels and Saw-Horses

Furnishing Improved

Household Gymnastic Exercise

1 2 3 4 5 6 7 8 9 0

TYPE METAL.

BY CARL SCHRAUBSTADTER, JR.

LITTLE information can be obtained concerning the composition of the metal of which the first type was cast. In the cost book issued by the directors of the Ripoli Press in Florence, for the years 1474 to 1483, the cost of lead and tin is given, so that there is scarcely any doubt that these metals were used. A third metal is vaguely mentioned, which was probably antimony, but that is only conjecture. In Jost Amman's "Book of Trades," published in Frankfort, in 1568, the ingredients are given as bismuth, tin and lead. Inasmuch as this composition would have resulted in an alloy which would melt at an extremely low temperature (in proper proportions at that of boiling water), and also be very soft, there could be no advantage in using the first named metal unless the matrices were made of lead, in which case the fusing point of the alloy, being lower than that of the matrix, would tend to lenghten its life. But as bismuth is very expensive, it is more than probable that the chronicler confused it with antimony. That there is reason to believe this is the case may be seen in the numerous mistakes made in modern books of the same caliber. One of these receipts, by no means the worst, gives the proportions as, lead, 7 parts; antimony, 4 parts; and tin, 4 per cent. Others name, besides these essential ingredients, copper (which is generally used), iron, zinc, and arsenic, which must be carefully avoided. The mistake in regard to iron may probably be traced to the method of refining antimony by melting it with iron turnings. Part of the ignorance on this subject is no doubt due to typefounders themselves. The life of the type depends upon the quality of the metal, and the typefounders' little secrets in metal-making are jealously guarded.

In mixing his metal, the modern typefounder usually calculates the amount of tin, antimony, and copper used in proportion to one hundred pounds of lead. For the sake of uniformity this method will be followed. The type cast at the beginning of the century probably contained, lead, 100 pounds; antimony, 15 pounds; and tin, 5 pounds — a mixture of about the hardness of modern electrotype metal. Since then the progress has been steadily upward, and the printer who has occasion to compare the type of twenty-five years ago with that of today can at once see the improvement. Until recently it was the practice of the foundries to make several grades of metal; soft for the large type, and gradually harder for the small ones. Thus, some foundries had nonpareil, bourgeois, pica and job metal, besides quad and script. But it is reasonable to suppose that if hard metal renders small type more durable it is preferable for large ones, and most of the type-foundries have adopted a standard metal for general use.

Lead, which is the largest ingredient, is the only component metal produced in this country. It must be of the best quality. Hard lead, which contains a small proportion of arsenicum, will not do, as that metal sublimates in the casting machine, and is deposited on the pump, and in the nipple and channel, soon obstructing the operation of the machine. This the typefounder who has attempted to use hard lead in order to economize antimony has found out to his cost. A peculiar property of antimony is that of slightly expanding on solidifying, thus insuring sharp faces. It gives the hardness, and at the same time brittleness, to the type. Native antimony has been produced, but it is so impure it cannot be used for type. The best grade (Cookin's) is imported via England, and comes packed in small kegs containing peculiar square pigs showing the granulations of the metal. Tin has also been produced to a slight extent here, but for type the former article is the best. Strait's tin is imported in long, heavy pigs. A peculiarity of these is that the pig often contains a small quantity of water in the interior, which makes its addition to the hot metal quite dangerous. This metal gives the type its toughness, and at the same time makes it flow easier. An alloy of antimony and lead would crumble under the pressure of the press and stereotype table. Copper is the last ingredient. The best is produced in this country, but enters into metals in such a small proportion that it is scarcely worth considering. It also hardens and toughens the metal, and in some manner renders the action of the metal on the matrix less injurious.

Before mixing his batch the metal-maker writes out a complete list of the ingredients. If none but pure metals are to be used this is but a few minutes' work, but when type, stereotype or electrotype is to be utilized careful calculations as to the relative proportions of the metals and the consequent additions have to be made. Experience in cutting small shavings from the type is the only guide to accuracy. Taking average metal, the mixer will make out a list in the following proportions: Lead, 100 pounds; antimony, 35 pounds; tin, 15 pounds; copper, 4 pounds. Part of the lead is first melted and the antimony added. Constant stirring slowly dissolves this, and the balance of the lead is now put in. Then follows the old metal, if any, and then the tin. The copper is usually melted with tin, and a portion of this alloy added to the whole mixture, which is now thoroughly stirred and then ladled into pans. Each pan contains about forty pounds, and by means of cross-bars the metal is divided into cakes of about four pounds each. Various devices for dispensing with the ladle are in use. Some metal pots have siphons, and others tubes at the bottom. And some metal-makers use a power stirring apparatus.

Script, on account of the many overhanging letters, must be tougher to stand the strain without breaking, and more tin is necessary. The small spaces, being liable to break, have also more than the usual proportion of this metal.

Much has been said about metal-making, but the principal secret in making durable type is not the hard metal — a comparatively easy task — but the casting of it. As in every other business, the secret, when sifted down, consists in the greatest care, the latest machinery, and the best workmen. As the typefounder develops his resources, he adds tin, antimony and copper to his metal, and the metal of each decade is superior to that of the last.

Archaic.

REGISTERED, No. 92,583.

PATENTED MAR. 6, 1888.

6 POINT.   NONPAREIL ARCHAIC.   36 A, 70 a, $2.70.

MESSIEURS ENROBE, GARNISH & WEARWELL
Dispensers of Fig Leaves
Galligaskins, Smockfrocks, Wraprascals, Farthingales, Inexpressibles
Gabardines, Mantillas, Kerchiefs and Moccasins
1234567890

9 POINT.   THREE-LINE EXCELSIOR ARCHAIC.   30 A, 50 a, $2.90.

EXTRAORDINARY ANNOUNCEMENT
Waggling Bustle Improvement Practically Illustrated
Moving Figures Shown at our Salesroom
1234567890

12 POINT.   PICA ARCHAIC.   25 A, 40 a, $3.10.

ECCENTRIC BEHAVIOUR
Fashionables Walking in Leading-Strings
Following the Bell-Wethers

18 POINT.   THREE-LINE NONPAREIL ARCHAIC.   14 A, 26 a, $3.75.

MUSICAL PRODIGY
Confusion of the Neighborhood
Donnybrook Saturnalia

24 POINT.   TWO-LINE PICA ARCHAIC.   10 A, 18 a, $4.25.

LOCOMOTIVE MACHINERY
Hardworking, Patient, Uncomplaining
Meritorious Deportment

30 POINT.   FIVE-LINE NONPAREIL ARCHAIC.   8 A, 14 a, $5.00.

CONTENTED SAURIAN
Tropical Sunshine Basking

36 POINT.   THREE-LINE PICA ARCHAIC.   7 A, 10 a, $6.00.

URBANE MANNER
Superior Characteristic

ALL COMPLETE WITH FIGURES.

The various sizes of the above series will line at the bottom with point justification.

THE MacKELLAR, SMITHS & JORDAN CO., PHILADELPHIA.   SHNIEDEWEND & LEE CO., AGENTS, CHICAGO, ILL.

❀ Hiawatha. ❀

PATÉNT APPLIED FOR.

12A Caps, $1.50.
36a L. Case, $2.60.

Pica (12 Point) Hiawatha.

No. 2, 36a L. Case, $2.35
Ornaments $0.55.

Thus the Youthful Hiawatha Said within Himself and Pondered,

Much Perplexed by Various Feeling, ❀ ❀ Listless, Longing, Hoping, Fearing,

Dreaming Still of Minnehaha, Of the Lovely Laughing Water,

123 ❀ In the Land of the Dacotahs. ❀ 678

1 2 3 4 5 6 7 8 9 10 11

Pica (12 Point) Hiawatha No. 2.

Wed a Maiden of your People, Warning said the old Nokomis;

Go not Eastward, go not Westward, ∘ ∘ For a Stranger, whom we know not;

Like a Fire upon the Hearth-stone Is a Neighbors homely Daughter,

Like the Starlight or the Moonlight ∘ ∘ Is the Handsomest of Strangers.

12A Caps, $2.80.
24a L. Case, $3.10.

Great Primer (18 Point) Hiawatha.

No. 2, 24a L. Case, $2.90.
Ornaments $0.65.

Thus they buried Minnehaha, and at Night

A Fire was Lighted, On her Grave four times was Kindled, For her

Soul upon its Journey to the Island of the Blessed

1 2 3 4 5 6 7 8 9 10 11

Great Primer (18 Point) Hiawatha No. 2.

As unto the Bow the Cord is, So unto Man is Woman,

Though she bends him, she obeys him, Though she draws him, she follows

123 Useless each without the other 456

SPACES AND QUADS EXTRA.

Dormer Series.

6A 12a   18 POINT DORMER   (3 line Nonp.) $2 50

American Government

The United States Minister to France

State Senators

67 Lower House of Congress 45

4A 8a   30 POINT DORMER   (5 line Nonp.) $3 15

Rocky Mountains

American Coast Steamers

Navy Yards

3 French War Vessel 5

Wide Black.

10A 30a   8 POINT WIDE BLACK   (Brevier) $2 70

Grand Scottish Athletic Meeting held in Chicago

23 Bonnie Lads and Lassies Finer 45

8A 25a   10 POINT WIDE BLACK   (Long Primer) $2 75

Two Bashful Little Maidens Sitting by the

23 Babbling Brooklet Dreaming 45

6A 18a   12 POINT WIDE BLACK   (2 line Nonp.) $2 70

The Evanston Express Company

32 Elevated Mountain 87

6A 16a   14 POINT WIDE BLACK   (English) $3 30

Superior Copper-Mixed Type

5 Best in the Market 6

5A 15a   16 POINT WIDE BLACK   (2 line Brevier) $3 45

Babcock Optimus Cylinder

4 Printing Press 8

5A 12a   18 POINT WIDE BLACK   (3 line Nonp.) $3 60

Printers Supply House

Chicago Illinois 6

4A 10a   20 POINT WIDE BLACK   (2 line Lg. Primer) $3 65

The Western Agents

Fifth Avenue 5

DARIUS WELLS.

INVENTOR OF THE ROUTING MACHINE.

WOOD TYPE is an important item in the equipment of every large printing office, and of late years competition has so reduced the price that it has come into quite general use. We present herewith a portrait and sketch of the life of the inventor of the machine which rendered the manufacture of wood letter on a large scale practicable, and trust it will prove of interest to our readers.

DARIUS WELLS.

Darius Wells was born April 26, 1800. He was apprenticed to learn the printers' trade with Mr. William Childs, of Johnstown, New York, but was released at the end of six years, before the expiration of his term, in consideratson of his abilities and faithful service. Soon after, he married and removed to Amsterdam, New York, where, in connection with Mr. Childs, his former employer, he established the first newspaper. In 1826 the partners removed to New York, where they continued the printing business in a small way. The sizes of type then furnished by the typefounders did not suit the increasing effort at display in theater posters and similar work. The largest type then made was only twelve-line pica, and cost more than the average printer could afford to pay. Besides this, there was a serious fault in the large size metal type then cast, as they shrank in cooling, so that the face was hollow and would not print well. They were also liable to serious damage and breakage if accidently dropped on the floor. It was while confined to the house when in a convalescent state, after a severe illness, that Mr. Wells made his first experiments with wood type. About this time (1828), a printer named Lomax, who was in the same predicament —a want of larger sizes of type—attempted to supply the deficiency by preparing wood type for his office, and exhibited much artistic taste. He, however, carved his type on the side of the wood, while Mr. Wells followed the engravers' method of cutting his on the end, or on the grain.

Soon after, Mr. Wells and Mr. David Bruce, inventor of the type-casting machine, formed a copartnership, with a view of furnishing printers with large type, but having more brains to project than to prosecute the business, they were soon compelled to discontinue it, but not before making some important experiments in their workshop. The advantage of wood type had been sufficiently established, but the difficulty of manufacturing it with greater rapidity and less labor was the main obstacle, and one that seemed insurmountable. However, Mr. Wells finally perceived the efficacy of a *lateral revolving* cutter for a more speedy removal of the white surrounding the letters. This revolving lateral cutter, under all its modifications, is now known as the *Routing Machine*, and is used in a variety of ways outside of those connected with the printing trade.

After the dissolution of his copartnership with Mr. Bruce, Mr. Wells remained in the city of New York, where he successfully established a wood type business. As an adjunct, he also made a specialty of the preparation of engravers' boxwood. In 1828, appeared the first specimen book of wood type ever printed — a small quarto pamphlet of about twenty pages. Only antiques, romans and italics were shown; the sizes ranging from seven to twenty-eight line. Eight cents was charged for the former, and 28 cents for the latter size. From some explanatory notes at the end of this book we extract the following:

The subscriber is enabled to state from experience that the use of wood type, when carefully prepared in the manner of those in these specimens, is in no respect objectionable; that they are more convenient in many respects; are more durable, and cost only from one-fourth to one-half as much as metal. Knowing, as the subscriber does, that printers will consult their own interests in patronizing his novel undertaking, and taking confidence from the perfect satisfaction his type has given to those to whom he is already known, he feels assured of their support.

Several years later, Mr. Wells formed a partnership with Mr. E. R. Webb, and the firm of Webb & Wells became widely known as manufacturers of wood type and printers' goods of various kinds. Mr. Wells retired from the business in 1856, and Mr. Webb continued in it until his death, in 1864, when Mr. A. Vanderburgh and Mr. Heber Wells (the younger son of Darius), formed a partnership in conjunction with a third party, and bought out the interest formerly held by Mr. Webb. The firm of Vanderburgh, Wells & Co. is still actively engaged in the printers' material business.

Darius Wells was an outspoken, communicative man, and although often urged to do so, could never be prevailed upon to secure his invention by patent. He had the erroneous notion that it had been too long before the public for his security. In 1861, Mr. Wells was appointed postmaster of Paterson, New Jersey, and held office thirteen years. He died May 27, 1875, of old age and diabetes.—*The Printers' Review.*

A PRINTER'S PARADISE.

Under the above title, Theodore L. De Vinne, the printer of the *Century*, writes in the June number of that magazine an account of Plantin and his museum at Antwerp, from which we quote as follows: " The printing room does not give a just idea of its old importance. What here remains is as it was in 1576, but the space then occupied for printing must have been very much larger. Plantin's inventory, taken after his death, showed that he had in Antwerp seventy three fonts of type, weighing 38,121 pounds. Now, seven hand presses and their tables occupy two sides of the room and rows of type-cases and stands fill the remnant of space. How petty these presses seem! How small the impression surface, how rude all the appliances! Yet from these presses came the great ' Royal Polyglot,' the Roman Missal, still bright with solid black and glowing red inks, and thousands of volumes, written by great scholars, many of them enriched with designs by old Flemish masters. ' The man is greater than the machine,' and Plantin was master over his presses. From these uncouth unions of wood and stone, pinned together with bits of iron, he made his pressmen extort workmanship which has been the admiration of the world.

" Plantin had this work done at small cost. His account books show that the average yearly earnings of expert compositors were 142 florins, and of the pressmen 105 florins. The eight-hour law was unknown. Work began at five o'clock in the morning, but no time is stated for its ending. His rules were hard. One of them was that the compositor who set three words or six letters not in the copy should be fined. Another was the prohibition of all discussions on religion. Every workman must pay for his entrance a *bienvenue* of 8 sous as drink money, and give 2 sous to the poor-box. At the end of the month he must give 30 sous to the poor-box and 10 sous to his comrades. This *bienvenue* was as much an English as a Flemish custom, as one may see in Franklin's autobiography.

" The presses cost about 50 florins each. In one of his account books is the record that he paid 45 florins for copper platens to six of his presses. This is an unexpected discovery. It shows that Plantin knew the value of a hard impression surface, and made use of it three centuries before the printer of the *Century* tried, as he thought for the first time, the experiment of iron and brass impression surfaces for inelastic impression."

CONCERNING SCRIPTS.

No jobbing outfit can be considered complete unless it includes several fonts of the script faces now so much in vogue. These are not only expensive in first cost, but soon become, to a man who is careful of his type, a prolific source of annoyance. Few printers know of any better plan than laying such fonts in an ordinary job case, where, despite the most careful handling, the fine connecting lines quickly get battered, so that a line set from the font has that broken appearance which is the *bête noir* of the good workman.

Sizes below double pica may be laid in a job case, the boxes of which have been partitioned off with strips of pica reglet, glued into place, into narrow divisions, so that in distributing the type can be put into the case with the faces all one way, and will stay in that position. For larger sizes, take a blank case, screw in the center of each half of the case strong partitions, similar to the one in the center and parallel with it, dividing the case into four sections of equal size. Cut a lot of pica reglet to fit these compartments, and arrange the type alphabetically, commencing at the front of the case, and putting a reglet between each line. Fasten the last reglet securely in place and divide the space remaining into suitable compartments for spaces and quads. If the type has a long bevel, making it difficult to pick out the letters when arranged in this way, put thicker strips between the lines, and have them two-thirds the height of reglet, so as to expose more of the body of the type. Of course it takes longer to set a line from such a case, but it pays in the end, for the type will last twice as long. Besides this, the type is arranged with greater compactness, and from four to six fonts can be put in a single case without crowding. Neither bodkin nor tweezers should be allowed to be used in setting from such a case, but a slip of wood can be kept in the case to assist in keeping the lines on their feet.

Only one man in an office should be allowed to use the script faces, and he should be held responsible for their condition. It is well to distribute every line of script as soon as the form in which it has been used is taken out of the chase, except when the form is to be used again within a day or two. Date lines and other lines which are in constant use should be electrotyped, and the type returned to the case. In fact, when an electrotyper is accessible, it will be found more economical to electrotype all script lines from which over a thousand impressions are to be taken. The type itself should be nickel plated when first purchased, as the cost is trifling. — *The Printers' Review.*

NEW FONT SCHEMES.

Since the advent of the first typefoundry each has apparently been a law unto itself in proportioning the relative number of each letter to a font of type, and while a few houses have acquired an almost unimprovable system, the majority seemed to put up their fonts with a view to exhibiting a large number of " A's," and with little attention to detail.

In order to do away with this uncertain plan, a competent committee was appointed in the Typefounders' Association to compile and draft a table or " scheme" from the best authority obtainable. This having been done to the entire satisfaction of the most experienced members, the new scheme was formally adopted by the association at the last meeting, and in future all fonts cast by American founders will be uniform in proportions.

While there have been a few changes made from the original scheme for job faces, it remains practically the same, and little, if any, alteration will occur in the prices of a limited number of fonts. In the point system the changes will be more noticeable, especially in the faces on long primer, great primer and double great primer, owing to the great difference between them and the old bodies.

While it is an impossibility to so construct a small font of type that some one letter will not occasionally run unexpectedly low, we think for all ordinary classes of work the new scheme will be found as near perfection as is attainable, and its general adoption will assist the printer in deciding the size and number of fonts he will require of any founder's production. — *Typographic Messenger.*

THE ADVANCE OF TYPOGRAPHY.

THE progress in the art of printing, within a somewhat recent period, has been marvelous in the extreme. The designers employed by the leading typefoundries in the United States have been fortunate in many instances in producing elaborate, beautiful and attractive faces, specially adapted for making striking and graceful combinations, and the artistic printers of the country, always on the alert, have been quick to seize the opportunity presented by the introduction of these ornate and valuable designs to make well-balanced, magnificent and happy displays, which are pleasing to the critical professional eye. While the artists of the typefoundries have luckily originated these elegant designs, it has been left for the proficient typographical artists to gratify the world, to utilize them by gratifying the laws of the beautiful with magnificent designs formed from the mute integers.

The improvement in all lines of printing has extended in every direction, but the job printer especially has steadily advanced in his profession, until he now justly ranks among the most prominent and cultured of artists. The typographical publications of today—splendid specimens of art—are both notable and gratifying evidences of his handicraft, and show to what a superior standard the ability of the skilled compositor can reach.

While the advance of printing and the kindred interests have been rapid within a comparatively short period, this progress is doubtless destined, in the near future, to be much greater, and certainly more satisfactory to all interested in the " art preservative of all arts," and the associated industries. With the continued improvement in type-making machinery, and the discovery and engagement of talented designers, the productions of the foundries will reach a more appreciative state of perfection. Job printers, as a rule, being men of fertile resources and taste, will naturally take advantage of the opportunity afforded, and the legitimate, or, rather, inevitable result will be the inauguration of an era of surprising and brilliant typography which will crown the American printers as unquestioned victors in the race with foreign printers for supremacy for anything that pertains to taste, beauty and correct art.

But, while cheerfully paying this tribute, we are not blind to the fact that there is still room for improvement in some quarters, or that in many of the specimens turned out there has been a proneness to run to the grotesque at the expense of utility, a failing, however, which we have reason to believe has been effectually curbed. Inflammatory rheumatic curves, and shapes fantastic as Doré's illustrations of Dante's Inferno, are not calculated to elevate the taste, or please either the eye or the judgment. Yet the evidence that they have already run their race, are being crowded to the wall and supplanted by designs possessing symmetry, use and beauty, proves that American taste is unwilling to endure or substitute the ridiculous for the meritorious, even if they are attempted to be palmed off as artistic productions.

LITHOTINT
PATENT APPLIED FOR.

8A, 16a,   Great Primer (18 Point). $4.75

AMATEUR BASE BALL PLAYERS

Regulation Score Sheets Supplied to all Free of Charge

453   Reserved Seats Extra   678

Excellent Batting and Fielding Exhibitions

6A, 12a,   Double Pica (24 Point). $5.50

MARDER, LUSE & COMPANY

Chicago Type Foundry

New and Useful Designs in Printing Type

139 East Monroe Street 141

4A, 8a,   Double Great Primer (36 Point). $6.75

THROUGH ROUTES

The Chicago and Northwestern

Railroad Company

FIGURES AND LOGOTYPES WITH ALL SIZES IN THIS SERIES.   SPACES AND QUADS EXTRA.

PRINCETON SPECIMENS.

12 A 20 a — 18 POINT PRINCETON (3 line Nonp.) — $2 75

SPLENDID MUSIC

Pretty Pieces Sung at Theatres

23 Little Fisher Maiden 45

10 A 15 a — 24 POINT PRINCETON (4 line Nonp.) — $3 40

PRINCIPALITY

The Hamiltonian House

78 United States 56

5 A 8 a — 36 POINT PRINCETON (6 line Nonp.) — $3 90

CHICAGO

National Leagues

5 Base Ball 8

SOLAR SERIES

15 A — 12 POINT SOLAR (2 line Nonp.) — $2 10

23 · LINCOLN · PARK · CONCERT

8 A — 18 POINT SOLAR (3 line Nonp.) — $2 60

ART · ACADEMIES · 67

6 A — 24 POINT SOLAR (4 line Nonp.) — $3 20

5 · WARM · HOUSE

5 A — 30 POINT SOLAR (5 line Nonp.) — $3 65

DRY · LAKE · 3

4 A — 36 POINT SOLAR (6 line Nonp.) — $4 60

6 · BANKER

3 A — 48 POINT SOLAR (8 line Nonp.) — $5 15

RAINS · 8

CASTLE SERIES.

25 A   12 POINT CASTLE (2 line Nonp.) $2 00

GREAT PORTION OF THE FINANCIAL DISASTERS OF THE WORLD GROW OUT

234 OF SPECULATION AND THE EFFECTS OF 567

15 A   18 POINT CASTLE (3 line Nonp.) $2 25

PLETHORIC UNITED STATES TREASURY ATTRACTS

462 AMBITIOUS CORMORANTS 837

10 A   24 POINT CASTLE (4 line Nonp.) $2 30

THE PATENT INDIA RUBBER OVERCOATS

57 FOR RAINY DAYS 83

8 A   30 POINT CASTLE (5 line Nonp.) $2 80

SUPERIOR COPPER - MIXED TYPE

115 FIFTH AVENUE 117

6 A   36 POINT CASTLE (6 line Nonp.) $3 60

PATENTED AND ORIGINAL

63 DESIGNS 79

Manufactured by BARNHART BROS. & SPINDLER, Chicago, Ill.

ANOTHER TYPESETTING MACHINE.

A typesetting machine has just been perfected by J. E. Munson, a well-known stenographer of this city. In the storing and preliminary treatment of the type it closely follows the Thorne machine, now in operation through the country, holding types that are nicked according to a graded system in long, narrow reservoirs, and releasing them one by one at the pressure of a lever. In Mr. Munson's machine the compositor is replaced by a perforator, who attends a little machine similar in appearance and action to those used in "rapid telegraphy." An endless tape of strong paper is run between rolls, which cut through it a series of arbitrary combinations of holes corresponding to the letters, capitals, numerals, and punctuation marks of a first-class job office. The tape, after the perforation, is read by the proofreader, who adds holes where they are needed, and blots out those that are incorrect, until the copy is perfectly justified. The perforations are produced by steel dies communicating with a keyboard similar to that used on the typewriter, but much larger and more complete. The justified tape is then placed in the receiver of the main machine, and the power, steam, electric or hand, applied. As it runs along, the perforations free the levers, as in the orguinette, and each combination causes the corresponding type to drop from the reservoir to the carrier and thence to the galley. If the take is correct, the galley is equally correct, so that the old style of galley-proof and page-proof revision is done away with completely. As there is almost no limit to the speed with which the main machine can be run, and as two dozen perforators can be used at once, it is easily seen that the new invention will do the work of a large number of compositors.

An experimental machine has been found to work successfully. The inventor is now finishing one for business purposes. It will be some time before the new idea will be put upon the market. As the types now in use are of varying and arbitrary widths, necessitating the insertion of "leads," "spaces," and "quads," it is not suited for the machine. Mr. Munson has therefore been compelled to devise a new system of types, based upon tenths of inches, which enables the machine when setting type to fill each line to the mathematical limit.

The machine will be quite costly, but, once in operation, it will involve little or no expense for maintenance and repairs. The claim is made that with it copy may be prepared up to within three minutes of going to press.—*New York Sun.*

CAREFUL SPACING.

A great deal has been said of late about the importance of good spacing in bookwork, and any suggestions that appertain to the subject ought to interest and be read carefully by all compositors who are anxious to excel in their chosen calling. It is a notable fact that the best workmen are those who subscribe for some good journal pertaining to their particular calling, and then intelligently read and put into practical use the suggestions that are therein given.

There are a great many things which might be written upon the subject, but space will not permit. In the first instance, it is absolutely necessary that great care should be exercised in the distribution of cases. Each letter, character, and space should be placed in its respective compartment. How many compositors carelessly "fire in their cases;" all they want is type, and lots of it. They do not separate their four and five em spaces, and some of them even consider themselves very painstaking fellows when they sort out and separate the en quads and three em spaces. Just look at their proofs. The matter is thrown together in precisely the same manner as they distribute their cases. The sole object of such compositor, if such he may be called, is to paste up a big string, caring nothing for the manner in which his matter is set. If the compositor has a clean case to begin with, it is a comparatively easy thing to do good work, and only needs a little care and attention to soon become accustomed to it, and, once started in the right way, ten to one the apprentice will come forth an accomplished workman and cast honor upon the office from which he graduated. In the composition of matter care should be taken to evenly space all lines, and after the letter " f " and before the letter " j " and before and after quotations, especially where there is a comma or other mark before the closing

quotation and the following word, the distance between the words should be carefully attended to. In thin spacing a line be particular to put a thinner space between words ending and commencing with such letters as "c," " a," " o," " w," etc., than between words ending and beginning with such letters as "l," " i," " t," " d," etc. If a word is quoted that has a comma or similar character after it the spacing is improved by placing a thin space before the inverted commas and the word to be quoted, and letting the apostrophes come close up to the comma, by so doing the space is evened up and does not appear to have it all on one side of the word.

Another fault very apt to occur is the trouble experienced in making even. What looks worse than to see an article evenly spaced and then where the matter has been made even to see the spacing all the way from one to three ems wide, immediately followed by good spacing again? Some compositors never give any attention to making even, but pound away at their take, and all at once discover they have to end even. Then they kick, and mentally curse the fellow who gave out the copy. Some of them have the nerve to ask who has the next take, and then spoil the spacing of the following take in order to have their own matter end nicely; others merely lay a few lines out in their case, and then make three lines spread to four, dump their matter and are ready for the fray again. It is an easy matter to end even if a little attention and care are taken. Upon first taking copy notice if the take ends even; if so, remember, and when you **have** it nearly finished, but perhaps six or seven lines, count the remaining words, see how many words average to the line, divide the remaining words accordingly, and the otherwise difficult task is overcome.

Still another point. A good practice to follow is never to divide a word at the end of a line when by running it over to the next line you can do so by not having to space too wide. Hyphens leave an open place at the end of the line and spoil the evenness of the matter; of course, they must be used and the word divided where otherwise the spacing would be too wide. But never divide a word on the first syllable if the syllable contains only two letters.

Matter may be carefully set and then its beauty spoiled or marred by carelessly correcting the galleys. Never take a thick letter out and replace it with a thinner one, but hold the thick letter between the thumb and forefinger and then take the thinner letter and enough thin spaces to even up the thickness and place the letter to be supplied where it belongs and divide the extra spaces where mostly needed. The same rule applies to the taking out of a large word and the insertion of a smaller one. In cases where outs have been made, and a paragraph exists down the matter a stickful or so, better time is made and vastly better results accomplished by running the whole over.

In quading out lines be sure to let the smaller spaces, en quads, etc., follow immediately after the last word in the paragraph and then end the line with larger quads. The matter not only looks better, but the trouble arising from spaces dropping off at the ends is also obviated. Much more might be written upon the subject, but if the above suggestions prove of benefit to the younger members of the craft, the *animus imponentis* of the writer will have been attained.—*Dashes.*

NOT CAST HIGHER.

We received some time ago a communication from a job printer, wherein he found fault with the manner in which all light faces were cast by leading founders, apparently of the impression that this class of letter was purposely cast higher to allow for wear of face. Any printer of ordinary intelligence must know that if he places a line of Athenian, Celtic, or Script in conjunction with, or even between two lines of heavier letter, the lighter face will invariably appear to have the stronger impression, for the very plain reason that there is not the surface to repel the impression, consequently it sinks into the paper. In such cases the equalizing must be done through the agency of underlays in the process of making ready. It would be a mechanical impossibility to graduate the height to paper of type in such a manner as to require no making ready on the part of the pressman; and one-half the objection to mixing different founders' productions on account of difference in height is traceable to this misconception.—*Typographic Messenger.*

GOOD FACE.

3 MONEY AND STOCKS ⚜

10 A 24 POINT YALE (4 line Nonp.) $2 00

8 A 30 POINT YALE (5 line Nonp.) $2 55

⚜ SOUND TEAMS 5

6 A 36 POINT YALE (6 line Nonp.) $2 65

6 BALL GAMES ⚜

5 A 42 POINT YALE (7 line Nonp.) $2 95

⚜ FINE RUGS 4

5 A 48 POINT YALE (8 line Nonp.) $4 00

8 BANNER ⚜

BARNHART BROS. & SPINDLER.

HANDY BORDER.

Cast on 9 and 18 Point Bodies.

Price per font, $2 50

ISN'T THIS A DANDY?

PIN, SCREW AND NAIL HEADS.

PRICE, 75 CENTS PER FONT.

30 A   6 POINT ARCADE No. 1 (Nonpareil) $1 60

GREAT WESTERN TYPE FOUNDRY

CELEBRATED SUPERIOR COPPER-MIXED TYPES

113, 115 AND 117 FIFTH AVENUE CHICAGO

25 A   6 POINT ARCADE (Nonpareil) $1 75

THE BABCOCK PATENT

AIR-SPRING STANDARD CYLINDER

394 PRINTING PRESSES 586

20 A   9 POINT ARCADE (Bourgeois) $2 00

THE HOMES OF WILD MEN

SIR RODERICK STRATHSPEY THE BRITISH PEER

23 RICH AUSTRALIAN GOLD MINES 45

15 A   12 POINT ARCADE (2 line Nonp.) $2 50

MOST DISASTROUS

RAILWAY AND MARINE INSURANCE

52 COMPANY OF MAINE 34

10 A   18 POINT ARCADE (3 line Nonp.) $3 25

THE IRON GUN

THE LILLIPUTIAN SHIPS

46 THE SAILORS 78

8 A   24 POINT ARCADE (4 line Nonp.) $4 00

PROUDEST

THE STREET CAR

3 ANCHORS 5

This Series lines at the bottom.

Manufactured by **BARNHART BROS. & SPINDLER**, Chicago, Ill.

CAST FROM COPPER AMALGAM METAL.

14 A   12-POINT FOSTER GOTHIC. $2.25

AS ⟨ THROUGH ⟨ THE ⟨ FOREST ⟨ DISARRAYED ⟨ BY ⟨ CHILL ⟨ NOVEMBER ⟨ LATE
WE ⟨ STRAYED ⟨ A ⟨ LONELY ⟨ MINSTREL ⟨ OF ⟨ THE
WOOD ⟨ WAS ⟨ SINGING ⟨ TO ⟨ THE ⟨ SOLITUDE ⟨ WE ⟨ LOVED ⟨ 406358

10 A   18-POINT FOSTER GOTHIC. $2.75

GAY ⟨ CAROLING ⟨ THUS ⟨ WE ⟨ SAID ⟨ WHEN ⟨ OVER
THY ⟨ PERCH ⟨ THE ⟨ LEAVES
WERE ⟨ SPREAD ⟨ SWEET ⟨ WAS ⟨ 375042

8 A   24-POINT FOSTER GOTHIC. $3.50

THY ⟨ SONG ⟨ BUT ⟨ SWEETER ⟨ NOW
THY ⟨ CAROL ⟨ ON ⟨ THE
LEAFLESS ⟨ BOUGH ⟨ SING ⟨ 5432

6 A   36-POINT FOSTER GOTHIC. $4.25

WHEN ⟨ VIOLETS ⟨ PRANKED
THE ⟨ TURF ⟨ WITH
BLUE ⟨ AND ⟨ MORNING ⟨ 58

THE UNION TYPE FOUNDRY, 337 and 339 Dearborn Street, Chicago.

DANTE SERIES.

30 A   8 Point Dante (Brevier) $1 85

THE WESTERN AGENTS FOR

BABCOCK * PATENT * AIR-SPRING * PRESSES

45 *STANDARD AND COUNTRY* 23

25 A   10 Point Dante (Long Primer) $2 00

THE GEM AND VICTOR

DIAMOND * SELF-CLAMP * POWER

586 *PAPER CUTTERS* 342

20 A   12 Point Dante (2 line Nonp.) $2 00

THE * CELEBRATED * SUPERIOR * COPPER-MIXED * TYPES

364 *FOR SALE BY ALL DEALERS* 752

10 A   18 Point Dante (3 line Nonp.) $2 50

GREAT * WESTERN * TYPE * FOUNDRY

34 *CHICAGO ILLINOIS* 57

8 A   24 Point Dante (4 line Nonp.) $3 00

THEIR * CHESTNUT * BELLS

2 *WERE RINGING* 6

6 A   30 Point Dante (5 line Nonp.) $3 50

GENERAL * MASTERS

9 *DOMESTIC* 8

5 A   36 Point Dante (6 line Nonp.) $4 00

FOREIGN * RESORT

3 *GARDEN* 5

Manufactured by BARNHART BROS. & SPINDLER, Chicago, Ill.

OUTING SERIES ✑ ✑ ✑

COMPLETE SERIES OF FOUR SIZES, $6.00
EVERY SIZE CAST ON 6 POINT BODY....
NO ORNAMENTS WITH THIS SERIES....
PATENT APPLIED FOR..........

40 A   6 Point, No. 45 $1.50

✑✑✑✑✑

TRULY BEAUTIFULLY DESIGNED
HANDSOMEST AND MOST STYLISH CLASS OF MATERIAL
THE ARTISTIC DESIGNING CO. LONGBRANCH
1 2 3 4 5 7 8 9 0

20 A   6 Point, No. 42, $1.75

METAL FURNITURE
BRASS CIRCLE CO. WORCESTER
LEAD AND RULE CUTTING
1234567890

@@@@
@@@@
@@@@

30 A   6 Point, No. 44 $1.50

PHELPS, DALTON & CO.
EVERY PRINTER SHOULD HAVE THIS SERIES
SIZES COMPLETE WITH FIGURES
1234567890

24 A   6 Point, No. 43 $1.75

ALLROUND COMPOSITOR
FASHIONABLE MUSICALE INVITATIONS
DESIGNING AND ENGRAVING
1234567890

ALL FONTS IN THE OUTING SERIES ARE COPPER-FACED.

SPECIMENS FROM
DICKINSON TYPE FOUNDERY
BOSTON, MASS.

JAGGED SERIES ✑

COMPLETED
IN THREE
SIZES, $5.
PATENTED

✑ EVERY SIZE CAST ON 12 POINT BODY
✑ ORNAMENTS ARE PUT UP WITH EACH
✑ SIZE AS HERE DISPLAYED........

18 A——12 POINT, No. 41——$1.75

COOL @ SHADES @ AND @ RAMBLES
WOUNDED VETERANS ADDRESS TO THE CONGREGATION
35 NOONS AMONG QUAINT ARCHITECTURE

12 A——12 POINT, No. 39——$1.75

POOR WORK UNKNOWN HERE

PHELPS, ✑ DALTON ✑ & ✑ CO. ✑ 150 ✑ CONGRESS ✑ STREET

THIS IS SOMETHING ENTIRELY UNEXPECTED

14 A——12 POINT, No. 40——$1.75

BRASS RULE & LEAD CUTTING CO

FLOWERS ✑ IN ✑ BLOOM ✑ 84 ✑ REMARKABLE ✑ PEOPLE

BOSTON MASSACHUSETTS

CURSIVE
SCRIPT

18 Point Cursive Script
40 Lower Case A, 10 Cap A, $6.00
Extra Lower Case, $3.25 . . . . . .

Boston, Mass., October, 1888

To Printers

This Cursive Script is an imitation of a fashion of writing which was popular in France during the Sixteenth Century. Nicholas Granjon, a French engraver, cut the first punches at Lyons, during the year 1556. The King gave him exclusive privilege to manufacture the Civilitie for ten years

The Cursive was then known as Civilitie, and was so called from the title of a book of precepts, which was frequently reprinted in these types with intent to teach French children to read the fashionable handwriting of the day

Admirers of eccentric characters will find in the Cursive pleasing varieties of Mediaeval forms in both the Capitals and Lower Case, models of shapes designed by the masters of early type printing

They have been displaced by reason of changes in taste, but they are being restored to favor, and will gratify those who delight in the quaintness and strength of the old=time master printers

Phelps, Dalton & Co.

50 A.   NONPAREIL (6 POINTS) EDITH.   PRICE $2.00   30 A.   BREVIER (8 POINTS) EDITH.   PRICE $2.25

TICKNOR & PHILLIPS
ENGRAVERS, + PRINTERS + AND + STATIONERS
CRESTS, MONOGRAMS, INVITATIONS, WEDDING CARDS, ETC.
34 UNION SQUARE, NEW YORK.

BEAUTIFUL + SCENIC + DISPLAY
NEBUCHADNEZZAR, OR BABYLON FALLEN
ST. GEORGE + STATEN-ISLAND
AUGUST 24TH, 1876

25 A.   PICA (12 POINTS) EDITH.   PRICE $2.50

JOHNSTON, LANGDON, THOMPSON, & COMPANY

WHOLESALE + GROCERS + AND + PRODUCE + COMMISSION + MERCHANTS

42 TO 50 CHESTNUT & 31 TO 37 WALNUT STREETS,

PHILADELPHIA + PENN

12 A.   PICA (12 POINTS) IRENE.   PRICE $4.00

NORMANDIE
SURF & STILL : WATER : BATHING
NEAR : SEABRIGHT
$82.545.761.73.

8 A.   THREE LINE NONPAREIL (18 POINTS) IRENE.   PRICE $5.00

CHICAGO
SUMMER : RESORT
NEW : AND : NOTABLE
$506379

LINDSAY TYPE FOUNDRY, NEW YORK.

 Mortised.

REGISTERED, No 11,265.
MECHANICAL PATENT, MAR. 31, 1885.

6 POINT.   NONPAREIL MORTISED.   Price, $1.45.

IMPORTANT INTELLIGENCE
POODLE'S BRASS COLLAR NEEDS REPAIRING
1234567890

9 POINT.   THREE-LINE EXCELSIOR MORTISED.   Price, $1.80.

MOURNFUL NEWS
SACRED ELEPHANT ABSCONDS
1234567890

12 POINT.   PICA MORTISED.   Price, $2.10.

TURNPIKE VIEW
FLOWERY HOMESTEADS

18 POINT.   THREE-LINE NONPAREIL MORTISED.   Price, $2.50.

PATIENCE
WAITING FATHERS

24 POINT.   TWO-LINE PICA MORTISED.   Price, $3.00.

MEDIEVAL WATCHMEN

36 POINT.   THREE-LINE PICA MORTISED.   Price, $4.30.

ADVANCED RUMORS

48 POINT.   FOUR-LINE PICA MORTISED.   Price, $5.70.

RECORDER

The Series used in Combination.

THE EIGHTH CHARITY FAIR CHECK.

The four larger sizes are cored or mortised, wherever practicable, to make even spacing, to allow their placement in the middle of a word, or to allow the insertion of a smaller size of the series. The Ornaments are furnished only with the Four-Line Pica. The founts are complete with figures.

MacKellar, Smiths & Jordan Co., Philadelphia.   **Shniedewend & Lee Co., Agents, Chicago, Ill.**

AMATEUR PRINTERS.

To the Editor   CANADA, October, 5, 1888.

You sometimes allude to the amateur printer nuisance, and have illustrated some of their abortions in masterly style. Still, do you not think that the complaints on the subject are hardly justified by the results as to the depressing effects of these interlopers on the business of professionals? I have a newspaper and job office in a town of less than 3,000 inhabitants. When the population was less than half that, the first amateur "printers" made their appearance. They were watch-makers as well. But one of the partners had a small do-your-own-printing card press, and by working and turning they professed to be able to print billheads and circulars. They made their own colored inks, and so you can imagine what formidable competitors they were. Certainly, I was rather surprised at the number of my friends who patronized them for their cheap cards, at first; but after all, the amateur, grotesque efforts at billheads and circulars proved too tough for the approval of even those with whom "cheapness" was the first consideration. So that amateur concern soon failed to capture even the small, cheap card business.

Then two youngsters, one of them having graduated as a stable boy, got hold of the smallest-sized presses and a few fonts of card type, and went round offering to do better work (!) at "cheaper rates" than the professional printer could charge. However, the professional did not hide his diminished head forthwith; and after a little time nothing more was heard of these amateur geniuses, or seen of their performances.

But the professional one day managed to tread upon the toes of a tradesman who had previously done business with him; and lo and behold, the angry tradesman forthwith invested in a press and a small stock of type, and canvassed everybody else for such small work as cards and envelopes — and rather than say "no," and lest the regular printer should get rich (!) in too great a hurry, he got quite a few jobs of this description. About the same time another tradesman thought he would do his own printing, and frankly told the regular printer of his intention, and asked him which was the best style of press for what was wanted. Knowing of no reason why anyone should not do his own printing, if so inclined, as freely as his own penmanship, the desired information was given as honestly as it was asked for.

Well, what was the result? What was an entertaining novelty at first, in leisure moments, was not long in becoming irksome as a matter of business, when other business had to be attended to; and now both of them come to the regular printing office when they want something neat, or in larger number in the printing line than can be accomplished with a limited amateur outfit; and they do not find fault with regular printing prices, either.

Experience has also been had as to the competition of "newspapers" run and edited by men who have no knowledge of the printing art beyond what they have learned from the instructions of the sellers of the cheap little card presses and amateur fonts, and without experience in journalism or reporting. They were going to break down the older concern in short order, by lowering the price for newspaper advertising and job printing. Well, the old concern never weakened on its established system and prices. Some of its advertising customers, of course, "tried it on"; they could get their "ad" of such a size, and for such a length of time, for so much less in the other paper. The reply to the proposition was that the proprietor of the other sheet knew of how much (or how little) value his sheet was as an advertising medium; that what he chose to take was no criterion for anyone who knew what business was — who could better afford to go without the advertisement altogether than to take it at less than it was worth, only to have to shut up entirely in the end. After some skirmishes on this line, as the old concern held firmly to its position, it got the advertising on its own terms, and the new one did not get it at all! Of the necessity of the other concern having finally to engage a regular printer and reporter, at a big figure at first — how the poor fellow was next cut down in his salary, bit by bit, till he could stand it no longer and left in disgust — how a substitute of some sort had to be found — your practical journalist can readily imagine; and what a lively and lovely time more than one such speculative concern had in keeping up till a purchaser could be found green enough to take hold of such "flourishing" ventures.

The "amateur" does not do the small country printer half so much injury as the grasping city "specialists," who send out travelers to grab up all the commercial printing they can — and who get it, by cutting prices, and by pestering tradesmen for orders till they are given, just to get rid of the drummers, as well as to save a few cents, and send money out of town to help the big city.

Lots of things in the world need   REVISING.

THE ABUSE OF BRASS RULE.
BY G. H. POWELL.

NO one thing in a printing office is more useful and more generally abused than brass rule. It is the target for incompetent compositors, as well as for the better class who are forever trying to outrival the true artist or the engraver. The outlay is always heavy, and any proprietor of considerable experience will testify that nothing perplexes him more than "where the rules all go to." Now and then will be found a proprietor who once worked himself at the case. He knows, in a measure, the abuse to which they are subjected, but a remedy he is not always sure of. In the majority of large city offices you will find all sizes and kinds huddled together, making blank work one of drudgery to the compositor and taking twice the time it should. This state of affairs will exist in any office as long as no system is carried out, and as long as the rule-cutter and mitering machine are allowed to run loose in the office.

There are several methods for the preservation of rules, but the following, if carried out in detail, will prove a success. There is but one man in the composing room capable of doing this — the foreman. He should arrange an alley for the special use of rule cases, the cutter and mitering machine, and allow no one to go there without special orders. In very large offices a small room would be better still. No compositor has use for rules until he receives his copy, and when the foreman gives it out he should select the proper set of rules. Suppose copy is given out for a title page which requires a double rule; the foreman or his assistant goes to the brass rule alley, selects a suitable set of labor-saving rules, and hands them to the compositor with the copy. By this means all mistakes are obviated and the compositor at once proceeds with his work. In case of legal or blank work which requires a large number of small rules, it would be necessary to send a case with the copy to be returned to the alley when through with. Where "fancy" compositors are employed, the use of the cutter and mitering machine will have to be at their disposal. As the rule used on such work is generally new, the foreman can supply a little at a time. The average "fancy" man would waste considerable if allowed a large quantity.

In stocking an office with rules only labor-saving should be bought. The foundry can do the work much better and cheaper than any compositor. In regard to double and parallel rules, an exception might be made which is now in vogue in many small offices. By purchasing two or three faces of this class of rules, the foreman can have the strips cut into solid pieces, varying in length from four to sixty ems pica and mitered at both ends. If a good supply is provided at the start, almost any job can be set up. The solid picas look better and waste less time in making good joints than several picas of labor-saving rules possibly can. A little study will enable almost anyone to see that a few picas will cover a good many sizes. The expense, however, is greater, and is not so practicable as that of labor-saving.

For legal and blank work it is a mystery why so many do not realize the utility and the money that can be saved by using fine dot leaders. Where such work is done to any extent, nothing can take the place of the old, reliable Caledonian or copperplate italic. Fine dot leaders are cast like spaces and quads, to line exactly with these types as well as scripts, and cost but a trifle. To do without them is folly. Two or three large jobs will pay for them.

Leads are subjected to almost, if not quite, as much abuse as rules. The remedy consists in refusing the use of the cutter to every compositor. Foundry-cut leads are generally better, but where it is necessary to do the cutting in the office one man only should do it. The only correct way is to cut them to the exact length of quads or rules, and not a shade longer, as many think necessary.—*Dashes.*

TRINAL

SERIES ONE.

PATENTED
OCTOBER 9, 1888.

10A,   Pica (12 Point). $2.50

PEOPLES ABSTRACT COMPANY
EXAMINATION OF ABSTRACTS OUR SPECIALTY
34 TITLES BOUGHT 12
IMPROVED FARM LANDS FOR SALE

8A, $2.85.   Great Primer (18 Point).   Initials, 4A, $1.15

MUTUAL UNION BANK
LETTERS OF CREDIT FOR TOURISTS
FOREIGN EXCHANGE
A B C D E F G H J K L M N

6A, $3.00   Double Pica (24 Point).   Initials, 3A, $1.50

PENSION BUREAU
12 CIVIL SERVICE REFORM 34
MOVEMENT
P Q R S T U V W Y Z

SPACES AND QUADS EXTRA.

12 A, 20 a. PICA (12 POINTS) GRETCHEN. PRICE $2.50.

LONDON ❋ PARIS ❋ BERLIN ❋ VIENNA
Pleasant and Invigorating Wanderings on Summer Mornings through Central Park
Metropolitan Museum ❂ Obelisk ❂ Grotto ❂ Terrace ❂ Belvidere ❂ Ramble
SEPTEMBER 1874-76

8 A, 15 a. 3 LINE NONPAREIL (18 POINTS) GRETCHEN. PRICE $3.75.

THE YEOMAN OF THE GUARD
Gilbert and Sullivan's New Comic Opera
Produced ❂ at ❂ the ❂ Savoy ❂ Theatre, ❂ London ❂ October ❂ 3rd.
A ❋ GREAT ❋ HIT ❋ 1884

7 A, 12 a. DOUBLE PICA (24 POINTS) GRETCHEN. PRICE $4.50.

SENATE CHAMBER
Evening ❂ Sessions ❂ held ❂ at ❂ Washington ❂ D.C.
SUMMER ❋ 1867

5 A, 8 a. THREE LINE PICA (36 POINTS) GRETCHEN. PRICE $6.50.

WEST POINT ACADEMY
Flirtation ❂ Walk ❂ by ❂ Moonlight
CLASS ❋ OF ❋ '84

LINDSAY TYPE FOUNDRY, NEW YORK.

4 A, $2.35. 4 A, $1.35. 36 POINT NERO. 6 a, $1.90. $5.60.

The Manhattan Riding Academy.
Graceful Maneuvers. Cantering Steeds
46 DARING HORSEMEN 73

4 A, $3.25. 48 POINT NERO. 6 a, $2.30. $5.55.

Modern Times 63 Galley Slaves
RECORDS--WONDERS

3 A, $3.50. 60 POINT NERO. 5 a, $2.35. $5.85.

Standard Printing Materials
72 MUNIVERSAL 43

3 A, $4.15. 72 POINT NERO. 5 a, $3.00. $7.15.

Railroad 372 Express
WICKED COMEDIES

JAMES CONNER'S SONS, NEW YORK.

THE BOSS PRINTER.

BY HERBERT L. BAKER, ST. PAUL, MINN.

IN all this talk about the rights of the poor printers and all this planning for the betterment of the laborer's condition, why doesn't someone say a word for the boss printer, too? When a printer yields to the insane itch to hustle for wages for other printers, does he thereby become transmogrified into another sort of being?—one who hasn't any rights worth speaking of; one who, whatever his former character as a workman, is instantly changed by the magic of that word "employer," to a tyrant, an oppressor, a villain, a schemer, against whose arts and wiles and inherent rascality his employés must always be on the alert? The writer knows what a delightful thing it is to be a boss printer—has sipped all the saccharine quintessence of pleasure this experience affords—has bathed his soul in all the floods of glory that independent business brings; but his debts and the patches on his pantaloons (earned during his last year at the case) are about all he has to show for all this sipping and bathing business. When he finds, from his yearly balance sheet, that he has made less money than some of his employés, while he has put in all the capital, taken all the risk and worked harder than any other man in the shop, he begins to think a word for himself would not be out of place — to him the betterment of his own condition becomes of some trifling importance.

As a kid, he beheld the portly, pursy prosperity of his employer, the grasping embodiment of selfishness and greed, who heartlessly refused to pay him $5 per week for 50 cents worth of work; and his soul yearned for the time when he would no longer have to be pi manipulator, roller cleanser, spittoon wrestler and lord high chambermaid to the office cat. He slapped his swelling chest over where his youthful lung ought to be, and resolved a deep bass resolve not to jeff with the boys, not to yield to the seductions of penny ante, not to bet his old boots on the election, nor squander his substance on hot wiener wurst and riotous living, but, at first opportunity, go into business on his own hook. Alas! the significance of that phrase did not strike him till he was hung so confoundedly high "on his own hook" that there was no getting down with either dignity or profit. Now he daren't attempt to come off the perch, for fear it will end like Darius Green's flying:

> The flyin's all well enough; but ther' ain't a darn sight
> O' fun in't when you come to light.

All this rot about business making a man free and independent makes him weary. Like all the rest, his caged soul wearied of drawing a snug salary Saturday night, and longed for freedom and independence. He finds them — an astonishing amount, but of rather an unexpected sort. He is now free — to take in smiling, silent rage, the abuse of cranks whose custom is valuable; free — to help himself Saturday night from a money drawer as dry as a sucked lemon after the pay roll is squeezed out; free — to work night and day with scarcely time to kiss his wife or spank his babies; free — to pay scale wages to every incompetent loafer whom the union has been careless enough to take in; free — to worry his soul gray-headed for fear the sheriff will get a clutch on him. Oh, yes! there's plenty of freedom in business; and, when he gets tired of this sort of freedom, he is free to take himself by the nape of the neck, carry himself out behind the woodshed and bump his fool cranium on the wood pile for expecting anything else.

But life is not all a dreary waste, even for a boss printer. He has lots of fun. The most amusing oversights slip by the proofreader, and it is such a joke to do the work all over again; the trimmer, in such a hilariously funny way, has the top sheet turned wrong side around, cutting the whole job down through the middle, and that makes the boss ha, ha! He estimates on a job, to find when he gets it that he only figured in half enough paper, and that is deliciously amusing; he has a large account against some concern which unexpectedly fails — on the theory of the rhetorics, that the element of surprise is the foundation of humor, this is deliriously humorous; he gets in the middle of a job that promises to be profitable, and the men walk out, and he finds that too laughable for any use. Finally, perchance, his Damocles' sword, the sheriff, drops in, and the printer finds this action so oppressively funny that it is too much for him, and he never goes into his office again. One would suppose that with so much laughter he would grow fat, but, with a contrariety peculiarly his own, he gets poorer and thinner, till it is doubtful if he could throw his own shadow if he should meet it on the street. Why this is so, is hard to understand. True, the employer knows too well that rent, interest, pay-roll, power, expenses, etc., go right along with remorseless regularity regardless of the business done — but why should that worry him? True, foolish competition has reduced prices below living figures, so that his profits are scant on the business he does get—but what does that matter? True, he often finds it very difficult to collect his hardly-earned money, and the pay-roll makes him "scratch gravel" with all his might — but that is a trifle! True, he devotes so much time and money to keeping his business on foot, that his wife has reason to complain that he has so little to devote to her pleasure and comfort — but why should that affect him? True, claims for money and thought and energy press upon him night and day till he is fairly frantic, and often knows not which way to turn — but anyone can see with half an eye that there is nothing in this to interfere with his life being one round of pleasure unalloyed. He is a strange creature in some respects, for all these pleasant things somehow fail to satisfy him, and he often would find a word of encouragement and cheer very agreeable. He works on, hopes on, his vivid imagination ever picturing the "good time coming" just ahead, which too often proves at last a mirage of his own tropical fancy.

But whether he succeed or whether he fail, so long as he is an employer he is tabooed by the craft. If he show himself friendly, he is said to have an ax to grind; if he appear indifferent, he is selfish and cares nothing for the welfare of other craftsmen; if he have vigorous ideas of his own rights and is making a hard struggle for existence against all odds, then he is an enemy to the craft and must be humbled at all hazards. What effects this marvelous change in the status of a printer when he becomes an employer? Who knows? It strikes "the blind man up a tree" that there is something wrong about this; that since all are working together to reach the same result, and since all are brothers of a common blood, the employer is certainly entitled to his share of the encouragement and kindly sympathy and helpfulness that there is to distribute.

PROGRESS IN LETTERPRESS PRINTING.

BY ALFRED PYE.

NOTWITHSTANDING all that has been written and said about the spread and increase of amateurism and blacksmithing in the printing trade, it cannot be denied that, as a whole, the jobwork of the present time is vastly superior to anything accomplished in the line of beauty and effectiveness in the past, even so recently as five years back. Every printer deserving of the name has done his best to outvie his fellow in originality of design and care in the presentment of ideas, with the result that work is produced which is often a surprise to those who have hitherto considered themselves acquainted with the possibilities of type-metal and brass rule. Yet many specimens of work that excite our admiration do not owe their worth entirely to the ingenuity and artistic skill of the compositor and the pressman. The productions of the typefoundries play an important part in the general improvement, for, almost as soon as a design in brass rule of any merit is evolved by a first-class printer, one or other of the typefoundries straightway reproduces the same in metal, in sections for convenience of handling and adaptability to all descriptions of work; and that which cost the designer many hours of painstaking labor is placed at the command of the whole fraternity in such shape that any printer possessed of an ordinary amount of intelligence can get up an elaborate piece of work, embellished with curlicues and flourishes, with the expenditure of an hour or two in the arrangement of the various pieces to form a complete design. Instead of using up yards of brass rule—cutting, twisting, filing and hammering it into the shape that best pleases the fancy of the compositor—an order is written out and sent to the founder, and in a short time a complete set of intricate designs, mortised for setting around and between lines of type, are at the disposal of the compositor, at an outlay of less than the bare cost of the rule for making the same design, without counting the cost of time saved in the production of the work. Of course, there is not the pride felt by the compositor in getting up a job in this manner that he would feel if he had made the design as before referred to, but the result is as satisfactory to the customer, while the charges are so much less. Then, again, the type ornaments can be used over and over again in endless variety, while the brass rule designs are not so easily adapted for changing from one job to another.

Much economy, however, can be practiced in many offices where it is not possible to get material on short notice, by using many pieces of rule and old type that were formerly considered useless. An old, battered piece of brass rule can be nicked and trimmed up with a pocket-knife or file, and form a respectable ornament to fill out a line or a blank space in a job. Old type, melted and poured into type-high molds laid upon the imposing stone, will furnish tint-blocks for use in many jobs where a streak or two of color will greatly enhance their effect. Leather or cardboard, or, in fact, any material with a surface that will take ink from the roller, can be made available for a variety of purposes in connection with job printing, and the use of them is only limited by the genius of the printer who handles them.

Previous to the introduction of so many brass-rule embellishments in jobwork, one of the most prominent typefoundries in the United States stimulated and aided the artistic ideas of the letterpress printer by furnishing such ornate specimens of type as the "Arboret," "Harper," "Chaucer," etc., with their floral, medallic, and emblematic ornaments, which opened up an entirely new field for the compositor to work in. These artistic faces held their own for quite a long time, when other foundries began to place upon the market various delicate, unique, and handsome faces of type, until each seemed bent upon outrivaling the other in the production of some novelty that would supersede all others. The result has been a bewildering array of the English alphabet in such various forms that many of the letters have apparently lost their identity, and can scarcely be recognized apart from their fellows. Rarely does a month pass by, as the pages of THE INLAND PRINTER demonstrate, without some one of the typefounders displaying a new design in lettering, or a resurrection of an almost forgotten one of the past ages, each intended to catch the wary, or unwary, eye of the modern printer, with the purpose of inducing him to purchase various sizes thereof, be the first in the field with the new letter, and thus "scoop" his ambitious rivals for public favor.

The old style of display work, in which roman, antique, celtic, doric, gothic, etc., were the only types available—though considered good enough at the time, and in many instances thought to be the very height of the letterpress printer's art—has fallen into disuse; and the printer who has not a stock of the latest designs in his office can scarcely expect to get a very large share of the public's patronage. But there is danger of overdoing, even in the use of the most modern types available. Many faces of type—beautiful in their proper place—have failed entirely of their purpose by being used indiscriminately in various jobs, without regard to the fitness of their surroundings. A few printers have, unfortunately, an idea that because they have a new type in their office every one must know it; therefore it is used in every job they thereafter get, whether it be a letterhead or an "in memoriam" card, a dodger or a wedding invitation. Such indiscriminate use of fancy type is rather a detriment than a help to the acquirement of a steady patronage. The public, though sometimes condemned in terms more forcible than polite, has some rights which printers, in common with other caterers for its favor, are bound to respect; and, though long suffering and patient, will not forever submit to have inflicted upon it such abortions as some are pleased to term "fine art printing."

QUAINT·OPEN···

PATENT APPLIED FOR

$1.90   12 POINT   14 A

THE · OLD · HOMESTEAD
ESTABLISHED 1493   △ △   ALL REBUILT IN 1852
MODERN IMPROVEMENTS

$3.40   36 POINT   6 A

OPERA △ 88 △ COMIQUE
VARIETY · SHOW

$1.90   8 POINT   24 A

LEARNING TO HAVE AND WISDOM
LACK IS A LOAD OF BOOKS
ON AN ASS'S BACK △ △ △ △ △

$1.90   10 POINT   20 A

THE BIBLE IN PEQUOT △ △ △
JOHN ELIOT TRANSLATOR
CAMBRIDGE, 1663 △ △ △ △ △

$4.00   48 POINT   4 A

TYPE △ SPECIMENS

$2.25   18 POINT   10 A

OLDEST · PUBLICATIONS
PONY SPECIMEN   BEAUTIFUL TYPE
34 △ THOUSAND △ COPIES △ SENT

$2.90   24 POINT   8 A

PHELPS, DALTON & COMPANY
150 CONGRESS ST

Grace Script.

Mr. and Mrs. O. Grace

request your presence

at the marriage of their daughter

Maud Bell

to

Wilfred Herbert Sherwood,

Friday evening, December sixteenth,

eighteen hundred and eighty=eight

Chicago Illinois

Everett.

Maud Grace

Mr. Harry Everett,

Louisville,

27 Lane Place

Kentucky.

30 POINT GRACE SCRIPT.
PATENT APPLIED FOR.
5 A Caps, . . $3.45
15 a Large Lower Case, $3.35
15 a Small Lower Case, $3.50

Sansom Script.

REGISTERED, No. 110,406.

18 POINT.   THREE-LINE NONPAREIL SANSOM SCRIPT.   10 A, 50 a, . . . $9.30
50 a, Lower-case only, 5.75

Bonanza within easy Reach of the Enterprising

Formation of a new Company with very favorable Prospects

Dividends not less than a Hundred per Cent,

The demand for Rushlights having become universal, and the facilities we possess for their manufacture and distribution being above the average, we are forming a Company for that purpose. To a few of our most intimate friends we tender the privilege of coming in on the ground floor, with option of paying for the stock in monthly installments. Our capital has been fixed at $964,158. Par value of shares, fifty dollars. A limited number can be had, if applied for at once, at eighty-five cents each

Neglect not the Opportunity of a Lifetime

Take at its Flood the Tide which will Doubtless lead to Fortune

24 POINT.   TWO-LINE PICA SANSOM SCRIPT.   10 A, 50 a, . . . $12.50
50 a, Lower-case only, 7.50

Announcement to Stockholders!

Sinews of War are Needed to Promote our Enterprise

Important Bulletin from Headquarters,

Urgent financial necessities have compelled the Directors to order an assessment on each share of capital stock of the Umbrage Rushlight Manufacturing Company, of $286.93, payable on Thursday next, after which time all shares not having paid as above will be forfeited

Office in our Palatial Marble Building

Which will be Open at Sunrise for Reception of Cash,

THE MACKELLAR, SMITHS & JORDAN CO., PHILADELPHIA.   SHNIEDEWEND & LEE CO., AGENTS, CHICAGO, ILL.

PATENT APPLIED FOR.

10 A 20 a	12 POINT HURON (2 line Nonp.)	$2 00

COSMOPOLITAN

Building ❖ for ❖ Printers ❖ or ❖ Binders

23 ❖ Seven Stories High ❖ 48

8 A 15 a	18 POINT HURON (3 line Nonp.)	$2 95

NEBRASKA

Impertinent ❖ Messenger

2 ❖ Gold Mines ❖ 5

❖ Western Agents Babcock Patent Air-Spring Presses. ❖

Barnhart Bros. & Spindler

Superior ❖ Copper-Mixed ❖ Type

Great Western Type Foundry

❖ ❖ ❖ ❖ ❖ No. 115-117 Fifth Avenue. ❖ ❖ ❖ ❖ ❖

Displayed with Wave Ornaments.   Price, $3.75 per font.

6 A 10 a	24 POINT HURON (4 line Nonp.)	$3 35

❖ THE SUPERIOR COURT ❖

Sixteen Criminals   Joliet Penitentiary

34 ❖ Divorce ❖ Suits ❖ 25

7 A. 14 a.   THREE LINE NONPAREIL (18 POINT) MATHILDE.   Price $3.75.

KALAMAZOO & OSHKOSH

Startling Vagaries of a Brilliant Imagination

WISCONSIN & 1835

6 A. 12 a.   DOUBLE PICA (24 POINT) MATHILDE.   Price $5.00.

DAKOTA & BLIZZARDS

Flowers & From & The & Mountains

SUNDAY 1764

PICA AND THREE-LINE PICA SIZES WILL BE READY WHEN THIS APPEARS.

---

15 A. 55 a.   PICA (12 POINT) PRISCILLA.   Price $5.00.

TO USERS OF LEATHER BELTING.

We ask all who desire to purchase the best Oak-tanned Leather Belting to favor us with a trial order. To every consumer we recommend our Belting as an article upon which the fullest reliance can be placed. We guarantee every Belt to give entire satisfaction with fair usage, and will replace any that may prove defective.

Those who purchase of us may rest assured that there will be no misrepresentation, and that they will obtain a good article of Belting, which we warrant to be well stretched, and to run true upon the pulleys and to do good service.

Hoping to be favored with a sample order, we are,

Yours respectfully,

TANNER, LACEER & CO.

LINDSAY TYPE FOUNDRY, NEW YORK.

CONTOUR No. 1.

ORIGINAL.

MORTISED LETTERS WITH THIS SERIES.

16A, 32a,   Pica (12 Point).   3.25

EXPERIENCE PROVES THAT THE APPRENTICE

24   Foreshadows the Workman Just as Surely as the Bend   36

10A, 20a,   Columbian (16 Point).   3.45

MEANDERINGS IN THE COUNTRY

567   Tribulations of the Summer Boarders   213

10A, 20a,   Paragon (20 Point).   5.00

MERRYMAN, SMYLER & CO.

Dispensers of Joques and Konundrums

8A, 16a,   Double Pica (24 Point).   5.00

Beautiful MAIDENS Dancing

6A, 12a,   Double English (28 Point).   5.15

Elevated RAILROAD Schemes

5A, 10a,   Double Great Primer (36 Point).   6.90

Swift RUNNING River

4A, 8a,   Four-Line Pica (48 Point).   8.80

Fast RAILWAY Train

FIGURES WITH ALL SIZES IN THIS SERIES.   SPACES AND QUADS EXTRA.

OTHER STYLES OF CONTOUR IN PREPARATION.

AMERICAN SYSTEM OF
INTERCHANGEABLE TYPE BODIES.

CONTOUR No. 2.

ORIGINAL.

MORTISED
LETTERS
WITH THIS
SERIES.

8A,
Two-Line Bourgeois (18 Point).
1.65

TURNOVER CLUB STORIES
PURELY INSTRUCTIVE LITERATURE
645 AMUSING 213

6A,
Two-Line Pica (24 Point).
1.90

NOTED STATESMEN
DOUGLASS 1859 CONKLING
BIOGRAPHICAL

4A,
Two-Line Great Primer (36 Point)
3.30

MUSICAL FESTIVAL
HOME TALENT

3A,
Four-Line-Pica (48 Point).
4.70

NEAT DESIGN

FIGURES WITH ALL SIZES IN THIS SERIES.

OTHER STYLES OF CONTOUR IN PREPARATION.

SPACES AND QUADS EXTRA.

CONTOUR No. 5.
ORIGINAL.

MORTISED LETTERS WITH THIS SERIES.

6A, Double Pica (24 Point). 2.35

YARDSTICKE & Cº.
IMPORTED DRESS GOODS
24 CHEAP 56

4A, Double Great Primer (36 Point). 4.00

HARD METAL
UNIQUE DESIGNS
3 BEST 8

3A, Four-line Pica (48 Point). 5.40

GREAT MEN
READING

FIGURES WITH ALL SIZES IN THESE SERIES.

OTHER STYLES OF CONTOUR IN PREPARATION.

SPACES AND QUADS EXTRA.

AMERICAN SYSTEM OF INTERCHANGEABLE TYPE BODIES.

CONTOUR No. 6.
ORIGINAL.

MORTISED LETTERS WITH THIS SERIES.

32A,   Pica (12 Point).   2.00

TIME WITH SILENT FOOTSTEPS
THROUGH ANOTHER YEAR HAS PASSED
23 BEARING FROM US 45

18A,   Great Primer (18 Point).   2.10

BOOKS HAVE INFLUENCE
AND AFFECT THE CHARACTER

12A,   Double Pica (24 Point).   2.25

89 NATIONAL 67
MERCANTILE PRINTING

8A,   Double Columbian (32 Point).   2.75

EXHIBITIONS
LACROSSE GAME

5A,   Double Paragon (40 Point).   2.70

NOTIONS AND FINE DRY GOODS

4A,   Four-Line Pica (48 Point).   3.20

MAGNIFICENT SCENES

3A,   Five-Line Pica (60 Point).   3.75

HOME MADE PLEASANT

3A,   Six-Line Pica (72 Point).   5.40

HONOR TO HEROES

FIGURES WITH ALL SIZES IN THIS SERIES.   OTHER STYLES OF CONTOUR IN PREPARATION.   SPACES AND QUADS EXTRA.

ILLINOIS ✳ TYPE ✳ FOUNDING ✳ COMPANY.

Freak Series.

PATENT APPLIED FOR.

12 A 25 A	10 POINT FREAK (Long Primer)	$2 75

American Coast Steamers

The ✦ United ✦ States ✦ Minister ✦ to ✦ France

23 ✦ Lower House of Congress ✦ 45

9 A 18a	12 POINT FREAK (2 line Nonp.)	$2 85

Little Fisher Maiden

Sung ✦ at ✦ the ✦ Columbia ✦ Theatre

45 ✦ Splendid Music ✦ 67

6 A 12a	18 POINT FREAK (3 line Nonp.)	$3 35

Chicago ✦ National ✦ Base ✦ Ball ✦ League

59 In Our Annual Struggle for Glory

Superior Copper-Mixed Type.   Great Western Type Foundry.

Barnhart Bros. & Spindler

✦ ✦ Letter Founders ✦ ✦

No. 115-117 Fifth Avenue   Chicago Illinois

5 A 10a	24 POINT FREAK (4 line Nonp.)	$3 95

Beautiful Christmas Attractions

In Novel Styles of Type 67

A 8a	30 POINT FREAK (5 line Nonp.)	$4 50

Spirits of the Long Departed   ✦   ✦

✦   ✦   38 Wafted Homeward

Manufactured by BARNHART BROS. & SPINDLER, Chicago.

AZTEC SERIES.

THE UNION TYPE FOUNDRY
TRADE MARK
CHICAGO
1872 1884

PATENTED.

··· CAST · FROM · COPPER · AMALGAM · METAL ···

12 A   8-POINT AZTEC. $1.20

A YOUNG MAN GOES TO COLLEGE TO INCREASE HIS STORE OF KNOWLEDGE AND TO STUDY
FROM ALPHA TOWARDS OMAHA
* ALL * THE * CLASSICS * THAT * HE * CAN - BUT - IT - SOON - BECOMES - 521 -

12 A   12-POINT AZTEC. $1.60

HIS MISSION AND MOST LAUDABLE AMBITION TO MAKE HIMSELF A TRUE
GREEK LETTER MAN SIR
* AND * MORE * ESPECIALLY * DOES * HE * TRY * TO * JOIN * 34 *

10 A   18-POINT AZTEC. $2.00

THE ZETA PSI FOR THEN HE WOULD HIS STANDING MOST
* WOULD * HE * TRY * THE * GOAT * TO * RIDE * 246 *

7 A   24-POINT AZTEC. $2.25

ON THE GREASED PLANK WOULD HE SLIDE OH
* NO * OF * COURSE * HE * WOULDN'T * 253 *

5 A   30-POINT AZTEC. $2.60

BUT HE WOULD LIKE THE CHANCE
* TO * TRY * UPSILON * AND * 518 *

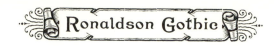 **Ronaldson Gothic**

REGISTERED, No. 114,768.

24 POINT RONALDSON GOTHIC.   10 A, 15 a, $3.70.

EXPECTED MERRY-MAKING
Frolicsome Youngsters and Patriarchs

6 POINT RONALDSON GOTHIC.   40 A, 60 a, $3.10.

WELCOME AS FLOWERS IN SPRINGTIME
Christmas Opportunities to Gladden the Face of Misfortune
Delightful Reunion of Widely-Scattered Families
1234567890

8 POINT RONALDSON GOTHIC.   38 A, 55 a, $3.10.

PROTESTATIONS OF KRISS KRINGLE
Difficulties Encountered in Descending Narrow Chimneys
Irksomeness of Crawling Through Stovepipes
1234567890

30 POINT RONALDSON GOTHIC.   8 A, 12 a, $4.95.

PLEASANT EXERTION
Osculation beneath Mistletoe

10 POINT RONALDSON GOTHIC.   28 A, 45 a, $3.10.
Furnished also on Long Primer Body.

AWAITING THE PATRON SAINT
Youths Determined to Discover his Appearance
Morpheus Defeats Laudable Efforts

12 POINT RONALDSON GOTHIC.   22 A, 34 a, $3.10.

STOCKINGS OVERFLOWING
Childish Prattle and Noisy Enjoyment
Displaying Acquired Treasures

36 POINT RONALDSON GOTHIC.   6 A, 9 a, $5.80.

Sportive PRANKS Abound

14 POINT RONALDSON GOTHIC.   18 A, 28 a, $3.15.

PERSONAL COMFORTS
Table Redolent with Savory Odors

18 POINT RONALDSON GOTHIC.   12 A, 18 a, $3.15.

DONATED BLESSINGS
Benevolent under Obligations

48 POINT RONALDSON GOTHIC.   5 A, 7 a, $7.15.

Bright EVENING Scene

The various sizes of the above series, caps or lower-case, may be justified with one another by using leads and quads of our Point System.

The MacKellar, Smiths & Jordan Co., Philadelphia.   Shniedewend & Lee Co., Agents, Chicago, Ill.

February 1889   267

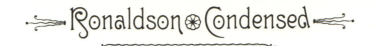

6 POINT RONALDSON CONDENSED.   36 A, 70 a, $2.50.

CONSTANTLY RISING IN PUBLIC APPRECIATION
Excellence in Quality and Material
Honorable Dealing with the Entire World Untainted by Duplicity or Equivocation
Fortune Crowning with Success the Deserving and Persevering
1234567890

8 POINT RONALDSON CONDENSED.   30 A, 60 a, $2.50.

SCIENTIFIC AND INVENTIVE INCONGRUITY
Cherished Theories Suddenly Explode after Years of Implicit Credence
Mechanical Appliances Ministering to Helplessness
1234567890

30 POINT RONALDSON CONDENSED.   8 A, 14 a, $4.15.

IMPORTANT PERSONAGE
Boasting Mediocrity Invested with Authority

10 POINT RONALDSON CONDENSED.   26 A, 52 a, $2.55.

INTIMIDATE, TERRIFY & BROWBEAT
Manufacturers of Ghost Stories and Ungraceful Scarecrows
Adapted for Farm, Office, and Household Purposes
1234567890

12 POINT RONALDSON CONDENSED.   22 A, 45 a, $2.70.

MAKING THE MOUTH WATER
Ronaldson Type Admired by Printers Everywhere
Readers Treading on Enchanted Ground
1234567890

36 POINT RONALDSON CONDENSED.   7 A, 12 a, $5.25.

SPACIOUS VAULTAGE
Railroad Tunnels through Mountains

18 POINT RONALDSON CONDENSED.   14 A, 28 a, $3.15.

LUXURY OF IDLENESS
Industry Enjoying Summer Pleasures
1234567890

24 POINT RONALDSON CONDENSED.   10 A, 18 a, $3.60.

SOLEMN PROTEST
Monarchies Crossing Bayonets
1234567890

48 POINT RONALDSON CONDENSED.   5 A, 8 a, $5.90.

CIRCUMSCRIBED
Happiness amidst Tribulation

The Point Bodies may be justified with one another by using leads and quads of our Point System.

The MacKellar, Smiths & Jordan Co., Philadelphia.   Shniedewend & Lee Co., Agents, Chicago, Ill.

PEERLESS SPECIMEN.

18A 36a 8 POINT WIDE PEERLESS (Brevier) $2 70	12A 25a 10 POINT WIDE PEERLESS (Long Primer) $2 35
LOOKING ❖ AT ❖ THE ❖ SPHINX	**❖ MERRY ❖ MASKERS ❖**
Dreaming of Days that Now are Past	Trip the Light Fantastic Toe
94 ·Worshipful Ancients 58	In Daintiest Step 43

10A 20a   12 POINT WIDE PEERLESS (2 line Nonp.) $2 50

HOURS OF UNALLOYED PLEASURES
One Smile One Glance and Love had Bound Their Hearts
And the Judge Looked Happy 86

6A 10a   18 POINT WIDE PEERLESS (3 line Nonp.) $2 85

THE IDES OF MERRY MAY
Over ❖ the ❖ Hills ❖ where ❖ Blossoms ❖ are
In the Greenwood ❖ 57

5A 8a   24 POINT WIDE PEERLESS (4 line Nonp.) $3 70

PEER ❖ OF ❖ ALL ❖ LETTERS
It Is Displayed Here ❖ 7

4A 6a   36 POINT WIDE PEERLESS (6 line Nonp.) $6 50

·WINTER ❖ IS ❖ HERE
6 ❖ Major Jim ❖ 4

Manufactured by BARNHART BROS. & SPINDLER, Chicago, Ill.

FARMER, LITTLE & CO., TYPE FOUNDERS.

The Attention of Printers is Directed to this Quaint and Unique Old Style Series,
Now for Sale, it Marks an Advance in Antique Printing.

QUAINT OLD STYLE FACES OF PAST AGES
RETURNING LIKE RIP VAN WINKLE
TO DELIGHT THE MODERN PRINTER.

PRINTERS CANNOT BUT ADMIRE
THIS NEW CANDIDATE FOR
ADMIRATION AND APPROVAL.

THE CADMUS OLD STYLE SERIES
Now Sold In Three Sizes,
SIX AND EIGHT POINT BODIES IN PREPARATION.

50 a 18 A 12 A   TWELVE POINT CADMUS OLD STYLE. $4 00

THE ETHIOPIANS affirme that Atlas, Hercules, Cadmus, and others, had from them the first light of all those Arts, Letters, Sciences, and civill Policies, which they afterward profest, and taught others: and that Pythagoras himselfe was instructed by the Lybians: to wit, from the South and superiour Egyptians: from whom those which inhabited neerer the out-let of

60 a 24 A 12 A   TEN POINT CADMUS OLD STYLE. $4 00

THE ETHIOPIANS affirme that Atlas, Hercules, Cadmus, and others, had from them the first light of all those Arts, Letters, Sciences, and civill Policies, which they afterward profest, and taught others: and that Pythagoras himselfe was instructed by the Lybians: to wit, from the South and superiour Egyptians: from whom those which inhabited neerer the out-let of Nilus, as they say, borrowed their Divinitie and Philosophie: and from them the

36 a 12 A 8 A   FOURTEEN POINT CADMUS OLD STYLE. $4 00

THE ETHIOPIANS affirme that Atlas, Hercules, Cadmus, and others, had from them the first light of all those Arts, Letters, Sciences, and civill Policies, which they afterward profest, and taught others: and that Pythagoras himselfe was instructed by the Lybians: to wit, from the South and superiour Egyptians: from whom those

36 a 12 A $3 50

Phœnicians first, if fame may credit have,
In rude Characters dar'd our Words to grave.

60 a 18 A $3 00

Phœnicians first, if fame may credit have,
In rude Characters dar'd our Words to grave.

50 a 12 A $3 25

Phœnicians first, if fame may credit have,
In rude Characters dar'd our Words to grave.

NEW YORK:
63 & 65 Beekman St.
CORNER OF GOLD ST.

IN FONTS OF FIFTY POUNDS AND UPWARDS AT BODY LETTER PRICES.

CHICAGO:
No. 154 Monroe St.
CHAS. B. ROSS, MANAGER.

24 A 50 a   6 POINT OBLIQUE GOTHIC $2 35

The Dreaded Arrival of the Quiet Lent

WHEN ALL THE WINSOME LASSIES RECUPERATE

42 For the Summer Coast Flirtations 68

18 A 36 a   8 POINT OBLIQUE GOTHIC $2 35

Let Loose the Savage Dogs

THE BOYS ARE IN THE MELON PATCH

75 Run Quicky For the Doctor 86

15 A 25 a   10 POINT OBLIQUE GOTHIC $2 30

THAT MERRY BACHELOR PLEASURE CLUB'S

First Grand Attempt at Arousing the Charming, Light-footed Terpsichore

534 Magnificent Modern Club House 928

12 A 20 a   12 POINT OBLIQUE GOTHIC $2 40

THAT'S WHAT THE DICKEY BIRDS SAY

Tuneful Erminie, Sweetest of all The Light Burlesque Operas

79 Presented by Eminent Artists 45

8 A 15 a   18 POINT OBLIQUE GOTHIC $3 15

GREAT ST. PATRICK'S DAY

When Snakes Took Hurried Departure

25 Irishmen are Happy 49

6 A 10 a   24 POINT OBLIQUE GOTHIC $4 05

OBLIQUE GOTHIC TYPES

5 The Latest Thing Out 8

Manufactured by BARNHART BROS. & SPINDLER, Chicago.

THE TRAMP PRINTER.

BY M. J. CARROLL.

TAKING the assertion of some very estimable people connected with the printing business as *prima facie* evidence of the truth of the proposition, many of the ills with which the fraternity is afflicted are to be traced in a more or less direct way to that most ubiquitous specimen of the human family, the tramp printer. But is the devil in this instance really as black as he is painted? I do not believe that he is, nor can I believe for a moment that one-half that is charged up to the debtor account of the tramp printer is really deserved, while many of his shortcomings are more than offset by his good qualities, of which we so rarely hear anything.

Of all the happy-go-lucky mortals that find an existence on this mundane sphere, this thoughtless, every-day sort of a Wilkins Micawber is unquestionably the most peculiar. Is there another human being that will so unconcernedly turn his back on the place that he has come to regard as his home, and in a too often penniless condition start out to "seek his fortune," a stranger in a strange land? He often throws up as good a situation as he hopes to find elsewhere, and without any preparation whatever goes on his way — he little cares whither. At the commencement of a journey he frequently finds himself without the means to purchase a meal, or to pay for a night's lodging. His linen may not be of the most immaculate description, and his general make-up not at all suggestive of dudish propensities; but his spirits are as buoyant, and his mind burdened with as little care, as any millionaire in the land. If he should in some unaccountable way find himself possessed of sufficient of this world's goods to provide for the necessities of the hour, he is perfectly happy. He does not propose to fret or worry for the morrow, having implicit faith that in its own good time "something will turn up" to supply his wants. As a general thing he is what is termed a good "all around" printer, and is familiar with the style of every prominent newspaper from Maine to Oregon. He is certain to be pretty well up in his information touching the leading questions of the day, and is ever ready to engage in a controversy, it making no material difference whether the subject is one of theology or politics, or on matters dramatic, musical or pugilistic.

In Richardson's "Beyond the Mississippi," a somewhat profusely illustrated work, may be seen an engraving termed "Evidences of Civilization," showing a boundless prairie, in the foreground of which is a newspaper, a whisky bottle and a cigar box. The two latter articles may not be necessary to prove that the tramp printer has gone over the scene, but the presence of the newspaper is evidence that among the pioneers was to be found at least one man who was as ready to undertake the editing of a newspaper as he was capable of setting the type for the same. It would doubtless be difficult to find that there has been a single frontier settlement in any part of America that did not contain one or more printers among its numbers. How they got there no one ever knew. The chances are that they did not originally start with the expedition formed to found a settlement or a colony. To use a popular though somewhat slangy phrase, they just "blew in" to the place, and they are just as likely to blow out of it again before anyone is aware of their intentions.

It must not be surmised, however, that the tramp printer is always a good-for-nothing or viciously inclined individual. The propensity to tramp and roam the country seems to have been a ruling passion among the disciples of Gutenberg and Faust from time immemorial. Did not that bright and shining light of the art preservative, the good Ben Franklin, indulge in this propensity when in early life he stole away from his home in Boston and went to Philadelphia; and did he not give way to the same restlessness later when he went to England in search of employment, and at a time when a visit to that country meant many weeks of toilsome and dangerous voyaging?

I must acknowledge that in many respects I have quite an admiration for the tramp printer. But I do not wish to be understood in this connection, or to have under consideration in any manner whatever, the lazy, worthless outcast, whose sole ambition is to "panhandle" an office for enough money to pander to an insatiable appetite for liquor. This excrescence on the craft is alike a nuisance, whether he tramps the country or confines his discreditable operations to a single city. Happily, this class of printers is becoming measurably less numerous year by year, and a firm resistance to their demands by all self-respecting printers will speedily make the practice a thing of the past.

But perhaps the most satisfactory results derived from this restless spirit on the part of so large a portion of the printing fraternity, is to be found in the fact that it has a tendency to equalize the supply with the demand for labor in different parts of the country. An overcrowded labor market in one city or section of the country, and a security of supply in another direction, are conditions that should not long exist among a people, so large a proportion of whom are ready to go so far for so little an inducement. I have frequently known of men who would resign a situation to take one hundreds of miles away, and when they knew they would not be benefiting their condition in any way by making the change. It would appear to be a part of their creed that life is made up of just about so much toil and labor, care and anxiety, and that if it can be relieved occasionally by a change of scene and associations, so much the better, and so much the easier it is to bear. And who can say after all that they are not right?

Another advantage to be derived from this practice of floating about is that it will improve the character of the work done in the country at large, and make the workman far more independent and self-reliant than would otherwise be the case. In the first instance, a superior line of work done by improved methods in a certain locality or city, would long remain an insurmountable task to printers in other places were it not from occasional visits from the roving craftsman. He picks up knowledge of the latest wrinkles in every quarter, and scatters it broadcast throughout the land, without money and without price. As to its making a workman more self-reliant and independent, there can be little question. Take a man, for instance, who has served his apprenticeship and remained for some years afterward in a certain establishment, and you will generally find him imbued with a morbid dread of leaving it. He has no confidence in his ability to give the same satisfaction elsewhere, and regards his removal from his old position in the nature of a calamity. Certainly, if a man can remain in one position for a lifetime, well and good. But how frequently do we see the most friendly relations severed by the most trivial occurrences. Is there a man employed in the printing business who has a mortgage on his position for a single day? Is there one who on going to work in the morning can tell but what by some misunderstanding, accident or mistake, he may not be compelled before night to seek a new situation? We cannot tell what a day may bring forth, and these things are among the most likely possibilities.

That the tramp is a constituent part of the printing fraternity, is beyond a question of doubt. But to determine the cause or causes that will drive a man to follow such an existence would lead to a great deal of speculation. Notwithstanding his apparent indifference and hopefulness, his lot must frequently be far from a happy one. He does not always dwell under a glorious sky and in a perfect atmosphere. His seeming jollity may often be a mask to cover blighted ambitions and dead and buried hopes. As a bright-faced, bright-eyed boy, he undoubtedly commenced life as the rest of us did. His hopes and ambitions were the same; his frugality and industry up to the average, until fate played him some scurvy trick that made him believe that there was nothing left worth working for, and nothing to guide him through life but an ungovernable restlessness, that relentlessly carries him from point to point, until his weary body finds its last resting place, and his spirit joins the silent majority. It will cost us very little effort to have at least a kind word and a kind wish for the tramp printer.

25 A   6 POINT WIDE SPENSER $1 50

HAIL TO FAIRIE QUEEN

SPENSER'S GREAT POETICAL FANCY

84 LOVED LITERATEURS 65

18 A   9 POINT WIDE SPENSER $1 60

HERBERT SPENSER

STUDENTS OF SOCIOLOGY

35 EVOLUTIONIST 46

15 A   12 POINT WIDE SPENSER $1 65

BEAUTIFUL WIDE SPENSER

ALWAYS GIVING COMPLETE SATISFACTION

89 PRAISED BY GOOD PRINTERS 75

10 A   18 POINT WIDE SPENSER $2 35

MYRTLE SCRIPTS

ATTRACTIVE AND HANDSOME

43 SPIRITED AWAY 56

8 A   24 POINT WIDE SPENSER $3 10

HELENE COMETH NOT

8 WONDERFUL 6

6 A   30 POINT WIDE SPENSER $3 70

FOUR LONG ACTS

3 WEARIED 5

Manufactured by BARNHART BROS. & SPINDLER, Chicago, Ill.

Also carried in stock and for sale by Minnesota Type Foundry Co., St. Paul, Minn.; Great Western Type Foundry, Kansas City, Mo.; Great Western Type Foundry, Omaha, Neb.; St. Louis Printers' Supply Co., St. Louis, Mo.

WAYSIDE ⌗ SERIES.

25 A,   10 POINT WAYSIDE. $1.50

INSTRVCTiVe : PaRaBLeS : aNDe : WiSe : SaYiNGS : oF : oVR :MoST : LEaRNeD : PEoPLe

GHoSTLie ⌗ LEGeNDS ⌗ DEPiCTeD ⌗ BY ⌗ MaSTeRLY ⌗ ViSioN ⌗ aND ⌗ FERTiLE ⌗ IMAGiNaTioN

⌗ Ye × CoRReCT × 88 × PoeMS × oF × LORD × BYRON ⌗

20 A,   12 POINT WAYSIDE. $1.60

Ye THRiLLiNG TaLeS FoR BLEaK aND WiNTRY DaYeS

A SELeCTioN oF SACReD BALLaDS FoR Ye ANNuAL SiNGiN SKEWL EXERCiSES

280   Ye × QuaiNT × OLDe × WaYSiDe × INN   162

20 A,   14 POINT WAYSIDE. $2.00

CuSToMS ⌗ AND ⌗ USaGeS ⌗ oF ⌗ EaRLY ⌗ ENGLiSH ⌗ PRiNTeRS

MUSiCaL CONCeRT oF THe CALVaRY HiLL SUNDaY SCHooL CLASSeS

HaPPie × XMaS × ANDe × NeW × YeAR

18 A,   16 POINT WAYSIDE. $2.05

GRAY'S QUAiNT OLD ELeGY iN A CouNTRY CHuRCHYARD

THe × CuRFeW × TOLLS × THe × KNELL × oF × PaRTING × DAY

15 A,   18 POINT WAYSIDE. $2.55

DouTFuL × TALeS × oF × THe × ANCieNT × CRuSADeR

618   LiTTLe × ReD × RiDiNG × HooD   261

10 A,   24 POINT WAYSIDE. $3.00

LEGeNDS ⌗ oF ⌗ GoLDeN ⌗ FaIRY ⌗ LaNDS

THE ∴ PaRSoNaGe ∴ SoCIeTY

JAMES CONNER'S SONS, UNITED STATES TYPE FOUNDRY, NEW YORK CITY.

8 A,   24 POINT VOLUNTEER. $3.75

SOLID FACTS FOR AGED MISERS
28 INVESTMENTS 65

12 A,   12 POINT VOLUNTEER. $1.75

CONVENTS OF EARLY TIMES   PAPER MONEY OF AMERICA
34 ROOT OF ALL EVIL 17

4 A,   48 POINT VOLUNTEER. $6.00

STEAM 3 PRESS

10 A,   18 POINT VOLUNTEER. $2.75

84 HANDSOME EQUIPMENT 62
BRAVE BOY IN BLUE ∴ SOLDIER OR SAILOR

5 A,   36 POINT VOLUNTEER. $5.00

7 VOLUNTEER 5
ORNAMENTAL BORDERS

FOUNDRY OF JAMES CONNER'S SONS, NEW YORK.

6 A, 36 POINT PILGRIM. $4.50

BEAUTIFUL ✤ & ✤ CHARMING
93 PRINCIPLE 54

12 A, 18 POINT PILGRIM. $3.10

LUCKY ✤ NUMBERS 853 CENTRAL ✤ PARK

45 ✤ PROGRAMME ✤ 78

4 A, 48 POINT PILGRIM. $5.00

SHARPS 47 COMEDY
52 GERMAN 63

8 A, 24 POINT PILGRIM. $3.35

MECHANICS' ✤ SCHOOL ✤ LIBRARY

34 ✤ FOUNDRIES ✤ 56

24 AND 18 POINT IN COMBINATION.

KOMICAL ✤ CONCERTS ∶∴∶ XCITING ✤ EXHIBITION

JAMES ✤ CONNER'S ✤ SONS, ✤ NEW ✤ YORK.

POINTERS FOR THE KID.

BY HERBERT L. BAKER.

HERE, Tom, you little twig of His Satanic Majesty, just stop teasing the cat long enough to gulp down a dose of instructions. Everybody else but you has instructions, advice and "pointers" till indigestion of the brain threatens; but, poor fellow, the only way you have to learn what is right is to do wrong, and welcome a kick for the information (not soon forgotten) which it conveys. Now, here is a nice little lot of "pointers" cooked *a la foreman d'shop* for your special delectation:

First pointer. Don't get down too early in the morning. If the printers should come in and find the place swept and warmed and cleaned, all ready for business, the shock would seriously disturb their nerve. They would not know what to do without their morning siesta waiting for the place to warm up, and some of them might die from the effects. You haven't made this dreadful error yet, and probably never will, but you might!

When you sweep, for heaven's sake don't pick up the type and material on the floor. Why, don't you know it will make your trousers bag at the knees to stoop so low? Then the printers despise distributing floor "pi," and since the office is run solely for their benefit, whatever they dislike they must not be asked to do. Then, too, where would the poor typefounder be if type was carefully saved and cared for — why, his business would soon be ruined! and it is your solemn duty to look after the typefounder and the printers. If the promptings of your tender little soul make it impossible to sweep out the type, by all means sweep them a long distance to a nice comfortable spot where it will be easy to pick them all up without skirmishing about under the cases. Take things easy as possible, my boy — don't break your back for a few pounds of sorts; they don't cost you anything, anyhow! This course will supply the office with a variegated assortment of hybrid letters, with small-pox faces and camel-backs, which any typefounder would gladly give as much as 8 cents a pound for; and if you are real diligent you can bring the office quite an income from this source. If the proprietor should find out how hard you were trying to add to his income, perhaps he would give you a raise — (with the soft end of his boot-toe!).

When you go out on an errand, don't get back too soon. You are paid just as much whether you run four errands or forty a day, and it isn't dignified to hurry. Don't the books on decorum say, "Gentlemen never hurry?" Your dinner will digest better if you will remember to saunter leisurely along the boulevard, with an occasional pause to witness canine pugilism, and frequent rests whenever the chance offers to "skin" another "kid" at the fascinating game of "keeps." This will improve your skill at marbles, while saving you from the imminent dangers of overexertion. Watch the punctuation of your errands: a short pause at anything commacal, a longer pause when you run across a man shoveling colon the walk, come to a full stop at any period of your jaunt, or dash up a side street when there is hy-fun ahead. If you see the proprietor coming while enjoying your heaven-given right to a life of leisure, it is a good plan to start off on a good trot, for these employers have such odd ideas about some things — besides, if you know he is out of the office, you are more likely to have a rest in it.

If you are set at putting away leads and slugs, be careful not to grab them too tight in your hand, for you might bruise them. If some fall on the floor occasionally, never mind, for you will only be aiding the "typographical artist." What! didn't you know that that is the way the artist in type gets his curves? Why, that ought to be plain even to you, after one glance at some of their productions. The easiest way (therefore the best) to sort leads, is to take a handful and jog them up on one end on the stone. It doesn't hurt the stone, and there are plenty of new leads at the foundry.

When finally put at learning the case, do not forget that you can know it in an hour as well as in a year, and your first duty certainly is to put the types in the right boxes. You will doubtless find the "p" box full of "d's," the "n" box full of "u's," etc. By all means regulate these little mistakes of the careless comps by putting together all letters that look the same, thereby earning the gratitude and good-will of the foreman. As soon as the case is learned you ought to have some cards; so when no one is about, go to the new script case and set up your name, tie a string around it and put it on the stone, then ink it, place a card on the type, put a piece of kindling wood on the card and hit it with a mallet. If it doesn't show enough on the card, hit it harder next time. This is a great scheme "never before published," except in "Hints to Amateurs," but observe one precaution: be sure to show the cards to the proprietor, for the rewards of genius are great, and his astonishment will be very funny!

Of course no bright boy in these latter days will be so foolish as to do without tobacco, so you will earn the admiration of all your elders by keeping a quid in one corner of your mouth and a cigarette in the other — as long as you can beg or steal them. Your first duty in this connection in the office will be to find some place on the floor where the gentlemanly compositors have not spat, then spit all over the spot. The floor doesn't look well with such spots of different color, and the proprietor will appreciate your efforts to add to the appearance of the place.

Above all things, don't forget to demand higher wages every few weeks. If you follow these instructions your services will soon be so invaluable that any price will be paid rather than lose you. The more diligently you follow them the sooner you will be taken into partnership by the proprietor or — FIRED!

THE GOOD OLD TIMES.

THAT "wise men change their minds, but fools never," is an aphorism as true as it is trite, and there is no better illustration than can be found in some printing offices. There are printers who, despite all argument, practical proof and even disastrous failure, still obstinately cling to old-fashioned methods and material that are heavy impediments to success and progress; to the exploded theory that whatever our grandfathers did is the only wise and sensible way, and glorify the ancient at the expense of the modern.

The old was well enough—when we knew no better. When we set up, corrected, made ready and worked off by the feeble, flickering dimness of a tallow candle stuck in a bit of wood or lead, we were content because we had to be. Then, kerosene, gas and the flame of electricity were unknown, and the light de luxe was made by chasing, killing and robbing whales, or in an hour of almost bankrupt extravagance by stealing wax from bees. The old press, that to work almost pulled one's arm from the socket, was good enough, for cylinder, power and perfecting printing machines were not even visionary dreams. We had little knowledge of paper manufacture, of the thousand improvements that now make the art luxury and work perfection. Steam hissed contentedly from the spout of the teakettle, with never a premonition of being enslaved and forced to labor. The lightning played unchallenged through black clouds, and laughed in its midst at the efforts of the pigmies of earth to bend and make it a servant of daring enterprise. The old "thorough brace" stage rattled on, dislocating joints, and brought mails when "the Indians did not murder the driver or the wolves eat him up!" Railway tracks, locomotives and vestibule cars were peacefully slumbering in the iron of mines and timber of forests. There was no conception of the might or majesty of matter, that when manipulated by genius would revolutionize the world. We had not the slightest premonition of the possibilities of the future, or a very discontented race would have inhabited the earth.

In the "good old times," so often and ridiculously boasted of, there was neither telephone, telegraph, ocean steamer, sewing machines, reapers nor any of the grander, almost inspired results following and to follow their inception and improvement. In old times, we froze by the fireplace in winter and roasted in summer. Our houses were of logs and we had no modern improvements. We ate the coarsest food from pewter dishes and by means of leaden spoons. The beasts of the field and fowls of the air were our thermometers and barometers, our signal service and weather prophets; we forded or swam bridgeless streams, and were often hopelessly mired in the depths of sloughs. Our guns would fire but a single shot without reloading, and our "Washington" and "Franklin" produce but a single impression without the flying and replacement of a sheet. We had the most primitive way of doing work, and the most unwieldy machinery for doing it. We were as children groping in the dark, and life was a continual battle, a hard and unrepaid struggle for its continuance.

Such and very much more of unpleasantness were the "good old times." Give them all possible credit, but in these later days of a new inspiration don't hanker after their return. They lived and died, that is enough to know; they are buried, disturb not their graves. Their dust can never again be quickened into life and usefulness. Better they should be forgotten than rise up ghosts of preposterous clumsiness and failure.

Particularly should this be the case in the modern printing office where every useful novelty is needed and every improvement stamped with availability demanded. Better throw out of the window or into the pi-box all relics of the past than cling to them, and endeavor to "make them answer." Time has become one of the most important factors in the race for wealth and the competition for patronage. It is whip and spur from the cradle to the grave, and a single moment lost often forbids the "breaking of the record." It is a wise man indeed who seizes upon every opportunity, and a fool who temporizes. By it more jobs and fortunes have been lost than can be enumerated; by clinging to the old more tempers have been soured and botched work turned out than should have been done in a century. In fact, it is a crime against labor and an imposition upon the laborer for the employer to neglect the opportunities furnished by the present. The art is worthy of it, and the craft should be worthy of the art. There should be no half way in the matter. Banish every antiquated, not up to the standard article from the office to the fire or the foundry. The new has no place for them. Show the youngest apprentice the stick, press and type used by your grandfather, the "brayer" and the shooting stick, and he would smile with supreme contempt at the stupidity incorporated in his body.

The new is ever growing to be the old. With today the things thereof pass away and others take their place. "Keep moving" is the motto of the world; "keep advancing" the order. Printing at the present day is no more like it was in the good old times than a matchlock musket is like a Gatling gun. One has to struggle to keep abreast of the tide; has to be supplied with new material and new inventions to compete with his neighbors. Good work cannot be turned out that will prove satisfactory without the means, and that does not belong to a former century or an earlier decade in this. Better burn your fingers with live coals than be digging among dead ashes. Tear off the musty, faded crape you are wearing for the good old times, keep up with and ahead of the requirements of the present. Let printing be your ambition as you hope it will be your profit, and it is only with the new can you tempt and command it.

Marder, Luse & Co., Type Founders, Chicago.

AMERICAN SYSTEM OF
INTERCHANGEABLE TYPE BODIES.

CONTOUR No. 4.
ORIGINAL.

MORTISED LETTERS  WITH THIS SERIES.

6A, 12a,   Double English (28 Point). $4.00

RED STAMPS
Four Hundred Sold
23 Daily 75

5A, 10a,   Double Columbian (32 Point). $4.90

BEAUTIFUL
Summer Resort

4A, 8a,   Double Paragon (40 Point). $6.00

WASHINGTON PARK
Beginning the Race Season

4A, 8a,   Four-Line Pica (48 Point). $8.20

2 Half MILE Dash 3

3A, 5a,   Five-Line Pica (60 Point). $9.45

For a GOLD Medal

3A, 5a,   Six-Line Pica (72 Point). $11.95

Free FOR Nine

30 A.   NONPAREIL (6 POINT) KATHERINE.   PRICE $2.25.

LADIES WALKING JACKETS, REEFING JACKETS AND NEWMARKETS
THE LATEST PRODUCTIONS OF THE MOST FASHIONABLE MAKERS ARE REPRESENTED
TAKE ADVANTAGE OF THIS OPPORTUNITY 1234567890

30 A.   BREVIER (8 POINT) KATHERINE.   PRICE $3.00.

I KNOW A BANK WHEREON THE WILD THYME GROWS
THE CELEBRATED AND POETICAL PRODUCTIONS OF THOMAS MOORE.
ALMOST PERSUADED 123456780

20 A.   PICA (12 POINT) KATHERINE.   PRICE $3.25.

CONCEITED DABBLERS IN LITERATURE
THE SHAKESPERIAN AND BACON CONTROVERSY
MEN OF LETTERS 24579

12 A.   THREE LINE NONPAREIL (18 POINT) KATHERINE.   PRICE $3.75.

WESTERN INDUSTRIES
THE CATTLE RANCHE OF KANSAS.
PRAIRIES 134567

10 A.   TWO LINE PICA (24 POINT) KATHERINE.   PRICE $5.00.

QUEEN OF THE AMAZONS
GRISELLA 5643

LINDSAY TYPE FOUNDRY, NEW YORK.

SPECIMENS FROM FARMER, LITTLE & CO., TYPE FOUNDERS.

NEW YORK—63 & 65 Beekman St.   CHICAGO—154 Monroe Street,
And 62 & 64 Gold Street.   Chas. B. Ross, Manager.

PATENT PENDING.

36 a   9 A—PRICE PER FONT, $8 00   THREE LINE NONPAREIL STATIONER SCRIPT—18 POINT.   LOWER CASE, $5 00

The Firm has much pleasure in returning their Thanks to

The American Printing Trade

For the Appreciation with which they have received the Stationer Script

And now Complete the Series with this New Size

Which they present to the Trade in Compliance with the Demand

Made for its Production

20 a   6 A—PRICE PER FONT, $8 00   TWO LINE PICA STATIONER SCRIPT—24 POINT.   LOWER CASE, $5 00

We Request the Attention of the Printing Trade to

This Elegant New Script Face

Designed Expressly for the Printing of Wedding and Visiting

Cards, Invitation Notes, etc.,

The Name Stationer Script will be appropriate

15 a   5 A—PRICE PER FONT, $9 50   THREE LINE PICA STATIONER SCRIPT—36 POINT.   LOWER CASE, $5 75

The Three Sizes in Combination are

Very Handsome in Appearance

Attractive and Useful in Character it will be

A General Favorite

FARMER, LITTLE & CO., TYPE FOUNDERS, CHICAGO.

Keystone Pen Writer

NINE-POINT.   12 A. 32 a. $3.45   32 a. $2.00

Its health-restoring qualities are becoming celebrated the world over
Little by little they go through a course of important reading
Do not try to make up the deficiency in price by the deficiency in workmanship; rather incur
loss than furnish inferior work of any kind
The severe gale which visited the coast during March. $1234567890

TWELVE-POINT.   12 A. 32 a. $4.64   32 a. $2.90

Do not marry until you are able to support a wife
Fun for fun. Business for business.
If any one speak evil of you, let your life be so that none will believe it
Push is the word for a world full of work as this is
Receipts $1,234,567,890

EIGHTEEN-POINT.   8 A. 20 a. $5.65   20 a. $3.25

An Account of my Experience
It is not well for one to have too many intimate friends
No Indication of being Discouraged
$1234567890

TWENTY-FOUR-POINT.   6 A. 14 a. $5.90   14 a. $3.40

Promoting Happiness
Several Celebrated Characters of this Age
Aid Given in the Right Direction
$1234567890

CAST FROM OUR NICKEL ALLOY TYPE METAL—SUPERIOR TO ALL OTHERS.

MATHER MANUFACTURING CO.
PROPRIETORS.

✠

734 TO 740 SANSOM STREET,
PHILADELPHIA.

Oldest and Largest Type Foundry in America.

THE MACKELLAR, SMITHS & JORDAN COMPANY,

Type Founders and Electrotypers,

606-614 Sansom St., Philadelphia.

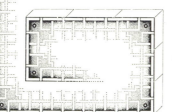

Ronaldson Title Slope.
6 Point, *30 A, 60 a,* $3.00
8 Point, *25 A, 50 a,* 3.15
10 Point, *22 A, 45 a,* 3.35
12 Point, *20 A, 40 a,* 3 55

Estimates for Printing-Office Outfits Furnished.

Graceful  Designs.

12 POINT GUTENBERG.   8 A, 20 a. $2.45

THE FINANCE COMPANY OF SPENDQUICK
≈ Charter · Perpetual, Capital · Unlimited ≈
Provides Methods to Speedily Reduce the Weight of Heavy Pockets
Secures · Opportunities · for · Seeing · the · Elephant

24 POINT GUTENBERG.   5 A, 10 a. $3.60

Commendable ✹ Principles
Promptness · in · Settling · with · Coachmen
1234567890

18 POINT GUTENBERG.   A, 14 a. $3.20

Everyday · Trials · of · Patience
Initiating Young Scholars into the Art of Printing
· · Spoiled · Jobs, · Squabbled · Types · ·
1234567890

The Ornaments displayed with the Gutenberg Series are from our Combination Border, Series 97.

18 A 36 a 6 POINT OLD STYLE EXPANDED (Nonpareil) $2 90

BEST TYPE MADE
Celebrated Copper-Mixed Type
89 Every Printer Uses 56

15 A 25 a 9 POINT OLD STYLE EXPANDED (Bourgeois) $3 05

BROWN BIRDS
Convicted and Hanged
67 Winter Dream 84

12 A 20 a 12 POINT OLD STYLE EXPANDED (2 line Nonp.) $3 10

TWENTY-ONE MAIDS
Waiting for their Fleeting Hopes Again
53 Romany Rum Rebellion 92

8 A 12 a 18 POINT OLD STYLE EXPANDED (3 line Nonp.) $4 50

KINGDOMS COMING QUICK
85 Will be There 73

6 A 10 a 24 POINT OLD STYLE EXPANDED (4 line Nonp.) $5 25

DANCING EVALENA
3 Fairy Dales 2

5 A 8 a 30 POINT OLD STYLE EXPANDED (5 line Nonp.) $6 25

GREAT CHICAGO
7 Metropolis 5

4 A 6 a 36 POINT OLD STYLE EXPANDED (6 line Nonp.) $7 35

BROWN PETE
3 Raiment 5

Manufactured by *BARNHART BROS. & SPINDLER*, Chicago, Ill.

SEMI GOTHIC.

AMERICAN SYSTEM OF INTERCHANGEABLE TYPE BODIES.

36A,   Nonpareil (6 Point). $1.10

LATEST RAILWAY SIGNAL INDICATES AUTOMATICALLY
THE TIME THAT HAS ELAPSED UP TO TWENTY MINUTES SINCE THE
123 LAST TRAIN PASSED NIAGARA FALLS 456

28A,   Brevier (8 Point). $1.15

SHADES OF PINK AND OTHER COLORS
LARGE ASSORTMENT OF THE SAME MAY BE FOUND
74 THE BLACK AND GREEN COMPANY 83

24A,   Long Primer (10 Point). $1.30

MICHIGAN CENTRAL RAILROAD
THE DIRECT ROUTE TO NEW YORK CITY
$38 ROUND TRIP $38

20A,   Pica (12 Point). $1.40

MARINE INSURANCE CO.
STRONGEST IN THE NORTHWEST

16A,   Two-Line Minion (14 Point). $1.60

HARTFORD FIRE INSURANCE COMPANY
RISKS ARE TAKEN ON ANY CITY AND SUBURBAN PROPERTY
253 ALWAYS CHEAPEST 674

16A,   Two-Line Brevier (16 Point). $2.10

RIVERDALE REAL ESTATE OFFICE
PROPERTY CAN BE HAD ON REASONABLE TERMS

14A,   Two-Line Long Primer (20 Point). $2.90

TRANSFER ASSOCIATION
7 FOR PROTECTION OF TARIFF RATES 9

12A,   Two-Line Pica (24 Point). $3.50

EAGLE PUBLISHING HOUSE
MAGAZINES BOUGHT

10A,   Two-Line Columbian (32 Point). $4.75

MORGAN & RAVENS
SUMMER NIGHT CONCERT

6 POINT LINING GOTHIC, No. 14.   60 A. $2.25

SUPERIORITY OF THE MODERN METHODS AND APPLIANCES
CALCULATIONS BY AN INVARIABLE AND CORRECT SYSTEM OF MEASUREMENT WITH IMPROVED APPARATUS
1 2 3 4 5 6 7 8 9 0

6 POINT LINING GOTHIC, No. 15.   60 A. $2.25

INSTANCES OF INACCURATE GEODETIC OPERATIONS
CIRCUMFERENCE OF TERRESTRIAL SPHERES CONSIDERED BY AN EXPERT MATHEMATICIAN
1 2 3 4 5 6 7 8 9 0

6 POINT LINING GOTHIC, No. 16.   60 A. $2.25

MICROSCOPIC VERNIER INDICATIONS COMPARED
CHANGES IN ATMOSPHERIC STRATA EXEMPLIFIED BY ASTRONOMY
1 2 3 4 5 6 7 8 9 0

60 A. $2.25   6 POINT LINING GOTHIC, No. 17.   70 a. $1.75

THEODOLITE REPEATING CIRCLE
Oblique Inclinations of Base with the Horizon Calculated
Zenith Distance Measured

36 A. $2.10   8 POINT LINING GOTHIC, No. 3.   55 a. $1.80

HONORABLE COMPETENCY
Basking in the Sunshine of Prosperous Days
Industrial Advancement

36 A. $2.10   9 POINT LINING GOTHIC, No. 3.   50 a. $1.80

THATCHED MANSIONS
Wonderfully Improved Roofing Materials
Artistic and Durable

25 A. $2.20   12 POINT LINING GOTHIC, No. 3.   40 a. $2.00

AIRLINE ROUTE TO SKYHIGH PEAKS
Excursion Organized and Guarded by Experienced Rangers

14 A. $2.40   18 POINT LINING GOTHIC, No. 3.   25 a. $2.55

Malcontented PATAGONIANS Emancipated

10 A. $2.70   24 POINT LINING GOTHIC, No. 3.   15 a. $2.50

Humane MEASURE Adopted

8 A. $3.50   30 POINT LINING GOTHIC, No. 3.   12 a. $3.10

ENAMOURED Companions

6 A. $3.90   36 POINT LINING GOTHIC, No. 3.   9 a. $3.20

ALL COMPLETE WITH FIGURES.

Advance MONEY

mmmmmmmm

HHHHHHHHHHH

MacKellar, Smiths & Jordan Co., Philadelphia.

Shniedewend & Lee Co., Agents, Chicago, Ill.

6 POINT LINING GOTHIC, No. 18.   50 A. $1.35

PROFESSOR LIGHTFINGER RESPECTFULLY RECOMMENDS
CARELESSNESS IN BOLTING FRONT DOORS, CELLAR WINDOWS, BACK GATES
1234567890

6 POINT LINING GOTHIC, No. 19.   50 A. $1.40

POLICEMEN HUNTING MIDNIGHT INVADERS
ANGRY HOUSEWIVES OVERHAULING BUREAUS AND JEWELRY CASES
1234567890

6 POINT LINING GOTHIC, No. 20.   50 A. $1.70

SCOURING THE COUNTRY FOR BURGLARS
HAY-FORKS AND THRASHELS BROUGHT INTO REQUISITION
1234567890

6 POINT LINING GOTHIC, No. 21.   50 A. $2.35

MOUNTED POLICE SUMMONED
LIGHTFINGER'S BRIGANDS TAKEN INTO CUSTODY
1234567890

50 A. $2.65   6 POINT LINING GOTHIC, No. 22.   70 a. $1.80

HAPPINESS AND SUNSHINE
Social Family Gathering around Welcome Fireside
1234567890

36 A. $2.00   8 POINT LINING GOTHIC, No. 4.   55 a. $1.80

INTERESTING LECTURES
Enforcing Stringent Household Regulations
Visitors Excepted

27 A. $2.10   10 POINT LINING GOTHIC, No. 4.   45 a. $1.95

MORNING RAMBLES
Tourists Inspecting Ancient Ruins
Unearthed Towns

2 A. $2.10   12 POINT LINING GOTHIC, No. 4.   40 a. $2.00

HILLSIDE SPORTS
Ascending Slippery Pathways
Taking Headers

14 A. $2.55   18 POINT LINING GOTHIC, No. 4.   22 a. $2.20

Competitive EXTRAVAGANCE Requested

10 A. $3.10   24 POINT LINING GOTHIC, No. 4.   15 a. $2.55

African MONKEY Houses

8 A. $3.75   30 POINT LINING GOTHIC, No. 4.   12 a. $3.20

PATHWAYS Ornamented

6 A. $4.40   36 POINT LINING GOTHIC, No. 4.   8 a. $3.25

Summer PATROL

ALL COMPLETE WITH FIGURES.

mmmmmmmm   nnnnNNNNNNNN

MacKellar, Smiths & Jordan Co., Philadelphia.   Shniedewend & Lee Co., Agents, Chicago, Ill.

July 1889 289

45 A. $1.45   6 POINT LINING GOTHIC, No. 23.

INTERNATIONAL CONGRESS ON FUTURE WARFARE
MOUNTED MEN FORBIDDEN, ARMIES NOT TO EXCEED ONE HUNDRED MEN
1234567890

6 POINT LINING GOTHIC, No. 24.   45 A. $1.55

YELLOWSTONE GEYSER WATER COMPANY
ABANDONMENT OF FUEL FOR COOKING, HEATING AND WASHING
1234567890

6 POINT LINING GOTHIC, No. 25.   45 A. $1.90

DINNER TIME AMONG INSURGENTS
PICTURES OF PARIS DURING THE FRENCH REVOLUTION
1234567890

6 POINT LINING GOTHIC, No. 26.   45 A. $2.10

STRUGGLING AGAINST POWER
ESCAPE FROM EMBRACES OF AFRICAN GORILLA
1234567890

45 A. $2.55   6 POINT LINING GOTHIC, No. 27.   70 a. $1.90

VETERAN SHOULDER THUMPERS
Quellers of Insurrection and Political Disturbance
Pensioned by Governments

36 A. $2.00   8 POINT LINING GOTHIC, No. 5.   55 a. $1.80

MIDSUMMER PLEASURES
Juveniles Rambling Through Shady Groves
Hammocks in Demand

25 A. $2.00   9 POINT LINING GOTHIC, No. 5.   45 a. $1.85

EXAGGERATIONS
Huntsmen Spinning Fishing Yarns
Unblushingly

20 A. $2.10   12 POINT LINING GOTHIC, No. 5.   30 a. $1.90

SIPPING BOHEA
Society Damsels Adopting
Latest Styles

12 A. $2.40   18 POINT LINING GOTHIC, No. 5.   18 a. $2.05

Deciphering NORWEGIAN Manuscript

8 A. $2.90   24 POINT LINING GOTHIC, No. 5.   12 a. $2.30

Saluting HEROIC General

6 A. $3.55   30 POINT LINING GOTHIC, No. 5.   9 a. $2.80

MIDNIGHT Adventures

4 A. $3.65   36 POINT LINING GOTHIC, No. 5.   7 a. $3.15

Baritone SINGER

ALL COMPLETE WITH FIGURES.

mmmmmmmm   nnnnnnNNNNN

MacKellar, Smiths & Jordan Co., Philadelphia.   Shniedewend & Lee Co., Agents, Chicago, Ill.

Lining Gothic  Extended.

MECHANICAL PATENT,
March 31, 1885.

25 A. $1.60	6 POINT LINING GOTHIC EXTENDED.	35 a. $1.40

IMMENSE REDUCTION
Regular Masculine Bargain Hunters
Presented with Nerve Tonic
1234567890

20 A. $1.60	8 POINT LINING GOTHIC EXTENDED.	30 a. $1.40

MONSIEUR TEARQUICK
Fashionable Gaskins Repaired
Charges Reasonable
1234567890

6 A. $1.60	10 POINT LINING GOTHIC EXTENDED.	24 a. $1.50

GRAND PAGEANT
Procession of Honorable
Townsmen

14 A. $1.70	12 POINT LINING GOTHIC EXTENDED.	22 a. $1.70

BEAU MONDE
Demands Continued
Notoriety

12 A. $1.80	14 POINT LINING GOTHIC EXTENDED.	18 a. $1.70

HANDSOME GROUPINGS
Nymphs Basking in Tropical Sunshine

10 A. $2.30	18 POINT LINING GOTHIC EXTENDED.	14 a. $2.00

FAMILIAR SAYINGS
Modern Phonograph Charged

7 A. $2.40	24 POINT LINING GOTHIC EXTENDED.	10 a. $2.10

CATALONIAN Masquerade

5 A. $2.80	30 POINT LINING GOTHIC EXTENDED.	7 a. $2.35

PAYING Brands

4 A. $3.80	36 POINT LINING GOTHIC EXTENDED.	6 a. $3.30

German FAVORS

ALL COMPLETE WITH FIGURES.

NNNNNNNNNN nnnnnnnnn

MacKellar, Smiths & Jordan Co., Philadelphia   Shniedewend & Lee Co., Agents, Chicago, Ill.

July 1889   291

USEFUL GOTHIC.

ORIGINAL.

40 A   6 POINT INCLINED LINING GOTHIC No. 4   (Nonpareil) $1 30

IN A SHADY NOOK, BY A BABBLING BROOK

THERE SITS MY LOVE SO FAIR. IN HER LAP A BOOK, IN HER

368 EYES A LOOK OF KISS ME IF YOU DARE 529

40 A   6 POINT INCLINED LINING GOTHIC No. 5   (Nonpareil) $1 55

OH PRINTER MAN WHEN YOU BEGAN

TO SEE THAT YOU WERE FIXED WAS WHEN YOU SENT OR

4 TO US WENT FOR SUPERIOR COPPER-MIXED 5

40 A   6 POINT INCLINED LINING GOTHIC No. 6   (Nonpareil) $1 75

THIS HANDSOME INCLINED LINING GOTHIC IS CAST

FROM OUR CELEBRATED SUPERIOR COPPER-MIXED TYPE METAL

289 THE BEST IN THE MARKET 754

GENERAL WESTERN AGENTS FOR BABCOCK PATENT AIR-SPRING PRESSES.

BARNHART BROS. & SPINDLER,

MANUFACTURERS OF

SUPERIOR COPPER-MIXED TYPE,

113, 115 AND 117 FIFTH AVENUE,

TELEPHONE 242.

CHICAGO, ILLINOIS.

40 A   6 POINT INCLINED LINING GOTHIC No. 7   (Nonpareil) $1 85

GENERAL WESTERN AGENTS

THE BABCOCK PATENT AIR-SPRING PRESS

475 OPTIMUS AND STANDARD 863

30 A   8 POINT INCLINED LINING GOTHIC   (Brevier) $1 85

IRON RAILROAD TRACKS

NORTH WESTERN STEEL COMPANY

294 CHICAGO ILLINOIS 536

20 A   10 POINT INCLINED LINING GOTHIC   (Lg. Primer) $1 65

AN INCLINED GOTHIC

USEFUL AND ORNAMENTAL

4 SURE TO WEAR WELL

20 A   12 POINT INCLINED LINING GOTHIC   (2 line Nonp.) $2 10

COPPER-MIXED

SUPERIOR TO OTHER

BOUND TO LAST 9

Manufactured by BARNHART BROS. & SPINDLER, Chicago, Ill.

Also carried in stock and for sale by Minnesota Type Foundry Co., St. Paul, Minn.; Great Western Type Foundry, Kansas City, Mo.; Great Western Type Foundry, Omaha, Neb.; St. Louis Printers' Supply Co., St. Louis, Mo.

SPECIMENS FROM FARMER, LITTLE & CO., TYPE FOUNDERS.

NEW YORK—63 & 65 Beekman St.
And 62 & 64 Gold Street.

CHICAGO—154 Monroe Street.
Chas. B. Ross, Manager.

15 A   TWENTY POINT CADMUS TITLE. $2 50

ANCIENT YET USEFUL CHARACTER

10 A   TWENTY-FOUR POINT CADMUS TITLE. $2 75

THE ORIGINAL CADMUS SERIES 8

25 A   TEN POINT CADMUS TITLE. $1 50

QUITE ORIGINAL DESIGN IN OLD STYLE
USEFUL CHARACTERS 467

20 A   TWELVE POINT CADMUS TITLE. $1 60

ARTISTIC PRINTERS MUST ADMIRE
NEW TITLE SERIES 825

10 A   TWENTY-EIGHT POINT CADMUS TITLE. $3 75

MEMORIAL ARCH 79-89

8 A   THIRTY-SIX POINT CADMUS TITLE. $5 00

OLD STYLE PRINTER

6 A   FORTY POINT CADMUS TITLE. $5 00

PRIMITIVE 46

20 A   FOURTEEN POINT CADMUS TITLE. $2 00

TYPOGRAPHICAL NOVELTIES
QUALIFICATION 185

18 A   SIXTEEN POINT CADMUS TITLE. $2 25

OUTFITS FOR PRINTERS
TYPOTHETÆ 284

4 A   FORTY-EIGHT POINT CADMUS TITLE. $5 25

DURABLE TYPE

4 A   SIXTY POINT CADMUS TITLE. $6 00

CADMUS 7

THE YOUNG FEMALE COMPOSITOR.

Oh ! but she's bonny and kind—
  A smart, cheerfu' witch o' a creature—
A lassie just form'd to my mind,
  Wi' a face beaming ower wi' guid nature.
And 'deed, the plain truth to declare,
  Few chaps ever turn up their nose at her,
The charms are sae catching and rare
  O' Nell, the young female compositor.

'Maist every five lines that she sets
  For sorts thro' the hale house she dances,
And a' that she asks for she gets,
  Returning her thanks wi' soft glances.
And though, ance or twice every week,
  The gaffer he threatens to closet her,
It ends wi' him patting the cheek
  O' this modest young female compositor.

But of a' the *frames* she seems to like mine ;
  And faith she's untrammeled wi' fetters,
For twice every hour in the nine
  She comes seeking capital letters.
Then up on a case she'lt play jump,
  And while I keep keeking richt close at her,
She fa's on my knees wi' a thump,
  This charming young female compositor.

A wee cockie cliquer sae braw,
  Wha' thinks he's a don 'mang the lasses,
Breaks a note or a headline or twa,
  Ilka time that the sweet lassie passes.
But he's out o' the hunt, that's quite clear,
  For a' the sly glances he throws at her
Are met wi' a cough and a sneer.
  By this handsome young female compositor.

A Beauregard jacket she wears,
  And a skirt neatly draped and brocaded ;
Yet she never puts on foolish airs,
  Though oft for her pride she's upbraided.
But though she might spit in my face,
  I'm sure I could never look cross at her,
Sae fu' o' saft, heart-winning grace
  Is this nymph, the young female compositor.

I'm on a grand volume—bourgeois,
  Wi' lots o' big wood cuts, and leaded—
And I'm certain, in sax weeks or so,
  I'll hae as much coin as is needed.
Then, low on my knees, I'll discharge
  O' Cupid's saft sawder a dose at her,
And *row* in the conjugal barge
  Wi' this darling young female compositor.

—*R. B.*, *in the Scottish Typographical Circular for June.*

REMINISCENCES.
BY JAMES BARNET.
"STEAM DID IT ! "

DID what ? There was one man who said that it cheapened job printing, while a great many others, good fellows, could not see it, for they had no boilers with which to raise the expanding force ; nothing but the tireless limbs of the youth who bore the ceaseless grind of the Gordon, the Ruggles or the Liberty. This was the boast, however, of the merchant who left the shores of the Mississippi and settled in Chicago, twenty years ago, as a book and job printer. "Steam did it !"

No doubt steam has done a great deal in cheapening many things, as I remember when it knocked aside the spinning wheels of the thrifty cottar wives, whose great aim was in getting up the linen for the daughter's outfit when she got married. Steam drove tne machines for heckling flax, and did away with combi-

nations and strikes of the hecklers by hand. When a country house was filled at one end with six looms, each one giving its click-clack, it was a busy house indeed, and if not quite musical, the sound had the advantage of the hundred pipers who all played different melodies—the looms had all one key. "Steam did it !" when the looms were all in large factories turning out one web each daily, instead of a week by hand. The country districts thereby were thinned of their inhabitants and driven into towns in search of work. "Steam did it !" when machinery turns out the finest bookwork instead of by the hand-press. Great is the power of steam ; but in cards and dodgers, the "Firefly" could not compete with the treadmill of the young man who drove the eighth medium job press.

While lying on my oars, as it were, I noticed an "ad" in one of the papers, of a foreman being wanted for the merchant already mentioned, and as active work was quite agreeable, I called on him to ascertain particulars. I found that his second in command was leaving to start business on his own account, and without much ado I agreed to fill the vacant post, as the salary was a temptation in itself.

As some tradesmen make a branch of their business a specialty, this idea was carried out by my new employer in printing cards and dodgers at ten per cent over cost, all other work being taken from my estimates. If a hustler happens to have a bee in his bonnet, and is willing to work out his scheme to a legitimate conclusion, it follows that he has both faith and courage. If failure meets his efforts, many will remark, "I told you so !" If success attends his endeavor, then others follow close after him.

When three or four small presses were kept going for a week, the ten-per-cent plan paid very well, and with glee the favorite phrase was seen in print, both by card and circular, that "Steam did it !" As a continued supply of cheap work did not come in all the time, a confession was in order, and an acknowledgment made that the estimated jobwork paid far better, besides more help being needed to meet its demands. Competition made my employer reduce his figures even on cheap work, but he was bound to lead. He began to doubt his figures when a smash was made on the quarto Gordon, costing $30 for repairs ; but, then, "Steam did it !"

As the composing room had been shifted to the fourth floor, and the office on the second, a tube was in requisition when orders were sent up. With no work on hand, and a quarter of the day spent, a whistle came up the tube with the inquiry, "What are your men doing ?" which was answered, "Distributing and clearing up." Then the order followed, "Lay them off ; there is nothing on hand." They were laid off. They put their coats on and walked downstairs, while some one with an order was going up. As soon as known, the wigless boss ran out and followed his men as if his house was on fire. "Come back," he cried, and they came back. This was only practiced once during my stay.

Meeting a customer whose printing I had done for nearly twelve years, he desired fifty dollars' worth as soon as possible. He would give his work to my employer if I made a commission on the first order. On taking this to my boss, I gave him the cost, and told him what my customer had said. "Well, then, I will give you twenty per cent," he answered. If it had been ten per cent, it would have pleased me as well. He delivered the printing and received his pay, but failed to turn over the twenty per cent commission as promised. On my customer learning who he was dealing with, he said, "He will not get another order from me." On asking what reason he had in not complying with his own arrangement, he opened my eyes with the remark, "Why, sir, I will charge you with obtaining orders for printing without a license from the United States." This was original if not satisfactory. He cut his nose off to spite his face.

My term of office was nearing an end, as the former holder of the position concluded to return and bring his material and presses with him. This seemed beneficial for both employer and foreman, and was carried out. The fire of 1871 squared all accounts, and there was no more heard of cheap printing by steam.

AMERICAN SYSTEM OF
INTERCHANGEABLE TYPE BODIES.

CONTOUR No. 7.

ORIGINAL.

MORTISED
LETTERS

WITH THIS
SERIES.

5A, 10a, Double Columbian (32 Point). $3.35

WESTERN LAND INVESTMENT CO.

Excellent Facilities for Reducing Bank Accounts

25 Enormous Liabilities 78

4A, 8a, Canon (44 Point). $4.40

MUNCIE NATIONAL BANK

Foreign Exchange 246 Cable Transfers

3A, 6a, Five-Line Pica (60 Point). $5.90

MARINE INSURANCE

Navigation Opened on Salt Lake

3A, 6a, Six-Line Pica (72 Point). $7.85

League BASE BALL Games

SPACES AND QUADS EXTRA.

Dearborn Series

PATENT APPLIED FOR.

24 POINT INITIALS, 3A $1 50

12 POINT CAPS, 15A $2 10

A E F B G H I J K L

THIS HANDSOME SERIES IS CAST FROM

Celebrated Superior Copper-Mixed Type Metal

BARNHART BROS. & SPINDLER

N D O R P U V W X

36 POINT INITIALS, 3A $2 50

18 POINT CAPS, 8A $2 00

A C E H I J K P

PAPER AND CARD CUTTERS

Great Western Type Foundry

PRINTING MACHINERY

L O M N R U S

MANUFACTURED BY BARNHART BROS. & SPINDLER, CHICAGO, ILL.

ALSO CARRIED IN STOCK AND FOR SALE BY

MINNESOTA TYPE FOUNDRY CO., ST. PAUL, MINN.,
GREAT WESTERN TYPE FOUNDRY, OMAHA, NEB.,

GREAT WESTERN TYPE FOUNDRY, KANSAS CITY, MO.,
ST. LOUIS PRINTERS' SUPPLY CO., ST. LOUIS, MO.

TUDOR BLACK.

5 A, 15 a.   24 POINT TUDOR BLACK. $4.75

Leading Features of our Advancement
8 Steamships and Railroads 6

15 A, 50 a.   6 POINT TUDOR BLACK. $2.25

While the Lexicographer is Hesitating, Weighing,
Suspending, Harshly Rejecting, or Tardily Admitting, a Language is being
Worked out, which will react again upon our literature.
Chronicles of Canongate, July, 1234.

15 A, 50 a.   8 POINT TUDOR BLACK. $2.75

The Periodical Press, though it Embodies
Some of the most Classical Compositions in our lan=
guage, is not accepted as academic authority.
Panegyric on Agesilaus 1876.

4 A, 12 a.   33 POINT TUDOR BLACK. $5.50

Chronicles of England and Scotia
3 Academy of Sciences 2

12 A 36 a.   10 POINT TUDOR BLACK. $2.75

1497 Jean Grolier de Servier 1565
Vicompte d'Aguisy, Treas.=Gen. of France
Ambassador to the Court of Rome
Bibliophile and Bookbinder

9 A, 30 a.   12 POINT TUDOR BLACK. $2.75

The Periodical Press forms the
Connecting Link between the Written
and the Spoken Language
1234567890

4 A, 12 a.   40 POINT TUDOR BLACK. $6.00

Mechanical Engineering
8 Turnpike Roads 4

8 A 25 a.   18 POINT TUDOR BLACK. $3.40

Ringwalts Transport
Encyclpædia of Technology
Fifth Edition 1876

5 A, 15 a.   20 POINT TUDOR BLACK. $3.50

East Indian
Inland Transportation
74 Flat=Boats 53

3 A, 8 a.   48 POINT TUDOR BLACK. $8.50

Continental Travelers
6 Railroads 7

FRENCH DORIC.

4 A, 8a.   36 Point French Doric. $6.00

SOCIETY RECEPTIONS
Magnificent Wedding Ceremonies
34 Elegant Trousseaux 56

20 A, 38 a.   12 Point French Doric. $4.00

BUSINESS PROSPECTS
Experienced Real Estate Boomer Wanted

Magnificent Sandhill Homesteads

23 Milkranch Avenue 45

10 A, 16 a.   18 Point French Doric. $4.50

MINING COMPANY
Monthly Dividends Guaranteed

Astonished Manipulators

7 Crafty Operators 8

4 A, 6a.   40 Point French Doric. $6.75

SWEET MELODY
Winter Lovemaking Rambles
2 Button Machines 7

8 A, 14 a.   22 Point French Doric. $4.75

SCHOOL LANDS
Handsome Maid Servant

Fondness for Labor

5 Proverbial 4

6 A, 12 a.   28 Point French Doric. $5.00

WONDERFUL
National Prosperity

8 Free Lunch 5

3 A, 5a.   48 Point French Doric. $7.50

5 INDEPENDENT 3
Traders' Trust Company

THE NOMENCLATURE OF TYPE FACES.

BY CARL SCHRAUBSTADTER, JR.

THE nomenclature of type faces apparently follows no law. The most common of faces, and the standard from which most of the others are drawn, is appropriately called roman, and, in contradistinction to the long serifed and stiffer faces which became popular during the early part of this century, old style is perhaps well named, and italic having originated in Italy, the name answers very well. If we confine ourselves to the old faces, the blacks are well named. These occupied so much of the paper as to produce a very black effect as compared with the roman, but some of the modern blacks are far lighter than the average face. Condensed, extended, expanded, lightface, etc., are usually properly used to qualify the name of the face. The titles (heavy romans, which were formerly used for the purpose indicated by the name), do not belie their name. One or two foundries call such styles Full-Face, and this is also appropriate ; but when we leave the plain letter apparently all laws cease. While some job faces possess good names, by far the greatest number seem to have been selected hap-hazard. This is, perhaps, not to be wondered at. The method adopted by one prominent foundry of numbering its faces consecutively has always proven unpopular. Numbers are difficult to remember, but the printer can readily keep in mind a name, even if it is not descriptive. For that reason short, euphonious words are preferred. With the host of modern job faces which have been poured on the market a supply of good names has become scarce, and it is almost as difficult to name as to originate a new and useful face. While perhaps the heavy serifs of the old faces may have suggested the name of Antique, the idea of such faces is essentially modern, and the name Block, as applied by sign painters, seems far more appropriate. Gothic could hardly have been suggested by the Gothic architecture, but it is barely possible that the name was suggested by the simplicity and rudeness of the Goths. They are called Egyptian by sign painters, and the European name of Sans-Serif, though not particularly euphonious, is certainly the most correct. Nevertheless, by popular consent these names have been adopted, as has also the name of Latin for faces which possess the main characteristics of the Antique, but have three-cornered serifs. But why a condensed face of this character should be called Latin Condensed, and the extended one Latin Antique, is difficult to say. The faces having these same characteristics, but much lighter lines, are generally called Celtic. Surely nothing in the history of that nation could warrant the selection of this name, and Romanesque, adopted by one or two, seems more appropriate. The confusion which this hap-hazard nomenclature sometimes occasions is well exemplified by such names as Old Style Antique, descriptive of an old style having very heavy serifs, and Modern Old Style, having its letters modified to suit modern tastes. Yet such a name as Modern Antique seems a palpable self-contradiction, although, perhaps there is as much reason for this name as for many of the others. Ionic, Doric, Clarendon and Caledonian, as applied to several Antiques, have become standard names, but why they were chosen would probably tax the reason of the man who first applied them. French Clarendon, applied to letters which have upper and lower serifs heavy, and perpendicular lines light, hardly seems as appropriate as Egyptian, used by one or two foundries, faces of this character having something suggestive of the heavy architecture of that nation. Another face, variously known as Law Italic and Caledonian Italic, is certainly better known by the former name, the face being very often used in printing legal documents, whereas there is nothing in the character of the face to suggest either the nation or the Caledonian face—a heavy Antique which preceded it by a number of years. There is nothing to suggest a monk in the Monastic, nor a seal in a Signet. Venetian, Chameleon, Alpine, Moslem, Altona, Teniers, Stencil, Esthetic, Ruskin, may be mentioned as examples of a great many which give the reader no idea of the face. Some foundries have taken the names of cities or states, others, of printers, artists and other well-known men, while the majority select them hap-hazard, the main thought being to get some euphonious two or three syllabled word which the compositor can easily remember.

Occasionally some strong departure is made, as in Mother Hubbard, Santa Claus or Morning Glory, but usually the titles are short and characteristic. Occasionally a modern face is appropriately named, as Typewriter, Filagree, Mortised, or Pen Text, but in general nothing of the kind has been done. The writer is far from believing that this system is in any way pernicious. The only alternative would be to number the faces consecutively by mutual agreement between the different producing typefounders, or to give a long descriptive title, either of which is certain to give dissatisfaction ; but there are certain anomalies which could and should be avoided.

WE show in the present issue two specimen pages from the Dickinson Typefoundry, Boston, Massachusetts, which will meet the approval of printers who desire to obtain new and handsome faces of type. The Typothetæ is original in design and really artistic, is made in nine sizes, with figures and ornaments for each size, and will be useful in any job office. The French Elzevir, although imitating somewhat the French Old Style, will still be wanted by many offices who secure everything that is new. We predict for the Typothetæ as large a sale as accorded the popular Quaint and Quaint Open.

FRENCH ELZEVIR

Complete Romans, $33.00   **Complete Italics, $13.25**

Italics for Three Larger Sizes will follow later.

Printers who have our FRENCH OLD STYLE need buy only FRENCH ELZEVIR LOWER CASE, on the three larger sizes, as they line together; the four smaller sizes line with our ELZEVIR ITALICS. Prices specified with each size. . .

Lower Case, $1.12   24 Point French Elzevir   10 a, 8 A, $4.00

This Letter is Exact Reproduction
From Works Printed During 1659 at Leyden

Roman, $4.00   8 Point French Elzevir   Roman, 90 a, 40 A, 20 A
Italic, $3.00...   Italic, 80 A, 28 a . . . .

By ceaseless action all that is subsists.
Constant rotation of the unwearied wheel
That Nature rides upon, maintains her health,
Her beauty, her fertility.   She dreads
An instant's pause, and lives but while she moves.
Its own revolvency upholds the world.
Winds from all quarters agitate the air,
And fit the limpid element for use,
Else noxious.   Oceans, rivers, lakes, and streams,
All feel the fresh'ning impulse, and are cleansed
By restless undulation : ev'n the oak
Thrives by the rude concussions of the storm :
He seems indeed indignant, and to feel

Th' impression of the blast with proud disdain;
Frowning, as if in his unconscious arm
He held the thunder: but the monarch owes
His firm stability to what he scorns.

Roman, $4.75   10 Point French Elzevir   Roman, 80 a, 40 A, 20 A
Italic, $3.80...   Italic, 80 a, 28 A . . . .

LAMARTINE was born of aristocratic parents at Macon, on the 21st of October, 1791. His father, whose name was De Prat, was major of a regiment of cavalry in the service of LOUIS XVI, and his mother was companion to the sister of Louis Philippe, her mother being Madame des Rois, under-governess to the family of the Prince of Orleans. The Revolution, which first swept away the crown and sceptre of France, reduced the family of De Prat from rank and opulence to grief and poverty, and consigned the father of Lamartine to a prison. The first

recollections of the poet are reflected in tears. When his father, whose name he has exchanged for that of his maternal uncle, was incarcerated in prison by

---

Lower Case, $2.66   48 Point French Elzevir   5 a, 4 A, $7.34

Old 17th Century Styles

Roman, $5.00   14 Point French Elzevir   Roman, 50 a, 20 A, 10 A
Italic, $3.90...   Italic, 36 a, 16 A . . . .

LAMARTINE was born of aristocratic parents at Macon, on the 21st day of Oct'er, 1791. His father, whose name was De Prat, was major of a regiment of cavalry in the service of LOUIS XVI, and his mother was companion to the sister of Louis Philippe, her mother

being Madame Rois, under-governess
to the family of the Prince of Orleans
The revolution, which first swept away

Roman, $5.00   12 Point French Elzevir   Roman, 62 a, 28 A, 16 A
Italic, $3.94...   Italic, 50 a, 20 A . . . .

The sun's last rays are on the hill,
And sparkle in the fountain rill,
Whose welcome waters, cool and clear,
Draw blessings from the mountaineer:
Here may the loitering merchant Greek
Find that repose 'twere vain to seek
In cities lodged too near his lord,
And trembling for his secret hoard:
Here may he rest where none can see,—

In crowds a slave, in deserts free,—
And with forbidden wine may stain
The bowl a Moslem must not drain.

Lower Case, $1.76   42 Point French Elzevir   6 a, 5 A, $5.66

Particular Attention Given Italics

Original Designs from Dickinson Type Foundery, Boston Mass.

[From the President of the UNITED TYPOTHETÆ]

MESSRS PHELPS, DALTON & CO., Boston.   Chicago, July 15, 1889.

Gentlemen: In reference to the series of type which you intend to issue under the name of "Typothetæ" . . . . if printers want artistic faces of type, the proof you sent me would, I think, meet with favor.

A. McNally

24 Point — 8 A — $4.50

NEW SPECIMEN SHEET FOR THE &

10 Point — 16 A — $2.00

53 DIFFERENT STYLE NEWSPAPER FACES TAKEN FROM ORIGINAL DESIGNS

36 Point — 6 A — $4.90

PRINTER OF 1890

16 Point — 12 A — $2.60

RUNNING OVER WITH 2643 DESIRABLE FACES SUCH AS EVERY

60 Point — 4 A — $5.90

BOOK AND JOB

12 Point — 14 A — $2.30

CONCERN SHOULD HAVE ON HAND
CORRESPONDENCE AND ORDERS ATTENDED AT ONCE

48 Point — 4 A — $5.40

THE $47 PRIZE

8 Point — 18 A — $1.90

EVERY VARIETY OF
SOCIETY AND MISCELLANEOUS CUTS
FURNISHED AT SHORT NOTICE

18 Point — 10 A — $3.25

GIVEN TO LARGEST
BUYER FOR 1872 &&&&

Original Designs from Dickinson Type Foundery, Boston, Mass.

THE HAMILTON MFG. CO.

Successors to HAMILTON & BAKER,

MANUFACTURERS OF

WOOD · TYPE

... AND ...

PRINTERS' WOOD GOODS, AND DEALERS IN MACHINERY AND SUPPLIES,

TWO RIVERS, WIS.

259 DEARBORN STREET, CHICAGO.

❖ ❖ ❖

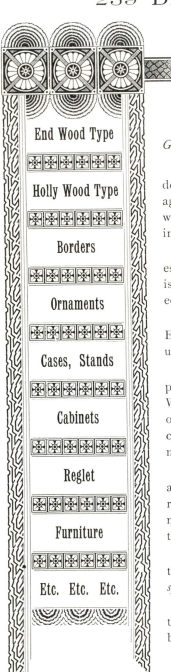

End Wood Type

Holly Wood Type

Borders

Ornaments

Cases, Stands

Cabinets

Reglet

Furniture

Etc. Etc. Etc.

CHICAGO, September 1, 1889.

Gentlemen :

We have for several years past felt the necessity growing upon us of having a depot for our goods in Chicago. Our business has increased so rapidly and our patronage has been so widely extended that the demand for a central distributing point, from which we could reach our customers with as little delay as possible, has seemed imperative.

We have now accomplished the object we have had in view so long, and have established our **Chicago Branch House at 259 Dearborn Street.** Our location is a choice one, situated between the two great printing districts of the city, it is equally as convenient to one as to the other.

We shall endeavor to carry at all times a complete stock of Wood Type, both End Wood and Holly, Printers' Wood Goods and Furniture, all of our own manufacture; and also handle Metal Type, Machinery and Printers' Supplies of all kinds.

We would *especially* direct your attention to our **End Wood Type,** upon which we pride ourselves. We have recently doubled our capacity for the manufacture of End Wood Type, by the addition of the latest improved machinery, and are now able to fill orders promptly. This type in material and finish has never been equaled in this country, nor in any other country. We say this without fear of contradiction. The material used is thoroughly seasoned *Rock Maple.*

We make the **Hamilton-Boss Lower Case.** In this case the spaces and en quads are all brought down directly under the hand of the compositor, an advantage that is readily recognized by the progressive printer. Hamilton's Brass Leader Case is another new feature that we are introducing, and is a great convenience, especially in offices that do much blank work.

Our plant for the manufacture of Printers' Wood Goods and Furniture is probably the most extensive in the country. We would be pleased to give you figures on any *special* Cabinet or article of Furniture that you may need.

Come and see us at our new Chicago House, or write to us for figures on anything in the Printers' Supply line. As to prices, we simply say that we can do as well by you as any house in the business.

Respectfully yours,

THE HAMILTON MFG. CO.

MECHANICAL PATENT, MAR. 31, 1885.

6 POINT OLD STYLE ANTIQUE.   36 A, 70 a, $2.85.

WARDROBES FOR EVERYDAY WEAR
Suitable for Embezzling Apprentices, Dashing Clerks and Saleswomen
Absconders' Leggings and Daredevil Road Dusters
1234567890

8 POINT OLD STYLE ANTIQUE.   36 A, 70 a, $3.40.

OUR GRANDFATHERS' DAYS
Carefully Providing for the Future with Economical Prudence
Like Newtown Pippins, Sound to the Core
1234567890

10 POINT OLD STYLE ANTIQUE.   36 A, 52 a, $4.05.

THE PROGRESSIVE AGE
Extravagant Young Spendthrifts and Mendshifts
1234567890

12 POINT OLD STYLE ANTIQUE.   25 A, 32 a, $3.65.

ORIENT AND OCCIDENT
Atlantic and Pacific Wedding Ceremony
1234567890

18 POINT OLD STYLE ANTIQUE.   14 A, 20 a, $4.10.

DICTIONARY OF DIFFICULTIES
Minding my own Business to Avoid Useless Trouble

36 POINT OLD STYLE ANTIQUE.   6 A, 9 a, $7.10.

MONOCHROME
Eastern Landscape Scenes

24 POINT OLD STYLE ANTIQUE.   10 A, 15 a, $5.00.

LOVINGLY WAITING
Snowbound Honeymoon Travelers

48 POINT OLD STYLE ANTIQUE.   4 A, 6 a, $8.00.

MONKISH Departure

30 POINT OLD STYLE ANTIQUE.   8 A, 12 a, $6.00.

IMPEDIMENTAL
Contrary Breeze and Current

MacKellar, Smiths & Jordan Co., Philadelphia.   Shniedewend & Lee Co., Agents, Chicago, Ill.

September 1889   303

10 A 15 a   18 POINT LaSalle (3 line Nonp.) $2 70

GREAT MEN ARE NOT ALWAYS WISE

Virtue is better than Riches

He Loves no other Land so Much as That of His Adoption

465 Native Born & Foreigners 273

8 A 12 a   24 POINT LaSalle (4 line Nonp.) $3 50

THE NATION IS POWERFUL

Great National Game

Sweet Flowers grow slow Weeds make Haste

25 Sun warms the Earth 34

6 A 10 a   30 POINT LaSalle (5 line Nonp.) $4 35

MONEY MAKES FRIENDS

Pure Gold & Silver

Were it not for Hope the Heart would

38 Surely Break 49

Manufactured by BARNHART BROS. & SPINDLER, Chicago, Ill.

Carried In stock by Minnesota Type Foundry Co., St. Paul, Minn.; Great Western Type Foundry, Kansas City, Mo.; Great Western Type
Foundry, Omaha, Neb.; St. Louis Printers' Supply Co., St. Louis, Mo., and for sale by all
Type Founders and Dealers In Printers Material.

PICA CAXTON OLD STYLE.

Alphabet, a to z, 14⅛ ems.

Pick and click
Go the types in the stick,
As the printer stands at the case;
His eyes glance quick, and his fingers pick
The types at a rapid pace,
And one by one as the letters go,
Words are piled up steady and slow—
Steady and slow,
But still they grow,
And words of fire they soon will glow;
Wonderful words, that without a sound
Traverse the earth to its utmost bound
Words that shall make
The tyrant quake

But the printer smiled
And his work beguiled
By chanting a song as the letter is piled;
While pick and click
Went the types in the stick,
Like the world's chronometer—tick, tick,
Oh, where is the man with simple tools,
Can govern the world like I?
A printing-press, an iron stick,
And a little leaden die;
With paper of white, and ink of black,
I support the right and the wrong attack.
I pull the strings
Of puppet kings,

ABCDEFGHIJKLMNOPQRSTUVWXYZ

1 2 3 4 5 6 7 8 9 0

The correctness of the propositions stated in our last article will be at once admitted by the reader who has been able to visit such an institution as the library of the British Museum, where literary productions of almost every conceivable size and shape, and with an endless variety of topics, are preserved so happily that they are easily found when needed for reference.

Here side by side are ancient manuscripts centuries old, the literary excellences of their time, and the new book of yesterday. The one on worn and yellow parchment with fading ink, and letters almost illegible, because the hand that had traced them in slow and crooked succession was more accustomed to guide the steed and clench the massive axe; the other brand-new, its corners and gilding untarnished, and its pages clear and fresh from the rapid and precise manipulations of modern printers.

These are the extremes, but they are united together by a thousand specimens, each of which has been the best

of its kind in its day; has asserted its supremacy, to be superseded in its turn until the chain is perfect.

Many who glance over them note the striking distinctions of form and character only, but the student finds in them a story plainly told. As it has been with the stones of the earth so it is with these. Boys have gathered them from the fields, have played with them by the ocean, and cast them in mischief or in strife; men have for ages quarried, cut, carved and ground them, but only to such as Miller and Lyell have they told the story so long hidden in them.

These manuscripts speak to the student, and as he slowly turns them over one by one, they relate to him their story; now of studious monks, with rare missal lore—now of learned barons, affecting the art of the scribe—now of clumsy first attempts to make printing an art for the speedy and cheap multiplication of copies; of these, but not of these alone, they are hieroglyphic chapters of British history—chronicles, not of kings and crowns and thrones, wars *and political machinations, but of the aspirations of the British mind and its long and earnest struggles 123456*

MARDER, LUSE & CO., CHICAGO, ILL.

Pica Caxton Old Style, fonts of 25 lbs. and over, 42c per lb.

Pica Caxton Old Style Italic, Card Fonts, 18A, 100a, $5.70

Marder, Luse & Co., Type Founders, Chicago.

Banquet

PATENT APPLIED FOR.

American system of
Interchangeable type bodies.

·

6A, 16a,   Paragon (20 Point). $3.75

Meeting of the National Editorial Association

Many Valuable and Practical Papers were Read, the more Worthy

25   Will be presented   38

To our Readers in the near Future

6A, 12a, $4.90   Double English (28 Point).   Ornamental Caps, 4A, $1.70

The Minnesota and Northern Railway

Vestibule ⚹ Trains⚹   ⚹Pullman ⚹ Sleepers⚹

25 Harvest Excursion 38

4A, 8a, $5.00   Double Great Primer (36 Point).   Ornamental Caps, 3A, $2.50

American Furnishing Emporium

Art Decorations⚹

Quaint English Ornaments

AMERICAN SYSTEM OF INTERCHANGEABLE TYPE BODIES.

RIVET.

ORIGINAL.

MORTISED LETTERS WITH THIS SERIES.

12A, Two-Line Nonpareil (12 Point). $1.00

POINTS ARE NOT OF EQUAL ANTIQUITY WITH

➤ PRINTING THOUGH NOT LONG AFTER ITS INVENTION THE NECESSITY OF ◄

234   INTRODUCING STOPS OR   689

10A, Two-Line Bourgeois (18 Point). $1.50

READERS BROUGHT FORWARD ◄

369   THE COLON AND FULL POINT   248

➤ THE FIRST TWO INVENTED

MARDER, LUSE & COMPANY

➤ CHICAGO TYPE FOUNDRY ◄

139-141 MONROE ST.

8A, Two-Line Pica (24 Point). $2.00

➤ INFANT PUNCTUATION ◄

CAPS FIGURES   SPACES QUADS

23   RULE WORK   45

ORNAMENTS WITH ALL SIZES   SPACES AND QUADS EXTRA.

Specimens from FARMER, LITTLE & CO., Type Founders.

NEW YORK—63 & 65 Beekman St.
And 62 & 64 Gold Street.

CHICAGO—154 Monroe Street,
Chas. B. Ross, Manager

NEW GOTHIC CONDENSED No. 9.

8 A   28 Point Gothic Condensed No. 9. $2 25

WE AIM FOR DURABILITY AND USEFULNESS 385

40 A   10 Point Gothic Condensed No. 9 $1 75

HAVE USED COPPER IN OUR TYPE METAL FOR YEARS
FRENCH ELECTION EXCITEMENT 573

35 A   12 Point Gothic Condensed No. 9. $2 00

COMMERCIAL RELATIONS WITH AUSTRALIA
MUTUAL ADVANTAGES 473

8 A   30 Point Gothic Condensed No. 9. $2 75

ANCIENT GOTHIC CATHEDRALS 492

24 A   14 Point Gothic Condensed No. 9. $1 75

PLEASANT REMINISCENCES OF SPRING
MOUNTAIN SCENES 856

16 A   18 Point Gothic Condensed No. 9. $1 80

THE WESTERN WHEAT HARVEST
EXPORT FREIGHTS 985

6 A   40 Point Gothic Condensed No. 9. $3 00

ELEGANT GOTHIC ORNAMENTS 329

12 A   20 Point Gothic Condensed No. 9. $1 80

GRAND HOLIDAY OPENING
AMUSEMENT 638

12 A   24 Point Gothic Condensed No. 9. $2 25

THE WEDDING PRESENTS
CHOICE GIFT 658

5 A   48 Point Gothic Condensed No. 9. $3 75

BEGONE DULL CARE 687

8 A 15 a without Initials, $4 00   18 POINT ANGLO (3 line Nonp.)   8 A 15 a with 3 A Initials, $6 00

15 a lower case only, . 2 25   WITH 24 POINT INITIALS (4 line Nonp.)   3 A Initials 2 00

BARNHART BROS. & SPINDLER

Manufacturers of Useful Novelties for Printers

Celebrated Superior Copper Mixed Type

In the art of Printing, the greatest discovery was that of forming every letter or character of the alphabet separately, so as to be capable of rearrangement, and forming in succession the pages of a work, thereby avoiding the interminable labor of cutting new blocks

5 A 10 a without Initials, $4 30   24 POINT ANGLO (4 line Nonp.)   5 A 10 a with 3 A Initials, $6 80

10 a lower case only, . 2 30   WITH 36 POINT INITIALS (6 line Nonp.)   3 A Initials, ... 2 50

REVENUE DEPARTMENT

American National Supply Company

Financial Committee

Stock for the Great Fair of eighteen hundred and ninety-two will be on sale at the rooms of the Subscription Committees for the next seven hundred days, at forty dollars a share.

COMPLETE WITH FIGURES.

20 A 40 a.   BREVIER (8 POINTS) ELIZABETH.   PRICE $3.00.

METROPOLITAN ✳ MUSEUM ✳ OBELISK ✳ BELVIDERE
Numerous and Pleasant Reminiscences of Delightful Saddle Excursions to the Blue Ridge Mountains
Invigorating Wanderings Through Central Park on Summer Mornings
OCTOBER ┆ NOVEMBER ┆ DECEMBER ┆ 429

15 A 30 a.   PICA (12 POINTS) ELIZABETH.   PRICE $3.00.

BEAUTIFUL FLOWERS FROM THE PRAIRIES
Startling ✳ Vagaries of a Singularly ✳ Brilliant ✳ Imagination
Representatives of the United States of America in General Congress Assembled.
WISCONSIN ┆ KALAMAZOO ┆ OSHKOSH ┆ 1385

8 A 15 a.   THREE-LINE NONPAREIL (18 POINTS) ELIZABETH.   PRICE $3.75.

FIELDS ┆ OF ┆ NEW ┆ SWEET ┆ CLOVER
Blackmore's New and Improved Agricultural Implements
Estimates Furnished 156

6 A 12 a.   TWO-LINE PICA (24 POINTS) ELIZABETH.   PRICE $5.25.

PRESIDENT ┆ HARRISON
Opinions ✳ of all ✳ Constitutional ✳ Writers
United States 34

6 A 10 a.   FIVE-LINE NONPAREIL (30 POINTS) ELIZABETH.   PRICE $6.75.

CABLE ✳ TRANSFERS
Reliable Circular Letter of Credit

Manufactured by BARNHART BROS. & SPINDLER, Chicago, Ill.

Carried in stock by Minnesota Type Foundry Co., St. Paul, Minn.; Great Western Type Foundry, Kansas City, Mo.; Great Western Type
Foundry, Omaha, Neb.; St. Louis Printers' Supply Co., St. Louis, Mo.; and for sale by all
Type Founders and Dealers in Printers' Materials.

THE THORNE TYPESETTING MACHINE.

We herewith present to the readers of THE INLAND PRINTER a description of the Thorne Typesetting Machine, accompanied with an illustration engraved expressly for its columns, a machine which beyond doubt is the most perfect of its class yet devised, and which needs only to be seen in practical operation to convince the confirmed skeptic it has come to stay. After years of laborious study, experiment and improvement, a result has been achieved which justifies the company offering it to present it with the utmost confidence to the employing printers of the United States; satisfied that a thorough test— and the more thorough the better—is all that is required to secure its almost universal adoption. Its mechanism, which is simple, consists primarily of two cast-iron cylinders fifteen inches in diameter, placed one above the other on the same axis. In the surface of these cylinders are cut ninety longitudinal channels, in depth nearly equal to the length of a type, and corresponding in width to the body of the type to be used. The channels of the lower cylinder or "setter" are fitted with wards corresponding exactly with nicks on the edge of the type, no two characters having the same combination of nicks. The upper cylinder is the distributer, and into its channels is loaded type, face out, from a special galley. The operation is very simple and rapid, less than five minutes being required to "load" 6,000 ems of minion. The distributing cylinder revolves above the "setter" with an intermittent movement, pausing an instant at the points where its channels coincide with those of the lower cylinder. The lowest type in each channel soon finds a combination of grooves corresponding to its nicks, and drops down. They cannot, under any circumstances, go into any but the proper groove, and as each of the ninety channels coincide or match one hundred and fifty times per minute, the speed of this automatic distribution is equal to 10,000 ems per hour. Over 7,000 ems can be "loaded" in and distributed within an hour. Provision is made for taking out surplus type in any channel when an excess of a particular letter has accumulated, and for replenishing when a sort is exhausted before distribution supplies it, the latter, however, being a rare occurrence. These sorts are kept in typefounders' galleys placed in a cabinet convenient to the machine.

The keyboard resembles that of a typewriter, except that it is larger, and has more keys. Each key is attached by a lever to a plunger or ejector which, when a key is depressed, forces out the lowest type in the corresponding channel of the setting cylinder. Each type is pushed out upon a rapidly-revolving horizontal disk, a short curved guide starting them in the right direction. The disk, the axis of which is the same as that of the cylinders, carries the type quickly to the right hand front of the machine, where it is received on an endless belt, which transfers it to a lifting apparatus or packer, where each successive type is placed in proper position on the line. The marvelous accuracy and nicety of this operation is one of the phenomenal features of the machine. As one type follows another, the line is pushed along across the front of the machine between the keyboard and the "setting" cylinder to the justifier who, with a "grab," set to the required measure, breaks up the long line coming from the "packer." As each line is justified, a lever operated by the foot pushes the distance of one line into the galley. Between the operator and justifier is placed a double case for sorts, etc., containing on the

THORNE TYPESETTING AND DISTRIBUTING MACHINE.
Engraved Expressly for THE INLAND PRINTER, from a Photograph of Machine in the Office of the Chicago *Evening Journal.*

operator's side italics, reference marks, etc., and on the justifier's side duplicate sorts of the type played out on the machine. Under this double case, convenient to both operator and justifier, is a third case containing small caps. Any character not played out from the keyboard is placed in a chute which delivers it to the disk, and it is carried into the line the same way as any letter played out from the machine.

In an iron case in front of the justifier are held the spaces required for properly justifying the lines. This case is so arranged that one, two or three of any particular space can be drawn out by a single motion. The machine is driven by two small belts, one of which transmits power to the revolving disk, packer, and ejector apparatus, and the other by means of an eccentric shaft operating an index pawl, produces the step by step motion of the distributer.

Three persons are required to operate the machine, namely, one operator, a justifier and a boy to distribute. Proof corrections are made in the ordinary way.

The capacity of the machine depends entirely upon the expertness of the operator and justifier, and under favorable conditions from 4,000 to 6,000 ems per hour can be turned out. A short experience will enable any intelligent compositor to attain a speed of over 3,000 ems per hour. Expert operators have set *over* 6,000 ems per hour. The letters on the keyboard are arranged with reference to the frequency of their use, such as "and," "the," "ing," "if," etc., and which combinations may be played at one stroke. The channels are numbered from 1 to 90, beginning at the point where the letters are transferred from the disk onto the carrying belt, and in playing out combinations each succeeding letter is from a channel bearing a number higher than its predecessor. Several keys may be struck simultaneously, and the letters will take their proper order in the line.

Among other decided advantages possessed by the machine are (1) that it sets and distributes *simultaneously or separately*, at will; (2) it only requires five feet square for the machine, operator and justifier; (3) it is simple in construction, and made to the highest standard of mechanical excellence.

For over a year past the entire reading matter for the *Evening Post*, an Associated Press daily, located at Hartford, Connecticut, has been set on brevier Thorne machines. A minion machine is doing very satisfactory work in the office of the Chicago *Evening Journal*, and a long primer machine has for some time past been employed on novel work in the office of Street & Smith, the well-known publishers of the New York *Weekly*. The West Publishing Company of St. Paul, Minnesota, leading law publishers, employing over one hundred compositors, are using two brevier machines, and they have ordered five more for brevier and two for minion In the office of the Publishers' Printing Company, 157 William street, New York, six of these machines are now in operation, and others have been ordered. At this establishment several leading magazines, such as the *Forum, Current Literature, Wood's Medical Monographs*, etc., are likewise set by the Thorne, as have been three hundred books varying from cheap novels to such high class works as Clarence Cook's "Art and Artists of our Time." Several of the offices referred to are under the jurisdiction of the typographical union, and such machines are operated by union compositors, while in others they are operated by girls.

Two Thorne machines are now on exhibition at the Exposition Universelle at Paris, one having Edison's phonograph attached thereto. In England and Ireland nearly twenty are in actual operation in newspaper and book offices. Over forty have been built and sold during the past two years, the manufacturers having on hand orders for thirty more, several of which are from Chicago publishers. Diagrams showing the arrangement of its keyboard will be sent free, upon application, to printers who wish to familiarize themselves with the operation of the machine.

The Thorne is manufactured and sold in the United States by the Thorne Typesetting Machine Company, Hartford, Connecticut, of which R. W. Nelson is president and John N. Woodfin treasurer, and abroad by the Tyesetting. Syndica te, Limited, No. 2 Copthall Buildings, London, E. C., England.

BRAIN WORKERS.

The *Medical Age* says that the most frequent fault of the brain worker is excessive application to work. "The most intense and fatiguing of toils is pursued almost uninterruptedly, food is neglected, and the claims of exercise and sleep are but imperfectly admitted. Two hours' exercise in the open air, daily, is probably a minimum, and might prudently be exceeded. The brain worker must live sparingly rather than luxuriantly, he must prefer the lighter classes of food to the heavier, and he must be very prudent in the use of alcohol. Tobacco and tea are apt to be favorites with him, and their immoderate use may require to be guarded against. It is a nice question whether he needs more or less sleep than other men. Many men of genius are light sleepers, probably in some cases a misfortune, but there seems some ground for the notion that more than a moderate indulgence in sleep is unfavorable to successful mental effort."

A commentator upon the above remarks says that he cannot fully agree with them. "Mental effort," he says, and the Cincinnati *Medical News* agrees with him, "causes waste of tissue elements quite as much as bodily exertion, and this demands a full supply of food. What with dyspepsia and absence of appetite, the results of deficient exercise, and the influence of preconceived ideas as to the use or disuse of special articles of food, the brain worker is very apt to receive too little nutriment to make up for the waste. Especially is this the case when he, unconsciously, perhaps, replaces food by the use of tobacco, tea, alcohol, or opium."

Some advise to go supperless to bed. This most medical authorities of the day think is a wrong notion. It is a fruitful source of insomnia and neurasthenia. The brain becomes exhausted by its evening work, and demands rest and refreshment of its wasted tissues, not by indigestible salads and "fried abominations," but by some nutritious, easily digested and assimilated articles. A bowl of stale bread and milk, of rice, or some other farinaceous food, with milk or hot soup, would be more to the purpose. Any of these would insure a sound night's sleep, from which the man would awaken refreshed.

BRAINS NEEDED IN MANUAL LABOR.

There are too many lawyers, and there will be so long as the present state of society exists. No other business requires a smaller capital; none offers such glittering temptations; in none are there so many precedents to show that merit will rise to high distinction notwithstanding the humblest beginnings. Thousands of young men with very imperfect educations, scorning the honest manual labor of their fathers, rush into professions for which they are unfitted by their qualities of mind and by their early training. A foolish notion that their education unfits them for manual work, and that such work would bring with it some sort of degradation, has ruined and will ruin thousands of them every year; this will continue until the bulk of our people have learned that nothing can be more honorable than honest and intelligent manual labor. Such labor, to be successful, requires brains, industry, courage, self-denial, and other qualities which nowhere meet with greater or readier recognition than in this country of ours. There is no reason why a paper maker should not read Horace's Odes in the original; nor anything to prevent a pattern maker from mastering Euclid. Each will do his work all the better for having exercised and refined his intellect in such pursuits. Indeed, the opportunities of the paper maker and the pattern maker are daily becoming greater than those of the professional student to master the sciences, the arts, and the literature which forms so important a factor in the charm and beauty of life. The legislation of our day, as well as a growing public sentiment, both concur in shortening the hours of labor. What the workingman will do with his sixteen hours that belong to him out of the twenty-four is a problem for him to solve, and upon the solution of which the greatness and prosperity of our country must to a considerable extent depend.—*Exchange.*

LADY COMPOSITORS.

BY F. M. COLE.

WERE one to visit the printing offices in Chicago, or any other city where female compositors are employed, a pale, worn-out set would be seen. Many there are, 'tis true, who have their usual robust appearance ; but many, and a majority, wear that peculiarly pale, determined expression which follows a term at the case. The average time a young woman can endure continuous work at the case is considerably less than five years. Some go over that time, but when they leave the case at five years, headaches, backaches and other aches have played sad havoc with their constitutions, unfitting them for other employment.

The agencies which contribute mainly to this destruction of health are lead poison, heat, confinement and the almost invariably poor ventilation.

Printing offices through the country are generally free from the main objectionable features so abundantly possessed by city offices ; and, too, a much smaller proportionate number of female compositors are found in the country offices. The reason of this is the fact that a country printer must be able to do all classes of work — composition, presswork, and frequently editorial writing.

Another interesting fact would be noticed in a visit to the offices. A majority of the girls are between eighteen and twenty-two years of age. Very few are over twenty-five, though fully two-thirds appear much older than the age they give. The number now employed in Chicago, computed after a careful canvass, is between four and five hundred. There are a few employed on the morning papers to distribute type ; but the majority will be found in book and periodical printing houses. A large number are also employed in the offices of the various trade journals, where the pay is the lowest and men cannot be found to do the work. Some have adopted the profession out of necessity ; others to satisfy a taste for dress, while a few, a very few, have taken up the "stick" solely because they love the work.

The foreman in the offices where women are employed is generally courteous and kind out of a regard for the sex and their proverbial dependency. The work assigned them is invariably straight composition, the belief prevailing that they lack the confidence in themselves and the strength to do jobwork.

An old foreman said, regarding women in the profession : "Girls cannot continuously set more than five thousand 'ems' per day, while men will set from seven to eight thousand ; not because the girls are not quicker in movement and perception, for they are, but because they cannot stand it, they are not strong enough. It seems to be the back that gives out. Girls cannot work more than eight hours and keep it up. They know it, and they rarely will. Even this seems to pull them down, so that it is extremely rare that a girl continues more than five years at the business."

The average pay of women engaged in setting type is about $8 per week, while men make from $12 to $14 on piecework, except on the morning papers, where their pay runs from $18 to $25. Notwithstanding this meager pay, there are a number of young ladies engaged in the city who are saving up handsome amounts each year. Some are investing in real estate, some in building and loan associations, while others are laying the foundations to prospective homes by weekly depositing their money in banks. The majority of female compositors, though, at the close of their term at the case will have nothing to show in return for their shattered health and lost time.

The tramp printer has been a conspicuous figure in newspaper life since long before the days of Artemus Ward. He has penetrated the borderland of civilization and darkened the threshold of every known printing office. Yet as long as he has been extant the number of known female tramp printers have not reached a score.

Several years ago there passed through western Ohio, riding when fortune favored, walking when fortune frowned, a young woman tramp apostle of Franklin. She was dressed plainly but neatly in what might be called a cross between a traveling and office suit of brown color. The toughened expression on her face indicated that she was familiar with the tricks of the profession, versed in the study of vulgarity. No tender, trusting female was she, but a hardened, suspicious, masculine woman. She understood job printing and was remarkably rapid on straight matter, and to this more than anything else is to be attributed her good success in a generally unsuccessful venture.

Undoubtedly, the chief reason why the walks of the tramp printer are so infrequently invaded by the female compositors, is their inability to endure the hardships suffered by the men.

A USEFUL SUGGESTION.

To the Editor :   OMAHA, November 5, 1889.

It seems to the writer that the little thing of sweeping out in a printing office is the cause of much more discomfort, waste and worry than is generally supposed. Having graduated from the broomstick to the composing stick himself, he knows whereof he writes. He has observed that in time hundreds of dollars' worth of valuable stock is absolutely ruined in being exposed to the dust which is daily stirred up by the "kid." Who ever heard of the counter-jumper in a dry goods or clothing store sweeping out without covering up the stock ? He would be fired in short order should he do so. He is also required to have the store swept out after business hours, instead of kicking up a dust on opening up in the morning. This is the point. Have your office swept out immediately at the close of the day's work, covering up the stock the while. The dust then has all night to settle, and your workmen have a clean room in which to begin work in the morning. No irritating dust assails the nostrils just as the day's labors are begun. The "kid," instead of crawling around the alleys and stones for an hour or so, compelling a man here and another there to stop work while he sweeps, has time to remove the covers from the stock and carry that rush proof over to Grumbler, Jones & Co. without delay.   WILL.

REGISTERED, No. 123,334.
MECHANICAL PATENT, MAR. 31, 1885.

PATENTED MAY 21, 1889.

30 POINT NYMPHIC.
With 48 Point Initials.

3 A Initials, $5.45
5 A, 9 a, . 6.05

Usual Number of Fancies
+ + Shown + by + + +
Huntup, Gabbler, Dazzlem & Co.
Contrivers + of
Rarities and Museum Goods

THE NYMPHIC SERIES SHOWN IN COMBINATION.

$7823.00

Cashton, May 4, 1956

Three hundred days after sight pay to the order of the

National + Bank + of + Atco

Seven thousand eight hundred and twenty-three Dollars

No. 124

Brown & Robinson

ALL COMPLETE WITH FIGURES.

MacKellar, Smiths & Jordan Co., Philadelphia.

Shniedewend & Lee Co., Agents, Chicago, Ill.

USEFUL GOTHIC.

ORIGINAL.

40 A 6 POINT INCLINED LINING GOTHIC No. 4 (Nonpareil) $1 30

IN A SHADY NOOK, BY A BABBLING BROOK
THERE SITS MY LOVE SO FAIR. IN HER LAP A BOOK, IN HER
368 EYES A LOOK OF KISS ME IF YOU DARE 529

40 A 6 POINT INCLINED LINING GOTHIC No. 5 (Nonpareil) $1 55

OH PRINTER MAN WHEN YOU BEGAN
TO SEE THAT YOU WERE FIXED WAS WHEN YOU SENT OR
4 TO US WENT FOR SUPERIOR COPPER-MIXED 5

40 A 6 POINT INCLINED LINING GOTHIC No. 6 (Nonpareil) $1 75

THIS HANDSOME INCLINED LINING
GOTHIC SERIES IS CAST FROM OUR FAMOUS
54 SUPERIOR COPPER-MIXED METAL 89

40 A 6 POINT INCLINED LINING GOTHIC No. 7 (Nonpareil) $1 85

GENERAL WESTERN AGENTS
THE BABCOCK PATENT AIR-SPRING PRESS
475 OPTIMUS AND STANDARD 863

30 A 8 POINT INCLINED LINING GOTHIC (Brevier) $1 85

IRON RAILROAD TRACKS
NORTH WESTERN STEEL COMPANY
294 CHICAGO ILLINOIS 536

20 A 10 POINT INCLINED LINING GOTHIC (Lg. Primer) $1 65

AN INCLINED GOTHIC
USEFUL DURABLE STRONG
4 SURE TO WEAR WELL

20 A 12 POINT INCLINED LINING GOTHIC (2 line Nonp.) $2 10

INTERNATIONAL EXPOSITION
THE WORLDS FAIR 1892 CITY OF CHICAGO
MMMMMMMMMMMMMMMMMMMMMMMMMMMMMMM

30 A 6 POINT WIDE LINING GOTHIC No. 20 (Nonpareil) $1 30

KNOWLEDGE AND TIMBER SHOULD
NOT BE MUCH USED UNTIL THEY ARE SEASONED
1234567890

30 A 6 POINT WIDE LINING GOTHIC No. 21 (Nonpareil) $1 60

THE REPUBLIC OF SPARTA
HAD TWO MAGISTRATES CALLED KINGS
1234567890

30 A 6 POINT WIDE LINING GOTHIC No. 22 (Nonpareil) $1 75

GRANDEUR AND MAGNITUDE
WESTERN THEORETICAL COMPANY
1234567890

30 A 6 POINT WIDE LINING GOTHIC No. 23 (Nonpareil) $1 95

BEAUTIFUL SUNBEAMS
WE SHOULD RESPECT OLD AGE
1234567890

20 A 8 POINT WIDE LINING GOTHIC (Brevier) $1 80

STOCK SHOWS
CHICAGO AND NEW YORK
123456789

15 A 10 POINT WIDE LINING GOTHIC (Long Primer) $1 75

CHESTNUTS
AND CIGAR STANDS
234567

15 A 12 POINT WIDE LINING GOTHIC (2 line Nonp.) $2 20

GEORGE HENRY BANGOR
THE ENGLISH 456 AND FRENCH
MMMMMMMMMMMMMMMMMMMMMMMMMMMMMMM

Manufactured by BARNHART BROS. & SPINDLER, Chicago, Ill.

No. 190. 4 Line. — 4 Cents per Letter.

Old Faces

No. 190. 6 Line. — 6 Cents per Letter.

Hange

No. 190. 10 Line. — 9 Cents per Letter.

Pug

No. 208. 3 Line. — 4 Cents per Letter.

Usually

No. 208. 6 Line. — 4 Cents per Letter.

MINE

No. 208. 10 Line. — 5 Cents per Letter.

UAI

No. 201. 4 Line. — 3 Cents per Letter.

Hang 5

No. 201. 6 Line. — 3 Cents per Letter.

KEG

No. 201. 10 Line. — 5 Cents per Letter

RA

No. 202. 4 Line. — 3 Cents per Letter.

New Style

No. 202. 6 Line. — 4 Cents per Letter.

Hamlet

No. 202. 10 Line. — 5 Cents per Letter.

Paid

THESE STYLES MADE ANY SIZE DESIRED.

259 DEARBORN ST., CHICAGO.   **TWO RIVERS, WIS.**

THE CIGARETTE PRINTER.

BY M. STANISLAUS MURPHY.

NEXT to the typical dude in the matter of cigarette smoking comes the precocious small boy. Following him, as far as my observation goes, is a third class, composed of a miscellaneous gathering, and in this latter class we find the "cigarette printer."

> "The 'cigarette printer' may be hungry and broke,
> He may think for the want of a 'smile' he will choke,
> But all his hard luck he will quickly forget,
> In the lung-sapping puff of the vile cigarette."

Where cigarette smoking had its origin is a profound mystery, and as far as I am concerned shall always remain so. It is an indisputable fact that much agony would have been spared fathers and mothers if the pernicious habit had died with the originator. How many incorrigible youngsters would have full miniature savings banks, if Sweet Caporals and other brands of cigarettes were unknown.

Much has been said and written upon this evil, but considerable more will have to be said, and many new paragraphs written, before the last cigarette disappears in smoke. The subject is broad and inviting, and there is always something new to be said in the matter. How often do we read in the newspapers an item bearing the familiar headline, "Another Cigarette Victim," and generally what little attention is paid to it! Perhaps the printer who set up the paragraph had a package or two of the diminutive cheroots in his inside pocket at the time, and, if the rules of the office didn't prohibit smoking during composition hours, possibly he might have been blowing the obnoxious smoke of a cigarette into the faces of his indignant alley mates at that very moment. If there is anything more disagreeable than to have your upper story immersed in a cloud of this infernal smoke, I haven't as yet experienced it, and I hope I never shall.

With the typical dude the habit is partly excusable, for the cigarette seems to be part of the dear fellow's make-up, and to him is really indispensable.

But it is chiefly in regard to the "cigarette printer" that I wish to confine my writing. It seems he ought to have better sense, but he will tell you it is his own business. So it is, so long as he keeps by himself when he smokes ; but when the obnoxious fumes arising from that which he calls a cigarette are filling the room, and the lungs of those he is mingling with, then it becomes the business of the ones who are being slowly smothered. To them it is extremely disagreeable and offensive, and if they are forced to file a protest occasionally they are more than justified in doing so. A victim of this injurious habit was working on a morning paper recently, and for every other take he lifted from the copy-hook he would light a fresh cigarette, to the disgust of those working in the immediate vicinity. The next day, the foreman, in measuring the strings, found one considerably shorter than his arm, and on investigation found it belonged to Mr. Cigarette Smoker. He eyed it contemplatively for a moment, then remarked, "Well, its all you can expect from a printer who smokes cigarettes."

A novel and striking picture met my gaze recently. The galley boy in a newspaper office and a gaunt six-footer, a "cigarette printer," were ambling along the street together, each smoking a "sweet cap." There was a noticeable disparity in their statures, the boy being a couple of feet shorter than his companion. In the matter of intellect I thought they were about on a par, with the percentage in favor of the youngster. The typo looked old enough to be the young man's father, but he wasn't. Imagine a father and a son, not any older than this boy, walking along the street side by side, smoking cigarettes ! It would be a picture for an artist, and a subject grave enough for an undertaker. If the "cigarette printer" does not want his boy to tumble into this vile, disagreeable and injurious habit, let him give up the pernicious practice himself. I have a young descendant bearing my name and features, who is just three, and he does not know what a cigarette is yet ! I hope he will be three years older than his father is at present when he finds out, and that he will have seen as many summers and winters as his aged and respected grandsire when he makes up his mind to smoke one.

Why it is that a printer, possessing the intelligence which is necessary in his business, should allow himself to become a victim of this abominable practice, I never could see, even with two pairs of spectacles. I have seen a tourist come into an office from the road shivering with cold, being both thinly clad and hungry ; I have seen him go out with money tendered him by his fellow-workmen, and, despite his hunger, have seen him pass a restaurant, go to a tobacco store and invest part of his money in a package of cigarettes before he gratified the inner man.

> "Oh for an influence mighty and grand,
> That will forever drive from this glorious land,
> Cigarettes of every conceivable brand !"

QUADRATS.

BY PICA ANTIQUE.

"THE five hundred women compositors in Boston are to be taken into the union," says an exchange. While questioning the correctness of the number, we do not discover anything so strange or alarming in the fact as to require its being blown over the world by telegraphic trumpets. Once it might have been an astonishing proceeding ; now it has become a matter of course.

Women as compositors are no longer an experiment. They have clearly demonstrated their capability and fitness to handle type ; the bars of typographical unions have been let down in other cities, and why not in Boston ? The only surprising part of the matter to our mind is that they ever were kept out ; ever debarred the privileges, the protection, the encouragement, to which they were justly entitled.

22 A, 35 a.   6 POINT UNIQUE CELTIC. $2.50

DINNA YE HEAR THE SLOGAN?
Listen, while we tell you what is
going on in our sleepy old town.
We, HUMDRUM & CO., are just
waking up with the intention of
stirring business in our locality
1234567890

10 A, 14 a.   18 POINT UNIQUE CELTIC. $3.60

HOLIDAY PRESENTS
Santa Claus Arrived
Unloading at our Door

20 A, 32 a.   8 POINT UNIQUE CELTIC. $2.60

OUR WINDOWS HAVE BEEN
Cleaned by an Expert, our
Store walls Whitewashed in
the highest style of the art,
and Cobwebs are abolished
1234567890

7 A, 10 a.   24 POINT UNIQUE CELTIC. $4.05

PURCHASERS
Returning Home
Smiling Sweetly

18 A, 28 a.   10 POINT UNIQUE CELTIC. $2.90

PAVEMENTS ARE KEPT
clear of Loafers and no
truant hog has rooting
or spitting privileges in
the vicinity of our shop

6 A, 8 a.   30 POINT UNIQUE CELTIC. $5.35

BUSINESS
Conducted
Honorably

15 A, 22 a.   12 POINT UNIQUE CELTIC. $3.00

POLITE SALESMEN
are ready to fawn
around and deftly
clutch your money

4 A, 6 a.   36 POINT UNIQUE CELTIC. $6.20

ACTIVITY
Becoming
Epidemic

12 A, 18 a.   14 POINT UNIQUE CELTIC. $3.25

IMMENSE STOCK
ready for buyers
who value worth

MacKellar, Smiths & Jordan Co., Philadelphia.   Shniedewend & Lee Co., Agents, Chicago, Ill.
318   *December 1889*

Hazel Script.

PATENT APPLIED FOR.

Mr. and Mrs. Y. F. Montague,

At Home
Friday, October 12th & 19th
3465 North Park Lane.

Mr. and Mrs. Rochester
request your presence
at the marriage of their daughter
Georgiana
to
Vincent Tavin Montague,
Wednesday evening, October eighth,
Eighteen hundred and ninety-three
at eight o'clock.

14 Point :—
9 A 30 a $5 50

18 Point :—
9 A 25 a $6 40

24 Point :—
7 A 20 a $8 00

Mr. & ·Burlington,

Los Angeles,

1657 Belthino Avenue.

California.

Manufactured by BARNHART BROS. & SPINDLER, Chicago, Ill.

THE "LINOTYPE" COMPOSING MACHINE.

THE INLAND PRINTER herewith presents to its readers a cut of this wonderful machine, which will give a very correct idea of its appearance. To describe its entire mechanism, so as to give the reader an understanding of it, is almost, if not quite impossible, but a short description, in a general way, may not be devoid of interest. It resembles a typesetting machine, in that it has a lettered keyboard. These keys are connected with a number of perpendicular tubes, shown in the cut, directly in front of the operator. In these tubes are placed the matrices, no type being used in this machine, representing all the characters of a book or newspaper font. When a key is touched one of these matrices

shaped, perfectly even spacing and justification is accomplished by these being pushed up between the words until the line-gauge is filled. The line of matrices is then carried just a little forward to the metal pot when the metal is forced in and the work of casting is accomplished. Enough time is allowed for the metal to cool, after which the line is trimmed to thickness and height to paper, and when completed resembles a line of solid type. In this resemblance originated the name, i. e., Linotype, or "line o' type." Herewith we show three lines cast on one of these machines in the office of the Providence, Rhode Island, *Journal.*

THE INLAND PRINTER
Leading Trade Journal of the World in the
Printing Industry.

drops into an inclined channel, along which it is carried by an air-blast to its proper place in the line-gauge where the line is formed. Spaces, or more properly speaking, spacers, are automatically placed between the words simply by touching a key, the same as for a matrix. When the line-gauge is full, or as nearly so as a line of type usually comes to proper justification in an ordinary composing stick, the operator touches a lever-key, shown just to the left of the keyboard proper, and the line of matrices is carried off to be properly justified and cast. The spacers being wedge-

After the casting of each line has been accomplished, the matrices are sent back mechanically and distributed into their respective tubes with unerring correctness. All these operations are performed automatically, without in any way detracting the attention of the operator from his work at the keyboard, this work consisting of manipulating the keys and pressing down the lever, at the completion of setting each line of matrices, to set the various mechanism in motion.

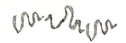

40 A $1 75   6 POINT RACINE No. 1 (Nonpareil)

FIRST GRAND OVERLAND FIREFLY MAIL
TRAIN RUNNING THROUGH MANY ZIGZAG ROCKY CANONS
23 EIGHTY MILES AN HOUR 45

6 POINT RACINE (Nonpareil)   32 A $1 75

GREAT WESTERN TYPE FOUNDRY
CELEBRATED SUPERIOR COPPER-MIXED TYPES
56 CHICAGO ILLINOIS 78

30 A   8 POINT RACINE (Brevier) $2 00

COUNTY JUDGES FINAL DECISION
INCONSISTENT TESTIMONY INTRODUCED
CRIMINAL EXECUTION

25 A   10 POINT RACINE (Long Primer) $2 25

GRAND SMOOTH ROADS
SCULPTOR POET AND PAINTER
TOURNAMENTS

24 A   12 POINT RACINE (2 line Nonp.) $2 50

FEDERAL SUPREME COURT JUDGESHIP
GRAND JURY CHAMBER   EIGHT   INDICTMENTS FOUND
CRIMINAL COURT BUILDING

10 A   24 POINT RACINE (4 line Nonp.) $3 25

CONCORD STUDENT
CHARACTER FOR HISTORIANS

15 A   18 POINT RACINE (3 line Nonp.) $3 00

DANGEROUS CROSSINGS
PASSENGERS ESCAPE DESTRUCTION

8 A   30 POINT RACINE (5 line Nonp.) $3 75

EMERGENCIES
PURCHASED EXPERIENCE

Manufactured by BARNHART BROS. & SPINDLER, Chicago, Ill.

Kept in stock by the Minnesota Type Foundry Co., St. Paul, Minn.; Great Western Type Foundry, Kansas City, Mo.; St. Louis Printers' Supply Co., St. Louis, Mo.; Great Western Type Foundry, Omaha, Neb., and for sale by all Type-Founders and Dealers in Printers' Material.

FRENCH OLD STYLE.

40 A   8 POINT FRENCH OLD STYLE (Brevier) $1 75

SUPERIOR COPPER-MIXED TYPES

GREAT WESTERN TYPE FOUNDRY CHICAGO

1234567890

24 A   12 POINT FRENCH OLD STYLE (2 line Nonp.) $1 75

ARTISTIC PAINTERS

DISH-WASHER AND CHAMBERMAID

18 A   16 POINT FRENCH OLD STYLE (2 line Brevier) $2 20

MUSICAL HISTORY

BRIGHT SUMMER NIGHTS

10 A   4 POINT FRENCH OLD STYLE (4 line Nonp.) $2 65

SPECIMEN

CONSTRUCTED

32 A   10 POINT FRENCH OLD STYLE (Long Primer) $1 75

HISTORY OF MODERN MUSIC

GREAT ITALIAN AND FRENCH COMPOSER

1234567890

20 A   14 POINT FRENCH OLD STYLE (English) $2 00

LOVERS PARADISE

BEAUTIFUL BRIDAL PRESENTS

12 A   20 POINT FRENCH OLD STYLE (2 line Lg. Primer) $2 35

BEETHOVEN

MUSICAL MOMENTS

8 A   30 POINT FRENCH OLD STYLE (5 line Nonp.) $3 00

GRAND

ENTERPRISES

6 A   36 POINT FRENCH OLD STYLE (6 line Nonp.) $3 45

INDIAN STORY

ENGLISH AND FRENCH

5 A   48 POINT FRENCH OLD STYLE (8 line Nonp.) $4 85

FURNISHERS

GRAND OPENING

Manufactured by BARNHART BROS. & SPINDLER, Chicago, Ill.

Kept in stock by the Minnesota Type Foundry Co., St. Paul, Minn.; Great Western Type Foundry, Kansas City, Mo.; St. Louis Printers' Supply Co., St. Louis, Mo.; Great Western Type Foundry, Omaha, Neb., and for sale by all Type-Founders and Dealers in Printers' Material.

TASSO SERIES.

40 A   6 POINT TASSO (Nonpareil) $1 75

POTATO MASHERS AND FLAT IRONS
SEVENTEEN MONTHS AFTER THE HONEYMOON
FLYING IN EVERY DIRECTION
WOULD YOU CONSIDER MARRIAGE A FAILURE
1 2 3 4 5 6 7 8 9 0

32 A   8 POINT TASSO (Brevier) $1 90

AMERICAN REFORMERS
MORE BLESSED TO GIVE THAN TAKE
THE LITTLE GIRLS AT HOME
1 2 3 4 5 6 7 8 9 0

25 A   10 POINT TASSO (Long Primer) $2 00

BEAUTIFUL GARDEN PLANTS EXHIBITED
PLEASING TOURNAMENTS   INSTRUCTIVE LECTURES
YEARNINGS AFTER LOVELINESS

26 A   12 POINT TASSO (2 line Nonp.) $2 00

BOSTON BROWN BREAD AND BEANS
TURKEY AND GOOSE   STUFFED   CRANBERRY SAUCE
PINEAPPLE FRITTERS

15 A   18 POINT TASSO (3 line Nonp.) $2 35

ROASTED PRAIRIE CHICKEN
PORK AND BEANS   SWEET POTATOES
SERVED OYSTERS

10 A   24 POINT TASSO (4 line Nonp.) $2 85

ABRAHAM LINCOLN
FAMOUS AMERICAN AUTHORS

THIS SERIES LINES AT THE BOTTOM. COMPLETE WITH FIGURES.

Manufactured by BARNHART BROS. & SPINDLER, Chicago, Ill.

Kept in stock by the Minnesota Type Foundry Co., St. Paul, Minn.; Great Western Type Foundry, Kansas City, Mo.; St. Louis Printers' Supply Co., St. Louis, Mo.; Great Western Type Foundry, Omaha, Neb., and for sale by all Type-Founders and Dealers in Printers' Material.

Printing Designs
Original & Striking
Superb Material

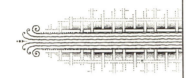

CRAYON SERIES

PATENTED FEB. 9, 1886.

THREE SIZES

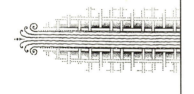

Lecture & Concert
Beechtown Forestry Association
Coming Thursday Evening
1234567890

Damon & Pythias
Friendly Toward Mankind
1234567890

Overland Merchandise Insured

The Atlantic & Pacific Co.

Charter Perpetual

MacKellar, Smiths & Jordan Co., Philadelphia.   Shniedewend & Lee Co., Agents, Chicago, Ill.

Grady  Series

Patent Pending

18 Point, 8 A, 12 a, $2.75

SUPERIOR WRITER STRICKEN DOWN WITH PNEUMONIA

Career of Unusual Interest Terminated Suddenly by Dreaded Disease 368

24 Point, 6 A, 10 a, $3.30

SILVER TONGUED SOUTHERN POLITICIAN

Quoted by Leading Newspapers Throughout the Country $754

Dodson's Printers' Supply Depot

23 East Mitchell Street

Atlanta, Georgia

. . . . . *The Grady Series was designed and named for the late Henry W. Grady, previous to his recent visit to Boston, Mass., and made its first appearance in Mr. Grady's paper, "The Atlanta Constitution," the type for which has been supplied for several years by the Dickinson Foundery, through its agent, Mr. Dodson . . . . The Grady Series now goes out to the Printing Fraternity as a modest reminder of the worth and greatness of a noble man. . . . . . .*

36 Point, 5 A, 8 a, $4.90

PATRIOTIC CITIZENS SHOCKED

Gallant Democrat with Brilliant Future 86

42 Point, 4 A, 6 a, $5.40

Golden HEARTED Gentleman 94

EBONY.

PATENT APPLIED FOR.

AMERICAN SYSTEM OF
INTERCHANGEABLE TYPE BODIES.

8A, 16a, Great Primer (18 Point). $4.75

NIGHT, SABLE GODDESS

From her Ebony Throne, in Rayless Majesty Stretches

234 Forth her Leaden Scepter 567

6A, 12a, Double Pica (24 Point). $4.75

MANNING & WOOD

Railroad and Commercial Printers

26 Broadway 28

4A, 8a Double Great Primer (36 Point). $7.25

WORLD'S FAIR

Chicago the Peoples Choice 93

3A, 6a, Four-Line Pica (48 Point). $9.75

Anniversary
Discovery of America

FIGURES AND LOGOTYPES WITH ALL SIZES.   SPACES AND QUADS EXTRA.

18 A $1 75   12 POINT CLIMAX (2 line Nonp.)

MONDAY MORNING

GRANDEUR AND SPLENDOR

1234567890

18 POINT CLIMAX (3 line Nonp.)   12 A $2 25

IMPRESSION

FOREIGN HOUSES

12345678

10 A   24 POINT CLIMAX (4 line Nonp.) $3 00

FANCY BOOK MAKERS

DESIRABLE SEWING MACHINES

A   30 POINT CLIMAX (5 line Nonp.) $3 65

UNIQUE DESIGN

ENGRAVING FURNISHED

6 A   36 POINT CLIMAX (6 line Nonp.) $4 05

BANKERS CASHIERS

4 A   48 POINT CLIMAX (8 line Nonp.) $4 50

SIBERIA PRISON

THIS SERIES LINES AT THE BOTTOM.   COMPLETE WITH FIGURES.

Manufactured by BARNHART BROS. & SPINDLER, Chicago, Ill.

Kept in stock by the Minnesota Type Foundry Co., St. Paul, Minn.; Great Western Type Foundry, Kansas City, Mo.; St. Louis Printers' Supply Co., St. Louis, Mo.; Great Western Type Foundry, Omaha, Neb., and for sale by all Type-Founders and Dealers in Printers' Material.

10 A, 35 a, $4.00.   12 POINT FRENCH SCRIPT.   35 a, Lower-case only, $2.40.

Profitable Business Opportunity

Everywhere Salable and Everywhere Useful

Agents Wanted to Canvass the Globe

Recent Improvements in Delusive Appliances have brought them so near perfection that fleeing cashiers or fraudulent debtors can be caught on the wing, voters entrapped for office-seekers, subscribers obtained for uninteresting publications, wealthy verdants corraled without using stool-pigeons, lovers secured for confirmed old maids, recruits rallied around kingly aspirants, or frogs and fish drawn from the pond at the back door

Apply before 11.59 p. m.

9 A, 30 a, $5.00.   14 POINT FRENCH SCRIPT.   30 a, Lower-case only, $3.05.

Hoodwink Manufacturing Co.   *Private*

Notice is Given

That Mrs Vulpine is Agent for our traps, which are adapted to catch mice or millionaires, elephants or heiresses, She can clearly explain their merits, (as her late husband, a man of much wealth, was ensnared in one of them,) and we ask a trial, either in forest or parlor, of the goods she will present

February 2, 1894.

6 A, 18 a, $8.90.   28 POINT FRENCH SCRIPT.   18 a, Lower-case only, $4.90.

Salesroom, No. 64 Decoy Place

Appliances for Luring and Entrapping the Unwary

Quadruped, Biped, Ichthyic, Ornithologic

January 31, 1897.

We this day Exhibit a few of the "Queer Fish" caught in traps made by the Hoodwink Manufacturing Co. of Lurem

Miss Tuberose

The American Naturalist

Gives Lectures Hourly

8 A, 24 a, $6.00.   18 POINT FRENCH SCRIPT.   24 a, Lower-case only, $3.40.

No. 5427

Arrests, tries and convicts chicken thieves without the help of either judge or jury

And Guards

Watermelon Plantations

From Depredation

22 POINT FRENCH SCRIPT.   22 a, Lower-case only, $3.90.

7 A, 22 a $7.25.

The MacKellar, Smiths & Jordan Co., Philadelphia.   Shniedewend & Lee Co., Agents, Chicago, Ill.

18 a 12 A   THREE LINE NONPAREIL DORIC CONDENSED—18 POINT. $3 00

PRINTERS MUST BUY CONDENSED TYPES
Another Condensed Face Introduced to Aid and Please the Job Printer
Columbian Celebrations 240

12 a 8 A   TWO LINE PICA DORIC CONDENSED—24 POINT. $3 50

THE FAST OCEAN STEAMERS
Our Commercial Relations with South America
Doric Architecture 158

10 a 6 A   FIVE LINE NONPAREIL DORIC CONDENSED—30 POINT. $4 25

ANCIENT DORIC TEMPLES
Many Pictures of Ancient and Modern Buildings
Household Charms 379

10 a 6 A   THREE LINE PICA DORIC CONDENSED—36 POINT. $4 50

NEW DORIC CONDENSED
Dealers in every Requisite used by
Printing Trade 259

PATENT PENDING.

10 a 6 A

Three Line Nonpareil Crystal—18 Point.

$3 50

Country Board at Gowanus

Enchanting Scenes among the Mountains

GOBLETS 520

8 a 5 A

Two Line Pica Crystal—24 Point.

$4 50

When Summer Comes

Our Crystal Ice! What may be its Cost?

COLUMBIA 302

6 a 4 A

Three Line Pica Crystal—36 Point.

$6 00

Eastern Customs

Storms on Sea and Land

BOAST 250

DECLINE OF THE BOOK PRINTER.

BY F. J. HURLBUT.

THE father of the art, he is no longer a leader, nor even a prominent factor in the craft. His decline from the high place he once held in the esteem of the public and his fellows is almost pathetic, because he has done nothing to merit his loss of prestige, but other branches of the trade have crept forward and passed him, and his place in the lead of the procession has been appropriated by others who were no more worthy than he, but whose labors were more productive of profit and therefore commanded a greater degree of respect and admiration from all parties concerned. The career of the book printer has been degraded and his ambition paralyzed by the wonderful progress in printing machinery, type, inks, paper, rollers, etc.

When we examine the works of the early printer, note the faultless register of folios, running heads and even the lines of reading matter, the uniform color, clean impression, etc., and then consider that this perfect work was done on a wooden press, that the form was inked by hand with inkballs or "daubers," that the printer made his own type, press, inkballs, etc., set the type and did the presswork, we have only to glance at the unhappy condition of the book printer of the present time to realize how far he has fallen. It was the death knell of the book printer when some of the commercial uses of printing were discovered, and as these uses have become more apparent and books have been to some extent supplanted by the newspapers, while labor-saving machinery and modern type and material have reduced the labor of the book printer to a very simple process, he has been sinking out of sight, while his younger brother, the job printer, has come to the front and will there remain, for the reason that his is the artistic department of composition, where the artist can surely stamp his individuality upon his work, and where routine is secondary. The improvements referred to have rendered what were the most tedious and skillful labors of early printers almost a matter of routine. In addition to this fact, the high degree of accuracy in some departments of bookwork is no longer exacted by printers nor cared for by the public. Other elements of the work, the engravings, paper, clear type, etc., are now considered of greater importance. While a perfect register was one of the most difficult feats in bookwork, printers vied with each other to produce it. Now, since it is an easy matter, unless the register is very bad, no one notices it particularly.

In spite of the well settled proposition that labor-saving machinery and material is a benefit to the worker, we must therefore admit that the book printer has suffered by it—in caste and in pay, at least. A larger number of them can undoubtedly find employment, but what miserably paid employment it is. The highest average wages for a book printer who works by the piece in any large American city is, perhaps, $12 or $14 per week, and his work is seldom steady. It is within the memory of the writer that book compositors who thoroughly understood their branch of the trade, made more money than the job men, and were the stronger element in the trades unions.

The proprietor of one of the largest book printing offices in this city once said to me:

"What is a book compositor, anyhow? He is little better than a common laborer."

I felt called upon to resent the remark, for it was untrue. The speaker, however, did not refer to such men as had charge of bookwork in his own office, even; but to the majority of those who call themselves book printers, though they could not cast up a table properly to save their lives, and to whom make-up and imposition are an unknown art. But one or two men can perform the two latter duties for twenty or more compositors, so there is little future in store for the book compositor, and little hope that he will be able to better his condition. There was really a grain of truth in the harsh remark quoted, and that unhappy truth is that the book compositor *is, in fact,* little better than a common laborer so far as his pay is concerned.

Gutenberg would have been amazed could he have foreseen the consequences of evolution in the printing business. In his day, printing was little, but the printer was great. In ours, printing is the mainspring of our civilization, and has made that civilization possible, while the printer is — well, he is relegated to the domain of a common wage worker, and that would be enough to horrify the father of typography.

Printing has passed through a natural process. Modern genius has developed it, but during the process of its development it has lent to that genius its invincible power, and the result is that its original object, the dissemination of literature, is now only a branch of its usefulness. Its beneficiaries are commerce, trades, arts, sciences and every department of human life. Was there ever a calling whose influence upon the human race was so extensive or so uniformly good? Gutenberg might have cried "prostitution!" if he had seen his beloved art blossom into a railroad tariff. But there were many things in his day which were dedicated to the "love of God," which are now applied, with great benefit, to the "use of man." In other words, we have come to know that both expressions mean the same thing when properly interpreted.

The brutal truth of the remark made by the Chicago "master" printer is one that cannot be denied. It would be better for the book compositor if he would abandon the job offices and persistently seek employment in a newspaper composing room, where the pay is much better and the exactions as to quality of his work much less. Jobwork, presswork and newspaper composition are the only branches of printing that are to be depended on for decent remuneration, and with all of these, even, the reduction will inevitably come.

 STIPPLE

REGISTERED, No. 141,360.

THREE-LINE PICA.   36 POINT STIPPLE.   7 A, $5.35.

FOUR-LINE PICA.   48 POINT STIPPLE.   6 A, $6.90.

STIPPLE SERIES SHOWN IN COMBINATION.

The MacKellar, Smiths & Jordan Co., Philadelphia.   Shniedewend & Lee Co., Agents, Chicago, Ill.

| NEW YORK—63 & 65 BEEKMAN ST. AND 62 & 64 GOLD ST. | Established 1804. | CHICAGO—154 MONROE STREET. CHAS. B. ROSS, Manager. |

PATENT PENDING.

10 A   THREE LINE NONPAREIL WAVE—18 POINT. $2 25

BORNE * AMIDST * WAVING * FLAGS
ENCHANTING 829

8 A   TWO LINE PICA WAVE—24 POINT. $2 75

ANY * GREAT * IMPROVEMENT
ORIGINAL TASTE 52

5 A   THREE LINE PICA WAVE—36 POINT. $3 50

THE * NEW * STATE
CHAIRS 38

4 A   FOUR LINE PICA WAVE—48 POINT. $5 00

HOW * TO * VOTE
RIGHT 23

ALGONQUIN SERIES

The Algonquin and Algonquin Ornamented are effectively used when printed in different colors, one over the other, as shown on next page. As initials and in combination they can be admirably worked.

$4.32   42 POINT ALGONQUIN   6 a, 4 A

HEADLINE FOR ARTISTIC

Beautiful and Illuminated Timetable 28

$4.85   48 POINT ALGONQUIN   5 a, 4 A

BOSTON Conventions Arrived 97

$5.70   60 POINT ALGONQUIN   4 a, 4 A

LEARNED Proffessors 24

ALGONQUIN ORNAMENTED SERIES

$4.32   42 POINT ALGONQUIN ORNAMENTED   6 a, 4 A

HEADLINE FOR ARTIST

Beautiful Illuminated Timetable 3

$4.85   48 POINT ALGONQUIN ORNAMENTED   5 a, 4 A

CHICAGO Excursions Arrive 2

$5.70   60 POINT ALGONQUIN ORNAMENTED   4 a, 4 A

LEADING Designers 42

ORIGINAL TYPE DESIGN FROM DICKINSON TYPE FOUNDERY, BOSTON, MASS.

Specimens from Farmer, Little & Co., Type Founders.

| NEW YORK—63 & 65 BEEKMAN ST. AND 62 & 64 GOLD ST. | Established 1804. | CHICAGO—154 MONROE STREET. CHAS. B. ROSS, Manager. |

50 A   Six Point Gotham. $2 00

THE BUSY HAUNTS OF GOTHAM STARTLED BY AN EXPLOSION

GREAT DESTRUCTION OF PROPERTY IN THE WEST CAUSED BY ALARMING AND DANGEROUS CLOUDBURSTS

DANGER IMPOSSIBLE TO FORESEE

DAMAGE TO BUILDINGS BY FIRE $12,345   GOODS DAMAGED BY FIRE & WATER $67,890

40 A   Eight Point Gotham. $2 25

RAPID TRANSIT IS THE QUESTION OF THE DAY

INCREASED FACILITIES REQUIRED FOR   SCHEME OUTLINED BY THE COMMISSION

EXPEDITIOUSLY HANDLING   THE COST $1,234,567,890

THE PASSENGERS BY RAILROAD   ADVANTAGES WORTH THE MONEY

THE TRADE AND COMMERCE OF CHICAGO RAPIDLY INCREASING

30 A   Ten Point Gotham. $2 25

THIS NEW TYPE IS NAMED GOTHAM

ISSUED IN THREE USEFUL SIZES, HAVE YOU GOT THEM?

OLD TYPE FOUNDRY

REAL ESTATE SALES FOR YEAR $1,234,567,890

MMMMM   MMMMM

THESE FONTS LINE AT TOP AND BOTTOM.

FARMER, LITTLE & CO., TYPE FOUNDERS, CHICAGO.

THE LINING ANTIQUE SERIES.

35 A $1 25   SIX-POINT LINING ANTIQUE NO. 1.

THE PURIFICATION OF POLITICS UNDER EXISTING CONDITIONS
IS AN IRRIDESCENT DREAM
GOVERNMENT IS FORCE. POLITICS IS A BATTLE FOR SUPREMACY. PARTIES ARE THE
ARMIES. THE DECALOGUE AND THE GOLDEN RULE HAVE NO PLACE IN A
POLITICAL CAMPAIGN, THE OBJECT IS TO SUCCEED

SIX-POINT LINING ANTIQUE NO. 2.   30 A $1 25

TO DEFEAT THE ANTAGONIST AND EXPEL THE PARTY IN
POWER IS THE OBJECT AND
MUST BE ACCOMPLISHED AT ANY HAZARD. THE REPUBLICANS AND DEMO-
CRATS ARE AS IRRECONCILABLY OPPOSED TO EACH OTHER AS
WERE GRANT AND LEE IN THE WILDERNESS

SIX-POINT LINING ANTIQUE NO. 5.   30 A $1 75

THEY USE BALLOTS INSTEAD OF BULLETS BUT THE STRUGGLE
IS OFTEN AS UNRELENTING
AND DESPERATE AND THE RESULT SOUGHT FOR THE SAME AS ON THE GORY FIELD
IN WAR IT IS CONSIDERED LAWFUL TO DECEIVE THE

30 A $1 25   SIX-POINT LINING ANTIQUE NO. 3.

ADVERSARY, TO HIRE HESSIANS, TO PURCHASE
MERCENARIES, TO DESTROY
TO MUTILATE, TO KILL. THE COMMANDER WHO SHOULD LOSE A
BATTLE THROUGH ACTIVITY OF HIS MORAL NATURE
WOULD BE THE DERISION AND JEST OF

SIX-POINT LINING ANTIQUE NO. 4.   30 A $1 50

HISTORY. BUT THE BEST CITIZENS USUALLY
CARE MORE FOR GOOD
GOVERNMENT THAN FOR THE SPOILS OF OFFICE. THIS
IS THE HOPE AND SALVATION OF THE REPUBLIC
AND SAFEGUARD OF CIVIL LIBERTY

TWELVE-POINT LINING ANTIQUE NO. 3.   20 A $2 80

THE ENORMOUS SALE OF THAT
STARTLING BOOK
CAESAR'S COLUMN, SURPASSES ALL RECORDS IN THE
BOOK-PUBLISHING BUSINESS. CERTAIN

20 A $1 70   TWELVE-POINT LINING ANTIQUE NO. 1.

IT IS THAT THE AUTHOR HAS
SOUNDED A LOUD
TRUMP THAT WILL AROUSE MILLIONS OF
HONEST TOILERS IN EVERY FIELD

TWELVE-POINT LINING ANTIQUE NO. 2.   20 A $2 30

OF INDUSTRY. IT WILL
IMPRESS THEM
WITH THE ERRORS OF CLASS
LEGISLATION AND POINT

EIGHTEEN-POINT LINING ANTIQUE.   10 A $2 70

TO THE PRESENT INEQUALITIES
BETWEEN OUR WEALTHY AND POOR

TWENTY-FOUR-POINT LINING ANTIQUE.   8 A $3 40

A REVELATION AND
PROPHECY BASED ON FACTS

THIRTY-POINT LINING ANTIQUE   6 A $3 75

UNSOLVED
THE LABOR PROBLEM
34343434343434343434**3456565**65656565656565656

THE ILLINOIS TYPE FOUNDING CO., 200 CLARK ST., CHICAGO.

MARINE.

8A, 16a   Pica (12 Point). $2.70   6A, 12a,   Great Primer (18 Point). $3.40

ENGLISH LANGUAGE
Points are not of Equal Antiquity
7 with Printing 8

THOUGH NOT LONG
After its Invention the 93

5A, 10a,   Double Pica (24 Point). $4.60

NECESSITY OF INTRODUCING
Stops or Pauses in Sentences for the 35

4A, 8a,   Double Great Primer (36 Point). $6.70

GUIDANCE
Of the Reader Brought

3A, 6a,   Four-Line Pica (48 Point). $7.30

3 FORWARD 5
The Colon or Full Point

3A, 5a,   Five-Line Pica (60 Point). $10.50

FIRST 2 Invented

SPACES AND QUADS EXTRA.

FOR SALE BY MARDER, LUSE & CO., MINNEAPOLIS, MINN.; THE OMAHA TYPE FOUNDRY, OMAHA, NEB.;

PICA.   12 POINT JENSON.   16 A, 25 a, $2.85.

INFORMATION WANTED
Conspicuous Newspaper Advertisement
1234567890

14 POINT JENSON.   14 A, 20 a, $3.05.

CHARMING PROSPECT
Juvenile Cogitations on Maturity
1234567890

THREE-LINE NONPAREIL.   18 POINT JENSON.   12 A, 18 a, $3.85.

EXPERIMENTAL
Neighborly Chitchat Analyzed

TWO-LINE PICA.   24 POINT JENSON.   10 A, 15 a, $4.60.

DISTRACTED
Mountebank Bewildered

FIVE-LINE NONPAREIL.   30 POINT JENSON.   7 A, 10 a, $5.20.

QUAINT COSTUMES
Promenading Thronged Sidewalks

THREE-LINE PICA.   36 POINT JENSON.   5 A, 8 a, $6.15.

VERNAL EQUINOX
Contagious Springtide Lassitude

FOUR-LINE PICA.   48 POINT JENSON.   4 A, 6 a, $7.40.

HUNTING SCENE
Dangerous Adventures

The MacKellar, Smiths & Jordan Co., Philadelphia.   *Shniedewend & Lee Co., Agents, Chicago, Ill.*

338   *July 1890*

Marder, Luse & Co., Type Founders, Chicago.

PATENTED
OCTOBER 8, 1889.

MANSFIELD.

AMERICAN SYSTEM OF
INTERCHANGEABLE TYPE BODIES.

10A, 20a,   Pica (12 Point). $3.00

In the Journey through life the
Farther we Speed the Better we learn that
32 Humanitys Need 56
Is Charitys Spirit that Prompts us

8A, 16a,   Great Primer (18 Point). $3.50

The Commendable Deeds
Are recorded with bright type
But the Evil men do

CA, 12a,   Double Pica (24 Point). $4.00

The Thomas Pheline Quartette
Songs that Chill the Blood and Harrow the Soul
Wearisome Pleasures

4A. 8a,   Double Great Primer (36 Point). $6.00

74 Original Designs 25
The Best of Materials
Superior Workmanship

3A. 6a,   Four-line Pica (48 Point). $8.50

Printing Machines
Describe 436 Revolutions

SPACES AND QUADS EXTRA.

FOR SALE BY MARDER LUSE & CO., MINNEAPOLIS, MINN.; THE OMAHA TYPE FOUNDRY, OMAHA, NEB.; JOHN CRESWELL, DENVER COLO.;
KANSAS NEWSPAPER UNION, TOPEKA, KANSAS.

August 1890   339

NEW YORK—63 & 65 BEEKMAN ST. AND 62 & 64 GOLD ST. | Established 1804. | CHICAGO—154 MONROE STREET. CHAS. B. ROSS, Manager.

PATENT PENDING.

10 a 6 A   THREE LINE NONPAREIL ASCOT—18 POINT. $3 00

SALVATOR WINS THE RACE

Great Excitement on the Race Course during the Contest

Westchester Home 465

8 a 5 A   TWO LINE PICA ASCOT—24 POINT. $4 00

THE ASCOT SERIES

Characteristic and Original Designs for the Printers

Beautiful Saratoga 95

Handsome and Elegant Appearance

6 a 4 A   THREE LINE PICA ASCOT—36 POINT. $5 75

ASCOT HEATH

Racing for the Royal Hunt Cup

Mascots 68

FOUR LINE PICA—48 POINT—ABOUT READY.

EUCLID.

10 A $1 35   18 a $1 40   TEN-POINT EUCLID   18 Point Initial Caps, 4 A, $1 10

Remorseless Landlords Swooping DOWN ON IRISH TENANTS 345

10 A $1 55   18 a $1 55   TWELVE-POINT EUCLID   24 Point Initials, 4 A, $1 65

Handsome Sagacious Compositors

COSMOPOLITAN 456

8 A $2 40   14 a $2 35   EIGHTEEN-POINT EUCLID   30 Point Initials, 3 A, $2 00

Special Ornamented Lithographs ALL COLORS 234

6 A $2 60   10 a $2 45   TWENTY-FOUR-POINT EUCLID   36 Point Initials, 3 A, $2 55

Latest TYPE Designs 234

THIRTY, THIRTY-SIX AND FORTY-EIGHT-POINT EUCLID ALSO IN STOCK.

THE PAST HAS TAUGHT ITS BITTER LESSON

THE PRESENT

HAS ITS OPPORTUNITY,

THE FUTURE ITS HOPE

EUCLID INITIALS IN COMBINATION WITH ALPHA.

EXTRA HARD DURABLE METAL

MADE BY THE

ILLINOIS TYPE FOUNDING CO.

ALL OUR FACES NOW CAST

ON THE POINT SYSTEM.

NOS. 200 AND 202 SOUTH CLARK STREET, CHICAGO.

PATENT APL'D & FOR. CITY WESTERN TYPE FON'RY, CHICAGO.

20 A 30 a $2 25   10 POINT GRANT NO. 2   (Long Primer)

MONTREAL REAL ESTATE BROKERS

Shakerville Locomotive Manufacturing Companies

1234567890

12 POINT GRANT NO. 2   (2 line Nonp.)   15 A 25 a $2 50

BRIGHT WINTER NIGHTS

Sweet Flowers Covering the River Banks

1234567890

10 A 20 a   18 POINT GRANT NO. 2   (3 line Nonp.) $3 00

PLEASANT EVENING

North Chicago Dashing Maidens

8 A 15 a   24 POINT GRANT NO. 2   (4 line Nonp.) $3 55

BRIGHT NIGHTS

Warm and Cold Weather

6 A 12 a   30 POINT GRANT NO. 2   (5 line Nonp.) $4 10

UNIVERSAL

Marble Court House

6 A 12 a   36 POINT GRANT NO. 2   (6 line Nonp.) $5 25

SLIPPERS

Little Glass Shoe

5 A 8 a   42 POINT GRANT NO. 2   (7 line Nonp.) $5 25

CHICAGO BROKERS

Corrupt Custom House Officials

5 A 8 a   48 POINT GRANT NO. 2   (8 line Nonp.) $6 30

PRESIDENTS Proclamation

THIS SERIES LINES AT THE BOTTOM.   COMPLETE WITH FIGURES.

8A, 16a, Pica Hexagon (12 Point). 3.05

APPRECIATIVE PRINTERS
Will show Approval
Of this Original and Beautiful Series
By Sending their Orders for
Three Different Sizes
1234567890

Hexagon.

AMERICAN SYSTEM OF
INTERCHANGEABLE TYPE BODIES.

4A, 8a, Double Pica Hexagon (24 Point). 4.40

Marder, Luse & Co
Chicago Type Foundry
139 Monroe St.
Chicago,

FIGURES
with
All Sizes.

6A, 12a, Great Primer Hexagon (18 Point). 4.25

SWEET MUSIC
Listen to the Mocking Bird
Early Morning Hours
8 Dewdrops 4

ALASKAN.

ALL SIZES IN THIS SERIES LINE AT BOTH TOP AND BOTTOM.

AMERICAN SYSTEM OF INTERCHANGEABLE TYPE BODIES.

24A, Nonpareil (6 Point). 1.50

MEN WITH ASPIRING MINDS SEEM FROM
THE EARLIEST TIMES TO HAVE BEEN DISSATISFIED
WITH THEIR NATURAL ALTITUDE AND TO HAVE
295 ENVIED THE ELEPHANT 384

16A, Brevier (8 Point). 1.70

THE ORDINARY TOILER FOR
DAILY BREAD HAS NOT SHARED THIS
4 EMULATION FOR THE 6

4A, Double Great Primer (36 Point). 6.00

5 GIANT 2

12A Long Primer (10 Point). 1.70

THIS SWELLING DESIRE
FOR IMPORTANCE SEEMS TO
35 MANIFEST 48

10A, Pica (12 Point). 2.05

ITSELF IN ANCIENT
LANDS OF EGYPTIANS

3A Four-Line Pica (48 Point). 7.30

NEATEST

8A, Great Primer (18 Point). 3.65

DESIGNS IN NEW ORIGINAL
35 TYPE FACES 48

6A, Double Pica (24 Point). 4.50

GRACEFUL
AMERICAN IDEAS

ALL SIZES IN THIS SERIES LINE AT BOTH TOP AND BOTTOM. SPACES AND QUADS EXTRA.

FOR SALE BY MARDER, LUSE & CO. MINNEAPOLIS, MINN.; THE OMAHA TYPE FOUNDRY, OMAHA, NEB.; JOHN CRESWELL, DENVER COLO.;
KANSAS NEWSPAPER UNION, TOPEKA KANSAS.

FILLET

REGISTERED, No. 153,671.

THREE-LINE NONPAREIL.   18 POINT FILLET.   9 A, $3.25

BILL OF FARE

ROAST TURKEY

CRANBERRY SAUCE

ROMAN PUNCH

4   3   2   1   1234567890   5   6

TWO-LINE PICA.   24 POINT FILLET.   A, $3.85

WINE LIST

ICED TOKAY

FRENCH PORT

MONTEBELLO

10   9   8   1234567890    11   12

THREE-LINE PICA.   36 POINT FILLET.   4 A, $4.85

CIGARS

MADURO

CONCHAS

22   15   14   13   123456    23   24

MacKellar, Smiths & Jordan Co., Philadelphia.   Shniedewend & Lee Co., Agents, Chicago, Ill.

8 Point, 32 a, 18 A, $3.00—L. Case, $1.10
10 Point, 32 a, 16 A, $3.50—L. Case, $1.50
12 Point, 24 a, 14 A, $4.00—L. Case, $1.70
18 Point, 14 a, 10 A, $5.00—L. Case, $2.00

24 Point, 10 a, 8 A, $5.50 — L. Case, $2.00
36 Point, 8 a, 6 A, $7.50 — L. Case, $3.00
48 Point, 5 a, 4 A, $8.65 — L. Case, $3.25
60 Point, 5 a, 4 A, $10.35 — L. Case, $4.45

THE SKJALD SERIES

Printers having the Typothetæ only need buy Skjald lower case. Caps are identical. . . . . This Series lines at the bottom accurately.

Eureka for

Skjald. ☞ This is Invariably Exclaimed by Superior Printers When Using the Series

Durable and Nice Looking

By using this Letter you not only save much Valuable Time in justification, etc. but Please Good Customers in delivering to them a job that is rapidly as well as

1234567890

☞ Stylishly

Gotten Together ☜ Printing Offices

Are Advanced 25

Per cent. in value, by adding these very Attractive Faces and discarding those ancient, dust-covered styles ✿ ✿ ✿ ✿

Everything Required to Furnish a Printing Office

Our Material will Prove Itself as Represented Every Time

Dickinson Type Foundery

150 Congress Street Boston, Mass.

GRADY SERIES

18 Point—12 a 8 A—$2.75
24 Point—10 a 6 A—$3.30
36 Point— 8 a 5 A—$4.90
42 Point— 6 a 4 A—$5.40

SERIES COMPLETE WITH FIGURES

UNIFORMITY IN TYPE BODIES.

The following is the report of the committee consisting of Messrs. DeVinne, Woodward and Pugh, appointed at St. Louis session of the Typothetæ to consider the subject of a possible greater uniformity in the bodies of types from different foundries. The accompanying letter was addressed to all the typefounders in the United States.

DEAR SIR,—At the third annual meeting of the United Typothetæ of America held at St. Louis, October 9, 1889, a special committee was appointed to consider the question of a possible greater uniformity in the bodies and in the lining of types made under the point system, with instructions to report at or before the next meeting to be held in Boston in September, 1890.

Master printers are already fairly informed as to the relative sizes of types made under the point system, as shown by the diagrams of Messrs. Marder, Luse & Co., of Chicago, and by other typefounders.

The unitary base of the system as explained by the MacKellar, Smiths & Jordan Company in their *Typographic Advertiser*, Nos. 119 and 120, 1884, is understood by all who have examined the subject.

It is also well known that a majority of American typefounders are making types by the point system; that this system is growing in favor; and that types of the same name from different foundries are more uniform as to body than they have been.

This marked improvement is thankfully acknowledged, but perfect uniformity has not yet been reached. There are differences of body in types of the same name from different foundries which lead us to ask :

1. Is the point system of your foundry established on the basis of 83 picas to 35 centimeters, and of 12 points to this body of pica ?

2. Do typefounders who adopt this system use a properly verified common measure ?

3. What measures have been taken by the associated typefounders to make accessible, for purpose of testing or verification, the standard meter on which the common measure depends ?

4. Is there a defined and observed agreement among the associated typefounders as to the best methods to be employed in the testing of molds, and in the casting and finishing of type, for the purpose of securing uniformity ?

5. Considering the large number of justified matrices now in use by different founders, and of types already cast therefrom from which future sorts will be wanted, as well as the increasing demand for text types and display types that fill the body unequally — some with short, and others with long descenders — is it practicable to attempt a new system which aims to put all faces on one line, or even on two or three established lines ?

6. Have you any trustworthy information as to the degree of uniformity reached by different European typefounders, all of whom (those of Great Britain excepted), we are told, cast type by the Didot point system ?

7. Why was not this point system adopted by American typefounders ?

We trust that you will not consider our questions unnecessary or hypercritical. The information asked for is needed by printers to prevent erroneous conclusions and possible erroneous action. Any suggestions or information that you can offer on this subject will be thankfully received.
[Signed by the Committee.]

From the many courteous replies received, and from personal interviews and correspondence with many typefounders (for which the committee here renews its thanks), it appears that most of the typefoundries in the United States are represented in the United States Typefounders' Association and are practically agreed in the maintenance of the point system of type bodies, first introduced to this country in 1878, and afterward modified by general agreement in 1886.

One prominent typefoundry, not a member of the United States Typefounders' Association, declines the point system entirely, and will make bodies on this system only to special order.

The members of the United States Typefounders' Association who have agreed upon the point system are : A. Foreman & Son, San Francisco, Cal.; Allison & Smith, Cincinnati, Ohio; Barnhart Bros. & Spindler, Chicago, Ill.; Benton, Waldo & Co., Milwaukee, Wis.; Boston Typefoundry, 104 Milk street, Boston, Mass.; Central Typefoundry, St. Louis, Mo.; Cincinnati Typefoundry, Cincinnati, Ohio; C. J. Cary & Co., Baltimore, Md.; Collins & McLeester, 705 Jayne street, Philadelphia, Pa.; Curtis & Mitchell, 15 Federal street, Boston, Mass.; Farmer, Little & Co., New York; H. H. Thorp Manufacturing Company, Cleveland, Ohio; Illinois Typefounding Co., Chicago, Ill.; James Conner's Sons, New York; Jno. G. Mengel & Co., Baltimore, Md.; Jno. T. Reton & Son, Kansas City, Mo.; L. Pelouze & Co., Philadelphia, Pa.; Marder, Luse & Co., Chicago, Ill.; Palmer & Rey, San Francisco, Cal.; Phelps, Dalton & Co., 150 Congress street, Boston, Mass.; St. Louis Typefoundry, St. Louis, Mo.; the Jno. Ryan Company, Baltimore, Md.; the MacKellar, Smiths & Jordan Company, Philadelphia, Pa.; Union Typefoundry, Chicago, Ill.

The types of the point system that are most in use are those of the newer fashions of ornamental type. The new bodies have not entirely displaced the old. All printers who have large stocks of text type continue to have sorts and additions made to the old bodies. The introduction of the new system before it has fully displaced the old, just now tends to increase existing irregularities.

The first attempt at uniformity by means of points began with the theory that the pica should be one-sixth of the American inch, and that there should be twelve points to this pica. This method of making a basis was not approved of by the founders whose pica was less than one-sixth of an inch, and these founders were in the majority. It was finally decided that the standard pica should be the pica of the MacKellar, Smiths & Jordan Company. It was claimed by the advocates of this standard that this body of pica, made by the oldest foundry in the United States, had already been adopted by many other founders, and was used by more printers than any other body of pica ; and that a system of points based on this pica would inflict the least loss on founders and printers who had to change from the old to the new system. These conclusions were accepted reluctantly by those who had made pica of a larger body. They objected to the new standard as capriciously and unscientifically selected, not based on any regular fraction of the foot or meter.

The need of a more definite standard than an accidentally selected pica led to the discovery that 83 picas of the accepted body were equal to 35 centimeters. It was also found that by making a very slight alteration in the height that 35 centimeters would exactly meet 15 heights of type. The old standard of height was eleven-twelfths or $\frac{916}{1000}$ of an inch. The new standard is one-fifteenth of 35 centimeters or $\frac{918}{1000}$ of an inch.

It does not appear that every typefoundry owns or has ready access to an official meter, on which the common measure of 35 centimeters depends. We cannot learn that all founders have procured this common measure. Some of them seem to depend entirely on a smaller measure of centimeters, by which they test their types. It has been claimed that there is no special reason why frequent recourse should be had to an official meter, as the meter is of a fixed and unalterable length, which can be determined by pure mathematical calculation.

The methods agreed upon by the United States Typefounders' Association for the purpose of securing uniformity under the new system seem to be theoretically satisfactory. A properly graduated measuring rod of steel, 35 centimeters or 83 picas in length, made or provided by the MacKellar, Smiths & Jordan Company, is accepted as the common measure. Each pica is divided into twelve points. The distance between the bodies of text types most used is kept in regular graduations of one point; in the smaller sizes of one-half point; in the larger sizes of two or more points. The typefounders who use the same measuring rod, and agree upon the same system, should make types uniform as to body.

Typefounders are agreed as to the best methods of casting, testing and finishing types, but at this point the agreement of the United States Typefounders' Association ends. It does not pretend to have any control over any member in his use of the point system or in his methods of making type. The quality of the metal selected, the degrees of heat employed, the care given to the testing of molds, or to the finishing of the cast type, are matters of individual right.

Your committee have been asked to get information concerning the irregular linings of types of the same body from the same foundry, and to find whether this irregularity is entirely or partially avoidable. We have to report that it is not practical to attempt extended alterations in the lining of the old and approved standard faces of type so that all shall be on one line, or even on two or three lines. The varieties of line already made are too many, and the expense of alteration would never be repaid. The evils of irregular linings are well understood by typefounders, and in the getting up of new faces will be avoided as much as possible.

Your committee have also been asked why the United States Typefounders' Association did not accept the point system which now prevails in Europe, generally known in France and southern Europe as the Didot system, and in Germany as the Berthold system. The Didot system was intelligently considered, but was rejected for good cause. The Didot point is too large: it makes the distance between bodies too great. The adoption of the Didot point would have compelled the retirement not only of all existing molds and matrices, but would have required the recutting of new punches for too many sizes. The point adopted by the United States Typefounders' Association is .0351 centimeters. This is almost identical with the point devised in 1737 by Fournier le jeune, of Paris, the true inventor of the point system. The point substituted afterward by Ambroise-Firmin Didot is .0376 centimeters. Eleven points of the Didot system are almost as large as twelve points of the American system. French typographers of the highest authority have recorded their regret at the change in size from the Fournier to the Didot point. Sharing this belief we think the United States Typefounders' Association acted wisely in preferring that system which allows of nicer subdivision and does not materially disturb existing sizes.

Whether this new American system is the best that could have been devised; whether the new point should have been a regular fraction of a foot or of a meter; whether the standard measure on which this unitary point is based should not be more readily accessible to all founders and printers; whether the Bruce system of a geometrical progression of bodies instead of an arithmetical extension of lines, is not more scientifically accurate — all these may be questions of speculative interest, but they are not now of practical import. The American point system is here to stay, and we are to make the best we can of it. That it will be of advantage in bringing the sizes of different founders in closer agreement is apparent. That it will ever be so perfect that types of the same body from different founders can be mixed and used together is not so clear. No perfection in the system can ever make care or skill in the manufacture of secondary importance. Under the new system good typefounding will exact as much

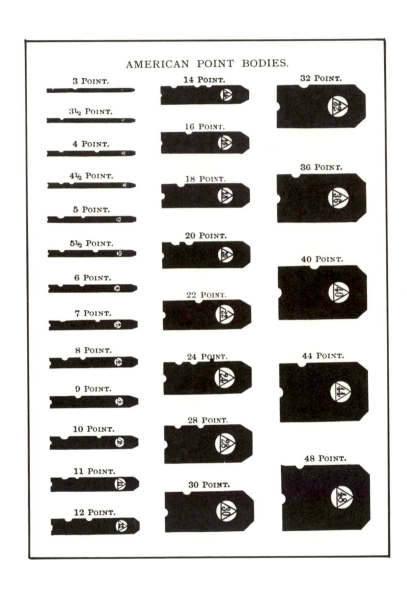

AMERICAN POINT BODIES.

3 POINT.
3½ POINT.
4 POINT.
4½ POINT.
5 POINT.
5½ POINT.
6 POINT.
7 POINT.
8 POINT.
9 POINT.
10 POINT.
11 POINT.
12 POINT.
14 POINT.
16 POINT.
18 POINT.
20 POINT.
22 POINT.
24 POINT.
28 POINT.
30 POINT.
32 POINT.
36 POINT.
40 POINT.
44 POINT.
48 POINT.

watchfulness as ever. The irregularities that follow from overheated metal, from sprung or untested molds, or from careless rubbing are as possible now as they ever were. "The man is more than the machine," or the system.

Your committee have been asked "to request of the leading typefounders specimens of all sizes of body letter made by them under the point system with the view to the adoption of that measurement and such faces as are used in the production of the largest amount of type." Compliance with this request is impracticable. A comparison of bodies would not lead to any useful result. The discrepancies would be slight and the conclusions derived therefrom might be misleading. A comparison of faces is still more impracticable because there is no accepted standard of taste. The style approved by one printer would not be accepted by another. Types are made to suit different tastes and different mechanical requirements. The face which is most useful and most durable in a newspaper is often highly objectionable in a book. The face used with advantage in jobbing is not good for many forms of fine printing. There must be a variety of faces. It would be impolitic to attempt to control individual taste in selection.

Your committee have been asked to consider the advantages of a distinct series of roman and italic, to be known as the Typothetæ series, matrices of which should be in every typefoundry. The object desired is to enable any printer to quickly get in any foundry sorts or additions to a font previously bought from another founder in another city. No doubt this arrangement would be of value to printers, but the difficulties of agreeing upon a common face, and of getting the coöperation of typefounders, are insuperable. The proposition does not meet with favor from the foundries.

The subject of accurate bodies cannot be dismissed without adverting to the wear of the printing house which often makes types from the same foundry and from the same casting irregular. All worn types have a thin film of adhering dust or gummy matter which makes them larger than new types. New sorts always seem smaller in body. The wearing types get from over-heating in one process of stereotyping, and the squeezing they often get from violent screw quoining, necessarily distort their bodies. For these faults the typefounders cannot be held responsible.

NEW FIXTURES FOR THE COMPOSING ROOM.

BY THEO. L. DE VINNE.

A NEW STAND.

THIS form of stand is the result of attempts to overcome certain difficulties encountered in trying to compose the Century " Dictionary." For this work the compositor was required to have before him or readily accessible : Brevier, upper and lower, 2 cases ; brevier italic, 1 cap case ; accents for brevier, 1 cap case ; brevier antique, for side-heads, 1 job case ; nonpareil, upper and lower, 2 cases ; nonpareil italic, 1 cap case ; accents, etc., for nonpareil, 1 cap case ; nonpareil antique for sub-heads, 1 job case. The copy called for changes of cases so often that it was not practicable to have one or even a dozen common cases of antique or italic. Compositors working from common cases would interfere with each other ; they would have to impatiently wait their turns ; there would be just complaint at probable bad distribution, for which no one could be held responsible. It was decided that every compositor should have his own set of separate cases. Greek and Hebrew, rarely used, were to be the only cases in common. This decision made a new difficulty. Ten exposed cases would fill two sides of an alley. The space occupied by a double alley would take a great deal of room. Each compositor would want about sixty-seven square feet of floor space ; twenty-five compositors, stone-men and makers-up, the galleys and chase rack, and proof presses and other equipments for the work, would be really huddled in a room of 2500 square feet. Many compositors would have to work in dim light, for not every one could have a separate window. Widely separated, they could not support or aid each other and the maker-up, as might be done if they were closer together. This would not do. The space was too valuable ; the compositors would lose too much time by constant walking up and down an alley ; they could not be readily directed by the foreman.

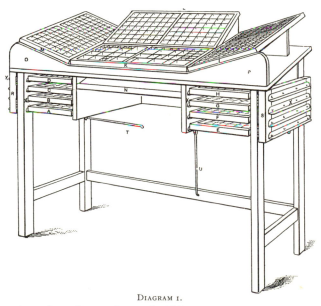

DIAGRAM 1.

A new form of composing stand, which permits the compositor to have ready access to more than eight hundred boxes This diagram shows the cases in racks, out of use, with swinging side frame put back.

DIAGRAMS 1 AND 2, A and B, Cases for extra sorts ; C, Nonpareil accents ; D, Nonpareil antique ; E, Brevier antique ; F, Nonpareil roman upper ; G, Nonpareil roman lower ; H, Nonpareil italic ; K and L, Brevier roman, upper and lower ; M, Brevier accents ; I, Brevier italic ; N, Drawer, containing galley ; O and P, Angled support for cases ; R and S, Swinging frame with racks ; T and U, Iron rods that hold the swinging side frame.

To put these ten cases, four on the top of a double stand and six in the rack below, would contract the space seriously, but this plan would increase and not lighten the work of the compositor. He would have to change his position with every

change in the style of type ; he would frequently have to take down and put up cases.

Could not this be avoided ? Could not more boxes be brought within easy reach of the compositor's arm ? Could not words in italic or side-heads be set without taking down and putting up cases, or making a complete change of position ?

The first step was to select the "rooker" case, 14 by 28 inches, smaller than the regular case, but large enough for a day's work on the sizes of brevier and nonpareil. The next was to

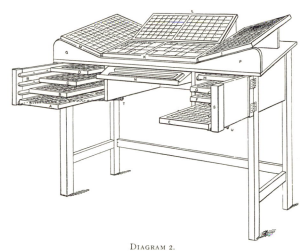

DIAGRAM 2.

This diagram shows the swinging side frames drawn out and locked the under cases made accessible to the compositor, and the position of the galley under the frame.

put two more rooker cases at right angles on either side, tilted upward as shown in the diagrams. The compositor, who stands before the case in the usual position, can readily reach all the boxes of the four cases, except those in the extreme outermost corners. A long-armed compositor can reach all without even swaying his body. This arrangement provides for the brevier upper and lower in the usual position (K and L in the diagram), with the accents to the extreme left (M) and the italic to the extreme right (I).

The framework of the stand below the extreme right and left was utilized by constructing racks with cleats so that the cases least used could be put in sidewise, and yet be kept within easy reach. A swinging side frame, firmly hinged, was then attached on either side, with cleats parallel to those in the stand. This side frame is kept firmly in position by the swinging iron bar T. When this bar is locked, the cases in either side can be drawn out at full length, exposing every box to view and touch. The compositor is in the center of three sides of a small square, and can pick out any type he wants from about eight hundred boxes, without leaving his frame, and for most of them without change of position. When the lower cases in the side racks are not needed, the swinging side frame can be put back as shown in diagram 1. To prevent the cluttering up of stands, and to save needless travel, the galley is put on an inclined plane in a drawer under the roman case. When the compositor wishes to empty his stick, he pulls out the drawer, empties his stick, and then shoves in the drawer. It is entirely out of the way, and not as liable to accident as in the old position on an exposed stand.

Two of the job cases have been arranged for capitals to the left, and two, with capitals to the right. This is to keep the most used division of lower case nearest to reach on right and left hand sides.

The roman cases have all the spaces and en-quadrets directly under the compositor's hand. This arrangement is made by putting the en-quadret next to the three-to-em space box on the other side of the broad bar ; and by putting the four and five-to-em space and hair-space next to the three-to-em space box. Not many other boxes have to be disturbed to so place these spaces. This arrangement saves time in spacing ; it is an aid to better work and is much approved by all compositors. The cost of these stands and cases is not much more than those of the old form. That they are much more economical in saving space and in giving greater ease in the management of work will be admitted by every one who sees them. Thirty compositors work in better light, more pleasantly and profitably to themselves, and more efficiently for the office in a space of 1000 square feet than they could do in 2500 square feet from cases laid out on the old plan.

This form of stand, which is not covered by any patent, is fully recommended to any printer who has work, like dictionaries or catalogues, which requires the frequent use of many styles of type.

A NEW CASE FOR QUADRATS AND SPACES.

Every printer who has many fonts of small display type in cabinet cases is annoyed by their lack of proper boxes for spaces and quadrats. The usual practice is to put spaces and quadrats in the two right hand corner boxes. It is not a good method. Too much time is lost in fumbling over the mixed spaces if there are any in case ; the work of spacing is done in an inconvenient position. But the spaces wanted are too often absent, and drawer after drawer has to be pulled out before they are found. Many foremen refuse to allow the distribution of spaces and quadrats in cabinet cases. They require them to be put in the regular cases of text types, where they can be assorted properly. This is better practice, but it has this serious disadvantage : it compels the compositor who is hunting spaces from alley to alley to stop another workman at case while he is spacing out his line.

To prevent this I had made a little case which holds nothing but spaces and quadrats of the sizes that are most used. It can be

DIAGRAM 3.

readily put on the top of any broad cabinet case or can be made longer or shorter to hold more or less sizes of quadrats.

This case has twelve large divisions each of which contains quadrats and spaces for each size, from pearl to great primer, 5-point to 18-point. Each division is again subdivided into six boxes, thus providing a proper box for the two-em, one-em and en-quadrat, and the three-to-em, four-to-em, and thinner spaces. All are exposed, accessible, and at convenient height to the compositor, who can space or distribute without interfering with his mates. It prevents no small waste of time, and keeps these constantly needed sorts in the place where they are the most needed.

The boxes are big enough for larger sizes, but I prefer to keep quotations in still larger boxes at the sides of cases and stones.

A LEAD RACK.

This rack has been used, and is approved of, by several printers ; but it is not, I believe, kept on sale by any printers' furnishing house. It deserves more publicity.

It is an oblong framework of pine, 26 inches wide, 48 inches long, 62 inches high, placed in the center of a room so as to be accessible on all sides. Made to hold a great weight in a small compass, it calls for a broad base and some unused space in the interior. As a further protection against toppling or bulging, the center is strengthened by a broad middle band. It is made to hold all needed sizes of leads, from 10 to 60 picas ; smaller lengths are graduated by half picas or nonpareils, the larger sizes by full picas. Each size is kept apart in a tall compartment, which will take the width of one lead only. Each compartment has its depth made exactly the length of the lead it is intended for, as will be more plainly seen in the next illustration. All lengths of leads are flush or even with the face of the rack.

The compositor who seeks any size finds its length shown at a glance by a strip of lead, of right length, which is tacked on the side of each compartment.

If too long a lead is put in one of these compartments, it will stick out and show it is out of place ; if too short a lead is put in, it will topple and spill the longer leads put above it.

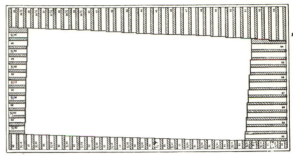

DIAGRAM 4.—LEAD RACK.

A sectional view, showing the provision made for one hundred different sizes of leads from 10 to 60 picas long.

In this rack the compartments are made for same length of leads below and above the cross-band, but they could be used for two thicknesses, like six-to-pica and four-to-pica.

A NEW FURNITURE CABINET.

In the ordinary book about one-half of the sheet printed on is devoted to print, and the other half to blanks and to margin. In ordinary jobwork the blanks are often twice and thrice as much as the print. Every printer understands this clearly, yet how few of us act on it. We buy types liberally, and furniture and blanking-out material sparingly. We grudge the cost. Typefounders, acting under general instructions from printers, furnish display fonts without quadrats and spaces. There seems to be a general belief that it is not really necessary to make a liberal provision of blanking-out material.

One reason why furniture is not more liberally bought is the fear that the compositor will waste it if he has an excess. So he will, if he is allowed or required to cut it, or if he is not provided with proper places to keep it in. In many offices all widths and lengths of furniture are thrown pell-mell into the drawer under the

DIAGRAM 5.—LEAD RACK.

stone. Out of this chaos one never finds what is needed. The maker-up has to fudge by piecing unequal lengths and widths, and too often has to use the saw to cut down pieces over-long. The time and the material wasted by fudging for furniture are serious losses in a composing-room. Bad workmanship is a common consequence. What is worst of all, the maker-up is encouraged in wasteful habits.

But it is of no advantage to buy furniture liberally unless it is cut to graduated lengths, and a proper place is made for every length. To keep everything in its place, it is necessary first to provide a place for everything. Even in a small office this provision must be made on a broad plan. Different lengths and widths should not be mixed, any more than different types should be mixed in a box. Each size should be kept apart, so that it can be selected without mistake, and all sizes should be readily accessible, and not liable to get in confusion. With this object in view, I submit, for the consideration of the typotheæ, a furniture cabinet which has been used in the composing room of the De Vinne Press with marked advantage. The general construction is but partially shown in the illustration. To make it accessible to all who work at the stone, it has been put under the stone.

This form of cabinet contains twenty-eight drawers; twelve on one side (not shown in cut), and sixteen on the other. The drawers are of unequal depth, to suit different lengths of furniture. Every length stands on its narrowest end; if too long a piece is put in,

DIAGRAM 6.

A new form of furniture drawer, containing proper places for fifty-six lengths of furniture, from 12 to 70½ picas, and for six widths of each length. The up-turned drawer shows the divisions of drawer, and the places for each width.

the drawer cannot be shoved in; if too short, its shortness is at once detected. This simple device effectually prevents the mixing of lengths.

Each drawer is divided into two compartments of proximate sizes, like 12 and 13 ems pica, so that the compositor can select either length when the drawer is open. Each compartment contains longitudinal trays for six widths; nonpareil, pica, two-line, four-line, six-line and ten-line. The pulling-out and shoving-in of the drawer does not throw the standing pieces into confusion, even when the compartments are but half full. All pieces of furniture are neatly planed and squared, and have the numbers of their length in picas stamped in their ends.

These drawers contain sixty lengths of furniture: beginning with 12 picas, advancing by one pica up to 60 picas, and from 61½ to 70½ picas. Properly numbered on the outside, the compositor who picks up an odd piece on the stone, knows at once in what drawer it belongs. The graduation of one pica each, from 12 to 60 picas, is found close enough for all purposes. No one has occasion to use a saw, for exact furniture is always at hand, and the pieces can be combined for lengths beyond 70½ picas. They are largely used, not only for jobwork, but as head bolts and gutter-pieces in book forms and for the blanking-out of open forms.

The cost of the stone, with cabinet and drawers, was $137.00; the cost of filling the drawers full of furniture, accurately cut and properly numbered, was $87.13; in all $224.13. The cost may seem large, but we should have spent more than twice this sum in wasted labor and material if the cabinet had not been in the office. Accurately cut and accessible furniture enables us to get more exactness and blanks and margins, and quicker and neater performance in making-up and stone-work. The cabinet saves a great deal of room. I do not think it possible to put more useful

furniture in smaller compass or in a more accessible place. It is not patented. Any one can make it.

As we do not print posters, I have made no provision for lengths beyond 70½ picas. A full assortment from 12 to 36 inches would call for much more space and more material. I would recommend a graduation by an advance of 2 picas up to 24 inches and of 3 picas beyond.

I do not favor any plan of case which has furniture lying flatwise, or which compels it to be shoved in a broad pigeon-hole. This invites disorder. I prefer that all furniture shall stand on its narrow end, and that it be kept in drawers which can be pulled out. In offices that are crowded, where space has to be economized, the unused space below the ordinary case rack could be utilized where it has an exposure on the side or back. But the best place of all for the shorter lengths is under the stone where the material is most needed.

JAMES WATT THE INVENTOR OF THE LETTER COPYING PRESS.

In his recent inaugural address before the University of Glasgow, Professor Archibald Barr, after speaking of Watt's steam engine discoveries, says:

Watt's other inventions are too numerous to mention, and most of them—such as the parallel motion, the governor, and the steam engine indicator—are well known to have come from him. But the very multitude of his inventions makes his name to be little associated with some of his most fruitful works. Had he made no other invention, or had he been of a more self-assertive disposition, his name would probably have become known wherever business is conducted, in connection with his invention of the method, still almost universally in use, of copying letters by means of the copying press.

It would seem to be the common fate of all great and novel inventions to raise a storm of opposition from those whom they are most calculated to benefit. Dudley's invention of the process of smelting iron by means of coal instead of charcoal brought him only persecution from the iron masters and the destruction of his works by rioters at their instigation. The steel makers of Sheffield attempted to get the government to prohibit Huntsman from working his great invention — the cast steel process — and nearly succeeded in driving the cutlery trade out of their own hands and out of Sheffield. David Mushet's discovery that the "wild coals" were ironstones of great value excited for years a strong prejudice against him in the minds of the iron masters of Scotland, who have since made not only their own fortunes, but in great measure the Scotland of to-day, through the working of those blackband ores. Neilson's invaluable invention of the hot blast for smelting furnaces was not only ridiculed by the iron masters, but so stoutly resisted that for years he was unable to get it even tried on a practical scale. So again the landed proprietors, who had perhaps most to gain from the opening up of communications through the country, strongly opposed the early railway projects. They supposed that they were to be reduced to beggary by the "infernal railroads," as one landowner called them, declaring that he "would rather meet a highwayman, or see a burglar on his premises, than an engineer!" Many more such instances might be quoted.

We need not, therefore, be surprised to find that Watt's copying process, though brought out practically in its present state of perfection, found little favor at first with many business men; but it is curious now, after the invention has for more than one hundred years been almost indispensable to the class of men who then resented its introduction, to read of the bitterness of the opposition which it met with. The fear that "it would lead to the increase of forgery" ran so high that on one occasion when Smeaton and Boulton (Watt's partner) were sitting in a London coffee house, they heard a gentleman exclaiming against the copying machine, and "wishing the inventor was hanged and the machines all burnt." No one could attempt to estimate the value to the world of this single invention, and still comparatively few people now know to whose labors and knowledge they owe the boon.

REGISTERED, No. 151,343.

12 POINT SPIRAL.   9 A, 18 a, $3.20

But, while helping us, it may be a charity to many
half-naked unfortunates.   Our store is piled
up with neatly-fitting Clothing, made of high-
grade material.   We are anxious to get rid of
it, and therefore ask you to carry away enough
for your use: you can do so for a mere song

WE * * * *
MEAN * *
BUSINESS * *
NOT * * *
CHARITY *
∴ 1 2 3 4 5 6 7 8 9 0 ∴

24 POINT SPIRAL.   5 A, 10 a, $5.00

Lying Useless on Shelves
While ∴ Rags ∴ are ∴ Patrolling ∴ the ∴ Streets

18 POINT SPIRAL.   6 A, 12 a, $4.25

DRESS * LIKE * NABOBS

And your friends will reverence you!   Step
up to our Counter and we will load you
down with Garments that will enable you
to cut a figure in polished Social Circles

* * *
∴ 1 2 3 4 5 6 7 8 9 0 ∴
* * *

36 POINT SPIRAL.   3 A, 5 a, $6.50

Shabby Arrivals
Depart ∴ in ∴ Princely ∴ Costume

ALL COMPLETE WITH FIGURES.

MacKellar, Smiths & Jordan Co., Philadelphia.   *Shniedewend & Lee Co., Agents, Chicago, Ill.*

Ronaldson Title Slope.

ESTABLISHED A. D. 1796.

NONPAREIL.   6 POINT RONALDSON TITLE SLOPE.   30 A, 60 a, $3.00.

ETHNOLOGICAL DISCOVERIES
Recently Published
Manners and Customs of our Neighbors Across the Street
Pleasant Episodes in Family Management
1 2 3 4 5 6 7 8 9 0

BREVIER.   8 POINT RONALDSON TITLE SLOPE.   25 A, 50 a, $3.15.

BANKRUPTED BUSINESS CONCERNS
Suddenly Depleted Exchequers
Caused by Reduced Earnings and Increased Expenses
Waiting for the Good Time Promised
1 2 3 4 5 6 7 8 9 0

LONG PRIMER.   10 POINT RONALDSON TITLE SLOPE.   22 A, 45 a, $3.35.

UNPLEASANT PREDICAMENT
Delivering Lectures Before the Ambidextrous
After Donning Misfit Coats

PICA.   12 POINT RONALDSON TITLE SLOPE.   20 A, 40 a, $3.55.

INFREQUENT HAPPENINGS
Accidental Triumph Without Exultation
Failure Without Murmuring

THREE-LINE NONPAREIL.   18 POINT RONALDSON TITLE SLOPE.   12 A, 22 a, $4.15.

TOURISTS' MIDSUMMER PROGRAMME
Refreshing and Invigorating Promenades Through Manitoba
Ascending Snow-capped Mountains

TWO-LINE PICA.   24 POINT RONALDSON TITLE SLOPE.   8 A, 14 a, $4.50.

MUNIFICENT PERSONS
Philanthropists and Humanitarians

FIVE-LINE NONPAREIL.   30 POINT RONALDSON TITLE SLOPE.   6 A, 10 a, $5.25.

SIBERIAN BREEZES
Furnished Regular Summer Visitors

THREE-LINE PICA.   36 POINT RONALDSON TITLE SLOPE.   5 A, 8 a, $6.00.

TRIUMPHANT
Municipal Athletic Contest

MacKellar, Smiths & Jordan Co., Philadelphia.   Shniedewend & Lee Co., Agents, Chicago, Ill.

THE PRINTER AND THE MACHINE.

BY THE WALKING DELEGATE.

IT is a sorry commentary on the social state of man that a true and correct line of reasoning, as well as the light of experience, should bring him to the absolute conclusion that a machine, calculated and designed to make a certain kind of work easier and quicker to perform, is, in however so small a degree, detrimental to the interests of him or her who erstwhile performed this work with the hand. The setter of type, whose position as a craftsman was thought but a few years ago to be impregnable for all time to come, as it had been since the days of Gutenberg and Faust, finds himself confronted with a machine which today threatens and menaces the source of his daily bread — a machine, good people, to invent which, Horace Greeley has said, would be to invent a human being!

Now and then one yet finds a poor fellow who hopes against fate, and tries as best he can to convince his unbelieving self that the machine will be a source of great good — a regular godsend, in its way. Why, the cost of composition will become so cheap that there will be an immense amount more of printing done; will have a printing office on every corner of a block; every lawyer will have a little printing office attachment to print his briefs in; newspapers will double in size; books will be printed ten to one, and so on, and so on. Others, again, who underrate and undervalue the human intellect, place a stray chip of hope on the failure of the machine, and as sure as fate they bet to lose.

It takes no giant mind to grasp the folly of the one and the hopelessness of the other of these two theories: (1) That the machine will be beneficial, and (2) that it will be a failure.

The first of these two theories is set forth in the tiresome and silly twaddle of a member of the New York union. He says: "Of course, some members of the union are a little skeptical as to the benefit these machines will be to the followers of the craft, but the whole history of labor-saving machinery teaches us that nothing has yet been invented that will lessen the need of good workmen." He is the first one that has yet been heard from that is not skeptical at all; and I have heard of but a very few beside him whose skepticism was not of the most pronounced type. The "whole history of labor-saving machinery" is something he knows nothing of, or perhaps he would not father a statement so untrue and false. If there was on record a solitary case, perhaps it wouldn't have been very troublesome for him to cite it. On the other hand, I can point him to the harvest field, the planing mill, the woolen mill, the shoe factory, the twine factory, the shirt and overall sweat-box, or whatever other place his fancy may dictate where machinery is chiefly employed, and show him that the machines are operated, not by the heads of families, at shorter hours and greater pay, but by old women, young girls and boys in their teens, at longer hours and less pay by half than when these different kinds of work were performed by the human hand. And when he says that "nothing has yet been invented that has lessened the need of good workmen," he seems to revel in a sort of ghoulish glee that something has been invented to help along Darwin's law of the survival of the fittest. There are those among my fellowmen who are, for physical or mental reasons, incapacitated for being at the "head of the class," and, of course, these fellows have no business on earth, and we must needs have a typesetting machine to rob them of their already scanty proportion to eat and drink, that they may the sooner go to the realm of the dear departed, where, as angels, they need no clothes, and, as simply souls, they have no use for food. Again, he says: "When typesetting machines have been introduced into every office in the country, it will lessen the cost of composition to such an extent that papers which now contain eight pages will have twelve, and four-page papers will be increased to eight." You bet — in your eye. The late Congressman Burns, of Missouri (if my memory does not mislead me, it was he), predicted in his paper some time before his death that the era of twenty-page dailies would in the near future come to a close, citing therefor the best of reasons. The four-page penny paper is growing in popularity too fast to assure a long lease of life to the unwieldy daily of two dozen pages. But, even count the dead congressman's prediction as a false one, and figure for yourselves. It is safe to say every machine, if it is of any value at all, will throw out of employment one printer; that is certainly moderate. Then, to provide employment for every man thrown out, it is necessary to have again as many newspapers, again as many magazines and periodicals, again as many books, and again as much of everything else set in straight type. Suppose such a colossal increase in the production of printed matter, with no decrease in the wages of the operator below those of the printer, and adding to the expenses of the proprietor the cost or rent of the machine, and then tell us who derives any benefit from the machine! Every particle of pecuniary benefit that this machine is to produce is for the employer, and must come out of *our* respective pockets, or there would be no object in putting the machine in operation. But the supposition is preposterous. Even an increase in the size of the present newspaper from eight to twelve pages is an unreasonable probability, and, besides, it would prove of no benefit whatever, for the simple reason that these immense editions would so encroach upon the territories of the weeklies devoted to special objects as to make engagement in the publication of them exceedingly unprofitable, and rapidly drive them out of existence. As a single instance, the Chicago *Times* devotes every Sunday a whole page to union labor affairs, and thereby does what it can to ruin the business of the labor papers, and throw out of employment the men and women unfortunate enough to have to make a living on them. And the plates! What will they cost?

One column of brevier plate matter costs now about twenty cents. The machine would reduce the price of them to ten cents. A page of seven columns full of plates at a total outlay of seventy cents. Now, then, these plates may certainly be classed among the great inventions in the printing trade, but who ever had the folly to attempt to argue that the plates were beneficial to the craft? But, according to this fellow from New York, and his "history of labor-saving machinery," the printer's time of plenty and joy and bliss is near at hand. Fudge!

The second theory (and a desperate theory it is), that the machine will, after all, prove a failure, has for it no good reason. It seems never to have been discovered, but it is a fact, nevertheless, that copy can be prepared correctly before the printer takes hold of it, as well as after the printer is through with it. The proofreading on machine matter will be largely done in the copy. Paragraphs may be made to occur more frequently, and callow reporters who cause the resetting of a whole paragraph on a "ring" will become more scarce when the cost of resetting comes out of their wages. So all the silly talk about failure will cease.

And, in the contemplation of these facts, is it not a sorry commentary on the social state which makes absolutely detrimental that which was designed to be of great good?

But it is not the purpose of my writing to oppose in any way the advent of the typesetting machine. I am not agitating a disposal of the inventor and his machine in the river, or the organization of a walk-out in every office where the machine is put into operation. Typesetting by machine, it is now beyond all doubt, is one of the inevitable things. It will be as much a milestone in the progress of the world as was the invention of printing itself. It is but a faint indication of the goal to which the human race aspires. But it *is* my purpose to do what little I can that you and I shall have our fair proportion of whatever benefit this machine affords. I desire that my fellow craftsmen shall awake to the necessity of being up and doing. It will not do for us to drown the ominous click of the machine with the snore of apathy.

The machine shall not rob me and mine of food and clothing; it shall not steal from me honorable employment; it shall not drive wives to the sewing needle; it shall not shove boys into the penitentiary; it shall not force budding womanhood upon the street to gain a livelihood in shame; it shall not be a machine to make the rich richer and the poor poorer; it shall not throw into idleness and want my fellowman, because idleness and want is the mother of bad citizens, and a most prolific mother she is, indeed. I wish this machine to be regarded in the nature of a "fat take," and what I am after particularly is a square deal all around. "What is sauce for the goose is sauce for the gander."

The printer's trade is not one conducive to good health, and if, with a machine, it is possible to accomplish again as much work as with the hand, we may derive our benefit from its use in the shape of shorter hours and consequent better health, without throwing men into forced idleness by the dozen and score. Making a fair allowance for the increase in the production of printed matter, perhaps two hours knocked off the present work day of ten hours would even the thing up.

In opposition to us, however, are the proprietors in whose workshops we are employed. At a recent convention of a number of these proprietors, it was

Resolved, That in the opinion of the Typothetæ of America there is nothing in the state of the printing trade of the country at this time which renders it wise to take any action in regard to the reduction of the hours of labor.

Here we have it. When the typothetæ declares that in its opinion there is nothing which urges the necessity for a shorter work day, then it virtually declares that it proposes to "wolf" all the "fat." Of course, I understand that when this resolution was adopted not a word was thought or said about the machine, but understand me this: Were every proprietor of a printing office to put in a machine tomorrow, thereby throwing out of employment half of all the printers in the country, do not doubt that he would hesitate one moment to go to the convention in Cincinnati next October and help to resolve to the same effect.

It may, to be just and fair with the gentlemen who compose the typothetæ, be true that there is nothing in the state of the printing trade to warrant a change of from ten to eight hours, and, they might have added, "there never will be"; but there is something in the state of the social condition of he who works, and there is a meaning to the word "justice," which absolutely demand it.

In view of the dire necessity for a shorter work day in the very near future, I feel half inclined to be angry with our International for disposing of the machine question with a force resolution which in effect says, "This machine is a bad thing; but it's bound to come; so stand back, boys, and don't make any fuss about what just can't be helped."

In closing I wish to present three methods which will give us relief from whatever injury the machine may inflict, and these are:

1. Raise a fund of as many millions as required and buy the invention up.

2. Kidnap the inventor and swipe the machine and drop both to the bottom of the deep blue sea.

3. Decrease the hours of labor in proportion to the time saved by the machine.

My preference inclines to the last method by a big majority as the most practicable one of taking the bull by the horns.

A PHILIPPICA.

SOME SUGGESTIONS FOR CONSIDERATION FOR THE WELFARE OF BOTH
EMPLOYER AND EMPLOYÉ — PICTURES FROM LIFE — A SPECIMEN
OF ORDER AND DISCIPLINE — THE "HUMAN SMOKESTACK" —
THE "PRESS SLOB" — THE "BULLY" — FRIENDLY ADVICE.

BY GUSTAV BOEHM.

I HAPPENED to call at the large printing house of Messrs. De Vinne & Co., corner of Lafayette place and Fourth street, New York City, a short time ago, and although I have often heard of the neatness and discipline governing this establishment from ground (or, better, underground) to the top of the building, yet I was overcome by surprise in noting the cleanliness and order prevailing. I have visited a great many printing offices, small, medium and large, and my experience teaches me that it does not require a five-story building or the employment of a few hundred men to keep up order, cleanliness and discipline. I have seen material wasted, inks dried up, dirt accumulating, to make one's heart bleed, and create some sort of a sorry feeling for the poor soul of a proprietor who is thus trifled with by his "regularly paid" but irresponsible employés, who seem to be utterly devoid of every particle of moral feeling, without *any* realization of common decency in respect to time wasted and material spoiled. I have seen this state of affairs in all sizes of offices. Some people do not care a continental whether they earn their wages or not. They seem to be absolutely devoid of every atom of calculative sense, and can evidently not understand why they should do their work more promptly, as long as they work at all. They cannot see the difference between working and *working*, and seem incapable of comprehending that a job for which the proprietor's competitor charges one hour's time, and which actually only takes one hour's time to produce, should be done in *such* time. They declare, if told so, that they are doing the best they can, and are working continually on the job.

Now, let us see how this "continually" appears in reality. They take hold of the copy; they examine it; they criticise it. So far, so good. They decide to set it up. But before so doing, they must strengthen themselves for the labor in view. The boy is called away from his work, and "a pint" is ordered. During the wait for the strengthening draught, a pipe is slowly hauled out. Mind you, this class of workmen can never be seen without a pipe. They claim they can not work without smoking, and declare openly that they do not care a "snap" whether the insurance policy of the proprietor prohibits smoking on the premises or not. This enemy of every well regulated office, the "pipe," is now scraped out, the superfluous ashes are emptied on the edge of the case, so that they are equally divided between the top case, the cases in the rack and the floor. This done, the pipe is slowly stuffed, stuck between the lips, and lighted. How is it lighted? It is the rule of the office that all lamps and lights should be lighted with the aid of sulphur matches, and that

such should be sent for in case there are none in the office. Mr. Irresponsible cares as much for the rules in this special case as in all the others, and invariably uses a big chunk of paper, lights it at the stove or lamp, and with it his dirty, thieving pipe. I say thieving, because it is not much less to steal a man's time in that way than to steal his money out of his pocket. These people are paid to utilize their time in a practical manner, and in these days of close competition, it can not appear small to speak about a waste of time which, as my experience teaches me, consumes fully ten per cent, if not more, of the smoker's working hours, not considering the danger the office is continually in to burn to ashes. I do not think it is fair that these human smoking-stacks should assume the right to endanger thousands of dollars of property simply to cater to their personal whim of smoking from morning to night. No matter how careful the precautions taken, a printing office is no place to indulge in smoking.

This is one of the leeches sucking up the healthy condition of business enterprise in our line. A second and more dangerous one is the disorderly workman, vulgarly called "slob." This species is very often met with in the pressroom. He is worse than acid to the machinery, and more dangerous to the prosperity of the business than the firebug. He is frequently a quick worker, and often has the luck to pass as a good hand. But, oh Lord, only too soon the proprietor finds out at what cost he is running his presses. Inks are only half used up; the other half is scab, which is the natural consequence of leaving the cans continually open. "This is black, or insurance ink; it will not scab," is the answer you get, if you call his attention to the often repeated rule, that inks must be covered as soon as the necessary quantity has been taken from the can for immediate use. He also, as a rule, takes enough ink on the slab to last for several days. He has, apparently, not the slightest desire to save in little things, thereby studying his employer's interests — a duty which ought to be appreciated by every respectable workman. This fellow will not be able to give you a respectable red print, all of them appearing of a brownish hue, a natural consequence of the dust which has settled in the color from being exposed to the open air. He has the habit of knowing everything better than anybody else, and will tell you in a stubborn, insulting manner that HE is running the presses. You may be sure that you never find a wrench, a roller, a socket, or any of his tools in place. It frequently occurs that a number of wastepaper bags must be searched to find his eraser or other tools. He has no system of working; forms coming from the press are slung in some place between or behind the presses, usually unwashed, so that the ink has every chance to dry on the type and fill the outlines and spoil the hairlines. He never oils the presses at certain times of the day, as should be done, but merely squirts oil over the frame, and accidentally places some in the oil-holes, when the poor, dry-running, burning metal is squeaking of pain and threatening to revenge itself upon the proprietor — alas! the very wrong victim for revenge — by simply going to the d—l.

This cited specimen of a slovenly, irresponsible workman generally belongs to the class that have no appreciation of the value of time. He appears late in the morning four times during the week, but is very careful to hand in his overtime when the week is over. His department is one large field of dirt, disorder and dissatisfaction, and the greatest wonder of all is that he gets as much good work out as he does. For, although complaints about dirty work, short counts, unsatisfactory workmanship are a daily occurrence in an office employing this specimen of pressman, it still happens that some good work is turned out.

Another dose of bad blood in the constitution of an office is — the bully. This "terror" generally appears in the shape of foreman or something like it. He is in the habit of using vile language, of having absolutely no respect for his superiors, and has continually phrases upon his vulgar lips which disgrace both him and his calling. He has a good time in general and makes himself "feared" and despised by all under him. He forgets frequently that he is to represent the proprietor in the absence of the latter, and if he feels like it, is at the head of a frolicking time in such cases. Instead of seeing that every employé does his duty, he heads the line of idlers and is in every respect a bad example to other men and a danger to the discipline of the office. He is often heard to use the vilest language possible to the proprietor in presence of all the men, and so in an outrageous manner undermines the respect which is due to the proprietor of even the smallest office. He is the sorest spot in the whole office, the greatest danger to the welfare of the concern. He forgets that he is expected to form the bridge from the office to the workshop, between employer and employés, with a natural inclination toward the office, and by his bullying actions gives the plainest testimony that he is absolutely unfit for the position he occupies.

There is nothing more dangerous to the carrying on of business than the undermining of discipline. There may be cases in which the subordinate is apparently in the right, still he cannot judge the motives of the action of his superior, and it is, even in such case, good policy and proper behavior to follow the instructions of the firm. To oppose openly, or to act or speak improperly, is the worst thing a would-be foreman can do and ought to be invariably resented on the part of the firm. It is simply an act of revolt, of which no thinking man will make himself guilty. There are various ways to reach the end; no employer will be deaf to the just requirements of a worthy and valued employé, but every employer will take *ad notam* the bullying behavior of his subaltern, and the time will arrive when such will have to be accounted for. This is generally the time when the workman expect it the least. I could add several other "dangers" to the series mentioned above,

but these are enough for *this* philippica. It remains yet to enlighten the astonished reader about the sanity of the firms who keep such men in their employ. It is hardly credible that it can occur, still there are circumstances which induce to leniency: for example, if a workman has been with the firm for a long time. Few firms find it desirable to turn a man out on the street who has been in their employ for many years, who has entered as a youngster, has grown up with the house and is at the present time a married man, the provider for a family. It is true that the behavior of the workman deserves no better treatment, and that neither time nor age gives him any right to forget the interests of those who are providing him and his family with the means of subsistence; but still we are human and consider. I therefore recommend all such houses to give their men — such men as I have described — a chance to view themselves in the looking-glass of my philippica; and I candidly admit that to give them a chance to change their behavior, to save some one a "good job" and others disappointment and anger, were the main objects in writing this article.

To those who believe I have looked at the matter through smoky glasses, I can give the assurance that I have followed the prescription of the best of our fiction writers: to take the material direct from life.

It is unnecessary to say that the respectable, self-esteemed workman need not find fault with the author of this paper — it is not he to whom this philippica is addressed, but to him who fills a place which by rights belongs to the decent workman.

YOUNG MAN! THIS IS FOR YOU.

1. Save a part of your weekly earnings, even if it be no more than a quarter dollar, and put your savings monthly in a savings bank.

2. Buy nothing until you can pay for it, and buy nothing that you do not need.

A young man who has grit enough to follow these rules will have taken the first step upward to success in business. He may be compelled to wear a coat a year longer, even if it be unfashionable; he may have to live in a smaller house than some of his young acquaintances; his wife may not sparkle with diamonds nor be resplendent in silk or satin, just yet; his children may not be dressed as dolls or popinjays; his table may be plain but wholesome, and the whiz of the beer or champagne cork may never be heard in his dwelling; he may have to get along without the earliest fruit or vegetables; he may have to abjure the clubroom, the theater and the gambling hell, and to reverence the sabbath day and read and follow the precepts of the Bible instead; but he will be the better off in every way for this self-discipline. Yes, he may do all these without detriment to his manhood, or health, or character. True, empty-headed folk may sneer at him and affect to pity him; but he will find that he has grown strong-hearted and brave enough to stand the laugh of the foolish. He has become an independent man. He never owes anybody, and so he is no man's slave. He has become master of himself, and a master of himself will become a leader among men, and prosperity will crown his every enterprise.

Young man! life's discipline and life's success come from hard work and early self-denial; and hard earned success is all the sweeter at the time when old years climb upon your shoulder and you need propping up.—*Typographic Advertiser.*

EIFFEL SHADE.

18 A   12-Point Eiffel Shade. $3.00

MICROSCOPIC ORGANISMS
BACTERIOLOGICAL LABORATORY
2 CHRYSANTHEMUM 3

16 A   16-Point Eiffel Shade. $3.50

MEDICAL SCHOOLS
PHYSIOLOGY AND HYGIENE
4 PHARMACY 5

12 A   20-Point Eiffel Shade. $4.00

WHITE SULPHUR SPRINGS
EASTERN OREGON, WASHINGTON, MONTANA
8 VALLEY OF THE YELLOWSTONE 5

10 A   24-Point Eiffel Shade. $4.50

SOLOMON GOLDSTONE
BANKER AND COMMISSION MERCHANT
54 WALL STREET, N. Y. 76

8 A   36-Point Eiffel Shade. $6.00

CHRISTMAS CHIMES
BOYHOOD'S HAPPY DREAMS
7 NEW YEAR 5

PALMER & REY, Manufacturers, San Francisco, Cal.   Carried in stock by MARDER, LUSE & CO., Chicago

FOR SALE BY ALL TYPE FOUNDERS IN THE U. S.

THE OPAL SERIES—PATENT PENDING.

24 Point Opal.   8 A—$4 25

INTRODUCING NEW TYPES
EVERY MONTH 5

30 Point Opal.   6 A—$5 00

DELIGHT THE THOUGHTFUL
WHOLESOME 4

36 Point Opal.   6 A—$6 00

THE GOLD MINER
WEIGHT 6

48 Point Opal.   4 A—$6 50

ENERGETIC MEN
COMBINE 8

PATENT APPLIED FOR

The Erratick Series lines accurately at the bottom.   Justify with Point system leads and slugs. . . . Complete with figures.

---

30 POINT ERRATICK   8 a, 6 A, $5.50

DICKINSON TYPE
Foundery Specimen

10 POINT ERRATICK   32 a, 16 A, $2.75

PRINTING OFFICE
Material of All Kinds
and Styles, Found in
Our Warerooms . . . .

18 POINT ERRATICK   18 a, 10 A, $3.50

PHELPS, DALTON & CO
No 150 Congress Street, Boston, Mass.

6 POINT ERRATICK   40 a, 20 A, $2.25

LOOK IN EVERY BOSTON DAILY PAPER
The leading Dailies and Weeklies
of New England, and Books from all

8 POINT ERRATICK   32 a, 20 A, $2.50

THE LARGE PUBLISHERS IN
the Country for Specimens of
Roman Faces made by this Concern

48 POINT ERRATICK   5 a, 4 A, $7.50

ORIGINAL
Designing

24 POINT ERRATICK   12 a, 8 A, $4.00

REFITTED COMPLETE
Dickinson Electrotype Department

42 POINT ERRATICK   6 a, 4 A, $6.00

Our Facilities
UNLIMITED

12 POINT ERRATICK   24 a, 14 A, $3.00

YOU WILL FIND OUR
Material Just as Repre-
sented Every Time . . . .
1234567890 $ £

ORIGINAL TYPE DESIGN FROM THE DICKINSON TYPE FOUNDERY, 150 CONGRESS STREET, BOSTON, MASS.

Know all men by these presents:-

That the Connecticut Life Insurance Company, of New Haven, Connecticut, for and in consideration of Nine Hundred Dollars, to it in hand paid, and for other good and valuable considerations, the receipt whereof is hereby confessed, does hereby Grant, Bargain, Remise, Convey, Release and Quit Claim unto John Homer of the County of Boone and State of Iowa, all the right, title, interest, claim or demand whatsoever, it may have acquired in, through or by a certain indenture or mortgage deed, bearing date the 12th day of May, A. D. 1885, and recorded in the Recorders office of Boone County, and State of Iowa, in Book 25 of Mortgages.

12 POINT HAZLETT.

16A 80a . . . $8.60
8A 40a . . . 4.40

Boonesboro, April 26, 1889.

Mr. Ed. Cowles,

My Dear Sir:--I send you herewith writings as requested in your letter of the 19th instant. I do not know how I acquired my style of writing but presume that it is a sort of a combination of different writings that I have seen and it may not contain enough individuality to justify its conversion into type, and it may be similar to some scripts already in use.

I regret that I am compelled for want of time to prepare the copies hurriedly; they are not as smooth as I wish they were but will probably answer your purpose. Very truly yours

Chas. S. Hazlett.

18 POINT HAZLETT.

12A 80a . . . $10.85
6A 40a . . . 5.50

Manufactured by BARNHART BROS. & SPINDLER, Chicago, Ill.

Registered, No. 151,417.

PATENTED AUG. 12, 1890.

EQUIPMENTS

Three-Line Nonpareil.   18 Point Luray.   6 A, $2.70

MATERIAL MODERN
DESIGN ANCIENT
1234567890

PUDDINGS

Two-Line Pica.   24 Point Luray.   5 A, $3.35

BAKED BROWN
SERVED HOT

SUPPER

Five-Line Nonpareil.   30 Point Luray.   4 A, $4.30

NUTRICIOUS
PLEASING

LUNCH

Three-Line Pica.   36 Point Luray.   3 A, $5.40

DELICATE

ALL COMPLETE WITH FIGURES.

The MacKellar, Smiths & Jordan Co., Sansom Street, Philadelphia.

| 4A | 48-POINT MURAL. | $5.25 |

MODERN

| 5A | 42-POINT MURAL. | $4.75 |

CHARMER

| 6A | 36-POINT MURAL. | $4.25 |

DEMANDED

| 30-POINT, 6A, $3.50 | 24-POINT, 8A, $3.25 |

BOARD | ROMAN

| 20-POINT, 9A, $2.50 | 18-POINT, 10A, $2.50 |

STEAMER | DOMINION

| 12-POINT, 18A, $2.25 | 10-POINT, 20A, $2.00 |

SEND HOME 27 | BROWN BREAD 35

| 26A | 8-POINT MURAL. | $1.75 |

RELIABLE AMERICAN HISTORICAL SCENES 48

| 26A | 6-POINT MURAL. | $1.50 |

FURNISHES APARTMENTS WITH BOARD REASONABLE 69

FIGURES WITH EACH SIZE.

THE NEW SIZES

of the

MURAL SERIES

AS shown on this page, and which, with the other sizes, now makes the series complete, are

48-POINT,   42-POINT,
30-POINT,   20-POINT.

You have the other sizes now in your office: order the new ones and have a complete series of this ever-popular face.

Cadet Series

The full series is in process of manufacture.

| 6a 3A | 36-POINT CADET. | $4.50 |

Evening Globe

| 8a 5A | 24-POINT CADET. | $3.50 |

Bangor Times

| 12a 7A | 16-POINT CADET. | $3.00 |

Sunday Morning Chronicle

HARVARD ITALICS

| 16a 8A | 24-POINT HARVARD ITALIC. | $3.50 |

FISHING STORIES
Present Ready 58

| 20a 12A | 18-POINT HARVARD ITALIC. | $3.25 |

HOME BOUND SAILOR
Life on the Ocean 23

| 26a 18A | 12-POINT HARVARD ITALIC. | $3.00 |

BEST MECHANICAL DESIGNS
Practical Engineering 26

| 30a 20A | 10-POINT HARVARD ITALIC. | $2.75 |

ELECTROTYPE AND STEREOTYPE
Fine Specimen of Casting 75

| 34a 20A | 9-POINT HARVARD ITALIC. | $2.50 |

BEAUTIFUL LETTER-PRESS PRINTING
Send Illustrated Catalogue 35

| 32a 24A | 8-POINT HARVARD ITALIC. | $2.50 |

PURCHASED MEDIÆVAL MANUSCRIPT
Remarkable Collection Secured 29

Never in the history of printing has there been such a marked advance in the improvement

MANUFACTURED BY BOSTON TYPE FOUNDRY

PATENT PENDING.

NEW FACADE CONDENSED

9A   B   72-Point Facade Condensed. $7.25

CHARMING MAIDENS AND RURAL SWAINS

12A   B   60-Point Facade Condensed. $6.75

ANNUAL CASH BALANCE

12A   B   54-Point Facade Condensed. $6.00

DEMANDS EXAMINATION

12A   B   48-Point Facade Condensed. $5.25

STRANGEST ATTACHMENT FORMED DURING WARTIME

14A   B   42-Point Facade Condensed. $4.50

THE SPACE IS VERY LIMITED

16A   B   36-Point Facade Condensed. $4.00

RETURNING GREATLY REFRESHED

16A   B   30-Point Facade Condensed. $3.50

WHEN OLD NEPTUNE SEEMS ENRAGED

20A   B   24-Point Facade Condensed. $3.00

UNAVOIDABLE BUT LAUGHABLE SITUATION

28A   B   18-Point Facade Condensed. $2.75

GENEROUS AMERICANS BRING LARGE CONTRIBUTIONS
SECURING REWARDS FOR SOLDIERS 76

30A   B   16-Point Facade Condensed. $2.50

LEAVES ARE TURNING BROWN AND SWALLOWS HOMEWARD
SWIFT RETURN TO DISTANT SUNNY CLIME 59

40A   B   12-Point Facade Condensed. $2.25

ANNUAL MEETINGS OF THE OLD FRANKLIN TYPOGRAPHICAL CLUBS
LESSONS IN AGRICULTURE AND HORTICULTURE 28

46A   B   10-Point Facade Condensed. $2.00

LIVES OF MANY CELEBRATED CHARACTERS IN ANCIENT AND MODERN HISTORY
BEAUTIFUL LETTER-PRESS PRINTING AND SUPERB BINDING 43

ALL SIZES COMPLETE WITH FIGURES.

MANUFACTURED BY BOSTON TYPE FOUNDRY

Fancy  Outline

Crayonette Open

❋

10 A. 30 a.   TWELVE-POINT CRAYONETTE OPEN. $3.50

Inter-State Farmers' Political Alliance Clubs
Uniformed and Mounted
Organized for Representation in the Government of the Nation
9,876,543 Active Members Enrolled

8 A. 20 a.   EIGHTEEN-POINT CRAYONETTE OPEN. $4.50

American Maritime Association
Transatlantic Sailers and Steamers Insured
Losses Paid, $1,234.56

5 A. 15 a.   TWENTY-FOUR-POINT CRAYONETTE OPEN. $5.00

Pennsylvania Railroad Company
Western Division

4 A. 10 a.   THIRTY-SIX-POINT CRAYONETTE OPEN. $6.75

Atlantic Mail Steamers

COMPLETE WITH FIGURES.

MMMM   mMMM

FITS EXACTLY OVER CRAYONETTE, FOR ILLUMINATED WORK

CAST FROM OUR CELEBRATED NICKEL ALLOY TYPE METAL. BEST IN THE WORLD.

Keystone Type Foundry.   734 to 740 Sansom St., Philadelphia.

CARRIED IN STOCK AND FOR SALE BY JULIUS HEINEMANN & CO., CHICAGO.

| NEW YORK—63 & 65 BEEKMAN ST. AND 62 & 64 GOLD ST. | Established 1804. | CHICAGO—109 QUINCY STREET. CHAS. B. ROSS, Manager. |

IN PREPARATION 8, 10, 14 AND 16 POINT SIZES.   THE OBLIQUE GOTHIC SERIES.

12 POINT OBLIQUE GOTHIC.   36 a 20 A—$3 00

CURRENTS BROUGHT THEM ASHORE IN AN OBLIQUE DIRECTION

The Holiday Season is now at hand when Santa Claus makes the usual visit to his Youthful Friends

Figures with each Size 1234567890

20 POINT OBLIQUE GOTHIC.   20 a 15 A—$4 00

DESTRUCTIVE CYCLONES SCARE THE NORTH-WEST

After the Storm comes the Calm, but Wrecks and Destruction mark its Deadly Track

24 POINT OBLIQUE GOTHIC.   18 a 12 A—$5 00

THE COLLEGIATE CHAMPIONSHIP

Collegiate Rivals contend for Supremacy on the Athletic Field

28 POINT OBLIQUE GOTHIC.   12 a 8 A—$4 50

HANDSOME OBLIQUE GOTHIC SERIES

Condensed sufficiently to secure for Printers a Useful Jobbing Letter

36 POINT OBLIQUE GOTHIC.   10 a 6 A—$4 50

POWERFUL ARMOURED SHIPS

Thanksgiving Turkeys now Decorate the Markets

THE LEGIBILITY OF TYPE.*

NOTWITHSTANDING the intimate relation of literature with the foundry and printing house, by a singularity, which it may not be useless to note, the foundry and printing house have never consulted literature for enlightenment in their march and progress. Even at the present time, the printers and founders, anxious to proceed without the aid of authors, and the authors content to be brought to light by the printers, have never approached each other in consultation upon the means of preserving and perfecting an art which has the authors for principal base and the readers for chief end. Writers are, without doubt, the class who read most, consequently the most capable of judging of the manner of treating the characters and impressions to acquire the maximum of utility, convenience and agreeableness.

Since we are entered upon this subject, let us say what we think concerning the art of the engraver of letters and its natural auxiliary, the founder of characters.

The artist in letters ought to consult the *savants* concerning his work. He ought to submit his attempts to men of letters for advice, should he fail in attaining success ; for approbation, should he reach the desired end. This intercourse could not fail to result in benefit, and too much praise could not be given to the zeal and modesty of gravers, printers and founders who will carry out the idea practically.

In order to judge of the value of an innovation in type, it is necessary to ask what is the end or aim of the printing office : Is it the beauty of a picture, or the facility of reading ? Is it the delicacy of the form of the letters, or the evidence of that form ? It is neither the one nor the other absolutely, and it is the one and the other concurrently. It is necessary that the two intentions should be combined. To reach the perfection of printed letters is to solve the problem of uniting beauty of forms with the strength of these forms, in a manner to produce the best effect upon the eye.

The letters destined to compose the writing of extreme length should be letters graven for the effect and not merely some lines in which fineness constitutes the essential feature. It is a fact that if one wishes to make some fine strokes, very thin and true, the alphabet does not offer such difficulty but that a good engraver can easily introduce some perfect strokes. This is what the engravers and English and American founders have commenced to do, and the French after them, the past forty years ; they have adopted some superfine strokes. But the gravers and founders of former times did precisely the contrary. In perfecting the roman letter, which, it may be remarked, is a French character, Garamond, among others, discarded the thin, sharp lines which had previously distinguished the italic. This last was exclusively employed by the Aldis, of Venice ; the Grifes, of Lyons, and Robert Estienne, of Paris. But the italic was abandoned because of the fatigue to the eye in reading in comparison with the roman, and was laid aside as soon as the roman system was established. The Vascosans, the Posuels, the Cramoisy and Anissons adopted it exclusively.

In other countries, artists of the greatest merit had pushed the art of printing to its greatest perfection, and nothing equals the beauty of style which the Elzévir and Janson gave to their books in the Pays-Bas. These celebrated printers were made a special means of assuring to posterity the transmission of literary monuments. Their system was to render the reading of books as easy as possible. Such was the spirit of edification which animated these generous printers, commendable also by the correctness, fidelity and fine harmony of their learned pages. Brindley, Faulis and Baskerville did not surpass these good French printers, who were able to oppose them with advantage. If any one surpassed our ancient *chefs d'œuvre*, the glory should be given to Bodoni, of Parma. But these illustrious printers did not employ the system of thin letters. Bodoni, moreover, embellished his letters by enriching them with the heavy strokes of the French letter. When the system of fine letters began to grow in favor in

*Translated from *L'Imprimerie* for THE INLAND PRINTER by Miss Ella Garoutte.

France, the last of the Anisson, who always refused to adopt it, established a comparison destined to enlighten the public upon the defects of this innovation. Anisson took a page of impression of this system, executed it with the same spacing in letters of the same size of the Garamond system. He placed the two pages side by side upon a reading desk in front of the experts. At first they read the two pages without perceiving any marked difference. Anisson caused the reading to be repeated while stepping further away, so that it could be no longer distinguished. It happened that the Garamond page could be read several times after the other had become undistinguishable. This experience is a fact which decides peremptorily the question between the old and new types.

But it is not sufficient to know this fact. The cause which produced it must be developed. We must know why the eye, falling upon a line of the Garamond system, runs across it without difficulty, with rapidity, without thinking of the letters, and only occupied with the text, while the eye scanning a line of the fine letters, moves more slowly and exercises a species of inspection which fastens upon the characters instead of the ideas which the characters represent, which is a great inconvenience, for one should only be occupied with the subject matter, and it is not necessary for him to even be conscious that he reads.

It is because Garamond took care to bring the strength of his letters into the parts of their forms which distinguished them one from another, such as the attachments ; while in the most of modern type, the heavy stroke of the characters is carried only in the part of their form common to all, such as the pot-hooks. Accordingly, when one sees the *u* or *n* of Garamond, the force of the full stroke being carried from the top or the bottom of the letter, even when the two strokes unite to form a particular letter, there is not a moment of doubt before distinguishing the exact character. On the other hand, when one sees the *u* or *n* of the modern type, the lines of attachment are so fine that the eye must be continually exercised in order to distinguish one from the other. It frequently happens that in removing the page a short distance the *u*, the *n* and the *m* only form some parallel lines. In adopting these fine strokes the founders have not only weakened the forms of the letters, but also the color. In the management of these letters, it is necessary to use lighter tints of ink, a circumstance which has made the books of perfect impression exceedingly rare, and introduced the pale tints which give to the books thus printed a delicate beauty of a faint type, which makes one almost afraid to handle them. The letters of the Garamond type unite, on the contrary, beauty of form with force of outline, taking always a deep black, which catches the eye and invites a reading.

The books of Vascosan, Cramoisy and Anisson, all distinguished by this strong tint, are still the charm of readers. They will always be sought for on account of this essential merit of the impression, which is the legibility, and the gravers, founders and printers of our time cannot be too strongly urged to promptly reëstablish this prime quality in the works which they prepare for us.

The fashion is a thing which imposes itself, but the fashion is not always perfection ; in many cases it is more rational to consult principles rather than taste.

It is fatiguing to read these pale thin letters continuously, and many persons are not able to read them at all. It may be remarked here, that printing, which is only an art expedient for supplying the place of writing and engraving, has finally taken the preference over both.

Printing owes this preference to the regularity, the continuity, the evidence and fine ensemble of its features. This quality must be faithfully guarded and preserved. It results from this development of the principles of book printing that the greatest perfection was attained by Garamond and his followers. Moreover, it is evident that those who have followed the modern style have done as well as their contemporaries, but they have not done as well as Garamond and his imitators.

The science of printing will very soon be restored to its former splendor if the artists will undertake the task of leading it back to its principles by discarding the fatal style of beauty which has been introduced only to cause a visible degeneration.

THE ROGERS TYPOGRAPH.

Among the many typesetting machines which have recently been brought to the attention of the printing trade, none have attracted more attention than the Rogers Typograph, illustrations of which are herewith presented. This machine has what is well known in all English-speaking countries as the Remington keyboard. The operator touches the key for the required character, the proper matrix is released and slides down an inclined wire guide until it reaches its position opposite the casting box. When the line is filled by touching letter keys and space keys, exactly as in the Remington typewriter, a pressure of the foot justifies and spaces the lines by rotating all the spaces, which are compensating twin disks, until the matrix line is just full. The line is cast by the machine itself, and the frame which carries the matrices is tilted

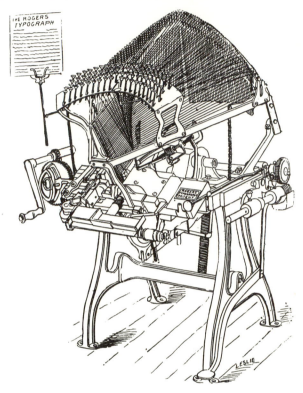

THE ROGERS TYPOGRAPH.

back by about the same motion as is used in the Remington typewriter to raise the carriage to inspect the work. The frame is dropped as the Remington carriage is dropped, and another line is set. The matrices are suspended on wires attached to a frame, and are released one at a time by touching the proper keys; but no matrix ever leaves its guide. The operations of justifying, aligning, casting, releasing and depositing the type-line on the galley take about five seconds in the foot-power machine, but if the machine is driven by belt, carrying about one-eighth horsepower, three seconds suffice, during which time the operator is "getting his line" from the copy, so that the working of the machine is practically continuous. The spacing may be by the spacing disks alone, the thinnest portions of which are thinner than a three-to-em space, so that closer justification can be obtained than by any other method; or ordinary three-to-em spaces may be interspersed by the machine if desired.

The melting-pot will hold and keep melted about thirty pounds of metal, requiring about eight cubic feet of gas, costing a cent an hour, or an amount of gasoline costing even less. The operation by foot-power is not fatiguing, and the speed only about ten per cent less than where power is used.

The speed of the machine is limited only by that of the operator, as is proved by the fact that from memorized matter over 7,000 ems of minion an hour have been set, in 16-pica em meas-

ure. On the same machine which did this C. W. Thullen has set from copy 4,700 ems of minion an hour; and on the same machine, also, A. V. Phister, of Typographical Union No. 18, of Detroit, set up, after a week's steady practice, 3,000 ems an hour, with less than half a dozen errors per 3,000 ems.

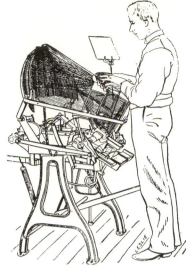

ASSEMBLING THE MATRICES.
(in effect setting the type.)

The length of line and the body of the type bar may be altered in twenty minutes, and the machines converted in that time from minion to nonpareil, or to any other face for which matrices and casting boxes have been provided. The machine, which is shown in the accompanying illustration, takes up only 4 by 4 feet on the floor, and stands about 4 feet 6 inches high over all; its weight being but 450 pounds. Its running makes less noise than that of a Remington or caligraph typewriter.

There is no book composition so large that the user of these machines cannot accept it. Publishers of directories may keep the matter standing any length of time at but nominal cost, and alter any one address line in it at any time. Mailing lists, regular or temporary, of any desired length, may be kept standing as long as desired, with but trifling outlay.

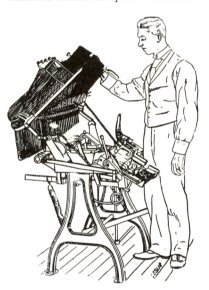

RELEASING THE MATRICES.
(in effect distributing the type.)

Thousands of small towns which have not been able to support even a weekly newspaper can now boldly enter upon the support of a daily, without risk to the publisher. This feature alone will cause an increase in the amount of composition done, far in excess of the increased amount over what every compositor can do by hand; thus paying employment will be found for everyone capable of running the machine. Compositors and proofreaders will also find the machine work beneficial to their eyesight, particularly where the type face is small, and in German offices. The public will profit by the ability to have more local papers, to make the present local press local in fact as well as in name, and by being able to print more "locals"; and by the mere fact of every paper using this machine having a new dress every day, the good accruing to the public eyesight will be no small one.

The machines are put out at a uniform rental of $1 per day for each working day, or $300 per year for weekly papers, for which price the company agrees to keep them in repair. The company has taken unusual care in the matter of patents, and will assume at its own expense all suits that may be brought for any alleged infringement.

PATENTED.

---

12 A, 16 a.   10 POINT CAXTONIAN. $3.00

HAVE RISKED OUR LIFE in crossing the Atlantic to select goods that will tickle your fancy, and have suffered the horrors of sea-sickness that you may strut about in Silks and Satins
1234567890

7 A, 10 a.   18 POINT CAXTONIAN. $4.00

SLEEPLESS Nights we endured, and strange bed-fellows made, in efforts to gratify you

4 A, 6 a.   36 POINT CAXTONIAN. $7.40

YOUTHS no longer need go in Rags

18 A, 20 a.   6 POINT CAXTONIAN. $2.50

WE INVITE YOU TO EXAMINE, at our Store, an immense variety of marvels in woven goods, produced by the brain and brawn of our own and other lands. We have ransacked every corner of the earth for such novelties as will enable our townspeople to outshine in personal appearance our rivals across the Creek SEVEN IN THE MORNING TO MIDNIGHT

THE CAXTONIAN IS A STANDARD JOBBING FACE OF MODERN TIMES. IT IS VERY BRIGHT AND ATTRACTIVE IN APPEARANCE, AND IS ALSO A GOOD MONEY EARNER.

LADIES will find unique dress goods

THIS SERIES SHOULD BE IN EVERY PRINTING OFFICE, AS OPPORTUNITIES ARE EVER PRESENT IN WHICH IT MAY BE USED TO MAKE THE JOB IN HAND MORE PLEASING.

14 A, 18 a.   8 POINT CAXTONIAN. $2.90

NATIONS MAY RISE AND FALL, Rulers govern and die, but while we clothe the people of this town it shall be done in a sumptuous manner, and no sacrifice will we hesitate to make in the accomplishment of the object we have set before us

MEN'S wear at very low prices now

5 A, 7 a.   24 POINT CAXTONIAN. $5.10

OUR STORE has been refitted for these occasions

10 A, 14 a.   12 POINT CAXTONIAN. $3.55

WHEN VISITING US don't forget your pocket-books, as our ambition also points towards the accumulation of a reserve fund adequate to emergencies

---

The MacKellar, Smiths & Jordan Co., { 606-614 Sansom Street, Philadelphia. Western Branch: 328-330 Dearborn Street, Chicago.

A TYPEFOUNDER GONE HOME.

It is always a sad duty to chronicle the death of an upright citizen whose prominence in commercial life, whose energy and sterling integrity, have united to give him a high position in the esteem of his associates and the general public. Such a man was Mr. A. P. Luse, of Marder, Luse & Co., typefounders, Chicago, whose portrait appears on this page, and who departed this life at Los Angeles, California, on Friday, January 16, while sojourning there for the recovery of his health.

Those whose business relations with the concern began within the last five or six years will not realize the truth of this so well as the earlier patrons of Marder, Luse & Co., for Mr. Luse has not been actively engaged in the affairs of the house since 1883. Up to that period he had led a remarkably busy life, but was then compelled to yield to the imperative demands of failing health.

The deceased was born at Indianapolis, April 3, 1831, and learned the printer's trade in the office of the *Sentinel,* of that city. He attended Wabash College from 1849 to 1851, but did not graduate there. In 1852, in company with his brother, he purchased the Lafayette *Journal,* and entered into business on his own account. In 1854 he was married to Miss Sarah Wade, of that city. Mrs. Luse died in 1884.

In the fall of 1854 Mr. Luse went to Davenport, Iowa, where for fourteen years he was engaged in the printing and stationery business, and wherein he was eminently successful. He first entered into partnership with the Hon. Hiram Price, under the firm name of

A. P. Luse & Co. Soon afterward the style of the concern became Luse & Scott, then Luse, Lane & Co., the partners in the latter firm being Mr. Luse, Mr. Price and E. Y. Lane. Later it was Luse & Griggs, F. H. Griggs being the partner, and this was the name of the house when Mr. Luse withdrew to enter a wider field of usefulness in the great metropolis of the West. It was in 1869 that he purchased an interest in the firm of Schofield, Marder & Co., proprietors of the Chicago Typefoundry, and the style of the house became Marder, Luse & Co. Under this proprietorship the house has made its greatest strides in growth and prosperity, and it is in no small degree due to the enterprise and business sagacity of A. P. Luse that the firm of Marder, Luse & Co. stands today as one of the pillars of the typefoundry interests of the world.

When the firm was incorporated, in 1883, Mr. Luse was obliged, from the precarious condition of his health, to withdraw from active participation in business, and for four years made his residence in Crawfordsville, Indiana, where he has won many friends. After that time he traveled extensively in Europe, Florida and California, and made his last visit to the latter state in the hope of bettering his physical condition. The hope, however, proved to be in vain, and his friends were soon called upon to mourn his demise.

The attendance at his funeral affords some indication of the esteem in which he was held and the wide circle of friends which he had made. His remains were interred at Crawfordsville, Indiana, on January 26. In addition to the local attendance a special car conveyed Chicago mourners to participate in the last sad rites. Among these were Mr. and Mrs. John Marder, J. W. Marder, Walter and Clarence Marder, Miss Amy Marder, Herbert Luse and Miss Alethea Luse, of Chicago, and Mr. Cyrus P. Luse, of Minneapolis.

Mr. John Marder, his partner of many years, was one of the pallbearers, and a clear idea of the mutual faith that existed between the two partners is furnished in the fact that John Marder was made executor of Mr. Luse's estate, without bond.

Mr. Luse was a man of modest and unassuming deportment, irreproachable character, unswerving integrity, iron will and the kindliest of sympathies and impulses. He had acquired a moderate fortune, and those who know of his energy and strict business methods will cheerfully acknowledge that he was fully entitled to it, and add the wish that he might have lived many years in the enjoyment of an independence which he had so honorably earned.

In the death of Mr. Luse the typefoundry business loses one of its stanchest promoters, one who has made his influence widely felt in its growth and prosperity, and who would now have been prominently identified with its development had not disease compelled him to relinquish the harness of business activity while yet it sat upon him with honor and credit, and when he should still have had many years of effective labor before him.

THE Key West (Fla.) *Equator-Democrat* has evolved an ingenious plan for preventing unscrupulous newsboys from reselling copies of papers belonging to subscribers and wrongfully diverted from their intended destination by ways that are dark. At the head of its editorial columns it has a notice in large type requesting the public not to buy from any newsboy an *Equator-Democrat* having the following printed warning: "Subscriber's Paper. Do Not Buy It."

WHAT IS THE REMEDY?

HAVING in a previous number condemned the unbusiness-like and senseless competition which has too long prevailed among the typefounders of the country, and its injurious effects upon the printing trade at large, we propose in the present issue to suggest what, in our judgment, seems a practical remedy for the same. Experience is the best though frequently the most expensive teacher, and experience has proven that *promises* of reform in this connection have been like pie crust — made but to be broken. In view of this fact some importance has been attached to the rumor prevailing for some months past that a new combination was to be formed among the founders, although no one seems to know exactly on what lines. It appears certain, however, that the larger establishments will not entertain the idea of any more *agreements* which experience has demonstrated have been more honored in the breach than in the observance. Under these circumstances it seems to us the most rational and feasible means out of the dilemma is the consolidation of most, if not all, the typefounders into one large corporation. This, we have reason to believe, is and has been the desire of several leading founders, who are anxious to quit a warfare which not only injures themselves, but is cruel and heartless to their competitors, and at the same time fraught with larger harm and loss to their patrons. It is impossible to learn definitely why this consolidation has not been projected ere this, but Dame Rumor says that at the last annual meeting of the typefounders all heretofore existing difficulties were overcome, with the exception that a small minority interest obstinately refused to join with the others unless it had its own way, to the injury of all the rest. We believe, however, that cool consideration, and the realization of the harm being done to so many thousands of the fraternity, will soon eliminate this opposition.

We have little fear that a consolidation of the typefoundries will create a monopoly in the sense of imposing burdensome prices. In fact we do not believe that prices would be much if any higher than most established printers now pay; but it would most effectually put a stop to the unrighteous discrimination which at present writing allows a new customer to buy his outfit at less than cost, and enables and encourages him to enter upon a career of price slashing which, if even temporarily successful, can only result in injury and undermining of those now in the business, and utterly demoralizing any fair schedule of rates. Who is benefited thereby? The founder is not, for he not only sacrifices his profits, but knows he is taking the surest course to destroy the financial responsibility of his customers; the established printer is certainly not benefited, for it is only the latest comer who gets the benefits of those high discounts, and the encouragement thus afforded to such to start in business is surely no benefit to those already in; and lastly, the public are not benefited, for though the prices of printing are spasmodically slaughtered, it can only be temporarily, as it is a well understood fact that no commodity will long continue to be sold at a figure which will not fully cover all the expenses of production, and keeping up the plant, and also interest on the capital invested. And whatever benefit the public would realize while prices were low or irregular would be more than offset by a depreciation in the value of the stock of printed matter on hand, and the disarrangement of long established and satisfactory connections.

We are aware the bugbear of monopoly has been raised as an objection to the proposed scheme. While we do not claim to be an authority on political economy, we think the plain truth is too frequently lost sight of. From our standpoint no monopoly, *per se*, can exist under present circumstances, unless (1) protected by secret processes; (2) protected by patents; (3) protected by a tariff, or (4) protected by exclusive and comprehensive ownership. An instance of this last named species of monopolies is that of the Standard Oil Company, which is understood to own or control directly or indirectly all the oil wells in this country, whose products are of commercial value in the trade centers. This sort of monopoly is doubtless against public policy, and should be prohibited, if possible. But why should a large typefoundry be any more a monopoly than the large stores in our great commercial centers. Is it not true that because of their size they have economized in their expenses, and shared this saving with the public by virtue of lower prices? And why should not printers share in like manner in the many economies a consolidation of the typefoundries would bring about? No, we cannot see how such a combination as referred to would be a monopoly; lead, antimony, tin and copper are free to all who can pay market prices, and there are now no patents to protect any necessary process in the manufacture of type.

But, for the sake of argument, let us suppose that consolidation should, through greed or shortsightedness on the part of the founders, result in an unwarranted advance in prices. For a short time, no doubt, printers would be compelled to submit, but the comparatively small amount of type they must needs buy at such prices would practically cut no figure in comparison to the increase in the market value of their plants — their restoration to normal value — and it would not be long before new typefoundries sprung up, because the natural laws of trade, of supply and demand, would inevitably soon bring prices down to a fair basis. Indeed, we are satisfied the founders are well aware of the fact that in every large city in the United States there are numbers of progressive, enterprising printers who could and would establish typefoundries in abundance if any of the evils of monopoly should show themselves; and such establishments would be certain to be self-supporting, because of the assured patronage of the trade at large. Again, in case of necessity, the printers and press would undoubtedly raise their united voices, either through self-interest, or principle, or both, and demand the repeal of all duties on foreign manufactured type; and it would take only a few years to introduce type from new or foreign foundries in sufficient quantity to bring any monopolist foundry or combination of foundries to their senses.

Our deliberate conclusion, therefore, is that the interests of the printing fraternity will be best subserved, as well as those of the public at large, by the stoppage of the type war through the consolidation of the foundries. This seems to be the best, quickest and cheapest way back to honest prices, and we believe that this conclusion is indorsed by every intelligent printer.

THE INVENTION OF PRINTING.

BY O. S. JENKS.

TO China, the birthplace of so many of the useful arts and inventions, we must look for the origin of the "art preservative." Early in the tenth century, five hundred years before Gutenberg contrived the movable metal types which have rendered his name imperishable, an imperial edition of the sacred books was published in that far oriental country. But on the same principle that the glory of America's discovery rests with Columbus and not with Lief Ericson, must the honor of the invention of the most powerful factor in civilization be ascribed to Gutenberg and his contemporaries.

No advancement commercially or politically of the civilized nations of Western Europe resulted from the discovery of America by the Norsemen, and had these early explorers exerted themselves to permanently colonize the western hemisphere, their semi-barbarous character affords no indication that civilization would have been promoted by their conquests. So, had the knowledge of printing remained the sole property of the inhabitants of the Flowery Kingdom and neighboring countries, the progress of civilization would have been retarded centuries, as it was not until a comparatively recent date that western energy and perseverance succeeded in penetrating their exclusiveness and in acquainting us with their peculiar customs and modes of living. The history of printing properly begins with the employment of movable metal types by Europeans.

Few inventions are the spontaneous conceptions of individual minds. An invention is generally the climax to a series of efforts of different individuals at different times, and the inventor is he who embodies the conclusions of himself and others in something that shall be serviceable to man.

The desirability of a method of rapidly multiplying copies of law records and the works of eminent writers was probably practically manifested with the first written law and literature.

Block printing was practiced in China, Japan and Corea centuries before the time of Coster and Gutenberg, and was occasionally employed by early European sovereigns for impressions of seals and coats of arms. Books printed by this process were quite common in China in the tenth century, and it is said that the Chinese printed from movable types of clay as early as the middle of the eleventh century; the Coreans are credited with the invention of copper types in the beginning of the fifteenth century. Yet, until the middle of the fourteenth century the laborious process of multiplying copies of manuscripts by handwriting was universal in Europe.

"Necessity is the mother of invention." The first books printed were impressions on paper or parchment from blocks of wood on which the letters or designs to be reproduced had to be cut in reverse. If an error that required correction was made in carving the block, it was generally necessary to substitute a new block and do the carving over again, and the desirability of obviating the extreme difficulty of correction led doubtless to the invention and employment of movable wooden types by Laurent Coster, of Haarlem.

But a great deal of labor was involved in the cutting of these letters, and as it was impossible to make any two exactly alike (being engraved one at a time), they made a very irregular and uneven impression.

A process of producing types which should be uniform, durable, not easily broken, and produced with less expense and labor, was the object of the researches of the early printers.

For a long time Coster endeavored to perfect his invention by the discovery of such a process, and, according to Hadrian Junius, actually invented metal types. The same authority states that a workman in Coster's employ discovered the secret of their manufacture and fled to Mayence. This workman's name is said to have been John. If we assume the correctness of the above account, which, however, is a matter of controversy, the John spoken of may have been John Fust or John Gaensefleisch (who afterward assumed the name of Gutenberg), who is said to have communicated the secret to his nephew, later the partner of Schöffer. There are good reasons, however, for believing that neither Gutenburg nor Fust were ever in Coster's employ. As M. Bouchot says, in his excellent work — "The Printed Book" — "But it is not at all apparent that Gutenberg, a gentleman of Mayence exiled from his country, was ever in the service of the Dutch inventor. As to Fust, we believe his only intervention in the association of printers of Mayence was as a money lender, from which may be comprehended the unlikelihood of his having been with Coster, the more so as we find Gutenberg retired to Strasburg where he pursued his researches. There he was, as it were, out of his sphere, a ruined noble whose great knowledge was bent entirely on invention. Doubtless, like many others, he may have had in his hands one of the printed works of Laurent Coster, and conceived the idea of appropriating the infant process."

A FORECAST

THERE is a disposition shown by the unthinking to "fight" the typesetting machine, and the changes its advent will occasion. Arguments have been made in the past that no degree of perfection in machinery could be reached that would interfere with hand composition—"until a machine could be made to think, there was no need for compositors to be uneasy." This view has been abandoned to a large extent as further improvements have been made, and as the inevitable supremacy of the typesetting machines has become manifest printers are bestirring themselves to study the mechanism and methods of operating them. This is as it should be. The time for wrecking looms and destroying steam printing presses has gone by, and any attempts to hold back the inventive genius of the age need only be hinted at to be denounced.

If the machine enables a compositor to set twice as much as by hand and he should receive a correspondingly reduced price per thousand, he would lose nothing. In fact he indirectly would be a gainer, for all his attention being concentrated on typesetting he will acquire a degree of skill and accuracy that would not be possible were his labors divided with the irksome task of distribution. The swiftest compositors are those employed on the daily press, and they as a rule prefer to pay for distribution. The contention that women will take the place of men as compositors when the machines are an assured success, is one that looks portentous enough, the difference between running a typesetting machine and a typewriting machine being very small; and the number of applicants for situations as typewriters, it needs only a glance at the advertising columns of the daily papers to show, far exceeds the demand. But take the average typewritten page, and what degree of knowledge of composition, punctuation capitalization, or orthography does it show? Manual dexterity in punching a bank of keys will not comprise all the requirements from an operator of a typesetting machine, and employers will find out as they ever have done that economy beyond a certain point is extravagance. It will be found that the employment of women to run machines will not be greater, if as great, as their employment in hand composition. We gain some encouragement in the belief that an increased output will result from the additional facility with which work can be turned out and from the greater cheapness resulting. Many a convention's proceedings, and hurried work of similar character, is withheld from the printer, for lack of time and money. Then again, our public libraries· are flooded with the books of foreign manufacture. The editions of Bernard Tauchnitz, of Leipsic, abound in the libraries of America because almost any work in fiction can be obtained from them and because they are cheaper. The passing of the copyright law, defending the compositor from foreign competition, and the cheapening power of the typesetting machines will cause a condition of affairs that will put the American printer at the head of the line of the mighty army of workmen who have profited from improvement in machinery.

March 1891

THE MANUFACTURE OF WOOD TYPE.

One of the essential needs of the modern printing office is a supply of wood type, large or small, according to the class of work turned out. There is probably no article used by printers the manufacture of which is so little understood. There being but four manufactories in the United States and these, with one exception, being located in comparatively small cities, the opportunity of the average printer to become acquainted with the details of its manufacture are limited indeed. Until recent years the prices for this material were so excessive that the poster printing business was confined to a few large houses who had fortunes invested in wood type; but strong competition among the manufacturers has resulted in new methods of manufacture, and today wood type is selling at about one-third the price received for it ten years ago. This state of affairs has had a pronounced effect upon the number of houses engaged in poster printing. The low price has enabled printers of moderate means to stock up on wood type and compete for this class of work.

Originally all wood type was cut by hand. The design was made upon the block of wood, and the workmen with their carving tools would remove the surrounding wood leaving the letter raised. This process was necessarily slow and tedious, and the class of work produced would not compare favorably with the beautifully cut and artistically designed wood type offered to printers today.

Wood type was first cut by machinery in the year 1846 at South Windham, Connecticut, by Edwin Allen, who continued its manufacture there for six years, and in the year 1850 his works fell into the hands of J. G. Cooley. Cooley continued to manufacture at South Windham until the year 1859, when he removed to New York City and, in 1868, sold out his entire plant to William H. Page, then of Greenville, Connecticut.

William H. Page first began the manufacture of wood type in 1854, and was then twenty-five years old. Located at that time at South Windham, he continued there until 1857, when he removed to Greenville and manufactured there for about twenty years moving thence to Norwich, Connecticut, where his works have been located up to the present time. On January 4, of this year, the William H. Page Wood Type Company sold its entire plant to the Hamilton Manufacturing Company, located at Two Rivers, Wisconsin.

About July 1, next, the entire plant will be removed from Norwich to Two Rivers, and a business of forty-five years standing in the old State of Connecticut will, like the proverbial star of empire, take its way westward.

Mr. Page has done more than any other man toward the development of the manufacture of wood type. As a letter designer his equal has never appeared. About the year 1872 he issued a catalogue of chromatic border and type that at once placed him at the head of the business in the world. The intricate and artistic designs of this color work have never been equaled by our best printers to this day. Mr. Page issued a thousand of these catalogues at a cost to his firm of $10,000. All the designs in this magnificent catalogue emanated from Mr. Page's fertile brain. He has taken many patents upon type faces and type-making machines, and is also an inventor of distinction in other branches of trade. A few years ago he secured letters patent for producing type by the new stamping process, and now has this style of type protected by nine domestic and four foreign patents. The machines for producing type under this process are wonderful pieces of mechanism which can stamp no less than 100,000 letters per day, and will eventually revolutionize the manufacture of wood type in the plain and standard faces.

By the transfer of his plant to the Hamilton Manufacturing Company Mr. Page does not retire from the business, but becomes a stockholder in the western company, and while he will not hereafter be directly identified with the manufacturing process, the benefit of his vast experience will still be enjoyed by the men in charge.

The Hamilton Manufacturing Company, which now becomes the greatest producer of wood type in the world, and probably manufactures more than all others in the world combined, has had a most phenomenal growth Its first appearance as J. E. Hamilton was in 1880. Mr. Hamilton was at that time a mechanic, working at the bench in Two Rivers, without money or business experience. Receiving a call from the local printer, whose stock of wood type was limited, for the words "Turner Hall" in a line of type mounted on one block to run across a half sheet bill, the result was so satisfactory that Mr. Hamilton began to do a little thinking, and he soon produced several fonts of wood type for this same printer. Having no knowledge of the requirements of type as to accuracy, etc., these fonts of type were necessarily very defective and would hardly stand comparison with the goods produced by this firm today. After producing these fonts of type an order was received from a neighboring printer, and thus the business started.

Mr. Hamilton deserted his bench, and, setting up a small foot-power saw in the loft of his dwelling house, he issued circulars at first to the printers in his immediate vicinity, soliciting a share of their patronage. The type produced was called holly wood type, and the process of manufacturing it was essentially different from any heretofore known. The faces of the type were sawed out of thin strips of holly wood and then mounted on their bases. While not so good an article as the old style of end wood type, it made a cheap article and enabled printers of moderate means to compete for the trade of poster printing. In a short time the business increased so rapidly that a little capital was required and also more room, and in 1881 the firm of Hamilton & Katz appeared,

J. E. HAMILTON.

a factory building was erected, more machinery purchased and set up, and the sale of holly wood type was pushed until the term became familiar to printers throughout the country.

The firm ran along under this name until 1885, when Mr. Katz sold his interest, and the firm became Hamilton & Baker ; meanwhile trade had been constantly on the increase, and in 1887 a new plant was purchased and the firm began the manufacture of a complete line of printers' wood goods.   In 1888 Mr. Baker severed his connection with the firm and the business was reorganized as a stock company under its present name, with J. E. Hamilton as president and general manager, and has since continued under this style.   Mr. Hamilton has been the soul of the concern since its infancy.   He has superintended all the details of the manufacturing and financial management, and designed and constructed intricate machines at the company's own machine shops which have greatly cheapened the cost of production of all articles in the firm's line, and have placed the firm at the head of the business in the world.   For the past two years the company has kept constantly employed two experienced machine builders in constructing the special machines designed by Mr. Hamilton. In many instances these machines produce fully ten times the amount formerly turned out by the best machines in use. From the small order of eleven years ago the business of the firm has grown to the aggregate of nearly a quarter of a million per annum, employing one hundred and fifty skilled workmen in the manufacture of its goods.

One peculiarity, and an astonishing one it is, is the fact that until recently purchasing the Page business, the firm derived no benefit from the long experience of its competitors. Entering the field unaided and alone in the West, it never sought the services of one of their workmen, but proceeded to unravel the problems of the manufacture of wood type and wood goods, gathering its experience by hard knocks, and always triumphing in the end.

In 1889 a Chicago branch was established under the management of W. C. Luse, who has since continued in charge.   Previous to removing the works of the Page Company at Norwich to Two Rivers, the firm will establish a branch at New York City under the management of one of the most experienced printers' supply men in the United States.   Liberal and aggressive in his policy, Mr. Hamilton has guided his company safely over the dangerous places which occur in the career of all business ventures, and placed it upon a substantial basis, enjoying the full confidence of its friends and respected by its competitors.

The manufacture of wood type is quite intricate, requiring considerable skill in its production and the use of accurate machinery. Very little holly wood type is now produced by this firm.   Its perfected machines enable it to produce end wood type at prices very little in advance of the cost of holly, except in the larger sizes, which the firm still continues to manufacture under the holly system, as they claim it to be more durable and less liable to warp than the end wood.   The timber from which the type is cut is sawed from the end of a log to a thickness somewhat more than type-high in the winter months when the weather is cold to enable the timber to freeze and remain so for some time.   As the season advances and the weather grows warmer, the timber dries out and should season at least two years in this manner before being prepared for the manufacture of type.   After being thoroughly seasoned it is dressed by hand with smoothing planes and planed type-high, which is $\frac{921}{1000}$ of an inch.   The smooth and even face so often admired on wood type is then applied, after which the process of cutting type on the block is proceeded with.   The machines for doing this work are quite a novelty ; they enable the operator to cut a twelve-line letter from a thirty-line pattern, or an eighteen-line letter from the same pattern, as he desires, and also other sizes.   The cutter which removes the wood runs at a high rate of speed, being no less than 18,000 revolutions per minute.

After the machine work on the type is completed it goes to the trimming department, where each type is closely examined, the corners cut out with carving tools, the edges smoothed off to give a clear impression and all imperfections removed.   It would be impossible in a short article to give all the interesting details of the manufacture of wood type and wood goods, and it is a pity the works are so far removed from the average printer as to bar him from observing the details of a business in which he is so deeply interested.

The works of this company at present occupy three distinct plants, two situated at Two Rivers and the one recently purchased at Norwich.   Operations are in active progress looking to the consolidation of the whole business of manufacturing in one plant.   The present type factory and office will be abandoned and sixty feet

WILLIAM H. PAGE.

east of the case factory, which is 67 by 125 feet and three stories high, will be constructed a new factory building 40 by 100 feet, two stories, to be used for type purposes.   This will be connected to a brick fireproof office building 30 by 38 feet, with pattern room in second story.   Adjoining this building will be a new warehouse and finishing department 40 by 100 feet and three stories high.

The machines of the entire plant will be driven by an improved Corliss engine of 250-horse power, located directly between the two factory buildings.   The plant will be lighted by electricity under the Edison incandescent system, generated by its own dynamos.   It will be protected against fire by a complete system of sprinklers and steam fire pumps connected by hydrants with all parts of the works, and heated by the Sturtevant hot air blast system.

The works are situated on lots having several hundred feet of river frontage which are docked and capable of floating the largest vessels to the factory door.   Taken as a whole, this plant will constitute the most complete one in the country for the manufacture of printers' wood goods.

THE TYPEFOUNDRIES OF THE UNITED STATES.

— THE CENTRAL TYPEFOUNDRY, ST. LOUIS.

Prominent among the manufacturing and business houses of St. Louis is the Central Typefoundry, situated on the southeast corner of Fourth and Elm streets. It is a new building five stories high, with a frontage of fifty feet on Fourth street, and is provided with every facility for conducting an extensive and constantly increasing business.

As they feel perfectly comfortable and content in their quarters, an outline description of them and what they contain may be of interest to our readers.

In the basement is a fifty-horse power boiler, which furnishes steam for the engines and heaters, and a thirty-horse power engine furnishes power for all the floors. Two elevators, each having its separate engine, communicate with every floor, and facilitate the handling of freight. The building extends from Fourth street to an alley one hundred and fifty feet, and all goods are shipped from the back doors of the basement, which is on a level with the alley. In the basement are also stored the different metals used in the composition of their unexcelled and world-renowned "copper alloy."

The first floor is devoted to office and salesroom. It is handsomely fitted up, and most convenient for the display and sale of all articles required by printers. Here, on shelves and compartments is stored an immense stock of types, borders, cuts, ornaments, rules, etc., of their own manufacture and from other foundries, arranged for the greatest facility in filling orders. A full assortment of inks, bronzes and varnishes, is also placed within easy reach, as are all other articles required in the outfit of a well-appointed printing office. Speaking tubes and a dumbwaiter connect with all the floors, giving quick communication between the office and salesroom, and the employés in their manufacturing departments. Their immense salesroom is thoroughly lighted, producing a comfortable and cheery effect, in addition to displaying goods to the best advantage.

The second floor is used as a stockroom. It is fifty by one hundred and fifty feet and contains a large display of cabinets, stands, cylinder presses, paper cutters, and printers' machinery of all kinds.

On the third floor is the electrotype and stereotype foundry, the largest and most complete and commodious in the Southwest; also the brass rule department, and the department for the finishing of brass type for bookbinders' use; likewise the department for the manufacturing of brass galleys, leads and slugs.

On the fourth floor — fifty by one hundred and fifty feet in area, lighted by large windows on all sides, and conveniently arranged throughout — is the finishing and dressing department. In this room all their type is given the finishing touches — rubbing, setting, dressing, picking and paging. The finished type is then taken to the dividing department, where it is separated into fonts and put up in wrappers for the salesroom, to which it is then transferred. In this dividing the strictest attention is paid to giving the proper proportions of the various characters to each font, and their system has been so perfected that errors in the putting up of fonts are almost impossible.

On the same floor are the fire and burglar proof safes, which contain an extensive and valuable collection of matrices, the increasing number of which has necessitated the purchase of several new safes of larger capacity. The engraving and punch-cutting department, in which their beautiful original patented faces are produced under the hands of skillful and artistic designers and engravers, is situated on the fourth floor, as is also the matrix-making department, in which superior workmen are engaged in following up the work begun by the engravers, in the process of getting out the new styles of type for the novelty, beauty and utility of which the Central Typefoundry has achieved such a world-wide reputation. As all the matrices have to be made to withstand the intense wearing action of the "copper alloy" metal in casting — against which the ordinary matrices of other foundries cannot hold out — this is in itself a very costly branch of the business, requiring superior methods and more than usual skill on the part of the matrix-makers.

On the same floor is also the specimen department and printing office, from which emanate the *Printers' Register* and the books, pamphlets and cards which are issued from time to time. Here the cases are well stocked with all their new designs in type, and orders for sorts from these are filled immediately. In the printing of the specimen sheets they use the same type as is sold from their shelves, no better care being exercised to cast more perfect type for their own use than is cast for their customers.

The office of the superintendent of the manufacturing departments of the foundry is on this floor, being neatly fitted up and in convenient position to oversee all work under his charge.

On the fifth floor is the casting department, where they have now thirty-five machines, including the wonderful Foucher French type casting and finishing machine, all of which are supplied with the improvements which they have found it necessary to make on the old-style casting machine, in order to enable them to use their metal, the "copper alloy."

Near the casting machines are placed the tables of the "breakers," who break off the jet formed at the foot of large type during the casting process. A large force of girls are employed at this work, as well as in that of rubbing, setting and paging on the floor below.

On this floor are four large furnaces for casting brass type. The Central is the only foundry in America casting brass type, and is now not only supplying the bookbinders of America, but does a large export business with England and Australia. The demand for "copper alloy" type and patent faces abroad has compelled them to establish agencies in England and Australia, and in both countries the "Central" does a large and increasing business.

On the fifth floor is also the metal-mixing department, where every pound of the famous "copper alloy" is compounded. This is a process requiring the closest attention, and peculiarly is this the case with their metal, in order to have the proper proportions and the proper methods carried out. The proportions of the different metals in the "copper alloy," and the secret of combining them are known only to them.

On the fifth floor is the machinists' department, where superior casting machines, molds, etc., are constructed under the hands of the most skillful workmen. In each division of their foundry they have endeavored to obtain machines and tools which combine labor-saving qualities with the ability to turn out superior products. We believe that they have been successful and have secured the best facilities for obtaining the highest results.

A cordial invitation is extended to visitors to inspect their new building and look through the various departments, of which they are justly proud, being satisfied that when their inspection is over they will be convinced that the ability of the "Central" to furnish the best of everything wanted in a printing office is unsurpassed.

CHICAGO CABLE TRAINS CROWDED

Morning Noon and Evening

Conductors · and · Drivers · Benevolent · Association

1 2 3 4 5 6 7 8 9 0

Electric and Cable Street Railroad Company

Handsome · ·

and

· · Useful Series

Barnhart Bros. & Spindler

· · ·

SUPERIOR · COPPER-MIXED · TYPE

· · ·

Great Western Type Foundry

12 POINT (2 line Nonp.)
    10 A 20 a $2 90

18 POINT (3 line Nonp.)
    6 A 12 a $3 35

24 POINT (4 line Nonp.)
    5 A 10 a $4 25

PRESIDENT'S PROCLAMATION

Inviting · the · Nations

Worlds Columbian Exposition Chicago

Foreign Governments Exhibit

ZINCO.

REGISTERED, No. 165,803.

12 POINT ZINCO.

10 A, 28 a, $3.50

· CURIOSITIES ·
· · OUTSIDE · ·
· · OF · THE · ·
· DIME · MUSEUM ·

Persons Accepting Misfortune with Smiling Countenances
Cheerfully Arising when Knocked Down by Adversity
Blithesome, Vivacious, Laughter-provoking Associates
Ever Finding Brightness in Character and Surroundings

24 POINT ZINCO.

5 A, 14 a, $4.30

Unobtrusive · Specimens · of · Benevolence

Opulence and Penury Walking Arm-in-Arm

Missionaries Labouring Among Politicians

· 1234567890 ·

18 POINT ZINCO.

8 A, 20 a, $3.95

· PAUL · PRY ·
· · THE · ·
· VILLAGE ·
SIR · ORACLE

Thoroughly Acquainted with Family History
Retailer of Gossip Probable and Improbable
Counsellor in Matters Trivial or Momentous
Author and Publisher of Fictitious Incidents

36 POINT ZINCO.

4 A, 10 a, $6.25

Kettle-Drumming and Locomotive Whistling

Calithumpia · Banging · Association

ALL COMPLETE WITH FIGURES.

The MacKellar, Smiths & Jordan Co. { Nos. 606-614 Sansom Street, Philadelphia.
Western Branch: 328-330 Dearborn Street, Chicago.

Typo.

Registered, No. 165,807.

PATENT PENDING.

18 Point Typo.   10 A, 14 a, $2.40

EPICUREAN RESTAURANT
Delicious Eatables for Hungry Bipeds
1 2 3 4 5 6 7 8 9 0

24 Point Typo.   8 A, 10 a, $2.85

INSURANCE COMPANY
Tornado, Lightning, Earthquake
1 2 3 4 5 6 7 8 9 0

30 Point Typo.   6 A, 9 a, $3.55

Ornamental Window-Shade Manufacturers
FABRICATE AND DECORATE

36 Point Typo.   5 A, 7 a, $4.70

Printing-Office Enigma, Compositor Puzzler
UNREADABLE MANUSCRIPT

48 Point Typo.   4 A, 6 a, $5.25

NATIONAL Household LAUNDRY

60 Point Typo.   3 A, 4 a, $7.00

Resolute COUNTRY Merchant

ALL COMPLETE WITH FIGURES.

The MacKellar, Smiths & Jordan Co. { Nos. 606-614 Sansom Street, Philadelphia.
Western Branch: 328-330 Dearborn Street, Chicago.

12 POINT DYNAMO. 16 A, 25 a, $2.25

CONFISCATION OF TELEGRAPHS
Messages Between Lovers
Forwarded Without Charge
Length or Distance Unheeded
1234567890

18 POINT DYNAMO. 10 A, 14 a, $2.45

NATIONAL PURCHASES
Silver, Gold, Pumpkins
Oysters, Bricks, Hosiery
1234567890

24 POINT DYNAMO. 8 A, 10 a, $3.00

SEQUESTRATION OF RAILROADS
Gratuitous Summertime Excursions
Pullman and Sleeping=cars Included

36 POINT DYNAMO. 4 A, 6 a, $3.60

LEGISLATIVE PAWNSHOPS
Loans on Mushroom Security

48 POINT DYNAMO. 3 A, 4 a, $4.55

ROTATION IN OFFICE
Ten=day Service Pension

ALL COMPLETE WITH FIGURES.

The MacKellar, Smiths and Jordan Co. { Nos. 606=614 Sansom Street, Philadelphia.
Western Branch: 328=330 Dearborn Street, Chicago.

ABBEY SERIES.

NEW YORK—63 & 65 BEEKMAN ST. AND 62 & 64 GOLD ST.

ESTABLISHED 1804.

CHICAGO—109 QUINCY STREET. CHAS. B. ROSS, MANAGER.

OLD STYLE ALDINE

8 POINT. PATENT PENDING.

MANY READERS REMEMBER THE STORY

CHILDREN OF THE ABBEY 259

36 A—$2 25

10 POINT.

POETS' CORNER IN WESTMINSTER ABBEY

THE POPULAR ROMANCE 354

24 A—$2 00

12 POINT.

HANDSOME OLD STYLE TYPES

ABBEY FACES 36

18 A—$2 00

18 POINT.

THE CANTERBURY TALES

ARCHITECTS 35

12 A—$3 00

24 POINT.

SERIOUS EVENTS

NAME 56

10 A—$3 25

36 POINT.

OLD PRINTER

STYLE 5

6 A—$4 75

---

10 POINT. PATENT PENDING.

THE POPULAR OLD STYLE ALDINE

The History of the Roman Republic by Goldsmith

Amount 1234567890

40 a 20 A—$2 75

12 POINT.

THE AMERICAN PRINTERS

Marked Advancement in Design of Old Style Types

Artistic Printers Rejoice thereat 257

36 a 18 A—$3 00

18 POINT.

WASHINGTON CITY

Seat of Our National Government

Navy Department 1835

24 a 12 A—$3 75

24 POINT.

REVOLUTIONS

Antique Furniture to be Sold

Election Printings 28

16 a 10 A—$4 50

36 POINT.

OLD STYLE

Never will Despair

Aldine 85

10 a 6 A—$6 00

One of the Trade Journals recently contained a criticism of OUR ABBEY SERIES which leads us to reprint the entire Series in THE INLAND PRINTER. Notice that two smaller sizes, viz: 8 point, and 10 point, or Long Primer, have been recently added. We desire to say that many *imitations* have appeared since OUR ABBEY SERIES WAS FIRST BROUGHT OUT.

REGISTERED, No. 165,804.

PATENTED MAR. 3, 1891.

8 POINT GIRAFFE. 30 A, $1.30

COLLEAGUES OF THE GOLDEN RULE
PRODUCERS OF HONEST TRADESMEN
CONSTRUCTORS OF HAPPY HOUSEHOLDS
1234567890

25 A, $1.60 12 POINT GIRAFFE.

SHOTGUN SWORD COMPANY
RUTHLESS DEVASTATORS
MALEVOLENT DESTROYERS
1234567890

18 POINT GIRAFFE. 18 A, $2.00

QUADRANT AND COMPASS
TRUSTWORTHY STEERSMEN

12 A, $2.30 24 POINT GIRAFFE.

SHOULDER-STRAPS
STRATEGY CONDUCTOR

30 POINT GIRAFFE. 10 A, $2.70

BROTHERHOOD OF THOROUGHBREDS
GRACEFUL DEPORTMENT TEACHERS

36 POINT GIRAFFE. 8 A, $3.30

DOWN-SOUTH ORANGE-GROVE
PERFUMED REFRESHMENTS

48 POINT GIRAFFE. 5 A, $3.55

PERMANENT INVESTMENTS

ALL COMPLETE WITH FIGURES.

The MacKellar, Smiths & Jordan Co. { Nos. 606-614 Sansom Street, Philadelphia.
Western Branch: 328 and 330 Dearborn St., Chicago.

NEW SIZE ʙ 72-POINT RUBENS. 6a 5A, $10.25

Monogram HARBOR Nobleman

6a 4A ʙ 60-POINT RUBENS. $7.50

Remain for Generations 35

NEW SIZE ʙ 54-POINT RUBENS. 8a 6A, $6.75

GENERAL REMARK

Machinery 68

11a 7A ʙ 36-POINT RUBENS. $5.00

ORIGINAL COMEDY COMPANY

Evening Concert 83

NEW SIZE ʙ 30-POINT RUBENS. 14a 10A, $4.50

MUSIC AND DRAMATIC READINGS

Magnificent Performance 92

20a 13A ʙ 18-POINT RUBENS. $3.25

ENCHANTING SUMMER BEAUTIES ARE PASSING

Extraordinary Attractions Furnished 27

7a 5A ʙ 48-POINT RUBENS. $6.00

SECURE CAR BRAKE

Associations 26

NEW SIZE ʙ 42-POINT RUBENS. 10a 7A, $5.50

WONDERFUL MONUMENT

Second Game 49

15a 11A ʙ 24-POINT RUBENS. $4.25

EXHIBITION OF EUROPEAN INDUSTRIES

Northern Townships Settled 37

30a 20A ʙ 12-POINT RUBENS. $3.00

CHEERFUL CANDIDATES RECEIVING BOISTEROUS DELEGATIONS

Strongest Arguments Remaining Unanswered 174

PATENTED BY BOSTON TYPE FOUNDRY.   FOR SALE BY ALL DEALERS

**OBELISK**

16 Point Obelisk.

10 A, 14 a, $2.50

NORTHWEST EGYPTIAN AIRLINE RAILROAD

Luxurious Equipments, Safety, Unique Scenery, Fast Time, Courteous Attendants

1234567890

24 Point Obelisk.

7 A, 10 a, $3.20

FIFTEEN MINUTES AT PYRAMID OF CHEOPS

Ancient Rivers, Sand-clad Plains, Ruined Temples and Mummy Tombs

36 Point Obelisk.

5 A, 7 a, $5.15

MONUMENTS OF NINEVEH

Noontide Rambles amid Crumbling Buildings

48 Point Obelisk.

4 A, 6 a, $5.75

ROMANTIC MEMORIES

Eating Dinner with Sphinx and Centaur

60 Point Obelisk.

3 A, 5 a, $6.50

Mozambique MOUNTAINS

The MacKellar, Smiths & Jordan Co. { Nos. 606-614 Sansom Street, Philadelphia.
Western Branch: 328-330 Dearborn Street, Chicago.

TYPESETTING MACHINES.

THE problem as to how far typesetting machines will accomplish the work for which they are designed, and thereby replace the present typographic system, is one that is now fully before the printers of the country for their consideration. While it will be acknowledged that remarkable progress has been made in the direction of perfecting these machines, considering the inherent difficulties attending the subject, it is still a doubtful question whether the gloomy and nervous expectancy displayed by so many of the craft as to future prospects is fully warranted or not. That a large amount of the type now set by hand will, in the immediate future, be done by machines, is a foregone conclusion. Admitting this, it does not follow by any means that great hardship will attend their introduction, or that any large number of men will be deprived of employment as the result of their instantaneous adoption throughout the country. This difficulty will be avoided to a great extent by the fact that the machines are intricate in their mechanism, and therefore costly and slow of manufacture.

This view of the case will be strengthened when we remember that while absolute perfection has been claimed for each distinct machine while it was in a constructive state, practical demonstrations have proven in every case that the perfect typesetting machine has not as yet made its appearance. About a dozen separate machines have so far been placed upon the market, differing widely as to their speed and accuracy in every instance. Of these, the Thorne machine, for bookwork, and the Mergenthaler linotype machine, for newspaper work, seem so far to have gained the greatest favor in this country, to judge by the number of machines of different patent and style of manufacture now in actual operation. The Paige machine, though operated to some extent in private, has not as yet been placed upon the market. It is claimed for this machine that it is capable of setting 10,000 ems an hour, at a cost of about 5 cents per thousand. The cost of this machine will approximate some $12,000 or $15,000, a circumstance that may have some restricting influence on its universal adoption. Another machine, the advent of which is awaited with considerable interest, the most wonderful reports of its capacity having been freely circulated, is the one now being manufactured by the Chicago Matrix Machine Company. The projectors of this machine appear to have the greatest confidence as to its ability to outclass all other inventions of a like nature so far brought to public notice.

But, so far as this whole subject is concerned, the interest of the journeyman printer undoubtedly centers around the main question as to how far the projected innovation will revolutionize existing conditions, and to what extent it will curtail the amount of labor that will be required in the printing office of the future as compared with that of the present day. Perhaps a brief review of the marvelous transformations that have taken place in the construction and capacity of the printing press during the past fifty years, will answer the purpose of a possible comparison between past events and the probabilities of the future as well as anything that could be suggested at the present time.

When the primitive hand press was about to be superseded by the steam-power press, the prediction was made that a large amount of labor would necessarily be dispensed with, and that fast running machinery would supply every want with a modicum of the labor formerly found indispensable. This prediction was verified but to a very limited extent. It was quickly ascertained that the improved facilities brought the cost of printing within the reach of a larger mass of the public, and that workmen of fully as high a grade of skill would be required under the new method as under the old. Improvements in the printing press came thick and fast, and in the course of time the newspaper pressrooms were equipped with the mammoth six, eight and, in a few instances, ten-cylinder presses. These machines were considered marvels of mechanical skill and inventive genius. It was believed that the acme of perfection and speed had been reached, and that no further improvements would be possible. As a matter of fact, it would be a difficult matter to find one of these machines in operation in any part of the United States today. They have been completely driven out of existence during the past twenty years by the web perfecting press, a much faster and better machine in every way.

But what has been the result of these vast improvements in the printing press? Simply, that fast running machinery and improved methods have placed the daily newspaper within the reach of all, and this circumstance has been taken advantage of to so large an extent that the newspaper pressroom of today requires just as large a force of men and fully as much room as they formerly did. We do not have to seek far for the reason of this condition of affairs. Every measurable reduction in the cost of production has increased the consumption in a ratio that about equalizes matters all around in the end. It is said that history repeats itself, and why may not this be another instance where this interesting phenomenon is about to occur, and where the experiences attending the evolution of the printing press may be repeated in connection with the introduction of the typesetting machine. In the meantime, it will be the part of wisdom for every printer to make himself master of the details necessary to a successful operation of these machines. This much he owes to himself and those depending upon him.

RULEWORK.

BY A. R. A.

COGNIZANT of the fact that some printers have an idea that rulework is on the decline, I will endeavor to convince them to the contrary. If they will but "look backward" a few years — not necessarily a half a century, a score of years or less will suffice — they will see the vast strides rulework has taken. A few years ago the old brass flourishes were about the only ornamentation in rule that was

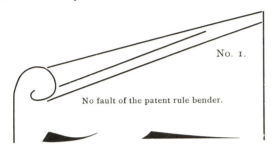

No. 1.

No fault of the patent rule bender.

attempted, and those were shaped at the foundry, except, perhaps, the plain straight rule used for borders around pages and labels, nearly all of which were also mitered and cut at the foundry; and the "artist" who could combine these already-manufactured designs in rule into "fantastic shapes" was indeed a "great artist," and looked upon by his fellow workmen with envy. But time brings many

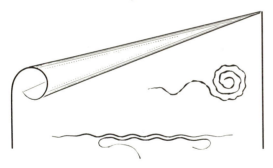

changes, which it undoubtedly has in rulework, and the artist of the past would have to do more than "build block houses" if he would want to keep pace with the artist of today. Go into any job office, large or small, and you will find printers with some pretensions as to rulework; even in the newspaper offices can be found the individual who, in a modest way, will resort to some original and appropriate design in rule when he gets the opportunity. Compare the foundry

specimen sheets of today with those of a few years ago, and see the varied designs in rule faces which have made their appearance of late, many of which

were copied from the work of the printer with original ideas, while some of the latest productions in metal can also be traced to his ingenuity; and still they say rulework is on the decline. Look over the field carefully, and I am sure that you will agree with me when I claim that rulework is on the increase instead of

on the decrease, and that rule is now more generally used for ornamenting jobwork than ever before.

Rulework is really the only branch of the printing business where a printer of artistic inclinations has an opportunity to show his good taste, because there is nothing that pleases the eye better than a well executed piece of rulework; and, then again, what is more abominable than rulework poorly done? There

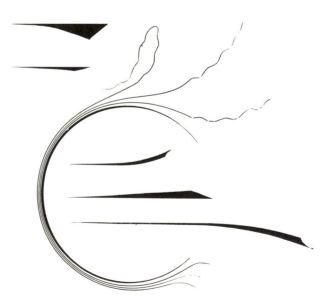

is no work, perhaps, in the printing line that will receive as much criticism as rulework (unless it be presswork), therefore, whatever is attempted with rule should be as near perfection as possible, and not hurried and thought "good enough." If you have not the time to do it right, if your foreman or employer will not give you the time to do the work, why, give them a good, plain job, which is ten times more preferable than a "poor ornamental job."

"Curves are really easy to make," so certain individuals claim ; but, judging from the efforts made at rule curving in the pamphlet from which the above quotation is taken, one would naturally think that

the "artist" could not have been sincere when he made the statement, as his specimens certainly do not look as though *he* found rule ornaments "really easy to make." Design marked No. 1 is a reproduction of one of his efforts — an improvement upon it, if anything — what do you think of it ? It is but one of many similar efforts with like results shown in his pamphlet.

No very extensive kit of tools is necessary to do your work. Nearly all offices are equipped with a mitering machine, rule cutter, curving machine and a vise, so that all that is necessary for a printer to supply

himself with is about three good files, tweezers, knife, small plyers, an old key or a saw set (which I find the best tools for kinking or waving rule). There are many new devices on the market to facilitate rulework, but with the above outfit you can accomplish as good results as desired ; if you cannot, the latest improvements will avail you nothing.

By glancing over the few specimens of rulework shown on this page, you will notice that we do not

have to rely entirely upon the products of the type-foundry to enable us to ornament our work. Dashes in great variety can be made, which you cannot buy at the foundry. Useful designs in all kinds of rule can

be made. Perhaps the most useful rule for light ornamentation is twelve-to-pica, it being the cheapest and easiest handled. It is unnecessary to anneal it, unless you want to make a very small curve. Heavier rule is, of course, better to work with when the temper is taken out of it. To do this hold it over a flame until it has a dead sound when struck by a piece of metal — in

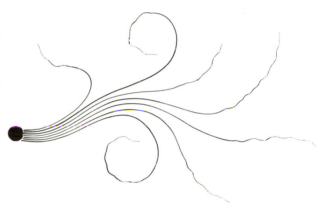

other words, when the ring is out of it — then lay it aside until cool.

When you get your curves or scrolls made, don't get them out of shape by locking up ; merely tighten sufficiently to keep them in place, being sure to get all the rule resting squarely on the stone, and then use plaster

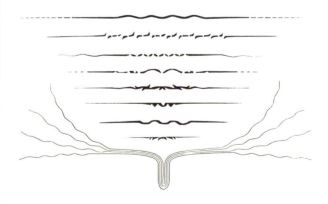

of paris ; don't be foolish and try to do without it ; it is cheap and saves time, and has no substitute.

The accompanying designs are not intended as great masterpieces, but only to show a few rule-curving designs which are useful, and may be used over and over again as long as properly taken care of.

ᴍMMᴹᴹ FARMER, LITTLE & Co., TYPE FOUNDERS, N. Y. ᴍMMᴹᴹ

NEW YORK, 63 & 65 BEEKMAN ST.
CORNER GOLD ST.

PATENT PENDING.

CHICAGO, 109 QUINCY STREET.
CHAS. B. ROSS, MANAGER.

FASHION EXTRA CONDENSED—12 POINT.   24 a 18 A—$3 00

EXTRA CONDENSED LETTERS ARE CONSTANTLY REQUIRED
We again Lead the Fashion with this Handsome New Addition to our Extra Condensed Jobbing Faces
The Fashion of the Hour 1234567890

FASHION EXTRA CONDENSED—18 POINT.   18 a 12 A—$3 50

JOB PRINTERS STILL ADMIRE THE FASHIONS
Fashions of Our Forefathers, dead and turned to clay, become again the Fashions of to-day
Triple Condensed 1234567890

FASHION EXTRA CONDENSED—24 POINT.   12 a 8 A—$3 50

THE FASHION FOR JOB PRINTERS
Experienced Printers know the Value of Extra Condensed Letters
Liabilities $12,345,678.00

FASHION EXTRA CONDENSED—30 POINT.   8 a 5 A—$3 50

NEW FASHION EXTRA CONDENSED
Extra Condensed News Items have lately become the Fashion
Mortgage $12,345,678.90

FASHION EXTRA CONDENSED—36 POINT.   6 a 4 A—$3 75

THE VERY TYPE OF FASHION
Swift Driving to the Race Course at Saratoga

THE TYPEFOUNDERS' TRUST

To the Editor :   BOSTON, Mass., September 8, 1891.

The newspapers this afternoon printed a dispatch from the Exposition City to the effect that a deal would be completed within the next twenty-four hours, whereby a trust would be formed, representing $18,000,000 in original sureties. It is to be a typefounders' trust, backed by an English syndicate. All the typefounders, the despatch said, of any consequence in America are in the deal, with the exception of one establishment in Chicago and perhaps two concerns in New York. The smallest concerns are to be squeezed out of existence.

This was shown to J. W. Phinney, of the Dickinson typefoundry of this city, who used some vigorous language when talking about the matter. He denied that any trust would be able to get control of the typefoundries in the United States and did not know anything about the English syndicate. He then went on to say : "We notice that about all the reported combinations of typefoundries come from Chicago, and we have thought it probable that with poor business pressing upon a concern, this concern takes this method to get a general advertising gratuitously. The public has had so many of these reports that have never materialized that it is hardly worth any paper's time and space to give this dispatch any extended consideration. We can quickly tell all we know about this so-called biggest of big deals : First, no deal has been completed for a trust. Second, no deal representing a trust will ever be completed in twenty-four hours or ever. Third, no trust has ever been thought of or considered. The truth and the whole truth of the matter is that in view of the large losses under which type has been manufactured and sold for the past two years, some year or more ago a meeting of the typefounders of the United States was held in New York, at which every typefoundry was represented, and, as a result of that meeting, a committee was appointed to devise some method for the general betterment of the business and to place it upon a secure and permanent foundation. In the report of this committee it was proposed to form one corporation for the purchase of all the typefoundry plants and businesses. The meeting accepted the report, discharged the committee and up to the present time no corporation has been formed, no application for one has been made and not a dollar has been promised or secured for such a purpose. That it is the one way out of the present business trouble all believe, but it is a big operation to successfully develop and complete, and no financial Moses has as yet appeared."

Mr. Rogers, of the Boston typefoundry, said there was some truth in the story of a type trust. He said : "I do not know who the English capitalists are behind this move, but the whole affair is being managed by a New York broker, C. De H. Brower, of 10 Wall street. He offered options which expired August 1, and which promised to be a good thing for the founders who might enter the combine. Our firm signed the agreement, but the whole matter fell through. Mr. Brower is now offering new options, but whether we will enter it now I do not know. We are holding it under advisement. I fancy there may have been greater difficulty in raising the necessary capital in England than the original projectors expected there would be. There are perhaps fifteen or twenty typefoundries in the United States of considerable importance. I should say $18,000,000 was an excessively high figure to value them at. Seven or eight millions would come nearer to it. It is all nonsense, however, that there is any combination contemplated that will squeeze the small concerns out of business."

This is what the two big Boston type concerns think about the matter. The wide divergence of facts and opinions are given not only for the information of your Chicago readers, where the news originated, but also for their amusement as well.   C. F. W.

[We subjoin an extract from the Chicago *Tribune* of September 8, giving the result of an interview with an official in one of the largest typefoundries in Chicago, which though almost a repetition of the matter above given, will not be without interest :

* * * * "I am not fully posted as to the recent developments, but it was originally intended that the English syndicate should advance $4,000,000 in cash. For this it was to get practical control of the combination. The owners of the foundries in the trust were to get this money, which represents two-thirds of the cash value of their plants. Then the foreign stockholders were to get the preferred stock of the trust, amounting to $4,000,000. Part of the common stock was to go to the original holders of the foundries. In addition to this they were to get two-thirds of the bonds to be issued, amounting to $6,000,000, these bonds to bear six per cent interest. The preferred stock was also to bear six per cent interest, and after this was paid the capital stock holders were to take whatever remained of the earnings. If this amounted to more than six per cent the preferred and capital stock were to participate equally up to the amount of eight per cent. If any remained over and above this it was to go to the holders of the capital stock. There may have been a few minor changes made in this, but I hardly think so. The amount of the whole deal is that the Americans are to take the minority of the stock and in a general way be retained as managers. The ultimate aim is to advance prices. Of the twenty-three typefoundries in the United States I don't think more than four or five have been making any money. The balance-sheets of some of the largest and oldest concerns in the East have shown a loss for years. This, of course, is what induced the formation of the trust."—ED.]

October 1891

Dickinson Type Foundery, Congress Street, Boston, Mass.

VIRILE SERIES
PATENT-APPLIED FOR
Virile Series lines accurately at the bottom. Justify with Point Leads and Slugs.

$3.00   12 POINT VIRILE   30 a, 16 A
OLD-FASHIONED MORNING GLORIES
Boarding Large Family for Summer Month 62

$3.50   18 POINT VIRILE   20 a, 12 A
MECHANICAL CONTRIVANCE
Disposed of £27 in British Golds

$4.00   24 POINT VIRILE   16 a, 10 A
NORTH CAMBRIDGE
Condensed Type Exhibited 8

$5.50   30 POINT VIRILE   12 a, 8 A
LARGE SQUADRON
Ruffian 4 Electrocuted

6.00   36 POINT VIRILE   10 a, 6 A
SEWING WORK
Quick Carpenters 5

$6.50   48 POINT VIRILE   8 a, 6 A
DICKINSONS
United States 7

$7.50   60 POINT VIRILE   6 a, 4 A
Quaint TAR 3

ERRATICK AND ERRATICK OUTLINE
PATENT APPLIED FOR
Erratick and Erratick Outline Series line accurately at the bottom.

40 a, 20 A 6 POINT $2.25	40 a, 20 A 6 POINT $2.25
BLOODLESS SHEEP	**BLOODLESS SHEEP**
23 Dilapitated Boneyards	23 Delapitated Boneyards

32 a, 20 A 8 POINT $2.50	32 a, 20 A 8 POINT $2.50
MISCHIEVOUS	**MISCHIEVOUS**
Established Itself 42	Established Itself 42

32 a, 16 A, $2.75   10 POINT   32 a, 16 A, $2.75

WIDE-AWAKE ADVERTISERS
Quickly Appreciate Attractive Type 8

24 a, 14 A, $3.00   12 POINT   24 a, 14 A, $3.00

ARTISTIC DESIGNER
Have Discovered the Adaptability

18 a, 10 A, $3.50   18 POINT   18 a, 10 A, $3.50

CRAZY RAVING
Enthusiastic Printers 7

12 a, 8 A, $4.00   24 POINT   12 a, 8 A, $4.00

WONDERFUL
Artistic 9 Advance

8 a, 6 A, $5.50   30 POINT   8 a, 6 A, $5.50

DESIGNING
Unique Style 2

6 a, 4 A, $6.00   42 POINT   6 a, 4 A, $6.00

AUCTION
Sunshade 4

5 a, 4 A, $7.50   48 POINT   5 a, 4 A, $7.50

CEASE
Heraldic 5

THE CONTEST OF COMPOSING MACHINES.

As arranged for by the American Newspaper Publishers' Association at its last annual meeting in New York City, last February, the test of devices for machine composition was held in the *Evening Post* Building, Chicago, October 12 to 24, 1891. The first week was devoted to the contest proper, and none were admitted but the committee in charge, and those connected directly with the test, or especially invited. During the second week the exhibition was open to the general public, and the attendance of printers, publishers and others interested was one of the largest that has ever gathered to witness a display of this kind. But four machines were entered and on exhibition, although it had been anticipated that twice this number would participate in the trial, they being the Mergenthaler "Linotype," the Rogers "Typograph," the McMillan Typesetting Machine, and the St. John "Typobar."

The committee appointed by the American Newspaper Publishers' Association to look after details of the tournament and determine which of the machines was "capable of producing the best practical results under ordinary newspaper conditions in well-managed offices," consisted of Frederick Driscoll, secretary and manager of the St. Paul *Pioneer Press*, W. J. Richards, business manager of the Indianapolis *News*, and E. H. Woods, president of the Boston *Herald*. These gentlemen were assisted in passing judgment on the work of the machines, and in keeping tally of the matter set by each, by Frank B. Moore, foreman of the St. Paul *Pioneer Press*, William Quinn, foreman of the Boston *Herald*, E. H. Perkins, foreman of the Indianapolis *News*, and Frank H. Ehlen, foreman of the Chicago *Herald*.

On the first day of the contest Mr. Moore was put in charge of the work of supplying copy to the operators and in looking after the make-up of the matter set, and Mr. Hugh T. Fisher, a compositor of large experience connected with the Chicago *Herald*, was assigned the work originally intended for Mr. Moore, which was the same as that of the other foremen, namely, to supervise each machine and note the actual time that the machine was in operation, the time it was stopped for repairs and the nature of such repairs, the speed of composition attained by the operator and the class of labor required to run the machine, the cost of maintaining and operating the machine, and to make a careful study of its mechanical construction with a view to learning its present and probable possibilities for doing the various kinds of newspaper composition. Remarks on these and other points of observation, together with the proofs and measurement of the composition of the operator were submitted daily by the foreman in charge of each machine to the committee. No foreman looked after the same machine two days in succession, and every endeavor was put forth by the committee to have the trial as fair and impartial to all concerned as lay in their power. The reports are now in the hands of the committee and the result of the trial will not be announced for some time, that a carefully revised statement may be rendered and presented to the members of the American Newspaper Publishers' Association before making the same public.

Although a full description of all the machines on trial, with the exception of the St. John Typobar, has already been published in the columns of THE INLAND PRINTER, it will no doubt be of interest to our readers to give a brief description of each at the present time, and in connection therewith a cut of each machine is shown. The gentlemen in charge of the four machines have kindly furnished a few lines of matter which are appended to the descriptions of the machines.

Following is a description of each machine taken from the report in the Chicago *Herald* of October 18.

MERGENTHALER LINOTYPE.

The "Linotype" (line of type) is the invention of Ottmar Mergenthaler, of Baltimore. The first patent was issued March 17, 1874, and there have been over a dozen issued to it since. A linotype machine is a type-making rather than a type-setting machine. Instead of using movable type it uses movable matrices, which are placed automatically to form a line of matrices, by which a solid line of type is cast. Each letter, space and punctuation mark has its individual matrix, which is made of brass. The die is cut into the edge of

the matrix at a certain distance from the bottom, so that when the matrices are in place the alignment of the dies is perfect.

The operator places the matrices in position by fingering a keyboard which resembles that of a typewriter. When a key is depressed, it permits the corresponding matrix to drop from the particular tube which contains a number of similar matrices and takes its proper position in the line formed in a holder on the left of the machine. A mark cut into the holder designates the

full length of the line of type which the machine is gauged to make. When the operator sees that the line is complete he presses a lever, and the assembled line of matrices and spaces is transferred to the face of the mold.

Sometimes the line is not quite long enough, and then the ingenious devices used to separate words come into play. These "justifiers" are slender wedges of steel. As the line of matrices moves toward the face of the mold the steel wedges are pushed up, and thus spread the matrices enough to make a full line.

Connected with the mold is a melting-pot containing molten type-metal, which is kept in a fluid condition by a Bunsen gas-burner. When the matrix for a line of type is in position the molten metal is fed automatically against its face, filling the mold, where it solidifies and becomes a linotype bar bearing on its edge in relief the characters corresponding to the line of matrices. An automatic stripping device withdraws the linotype bar, which is then placed automatically and trimmed to the right proportions and ejected onto the pile of linotypes previously made.

While all this is going on another automatic device lifts the line of matrices and justifiers and carries it to the top of the machine, where it is made to travel back over the row of tubes. As the line travels along the matrices are distributed automatically, each matrix finding its own tube, into which it drops, ready to be used again.

The editor of the Inland Printer having requested the operator of the "Linotype" in use at the exhibition in Chicago to "set" a few lines to show the working of the machine, these lines are herewith submitted as specimens of the average every-day work produced by that machine.

ROGERS TYPOGRAPH.

The Rogers Typograph was invented by J. R. Rogers, of Cleveland, Ohio, September 4, 1888, many improvements having been made on the machine since. Of these a number have been suggested by Mr. F. E. Bright, the superintendent of the Rogers Typograph Company's factory. In its latest improved form it consists of two parts, an assemblage and distributing mechanism, and the casting mechanism. The assembling and distributing mechanism consists essentially of wires, which spread out in fan shape at their rear portion and converge into a common vertical plane in front. These wires are fastened to a light iron frame, which is pivoted so as to tip forward and back something like a Remington typewriter carriage. This frame and the wires it supports stand at an angle of about thirty-five degrees. On these wires, at their upper or rear extremity, are the matrices suspended by an eye. They are strung on the wire like beads on a string, all those of the same letter being on one wire. By a very simple mechanism the matrices are released by touching a key on the keyboard, precisely like a typewriter. The matrices then by their own gravity slide down the wires to the forward portion of the machine, where the wires are in the common plane before mentioned. When a line is assembled, the casting mechanism comes into play. This consists of two parts. First the mold, which is brought forward against the matrices, or female type. This mold has an aperture just the size of a line of type. The secondary part of the casting mechanism is the melting pot, which contains about thirty pounds of stereotype metal, kept in a liquid state by a small gas burner. The melting pot has a spout adapted to fit into the mold, and also a force-pump attachment which ejects the metal into the mold and the faces of the matrices by the operation of the machine. When the line has been assembled by touching the keys on the frame before described, thereby assembling into a line side by side the matrices, the mold comes forward against these matrices, the spout of the melting pot closes into the mold, the force pump in the melting pot ejects just enough metal to fill the aperture in the mold, making a typebar, or stereotype line plate, or, in printers' phraseology, a "slug" bearing the characters on its edge to print a single line. The melting pot is then withdrawn, the mold opens and the completed line, hard and solid, though still warm to the touch, is shoved by a mechanical finger into a galley. The wire

frame containing the matrices is then tilted back and the matrices slide back simultaneously by their own weight, so that the assemblage and distribution are both accomplished by gravitation. This is the simplest possible method of assemblage and distribution, and is the most prominent feature of the machine. The spacing is automatically accomplished by little discs about an inch and a quarter in diameter, which are thrown in by the action of a key between each word. These spacers are composed of two screw-shaped faces, which, when the cam is caused to revolve, spread the line to a pre-determined limit. This is done entirely by the machine, and the operator pays no attention to it. There are a number of other devices upon the machine, one of which is very simple and yet important. By its action the machine will not work unless the operator has put in the right number of spaces and letters to fill the line. In case too many or not enough are put in, the machine refuses to work, so that accidents upon it are almost impossible.

The Rogers Typograph casts lines or "slugs" o metal. These lines are shown as specimens o those turned out by that machine, and were produced at the request of the editor o the Inland Printer on October 22, 1891.

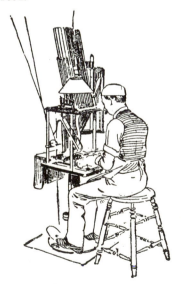

M'MILLAN TYPESETTING MACHINE.

The McMillan typesetting machine was invented by J. L. McMillan, of Ilion, New York. The inventor is a native of New York, having been born at Cambridge thirty-two years ago. The McMillan system of mechanical composition has been a growth from a small beginning, which dates back to the year 1883, when the first attempt to set type mechanically was made by the present company. The first machine which left the works was sent to the office of the Utica *Morning Herald* in 1885. An important feature of the typesetting machine is that the keyboard is an exact reproduction of the

Remington typewriter, an advantage that can be enjoyed by no other company. Owing to the small number of keys used and the consequent conciseness of the keyboard, operators acquire skill in much less time than is required to learn large keyboards. Remington stenographers readily adapt themselves to the machine. The forty keys of the board communicate with the eighty characters in precisely the same manner as a typewriter. The typesetting machine is quite compact, the parts are all accessible, the motions seem positive and safe, the pressure of the keys very easy, approximating a typewriter in this respect. The line of set-up matter is directly in front of the operator, and he may see every letter take its place, add any character not in the machine or make a correction when wrong keys are struck. For daily newspaper work the machines are made with the justifying attachment fastened to the frame and the type is justified as fast as set up, but for book, magazine and periodical work not requiring special dispatch a separate justifying machine is provided. On this latter class the operator of the typesetting machine sets the matter into a "storage galley," which is provided with a number of walls about 24 inches in length which serve to separate the lines. As soon as a galley is filled it is removed and a fresh one put on the machine. The filled galley is then proved, corrected and taken to the justifying machine, which feeds the long lines automatically to the spacer, who justifies it into lines of the required length. The distributing machine occupies perhaps a little more room than two ordinary type frames. It distributes from 10,000 to 25,000 ems per hour, owing to the size of the type. The distributor consists of a rotary disk which has eighty-five inside distributing radial channels. The type are distributed, by means of nicks on their side, directly into removable brass channels, and are all ready for use on the typesetting machines. The wards that make the combinations for the nicks are small rolls at the mouths of the outside or receiving channels. The rolls, like the outside and inside sectors, are of hardened steel. The inside channels are straight grooves in which the type is placed with a follower and spring to hold the type against the rolls or wards by which the type passes into the receiving channels. Where the machine is used as an adjunct to hand composition the type are deposited into tin boxes which are emptied

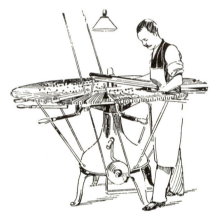

M'MILLAN TYPE DISTRIBUTING MACHINE.

into the compositors' cases. When so used the size of the distributor is reduced one-half. The type is specially nicked for the distributor, and each type has two little nicks on its body. They vary in depth from two hundredths of an inch on the nonpareil bodies up to three hundredths of an inch on small pica. When new fonts are used they are cast with a nick near the heel of the type, and the machine nicks are made at intervals on the same side, but old fonts have to be nicked on the opposite side. The face of the type does not come in contact with anything in either the typesetter or the distributor, and it is probable that fine text types will wear much longer than when "thrown in" by hand compositors.

These lines are set and furnished THE INLAND PRINTER as a sample of the composition done upon the McMillan Typesetting Machine, at the public exhibition given in Chicago, in October, 1891. The McMillan was the only typesetting machine in the contest held at the above time.

ST. JOHN TYPOBAR.

The St. John Typobar is the construction of R. H. St. John, of Cleveland, Ohio. Mr. St. John is a native of the Buckeye State and is fifty-nine years old. When a boy he learned the trade of watchmaker and jeweler, which he followed for fifteen years, since which time he has been a mechanical engineer. The "typobar" constructed by him was first patented September 2, 1890. Many improvements have since been patented, but the principle and general form of the machine remains as his mind first conceived it. The typobar is the only exponent of the cold metal process or cold type bar. The producing of the line of matrices which form the type, the justification of the line, and the distribution of the matrices after use, are done automatically, and require only one second in the operation. The action of assembling the matrices is positive and practically instantaneous; they all travel the same distance, guided to their positions by the same kind of mechanism and the same amount of force, and only in the order of their releasing. In case the wrong matrix is released an ingenious device permits of a correction being made before completing the line. The absence of all heat above the machine avoids all danger of molecular adhesion of two metals brought together in a heated condition whereby the line of type would be made defective. Likewise there is an absence of all evils attendant upon continual heating and chilling of the matrices and the parts surrounding the impression chamber. As the line of type is formed from cold metal, by compression, there is no expense for gas or other means for melting metals. The type bar is made up

of two parts; one, a permanent base or blank, to be used over and over, and is in theory part of the machine, the other part being a slight strip of type metal, in the nature of a supply, which is mounted upon the edge of the blank simultaneously with the operation of impressing the characters upon it. This type-metal strip is removed from the bar after use and may be remelted and reformed for further use at a very slight expense and without appreciable loss of metal. Moreover, the compression process insures with absolute certainty that every type-bar shall be perfect, as there can be no air bubbles, blisters, chilled metal or defect of impression. The machines are built of the best materials to be obtained for the several parts, and are especially reënforced at points bearing the greatest strain. All the operations of the machine being positive, direct and automatic, the speed and correctness of the results depend only upon the skill and intelligence of the operator, as the machine will respond to all the demands of the operator. The machine is operated with a keyboard, on the principle of the Remington typewriter. The adoption of the point system of types allies the type bodies to this generally accepted principle. The spacing is done on an entirely new principle, which opposes to the adjacent matrices two sides, which are held as immovable as the matrices themselves, and between which the movable part of the spacer is pushed, thereby avoiding any displacement of the alignment, or of the impression surface of the bar. The company is thoroughly protected by numerous patents.

> **The St. John Typobar produces lines of type by the cold process, these few lines show the character of the slugs made by that machine. The date on which these slugs were made was Oct. 22, 1891, being one of the days of the public exhibitino. The machine on which they were made was the first or experimental machine.**

As will be noted by reference to the illustrations and by a careful reading of the descriptions, the four machines vary considerably in appearance and in manner of producing results, the two nearest alike being the "Linotype" and the "Typograph." In justice to the inventor of the "Typobar" it is only proper to state that the machine on exhibition was the first one built and was really an experiment to a certain extent, so that the results attained by that machine in comparison with the others are not to be taken as a guide to what may yet be accomplished when it is more nearly perfected.

THE SPEED OF TYPESETTING MACHINES.

We are indebted to *L'Imprimerie*, says the *British and Colonial Stationer and Printer*, for the following details respecting typesetting machines : The Kastenbein machine can compose 70,000

letters a day at a cost (for wages, etc.) of 9s. 2d.; the Burr, 90,000 letters, at a cost of 20s. 10d.; the Thorne, 90,000 letters, at a cost of 10s. The price of the Kastenbein, with two distributers, is £300, and it requires five attendants—a compositor, a justifier, two distributers, and an assistant. The Burr, with two distributers, costs £1,000, and requires four attendants—a compositor, a justifier, and two assistants. The Thorne, with one distributer, costs £340, and requires three attendants—a compositor, a justifier, and an assistant. The price of the Winder composing machine is £20, and it is advertised as being able to compose 5,000 letters an hour. The distributing apparatus for the same machine is said to be able to distribute 9,000 letters an hour, and costs £100. The production of the Rogers typograph machine, constructed after the Linotype pattern, is limited only by the ability of the operator. The inventor asserts that it is easy to attain a speed of 8,000 to 8,500 letters an hour. The machine occupies but little more space than a sewing-machine. The metal pot contains about 30 lbs. of metal, and 6 cubic feet of gas per hour are needed to keep it in a state of fusion. The operator can work the machine with the pedal, when the production is half less than when driven by steam.

THE EFFECT OF TYPESETTING MACHINES.

To the Editor :   PRINCETON, Ind., October 18, 1891.

"Who can doubt but what the art of printing, so far as the compositor's relation thereto, is on the verge of a revolution or radical change?" asks Mr. S. K. Parker in the October INLAND PRINTER.

There seems to be a unanimity of opinion upon the question of the great change coming, but quite a diversity as to what will be the result as affecting the compositor.

The outcome of the contest of the several machines for typesetting, in progress in Chicago at the time of this writing, is awaited with the deepest interest by printers and publishers the world over. Whether or not these machines now on trial prove the practical success hoped for by their respective owners, it seems to be a foregone conclusion among printers everywhere that typesetting by machinery is bound to come, and come to stay, and that its coming is very near at hand ; and also that if the machines now under trial do not fill the bill, others will be made, or these improved, until "just the thing" is found. Then will the revolution take place ; in all the offices of the whole country, where any considerable amount of type is to be set, these machines will be put to work in place of the compositor. As far back as twenty years ago, to my knowledge, printers conceded that the typesetting machine had cast its shadow before and was certainly one of the coming events, and at that time the average compositor looked upon its coming with more or less fear and trembling, lest his occupation should go glimmering with the advent of the machine.

Now, however, I believe the hand workmen in general look in a different light upon the invasion ; many think it does not come as a menace, though others do. So far as my individual opinion goes I would welcome its coming as a relief from the tedious monotony of every-day sameness, the bane of the compositor's life, namely, the composition and distribution of "straight matter." With the machine typesetter in practical service, the hardworking typo's life will contain more of the spice of change, his labor will be more varied and therefore more cheerful, nor will there be any material lessening in the demand for his labor. The machine will never be made to set display advertisements nor job forms ; nor will it in the next thousand years be able to set even straight matter complete, without the assistance of the compositor, that is, to "justify" the lines, correct errors and make the matter absolutely ready for the forms.

In short, the occupation of the compositor is, in my humble opinion, improving in aspect, and it will never wane until they *get to making machinery with brains in it.*   D. McD. K.

Columbian.

Registered, No. 178,262.
Mechanical Patent, March 31, 1885.

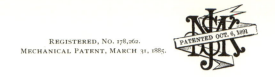

24 Point Columbian.   8 A, 28 a, $4.40

Important Notice
from the
Fool-killer Co.

We have labored heroically to rid the world of fools, but must abandon the impossible task. Still wishing to assist in reforming mankind, we have bought some heavy, hobnailed Boots, and ask those whose conduct has been culpable, and who wish to be kicked, to call on us after 12 m. and we will perform the job Gratuitously

48 Point Columbian.   4 A, 6 a, $6.70

Thirty=fourth Centennial Jubilee
Landing of Icelanders in North America
Wednesday, September 29

30 Point Columbian   6 A, 16 a, $5.10

Attention, ==
Marriageable ==
Damsels! ==

Having squandered his Fortune
the subscriber is
Anxious to Reform, but Needs the Help
of a young woman with
Wealth to Carry on the Process

The MacKellar, Smiths & Jordan Co. { Nos. 606-614 Sansom Street, Philadelphia.
Western Branch: 328-330 Dearborn Street, Chicago.

BOSTON SCRIPT.

AMERICAN SYSTEM OF
INTERCHANGEABLE TYPE BODIES.

9A, 25a,   18 Point Boston Script.   6.00

Yourself and friends are cordially invited to attend the

Opening Exercises of the Northwestern Conservatory of Music, which will be

345   Held at the Auditorium 678

Friday Evening, September Twenty-fifth, at eight

7A, 20a,   24 Point Boston Script.   8.00

In the Selection of a Series of Script

Printers should choose one suitable for all kinds of work

None better than the Boston Script

5A, 15a,   36 Point Boston Script.   10.00

Adapted to all Requirements

Graceful Curves and Perfect Shading

$1234567890

4A, 10a,   48 Point Boston Script.   12.00

Specimen of Writing

Gem City Business College

Fall term 1891

MARDER, LUSE & CO., CHICAGO, MINNEAPOLIS and OMAHA.

A TOPOGRAPHICAL DESCRIPTION OF EVERY COUNTY, TOGETHER WITH THE
ANTIQUITIES OF THE SAME. FULL OF CURIOUS REMARKS.
RESULTS OF PERSONAL EXPERIENCE. 1891.

$3.50.　　　　TWO-LINE BOURGEOIS ORNAMENTED, NO. 1,091.　　　　12 A

NUMISMATIC AND OTHER CRUMBS.
AN EXMOOR SCOLDING AND AN EXMOOR COURTSHIP.
ARTIC NAVIGATORS. 123456.

$4.95.　　　　TWO-LINE PICA ORNAMENTED, NO. 1,091.　　　　10 A

ORGANISMS IN ORGANIC INFUSIONS.
ACHROMATIC TELESCOPES.
ISOMETRICAL PERSPECTIVE. $827.

$7.35.　　　　TWO-LINE GREAT-PRIMER ORNAMENTED, NO. 1,091.　　　　8 A

LITERARY AND SCIENTIFIC.
OLD MORTALITY. 1891.

$6.85.　　　　FOUR-LINE PICA ORNAMENTED, NO. 1,091.　　　　5 A

ELECTRO-MAGNETS.
DECEMBER. 148.

GEORGE BRUCE'S SON & CO., TYPE-FOUNDERS, NO. 13 CHAMBERS-STREET, NEW-YORK.

$1.45. Two-line Nonpareil Orna'd, No. 1,089. 15 A

REPERTORY OF ARTS AND MANUFACTURES.

XPERIMENTS TO MEASURE THE VELOCITY OF LIGHTNING.

OBSERVATIONS OF COMETS.

ON REAL AND IMAGINARY ROOTS OF ALGEBRAICAL

NOTES. BAROMETER MANUAL. 123456.

$1.75. Two-line Bourgeois Orna'd, No. 1,089. 12 A

JOURNAL OF SCIENCE AND ART.

MANUAL OF LAND AND FRESH WATER SHELLS

LETTERS AND EXTRACTS.

13 CHAMBERS-STREET, NEW-YORK,

$2.25. TWO-LINE PICA ORNAMENTED, NO. 1,089. 10 A

FOREIGN MEDICAL AND CHEMICAL SCIENCE.

MICROSCOPIC ILLUSTRATIONS OF LIVING OBJECTS. INSTRUCTIONS AND EXPLANATIONS.

SANDSTONE OF THE ATLANTIC SLOPES. 1891.

$3.45. TWO-LINE GREAT-PRIMER ORNAMENTED, NO. 1,089. 8 A

NEW EXPLANATIONS OF THE EBBING AND FLOWING OF THE SEA.

THOUGHTS ON A PEBBLE. $786.

$3.05. FOUR-LINE PICA ORNAMENTED, NO. 1,089. 5 A

THE LIVES OF THE NOBLE GREEKS AND ROMANS

A PILL TO PURGE STATE MELANCHOLY 1891.

GEORGE BRUCE'S SON & CO., TYPE-FOUNDERS, NO. 13 CHAMBERS-STREET, NEW-YORK.

Lack of Steam Communication.

All Consular Reports from South America

agree upon the lack of Direct

American Steam Communication to the

United States.   1891.

Topographical Engineering.

Annual United States Register

National Insurance Co.

Did it ever Occur to You? 92.

Genealogical Memoirs of Celebrated Families.

The Ninth Annual Report of the Board of Education.

Bank Report.   Dividend, $2,500.

My son, Emulate the Mule: it is backward

in Deeds of Violence.

A Pickle for the Knowing Ones. 1892.

Lives of Eminent Americans.

Weeping Water. 1891.

$2.90. TWO-LINE NONPAREIL ORNAMENTED, NO. 1,090. 15 A

ENVOYS EXTRAORDINARY AND MINISTERS PLENIPOTENTIARY.
RULES OF THE COLUMBUS, CINCINNATI AND INDIANAPOLIS RAILROADS.
POPULATION OF THE UNITED STATES. 1891.

$3.50. TWO-LINE BOURGEOIS ORNAMENTED, NO. 1,090. 12 A

MANUFACTURERS OF PRINTING TYPES.
OUR BALANCE OF TRADE AND FOREIGN INDEBTEDNESS.
DOLLARS CAN BE SAVED BY CALLING ON US. 1891.

$5.60. TWO-LINE PICA ORNAMENTED, NO. 1,090. 10 A

THE BOOK PUBLISHING TRADE.
PLANS OF RAILROAD CONSTRUCTION.
COMMERCIAL BANKERS. $28,900.

$8.40. TWO-LINE GREAT-PRIMER ORNAMENTED, NO. 1,090. 8 A

BITUMINOUS SUBSTANCES.
MOOR OF VENICE. 1891.

$7.75. FOUR-LINE PICA ORNAMENTED, NO. 1,090. 5 A

BUSINESS CAPITAL
NEW-YORK, $18.

GEORGE BRUCE'S SON & CO., TYPE-FOUNDERS, No. 13 CHAMBERS-STREET, NEW-YORK.

Black Cap.

30 A. 8 POINT BLACK CAP. $1.60

AERIAL DETONATING COMPANY
FERTILIZERS OF PARCHED PLANTATIONS
RAINBOW MANUFACTURERS
1234567890

22 A. 12 POINT BLACK CAP. $1.85

FURNISHED ON DEMAND
DRIZZLE, OR DRIVING RAINFALL
1234567890

16 A. 18 POINT BLACK CAP. $2.35

FIELDS WATERED
BOULEVARDS DRENCHED
1234567890

12 A. 24 POINT BLACK CAP. $2.95

GROUND SPRINKLED

9 A. 30 POINT BLACK CAP. $3.15

AVENUES SOAKED

7 A. 36 POINT BLACK CAP. $3.70

INUNDATIONS

5 A. 48 POINT BLACK CAP. $4.65

RAIN DROPS

Giraffe Extended.

PATENTED.

8 A. 18 POINT GIRAFFE EXTENDED. $2.15

BRIGHT RUBIES

6 A. 24 POINT GIRAFFE EXTENDED. $2.70

ARABESQUES

5 A. 30 POINT GIRAFFE EXTENDED. $3.20

GARNETS

3 A. 36 POINT GIRAFFE EXTENDED. $3.75

MINERAL

25 A. 6 POINT GIRAFFE EXTENDED. $1.50

SPANGLE, BEDIZEN & GARNISH
DIAMONDS FOR SUMMER RESORT VISITORS
PECUNIOUS PEOPLE EMBLAZONED
1234567890

20 A. 8 POINT GIRAFFE EXTENDED. $1.50

BOMBASTIC CHARLATANS
JUBILANT DAMES AND DAMSELS
DRESSED FOR PARADE
1234567890

12 A. 12 POINT GIRAFFE EXTENDED. $1.55

PERTURBATION
BEAUTIFUL SAPPHIRES
CONFISCATED

The MacKellar, Smiths & Jordan Co. { Nos. 606-614 Sansom Street, Philadelphia.
{ Western Branch: 328-330 Dearborn Street, Chicago.

THE TYPEFOUNDERS' COMBINATION EFFECTED.

The long talked of combination of American typefoundries has culminated in the incorporation under the laws of the state of New Jersey of the American Typefounders' Company, for the purpose of uniting and controlling the different foundries of the United States. This combination is expected to include every prominent foundry in the country, eighty-five per cent of the foundries now composing it. The capital stock of the company will be fixed when operations commence. The following gentlemen have been elected directors: Robert Allison, president; William B. MacKellar, vice-president; G. Frederick Gordon, eastern manager; John Marder, western manager, and A. T. H. Brower, secretary. It had been considered that incorporation papers would be applied for under the laws of the state of Illinois, but the frequent and radical changes in the incorporation laws of the West and of Illinois in particular rendered the more stable legislation of New Jersey preferable. It is anticipated that the price of type will be advanced in the near future.

AMERICAN TYPEFOUNDERS' COMPANY.

SINCE the announcement in the daily press last month that the long-talked-of combination of typefounders had been consummated, numerous letters have been received at this office from employing printers in which the fear is expressed that the combination will be detrimental to their interests. This anxiety is perhaps natural enough, but it is anxiety previous to inquiry and investigation. The foundries in the combine are reticent as to the progress and development of the operations of the association beyond expatiating on the benefits to accrue to the printers from its incorporation, but this does not soothe the feeling of uneasiness that prevails. Much of this feeling was expressed in a well-written article on page 722 of the May issue of this journal in 1891, the leading idea in which was a deprecation of the typefounding industry in America being dominated by British capital and British brains. The benefit of bringing under one corporate ownership all the typefoundries of the United States, it was stated, would consist in a simplification of business whereby production would be governed and expenses reduced in the aggregate, but that the greatest item of economy would be found in contracting the output of individual foundries or confining each to certain special lines. Two or three good series of old style and modern would be standard, and could be purchased from any branch of the corporation in the United States, and by this method, said the writer, sorts of every description could be kept in stock in large quantities, and be a great convenience to printers.

To these anticipated advantages we might add, for the purpose of a disinterested review of the situation, that the present method of extending credit to irresponsible parties so perniciously common at the present time might be controlled. It also might not be considered advisable as good policy to carry on the business of an inextricably involved debtor and compete actively with the patrons of the typefoundry branch, as is the custom at present with some foundries. It might prevent the fluctuation of prices of type, so that an employing printer might have an approximate idea of the value of his plant, though it might not govern the practice of charging the cash customer the full rate, and giving the long-time man a cut price.

If the monopoly, combine, trust or association becomes oppressive, it may be possible to establish other foundries despite the "enormous cost of the plant, and the extremely low profits." Organization is applicable to all industries, and the Typothetæ might find it expedient to devise means of procuring type supplies at a moderate rate. An effectual check might be thus placed upon exorbitant prices.

SPECIMENS OF TYPE FROM THE DE VINNE PRESS.

When the Prince of American Printers sets out to compliment a customer he does it handsomely. In issuing his very elaborate catalogue of Roman and Italic Printing Types, Mr. Theodore L. De Vinne has far surpassed all his previous efforts in the souvenir line, painstaking and tasteful as those were. The undertaking must have been a costly one. It is not simply a dry catalogue enumerating the different fonts of type in use by the De Vinne Press, but an exceedingly handsome volume of 145 pages, including title, of page selections, gathered from a great variety of sources, from Richard de Bury to the New York *Sun*, and printed from as many varieties of type. Some idea of the magnitude of the work may be given by stating that there are ninety-four illuminated initials beginning as many different selections, and printed in every conceivable color. The writer has examined at least two copies of the work very carefully, and is unable to detect a single fault in the printing of these illuminated initials. The title-page is all in black, except the printers' device, which is illuminated. Then follows on third page a note from the printers, in which they state, among other things, that "an effort has been made to contrast the old style and modern cuts of letter on opposing pages. To facilitate a comparison of effects the sizes most frequently used are shown in three forms — solid, leaded, and double-leaded. Initials have been inserted to show how an otherwise unattractive page may be brightened." This is sufficiently modest, surely. Following, on the fifth page, we find some very pertinent information in the nature of general rules on "the number of words in a square inch"; "make-up of a book"; "relative sizes of types"; "relative values of bindings"; "customary sizes of books"; "about manuscripts"; "title-page and preface"; and "the expense of printing a book." The editor must be a scholarly reader, else he could not have filled so many pages with selections, all bearing directly on the subject of type, paper, engraving, ink-making and bookmaking generally. In these selections is a vast fund of useful information culled from the most authoritative sources. One is often struck by the appropriateness of the type used to the selection chosen — as, for instance, what could lend greater dignity and impressiveness to the quotation from Swift, "When a proud man keeps me at my distance, it is comforting to see him keep at his, also," than the use of "Four-line Pica Roman, Quadruple Leaded"? But was it not a sly touch of humor that led the editor to print on page 97 a long quotation from the *Saturday Review* (London) anent tall copies, editions de luxe, etc., and then follow it on page 117 with an almost verbatim reprint (unacknowledged) from *Paper and Print*. Aside from its value as a guide to the "trade" and the customers of the De Vinne Press, the Specimen Book of Printing Types would be invaluable to the general book-loving public, but we must inform the gentle book-lover that he is likely to be disappointed if he tries to procure a copy, as it is reserved only for the elect. But few copies have been printed for private circulation, and it is not for sale. A free translation of the Greek in the De Vinne Press device may interest the curious.

> "The wealth of Numbers to the world I gave,
> With Letters ranged in mystical array;
> And Memory with sweet mother-care to save
> All art — all wisdom — changeless and for aye!"

Cast by the Dickinson Type Foundery, Boston, Mass.

SIX NEW SIZES OF DE VINNE ARE NOW BEING CUT

THE DE VINNE,— COMPANION SERIES TO HOWLAND

$2.25   6 POINT DE VINNE   36 a, 24 A

RELIABLE PHELPS, DALTON AND COMPANY

Dickinson Electrotype Foundery, 150 Congress Street, Boston
Wide awake and Enterprising Concerns

Cast by Dickinson Type Foundery

$3.00   12 POINT DE VINNE   20 a, 16 A

SPECIALLY DESIRABLE

Companion of Great Durability 73

Latest Production Howland

$2.50   8 POINT DE VINNE   30 a, 22 A

TYPE OF BUSINESS BRINGING POWER

Fresh Productions in $495 Borders and Ornaments
Send for Latest Specimen Book

Cast by Dickinson Type Foundery

$2.75   10 POINT DE VINNE   26 a, 20 A

PRESENT TREMENDOUS SHIPMENTS

Taking Designs Quickly Utilized by Printers
Renowned Reputation Gained 1892

Cast by Dickinson Type Foundery

$3.25   18 POINT DE VINNE   16 a, 10 A

LONGLIVED AND HONEST DEALING

Manufactured and Sold 47 Dickinson Type Foundery

Laborsaving Advertising Letters

Cast by Dickinson Type Foundery

$4.00   24 POINT DE VINNE   10 a, 8 A

SERVICEABLE MANUFACTURE

Howland De Vinne 36 Furnish Outfits

Cast by Dickinson Type Foundery

$5.50   36 POINT DE VINNE   8 a, 5 A

GREAT WONDERS

Continued $82 Prosperity

Cast by Dickinson Type Foundery

$7.75   48 POINT DE VINNE   5 a, 4 A

RELIABILITY

Numerous Devices 4

Cast by the Dickinson Type Foundery, Boston, Mass.

THE HOWLAND,— COMPANION SERIES TO DE VINNE

$2.25   6 POINT HOWLAND   50 a, 30 A

RELIGIOUS AND BUSINESS COMBINATION FORMED

Reducing Cost of Manufacture   3902   Labor Controlled Wholly

$2.50   8 POINT HOWLAND   40 a, 28 A

NONSENSICAL PRESIDENTIAL ABSURDITY

Womans Rights Advocated   43   Hopeless Contest Opened

$3.00   12 POINT HOWLAND   30 a, 20 A

BEAUTIFUL SPRINGTIME

Holiday Attire of Boston Public Park 5

$2.75   10 POINT HOWLAND   36 a, 24 A

ELEVATED RAILWAYS CONDEMNED

Advancing Civilization Demands Improvement 12

$3.25   18 POINT HOWLAND   20 a, 12 A

MANUFACTURED BY DICKINSON TYPE FOUNDERY

Plain, Strong, Clear, Eye-Delighting   92   Suitable for Great Variety of Work

$4.00   24 POINT HOWLAND   16 a, 10 A

REDUCING EXPENSIVE BLUNDERING

Deserving Chastisement   £64   Unreliable Engravers

$5.00   30 POINT HOWLAND   12 a, 8 A

ANTIQUATED STYLES DISCARDED

Desirable Selection $50 Companion Series

$6.00   42 POINT HOWLAND   10 a, 6 A

HORIZONTAL MECHANISM

American Youth 23 Conquor Ambition

$7.00   48 POINT HOWLAND   8 a, 5 A

PHELPS AND DALTON

Enterprising 48 Manufacturers

FARMER, LITTLE & CO.,

NEW YORK, 63 & 65 BEEKMAN ST.
CORNER GOLD ST.

TYPE FOUNDERS.

CHICAGO, 109 QUINCY STREET.
CHAS. B. ROSS, MANAGER.

THIS ABBEY SERIES was issued by our Firm—Caps only—several years ago. We now add the Lower Case Characters. Customers who desire to complete their Fonts can order to suit, as the New Lower Case "Lines" with the Original Caps.

8 POINT ABBEY No. 2.   PATENT PENDING.   30 a 20 A—$2 50

GREAT EXCITEMENT IN THE COAL MARKET
Tintern Abbey seems Far More Beautiful in Decay than in its Time of Prosperity
Held in Abeyance until 1893

10 POINT ABBEY No. 2.   24 a 18 A—$2 75

MONUMENT IN WESTMINISTER ABBEY
Rapid Transit Obstacles and Obstructions Disappearing before the Electric Motor
Columbian Fair of 1893

12 POINT ABBEY No. 2.   18 a 12 A—$2 75

NOVELTIES FOR THE JOB PRINTER
The Sterling Character of Our Job Faces Insure their Popularity
Leap-Year 1892

18 POINT ABBEY No. 2.   12 a 8 A—$3 25

HANDSOME OLD STYLES
The History of the Ancient Abbeys of the Old World
Published in 1892

24 POINT ABBEY No. 2.   10 a 6 A—$4 00

OUR ORIGINAL FACE
Hospitable Reception at Abbey Gate
Time 1298

36 POINT ABBEY No. 2.   6 a 4 A—$5 50

MELROSE ABBEY
Famous in the Olden Days
Charm 826

10A, $1.20. 16a, $1.20.   12 POINT WHITTIER.   Complete Font, $2.40

LAUGH AND THE WORLD
Laughs with You Weep and You Weep
$1234567890

8A $2.00. 12a, $1.75   18 POINT WHITTIER.   Complete Font, $3.75

ALONE BE GLAD
And Your Friends are all
$1234567890
Happy

Artistic Type Faces .

Cleveland Type Foundry,
THE H. H. THORP MANUFACTURING CO.
CLEVELAND, OHIO.

Type
Printing Material
Presses

6A, $2.35. 10a, $2.40.   24 POINT WHITTIER.   Complete Font, $4.75

BUT ALONE
You Must Drink $19

4A, $2.90. 6a, $2.35.   30 POINT WHITTIER.   Complete Font, $5.25

ORIGINAL DESIGNS
348 In Type Faces 509

4A, $3.30. 5a, $2.00.   36 POINT WHITTIER.   Complete Font, $5.50

THE ART
30 Preservative of Arts 45

PRINTING IN THE FUTURE.

BY O. V. L.

THE hand compositors on straight composition may as well recognize at once that the typesetting machine will make great inroads into their occupation in the near future. It is useless for the compositors or others to deny this fact, even to themselves, and hug the delusion that the machines cannot be made a success. It is within the nature of progress in the perfecting of machinery that reasonably perfect and practical typesetting machines will soon be quite extensively introduced.

Then what is the long-headed and far-seeing compositor of the present to do to keep up with the progress of the world, and not to become a "back number"? Let him make a study of the different typesetting machines theoretically, and gather such information as he may be able to gather from printed descriptions and instructions. It, of course, would be better still, if he has the opportunity, to make a practical study of a machine, and become an operator upon it. The progress of the machine will resemble, in many respects, the progress made by the typewriter, and the persons who first become operators upon them will be the ones to reap the most benefit from their introduction. And who is more fitted to become operators than the hand compositors?

Already, even though the present typesetting machines are crude samples of mechanism, they are being very extensively experimented with in the larger offices and with quite satisfactory results as to saving in cost of composition and gain in speed.

No fear may be entertained, I think, that the typesetting machine will affect job composition further than as to bookwork. And, also, the compositor of display advertisements and setter of headings upon the newspaper need not fear the machine, as it is conceded that the machine is not capable of doing such work as theirs. But another art is menacing the job compositor, and that is the art of photo-engraving or zinc etching. More and more will the products of the pen and ink designer and artist, assisted by the etcher, take the place of curve line and "fancy" job composition. Soon the job printer will rely more upon the zinc etchings for attaining pleasing effects than he will rely upon rule twisting, bending, or whatever you may term it. The compositor will have appropriate illustrations of suitable size to intersperse in the body of the job, work off the edges of the paper, work in tints, etc. The type line then will be plain and straight. Not only will the compositor have illustrations and cuts at his disposal, but he will have initial letters, "curliques," etc.; and even it will in some cases be found cheaper, quicker and more satisfactory for the proprietor to have a piece of work reproduced in its entirety. The process of zinc etching has already revolutionized some branches of the trade, such as wood engraving, lithography, etc., to a certain extent, and it will affect them to a still greater extent, and its circle of influence will constantly increase. The cost of the production in zinc etching is

rapidly moving toward the minimum, and the capacity and rapidity toward the maximum. Whole books may be reproduced cheaply, rapidly, and the size of page to be the same or different at the will of the producer, and all this without any damage occurring to the original book. This will do away with much composition, and at the present time we can see the effects of this mode of reproduction in the case of the recent reprints of a dictionary and of an encyclopedia.

As I have offered suggestions to the straight matter compositor, I may now venture to offer a few words to the job hand. Study the use of cuts as a means of display in work, and collect samples and keep posted upon the cuts, more or less artistic, which are produced by the different zinc-etching establishments. It might not be far wrong to advise a job compositor who may have a bent in that direction to become a practical zinc etcher. There are as yet comparatively few men engaged in that calling and the demand is sure to increase.

TRANSLATED NOTES FROM FRENCH EXCHANGES.

AN Italian doctor recommends the following preparation for the use of compositors with weak eyes: To one pint of water add a spoonful of brandy and a pinch of cooking salt. It is said to relieve "that tired feeling" in the eyes wonderfully, if they are given a bath in the mixture every morning.

THE association for encouraging the study of Greek in France has offered a prize to be given annually to the printer who is most proficient in Greek. The competitors are divided into two classes, one for journeymen, etc., and another for apprentices, and the task is to set a page of Greek from manuscript.

IT was not till many years after newspapers were first printed that a doctor named Theophrastes Renaudot, in 1631, obtained from Cardinal Richelieu permission to advertise in the *Gazette*, in Paris. It was not till eighteen years later that an advertisement for two stolen horses appeared in an English paper, in 1649, but this style of announcement did not become popular till 1658, when the proprietor of the London coffee house, "The Sultan's Head," made use of the columns of the newspaper to spread a knowledge of the virtues of the new beverage then called *teha, tay* or tea.

SPEAKING of the origin of italic characters, Bodoni, the celebrated engraver and typefounder, in his *Manual Typographique*, Volume I, page 41, says that at first this style of type was called "aldin," and then "italique," by the French printers, and "cursif" by the Italians. Petrarch wrote so admirably that Alde Maurice resolved to get a font of type made to imitate that writing, and at the end of his edition of Petrarch, in a note to the reader, said that: "The writing of Petrarch is so perfect that the engraver to whom I entrusted the execution of the punches had only to follow their outlines, stroke for stroke." By the force of circumstances Petrarch was the designer, Alde conceived the idea of having the type made, Francois de Balogne, an ancient goldsmith, engraved the punches for the first font of this style of letter. Alde obtained from the Venetian senate the sole right to use this letter in the territory of that republic. The first volume printed in this type appeared in 1501, and was an edition of Virgil; this was followed by several other works, but the fancy for printing in italic did not last long. Foreign printers soon imitated this style of type, but much of the engraving and presswork done by them was so badly executed that it could only be read with difficulty. In 1737 small capitals were added to italic fonts by Fournier, but when fantastic or display type came into use these dropped into desuetude.

ONE OF THE FINEST AND LARGEST TYPECASTING FOUNDRIES IN THE WORLD.

A visit to the premises of Messrs. Barnhart Brothers & Spindler at 183 to 187 Monroe street, Chicago, into which they have recently moved, is surprising even to those who are well acquainted with this eminent typefounding firm's history, enterprise and business energy. To the readers of THE INLAND PRINTER, the wares of this firm are well and favorably known, and it will consequently be interesting to trace its evolution to the occupation of its present immense and thoroughly equipped establishment. Back in 1868, the foundry was established under the title of the Great Western Typefoundry, but although still distinguished by that name, it was reorganized a year later under the name of Barnhart Brothers & Spindler, and the business rapidly increased — the methods of the

firm together with the quality of their products, superior copper-mixed type especially, meeting with general appreciation. The tremendous holocaust of October, 1871, which swept Chicago's business center, included the foundry of Messrs. Barnhart Brothers & Spindler ; but like many of their fellow Chicagoans their misfortune only seemed an incentive to renewed efforts, and but a short time elapsed before they were again established, this time at 49 West Randolph street, and filling rapidly increasing orders with their old-time celerity and satisfaction to their customers, the accumulation of whom it was soon found rendered necessary a removal to larger premises but a few months later to 107 and 109 Madison street, which in turn the year 1876 saw them compelled to abandon for the same reason, and at 146 Fifth avenue (taking the entire building) the firm considered they would have ample accommodation for

many years to come. They were "building better than they knew," it would seem, for but four years elapsed until another change was necessary, and in 1880, the establishment was moved to 115 and 117 Fifth avenue, these quarters in turn being enlarged, in 1887, by the addition of five stories of adjoining building, known as 113 Fifth avenue. Each year that the firm has been in business has been a year of progress, and the beginning of the present year found them engaged in preparing the premises at 183 to 187 Monroe street for their occupation in the early spring. These buildings consist of a front building six stories in height and 60 by 125 feet in area and a rear building of the same height 60 by 50 feet. The forepart of the first floor of the front building is occupied by the business offices, which are finished in black walnut throughout, and are commodious and well equipped — in themselves, with the large clerical force, significant of the volume of the trade done. Slightly to the rear on each side of the lofty room is arranged an expansive array of packages of type ready for shipment on short notice. The balance of the floor space is taken up with a display of new machines of every description and manufacture, including the different makes of job presses, Babcock air-spring presses and Howard Iron Works paper-cutting machinery. Leaving the counting room and the large and interesting exhibit of mechanical ingenuity and skill, the visitor takes the passenger elevator run by an independent sixteen horse power engine at the front of the building to *the largest and finest typecasting room in the world.* This is situated on the sixth floor and the spectacle disclosed to the visitor is of supreme interest — the rapid play of the typecasting machines which seem almost sensate in their automatic perfection, the flicker and flash of the flame in the fire pots, the silvery type falling in continuous streams, the neatly attired girls setting the type with a rapidity beyond belief, all conspiring to produce a busy and cheerful scene not easily forgotten. The room is lit from above with a skylight 20 by 68 feet, and it is convenient to here state that for daylight there has been made ample provision, both the buildings being lighted on three sides from street and alley. Descending to the fifth floor the visitor witnesses the process of finishing the type and dividing it into fonts. On the fourth, fifth and sixth floors of the rear building are carried on the processes of the manufacture of brass rule, matrix fitting, mold making, etc., in addition to type making. The third floor is the home of the *Typefounder,* well known to the printers throughout the continent, and in this neat composing room the handsome specimens of the firm's wares are produced. The second and third floors, devoted to the machine shops and repairing, are in charge of a large and competent staff of workmen, and every appliance known for such work may be here seen. The basement of the rear building is used for the engine and dynamo room and here also the metals are mixed, the basement of the front building giving storage for boxed machinery, cases, stands, etc. Both buildings are heated with steam and supplied with light from the firm's own electric light plant with six hundred lamp capacity, the power used being one eighty and one seventy horse-power engine of latest pattern. Due precautions are taken for the preservation of the firm's valuable matrices and molds, no less than three separate vaults being used for these, as well as papers, books, etc. All the departments are admirably equipped, electric bells and speaking tubes connecting them all. Special attention is paid to the accommodation and convenience of customers, writing desks and other facilities being placed exclusively for their use.

Messrs. Barnhart Brothers & Spindler owe no allegiance to any trust or syndicate nor do they contemplate doing so, their past success and present progress giving them sufficient confidence for their future, and, employing in round numbers some three hundred hands they are quite able to meet all the requirements of their numerous customers.

FRENCH OLD STYLE.

H. C. HANSEN, - TYPE FOUNDER,

24-26 Hawley Street. - - - - Boston, Mass.

8 a 4 A   48-POINT FRENCH OLD STYLE. $8.00

COMPLIMENTARY
Ticket 12734.2

10 a 5 A   36-POINT FRENCH OLD STYLE. $6.00

PERFORATING MACHINE
Sold to Printers for $75

12 a 6 A   30-POINT FRENCH OLD STYLE. $5.30

MORE WONDERFUL PRINTERS
In the City of Boston than 163

20 a 10 A   24-POINT FRENCH OLD STYLE. $5.50

CURVING RULE FOR CITY PRINTERS
Makes work for many men 2158

28 a 14 A   20-POINT FRENCH OLD STYLE. $5.50

IMPROVED SOCIETY
Admired by man 32

36 a 18 A   16-POINT FRENCH OLD STYLE. $4.50

BOSTON WAS CONSIDERED
Next to the garden in 1892

60 a 10 a 20 A   12-POINT FRENCH OLD STYLE. $4.40

NEW YORK AND LONDON RAILROAD
NEW YORK TO LONDON TWO HOURS
Rapid Transit between the Capitals 231937

75 a 12 A 24 A   10-POINT FRENCH OLD STYLE. $4.10

DREADFUL RESULT OF IMBIBING FLAVORED
WATERS WITH HILARIOUS ROYSTERERS
Sportive Blizzards come gaily Prancing into $2136794

90 a 15 A 30 A   8-POINT FRENCH OLD STYLE. $4.05

I STAND BESIDE A SUMMER SEA AND LAUNCH
A TINY SHIP UPON THE SHINING CRESTS
Happy to see it Sail so Gallantly and free, away to where an
Island fair amid the blue 2130578

100 a 20 A 30 A   6-POINT FRENCH OLD STYLE. $3.50

NUMBERLESS TORRENTS, WITH CEASELESS SOUND, DESCEND
TO OCEAN, LIKE GREAT CHORDS OF A HARP, IN LOUD VIBRATIONS
There Entered into the Little Camp an Indian Woman, whose Features wore
Deep traces of sorrow and patience 321589056

HHHHHHHHHHHHHHh

ROUTINE OF A MERGENTHALER OFFICE.

BY E. L. MARSTERS.

THE surprise exhibited by many printers at the changed conditions of office routine, on their first entrance into an establishment that uses typesetting or typecasting machines, has been so marked, that an article explaining the workings of " machine offices " cannot but be of interest to the great number of printers who never saw a typesetting or typecasting machine in actual operation.

Being employed in such an office, the Albany *Evening Journal*, I will endeavor to give an outline of the routine daily work as it exists.

There are five Linotype or Mergenthaler machines which set the body-matter of the paper ; the ads are set by the regular ad men, and the stock quotation tables and similar tables subject to frequent changes are kept standing in type and changed by the commercial men.

The machinist arrives first and visits each machine. He " assembles " a line of matrices, casts a slug, and looks over each machine to see that everything is all right. " Time " is called at eight, and the old system of " shaking up the balls " gone through with. Each operator takes copy in his turn. The takes average in length four or five stickfuls, and in most cases the articles go out whole. The smallest takes, with rare exceptions are about ten lines. " Two-liners " are unknown, and one bane of the fast compositor when he comes to paste up is done away with. A machine stick will hold about six stickfuls.

After the first taking out of copy by the operator, that is the last time he takes copy himself during the day. A boy carries his other takes to him ; returns with the stick of set matter, and deposits it on the bank. All matter at the bank is leaded, according to the style prevailing, and the first half on all triple and double headed articles put on ; the hangers on all triple and double heads, and all single heads are set in caps on the machines. A great many of the galleys have no lines of type on them, and all such are proved without locking up, at this point a little time is gained over the previous way.

As the proof returns from the proofroom it is carried from the foreman, by the boy, to the operator to whom it belongs. All proofs are corrected immediately upon receipt and returned to the stone.

It is hardly necessary to add that if the takes are cut short (10 lines), in view of an approaching edition, the boy has to hustle and has no sinecure.

The " head " man substitutes the lines with errors in them with the corrected lines. The bother that foremen experience with bad proofs, and all offices at times have such, on an afternoon paper of numerous editions that uses type, in having to wait until the forms return from the stereotyping room before they can be corrected, is here partly overcome by having the corrected lines all set and ready to be inserted. This last task is rapidly done without removing the matter from the forms. Care must be taken, though, as the type lines are frequently " off plumb " and are liable to fall against one another and close the hole made by the line taken out, and thus get the corrected line in the wrong place, and consequently have a transposition of lines. By leaving all matter in the forms after a first or second edition the liability of getting articles " mixed " is lessened.

After the last edition is out and the matter wanted for the weekly, semi-weekly and the morrow's early edition is picked out, the rest of the type lines are separated from the leads and dashes and returned to the " dead " boxes, of which each machine has one. The form is not wet, as all the metal slugs must be perfectly dry when put in the melting pot to be again used. To anyone who has had experience in " mixing " water and hot metal the above explanation is not necessary. All wet slugs are put on galleys and dried on the steam table in the stereotyping room. One must not use good galleys for this purpose, as it is liable to ruin them. The *Journal* office uses some solid brass galleys that did good service with the turtle form of years gone by. The " sweepings " and shavings from the machines are melted, purified and cast into " pigs " for use again.

The above is the routine of one machine office and the writer sincerely trusts that it will be of some interest to the printing fraternity and enable " strangers to machines " to better comprehend the routine work when an opportunity arises to secure employment in a Mergenthaler office.

THE springtime number of the *Typographic Advertiser*, published by the MacKellar, Smiths & Jordan Company, of Philadelphia, has come to hand, and presents a number of bright and new type designs for printers. The latest face produced by this foundry is the " Childs " series, two pages of which are shown in this issue of the *Advertiser*. This letter is quite a handsome face, resembling the " De Vinne " somewhat, but still enough different to make it an entirely new letter. Another new letter is the " Newfangle." A page of " Johnson " is also shown, made in six sizes, in upper and lower case, all complete with figures. Samples of " Dynamo," " Gutenberg," " Columbian," " Typo," " Zinco," " Koster," and other series also have a place in this number. The penchant this foundry has for making new faces does not seem to be on the decline by any means.

THE specimen book of the Boston Typefoundry received last month, shows also the faces of the Central Typefoundry, of St. Louis, and a complete line of printing material. The two foundries being under one management, all the jobbing faces, borders, ornaments, etc., made by both can be supplied by either at the shortest notice. The work contains over three hundred pages, printed in a style that does credit to the faces exhibited, and is neatly bound in cloth. To even enumerate the names of the various faces in the catalogue would take up more space than we have at our disposal. We can with truthfulness say that a printer desiring to be up with the times cannot afford to be without a copy of the work, and might as well go out of business as to attempt to get along without some of the material therein shown.

60 POINT JOHNSON.

3 A, 5 a.

Rompish Jaunting

48 POINT JOHNSON.

3 A, 6 a, $7.60

Hunting Mountain Caverns

36 POINT JOHNSON.

4 A, 8 a, $6.20

Enchanting Landscape
Unbounded Admiration

30 POINT JOHNSON.

5 A, 10 a, $5.75

Divertisement that Conquers
Drowsiness and Lassitude

24 POINT JOHNSON.   6 A, 12 a, $5.05

SPRING TOURS
Arranged for Pleasure
1234567890

18 POINT JOHNSON.   8 A, 16 a, $4.35

PERAMBULATING
Through Meadow and Field
Amidst Budding Plants
1234567890

The MacKellar, Smiths & Jordan Co.   Nos. 606-614 Sansom Street, Philadelphia. Western Branch: 328 and 330 Dearborn Street, Chicago.

WOMEN TYPESETTERS.

To the Editor: CHICAGO, Ill., June 3, 1892.

As long as there are women employed as typesetters, so long will the printers' union be obliged to combat non-unionism. This is a direct statement meaning that from a union standpoint women as printers are not a success. In allowing women to become members of the typographical union we totally ignore the apprenticeship system. There are no women who can truthfully say they have ever considered themselves apprentices for the required length of time prescribed by the rules and regulations of the International Typographical Union. Ask a non-union employing printer : "How long does it require to make an ordinarily intelligent woman a compositor," and nine chances to one the answer is, "a woman can learn the 'case' in an hour !" and that simple *hour* is all the apprenticeship they serve. From the start women receive so much per stated thousand ems — as printers ! In any trade, no matter which, it is understood that women are *underpaid*. Are they underpaid in the printing business? We think no more so than men ; but this involves a proposition : a boy goes into a printing office to learn the trade, at the same time that a young woman does. For six months the boy runs errands and sweeps the floor and receives for his compensation $2 per week. The woman is placed before a case and after being shown the "lay of the boxes," is given a piece of reprint copy and straightway begins to compose. The first week she gets nothing, perhaps ; the second week she makes something ; at the end of six months she manages to draw a salary of "from $9 to $12 per week in non-union offices." Our "cub" does not earn (for himself) $12 per week, in a union office, until he has served two-thirds of his time. In quoting figures I have strict reference now to the present Chicago scale governing union printers. Thus, it will be seen, the girl receives from $1 to $10 per week more than does the boy apprentice. In this case you will admit that women are not underpaid, not even if a man working by her side should receive one-third again as much per thousand ems for the same class of work as she does — why? because she is, in justice to our apprentices, only entitled to a two-thirder's wages. In proving that women are paid according to their dues I have somewhat proved that women *are a success*. What have they gained? They have learned a business where they can make a pittance — one simple branch out of four prominent branches in the printing business, and we doubt that they have learned it well, for the simple reason that they have never learned the rudiments of printing. The "cub" in the meantime has a practical knowledge of everything concerning printing. He can set type, perhaps has had a chance to set "ads," can impose a four or an eight page form, and can make-up (not over intelligently, may be) an ordinary book or newspaper. The woman has not gained respect, the employer who pays her her salary does not honor her — she is simply turning the grindstone for him to grind his axe. The boy is looked up to for his perseverance under difficulties and is respected for his manliness, and in time will earn $3 where the woman will earn but two.

We hardly think that any reader of a printer's journal of the character of THE INLAND PRINTER believes that women are a success as compositors ; but the uninitiated reading an elaborately worded article in some household magazine, which quotes New York maximum salaries as an *average*, are no doubt deluded into believing that women are achieving moneyed success, and that there are situations open for more women to perform the same duty for the same money. Twenty to twenty-seven dollars per week is not the average in any single town in the United States, and there are places where a compositor would have to set 50,000 ems per week to make $11.25, and that, too, right in Chicago. No doubt there are like places even in the city of New York, and women are the typesetters who hold such cases. We are willing to concede the fact, under existing circumstances, that it does not pay to serve five years' apprenticeship to learn any *trade* which does not pay better than an average of $9 per week. We will concede that "it is the opportunity which keeps women from the ranks of unionism," and one of the reasons is : "most women regard the business as but a make-shift until married," and being of a marriageable age when they enter an office have neither the time nor the inclination to master it sufficiently well. We have a few union woman printers in the International. Where did we get them? By allowing them to become members by recognizing *time* instead of service. We show partiality to women. We would be glad to see more partiality shown in this respect, for every friend we make is an enemy the less, and those that are not with us are against us.

Of the 5,500 printers in New York city, 5,000 are union, including 200 women (over sixty work on a single paper) ; 500 non-union, including 200 women. These are terrible figures, for they show conclusively that in trying to get the upper hand of non-unionism we are fighting the women in a greater proportion than we are men ! In Chicago the proportion is even greater — 2,200 union printers, including, we believe, less than 100 women, with 400 non-union printers, including fully 200 women (from twenty to sixty, including two forewomen, are employed in one institution). There is not a union house in Chicago that employs women as compositors.

The women have no natural protectors but themselves. They are not asked to join the union until they have brought themselves into prominence either as an enemy to be conquered or as a valuable ally. The union is not a charitable organization, though perhaps a just one, protecting all alike, though our non-union printers do not seem to realize the fact.

We are compelled to fight women, because woman never can, nor never has, shown herself the equal of man in the printing business. It is a deplorable condition of affairs, but it is true. If we wish to reduce the fighting force that is pitted against us we must frame some more lenient rule that will make it still more easy for women to join our organization. If, however, we cannot raise them to our standard we must not lower ourselves to their standard. Be not deluded, from a union standpoint women as typesetters are not a success.

B. C. M.

A. D. FARMER & SON.

Our advertisement columns last month contained the notice of the dissolution of partnership of Messrs. Farmer, Little & Co., the well-known typefounders, and our readers will notice that the old advertisement of Farmer, Little & Co., on page 856 of this issue, now reads A. D. Farmer & Son. This "Old New York Typefoundry" was established in 1804, by one Elihu White, to whom, after some changes, the late firm succeeded about forty years ago. The termination of this long partnership has not been caused, we are happy to say, by the death or advancing years of any of the late partners, but is due solely to the differences which arose among them over the recent attempt of some of the principal typefounders of Philadelphia, Chicago, St. Louis and New York to form a trust in order to raise the prices of printing materials, etc., after the usual manner of such combinations. Mr. Andrew Little and Mr. John Bentley, two of the partners, were favorable to the proposed measure, which on the other hand was opposed by Messrs. A. D. and W. W. Farmer. The last named gentlemen (the senior and junior members of the firm) considered such action to be not only illegal, but opposed to sound business methods, and they declined to hand over their customers in the printing trade, from whom they had received so many favors, to the tender mercies of the proposed monopoly. The business will be carried on in future under the firm name of A. D. Farmer & Son, and will no doubt be characterized by increased enterprise and vigor, the management being now in the hands of men united in ideas and interests.

BUSINESS COURTESY.

BY F. W. THOMAS.

CLASSIFY business men according to their manners and there are three kinds. There is the man who has no manners in particular, who has no individuality, in short, only an every-day sort of a fellow. There is the abrupt, bluff man, often so short spoken as to be impolite ; never puts any extra polish in his manner ; makes you feel in a hurry the instant you look at him. Last and best comes the polished gentleman — none the less a business man — but possessed of a regard for the propriety of things sufficient to enable him to greet everyone courteously. He treats his customers with the utmost politeness, even in their most unreasonable demands.

To my mind, there are two elements in business success. One is to so conduct your business as to acquire the respect and confidence of business associates. The other is to make money. The man who is entirely successful in these two points, may be spoken of as a model business man.

I desire to show in this article that business courtesy is a strong point in reaching success in both of these particulars. That it is, in fact, necessary if you would be a typical modern business man. And further, that there is no place where it pays better than in a printing office. And by "paying" I do not, for one moment, wish to be understood that the profit is to come simply in a vague, indefinite way, but that it can be seen in good hard cash every month.

Printing office proprietors are not an impolite set of fellows. Many of them could shine in society. But when they reach their office, they seem to think it is a place solely for close figuring and hard work and that courtesy is an immaterial matter. The principal reason for this lies in the fact that but comparatively few printing offices are arranged for the proper reception and treatment of customers. Few printers have what can, with any propriety, be termed a business office. Usually a corner of their workroom is fenced off by a railing or pine partition a little too high to look over. This place contains a common desk and perhaps the proprietor's chair. It is dignified by the title "office" and the customer is allowed to hang over the railing and make his wants known. Little attention is paid to the proper arrangement of specimens from which to select. In short, nowhere is there apparent that solicitude for the comfort and care of the customer which has become a necessary and profitable feature in other lines of business. It is difficult to use reception-room manners amid such surroundings.

You have possibly read of the miser, the floor of whose one-room shanty was chalked off into the parlor, banquet-hall and bedrooms of his imaginary palace. He would place a chair in his reception room and with a pompous wave of his hand, beckon his guest to be seated. If a meal (?) were to be served he would set his old kitchen table in the space called the banquet-hall — draw the chairs over the line — and invite his friends to dine. His manners were those of a prince, his language that of an orator. The effect — was simply amusing. Is it any more amusing, brother printers, when you look at it from away up a tree, to talk art printing over a railing ? Will not an effort at personal gentility be equally as incongruous — with a dusty floor — dirty walls and unkempt surroundings. Fit up your offices. Have a place for the proper reception of your customers ; furnish it in style ; cover the floor ; decorate the walls and fill the blank spaces with neatly framed specimens of fine work. Let the whole arrangement and furnishing of the place demonstrate that you are a man of taste. Welcome your customers as you would a caller at your home. Keep a box of good cigars in your private desk. When Jones comes in with the serious intention of trying to beat you down on that last bill, hand out the box, treat Jones with the utmost courtesy, and he'll forget all about that bill. Although the bill was a just one you might have had to knock off a dollar or two to keep him from becoming dissatisfied. Cigars cost 10 cents. Which is cheapest ? An amusing illustration of this point was the case of a Chicago man who borrowed $100 from a hotel keeper when attending a banquet with his old college associates at an outside town. The $100 was never paid and finally the hotel man in desperation wrote the Chicago man he was coming and boarded a train for the windy city. The borrower met him at the depot with the blandest smile and in the most courteous manner invited him to dine at his club and then outdid himself showing the sights. So great was his affability and so assiduous his attentions that in very admiration of his style the $100 was entirely forgotten and the visitor returned without a mention of the debt.

Courtesy is far more profitable than bluff.

A nicely fitted-up office and the genial treatment of your trade will attract to you a class of customers who are fond of nice things and who are willing to pay for them. You will then have a pleasant place for your own work. The best hours of a man's life are spent in his office. Why should it not be nice ? Why should he not strive to make his dealings of a character which will be a source of pleasure to himself ? There is one more characteristic of a truly courteous man which I desire to mention. No such man will delay the fulfilling of an appointment or the answering of a letter or the acknowledging of a favor. It is the greatest discourtesy to the other party. The man who is known to be punctual is always favored when an order is wanted quickly. The appreciative man is remembered a second time. Often some friend sends you a customer and never hearing you speak of it — thinks the kindness forgotten. An acknowledgment of such good offices should be made in such cases *at once*.

The courtesy is always appreciated.

8A, 26a. 18 POINT PALO ALTO. $5 00

SUMMER RAMBLE NEAR THE SEACOAST

Recreation and Pleasant Loitering by Numerous People from our Large City

$ 1 2 3 4 5 6

6A, 20a 24 POINT PALO ALTO. $5.50

AMONG THE LAKES OF WISCONSIN

The Delightful Resorts will soon Ring with Merriment of the Tourist

$ 1 2 3 4 5 6

PATENT APPLIED FOR.

10A, 32a. 18 POINT RAMONA. $4.50

TO THE TOP OF PIKE'S PEAK BY RAIL

Snowball Sandwiches, Snowflake Cake, Ice Cream, Frozen Buttermilk, etc., served at Toocold's

Ch Th ng ly 1 2 3 4 5 6

8A, 20a. 24 POINT RAMONA. $4.60

MISSOURI RIVER FISH

Piscatorial Amusement on this Stream is limited to Catfish, Bullheads and Dogfish

Qu Th Ch ly and ng 678

6A, 14a. 30 POINT RAMONA. $4.75

A BIG FLOWER HOUSE

The Finest in the Country and Situated nicely on Mount Taraboomding

$ 1 2 3 4 5 6 7

PATENT APPLIED FOR.

PALMER & REY, TYPE FOUNDERS,

SAN FRANCISCO, CAL., and PORTLAND, OREGON.

18A, 36a. 12 POINT EXTRA CONDENSED No. 4. $2.50

IN THE YEAR 1492 COLUMBUS Sailed the Ocean Blue. Chicago, '92.

16A, 32a. 14 POINT EXTRA CONDENSED No. 4. $2.65

BIG TIME AT THE WORLD'S FAIR! Only $1892 to See the Sights.

14A, 28a. 16 POINT EXTRA CONDENSED No. 4. $3.00

CHICAGO'S BIG ELEPHANT at Lincoln Park cost $95342

12A, 24a. 24 POINT EXTRA CONDENSED No. 4. $3.75

CALIFORNIA FRUIT for Jack Bull & Co., $7498

10A, 20a. 30 POINT EXTRA CONDENSED No. 4. $4.50

DAKOTA as a Summer Resort 98 in Shade

8A, 16a. 36 POINT EXTRA CONDENSED No. 4. $5.50

FISHING at South Chicago, No. 86

8A, 16a. 42 POINT EXTRA CONDENSED No. 4. $6.00

RED HOT Summer Weather, '92

6A, 12a. 60 POINT EXTRA CONDENSED No. 4. $8.00

BIDWELL is Out of Sight and Can't Get In 1892

5A, 10a. 72 POINT EXTRA CONDENSED No. 4. $10.50

WEAVER says that He will Get There 1892

4A, 8a. 96 POINT EXTRA CONDENSED No. 4. $11.00

HARRISON is also very Confident 1892

3A, 6a. 120 POINT EXTRA CONDENSED No. 4. $12.50

GROVER thinks it's Sure 1892

SPANISH ACCENTS TO ALL FONTS OF THIS SERIES

Carried in Stock by { UNION TYPE FOUNDRY, Chicago, Ill.
H. P. HALLOCK & CO., ATLANTIC-PACIFIC TYPE FOUNDRY, Omaha, Neb.

Other Type Founders and Dealers can procure these faces from the UNION TYPE FOUNDRY at the regular discount.

PALMER & REY, TYPE FOUNDERS,

SAN FRANCISCO, CAL., and PORTLAND, OREGON.

24A, 48a.　　　6 POINT ART OLD STYLE.　　　$2.00

BELIEVE NOT AMBITION WISE BECAUSE 'TIS BRAVE!

Soar Not too High to Fall but Stoop to Rise.

1 2 3 4 5 6 7 8

20A, 40a.　　　8 POINT ART OLD STYLE.　　　$2.10

PRACTICE OR THEORY IN HORTICULTURE!

Plowing Deep into the Mind.

1 2 3 4 5 6 7

20A, 40a.　　　9 POINT ART OLD STYLE.　　　$2.25

DAILY MEANDERINGS IN SHADY GLENS

Enjoying Nature's Sweet Solitude.

1 2 3 4 5 6

18A, 36a.　　　10 POINT ART OLD STYLE.　　　$2.35

THE ASCENSION OF ALPINE HEIGHTS

Tourists in Switzerland.

The Mountain-Climbers' Paradise.

1 2 3 4 5 6

16A, 32a.　　　12 POINT ART OLD STYLE.　　　$2.65

PRETTIEST FRAGRANT ROSES

Sweet Scented Flowers.

Forms of Leaves and Buds.

1 2 3 4 5

14A, 28a.　　　14 POINT ART OLD STYLE.　　　$4.00

COLLECTION OF SPEECHES BY EMINENT MEN AND WOMEN

With Original Maps and Portraits.

12A, 24a.　　　18 POINT ART OLD STYLE.　　　$4.30

POLITICAL MEETING AND PIE-EATING CONTEST

Republicans and Democrats.

10A, 20a.　　　22 POINT ART OLD STYLE.　　　$4.75

LESSONS IN DANCING AND SITTING UP

287 Lightfoot Street.

8A, 16a.　　　30 POINT ART OLD STYLE.　　　$6.00

NORTH POLE ICING COUNTRY

180 Miles from Freeze.

6A, 12a.　　　36 POINT ART OLD STYLE.　　　$8.15

POOR BOB'S Dinner 1762

SPANISH ACCENTS TO ALL FONTS OF THIS SERIES.

Carried in Stock by { UNION TYPE FOUNDRY, Chicago, Ill.
{ H. P. HALLOCK & CO., ATLANTIC-PACIFIC TYPE FOUNDRY, Omaha, Neb.

Other Type Founders and Dealers can procure these faces from the UNION TYPE FOUNDRY at the regular discount.

ANARCHISTS, SOCIALISTS AND WORKINGMEN.

BY THE LATE O. S. JENKS.

ANARCHY is defined as "absence of government; the state of society where there is no law or supreme power." An anarchist, therefore, is one who advocates the abolition of law and government. That this is his object is evident, for the significations of the words "anarchy" and "anarchist" have not changed; that he seeks to accomplish his object by the employment of force, everyone knows who is informed as to the events of our time and has heard of the admitted remarks of anarchistic orators.

It is a common mistake to confound the socialist and anarchist. The socialist seeks to bring the government to his ideal by a greater paternalism and concentration of power (comprehending, of course, the contentment of the individual). The anarchist endeavors to bring about the overthrow of government and social order. Socialism, whatever its merits or demerits, works with a definite purpose in view, and it seeks to attain to the realization of its purpose by lawful agitation and legitimate means. If the anarchist has any formula of government or society to substitute for existing conditions, it is seldom if ever enunciated. It can hardly be that he has, else his appellation would be a misnomer.

Many persons who have never studied the works of Karl Marx are socialists in a degree at least. That part of the socialistic plan which comprehends the acquirement of the railroads, lighting plants and other public industries by national, state or municipal government finds favor with many whose socialism extends no further.

The socialist has suffered from associating with the anarchists. The anarchist has often found it to his advantage to take upon himself for a time the mantle of socialism with the object of propagating his malevolent teachings more safely and effectually. The socialist now sees the disadvantage to him and his cause of such an association. On a number of occasions of late, socialists have made expressions of their repudiation of anarchists and anarchy.

The tendency of the world is for the better. Every century, every decade, witnesses great triumphs of right and of genius. Labor, looking upward to a greater independence, and a larger enjoyment of the higher, the better things of life and nature, has gathered its forces for a conquest, guided by convictions of justice and right. With many victories gained and future triumphs assured, its advance is becoming steady and its forces unified — when there appear the advocates of the bomb and firebrand policy. Blind to the victories already achieved, they madly counsel violence as the only method of redress for labor. Destitute of any moral code, they have no compunctions of conscience in urging to pillage and murder.

These disciples of chaos in the pursuit of their reckless policy come in conflict with those appointed for the enforcement of law and the preservation of the public peace and order; meetings are disrupted, and forthwith there is a storm of protest, charges and countercharges, and many citizens see, in the large discretion allowed the police in determining the character of meetings, a serious menace to the right of free assemblage and of free speech.

It has been suggested that in the case of meetings of an anarchistic character, officers should be present to write down any violent or unlawful language on the part of the speakers, and have the latter arrested by due process of law. This method, clearly, would be unavailing to put a stop to anarchistic agitation. It would be as fallacious as for a town board to ordain that in case of fire the marshal should make requisition for a hosecart on the treasurer of the town. When the wily speaker has convinced his ignorant auditors that they have a moral right to the homes of the wealthy, when (though perhaps in guarded language) he has justified the use of the bomb and firebrand, when words of treason have moved the audience to a fever heat of hatred of our government and laws — then is the time for police interference.

Workingmen should in no way identify themselves with these revolutionists. There is a widespread misconception as to the attitude of labor toward the law. This misconception, fostered by occasional arbitrary and illegal acts on the part of organized workingmen, has retarded the progress of labor reform legislatively and in popular favor. Any act or expression of affiliation with men who preach murder and riot will seriously embarrass and hinder all legitimate efforts.

Though the methods of the anarchists cannot be too forcibly denounced, we should look beyond the speaker and his wild harangue, and the chafing, lawless, impatient audience, to the causes of the trouble, for the complaints of the anarchists are not entirely without foundation. Anarchy is the outgrowth from the seeds of discontent sown among the vicious and ignorant. The causes which give rise to this discontent (which pervades all society) are found in "man's inhumanity to man"; and, if we go back of this, we find the most fruitful cause in the love of money — the root of all evil. The penurious employer who takes advantage of the poverty of little children to enforce a service of labor extending from early morning into the hours of the night, for a mere pittance; the unscrupulous capitalist who employs the imported, downtrodden creatures of other lands to the exclusion of American workingmen; the "public benefactor" who reduces the wages of already underpaid workingmen in order to establish universities and libraries — these are some of the disturbing factors in society; these are *breeders* of anarchists.

There is one fact, however, that cannot be too often reiterated for the benefit of the anarchist. It is, that the foundation stone of our government is the right of the majority to rule.

Douglas.

18A, 36a   Long Primer (10 Point).   2.40

ENGLAND HAS TO UNDERGO THE

Revolt of the Colonies to Submit to Defeat and

Separation to Shake under the

Volcano of the French Revolution to Grapple

12A, 24a,   Pica (12 Point).   2.10

THE SHADES OF NIGHT

Falling Fast as Through the Sanctum

Door there Passed 38

10A, 20a,   Great Primer (18 Point).   3.30

THE NORTHWESTERN INK COMPANY

Manufacturers of Black and Colored Lithographing Inks

485 Printing House Square

8A, 16a,   Double Pica (24 Point).   4.30

RAPID TRANSIT COMPANY

New York City to London in Thirty-Six Hours

234   Watered Stocks For Sale   567

6A, 12a   Five-Line Nonpareil (30 Point).   4.45

MEXICAN REPUBLIC

Daily Exercise of the Flexible Tensors

4A, 8a,   Double Great Primer (36 Point).   4.90

MAGNIFICENT FACE

Useful and Excellent Series 38

SPACES AND QUADS EXTRA.

MARDER, LUSE & CO., Chicago, Minneapolis and Omaha.

THE UNION TYPE FOUNDRY,

337 DEARBORN ST., CHICAGO.

15A 20a $3.00   12 POINT AMERICAN OLD STYLE NO. 2.   20a Lower Case $1 00

THE INDIAN AND HIS HUNTING GROUNDS
Are fast disappearing. the one by various paleface refreshments. the other by civilized landgrabbers.

12A 18a $3.50   18 POINT AMERICAN OLD STYLE NO. 2.   18a Lower Case $1.25

AMERICAN TWO-LEGGED COONS
Plenty south of Mason and Dixon Line. 92

10A 15a $4.00   24 POINT AMERICAN OLD STYLE No. 2.   15a Lower Case $1.50

BALLOON ROUTE 76
To top of Chicago Sky-Scrapers

30, 36 AND 48 POINT READY SOON.

JOB FONT $2.50.   **LITTLE REBELS.**   CARD FONT $1.50.

JOB FONT $5.00.   **LITTLE REBELS No. 2.**   CARD FONT $3.00.

THIRTEEN CHARACTERS TO EACH FONT.

A. D. FARMER AND SON

TYPE FOUNDING CO.

— NEW YORK —
63 & 65 Beekman Street and
62 & 64 Gold Street.

— CHICAGO —
Warehouse, 109 Quincy Street.
Chas. B. Ross, Manager.

— ESTABLISHED 1804 —

6 Point Bold Face Old Style.   60 a 30 A—$3 25

BOLDFACE OLD STYLE A USEFUL LETTER FOR THE JOB PRINTER

European Visitors to the Columbian Exhibition at Chicago should beware of the Bunco Man, who

still works the Game in the same Boldfaced Old Style

Disastrous Collisions on the Ocean caused by Fogs and Racing for Records

$1234567890

8 Point Bold Face Old Style   50 a 24 A—$3 25

SOME ASTRONOMERS DECLARE THEIR BELIEF

That the Planet Mars is Inhabited and therefore capable of Supporting Life, this is a fortunate

and timely announcement at present

Where is the Marian Columbus to Start the First Air Ship for the Planets

$1234567890

10 Point Bold Face Old Style.   36 a 18 A—$3 15

CONTENDING IN THE SAME OLD STYLE

Educational Campaigns are welcome and profitable to the Printing Trade

Presidential Aspirations Blooming

Grand Musical Torchlight Parades delight the Small Boy

$1234567890

12 Point Bold Face Old Style.   24 a 12 A—$2 80

PRINTERS ADMIRE THIS OLD STYLE

Handsome and Original Characters Designed to meet the Demand

for a New Job Face in Old Style

Now for Regular Old Fashioned Summer Weather

$1234567890

ADVERTISEMENTS WITH IDEAS.

BY BURT. H. VERNET.

DO you grasp the idea? Perhaps you do; perhaps you think you do — probably you don't. I say probably, for I am of the opinion that not one good printer in five gets the advertiser's idea, or even tries to.

In getting up ads. for the better class of publications, such for instance as elaborate programmes, high-class magazines, souvenir books, trade journals, etc., where a reasonable amount of time is obtainable for the purpose, the average printer-artist is too apt to indulge his fancy to extremes in turning out something very elaborate, and no doubt artistic from a printer's standpoint; something he is inclined to think will eclipse former efforts and rouse the dormant envy of "the fellow in the next alley." This will be the case more especially when he gets a half or full page marked "handsome display" or "get up something striking."

If you are in a rut get out of it. What is needed above anything else in the average ad. work is more character — more *individuality* — ideas. If you feel yourself drifting toward the same old long-line-and-a-short-line style, or getting up the same old panel and band, "break away," give it up. Try and rake up something new — if not entirely original. See if your copy won't give you a cue.

Of course every advertiser doesn't have an idea all ready for you to work out, but as a rule you will find that the majority of the best advertisers have some prominent feature they wish brought out in every ad., or some especial mode of display, and have also a vague conception of what their matter should look like when put in type.

If your copy contains no given idea, try and supply the omission. If you are wide-awake and have an interest in your work, two or more ideas will probably at once suggest themselves — *one* is enough. Don't make the mistake of trying to crowd four or five ideas from your fertile brain into one ad., for it will prove a failure, sure.

Given the idea, try and look at your work for the moment from the advertiser's standpoint. That ad. has been solicited with the understanding that it is to cost so much, and you as an advertiser expect to get the return of your money through the ability of the ad. to attract the attention and custom of the public. You expect the printer to give you something a little better than is given the rest of his advertisers in the way of display, and you are displeased if disappointed.

Now, you, as a printer, should take a more or less individual interest in that ad.— every ad. in fact that passes through your hands. Learn the tastes of advertisers who do not draft their copy exactly as they want it. Find, if possible, what does and does not please them. Some advertisers will get "caught," and be your everlasting friend by some inserted happy thought or unique display of their apparently poorly written ad. or job. Why, I have known advertisers to patronize comparatively obscure journals and special publications for years simply because their matter was always well displayed and nicely printed. This is a point many publishers could pursue with profit to themselves.

Now we will suppose you have your idea. If its going to be something elaborate in the way of a page ad., with panels or other rulework, draft out a rough sketch of it. If you are not handy at sketching it is something you should try your hand at during spare moments or evenings — not in the summer! It is a necessary "trick" of the tasty printer's trade of today. Unless you are working on a typefounder's publication or printing trade journal don't indulge your fancy for rulework to an "indecent" extent. Your audience, the public, won't appreciate it, and doubtless your employer will frown. Remember the shop has to make some money on that ad. as well as the advertiser.

If you insist on something in the way of rulework try and grasp something with an idea in it, and not so cumbersome that a few leading lines will be "out of sight." Try and not get in "too deep," and go floundering around for ten hours and finally prove up "a something" which neither pleases the eye nor the man who locks it up.

Don't chop up four or five feet of rule for every fancy ad. Did you ever stop to wonder where all the pins go to? Chopped rule finally goes to the same place. Learn to utilize rule that has already been introduced to the mitering machine and curver. Do as your tailor would with an old coat — put on a new binding or new buttons; dress it up a little here and there and it passes for a new garment.

But above all, work out that *idea*. Don't lose sight of the fact that there will be at least *one* person who will scan that ad. with a look of pleasure or pain — the man who wrote the copy. If he should happen to be a professional ad. writer he will probably be disappointed, anyway.

TYPECASTING VS. TYPESETTING MACHINES.

BY EMORY L. MARSTERS.

THE rapidly increasing output of typecasting machines is further evidence of the view held by the writer several years back that the practicable "coming machine" would be a typecasting one as against the typesetting machine. I am not prejudiced against typesetting machines, for I admire their work, and I know that the even and clear face of type is far superior in looks to the product of the rapid typecasting machine.

Several typesetting machines are in existence, either in theory or as models, while the Thorne principally and the McMillan are now being used very acceptably in various newspaper and book offices. In the latter establishments I think the results are more satisfactory. In newspaper offices they are not so practical, and are not the "economical ingenuities" that some people would try to make one believe. This idea is not based on superficial knowledge, but rather on practical observation and information in reference to the operating expenses.

Inventors and newspaper men have been looking for a machine that would do away with that costly item — type. In the typecasting machines they have succeeded in obtaining that result. To give the reader a better and more practical idea of the difference between the workings of the two machines, I will compare them in a general way.

As regards power and the services of a machinist, the difference is not material. The difference in the cost of type for the setting and metal for the casting machine is a large item, and the price of each is familiar to all printers. The waste, perhaps, is larger in quantity with the metal, but the cost being so much less, it does not equal in value that of type broken, the latter being done mostly by the machine distributer. The destruction of type used by setting machines has been one of the greatest drawbacks of all the efforts at mechanical composition. The McMillan machine has a distributer separate from the type-setting machine, while with the Thorne the work of distributing "dead matter" is carried on coincidently with the composition of new matter. In addition to the original cost of type, certain machines require an extra "nicking" for each character, which adds about 5 cents per thousand ems.

Besides the keyboard operator the typesetting machine requires a justifier, which doubles the cost of composition. The one who runs or feeds the distributer is also an extra expense, and generally a boy or girl is employed to keep the dust off the type, for if the type is the least dirty it does not move easily in the channels. Three or four persons' work — the product of one machine — costs too much to be practical.

With the typecasting machines a great amount of this expense is avoided and the results are larger. For either the Mergenthaler linotype or the Rogers machine — these two being the leading ones — but one operator is required. No distributer is needed. The Schuckers machine — whose owners have recently combined with the Rogers people — is also a typecasting machine, but it has never been put on the market. Its projector is the original inventor of the "double-wedge justifying device," used by both the Mergenthaler and Rogers machines. The Schuckers differs from those machines in that it uses "male" instead of "female" dies and the casting is done outside the machine. The line is indented into a lead slug and the slug is passed automatically into a casting box external of the machine proper, where it is cast and trimmed.

The Mergenthaler has an automatic distributer, and the operator of the Rogers distributes the matrices after the casting of each line by elevating the forward end of the machine. These two machines require no help outside the operators, and it is patent to all that the cost of running them is small as compared with the typesetting machines. The product is much larger, especially so in the case of the Mergenthaler, where the operator has nothing to do with the distribution. The Rogers operator is handicapped by having to wait until a line is cast, and then distribute that line before he can start a new one.

Another point in favor of typecasting machines is the utility in handling the type-bars. Less care is required, which is a gain of time. If type gets bent or broken it goes into the "hell box." The type-bars can get bent and dirty and not lose their value. They are remelted. After a form is dead the type-bars can be taken out in five minutes and put in a box for use in again supplying the machine's metal pot. But how different with type! The form requires care and is frequently in the way, as it crowds your stone-room.

Printers, and especially newspaper publishers, are finding availability and practical results in typecasting machines. Although the face of the type-bar is not all that could be desired, it is improving with the constantly added improvements to the machines.

The typesetting machines are not advancing with the same stride, and it is due to the *fact* that they have no practical automatic or mechanical justifier. It has been stated in the trade papers that the McMillan inventor has finally succeeded in devising such a scheme; but there are many who are asking: Will it do practical work? The writer is in doubt. The typecasting machine of today is vastly better than that of even a year ago. It has come to stay.

$4.05.   12-POINT ORNAMENTED, NO. 1,562.   30 a and 15 A   3 lb. 8 oz.

The Property which characterizes Capital, of Lending itself any
Number of times to Facilitate Production, does not appear to be Sufficiently Appreciated.
STATISTICAL ACCOUNT OF STATE DEBTS. $122,765.

$5.35.   18-POINT ORNAMENTED, NO. 1,562.   25 a and 12 A   5 lb. 6 oz.

Invention of Paper.   According to Varro, Paper was
First Invented after the Conquest of Egypt by Alexander the Great.
BRUCE'S SPECIMEN BOOK OF 1882.

$6.95.   24-POINT ORNAMENTED, NO. 1,562.   20 a and 10 A   7 lb. 12 oz.

The Triumph of the Wise Man over Fortune.
Doctrine of the Stoics and Platonists Exemplified.
PROMISSORY NOTES. 1892.

$11.25.   36-POINT ORNAMENTED, NO. 1,562.   15 a and 8 A   13 lb. 12 oz.

Opening for American Enterprise.
TRANSPORTATION, 1234.

$8.25.   48-POINT ORNAMENTED, NO. 1,562.   5 a and 5 A   11 lb. 8 oz.

Commerce of the World.
POINT SYSTEM, 92.

GEORGE BRUCE'S SON & CO., TYPE-FOUNDERS, 13 CHAMBERS STREET, NEW YORK.

The Steady and Rapid Advancement of
the Colonies of Australasia is interesting to Statisticians.
COMMERCE OF AUSTRALASIA. $123,45.

PAT. PENDING. BRUCE'S N.Y. TYPE FOUNDRY

$3.90.   18-POINT GOTHIC EXTENDED, NO. 251.   12 a and 12 A   6 lb. 8 oz.

Special Imports and Exports of the
Countries of Europe and the United States.
CONSULAR REPORTS. 1892.

$5.35.   24-POINT GOTHIC EXTENDED, NO. 251.   10 a and 10 A   9 lb. 8 oz.

Steam Communication.
Secure Life Assurance Policies.
MARINE ENGINES. 4567.

$8.80.   36-POINT GOTHIC EXTENDED, NO. 251.   8 a and 8 A   15 lb. 12 oz.

Tools and Implements
THE MIKADO. 1892.

$9.45.   48-POINT GOTHIC EXTENDED, NO. 251.   5 a and 5 A   17 lb. 8 oz.

Central American
REPORT. $84.

GEORGE BRUCE'S SON & CO., Type-Founders, 13 Chambers Street, NEW YORK.

A. D. FARMER AND SON

TYPE FOUNDING CO.

NEW YORK
NOS. 63 AND 65 BEEKMAN STREET, AND
NOS. 62 AND 64 GOLD ST.

ESTABLISHED 1804.
LATE FARMER, LITTLE AND COMPANY,
TYPE FOUNDERS.

1

3

5

7

2

4

6

8

12 POINT FONTS—ONE NO. ONLY—5 FEET, $2 00

6 POINT FONTS—ONE NO. ONLY—5 FEET, $1 75

12 POINT TYPAL.   36 a 18 A—$3 00

THE GRAND MILITARY CELEBRATION
Astronomer on the watch for Change in the Heavenly Bodies
Wonderous Fancy 1892

18 POINT TYPAL.   24 a 12 A—$3 75

HONORS FOR COLUMBUS
Great Discoveries made Four Hundred Years ago
San Salvador 1492

24 POINT TYPAL.   16 a 10 A—$4 50

HANDSOME ITALICS
Erection of the Columbus Statue
Honduras 580

Chicago—Warehouse, 109 Quincy Street—Chas. B. Ross, Manager.

20 A 30 a   12 POINT FAIR (2 line Nonp.) $2 50

DRYQUICK PRINTING INK COMPANY

1234567890   Black and Colored Writing Printing and Lithographic Inks of all Kinds

Colored Inks Guaranteed to Dry Instantly after Using

12 A 25 a   18 POINT FAIR (3 line Nonp.) $3 60

FINE PAPER STOCK
Linen Ledger and Record Paper

Established 1868.

BARNHART BROS. & SPINDLER,

Manufacturers of **SUPERIOR COPPER-MIXED TYPE**

Great Western Type Foundry.

183 to 187 Monroe Street, CHICAGO, ILL.

24 POINT FAIR (4 line Nonp.   10 A 15 a $4 05

UNITED STATES
American Telegraph Districts

6 A 10 a   36 POINT FAIR (6 line Nonp.) $5 40

CELEBRATED
Superior Copper-Mixed Type

COMPLETE WITH FIGURES.

Smiles may be Bright while the Heart is Sad,
the Rainbow is Beautiful in the Air, while beneath is the Moaning of the Sea.
PHENOMENA AND IMPORTANT EVENTS. 1892.

PAT.
PENDING.
BRUCE'S N.Y. TYPE FOUNDRY.

$5.00.   18-POINT ORNAMENTED, NO. 1,563.   25 a and 12 A   5 lb.

Every Part of the Human Frame contributes to Express the
Passions of the Mind, and to Show its Present State to the observer
RISING AND SETTING OF THE SUN. 1892.

$6.05.   24-POINT ORNAMENTED, NO. 1,563.   20 a and 10 A   6 lb. 12 oz.

Printers Supplied with Everything
pertaining to the Business, from a Bodkin to a Press.
GEO. BRUCE'S SON & CO., NEW YORK. 1892

$9.10.   36-POINT ORNAMENTED, NO. 1,563.   15 a and 8 A   10 lb. 2 oz.

Essay on the Origin of Stereotype Printing.
NEW YORK DIRECTORY. 1892.

$5.75.   48-POINT ORNAMENTED. NO. 1,563.   5 a and 5 A   8 lb.

New Explorations and Discoveries.
MORNING EXPRESS. $1845.

GEORGE BRUCE'S SON & CO., TYPE-FOUNDERS, 13 CHAMBERS STREET, NEW YORK.

IGNORANCE OF THE LAW EXCUSES NO ONE.

THERE IS NO QUESTION BUT HABITUAL CHEERFULNESS IS A GREAT BLESSING.

DO NOT BE ABOVE YOUR BUSINESS, NO MATTER WHAT IT IS. 1892.

$3.00. 18–POINT ORNAMENTED, NO. 1,092. 12 A 3 lb.

VARIOUS ORNAMENTS AND MONOCHROME DESIGNS.

SELECT SPECIMENS OF ORNAMENTAL ART AND COLORING.

ART IN THE UNITED STATES. $6,343.

$3.80. 24–POINT ORNAMENTED. NO. 1,092. 10 A 4 lb. 4 oz.

DRAWINGS BY THE OLD MASTERS.

RARE OLD BOOKS AND MODERN WORKS.

BALANCE ON HAND. $125.

$6.35. 36–POINT ORNAMENTED, NO. 1,092. 8 A 7 lb. 12 oz.

NEW ENGLAND EXPRESS CO.

SAVING BANKS. 1892.

$6.30. 48–POINT ORNAMENTED, NO. 1,092. 5 A 8 lb. 12 oz.

NOTICE TO SHIPPERS

PREPAID. 1892.

GEORGE BRUCE'S SON & CO., TYPE-FOUNDERS, 13 CHAMBERS STREET, NEW YORK

TYPEFOUNDERS' COMPETITION.

BY AN EMPLOYING PRINTER.

EMPLOYING printers throughout the country have watched with much interest the development of the American Typefounders' Company, the first intimation of its projection causing an uneasiness which has since been largely dissipated by the soothing explanations of its members, and from the inability of the company to complete the solidarity contemplated, though it is doubtless quite sufficiently strong to carry out the reforms proposed, the bringing about of which is its excuse for existence. "Trust" and "combine" are distasteful words to American citizens who are not "in it," and I have no desire to use these terms in connection with the American Typefounders' Company — as there are perhaps sufficient founders outside of the corporation to serve as a wholesome check on the concern assuming the complexion of a combine.

Printers have generally come to the conclusion that they have not much to fear but a good deal to gain from the new order of things which the company proposes to bring about, and not the least of these is the restraint of credit to proper channels. A prominent official of the concern says : "The causes that brought about the amalgamation of the twenty-three foundries into one company were that under the various ownerships of the foundries the prices for type and printers' material were being cut to a ruinous extent. Middlemen were also increasing in number and pitting one founder against another until they got their goods at sometimes less than the cost of production, and all along the line there was a continuous strife between the founders and the middlemen to sell type and material upon any terms to printers. . . The policy of the American Typefounders' Company is not to raise prices on type ; on the contrary, the making of type will be centralized into a few centers, and at these centers type will be manufactured on such a large scale, with the most improved machinery, that it can be made and will be sold to the trade cheaper than ever before. The American Typefounders' Company are determined to deal with the printing trade direct, and not through middlemen ; and the printer will get the full benefit of the new methods of manufacture, in lower prices and in better material."

This seems very satisfactory, and would do much to encourage the trade in placing its belief in the company conserving the interest of printers, but many would like to be satisfied with regard to the editorial in THE INLAND PRINTER for December to what degree the company has control of its membership. The name of a gentleman of prominence in the company has lately been given in letters of incorporation as the chief promoter of a printing firm lately incorporated to do business in Chicago, the ostensible principal of which has a disastrous record of failure, and this it must be confessed is rather disappointing to believers in the company from the outside. Owners of large offices will not look with very lively satisfaction on the depreciation in the value of their plant when they "get the full benefit of the new methods of manufacture in lower prices and in better material." Though the middlemen be done away with, there are enough of the founders on the other side of the fence (with whose reasons for being there we have nothing logically to do) who may make an interesting demonstration if the company puts a squeeze on them under cover of its "superior facilities and giving customers the benefit," etc. In such event, between the two factions cheap john printers will be jubilant, but the legitimate trade will be made very, very tired.

A NEW TYPESETTING MACHINE — THE FORMOTYPE.

A CORRESPONDENT in Akron, Ohio, writes under date of December 20 :

"The December number of THE INLAND PRINTER announced that a patent upon a new typesetting machine had been issued to Louis Ransom and Alexander W. Maynus. These gentlemen are Akronians, the former an artist and well-known inventor, the latter assistant manager sales department, The Werner Printing and Lithographing Company, and their machine, the "Formotype," will be put upon the market shortly by a syndicate of Cleveland and Akron capitalists, who have been behind the enterprise for the past three years.

"The Formotype is an entirely new departure in the line of typesetting machines, occupying a sphere peculiarly its own, and by it the ultimate result is expeditiously reached, the many intermediate processes that make other machines so clumsy, slow and unsafe being eliminated entirely. Your correspondent has examined this machine and finds that the letters are stamped directly upon the edge of a strip of soft metal that has been prepared of proper dimensions. A keyboard, not unlike that of the usual typewriter, projects from the front of the machine and by pressing upon one of the keys mechanism is actuated that brings the die, which is in intaglio form, immediately beneath an impression orifice, and by the operation of a reciprocating plunger the die is impressed upon the metal forming the proper letter. The machine is so constructed that this operation can be repeated as rapidly as the compositor can play upon the keys, and it will not be impossible to attain the speed of the usual typewriter upon the Formotype. Of course there are spacing keys, enough metal being removed from the line between words by a chisel to make the spaces. The most ingenious part of the machine is the justifying mechanism which works like a charm. It is based upon the principle that by compressing a line of impressible material the line is elongated. A pair of jaws grip the line automatically, at the spaces, after the words are formed upon it and while another line is being made, and a certain amount of compression being given between each word the line is squeezed out to its proper length, which is column width.

"Proofreading with the Formotype is easier than in hand composition. It is not necessary to form an entirely new line when an error is made, as is the case in other machines, this being hazardous work, as the operator is liable to make the same or some other error when the line is formed anew.

"The International Formotype Company, which controls the foreign patents, has protected this machine in the most desirable countries, and they are now negotiating with eastern capitalists who are anxious to control certain foreign rights. It is reported also that a company now manufacturing a well-known typesetting machine have made overtures to the home company."

A. D. FARMER AND SON

TYPE FOUNDING CO.

— NEW YORK —
63 & 65 Beekman Street and
62 & 64 Gold Street.

— CHICAGO —
Warehouse, 109 Quincy Street.
Chas. B. Ross, Manager.

This Firm is not connected in any way with THE AMERICAN TYPE FOUNDERS' TRUST.

12 POINT BOREAS—PATENT PENDING.   18 A—$3 00

GREAT NAVAL PARADE ON THE HUDSON

THUNDEROUS SALUTES FROM THE GREAT IRONCLAD SHIPS

CHARMING WEATHER 1893

18 POINT BOREAS.   12 A—$3 75

COLUMBIAN EXHIBITION

DEDICATION OF THE BUILDINGS

BOREAS TYPE 293

24 POINT BOREAS.   8 A—$3 75

THE WESTERN STARS

NOW BOREAS RULES THE SEA

CHEMISTRY 584

A. D. FARMER & SON   (Late Farmer, Little & Company.)   TYPE FOUNDING CO.

Ferdinand

Mechanical Patent, March 31, 1885.

3 A, 5 a. 60 Point Ferdinand. $9.85

Harlequinade

Frolicsome

Recreative

4 A, 10 a. 36 Point Ferdinand. $5.30

Convulsed with Laughter

Amusing the Overworked with Burlesque

Scaramouch Performances

1234567890

3 A, 8 a. 48 Point Ferdinand. $7.35

Knowledge and
Genius avoiding

Beaten Tracks

ALL COMPLETE WITH FIGURES.

The MacKellar, Smiths & Jordan Co., { 606-614 Sansom Street, Philadelphia.
Western Branch: 328-330 Dearborn St., Chicago.

430   January 1893

THE DE VINNE SERIES

CAST BY
H. C. HANSEN,

24 and 26 Hawley Street, = = Boston, Mass.

---

36 a 24 A   6-POINT DE VINNE. $2.25

DISTINGUISHED PERSONS WITH GOOD MANNERS
Circumstances Brought into Subjection by a Tenacious Adherence

26 a 20 A   10-POINT DE VINNE. $2.75

RECEIVED CHRISTMAS PRESENTS
Amounting to Eighteen Cents Expended Almost

18 a 12 A   14-POINT DE VINNE. $3.25

DEBASING MANHOOD
Pugilistic Affairs Tend to Vitiate

10 a 8 A   24-POINT DE VINNE. $4.00

FRENCH DAME
Breath 67 Perfume

30 a 22 A   8-POINT DE VINNE. $2.50

PRIDE CAUSES MORE WRETCHEDNESS
Fluent Speaking Should be Regulated and Modulated

20 a 16 A   12-POINT DE VINNE. $3.00

COMPOSITION REQUIRES
Constant Study Thorough Knowledge

16 a 10 A   18-POINT DE VINNE. $3.25

SUPREME ENDURE
Admire Mundane Courage

9 a 6 A   30-POINT DE VINNE. $5.00

CONDENSE
Manly 25 Eolian

8 a 5 A   36-POINT DE VINNE. $5.50

PRINTING COMPANY
Friendship 364 December

6 a 4 A   42-POINT DE VINNE. $7.25

HONEST DEACON
Straight 298 American

5 a 4 A   48-POINT DE VINNE. $7.75

DARING 56 Comely

HHHHHHHHHHHHHHHHHHHH

WOMEN COMPOSITORS.

THE New York *Sun*, a few weeks ago, printed an article giving the experiences and observations of a woman who has worked at the printing trade for thirty years and made a success of it. "The girl who is thinking about an occupation, with a view to making it support her, might do a great deal worse than to learn the printer's trade," such is the negative encouragement of the opening sentences of the article. The reporter who interviewed the woman is frank enough. After stating that "she is one of the few women who have proved that women can and do rise above the ranks, and is one of about four women in New York city who are forewomen in printing establishments, he goes on to say of her work, "she has charge of the book department of her house, and is responsible for the work done by from seven to fifteen employés, according to the amount of work on hand." The frankness comes in at the statement: "Her pay is $18 a week, which is a very good salary indeed, as women's wages run, *though it may be remarked in passing that she replaced a man at $22*." Just merely in passing! "The wages paid women in the printing trade range from $9 to $25. Twelve or fourteen is about the average. Women would be more valuable, of course, if they didn't require so much waiting on. If an office employs five or six women, it has to employ a boy to do odd things for them, or they will bother the men employés so much asking to have things lifted or carried that the men won't work in the office." After accepting lower wages to get a position which this last sentence admits they are not capable of filling satisfactorily, it *does* seem rather too much to ask the men employés to assist in lowering their own wages.

But then the "forelady" says in palliation of the men objecting: "The men, of course, are hardly to be blamed for disliking to see girls come into the offices. They do injure the trade, because they accept far less wages than a man can support his family on. As compositors they are fully as competent as men. They carry out instructions more accurately. Their home training in neatness has its effect on their work. They are steadier workers, too, and they don't run out every few hours to see a man."

To the claim that women are as competent as men, we offer in rebuttal, the words of no less an authority than Mrs. Annie Besant, who, with her coadjutors, employs female help in doing the work in their printing office. Mrs. Besant says they could get the work done as cheaply if they employed union men, but she preferred to employ women, because they were, as a rule, underpaid.

This is an admission of the inferiority of women, generally speaking, as workers in the printing office. If Mrs. Besant's experience proves anything it is that while women are not paid so much as men, yet the result shows that men, although paid higher wages than women, turn out the work as cheaply. In regard to the claim of superior "neatness" on account of home training, etc., which, it is claimed, has its effect on women's work, we doubt if women are generally any less slovenly than men. If they are steadier workers, which is doubtful, they are indefatigable talkers, and if they don't run out every few hours to see a man they do to see a woman — besides making a practice of coming late to their work in the morning and at noon.

We are not desiring to belittle or discourage women workers in the printing office, but are merely desirous of putting matters in a plain light and on a proper basis, letting the sentimental part of the matter take care of itself with the assistance of the space-fillers on the daily press. Let us give women all the recognition and help possible, but do not let us encourage her when endowed with energy and talent to waste them in climbing to the dizzy pinnacle of the position of a "forelady" of a female printery at $18 per week. Let us paraphrase the *Sun* and tell our women that "the girl who is thinking about an occupation with a view to making it support her might do a *great deal better* than to learn the printer's trade."

THE NEED OF A COMPETENT FOREMAN.

To the Editor:　　　　OAKLAND, Cal., January 12, 1893.

Occasionally there is a printing office with the jobroom under the supervision of a foreman that knows comparatively nothing about good job printing nor how a jobroom should be managed. In such an office the foreman is a source of continual annoyance to a job printer who understands his business and is trying to keep up with the times in fine jobwork. He can't set a line of script and space it correctly, and any job he sets would be a first-class specimen for a collection of monstrosities. When he attempts to criticise and mark a proof of a job set by a competent printer it is spoiled every time.

Under such a foreman an ambitious artist will progress like a boy climbing a slippery pole — he will never get on top. Such an office generally runs behind at the end of the year, and all caused by the ignorance of the foreman, whereby jobs are dragged along, material wasted, etc.

In this office a printer may work hard all day setting a job that the foreman couldn't duplicate in the same time; then he takes a proof; it is read, corrected and another proof taken; the foreman thinks it might be improved some by changing two or three lines, and, of course, they have to be changed. A revise is then taken, which is handed to the respective solicitor who took the job to submit to the customer, but the solicitor thinks that a line or two ought to be set in lighter type or something else. Well, the foreman doesn't know the difference, so he has the change made and another clean proof taken. When finally they are all satisfied it is taken to the customer, who tears his hair and howls and wonders why they can't hire some printers that can set a job right side up. And he won't have the job, so it has to be all set over again. Now, I want to ask, why wouldn't it have been better to have sent the first good proof to the customer, and save all that time wasted in making useless changes?

In an office in this city, on all the jobs that are printed, one-third of the profit is lost before the job is ready for the press by trying to suit everyone with the job before it is shown to the customer, and a number of other items might be mentioned where time is lost and the patience of the printers worn, but suffice it to say that money would be made by putting a competent man in charge of such a jobroom.　　ANT IQUE.

Astoria  Series

NEWEST SPECIMEN SHEETS

Cheap Newspaper Press

Printers Standard Nonparell Emerald

1234567890

AMERICAN MACHINIST

Brand New Shaft

Repairs Given Extra Attention

1234567890

SIXTEEN HUNDRED

Tourists Exploring Africa

Starve to Death

USFEUL SERIES

Includes Nice Figures

Eighty Seven

UNITED STATES CADET

Torpedo Boats Quickly Repaired

French War Vessel

CENTRAL BUILDING

Manager Desires Agents

Womans Temple

DEARBORN

Street Milk Depot

Manufactured by BARNHART BROS. & SPINDLER, CHICAGO. Kept in stock and sold by Great Western Typefoundry, Omaha ; Great Western Typefoundry, Kansas City ; Minnesota Typefoundry, St. Paul ; and St. Louis Printers' Supply Co., St. Louis.

IVANHOE SERIES.

8 Point Ivanhoe.

12A, $1.20. 20a, $1.20.   Complete Font, $2.40

LAUGH AND THE WORLD SNICKERS

With You, But Weep and You Will Weep Quite Alone

When Glad Your Friends Will Be Many

$123456   Be Sad and You Will Lose   67890

10 Point Ivanhoe.

10A, $1.15. 18a, $1.20.   Complete Font, $2.35

WITH THEE, MY BARK, I'LL

Swiftly Go Athwart the Foaming Brine, Nor

Gare What Land Thou Bearest

$3245   Me to, So Not to Mine   16789

12 Point Ivanhoe.

10A, $1.20. 16a, $1.20.   Complete Font, $2.40

EVERY ONE OF THE SUNSHINE

Friends Who Stuck to Him While His

Ducats Lasted, Alas! Have

$12345   Faded and Gone   167980

16 Point Ivanhoe.

8A, $1.50. 14a, $1.55.   Complete Font, $3.05

HE IS A PLAIN HONEST

Man in the Parliament of Man

The Federation of the

$12345   World!   567890

8A, $2.00. 12a, $1.75.   18 Point Ivanhoe.   Complete Font, $3.75

THE MORNING WATCH WAS COME

The Vessel Lay Her Course and Gently Made Her Way

67889   The Cloven Billows Flashed   12345

6A, $2.35. 10a, $2.40.   24 Point Ivanhoe.   Complete Font, $4.75

FRIENDS ARE MANY, BE SAD

$12356   And You Lose Them   67890

4A, $2.90. 6a, $2.35.   30 Point Ivanhoe.   Complete Font $5.25

BUT ALONE YOU MUST

$1234   Drink Life's Gall   67890

4A, $3.30. 5a, $2.30.   36 Point Ivanhoe.   Complete Font $5.50

IN THE HALLS OF

$1234   Gaily Sing   5688

CAST BY CLEVELAND TYPE FOUNDRY, CLEVELAND, OHIO.
For Sale by all Foundries and Branches of the American Typefounders' Company.

Isabella Series

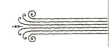

8 A, 32 a.　　　　12 POINT ISABELLA.　　　　$3.80

Falltime Invitation to Fastidious Womankind

Display of Shapely Parisian Styles

The undersigned, Artist Milliners from Paris, beg leave to inform the ladies of Fadville that they have opened a Grand Emporium for the sale of Fashionable Millinery and Ostrich Plumes calculated to heighten attractiveness of form by producing graceful effects. Every requirement of good style and superior service can be relied upon when purchasing from us

Cagliostro, Tartufe & Company

2637 Maiden Lane, Fadville

5 A, 20 a.　　　　18 POINT ISABELLA.　　　　$4.15

Headquarters Ladies' Dress Reform Club

Special Circular to Members

In pursuance of Resolution adopted at the November meeting, members will hereafter, when visiting places of amusement, refrain from wearing towering bonnets and hats decorated with soaring plumes and glaring flowers

Tasteful and Original Design

10 A, 35 a.　　　　9 POINT ISABELLA.　　　　$3.45

Enforced Sale of Fashionable Headgear and Trimmings

Entire Stock to be Sold without Reserve

Owing to resolutions recently passed by the Ladies' Dress Reform Club, and the unexpected demands from our creditors, we have this day decided to sacrifice our large stock of Ladies' and Misses' Headgear, consisting of

Fashionable Bonnets　　　Crinkled Feathers
Silk and Satin Ribbons　　Colored Ostrich Plumes
Hamburg Edgings　　　Artificial Flowers

As no reasonable offers will be refused for these pretty and stylish goods, ladies should not hesitate to call on us and avail themselves of this chance

December 24, 1985　　　Richwine, Jackson & Company

MULTIFORM SPECIMENS.

ORIGINAL.

4A 36-Point Multiform No. 1. $4.25

COURTEOUS JUNIORS
OLD ❖ ACADEMY

5A 30-Point Multiform No. 1. $3.75

RELATED SAD ROMANCE
❖ SENTIMENTALIST ❖

6A 24-Point Multiform No. 1. $3.25

GOLDEN HOUR
CHILDHOOD

8A 18-Point Multiform No. 1. $2.75

FAIR ❖ MARGUERITE
EYES LIKE FATE

4A 36-Point Multiform No. 2. $4.25

COURTEOUS JUNIORS
OLD ❖ ACADEMY

5A 30-Point Multiform No. 2. $3.75

RELATED SAD ROMANCE
❖ SENTIMENTALIST ❖

6A 24-Point Multiform No. 2. $3.25

GOLDEN HOUR
CHILDHOOD

8A 18-Point Multiform No. 2. $2.75

FAIR ❖ MARGUERITE
EYES LIKE FATE

CAST BY CENTRAL TYPE FOUNDRY, ST. LOUIS, MISSOURI.

For Sale by all Foundries and Branches of the American Type Founders' Company.

ORIGINAL.

5a 3A   54-POINT ANTIQUE No. 6. $10.00

REND FORMS
Inducement

5a 3A   48-POINT ANTIQUE No. 6. $8.00

STRING BANKS
Note Cashed

6a 4A   42-POINT ANTIQUE No. 6. $7.00

SELFISH
Market

8a 5A   30-POINT ANTIQUE No. 6. $4.50

FINE SUGAR
Plantations

16a 10A   18-POINT ANTIQUE No. 6. $3.25

ADMIRING ROMAN
Church and Palace

6a 4A   36-POINT ANTIQUE No. 6. $5.00

DESIGNER
Complete

10a 6A   24-POINT ANTIQUE No. 6. $4.00

ADMIRE MINES
Silver Bullion

20a 14A   14-POINT ANTIQUE No. 6. $3.00

HISTORIANS OF FRANCE
Government Property

HHHHHHHHHHHHHHHHH

CAST BY CENTRAL TYPE FOUNDRY, ST. LOUIS, MISSOURI.
For Sale by all Foundries and Branches of the American Type Founders' Company.

A. D. FARMER and SON

TYPE FOUNDING CO.

— NEW YORK —
63 & 65 Beekman Street and
62 & 64 Gold Street.

— CHICAGO ---
Warehouse, 109 Quincy Street.
Chas. B. Ross, Manager.

PATENT PENDING.

12 POINT LOCKWOOD.

18 a 12 A $3 50

HANDSOME SERIES NAMED LOCKWOOD

Thirty-six Point, the New Size, is now ready and is shown below
The Fonts are cast to Line 1893

18 POINT LOCKWOOD.

12 a 8 A $4 00

THE SLEIGH BELLS RING OUT

Old Fashioned Wintry Weather will Delay Business

Saratoga 1893

24 POINT LOCKWOOD.

10 a 6 A- $4 50

THE LOCKWOOD SERIES

Bookmaking by Authors and Workmen

Monmouth 1893

30 POINT LOCKWOOD.

8 a 5 A—$5 50

PLEASANT TIMES

Reliable Stories of Fishing Exploits

Students 1685

NEW SIZE—NOW READY.

36 POINT LOCKWOOD.

6 a 4 A $6 25

METROPOLITAN

Capital Cities of the World

Printers 1893

Royal Script.

ORIGINAL.

Annual Meeting State Board of Public Charities

Official Investigating Committees

Daily Excursion Train to Jefferson Barracks and Vicinity

First Class Refreshments to be Furnished

Directory of the Island of Cuba, Porto-Rico and St. Thomas

Matter Relating to the Spanish Government

Displaying Admirable Specimens of Superior Modern Script Faces

Artistic and Durable Type for Circulars and Invitations

Superior Design and Masterly Execution of American Workmen Highly Praised

Miss Rita Hosmer Desires Your Presence Thursday Evening

Fourteenth Annual Dance of the Hibernian Society   *Spending Much Time in Writing Sonnets to her Beauty*

Pleasant Evening Entertainment   *Meandering on Summer Evenings*

Celebrated Soloist of Musicville will Appear   *More Practical Suitor Monopolizes Her Time*

Enlarged Orchestra Furnished Music   *Records Many Nice Little Quiet Strolls*

CAST BY CENTRAL TYPE FOUNDRY, ST. LOUIS.

For Sale by all Foundries and Branches of the American Type Founders' Co.

4a 3A 72-POINT NOVELTY SCRIPT. $16.00

Beatrice Granger
Nature's Child

5a 3A 60-POINT NOVELTY SCRIPT. $11.75

Whistling Heathens
Love is Blind

6a 3A 48-POINT NOVELTY SCRIPT. $9.00

King's Lake
Cat Fish

8a 4A 36-POINT NOVELTY SCRIPT. $7.25

Happy Dreams
Night Time

12a 5A 24-POINT NOVELTY SCRIPT. $5.25

Beauties of the Vintage
Pure Grape Juice

16a 5A 18-POINT NOVELTY SCRIPT. $4.00

Vice Stings Even in Our Pleasure
Field of Golden Clover

CAST BY CENTRAL TYPE FOUNDRY, ST. LOUIS.
For Sale by all Foundries and Branches of the American Type Founders' Co.

EPITAPH SERIES

PATENTED.

MANUFACTURED BY BOSTON TYPE FOUNDRY, BOSTON, MASS.

(Canon)   48-POINT EPITAPH.   3A, $6.00

MODERN CASKETS UNDERTAKERS

(Dbl. Gt. Primer)   36-POINT EPITAPH   5A, $4.25

HANDSOME CEMETERIES THE GRAVE DIGGER 85

(Dbl. Pica)   24-POINT EPITAPH   7A, $3.25

DEPARTED ❖ FRIENDS ❖ EULOGIZED
◄BIRTH AND DEATH►
GLOOMY RESTING PLACE 43

(Gt. Primer)   18-POINT EPITAPH   9A, $2.50

MORTUARY EMBELLISHMENTS MANUFACTURED
◄EVERLASTING AND BEAUTIFUL►
CROSSES ❖ AND ❖ MARBLE ❖ ORNAMENTS ❖ 28

(Pica)   12-POINT EPITAPH.   14A, $2.25

IMPROVED PROCESS AROMATIC EMBALMING SKILFULLY PERFORMED

◄TRUE FRIENDSHP AND SINCERE AFFECTION►

CAST BY CENTRAL TYPE FOUNDRY, ST. LOUIS.

For Sale by all Foundries and Branches of the American Type Founders' Co.

4A 48-POINT QUAINT ROMAN. $6.75

VESPER HYMNS
GLOAMING 87

4A 36-POINT QUAINT ROMAN. $4.40

BLOW WINTER WINDS
ROUGH NIGHTS

6A 24-POINT QUAINT ROMAN. $3.00

HUNGRY AND THIRSTY TRAMPS
ENJOYING HOT DINNER $5

8A 18-POINT QUAINT ROMAN. $2.80

SOCIALISTIC INCENDIARY HARRANGUES
DESTROYING HAPPINESS 90

14A 12-POINT QUAINT ROMAN. $2.00

GOOD CONDUCT RECEIVES RESPECT OF ALL HONEST PEOPLE
LET TRUTH AND JUSTICE ALWAYS LEAD
INSINUATIONS CONSIST OF ARTFUL WINDINGS £20

14A 10-POINT QUAINT ROMAN. $2.00

COUNTLESS SHOALS OF SHRIMPY TRIBES ABIDE BY SOLWAYS FALLOW TIDE
RUGGED CLIFFS AND CASTLES 13

HHHHₕₕ   The various sizes of the QUAINT ROMAN Series can be easily
lined in combination as Caps and Small Caps,
with Point justification.   ₕₕₕₕₕHH

CAST BY CENTRAL TYPE FOUNDRY, ST. LOUIS.

For Sale by all Foundries and Branches of the American Type Founders' Co.

PATENTED NOVEMBER 29, 1892.

Price per Sont.
36 Point . . $2.00
48 Point . . 3.00
60 Point . . 4.00

3 A.   60 POINT COLUMBUS. $7.80

REMARKS

3 A.   48 POINT COLUMBUS. $5.60

FOUNDER

5 A.   36 POINT COLUMBUS. $4.35

STEAM YACHTS

10 A.   24 POINT COLUMBUS. $3.90

MOUNTEBANK
AUTUMNAL EXCURSION

15 A.   18 POINT COLUMBUS. $3.45

AMUSING ORATIONS
FURNISHED FOR COMEDIANS
1234567890

24 POINT COLUMBUS WITH 48 POINT INITIALS.

THE FIRST CRUISE

B C E F K L Q R S T V W

American Type Founders' Company
MACKELLAR, SMITHS & JORDAN FOUNDRY
Philadelphia—Pittsburgh—Buffalo—Chicago

24 A 50 a   6 POINT MONARCH (Nonpareil) $2 30

MAGNIFICENT AND VERY FASHIONABLE
Black Walnut and Rosewood Drawing Room Furniture
1234567890

20 A 40 a   9 POINT MONARCH (Bourgeois) $2 55

SECOND REGIMENT ARMORY
Uniforms for Military and Naval Officers

18 A 36 a   11 POINT MONARCH (Small Pica) $3 00

NATIONAL COMMITTEE
Important Telegraph Communications

9 A 18 a   18 POINT MONARCH (3 line Nonp.) $3 25

CONDENSED
Useful Accented Letter

20 A 40 a   8 POINT MONARCH (Brevier) $2 30

MONARCH OF ALL IT SURVEYS
Copper-Mixed Type Throws Its Luminous Rays
1234567890

18 A 36 a   10 POINT MONARCH (Long Primer) $2 70

CENTRAL LOAN COMPANY
Chicago Milwaukee and New London

18 A 36 a   12 POINT MONARCH (2 line Nonp) $3 20

GRAND UNION HOTEL
Elegantly Furnished Front Suite

6 A 12 a   24 POINT MONARCH (4 line Nonp.) $3 50

MOUNTAINS
Deserts and Camels

5 A 10 a   30 POINT MONARCH (5 line Nonp.) $4 05

THE MORNING SUN
Dederick Center Evening Beacon

4 A 6 a   36 POINT MONARCH (6 line Nonp.) $5 00

FRENCH PRISON
Soldiers Building Society

4 A 6 a   48 POINT MONARCH. (8 line Nonp.) $6 95

HOUSEHOLD
Furniture Merchant

Manufactured from superior copper-mixed metal by Barnhart Bros. & Spindler, Chicago. Carried in stock by Minnesota Typefoundry, St. Paul; Great Western Typefoundry, Omaha; Great Western Typefoundry, Kansas City; and St. Louis Printers' Supply Company, St. Louis.

25 A, 40 a.   12 POINT OLD STYLE COND. No 4 $2.40

A FISHER'S CHILD WITH TRESSES WILD
Was Quickly Unto the Smooth, Bright Sand Beguiled
1 2 3 4 5 6 7 8 9 0

15 A, 20 a.   24 POINT OLD STYLE COND. No. 4. $3.60

Handsome MAHOGANY Furniture

6 A, 10 a.   40 POINT OLD STYLE COND. No. 4. $4.05

Amazon RIVER Station

20 A, 30 a.   18 POINT OLD STYLE COND. No. 4 $3.30

MY DREAMFUL SPIRIT FLIES
Where Bright Summer Sunshine Never Dies

10 A, 15 a.   36 POINT OLD STYLE COND. No. 4. $4.50

Monster MILITARY Parade

6 A, 10 a.   48 POINT OLD STYLE COND. No 4. $5.60

Dress REFORM Club

CONDENSED RUNIC No. 2.

25 A, 42 a.   8 POINT COND. RUNIC No. 2. $2.25

ALL THEY THAT TREAD THE GLOBE
Are but a Handful to the Tribes that Slumber in its Bosom
1 2 3 4 5 6 7 8 9 0

18 A, 24 a.   12 POINT COND. RUNIC No. 2. $2.65

Unprofitable MOUNTAIN Explorations

12 A, 18 a,   22 POINT COND. RUNIC No. 2. $4.20

Village SCHOOL Ground

8 A, 10 a.   36 POINT COND. RUNIC No. 2. $6.75

Fine SILK Hats

22 A, 32 a.   10 POINT COND. RUNIC No. 2. $2.40

SO LIVE, THAT WHEN THY
Summons Comes to Join the Innumerable Host

14 A, 20 a.   18 POINT COND. RUNIC No. 2. $3.50

Striking HANDSOME Display

10 A, 14 a.   28 POINT COND. RUNIC No. 2. $5.35

Jolly LITTLE Maid

6 A, 8 a.   43 POINT COND. RUNIC No. 2. $8.40

PURE water

4 A, 6 a.   60 POINT COND. RUNIC No. 2. $9.25

Daily BOOK Sales

ALLISON & SMITH,   FRANKLIN **TYPE** FOUNDRY,   *168 Vine St., Cincinnati, O.*

For sale by all Foundries and Branches of the American Type Founders' Co.

GOTHIC ITALIC No. 3.

STEEPLE TOWERS AND GLOOMY BOWERS
Moneyed Husbands Without Brains Supplied Cheap on Short Notice

SOMEWHAT BACK FROM THE VILLAGE STREET

Stands the Old-Fashioned Country-Seat, and Across Its Antique
Portico Tall Poplar Trees Their
Shadows Throw, and From Its Station In the Hall 246

GRAND DISPLAY FOR NEW YEAR'S DAY

Beautiful Ornaments, Charming Music and Good Singing
American Dance Hall, Tickets Five Dollars 357

Eastern QUINCE Mashers

DREAD THUNDER'S AMPLE VOICE

Lightning Flashes Around the Mountain Range
Miners Seek Their Home in Haste

NATIONAL IRON COMPANY

Malleable Iron and Steel Manufacturers

HANDSOME FURNITURE
Elaborate Silk, Satin and Plush

BEAUTIFUL YOUNG MAIDENS
New Patent Skirts for Street Admiration Just Made

Heard ORGAN Music

CAST BY MARDER, LUSE & CO. FOUNDRY, CHICAGO.
For Sale by all Foundries and Branches of the American Type Founders' Co.

GRAND GUTTEMBURGH FESTIVAL
Commemorating the Four Hundred
and Fiftieth Anniversary of the—450

DISCOVERY OF PRINTING
Was Inaugurated in Mayence
lately. In 1837 the Statue in

GUTTEMBURG PLACE
Was erected in Honor of
The Discoverer of Types

UNIQUE PRINTING
Specimens have been
Placed on View in the

OLD MUSEUM
Inspection Hall
and Citizens of

MAYENCE
Often Point
out the Old

HOUSE
in which
he dwelt

Abbey  No. 2.

The following additions to this popular Series—48 and 60 pt.—
are now ready for delivery.

NEW ABBEY

LETTERS

Band Masters

Figures supplied with all Fonts.

THE LAST

FLIGHT

Gay Homes

Since this Foundry first issued the Abbey Series many grotesque imitations of
it have been made, the Original Abbey, however, is still incomparable.

A. D. FARMER and SON
TYPE FOUNDING COMPANY.

Not in the Trust.   — Established 1804 —   Beekman St., N. Y.

May 1893   447

5A, 10a, Double Great Primer (36 Point). 4.75

CLEARING SALE
Shaggy Fur Beaver
Calamity Clothing

12A, 24a, Pica (12 Point). 2.25

SIX THOUSAND CARATS WEIGHT OF SOUTH
AFRICAN DIAMONDS WASHED OUT

Exhibit of Diamond Cutting Machines
Precious Stones from Mines in Brazil
Everything Realistic in the Extreme
Noticeable Feature: Tiger-Eye Gems

4A, 8a, Four-Line Pica (48 Point). 6.00

Merchants INSURANCE Company

Seven-Line Nonpareil in Preparation.

20A, 40a, Long Primer (10 Point). 2.00

IN THE CHURCH OF SAINTED LAWRENCE STANDS
A PIX OF SCULPTURE RARE

This Pix, or Tabernacle for the Vessels of the Sacraments
Is an Exquisite Piece of Sculpture, in White Stone.
It Stands in the Choir, Whose Richly Painted
Windows Cover it with Varied Colors.

1 2 3 4 5 6 7 8 9 0

8A, 16a, Double Pica (24 Point). 3.50

FAT FOLKS REDUCED
Patients Treated by Mail
Freckles, Moth Patches, Spots
Complexion Restored 1234

ALL COMPLETE WITH FIGURES.

6A, 12a, Five-Line Nonpareil (30 Point). 3.75

GREEK ARCHITECTURE
Collection of Sculpture
Before the Christian Era

10A, 20a, Great Primer (18 Point). 2.75

VENETIAN GONDOLIERS
Aquatic Pastimes
Grand Canal Illuminated
Imitations of Water Monsters
1 2 3 4 5 6 7 8 9

CAST BY MARDER, LUSE & CO. FOUNDRY, CHICAGO, ILL.
For Sale by all Foundries and Branches of the American Type Founders' Co.

6A, 12a, Double Pica (24 Point). 4.75

INTRODUCTION

Honorable Competency

Popular Decision

Thatched Mansion

$1234567890

EBONY.

12A, 24a, Pica (12 Point). 4.00

NOTHING WAS HEARD
In the Room but the Hurrying
Pen of the Stripling
Or an Occasional Sigh from
The Laboring Heart.

FIGURES AND LOGOTYPES WITH ALL SIZES.

3A, 6a, Four-Line Pica (48 Point). 9.75

Public Expense

SPASM CHARMS

Thatch Company

SPACES AND QUADS EXTRA.

8A, 16a, Great Primer (18 Point). 4.75

HAVE LABORED
Heroically to Rid the
World of Fools, but
Must abandon the
Impossible Task.

4A, 8a, Double Great Primer (36 Point). 7.25

SUBDUED
Unreadable
Specimens
$1243567

CAST BY MARDER, LUSE & CO. FOUNDRY, CHICAGO, ILL.

For Sale by all Foundries and Branches of the American Type Founders' Co.

Foster Gothic.

ALL COMPLETE WITH FIGURES.

7A,   Five-Line Nonpareil (30 Point).   3.75

RACES METROPOLITAN SUBURBAN

10A,   Great Primer (18 Point).   2.75

IMPROVED METHODS

ELEVATING THE EYEBROWS
WINKING THE EARS   1234567890
SALUTING ACQUAINTANCES

4A,   Four-Line Pica (48 Point).   4.75

STIRRING 1893 EVENTS

8A,   Two-Line Pica (24 Point).   3.50

MONEY

MUSHROOM SECURITIES
UNCOLLECTED BILLS

6A,   Two-Line Great Primer (36 Point).   4.25

PRINTERS' FAREWELL OVERTURES

14A,   Pica (12 Point).   2.25

A LOVER HANDSOME AND TRUE,
SHE SAYS SHE'D LIKE TO GET;
HOW VERY LUCKY FOR US TWO
THAT YOU AND I HAVE MET.
1234567890

CAST BY MARDER, LUSE & CO. FOUNDRY, CHICAGO, ILL.

For Sale by all Foundries and Branches of the American Type Founders' Co.

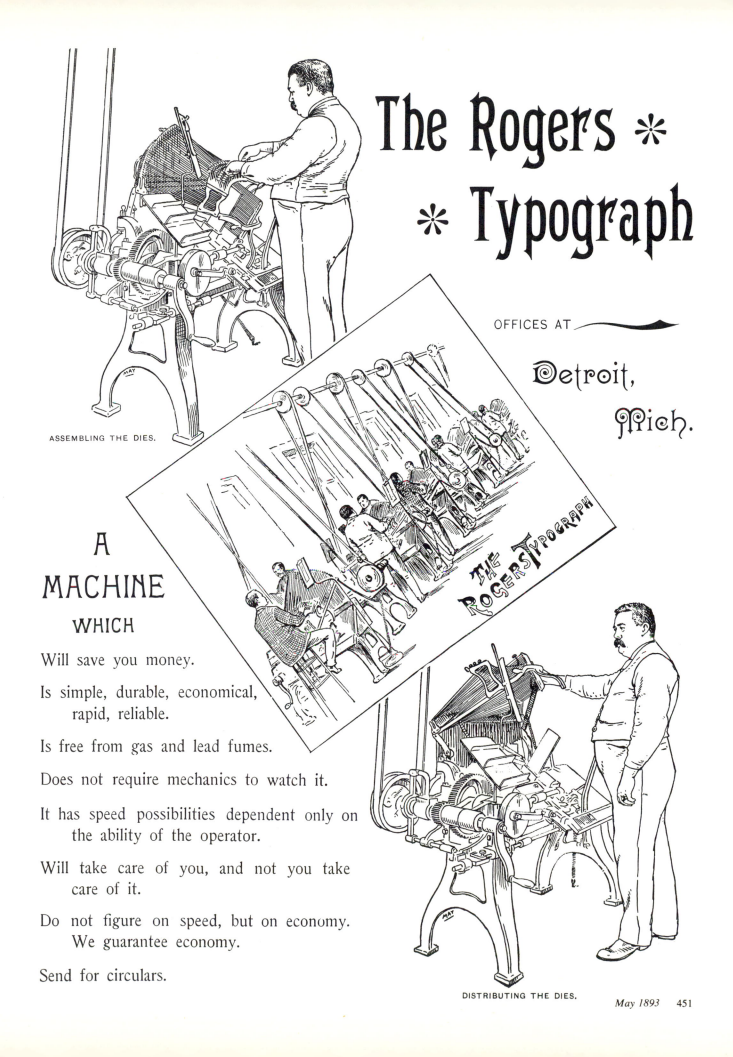

The Rogers * * Typograph

ASSEMBLING THE DIES.

OFFICES AT

Detroit, Mich.

A MACHINE WHICH

Will save you money.

Is simple, durable, economical, rapid, reliable.

Is free from gas and lead fumes.

Does not require mechanics to watch it.

It has speed possibilities dependent only on the ability of the operator.

Will take care of you, and not you take care of it.

Do not figure on speed, but on economy. We guarantee economy.

Send for circulars.

DISTRIBUTING THE DIES.

THE TYPEFOUNDERS' WAR FROM THE PRINTER'S STANDPOINT.

BY TYPOGRAPHICUS.

IT may be fairly presumed that, for the present at least, there will be no change in the prices of type and printing material. The new list forever abolishes the old. It would require a "trust" indeed of the most pronounced type which absolutely controlled every casting machine in America, to restore the old list ; and, as the new company declare that they have sufficient field for operation in the line of economy, and the outside foundries are equally vigorous in their oft-repeated declaration of independence, the purchasers of type need have little fear that competition of a healthy nature will be eliminated from the market. So long as this can be maintained there is no danger.

To the printer who is also a business man, the fixture of prices at a point near the actual selling value, and consequently the abolition of margins so large that they afforded ample room for elastic discounts, will be hailed with satisfaction. For the first time in many years he can accurately estimate the value of his plant, and can fix his insurance at a figure which will at the lowest cost protect him against the eighty per cent co-insurance clause which is generally made a con dition of printing-office risks. He knows he is buying type as cheap as his competitor, and as cheap as his shrewd country cousin who "knows the ropes" and has a few hundred to lay down for printing material.

These points settled, other possibilities of great good to the printing fraternity suggest themselves, and these possibilities are all in the hands of the great company. Perhaps the next and most interesting field is that of type faces—the production of new ones and the abolition of useless old ones. In the past every foundry has persisted in showing its antiquated faces in each succeeding specimen book, and the result has been rapidly growing volumes composed of some new faces, some standard ones that are always needed, and then a lot of riffraff and experiments which no one but a backwoods printer would ever think of buying. But they made the specimen books bulky, and therefore annoying to the business man who was compelled to look through hundreds of useless pages to find the one he wanted. The American Typefounders' Company can issue specimen books which contain all that is good from their combined product, and leave out the hundreds of series which are neither ornamental nor useful, and the printer who receives such a book will rise up and call them blessed. What a royal compilation it would be—a volume containing, besides the regular array of standard faces like the gothics, antiques, etc., all the cream of such great foundries as MacKellar, Smiths & Jordan Company, the Dickinson, Boston and Central Type Foundries, and Marder, Luse & Co. The printers never demanded the useless

faces. They were the one result of competition that was of no benefit to anyone, and for years the printer has been turning over the pages containing their unsightly faces without buying them. This proposition is true of body type as well as display, though in less degree. The founders could retain the matrices of old faces, so that printers could procure sorts or additional fonts for the offices when they were already in use, but the call would soon die out, and the undesirable faces would then be dead forever. Perhaps the same objections to this course would be made as were offered against the point system. There is always an ultra-conservative class which tries to stay the hand of progress, but as in the former case, they will be dragged along with the procession, and will afterward declare that they were "in it" all the time.

In the arguments of the new company the promise to reform type faces and the manner of showing them has frequently appeared. The thoughtful printer, who regards the recent history of typefounding and the advent of the company from a business point of view, and who is not moved by the rattle of small arms fired by struggling newspapers and the natural enemies of the combine, is watching the actions of the American Typefounder's Company with much interest. He does not join the hue and cry, for he knows that is all incited for an advertising scheme by the competing founders, and that its effect will have no lasting value to its promoters nor injury to the company. He was gratified at the fixing of values. He now looks to see the company continue in its efforts toward a lifting up of the printing business to a higher commercial plane, and for the fulfillment of its promises to render to printers services which would be impossible under a separate management of the foundries. He has held his peace and sawed wood in spite of frantic appeals to withdraw his patronage from the dreaded "octopus," nor has he withdrawn the same. He has seen two glorious events in the history of typemaking take place, namely, the adoption of the point system, under separate foundry ownership, and the reduction of the published price list to a nearly net figure under corporate ownership. He is now waiting for the third number of the great triumvirate to appear, i. e., specimen books which, *while complete*, make useless faces conspicuous by their absence, and withdraw them from the market forever.

The point system.

The reduced price list.

The abolition of useless faces.

These three shall constitute a historic record of progress and enterprise for the typefounders of America, and the new company can justly claim the honor of inaugurating two of them if it will soon carry out its implied promises as to the third.

The business element in the printing fraternity look for it, and they have the right to expect it.

THE PAIGE TYPESETTING MACHINE.

BY W. C. ROBERTS.

THE Paige typesetting machine, which is controlled by the Connecticut Company, with headquarters in New York city, though incorporated in Hartford, Connecticut (capital stock $15,000,000), is manufactured by the Webster Manufacturing Company, of Chicago. A private exhibition of the working of the machine was recently given, which proved the invention a marvelous success. This machine will be on exhibition in all probability at the World's Fair, in the summer, at which time the trade will begin to be supplied. Extraordinary speed is claimed for the machine. In fact it can produce as fast as anyone can operate it. The speed of the apparatus itself is practically without limit. The keyboard — in appearance as simple as that of an ordinary typewriter — is half of the invention, and the inventor, after ten years of study of the difficulties to be overcome, has succeeded in so arranging the keys that, although each one commands a certain letter, the operator is able to strike every letter in a word at the same instant, or, at least, do so without more than one perceptible movement of the hands. The keys are close together, and when both hands are brought into play, they command every lower-case letter. When it is known that the operator produces whole words with a single pressure of one hand, or both at the same time, and that the machinery takes charge of the grouping and spacing, the marvelous speed achieved in setting movable types on this machine can be understood. It distributes, spaces and "leads" automatically. It automatically rejects and disposes of broken or battered type. An indicator on the keyboard shows the operator when a line is full, which is also announced by the tap of a tiny bell. The justification is absolutely perfect and the spacing so even as to be faultless. The operator at work on the machine, at the private exhibition mentioned, stated that after five months' practice he was able to produce 12,900 ems per hour of solid nonpareil. The type in use on the machine is very lean.

The following is as close a description as can now be given without drawings :

The Paige machine is about nine feet long, weighs three tons, and is substantially made of the finest steel, finished with the smoothness of the machinery of a watch. A machine must be made for each kind of type to be used — a nonpareil machine will only set nonpareil ; minion only minion, etc. It uses the same kind of type usually set by hand, only there must be a special nick on each letter, as is the style with the Thorne machine. The type of any foundry can be used or the type in use in any office, only it must be specially nicked.

The keyboard contains 109 characters, arranged in five rows running from left to right. The keys are about three-quarters of an inch square and appear to be made of celluloid. The lower-case letters are at the left. The type case is above the keyboard, each letter being in a channel directly in line with the key which governs it. The case is about three feet long by two and a half wide, and is slightly inclined back from a perpendicular position. It contains 109 channels about half an inch apart, which run up and down, each the size of the letter for which it is used when placed with the nick up. At the extreme left on top of the machine is the space case, eleven different sizes being used. When a letter is called for by touching the keys, it drops out of the case from the bottom and is pushed along to a finger which draws it into a space where it remains until all the letters in the word being set are there, when the operator touches what is called the word key, and another finger moves it along. The machine records the length of the word and then moves it out of the way of the second word, already on its way to join the first. Each word is automatically measured without assistance from the operator. An indicator tells when the line can receive no more words, or parts of words, and a line key is then touched and the machine automatically justi-

fies the line, after which it is dropped into a galley. The machine is spacing the first line while the third is being set. When this galley is filled, it automatically locks the keys, thus calling the operator's attention. The duty of the operator is simply to touch the proper keys ; the machine automatically does the remainder of the work, and it looks to the observer as though the machine regulates the operator instead of vice versa.

What is called the brains of the machine is a wonderful device, and is the result of eighteen years of hard study. It controls the working of every part. For instance, if a key is touched and there is some part of the machine which is not ready to perform its duty, this piece of mechanism locks every other part, until it is time for them to continue working ; and although the letter called for cannot leave the case without the permission of this device, it is not retarded for but a fraction of a second, and then, without a further touching of the key, takes its proper place.

To the left of the operator is the distributor. Three columns of matter placed side by side and about a foot long are placed on a sort of a shelf standing nearly perpendicular. The machine takes the first line, which is, in fact, three, and automatically distributes it. The shelf then moves up and the next line is distributed and so on. It removes any type which may have been damaged by stereotyping or turned end for end by the hand compositor in correcting or otherwise, and drops it in a box provided for the purpose. It takes the spaces out of the line and distributes them in the proper case. The types are then built up one on another from the bottom. On top of the type in each channel is placed a piece of metal resembling a common slug, the thickness varying with the width of the channel. When any one of the channels of type reach up to a certain point in the case, the metal comes in contact with a bar which stops the distribution, thus preventing an overflow of the case. All this of course is done automatically. If the operator should be called away from the machine, it would not matter, as it takes care of itself.

The machine sets and distributes at the same time, and a type can be put in and one taken out during the same revolution of the machine, and although the last letter distributed is the first letter out, there is no chance for conflict.

Here is the explanation of their method of justification : " While this has always been considered impossible of accomplishment its practicability will be clear to anyone, if considered from the mathematical side. Of course, to make any number of things the same length one must start with some length as a standard unit. This unit can be made whatever length the work to be done requires, as the width of any book page or newspaper column. With this length known, the problem is simply this : Take the length of any number of words which are to compose a line and subtract their sum from the unit or standard and the remainder will be the length, which is to be filled out by spaces to separate the words of the line." And this mathematical problem is automatically worked.

The machine runs very lightly, an ordinary sewing machine belt being used on the pulleys. The only machine now in running order is the result of twenty-two years' work. While there will be no change in the principle, the new machines will be different in some respects, some parts made lighter and others heavier, but the whole will weigh considerably less. It oils itself. It adjusts itself to any wear, and it is claimed that the machine can be run constantly for years.

Tables can be set with this machine much quicker than they can be corrected by hand.

All in all, it is a great piece of mechanism, and the inventor can well feel proud of the outcome of his many years' work.

As to the printers — that is another question. For one of the craft to publish what he really thinks of the future would call down upon him the wrath of thousands who do not or will not realize what is in store for them.

AN ELEMENT OF SUCCESS.

BY H. A. B.

AS a young man who has achieved a moderate success by my own efforts I have a message to young men who are hunting the same elusive game. Printers are of more than ordinary intelligence, and hence the only necessity is to get them started right.

The curious thing about this phantom, success, is that it will not come unless you try for it, and make up your mind that you are going to have it. The same truth holds good in any business, but especially in printing, which is making such vast strides forward year by year.

A young friend of mine who is bright, has good habits and ability to hustle, is always finding fault and cursing his luck because he has not been advanced faster. Yet he has not far to seek for his failure. It lies with himself to succeed or not, if he is but willing to pay the price of success. So far he has evinced no willingness to pay the price and is lagging behind in the race, being now employed as pressfeeder in a small office, at $10 a week, while others less favored by nature, perhaps, are forging ahead and will make a goal before long.

His difficulty is in being afraid to put in a little work in acquiring information on the art of printing and studying for new ideas. Though having no connection with the mechanical department of an office, apart from the necessary oversight of the office where the type for the magazine of which I am editor is set, I rejoice in the fact that I could go into the composing room and do anything from washing a form to setting a display ad., slowly, it is true, because out of practice, yet the knowledge makes direction easier.

Further, all the leading trade journals, headed by THE INLAND PRINTER, come to my desk regularly, and I try to keep abreast of the progress of the trade. My young friend, who has had superior advantages in many respects, prefers to enjoy an excess of card playing and other social diversions, harmless in themselves, but doing damage because they take one's attention. One cannot do business and attend card parties and dancing assemblies every night. Now do not construe this as being a phillipic against sociability. It is not. It is simply a warning to "kickers" of one cause of their inability to get ahead faster in the world.

It pays a young man to study, to learn all he possibly can about his business, and when it comes to printing he has much to do to keep up with the progress after he is once a printer. How much better to have the ability and cultivation to aid in that progress. Almost everyone can have it, if they are willing to pay the price.

In addition to what has been said, I would add, throw away the cigar. It does you no good, and the price of cigars for a month would pay for THE INLAND PRINTER a year. The other months can be invested in something else equally as beneficial.

Keep off the street corners. A boarding house is not the best place to pass an evening ; but it is infinitely better than loafing on corners and getting a hard reputation. The free reading rooms in every city can be utilized to good advantage in these days.

Keep away from the pool table. Pool ruins young men, not because the game itself is harmful, but because it distracts their attention.

Pass by the beer mug. The remark I once heard a hotel man make, that if the printers would pay their beer bills he would board them free, had a world of meaning.

Do not be afraid to do some work for nothing. Every man has to do it, and will to the end of time.

Attend to your own business, and always do just as well as you can under all circumstances. That is the winning number. Attention is what wins, and the man who is attentive, sober, industrious and willing to work overtime or for nothing has a sure road to prosperity and advancement.

THE PRINTER THAT I WANT.

BY AN EMPLOYER.

THE printer that I want around my office is a man who has correct and careful habits of thought ; who is possessed with a mental determination to do everything well. The boy who will always be found sweeping the dust and dirt from the corners will be far more likely to make a careful and artistic printer when he arrives at manhood, than one who shirks his work of sweeping when he is not being carefully watched. Nature produces so much that is second rate, and below that grade, that it is no wonder a great deal of her bad work is found in the ranks of the printing fraternity. I had a young man working for me a short time ago, whose antecedents were of the best. He came of a good family ; was well educated. But his experience as a printer had evidently been in offices where slovenliness did not offend the eye of the management. After he had worked for me a month, he came to me one day and thanked me that I had time and again insisted that he should slight nothing — the smallest job was to be done as well, as to presswork, proofreading, etc., as the largest. Dirty sheets of paper were to be rigorously thrown out ; a full count I insisted on, even if a new package of paper had to be broken into for a dozen sheets or less ; no trouble was to be spared to make every job worthy of the office, whether the imprint was on it or not. He had been unaccustomed to this. His youthful training and education taught him that this was right. He realized that that was the proper way to do business, but evidently he had never before seen it work in a country printing office.

FRAUDULENT ADVERTISING MANAGERS.

THE science or art of advertising fills a large place in the public interest at the present day, and has led to a discriminating knowledge on the subject that makes the manipulator of fakes a pariah in the business world. For defense against the false representations of these men, business men usually give to a trusted employé, or to an advertising expert, the office of looking after their advertising interests. It is here, though rarely, we are glad to say, that the employer is sometimes defrauded in a despicable way, by his employé giving out his advertising on the inducement of private commissions. An advertising manager who is capable of such treachery is beneath contempt. The difficulty is that his operations can be concealed so successfully that his vampire tactics may be long continued secretly. It occasionally happens, however, when his evil star is on the ascendant that he allows his greed to overmaster his discretion and his methods are discovered. His punishment is then rarely more than the loss of his position, for the law cannot reach him. Public opinion can reach him though, and his skulking methods blacklist him, while he fancies himself secure in the good opinion of his fellow-men. He is a marked man, and truculency will not save him from his just deserts.

INVENTORS AND HARD-TACK.

To the Editor: WASHINGTON, D. C., July 17, 1893.

It is not my purpose to reiterate the oft-told tales in story and song of the hardships and miserable vicissitudes, to say nothing of the wholesale robberies of the inventors of this country for the last century, but a mere reference to some of them may not be inopportune, even though I should refer to some facts not yet reduced to history.

Let us look at that colossal pyramid at our national capital, known as the Patent office — built and sustained by the inventors of the dead past and the live present, with about $4,000,000 now in the Federal treasury to their credit, and so lax have been the national representatives that all appeals for better facilities and more help have been "sung to deaf ears," and it is not only a fact, but a burning shame, that there are cases now pending nearly a quarter of a century old. Of course, these are exceptional cases, but it is notorious that the Patent office, built by the inventors of the country, is in some departments months behind their work, while the Interior and Land offices are crowding out the Patent office, and causing much unnecessary and expensive delays to that class of our people — the inventors — who are entitled to better treatment.

Let whom that doubts this make a voyage of that industrial caravansary, if he has a few weeks to spare, and behold the myriads of wonderful mind creations that have added more wealth to the country as labor-abettors and labor-savers, than a dozen other causes combined. The inventors of the vast improvements in railway transportation and their successors are virtually almost kicked out of the vast building they have erected; but the now possessors of these inventions, obtained at a nominal cost, are loaded with federal and state muniments, in the gifts of vast tracts of lands, large enough to form empires, and are permitted, without legal restraint worthy of the term, to charge all such tolls as their blank consciences and "the trade will bear."

The lords of the looms and spindles, whose fortunes are bottomed on ill-requited inventions — without which not a wheel of their mills could turn — these lords are arrayed in all the glory of Solomon, yet they neither toil nor spin, but they manage to have a "pull" on congressmen for all the tariff legislation their consciences will allow, while those whose brains worked out the peculiar mechanism, by which large profits are assured, as triumphs over tardy labor—these, when they humbly petition that their own dearly earned money may be used to their own and the public weal, they are turned off without even a secondhand apology. This is not only base ingratitude—more—it is robbing poor Peter to enrich opulent Paul.

Both the government and the reading masses have treated our greatest inventors as crooks and cranks, deserving of no higher grade than allotted to mendicants and cracksmen.

What geometrician can estimate in dollars the benefits to the world of the invention of steam navigation? And yet when the great Fulton was beseeching his countrymen to lend him aid to build the first trial craft that yielded to the pulsations of steam as a motive power for water navigation, he was insulted as a "crank," an "old fool," to think of succeeding where so many had failed. Derided and snubbed at home, this man of small means, yet possessing more than Alexandrian heroism, turned his sad face to a foreign land for the aid denied him at home. When he reached the strand of old England, he met an American, the representative of his own government, to whom he made known his troubles. Robert Livingstone was too high-spirited to thus risk the reputation of his own country, and though he knew nothing of the nature of the enterprise, as a success or failure, but rather than run the chance of turning all the glory over to a foreign land, he would take the chances of failure, whatever they might be, to furnish the necessary means. In spite of hundreds of prior failures, Fulton succeeded, though he was called an "old fool" up to the last moment before starting his boat up the Hudson. There are in all like cases of great ventures, failures in first efforts, but so far, in every case, where undertakings have not essayed to violate natural laws, as in the perpetual motion quest, etc., success has finally followed.

This was the case in the grain binder, which was declared impossible by a reapermaker who three years thereafter was ready and anxious to buy what he had denounced as impossible. But in all these cases the inventor — except in rare, exceptional cases — stands no more show than a thistledown in a tornado.

Though Professor Morse was mocked as an "old fool" and "star gazer," and denied all aid from the rich men of Gotham, and was forced by the stress of poverty to congress for aid, he finally succeeded in securing to the world an invention which all the gold on this planet would not be a compensation for its suppression.

The sewing machines and typewriters, whose inventors, with rare exceptions, failed of any compensation worthy that term, have served vast and valuable purposes.

The telephone, with its millions of accumulated capital, is enjoyed by not one of the inventors.

The power loom and the spinning jenny, by increasing hand speed some 800 to 1, and the improved agricultural machinery make it possible, and only possible, to clothe and feed our vast population; and yet the inventors are treated as noodles, only fit for the jibes and jeers of the beneficiaries.

Is it not time we had a national bureau devoted to the protection of inventors from the insolence of those they have enriched, and also to provide that a certain per cent of all inventions shall be inalienable, and that the reserved amount shall be paid to the inventor at stated intervals on pain of forfeiture of the part sold? Whether this is practical or not, it is safe to say that no sane man will deny its justice.

LEX JUSTICIA.

TYPE MAKING AND SETTING BY MACHINERY.

AS a chronicler of inventions for composing, and making and composing printing types, THE INLAND PRINTER aims to be scrupulously fair in presenting the special claims set forth by each inventor, without prejudice, that the craft, which is most interested, may judge the merits of all from their own best formed judgments.

Accompanying this article is an illustration of the recently allowed patents on the Logo-Typer, the invention of S. D. Carpenter, an old-time western printer-editor. The thesis of this invention sets up principles of construction, operation and effects differing from all other cognate machines.

The whole mechanism, aside from the galley table, is about twenty inches square, and some thirteen inches high, weighing about two hundred pounds. The parts are few — several of which perform dual or multiplex movements, synchronously, really resolvable into a unity of motion, so that it may be said there are really but two motions required, one to set the cylinder, the other to make the cast and remove it to alignment in the line being composed; the entire results of closing the mold, comprising the proper intaglio of the cylinder at the mouth of the casting mold, percussively injecting the metal, then suddenly opening the mold and removing the character cast to place, constitutes practically but one motion by one

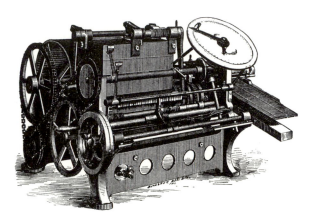

wheel, and the movements thus described constitute the whole movements necessary, except to turn the line from a horizontal to a vertical position, as the types should stand on a galley, and this will be done automatically — leaving nothing to do by hand except to transfer the types from the galley when full to a standing galley, in the usual way.

Patents have been allowed for two modes of operation, one by two levers (sufficient to secure any character instantly, from many thousands on the cylinder); the other made by keys, each key controlling sixty characters, without extra motion or mechanism — the keys being arranged in cognate circles — all having the same arrangements of the unit on the left, by tens; the tenth key in the center of each circle will enable the novice to select any key from a large number in five minutes of pupilage. Either of these modes may be used, the effect being the same in both cases.

It is believed that the lever system secures the greater rapidity, since the cylinder may be more safely manipulated by hand, to ease up for and protect the stops, etc. In this system the average per motion of the hands will give seven ems, ranging from one to fourteen ems. Thus, an expert, who by force of constant habit has memorized a large portion of the most useful and common words, by sixty movements per minute will score 25,200 ems an hour, or 252,000 ems in ten hours. One less trained, at thirty movements per minute, would score 126,000 ems in ten hours; at fifteen motions per minute, the result would be 63,000 ems in ten hours; while the beginner, before the close of the first day, ought to make an average of ten movements per minute, or at the rate of 42,000 ems in ten

hours. Even five movements per minute, average, would give 21,000 ems per day, without any memorization, since a full diagram of the intaglio cylinder matrices is placed before the operator, in bold black-faced type, the diagram being arranged, not only in alphabetical, but in rhythmetical order — whole words and many fragmentary sentences being available by one movement. As soon as the eye catches the word, part of word or character required, he will find on the right and left the exact number on the key, or on the sector for stops. The following, which the inventor claims to be the best feature of his invention, will give an idea of the whole scheme .

15	Able.......	1	24	Ailed	12	24	Accrete....	2	20	Ability	1
22	Babble...	3	24	all told	17	42	all complete	18	30	absurdity..	2
24	boggle.....	13	13	Bald.......	7	38	By the heat	9	30	Barbarity .	6
20	bicycle	14	13	bold	9	13	beat	6	33	bombasity.	7
31	charitable .	15	17	called	13	12	beet	7	22	Celerity ...	8
29	constable..	17	16	could	15	18	Conceit....	11	22	charity	9
24	Dabble	17	17	culled	16	25	concrete..	12	25	chastity ...	10
16	Edible.....	22	16	Doled	12	18	Defeat.....	13	22	Declivity ..	12
23	eligible	23	18	dulled	14	18	discreet ...	15	23	docility...	13

It will thus be seen that as each word, part of word or phrase is in some line and some column on the cylinder, and as the column is numbered on the left of each character and the line on the right thereof, that if the cylinder be moved longitudinal or rotarial to those numbers on the keys or the sectors, the exact character desired will be obtained. These motions are instantly made. Having all characters in rhythmic sound and alphabetical order before the operator, on this system the time necessary for selection must be very scant, and more than compensated by the width of cast at each selection, for the average on the exposed gamut would be about seven ems to an impulse of the hand ; whereas, by single letter selection, including spacing, the number of movements would be twenty-one. In the course of a few months' practice, a large memorization will have been assured, when the speed would be phenomenal. In the use of parts of words, whole words and phrases, no attention to spelling need delay the operator, for the maker of the machine sets the types, and secures absolutely correct orthography.

Logotype figures are also provided, from 1 to near 400 consecutively, and in the use of round numbers the operator may set from 500, 1,000, etc., up to 500,000,000,000 by a single motion, while space rules are cast with figures on the right and the left, from 1 to 0, so that rule and figure work may be rapidly and correctly composed in any width from half an inch to ten inches.

The inventor has secured patents on arrangement and operation for "long distance" type making and setting, so that telegraphic dispatches may be transmitted any required distance, to 1,000 miles, and produced in ready-set types in the various offices that may enter the association. This is claimed to be as simple as telegraphy, and requires no machinery extra — nothing but to attach certain magnets and provide a suitable cable for the transmission of sufficient power to move stop pins, the size of a lead pencil — the machines being run by local power, and when the dispatches are transmitted, the current to be switched off from the common line, and the machine used for other work. The inventor has one simple rule for "spacing out," which, while he does not claim it dispenses with all and any hand work, believes that one corrector can keep pace with ten operators at their best.

The inventor vouches that any of his work can be corrected or "run over," as well as in hand-set types, and that his invention is suited to all classes of work in any sized types, from pearl to pica.

Only one operator is required to work this machine.

These claims are certainly extraordinary, and it seems they are worthy of investigation by those interested.

Mr. Carpenter, the inventor, is an old western publisher and a life-long printer, and besides has been an inventor of considerable note. He has long been a publisher in this state and Wisconsin, and is well known throughout the northwest. He anticipates exhibiting the machine at the World's Fair.

THE LANSTON MONOTYPE.

THERE is no machinery at the World's Fair that commands more attention than the typesetting devices. The inventions there represent several different principles, all radically opposed to each other. A machine little known to the craft at large, but which is apt to create a furor some day, is the Lanston monotype, which casts separate type of the usual commercial form, at the same time setting them in justified lines, the operation being controlled by strips of paper containing small round holes which have previously been punched by another machine or keyboard. This keyboard is separate from the casting machine, the operations of which it governs, and may be located in another room if necessary. It contains 245 keys, 225 of which are for caps, small caps, lower case, italics and punctuation marks, each division being of a different color. The remaining keys are for spacing and justifying. During the process of perforating the roll of paper, lines are completed in the same manner as on the Paige. An indicator and a tiny bell call attention to the line being nearly full. A little dial just above the keyboard registers the number of spaces that have been used in the line. By another dial the operator learns just how many thousandths of an inch the line is short, and by touching the proper justifying keys swells the size of each space already used, and perfectly fills the line. Spaces can be increased or decreased, this being the only machine known which will thin-space a line as in hand composition.

The roll of paper is placed in the casting machine backward, the period at the end of a paragraph being the first character cast, and so on. As each letter is cast, by an ingenious device it is placed into a galley. The justification of the lines is as perfect as the average justification by hand.

The keyboard is simply a typewriter, and can be operated by anyone after a few hours' instruction in justification, which is mechanical, the operator following the indications made by the machine itself.

The keyboard performs its work independently of the size or kind of type the copy is to be set in. To do this the operator must know in advance the number of ems required to each line, and the machine is set to the required length, measured in ems, regardless of the size of type used. With thirty ems to the line, the matter cast in pica will be represented by a line five inches long. Nonpareil type with the same number of ems gives a line 2½ inches long, and so on in proportion for every size of type between the above. If a combination of sizes in one page is required, the operator can arrange spaces to permit two lines of one size, or parts of lines, to be placed end to end, thus making the line the same length as that of the larger type.

The speed of the machine is as great, if not greater, than the ordinary typecasting machine running on the same size of body, the number of face molds presented to the one body matrice favoring cooling.

The perfected Lanston keyboard is operated by electricity, and has the power to repeat the same letter or space continuously so long as any one key is held down, on the same principle as the Mergenthaler. In a day of eight hours it is claimed that a fairly good operator can perforate the holes for at least 38,000 ems. One keyboard will more than feed one casting machine, which can cast and justify into lines 35,000 ems in ten hours. The casting machine, being merely mechanical, will run continuously. One machinist can superintend four machines.

The Lanston seems to be adapted especially for bookwork and circulars. The inventor has in view the working of the keyboard by telegraph, one operator working the keys in Chicago, say, and the machine perforating the holes in all newspaper offices within a radius of 500 miles.

The principle on which the Lanston works is a good one and worthy of investigation.

A machine is being constructed which will cast from four different rolls of paper at once. Four sizes of type can be cast at one time, at a speed of 12,000 an hour.

The perforated rolls of paper after being used can be deposited in a vault, the same as is now done with electrotype plates, and if needed in the future can be placed in the casting machine and the same work again accomplished.

KEYBOARD OF THE LANSTON MONOTYPE MACHINE.

```
!   ||   J  k  x  z      &   J  Z  Q  &   ⅔
:   ‡    q  s  y  T  Q   v   S  P  T  Œ   ⅓
;   °  †  v  o  h  c  P  Y  x   L  G  Æ   ⅛
!   [  ?  r  9  d  p  L  U  K   C  F  Y   ⅞      Œ
'   *  g  8  a  u  F  R  H  M   D  V  ⅝   ⅜      Æ
,   (  "  b  7  q  n  G  D  ff  œ  B  U  ⅜       Œ
l   )  "  f  6  v  J  B  N  æ   m  E  R  ¾       Æ
:      z  o  5  y  x  o  A  Q   &  w  N  ¼
-  j  s  I  4  p  fl  E  w  R   V  X  D  ½       ..
;  t  c  I  3  g  fi  fl  P  O  U  K  A  X       W
.      i  z  2  d  k  fi  T  G  Y  H  ffl K  M
,  ?  e  s  I  b  h  Z  L  E  N  ffl  ffi H  W
l  j  I  r  $  o  u  S  F  B  D  ffi  —  th ed
i  f  t  c  e  a  n  ff  C  w  A  m  M
```

The sets of characters are readily distinguished by a special coloring of the keys of each set.

AMERICAN OLD STYLE

15A,   Pica (12 Point). $2.00

LEGISLATIVE COMMISSIONS
EMPOWERED WITH GREAT AUTHORITY
$1234567890
PURCHASED FOR THE LOBBYISTS

12A,   Great Primer (18 Point). $2.25

RAILWAY COMPANY
PASSENGER EXCURSIONS
$1234567890

10A,   Two-Line Pica (24 Point). $2.50

MAGNIFICENT INTERNATIONAL EXHIBITIONS
123 GORGEOUS COSTUMES 456

8A,   Five-Line Nonpareil (30 Point). $2.75

TYPOGRAPHIC 892 CONVENIENCE
PRINTERS REPORTED

6A,   Two-Line Great Primer (36 Point) $3.00

GENEROSITY 45 PRODUCERS
GREATER CHANCES

4A,   Four-Line Pica (48 Point). $4.00

HOLIDAY 123 BARGAIN

CAST BY MARDER, LUSE & CO. FOUNDRY, CHICAGO, ILL.

For Sale by all Foundries and Branches of the American Type Founders' Co.

12A, 18a,   Great Primer (18 Point).   3.50

DELEGATE MOVING HOMEWARD
American Foundries Building Large House
Honoring American History
$1234567890

10A, 15a,   Double Pica (24 Point).   4.00

BOSTON RECRUITS
Pittsburg Machine Operator
$1234567890

8A, 12a,   Six-Line Nonpareil (30 Point).   4.70

WASHINGTON MANUFACTURER PROMOTED
234 Direct Telegraphic Returns 567

6A, 10a,   Double Great Primer (36 Point).   5.50

EXCHANGE HANDPOWER MACHINE
Agricultural 754 Products

4A, 8a,   Four-Line Pica (48 Point).   7.00

POWERFUL ENGINE DEVISED
Scientific 435 Knowledge

3A, 6a,   Five-Line Pica (60 Point).   10.00

HANDSOME Imposition

CAST BY MARDER, LUSE & CO. FOUNDRY, CHICAGO, ILL.

For Sale by all Foundries and Branches of the American Type Founders' Co.

DE VINNE CONDENSED.

PATENT APPLIED FOR.

6A, 9a. 30-Point De Vinne Condensed. $4.50

FIGHTING ROMAN

Bombards the Fort

Serious Imbroglio

22A, 30a. 10-Point De Vinne Condensed. $2.75

GENERAL EUROPEAN BLOCKADE

Purchase Ten World's Fair Souvenir Half Dollars

Conservatory of Music $74

12A, 20a. 14-Point De Vinne Condensed. $3.25

METHODICAL SPINSTERS

Tabby Cats and Green Tea

5A, 8a. 36-Point De Vinne Condensed. $5.00

SEVENTH EDITION

History of the United States

OTHER SIZES IN PREPARATION.

4A, 6a. 42-Point De Vinne Condensed. $5.50

MUTUAL BENEFITS

Southern California Resorts

18A, 22a. 12-Point De Vinne Condensed. $3.00

LIBERAL SAMPLES GIVEN

Delivered in Fancy Packages

Riding Habits and Coats

10A, 16a. 18-Point De Vinne Condensed. $3.25

SONGS OF SEVEN

Sonnets by Famous Poets

8A, 12a. 24-Point De Vinne Condensed. $4.00

EVENING STROLLS

Questions in Modern Science

Holiday Books

Manufactured by CENTRAL TYPE FOUNDRY, St. Louis, Mo.

DE VINNE ITALIC.

PATENT APPLIED FOR.

CHOICE ROSE
Flower Garden
Ship Ferns 45

MINIATURE STEAMSHIPS
Secured Choicest Staterooms in Advance

Rates only $83 Per Day

ROMANTIC MAIDEN
Hath Practical Papa

TRUNK LINES
Take Through Trains

OTHER SIZES IN PREPARATION.

EXPERT SHOT
Hunting Bengal Tigers

BARGAINS IN DRUGS
Fashionable Perfumery

Fine Toilet Requisites

RICH MINERS
Form Shooting Clubs

FRENCH SOUP
For Christmas Dinner
Mock Turtle

Manufactured by **CENTRAL TYPE FOUNDRY**, St. Louis, Mo.

For Sale by all Foundries and Branches of the American Type Founders' Co.

THE PURPOSE OF THE TYPOTHETÆ.

A SPONTANEOUS remark is often the utterance of a significant truth, revealing facts which were generally suspected, but the avowal of which is neither desirable nor judicious. Such a remark the *American Bookmaker*, in its report of the Typothetæ proceedings, credits to Mr. J. J. Little, of New York.

A motion to appoint a committee to consider the question of reducing the hours of labor, and report at that meeting, was before the convention, and the opponents of a reduction evidently considered that the merits of the question were before them. Indeed, the point of order was raised, whether the question could be discussed on its merits when the motion was only to appoint a committee to consider it, and the president decided to admit a general discussion before putting the motion to a vote.

Mr. Little opposed the reduction of hours, and it was in the course of his argument that he uttered the remarks referred to by the *Bookmaker*.

"Why should we consider the question of reducing hours of labor?" asked the gentleman from New York, "was not the Typothetæ first organized in this city six years ago to combat this very question?" Then he said, substantially, "You may turn this subject around as you like, but the plain truth is that the Typothetæ found its origin in a united purpose to oppose a shorter day, and now you come here and ask us to assist in defeating the purpose for which we are organized."

This, then, is the beginning of and the reason for continuing the organization of the society known as the Typothetæ. It is for this high and holy purpose that these solid-appearing, gray-haired business men come together annually, and listen to reports which report nothing, squabble over motions which would accomplish nothing if they were passed, recommend a dozen things for the consideration of its members, but adopt nothing, pass glowing resolutions of thanks to their local entertainers and the retiring officers, and then elect a new set of officers and appoint a day to go through with the same fruitless performance. They talk much, and they feast much, but neither they nor the men whose labor is their commerce are better off because they have met. They are evidently waiting. They are a sort of standing army, acknowledging no weapon but the sword, unwilling to entertain any argument except physical force.

"The workmen tried to force the eight-hour day upon us once," they say, "and we beat them. They did not ask for a conference then. They simply declared that on such a day and thereafter eight hours would constitute a day's work. We organized and beat them. Now they want to discuss the question with us, and we'll none of it. They began with force, we opposed and beat them with force, and now force it shall be to the end."

The Typothetæ is like one of the great European nations. It has an expensive standing army, but dare not disband it for fear of the enemy.

What a noble spectacle for the close of this pregnant century! What a splendid purpose for such men as De Vinne, Little, Taylor, Wright, Todd, Ellis, Morehouse, Houghton, Matthews, Morgan, Woodward, Donnelley, McNally, Blakely and Pettibone, whose names will be forever linked with the history of printing in America! The nations of the earth, even, are substituting arbitration for powder and ball; but these high-minded gentlemen belong to the old school, they believe in force.

They are individually and collectively endeavoring to better their condition in life, which means shorter hours and greater ease. They are meeting with a fair success in the effort.

The toilers are also trying to better their condition in life, but their efforts are not united. They stumble and waste their strength, because having to labor many hours, having less education and less facilities for forming accurate judgment of men and forces than their employers, they do not proceed intelligently. They are children or raw recruits, while their opponents are trained soldiers, skilled in the arts of diplomacy, of manipulation, of organized warfare.

Yet the handwriting is on the wall. Humanity in every stage of life is emancipating itself to a higher plane. Labor has pruned its hours from sixteen and fourteen to ten. It will continue to prune until the doctrine of the thirds prevails — one-third for labor, one-third for recreation, and one-third for sleep. With no other arrangement of his time can man approach his best condition. It is nothing for Mr. Polhemus to say and others to attest that they have worked eighteen hours a day as employers, and it cannot therefore injure their employés to work ten. Some men like drudgery, but that does not prove that it is best for all.

The great truths that the laborer is growing in mental stature, that he is aspiring to a higher and broader life, that he is realizing the dignity of labor through realizing the dignity of man, and that it is in him to attain his deep purposes sooner or later — these are the imperial facts that the Typothetæ cannot or will not see.

These men whose names I have written are all past the meridian of life. Most of them know by experience the story of the printer from apprentice to master. Their names are upon the honor roll of printerdom. But they may add a new luster to its glowing column if they will come out from themselves to the consideration of this subject — out from the narrow walls of partisan selfishness, out from the musty atmosphere of commercial usage, out from the bitterness of resentment and spite — out into the generous sunshine of justice and philanthropy, out where they can see that the man with the powerful weapon of money in his hands is a coward if he overwhelms his opponent who has only his empty hands to oppose its irresistible force.

15 A   12–POINT ORNAMENTED. NO. 1,010. $2.05.

AMERICAN DICTIONARY OF THE ENGLISH LANGUAGE,
LECTURES BEFORE THE ASSOCIATION FOR THE ADVANCEMENT OF SCIENCE AND ART.

12 A   18–POINT ORNAMENTED, NO. 1,010. $3.00.

AMERICAN FRUIT AND FLOWER GARDEN, 1893.
PRINCIPLES AND RULES FOR THE CULTIVATION OF FLOWERS,

10 A   24–POINT ORNAMENTED, NO. 1,010. $3.95.

ENGLISH AND GERMAN LITERATURE,
BEAUTIFULLY PRINTED IN TWO COLORS, 189

8 A   36–POINT ORNAMENTED. NO. 1,010. $6.15.

EXHIBITION BUILDINGS,
18 WORLD'S FAIR DIRECTORY 93

5 A   48–POINT ORNAMENTED, NO. 1,010. $6.10.

POPULAR MUSIC,
3 NEW AND ORIGINAL 8

GEORGE BRUCE'S SON & CO., Type-Founders, NEW YORK.

DE VINNE SHADED

PATENT PENDING

ORIGINATED BY DICKINSON TYPE FOUNDERY, BOSTON, MASS.

5 a 4 A · 48 POINT *(Eight Line Nonpareil)* · $7 75

Morning 5 Rambles
PROMENADE

6 a 4 A · 42 POINT *(Seven Line Nonpareil)* · $7 50

Discovery 14 Rewarded
CONGREGATION

8 a 5 A · 36 POINT *(Six Line Nonpareil)* · $5 75

Gluttonous $9 Delegations
ORIGINAL OUTLINES

10 a 8 A · 24 POINT *(Four Line Nonpareil)* · $4 50

Artists Appreciate 78 Later Productions
SERVICEABLE MANUFACTURE

16 a 10 A · 18 POINT *(Three Line Nonp)* · $3 75

Wandering 3 Grimalkin
FELINE CONCERT

20 a 16 A · 12 POINT *(Two Line Nonp)* · $3 25

Champion Heavyweights Defeat 90
INTERNATIONAL DISPUTES

For Sale by all Foundries and Branches of the American Type Founders' Co.

French Old Style Extended.

3A, 6a,   Four Line Pica (48 Point). $8.25

Sending 85 Medals
EXCURSION

4A, 8a,   Double Great Primer (36 Point). $5.25

Remarkable 97 Advertising
MISCONCEIVING

6A, 12a,   Double Pica (24 Point). $4.00

Rehearsing $265 Melodrama
Unconsciously Absorbing Information
NUMBERS COMPARED

8A, 16a,   Great Primer (18 Point). $3.00

234 Dead Nations Never Rise Again 567
Many Egyptian Ornaments Received Wednesday
Champagne Excursions
RENOWNED ENGLISH DICTIONARY

CAST BY MARDER, LUSE & CO. FOUNDRY, CHICAGO, ILL.

For Sale by all Foundries and Branches of the American Type Founders' Co.

Pantagraph Specimens.

. . . PATENT PENDING. . .

9 A 25 a   18 POINT PANTAGRAPH (3 line Nonp.) $5 25

Barnhart Brothers & Spindler Superior Copper = Mixed Type

Manhattan Savings Bank   1234567890   Hamilton Printing Company

7 A 20 a   24 POINT PANTAGRAPH (4 line Nonp.) $5 30

Several Milwaukee Corporations Financially Embarrassed

First Chemical Bank $34,297,536.80   Home Insurance Agents

5 A 15 a   36 POINT PANTAGRAPH (6 line Nonp.) $7 00

Beautiful Samples of Wedding Cards

Employing Lithographers and Electrotypers Associations

4 A 10 a   48 POINT PANTAGRAPH (8 line Nonp.) $8 20

Economical Printing Machinery

Specimens of Handsome and Durable Type

4 A 10 a   60 POINT PANTAGRAPH (10 line Nonp.) $9 25

Merchants Safe Depository

Eastern Publishers Protective Society

COMPLETE WITH FIGURES.

Manufactured by Barnhart Bros. & Spindler, Chicago. Carried in stock by Great Western Typefoundry, Omaha; Great Western Typefoundry, Kansas City; Minnesota Typefoundry, St. Paul, and St. Louis Printers' Supply Company, St. Louis.

$3.50.   10-POINT ANTIQUE, NO. 311.   40 a and 20 A
4 lb. 12 oz.

Geological Survey of the Whole Earth
Spanish Conquests in Mexico
HABITS OF MASTODONS.   1894

$3.30.   12-POINT ANTIQUE, NO. 311.   30 a and 15 A
5 lb.

Meditations on social Revolution
Court of Common Pleas
NEAT TYPE, ON SALE 1894

$5.10.   18-POINT ANTIQUE, NO. 311.   25 a and 12 A
8 lb. 8 oz.

Fast Express Trains
Quick Sales
Investor and Speculator
HEAD LINES 1894

$6.70.   24-POINT ANTIQUE, NO. 311.   20 a and 10 A
12 lb.

Law Reports
Commercial Style
STOCKS $20

$7.70.   36-POINT ANTIQUE, NO. 311.   15 a and 8 A
13 lb. 12 oz.

Mutual Insurance.
Wholesale and Retail Dealers
NATIONAL BANK 18

$8.90.   48-POINT ANTIQUE, NO. 311.   5 a and 5 A
16 lb. 8 oz.

American Newspapers
NEW TYPE 94

GEORGE BRUCE'S SON & CO., TYPE-FOUNDERS, 13 CHAMBERS STREET, NEW YORK.

12-POINT ORNAMENTED, No. 1,566.   30 a and 15 A
2 lb. 4 oz.

Manual of the Corporation of the City of New York, with Maps, Plans and Specifications

The American Magazine and Repository of Useful Literature, devoted to Science, Literature and Art, Embellished with many Engravings

PERSONAL RECOLLECTIONS OF THE STAGE.   NOTICES OF ACTORS.   AMOUNT DUE $2,679

$4.00.   18-POINT ORNAMENTED, No. 1,566.   25 a and 12 A
4 lb.

Exploration of the Valley of the Amazon River made under the Direction of the Navy Department

AMERICAN LIFE INSURANCE COMPANY OF PHILADELPHIA, $75,000.

$5.15.   24-POINT ORNAMENTED, No. 1,566.   20 a and 10 A
5 lb. 12 oz.

Medicines in themselves are really Mischievous and Destructive of Nature.

AMERICAN SAVINGS INSTITUTE.   BALANCE 1894

$6.35.   36-POINT ORNAMENTED, No. 1,566.   15 a and 8 A
7 lb. 12 oz.

Special Departments to Represent each Branch of our Business

ARTICLES SUITABLE TO THE TRADE, 1894

$8.80.   48-POINT ORNAMENTED, No. 1,566.   12 a and 7 A
12 lb. 4 oz.

Printing Types at Reduced Prices. Estimates given

TYPE-FOUNDRY, 13 CHAMBERS-ST.

GEORGE BRUCE'S SON & CO., TYPE-FOUNDERS, 13 CHAMBERS STREET, NEW YORK.

ACQUIRING SPEED ON THE MERGENTHALER LINOTYPE MACHINE.

BY LEE REILLY.*

THE editor of THE INLAND PRINTER having asked me to contribute an article giving my personal views and experiences regarding typecasting machines, I have pleasure in complying, in the hope that some benefit may be derived therefrom by some of my brother printers who may be struggling as beginners with the mysteries of machine composition.

In reference to attaining speed on the Mergenthaler machine, printers should bear well in mind that with this machine as in hand composition, speed depends upon the printer or operator himself — the mechanism responds instantly to the skill and celerity of the operator — and in this connection I will take the opportunity to say that the assertions often made of remarkable speed as machine operators being attained by persons other than printers is a hoax. An operator requires to be a *printer* to be rapid and competent. The assumption has been that typewriters — or typewritists — as a rule, make competent operators of composing machines. This is a complete delusion. Such operators are failures in every sense of the word, and I speak from practical observation.

A fast compositor at " case " is usually blessed with clean proofs — and the same holds good in machine operating. Printers are now convinced of the practical character of machines and regard them no longer as experiments. The Mergenthaler machine in my opinion is the *only* machine. I say this not because I have made several records on it, but for the very sufficient reason that it is the only machine which has displaced a large number of our craft today — a poor recommendation, some will say, but certainly a strong guaranty of the machine's efficiency. Among the machines I have examined are the Thorne, McMillan, Rogers, Burr and Empire, but I have found no grounds to change my belief as above expressed.

In regard to women operating the machines I do not think they are a success, and as I have worked in offices where they were engaged I have the benefit of speaking from experience. The difficulties which the touring printer experiences in learning the styles of the various newspapers cannot be compared to the difficulties encountered by the lady typewriters who endeavor to operate composing machines. There is a paper in New York city today that employs several women, but it is difficult to see why their services are retained except for sentimental reasons, as without

them the paper would get more type set up — candidly, the matter composed by the ladies has to be reset.

It is somewhat difficult for me to tell exactly what steps a beginner should take to acquire swiftness in machine operating. A thorough knowledge of the machine is the first requisite — study the mechanism from the foundation to the distributor. This is far more important than a study of the keyboard. It is folly — though you will see it often done — for a printer to get a keyboard to practice on before he has made any study of the machine. Such study is waste of time. The keyboard is the simplest part of it all. But what is of importance is, when anything goes wrong in the machine, to be able to discover the trouble. You can learn the keyboard with the operating of the machine. Don't try to become an operator unless you have your mind made up to master the work thoroughly. You must put all the ambition you have in your work. When I started on the machine I was deeply interested in the work. So much so that even when in bed before I went to sleep I would study out how the keys on the board were located and make combinations of words and sentences. I have tried often to dispel such thoughts, but it seemed impossible to do so. I would think of a word or a series of words, for instance " when," " where," " the," " this," " at," " interesting," " consideration," etc., and the next day I would go to the office and try a combination on any of these or other words, until finally I ran over the keyboard like a racehorse. Then I took up the idea of reading copy, not in long sentences but by reading two or three or perhaps half-a-dozen words, and still " finger " the keyboard without looking at it. The result of this practice was such that I finally found myself so familiar with the location of the keys that I only required to look at the keyboard when I had to " travel," that is, to set caps, figures, etc. Operating does not seem to be any exertion to me now, in fact it has not been for the last three years. I have been operating for five years.

I could say much more on the subject of machine operating, which is now a matter of paramount importance to printers, but fearing that I have already overstepped the space at my disposal I will defer anything further for the present in the hope that an opportunity will present itself later to give some more details for the benefit of the craft.

THE BUZZ OF THE MACHINE TYPESETTER.

The *Press* composing room has been equipped with typesetting machines. The operation of these machines will be given to the old compositors of the paper, who will soon be adepts therein. The machines are new, and the workmen will not for a time be familiar with their working, and it is possible a great many mmmstakes, some of them doM ridicyyouls, will creep into the paper, to the annoyanncccceee of our readers, but this trouble will only be tempqquifquily, and we hope our condeMned setters will be able to set alllll wwwrigghtt ppppretty sqqn. Mean While we beg the kkind indulgdulggggence of our fffriendz. — *Cleveland Press.*

---

* NOTE. — Mr. Lee Reilly is a compositor in the office of the New York *Tribune.* During the week ending December 20, 1893, he set on a Mergenthaler machine, taking copy from the hook in the regular course of business, four hundred and eleven thousand two hundred ems of nonpareil matter, all of which appeared in print, the actual working time being forty-eight hours and five minutes. All of this matter, except that of the last day, was corrected by him within the time named. Seventy-five per cent or upward of the matter was set solid, and no handwork, such as heads or leads, was counted, and no special preparation was made for doing the work.

Written for THE INLAND PRINTER.

A PRINTING OFFICE AND ITS PRINTERS.

BY A PIECE HAND.*

THE office of Rush & Botchit is probably one of the best object lessons to be found in the United States for the young printer who wishes to find out what to avoid, for everything about the establishment seems to have been arranged with a view of combining the maximum amount of exertion with the minimum of results, and the life of a chattel slave would be a picnic to a man after working there a few days. The firm has a large patronage, employs about forty compositors and do considerable work; in size the office is a

Plate by Illinois Engraving Co., Chicago. Photo by Randall, Ann Arbor, Mich. Copyrighted.

NIGHT.

The manager, Mr. Rush, the moneyed man of the firm, is a lawyer with a prodigious ignorance of the rudiments of the craft and an all-pervading idea that nothing can go right without his personal supervision. He can give more conflicting orders on a subject in a given space of time than any man in the business, and his memory is of such a character that he would be better without it. The foreman, a choleric German, with a Wagnerian voice like Paddy Whisky filing a bucksaw, has fifty places for everything and half a dozen boys to try to find which one it is in. When these embryo prints are not hustling for something that has been mislaid, they have a stock job of setting pi, which no one ever distributes, for by the time one of them has accumulated a stickful, the stick is needed by someone, and the contents, ranging from pearl to pica, are dumped back into the barrel for another occasion.

The lead and slug racks have a perfect sinecure, for no one ever recollects seeing anything in them; but to offset this, each compositor has a miniature outfit, consisting of leads, slugs, ornaments, quoins and rules, under his case for his own private use; as a natural consequence a green hand can do little or nothing until he has accumulated an outfit of his own, and probably spends the greater part of the first few days hunting for the pica quad or the long primer space, for although at least one of each of these necessaries was furnished with the outfit when it was new, no one recollects seeing either of them of late years and resort is had to all kinds of contrivances to get along without them. On the other hand, there are tons of straight type on the boards, tied up and loose, with enough job type in chapter and running heads to fill the cases, and sufficient leads and slugs to flood the racks if they had been taken out before the matter was put away, but it would have taken too much time to have removed them, and when they are needed the leads can be pulled and a piece of furniture shoved in to brace the string.

The dead-stone man has his hands so occupied in pulling sorts and leads that he has no time left for distribution, and every case in the shop is empty — except the quad box, which is invariably filled with pi. When a man sets a job he has to take what type he can get sorts in, irrespective of whether it is suitable or not, hence most of the work turned out can only be characterized as abortions. The artist who laid out the office intended that all the cases should be kept in racks against the wall, each size and style by itself, and to prevent them being shoved into the frames had the latter made without slides, and now the cases are all kept piled on the floor and serve as foot rests, when not otherwise engaged. The cases are kept in no particular place, for nothing is particular here, but have to be hunted for from one end of the room to the other, and when found are either empty or pied. Piece hands have no particular cases, and every time they get a take have to throw in just enough to set it or beg sorts, for the chances are the next take will be in some other type, and no one wants to have a full case to be picked up by the first man who needs it; hence every-

decent one, but that is the only thing decent there is about it. The composing room occupies an entire floor, with good light and plenty of room, and there would be abundance of material if it were only kept in such a manner as to be available, but owing to the peculiar want of system that obtains, nothing can ever be found till the printer has done without it, and then dead loads of it are forthcoming from some out-of-the-way corner under an accumulation of waste paper and the dust of ages. So it frequently happens that when a job that runs on sorts is about completed there are more sorts in sight than at any other stage of the transaction.

* NOTE. — This is no fancy sketch. It is a fair description of a well-known printing office in the city of Chicago. The establishment is a factory for the development of botch workmen. — "PIECE HAND."

one is setting off the bare boards all the time and $1.25 a day is a fair average for a piece hand.

The frames are of a peculiar construction, having been made specially, on scientific principles, for the accommodation of the rush compositor, who can hold the stick in his mouth while he uses both hands to set type, with a pile of cases at his feet, so that by the time his case is empty he can take up a full one from the floor. Owing to this peculiar construction it is almost impossible for a novice to move his case without "pieing" it, and it is a standing joke in the shop to watch a new man try to change his case; the pi is gathered up by a boy and put into the ever-ready barrel — or rather on the top of it, for all the barrels have been full of pi as long as anyone can remember. It is looked upon as the most natural thing in the world for cases or matter to be pied, and no one takes any notice of such an occurrence except to laugh at it, when a case slips off a frame or a pile of cases on the floor topples over. The foreman will offer a piece hand a pied case to set out of with the utmost equanimity, and gasps with astonishment if the man prefers putting on his coat to commencing work under such auspices. The devil, who has hunted up the case, will also feel aggrieved that the man did not take it, and will observe "it wasn't such a bad case either, the main of the type in it was modern." If a day hand gets hold of such a case he has to rush himself black in the face and then cannot do half a day's work. This would be a serious matter in any other shop, because the men have each a ten-hour ticket to fill out; but at R. & B.'s this difficulty is overcome by charging up the time it ought to take to do the job and balancing the ticket by adding a sufficient number of hours for distribution to even it up, although not a minute has been spent distributing the entire day. But the foreman and everyone else seems to understand what that item is there for, and it goes.

In giving out a job, the foreman rushes in with something and hands it out to be set up. "What size is it to be?" is the natural inquiry. "Oh, I don't know," is the reply, "but hustle along and set it up in something; I'll go and find out whether it is to be a business card or a dodger."

The only instructions a man gets with his copy is to rush it through and not be particular about it, for nothing is particular at Rush & Botchit's. The stock is to be cut out of waste, and it is to be set in no particular style nor of any particular size, so that the compositor is left entirely to his own discretion, with the certainty that when he has got it up it will be all wrong and have to be reset the other way.

The foreman seems to be afraid to keep a good printer around for fear he might be supplanted, and poor ones are not wanted — so between Scylla and Charybdis the staff is continually changing. One week it is a union shop, and another it is "ratted;" then again it will be open to all. As a refuge for destitute printers it is a success, for a man can always get a job there on piece — on small pica leaded with pieced leads, fourteen ems wide, measured as Lord only knows what, but it

always comes out a couple of dollars short on pay-day. This event occurs semi-occasionally about every two weeks, and by the time it arrives the boys are all strapped; those who have not "shved" their dupes are then on the verge of desperation, and so hard up that they would be almost willing to compromise for 50 cents on the dollar.

All this time the proprietors are complaining that they can't get good men, and wondering how it is printers — that is, those in their office — are such botches.

THE biggest literary work ever undertaken in America is the military history now being produced by the United States government under the title of "War of the Rebellion." It was begun twenty years ago. The whole work will embrace 120

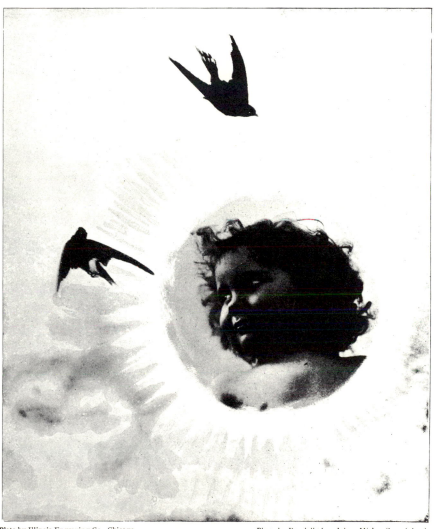

Plate by Illinois Engraving Co., Chicago. Photo by Randall, Ann Arbor, Mich. Copyrighted.
MORNING.

huge royal octavo volumes of 1,000 pages each, and a gigantic atlas, and the cost will be about $2,500,000. Each separate book in a set is three inches thick and weighs from fifty to sixty ounces and the combined weight of an entire set will be 520 pounds. The volumes, if set up in a row on a single shelf, will extend a distance of thirty feet. Eleven thousand copies will be printed, so that the edition will comprise 1,320,000 books of 1,000 printed pages, aggregating 1,320,000,000 pages of matter, exclusive of the atlas. Up to this date eighty-nine serial volumes have been published, and about $1,800,000 has been spent in all branches of the work, or about $20,000 a volume. The printing and binding alone cost $10,000 a volume, while the previous preparation of each volume for the printers' hands cost an equal sum.

HOWLAND OPEN AND HOWLAND

ORIGINATED BY THE DICKINSON TYPE FOUNDERY, BOSTON, MASS.

Howland 5 a 4 A $9 00 —— 60 POINT —— Howland Open 5 a 4 A $9 50

CONSENT Hard Knock 5

Howland 6 a 4 A $8 00 —— 54 POINT —— Howland Open 6 a 4 A $8 50

Hair Cutting AESTHETIC 73

Howland 8 a 5 A $7 00 —— 48 POINT —— Howland Open 8 a 5 A $7 50

Foundation for 19 High Churches
BRIGHTEST DECORATION

Howland Open 10 a 6 A $6 50   42 POINT   Howland 10 a 6 A $6 00

Artistic 42 Designs
QUAINT OPEN

Howland Open 16 a 10 A $4 50   24 POINT   Howland 16 a 10 A $4 00

Workmen Triumphant 28
DELICATE QUESTION

Howland Open 30 a 20 A $3 00   12 POINT   Howland 30 a 20 A $3 00

Large Commission 90 Investments Safely
DECISIVE ACTIONS ATTAINED

Howland   8 POINT   40 a 28 A $2 50

Mourning for the Departed £2345 Rescued from Shipwreck
NUMEROUS AND BLOOD-CURDLING DISASTERS

Howland 12 a 8 A $5 00   30 POINT   Howland Open 12 a 8 A $5 50

Greatest 2 Bargains
LARGE STOCK

Howland 20 a 12 A $3 25   18 POINT   Howland Open 20 a 12 A $3 50

Educate Laborers 75 Struggle Along
WORKING QUIET SCHEME

Howland 36 a 24 A $2 75   10 POINT   Howland Open 36 a 24 A $2 75

States Health Reports 64 Large Contracts Awarded
TORPID STATE OF BUSINESS AFFAIRS

Howland   6 POINT   50 a 30 A $2 25

Grand National Peace Jubilee £2,349 Consolidated Musical Chorus
Vociferously Applauded the Yankee Doodle
FOREIGN COUNTRIES REPRESENTED CONSPICUOUSLY

Showing the Howland and Howland Open printed in combination.

For Sale by All Foundries and Branches of the American Type Founders' Co.

THE EMPIRE TYPESETTING MACHINE.

A machine which will set type and make an actual saving of forty-five per cent over hand composition is certainly a refutation of the claim that the future of machine composition will be confined to the typecasting mechanisms alone. In

COMPOSER AND JUSTIFIER.
EMPIRE TYPESETTING MACHINE.

a recent test of the Empire typesetting machine, lasting for one week, and conducted under no special conditions favorable to the result, but rather inclining to unfavorable circumstances, after careful calculation and deduction and in the most conservative spirit, the above estimate was ascertained as the minimum of the machine's operation. As to the perfection of the work turned out from it, the pages of the *New York Weekly* form a sufficient illustration. Briefly enumerated the advantages of the Empire are, first, that each machine will handle two bodies of type; thus one machine sets and distributes nonpareil and minion, one brevier and bourgeois, and one long primer and small pica. It requires no machinist to look after it. As a movable-type machine it is adapted alike to newspaper work and the finest kind of bookwork, no style of composition excelling its output. The company have a special contract to supply the highest grade of type at the lowest cost, nicked and ready for use on the machine.

The face of the type is not touched in manipulation in the composing or distributing machines, and the distribution of type is entirely automatic. *The machine does not break type.* The "nick" in the type is only $\frac{1}{100}$ of an inch in depth — much shallower than that used for other machines — and does not practically weaken the body of the type; and the

mechanism of both the setter and distributer is such that there is no strain upon the type. The justifying of the type directly from the setter saves much time — the space channels and other appliances used in connection therewith rendering it exceedingly convenient and easy.

The type cases or hoppers are more quickly and easily transferred from the distributer to the setter and vice versa than in any other machine, and being made of corrugated metal are much lighter in proportion to their strength.

The position of the keys and the convenient arrangement on the keyboard of the letters and figures, as will be seen from the diagram, very materially assists the operator in their manipulation.

The parts of the machines are made interchangeable and easily transferred from one to another, or replaced in case of accident.

It is not necessary, in placing a page of type on the distribution table, to raise the same from the galley, as the table and galley are so adjusted as to allow the type to be moved from one to the other without danger of disarrangement.

All the small parts of the machines are made with a regard to strength as well as utility, and not liable to break or get out of order.

The price paid to operators on these machines per 1,000 ems is very much lower than that for hand composition; in this respect there is naturally a great saving to the employer, while the operator earns larger wages than by hand composition.

DISTRIBUTER.
EMPIRE TYPESETTING MACHINE.

Space does not permit a full description of the interesting mechanism by which the above means are attained, as like all successful inventions it must be seen to be fully understood. For further particulars and detailed explanation address the Empire Typesetting Machine Co., Mail and Express Building, 203 Broadway, New York.

CAP
N K R G L fi ff

H D Y Q E J S

M U A B C Z F

W X V O P I T

LOWER
l l . ' l p b

v u f l l e g
    SPACE SPACE

m o c s a n d

w r i t h e y

POINT
z , ' 1 2 3 –
  TURN   APOSTROPHY   EM.DASH
  COMMA

x : ; 4 5 6 ffl

q ! ? 7 8 9 ffi

k j – l o fl &
  HYPHON 4-m. SPACE

EN. QUADS   COMMA

KEYBOARD — EMPIRE TYPESETTING MACHINE.

THE EMPIRE TYPESETTER.

Now that the fire of criticism which so fiercely assailed the introduction of typesetting machines has died almost entirely down, their points of real practical utility are being made more manifest with the constant broadening of the field. However, even though the issue is being so generally accepted, the writer believes it to be a fact that a great many well-informed members of the printing and publishing fraternity are not yet fully aware of the marvelous work that is being done upon them. Some observations were recently made with a view to ascertaining just what is being accomplished in this line, which are of value because they were made entirely upon work done under ordinary

circumstances, with no preparation whatever for the trial. The machine noted was an Empire typesetter in the office of the New York *Observer*. Copy was given to the operator on a Thursday afternoon, at thirty minutes past four. Closing-up time came an hour later, and work was abandoned until 8:05 the next morning. The machine was started again at that time, and with the exception of a wait of nineteen minutes for copy, was kept in motion until fourteen minutes past twelve. The average per hour for the two operators was 6,336 ems, the total amount set being 30,621 ems. The type set had been nicked six months before, and was in constant use since that time. The usual amount of dust and printing ink adhered to it, retarding its motion to a certain degree, but notwithstanding this fact and the speed at which the machine was run, not an ounce of type was broken.

A NEW TYPESETTER — THE UNIVERSAL.

A NEW machine just placed upon the market, called the Universal Typesetter, has several features to recommend it, among which might be mentioned its low cost, small space occupied and no change required in type, material, etc., used in hand composition. The object is to facilitate rather than to revolutionize existing methods.

It is used in connection with a printer's case of the ordinary make, and is placed on a support directly under the top case, and has a funnel attached which comes up even with case;

into this the compositor drops the letters, using both hands in the operation, and facing the case in the ordinary manner.

As it matters not whether the letters are wrong side up or face about when dropped into the funnel, and as both hands are brought into service, the work is greatly facilitated. The funnel is large at the mouth, converging at the lower end, so that as each letter passes through, it takes its place upright in a groove; here it encounters a pair of metal fingers, which turn it if it be upside down; a little further on it encounters another

set of fingers, which release it when the nicks are turned the proper way. The fingers, or clamps, remain inactive if the letters have dropped in the right position. After running this gauntlet, the letters enter that section of the groove from which they finally emerge, line by line, upon the galley.

A bell is arranged to ring when the line is within two or three ems of being filled, so that the compositor can complete or divide word, as may be necessary, when a gauge attached to the machine indicates the number of spaces required to justify line, which are thrown into the funnel and take their place at end of line, and are transferred when galley is filled. The line then automatically advances one step in the galley, not diverting the compositor's attention from his copy.

This typesetter has many features to recommend it, and has numerous advantages over the large and expensive machines, which can only be afforded by offices having large quantities of bookwork.

It is claimed for this machine that it adds enormously to the capacity of the compositor; does not disturb present arrangement of any printing office; brings into requisition the type

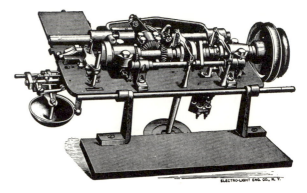

now in use, not requiring the casting of special fonts; does not break or injure the type; and leaves, in case of accident to the machine, the same facilities which the compositor now has.

A TYPOGRAPHICAL REFORM.

An occasional correspondent in Lynn, Massachusetts, of *Printers' Ink*, calls attention to a departure from old-time methods of composition introduced by the fortnightly *Liberty*, of New York. In ordinary composition the lines are made to observe a uniformity of length by adjusting the space between the words of a line along its entire length. This work requires the skilled workmanship of an experienced compositor, and the labor of justifying is computed as representing a considerable percentage of the cost of composition. By the *Liberty* system all attempts at justification are abolished, and when the compositor finds, in approaching the end of a line, that another word or syllable cannot be inserted he fills in the line with quads. The original and perfect spacing is not disturbed. Here is a sample:

> Does the absence of this straight edge
> ever disturb anybody? Let the reader ans-
> wer the question for himself by taking down
> a volume of Shakespeare or any other poet,
> examining the pages, and asking himself
> whether the ragged edge at the right had
> ever in the least offended him. Not one
> reader in a hundred thousand will answer
> yes.

A column thus set gives the reader an impression that he is looking at blank verse; but no one finds the reading at all inconvenient. From an economic standpoint this method of composition means the saving of labor. It is simply the method now made pretty familiar to everyone by the typewriter, which is compelled to use it from the limitations of its possibilities.

6A, 8a.

JUNE
ROSE

24-Point Quaint Roman No. 2. $5.00

REFRESHING
Mountain Scene
Grand River

14A, 16a.

PURCHASE
CAST STEEL
FURNACES

12-Point Quaint Roman No. 2. $3.25

ORIGINATORS AND DISTRIBUTORS

Retailers of Gossip Possible and Impossible   123

Traducing People Who Are Absent

Latest Show Printing House Equipments

4A, 5a.   48-Point Quaint Roman No. 2. $11.00

SECURITIES
Mushroom Plants

8A, 10a.

SILVER
MONEY

18-Point Quaint Roman No. 2. $4.50

CHANGE OF GOVERNMENT
Splendid Assortments
Wonderful Machinery Sold

4A, 6a.   36-Point Quaint Roman No. 2. $8.50

MONDAY
Consents
Designer

14A, 18a.   10-Point Quaint Roman No. 2. $3.00

SIGH NO MORE, LADIES.

Sigh no more, ladies, sigh no more;
Men were deceivers ever;
One foot in sea, and one on shore,
To one thing constant never:
Then sigh not so,
But let them go,
And be you blithe and bonny.

For sale by all Foundries and Branches of the American Type Founders' Co.

THE THORNE TYPESETTING MACHINE.

THERE can be no question as to the fact that printers and publishers generally are now thoroughly alive to the importance of the problem of typesetting by machinery. The rapid introduction of typesetting machines during the past year has awakened the most conservative, or one might say the most lethargic. No one state or section and no special line of offices has absorbed all the machines put out, but they have gone into every part of the union and into every kind of

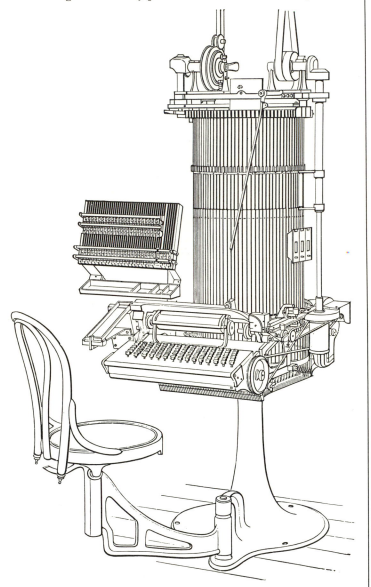

printing office from the small country weekly or book office to the largest of the metropolitan daily offices.

The careful, thorough-going printer or publisher has applied himself vigorously to the question of determining which is the best, which is the most practical, which is the biggest money-saver, which is the simplest of the machines offered on the market today.

The manufacturers of the "Thorne" typesetting and dis-

tributing machine contend that not only have they the simplest machine in use today, but that having demonstrated its practicability and profitableness of operation in the leading daily, weekly, magazine and book offices of the country (in many offices for several years past), it should not be classed among the experiments at accomplishing typesetting by machinery, but as a perfected machine, the simplest in construction and the most easily operated and controlled.

It does not require the services of a trained machinist to operate the Thorne machine, there being no delicate or difficult adjustments — no complex mechanism about its construction. The entire work of composition — setting, distributing and justifying — are done on the one simple, compact machine shown in the accompanying illustration. It needs to be understood, however, that the setting and distributing parts are independent of each other in so far as the distribution (which is automatic), can go on while the operator is calling out the type with the aid of the keyboard, or it can stop, and vice versa.

But as to the mechanism and method of operating the Thorne the printing public is already well informed and needs no detailed description. We will simply mention that several improvements or changes, in the direction of simplification, have been made since THE INLAND PRINTER last treated of this machine. While having just as many keys and the same characters the keyboard has been compacted into much smaller and more convenient space, and the operating and justifying parts brought very close together. The machine requires less space by considerable than formerly, and less than any other in practical operation. The swinging stool attached to the base of the machine is so arranged with reference to the justifying apparatus that the operator can, after filling out the line, swing around quickly and easily into justifying position, thus accomplishing the work of both operator and justifier.

It is a little out of the ordinary to be informed that in the prevailing business depression the Thorne Company is considerable behind its orders, running over one hundred men in its splendidly equipped factory at Hartford, and part of the force working overtime. Such is the case, however, and the company reports an even more promising outlook for orders in the near future.

Among the daily newspapers using the Thorne are the New York *Evening Post*, New York *Mail and Express*, American Press Association of New York, Hartford *Post*, Bridgeport *Post*, Portland (Me.) *Press*, New Haven *Palladium*, Atlanta *Journal*, Rome *Tribune*, Joliet *News; Daily Sportsman*, London, England; *Daily Guardian*, Manchester, England; *Daily Times*, Oxford, England; and among weekly newspapers and magazines we would mention the *Christian Register*, of Boston; New York *Churchman;* New York *Evangelist;* the *Interior* and the *Ram's Horn*, of Chicago; the *North and West*, of Minneapolis; the *Forum, Current Literature, Short Stories, Romance, Arena, Atlantic Monthly*, etc. Among the western establishments that have recently adopted the Thorne machine are the *Daily Michigan Volksblatt*, of Detroit, Mich.; *Daily News*, Mansfield, Ohio; *Daily News*, Norfolk, Neb.; J. C. Benedict, Chicago; Loomis & Onderdonk, Grand Rapids, Mich., etc.

The western office of the Thorne Typesetting Machine Company is at 139 Monroe street, Chicago, the factory and main office at Hartford, Conn.

Thorne Typesetting Machine. ✿

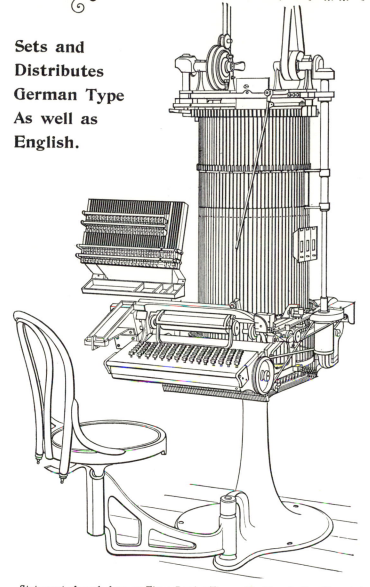

**Sets and
Distributes
German Type
As well as
English.**

Saves 50 per cent over Handwork.

Distributes Automatically.

**Produces First-class Typographical
Results.**

Does not Require a Machinist.

**Not an Experiment, but a Perfected
Machine.**

Simplest Machine in Use.

IN successful and profitable operation on best dailies, weeklies, magazines and in most prominent book offices in the country, as for instance: New York Evening Post, Hartford Post, Portland (Me.) Press, Watertown (N. Y.) Times, Richmond (Va.) State, Joliet (Ill.) News, New York Churchman, New York Evangelist, Boston Christian Register, Chicago Interior, The Ram's Horn of Chicago, Atlantic Monthly, Forum, Current Literature, Romance, American Press Association, Street & Smith, New York; Publishers Printing Co., New York; Charles H. Kerr & Co., Chicago, etc., etc.

**YOU CANNOT AFFORD TO BE WITHOUT
THESE MACHINES.**

**We Furnish our Newspaper Customers with
Superior Type, all Nicked for Machines.**

Statement of work done on Three 7-point Thorne Machines in the office of the New York Evening Post, during four weeks of December, 1893:

DATE.	TEAM NO. 1.		TEAM NO. 2.		TEAM NO. 3.		DATE.	TEAM NO. 1.		TEAM NO. 2.		TEAM NO. 3.	
	Time run.	Ems set.	Time run.	Ems set.	Time run.	Ems set.		Time run.	Ems set.	Time run.	Ems set.	Time run.	Ems set.
	h. m.		h. m.		h. m.			h. m.		h. m.		h. m.	
December 1........	8 30	57,750	8 40	58,500	8 15	51,500	December 15.......	7 30	53,500	7 15	48,500	7 00	43,750
" 2.........	6 40	46,000	6 40	44,500	6 40	40,000	" 16.......	5 30	37,250	5 35	37,500	5 20	34,500
" 4.........	7 15	52,000	7 50	50,000	7 35	46,750	" 18.......	7 20	52,750	7 20	47,750	7 45	46,000
" 5.........	5 20	40,750	5 45	38,000	5 10	34,750	" 19.......	6 30	48,250	6 50	45,500	6 45	44,750
" 6.........	6 15	48,000	6 30	46,000	6 30	45,250	" 20.......	7 10	50,500	7 10	45,250	6 50	44,000
" 7.........	6 50	52,000	6 30	45,500	6 45	42,000	" 21.......	7 10	52,000	7 10	49,000	7 20	45,750
Total for week..	40 50	296,500	41 55	282,500	40 55	260,250	Total for week....	41 10	294,250	41 20	273,500	41 00	258,750
December 8........	7 35	55,500	8 00	32,750	7 45	49,750	December 22........	7 10	53,500	7 30	52,750	7 30	49,500
" 9.........	5 10	38,500	5 00	32,750	5 00	33,250	" 23........	4 20	32,000	4 25	28,250	4 30	25,750
" 11.........	7 30	53,000	7 15	48,000	7 35	46,000	" 26........	6 10	44,250	6 25	41,250	6 30	39,750
" 12.........	7 25	55,250	7 30	51,250	7 15	47,000	" 27........	6 00	46,500	6 10	44,750	6 05	39,750
" 13.........	7 35	55,250	7 40	52,750	7 20	46,750	" 28........	6 10	46,500	6 30	43,500	6 15	40,750
" 14.........	7 10	52,750	7 00	48,500	7 05	43,500							
Total for week..	42 25	310,250	42 25	266,000	42 00	266,250	Total for 5 days....	29 50	222,750	31 00	210,500	30 50	195,500

For Terms, Circulars, etc., address # Thorne Typesetting Machine Co.

**FACTORY AND GENERAL OFFICE,
HARTFORD, CONN.**

139 Monroe Street, CHICAGO.

THE POINT SYSTEM IN TYPEFOUNDING.

BY R. COUPLAND HARDING.

SOME headway is just beginning to be made in the fundamental idea underlying all labor-saving improvements in typography — that each individual type, having three dimensions, should have each of those dimensions in a recognized proportion to one common standard measure. As one of those who have, in season and out of season, for more than seven years past, advocated a systematic scheme of typometric unity, it is with no little gratification that I see the idea, so long treated by manufacturers as a printer's "fad," coming more and more into practical effect. Since the first article of this series was written, I have received, from two different quarters, prospectus and specimens, anticipating some of the points raised in this paper. Having, however, dealt with them very fully as long ago as the year 1887, I will scarcely be suspected of deriving in any way from these sources my present suggestions, more especially as they are not in either case fully carried into effect. The printer of the next generation will scarcely be able to credit the fact that for four centuries after the invention of movable type, printers were compelled to deal with material adjusted on endless variety of standards, and often to no standard at all; and that at the cost of incalculable drudgery, loss of time, and waste of material, the compositors were compelled to adjust, as accurately as they might, the heterogeneous and incommensurable bodies and "sets" supplied by the typefounder, which might far more easily have been cast at first to a rational scheme of mathematical proportions.

It is true that at the outset a difficulty has to be faced. The first question is : Shall the scheme of proportion be geometrical or arithmetical? The artist, the author, the booklover — all but the practical printer — will answer at once : The geometrical, of course. It is the only perfect scheme. By no other means can a just gradation both of size and proportion be attained.

True, answers the compositor. But do you see what this implies? Type composition is a process of simple addition. The whole of our work consists in the aggregation of units of a definite magnitude. We have what we call a "measure" — the standard width of our page or columns. It is necessary that these should be to a common and regular standard. Given a geometrical increase in the size of bodies, doubling, say, in every seven steps, and at the same time a uniform proportion of "set," we have absolutely no fixed standard — every page and every column must bear a fractional relation to every other. We can understand a type differing in the proportion of one-half, one-fourth, one-sixth, one-twelfth or any other aliquot part, from its neighbor ; we can, with a reasonable proportion of justifiers made to these regular fractions, at once adjust one size to another — but what can we do when the unit of each size differs, say, 12.2462+ per cent from its fellow? Who is to cast a series of leads ascending by geometrical progression, to justify minion with brevier, brevier with bourgeois, and so on? or who could recognize such measures even if supplied? We can understand a brevier running 108 lines to the foot, and have no difficulty in justifying it with a pica which equals seventy-two lines to the foot. But what can we do with a pica 71.271+ and a brevier 113.137+ ? No one could remember such proportions ; no one could make any practical use of them. The very nature of our work demands that we deal with commensurable units, in the simplest possible proportions. On the basis of arithmetical progression, and especially on a duodecimal system, we have this advantage. Geometrical progression at once brings us among the incommensurables.

As the readers of THE INLAND PRINTER are aware, an attempt (the only attempt, so far as I know) was made by a great American firm to introduce a system of geometrical proportions of bodies. It was brought out in 1822, and has had a trial of seventy years. Beautiful as it undoubtedly was in theory, it met with no general acceptance, and has lately been definitely abandoned. I have no doubt that the firm who tried the scheme, and who have invested large sums in borders, etc., engraved and cast to their own special bodies, have suffered loss by their long persistence in a scheme which had so many drawbacks in practical use.

In investigating this subject seven years ago, after collating many tables, the writer found, a little to his surprise, that every systematic scheme now in use, English, American or Continental, was based originally on the national duodecimal standard of the inch and foot, and was a continuation in miniature of the same system. The old scientific measure of the "line" ($\frac{1}{12}$ inch) corresponded with the nonpareil of Fournier, who, in 1737, devised the first "interchangeable" system — in all essential details precisely the same as the American point system of today. After his death Didot modified it, as regarded the unit of measurement, by adopting the "royal" foot of France, about one-twelfth larger than the English foot, as his standard. This difference of about one-twelfth represents the discrepancy existing to the present time between the foreign "Cicero" (= two-line emerald in English phraseology, and two-line minionette in American) and "pica." The body is used by English-speaking printers almost exclusively for combination borders. These being nearly all at first of French, and afterward of German origin, were necessarily cast to the standard body for which they were designed.

It may seem late to complain of the standard adopted by the American founders for the point system, but it was a serious mistake to depart from the inch-and-foot national standard. As originally carried out by Marder, Luse & Co., the system was perfect in the first essential — it conformed to a recognized national standard. The vested interest of two large foundries in a nondescript body of pica ultimately prevailed, and an altogether arbitrary and irregular basis of 72.2892 ems to the foot was adopted as the basis. The English point system, as followed by Caslon and the Patent Typefounding Company, takes seventy-two lines to the foot as its basis; and we have (in the former) a regular duodecimal series from the point, $= \frac{1}{72}$ inch, up to the standard fathom measure $= 72$ inches.

Somebody will probably here correct me: "You forget that the American point, and the German point also, *do* conform to a national standard. They are based upon the great coming international system — the metric scheme, to which inches, feet and yards, degrees, hours and minutes — all effete duodecimal and sexagesimal systems — must soon give way." I have read something to this effect, but it is entirely fallacious. I know that some of the American founders assert that their point system is based on the metric system — everything is tested by "a steel rod 35 centimeters long." (Very likely it is.) I also find the leading German houses claim for *conflicting* standards approximating to the Didot point that they are based upon the meter. With all respect to these gentlemen, I submit that the claim, not in one case only, but in all, is sheer nonsense.

What is the essence of the vaunted metric system? *Not* its unit of measurement, certainly. That is founded on an admittedly erroneous geographic measure. It lies in its consistent use of the one decimal division in all measures of length, superficies and capacity. From the highest to the lowest, all values may be expressed in one series of figures, divided where required by the decimal point. All vulgar fractions, no matter how convenient, have to give way to this method. We must not write $\frac{1}{2}$, but .5. A system of type standards *based on this scheme* must necessarily have a decimal fraction of the meter as its base, and be *divided decimally*. A duodecimal division of the meter would be absurd enough — it would be the old inch and foot in another form. Still more absurd would be the grafting on the beautiful decimal simplicity of the metric system such exceedingly vulgar fractions as $\frac{60}{133}$, $\frac{300}{798}$ and $\frac{35}{83}$. Yet these are the precise relations of three of these "metric" schemes, while the neater fraction $\frac{3}{8}$, on which the Berthold system is founded, is equally foreign to the metric system. In fact, the simple method by which one and all (save Berthold) of these gentlemen seem to have proceeded, has been to lay two totally incongruous scales side by side, mark off the first place at which two divisions appeared to coincide, note the coincidence, and then claim that one measure was *based* on the other!

The fact that such a claim is made, on such inadequate grounds, is proof of the general acknowledgment of my first principle — that the basis of measurement should be an aliquot part of a recognized national standard. Just here is where the American system falls short. And on this ground I doubt its permanence.

IT may reasonably be asked: Why did not the continental decimalists apply their fundamental principle to type division? Why not, indeed? The answer brings us to the root of the matter and discloses the inherent weakness of the whole system.

For constructive work of all kinds a system of aliquot division is a first essential. The number ten, divisible only by 2 and 5, is one of the worst divisions for practical work. It has acquired a fictitious value as the basis of the artificial notation in general use. Twelve is the best number for aliquot division, and therefore for practical purposes; and a notation of twelve ciphers, could it ever have been agreed upon, would have been immeasurably superior to the decimal system. Unfortunately for the world today, and for every branch of mathematical science, the first savage who used his fingers as tallies imposed a yoke upon all future generations.* Geometry, under a purely decimal system, would be almost impossible. Imagine the substitution of 1,000 for the 360 degrees of the circle! This has actually been tried by decimal enthusiasts, notwithstanding the fact that nearly all the divisions are useless, and that some of the most valuable angles disappear entirely and are replaced by incommensurables.

Just where the artificial metric system is weak, the old national inch-and-foot systems are strong. They are based on the rock of practical adaptability. In the thirty-six inches of the three-foot rule we have a number composed of the most useful divisors. In the sexagesimal division in use by astronomers, geographers and navigators from the most primitive times, and of which we have a familiar example in the clock-dial, the decimal and duodecimal schemes meet. This system, as the late learned Professor De Morgan (himself a prominent decimalist) has told us, can never be superseded; the astronomer's ledger, he says, goes back three thousand years, and the old entries must always be open for immediate reference.

In the mariner's compass-card we have a good example of the half-and-quarter scheme, familiar and most convenient in weight and measure; but as a universal system greatly inferior to the duodecimal. Compared with either of these, a hard-and-fast decimal scheme is clumsy and unnatural. Each has its own advantages, and can never be legislated out of use.†

It is a significant fact that no one has ever ventured to adopt a decimal standard of type division. The

* Mr. Isaac Pitman, of Bath, the well-known spelling reformer, devised two extra numerals, and for some years kept his accounts and paged his *journal* duodecimally. There is in London, I believe, a Duodecimal Society, the object of which is to substitute 12 for 10 as the basis of numeration. The task is too stupendous. It would involve not only the recalculation or translation of all books of tables, but the revising and rewriting of all the world's permanent literature.

truth is, that the inconveniences of such a scheme are so obvious that it would be a waste of time and money to try the experiment. All point schemes, save one, have twelve as their basis. The single exception is that of the Patent Typefounding Company, of London, in which the pica is divided into twenty points. The system is a defective one, and must prove a clog on the operations of the foundry. Ultimately the vicesimal division will have to follow the other costly experiment of geometrical proportion.

It is worth while, before passing from this subject, to examine the claim sometimes put forth that there is a practical relation between existing point systems and the metric standard. It must be a little puzzling to those who have not investigated the matter to find this claim made, with equal confidence on behalf of two conflicting standards, the Didot and the American, the respective units of which differ about one-twelfth; besides a third, to be noted hereafter. It is certain that both cannot be harmonized with the same decimal standard, and the truth is that neither can. I have already shown the absurdity of any attempt to graft a duodecimal scheme upon a system so consistently decimal as the metric. American coinage would scarcely be improved, nor would financial computations be greatly facilitated by the introduction of a coin value $\frac{7}{12}$-cent, in which all small reckonings would have to be made. If, however, some ingenious treasurer were to invent a new coin of which 83 should *exactly* equal in value 35 cents, and a smaller one just one-twelfth less in value, should compel their use, and stoutly maintain that they were based on the national decimal system of coinage, what would be thought of him? What would the distracted accountants say? Yet exactly such a preposterous claim passed almost without comment when the point system came into use. "We use a standard steel rod 35 centimeters long, which is divided into 83 parts, each part being equal to a pica body, and the twelfth part of pica (called a point) is the unit by which we measure our type." The parallel of the imaginary new currency is exact. Taking the meter as representing the dollar, we have the 35 cents as equivalent to the steel rod, and the two new coins (based on the American decimal currency) representing $0.0422 and $0.00351, respectively.

---

† The late Mr. Spurrell, a Welsh printer, ably advocated in the London *Printers' Register*, some years ago, the adoption of the sixteenth of pica as the typographic point. After reading his arguments carefully, I could find no more serious objection to the ordinary duodecimal division than the fact that in the smaller grades of type the half-point division became necessary. On the introduction of the English point system by the Caslon Foundry, Mr. Spurrell showed his appreciation of the reform by replacing all his letter with fonts cast to the new bodies.

Equally inexcusable are the claims of the two rival point schemes in use on the European continent to conform to the metric system. The Didot standard bears the accidental and perfectly useless relation of 133 Ciceros (picas) to 60 centimeters, or 66½ Ciceros (= 798 points) to 300 millimeters. The Berthold standard is 800 points (63⅓ Ciceros) to 300 millimeters — a simpler fraction, certainly; but quite destitute of practical value.

It is a mistake to suppose that this fundamental question of standard is of no practical concern. I do not believe that finality has yet been reached. Apart from the unsystematic bodies still produced, but gradually falling into disuse, in England, there are now four rival schemes, differing only in their unit. These are, on the one hand, the Didot and Berthold scales, differing in the infinitesimal proportion of $\frac{1}{395}$; on the other, the American and English points, differing only $\frac{1}{224}$; the latter pair about one-twelfth smaller than the former. Not until an international measure is agreed upon can we look for finality, and the first requisite is to realize that any supposed relation of any existing standard to the metric system is illusory and fictitious; and that as by universal consent the duodecimal division is the only practical one for type, it should be absolutely and definitely distinguished from any decimal standard whatever. As a plain conclusion it would follow that the scheme should be conformed to the international English-American inch-and-foot system, of which it is the natural corollary. On this latter point opinions will differ. It would only be a reversion to the original and scientific standard originally adopted by Marder, Luse & Co., and which was unfortunately forced to give way to an inferior and arbitrary scale supported by large vested interests.

The great difficulty in the way of the adoption of an international standard lies in the large and rapidly increasing amount of capital invested in the vulgar-fractional schemes. But each year, as international commerce expands and the demand for fine work increases, the necessity becomes more manifest. The partial reform already secured in the United States would have been deemed impossible ten years ago. To my mind it proves the possibility of a thorough and fundamental reform on scientific principles and world-wide in its adoption, which you and I, Mr. Editor, may live to see.‡

---

‡ In fact, the first step toward an international standard has already been voluntarily taken by the leading German houses, who are casting their new job faces to the English as well as to the German point system, in order to adapt their wares to the English market.

SOME NEGLECTED TYPE-BODIES.

BY N. J. WERNER.

IN discussing the usefulness of the nine-point body with a typefounder the other day, he told me that most printers he met with still associated it with the old bourgeois, and called it a "bastard"; it was therefore somewhat unsaleable, though it is really one of the most useful type-bodies made, if the printers only knew it.

As far as the "bastardness" is concerned, there is no valid reason whatever for considering any body of the point system entitled to the designation. Every body has a fixed and regular proportion to all the other bodies, can be readily justified with them, and each one has its legitimate uses as much as the others. If I made any exceptions at all, I would name the 5½-point, 11-point and 22-point bodies, which I think could have been left out of the scale without causing any inconvenience whatever.

Most old double small picas are now cast on 20-point, and a few on 24-point, instead of on 22-point. The same plan could have been pursued with small pica faces, which by measurement I find could have been easily cast on 10-point instead of 11-point bodies. I find, also, that nearly all the old long primer faces could have been just as easily cast on 9-point instead of 10-point. By doing this, not so much space would have been wasted on shoulders and in extra metal.

A study of the subject proves that the typefounders, in changing from their old systems to the point bodies, went to work in a very reckless manner, and gave no intelligent consideration, if any at all, to the fact that while making the change other improvements could have been incidentally effected which would have added doubly and trebly to the value of the point system. For one instance of such carelessness I refer to the fact that one size of a certain face is cast by the Johnson foundry on 36-point, by the Central foundry on 30-point and by the Dickinson foundry on 24-point; only one of the three can be right. The specimen books are full of evidence of such want of attention to the details which would have made the point system many times more serviceable to the printer than it now is. I may mention, also, that no founder seems to have considered the matter of uniform alignment, which hundreds of printers, as well as the Typothetæ, have been asking for.

But this is digressing. I started to speak of the value of the 9-point body, and to disabuse the printer of the "bastard" view he has about it. To note some of its features: It is half-way between pica (12-point) and nonpareil (6-point); it is the half of 18-point, which, next to 12-point, is the most useful size in every jobbing series; it is three-fourths of pica, and one-and-a-half times nonpareil. On account of these good proportions it is now used for a number of border faces, and might well be used for more. Mr.

J. R. Bettis, in an article on the arrangement of a printing office, says: "I consider bourgeois [9-point] the noblest Roman of them all." I coincide heartily with him in this view. 10-point is too large to be used for newspapers; yet many have it for body letter where 9-point should be the largest size permitted. Even for books I consider 10-point too large. I note that the typefounders of Germany in nearly all cases include the 9-point body in their various series of display and jobbing letters (11-point is omitted altogether), and I fail to see why our founders and printers should not give it the same proper recognition. The Johnson foundry, of Philadelphia, has cast a number of original faces on 9-point (3-line excelsior), and I hope it will continue the practice, and that it will become general. I would say, however, that when the 9-point size is made, neither the 8-point nor the 10-point should be omitted between the 6-point and 12-point sizes. We have use for all of these sizes. Nor do I believe in casting an 8-point face on 9-point body, as some founders do; it does not "fill the bill." Cut the face the proper size to match the body.

Before dropping the subject, I want to speak a good word for the 14-point body, which some printers, who don't know as much as they ought, also call a "bastard." We must have a size between 12-point and 18-point. Though there is an enormous "jump" between these bodies, most series are furnished without an intermediate size, and this makes them most awkwardly graded and proportioned. A fellow-printer told me the other day that he would also like to see a size between 18-point and 24-point in every series (and particularly in the "De Vinne"); but I am not asking to carry refinement that far. The need for the 14-point size in all series made as small as 12-point or smaller is, however, very apparent to every thoughtful and discriminative printer.

Ye considerate ones among the typefounders, please therefore let us by all means have the 9-point and 14-point sizes as permanent fixtures. Also bring them prominently forward, advertise them well, and teach the unwise printer the falsity of terming them "bastards." By pushing them you will "get your money back," and earn the gratitude of the progressive printers.

RECIPE TO DULL THE FACE OF TYPESETTING MACHINE SLUGS.

To the Editor: DETROIT, Mich., June 29, 1894.

In THE INLAND PRINTER, of a recent issue, I saw that a patent had been granted to someone for inking the metal slugs as they came from the typesetting machine, so that the glitter would not injure the eyes of the make-up.

A simple remedy for that is to dissolve a small quantity of black aniline in the lye pot, and when the galley is rubbed off after proving, the bars are dulled so that the face is almost as black as old type. This is a simple remedy and costs comparatively nothing. It does not hurt the type or lye in any way.

You might publish this if you see fit. It may do some poor make-up good.   RAYNOR & TAYLOR.

SPECIMENS OF MID-GOTHIC.

ORIGINATED BY CENTRAL TYPE FOUNDRY, ST. LOUIS, MO.

8a 5A   42-POINT MID-GOTHIC. $6.50

Noted Chief 78 Great Brave
MANCHESTER HOUSE

9a 6A   36-POINT MID-GOTHIC. $5.00

Medical Book 302 Tenth Edition
MUTUAL EXPRESS COMPANY

10a 7A   30-POINT MID-GOTHIC. $4.25

Choice 75 Supper
CHEAP MUSIC

12a 9A   24-POINT MID-GOTHIC. $4.00

Forward 54 Marched
HIGH BUILDINGS

16a 12A   18-POINT MID-GOTHIC. $3.50

Humourous $19 Magazines
MODERN EUROPE

18a 12A   14-POINT MID-GOTHIC. $3.25

Manufacturers $132 Blank Forms
GENERAL PUBLISHER

20a 16A   12-POINT MID-GOTHIC. $3.00

Financial Review 264 Member of Clubs

FROM BRITISH NORTH AMERICA

26a 20A   10-POINT MID-GOTHIC. $2.75

Instructions Are Given 375 Every Purchaser Shown

PRINTING AND PAPER WORKING MACHINE

30a 22A   8-POINT MID-GOTHIC. $2.50

Some Accumulated Science £895 Precious Stones For Sale

GERMAN INTRODUCTION TO ENGLISH COMPOSITIONS

36a 24A   6-POINT MID-GOTHIC. $2.25

Coupon Ticket Railway Machinery $783 Paper Cutter and Cylinder Presses

COLONIAL AND INDIAN EXHIBITION FULLY DESCRIBED

For Sale by All Foundries and Branches of the American Type Founders' Company.

CAXTON BOLD.

Nonpareil (6 Point). 2.60

PEOPLE ARE VERY OFTEN WARNED TO KEEP AWAY FROM MOBS
The New York Representative Seems to Desire that Some One Fire at the Target he Offers. And in View of the Recent
Revelations of a Police Department Flagrant in its Abuses

Brevier (8 Point). 3.20

AGAIN SPRINGFIELD BECOMES THE CENTER OF INTEREST
Many Eminent Republicans Assembled there in Convention will be Carefully Watched by Democrats
State Superintendent of Public Instruction and Trustees 427

Long Primer (10 Point). 3.00

ELBOW GREASE RECOMMENDED FOR IDLERS
Action of the Citizens of Hawaii in Formally Proclaiming the Establishment of a Republic
Representatives of Foreign Nations $485

Pica (12 Point). 3.40

SUCCESSFUL CURE FOR BROKEN HEARTS
Melancholic Lovers whose Hearts have been Shattered by the Hand of Others

Great Primer (18 Point). 3.85

GRAND RECEPTION TUESDAY
Brought Unreliable Circumstantial Evidence 584

Double Pica (24 Point). 4.90

MONTHLY HERALD
Destroying Ancient Exhibition Building

Five-Line Nonpareil (30 Point). 5.60

MODERN UNIFORMS
Remarkable Personal Advertising

SPACES AND QUADS EXTRA.

Cast by the MARDER, LUSE & CO. FOUNDRY, Chicago, Illinois.

For sale by All Foundries and Branches of the American Type Founders' Company.

WHAT MUST BE DONE FOR MACHINE-DISPLACED COMPOSITORS?

THE past twelve months have done much to clearly define the possibilities of the typesetting machine. The practical utility of this method of setting type can no longer be successfully disputed. The machine has been introduced into all parts of the country, the result being such as to settle the question of permanency beyond cavil. The most that can truthfully be asserted in disparagement is that the machine is not all that it should be, an objection that applied with equal force and truth to the web press during its introductory or probationary period. The difficulties with the press were due to certain mechanical crudities which were easily overcome in time. The same objections are noticeable in the typesetting machine, but the final result will no doubt be the same as with the press. Mechanical skill will triumph in the end. There is now no talk of going back to the hand press, while the desire to return to hand composition is received with less favor day by day. As a matter of fact, the typesetting machine is fast establishing its claim to recognition as a worthy companion to the web press.

In view of the changed conditions accompanying the introduction of the machine, it is well to inquire what provision, if any, is made for the hundreds of compositors who must necessarily be thrown out of employment, if only temporarily? We say temporarily, for past experiences prove that it is during the readjustment period attending the introduction of machinery, where hardship and suffering may be expected, and perhaps unavoidably so. Newspaper work in nearly all the more populous cities is now done largely by the machine. Hundreds, and perhaps thousands of compositors have been deprived of employment, many of them driven from situations which they have held the better part of their lives. In New York city a system of relief has been established by the union, which has accomplished a great deal of good. The practice of the newspapers of that city in doing outside composition, may or may not relieve the situation, but it is a fact that the eastern metropolis so far furnishes the only instance where an effort of any kind has been made to relieve the distress caused by the displacement of compositors by machines. True, coöperative newspapers have been established at various points throughout the country, but this was due more to the efforts of the displaced compositors than to any desire to aid them manifested by their more fortunate brethren who retained their situations.

In Chicago printers have been more fortunate than in other localities. The machine so far has made no serious inroads, the compositor following the even tenor of his way, harassed only by the general depression in business and a wage-scale not so liberal as in years gone by. But a speedy and radical change is promised in all this. The machine looms up as a certainty of the immediate future. If we are correctly informed, machines have been contracted for by a number of the more important daily newspapers, while at least one establishment is making the alterations necessary for their reception. It can, therefore, be accepted as a moral certainty that Chicago printers are not to enjoy immunity from machine competition for a much longer period. This being the case, we again inquire, What provision is being made for the large number of compositors who will inevitably find themselves without employment as a result of machine competition?

So far as can be learned, nothing is being done in this direction. The printer is a happy-go-lucky individual under all circumstances, and does not, as a usual thing, worry himself as to how he is to cross a bridge before he comes to it. Nevertheless, we believe that the gravity of the situation now confronting him will warrant a departure from his customary practices, and incline the printer to favor any policy promising even a modicum of protection in the future. What that policy is to be is a difficult matter to determine. In the absence of anything better, we would suggest that the benefit associations maintained in the newspaper offices be utilized for this purpose. Let a clause be inserted in the by-laws making provision for the maintenance for a stated period of those deprived of employment through a reorganization of the force incident to the introduction of machines. A special payment might be provided for under this provision, when all would gladly avail themselves of the benefit, for no one knows where the lightning will strike.

Measures of this character, supplemented by such aid as members of the typographical union will extend in the way of assessments, will prevent a world of suffering and misery. While we have addressed ourselves more particularly to the case as it exists in Chicago, there is no doubt but that like conditions prevail in other cities, where deserving printers will suffer as they will in Chicago unless immediate steps are taken to prevent it. Newspaper printers have always been generous, free-hearted, timely contributors to every project calculated to advance the craft, and there is no doubt but that others will now be liberal in contributing to their own protection. But newspaper printers will not be the only sufferers through the introduction of the machine, and all will have enough to do to provide for themselves and families. It is, therefore, the part of wisdom for those more immediately threatened to avail themselves of any and all means to weather the storm when that is sure to overtake them. It is foolish to await the arrival of the machines before anything is done. The plan outlined here is feasible and comprehensive. A liberal weekly contribution by one hundred members of a chapel, the fund to be eventually divided between, say, one-third of that number who will be deprived of employment under the new dispensation, will be a most welcome boon to the recipient.

ANTI-TRUST

Great Western Type Foundry

Only Type Foundry in the United States that manufactures the Celebrated

Superior Copper-Mixed Type

TYPE

❄

❄

FOUNDERS

BARNHART BROS. & SPINDLER

183 to 187 Monroe Street,

CHICAGO, ILL.

Send for Estimates and Specimens

COMPLETE NEWSPAPER and
JOB OUTFITS FURNISHED

ELZEVIR TITLE

6 Point, 24 A 50 a. $2.25	24 Point, 9 A 18 a $3.40
8 Point, 24 A 50 a. 2.50	36 Point, 6 A 12 a. 5.30
10 Point, 20 A 40 a. 2.50	48 Point, 5 A 10 a. 5.95
12 Point, 20 A 40 a. 2.80	60 Point, 4 A 6 a. 6.25
18 Point, 12 A 25 a. 3.35	72 Point, 4 A 5 a. 7.70

PATENT PENDING.

3 A, 5 a.   48 Point Telegraph. $5.50

Monthly Lectures
Resumed
Junior Course

5 A, 12 a.   24 Point Telegraph. $3.75

The noted standing of
Rush Physical Culture
Academy is due to the
inexorable energies of
. . Strike & Parry . .

Valuable as scientific
proficiency is to man,
the Board renews the
theoretical discourses

6 A, 15 a.   18 Point Telegraph. $3.25

To make the lectures more
comprehensible to students,
the Tutors and their worthy
Assistants have introduced
the original and renowned

Musical Automath . .
. . . and Harpsichord

Their object is to teach the
Junior Class all the popular
airs that generally emanate
from those Persons quietly
touched on sensitive spots

3 A, 6 a.   36 Point Telegraph. $4.25

Broadshouldered
Dexterous Autoharpist
Rehearsing
Medals Awarded

ALL COMPLETE WITH FIGURES.

Originated by MacKellar, Smiths & Jordan Foundry, Philadelphia.
For Sale by all Foundries, Branches and Selling Agents of the American Type Founders' Company.

PATENTED.

4 A, 6 a.   36 POINT UNIQUE CELTIC CONDENSED. $4.25

Handsome SEMINARIAN Enchanted
Remarkable Performance

8 POINT UNIQUE CELTIC CONDENSED.
25 A, 38 a, $2.25

PROVINCIAL GIMCRACK EXCHANGE
We need no greater evidence of the popularity of our gimcracks and appreciation of the bargains tendered than the great crowds that thronged our stores during the past eight weeks. We have reduced prices, and it has a telling effect on the enormous stock imported from Madeira

8 A, 10 a.   24 POINT UNIQUE CELTIC CONDENSED. $3.25

WINSOME VIRGINS
Sunshine Banishing Melancholy
1234567890

18 A, 30 a.   12 POINT UNIQUE CELTIC CONDENSED. $2.75

FASHIONABLE PARASOL EXHIBITIONS
If our efforts in this line are appreciated, we shall extend them more widely and with more handsome and pleasure-giving effects

20 A, 34 a   10 POINT UNIQUE CELTIC CONDENSED. $2.50

BLITHESOME AND HIGH-SPIRITED MAIDENS
For the Benefit of the Community at Large, we take pleasure in announcing that persons having original ideas can dispose of them to us at liberal prices, if adaptable to our contemplated purposes

12 A, 16 a.   18 POINT UNIQUE CELTIC CONDENSED. $3.00

ORATORICAL REFORMERS
Smockfrocked Blatherskites Gesticulating
1234567890

6 POINT UNIQUE CELTIC CONDENSED.
30 A, 45 a, $2.00

MAGNIFICENT EXPEDITIONS TO WONDERLAND
Neither language nor pencil can magnify the beauty of this wonderful isle, and in climate it may well be reckoned among the Isles of the Blest. It lies in an easily accessible part, and will belong to any member of the expedition who shall see it first. The island rises from the sea in magnificent outline, with lofty precipices and vast detached rocks of peculiar shapes, the peaks being grouped like the bastions and pinnacles of a gigantic fortress of recent architectural style

6 A, 8 a.   30 POINT UNIQUE CELTIC CONDENSED. $3.75

KINETOSCOPE EXHIBITION

Originated by MacKellar, Smiths & Jordan Foundry, Philadelphia.
For Sale by all Foundries, Branches and Selling Agents of the American Type Founders' Company.

Season Ticket

Autumnal Display

Oriental Fair Grounds

12 A, 32 a.   12 POINT STYLUS, No. 2. $4.00

Dress Goods, Curtains and La

Our several departments are fully stocked with fresh merchandise, which is matchless in quality, newness, variety and cheapness. It is now the high tide of the Fall Trade, and as in the Autumn all roads lead to Christmas, so all prospective purchasers find their way to our well-known establishment. Our buying power commands for the judicious buyer the most advantageous prices. The salesladies are gladsome and merry, just as you would expect them to be during these bright autumnal days, so full of life, hope and joy.

24 POINT STYLUS, No. 2.   6 A, 14 a, $5.00

Costumes, Furs

Wrappers

Infants' Cloaks

Jackets

Capes, Hosiery

Thursday, October 25, 1894

Grand Fall Opening

Australian Tailoring Company

Leading Styles

Exhibits at Main Entrance

8 A, 20 a.   18 POINT STYLUS, No. 2. $4.50

Our Ambition is to Give Entire Satisfaction

For the convenience of out-of-town buyers we issue daily an Illustrated Descriptive Catalogue, magnificently embellished with Photogravures, which will be mailed free upon application. Customers satisfactorily served from sam as if they were in our store. Address, Mail Dept.

Originated by MacKellar, Smiths & Jordan Foundry, Philadelphia.
For Sale by all Foundries, Branches and Selling Agents of the American Type Founders' Company.

4 A, 6 a.   60 Point Lippincott. $9.00

HAMBURG Retouchers

4 A, 7 a.   48 Point Lippincott. $6.50

Mountainhouse EXCURSION

6 A, 8 a.   36 Point Lippincott. $5.00

CROCKERY WIELDERS
Enthusiastic Midnight Demonstrator

7 A, 10 a   30 Point Lippincott. $4.25

IMPROVISED BACKGROUND
Beautiful and Enchanting Result Obtained

10 A, 15 a.   24 Point Lippincott. $3.75

CASINO TALKS
Delightful for Students

12 A, 18 a.   18 Point Lippincott. $3.25

MODERN OUTFITS
Automatic Miniature Camera

22 A, 35 a.   12 Point Lippincott. $3.00

UNIVERSAL ART EXHIBITION
Highly Complimented Marine Photography

28 A, 40 a.   10 Point Lippincott. $2.75

REFRESHING AND INVIGORATING
Hieroglyphical Studies of Celebrated Discoverers

30 A, 50 a.   8 Point Lippincott. $2.50

RENOWNED AMATEUR KODACK FRATERNITY

35 A, 52 a.   6 Point Lippincott. $2.25

THIRTY-SEVENTH CRUISE TO THE MEDITERRANEAN

Originated by MacKellar, Smiths & Jordan Foundry, Philadelphia.
For Sale by all Foundries, Branches and Selling Agents of the American Type Founders' Company.

PROGRESS OF COMPOSING MACHINES.

BY H. L. L.

FROM remarks heard in newspaper offices one would be led to believe that the typesetting machine question was finally settled — that the machine *par excellence* was discovered, and, on the other hand, from the list of machines that we hear and read of we could easily imagine that inventing a typesetting machine was of everyday occurrence and the easiest thing possible.

Up to date these machines can be classified as follows, namely : Slug or bar casters, movable typesetters, and type casters and setters. Of the bar casting machines we have the Mergenthaler, the Monoline, the Rogers and the St. John.

The Mergenthaler, after expending vast sums of money, is now placed before us in an acceptable shape and is reaping the reward which it so richly deserves for its perseverance. Newspaper publishers have become reconciled to its product and they have learned that their readers are not as critical as they had feared. That the Rogers and the Monoline will also come to the front goes without saying, but whether the St. John Typobar can be made a success with its steel base is as yet an unsolved problem.

Publishers of fine books and magazines look toward the movable typesetting machines as their hope of preventing a retrograde typographical appearance in their publications, and in this the inventive genius has not failed them, for here they find the Thorne, the Paige, the McMillan, the Lagerman, the Empire, and a few others, but in such an embryo state as to be nameless.

Of these, at the present time, the Thorne is preëminently in advance, not only in its capability for preserving our high grade printing, but also in its utility in the newspaper offices as well, while it is conceded that as a mechanical wonder the Paige is unrivaled in nineteenth century inventions and in time its commercial usefulness may equal its construction. All of the movable typesetting machines are bending their energies toward automatic justification, and it would appear that this has been at least approached by the patents of the Cox typesetting machine, illustrated in the patent review in the present issue of THE INLAND PRINTER. A machine in which perforated paper is placed, a button is touched and, without any further attendance, casts each type separate and places them in a galley, with lines exactly justified, is the type casting and setting machine. Of these we know of two, the Langston, of Washington, and Goodson, of Minneapolis, and both are now claiming perfection.

Other machines that are heard of as being in experimental stages are the Converse, of Louisville ; the Cox, of Battle Creek, Michigan ; Sears, of Cleveland, Ohio, who is experimenting with wood instead of type metal with favorable results, and an untold number of others which are yet in the inventor's brain.

The survival of the fittest will govern and an anxious public is awaiting results.

PRACTICAL WORKING OF COMPOSING MACHINES.

BY ALEX DUGUID.

THE advent of the typesetting machines has brought into prominence many peculiar traits of the morning newspaper printer. After the first scare is over, and the machines are in working order, the selected few who are fortunate enough to be put on as learners become objects of intense curiosity — often envy. Every movement is watched, and the gossips, in great glee, detail to willing ears every mishap. To the sensitive, life is made a burden ; to the hardened, an opportunity is afforded to get even.

It was hoped that the change from piecework to timework would bring about a truce between compositor and proofreader, and that the growling and grumbling, bickering and

strife, jealousy and rivalry would give way to peace and harmony, and that the much-needed era of good will and fairness to all would dawn upon the composing room. Alas, for the hope ! In many places it will take more than a mere change to the time system to eradicate the accumulated grumbling of years of work upon a morning newspaper.

Experience will demonstrate the wisdom of a time system, but until the machines become an old story there will be as much rivalry as under handwork, and everything that checks rapid work will be abused, such as bad proofs, machines out of order, etc.

Every printer will remember the youthful days when his ambition was to set the biggest string on the paper, and hope was high in his breast that he might be considered a "swift." Time went on, perseverance lagged, hope dimmed, and he began to pride himself rather on the correctness of his work than on the amount set — quality rather than quantity. By and by his standing as a workman becomes a fixture of the composing room. Now comes another learning of the trade — a new art — demanding youth's resources, when he has not the power to command at will the enthusiasm, vigor, hope and perseverance required to meet the issue. To fail now means disaster, and the chances are greater for failure. In the present condition of the trade, with daily accessions to the "outs," the fear of failure proves incentive enough to put every man on his mettle. Every nerve is strained and every point watched that success may result.

All these circumstances develop rivalry. To a certain degree this is commendable. Not so when trickery and underhand work are resorted to or unfair advantage taken of another. Men need watching almost as much as in the palmy days of "shirking the hook." And the backcapper finds a feast, instead of the famine he feared.

The glory of the composing room is gone forever, and soon will be but a reminiscence as it fades before the everyday, practical typesetting machine. Who does not recall the good old days when a man could joke and talk and laugh all night long and set type just the same ? All the latest news, the ball score, the horse race, the election returns, union gossip, the last row out, the single land tax and prohibition all came in for their share of discussion, and each found an earnest advocate, for a printer is nothing if not partisan. When "time" was called a hush settled over the composing room, and there was a hustle to be the first done with the starting "take." The click-click of the type, as it "clothed the busy thoughts of the day in the garb of the morning newspaper," was the only sound in the well-conducted composing-room. Now the rattle and bang, the rumble and din of the machine shop takes the place of conversation, and the operator is alone among his fellows. The fascination of morning newspaper work for printers will surely disappear with handwork and the piece system. The old-time independence is gone. We are workingmen now, and realize that our trade has lost much of its distinctive features and become commonplace.

Let us hope that the increased care and responsibility of a machine position will influence for good the character of the operator, and be some gain where so much has been lost.

Will a rapid typesetter make a rapid machine operator ? is frequently asked. As a rule, yes. Both require the same faculties — good eyesight and quick mental action. Some rapid hand men learn more quickly than others, but I have yet to hear of a single instance where a rapid typesetter has failed to learn the machine, and the operator's speed can be gauged largely by his handwork.

Wonderful stories of the amount set on the machines have been circulated all over the country, and they have been promptly denied by printers who claim to know. Most of the measurements are taken as the matter appears in the paper, and the operator gets the benefit of heads, dashes, leads, etc. This is manifestly a very unfair way of measuring a man's work, and is little better than no gauge at all.

Clipper Extended No. 3.

CHRISTMAS | EMPEROR
MIDNIGHT HUMBUGS | FRANZ JOSEPH
POINTS | DENIS

MORNERS

SINGING

BRUNES

ROMES | SOUND
UNCHANGED | SUNSHINE
ECHO | HOME

CHIME MUSEUM

ART BORDERS.

No. 68.   No. 50.   No. 52.   No. 53.   No. 51.   No. 69.

Nos. 68 and 69, Fonts of Six Feet, $1 80.   Nos. 50, 51, 52 and 53, Fonts of 6 Feet, $3 00.
Small Fonts, $1 00.   Small Fonts, $1 50.

THE STANDARD TYPE FOUNDRY,

200-202 CLARK STREET, CHICAGO.

$2.90. 12-POINT ORNAMENTED, No. 1,569. 15 A / 2 lb. 8 oz.

RESOURCES OF SOLID INSURANCE
MANUFACTURERS AND REPRESENTATIVES FROM BOSTON
STAPLE GOODS FOR CASH ONLY. SPOT PRICE 1894

$4.00. 18-POINT ORNAMENTED, No. 1,569. 12 A / 4 lb.

REPRESENTING EACH BRANCH ONLY
VALUE OF PROPERTY THE STATE CLAIMED
COMMERCIAL DIRECTORY 1894

$4.85. 24-POINT ORNAMENTED, No. 1,569. 10 A / 5 lb. 6 oz

PRINTED LISTS OF ALL PRICES
CAPITAL INVESTED $12,376

$6.95. 36-POINT ORNAMENTED, No. 1,569. 8 A / 8 lb. 8 oz.

WORLD'S FAIR DIPLOMAS
MONTHLY SALES 1894

$6.50. 48-POINT ORNAMENTED, No. 1,569. 5 A / 9 lb.

COMMERCIAL RATE
PRICES FIRM 184

GEORGE BRUCE'S SON & CO., TYPE-FOUNDERS, 13 CHAMBERS STREET, NEW YORK.

BRUCE'S N. Y. TYPE-FOUNDRY.

<table>
<tr><td>$1.45.</td><td>6-Point Gothic, No. 205.</td><td>30 A
1 lb. 4 oz.</td><td>$2.00.</td><td>8-Point Gothic, No. 205.</td><td>30 A
2 lb. 4 oz.</td></tr>
</table>

WE SEE NO MORE REASON WHY THE SORDIDNESS OF

SOME WORKMEN SHOULD BE THE

CAUSE OF CONTEMPT UPON MANUAL

OPERATIONS. 1720.

TELEGRAMS FOR THE MILLIONS

ALL THE OLD AUTHORS AND PRINTERS

WHO GAVE THEIR DESCRIP-

TIONS AND APPLAUSE. £34,592

HOBART, TASMANIA

$1.75. 10-Point Gothic, No. 205. 20 A / 2 lb. 6 oz.

PARCHMENT PAPER WAS INVENTED IN PARIS.

A DESCRIPTIVE ACCOUNT THAT HAS JUST BEEN WRITTEN OF

THE FIRST SEVEN EDITIONS OF THE BIBLE IS AN INTERESTING PUBLICATION.

$1.65. 12-Point Gothic, No. 205. 15 A / ib. 8 oz.

UNITED STATES COMMISSIONER OF EDUCATION. 874

TO THE PRESIDENT, VICE-PRESIDENTS, AND ALL FELLOW

MEMBERS ATTENDING ON THIS "GREAT AND SOLEMN OCCASION."

$2.25. 18-Point Gothic, No. 205. 12 A / 3 lb. 12 oz.

WHITEFRIARS TO RED LION PASSAGE, 62

SOUTH FLEET STREET, EAST NORFOLK. 10

$3.10. 24-Point Gothic, No. 205. 10 A / 5 lb. 8 oz.

"TOPOGRAPHICAL ANTIQUITIES"

NEW BRADLEY CHURCH. 9009.

HHHHHHH   HHHHHH

GEORGE BRUCE'S SON & CO., TYPE-FOUNDERS, 13 CHAMBERS STREET, NEW YORK.

$3.05.   12-POINT ORNAMENTED, No. 1,567.   15 a and 15 A / 2 lb. 10 oz.

The Imperial Academy
Printing and its Accessories, Powerful
The Faustus Association, Paris
RUTHVEN'S PRESSES 1872

$4.40.   18-POINT ORNAMENTED, No. 1,567.   12 a ond 12 A / 4 lb. 6 oz.

Comprehensive Books
Information for Station Men
THE PUBLIC. 2793

$5.20.   24-POINT ORNAMENTED, No. 1,567.   .0 a and 10 A / 5 lb. 12 oz.

Eighty-one Tables of the Master-Printer's Charges
QUANTITY OF PAPER BOXES. CASH $193

$6.65.   30-POINT ORNAMENTED, No. 1,567.   8 a snd 8 A / 7 lb. 12 oz.

At Antwerp, Dedicated to Chas. Ruelens
TRANSLATED INTO FRENCH 1645

$7.40.   36-POINT ORNAMENTED, No. 1,567.   6 a and 6 A / 9 lb.

Account of many excellent People
ALEXANDER STEPHENS 1901.

$8.35.   48-POINT ORNAMENTED, No. 1,567.   5 a and 5 A / 11 lb. 10 oz.

The Royal Colonial Institute
COMMENTARIES. $17.84

HHHHHHH   HHHHHHH

GEORGE BRUCE'S SON & CO., TYPE-FOUNDERS, 13 CHAMBERS STREET, NEW YORK.

$2.45.   12-POINT ORNAMENTED, No. 1,568.   15 a and 15 A
2 lb. 2 oz.

**A monthly Literary and
Business Journal for Printers and Newspaper
Proprietors, St. Augustine 1866
LONDON, PROVINCIAL AND PRESS. PUBLISHED**

$3.35.   18-POINT ORNAMENTED, No. 1,568.   12 a and 12 A
3 lb. 6 oz.

**Every Printer to Register his name
and Residence; to have a Trade Mark
AS WELL AS HIS NAME. 4231**

$4.05.   24-POINT ORNAMENTED, No, 1,568.   10 a and 10 A
4 lb. 8 oz.

**Preston was originally a Printer's Devil, who Eventually became
A PARTNER WITH WILLIAM STRAHAN, KING'S PRINTER 17**

$5.15.   30-POINT ORNAMENTED, No. 1,568.   8 a and 8 A
6 lb.

**An Act concerning Printers and Binders of Book.
"THE OBEDIENCE OF A CHRISTIAN MAN. 19."**

$5.75.   36-POINT ORNAMENTED, No. 1,568.   6 a and 6 A
7 lb.

**The Fac-simile of the Letter of Indulgence
RUDENESS OF EARLY COMPOSITION 45**

$6.30.   48-POINT ORNAMENTED, No. 1,568.   5 a and 5 A
8 lb. 12 oz

**The Press of the Unknown Printer
COSTER LIVING AT HAARLEM. 98**

HHHHHHH   HHHHHH

GEORGE BRUCE'S SON & CO., TYPE-FOUNDERS, 13 CHAMBERS STREET, NEW YORK.

American Type Founders' Company

BOSTON, 144-150 Congress St.
NEW YORK, Rose and Duane Sts.
PHILADELPHIA, 606-614 Sansom St.
BALTIMORE, Frederick and Water Sts.
BUFFALO, 83-85 Ellicott St.
PITTSBURGH, 308 Wood St.

CLEVELAND, 239-241 St. Clair St.
CINCINNATI, 7-17 Longworth St.
CHICAGO, 139-141 Monroe St.
MILWAUKEE, 89 Huron St.
ST. LOUIS, Fourth and Elm Sts.
MINNEAPOLIS, 113 First Ave., South

ST. PAUL, 84-86 East Fifth St.
KANSAS CITY, 533-535 Delaware St.
OMAHA, 1118 Howard St.
DENVER, 1616-1622 Blake St.
PORTLAND, Second and Stark Sts.
SAN FRANCISCO, 405-407 Sansome St.

Harmonious TYPOGRAPHY

MMMmmmmmmmm
MMMMMMMmMMmmmmmmmmm
mmmmmmmmmmm
MMMMMMMMMMmmmmmmmmmm

NNNNNNNNNNnnnnnnnnnnnn

HHHHHHHHHH
HHHHHHHHHHHHHHhhhhhhh
hhhhhhhhhh
HHHHHHHHHHHHhhhhhhhhh

Mechanical APPLIANCES

American Type Founders' Company

CLEVELAND SERIES

STANDARD LINE

THE EXPLORING OF THE NILE

SWIMMING RIVERS

MASTER DAMEON

HOW LITTLE AFTER ALL WE KNOW OF WHAT IS ILL OR WELL--HOW LITTLE OF THIS WONDROUS STREAM OF CATARACT AND POOLS THIS STREAM OF LIFE THAT RISES IN A WORLD UNKNOWN AND FLOWS TO THAT MYSTERI-OUS SEA WHOSE SHORE THE FOOT OF ONE WHO COMES

HAS NEVER PRESSED-- HOW LITTLE OF THIS LIFE WE KNOW--THIS STRUGGLING WAY OF LIGHT BE-TWIXT GLOOM AND GLOOM--THIS STRIP OF LAND BY VERDURE CLAD BETWEEN THE UNKNOWN WASTES--THIS THROBBING MOMENT FILLED WITH

LOVE AND PAIN--THIS DREAM THAT LIES ALONG THE SHADOWY SHORES OF SLEEP AND DEATH--WE STAND ON THIS VERGE OF CRUMBLING TIME--WE LOVE WE HOPE WE DISAPPEAR--AGAIN WE MINGLE WITH

THE DUST--AND THE KNOT INTRIN-SECATE FALLS APART--BUT THIS WE KNOW--A NOBLE LIFE ENRICHES ALL THE WORLD--THE HAPPIEST DREAM IS ETERNAL REST FREE FROM PAIN.

A TRADE JOURNAL LATELY IS-SUED THE FOLLOWING TIMELY NOTICE RELATING TO A METAL MUCH USED IN TYPE MAKING:-

THE WORLD'S SUPPLY OF ANTIMONY SEEMS ABOUT EXHAUSTED. THE PRICES

HAVE BEEN GOING UP STEADILY FOR SEVERAL MONTHS

WHILE DEALERS ARE ANXIOUSLY

COMPLETE SERIES, Eleven Sizes, $23.95.

222222 HHHHHHH 444444

ART BORDERS

NO. 1271.

NO. 1272.

NO. 1273.

IN FONTS OF 2 FEET, 75 CENTS.

NO. 1806. NO. 1805. NO. 1807.

IN FONTS OF 2 FEET, $1.25.

CLEVELAND SERIES...6 Pt. No. 1, 35 A $1 25--No. 2, 30 A $1 25--No. 3, 30 A $1 25--No. 4, 30 A $ 150--8 Pt. No. 1, 30 A $1 75--No. 2, 30 A $2 00--12 Pt. 20 A $2 30--14 Pt. 20 A $2 80--20 Pt. 10 A $2 70. 24 Pt. 8 A $3 40--30 Pt. 6 A $3 75.

THE STANDARD TYPE FOUNDRY, 200 SOUTH CLARK ST., CHICAGO.

ROCOCO BORDER, No. 1809.
2 FEET, $1.25; 3 FEET, $1.90.

ROCOCO BORDER, No. 1808.
2 FEET, $1.25; 3 FEET, $1.90.

EVOLUTION OF THE PRINTER'S CRAFT

MUCH has been said and written regarding the rapid changes now going on in the printing business; so much, in fact, that to again refer to the matter in these columns might, under ordinary circumstances, justify an apology. But the circumstances are most unusual, and almost without a parallel in the whole industrial world. Thousands of skilled workmen are daily being deprived of the opportunity of earning a livelihood in a handicraft to which they have devoted the best years of their lives in an effort to attain proficiency, and if any apology were needed from us for again taking up this subject, it is furnished in the keen interest we have always taken in the welfare of printers, and the utter indifference with which scores upon scores of faithful men are now cast adrift without thought of their future, and without an effort on the part of those who are in a position to act to relieve the inevitable distress which must follow.

There is no one who depends upon the printing business for a livelihood who can afford to treat this matter with indifference. The changes which have already taken place, and which have proved so disastrous to the journeyman printer, may well be regarded as but a faint foreshadowing of the changes yet to take place. The whole industry is in an evolutionary state, with a strong possibility that the art of printing, as heretofore understood and practiced, may speedily become a thing of the past. In support of this theory it is only necessary to remind the reader that recently word has come from Paris to the effect that a device has been perfected, based upon the principle of the phonograph, by which newspapers can be printed in a way that will render unnecessary any coöperation on the part of compositors, pressmen, stereotypers, or other mechanics. It is further asserted that by the use of the telegraph a number of these devices, situated in different cities, can be made to do their work simultaneously. Although the more radical changes so far made have been confined to the production of newspapers, it will be seen by the foregoing that the evolutionary process is by no means completed. It may be accepted as a foregone conclusion that book and job work will also be seriously affected. No branch of the business will remain at a standstill in this age of progression. Close observers are of the opinion that the job printer of the future will be a man of some artistic attainments, who will design what is now known as the display portion of the work, and which will be reproduced by some of the rapid and cheap processes now being developed, after which the reading matter or solid portion of the work may be sent to the machine operator.

We refer to these circumstances merely to show that, although large numbers of men have been deprived of employment through the introduction of modern methods and devices, it must not be supposed that the period of evolution is at an end. On the contrary, every indication points to greater changes in the future than in the past. Mechanical labor will be less and less in vogue, and people who have devoted their lives to the mastery of a mechanical pursuit will awake to the fact that their services are no longer in demand. This has taken place to such an extent now that a united effort should be made to place unemployed printers in other vocations. It will be admitted that this will be a very serious problem to handle, but much can be done through well-directed effort. By way of illustration we will refer briefly to what might be done in Chicago, assuming that the situation here is not materially different from what it is in other localities. Here new industries are continually being opened up — elevated and surface railway lines, private industries and public corporations, which employ in the aggregate very large numbers of men. Now, as previously said, up to the present time it is newspaper men altogether who have been thrown out of employment by the introduction of machinery, and it is not unreasonable to suppose that the great influence of the newspapers could be brought to bear to secure the employment of idle printers by these new industries, where their services might be profitably employed as clerks, ticket takers and ticket sellers, conductors, etc. This could be done with profit to the employer, for we believe that men could be selected from the ranks of the printers who for intelligence, capacity and industry would average higher than if selected from the people who are usually, and we might say chronically, out of employment. In the long run the change may turn out to be very beneficial for the printers. The men who early leave the case are invariably the ones who prosper in the world. They will be found in all walks of life, in the professions, and in public life. A well-known and prosperous gentleman of this city, one who left the case thirty years ago, was recently heard to remark that the proper way to treat a young man who had served an apprenticeship at the case was to drive him out of the business as soon as he graduated. His experience and observation led him to the conclusion that the man was then well equipped to make his way in the world, while the opportunities for advancement in the printing industry were few, uncertain and illusive.

POINTS FOR PRINTERS.

A PRINTER seems to be most everybody's friend but his own. He supplies the bulk of the lubricant for the commercial machinery, but fails to use it properly in his own behalf. In his work he is progressive, and inventive genius has befriended him to a marvelous extent, but he figures advertising space with a type-measure, and not by the rules of trade. An important cause of the ineffectiveness of the ads. of most printers appears to lie in the fact that they do not realize the individuality of their equipment or else do not appreciate the value of calling attention to it. The chief cause is carelessness.

Long Run Presswork Our Specialty

Economy and speed are of utmost importance on a big job if the quality of work is not sacrificed. We are equipped with perfecting presses of the highest capacity, which turn out the best kind of rapid work in any quantity desired and at the lowest prices possible to anyone. Our composing room and bindery enable us to take care of any job from start to finish. We are always glad to furnish estimates and samples.

No. 1.

The invention of machine composition and perfecting presses for bookwork, together with increased illustrating facilities, have been the principal factors in cheapening the cost of every grade of work, and thereby greatly increasing the demand. A concern which proposed distributing a large number of cheap almanacs or catalogues would not find it profitable to patronize a printing office which devoted its efforts to producing high-class effects in typography and presswork. As the latter would be the chief item of expense, it might be desirable to have the composition done in such an office and the presswork done elsewhere. Yet, would not this concern be better satisfied to have its work done by such an establishment as could honestly advertise in manner of No. 1?

The Secret OF Fine Printing

Is a chain of many links. If one breaks, the effect is ruined. Long experience and true artistic taste are necessary in designing ; the best judgment in selecting paper and ink. A complete outfit of the most effective styles of type and borders and compositors who know how to use them to the best advantage ; pressmen who know thoroughly how to "make ready," one of the most difficult processes in printing, and press facilities of the very best, are links which have to stand the heavy strain. The price must also be considered, but not the first thing. We can satisfy you on every point. Booklets are now very popular, and we have made them a special study. Send for estimates and samples.

No. 2.

A Suitable Wedding

Invitation should be printed in the most careful and artistic manner. Nothing is criticised so sharply by one's friends as an invitation which is not neat and elegant. Depend on us to do the best kind of work at the most reasonable prices.

No. 3.

A Mean=Looking Letter=Head

Has lost many a dollar for business men. If a man is judged by the coat he wears, he is also judged by the letter-head he uses. An artistic and business-like letter-head has frequently been a basis of credit. It may be looked on as a good investment. Let us fit your business with a good coat.

No. 4.

On the contrary, if a handsome booklet, perhaps containing half-tones, is the desideratum, a differently equipped office might be expected to do the work better. Would not No. 2 be more likely to elicit a response ?

It would pay best to use different copy nearly every insertion, or, at least, to use a number of ads. in rotation, having regard for their timeliness.

Observing these requisites, it might be well to launch out in the way of No. 3. This suggestion is obviously intended for country printers. No. 4 will be more suitable for metropolitan printers.

Nos. 5 and 6 are the merest suggestions as to what can be done. and the available material is inexhaustible. Technicalities should be avoided, as the general public knows very little about the printing business. There is a class of work which could be greatly increased if a knowledge of its economy were more general. I refer to the kind of matter which is set solid, such as law printing, specifications, contracts, etc., of which, perhaps, only twenty or thirty copies are necessary, although each should be a perfect facsimile of the others. As composition has been the principal item of expense, this work was, until recently, done on the typewriter, which was a laborious process and offered continual opportunity for errors. Now, however, through the use of typesetting and typecasting machines, the cost of this kind of composition has been reduced to such an extent that in many cases it is cheaper to produce printed copies than typewritten ones. Would not an ad. of the nature of No. 7 attract business ?

The consideration of suitable mediums is a most important matter, and I may discuss it later.—*G. M. Brennan, in Printers' Ink.*

A Successful Entertainment

Is helped in no small degree by a programme handsomely printed on good paper by an artistic printer. If the performance is to be repeated next year the programme will be your best advertisement, as it will be kept by many of the audience who would hate to throw it away. Let us get one up for you when you need it, and you will see the point. We can also print your cards of admission so attractively that they will be irresistible.

No. 5.

A Pointer For Business Men

Circular distribution is an important factor in nearly every line of business, and its effectiveness could be immeasurably increased if the printer more generally knew his business. We have departed from ancient methods, and carry the latest and most artistic styles of type. We have every means of producing the best effects and know how to use them. Let us show what we mean by this. It may open your eyes.

No. 6.

PAPYRUS AND PAPER.

THERE is no evidence that papyrus was grown for commercial purposes outside of Egypt during the whole Roman period, and the industry of its growth and manufacture must have been a large and profitable one. In the time of Tiberius a sedition was nearly caused by a scarcity of paper, and a rebellious papermaker, in the days of Aurelian, boasted that he could equip an army from the profits of his business—and did it, too.

Parchment was invented by the Greeks when papyrus was scarce, and the middle ages reinvented it. There is evidence that linen rags were used in papermaking as early as the eighth and ninth centuries. In paper of that period the fiber was chiefly linen, with traces of cotton, hemp and other fibers. The known specimens are of oriental origin, and appear to have been clayed, like modern papers, the material used being a starch paste manufactured from wheat. The oldest manuscript written on cotton paper in England is in the British Museum, and dates from 1049 A. D., and the oldest on the same material in the Paris National Library is dated 1050. In 1085 the Christian successors of the Spanish Saracens made paper of rags instead of raw cotton, which had been formerly employed.—*All the Year Round.*

Printing Cheaper Than Typewriting

Lawyers, contractors and all who wish any kind of document copied so that clearness and accuracy are positively assured, and at less cost than typewriting, should have them printed by us on our typesetting machines. On more than 8 or 10 copies we can save you money, and you will have a neatly printed and uniform copy which will last. Estimates on application.

No. 7.

THE Los Angeles (Cal.) *Record* has placed an order with the Empire Typesetting Machine Company, New York, for a battery of four machines.

Originated by MACKELLAR, SMITHS & JORDAN BRANCH, PHILADELPHIA

48 POINT   5 A 8 a $8 35

Sprinkled or Renovated
BOARDWALKS

36 POINT   6 A 10 a $7 00

Quarterly Magazines Delivered
SPECIAL AGENTS

30 POINT   8 A 16 a $6 05

Seventy-seven Seconds for Breakfast
MISERLY CATERERS

24 POINT   10 A 20 a $5 00

Demonstrating Mysterious Occult Influences
PROMINENT MESMERISTS

18 POINT   14 A 28 a $4 65

Committee to Devise Means for Living Without Working
PROMOTERS OF INDOLENCE

12 POINT   22 A 45 a $3 95   10 POINT   25 A 50 a $3 55

Recognizing Friends and Enemies   **Fearful Landlords and Recreant Tenants**
CHEERFUL PERSONS   **WEEKLY MEETINGS**

8 POINT   30 A 60 a $3 45   6 POINT   36 A 70 a $3 35

Fortune-Seeking Adventurers' Silly Occupation   **Curfew Bell Signaling to Lovers the Hour of Separation**
CHASING GOLDEN SUNBEAMS   **RULES GOVERNING COURTSHIP**
1234567890   **1234567890**

AMERICAN TYPE FOUNDERS' COMPANY

BOSTON, 144-150 Congress St.   CLEVELAND, 239-241 St. Clair St.   ST. PAUL, 84-86 East Fifth St.
NEW YORK, Rose and Duane Sts.   CINCINNATI, 7-17 Longworth St.   KANSAS CITY, 533-535 Delaware St.
PHILADELPHIA, 606-614 Sansom St.   CHICAGO, 139-141 Monroe St.   OMAHA, 1118 Howard St.
BALTIMORE, Frederick and Water Sts.   MILWAUKEE, 89 Huron St.   DENVER, 1616-1622 Blake St.
BUFFALO, 83-85 Ellicott St.   ST. LOUIS, Fourth and Elm Sts.   PORTLAND, Second and Stark Sts.
PITTSBURGH, 308 Wood St.   MINNEAPOLIS, 113 First Ave., South   SAN FRANCISCO, 405-407 Sansome St.

Empire Type=Setting Machine Co. ❧ ❧ ❧

203 Broadway,
Mail and Express Building,
New York.

4,500 Ems per hour Guaranteed, or no sale.

(SOLID)

Change of face in
3 minutes.
No melting of metal.
No Gas.
No Machinist.
Measure adjustable
to any required
width instantly.

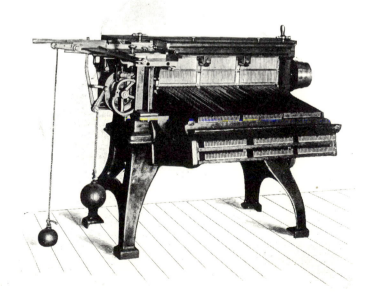

NOTICEABLE PROGRESS IN ADVERTISING METHODS.

ALTHOUGH much has been said and written on the subject of art in advertising, it is not due to that fact alone that so large a portion of the public have come to realize that, as now practiced, advertising is an art. The work speaks for itself; and it is not alone in words that the tale is told, for the designer shares in honor with the writer for the results attained. The ponderous platitudes by which the merchant of former days took the public into his confidence have given place to a most comprehensive blending of catchy phrases and artistic illustrations, brevity of expression and aptness of illustration being combined in the most remarkably effective and skillful manner. The effect sought by the illustrator is to attract the attention of all, old and young, while the writer endeavors in the fewest words and in the most attractive manner to convey the desired information to the public. By their combined efforts they appeal to the eye, to good taste and to reason, and have succeeded not only in reducing advertising to a science, but in elevating it to an art.

A recent writer says, "We cannot command success, but we can coax it along by judicious advertising." Even a superficial investigation will lead to the conclusion that advertising artists now depend largely upon their ability to please and coax the public. It is not in evidence that they have failed in their purpose, while it is manifest to even the casual observer that they have succeeded admirably in lending attractiveness to the columns of the daily newspaper, as well as to the pages of catalogues and miscellaneous works of all kinds where advertisements find a place. The newspapers especially have been benefited by the work of the modern advertisement designer, their advertising columns no longer being the dull and prosy receptacles for commonplace announcements which so long was their distinguishing and only feature. Readers can now turn to the advertisement columns of a daily or weekly newspaper with a certainty of finding something to admire, or at least to amuse them. And this is the way success is coaxed along, for when the advertiser can entertain or amuse the reading public he has accomplished his aim. The rest must be left to the discrimination of that self-same public, always taking into consideration the fact that a very large proportion of the public uses very little, if any, discrimination. The public likes to be amused, and always displays a kindly feeling for whosoever accomplishes the task.

Two prerequisites are necessary before the best results can be obtained by the people who devote their talents to the creation of artistic advertisements. These are brevity of expression in the description and good printing in the execution. The most artistically designed and happily worded advertisement will be ruined by slovenly printing. Printers know that poor printing will spoil any work, but the man who has an advertisement written to his taste, and then has secured a design which he regards as very striking, will often be at a loss to know why the whole thing has such a poor effect when it comes from the hands of the printer. Brevity of expression and aptness of illustration are indispensable qualities in the character of the work under discussion, but they lose half their force when poorly printed. Instances are not rare where large sums of money have been expended in preparing illustrations and reading matter for what was intended to be a superior work, but which, when it came from the hands of the pressman, was a disappointment, a poor excuse being offered instead of good work. This is a somewhat common experience; so common, in fact, that it is difficult to account for the fact that anyone can now be found who would be led into the error. Whoever desires good work, with the best possible effect from illustrations and reading matter, must pay as much attention to the selection of his printer as he does to the selection of his designer or writer. If one were about to erect a million dollar building on valuable land he would not be apt to select a builder whose only achievement was the laying of a drain. He would select a builder familiar with the kind of work planned by the architect, and the same rule will hold good in the selection of a printer for a choice work. It will be a saving to secure one whose experience and methods warrant the belief that he can do just what is desired of him.

However, we do not wish to be understood as harboring a desire to detract from the merit of the work done in recent years by those who are responsible for the great advances made in advertising methods. They have created a distinct art, and a pleasing and profitable one at that. They point a moral or adorn a tale with profit to some and pleasure to all. In short, they let the sunshine into business methods, and by their efforts the soil of publicity has been fructified beyond belief.

EMPLOYMENT FOR PRINTERS.

A mighty and irresistible influence is now being felt all over the land in the art or trade of type composition by the substitution of mechanical for hand methods, and printers everywhere are looking with dismay at the reception into their midst of typesetting machinery, knowing that it will mean a wholesale reduction in the number of employes in the office where the machines are placed, owing to their capacity for producing matter at a saving of about fifty per cent over hand composition. It is a self-evident fact to even the most casual observer who knows anything at all about the matter, that compositors, as a body, seem helpless to do the best thing for themselves under these conditions, or as individuals, to take the proper precaution to make an earnest endeavor to help themselves before they are actually driven out of employment by this iron hand of improvement.

To take up this condition of the trade in a general way, and point out what compositors might do to help themselves, is the purpose of the writer. Almost without exception every recognized trade or vocation during some course of its existence has had its hand methods changed or supplemented by the substitution of some mechanical labor-saving or ingenious device which for a period of time made a marked reduction in the number of employes who were affected by its labor-saving qualities. That there is a vast amount of suffering and distress among the men who have large families to support, and who have given the best years of their lives to following these trades, and have lost their situations by reason of the change in conditions thus brought about, goes without saying. However, it is gratifying to know that this sad decline in the necessity for labor, fortunately, only continues for a few years, as history proves that in time the use of this labor-saving machinery results in cheapening the product and increasing the demand for it to such an extent that just as many men, if not more, are required to carry on the operations of trade. It seems remarkable, but is nevertheless true, that the pressroom branch of the printing industry has received, for a long number of years, the close attention, study and thought of some of the brightest mechanical minds this country has produced, resulting in the amazing progress seen and appreciated in contemplating the difference between the old hand press and the latest perfecting machine in use today, while the composing room has gone along in the even tenor of its way and until the practical operation of the present typesetting machines its hand operation has seen fewer changes of a mechanical nature than any trade or vocation with which the writer is acquainted. But this is an inventive age and changes are bound to come. The old argument that no machine could be constructed which would space a line and properly distribute type has been exploded or refuted by the typesetting machinery in use today. A start has been made in the line of mechanical typesetting and distributing, and we are just on the threshold of some very remarkable improvements in the machinery already in use, for the strongest mechanical minds in the world are devoting their best efforts in this direction. Nothing can stop this march of improvement. It is everywhere in the air. Each year space is becoming more valuable. Quantity is demanded; speed is required. These essentials must and will be met, and the next twenty years will see a manifest change in the methods of producing printed matter compared with those of a few years back. Then again will history repeat itself. The demand will continue to enlarge as improvements continue to advance, and just as many men, or more, will be required to operate under these new conditions as were required by the old way. The device or machine, however, that causes an extreme or radical change in the methods of a trade or business is not generally the result of any instantaneous inspiration of genius, nor is it usually brought to perfection in secret to be sprung on the market without notice or warning to those whose labor and business it might affect, but the working out of its principle and details of construction is rather the result of long continuous experiments, very often attended by anxious thought and a large expenditure of money, and the machine is very well known and thoroughly discussed before it is completed for actual work.

The conception and completion of the present typesetting machines now in successful operation were no exception to this, and we believe that when they were first introduced for use their history and existence was known to every printer in the country. Assuming this to be true, was it wise for the compositor to wait until the very moment this march of improvement overtook his labor and crushed him out of the business, before giving some thought and action to his future? Without a doubt, when he is earning money and has not yet felt the sting of care and anxiety that non-employment brings in its train, he is better able to look around and consider his condition and make an effort to obtain some field of labor to which he can adapt himself. I would then say to the individual compositor: Do not wait until a typesetting or other machine takes your place upon the floor of the office where you are engaged, before seeking other employment, but take time by the forelock, and devote as much time as you can reasonably spare in an endeavor to secure other work, that it is within your ability and capacity to perform. A question might be presented right here, to wit: Suppose the printer be a man well advanced in years without any apparent ability for other than the trade to which he has devoted the best years of his life, what can he do?

In answer to this, I would say, if he is a man without any influence of a political character, which he might utilize to obtain some light employment for the city, then the positions which he might fill would be as janitor in an office building, a watchman in a banking institution, a salesman in a stationery or book store, especially one with a printing department.

These are only some of the occupations that occur to me, and are merely outlined as suggestions. For the younger and stronger men there is the police force, city work, conductors, motormen, solicitors for advertisements, etc.

I would also advise or suggest as a means of helping each other, that the printers' union form a paid committee of two men in each of the cities where there are machines at work whose duty it would be to make a list of the members of their organization thrown out of employment by the machines, and devote certain days in the week to assist these unfortunates in obtaining something to do. Let this committee interview those who have positions or employment to offer and make an appeal for their brother members, and I am sure, if the circumstances of the case were properly presented, it would be effective in many instances. Some such concerted effort on the part of the union in this direction, I am led to believe, would help to relieve, in a greater or lesser degree, the want and distress that is now pervading the ranks of the printers all over the country.

W. Ross Wilson.

THE EXTINCTION OF THE TRAMP PRINTER.

BEFORE the typesetting machines began to change the appearance of the composing room, the tramp printer was becoming more and more rare as the years went on, changed methods from those which used to encourage his class being the influence which made his mode of life more settled. With the advent of the machines he became

A Vanishing Type — Dixie Dunbar.

still more rare, and the younger printers of the present day, though they have heard their older companions talk of tramp printers, rarely if ever have the pleasure of meeting or conversing with one of the species. The tramp printer exists, however, in the more out-of-the-way parts of the country and occasionally invades the offices of the larger cities.

It was during a visit of one of these interesting reminders of the roving days of independent printerdom that the photograph was taken which is used to illustrate this article. Mr. Edgar White, city editor of the Macon *Times*, of Macon, Missouri, to whose courtesy we are indebted for the photograph, says that Dixie Dunbar is one of the best-known tramp printers of the country, and that he is proud of the fact.

"In a rather rambling conversation which I had with him," writes Mr. White, " he told me that he was born in Ireland and his parents removed to Macon, Georgia, shortly before the rebellion. He was an officer in Colonel Claiborne's confederate regiment and did some good service for the South. He was taken prisoner and transported to Johnson's Island, in Lake Erie, where he suffered extremely from the cold. For the last thirty years he has been a tramp printer, and has set up the copy of Horace Greeley and many noted editors. He refers to himself with pride as

' The King of Tramps,' a name bestowed upon him one day in an eastern printing office by the printers. In his pilgrimage he has traveled from ocean to ocean several times and worked in almost every town of consequence, he says, in the United States. He is now sixty-seven years old, well and hearty, and in his thirty years of tramping has never been seriously ill or required the attention of a physician. He admits the occasional use of a little whisky 'as a restorative,' but says he never takes too much to know what he is about. Until recently his inseparable companion has been a ferocious looking bulldog, but the coming on of old age to the latter deprived him of the ability of sharing with his master the pleasure and vicissitudes of his ceaseless wanderings."

EARLY CHANGES IN THE ART OF PRINTING.

FROM 1693 until about 1813 no improvements were seen in the art of printing, says the New York *Shipping and Commercial List*, of May 4. The workman toiled in the same old way; his tools were nearly as awkward and clumsy as those of Caxton and Day, and his speed was no greater. The largest printing office in 1809 was that of the Bruces. Its production, working at the maximum, would be surpassed by four hundred printers here today. The pay roll did not exceed $100 a week. The year after that typefounding was introduced here by an ingenious Yankee from Connecticut.  In 1813 Bruce and Watts simultaneously began making stereotype plates. In 1818 the wooden hand press began to give way for one constructed entirely of iron, thus enabling a sheet to be printed twice as large as before. Previously nothing could be employed which would print much larger than a page of the Herald. Ink had then been made here for a few years, and at about the end of the second decade of this century paper became cheaper and more abundant, for there were many more paper mills in America, and some importations were of paper which had been made by a much cheaper process than the old one of dipping a sieve into a vat of pulp, shaking the sieve so that the stuff would lie evenly at the bottom, the water escaping meanwhile, and turning out the thick substance upon a piece of felt, there to dry and assume the appearance of a sheet of paper. The causes, however, which led to the great increase of printing were a little later. The improvement in paper machinery began to have a very decided effect upon the market in 1825; in 1835 all paper manufactured here was substantially machine paper. Cloth bookbinding made its appearance about 1832, enabling books to be produced much cheaper; power presses were in use about 1826, the first one in New York being employed on Dwight's newspaper; penny journals of large circulation began to appear in 1833, and in 1817 we had for the first time book publishers of energy and skill, taste and commercial judgment. In that year James and John Harper began a little printing establishment which rapidly increased in magnitude. During the yellow fever year of 1822 they sought refuge in Captain Tylee's barn, in Newtown, but business did not stop. Ten years after they began they were the great printers of New York, as well as the great publishers, as their house still is. Only three other printers in the Union have so great an establishment, and one of these is the United States, at Washington.

15 A 40 a   12 POINT OLIPHANT (2 line Nonp. $3 00

Valuable Gold Bronzed Frames
New Brussles Carpet for Hardwood Floor
Durable Japaned Household Ware
1 2 3 4 5 6 7 8 9 0

10 A 25 a   18 POINT OLIPHANT (3 line Nonp.) $3 50

Latest Artistic Fancy
Beautiful Body Type Specimen
Borders and Fine Job Faces

8 A 15 a   24 POINT OLIPHANT (4 line Nonp.) $4 00

Handsome Colored Business Card Printres
Michigan Monthly Newspaper Publications Resumed

5 A 10 a   36 POINT OLIPHANT (6 line Nonp.) $5 50

Wholesale Shoe Department
Retailer of Childrens School Clothing

4 A 8 a   48 POINT OLIPHANT (8 line Nonp.) $7 25

Northern Medical Records

4 A 6 a   60 POINT OLIPHANT (10 line Nonp.) $9 25

Pleasant Lake Resorts

3 A 4 a   72 POINT OLIPHANT (12 line Nonp.) $9 50

Eastern Art School

MANUFACTURED BY BARNHART BROS. & SPINDLER, CHICAGO, ILL.

FOR SALE BY MINNESOTA TYPE FOUNDRY, ST. PAUL; GREAT WESTERN TYPE FOUNDRY, KANSAS CITY; ST. LOUIS PRINTERS SUPPLY CO., ST. LOUIS; GREAT WESTERN TYPE FOUNDRY, OMAHA.

5a 3A, \$7.50   48-POINT COSMOPOLITAN   L. C. \$2.90; C. \$4.60

Fashionable Production
Italic Character 28

6a 3A, \$5.50   36-POINT COSMOPOLITAN   L. C \$2.30; C. \$3.20

Handsomest Variety Advertized
Ornamental Novelties 36

8a 4A, \$5.00   30-POINT COSMOPOLITAN   L. C. \$2.25; C. \$2.75

Wonderful and Superior Yield of Cutters
Improvements in Manufacture 10

10a 5A, \$3.80   24-POINT COSMOPOLITAN   L. C. \$1.80; C. \$2.00

Knowing Printers Commend the Standard Line System
Adopted by the Inland Type Foundry 45

12a 5A, \$3.30   18-POINT COSMOPOLITAN   L. C. \$1.50; C. \$1.80   30a 8A, \$3.00   12-POINT COSMOPOLITAN   L. C. \$1.75; C. \$1.25

We have many other new designs under way, and desire your name and address for our mail list 26

Being cast on Standard Line, every italic, script or other face made by the Inland Type Foundry is available for date lines, as 2-Point Rule, either single or dotted, can be readily justified to line 75

60-POINT COSMOPOLITAN IN PREPARATION; READY ABOUT OCTOBER 1ST.

MANUFACTURED BY THE INLAND TYPE FOUNDRY, 217-219 OLIVE ST., SAINT LOUIS
DISCOUNT FOR CASH WITH ORDER, 30 AND 5 PER CENT

MMMMMMM Saint Louis_____ 189... mmmmMM

IN STOCK AND FOR SALE BY STANDARD TYPE FOUNDRY, CHICAGO
GOLDING & CO., BOSTON, PHILADELPHIA AND CHICAGO   CONNER, FENDLER & CO., NEW YORK
DOMINION PRINTERS' SUPPLY CO., TORONTO

IROQUOIS CONDENSED SERIES.

Originated by THE CRESCENT TYPE FOUNDRY, 358 Dearborn St., Chicago.

5A 8a.   36 Point Iroquois Condensed. $5.00

STANDARD LINE TYPE
Cast from the best Hard Metal

8A 12a.   24 Point Iroquois Condensed. $4.00

THESE BEAUTIFUL JOB FACES
Are Constantly in Preparation to Line 1895

10A 16a.   18 Point Iroquois Condensed. $3.25

→WHAT A NEAT NEW TYPE TO WEAR←
All are Handsome and Easily Read from any Poster

Other Sizes from 6 to 60 Point in Preparation.

YOST TYPEWRITER SERIES.

20A 90a.   10 Point Yost Typewriter Type. $6.75

                              Kalamazoo, August 12, 1895.

The Crescent Type Foundry,

        358 Dearborn St., Chicago.

Gentlemen:-

        Enclosed please find our order #7236 for the complete

series of "Iroquois" 6 to 36-Pt., also for series of "Iroquois

Condensed" 6 to 60-Pt. Ship same by U. S. Express as soon as pos-

sible and as we are in a great hurry for same. When are may we

expect that new typewriter type? An early reply will be con-

sidered a favor by   Yours respectfully,

                              MALLET & PLANER PRTG. CO.

Complete with Extra Characters and Spaces.

"IGNORANT ABUSE OF LABOR-SAVING MACHINERY."

IN a recent editorial under the heading quoted above, the Chicago *Tribune* condemns the utterances of certain labor agitators respecting labor-saving machinery, and reverts to time-honored arguments respecting the benefits which have accrued to workingmen and workingwomen by the introduction of labor-saving machinery. The conditions which might possibly govern skilled and unskilled labor without such machinery are pointed out, the miserably housed and miserably fed working classes of China, where hand-labor reigns supreme, being referred to as a contrast to the comparative comfort in which the American workman lives, the result of labor-saving machinery.

In so far as the printing trade is concerned, the history of labor-saving machinery sustains the contention of the *Tribune* that the workman has benefited — ultimately and indirectly ; but it is a matter of doubt if the advent of typesetting machines will be eventually as felicitous for printers as we would desire. The experience of one correspondent — Mr. R. M. Tuttle — whose letter appears in another column in this issue, is certainly not encouraging : "I used to believe," writes Mr. Tuttle, "that as typesetting machines came into use more type would be set by the newspaper proprietor, and that in the long run about as many printers would be employed. But my belief in that regard was not correct. There is a tendency to ridicule the enormity of the Sunday editions of the large dailies. It seems to be very generally considered by the public that there was enough reading matter put forth even before machine typesetting was in vogue. This clubbing together of country newspapers to buy and use a machine was something that I did not look for, and it is the means of throwing out a large number of good men."

The *Tribune* asserts that the advent of labor-saving machinery brought about the shortening of the workday, and that trades-unionism did not effect it. If this be true, it might logically be expected that the shortening process would continue and keep step with the advances or encroachments of the various machines in almost all lines of industry. No one can deny that labor-saving machines displacing workmen are for a time the cause of much individual distress. Yet American workmen, and those whom they elect to represent their interests, desire to place no obstruction in the way of labor-saving machinery.

OUT-OF-WORK PRINTERS.

To the Editor :   MANDAN, N. D., September 6, 1895.

The articles that have appeared in THE INLAND PRINTER on the subject of printers out of work must be of interest to everyone engaged in the printing business, whether as an employer or an employe. The fact is very apparent that with the advent of machines, there are too many men in the business. Daily, printers whom I hate to designate as "tramps," come to my office seeking work, and they give as an explanation of their being on the tramp that machines have driven them out of employment. They tell me that in many small towns two or three papers club together and get a machine, and thus cheapen their composition. I hate to believe that your Baltimore correspondent, who writes in the August issue of THE INLAND PRINTER, has solved the problem when he suggests that printers out of work should seek for positions as janitors in office buildings, watchmen in banking institutions or salesmen in stationery stores. These positions require no especial previous training. Any man of fair address and common-school education can fill such positions with satisfaction. It is always to be regretted when a man possessing a trade is obliged to go out into the market and compete with those who have none.

The printer, because of having followed his business for a number of years, gathers a vast amount of information which a bricklayer or stonemason would not acquire. If he must leave the printing business, it should certainly be to go into some occupation where this general store of information could be utilized. But where? That is the all-important question. All branches of labor seem to be occupied. Every now and again we see a new industry start up, such as the manufacture of bicycles, but the out-of-work printer cannot drop into that niche. It requires a different kind of mechanical knowledge and experience.

I used to believe that as typesetting machines came into use more type would be set by the newspaper proprietor, and that in the long run about as many printers would be employed. But my belief in that regard was not correct. There is a tendency to ridicule the enormity of the Sunday editions of the large dailies. It seems to be very generally considered by the public that there was enough reading matter put forth even before machine typesetting was in vogue. This clubbing together of country newspapers to buy and use a machine was something that I did not look for, and it is the means of throwing out a large number of good men.

It does no good to inveigh against labor-saving machinery. The country newspaper owner is unwise if he does not take advantage of every labor-saving contrivance that is within his means, and that would lessen the cost per week of putting out his paper. He must be in line with the age. It may be that when he puts in his new machinery he is obliged to discharge an employe or two who has worked for him for years. But what is he to do? Many a country editor with several thousands of dollars invested in his business, has struggled along for several years past against adverse conditions, barely able to clear expenses and live.

Experience and observation teach me that it behooves the printer who is working for wages to cultivate individual thrift. You may look for panaceas where you will — ever since the world began individual thrift is the thing without which men cannot rise above such conditions as now overtake the printer who loses his job through the introduction of the machine. When the thrifty man earns 50 cents a day he spends less than that. When he gets a rise of wage he spends more, but still less than he earns. What is capital but the surplus — what men have saved, instead of spent ? The man who is earning the wages that are now paid to the journeyman printer will ask how he can save anything. It can be done ; it is done. Those who do it are the men who are not worried all the time for fear their jobs will quit. It will take generations for the world to learn the lesson of individual thrift. Perhaps the world is going backward on the subject. However that may be, happy is the man, whether he is a printer or something else, who has learned the lesson of personal thrift.   R. M. TUTTLE.

SECOND ANNUAL SOCIAL

OF THE

BICYCLE BLOOMERS OF CHICAGO

IN COMMEMORATION OF THE

AMERICAN DRESS REFORM

JULY FOURTH
1895

40 A   6 Point Menu No. 1 $1.40

SKILLFUL MECHANICAL DRAWINGS
EVANSTON ACCIDENT INSURANCE COMPANIES
1234567890

40 A   6 Point Menu No. 2 $1.60

GREAT WESTERN EXPRESS
GOVERNMENT STAMP DEPARTMENT

40 A   6 Point Menu No. 3 $1.75

FOREIGN ART DISPLAY
GRAND WATER COLOR PAINTINGS

30 A   8 Point Menu No. 4 $1.75

OPERAS AND DRAMAS
CONTINUOUS PERFORMANCE

24 A   10 Point Menu No. 5 $1.75

POPULAR SONGS PRETTY ARMY MARCH

20 A   12 Point Menu No. 6 $2.00

ROUND HOUSE ILLINOIS CENTRAL

20 A   12 Point Menu No. 7 $2.25

CREDITORS RACINE BANKS

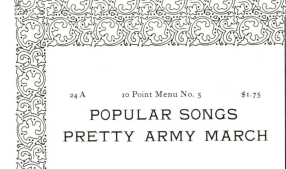

MENU

LITTLE NECK CLAMS

POTAGE SECRET   CONSOMME PRINTANIERE ROYALE

LETTUCE   CELERY   TOMATOES

BOILED SHEEPSHEAD, LOBSTER SAUCE
POMMES FARCIE

ROAST BEEF
YOUNG DUCK, APPLE SAUCE

SWEETBREAD PATTIES, A LA REINE
STUFFED GREEN PEPPERS, BELVIDERE

BOILED POTATOES   MASHED POTATOES
GREEN CORN   ONIONS IN CREAM   TOMATOES

CHARTREUSE PUNCH

CHICKEN SALAD

CHOCOLATE PUDDING, VANILLA SAUCE
APPLE PIE   CREAM PIE
BISQUE ICE CREAM   ASSORTED CAKE
CHARLOTTE RUSSE   CHAMPAGNE JELLY

ROQUEFORT AND AMERICAN CHEESE
CRACKERS

FRUIT   WATERMELON
RAISINS   NUTS

COFFEE

THE ABOVE IS SET IN 6 POINT NOS. 1, 2 AND 3, NO. 1 BEING THE SMALLEST.

MANUFACTURED BY BARNHART BROS. & SPINDLER, CHICAGO, ILL.

FOR SALE BY MINNESOTA TYPE FOUNDRY, ST. PAUL; GREAT WESTERN TYPE FOUNDRY, KANSAS CITY; ST. LOUIS PRINTERS SUPPLY CO., ST. LOUIS; GREAT WESTERN TYPE FOUNDRY, OMAHA

Quentell Series . . .

Originated by CENTRAL TYPE FOUNDRY BRANCH, ST. LOUIS.

36 Point   5 A 8 a $5 50

Proposals for Purchase Invited
ATTRACTIVE FACES

30 Point   6 A 9 a $5 00

Beautiful Dark Red Roses Have Long
THORNS TO PROTECT THEM

24 Point   8 A 10 a $4 00

Copper Alloy Type is Strong and Durable and
LEADS ALL OTHERS IN STYLE

18 Point   10 A 16 a $3 25

Wedding Invitations should be Printed in the most Artistic and
CAREFUL MANNER TO BE FULLY APPRECIATED

14 Point   12 A 18 a $3 25

Committee of Eight Appointed to Devise Means for Living Without Working
WEEKLY MEETINGS OF PROMOTERS OF INDOLENCE

12 Point   16 A 20 a $3 00   10 Point   20 A 26 a $2 75

Pouring Knowledge into Youthful Heads   Attractive and Novel Method of Advertising Business

PROFOUND PROFESSOR   QUAINTNESS AND LEGIBILITY OF FACE

8 Point   22 A 30 a $2 50   6 Point   24 A 36 a $2 25

Curfew Bells Signaling to Lovers the Hour of Separation   A Mean-Looking Letter Head has Lost Many a Dollar for Business

LATEST RULES GOVERNING COURTSHIP   USUALLY A MAN IS JUDGED BY THE COAT HE WEARS

AMERICAN TYPE FOUNDERS' COMPANY.

BOSTON, 144-150 Congress St.
NEW YORK, Rose and Duane Sts.
PHILADELPHIA, 606-614 Sansom St.
BALTIMORE, Frederick and Water Sts.
BUFFALO, 83-85 Ellicott St.
PITTSBURG, 308 Wood St.
CLEVELAND, 239-241 St. Clair St.
CINCINNATI, 7-31 Longworth St.

CHICAGO, 139-141 Monroe St.
ST. LOUIS, Fourth and Elm Sts.
MILWAUKEE, 89 Huron St.
MINNEAPOLIS, 113 First Ave., South.
ST. PAUL, 84-86 East Fifth St.
KANSAS CITY, 533-535 Delaware St.
OMAHA, 1118 Howard St.
DENVER, 1616-1622 Blake St.

PORTLAND, ORE., Second and Stark Sts.
SAN FRANCISCO, 405-407 Sansome St.
ATLANTA, 23 East Mitchell St.
TORONTO, CAN., 44 Bay St.
MONTREAL, CAN., 780 Craig St.
WINNIPEG, MAN., 286 Portage Ave.
LONDON, ENG., 54 Farringdon Road, E. C.
MELBOURNE, AUS., 395 Flinders Lane.

MORRIS OLD STYLE SERIES.

Originated by THE CRESCENT TYPE FOUNDRY, 349 & 351 Dearborn Street, Chicago.

A NEW DEPARTURE IN THE MANUFACTURE OF TYPE. &

STANDARD Lining System. A glance at specimen sheets issued during recent years clearly shows a constantly increasing demand for something of this description, which has led to ever recurrent attempts to solve the problem; these efforts have been sporadic and inconsistent, however, and failure to take into account all conditions has rendered the result unsatisfactory. All our types are on Standard Line, therefore faces of all letters on the same body line together perfectly. It is difficult to enumerate the advantages of this system, but can mention that it is now possible to line any Italic or Title

8 Point 24A 50a, $2.50
25 pound fonts $20.00.

24 Pt. Border No. 14, 3 feet $1.65.

AN EXPLANATION OF THE STANDARD LINE. &

STANDARD Lining System. A glance at specimen sheets of recent years clearly shows an increasing demand for a system of this description, which has led to ever recurrent attempts to solve the problem; these efforts have been inconsistent, however, and failure to take into account all conditions has rendered the result unsatisfactory.

10 Point 20A 40a $2.50. Font of 25 pounds $16.25.

THE MORRIS OLD STYLE SERIES & CRESCENT ART BORDERS. & & & &

SPECIMEN sheets issued for the past few years show a constant demand for types of this order, and as the aim of the Crescent Type Foundry is always keep at the head of the procession, this series has been produced. It will be completed in all sizes from 6 to 48 point, is made by skilled workmen, is cast from the hardest metal and on the latest improved machinery. All type faces made by this foundry are cast on the Standard Line invented by the Inland Type Foundry, of Saint Louis, Missouri, and adopted by their permission. & & &

12 Pt. Morris Old Style 18A 30a $2.75. 25 pound fonts $13.50.

36 Point Border No. 25, 1 foot $1.10.

24 Point Border No. 15, 3 feet $1.65.

24 Point Border No. 16, 3 feet $1.65.

Columbus Initials

36 POINT	$2 00
48	3 00
60	4 00

B C E F K L Q R S T V W

60 POINT   3 A 4 a $12 35

Cash ONE

36 POINT WITH 60 POINT INITIALS

Loud Song

48 POINT   3 A 5 a $9 35

FINE Horses

24 POINT WITH 48 POINT INITIALS

Fashion QUAINT

36 POINT   5 A 8 a $8 00

Guarded HOMES

18 POINT WITH 36 POINT INITIALS

Eleven Recitations

24 POINT   10 A 15 a $7 05

Reward BRAVE Soldier

18 POINT   15 A 20 a $6 10

Welcome ROMANTIC Authors
1234567890

...American Type Founders Co...

April 1896 531

COMPOSITION OF TITLE-PAGES.

BY ED S. RALPH.

TITLE-PAGES play a very prominent and important part in any catalogue or book, and the compositor is often at his wits' end to get up something artistic, attractive and sensible — a page, as it were, that will induce the prospective customer, or reader, to more closely examine the pages following. There are some beautiful type faces now, admirably adapted for this purpose, but care and good judgment should be exercised in their use.

Much depends upon the inside of the book or pamphlet as to the extent to which ornamentation can be employed with propriety. Should artistic lithographic inserts be used, the title-page should be plain and as few ornaments as possible used. The adoption of a reverse plan will lay the whole book open to adverse criticism from artistic judges, and these criticisms would be well founded, for the simple reason that these inserts are about all the ornamentation necessary.

In the illustration showing a De Vinne title-page used in the White bicycle catalogue, the ideas expressed above are carried out as far as it was possible to do. The two small ornaments were positively necessary in order to balance the page; otherwise they would not have been used. This catalogue has a number of lithographic inserts, besides the litho cover. In a case of this kind the type should be plain, and no texts or faces semi-fancy be employed in the construction of the title-page.

The title-page of the Dayton bicycle catalogue, set in Jenson, is, as will be seen, quite the reverse

Portfolio of Illustrations

showing

The White Bicycles

Then and Now

Illustrated by

Thulstrup
Veenfliet

Mente
Clarke

(In Colors.)

Lovers Will Meet. The Postman's Welcome. The Doctor's Hasty Call. Central Park New York Now. Vassar Girls Exercising. The Family's Country Outing. White Girl Coaster.

(In Black and White.)

Wheel of the Past and Present. Playing Tag on the Bike. Trio of White Girls Out for Fun.

The White Sewing Machine Co.

Principal Office and Factory.

Cleveland, Ohio, U. S. A.

Branches:

New York. Boston. San Francisco.

De Vinne title-page. Reduced one-half.

of the De Vinne page. The same conditions did not prevail and ornamentation was resorted to.

The catalogue was printed in colors. The main ornaments were printed in brown and the type

Was the Surprise of '95

The Dayton

Will be the Wonder of '96

Dayton Bicycles

Manufactured By

The Davis Sewing Machine Co.,

Dayton, Ohio, U. S. A.

Branches:

New York City,
76 Reade Street.

Chicago, Ill.,
338-340 Wabash Avenue.

Boston, Mass.,
159 Tremont Street.

London, England,
24 Aldersgate Street.

Jenson title-page. Reduced one-half.

in dark green. Half-tones were copiously used throughout the catalogue and the typework was to a large extent ornamental. The ornamentation was not at all out of place and was an essential feature in an artistic piece of work, because of its attractive nature. It had a pleasing effect on the eye and held the attention of the reader and inspired him to keep on turning the leaves and continue reading. This, however, was not the case in the White catalogue, the lithographic inserts performed that office, and extensive ornamentation would have produced a reverse effect.

It often happens in a title-page that the customer makes it a combination title-page and introductory. In cases of this kind it is more difficult

1896

Acme Cycle Co

High-Grade

Bicycles

Elkhart, Indiana, U. S. A.

THE TIME when two or three manufacturers could fairly claim the only high-grade Bicycle and command their own price, is gone. THE TIME when improved machinery and skilled mechanics shall produce the finest in the world, at prices all can afford, is come.

Combination title. Reduced one-half.

to get good results, but they can be obtained, as will be seen from the "Acme" cycle page and also that of the Dayton Church & Opera Chair Company. St. John and Jenson, together with the ornaments of the same name, are exceedingly useful in cases of this kind.

Where a title-page is made to serve a twofold purpose, it is a good idea to divide the page and put

Combination title. Reduced one-half.

the title part in one series of type and the introductory portion in another, as is done in the title-introductory page of the Dayton Church & Opera Chair Company. This method, provided the type thoroughly harmonizes, produces a pleasing effect, and serves to distinguish and separate the one from the other. But harmony and effect must be well considered, otherwise the result will be anything but satisfactory. Tons upon tons of printed matter — pamphlets and catalogues, alone — are annually wasted. That is, they find their way to the omnivorous waste-basket, many times without even having had their pages scanned. The reason is plain enough. Inferior work, lack of attractiveness, or a repulsive appearance seals their fate. The recipient cannot drop them quick enough, and instead of helping to sell the product which they advertise, they fail even to pave the way for the traveling representative, and make his task an extremely hard one. Thus it is that the work is wasted, postage squandered, and a desirable effect utterly annihilated. Many times the compositor is as much at fault as the firm for which the work is being gotten out, and it is no more than plain truth to say that lack of thought and no judgment whatever on the part of the compositor plays a very unwholesome part in the matter.

Too much care cannot be exercised in the title-page. The cover may be very attractive, but if the title-page is not in keeping, it has the effect of an ice-water douche. Therefore, use judgment and help the customer in attaining the end desired. This is as much to the interest of the compositor as it is to his employer and the customer, because it adds to his value. Very few employers are so blind to their own interests that they will allow a man to go unrewarded who is zealous in his endeavors to

look after the welfare of the firm and do his customers' work so well that they will, rather than let their work go to another concern, wait a reasonable time for it and even pay a larger price than the rival concern offers to do it for.

The compositor has a very important part to play in the work turned out of any office, and he should have enough energy and self-esteem not to let it be said: "If the compositor had done his work as he should, that job would have been a fine one throughout."

RECENT TYPE DESIGNS.

We showed last month a specimen page of a new face adapted from the German and called Gracilis, cast by the Pacific States Typefoundry, of San Francisco, a line of the

COMPANION SERIES to Latin Antique

GRACILIS.

18-point size being shown herewith. It is cast on the standard line from 8-point to 48-point, and makes a good companion face to Latin Antique and Latin Condensed.

We present a line of 54-point DeVinne Italic Outline made by the American Type Founders' Company. This series consists of eleven sizes, from 12 to 72 point. We also show a line of Chelsea Circular, which is made in 6, 8, 10, 12

America

DE VINNE ITALIC OUTLINE.

Future Terrace

DE VINNE EXTENDED.

American Type Founders' Company, HAS EIGHTEEN BRANCHES

7-POINT DE VINNE.

Chelsea Circular Series 34

and 18 point sizes. They have recently added to the DeVinne series a 7-point size, a sample line of which is here shown. The DeVinne Extended is also among the recent new letters, there being fifteen sizes in preparation, running from 6 to 72 point, and including a 7-point size. Among their new borders we mention the Caxton, a page of which is shown elsewhere.

Barnhart Brothers & Spindler have brought out the XIV. Century series, made in upper and lower cases, in seven sizes, from 8 to 48 point. We show a line of it which gives

Superior Copper-Mixed Type

XIV. CENTURY.

Monthly and Weekly Gazette

OPAQUE SERIES.

but a faint idea of what the letter is. It must be seen in massed effects to show off to best advantage. A page will be shown in our June number. Another of their new letters is the Opaque series, a heavy condensed letter.

SIERRA SERIES.

24 A 36 a 6-Point Sierra $2.15

JOB COMPOSITORS APPRECIATE STANDARD LINE TYPE
Annoying Complications of the Old Style Justification are Obviated $6789012345

22 A 30 a 8-Point Sierra $2.25

STANDARD LINE TYPE INCREASES IN POPULARITY
Delighting Printers Everywhere from Main to California Shore 2345

20 A 26 a 10-Point Sierra $2.50

ADVERTISERS BEAUTIFUL SERIES
Tasteful Faces Displayed Artistically Earn Money 987

16 A 20 a 12-Point Sierra $2.75

NORTHWESTERN PACIFIC RAILROAD
The Elevated Railroads in the City of Chicago

10 A 16 a 18-Point Sierra $3.50

EAST COAST SURVEY
United States Internal Revenue 3

8 A 10 a 24-Point Sierra $3.50

ARTISTIC SELECTION
The Modern Sciences 2567

5 A 8 a 36-Point Sierra $5.50

HAMBURGH
Beautiful Sierras

4 A 5 a 48-Point Sierra $7.50

HUBbard 45

Sold in fonts of 25 pounds at prices of Poster Caledonian. Cast to Standard Line by
PACIFIC STATES TYPE FOUNDRY, San Francisco.

For Sale by CONNER, FENDLER & CO., New York; CRESCENT TYPE FOUNDRY, Chicago: STANDARD TYPE FOUNDRY, Chicago; INLAND TYPE FOUNDRY, St. Louis; H. C. HANSEN TYPE FOUNDRY, Boston; KEYSTONE TYPE FOUNDRY, Philadelphia.

24-Point Pacific Border No. 245, 3 feet, $1.65.

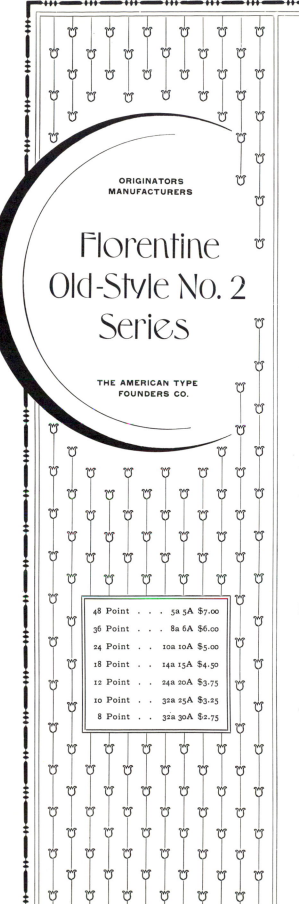

PATENT APPLIED FOR

Another Face for Art Work 5

48 POINT

Companion to the Florentine Old-Style

36 POINT

Send Your Orders to the Nearest Branch House 4

24 POINT

This is the Largest Concern in the World Manufacturing Type Faces $364,275,890

18 POINT

OUR Products are used in Every Printing Office in the Country. Forward Your Address to the Nearest Branch to be placed on the Mailing List 23456789

12 POINT

THE American Type Founders Company are Manufacturers and General Selling Agents for all of the High-Grade Printing Machinery and Material made in this Country £234567890

10 POINT

BRANCHES in Boston, New York, Philadelphia, Chicago, St. Louis, Baltimore, Buffalo, Pittsburgh, Cleveland, Cincinnati, Minneapolis, Milwaukee, Kansas City, Omaha, Denver, Portland, Ore., San Francisco, Atlanta, Ga., Dallas, Tex., Toronto, Montreal, Can., London, Eng., Melbourne-Sydney, Aus., Madras, India.

8 POINT

RAMONA SERIES

30 POINT   6 A 14 a $4 75

Theatrical Manager Organizing Famous Vaudeville Companies
Superior Acrobatic Performances Advertised

24 POINT   8 A 20 a $4 60

Dancers and Singers Entertaining
Grand Weekly Concerts
12345678

18 POINT   10 A 32 a $4 50

Quarters Secured at the Aldine Hotel
Arrival of Celebrated Persons
1234567890

SANTA CRUZ SERIES

24 POINT   18 A $3 75

PUBLIC REHEARSAL PROMISED BY AMATEUR MUSICIANS
INSPIRING ◆ MARCHES ◆ RENDERED

18 POINT   24 A $3 00

PRINTED INVITATIONS MAILED
RECEIVING ◆ PRESENTS
◆ 1234567 ◆

12 POINT   30 A $2 50

RURAL LANDSCAPE SCENERY ADMIRED
SURGING ◆ MOUNTAIN ◆ STREAM
◆ 1234567890 ◆

PALO ALTO SERIES

24 POINT   6 A 20 a $5 50

Storms Damaged Property
TORNADOES
12345678

18 POINT   8 A 26 a $5 00

Evidence Secured by Reporter
PUBLISH REPORTS
12345678

American Type Founders Company

For Sale at all Branches and Agencies

ECONOMY! SPEED! EXCELLENCE!

A Perfect Mechanical Substitute for Hand Composition of Types

THE LANSTON MONOTYPE MACHINE

Composition Absolutely Justified.

Capabilities those of the Compositor.

Types Equal to Foundry Letter.

The SIMPLEST, SMALLEST and MOST ECONOMIC MACHINE ever put into Practical Operation.

Note Its Advantages:

Makes and sets single types in justified lines at a maximum and unvarying speed.

Change to any desired measure effected in thirty seconds.

Change to any desired style of face instantaneous.

Change to any desired body size, from Nonpareil to Small Pica (6 point to 11 point) effected in less than ten minutes.

All fonts interchangeable in each machine.

Overrunning automatic. High-class typography insured.

Range—all the characters of a full font of type, including small caps and italic.

Address, for Terms and Specimens: **THE LANSTON MONOTYPE MACHINE CO.**

Central Power Station, WASHINGTON, D. C.

DISPLAY COMPOSITION.

ONE of the causes which aid in the depreciation of the value of the ad, compositor, and, incidentally, of the business, is the disposition to underestimate the value of instructions, and to ignore them unless proofs are demanded. The usual claim that the work has been done much neater than would have been possible if directions had been closely followed has no weight with the advertiser, and is not usually the real reason for failure to observe instructions. Careless or unintelligent scanning of the copy, technical difficulties, etc., are more often the cause. The demand for speed is also a factor.

No class of printing is more deserving of proper treatment than advertisements, and none in which the relative value of good and bad work is more pronounced. If tests could be made which would give the actual financial results respectively of good, bad and indifferent work, it is safe to say the effect would prepare patrons to pay for and demand the best, and enable employers to grant the time necessary in the execution.

In so far as the following of instructions is concerned, everyone should receive the same attention. The inexperienced advertiser knows what he desires placed most prominently before the public, and if he should have any peculiar ideas which he is willing to pay for, they should be respected.

When copy is furnished without marks to guide in its display, the compositor should view it in the light of an advertiser and treat it strictly with a view to utility. Any artistic effects which do not add to its money-earning power should be avoided.

The intention or object of the advertiser should receive careful consideration before any plan of display is decided upon. It is not wise to hastily conclude that the copy has been superficially prepared and demands no serious thought. The business of the printer is to execute orders, and the accuracy with which he interprets the same should be the first point in determining his standard of excellence. Failing in this first essential, the most artistic and painstaking of efforts will be misdirected. It is not for the printer to question the wisdom of any plan that may be submitted to him. It should be presumed that the same has been decided upon after due deliberation and with an inside knowledge of the necessity of the case, with which he may be unacquainted. And yet this is one of the most common as well as most inexcusable offenses with which the printer is charged. When difficulties of a technical character interfere with the easy execution of a presentable piece of work the disposition is to break away from the instructions, often resulting in thwarting the object of the advertiser and rendering the advertisement comparatively worthless.

Successful writers of advertisements exercise great care in the preparation of their copy. Their business is not only to furnish the copy, but also to direct which are its most important points; and even to select the series or combination of type faces which will be most suitable. They are, or should be, well equipped for such duties. Their view of the advertising field is much broader than the printer's, and their ads. are written and placed with a due consideration of the immediate necessity for advertising, the method to be pursued, the medium to be used, its location, character, and territory in which it circulates; the nature of the wares to be disposed of; location of advertiser, his reputation and prominence, etc. Assuming that method and intelligence have been exercised both in the writing and the placing of the ad., it is reasonable to suppose that the marks of emphasis have their meaning, and show what in his opinion is the line of display which will best answer his purpose. Ordinarily these marks of emphasis do not indicate the relative degree of strength between the display lines, and considerable room is left for judgment. The printer, having in hand a piece of copy thus underscored, and of which no proof is to be submitted, is placed in a position of trust, and if he disregards the underscoring it is an abuse of confidence. He should be sufficiently acquainted with methods, purposes and mediums of advertising to be able, with the assistance of ordinary underscoring, to separate an ad. into its proper divisions; and when the divisions are known, no idea of taste or style should interfere with the arrangement, and to permit technical difficulties to do so is a confession of incapacity.

The question of style is of secondary consideration, and the style that will best suit the purpose of the work in hand should be the one adopted. All styles have their merits, and when properly executed and adapted are equally commendable. The idea of old-time printers was to make every piece of display work conform to certain arbitrary rules, and the result was often anything but pleasing to the eye, although satisfactory to the patron, as the features were brought out strongly, and he had not yet learned that the power of the subject matter was impaired by a multiplication of minor display lines. The idea of the modern printers is to use the style or material that is most appropriate for the occasion; and, when the peculiar wording of his copy or technical necessities suggest such a course, he discards all conventional forms of display; and, if the result is satisfactory and catches the public eye, a new style is proclaimed, and for some time everything is made to conform to the new fad.

In some instances the effort is all directed toward producing a peculiar effect.

POSSIBILITIES OF MACHINE COMPOSITION.

BY HAROLD M. DUNCAN.

THE art of printing has passed through many stages on its road to present possibilities, all of which have not been equally conducive to upward progress. Despite such intervals, however, as have been decadent and such extremes of taste as have tended to deplete it of virility, it has experienced a fairly constant unfoldment from mediæval estheticism to the technical perfection of today. The excellence of its results gauges the utility of the conditions under which they were produced, and would also seem to furnish the indubitable right for those conditions to survive. The four and a half centuries during which typography has been slowly developing have eventuated in standards of the highest excellence, and have evolved methods that to abandon means to deteriorate. If an art is to be adjudged by its most advanced exponents, the printing of this decade compares favorably with that of the best periods, while, in facilities to production, it immeasurably surpasses it. At no prior time have the technical details of execution occupied so high a plane; the entire mechanical equipment, processes and auxiliaries of the modern printing office are being constantly expanded by inventive genius, with a view to both economy and quality. The trend of the movement, however, is all toward the provision of mechanical means to do what, heretofore, has been done alone by hand.

In any mechanical substitute for handicraft it is, first of all, essential that the standards of excellence raised by the latter shall be maintained; nor must the range of accomplishment proper to the machine be less than that of the same function, manually performed. In the precise degree that it lowers the quality resident in handicraft is a machine a retrograding influence. In quantity of output, it is self-evident that it must greatly transcend the hand operative.

The possibilities of machine composition is one of those pleasing questions about which no little prophesying has been done. The class journals in the field of printing have always, where progressive, dealt with the subject from a practical standpoint. Regarding the beauty of latter-day printing as the result of complex factors, each of which is sufficient to engross a lifetime of experiment and study, their editors have not been blind to the probable outcome of efforts made by inventors toward a wider scope of operation than the majority of machines embodied. The problem has been a progressive one, and it may interest the readers of THE INLAND PRINTER to learn the particulars of the latest perfected machine for superseding the hand composition of types, a machine which, after subjection to exhaustive tests and practical work in the printing office, is fairly launched upon its commercial way under very promising conditions. At the kind solicitation of the editor, I would present a few particulars about the perfected Monotype machine, the invention of Tolbert Lanston, Washington, D. C.

Some years ago, Mr. Lanston wrote me about his attitude toward the problem of mechanical type composition, and about the plan on which the Monotype machine is constructed. "In adopting this plan," he said, "it was accepted as an incontrovertible proposition that centuries of development of the art of printing had brought into use the very best conditions; that the artistic excellence of the publications of today, which are at once the surprise and delight of all cultivated minds, bears witness to the superiority of the conditions underlying it. Moreover, the entire equipment, the experience, the prejudices, if you will, of the craft, are adapted to and indisputably in favor of the continuance of the art as now practiced, and of the essentials which sustain its marvelous achievements. It was concluded that no lowering of the standard of excellence would

be tolerated, and that the mechanical substitute for hand composition should and must comprehend all the qualities of the latter, or it would fail of its purpose in a greater or lesser degree." Accordingly, it has been the aim to provide a machine, fully equal in range of functions to the compositor at the case, the output of which shall be in every respect the equivalent in excellence of foundry letter. In the manufacture of the latter, as is well known, modern mechanical art exhibits its finest accomplishments. Letter after letter, with unvarying precision, comes from the mold in the typefoundry with no appreciable variation in height to paper from the standard of .918, and with almost absolute uniformity, body-way or set-way, among themselves. It has been the perfect productions of the best foundries that have rendered it possible for printers to accomplish the beauty of impression now to be seen in our leading magazines and hand-set books; and it is a general, and I believe correct, impression among book and job printers that by the use of single types alone can the highest typographic effects be attained. To my own mind, no mechanical substitute for hand composition can ever hope to meet the conditions at the printing press, presented in dry printing, unless it equals the standards of quality, as to printing surface, etc., resident in foundry letter of the best class. The product of the Lanston Monotype machine is single types, normal as to body proportions, and up to the standard letter in other respects, the space types being made of justifying size as the individual types are made and composed into the line at the machine. The machine is, in fact, a complete typefoundry, in which a movable die case, carrying all the letters of the full font of types desired, replaces the single matrix employed in the foundry casting machine to make one letter.

The Monotype machine is divided into two parts, keyboard and type machine, in the first of which a record strip is perforated by a series of punches, operated in the usual manner by keys, while in the second, which is purely automatic, the composition, so perforated, is converted into perfectly justified lines of type, set in the galley, and sent to the imposing stone under the identical conditions of hand-set types. A very brief description will suffice.

The Keyboard. — This part of the mechanism is operated by hand, a compositor being the operative. He has absolutely nothing to do but attend to the work proper to his department, thus being accorded the entire speed possible by manipulating the keys. These latter correspond to all the characters in a full font of types, extending to caps. small caps and lower case, as well as italics, etc., with space keys for open or narrow spacing, as fancy or the demands of a job may dictate. The Monotype is alone in this range of characters, no other machine offering the free use of a complete font. The machine is about the size of an ordinary typewriter stand.

Upon depressing a key two round holes are punched in a paper ribbon, in such arbitrary position as to refer to the position of the matrix carrying that character in the die case at the casting machine. A word is thus perforated; the normal space (three to em or any other size selected) is made by a key-stroke, and word after word, and space after space, are thus progressively composed at the line, until the end thereof is approached. The ringing of a bell warns the operator of the termination; he glances up at a scale on which is recorded the number of ems set in the line and the number of space types, and sees before him the justifying number, which he records upon keys at the right of the keyboard, in a second of time, by merely depressing the suitable keys. This effects perforations at the end of the line previously perforated. He thus proceeds until his record strip is used up, which will be after about 23,000 ems have been composed. The spool is then lifted out, another spool of blank paper is inserted, and the same operation is repeated.

At the Monotype keyboard an operator can do anything that can be done by hand. He can overrun illustrations, set tabular work with perfect justification in any number of columns of figures, up to the measure for which the scale is set, and can set any desired face at will, in any body size.

The Casting and Composing Machine. — The two perforations made on the paper ribbon for each character, and the justifying perforations at the end of the line, govern the travel at right angles upon a compound slide of the square die case containing matrices of each of the types represented at the keyboard, so that the character indicated will be made at the casting machine, and the line justified by making the space types of justifying instead of initial size. The ribbon is unwound in opposite order to that in which it was perforated; the justifying holes are first presented and set the mold for the space types to a degree necessary to cast the spaces absolutely alike throughout that line, and the types are made consecutively, but backwards. The proper character is selected with unfailing accuracy, and when the galley is filled it will be with lines of types perfectly justified, equal in all respects to the hand-set product. As the die case is brought into position so that its proper matrix is centered over the mold, the latter incloses it to form the body of the type, which is cast, vertically, therein. The metal flows from a nozzle directly into the mold, which is first filled, and then instantly followed by the occupation of the body of the mold under pressure, thus insuring good casts. Regular foundry metal is used, giving clean, sharp faces, of toughness and durability. The types are then ejected from the mold into a carrier, and are positively held until placed in the line in the galley, which, upon the completion of any line, advances to receive the next. The entire machine weighs but 900 pounds, and occupies about 3 feet by 3 feet 8 inches.

Range of the Monotype System. — By working upon the square and by means of the peculiar principle underlying the system the scope of the perfected machine is raised to a degree quite remarkable. Whereas, in prior mechanical means for the composition of types, a single character could only be actuated by a separate mechanical movement, thus giving a complexity which prevented the use of fonts exceeding 100 characters; in the Lanston Monotype the mechanical movements are but double the square root of the entire number of characters employed. In a font of 225 characters the movement would only be fifteen plus fifteen, or thirty, as the die case is a square, containing the matrices in rows. By increasing the movements but two, the matrices would number 256; by increasing the movements five on a side, or ten, the matrices would number 400, a range it is entirely practicable to carry in machines designed to cast matter for display work, as the die case of such a machine would embrace a large number of alphabets with sorts, with different faces. The possibilities of such range will need no emphasis with practical printers.

One of the most interesting features of the Monotype machines is the interchangeability of fonts and its remarkable facility for change of measure. Thirty seconds suffices to accomplish the latter, and any style or size of letter may be used by the simple substitution of a die case and slight changes, occupying in all but about eight minutes.

For stereotyping and electrotyping, where such is needed, the types made by the perfected Monotype offer the best of advantages, being twenty per cent greater as to shoulder than foundry letter. By storing the spools of paper, moreover, future editions do not require to be electrotyped, as, after the first composition, the editions can be run off at one-fourth the cost of the original.

For corrections, etc., the same possibilities are presented as with hand-set types. The keyboard operator, who comprises three-fourths of the cost of production, is left free to continue with his work, while corrections are made from the proof-read galleys by a cheaper operative. Sorts are provided by the casting machine. Standing matter only embraces the cost of type metal. The types may be used in the jobroom for such work as require their use, as the machine will produce spaces of normal sizes, to be employed in corrections, etc.

As to speed of production, the makers claim that the capacity of their perfected machine is equal to that of any other system. It is, of course, self-evident that the limit of speed is the solidifying of the molten metal in the mold. As to cost of production, the makers assert that the peculiar nature of their system enables them to secure economies beyond those hitherto accomplished. They point to the separation of the mental and manual operations from the merely mechanical function as decidedly in their favor, the keyboard operator being thus enabled to get a speed that will enable him in seven or eight hours to feed a casting and composing machine for a ten hours' run, at belt speed. As but one-fourth of the cost lies with the automatic machine, the importance of the feature appears to be justified. The machines are thus placed where they will give the best results, the keyboard under pleasant conditions, away from noise and distracting elements, and the casting machine in a location suited thereto. A skilled mechanic is not required to supervise the latter, unless there are a number of machines employed, when one man can assume charge of a large number of machines. Hitherto, in the race for economic composition, the smaller offices seem to have been left entirely out of the calculation. As an important influence upon their business, typesetting by machine cannot be over-estimated. If they do not compete, the larger offices with machines secure their work; if they do compete, and depend upon hand composition, their margin of profits rapidly dwindles into one of losses. It would seem that these small offices need, most of all, the advantages offered by machine methods, for they work with cheap hand labor in an environment where a dollar possesses greater purchasing power than in the larger cities. They can, therefore, afford to bid against large offices without machines, but cannot underbid the latter where machines have been installed.

It is scarcely needful to enumerate the ordinary advantages which are well known to reside in a machine that makes its own types. New faces for every issue or edition; absence of loss from wear and tear of type; minimum of cost locked up in standing matter; maximum of economy by production of the types themselves! Such are the principal factors which such a machine conserves to the advantage of the user. If this saving be increased by guaranteeing a product equal in every respect to hand-set letter of the best class, perfect justification and an equal range of accomplishment to that of the compositor of most advanced skill, the possibilities of machine composition with regard to the perfected Lanston Monotype machine will become apparent. In my investigation of all mechanical substitutes for the manual composition of types, I have never found a system so promising in its application to the general needs of the printing office or so extensive in functions commonly believed to be solely the prerogative of the compositor. What I have frequently said before, it now gives me pleasure to repeat: The Monotype system and the Lanston machine embody capabilities which are not only of the widest, but are proper to themselves alone. I regard the invention as among the most marvelous achievements of this century.

The WOODWARD [48]

GROUP OF FACES [30]

MEDIUM, [36] OUTLINE, CONDENSED, EXTENDED

A Quartette of Useful Designs [18]

Woodward Series

60-Point, 4a 3A,	$9.50	L. C. $3.70	Caps $5.80
48-Point, 5a 4A,	7.25	3.10	4 15
36-Point, 7a 4A,	5 00	2.40	2.60
30-Point, 9a 5A,	4.30	2.15	2.15
24-Point, 9a 6A,	3.50	1.60	1.90
18-Point, 15a 9A,	3.20	1.60	1.60
14-Point, 18a 12A,	3.00	1 40	1.60
12-Point, 22a 15A,	2.80	1.35	1.45
10-Point, 26a 16A,	2.50	1.25	1.25
8-Point, 28a 20A,	2 25	1.05	1.20
6-Point, 34a 20A,	2 00	1.00	1.00

THE WOODWARDS

All Cast on Unit Sets

Designs of Woodwards   Patented Aug. 4, 1896

TO BE DONE AT ONCE:

Send for Specimens showing the four Series complete from 6-Point to 60-Point.

Woodward Outline

60-Point, 4a 3A,	$9.50	L. C. $3.70	Caps $5.80
48-Point, 5a 4A,	7 25	3.10	4.15
36-Point, 7a 4A,	5.00	2.40	2.60
30-Point, 9a 5A,	4 30	2.15	2.15
24-Point, 9a 6A,	3.50	1.60	1.90
18-Point, 15a 9A,	3 20	1.60	1.60
14-Point, 18a 12A,	3.00	1.40	1.60
12-Point, 22a 15A,	2.80	1.35	1.45

The WOODWARD and WOODWARD OUTLINE series are cast to the same widths, and one will register accurately over the other for use in two-color work.

MUCH ASTONISHED!

A Leading Printer Whose Ledger Showed He Was Actually Making Money

ALMOST BEYOND BELIEF!

Further Investigation Develops the Cause of His Establishment Giving Large Profits

REMARKABLE DISCOVERY MADE

Matter of Great Importance to the Printing Trades, Which Have Had a Hard Row to Hoe

WIDESPREAD SATISFACTION PROBABLE

Strange History of a Printer Who Bought an Outfit of Standard Line Type—What He Thinks of Its Money-Making Possibilities—Advice to Buyers of Material.

Special Dispatch to the Inland Printer.

ST. LOUIS, Sep. 1.—The above heading shows the utility and elegance of the Woodward and Condensed Woodward for newspaper columns

Condensed Woodward Series

60-Point, 5a 4A,	$9.50	L. C. $4.10	Caps $5.40
48-Point, 8a 5A,	7.25	3.55	3.70
36-Point, 8a 6A,	5.00	2.30	2 70
30-Point, 10a 6A,	4.30	2.20	2.10
24-Point, 12a 8A,	3.50	1.70	1 80
18-Point, 16a 10A,	3.20	1.60	1.60
14-Point, 22a 14A,	3.00	1.50	1.50
12-Point, 28a 18A,	2.80	1.40	1.40
10-Point, 34a 22A,	2.50	1.25	1.25
8-Point, 36a 25A,	2.25	1.10	1.15
6-Point, 40a 24A,	2.00	1.00	1.00

Send Orders Direct to Us or to any of the following Agents:

CRESCENT TYPE FOUNDRY, Chicago, Ill.
PACIFIC STATES TYPE FOUNDRY, San Francisco, Cal.
CALIFORNIA TYPE FOUNDRY, San Francisco, Cal.
FREEMAN, WOODLEY & CO., Boston, Mass.
GRANT C. SNYDER & CO., Denver, Colo.
PALMER'S PRINTING MACHINERY DEPOT, Buffalo, N. Y.
DOMINION PRINTERS' SUPPLY CO., Toronto, Canada.
MORGANS & WILCOX MFG. CO., Middletown, N. Y.
PRESTON FIDDIS COMPANY, Baltimore, Md.
HARRIS' PAPER HOUSE, Grand Rapids, Mich.
GOLDING & CO., Boston, New York, Philadelphia, Chicago.

Extended W'd

48-Point, 4a 3A,	$10.75	L. C. $4.15	Caps $6.60
36-Point, 5a 3A,	6.40	2.80	3.60
30-Point, 5a 3A,	4.70	2.10	2.60
24-Point, 7a 4A,	4.00	2.00	2.00
18-Point, 9a 5A,	3.20	1.65	1.55
14-Point, 14a 8A,	3.00	1.50	1.50
12-Point, 16a 10A,	2.80	1.40	1.40
10-Point, 18a 10A,	2.50	1.25	1.25
8-Point, 22a 14A,	2.25	1.10	1.15
6-Point, 28a 16A,	2.00	1.00	1.00

60-Point Extended Woodward in preparation.

HEADING AND JOBBING SERIES [24]

Cast [30] on Standard Line!

Originated and Manufactured by the [10]

INLAND TYPE FOUNDRY [36]

217-219 Olive Street, SAINT LOUIS [14]

THE Italic was first intended and used for the entire text of a classical work. Subsequently, as it became more general, it was used to distinguish the portions of a book *not properly* belonging to the work, such as introductions, prefaces, indexes, and notes; the text itself being in Roman. Later it was used in the text for quotations; and finally it served the double part of *emphasizing many words* in some works, and in others, chiefly translations of the Bible, of marking words not properly belonging to the text. In England it was first used by De Worde in 1524.

Jenson Italic Series

PATENT APPLIED FOR

20 A, 50 a   8 Point Jenson Italic $2.75

The Italic letter, which is an accessory of the Roman, claims an origin quite independent of that letter. It is said to be an imitation of the handwriting of Petrarch, being introduced by Manutius for the printing of his classics, which otherwise would have required bulky volumes. Chevillier informs us that a further object was to prevent the great number of contractions then in use, a feature which rendered the typography of the day unintelligible and unsightly. The execution of the Aldine Italic was entrusted to Francesco de Bologna. The font is lower case only. It contains tied letters, to imitate handwriting, but is free from contractions.

ALDUS PRODUCED SIX SIZES OF THE ITALIC, 1501

20 A, 45 a   10 Point Jenson Italic $3.00

Type ornaments and flowers began, like the initials, with the illuminators, and were afterwards made on wood. The first printed ornament or vignette is supposed to be that in the Lactantius, at Sabiaco, in 1465. Caxton, in 1490, used ornamental pieces to form the border for his Fifteen O's. The Paris printers at the same time engraved still more elaborate border pieces. The elaborate wood-cut borders and vignettes of the succeeding printers kept pace with the initial letters.

ORIGIN AND FIRST USES OF ORNAMENTS

18 A, 40 a   12 Point Jenson Italic $3.25

They had evidently been cast from a matrix; and the idea of combining these pieces into a continuous border or headpiece was probably early conceived. Mores states that ornaments of this kind were common before wood-engraved borders were adopted; and Moxon speaks of them in his day as old fashioned. In Holland, France, Germany and England these type flowers were in use during the eighteenth century, and every founder was supplied with a number of designs.

THE ORIGIN AND FIRST USES OF TYPE ORNAMENTS AND FLOWER DESIGNS

10 A, 25 a   18 Point Jenson Italic $4.00

They were cast on regular bodies, and some of the type specimens exhibit most elaborate figures constructed out of these flowers, and as late as 1820 these ornaments continued to engross a considerable space in the specimens of every English Type Founder of any note.

ORIGIN OF TYPE ORNAMENTS AND FLOWER DESIGNS

6 A, 15 a   24 Point Jenson Italic $4.50

A curious collection of these type ornaments can be seen in the Quincuplex Psalterium, which was printed by Henri Estienne, at Paris, France, about the year 1613.

DEVELOPMENT OF THE TYPE FLOWERS

DISPLAY COMPOSITION.

BY J. H. SODEN.

WHERE numbers of different advertisements are to appear on the same page of a newspaper or other publication, the compositor should endeavor to give to each a distinct individuality. Nothing in typography is more disagreeable to the eye than a page of displayed ads. in which the individual parts are all merged into one grand ensemble, "without form, and void" in so far as individual effectiveness is concerned. The constituent parts taken from the mass and proven separately may be commendable, and the make-up, with the exercise of patience, may alter the leading and change positions so as to give to the whole a creditable effect; but usually either the time, patience or judgment is lacking for such experimental work, and the demand is for display matter which may be taken from the galley as it is, without alteration, and which will preserve its individuality in any position in which it may be placed. It is not always possible to consider the question of environment, etc., as either its position or the character of the matter adjacent to the ad. may be an after consideration.

Each step in the composition of an ad. should have in view and may contribute toward its distinctive character, but the one feature which is always necessary, and cannot be slighted without vitiating any other commendable feature, is the proper separation of the ads. one from another. Next in importance is the leading of the matter, and then follows the question of side margins. With proper attention given to these three points, good results will be obtained from otherwise very ordinary composition.

It is impossible to propound any arbitrary rules with regard to display work, as tastes will differ, and circumstances which will not adjust themselves to any set form are continually arising. However, suggestions of a character which are adapted to the general run of work are certainly in order.

Comparison between different publications will demonstrate to anyone that those journals which have the most pronounced divisions between the ads. present the best appearance, and also give to each separate ad. the strongest distinguishing effects. One of the methods which never fails to give satisfactory results in this connection is to make the blank space at the head of the ad. from one and a half to twice the amount allowed between the lines; and the blank space at the end of the ad. to just equal the space between lines. This manner of separation is commendable for several reasons; the extra allowance of space at the head, besides strongly marking the beginning of new matter, presents a broad strip of white which adds to the strength of the display lines, and also assists in unifying the parts of the ad. as the smaller stripes of white between lines (if the leading is done properly) present a series of smaller streaks of uniform width, which, in contrast with the broad strip at the head, at once impress upon the eye the homogeneous nature of the matter between the rules.

In most periodicals the body of the column rules has been selected with a view to properly separating pure reading matter, and the demand of display ads. for relief by a broader strip of white paper is not considered. In single-column matter the need is not so noticeable, but as column after column is added to the width of the ad. the need becomes apparent. When practicable, the ad. might be set to a measure based on the width of the column, placing at the sides of the ad. slugs corresponding to the width of the column rules, and allowing the cut-off rules to pass by the slugs, close up to the bodies of the column rules. With a font of slugs cut to labor-saving sizes for the purpose, the compositor would incur no additional labor, and the make-up's task would not be increased. This would add very materially to the isolation of the ad., as the ad. rules passing through the white space at the ends would make a distinct cut-off. An ad. spaced off as above would have a liberal white margin at the top and on the two sides, while its ending would be well marked.

An effective way to space off ads. which are to be inclosed within rules or borders is to make the space between the column rules or other adjacent matter and the border at least one-half more than is placed between the border and the inclosed matter. The border is a part of the ad., but when set off close to the column rules at the sides and up to the adjacent matter at the top and bottom, while the inclosed matter is surrounded with a liberal showing of white paper between its outer margins and the inclosing rules or border, it has a wandering appearance, and its identity as a part of the ad. is not at all pronounced. The best results will be secured if the white spaces between the different lines of the ad. do not exceed, or are less than, what is placed between the ad. itself and the surrounding border. This, of course, will suggest that when an ad. which is open in character is to be inclosed within a border, both its outer and inner margins should be increased proportionately to correspond with the width of white space represented between the lines, and vice versa. The white space is a factor of more consequence than the style of face to be used, and should be considered of equal importance and in connection with the question of appropriateness of type sizes.

THE SUCCESSFUL AND UNSUCCESSFUL PRINTER.

BY W. ROSS WILSON.

THE men engaged in the printing business today can be determined as the successful and the unsuccessful printers. The line is not sharply drawn and it does not take much discernment to recognize to which class each belongs.

The successful printer is typical, and we recognize him as a man of some intelligence, good judgment, and persistent in his efforts to advance his business by right methods. He is a generous buyer, acts promptly where an improvement in his business is concerned, and keeps abreast of the times with his work; believes in himself, and recognizes that only by his own efforts applied in an intelligent and business-like way can he hope to succeed.

The unsuccessful printers can be divided into two classes, the Hustlers and the Procrastinators. Referring to the first of these two classes, I take exception to the popular assertion that if a man wants to succeed in the printing business nowadays he must hustle or be a hustler. A man may be a hustler and succeed pretty well as an oyster shucker, a paper carrier, or in any vocation or trade where mere manual labor only is required and speed is a desideratum, but to say that a hustler can succeed where cool, level-headed judgment, skill, taste and the best of business methods are required, is a fallacy to say the least.

You easily recognize the hustler in the printing business—you see him around you every day. He is the one who rushes out of the office doing a boy's errand, who says to his pressman, "Don't take any more time making that job ready, let it go as it is"; who hasn't time to stop to pick out soiled sheets, hasn't time to stop to clean up the office, hasn't much time to devote to making up an estimate, must guess at some items, meets a calling salesman with, "Really you must excuse me, haven't time to say a word." System—he hasn't had time to arrange one. Yes, you easily recognize the man as the hustling printer. But he don't succeed. Why? because he is hustling with his hands and feet, and giving his head a long vacation.

The second of the unsuccessful class is the man of slow action or the procrastinator. You know him; he is always ready to stop work and give you an hour's discussion on dull times, and what, if he had the influence and the opportunities of his competitor, he could do; who is always going to make a certain improvement in the office when he gets certain work off his hands, or who never makes the improvement because at one time he is too busy and at another too dull. Who always says to the type salesman that he needs that series of type and intends to put it in his office some day, who is always thinking about buying a certain press but rarely ever does it, because he never gets over that long spell of thinking. Some people are charitable and call this man conservative, but that kind of conservatism never succeeds in business.

Following are some of the practical reasons why some printers are successful and others are not:

THE SUCCESSFUL PRINTER believes in keeping his place thoroughly clean, for economic reasons if nothing else.

Has a regular rule bearing on his men coming to and quitting work, and insists on that rule being obeyed.

Keeps his machinery in good order and condition, and regularly and properly oiled.

Always has lubricating oil on hand to use when it is required.

Sees that the overhead fixtures and shafting are oiled, as well as the machinery on the floor.

Keeps a close eye over his men and their manner of doing work.

If he observes a leak stops it instantly, and if he sees he can save time or advance the work by the use of a labor-saving tool or appliance, gets it without delay.

If he sees an improvement can be made in the office to enlarge or better its work, he goes into it promptly and does not wait for dull times, the first of the year, next fall or spring, or when he makes up his inventory or trial balance.

Makes up an estimate with the view of getting a profit out of the work, and if for some reason does not get it, never duplicates the same job at the unprofitable figure.

Does not accept a job at his competitor's price without first estimating that there is a profit in it.

Never tries to save a few cents by getting cheap electrotyping and spending dollars of his pressmen's time making the job ready.

Never refuses to buy good type that he thinks he can use to advantage because the salesman cannot give him an extra five per cent discount.

Looks pleased when a salesman calls, and meets him with a cheery "What have you new this time?" or "I am glad you called, I want to ask your advice about the merit of a certain labor-saving tool or appliance I saw advertised," etc.

Doesn't haggle over the price of ten pounds of lead and give two prices for a machine because he can get it on long time.

Freshens up his office from time to time by adding a few new series of type, and discards his old and worn faces.

Tries to attract patronage by giving prompt and reliable service, and clean and attractive printing.

Never uses his time talking about hard times and trying to impress everyone that the printing business is about the poorest in creation.

=VOGUE=SERIES=

A. D. Farmer & Son Type Founding Co., Beekman Street, New York.

New Brass Rule No. 83.

6 POINT. 40 a 30 A—$

8 POINT. 36 a 24 A—$

6 AND 8 POINT NEARLY READY.

10 POINT. 30 a 20 A—$2 75

NOW ALL THE VOGUE
Many Leaders of the Fashions
1234567890

12 POINT. 24 a 18 A—$3 00

LIBERTY HALL
Opposed to Type Trust
1234567890

18 POINT. 18 a 12 A—$3 75

CONTENTION
Political Meetings
1896=7

24 POINT. 12 a 8 A—$4 00

WINTER
Rain or Snow
2586

30 POINT. 10 a 6 A—$5 00

SMILE
Homeward
2683

36 POINT. 8 a 5 A—$5 75

WATCHMAN
What of the Night?
2345678

48 POINT. 6 a 4 A—$7 25

TRUSTING
The Bunco Men
23458

60 POINT. 5 a 4 A—$10 25

DIGEST
Modern Life
3829

A. D. FARMER & SON TYPE FOUNDING CO.

NOT IN THE TRUST.

Branches: Chicago, Philadelphia, Detroit, San Francisco.

ESTABLISHED 1804.

Mazarin  Italic

Western Company

Manufacturers of Fine

>>>>>>>>>> Stationery

x x x x x

Orders taken for
all kinds of
FINE PRINTING

Seven Hundred and Twelve Broadway

Fine Wedding Stationery
A Specialty.

Superior
Copper-Mixed
Type

The Recorder Company

Printers

>>>>>>>>>> and Book

Publishers

Estimates furnished on
Book and Job Work.

365 Century Building
CHICAGO

Mazarin Italic.

6 Point,	30 A	60 a	$2 50		
8 Point,	24 A	50 a	2 75		
10 Point,	20 A	40 a	2 95		
12 Point,	18 A	36 a	3 10		
18 Point,	12 A	25 a	$3 90		
24 Point,	9 A	18 a	4 25		
36 Point,	5 A	10 a	5 50		
48 Point,	4 A	8 a	7 75		

Manufactured by BARNHART BROS. & SPINDLER, Chicago, Ill.

DIPLOMA SERIES

PATENT APPLIED FOR

8 A, $3.45   10 a, $2.55   24 Point Diploma $6.00

Original and Artistic Type Designing
Letter-Press Printing Imitating
Lithography. Stock $482 per Share
FIRST NATIONAL BANK

5 A, $4.75   8 a, $3.70   36 Point Diploma $8.45

California Type Foundry
San Francisco
Copper-Alloyed Metal
ROYAL SAVINGS FUND

4 A, $5.45   5 a, $3.85   48 Point Diploma $9.30

Life Insurance Co.
Agriculture
Board of Trade

18 POINT IN PREPARATION

In Stock and For Sale by
    KEYSTONE TYPE FOUNDRY, Philadelphia
    CRESCENT TYPE FOUNDRY, Chicago
    GREAT WESTERN TYPE FOUNDRY, Kansas City

CALIFORNIA TYPE FOUNDRY
San Francisco, California
November 1896   547

Caxton Black Series

This Series was originally designed by William Caxton, who introduced printing in England, at Westminster, in the year 1477. He was endowed with erudition and a sound judgment; and was persevering, active, zealous and liberal in his devices for that important art, laboring not only as a printer, but as translator and author

Caxton Black is made complete in eight sizes, now in stock and for sale by all Branches and Agencies. The finest printed magazines and papers in the country use our Type. We carry a large stock, and can ship a whole Printing Office in a day.

The American Type Founders' Company received five Diplomas and Medals of Award at the World's Columbian Exposition for the finest Type=Punch Cutting Machine, Type Casting Machine, Space and Quad Casting Machine, and Best Assortment of original Type Faces. Why buy the second=best Printing Material when the best costs you no more?

This Series of Letter is especially Suitable for all Occasions of Ceremony and High=class Typography

As largest Dealers in Cylinder and Platen Presses, we can quote the lowest prices on:

Cottrell's Triumph Country Press, for printing Newspapers, Folders, Posters, and Commercial Work

Gally Universal Press, for 25 years the Leading Platen Press of the World. Send for our Catalogue

Chandler & Price Old Style Gordon Presses, the best of their kind on the market. Send for Price List.

When placing Orders for Type, Machinery, and other Printing Material, printers should send to the Branch nearest their place of business, thereby saving much time and freight expense. All Branches are well stocked with the productions of our Manufacturing Branches, and are in a position to furnish Everything for Printers on very short notice. This Company is the largest concern of its kind in the world, having Branches in the principal cities of the United States, and Agencies in Canada, Europe, Australia and India. Its productions set the Fashions in Type Styles over the entire Continent

..American Type Founders Company..

THE CHADWICK TYPESETTER.

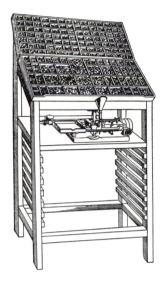

The printer who would put in typesetting machines if it were not for the fact that he is told in most instances that he must not only expend a large sum of money for the machines themselves, but must revolutionize his office to the extent of refitting it with specially nicked type — this printer will be interested in the subject of this article, the "Chadwick Typesetter." It is a machine which sets type dropped into the funnel right side up or upside down, with the nick in any direction in which it happens to fall. A lower case i following a capital W, or a thin space after an em quad will all be found lined up in their proper place in the galley. When a line has been set the machine pushes it along and makes way for a new one without a second's intermission for the operation. A line of brevier may be followed by one of nonpareil or long primer, suiting the convenience or necessity of the operator, without a change of mechanism. It sets any length of line. It requires almost no practice to enable the compositor to become a skilled operator. It requires no machinist. Expensive repairs or supplies are an impossibility. It increases the production of the compositor at least fifty per cent. The Chadwick Typesetter is so simply constructed and so unpretentious in appearance that its worth cannot be properly appreciated save by a careful inquiry into its possibilities. A thorough investigation is invited.

A COUNTRY PRINTER'S VIEWS ON TYPE STYLES.

To the Editor :   PETERSBURG, Mich.

I have noticed a tendency of type founders (nearly all are guilty) of imitating the styles of the fifteenth century. I am only a country printer, and perhaps my views are not worth printing, but it seems to me that the typographic art should advance instead of going backward. There are printers — and good printers, too — who will buy anything placed on the market by the founders, as they look upon them as leaders in the art preservative. A Worth in Paris could dictate what was correct for the women of two continents to wear, so also can a MacKellar dictate typographic styles to the printers of the land. Dresses are worn out and cast aside in a few short months, but the impressions from type last for centuries. This is a day of progression and invention. No manufacturer would dream of building a press after the pattern of those used in the fifteenth century. Why should not the founders do likewise — cast nothing but up-to-date nineteenth century type ?

I would like to hear from others on this subject.

A. P. FALING.

CREATION OF STYLES IN TYPE FACES.

To the Editor :   PROVIDENCE, R. I.

In the September number of THE INLAND PRINTER Mr. A. P. Faling has, I think, touched upon a point worthy of consideration, namely, changes in type faces.

That changes, not only in type faces, but in all branches of the allied arts, are continually going on is an ever-present fact; but in viewing such changes, if we look for

advancement, we shall, in the majority of cases, find but little cause for satisfaction. By what standard of beauty can it be judged ? Fixed standard we have none, and who shall say whether or not the highest development of a particular style is excelled by the highest development of another period upon antagonistic lines ?

In reviewing specimens of but a few years back we are occasionally somewhat surprised to find that our ideas of the artistic in relation to faces then extensively used have so changed that the result of our judgment upon them is decidedly different, indicating very clearly that our immediate ideas are largely governed (to a greater extent, I think, than is generally recognized) by present-day tendencies. Neither can it be said that there is possible a development of the more symmetrical, for that is exhibited in the highest degree in such older faces as the Gothics, Old Styles, etc. Indeed, can there be named any *new* characteristic that it should be the aim of the designer to inculcate in his productions ?

There can be found no possible parallel in the advancement of machinery which Mr. Faling suggests. Between facilitated mechanical operation and artistic development there is no analogy. The Parthenon, the "gem of the Periclean era," shows an artistic development we have never since obtained, while our mechanical ingenuity, as expressed, for instance, in the typesetting machine, the triumph of but a few years, was something absolutely unknown to the Hellene.

Let us see what are the bases of formation to which the originator of a new face must conform to produce a salable, or what is known as a taking product. That it should be thoroughly readable is the first and most important factor ; otherwise whatever "good points" it may contain, they are, through this lack of plainness, largely discounted in its commercial value. Symmetry follows in importance ; a perfect balance of the lettering appeals to the artistic sense, and often partially covers more or less serious faults which are not immediately apparent owing to its influence. Fully as much as this holds true in combinations — as in the completed work — it also holds true in the individual letter, whether it be on "Erratic" or a "Gothic," subject always to the necessary conformation of readableness.

Sentiment aside, then, the type founder must produce a face which, while possessing these two important features, shall also possess certain "new" attractions. That "a MacKellar can dictate typographic styles to the printers of the land" seems to me a decidedly erroneous view. It would appear that two, at least, are the most prominent among the general causes, as causes of deviation from existing styles — each modifying or accelerating the actions of the other. It has been shown by a writer * of considerable eminence that all change, whether we call it progression or not, is rhythmic. From the "periodicities of the planets" to the most minute terrestrial details the law is all-pervading ; and it is to this undulatory movement that we must look as the general cause of particular characters repeating themselves (that is in the main, not usually in detail), at intervals of longer or shorter duration — the strength of the repetition depending chiefly, though not wholly, on its former intensity. While in the variations of the productions of the type founder's art this must be ascribed as the general cause, the special causes by which the results are actually accomplished are probably as further suggested.

The first of the two causes above mentioned would appear to be the familiar law of "supply and demand." The type founder finds that there are certain tendencies in the demand ; that there are increasing orders for a certain

---

* Herbert Spencer's First Principles, Part II.

style of face, and correspondingly decreasing orders for other styles, and varies his product accordingly. By this means, in the course of time, faces bearing certain characteristics fall into disuse, while others bearing more or less unlike features supply the changing demand. The demand is, however, in many cases but a reaction upon the productions of the designers — whom I look upon as the second cause — the designers themselves being affected by a variety of causes more or less complicated. Thus a designer for a type founding company, observing development of a more or less distinct nature in the kindred arts, produces a face corresponding to those developments, which has a "run." The demand for letters of a similar kind increases, reacting upon the originator's productive genius, resulting in like designs. In describing the action of that which has a circular motion, it is difficult to give preëminence to any particular part and assign a principal cause. The movements of supply and demand, demand and supply, must, however, govern the results, whether by the methods indicated or not.

In advancing this argument against "the dictates of a MacKellar," I would say that it may not be *entirely* correct, though to me apparently so, and an easy explanation, and would be pleased to see the expression of contrary ideas should others entertain them.   HAROLD E. NOCK.

DESIRABLE JOB LETTER — A REPLY TO MR. FALING.

To the Editor :   THREE RIVERS, MICH.

I see Brother Faling, of Petersburg, in an article in the September issue of THE INLAND PRINTER, asks : "Why should not the type founders cast nothing but nineteenth century type ?" I think Mr. Faling judges all country printers by himself, that they all are progressive, and constantly share their dividends with the type founders, which I am sorry to say they do not. With an experience of only eight years, and after working in about thirty different shops in and out of the State, I am inclined to believe that the "fancies" of the average printer seldom reach beyond the old-style plain letter, a letter that will "wear until it will roll." Having been engaged in the job printing business for the past two years, I find that among the many new faces of type which have been placed before the printer "but few have been chosen." Type that will catch one eye will not please another, and there being hundreds, yes thousands, of printers in the land, and each " printer with an additional 1,000 of ideas," Mr. Faling cannot expect they all will leave the " rut " trodden by their predecessors. That the De Vinne series, in its different styles, is the most popular and meets the needs of the country printer best, there is no doubt. For my part I prefer a plain, neat, clear type to some of the new faces, that at first glance remind one of "German." Perhaps I may be in the rear of the procession, despite the fact that I carefully read THE INLAND PRINTER and several other good craft periodicals, but nevertheless I will stand my own ground, and think I can pick out type for an office that when in use will satisfy all. It matters not so much whether you use nineteenth century type or type that has been cast for twenty years, the appearance of neat, attractive work depends largely upon its position, ornamentation and the presswork. A good printer will do better work with old type and press (providing he has good rollers), than a poor workman can with the latest type and everything else in accordance. I think if Mr. Faling will give the matter a careful examination he will find the careful, judicious country printer as well as the city printer buying type that is neat, plain and will wear, and also stand handling by mechanics, not of the

best, of which there is such an overproduction. While I do not wish to reflect on the man from Petersburg, as I once worked for him and found him a good all-round printer, and also a progressive one, yet I think the man who has seen the interior of many different shops and labored under their inconveniences is the one who is better able to select material that is worth its " weight in gold," and one who is not apt to become fascinated by a new face of type on a defender cover simply because it looks neat and is up-to-date, without duly considering as to how it will look on a packet note-head or business card, in combination with the usual run of material.   C. K. SMEED.

PREVAILING TYPE STYLES VS. THE COUNTRY PRINTER.

To the Editor :   HAMILTON, N. Y.

Mr. A. P. Faling, of Petersburg, Michigan, asks in this month's issue of THE INLAND PRINTER why founders should cast fifteenth century faces in place of modern faces. As a country printer I am unable to answer the question, but for the country printer I would say from experience that they are to a large extent practically useless. What use our city brethren may put them to I cannot say. Certainly no foundry would cast that for which there is no sale or apparent demand. One cannot but admire some of the ancient effects produced by their use — but are they, as a rule, money-makers ? The country printer, as a rule, cannot afford to buy faces that he cannot use to a large extent in nearly all classes of work. Such a face as the Jenson and its imitations is therefore impracticable to him. But he may feel that he must have something in this line. I believe that the Ancient Roman is the type for such an one. While it gives much the same effect as the Jenson and imitations of it, it is not so black, and the characters are more pleasing to the average customer — for customers and not prevailing fads are to be considered. The Jenson lower-case " s " is to my mind the worst of its many oddities, being too condensed for either symmetry or beauty. The country printer will find, too, that he can set a job in the fifteenth century style that will be much more pleasing to the average customer by using French Old Style in the place of Jenson.

A few years ago we suffered from the fad whose chief exponents were the Erratic and Quaint, in both black and outline design. Many an office has full series of these faces little worn and now seldom used. A country printer cannot afford this expenditure.

Buy type with a view of its money-earning powers — not because type founders tell you it's all the rage. When about to purchase, carefully consider (1) the durability of the face, noting whether it abounds in kerned letters as do the De Vinne Italic and Victoria Italic; (2) whether it can be used to an advantage on *your* class of work; (3) whether cap lines are distinct and readable; (4) whether it is in harmony with the general style of faces you are now using, and (5) whether it will be as acceptable a few years from now as some of the standard faces that every office must have.

If your office is thoroughly equipped with gothics, old styles, the De Vinne or kindred series, two or three good circular fonts and plenty of modern rule and borders, then select a few of the most acceptable faces and set up a few specimens in tasty designs, print them in black or some subdued color and distribute among your patrons. In this way you can utilize faces that might otherwise prove fit only for the hell-box.

I would like to hear from some of our up-to-date printers in regard to these so-called up-to-date type freaks.

EDWARD A. KNIGHT.

PROGRAM

▽▽▽

FIRST PART

1. Overture: "Alessandro Stradella"...................Flotow
   String Quartette: Messrs. Link, Gross, Bend and Norton.

2. Song: "One little cot among the hills"...............Butterfield
   Tenor Solo: Mr. George Travers.

3. Reverie: "Moonlight in the glen"........................Mack
   Piano Duet: Misses Anna and Elizabeth Fairmount.

4. Song: "Non conosci il bel suol"..................."Mignon"
   Soprano Solo: Mrs. Susan Winterfield.

5. Fantasie: "Des Alpenhirten's Klagelied"...............Umlauf
   Zither Duet: Messrs. J. J. Koch and Frank E. Eichler

6. Comic Song: "I saw her first in
   Bass Solo: Mr. Ferdinan

7. Chorus: "Christmas Carol"..........
   Quartette: Misses Emma Jone
   Messrs. Wm. Barta an

SECOND PA

1. Barcarolle: "Gondellied"...............
   String Quartette: Messrs. Link, Gr

2. Song: "Joyful, joyful Spring".......
   Soprano Solo: Mrs. Susan

3. Nocturne: "Harp at Midnight"..
   Piano Solo: Miss Elizabet

4. Song: "My sighs shall on the b
   Duet for Soprano and Tenor: Mrs

5. Waltz: "Dance on forever"..........
   Violin Solo: Mr. Archib

6. Comic Song: "Courting in the r
   Bass Solo: Mr. Ferdinan

7. March: "Grand triumphal".........
   String Quartette: Messrs. Link, Gr

Carriages may be order

HANSEN OLD STYLE SERIES.

Manufactured by H. C. HANSEN, Type Founder, 24 and 26 Hawley Street, Boston, Mass.

❧ ❧ ❧ ❧ ❧

35 a 25 A 8 POINT HANSEN OLD STYLE. $2.75

FINE PRINTING MOST DESIRABLE

Reproduction of Old Style Types of Ancient Days

Leading Feature in Artistic Typography

30 a 25 A 10 POINT HANSEN OLD STYLE. $3.00

INVENTION OF PRINTING

There is now a Wide Spread Belief that

Printing was an Original Invention

30 a 18 A 12 POINT HANSEN OLD STYLE. $3.25

HUMOROUS COMEDIES

European Excursions to Germany

Conducted by Ryder Haggard

25 a 15 A 14 POINT HANSEN OLD STYLE. $3.50

MOONSHINERS

California Flying Machines

Successfully Operated

20 a 12 A 18 POINT HANSEN OLD STYLE. $4.00

SUMMER HOMES IN ❧ Sweetest Magnolia 43

15 a 10 A 24 POINT HANSEN OLD STYLE. $4.50

MODERNIZED ❧ Enlargements 958

10 a 6 A 30 POINT HANSEN OLD STYLE. $5.00

NICE HOUSE 27 Home Study

8 a 5 A 36 POINT HANSEN OLD STYLE. $5.50

HIGHER ❧ Elegant Boy 4

6 a 4 A 42 POINT HANSEN OLD STYLE. $6.00

REMINDS 6 Sampson

5 a 4 A 48 POINT HANSEN OLD STYLE. $6.50

BRINGS Harmonies

30 POINT BORDER NO. 153, 60c. PER FOOT.

Chas. H. Taylor.
BOSTON GLOBE

48 Point   4A 5a $7.75

Golden 8 Hours
ADVOCATE

36 Point   5A 8a $5.50

Boston Globe 1897 Advertisers
PROPOSED BANQUET

24 Point   10A 15a $4.50

Audiences Entertained 24 Gorgeously Costumed
Theatrical Benevolent Society
NOTICES PREVENTING TROUBLE

18 Point   12A 20a $4.00

Ordering Imported Specialties 18 Customers Demand Novelties
Trustworthy Manufacturing Enterprises
CHILDREN ROMPING THROUGH GARDENS

12 Point   16A 25a $3.25

Farmers Growing $49 Elegant Wheat
Merchant Likewise Delights
CALIFORNIAN EXCURSIONIST

10 Point   20A 30a $3.00

Lowest Market Rate £35 Special Agent Wanted
Celebrating Throughout Europe
GRAND HUDSON RIVER TRIPS

Originated by the American Type Founders Co.

Specimen Pisa Series.

48 Point Pisa, 3 A 6 a $6 25

Southern Banking Associations
Metropolis Furniture Company
Productions of Central America

24 Point Pisa, 5 A 15 a $3 90

12 Point Pisa, 9 A 30 a $2 75

Send for Specimen Book
Correspondence Solicited

Superior
Copper=Mixed
Jype

60 Point Pisa, 3 A 5 a $8 25

Annual Moonlight Excursions
Pleasure Grounds

For sale by

Minnesota Jype Foundry Co., St. Paul
Great Western Jype Foundry, Kansas City
St. Louis Printers Supply Co., St. Louis
Great Western Jype Foundry, Omaha

18 Point Pisa, 8 A 25 a $3 25

Manufactured by

Barnhart Bros. & Spindler

36 Point Pisa, 4 A 10 a $5 25

185 Monroe Street, Chicago

6, 8 and 10 Point in Preparation.

Bradley

is one of the most use=
ful as well as one of the
most stylish of modern
type faces. ● Based on
the lettering of ancient
manuscripts, it is one
of the most legible and
tasteful text letters of
the day. ●● Its several
imitations by other let=
ter founders attest its
worth and popularity.

18 POINT   8 A 25 a $3 25

18 Point Collins Border No. 223. Font measuring 30 inches, $1 50

Leads the Styles
in Black Letter ●
It is cast in eight
sizes and ranges
from six point to
forty=eight point.

48 POINT   3 A 8 a $6 75

Bradley Initials

54 Point . . 3 A $4 25
Single Letter, 25 cts.

42 Point . . 3 A $3 00
Single Letter, 20 cts.

The American Type
Founders' Company
have recently added
German Characters
to the Bradley Series
and introduced it to
the Trade under the
Name of Jhlenburg.

36 POINT   4 A 10 a $5 00

General application and
unsurpassed wearing
quality have made the
Bradley Series one of
the leading letters of the day.
No Printing Office should be
without it. ● Like all leading
type styles, this series is original with the American Type
Founders' Company, and is on
sale at all its Branch Houses
and Agencies, which are located in the principal cities of
the United States. ● In ordering send to the Branch nearest
your place of business to insure
promptness in filling orders.
The Branches carry a full line
of Type, all kinds of Printing
Machinery, in fact, everything
needed in the Printing Office.

12 POINT   15 A 45 a $3 00

18 Point Collins Border No. 198. Font measuring 30 inches, $1 50

AD. WRITING AND SETTING.*

BY W. C. CRANDALL.

THE ability to write an ad. is practically universal. Any individual who can compose a business letter, who is at all versed in the line in which he is employed, is able to write something which passes in the composing room as an ad. But the person who can write an ad. which shall be distinctive in its wording, that shall have directness, truth, strength and individuality, is not found in every place of business, nor indeed in every line of business. The man who can build ponderous, intricate, or delicate machinery, who plans and estimates, studies and accomplishes wonders in the productions to which his mind and thought has been given, generally fails completely when he comes to take his pen and plan an attractive ad.—something that shall attract the public to his invention or production. The scholar who writes an interesting novel, who can command the interest and close attention of the reader from cover to cover, fails when it comes to enumerating the advantages of a particular brand of soap. Chemists who have after long years of experiment and study succeeded in producing a medicine which will build up the wasted physical nature, are powerless to explain its merits with a pencil. Men who can talk on the merits of their particular line of goods, who can take a customer and demonstrate beyond a possibility of question that their goods are superior and cheaper by far than any other similar goods, fail to touch the public by the composition of their printed announcements. There was a time years ago, when competition was not so keen, that the simple announcement that Mr. John Smith manufactured horseshoes was sufficient to bring a maximum of trade. This condition no longer obtains. Many people manufacture horseshoes. Why is Smith's shoe better than Jones'? The American people are characteristic advertisers. They differ from their English cousins in this particular, and today in English periodicals you will observe those old-fashioned ideas predominating. The desire to acquire riches quickly is undoubtedly the occasion of the rise of the ad. writer. He took in the situation. He saw that the man who manufactured the article gave so much of his thought to the manufacture that he had nothing left to give to the advertising. He prepares himself by a study of the merits of the goods; he examines the claims made by the rival concern, and like an attorney looking for technicalities, he looks for the points which may be sprung on the public to advance the sale of the particular line which he is writing up. Having secured that, he makes the great public acquainted not only with its merits but also with the defect of the opposition.

Illustrations have always been an attractive feature in ads. Who does not know " Woodbury's Facial Soap" (the neckless head); "The Hoffman House Cigar"; "Pyle's Pearline"; and that latest success: "Wool Soap—'My Mama Uses It; I Wish Mine Had'"?

But the combination of ad. writer and ad. setter is rare. The ad. writer prepares his copy carefully and sends it to the printer, marked often as to the exact size and style of letter he desires to use. He does not leave much to the compositor, for before him he has the firm's specimen book which shows the contents of the office, and from this he plans his work.

Not so with the business man with whom the average compositor must deal. There is nothing but a mixed mass of copy—an underline here and there, and that usually in the wrong place.

It is an old rule of the printing office to "follow copy if

*Paper read before the Printers' Technical Club No. 1, of Rockford, Illinois.

you follow it out of the window." Once that might have held good, but today it does not. The compositor, by study of his text-book, by observation of the style set by the men who make the display of ads. a study, has learned that the average business man has little idea of how to write an ad. The basis of the argument is there, but proper display is a matter of judgment. In the first place, take the copy and set all the straight matter as small as you think it will stand, leaving all possible room for display lines. Many an ad. has been spoiled by the comp. setting the body too large, and leaving no room for a proper heading. If the matter has a border, that must be selected according to the character of the advertisement. If it has a cut, see if by sawing the wood you can obtain more space for a large display letter. When fixed sizes like straight matter and cuts are laid out, you know just how much room you have for display. In this, try and find from the copy what the man wants to advertise the most. When found, throw it in as big and black a type as you can get. Avoid fancy type in ads. It does not suit the public even though it suits the customer. De Vinne, Howland, large faces of old styles, Gothics, Jensons and such lines are almost entirely called for by the ad. writers who draw large salaries, to attract trade. It is not always necessary that the name of the firm who manufactures the goods should be large; in fact, in the late production of Fowler, Shumway, and others, the firm name is kept small, as it is the inference that if the article itself possessed enough merit to attract, the reader will naturally look to see who manufactures it. The spacing of ads. is one of the most important features. Let a two-thirder set an ad. according to instructions as to type and take a proof, and then an ad. man take the same type and space it properly, and his proof will show a marked change for the better. To sum up the subject, the compositor must look to these points in copy not designed: How small dare I place the body matter? What is the strong word or words to bring out? What type is adapted to the character of the ad.? See that the spacing shows the ad. to the best advantage. These points well followed produce an ad.

FIG. 4.

The font of type shown in Fig. 4 is the invention of John F. Cumming, of Worcester, Massachusetts, who has assigned to the American Type Founders' Company, of Newark, New Jersey. His grant is in the form of a design patent. The characteristic features of the respective letters of this font of type are mostly dissimilar, there apparently being no feature common to all the letters except the heavy face. The letters A, M and N have features in common, as also the letters B and R. An essential feature is said to be the curve.

5A 8a   42 Point $6.00

Where Lie Those Happier Times
OUR GUARDIAN OF TRUTH

10A 14a   18 Point $3.25

CHARMING COMPANIONSHIP

That of the Man without Pretensions

to Oppressive Greatness

8A 12a   24 Point $4.00

LITERARY MARTYRS

The World Knows Nothing of

its Greatest Minds

20A 26a   10 Point $2.75

THE BREVITY OF LIFE.

Swift as the arrow cuts its way
    Through the soft yielding air;
Or as the sun's more subtle ray,
    Or lightning's sudden glare;

Or as an eagle to the prey,
    Or shuttle through the loom—
So haste our fleeting lives away
    So pass we to the tomb.

J B McCullagh

LATE EDITOR GLOBE-DEMOCRAT, ST. LOUIS, MO.

16A 20a   12 Point $3.00

IMMORTALITY.

Beyond this vale of tears,
    There is a life above,
Unmeasured by the flight of years;
    And all that life is love.

Here would we end our quest;
    Alone are found in Thee
The life of perfect love—the rest
    Of immortality.

7A 10a   30 Point $4.25

Grand Army of Letters

ROYAL MEMBER

6A 9a   36 Point $5.50

Modern Language

GRAND RACE

4A 7a   48 Point $6.50

Death all Fetters Doth Unbind
MOTIVE POWER OF LIFE

60 Point and 72 Point Sizes in Preparation.

Barnhart Bros. & Spindler

Artistic Letter Founders

183 to 187 Monroe Street

Chicago

SUPERIOR
COPPER-MIXED
TYPE

Yourself and Lady are cordially invited by

The Lambchop Club

to attend a dinner to be given at the

Oak Club House

Friday evening, February the twelfth, 1897

at six thirty o'clock.

BANK SCRIPT.
18 Point, 9 A 25 a $7 00
24 Point, 7 A 20 a   8 90
36 Point, 5 A 15 a   10 80
48 Point, 4 A 10 a   13 15

No. _____   Burlington, Ill., _____ 189__

The Great Eastern Bank

Pay to the order of _____

_____ Dollars

$ _____   _____

Mr. & Mrs. Wesley Thompson

announce the marriage of their daughter

Theresa Lenora

to

Mr. Lester W. Livingston

Wednesday morning September the seventh

eighteen hundred and ninety-six

Chicago

Mrs. Lester W. Livingston

At Home

Thursday, October the thirty-second

from four until six o'clock

414 Madison Avenue

PLATE SCRIPT.

14 Point, 9 A 30 a $5 00
18 Point, 9 A 25 a 6 00
24 Point, 7 A 20 a 7 25
36 Point, 5 A 15 a 8 50
48 Point, 4 A 10 a 10 00

Horace B. Lee, President
Albert Long, Vice-President
George Dearborn, Treasurer
Edwin F. Clark, Secretary

Branch Houses
187 Liberty St., Toledo, Ohio.
234 Ontario Street, New York.
569 Lake Ave., San Francisco.

Horace Lee Printing Company

Manufacturers of

Blank Books and Anderson's Celebrated Printed Index

Telephone 235.

Chicago, Ill., _____ 189__

Barnhart Brothers & Spindler

Artistic Letter Founders

Wish to call the attention of their printer friends to the
great demand for their Plate Script. No series of type ever
received so cordial a reception from printers all over the world
as the Plate. This is undoubtedly the handsomest series of
script ever produced.

Soliciting your orders
Very respectfully yours
Barnhart Bros. & Spindler

183 to 187 Monroe Street
Chicago, Illinois.

Two impressions are made in
printing the two lower cards.

COVER DESIGN BY JOHN SLOAN.

One Hundred Years

TYPEMAKING, like printing, has a venerable history. The span of four hundred years of typefounding from Gutenberg to MacKellar has been marked by wonderful achievements in the typographic art, and by an even more marvelous diffusion of knowledge directly traceable to the development of type and press.

That an existing type foundry has for one of these four centuries played an important part in this history is a fact as interesting as it is new. The centennial of this event is fittingly memorialized by a sumptuous souvenir volume — a *chef d'œuvre* of the printers' art — recently issued by the MacKellar, Smiths & Jordan branch of the American Type Founders' Company. The crude beginnings of the infant industry with which the name of this firm must always be honorably associated are here vividly set forth in choice text and illustration, and the intelligent, industrious and resolute character of the pioneer artisans who laid the foundations for after success finds fitting delineation and tribute. History opens at a new page.

Liberty Bell had been stilled but a few years when a young printer and type founder of Edinburgh, Archibald Binny, essaying to try his fortune in the new world, landed in the Quaker City and settled near the shadow of Independence Hall. He came at an opportune time. The printers were importing their type from England, as the home industry, which had boasted but two type foundries, had become extinct. The scanty remains of these two pioneer establishments are represented by two sets of matrices carefully treasured to this day in the vaults of the MacKellar, Smiths & Jordan Company, whose predecessors acquired them by purchase long, long years ago. One package, marked 1764, of great primer, is a relic of the Christopher Saur foundry, established at Germantown, Pennsylvania, as early as 1735, the first one in the United States. The tools of Adam G. Mappa, a Dutch founder, who cast many unique alphabets, are the fragments of the second foundry. This was carried on in New York City for a few years after 1787, but without financial success.

Binny was a practical founder, and had his tools, his punches, his stock of metal, but no other capital. It is related that an intimacy growing out of a chance meeting in a Philadelphia alehouse led Binny to associate himself with James Ronaldson, also a native of Edinburgh, and an active young man of business, with some means. It is the formation of this partnership, November 1, 1796, in the closing year of Washington's last presidency, that the souvenir "One Hundred Years" is intended to celebrate.

In a reading of this book nothing comes out in such strong relief as the thorough practical knowledge and conspicuous business ability which have been combined so felicitously in all the long series of partnerships. Binny's inventive genius was demonstrated in the modification, patented by him in 1811, of the old mold, greatly increasing the rapidity of casting. Our picture represents him at work before the melting pot with mold in hand as he cast type in the first years of the young firm. He also endeavored to construct a machine for rubbing type, but in this was not successful. Ronaldson's keen business instinct is manifested in the energetic promptitude with which he avails himself of the offer of a loan of the matrices of Benjamin Franklin by Mr. Duane, a relative of the philosopher. We see him going at once to Mr. Duane's house and trundling home in a wheelbarrow, on a hot midsummer day, the superior tools which Franklin had bought in France and brought home for his own convenience in casting sorts. It would indeed have been surprising had men of such dexterous skill, of such far-sighted intelligence and persistence of purpose not succeeded.

BINNY MOLDING BY HAND.

The subsequent history of the firm in all its ups and downs is faithfully related, as well as many incidents entertaining to the printer. The biographies of Johnson and the Smiths — father and sons — strikingly exemplify the success that is founded on thorough practical training in the mechanics of the profession. Their histories furnish several inspiring and interesting chapters which the printer, young and old, will enjoy reading.

Of absorbing interest is the story of the career of one young man who was selected as a business associate purely on his merits as a thorough workman— Thomas MacKellar — than whom the history of type and printing in America has no more illustrious character. Mac-Kellar, like Binny and Johnson, brought into the firm years of technical knowledge. Born in 1812 in New York, he found his way at the early age of four-teen years into a weekly newspaper office and learned the case the first day. He soon became a

ARRANGING THE PARTNERSHIP.

peer of the best workmen, and all the work requiring inge-nuity, taste and skill was assigned to him. In 1833 he went to Philadelphia and entered the employ of L. Johnson, who speedily recognized his ability and raised him to the posi-tion of foreman of the entire mechanical department, includ-ing the composing rooms and stereotype foundry. In 1845 he was taken into the firm, but did not cease his efforts to bring its work up to the highest stage of excellence, often manipulating the type himself, and studying out the artistic display and combinations which entered into the specimen books of which he was the editor. When the *Typographic Advertiser* was established, one page of the first number of which is here illustrated, Mr. MacKellar was made editor, and the popularity it received among printers is due very largely to his care in filling it with valuable ideas on type composition and ornament. Mr. MacKellar was at one time president of the Philadelphia Book Trade Association, and also of the American Type Founders' Association of the United States, but is now living in retirement at Ger-mantown. In 1883, on the occasion of the fiftieth anniver-sary of his connection with the foundry, a beautiful Etruscan vase of solid silver was presented to him, of their own accord, by the employes. It is twenty inches high, is ornamented with designs symbolic of the art of typemaking and printing, and bears a vignette of the recipient. His "American Printer" is used as a work of reference in every office, but outside of his art his interest in books and life has led him to contribute to literature several volumes of poetry and prose. In recognition of this, and of his eminent service to the arts and crafts, Wooster College conferred upon him the de-gree of Doctor of Philosophy. The life of such a man is an inspira-tion to the ambitious youth and craftsman who would be assured that industry, excellence in work and integrity of character are the sure forerunners of reward and

honor. It is refreshing in these times of hothouse successes to read the career of a man who put his main reliance on hard work and good work.

Again was the practical side of the firm supplemented by the equally essential qualities of the mercantile manager when John F. Smith and later Peter A. Jordan, who had been promoted from bookkeeper to cashier, were added to the firm. These gentlemen, having an intimate acquaint-ance with business requirements and methods, the extension of credits and wide commercial relations—in short, the entire financial and business organization of the house—greatly strengthened its standing. Mr. Richard Smith was for a long time in charge of the manufacturing department and did much to promote its advancement.

The sons of MacKellar and Jordan who are now in charge of the business have, thanks to the foresight and wisdom of their parents, the advantage of a combined mechanical and mercantile education. Both have served their apprentice-ship in the foundry and in the office. Mr. William B. Mac-Kellar is now editor of the *Typographic Advertiser*, as well

BORROWING FRANKLIN'S MATRICES.

as of the specimen books, and performs the complicated and extensive secretarial duties. Mr. G. Frederick Jordan is manager of the manufacturing department, into which he has introduced many of the improvements in machinery and methods that are described at length in the second part of this comprehensive work.

The description of the foundry, in all its departments, is no less interesting than the historical section. All of the processes involved in cutting the punch, in fashioning the matrix, in making the mold, and in casting the type, are accurately and clearly explained, and at the same time lavishly illustrated with pictures of the men in the midst of their work, and of the shops nervously alive with busy hands and wheels. The full-page illustrations are supplemented by small cuts that carry along the story from one operation to the next. One can pass from the manager's office, in the center of this hive of industry, through the entire plant, and see every step in type founding and electrotyping with as much satisfac-tion as if the visit were made in person.

Through it all, the dominant impres-sion conveyed is orderliness. What stress is laid upon this cardinal principle is apparent from the following reference to the arrangement of the foundry stock room:

"The world is not so very old, com-pared with what it may be, and yet it is a great step from the receptacles of the

THE MACKELLAR VASE.

baked-clay records of the Chaldeans, the most venerable of preserved characters, to a modern foundry stockroom, fitted with every convenience and labor-saving device, including a system of arrangement that is the outcome of a whole century of practical experience.

"Portions of the papyri of early Egypt are still preserved as sacredly as the mummies in the sarcophagi; but in present living interest they do not compare in importance with stacks of pica and tiers of nonpareil that blink and wink in mute eloquence from the thousands of shelves of the main type repository, dumb as oysters, but waiting the hour when, in answer to the click of the compositor's stick and the roll of the press, they will speak to readers yet unborn.

"It was said of Darius, the great Persian king and commander, that he knew the name and identity of every man in his immense army; and similarly there is not one servitor in the metal-clad legion of this gigantic typographical army but is known and can be identified at a moment's notice. System prevails everywhere; not the ordinary system of a lawyer's office, nor of some miscellaneous store, but a system like that of a carefully conducted bank, where every coin and note and piece of value has its own place, according to its denomination and relation."

Every now and then there are bits of equally well worded information that greatly heighten interest in the narrative. Under the description of type sizes, for example, a valuable summary is given of the origin and development of these sizes, and their nomenclature. We learn that they were probably named at first by the early printers according to the works on which they were used. In England no definite scale was adopted until the 16th century, and in France not until a public decree, in 1725, regulated both the scale of bodies and the standard weight of the type as well. The italic letter is popularly understood to be an imitation of the handwriting of the famous Italian poet, Petrarch. Likewise the subject of music type, which is made only by this foundry in the United States, is accompanied by many facts new alike to musicians and printers, about the early printing of music.

In the chapters on Specimen Printing, considerable space is given to the description of the department for the publication of the voluminous specimen books issued by the company. Full-page half-tones illustrate the press and composing rooms, undoubtedly the "best equipped" job-room in the country, for in the cases and on the shelves are stored away, carefully numbered, thousands of pounds of type, comprising every one of the hundreds of sizes and styles made by the foundry.

The best artistic and literary talent has been employed to produce this exquisite memorial volume. It is bound in white buckram, stamped in gold, with a symbolic design

upon the side, typifying the genius of type founding. This is by the artist, John Sloan. The inside cover paper is a unique design made up from the idea of type scattered over a flat surface. The ninety-six pages of printed matter,

set up and arranged under the direction of Jacob Rupertus, are in 15-point Ronaldson Old Style, especially cut for the purpose. The designs, printed in a delicate shade of brown, are remarkably well executed in half-tone by the Electro-Tint Engraving Company, who prepared and arranged the entire artistic and illustrative work. The binding is by the Murphy-Parker Company. Mr. W. B. MacKellar, the editor, has occasion to be proud of this unique and handsome production, which is a distinct contribution to the printers' art. It adds to the literature of American typography a charming vista into the early days of this art, heretofore an unwritten page, and furnishes an intelligent and attractive description of the small city of machinery that constitutes a modern plant for type founding.

THOMAS MACKELLAR.

WILLIAM B. MACKELLAR.

G. FREDERICK JORDAN.

THE PROOFREADER'S RESPONSIBILITY.

BY F. HORACE TEALL.

STRICTLY speaking, the responsibility of a proofreader, on any kind of work, should be very narrowly defined. In an ideal state of affairs it would never go beyond close following of copy in every detail. Even that is by no means always easy, and for a reason that should cause writers to be very lenient with proofreaders. This reason is that writers make much manuscript that is almost positively illegible, and are often careless in many details that should be closely attended to in the writing. But, since there is little ground for hoping that writers will ever generally produce copy that can be reproduced exactly, the question remains open, How much responsibility must the proofreader assume?

A good illustration of the legal aspect of this question is found in Benjamin Drew's book, "Pens and Types," published in its second edition in 1889, as follows: "In an action brought against the proprietor of Lloyd's paper, in London, for damages for not inserting a newspaper advertisement correctly, the verdict was for the defendant, by reason of the illegibility of the writing."

"Illegibility of the writing" is a more serious stumbling-block even than most writers know it to be, although many writers do know that they are great sinners in this matter. Notwithstanding the fact that it has been a subject of wide discussion, much more might profitably be said about it, and it would be a great boon to printers if somebody could devise a way of instituting a practical reform in the handwriting of authors, editors, and reporters; but the incessant necessity of deciphering what is almost undecipherable is our immediately practical concern just now. What should be the limit of the proofreader's responsibility here?

Some time ago a New York paper had frequent articles in a handwriting so bad that the compositors were paid double price for setting type from it. One of the compositors, in talking with a proofreader, expressed the opinion that the readers had very easy work, and part of his reason for the assumption was the fact (as he put it) that all the copy was read for them by the compositors before the readers got it. That same evening this compositor had a take of the bad manuscript mentioned, and for what the writer had intended as "June freshets" the proofreader found in his proof "Sierra forests." Well, the compositor read the manuscript first, but how much good did that do the proofreader? If the latter had passed the "Sierra forests" into print, he would have deserved to be discharged; for any intelligent man should know that one of the quoted terms could not possibly be used in any connection where the other would make sense. That compositor prob-

ably knew as well as the proofreader did that what he set did not make sense, but he also knew that the proofreader would have to do better with it, and that, no matter how much correcting he had to do, it would pay him better to do it than to lose too much time in the effort to get it right at first. Again, the compositor had practically no responsibility in the matter, though the one who shows most ability in setting his type clean from bad copy is a better workman than others.

We have said that one who passed into print an error like the one mentioned should be liable to discharge. This is true, because no person reasonably fitted to read proof could fail to recognize it as an error. The best proofreader who ever lived, however, might in some similar cases fail to read what is written exactly as it was intended in the writing. Unfortunately, it is only too often the case that proper names or generally unfamiliar words are written more illegibly than common words, and names so written may easily be misprinted after the best proofreader has done his best with them. Where it is possible, it should be the most natural thing in the world for anything hard to decipher to be submitted to its writer. It does not seem necessary to say that a good reader will not do too much of such referring, but only when it is really needful. Commonly this cannot be done on daily newspapers; but even there, in extreme cases, and with caution in deciding when it is well to do so, the matter should be referred to an editor, for it is to the editors that final responsibility for the wording of what is printed belongs.

What has been said seems well calculated to indicate clearly the limit the writer would place in such matters upon the proofreader's responsibility. Naturally and equitably that limit is merely the exact reproduction of what is written, as to the wording, but including proper spelling and punctuation.

No careful author will allow his book to be printed without reading it himself in proof; but this must be mainly for the wording only, as the printer's bill includes pay for good proofreading. Here matters are more simple as to the responsibility for getting the right words, as even hurried work from manuscript can generally be referred to the author in cases of real doubt. Occasionally this cannot be done, but these occasions are comparatively rare exceptions. Submission of reasonable doubt to the author for his decision should be an important feature of the reader's responsibility. It hardly seems necessary to dwell upon the question with regard to book-work, because the distinctive peculiarities of such work in this respect are so generally amenable to consultation. It is in newspaper and job work that the greatest practical difficulty is encountered.

5 A 8 a   48 Point Topic $7 75

UNIFORM MAKERS
Bronzed Medal

24 A 50 a   6 Point Topic $2 50

EXHIBITION OF FAMOUS EGYPTIAN STATUARY
Lecture Delivered on Portraiture Illustrated with Stereopticon Views
Dowered with Ethereal Loveliness She Bewitched the Town
1 2 3 4 5 6 7 8 9 0

5 A 8 a   36 Point Topic $5 10

INTERNATIONAL
Government Situations

20 A 40 a   8 Point Topic $2 75

IMPORTANT COMMERCIAL INFORMATION
The Geographic Survey Department of the United States
Expensive and Unscientific Experiments Performed

4 A 5 a   72 Point Topic $9 60

BRICK HOUSE

18 A 36 a   10 Point Topic $3 00

PRINCIPAL INVENTIONS PATENTED
Experiments for Perpetual Motion Unsuccessful
Many Corporations Financially Embarrassed

15 A 30 a   12 Point Topic $3 15

IMPROVED CITY PROPERTY
Enormous Railroad Building Being Erected
Beautiful Boulevards and Driveways

Fine Mansion

10 A 20 a   18 Point Topic $3 50

TENNESSEE LEGISLATURE
Beautiful Paintings of Mountains
New Southern Plantation Song

8 A 12 a   24 Point Topic $4 10

CONCERT DIRECTOR
Experienced Music Teachers

4 A 6 a   60 Point Topic $8 50

SOUTHERN MICHIGAN
Milwaukee and Columbus

Manufactured by BARNHART BROS. & SPINDLER, Chicago, Ill.

CONDENSED ITF GOTHIC No. 1

MOST COMPLETE SERIES MADE—CAST ON STANDARD LINE

STANDARD LINE INVENTED BY INLAND TYPE FOUNDRY

5a 4A, $10.00   72-POINT CONDENSED GOTHIC No. 31   L. C. $4.10; C. $5.90

Narrow GOTHIC Face 6

8a 4A, $6.40   54-POINT CONDENSED GOTHIC No. 1   L. C. $3.25; C. $3.15

USEFUL Series 5

8a 5A, $6.00   48-POINT CONDENSED GOTHIC No. 1   L. C. $2.90; C. $3.10

Uniform LINING 72

9a 5A, $4.50   42 POINT CONDENSED GOTHIC No. 1   L. C. $2.25; C. $2.25

IMPROVED Letter 16

9a 6A, $4.00   36-POINT CONDENSED GOTHIC No. 1   L. C. $1.90; C. $2.10

Made in ALL SIZES 30

5a 4A, $8.75   72-POINT CONDENSED GOTHIC No. 1   L. C $3.50; C. $5.25

Modern SPECIMEN Lines 8

18-POINT CONDENSED GOTHIC No. 1
26a 16A, $3.00   L. C. $1.50; C. $1.50

SYSTEMATIC TYPE FOUNDING
Better Methods of Working 35

30-POINT CONDENSED GOTHIC No. 1
12a 7A, $3.50   L. C. $1.80; C. $1.70

SUPERIOR GRADING
Fine Proportions 92

14-POINT CONDENSED GOTHIC No. 1
38a 20A, $2.80   L. C. $1.40; C. $1 40

EVERY CHARACTER ON UNIT SETS
Particular Attention Given Widths 14

12-POINT CONDENSED GOTHIC No. 1
44a 24A, $2.50   L. C. $1.25; C. $1.25

DISPLAYS THE MOST COMPLETE SERIES
Fifteen Sizes of this Useful Face Shown 60

24-POINT CONDENSED GOTHIC No. 1
20a 10A, $3.20   L. C. $1.65; C. $1.55

STANDARD LINE FACES

10-POINT CONDENSED GOTHIC No. 1
44a 25A, $2.50   L. C. $1.25; C. $1.25

STANDARD LINE IS THE ONLY PROFITABLE TYPE
Printers Can Save Labor and Money by its Use 50

8 POINT CONDENSED GOTHIC No 1
40a 26A, $2.25   L. C. $1.10; C. $1.15

RECUTTING, REMODELING AND IMPROVING PLAIN FACES
Increasing the Merits of the Bread-and-Butter Styles $79

Welcomed by Printers 48

6-POINT CONDENSED GOTHIC No. 1
45a 28A, $2.00   L. C. $1.00; C. $1.00

THIS SMALL SIZE OF CONDENSED GOTHIC IS VERY DESIRABLE
Required for Box-Headings, Railway Time-Tables and the Like 26

6a 4A, $7.00   60-POINT CONDENSED GOTHIC No. 1   L. C. $3.40; C. $3.60

Complete FOUNDING System 3

Cut and Manufactured Solely by INLAND TYPE FOUNDRY, 217-219 Pine St., Saint Louis

25 A 40 a   6 POINT ARNO (Nonpareil) $2 50

LOCAL RAILROAD AND STEAMBOAT NEWS

2 Popular Novelties in Carriages for City and Country Driving

20 A 30 a   10 POINT ARNO (Long Primer) $2 75

SEVEN THOUSAND SOLDIERS

89 Monadnock Cash Register Company

10 A 15 a   18 POINT ARNO (3 line Nonp.) $3 50

CUSTOM HOUSES

4 Fashions for Summer

20 A 30 a   8 POINT ARNO (Brevier) $2 50

PRACTICAL VAUDEVILLE TRAINING

European Music Academy Headquarters at Stockholm 9

15 A 25 a   12 POINT ARNO (2 line Nonp.) $2 75

BRAVE SOLDIER BOYS

Second Regiment Camping Ground 3

8 A 12 a   24 POINT ARNO (4 line Nonp.) $4 25

TREASURER

Honest Cashier 5

6 A 10 a   30 POINT ARNO (5 line Nonp.) $5 25

HANDSOME BUILDINGS

6 Columbian Exhibition Closed

5 A 8 A   36 POINT ARNO (6 line Nonp.) $6 00

ADMINISTRATION

Republican Conventions 7

4 A 6 a   48 POINT ARNO (8 line Nonp.) $8 00

DRUM HEAD

8 Ninth Sham Battle

4 A 5 a   60 POINT ARNO (10 line Nonp.) $10 00

MUSIC Stands 9

Manufactured by BARNHART BROS. & SPINDLER, Chicago, Ill.

A MATCHLESS EXTENDED SERIES

De Vinne Extended

B 15

6A 10a $6 00

24 POINT

EXPOSITION
Home Manufacture

9A 12a $4 50

18 POINT

UNIFORM PRINT
Looks Plain and Artistic

10A 14a $3 75

14 POINT

BEAUTIFUL SCENE
Views From Excursion Boats

14A 18a $3 50

12 POINT

NINETEENTH CENTURY
Base Ball and Lawn Tennis Player

18A 24a $3 00

10 POINT

EUROPEAN BICYCLE EXHIBITION
American Products Receive Highest Awards
Enterprising Competitors

24A 36a $2 50

6 POINT

JUVENILE ORCHESTRA
Renders Popular Selections
Thursday Evening
1234567890

22A 30a $2 75

8 POINT

MODEST YOUTHS
Introduced to Director
Gratifying Result
12345678

De Vinne Extended

B 15

3A 4a $11 50

48 POINT

HOME
Fashions

4A 5a $10 00

42 POINT

FARMS
Fine Cattle

4A 6a $8 00

36 POINT

SPRING
Sugar Barrel

5A 8a $7 00

30 POINT

INDUSTRY
Missouri Firms

ELZEVIR GOTHIC SERIES.

Originated by the CRESCENT TYPE COMPANY, 346-348 Dearborn Street, Chicago.

3A, 6a, $8.00   48 Point Elzevir Gothic   Caps, $4.00   L. C., $4.00

LOAN OFFICE
Last Ray of Hope

5A, 9a, $6.00   36 Point Elzevir Gothic   Caps, $3.00   L. C., $3.00

36 ELZEVIR GOTHIC
A Beautiful Line of Type

6A, 12a, $5.50   30 Point Elzevir Gothic   Caps, $2.60   L. C., $2.90

REJUVENATING COSTUME
&4 Favorable Impressions Made&

8A, 16a, $5.00   24 Point Elzevir Gothic   Caps, $2.50   L. C., $2.50

ABBREVIATED BICYCLE SKIRT
Causes Disease Called Rubber Neck

18 Point Elzevir Gothic

12A, 24a, $4.50   Caps, $2.25   L. C., $2.25

TREATISE ON BEES
&Points to Remember&

12 Point Elzevir Gothic

18A, 36a, $3.25   Caps, $1.50   L. C., $1.75

PATENT BURGLAR ALARM
It Catches and Holds the Burglar

8 Point Elzevir Gothic

22A, 44a, $2.75   Caps, $1.25   L. C., $1.50

GRAND PYROTECHNIC EXHIBITION
Two-Thousandth Annual Purgatorial Housecleaning

14 Point Elzevir Gothic

15A, 30a, $4.00   Caps, $1.80   L. C., $2.20

ELEMENTS OF SUCCESS
&Fertile Brain and Iron Will&

10 Point Elzevir Gothic

20A, 40a, $3.00   Caps, $1.40   L. C., $1.60

MANY MEN OF MANY MINDS
Many Type of Many Kinds See Elzevir

6 Point Elzevir Gothic

25A, 50a, $2.50   Caps, $1.20   L. C., $1.30

& & INSTRUCTIONS FOR MAKING MONEY & &
Fold a Bill, Press It, Open It, and You Will Find It Increases

——FOR SALE BY——

Conner, Fendler & Co., New York City,   Scarff & O'Connor Co., Dallas, Texas,
And all Type Founders and Dealers in Printers' Supplies.

De Vinne Extra Condensed

B 15

PATENTED

6 A 12a $5 50

36 POINT

COLLEGE MONTHS

Bright Maidens in Attendance

8 A 12a $5 00

30 POINT

NUMEROUS LANDMARKS

Throughout Cumberland Discovered

10 A 16a $4 00

24 POINT

INNUMERABLE REQUISITIONS

Administration Upholding Monroe Doctrines

12 A 20a $3 25

18 POINT

DISPLAY BEAUTIFUL FLORAL DESIGNS

Seventh Annual International Chrysanthemum Exhibit

14 POINT

18 A 22a $3 25

NATIONAL CONVENTION

Mississippi Valley Metropolis

1 2 3 4 5 6 7 8 9 0

12 POINT

20 A 26a $3 00

VENEZUELAN COMMISSION

Arbitration Now Becomes Necessary

1 2 3 4 5 6 7 8 9 0

Can only be purchased from the Originators, the

AMERICAN TYPE FOUNDERS COMPANY

Makers of Type that Satisfies the Buyers of Printing

De Vinne Extra Condensed

B 15

PATENTED

4 A 5a $15 00

72 POINT

NOBLE Horses

4 A 5a $9 00

60 POINT

Brought ROCKER

5 A 7a $8 00

54 POINT

DURABLE Flooring

5 A 8a $7 00

48 POINT

Landscape IMPROVED

6 A 10a $6 00

42 POINT

MODERN CUISINE

Clothed in Deep Mystery

A GRACEFUL, STRONG AND USEFUL SERIES

LIVERMORE SERIES

PATENTED

60 POINT — 3A 4a $8 25

Denouncement

48 POINT — 3A 6a $6 25

Famous Workmen

36 POINT — 4A 10a $5 25

Determined Advertiser

30 POINT — 5A 12a $4 75

Reward Honest Merchants

24 POINT — 6A 18a $4 25

Scientific Explorations Postponed

18 POINT — 9A 28a $3 75

Enthusiastic Audience Became Ungovernable

12 POINT — 15A 50a $3 25

Dramatic Elocution Admired

10 POINT — 15A 55a $3 00

Patriotic Orators Arouse Natives

8 POINT — 15A 55a $2 75

Sensational News Eagerly Devoured

1234567890

8 POINT — 15A 60a $2 50

Conservatives and Radicals Join Hands

1234567890

Originated and Made only by the

AMERICAN TYPE FOUNDERS COMPANY

Whose Type is most valuable because made
with Brains and Good Taste

LIVERMORE OUTLINE

PATENTED

60 POINT — 3A 4a $8 25

Denouncement

48 POINT — 3A 6a $6 25

Famous Workmen

36 POINT — 4A 10a $5 25

Remunerated

30 POINT — 5A 12a $4 75

Determined Advertiser

24 POINT — 6A 18a $4 25

Generous Patrons

Reward Honest Merchants

Meritorious Investigation

Scientific Explorations Postponed

1234567890

36 POINT   5 A 8a $5 50

September Twilight Excursions Preachers 64 Camping

30 POINT   6 A 10a $5 00

National Bank of Iowa was organized at Cedar Rapids, May, 1872

8 POINT   15 A 50a $2 75

THE short stories should not exceed one thousand words in length, preferably eight hundred. They must be written on only one side of the paper and the name and address of the writer to accompany the same for publication. Brevity will be considered in all the awards. The sum of $24,180.35 will be awarded as prizes and will not be given to anonymous writers

24 POINT   6 A 15 a $4 50

Persons with bright thoughts and aspiring minds seem from the very earliest part of the 16th Century to have been dissatisfied

6 POINT   15 A 50a $2 50

WE have previously indicated in an article, published the 28th inst., our conviction that the present debased condition of the American stage is due chiefly to the greed, ignorance, and incapacity of a large majority of the men who have established a virtual monopoly in the control of the theatre, and, temporarily at least, have put an end to competition. One of the greatest obstacles in the way of reform is the inability of those same men, for obvious reasons, to discern the trend of intelligent, to say nothing of cultivated, public opinion, or to inform themselves of the craving for better entertainment

18 POINT   8 A 25 a $4 00

While $20,483 is an exceptional price for a meal, even among the wealthiest Americans, there are a few who allow their dinner bills to reach the three-thousand-dollar point

12 POINT   10 A 35 a $3 25

EARLY to-morrow morning the tents will be folded and, like the Arabs, the regiment will silently steal away to town, where once again the garb of citizens will be resumed and the ideal soldier life which 567 men have been living for the past week or ten days, will be at an end

10 POINT   12 A 40a $3 00

RELIEf of the poor is one of the many themes of life with which the people of a great city are constantly brought face to face. Like the people themselves, the question of their relief is always with us, not in an obscure way but insistently, demanding thought, awakening our sympathies, and inciting us to action. About 4678 men and women braver than the rest of us devote their lives in giving us the facts about the poor

Send orders to nearest Branch of the American Type Founders Company, Leaders of Type Fashions.

PATENTED

60 POINT   3 A 4 a $11 90

Morning Exercises Contemplations

48 POINT   3 A 5 a $9 25

Sparkling and Amusing Divertisement

36 POINT   3 A 7 a $7 50

Aeronauts Descend Gracefully

¹ ² ³ # Excited Citizens ⁴ ⁵ ⁶

24 POINT   4 A 10 a $4 50

Multitudes Witness Acrobatic Tournament
Frightened 456 Countrymen

....AMERICAN TYPE FOUNDERS COMPANY....

Boston, 150 Congress St.
New York, Rose and Duane Sts.
Philadelphia, 606-614 Sansom St.
Baltimore, Frederick and Water Sts.
Buffalo, 83-85 Ellicott St.
Pittsburgh, 323 Third Ave.
Cleveland, St. Clair and Ontario Sts.

Cincinnati, 7-13 Longworth St.
Chicago, 139-141 Monroe St.
Milwaukee, 376 Milwaukee St.
St. Louis, Fourth and Elm Sts.
Minneapolis, 24-26 First St., South
Kansas City, 533-535 Delaware St.
Denver, 1616-1622 Blake St.

San Francisco, 405-407 Sansome St.
Portland, Ore., Second and Stark Sts.
Dallas, 256 Commerce St.
London, E. C., 54 Farringdon Road
Melbourne, Australia, 395 Flinders Lane
Sydney, Australia, 37 Winyard Square
Adelaide, South Australia, 69 Grenfell St.

PROSPECTOR'S LUNCH

CONTAINS COLD BROILED CHICKEN OR GAME,
SANDWICHES, PICKLES, HARD-BOILED
EGGS, CAKE, PIE AND FRUIT.
PRICE, $2.50

RULES AND SUGGESTIONS

PATRONS OF OUR ESTABLISHMENT MUST HELP
THEMSELVES, OUR WAITERS BEING IN THE
MINES, AND UNDER NO CIRCUMSTANCES
WILL WE ENTERTAIN ANY COMPLAINT.
GRUB STAKES FURNISHED.

THE
KLONDYKE

CIRCLE CITY

ALASKA

BRUCE TITLE SERIES

24-POINT. 5A $2.50
20-POINT. 6A 2.25
16-POINT. 7A 1.80
12-POINT. 10A 1.50
10-POINT. 12A 1.40
9-POINT. 14A 1.35
8-POINT NO. 1. 15A 1.25
8-POINT NO. 2. 16A 1.00
6-POINT NO. 1. 18A 1.00
6-POINT NO. 2. 20A 1.00
6-POINT NO. 3. 20A 1.00
6-POINT NO. 4. 20A 1.00

BILL OF F

SOUP

OX TAIL, 25c

REINDEER, 25c   MOOSE, 25c

BOILED

SHORT RIBS OF BEEF, 75c

ENGLISH BREAKFAST SAUSAGE, 75c

ROASTS

PRIME RIBS OF BEEF, 85c

BILL OF FARE

VEGETABLES

MASHED POTATOES   GREEN CORN
BOILED POTATOES
SWEET POTATOES   BOILED RICE
BROWN POTATOES   SAUER KRAUT

FRESH FRUITS

PEACHES   ORANGES   APPLES
BLACKBERRIES   RASPBERRIES
BANANAS

DESSERT

PLE PIE   PEACH PIE
VANILLA ICE CREAM
PURE JAVA COFFEE WITH CREAM
EET MILK   BUTTERMILK

VEGETABLES, FRESH FRUITS AND DESSERT
SERVED WITH MEAT ORDERS.

MADE BY

INLAND
TYPE
FOUNDRY

SAINT LOUIS

FOR SALE BY

GOLDING & CO.
BOSTON, PHILADELPHIA, CHICAGO
AND NEW YORK.

DAMON-PEETS, NEW YORK.

WM. E. LOY, SAN FRANCISCO.

GWATKIN & SON, TORONTO.

GETHER & DREBERT,
MILWAUKEE.

TWO DESERVED PROMOTIONS.

EDWARD PAYSON SUTER has been appointed manager of the Philadelphia branch of the American Type Founders' Company, to fill the vacancy caused by the recent and lamented death of Mr. William Brashear MacKellar. Mr. Suter was promoted from the Baltimore branch of the same company, and Mr. W. Ross Wilson, who was Mr. Suter's chief assistant, succeeds as manager of the Baltimore branch. On this and the following page we have pleasure in publishing the portraits of these two gentlemen.

The customers of the Philadelphia branch may be congratulated on the appointment of Mr. Suter, whose long familiarity with the product of the Mac-Kellar, Smiths & Jordan Foundry, combined with his well-known respect for its fame and traditions, and whose extended experience in large business affairs furnishes the assurance that he will uphold its reputation, while his progressive character leads us to predict that he will extend the scope of its business usefulness.

Edward Payson Suter was born in Baltimore in 1849, and, losing his parents in early infancy, was brought up and educated as the foster son of Mr. John Ryan, owner of the John Ryan Type Foundry, who was for many years vice-president of the old Type Founders' Association of the United States. Although his earliest active connection with the type foundry was in 1881, as a lad he acquired a general knowledge of the art of type founding and the methods of disposing of the product. Completing his education in the public schools, young Suter developed a remarkable capacity for business, and at the age of seventeen handled large city and national government contracts. He then entered the real-estate business, and subsequently became a member of the firm of Sheeler & Ripple, a livestock concern doing an annual business of $2,000,000. Mr. Suter managed the finance and law department. Retiring on account of ill health, after a time Mr. Suter carried on business in New York City as an advisory commercial expert. The increasing years of Mr. John Ryan and mutual interests induced Mr. Suter to undertake the management of

the John Ryan Foundry in 1881, since which time it has steadily progressed. In 1892 it was acquired by the American Type Founders' Company, and Mr. Suter continued as manager. It has proved a successful branch, and the promotion of Mr. Suter to a more important branch indicates the high esteem in which he is held by the general management of the company.

Mr. Suter has been an active member of the Baltimore Typothetæ and chairman of its Entertainment Committee since its organization. During the period covered by his management of the foundry in Baltimore he has made many strong friendships among the newspaper men and printers of the Middle and Southern States. He is of an even temperament and pleasing address, and although of quiet demeanor, he gets into close touch with and secures the confidence and respect of his customers, who receive that courteous consideration which takes off the rough edges of business and brings it to a higher plane — in a word, he is an approachable man in the best sense of that term, with a kindly disposition. He devotes his leisure time to philosophical, historical and archæological studies, and has accumulated a valuable and interesting collection of ancient coins and antiquities.

W. Ross Wilson, the new manager of the Baltimore branch of the American Type Founders' Company, was born in Baltimore in 1855, received a public school education, and has always resided in that city. As a young man he acquired a knowledge of the construction of machinery, and in 1880 became associated with the firm of Bateman, Hooper & Co., dealers in type and manufacturers of printers' supplies, who also carried on a printers' machine shop. In 1883 the firm was changed to Hooper & Wilson, and in 1888 a type foundry was added to the business. In 1892 the business was purchased by the American Type Founders' Company, and Mr. Wilson was appointed assistant to Mr. E. P. Suter, the manager, and devoted his attention especially to the machinery department of the business with marked success, establishing a well-equipped machine shop for the rebuilding and repair of printing and bookbinding machinery, and developing business in all possible directions.

EDWARD PAYSON SUTER.
Recently appointed manager of the Philadelphia branch of the American Type Founders' Company.

IMPROVED TYPESETTING MACHINES.

BY CHARLES H. COCHRANE.

THE present activity of typesetting machine inventors means a good deal to the printers of the next decade. Notwithstanding the almost hopeless complexity of the average mechanism designed to supplant the compositor, yet the industrious inventor never tires, but goes on producing machines in embryo, some of which may form important parts of the machines which will become staple in the twentieth century. The Mergenthaler Company is steadily acquiring new patents, most of them for minor improvements, but many of them involving radical changes in mechanism, which suggest the truth of the rumor that they contemplate putting out a new style of machine whenever competition demands such a step on their part.

Philip T. Dodge, B. L. Fairchild, and others besides Otto Mergenthaler, have patented numerous improvements and assigned them to the Mergenthaler Linotype Company within a year. Mr. Mergenthaler has also made improvements which have been assigned, not to the company which bears his name, but to the National Typographical Company, of West Virginia.

The Empire Typesetting Machine Company is not standing still, either. Charles D. Hughes, of Brooklyn, has invented and assigned to them an improved distributer. R. J. Moxley has also made some improvements in the Empire distributer.

The Thorne Company have been busy in securing patents. Walter J. Ennison, William H. Honiss and E. J. Andrews have been conspicuous in assisting them. It is understood that they will add a type-justifying mechanism to their machines in the near future, doing away with one operator.

The Monotype Machine Company are busier just now in getting their perfected machine on the market than in taking out patents; still, Tolbert Lanston's name is seen occasionally in the *Official Gazette*.

The Chadwick machine, I believe, is considered perfected — at least no recent patents have come to my notice.

The Dow Composing Machine Company, of West Virginia, have obtained recent patents from Alexander Dow, on a type distributer, in the form of an upright cylinder with radiating pieces. The type is introduced in galleys, the leads being pushed out and lines elevated automatically.

The Alden Type Machine Company, of Brooklyn, is also heard from frequently at the Patent Office. L. K. Johnson and A. A. Low assigned three patents to them last fall, and there have been others this spring. They appear to be experimenting with type-channels and pushers.

Paul F. Cox, of Chicago, is very busy with his machine, which must be nearly perfected. The peculiarity of his mechanism is that he justifies the lines with crimped spaces, and leads the matter automatically. The compressible crimped space is entirely novel, and would appear to be practical, though it would seem to limit the machine principally to leaded composition. Every line is overset, and then compressed to the proper length, and it is evident that only the use of leads could prevent the lines in a column from being further compressed by the lockup. The machine sets ordinary foundry type, but the spaces are cut off from a reel and crimped as wanted. After printing, the spaces are melted down to form another reel. The general shape of this machine may be compared to a common roll-top desk, and it looks both simple and substantial.

W. E. Crane, of Hartford, is developing a machine for forming raised letters on a brass column strip. He uses only capitals and figures on the keyboard, as the machine is designed only for setting up mail lists or other coarse work. The formation of the raised letters is accomplished by coacting male and female dies, and there are blotting-out dies for use in correcting when a wrong letter has been struck. There is no justification of the lines.

The Johnson Typesetting Company of Portland, Maine, has had patents assigned by Frank A. Johnson, but that gentleman has been more conspicuous by the numerous patents which he has assigned to the Tachytype Company, of Minneapolis. First, he has patented a typesetting machine with a justifying device consisting of a lever with a series of fulcra, and means for rendering any one of said fulcra operative dependent upon the number of spaces in the line. Then a matrix-making machine (which was applied for away back in 1892, but only granted a few months since). This has a keyboard and calculating device. Then a typecasting and composing machine, very similar to the Monotype, having a square matrix-box or die-case, which contains the dies for the faces of all the characters, and is shifted about to form the face of the mold. Then a machine for making controllers for the typecasting machine. This is a sort of typewriter, with a form of punching device to make holes in a strip of paper. The typewriter prints a line simply as a proof of the matter set up, by which errors may be detected. And lastly, Mr. Johnson has assigned to the Tachytype Company a new form of linotype, in which the justification is accomplished by means of a dummy line, which assists in the proper selection of dies to give the right length of line.

A decided novelty in typesetting machines is the one patented by Alexander T. Brown, of Syracuse, last December, in which the type are all formed of one uniform size, as typewriter type, and, instead of being cast, are cut as blanks from a strip of metal on a reel, the faces being formed on the blanks by pressure, as selected by the action of the keyboard.

Joseph Sachs, an electrical expert of New York, has patented a device for releasing type in a typesetting machine. The touching of a key actuates an armature, which causes a pusher and gate to vibrate and discharge a type. There are persons who object to the use of electricity in a typesetting machine as being more subject to accidental stoppage than positive mechanical movements. It has certain advantages, however, which may cause its introduction one of these days.

There are others at work developing and improving typesetting machines, and it is fair to assume from the general activity that the perfect machine has not yet been devised, and that improvements on the present devices will continue to come for many years.

"FOLLOWING COPY" ON COMMERCIAL PRINTING.

BY J. R. BERTSCH.

USING the term in its broadest sense, "commercial printing" is all printing that enters in any way into the bringing about of an exchange of one thing for another, whether it be a handsome book, voluminously setting forth the merits of some new theory, to be received in exchange for old dogmas, or the dodger, so convenient to attract the attention of the public on short notice.

But strictly speaking, "commercial printing" is made up largely of letter-heads, note-heads, bill-heads, statement-heads, business cards, circular letters, circulars, pamphlets and catalogues. While this kind of printing is the least susceptible to changes in form and style, still there is a noticeable change going on continually, and that for the better in appearance and utility of the work turned out.

Nearly every customer for "commercial printing" knows just what he wants, and usually gives explicit directions as to how he desires his job done. Usually copy for such work is reprint with instructions to "make as before." In such a case the compositor should invariably "follow copy," no matter how strongly tempted he may be to improve the appearance of the job, which his sense of beauty and practical experience tell him can easily

be done by the substituting of another line of type or by rearranging the whole; for as sure as he changes it from that which the customer indicates, he is putting himself in the way of having his proof returned with the legend "make like copy" written on it, and may consider himself fortunate if he gets off so easily. Therefore in setting "commercial work" be sure to "follow copy" and you will get "O. K." proof, and the customers of the office will consider you accommodating because you do work just as they tell you to. You must remember that the customers of printing offices think they also know a thing or two, and nothing is gained by doing their work in such a manner as to arouse their antagonism to your methods, no matter how much more you may know about how it ought to be done.

You may think by this time that if all you have to do is to "follow copy" there is not much need for skill and originality. But there is, for not every user of "commercial printing" is included in the class of customers that I have mentioned, as many a job is taken with no further instruction than to make something neat or perhaps something fancy. Now it will depend on what you understand by "neat" as to what kind of work you will turn out. A job looks neat not because of the use of fancy type or intricate justifications. Usually such jobs are not neat but grotesque. A very commonplace type may, and usually does, make the neatest job, because neatness does not consist so much in the kind of type as in the manner of setting it. Proportion and symmetry are the two essential points to keep in mind in the setting of display matter, for on them depend the neatness of your work.

In setting commercial work avoid intricate justifications, or combinations that require the destruction of materials and more than the usual amount of time, for remember that on commercial work the price is already fixed, and your employer does not get any more for A's work, on which you may spend twice as much time as on B's.

As "commercial printing" is used in various kinds of business and professional enterprises, some regard should be given to the fitness of things. All printing to be used in the professions should be set in light-face type or small type, and ornaments used very sparingly, if at all, as the impression conveyed by the printed matter should be one of dignity. The same rule holds good in "commercial printing"; that is, the type and general arrangement should represent the business specified just as much as does the matter that is to be placed in type.

Hansen Vertical Script

Patent Applied for

12-Point

Economy is often attained by Printing under the
Dominant colors, strengthening them, and making them
forcible.   Blue under black makes the last
color stronger, and, generally speaking, black is deeper and better
from having another dark color under it, as purple,
dark green, or brown.   This quality enables
the first printing to be executed
in some ordinary, cheap ink, and the brilliancy

18-Point

Cutting Punches and making Moulds were
the first processes in the practice of Typography,
and demanded a degree of skill in the manipulation of tools and of Experience in the working
of Metal rarely found in any man undertaking
to learn the art of Printing.   They were never
regarded as proper Branches of the trade.

24-Point

Designed, manufactured
and for sale by
H. C. Hansen, - Type Founder,
24 & 26 Hawley Street,
Boston, Mass., U. S. A.

2-Pt., 32 a 10 A $4.00   18-Pt., 25 a 8 A, $4.75   24-Pt., 20 a 7 A, $6.00

Copperplate Roman.

Type that does not look like type. Successful imitation of Copperplate Engraving.

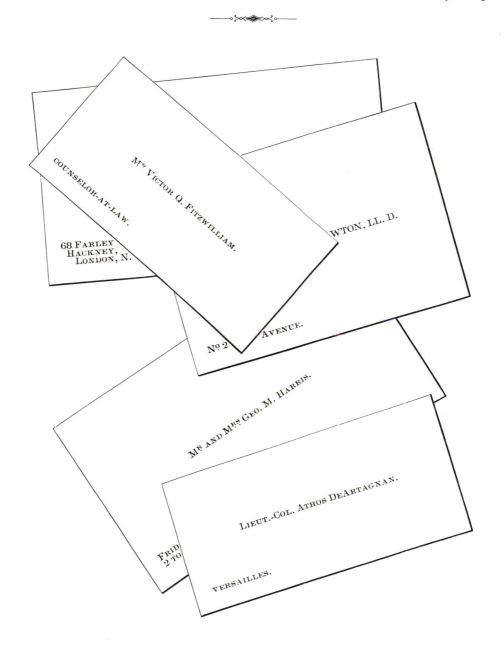

ABCDEFGHIJKLMNOℴPQRℲSℲTℲUVWXYZ.,-'&

ABCDEFGHIJKLMNOPQRSTUVWXYZ

1234567890

SPECIMEN OF

6-POINT COPPERPLATE ROMAN

30A 60A $3.00

MANUFACTURED EXCLUSIVELY

BY THE

AMERICAN TYPE FOUNDERS' CO.

48 POINT   4 A 7 a $8 00

Beautiful Finish
Design and Make

24 POINT   5 A 14 a $4 00

The Hercules
Gas and Gasoline
Engine
Best Made

72 POINT   3 A 5 a $12 00

Latest Italic Out

12 POINT   7 A 24 a $3 00

The little toy dog is covered with dust
But sturdy and staunch he stands
And the little toy soldier is red with rust
And his musket moulds in his hands

10 POINT   9 A 30 a $2 75

Saint Louis, Missouri, Eighteenth of September
Eighteen=ninety=nine
For Value received, I hereby subscribe for one share of stock in the
Klondike Sanitarium for Gold Incurables, subject to all the rules and
regulations   Dusty Rhodes   His X Mark

60 POINT   3 A 6 a $10 00

We Keep Abreast
Of the Times

18 POINT   5 A 18 a $3 25

Least Expensive Engine
Occupies Less Room
Comparatively Noiseless
in Operation

36 POINT   4 A 9 a $6 25

Nothing So Popular
Before the Trade

Made and For Sale Exclusively by

American Type Founders' Company

Send to Nearest Branch—Branches in Eighteen Cities

Harvard Old-Style Italic
8-2

30 POINT
6 A 12 a $4.25

American Type Founders Company
World's Leader in Type Fashions

12 POINT
18 A 30 a $3.00

HE sees the cattle in the fields,
The homestead farther back;
And memory wanders softly then
Along a hallowed track.

14 POINT
16 A 26 a $3.00

«GOLDEN sun of evening
Why so fair dost gleam?
Never without rapture
Do I see thy beam.»

24 POINT
7 A 15 a $3.50

Manufacturer of Type and Printing Office Furnisher
Branches in all Large Cities in the Country

10 POINT
20 A 34 a $2.75

«MARCH, march the heavy tramp,
Tentless field, the broken camp,
Friends meet friends in death's array,
Cannon peal, the sword shall slay,
Man, and steed, and riders, all,
Fame like theirs shall never fall.»

9 POINT
20 A 34 a $2.50

«THY work is o'er at last, proud gun!
Thy last red battle has been won,
And, rusting 'mong the flowers you lie,
The home of birds and vines;
Yet you that made the bravest die,
That broke the hostile lines.»

18 POINT
10 A 18 a $3.25

«We'll forget your mad endeavor to roll back the wheels of time,
And to curse the land forever with your statute-sanctioned crime,
Crime whose parallel was never since the earth was in its prime!»

8 POINT
24 A 36 a $2.50

WAR'S alarms were loudly sounding
Hearts of patriots madly bounding,
Songs of valor then were reigning,
Every eye was wildly straining,
Every tongue in martial numbers,
Roused the bravest from their slumbers.

6 POINT
32 A 42 a $2.25

«AND just below, the gathered throng
To eloquence did pay respect,
While Bruces talked, or Rays declaimed,
Or lesser minds in fashion decked,
Showed powers a Cicero to trance,
Demosthenes with art to thrall,
With listening senates wrapped in awe
And Elocution lord of all.»

6 Point	$2.25
8 Point	2.50
9 Point	2.50
10 Point	2.75
12 Point	3.00
14 Point	3.00
18 Point	3.25
24 Point	3.50
30 Point	4.25

$27.00 less discount

Originated and Manufactured
Exclusively by the

for sale by all Branches and
Agencies

American Type Founders Company

NOTES ON JOB COMPOSITION.

BY ED S. RALPH.

Under this head will appear, each month, suggestive comment on the composition of jobwork, advertisements, etc. Specimens for this department must be clearly printed in black ink on white paper, and mailed to this office, flat, marked plainly, "RALPH."

HENRY A. ANGER, Oshkosh, Wisconsin.—The work on your samples is excellent and fully up to standard for artistic merit.

JOSEPH DeCASTRO, with the *Illinois State Journal*, Springfield, Illinois.—We have nothing but words of praise for your ads. They are all good and reflect much credit.

C. H. JACKSON, Waukegan, Illinois.—The *Gazette* is certainly a neat and attractive country daily. The ads. show good common-sense treatment, and the make-up of the paper is neatness itself.

J. FAUNT LE ROY, San Rafael, California.—The composition on the entire concert programme, ads. and all, is excellent. The presswork, however, is susceptible of improvement. Your work, as a whole, shows up very well.

WALTER A. KING, Mason City, Iowa.—Your work is all excellent. The letter-head and card of the *Globe-Gazette* are beautiful and artistic. They are well balanced, correctly whited out, and harmonious in the color scheme.

THE TOWNSEND COMPANY, Pottsville, Pennsylvania.—Your blotter is a splendid one. There is not very much work on it, but for dignified simplicity, balance and finish, it would be hard to improve upon it. You should get trade from this blotter.

THE KEYSTONE PRESS, Portsmouth, Ohio.—Your new letter-head is very artistic, showing excellent composition and harmonious color arrangement. We think this last package of your specimens is very much better than the ones previously sent in for criticism.

ALEX L. FYFE, Chicago, Illinois.—As a whole your office stationery is excellent. On your bill-head, we think the street address is a trifle too prominent. You have accorded it nearly the same prominence as your name. The other four jobs are good as to plan, balance, finish and correct whiting out.

H. V. WATSON, Baldwinsville, New York.—The *Gazette* can well be proud of their ad. man. We have seen few better ads. anywhere than those collected in your neat little brochure, and you deserve credit for using your head as well as your hands. Excellent judgment was certainly used on every ad. in the collection.

MATT KUMP, Aldine Printing House, Xenia, Ohio.—Your jobwork is all excellent, and shows that Mr. Chew has a good man in his composing room. The blotters, which we had occasion to review some time ago, rank among the best we have seen. The work on the plat of the real estate poster is excellently well done.

AMSTUTZ MUSIC COMPANY, Bluffton, Ohio.—The composition on the cover page of the Public School Manual is only ordinary. There is nothing very striking or original about it. The words "Public Schools" should have no more prominence accorded them than the words "Manual of." They are all of equal importance, and consequently should have the same treatment as to prominence. The border around the line "Public Schools" did not add to the neatness of the page. The inside pages of the manual are very good, but there is room for improvement in the cover page. It would require very little change to make this page an excellent one.

"STAR" PRINTERS, Kewanee, Illinois.—There is decidedly too much border employed on the page ad. in the Premium List of the Kewanee District Fair. The border has taken up too much white. In advertisements it is always a good plan to give them as much white space as is consistent, in order to not hamper the display, and to serve the purpose of making the entire ad. stand out.

CHARLES W. ROLL, Manager, Lincoln Printing Company, Pittsburg, Pennsylvania.—The cover page of "The Heart of It" is your most artistic sample. We reproduce it (No. 1) as it is a good example of an excellent De Vinne page, showing correct whiting out, balance and finish. Some of your other

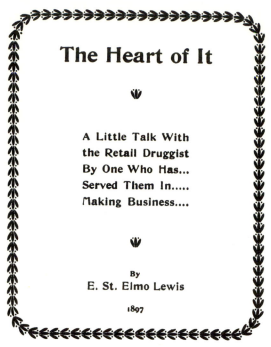

The Heart of It

A Little Talk With
the Retail Druggist
By One Who Has...
Served Them In.....
Making Business....

By
E. St. Elmo Lewis
1897

NO. 1.

work, however, has faults which you should strive to eliminate. The panel on the letter-head of Harry G. Bauman is entirely too large, and the border is so heavy that it renders it too conspicuous by far. Panel work, to be effective, should be in good proportion to the rest of the display, and special care should be taken or there is danger of its overbalancing the heading.

ROY T. PORTE, Hunter, North Dakota.—Your work, as a whole, is quite good. Your letter-head is up to date. The best two packet headings are those of J. H. McMullen and U. G. Miller. The first page of the statement for the Hunter State Bank is exceptionally good and shows the beauties of the plain gothic letter. The cover page for the programme of the North Dakota C. E. U. is quite artistic.

YORK PRINTING COMPANY, Brooklyn, New York.—The plan of the Remisio Lopez card is very good, indeed. The name, however, is in rather too heavy-faced type for use on an invitation in conjunction with light-faced type. To be sure, the name should have been accorded some prominence, but on invitation work it is always a good plan to avoid heavy results.

JAMES G. RICE, Manager Peerless Printing Company, Philadelphia, Pennsylvania.—The samples submitted for criticism are excellent and possess considerable individuality. There is, however, one sample to which we take exceptions, and feel that you will fully agree with us. In the bill-head of Charles D. Woods & Co. the words, or line, "House Painting" is too small, while too much prominence is given to the street address. The plan of the heading is all right, and with the alteration spoken of would make a most excellent heading.

A. L. FREEMOTT, Albert Lea, Minnesota.—There are many faults in your note-head. Take away the rulework around "Star Printing Office," and move the line about eighteen points, or a quarter of an inch, to the right. Leave off the word "for" and set the words "General Book and Job" in a little larger type to correspond with "Printing." Now, in the upper left-hand corner, place your name, set in small caps.

Browne & Maynard

request the honor of your presence at a

Grand Opening

of their newly enlarged and perfected stores,

displaying the very latest European fashions in

Millinery, Suits, Outer=garments, Furs,

Silks, Dress=goods, Laces, Trimmings, etc.

Handsome Lingerie Trousseaux

Infants Outfits, Childrens and Misses Dresses & Coats.

also the opening of the

New French Cafe

unlike any other Cafe outside of Paris.

Tuesday and Wednesday

November twenty=third and twenty=fourth.

BANK SCRIPT No 2.

14 Point,	9 A	30 a	$6 00	Extra lower case, 30 a	$3 50
18 Point,	9 A	25 a	7 40	Extra lower case, 25 a	4 00
24 Point,	7 A	20 a	9 30	Extra lower case, 20 a	5 00
36 Point,	5 A	15 a	11 00	Extra lower case, 15 a	5 75
48 Point,	4 A	10 a	13 30	Extra lower case, 10 a	7 00

The popular agitation in favor of Vertical Writing began some 15 years ago as a hygienic movement by German medical men.

School Committee.

Fourteenth
Masquerade Carnival
of the
Cawkering Humorous Society
to be held in
Mechanics Pavilion
August ninth
1904

Vertical Writing

B-1

PATENT APPLIED FOR

November 23.

Gentlemen: The system of Vertical Writing has found advocates in every part of Europe, and is now established in the German States, it having been introduced in very many of their schools.

C P Ralph, Principal.

Exclusively Manufactured by the American Type Founders Company
In stock and for sale at all Branches and Agencies

BINNER GOTHIC

72 POINT 5 A 8 a $9 00

REGIMENTALS 942 Entertainments

60 POINT 7 A 10 a $8 00

Handsome Borders 68 Combustible Material

BINNER PLATES MEAN PERFECT PLATES

48 POINT 8 A 12 a $7 00

Grand Columbian Exposition Demonstration Beautiful 257

EXPERIMENTS CONSIDERED SATISFACTORY

36 POINT 10 A 15 a $6 00

Enhance Boston Residence 63

DELIGHTED MAIDEN

30 POINT 12 A 18 a $5 00

Eastern Manufacturers Convention 89

ENGRAVING DECORATION

24 POINT 14 A 20 a $4 00

Eleventh Grand Annual Masquerade Carnival 14

EUROPEAN INFORMATION BUREAU

18 POINT 18 A 27 a $3 25

Handsome Christmas Presents Presented Obedient Children

MERCHANTS DONATING MANY GREENBACKS

MANUFACTURED EXCLUSIVELY AND FOR SALE BY ALL BRANCHES OF THE

AMERICAN TYPE FOUNDERS COMPANY

25 A 40 a   6 Point Southey (Nonpareil) $2 25

PHILADELPHIA CHARITY ASSOCIATIONS

Important Telegraph Communications to the Southwest Weekly Journal

423 Great Routes of the Northern Canada Steamboats 567

25 A 40 a   8 Point Southey (Brevier) $2 50

BEAUTIFUL EUROPEAN PAINTINGS EXHIBITED

89 Nineteenth Annual Convention of the Plumbers Union 23

20 A 30 a   10 Point Southey (Long Primer) $2 50

COUNTY CLERKS NEW OFFICE

45 Reception Given by Prominent Americans 67

20 A 30 a   12 Point Southey (2 line Nonp.) $2 80

EXCURSION STEAMBOAT

25 Dramatic Instruction Establishment 87

15 A 25 a   18 Point Southey (3 line Nonp.) $4 10

OPERA HOUSE

8 German Music Academy 9

10 A 15 a   24 Point Southey (4 line Nonp.) $4 80

NORTH HOTEL

9 Summer Resorts 4

8 A 12 a   30 Point Southey (5 line Nonp.) $5 45

GROUNDS

3 Surprise Parties

6 A 8 a   36 Point Southey (6 line Nonp.) $6 10

BOATS

Ohio Canal 2

5 A 6 a   48 Point Southey (8 line Nonp.) $7 25

KANSAS BANKERS

Six Million Business Men 9

4 A 5 a   60 Point Southey (10 line Nonp.) $8 75

BRANCH OFFICE

Northwestern House 5

MANUFACTURED BY BARNHART BROS. & SPINDLER, CHICAGO, ILL.

FOR SALE BY GREAT WESTERN TYPE FOUNDRY, KANSAS CITY; MINNESOTA TYPE FOUNDRY CO., ST. PAUL; ST. LOUIS PRINTERS SUPPLY CO., ST. LOUIS; GREAT WESTERN TYPE FOUNDRY, OMAHA.

NEWSPAPER GOSSIP AND COMMENT.

CONDUCTED BY O. F. BYXBEE.

Editors and publishers of newspapers desiring criticism or notice of new features in their papers, rate cards, procuring of subscriptions and advertisements, carrier systems, etc., are requested to send all letters, papers, etc., bearing on these subjects, to The Inland Printer Office, 212 Monroe street, Chicago, marked "BYXBEE."

HUNTINGTON, Indiana, has a new Sunday morning paper — the *Tribune*.

THE third international congress of editors will be held at London, May, 1899.

THE Middleburg (N. Y.) *News* has for its motto: "Keep to the right and keep moving."

A NEW sporting monthly, called *Outdoors*, has made its appearance in New York City.

AN interesting and creditable "Industrial Edition" is issued by the Lafayette (Ind.) *Journal*.

JASPER (Ind.) *Herald:* Your ads. are well displayed. Thanks for the curiosity inclosed.

THE Hinsdale (Ill.) *Doings* is a neat little weekly, well filled with interesting news, attractively presented.

A BRIGHT and fully illustrated "Mining Number" was recently issued by the Los Angeles (Cal.) *Times*.

La Ilustracion del Pacifico for October, published at Guatemala, Central America, shows some fine half-tones.

PAUL DANA, son of Charles A. Dana, has been appointed editor of the New York *Sun*, to succeed his father.

THE Syracuse (N. Y.) *Courier* has been sold by the receiver to John Francis Nash, the present managing editor, for $1,500.

THE Lee's Summit *Journal* celebrated its entrance upon its sixteenth year by publishing a "Souvenir Edition," embellished with over seventy cuts.

SOME papers seem to consider it unnecessary to mention the State, either in heading or date line, from which they emanate. The Mayfield *Mirror* and the Los Angeles *Times* are two of these. The former place, we learn from the "Entered as second-class matter" line, is located in Kentucky.

THE Sanilac County *Republican*, Sanilac Center, Michigan, is now comfortably situated in its own new building.

THE Ashland (Ohio) *Press* has added an extra column to each of its eight pages, and is now one of the largest weekly papers in Ohio.

W. R. FINCH, editor and publisher of the *Republican and Leader*, La Crosse, Wisconsin, has been appointed minister to Paraguay and Uruguay.

MR. W. F. DERFLINGER has been appointed editor of the New York *Industrial News*. This labor organ is set in both English and German type.

THE *Catholic Universe*, of Cleveland, Ohio, published an interesting and voluminous number commemorating the golden jubilee of the diocese of Cleveland.

A CHICAGO firm has furnished the New York *Herald* with a press with a capacity to print 96,000 copies of an 8-page paper in an hour, or 25,000 copies of a 24-page paper.

MR. WARREN C. BROWNE has accepted the management of the *American Craftsman*, of New York City, much to the gratification of that popular publication's many friends.

IT is evidently not considered "unprofessional" for physicians to advertise in Des Moines, Iowa. The *Saturday Review* has a "Directory of Physicians and Surgeons" containing forty ads. From two to four nonpareil double-column lines are used for each, and the name, office and residence, office hours, and telephone numbers appear in separate columns.

MR. JAMES SPRAGUE, the Ingersoll representative of the *Sentinel-Review*, Woodstock, Ontario, is doing some valuable work for that journal, covering a large territory.

THE COX TYPESETTING MACHINE.

THE well-prepared booklet issued by the Cox Typesetting Machine Company, descriptive and illustrative of the latest "one-man" typesetting and justifying device — the Cox Typesetting Machine — after giving a short review of typesetting machinery in general, points out the advantages of the Cox in economy and adaptability. We give the following condensed account for the convenience of our readers. Speed, economy and simplicity are secured by making the machine

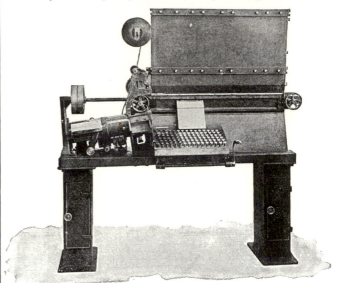

THE COX TYPESETTING MACHINE — FRONT VIEW.

virtually three machines. This prevents one part of the mechanism from limiting the operation of the others and increases the output of batteries without proportionately increasing the cost. Thus one distributer will serve two or more composing machines and one discarder will serve five composers. As will be noted in the illustration they are very symmetrical and compact. The keyboard has a sensitive action and convenient arrangement, and the copy is in the direct line of vision. The keyboard can be locked by the pressure of a button, prevent-

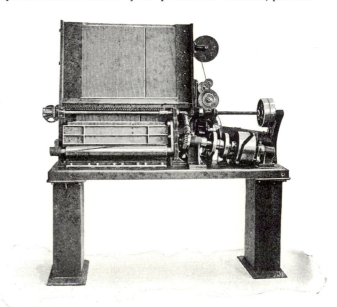

THE COX TYPESETTING MACHINE — REAR VIEW.

ing any type being ejected during any temporary absence of the operator. The assembled type is in a convenient position for the operator to scan and correct before justification. Leading is done automatically, and is a valuable feature of the machine, as matter can be set solid or leaded at will, and the change can be made almost instantly. The machine can be adjusted to set any length of line from 13 to 26 ems in a moment's time without readjusting cams or gears. An indicator in a convenient position assists the operator in determining the length of his line, and a bell announces when it has

THE COX SPACE DISCARDER AND LEAD EJECTOR.

reached its limit. Automatic throw-off devices are employed throughout the machine, thus guarding against breakage of type as well as injury to any part of the mechanism, thereby dismissing any strain on the operator's mind as to what might happen in the event of any mistake on his part in manipulating the machine. The most important function of justification is performed by the mere pressure of a lever. The assembling of type is not retarded in the least by this operation. An average speed of 4,000 ems per hour has been attained repeatedly, but the machine is limited only by the ability of the operator.

The justification is accomplished by the use of corrugated spaces, instead of the straight spaces of a foundered font. The spaces separate the words in the line more than is necessary,

ILLUSTRATION No. 1.
Showing line of type before justification has taken place.

ILLUSTRATION No. 2.
Showing line of type after justification has taken place.

but can be compressed laterally from their normal size when corrugated (which is about the thickness of an en space) to that of the thin space.

To accomplish justification by this method it is necessary that each line be overset — that is, longer than the measure desired. Then by suitable mechanism the line is compressed, the corrugated spaces yielding uniformly while the compression

is taking place until the line reaches the proper length. (See illustrations Nos. 1 and 2, showing line assembled with corrugated spaces between the words before compressed and after the compression has taken place.) This cut shows the limit before and after compression. This line would be accurately justified and rigidly spaced if its length had not called for the extreme limit of compression. The spaces are made from a lead ribbon fed from a reel placed on the typesetter immediately over the space-making device, which operates only when the spacebar is depressed.

To operate the space discarder the type is placed in the galley of the machine. The first function performed after the discarder is set in motion is to separate a single line of type from the dead matter in the galley and simultaneously eject the lead (if leaded) into the lead box, the line being moved along horizontally until it is directly in front of the mechanism which ejects the spaces and quads from the line of type. This is accomplished by the space discarders or "feelers," which insert themselves over the tops of the spaces and quads, forcing them from the line. It then passes out of the machine into the individual channels ready for the distributer. The quads are separated from the spaces and automatically stacked in channels ready for use in the typesetting machine. As spaces and quads average about one-fifth of the matter, it will readily be seen that a great portion of the distribution is accomplished by the discarder, which is capable of handling dead matter for five typesetters, having proved its capacity to be more than 30,000 ems per hour.

The distributer is simple in construction and speedy in operation, and has proven its ability to distribute for two typesetters. Ten thousand ems per hour is a conservative claim for its product. This speed can be maintained constantly. Test runs of one hour each have resulted in a distribution of over 17,000 ems for that limited period. This great speed is attained by the duplication of test wards of letters most used in the font, such as e, o, t, h, n, etc., so arranged as to catch all common syllables and short words in routine. A high

THE COX DISTRIBUTING MACHINE.

rate of speed is not necessary to insure a large product, as the machine is so constructed as to enable the operator to load it with matter to be distributed while it is in operation.

A most important feature embodied in this machine, not to be found in other distributers, is the mechanical means for automatically cleaning the test wards while the distributer is in operation. This is a most important function and has reduced the breakage of type to a minimum.

Arrangements are now being perfected to manufacture the Cox machine on a large scale. Special machinery will be required in order to turn out machines economically, and to enable the company to place the machine on the market at a moderate price. Particulars will be given concerning these matters within a short time.

MACHINE COMPOSITION NOTES AND QUERIES.

CONDUCTED BY GEORGE E. LINCOLN.

Under this head will be given, from month to month, practical information, notes and queries, relating to type composition by machinery. The latest inventions will be published, and the interests of manufacturers, printers and operators sedulously cultivated.

LINOTYPE operators in Spokane receive $4.50 a day of 7½ hours.

THE San Bernardino (Cal.) *Sun* recently installed Thorne machines.

OVER 300 dailies of medium size and circulation use from three to six linotype machines each.

THE Thorne Typesetting Machine Company has entered suit against the Richmond (Va.) States Newspaper Company for $511.40.

THE automatic justifier for the Empire Typesetting machine is reported to be completed, and is on its way to Europe to secure foreign patents.

BOOK machine offices in New York City are quoting 30 to 65 cents per thousand ems for composition — including proofreading and correcting.

OTTO MERGENTHALER, the inventor of the linotype, arrived in America when eighteen years of age, penniless. His invention has made him wealthy.

THE Mergenthaler Linotype Company is perfecting a very simple method by which italics and roman can be set with equal facility upon the same machine.

FONT DISTINGUISHERS.—"Bob," Baltimore, Maryland: In answer to your question whether machines are ever run without the font distinguisher, we reply that in quite a number of large dailies they are run in this manner, but it is not a desirable plan.

THE Riverside (Cal.) *Enterprise* lately purchased a linotype, and in addition to doing its own composition upon it, is also doing much of the *Globe's*.

MIKE MORIARITY, a linotype operator upon the Kansas City *Journal*, was threatened with blood poisoning from getting a squirt of hot metal in his hand recently.

IT is reported that D. O. Mills, father-in-law of Whitelaw Reid, has purchased a controlling interest in the New York *Sun*. If this report is correct, the Linotype will soon be installed in that office.

OVERHEAD BELTING.— G. G., New York City: The chief objection to overhead belting a linotype machine is that the belts so arranged will carry so much dirt into the distributers and magazine.

NEW officers of the Empire Typesetting Machine Company, who were recently elected, are: Hammond Odell, president; Henry Thrush, vice-president; Charles Lowenstein, treasurer, and Albert Salomon, secretary.

THE Washington (D. C.) Typographical Union is having trouble with a machinist society, the latter claiming the exclusive right to be employed in offices, even though but one or two linotype machines are operated.

A. S. ORCHARD, 14 Frankfort street, New York City, has issued a circular of his linotype burner. From the quality of the testimonials it contains, quite a large number of prominent offices have already profited by its use.

THE ORCHARD GAS BURNER.— P. M., of Albany, wishes to know "if the Orchard linotype gas burner is a benefit?" *Answer.*— We judge from the number of offices that are adopting this burner that it must have considerable merit.

CHICAGO Typographical Union, No. 16, has established the following scale for operators and justifiers upon the Empire machines: $20 per week for ten hours per day; $19 per week for nine hours per day, and $22 for nightwork of eight hours per night.

HIGH LINOTYPE LINES.— T. S., of Lancaster, Pennsylvania, asks why his linotype slugs are high. *Answer.*— If all the lines are high, your back knife requires adjustment, or it may have become nicked and scratched, the back of the mold thus forming a foothold for specks of metal to accumulate, and cause high lines.

SQUIRTS AND STICKS IN LINOTYPE MOLDS.— "Linotype," St. Louis, Missouri, asks us why he is at times troubled with "squirts" and "sticks in the mold," and at other times he has no trouble with them at all? *Answer.*— You allow your metal to get too hot at times, and this is undoubtedly the cause of your trouble.

METAL AT LOW TEMPERATURE.—Operator, St. Louis, wishes to know "if a uniformly high temperature does not insure a better face than a low temperature?" *Answer.*— No; keep your metal at as low a temperature as possible to obtain the best results. High heat is productive of squirts and sticking of the slugs in the mold.

THE Newton Copper-Faced Type Company is now profiting from the use of both the movable-type setting and slug-casting machines, as quite a large number of purchasers of both the Thorne and the Empire machines have the type to accompany them copper-faced, and book offices which are using linotypes are adopting the same method upon the slugs that are to have a long run upon their presses.

BURRS ON MATRICES.— H. A., Lancaster, Pennsylvania, asks "the cause of burrs showing upon matrices only three months in use?" *Answer.*— This is nearly always due to the improper care of the space bands. These must be kept dry and smooth and cleaned at least once a day, using only oil and graphite, being careful to wipe entirely dry before using. Remember that a small adhesion upon only *one* space band will, within a short time, injure the entire font of matrices.

IT is pleasing to note the vast improvement in the appearance of the literature, circulars, booklets, etc., which is being issued by the Linotype Company over that which they formerly indulged in. Their present class of literature is not excelled by any firm and is the direct result of having it printed by Redfield Brothers.

W. J. MÜLLER, the representative of the Chicago and Aurora Smelting and Refining Company, Chicago, reports that the linotype metal made by his firm is meeting with great success. It has qualities that specially commend it, and numerous letters have been received testifying to its excellence. The works of this company are at Aurora, Illinois, and Leadville, Colorado.

THE Empire Typesetting Machine Company have recently placed machines in the offices of the W. B. Conkey Company and R. R. Donnelley & Sons Company, of Chicago; Edwards & Boughton, Raleigh, N. C.; Gospel Trumpet Publishing Company, Grand Junction, Mich.; *Herald*, Carbondale, Pa.; G. W. Hansauer, Buffalo, N. Y.; Printing & Publishing Company, Cleveland, Ohio.

DO NOT OIL CAM OR GEAR WHEELS.— A. G. asks if the cams and gear wheels of the Linotype would not wear less if they were kept oiled, stating that he has adopted this course, but has been told not to do so. *Answer.*— These parts should not be oiled; it does them no good whatever, but causes accumulations of dirt, and is injurious. Oil the journals only, and with good oil, about once a week.

TIGHTENING FRICTION PULLEY.— J. A., Philadelphia, writes: "How often must the friction pulley of the linotype be tightened? I am having considerable trouble with this particular part." *Answer.*— The friction pulley is to prevent breakage, and you must not tighten up the pressure. You must ascertain the cause of the extra resistance and remove it or you will have a break. Possibly some oil may have gotten between it and the pulley. Wipe it with a dry cloth to remove any oil or dirt and leave the pressure alone.

B-1

Patent applied for

48 Point   4 A 5 a $7.75

Historical 8 Remedies STRONG DESIGNS

36 Point   5 A 8 a $5.50

North Winds 65 Grow Colder VETERAN CAMPERS

24 Point   8 A 10 a $4.50

Latest Heavyface $829 Artistic Displaying COMMERCIAL PROGRESS RETURNS

18 Point   10 A 16 a $4.00

**Circulation 92 Numbers
Expert Decides
CUTS HIGH PRICES**

12 Point   ·16 A 20 a $3.25

**Wheat Grower 37 Signing Check
Purchased Clothing
AMERICAN FARMS PROSPER**

10 Point   20 A 26 a $3.00

SELECTIONS from many operas will be
rendered during the winter months,
by the Metropolitan Stock Company,
which opens here on November 29

8 Point   22 A 30 a $2.75

TELEPHONE MESSAGES have been sent to active
members, informing them that the Business
Meeting of the Horticultural Societies will be
held next Saturday Afternoon, December 30

6 Point   24 A 36 a $2.50

GREAT TEMPERANCE MOVEMENT
Preparations are already on foot for the large Temperance
Convention to be held in this city next summer.
Delegates will be present from Australia

5 Point on 6 Point Body   24 A 36 a $2.50

OCEAN VOYAGERS CANNOT EMBRACE FRIENDS
Passengers arriving from Europe and other foreign ports cannot
greet their waiting friends until their baggage has been
inspected. This is practically against kissing

Originated and Manufactured by the American Type Founders Co.
In stock and for sale at all its Branches and Agencies

Type Founders Electrotypers

48 Point Trenton   5 A 8 a $5 95

SPECIAL OFFER LADIES' GLOVES.

Here are values that all comers will appreci-ate--choice from an immense line of two-clasp Genuine Kid Gloves, out seam or pique sewn, with heavy embroidered back, in tan, brown, modes, greens, black, English red, white, butter and white embroidered--also a superb quality in two-clasp Mocha Gloves, with three rows of stitching, all the good colors--these gloves should sell and would be good values at $1.35, but for the next week will offer them for $1.00.

Ladies' Kid Gloves at 75c. Nothing can com-pare with them in the city at the price--the demand for them is enormous. Our stock is still complete, but we advise early purchasing to insure all sizes and colors. They come in 4 button, 5 hook and 2 clasp, choice of the em-broidered or plain backs, and are of such quality as you would expect to pay $1.00. The price of this choice selection of Kid Gloves for this

6 Point Trenton   24 A 50 a $2 05

FUN IN TYPE LABELS.

Long before the memory of the oldest living typo the type founders started the fashion of printing trite phrases in illustrating samples of their type for sale. Naturally enough, printers took to past-ing these impressions from display type on the front edges of the cases, to show at a glance what type was contained in the respective cases. This labeling of the type cases with suggestive or ridic-ulous sentences afforded a precedent when it be-came necessary in any office to label cases in use, and the printers took to setting up original prov-erbs and more or less witty notions which flitted through their brains at the time of setting up lines from the cases for use as labels. The typos have

10 Point Trenton   18 A 36 a $2 30

Happy New Year to All

72 Point Trenton   4 A 5 a $8 80

NO DISAPPOINTMENT IN BUYING OF US.

There is no risk of disappointing the re-ceiver if the present is purchased from a house that is recognized as Headquarters for Gentlemen's Apparel, and is patronized by the class of men for whom the present is intended. The splendid preparation we made for our holiday trade, enables us to start into this week with absolutely the most satisfactory assortments in town, of Gentlemen's Fashionable Apparel, as our

12 Point Trenton   15 A 30 a $2 50

ART IN ANCIENT AND MODERN PRINTING.

About the year 1450, there was an in-finite abundance of beauty and richness scattered through the writing rooms of Europe. There were gigantic mass books or missals, with letters of large dimen-sions, legible at long distances; codices of elegant lettering and finish, plain books for daily use, and, last of all, the many different documents in public offices. The aim of the first printers was to have their work make the impression of writ-ten books; this is why the technic and ornamentation of the early days of print-ing were borrowed from manuscripts, and

8 Point Trenton   20 A 40 a $2.15

Barnhart Bros. & Spindler

60 Point Trenton   4 A 6 a $7 60

Kate Greenaways Mignonettes

8-1
Manufactured by the American Type Founders Company

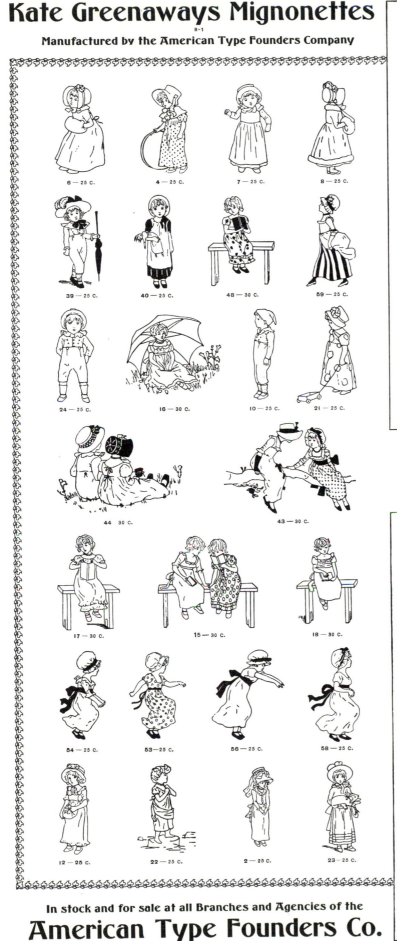

FIRST ARRIVALS

It is a party, do you know,
And there they sit, all in a row,
Waiting till the others come,
To begin to have some fun.

Hark! the bell rings sharp and clear,
Other little friends appear;
And no longer all alone,
They begin to feel at home.

To them a little hard is Fate,
Yet better early than too late;
Fancy getting there forlorn,
With the tea and cake all gone.

Wonder what they'll have for tea;
Hope the jam is strawberry.
Wonder what the dance and game;
Feel so very glad they came.

Set in 8-point Cushing Italic (1)
Series complete in four sizes

Send to nearest Branch of the American Type Founders Company for a complete Specimen of the Kate Greenaways Mignonettes, showing sixty characters

Some children are so naughty,
And some are very good,
But the Genteel Family
Did always what it should.

They put on gloves when they went out,
And ran not in the street;
And on wet days not one of them
Had ever muddy feet.

Then they were always so polite,
And always thanked you so;
And never threw their toys about,
As naughty children do.

Set in 8-point Tristan Italic (15)
Series complete in six sizes

In stock and for sale at all Branches and Agencies of the
American Type Founders Co.

Choicest Lyrics

From

The Realms of Love

Delineating

Cupids Charms and Snares, and Hymen's Joys and Cares,

and Depicting the Gaieties and Gravities

Courtshi

in ev

Gathered from the standard

most popular epic

Idyllic Poets

CHICA

Printed by W

MDCCC

Sizes and Prices.

8 Point,	24 A	50 a	$2 80
10 Point,	20 A	40 a	3 00
12 Point,	18 A	36 a	3 25
18 Point,	12 A	25 a	4 30
24 Point,	9 A	18 a	4 75
36 Point,	6 A	10 a	6 30
48 Point,	5 A	8 a	8 90

SPREAD OF PRINTING.

BOOK VII.

THE FIRST BOOK
PRINTED IN THE ENGLISH LANGUAGE

HE first book printed in the English language, the *Recuyell of the Historyes of Troye,* a stout folio of 351 leaves, does not contain the date of printing, nor the name and place of the printer, but it appears from the introduction that it was tranflated from the French by William Caxton between the years 1469 and 1471. When and where it was printed is a vexed question. Blades thinks that it was printed at Bruges by Colard Manfion and William Caxton, about 1472. Madden thinks it was printed at the monastery of Weidenbach by Mansion and Caxton, who went there about 1474 to learn practical typography. Other bibliographers say that it was printed by Zell at

INVENTION OF TYPOGRAPHY.

The character of typography is not pressing and printing, but mobilization. The winged A is its symbol. The elements unchained, the letters freed from every bond in which the pen or chisel of calligrapher or xylographer held them entangled; the cut character rifen from the tomb of the solitary tablet into the substantive life of the cast types—that is the invention of printing.

MANUFACTURED BY
BARNHART BROS. & SPINDLER.

THE FIFTEENTH CENTURY
Italic Series · is now ready as promised

36 Point Fifteenth Century Italic   5 A   8 a $5 80

PRINTERS WHO HAVE ALREADY PURCHASED THE
Fifteenth Century, will find by using this Italic Series in connection with the Fifteenth Century, they will have two of the most useful series that can be produced for an up-to-date class of work

8 Point Fifteenth Century Italic   24 A   50 a $2 95

COPPER THIN SPACES ARE BECOMING
more popular with printers every day, and those who have ufed them say they are the biggest little thing ever manufactured for the printer.   They are accurately cut by machinery and never break or wear out

10 Point Fifteenth Century Italic   20 A   40 a $2 80

THE GHOST
OF
CAPTAIN BRAND:
OR, a true
ACCOUNT
OF THE
Moft remarkable Appearance
of that renouned *Freebooter* off the Harbor of
NEW YORK
and the laft Time he was ever beheld by the
Eyes of a Living Man.

Being a Narrative of certain
Extraordinary Adventures that befell *Barnaby True, Esq.,*
of the Town of *New York* in the year 1750, or thereabouts.

Written originally by Howard Pyle for Harper's Christmas Number.   Now firft imprinted in this form for the pleafure of thofe friends of the Author, whofe names appear below.

WILMINGTON: Printed for *Annie Poole Pyle, Henry A. du Pont, J. Henry Harper* and *Theodore Roofevelt,* by *John M. Rogers,* on *Orange Street,* oppofite the *Old Malt Houfe.* 1896.

CHINESE METHOD OF PRINTING
Many eminent authors are of the opinion that we are indebted to China not only for playing cards, but for the means of making them. They tell us that playing cards could not have

12 Point Fifteenth Century Italic   18 A   36 a $3 10

STUDENTS ENROUTE
for their homes to enjoy their holiday vacation with parents, relatives and acquaintances

18 Point Fifteenth Century Italic   10 A   20 a $3 75

FIRST NEW YEAR
Ball at Utica Hall, will be held January the twelfth

24 Point Fifteenth Century Italic   6 A   12 a $4 00

Fac-Simile of the type used in
THE XVth CENTURY

48 Point Fifteenth Century Italic   4 A   6 a $7 60

MANUFACTURED BY BARNHART BROS. & SPINDLER, 183-7 MONROE ST., CHICAGO.

FOR SALE BY MINNESOTA TYPE FOUNDRY CO., ST. PAUL; GREAT WESTERN TYPE FOUNDRY, KANSAS CITY; ST. LOUIS PRINTERS SUPPLY CO., ST. LOUIS; GREAT WESTERN TYPE FOUNDRY, OMAHA.

Commercial Script

Made in Four Sizes, by

Inland Type Foundry.

PRICES OF JOB FONTS
18-POINT, $6.00 24-POINT, $7.50
36-POINT, 9.50 48-POINT, 12.00
PRICES OF CARD FONTS
18-POINT, $3.25 24-POINT, $4.25
SPACES AND QUADS ARE
INCLUDED IN SCRIPT FONTS

Wishing You a Happy
and Prosperous New Year.

AGENTS FOR INLAND TYPE

GOLDING & CO.
  BOSTON, PHILADELPHIA,
  NEW YORK AND CHICAGO
WILLIAM E. LOY
  SAN FRANCISCO
DAMON-PEETS CO.
  NEW YORK
GETHER & DREBERT
  MILWAUKEE
PRESTON FIDDIS CO.
  BALTIMORE
GWATKIN & SON
  TORONTO, CANADA

Inland Type Foundry

Inventors of Standard Line Type

217-219 Pine Street   Saint Louis

Bradley ~ Outline ~ Series
Leads all Contour Styles

Beautiful Color Effects are produced
by printing the Bradley in a Delicate
Tint and then registering the Bradley
Outline over it in a Darker Color Ink

Chromatic Type Designs Give Life and
Lustre to Otherwise Commonplace Jobs

Bradley Outline is submitted as an aid to printers
who desire to give their customers artistic effects
in color harmonies. ~ That office which does not use
our beautiful and very useful Bradley Series has
deprived itself and customers of a great pleasure

Makes an Attractive Showing
Combining Beauty with Utility

~ Originated by the American Type Founders Company ~

SCHŒFFER OLD STYLE & INITIALS

HELP the printer to please those desiring neat work.

HORSELESS WAGONS AND TRICYCLES ARE

UPON the market for persons who desire to get them. These will be popular in Summer.

COAL THAT WILL NOT HEAT IS VERY DEAR AT ANY PRICE

AND is not worth the room it occupies.   Two points are to be considered when coal is needed: "Quality and Weight."

SCHŒFFER OLD STYLE INITIALS

A B C D

E F G H I

J K L M N O P

Q R S T U V W X Y Z

DRESSES

FOR SMALL CHILDREN

We have the largest assortment of Clothing for Children of any house in the city.   Prices are the lowest.

 THE **HIGHEST** GRADES OF

Beautiful

Dress

Goods

We are prepared to furnish a complete line of up-to-date patterns in the way of Dress Goods, at prices within reach of all.   Our

$2.00

Goods are most beautiful, and can be recommended.

Fashions & Co.

80 STYLISH AVENUE

LADY SPEAKERS

SOLD BY ALL BRANCHES OF THE AMERICAN TYPE FOUNDERS CO.

The Latest Candidate for the Printer's Favor
A Popular Old Face Entirely Recut

GOTHIC No. 8

Now Ready in Thirteen Sizes, from 5-Point to 60-Point
And Three More Sizes are in Preparation

SIZES AND PRICES OF FONTS

60-Point,	4a	3A,	$13.00	12-Point,	25a	15A,	$2.80
48-Point,	4a	3A,	8.00	10-Point,	28a	16A,	2.50
36-Point,	6a	4A,	5.75	9-Point,	30a	18A,	2.40
30-Point,	7a	4A,	4.30	8-Point,	34a	20A,	2.25
24-Point,	9a	5A,	3.50	6-Point,	38a	22A,	2.00
18-Point,	14a	8A,	3.20	5-Point,	34a	20A,	2.00
14-Point,	20a	12A,	3.00				

Discount, 30 and 5 Per Cent

PRINTERS PLEASE OBSERVE
That the Whole Series is

Uniform in Design

In all the Various Sizes, from the Largest to the Smallest
Notice also that the Face, one of the Most Useful known, has been

IMPROVED THROUGHOUT

The Series is Cast on STANDARD LINE and UNIT SETS
All Sizes from 14-Point to 60-Point are also on Point Sets and all from
8-Point to 12-Point on Point and Half-Point Sets

AGENTS FOR

GOLDING & CO., Boston, New York,
    Philadelphia and Chicago
DAMON-PEETS CO., New York
WM. E. LOY, San Francisco
GETHER & DREBERT, Milwaukee
PRESTON FIDDIS CO., Baltimore
GWATKIN & SON, Toronto, Canada

THIS SERIES

Gothic No. 8 Originated and Cast by the

INLAND TYPE FOUNDRY

217-219 Pine Street, SAINT LOUIS

THE AUTOMATIC JUSTIFYING OF TYPE.

BY C. H. COCHRANE.

TWENTY-FIVE years ago if the average compositor had been told that a machine could be made that would justify lines of type automatically, he would have smiled incredulously, and replied that it required something more than mere mechanical motions for such work — that brains and judgment were essential to the justification of lines, and that no machine could furnish these. Today we know that automatic justifying can be done in at least four radically different ways, all of which may be more or less differentiated, and we can readily believe that four more practical methods may be developed.

The first method to suggest itself was naturally the wedge principle, adopted by the Linotype, and characteristic of most of the type-slug machines that have been patented. Each space consists of two beveled surfaces, which may be closed up like a Hempel quoin, and thus expanded to fill the line.

The next most simple method is that of the crimped compressible space, as used in the Cox machine. The line is simply overset and squeezed down to measure, the spaces being made of sufficiently stiff metal to withstand the side pressure of lockup.

Then we have the MacMillan principle, in which the line is set short, and taken up in a carrier, the spaces being removed by feelers, and larger ones substituted until the line fills the carrier, when no more are admitted. This is the closest approximation to the method of hand composition. Each size of space bears a different nick, into which its appropriate feeler drops, making an electric connection that sets in operation pushers for removing the space and inserting a larger one.

But the most interesting, from a mechanical point of view of the self-justifying mechanisms, are those that accomplish the result by the aid of calculating mechanism. Among these are the Lanston, the Dow and the Thorne. It may be interesting to those who have not studied the matter to explain how it is that a mere machine can perform a calculating operation. The basic principles of calculating mechanism will be the best understood by printers by reference to the familiar printing-press counter. This has a series of wheels, geared one to ten so that when certain wheels bearing figures are brought to the front by the turning of the gears, the number of times the lever has been pulled will appear. Most calculating machines also make use of the one-to-ten gear arrangement, and operations of addition, subtraction, etc., are performed on them by setting the figure-wheels to read one element of the problem, and whirling them around a certain number of times to add, subtract, etc., the other element. In the justification of type it is customary to take a thousandth of an inch as a unit, that being an amount so infinitesimal that it does not matter if a justified line be a half thousandth too long or too short. A calculating device, on the principle of a counter, is then supplied, to count and add up the body-width of each type as set for the line. Suppose that 8-point is being set, and that the " t " represents .040 of an inch, the " h " .050, and " e " .045. As each of these letters is released by its appropriate key, an impulse is sent to the calculator that turns the figure-wheels to register so many thousandths, so that when " the " is set, 145 units are registered. If the measure is 2,167 units wide — 13 ems pica — the compositor will perhaps cease composition at somewhere between 1,600 and 2,000 units. Suppose that he finishes his last word when the calculator registers 1,867, and that there are seven words in the line, requiring six spaces of a size to fill the vacant 300 units. If spaces of any width can be obtained this would give just 50 units to a space, about an en quad of 8-point, and the calculator in recording that fact would be set to deliver spaces of that size.

In the Lanston Monotype machine the thickness of each character, expressed in units, is added in turn to those preceding it, and the total at any time during the composition of the line is shown on a dial before the operator. At the same time the number of spaces is being recorded, and at the completion of the line is also shown. It is obvious the dial could be so constructed with concentric circles and radial lines — the radial lines representing the added units of the line, and the concentric circles numbers of spaces — that by certain figures contained in the areas between the radial and concentric lines the thickness of the necessary spaces in units could be expressed. The operator would have then to refer to this dial at the end of each line, select the proper figure, and operate keys on the keyboard in accordance therewith, to record the thickness of the spaces to be cast. This system differs from the automatic justifying machines in that they are designed to select the proper spaces without any effort whatever on the part of the operator. This is practically what is done in the Monotype mechanism, where the calculator adds up the thousandths, and the operator takes note of the number of spaces required, strikes certain justifying keys, and thus punches holes in a record strip, which gives information to the casting machine to cast spaces of just such a width for that line.

In other patents, as the Thorne, where spaces of ordinary proportion are to be used — about four sizes of spaces — it is obviously impractical to select a certain size, and space the whole line therewith, because there are not enough sizes to permit of even justification in this manner. For instance, a three-em space of 8-point is equivalent to about .037 of an inch, and if these alone were used in justifying a line it might fall .020 long or short. To overcome this difficulty a selecting mechanism is required, which is also a partial calculator, and this takes note of the tendency of the spaces used to overspace or underspace the line, and in either case sets a switch to supply the next size thicker or thinner spaces, as the case may require. Thus the line, as finally justified, lacks in accuracy only a fraction of the difference between the thickness of the last space used and the next size, which is the same result that would be obtained in justification by hand.

In the Dow machine, which is capable of setting and automatically justifying all the different sizes of type in the same machine, from agate to pica, it is obvious that no unit system would be applicable. Any unit system must be arbitrarily prearranged, and the slightest alteration of the body of any of the characters would vitiate the justification. In the practical handling of type also slight changes due to dirt occur, and when fifty or sixty separate letters are assembled in a line these variations are so multiplied that the line is not likely to aggregate the amount previously predetermined. Loose or tight lines may result if the length of the lines are assumed by predetermined standards. In the Dow machine the lines as set are, therefore, separately gauged, and the result of such gauging controls the selection of the combination of spaces necessary to perfectly justify the lines. As has been previously stated, where a limited number of spaces are used, which is absolutely necessary in any practical machine, two adjacent sizes of spaces are likely to be required to justify most of the lines. The problem presented to the automatic justifier is therefore this : Suppose the space to be occupied by the aggregate width of the spaces be .565 of an inch, and eleven spaces exist in the line. By dividing .565 of an inch by eleven, we obtain the result that uniform spaces .051₁₁ of an inch in thickness would justify the line perfectly. Assuming, however, that spaces of .050 of an inch and .055 of an inch only are obtainable, how many of each size are required so that eleven of the two sizes amount to .565 of an inch?

The problem at once becomes one of dividing a quantity *not* into a certain number of *equal parts*, but into a certain number of *unequal parts*, a kind of division out of the ordinary. With the aid of a little calculation not readily done mentally, we find that in this case :

$$8 \times .050 = .400$$
$$3 \times .055 = .165$$
$$\overline{}$$
$$11 \text{ spaces} = .565 \text{ of an inch,}$$

the amount required.

In the Dow machine this problem of *equal or unequal division*, as the case may be, is at once automatically performed without the aid of the operator in any way, and the proper combination of spaces is determined and inserted in their respective places in the line. At the same time the mechanism is recording and preparing to select the spaces necessary to the justification of the line next to follow.

Perhaps this sounds very complex, but in reality the operation is accomplished positively and with little effort. In the astronomical calculating machines, it is only necessary to give the calculator the multiplier and the multiplicand and you get the product. In much the same way in the automatic justifier, you give the calculator the number of units and the number of spaces required in the line, and obtain the desired result with equal accuracy.

There may be other methods of mechanically expanding or contracting a line, or of calculating the size of justifying spaces, and if so time will develop them, and the fittest will eventually survive.

EVEN old-timers in typesetting machines may be surprised, as was the writer, in making a list of all the typesetting machines, to find how many there are which have sought or are seeking approbation. No less than thirty-two of them have come prominently before the public, including the "has beens," the "is's," and the "would-be's." The list includes thirteen or fourteen of the past, seven or eight of the present, and fourteen or fifteen of the future, which latter may or may not come into extended use. It does not include about two hundred patents for typesetting machines, which never existed except on paper or in an incomplete form, and which were presumably all impractical. So far as known, each machine was developed only after long and expensive experimentation, and many of them have yet before them a long course of costly trials before they will be ready for commercial use. The average cost of marketing a typesetting machine is probably to be counted in the hundreds of thousands of dollars, and the one that has found the largest sale is credited with spending over a million in establishing itself. There are seven general mechanical systems employed in typesetting machines (or machines designed to replace hand composition), namely: 1, those machines in which the type is specially nicked, each character being different, in order that each may be dropped automatically in a similarly grooved channel, and pushed out or dropped by levers actuated from a keyboard; 2, those in which a line of matrices are assembled, and a slug or linotype cast therefrom; 3, those in which type are cast as wanted, the selection being determined by the manner of punching a continuous strip of paper; 4, those in which a matrix is impressed with characters, and a stereotype taken therefrom; 5, those which raise letters on a previously formed metal plate; 6, those which form type as wanted from soft metal by compression; 7, those which assist the manipulation of type by hand. Two of these systems are already largely in use, two are partially in use, and the rest are in the experimental stage. The printing fraternity is vitally interested in the determination of which of them will stand the test of time and survive its fellows.

MR. COX, of the Cox Typesetting Machine Company, is feeling happy just now over the consummation of his efforts as inventor of the typesetting machine bearing his name. For five long years he has labored to bring his mechanism to perfection, and has had to encounter and overcome the many usual obstacles that attend the achievement of a new principle in machine composition. The new machine that he has just finished and that will soon be on the market is planned to do the most difficult class of bookwork. It has been in operation for some little time in one of the leading law printing offices of Chicago, and has more than performed the requirements. A speed of 4,000 ems per hour is claimed for it under the most favorable circumstances, and 3,500 ems per hour as the average capacity. We show below a specimen of work by the new perfected machine. With the success now attained Mr. Cox feels convinced that there will be no perfecting "in the field" necessary, and that purchasers will, therefore, be spared considerable expense.

This article was set and automatically justified on the Cox Type-Setting Machine, to show the uniformity of the spacing by the use of the corrugated space. The justification, as can be observed by the even lines, is equal to that of hand composition.

60 POINT   4A 5a $12 25

Convention Nominates
ENTHUSIASM

36 POINT   4A 8a $5 50

Dishonest Speculator Refused Advice
MARKETS CHANGING

10 POINT   20 A 45 a $3 00

SPARKLING AND BRIGHT

Sparkling and bright in liquid light
Does the wine our goblets gleam in ;
With hue as red as the rosy bed
Which a bee would choose to dream in.
Then fill to-night, with hearts as light,
To loves as gay and fleeting
As bubbles that swim on the beaker's brim
And break on the lips while meeting.

8 POINT   20 A 50 a $2 75

COME, SEND ROUND THE WINE

Come, send round the wine, and leave points of belief
To simpleton sages and reasoning fools ;
This moment's a flower too fair and brief
To be withered and stained by the dust of the schools.
Your glass may be purple, and mine may be blue,
But while they are filled from the same bright bowl,
The fool who would quarrel for difference of hue
Deserves not the comfort they shed o'er the soul.

24 POINT   6 A 15 a $4 50

Peculiar Business Methods Hastened Complete Failure
INJUDICIOUS ADVERTISERS

54 POINT   4A 5a $10 25

Constituents Discouraged
MISREPRESENT

For sale at all Branches of the
AMERICAN TYPE FOUNDERS COMPANY

Circular Black—A Dainty Design....

PATENTED

Spring Opening

•• Prices ••

24 Point . . . 5 A 10 a	$4.00
18 Point . . . 6 A 14 a	3.20
12 Point . . . 8 A 20 a	2.55
9 Point . . . 10 A 28 a	2.35
6 Point . . . 12 A 32 a	2.10

Housekeepers should attend this most extraordinary Ingrain Carpet Sale of the Season. The Goods are fresh from the loom and the products of the most celebrated mills. All are the newest patterns and most exquisite colorings.

Our "Dundee" Reversible Rug is sure to meet with popular favor. These floor coverings are suitable for large rooms and are exact reproductions of the finest Egyptian Body Brussels.

Hartshorn & Cunningham
•• London • Paris • New York ••

March 6, 1898

MENU

Tomato Soup	Mock Turtle

Creamed Corned Beef

Broiled Sirloin Steak

Sweetbreads, Buttered

Fried Potatoes   New Green Peas

Celery Salad

Crackers   Cheese

Cucumbers

Home-Made Mince Pie

Cottage Pudding   Floating Island

Coffee   Ice Cream   Fruit

$1,900,051.00   Germantown, March 4, 1898

First National Bank of the Universe

Pay to the Officers of the Monmouth Physical Culture Society, or order, the sum of One Million, Nine Hundred Thousand and Fifty-one Dollars.

Ida Clare, Cashier   Timothy J. Graball, President

Concert and Ball

given by the

·:· Harmony Legion ·:·

Monday Evening, April 4, 1898

·:·

Elks Hall

·:·

Dancing until 3 A.M.   Ladies' Ticket, $1.50

Program   Dancing

Overture · · Orchestra	Grand March · · Sousa
Flute Solo · W. Cooke	Waltz · · · · Straus
Duet · · · Dare Bros.	Polka · · · · Roller
Recitation · · J. Jones	Plain Quadrille · Downs
Songs · · · Glee Club	Galop · · · · Werner
Piano Solo · A. Prides	Waltz · · · · · King

M. Peter Voigt, Master of Ceremonies

·:· Sold at all Branches of the American Type Founders Company ·:·

Tell Text Series.

4 A 10 a   36 Point Tell Text $6 25

Cast from Copper-Mixed Metal

12 A 40 a   6 Point Tell Text $2 50

On February the 10th, 1898, the Metropolitan Opera House, Corner Potomac and Conococheague Streets, will be opened by Spielman Brothers as a first-class Theatre in every respect, and patrons can rest assured that the best companies traveling can be seen at the Opera House any time after the date mentioned above. For the first three nights the admission will be free in order to let the public know that we have the best talent as well as the finest theatre in town. We invite one and all to take advantage of the free admission tickets.

10 A 30 a   10 Point Tell Text $3 00

William Shakspeare, the great dramatic poet, not of England only, but of the world, was born at Stratford on the Avon, in the county of Warwick, April 23rd, 1564. Of his early life, of his education, of his personal appearance, manners

5 A 12 a   24 Point Tell Text $4 75

Improved Commercial Conditions
Discouraged Explorers Returning

3 A 6 a   60 Point Tell Text $9 60

Printers Machinery

5 A 15 a   18 Point Tell Text $3 60

Northwestern Life Insurance Associations
Coal Merchants are Complaining Terribly

8 A 25 a   12 Point Tell Text $3 00

Commencing May 15th, 1898, Excursions will run from Chicago to Milwaukee every Wednesday and Saturday night. Tickets can be purchased at the River Front Office.

12 A 40 a   8 Point Tell Text $3 00

The name of William Caxton will ever be held in grateful remembrance by the world of letters for he it was who introduced the art of printing into England. He was born in the county of Kent in the year 1413, and at the age of fifteen was put as an apprentice to a merchant of London. In consideration of his integrity and good behavior

3 A 6 a   48 Point Tell Text $7 25

Useful Attractive Letter

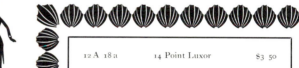

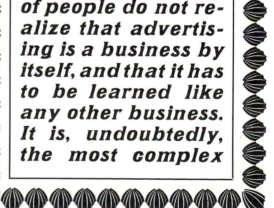

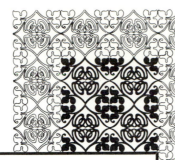

C. E. KING, PRESIDENT.   D. K. TICE, VICE-PRES.
GRASON BEACHLEY, SEC. AND TREAS.

THE GRAND CHAINLESS BICYCLE COMPANY

MANUFACTURERS OF THE

GRAND CHAINLESS BICYCLES

AND SOLE MANUFACTURERS
OF THE FAMOUS

"ARLINGTON"

OR

TANDEM WHEELS.

AGENTS: AGENTS:
ARNO BICYCLE CO.,   HUGO BICYCLE CO.,
NEW YORK.   PHILADELPHIA.

FACTORY AND GENERAL OFFICES

CHICAGO, ILLINOIS.

SIZES AND PRICES.

6 Point Menu No. 1	40 A	$1 40
6 Point Menu No. 2	40 A	$1 60
6 Point Menu No. 3	40 A	$1 75
8 Point Menu No. 4	30 A	$1 75
10 Point Menu No. 5	24 A	$1 75
12 Point Menu No 6	20 A	$2 00
12 Point Menu No. 7	20 A	$2 25

THE DISCOVERY OF PRINTING.

It is not a little singular that the history of printing, that art which commemorates all other inventions, and which hands down to posterity every important event, is so enveloped in mystery that the ablest minds in Europe have had long and acrimonious disputations respecting the question to what place and to what person the invention is rightfully due. There is not space here to give even an outline of these controversies; we can merely give the result. The two cities which claim the discovery are Haarlem or Haerlem, a city of North Holland, and Mentz, in Germany on the Rhine. The dispute, however, as Mr. Timperley properly observes, has turned rather on words than facts, arising from the different definitions of the word printing. If the honor is to be awarded from the discovery of the principle, it is

25 A 150 a   6 Point Marshall Italic $4 90

WILLIAM CAXTON

The name of William Caxton will ever be held in grateful remembrance by the world of letters, for he it was who introduced the art of printing into England. He was born in the county of Kent in the year 1413, and at the age of fifteen was put as an apprentice to a merchant of London. In consideration of his integrity and good behavior, his master bequeathed him a small sum of money as a capital with which to trade. He was soon chosen by the Mercer's Company to be their agent in Holland and Flanders, in which countries he spent about twenty years. While there, the new invention of the art of printing was every-

20 A 125 a   8 Point Marshall Italic $5 00

IMAGE PRINTS OF THE FIFTEENTH CENTURY.

One of the purposes to which early printing was applied was the manufacture of engraved and colored pictures of sacred personages. These pictures, or image prints, as they are called by bibliographers, were made of many sizes; some of them are but little larger than the palm of the hand, others are of the size of a half sheet of foolscap. In a few prints there are peculiarities of texture which have provoked the thought

20 A 100 a   10 Point Marshall Italic $5 25

MANUFACTURED BY BARNHART BROS. & SPINDLER, CHICAGO, ILL.

FOR SALE BY MINNESOTA TYPE FOUNDRY CO., ST. PAUL; GREAT WESTERN TYPE FOUNDRY, KANSAS CITY; ST. LOUIS PRINTERS SUPPLY CO., ST. LOUIS; GREAT WESTERN TYPE FOUNDRY, OMAHA.

PRINTERS AND TEMPERANCE.

EACH trade or profession as well as each nation has its accepted typical characteristics. It does not matter that the accepted type no longer in any way represents those who follow the trade supposed to be characterized by it. It is all one. Our great-great-grandfathers were amused with the idea that all printers were drunken, and it is still considered a pleasant thing by those not acquainted with the sentiments or aspirations of the modern printer to class him and his morals with the printers of generations back at a time when both drinking and profanity and loose living were common among the people because approved of by the fashion of the day. At the recent banquet of the Old-Time Printers, of Chicago, Mayor Harrison jestingly spoke of the drinking habits of printers and among other things said that on the night of his father's last election to the mayoralty there were only two sober printers in the *Times* composing room, and they were two who had taken the Keeley Cure. Some fifty years ago possibly this would have been thought a pretty stroke of wit, and there is of course no doubt that Mayor Harrison, on this occasion, had no wish to be otherwise than amusing. But the Old-Time Printers did not like the pleasantry, and have not been slow in expressing their disapproval. Printers have their faults like other human beings, but they are no more given to dissipation than editors, lawyers or other professional men or tradesmen. If the printers were all drunk on the night of the last election of the late Mr. Carter Harrison, one is forced to the conclusion that they were unable to keep pace with the conviviality of the occasion, and being unaccustomed to stimulants they were more readily overcome than the rest of the town.

NEW METHODS, NEW IDEAS, AND SOME PRINTERS.

AN old printer, who has had much to do with the business end of the printing trade, arraigns printers generally for their lack of appreciation of the new devices and new methods sought to be introduced to the trade from time to time. He claims that probably nothing stands more in the way of the introduction and adoption of new and labor-saving devices than the old-fogyism of the workman, and possibly in no industry is this more apparent than in that of printing. So well understood is this among those who have dealings with printers that they ridicule the oft-quoted term of printers being the "most intelligent of all the craftsmen." It is an undeniable fact that the majority of printers will continue to use old, antiquated methods and means of accomplishing their work rather than adopt the many more useful devices which are constantly being perfected, and if any new device is adopted at all it is rarely by their sanction.

Take, for instance, the introduction of the Hempel quoins. They were condemned in many offices. They have been thrown under the imposing stones with epithets thrown after them, with gratification shining upon the face of the printer driving up the old wooden quoins a moment later. Had it been left to the printers, wooden quoins would still be in demand.

A veteran salesman of printers' material declares that he would under no circumstances permit a new device, however. meritorious, to enter an office the sale of which depended upon the decision of the printers. His experience has taught him that the slightest derogatory remark made against the device by any one of the employes, even before the merits of the device are understood, will have the effect of the article being condemned or rejected.

A case came under notice lately. A salesman left a new mailing machine subject to acceptance, if found satisfactory. A number gathered around, looked contemptuously at it and pronounced it "no good." It was returned without even having had a trial. If they had known that a large number of these same mailers were in successful use their verdict would have been different.

Printers, apparently, do not stop to think that the manufacturers looked well into the merits of their products, and that skilled, up-to-date craftsmen and mechanical engineers had been consulted and had recognized the usefulness, utility, convenience or economy of the goods offered for sale before money had been invested in the manufacture. They simply see a new article or method which is different from what they are accustomed to and condemn it. Some condemn it through a disinclination to investigate ; others because they had always gotten along without it, and others again because they think it a new-fangled idea gotten up by some "jay shoemaker," who should not be encouraged anyway.

Having worked in quite a number of offices I have noticed that when a new article would be sent to the composing room without instructions that that article would be used without a comment, or if a comment was made it would be one recognizing its advantages. But should it be delivered with the request that a report be made upon its utility, then every member of the force would imagine himself an expert and alleged imperfections would be dilated upon until no one would have the hardihood to speak a word in its favor.

This is not done with malice, but is usually the result of the desire to prove to their employers that they have a knowledge of what is required to do their work, that superior to that of any inventor, manufacturer or dealer in the land.

This state of affairs exists to such an extent that it works many financial hardships and much perplexity to the one who has money invested in these manufactured articles, and were it not for the competition which exists and which compels the owners of printing offices to adopt these new devices, it is safe to say that no improvement in our offices would be in evidence today over the times when Gutenberg first invented the art of printing.

KELMSCOTT SERIES

Morris' Famous Face Cast on Standard Line

5a 4A, $7.25   48-POINT KELMSCOTT   L. C. $2.90; C. $4.35

RELICS OF OLD TIMES
Excellent Styles Revived 28

8a 4A, $5.00   36-POINT KELMSCOTT   L. C. $2.45; C. $2.55

COPYING SUPERB PRINTS
Ancient Typography Good 35

10a 5A, $4.30   30-POINT KELMSCOTT   L. C. $2.10; C. $2.20

UNIQUE AND HANDSOME LETTERS
Designed by Early Followers of Gutenberg 14

12a 6A, $3.50   24-POINT KELMSCOTT   L. C. $1.65; C. $1.85

SUPERIOR MAKE
Improved Fonts 60

18a 9A, $3.20   18-POINT KELMSCOTT   L. C. $1.60; C. $1.60

GOLDEN TYPE FONT
Copy Kelmscott Press 72

24a 12A, $3.00   14-POINT KELMSCOTT   L. C. $1.50; C. $1.50

EDITIONS DE LUXE PUBLISHED
Artistic Printing of Unique Books Liked
Gratifies the Highest Esthetic Taste 83

30a 15A, $2.80   12-POINT KELMSCOTT   L. C. $1.40; C. $1.40

MEETING A DEMAND FOR NOVELTIES
Old Wine Poured from New Bottles Satisfactory
Palates of Exquisite Change-Lovers Tickled 64

30a 16A, $2.50   10-POINT KELMSCOTT   L. C. $1.25; C. $1.25

REJUVINATION OF THE ANTIQUE MANNER
William Morris' self-imposed task as a worker in the fields of political science, literature and typography, gave him ample pleasure, and it is likely that the results of his artistic labor will not be so very quickly forgotten. 175

35a 18A, $2.25   8-POINT KELMSCOTT   L. C. $1.15; C. $1.10

INJUNCTION THAT SHOULD BE GENERALLY HEEDED
The Chicago Society of Proofreaders recommends the abrogation of the diphthongs in words which have become incorporated in our language, including legal and medical terms, and the substitution of e for them; hence, spell archeological, diarrhea, subpena, eolian, etc.; also in proper names, thus: Cesar, Etna, Esculapius, Linnean, etc. $205

INLAND TYPE FOUNDRY,

Manufacturers of the Kelmscott Series   217-219 Pine Street, SAINT LOUIS

STANDARD LINE AND UNIT SETS
HHHHHHHHH HHHHHHHHH

THE SLUGMAKER, TYPECASTER OR TYPE-SETTER.

AN experienced observer has contributed his views on the status of machine composition to THE INLAND PRINTER. No subject is interesting employing printers more than the matter of composition, and the benefit of this expert opinion will be appreciated by our readers.

There are three natural divisions into which composing machines are often classed by those interested in their present and future, namely: The slugmaking or lineforming machines, the typecasting and composing machines, and the typesetting machines proper, that serve simply to compose foundry type. Each of these systems has its friends and advocates, and each is represented by several machines now on the market or actively engaged in seeking a place on the market. The next decade will undoubtedly determine whether each and all of these systems will survive, or whether one or more of them may die, and the printing public is almost as vitally interested in the outcome as are the inventors, promoters and capitalists who are backing the respective machines. The composing machine is making history rapidly nowadays, and all persons connected with the printing trades are vitally interested in the sort of history made.

The inventors of composing machines turn things over with their innovations, and the companies who market the machines make war upon each other, which war will continue until standard types of machines are developed, and the makers combine and form a trust to regulate the output. In the meantime every proprietor of a printing office desires to know what machines are coming out on top or near the top, that he may provide himself with those that shall prove the fittest, or be able to "get from under" in case he is interested in a machine liable to take a financial tumble.

Without favor or prejudice toward any, it seems to me that it is possible to look into the situation somewhat and predict with some certainty a little of the future, and arrive at conclusions as to the prospects and field open for the three classes of machines as we have divided them. Each class presents special advantages of its own, and special disadvantages, which are so fully known that a statement of them here can injure no one, yet may help those who are studying the machines, and wondering which are best for their use. The slug machines, or linecasting machines, or linotypes, or whatever they may be called by the printers of the future, may naturally be considered first, as being the first in the field, and as having outsold all other machines combined, this success being attributable almost wholly to the fact that they have cheapened the product — that is, reduced the cost of typesetting more than any other machine up to the present time. The outcry raised against this class of composing machines, by those interested in other classes, is that they reduce the quality of the product, and have given a setback to

fine printing, which has been a damage to the art. It must be admitted that the slug machines have in many cases reduced the quality of the printing, and on the other hand, their universal adoption is proof positive that they have more than offset this by other advantages. But the question just now is — Will they hold their own in the face of incoming machines producing a perfect product at the same cost as the slug product? If so, how will they do it?

There are good reasons for believing that the slug machine will remain, and that the line system, introduced by Mergenthaler as a substitute for Gutenberg's individual type system, will retain a permanent place in printing. If the slug machine were coming in now, just as the one-man typesetting machine is coming on the stage, it might be that the slug machine would fall out of the race; but it has been with us for a decade, and its faults and shortcomings have been recognized and dealt with by the manufacturers in such an intelligent manner that the quality of the work has steadily improved, and today some of the best publications in the country are using the linotype. The enterprise and ability manifested in the production of new type faces, and the constant simplification and improvement of the machinery, have made the linotype available for a better class of work with each succeeding year, and it is evident that further improvements will come, and that within a few years there will be little criticism of the quality of the product. Possession is nine points of the law, and the slug machine certainly has possession of the field, and cannot be driven out until something both better and cheaper, backed by ample capital, is offered in its place. The only natural conclusion is that this class of machine is here to stay, and that the linotypes will go right on doing business regardless of the success or failure of other machines, and it is also probable that several other slug machines will eventually find something of a sale, on the strength of the market made for them by the Mergenthaler.

The typecaster, or machine that casts its type as it is set, is a unique production, with manifest advantages, but as yet largely experimental. Though a number of them have been built, and used more or less, yet, at the present time, there is no authentic knowledge in the trade of the quantity, quality, and general character of the product that can be obtained from them. With the exception of a very few, who have had personal experience with them, the commercial possibilities of the machines are as unknown as they were when this system was first projected some twelve years ago. That they are capable of casting really good type, at a sufficient speed for commercial purposes, and of setting and justifying it in a satisfactory manner, has been demonstrated; but whether they can do this day in and day out, in competition with slug machines and typesetting machines that deliver foundry type, is something that no one absolutely knows. Those interested in the machines say that they can, and have backed their opinion with their money; their competitors say they cannot. Time alone can determine.

The advantages peculiar to these machines — we refer now principally to the Lanston and Goodson systems — are that by separating the keyboard from the rest of the work they make it possible for small printing offices to own low-priced keyboards on which they can do composition, which may afterward be set and cast at some central plant in any size or face of type provided at the central plant. Thus the small printer may obtain the advantages of a composing machine with no great outlay of capital. This advantage would seem to open a wide field for these machines — a field which they could control regardless of the slug machines and of the machines that set foundry type. If they ever occupy this field, doubtless they will retain it; but as yet there are no central plants to cast and set the type for such keyboards, neither are there more than three or four type faces cut as a working basis for such central plants. Until some concern spends a fortune in cutting and perfecting faces and sizes of type for the use of typecasting machines the system is minus its greatest advantage, and while waiting for such faces the typecaster, in my opinion, must be regarded as an experiment. When I add that my knowledge of typecasting machines cost me in its acquirement fully $1,000, it will be admitted, I think, that I speak advisedly.

The one-man typesetting machine, setting foundry-made type, and justifying and delivering it on the galley, is the last class of machines for our consideration. It was the first machine thought of, and no other machine would be in existence today if a full-fledged automatic typesetter had made its appearance thirty years ago. The thing sought by all inventors has been the reduction of labor in setting type. The formation of line slugs and attaching of a typecaster to the composer have been done merely as a means toward the desired end. No maker of a composing machine has cared to go into a competition with the typefoundries in the manufacture of type faces — they have simply been forced into cutting faces by circumstances. Therefore, if these conclusions be just, the typesetting machine handling foundry type is the ideal machine — mechanically, because it does the real thing aimed at; and commercially, because it does not interfere with the manufacturers of type.

The success of the typesetting machine, however, has been limited heretofore, because it was necessary to employ two or three operators to a machine, thus rendering the saving quite moderate. It could not produce matter at a price to compete with the slug machine, but it could produce matter of a quality equal to hand-set type. Here it found its field, necessarily limited in comparison with the slug machine, which cut the cost in half.

But now a new era is dawning in typesetting machines. Within a year the printing public will have their choice of buying no less than five kinds of machines that set, distribute and justify type, employing but one man to the composing and justifying, and a part of a boy's time to the distributing. These are the McMillan, Thorne, Empire, Dow and Cox. McMillan was the first to put a justifier in operation, the Dow and Cox machines have been before the public but a few months, and the Thorne and Empire justifiers are understood to be coming along soon. Just how warm a reception these will meet with from the trade is yet a matter of conjecture. Probably all of them will have some sales, and, as their respective merits or demerits become known, some one or two will begin to outsell the rest, and thus become the recognized occupant of this field. They will doubtless set type at about the same cost per 1,000 ems that matter is produced on the Mergenthaler. They will not drive out the latter, because it is too valuable a machine to be cast aside, and too many interests are involved; and further, the linotype slug has some advantages in the way of keeping matter standing, etc., that type has not.

Thus it appears, if we have reasoned correctly, that in the future we are to count upon both slug machines and one-man typesetters, but that the typecaster has yet to prove its fitness to survive. It may have its test very soon, as rumor has it that a battery of forty of these machines is to be placed on trial in the office of the New York *Sun*. If they survive the ordeal in that office, where nothing but high-class typography will pass muster, then the typecaster must also be accepted as an element to be counted upon in the future of composing machines.

What will be the prices of these machines when competition becomes fierce among the various companies and systems? This is almost as interesting a problem to the printers who will buy them as is the question of the productive excellencies which we have been discussing. One maker has informed me that the shop cost of producing his machine is less than $400, and that he expects to be able to undersell the market, if necessary. But if experience goes for anything, the makers of composing machines are not price-cutters, and the man who buys an A No. 1 composing machine, up to date, in 1900 may expect to burn a hole in his pocket for larger figures than those represented by that date.

———

THE CONVERSE TYPESETTING AND JUSTIFYING MACHINE.— It appears that something less than justice has been done this mechanism in our note on the British patent last month. Next month we hope to give further attention to the matter and to give the machine its full meed of critical notice.

MACHINE COMPOSITION

CONDUCTED BY GEORGE E. LINCOLN.

IN the employ of the Mergenthaler Company are some of the brightest mechanical geniuses of the age, and in consequence of this fact we naturally expect some day to see constructed a spaceband which will not always present the same surface to the mold when the lines are cast. If such a device could be made, the trouble with burs would be quite a thing of the past. With the present spaceband it matters not whether a thick or thin spaced line is cast; the same spot on the slide is always in contact with the mold. No metal ever collects on the wedge side of the spaceband. While the Baltimore machines have not this objectionable slide, still, for various reasons, they are not recommended. But whether it will be a step wedge, a split wedge, an inner wedge driven from the bottom, or a wedge at all, or whatever the nature of the device, all can rest assured that the talent which overcomes these obstacles will do so in the most practical and intelligent manner when they do accomplish it.

————————

THIS age of speed and economy, in which the typesetting machines are playing such an active and prominent part in the printing industry, is being greatly assisted by auxiliary methods, one of these being the copper-facing of body type for the use of the movable typesetting machines, and the same means applied to the slugs of the linotype, thereby, in the one case, doubling at least the durability of the type, and in the other guaranteeing the slugs from disastrous wear during long runs upon the press. Although we occasionally notice that a linotype metal manufacturer states that his metal will withstand a run of 100,000 impressions, still it is hardly probable that any book printer would knowingly have the hardihood to attempt such an experiment, fearing the costly result should it prove a failure. As to its economy for the purposes of the movable typesetting machines, it is quite probable that had the promoters of this class of machinery insisted that type for their use should be thus treated, their machines would be more in evidence today in the book offices, and the linotype would not have such a virgin field to invade. It is a curious fact that the movable typesetting machine companies permitted the printer to discover the financial saving of copper-facing whereby he would not be required to purchase a new font of type in years by the expenditure of less than one-fourth its first cost. And it is also singular that the type founders do not recognize this fact and encourage its use, and thus lessen the jeopardy which confronts them today of eventually losing the entire body-type trade in the book offices, as they already have in the newspaper offices.

————————

WE believe our readers will appreciate the opportunity accorded them of viewing the Converse machine, which shows the rapid progress made in its construction and also gives general appearance of the machine. Lest anyone should have been misled by our description of the automatic justifier given in our April issue we here give its operation in full: The depression of the space key, following the setting of a word, causes the insertion of a wedge into the line, the thin edge of the wedge being between the type and maintaining a separation between it and the following word. When as many type are thus assembled as the completed line will properly contain, the depression of the "line lever" by the operator sets into operation the justifying mechanism, from which point on, the operations of justification are entirely automatic. First, the wedges contained in the line are driven in to spread the words apart until the line is expanded to the length of the containing lineholder, which is the width of the desired column. The

distance that the wedges are driven through the line determines the selection of the proper sizes of spaces necessary to the exact justification of the line. Nine sizes of spaces are provided as the machine is now constructed, which gives a range

CONVERSE TYPESETTING MACHINE.

from about the thickness of a four-em space to an em quad; though the machine might be made with either a greater or less number of sizes of spaces, if desirable. Most lines of type cannot be justified by the insertion of a single size of spaces. Two sizes must be used, and a very simple arrangement enables the machine to select the proper number of each of two adjacent sizes of spaces and cause their substitution for the wedges in the line. In such lines the first space, or spaces, inserted are a little less in thickness than the space between the words, resulting in a looseness of the line; after the insertion of each space and the withdrawal of the corresponding wedge, the wedges remaining in the line are again driven in to take up this looseness, distributing it between the spaces still occupied by wedges. As this looseness accumulates it will become sufficient to allow the wedges to pass through the line enough further to cause the space-selecting mechanism to insert the next larger size of spaces, with which the justification of the line will be completed. Thus if a line is .24 of an inch too short before justification and requires six spaces, the spaces inserted will be each .04 of an inch in thickness, exactly justifying the line; but if this line is .26 of an inch too short, the selecting mechanism will insert four spaces each .04 inch thick, and two spaces each .05 inch thick, making up the .26 inch. The justification proceeds automatically while the operator is assembling the next line. It is very rapid — the justifier in the present machine being geared to a speed of about eight thousand ems per hour, but is capable of a higher speed it desirable. The lineholder and the spacing wedges are, after use, returned to the point of assemblage to be used again, the line delivered on the galley, either with or without a lead, as desired, all these operations being entirely automatic.

Rountree Brothers

announce the autumn show
of the latest foreign fashions in their new

Dressmaking

reception parlors, on Wednesday,
August the twenty=fourth.
There will be a recherché display of the Paris
and London tailors' and dressmakers'
richest and rarest creations in

Light Wraps, Gowns, Costumes,

Fabrics and Garnitures,

elegant laces and lingerie, fashionable fancies, etc.

It will be an exceptional exhibition of exclusive
novelties = the handsomest freshest foreign fancies in
feminine fashions and furnishings.

Rountree Brothers

NESTOR SCRIPT.
18 Point, 9 A 25 a $ 6.00
24 Point, 7 A 20 a 8.00
36 Point, 5 A 15 a 9.50
48 Point, 4 A 10 a 11.00

MANUFACTURED BY BARNHART BROS. & SPINDLER, CHICAGO, ILL.
FOR SALE BY MINNESOTA TYPE FOUNDRY CO., ST PAUL; GREAT WESTERN TYPE FOUNDRY, KANSAS CITY; ST. LOUIS PRINTERS SUPPLY CO., ST. LOUIS; GREAT WESTERN TYPE FOUNDRY, OMAHA.

Faust Text.

ANGLO-SAXON
BOOK OF POEMS

by

Several Distinguished Poets.

Barnhart Bros. & Spin

Chicago, Illinois.

Faust Text.

8 Point, 24A 50a $2.50
10 Point, 20A 40a 3.00
12 Point, 18A 36a 3.50
18 Point, 10A 20a 3.75
24 Point, 8A 12a 4.00
36 Point, 5A 8a 4.50

Electrotype cut of Flag, 75 cents.

A Plea for an Anglo-Saxon Alliance.

By Alfred Austin.

What is the voice I hear
  On the winds of the Western sea?
Sentinel, listen from out Cape Clear
  And say what the voice may be.

'Tis a proud, free people, calling loud to a people
    proud and free.

And it says to them: "Kinsmen, hail,
  We severed have been too long.
Now let us have done with a wornout tale--
  The tale of an ancient wrong;
And our friendship last long as love doth last,
  And be stronger than death is strong."

Answer them, sons of the self-same race,
  And blood of the self-same clan,
Let us speak with each other face to face,
  And answer as man to man;
And loyally love and trust each other as none but
    free men can.

Now fling them out the breeze,
  Shamrock, thistle, and rose;
And the star spangled banner unfurl with these--
  A message to friends, to foes,
Wherever the sails of peace are seen, and
    wherever the war wind blows--

A message to bond and thrall to wake
For, wherever we come, we twain,
The throne of the tyrant shall rock and quake,
  And his menace be void and vain,
For you are lords of a strong, young land, and we
  are lords of the main.

Yes, this is the voice on the bluff March gale,
  We severed have been to long,
But now we have done with a wornout tale--
  The tale of an ancient wrong;
And our friendship last long as love doth last, and
    be stronger than death is strong.

Manufactured by BARNHART BROS. & SPINDLER, CHICAGO, ILL.
FOR SALE BY MINNESOTA TYPE FOUNDRY CO., ST. PAUL; GREAT WESTERN TYPE FOUNDRY, KANSAS CITY; ST. LOUIS PRINTERS SUPPLY CO., ST. LOUIS; GREAT WESTERN TYPE FOUNDRY, OMAHA.

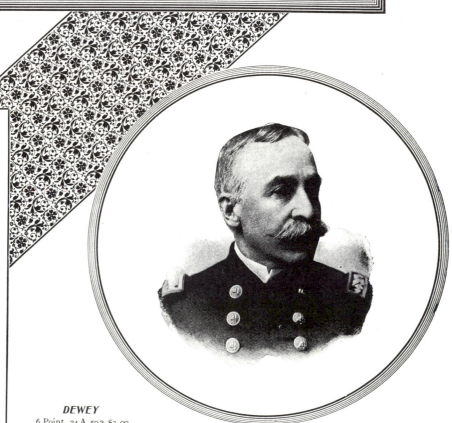

Standard Line

MOSSBACKS
Fight Order 9

That a perfect system of spelling English is needed is a fact none can strongly deny. 92

Progress in amending the current modes of spelling is opposed mainly by the fossils occupying chairs in back-number colleges. 45

BETTER ORTHOGRAPHY
Desired by Everybody $60

OSBORNE ❧ SPECIMEN

SUGGEST REFORM
Faults Eradicated 75

With barely an exception, the foremost philologists, as well as the makers of the leading dictionaries, are advocates of scientific, precise and perfect ways of indicating sounds. 83

Why not abolish the present illogical and misleading orthography, which makes it an impossibility for anyone to ascertain correct pronunciations from printed speech, and is a stumbling block to foreigners as well as to ourselves in studying English? $46

NEW SPELLINGS
Easier System 28

Unit Set Type

INLAND
TYPE
FOUNDRY

OSBORNE SERIES
Prices of Fonts

48-Point	5a	4A	$7.25
36-Point	6a	4A	5.00
30-Point	8a	5A	4.30
24-Point	9a	6A	3.50
18-Point	12a	8A	3.20
14-Point	18a	10A	3.00
12-Point	22a	15A	2.80
10-Point	25a	16A	2.50
8-Point	28a	18A	2.25
6-Point	32a	20A	2.00

6-Point Border No. 601
Fonts of 48 inches, each, $1.25

INLAND AGENTS

DAMON-PEETS CO.,
New York
PRESTON FIDDIS CO.,
Baltimore
WILLIAM E. LOY,
San Francisco
GETHER & DREBERT,
Milwaukee
GWATKIN & SON,
Toronto, Canada
GOLDING & CO.,
Boston, Philadelphia,
New York and Chicago

OSBORNE SERIES
Patent Pending
Cast on Standard Line and Unit Sets
Originated and Made by the
INLAND TYPE FOUNDRY
217-219 Pine Street
SAINT LOUIS, MO. U.S.A.

June 1898 617

44 Point American Flags, $2.50 per Dozen

24 POINT   6 A 10 a $5 00

Doric Italic—For War Scare-Heads

Made also in 6, 8, 10, 12 and 18 Point Sizes

60 POINT   4 A 5 a $15 50

CUBA FREED

36 POINT   5 A 7 a $8 75

Spanish Flags Driven from Western Seas

48 POINT   4 A 5 a $10 75

BIG INDEMNITY

48 POINT   4 A 5 a $10 75

Patriots Happy!

36 POINT   5 A 7 a $8 75

PHILIPPINE ISLANDS

30 POINT   5 A 7 a $6 50

And Porto Rico Held under Stars and Stripes!

AMERICAN TYPE FOUNDERS COMPANY

Chamfer Condensed—For War Scare-Heads

72 POINT   7 A $9 90

SECOND EDITION!

96 POINT   5 A $12 80

SURRENDERS

No. 5142C (one color) $1.25
No. 5143C (two colors) $2.00

40 POINT   10 A $4 90

BESIEGED COAST TOWNS FORCED TO CAPITULATE

EXTRA

SPANISH

48 POINT
7 A $6 15

60 POINT   7 A $7 15

ACCURATE GUNNERY

ARMADA CAUGHT

36 POINT   10 A $3 75

ARMY AND NAVY FORCES COMBINE

22 POINT   18 A $3 00

FIERCE FIGHTING REPORTED NEAR BAHIA HONDA

18 POINT   30 A $3 60

THE FLYING SQUADRON POUNDS THE FORTIFICATIONS AROUND HAVANA AND GENERAL MILES LEADS THE ARMY

28 POINT   14 A $4 00

AMERICAN TRIUMPH

SOLD AT ALL BRANCHES OF THE

...AMERICAN TYPE FOUNDERS CO...

36 Point No. 2   5 A 8 a $6.00

Words from Manchester, being the true relation of the battell fought, wherein the Lord Strange lost many men, as sent in a private letter.

12 Point No. 2   8 A 24 a $3.19

An ordinance concerning the late rebellious insurrections in the County of Kent, whereby a committee is appointed from the said County, to seize all armes forthwith.

12 Point No. 1   12 A 32 a $3.08

Sure methods of improving estates, by planting oak, elm and numerous other timber trees : necessity and advantage thereof, and their manner of raising and cultivating in all kinds of soil.

10 Point No. 1   16 A 40 a $3.42

Bannad Art of Husbandry contained in seven large books; notes on the bettering and improving of all degrees of land, fertilizing the most barren soil, recovering it from all weeds, brushes, briars, and overflowing of unwholesome waters.

8 Point No. 1   16 A 44 a $3.00

The History of the Holland Republick, from its original foundation to the death of King William, including also a particular description of the two United Provinces; profusely illustrated by the insertion of many old engraved portraits. Two volumes are bound together.

30 Point No. 2   6 A 10 a $5.00

Declaration that all colonels, captains, and other officers inhabiting the County of Kent, shall associate themselves in the mutual defence of each other.

18 Point No. 2   8 A 20 a $4.00

History of that incomparable thief, known as Richard Hainam, relating the several robberies, mad pranks, and handsome jests by him performed. As it was taken from his own mouth, not long before his death. Also with his confession concerning his robbing of the King of Scots, and the Duke of Normandy.

14 Point No. 1   8 A 24 a $3.64

Copy of an interesting dialogue between Experience and a Courtier, compiled in the Scottish tung, first turned and made perfect English, and now the second time corrected and amended according to the first copie, a work very pleasant and profitable to all estates, but chiefly to gentlemen, and such as are in aucthorite: hereunto also are annexed certain other works.

FOR SALE AT ALL BRANCHES OF THE AMERICAN TYPE FOUNDERS CO.

42 Point   4 A 6 a $7.25

Proofs from some type lines of Touraine Old Style Italic Modeled by Jean Goujon, a celebrated French artist 152

36 Point   4 A 8 a $5.50

Other Sizes of the Touraine Old Style Italic are now being made For Sale at all Branches of the American Type Founders Co.

30 Point   5 A 10 a $5.00

LES CARACTÈRES "TOURAINE" sont coupés d'après le genre de lettres dont se servait le sculpteur français Jean Goujon, qui se trouvait à la hauteur de sa gloire au commencement du 15ᵉ siècle. Ses meilleurs ouvrages se trouvent dans et aux en

---

FOR SALE AT ALL BRANCHES OF THE AMERICAN TYPE FOUNDERS CO.

SLUG FIVE.

BY OPIE READ.

 BLAZING day in June, a railway trestle through the yellowish scum of a cypress swamp. Hour after hour I trudged along, straining eye to search out the end of the timbered highway. A distant roar, a train, a tremulous cling to timbers below, lizard-like, to give the train full right of way. A green frog on a yellow lily pad. I thought of frog legs, fried, and hunger-water moistened my mouth. My tramping companion and I had separated to forage. At some wayside place, in the near edge of the shady future, we were to meet and divide contributions — corn bread and the rancid belly of the razor-back hog. I had chosen the railway, to entertain section hands with stories of adventure, sad lies tipped with the gild of sarcasm. But there were no section hands, nothing but the desolate stretch of trestlework.

Far down the track I saw a man coming. How picturesque was the sight of a human form — for a moment, and then there came distress. I saw that in his hand he was swinging something that looked like a slungshot. I halted and looked back. The way was long, and I said to myself aloud: "He's going to knock me on the head with that thing. If I run he can catch me before I can reach the hard ground."

Reason strove to assert itself: "Why should he want to hit you? He can see that you have no money. Men who have money don't walk through a cypress swamp."

"Yes, I know, but the other day a tramp was found dead not far from here, with his pockets turned out. A fellow like that one coming yonder would kill a man for 10 cents."

"Perhaps; but you are as strong as he is. You can throw him off into the ooze."

"Yes, but ——"

As he drew nearer I saw that the thing he was swinging was too bulky for a slungshot. I advanced to meet him, gazing eagerly. A gleam of white across his face told that he was smiling. He called out cheerfully, and I saw that he was swinging a bit of bacon tied with a shoestring. I wanted to grasp him, so strong was my gratitude; but my eye fell upon the bacon, and I then became more of an appetite than a soul.

"Which way?" he asked.

"Down this way. Which way with you?"

"Up this way. Where from?"

"Nashville," I answered. "Where are you from?"

"Memphis."

It was of no use for one to ask what line of business the other had followed. Intuition settled that question before it was asked.

"How's work in Nashville?"

"Bad. They've got a sub-list and all sorts of scol-lops. Two dailies have consolidated. How is it in Memphis?"

"Tough. By the way, I am just about to have dinner. Join me, if you ain't in a hurry."

I told him that I was a man of leisure. He bowed and said that he had presumed as much. He cut his bacon half in two, dividing it with the utmost precision, and we sat down on the cross-ties. We chewed and talked, the grease streaming between our fingers. I shall never forget the picture of his great red head bobbing in the sun. When the meal was over he shoved his head toward me and said:

"Napkin?"

I hesitated, but he insisted, and I wiped my hands on his shock of hair.

"Well," he said, getting up, "I have an engagement and must be moving on. If you ever come my way, drop in."

"I hope to meet you again. By the way, what is your name?"

"Haven't any — I'm a sub."

"But what do they call you?"

"Slug Five. So long."

.   .   .   .

The long road had a turn. The years went by, and I often thought of Slug Five, in the cool shade of a garden with roses nodding about me, at a banquet where a fortune had been spread upon the table. I was at the head of a large newspaper interest. One night, just before going to a ball, I had to step into the composing room. I hesitated a moment, almost afraid to let the printers see me in a swallow-tailed coat. But I went in, bracing myself for the fight. One glance made me forget all embarrassment. At a case I saw a red head bobbing in the gaslight. I stepped up to the case and tapped upon it. Up came the countenance of Slug Five.

"You can't work here," I said.

He put down his stick and looked at me. His countenance fell. He had walked many a weary mile. His hope had been centered upon reaching my office. Now it was fallen. "No, you can't work here."

"Well, sir, I'm mighty sorry. But I don't know what harm I've ever done you. I did want to get enough work to help me out. I am ragged and — but it's all right. I'll go."

In my mind I saw what was soon to be. I saw his rags fall off; I saw him well dressed and happy; I saw him a useful citizen; I saw him develop the first opportunity that had ever been given to him, the first chance to become a man.

"But I wish you'd tell me what harm I've done," he said.

"Slug Five, don't you know me? Don't you remember dividing your bacon with me in a swamp? Don't you ——"

A smile broke through the red stubble on his face, and shoving his head toward me, he said: "No, don't believe I will work tonight. Napkin?"

Printers Supplies

American Type Founders Company

No. 270 Congress Street

Geo. F. Mahoney
Representative

Boston, Mass.

"A drop of ink makes millions think."

The American Type Founders Company
Is general selling agent for the celebrated
German printing inks; and, using them
To the exclusion of all others on its
Specimen work, can guarantee density
And uniformity of color; moderate prices.

CARD SET IN
12 AND 8 POINT
DEVENS SCRIPT

New Character Script

This italic is a reproduction in type of the handwriting of Rev. Richard M. Devens. In cutting the various letters, absolute fidelity to the original penmanship of Mr. Devens was adhered to, even when in so doing the taste of the type founder was violated, and the result is a most delightful and harmonious symphony in type.

CARD SET IN
18 POINT DEVENS SCRIPT

Devens Script Series

PATENT APPLIED FOR

ORIGINATED BY
AMERICAN TYPE FOUNDERS CO.
SOLE MANUFACTURER

Dance

Quadrille

Waltz

Schottische — Twilight

Polka Redowa — Rubinstein

Mazurka — Tschaikowsky

Galop — Schubert

Intermission

6 Point, 20A 50a, $3.50
8 Point, 18A 44a, 3.75
10 Point, 16A 40a, 4.00
12 Point, 12A 30a, 4.25
18 Point, 8A 24a, 4.50

CARD SET IN
8 AND 6 POINT
DEVENS SCRIPT

My Dear Madame:
It affords me great pleasure to announce that I have leased the apartments at 2308 Columbus Avenue, and have now ready for inspection a complete line of

French Designs

combining the latest Parisian fashions for the approaching season. Your presence at the opening on Friday, the 25th instant, at 3 o'clock, is requested.

Madame Fallfashions

CARD SET IN
10 AND 18 POINT
DEVENS SCRIPT

Originated and Manufactured by

American Type Founders Company

For sale at all Branches

624   *August 1898*

CASLON OLD STYLE

THIS FACE WAS CUT ANNO DOMINI 1722

The oldest Type face now in use in America
It survived on account of its exceptional merit

40 POINT OLD STYLE NO. 71   5 A 10a $8 35

HINTS for Advertisers to consider

22 POINT OLD STYLE NO. 71   14 A 10 A 28a $7 65

A GOOD ADVERTISEMENT should contain language as easily understood by a cowboy as by a lawyer. Never lay claim to more than you can substantiate, but be forcible in your arguments to the consumer

24 POINT OLD STYLE NO. 71   10 A 7 A 20a $7 65

DON'T BE SATISFIED with any old type when there are so many styles that will please the most fastidious tastes. A distinctly attractive, popular letter is admired and noted by everybody. To use poor type is WASTING MONEY

48 POINT OLD STYLE NO. 71   4 A 6a $8 50

SELECT the design to be used

36 POINT OLD STYLE NO. 71   7 A 4 A 14a $9 35

HANDSOME Faces Produce Grand Results

18 POINT OLD STYLE NO. 71   18 A 14 A 52a $8 30

The type styles used to-day by many of the leading publishers and printers are Jenson Old Style, Bradley, Cushing, Schœffer Old Style, Jenson Italic, Doric Italic, Livermore, Satanick, Columbus, Cushing Monotone, and Cushing Italic. They are exclusive leaders in their class

FOR SALE AT ALL BRANCHES OF THE

American Type Founders Company

THE WAGES OF COMPOSITORS.

PESSIMISM among workmen in the printing trades would seem to be excusable enough, judging from the views expressed by Mr. Silas W. Read, of Montreal, Canada, who, referring to a tabulated statement recently published in the *Typographical Journal*, giving the wages of compositors in the United States and Canada, points out that, with the exception of a few cities, operators are employed for as low as $18 per week on morning papers and $15 on evening papers. Why this should be so, Mr. Read says, is hard to understand: "One hundred and eighty thousand ems constitute a week's work. Nearly everywhere in Canada, and many places in the United States, operators are practically on piecework. If I am employed on a paper paying $18, and I cannot set 180,000 ems a week, my services will be dispensed with; but 10 cents per thousand for all matter over that amount is paid as a bonus in many instances. Operators should be compensated much better than they are. Before the introduction of the Mergenthaler, newspaper printers were seldom, if ever, displaced on account of age. The old man may have grown slow, but that was not a sufficient reason for an employer to dispense with the services of a faithful employe. There was, to the employer, no material loss attached to the old man's slowness, and why should he be removed? But with the operator it is different. The machines have cost the publisher $3,000 each, and if the operator is slow it is at his employer's expense. The publisher desires to earn as much money as he can, and to make the machine a profitable investment the operator must be fast. Thus it is that, although the old-style compositor may not be more than forty, he is turned down. He is told that younger men possess better eyesight, more speed and endurance than those who have spent their youth in the old-fashioned composing room. It is not the employer's intention to lose money, consequently he engages compositors who are naturally the best fitted to be operators, and the young man is in demand; but he will not always be young. At forty years of age he, too, will be on the ragged edge. At one time he may have been a record-breaker, but a 'has been' is not wanted on machines. Already there are many operators who know nothing about setting type, and in a short time our newspaper printers will be made up of young men who have never learned the case, and when through natural weakness they lose their employment, their condition, unless they have provided against destitution, will be even worse than that of the old stick-handlers. The working life of the operator is short, and that fact should cause him to demand a proper value for his services. If he is a cheap worker, when his time comes to make room for a younger expert, and he has not been able to provide for a retirement, he will discover to his sorrow what a fool he has been."

MACHINE COMPOSITION NOTES.

CONDUCTED BY GEORGE E. LINCOLN.

BUSINESS MANAGER THRUSH, of the Empire Typesetting Machine Company, is combining business with pleasure in an extended trip through Europe.

ON the introduction of typesetting machines at Muncie, Indiana, the printers presented a scale of prices calling for $17 and $19 per week for day and night work, respectively, forty-eight hours to constitute a week. A learner's scale was also provided, which proved acceptable to the proprietors of the papers.

IT is stated that the Des Jardins Type Justifier Company has recently been incorporated under the laws of New Jersey with an authorized capital of $200,000. The company will have a factory at Hartford, Connecticut, for the purpose of designing and manufacturing various automatic justification devices for existing or contemplated typesetting machines.

MESSRS. OTTMAR MERGENTHALER & CO., of Baltimore, Maryland, have issued a list of the parts of the linotype which they are prepared to furnish to users of that machine. The book has been carefully compiled, and is illustrated with fine half-tones. This firm has entered into the supply industry for the purpose of keeping their finely appointed factory busy.

WE take pleasure in presenting to our readers the picture of Mr. Ottmar Mergenthaler, the inventor of the linotype. To him is largely due the present revolution in our method of printing, and consequently his name has become familiar wherever printing is done. From a very interesting pamphlet which

OTTMAR MERGENTHALER.

he has kindly sent us, entitled "Biography of Ottmar Mergenthaler and History of the Linotype, Its Invention and Development," we learn that Mr. Mergenthaler was born in the Kingdom of Wurtemberg, Germany, on May 10, 1854. At the age of fourteen he was apprenticed to a watch and clock maker at Bietigheim, and in October, 1872, at the age of eighteen, he landed in Baltimore with a trunk and $30 in cash. He went direct to Washington, D. C., where, in connection with his trade, he worked largely upon electrical instruments for the United States Signal Service. From 1876 to 1879 he devoted considerable time in attempting to develop other people's ideas of printing by machinery. During the latter year he abandoned all others' ideas and commenced work upon what he has since developed into the linotype machine.

60 POINT

3 A 4 a $12 00

Novel Series
REFINED

24 POINT

5 A 10 a $4 50

SUITABLE FOR ADVERTISERS
Who desire the bold and striking effects in display lines which catch the daily readers

8 POINT

15 A 30 a $2 10

COMPLETENESS MAKES IT VERY USEFUL IN THE PRINTING OFFICE

THE Iroquois Series is made in ten sizes, from 6 to 60 Point. It is a strong and legible type and appeals with force wherever used, being at once pleasing to the eye and neat in design. These features make it an admirable letter for newspaper or magazine advertising of the finest order. The job compositor will find it a useful and valuable Type Series

18 POINT

6 A 12 a $3 30

MAGNETIC RESULTS
OF PROMINENT TYPE

must be calculated by their power to attract the customer and command attention. Every space buyer pays for this effectiveness in advertising

36 POINT

3 A 6 a $6 50

SUPERIOR PRINTING
Material for Printers

⇢ American Type Founders Company ⇠

The Elandkay Series

ALL SIZES LINE PERFECTLY ONE WITH ANOTHER BY POINT SYSTEM JUSTIFICATION

36 POINT 6 A $3.25

HANDSOME DESIGNS

36 Point and 24 Point are New Sizes

12 POINT NO. 27 16 A $1.50

ABOUT RIGHT FOR
NEAT BUSINESS PRINTING

12 POINT NO. 26 18 A $1.50

NOTHING FINER FOR
LEGIBLE OFFICE STATIONERY

18 POINT NO. 29 12 A $2.00

GRACEFUL 295 CHARMING
BEAUTIFUL

6 POINT NO. 23 30 A $1.50

PROFITABLE TYPE BECAUSE
IT CAN BE USED ON THE VERY BEST
GRADE OF PRINTING

6 POINT NO. 21 40 A $1.25

ALL OTHER VALUABLE FEATURES
APPARENT TO THE
OBSERVING JOB PRINTER

6 POINT NO. 22 40 A $1.25

ELEVEN SIZES ON FIVE BODIES
SHOULD BE LAID IN TRIPLE TYPE CASES
FOR CONVENIENT USE

18 POINT NO. 28 14 A $1.75

REQUIRING LESS THAN FOUR CASES
UNIQUE 34 EFFECT

12 POINT NO. 25 24 A $1.50

GOOD TITLE PAGE TYPES
DANCE ORDERS AND NEAT PROGRAMS
COST £280 EACH

6 POINT NO. 24 30 A $1.50

TWO STYLES OF SOME LETTERS
COSTING NOTHING AND WORTH SURELY $25
EVERY SIZE COMPLETE

24 POINT 8 A $2.50

OBSERVE THEIR HARMONY

Observe their Font Prices

MANUFACTURED EXCLUSIVELY BY

American Type Founders Company

SELLING POINTS THROUGHOUT THE WORLD

HENRY LEWIS BULLEN.

WE take pleasure in publishing the portrait of Henry Lewis Bullen, a man who is perhaps more widely known in a personal sense than any other in touch with printers. The accompanying likeness will be recognized by his many friends all over the United States, in Great Britain, Europe and Australia.

For three years Mr. Bullen has been advertising manager of the American Type Founders Company, and every printer who reads THE INLAND PRINTER, or who has received the beautiful pamphlets, specimen books and catalogues of that company, will concede that Mr. Bullen has established a very high standard of excellence in such work. Three years ago the American Type Founders Company was subordinated in the public mind to the prestige of the old local names, but Mr. Bullen's work has left no doubt as to who sells "Everything for the Printer," and "Leads the Fashions in Type."

The value of his services in the advertising department was increased by his intimate knowledge of the wares he advertised, and this knowledge will now be used as manager of the Buffalo branch, to which position he has been appointed. On assuming the duties of this position the advertising department of the American Type Founders Company was closed, and Mr. Bullen has returned to a field in which few have had more experience or have been more successful. We predict that his services will be as valuable in the new as in the old position, and our best wishes go with him.

Henry L. Bullen was born in Australia, of American-Scotch parentage. His father was of old New England stock. The first Bullen arrived in the vicinity of Dedham, Massachusetts, in 1640, and to this day the family claim a homestead in that part of the country. After receiving a common school education in Australia he learned the printing business under the late Alexander Anderson, of Ballarat, and W. S. Mitchell (now of the firm of A. H. Massina & Co.), Melbourne, Australia. He came to America before he was of age, and first worked as a printer in Davenport, Iowa, and after that in St. Louis, Cincinnati, Philadelphia, Trenton, New York and Boston. In this tour he developed into a good printer — the one thing he is most proud of — besides contributing to various journals more or less regularly. While working in Boston he was engaged to set up and edit a trade publication for Golding & Co., and, succeeding in this, was offered the management of the selling department of that concern, which was then comparatively small. Developing a peculiar fitness for the position, he

increased the business rapidly, until it entered the front rank. Buildings were added year by year to keep pace with the demand, and Mr. Bullen was recognized by the trade as one of its leading men. This was at the time the point system of type bodies was coming into general use in the West, and Mr. Bullen, appreciating that reform to the fullest degree, was the first to introduce the new system in the East. The first point system outfits in New England were sold by him. The first point system office in New York City was also sold by him. The great development of Golding & Co's business in type at that time was primarily due to advocacy of the point system, and their success had a great deal to do with convincing the eastern type founders that "lack of system" type had to go. Several appliances in common use in printing offices were introduced at the suggestion of Mr. Bullen, among them the Polhemus cabinet, the best selling high-grade cabinet of the present time, first constructed from his drawings in 1887, and put on the market in 1888 by the Hamilton Manufacturing Company, and now made by all manufacturers of printers' wood goods.

In pursuance of a strong desire to return to Australia, Mr. Bullen in 1888 secured an appointment to establish a printers' supply department for Alex. Cowan & Sons, papermakers, of Melbourne and Sydney, Australia. Before leaving for the antipodes, he visited Great Britain in order to acquaint himself with foreign machinery, type and supplies, and as a result of his experience here and across the Atlantic, obtained agencies from the leading manufactories; several American manufacturers thus secured an established growing market in Australia where before they had practically no business. Mr. Bullen arrived in Australia while the great Australian land boom was at its height,

HENRY LEWIS BULLEN.
The new Manager of the Buffalo Branch of the American Type Founders Company.

and established his department under very favorable conditions, to the complete satisfaction of Alex. Cowan & Sons. He was under a contract for three years, but at its expiration the great panic which followed the land boom was coming on, and Mr. Bullen believed that the opportunities in the United States were better than in Australia, and decided to return here. Upon leaving he received very substantial evidences of the good opinion in which he was held by that highly respected firm and its employes, mementoes that are highly prized by him. Leaving Australia, the return was made via Ceylon and the Suez Canal to Naples. A trip through Italy, Switzerland, France, England and Scotland occupied several months, and Mr. Bullen arrived in New York in October, 1891, and, according to arrangements made while in Australia, immediately established the New York warehouse of the

Hamilton Manufacturing Company, controlling the business of that company in the States east of Pittsburg. The business at once assumed good proportions, but its development was hampered by the uncertainties incident to the organization of the American Type Founders Company. In 1893 the stock of the Eastern branch of the Hamilton Manufacturing Company was sold to the American Type Founders Company and Mr. Bullen became acting manager of the New York branch of the

TESTIMONIAL TO HENRY L. BULLEN.

We, the undersigned, employes of the specimen printing department of the American Type Founders Company, Philadelphia, Pennsylvania, hereby express our sincere appreciation of the courteous and gentlemanly manner in which

HENRY L. BULLEN

at all times coöperated with us while manager of the advertising department. We congratulate him on his promotion to the position of manager of the Buffalo branch of the American Type Founders Company, and extend to him our hearty good wishes for his success.

Jacob J. Rupertus,	Charles W. Berner,	Harry L. Sullivan,
John C. Soby,	M. Peter Voigt,	Gustave Goette,
William Kohler,	William P. Mayhew,	Gustavus Rickets,
William Crossin,	George Bastian,	James Cunningham,
William H. V. Jackson,	Louis Ficarotta,	John Riley,
J. W. Richwine,	John B. McCullough,	Frank Riley,
Joseph Combs,	Thomas Brown,	S. A. Keller,
George M. Thorn,	Thomas MacKellar,	Frank Rupertus.
	George Snyder,	

latter company, and afterward assistant manager under Mr. L. B. Benton, holding that position for nearly two years. The New York branch was moved into new quarters, its staff reorganized and its business increased largely and steadily. With the advent of Mr. R. W. Nelson as general manager of the company, there was a reorganization of the personnel, and Mr. Bullen was selected as advertising manager, in which position he has substantially increased his reputation, his principal work being the production of the type specimen books, machinery and material catalogues and pamphlets, which are familiar to all printers. In its early days Mr. Bullen was a contributor to THE INLAND PRINTER, and has always been a helpful friend and adviser to it. When manager for Golding & Co., he was the first to suggest that it be sold through supply houses, and through his energetic influence in those days hundreds of subscribers were added. His friendly interest in this publication was continued in Australia, where in 1888 very few

copies were sold. In 1889 the sales ran into thousands, and a large and permanent list of subscribers was added. It is characteristic of Mr. Bullen to go out of his way to benefit all whom he knows, and to do the service in an entirely unselfish manner.

As showing the good feeling existing between Mr. Bullen and the employes of the printing department of his company at Philadelphia, we have pleasure in presenting a miniature reproduction of a very handsome testimonial given him by the gentlemen whose names are subscribed thereto.

A COSTLY MECHANISM.

MR. PHILIP T. DODGE, president of the Mergenthaler Linotype Company, has presented to Cornell University, through Doctor Thurston, of Sibley College, what is said to be the costliest piece of machinery ever constructed. It is the original Paige typesetting machine, the only one of its kind ever built, which was constructed at an expense of nearly $2,000,000. Besides being the costliest piece of machinery in the world, it is, at the same time, one of the most remarkable and ingenious. It consists of over 19,000 parts and has 800 bearings for shafts, about half of the shafts rotating continuously and the rest intermittently. The students of Cornell can here study the cam in all its glory. This machine will select the type, place them in a raceway and move them along until a line is set up; it then inserts the exact spaces required and conveys the justified line to the galley, either leaded or solid, and registers each line as set. In distributing, it advances the column of type line by line to a testing mechanism, where all defective type are cast out. The perfect type are advanced to a selecting mechanism, where type which have been turned end for end or otherwise disarranged are removed; then all such characters as the asterisks, daggers, etc., are separated and the regular characters are advanced to their proper channels. The most complex part of the entire machine is the justifying mechanism. Each key upon the keyboard when pressed averages four and one-half type, and no person short of a college professor could hope to become an expert operator. Anything not right, even of the minutest kind, causes the keyboard to lock, thus giving instant warning to the operator. The original application for patent contained 204 sheets of drawings, having over 1,000 separate views. The justifying part was made the subject of a second patent which contained 81 sheets of drawings. The case was eight years pending in the Patent Office, and the Government lost thousands of dollars in examining, printing, etc., before the patent was granted. The invention was a failure in a commercial sense, for, even after the first machine was perfected, it was impossible to build the machine so that it could be sold. The machine occupies floor space 11 feet 6 inches by 3 feet 6 inches, has a maximum height of 6 feet 6 inches, and weighs about 5,500 pounds. The new gift to Cornell is all the more interesting inasmuch as it was in the construction of this machine that Mark Twain sank some of his fortune.

LARGER sizes of the Cushing Types made on 15, 18 and 24 point bodies. Originated and manufactured by the American Type Founders Company, being carried in stock and for sale at its branch houses and agencies throughout the world.

TWENTY-FOUR POINT

JOSIAH STEARNS CUSHING, President of the Norwood Press Company, Norwood, Mass., was born in Bedford, on May 3, 1854, and comes of the old New England stock, of scholarly instinct and inheritance. Leaving the public high schools, he commenced the printer's trade at the University Press in Cambridge as a boy of fourteen, later working in various printing offices in Boston and Cambridge, and becoming an expert printer. In 1878, with a modest capital saved from his personal earnings, he established a book-printing office at the corner of Milk and Federal streets, Boston. In 1895 he removed to Norwood, where he occupies one of the largest and best equipped printing plants in the country. As a designer of types now in use by bookmakers, Mr. Cushing has been very successful. The Cushing is one of his best examples in this direction. His special line of work is college text-books and standard educational work in numerous languages. His fonts of Greek, Hebrew, Latin, Spanish and other alphabets are exceptionally complete. All the mathematical type used in his office is made under his immediate supervision.

TEN POINT

CUSHING SERIES CONCEIVED BROADER USAGE

When the formation of the Cushing types was first conceived they had no broader purpose than the providing of a letter particularly adapted for book work, printing clearly and readably, and making a sharp, durable electrotype plate. Coupled with these features was the departure in Romans that they represented, and which quickly attracted the attention of book printers and publishers. With the additions above noted, Cushing now becomes a series of seven well-graded sizes, and a most useful adjunct to any composing room. A casual examination cannot but disclose the possibilities of this beautiful face as a display letter, and we confidently predict for the added trio of sizes an even greater patronage than has been accorded the original showing. 1234567890&$£

FIFTEEN POINT

CUSHING TYPES

60 POINT BINNER 4 A 5 a $12.25

BINNER

BRANCH 1

36 POINT BINNER 5 A 8 a $5.50

Printers
ADOPTING
Unique

30 POINT BINNER 6 A 9 a $5.00

AMERICAN
Type
Founders

12 POINT BINNER 16 A 20 a $3.25

COMPANY, leader in type fashions, and exclusive manufacturer of Binner and Binner Open types, wishes to call the attention of printers and laymen to the remarkable excellence of these letters

72 POINT BINNER 4 A 5 a $17.00

Binner Series

PATENT APPLIED FOR

48 POINT BINNER 4 A 5 a $7.75

CLEAR
Send Much

THE 6, 8 AND 10 POINT SIZES OF BINNER
ARE IN PREPARATION

18 POINT BINNER 10 A 16 a $4.00

SELDOM DIFFICULT to secure catchy and pleasing results with

24 POINT BINNER 8 A 10 a $4.50

LEAST AMOUNT of work on part of compositors 4

and the design is such as will insure a most extended service

54 POINT BINNER 4 A 5 a $10.25

ORDERS

BINNER OPEN SERIES

PATENT APPLIED FOR

48 POINT

COMPANION

36 POINT

OPEN FACE

12 POINT

INTENDED TO ACCOMPANY
THE BINNER TYPES SHOWN
ON PAGE PRECEDING THIS

60 POINT

DESIGNS

18 POINT

BY AMERICAN TYPE
FOUNDERS CO.
AMERICA

24 POINT

HANDSOME, USEFUL
DURABLE

72 POINT

BINNER

---

48 Point   4 A 5 a $7.75

Binner

SEVEN SIZES
FIGURES COMPLETE WITH EACH

36 Point   5 A 8 a $5.50

Unique

12 Point   16 A 20 a $3.25

Designed to surpass
by the world's great
type fashion makers

60 Point   4 A 5 a $12.25

Gold

18 Point   10 A 16 a $4.00

For the printer
who makes use
of latest faces

24 Point   8 A 10 a $4.50

All printers
should have

SEVEN SIZES
FIGURES COMPLETE WITH EACH

72 Point   4 A 5 a $17.00

$18

See Binner Series Opposite

Manufactured by American Type Founders Co.

FOR SALE AT ALL BRANCHES AND AGENCIES

HANDSOME SHOWING
USEFUL DESIGN 15

SPECIMEN OF OLYMPIA

15A   12-Point Olympia $1.50

REWARD OF PROGRESS
TYPOGRAPHICAL 95

18A   10-Point Olympia $1.40

SAVING LABOR AND WORRY
MODERN INVENTION 40

12A   14-Point Olympia $1.75

RELYING ON THE EXACTNESS OF LINING
SECURING BEST JUSTIFICATION 18

20A   8-Point Olympia No. 2 $1.25

PRECISENESS IN MANUFACTURE
SCIENTIFIC PRODUCTION 76

22A   8-Point Olympia No. 1 $1.25

EXCELLENCE OF SYSTEM RECOGNIZED
LONG FELT WANTS SUPPLIED 84

4A   30-Point Olympia $3.00

IMPROVED LINING 12

22A   6-Point Olympia No. 4 $1.00

MODERN METHODS CROWDING OUT THE OLD
WASTEFUL MATERIAL IS DISCARDED 25

24A   6-Point Olympia No. 3 $1.00

DISPENSED WITH CARD AND PAPER JUSTIFICATION
LITTERING-UP OF THE CASES AVOIDABLE 38

8A   18-Point Olympia $2.00

QUICKNESS IN COMPOSITION
USING BETTER TYPES 36

26A   6-Point Olympia No. 2 $1.00

COMPLETE ASSORTMENT OF SYSTEMATIC TYPES PROCURABLE
ALL THE MOST USEFUL FAVORITES ARE NOW MADE 46

28A   6-Point Olympia No. 1 $1.00

OLYMPIA SERIES IS PLACED ON STANDARD TITLE LINE AND UNIT SETS
FOUR SIZES ON 6-POINT, 2 ON 8-POINT AND 1 ON 10-POINT

INLAND TYPE FOUNDRY

217-219 Pine, SAINT LOUIS

NICKS ARE DIFFERENT ON THE SIX SIZES CAST ON 8-POINT AND 6-POINT

HHHHHHHHHHHH   HHHHHHHHHHHH

ERRORS IN LINOTYPE COMPOSITION.

BY F. HORACE TEALL.

WITH the use of linotype bars a problem in connection with proofreading has arisen, that has not yet received sufficient attention, in newspaper offices especially. The problem involves also the making of corrections in the bars. Probably in a majority of offices the proofreading force has been increased somewhat with the enlargement of the product, but seldom adequately, if good work is desired. It seems reasonably certain, judging from examination of many newspapers, that the real necessity of careful revising of proofs is not commonly recognized.

How many newspapers are printed every day replete with errors of all possible kinds — nay, with many that would seem impossible if they did not stare us in the face? Such newspapers need not be counted; their name is legion. But does any one think that all these errors are the result of careless proofreading? Some of them are, certainly, but probably only a small proportion. Many errors find their way into print notwithstanding their correction on the proof, especially if no revising of proofs is done, and errors often appear even when proofs are revised. Experience seems to prove that the most careful and intelligent workers, those who would very seldom leave a marked error uncorrected in type, will often put a new bar in the wrong place, thus increasing instead of diminishing the number of errors. The bars are not so easy to read as type is — or at least any but the newest white-faced type — and for each correction, no matter how slight, the whole line must be replaced.

For practical illustration and enforcement of the point, or points, nothing else seems so promising as a statement of experience in one establishment. On a certain evening newspaper all the composition, including advertisements, used to average about 2,500,000 ems weekly when done by hand, and now the Mergenthaler machines produce an average amount much larger than that, and the type-work, consisting of tables and displayed advertisements, amounts roughly to 2,500,000 ems, making nearly 6,000,000 ems in all. Notwithstanding this increase in production, the force of proofreaders remains to this day the same — even the same persons — and there is probably not a newspaper in the country that is printed with fewer errors. One great difference between the present and the old-time conditions is seen in the fact that the proofreaders now work many more hours in the week than they did originally, but their wages is increased only by an occasional allowance for overtime. The regular weekly wages is the same, but the readers, who seldom used to work all the hours that could have been demanded as a full week, now seldom work less than the full number of hours. Their pay was not originally considered by their employers as being too much, or it would never have been so much. Surely it should have been increased with their work. But that is only incidental; this writing is not a plea for increased pay, but an inquiry as to method, with a view to improvement in the work.

No editors were ever more solicitous of accuracy than those of the newspaper we are considering; yet we may hope to be pardoned for pointing out what may be called false economy on their part, possibly creating increased likelihood of error. One example may suffice for this. In a reprint article the managing editor made three new paragraphs on his proof. This necessitated the resetting of thirty lines, use of a few minutes of time for substituting the new bars for the old ones, the reading of the new matter in proof, and then a little more resetting and another revision, besides the waste of material, or wear and tear. All this, of course, is not much in one instance, but similar things happen with sufficient frequency to add considerable expense. It does not seem unlikely that their avoidance, through more careful preparation of copy, would be good economy, even at the cost of increasing the editorial force. Composing-room workers are not so expensive individually as editors are; but one experienced proofreader employed in the editorial room in preparing copy so that it could be followed literally, and with the special duty of making everything plain, might be found very helpful. Of course much copy must be rushed through without such careful preparation, but there is enough of it that need not be. It would be an almost impossible accomplishment to tell the full amount of increase in liability to error over that of type-work, but a few examples of errors that never could occur in handling type instead of bars are worth stating.

In a collection of **related** paragraphs one of them began with the line, "All canned goods should be opened for," and the next one with the line, "A correspondent asks for a formula for." The editor struck out, on proof, "for" on the end of the first of these lines, and two lines had to be set in making the correction. In changing the bars the second line ending with "for" was removed, together with the next line, and the two new bars, belonging to the preceding paragraph, were inserted there. This is a very common kind of occurrence, and a fair amount of certainty in avoiding it would demand very deliberate work, which is just the one thing that cannot be had in the rush of getting out an evening newspaper.

Another way in which serious errors are sometimes made is by removing an extra bar, as in the following instance: A sentence was omitted from the very beginning of a short item just before edition time, when it was impossible to revise anything; in fact, just when it is not uncommon to put the matter right into the form without reading. Three lines had to be set, and the man who changed the bars in the form, amid the utmost haste, and with four or five men working over the page, did not realize that the three bars handed to him were to take the place of only two original ones, and removed three instead of two, thus making a new "out" in the very act of inserting the first one. And this could not reasonably be held very censurable on the part of any man but one who did it often enough to prove that he was habitually careless. The man who did it in this instance had previously proved himself beyond doubt a careful and accurate workman.

In the office we are considering there are fifteen machines, and the operators take turns in setting the new lines for office corrections. For this they measure twice the number of lines set. One operator asked the foreman, who leaves all the correcting as a special department in charge of one man, why he was passed by when his turn came, and orders were given that he must have this work in his turn. His first line of correction occurred in an article for which the form was waiting. Its last word was "companion," and he set "campaign." Something happened that is unusual under the circumstances; the floorman noticed the error in the bar and had the operator reset the line with the right word — all of which wasted valuable time, for it kept the form waiting.

Proofreading details have been multiplied almost beyond conception by the change from type to linotype. We may well enough keep to the one establishment, though there is no reason to suppose that the consideration might not with equal force be placed on a general basis. In the first place, all advertisements have always been and still are read twice by copy. This was not nearly so burdensome in the old time as it is now, as the advertising matter has at least doubled in quantity. Revises were always taken, but in the type-work mere comparison of the changed letters or words often sufficed, though the reviser even then was supposed to read advertisements all through for possible errors not noticed in the other reading; but now not a letter of them can be allowed to escape his scrutiny with any degree of safety. By this is meant the linotype matter. There never was any real certainty in handling display except through careful reading.

As the slightest change now involves substitution of an entire new line, any error, even of a single letter, may lead to the making of a new error, so that revising becomes a matter not merely of looking at the word in which a letter is changed, which could be done sometimes on a proof from type. Again, not only are new errors often made within the line, but, as we have seen, lines are likely to be dropped or misplaced in changing the bars. Certainty cannot be fully assured without reading through at least three lines for even the slightest change, so that the reader may not only see that the new line is free from error, but may be sure that it is in its proper place.

Even the reading of three lines is sometimes not sufficient. Let the reader, in revising, find an error uncorrected, so that he might be sure in type-work that it had been overlooked; it will never do merely to repeat the mark in handling linotype matter. Instances of this kind frequently result from substitution of the new bar in the wrong place — so frequently that the reviser, on coming to one of them, should instantly expect to find the corrected line somewhere else, and another line missing where the bar has been inserted. With this likelihood in mind, it must be apparent that every revise demands reading all through, if accuracy is to be required with any semblance of justice.

Again, on the paper alluded to all editorial articles have to be read carefully by the reviser, who usually gets them all in a heap — often within half an hour of going to press; and not only this, but editors' proofs must be carefully revised also. This alone may easily be recognized as no slight task, but it is not all. Frequently in the same half-hour this reviser has had in addition a number of advertisement proofs that must be attended to immediately. He has good help, but the news matter often flows in at that same time in a regular deluge, and the editorial and advertising matter he must handle alone. It is more than the quickest and most accurate reader living can turn out in the time allowed without feeling that he may pass a very bad error at almost any instant.

Even what is here said does not come anywhere near to telling the whole "tale of woe." It is told of only one establishment, but that one is undoubtedly typical of those that may be classed as careful. Newspaper publishers, and even composing-room foremen, have not yet begun to realize the full demand of the proofreading work caused by the linotype.

THE ELECTRIC MOTOR.

WHEN we consider that a printing press for a daily newspaper is in use only a few hours out of each twenty-four, that its output may vary within very wide limits, and that under the old system steam was kept up and belting running for a considerable time before and after the edition was actually printed, it is seen that the starting or stopping of a press by the turning of a hand switch results in a much more economical output of power. Among the practical difficulties which always existed in the pressroom of a large daily newspaper run by belting was the fact that two men were always required to put the press in motion, if only for oiling purposes. This was because one man had always to stand by the belt to slip it on the pulley, while the other climbed up to oil bearings or to the semi-cylindrical stereotype plates on the printing cylinder. As the belt had only one invariable speed, and it took perceptible time for the man at the press to call out to the man at the belt, and for the man at the belt to throw it on to the idle pulley, the press was frequently turned past the desired mark, and had to be put through another revolution to again reach it. The electric motor, with twenty different rates of speed, between "dead slow" and full speed, and with "stop" buttons placed within reach of a man's hand in every part of the machine, has changed all this, so that what is now comfortable for one man to do, was formerly a thankless job for two men to attempt together.

60 POINT

3 A 4a $10 50

Merry Christmas

24 POINT

6 A 16a $5 50

15 POINT

12 A 36a $4 50

Patriarch & Youngsters Under Mistletoe Bough

Saint Nicholas Welcomed by Children Large and Small

Cable Address: Universe

Telephone, No. 810, North

Kriskingle Brothers

Distributers of

Fancy Goods **Toys** and Novelties

No. 5 Reindeer Avenue

Fairyland Borough

Open Every Day

Mail Orders Receive Special Attention

18 POINT

10 A 28a $5 00

30 POINT

5 A 12a $6 00

Delectation Tables Redolent with Savory Odors

Compliments of the 1898 Season 1899

Originated by the

American Type Founders Company

Magnificence Unadorned!

The Bradley Italic Series

Patented, 1898

This handsome and useful series of letter is exhibited here for the first time, and is shown in practical display on the following page. The Series comprises ten sizes, which are sold as follows:

8 Point,	16 A	48 a	$2.75	24 Point,	6 A	18 a	$4.50
10 Point,	14 A	45 a	$3.00	30 Point,	5 A	12 a	$5.00
12 Point,	14 A	40 a	$3.25	36 Point,	4 A	10 a	$5.50
15 Point,	12 A	36 a	$3.50	48 Point,	3 A	7 a	$7.25
18 Point,	9 A	26 a	$4.00	60 Point,	3 A	5 a	$9.00

Now Ready and in Stock at all Branches of the

American Type Founders Co.

Order from Branch nearest your place of business

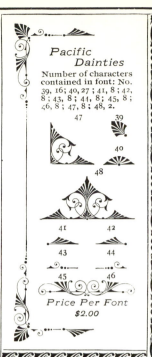

Regal Italic Series

ORIGINATED BY THE
American Type Founders Co.
For Sale by all its Branches

Charles Roth 14

**WHOLESALE FARM MACHINERY
AND SUPPLIES**

2341 South Fulton Street

≈ ≈

Telephone:
Main 2237 M

Caxton,_____1899

No._____ 12

14 Duplex,_____1899

36 **Bank of Regal**

Pay to the
10 Order of_____

18
100 Dollars

12 Ozark Mercantile Company

8 By_____

6 President

Menu 30.

♣♣

Blue Points

Celery   Mangoes   Salted Nuts

SHERRY

Clear Green Turtle

Pompano a la Marguerite

Cucumbers   Curled Potatoes

CHAMPAGNE

Supreme of Chicken

French Peas

Southern Hotel Punch

Frozen Tomatoes

VEUVE CLIQUOT

Cake   Fruit   Cheese

Coffee   Cigars   COGNAC

Grand 18 Opening

Feathers
Cleaned

24 **Fine Millinery**

UP-TO-DATE STYLES

12 612 Elm
Street

Tuesday Evening 10
May 2, 1899

REGAL ITALIC

6	POINT	24 A	48 a	$2 50
8	"	18 A	36 a	3 00
10	"	14 A	28 a	3 50
12	"	12 A	24 a	4 00
14	"	9 A	18 a	4 20
18	"	7 A	14 a	4 50
24	"	6 A	12 a	5 25
30	"	5 A	10 a	6 00
36	"	4 A	8 a	6 50

RULES FOR WINNING SUCCESS IN THE PRINTING BUSINESS.

WHILE it may be true that no man can pull through life successfully if tied to an absolute set of rules, since he thus becomes a creature of red tape, yet there are many principles of conduct that it is well to bear in mind, and make use of whenever the judgment of the time does not demand an exception. Probably there are few rules that should be followed blindly, because circumstances alter cases, and call for modifications of one sort or another, yet it is thought that the rules that are gathered together here will be found to contain the leading elements calculated to contribute to success in the printing industry, because they represent something of the methods of some of the foremost printers in America, and we ought to be able to gather somewhat from the fruits of their experience.

It may occur to some readers that these rules consist largely of "don'ts," but it should be remembered that success is largely dependent upon the things that we refrain from doing. Men fail more often through omission than commission, and they succeed often largely through ability to keep away from the hundred and one seductive paths that lead to failure.

1. Don't start in business unless you have enough money to do it properly. If you cannot command sufficient capital to make a fair start, wait and save until you do have enough.

2. Don't start a business in a place because you happen to want to live there. Start in a place where there is some sort of an opening, or some reason for believing that trade can be developed.

3. Don't buy out an old run-down concern. Its "bad will" will more than offset its "good will," and its old material will be a halter around your neck.

4. Don't buy secondhand material; it is dear at any price. This is one of the most common mistakes of the printer who begins with small capital. Because he has not enough to buy what he needs, he takes the secondhand, and the quality of his work suffers, or he loses time, which is money.

5. It is bad to run in debt, but it is better to owe money for new material than to fuss along with old type and rattle-trap presses.

6. In selecting a location for business, don't think that the lowest rent is sure to be the cheapest, or that you can get to your customers even if you are too far out of the way for them to call. It is cheaper to pay more rent than to waste your time running around. Of course, you must take a rent within your means; but choose a central location.

7. In choosing a place of business in a city, give preference to one near other printers. It will then be easy for their customers to run in on you when they desire to make a change.

8. Rent as light rooms as you can get. A dark place is a great drawback and expense, and adds to your lost time.

9. Choose your type for usefulness and not for novelty or ornament. The standard faces are the money-earners. Restrain your longing for the fanciful and bizarre. Buy in series, and prefer a few large fonts to a number of small fonts.

10. Buy good, up-to-date presses that will stand being speeded up. The machine that will turn out the greatest number of tokens in a day is worth a lot more than a slower machine.

11. Don't be stingy in buying labor-saving conveniences. Labor is your heaviest item of expense, and it is good economy to save it wherever you can.

12. Don't be in too much of a hurry to buy more machinery and material when rushed with work. The rush may not last.

13. Demand a fair price for your work, and don't be afraid to let go the customer who will not pay it. You could remain poor all your days working for some people.

14. Do not be too anxious to get work by cutting under your competitors. If you cut them in price, they may cut you, and then both will be worse off.

15. Remember that you are in business to get the highest legitimate price you can for your work. This rule perhaps is forgotten more often than any other.

16. Treat your competitors as honorable men, and don't believe all that your customers tell you about them. Customers are human, and it is business for them to offset printers against each other.

17. Try to agree with your competitors in maintaining prices, and let the competition be as to quality of work, not cheapness.

18. If you are asked to figure on a big job that is being done by a competitor it is a very good plan to go and have a talk with your brother printer before making a price on it. Ten to one the customer is only trying to use you to beat down the other fellow in price, and you cannot get the work at all, though you may hurt your brother printer. By going to him, and frankly talking it over, you prevent this, and he is apt to reciprocate, and this prevents your customers from using the brother printer to hammer your prices. There is more wisdom in this than a good many may think. It is practiced by only a very few. Were it common, the printing business might be more remunerative for all.

19. Treat your customers honorably and fairly. Never lie to them, but do not construe this to mean that you should expose to them trade secrets.

20. Do not slight a job because you find that you have given too close a price on it. Do it as well as you would any other job, but tell your customer that you made a mistake, that he may feel like giving you other work to make it up, and that he may not expect the job again at the same price.

21. Don't be afraid to charge all that work is worth, and strive to do every job in the best style. Get up a reputation for good work, promptly delivered, and not for low prices. There is money in the former, and none in the latter.

22. Insist on cash from strangers, and on short credits from everybody. Out of eight men who want too much credit, one will stick you, and you will lose more than you made on the seven. Be especially on your guard against the new customer, who pays prompt cash for several small jobs, and then gives you a large job without cash advance.

23. Don't lend money to your customers, as by purchasing postal cards, stamped envelopes, etc., without charging a commission. If they want to save the commission, let them buy the goods.

24. Don't figure on paper stock or anything else at cost; charge an advance. There is no money in selling paper or anything else at cost price.

25. Talk to your customers as a salesman should. Make suggestions to them to add to the business-bringing qualities of the printing. Try and make them understand that their standing is often judged by the quality of the printing they send out, and that they cannot afford to take poor work.

26. Cultivate the capacity of writing clever circulars, etc., for the benefit of customers who cannot do it for themselves. If you can do this better than your competitors you will get more trade.

27. Don't try to perform all your own labor. Look after your customers and develop trade. You can hire others to do the actual work. It is your place to see that it is done at a profit. You can never make much by selling your own labor, but you may by exacting a profit from the well-directed labor of a number of others.

28. Hire good workmen, and pay them enough to keep them satisfied. Be friendly with them, and make them like you, that they may have the spirit to work for your interest. Be liberal with them, but exact what you pay for. Learn to know just what each man can do in a week, and see that he does it.

29. Keep books and time-slips in such a way that you know the exact cost of every job you do.

30. Learn what it costs to do work, and don't be too sure that you know it all. Many clever men have failed because they did not know what work cost. The indirect items of cost are often fifty to sixty per cent of the total, and it is all too easy to forget them.

31. Use estimate blanks that will remind you of all possible items of cost, and never chance things or leave out a portion of the charge against general expenses.

32. Do not give customers estimates in detail. It only furnishes them with knowledge to be used against you. For instance, if one saw your charge for electrotypes was so much, and learned that he could get them of the electrotyper for fifteen per cent less, he would fix things so that you would lose that fifteen per cent.

33. Pay your bills promptly, and save all discounts for cash.

34. Don't promise work before you can deliver it; better lose the work. When a job is promised, get it done on time, even if it costs extra to fulfill your promise. This course will pay in the long run, and many customers will pay beyond the price agreed when they understand that circumstances have caused you to pay more for the work to get it done on time than you agreed to charge.

35. See to it that none but good work leaves your premises.

36. Don't take in work that you have not the facilities to execute. There is lots of bother and no profit in that sort of thing.

37. Never take work just to keep the presses running, or to keep the hands employed. It is false philanthropy, and hurts employes as much as employers in the long run.

38. See that your office is always orderly; that the machinery is kept clean, and that dead type is never allowed to accumulate. Provide plenty of sorts, as time spent in picking sorts is a total waste.

39. Don't forget that the imprint is an advertisement that costs nothing.

40. When you get to running several cylinder presses, the vibration may annoy your landlord and fellow-tenants. Make calculations ahead to avoid this and you will save trouble and expense.

41. Don't brag about how much money you are making. It invites competition.

42. When you have made your pile, be liberal with young competitors, and let them reap knowledge from your wisdom.

THE INLAND PRINTER AND THE UNION LABEL.

SOME inquiries have been received with reference to the use of the union label in the pages of THE INLAND PRINTER. We are advised that some have zealously tried to injure the circulation of this paper by making attacks upon it for the nonuse of the label. THE INLAND PRINTER has not sought the label, as it has desired to preserve an impartial attitude in all matters affecting trade conditions. It would be equally competent for the master printers or the Typothetæ to seek to injure this publication because it used no insignia indicative of its fair dealing. The union label, within certain bounds, is, perhaps, a great aid to the spreading of the broad principles of trades-unionism, but its aid has in some cases been used in a way to force the unions into a false position. And the union can well say: "Better an open opponent than a foolish friend," as between some of its overzealous friends and the United Typothetæ. If THE INLAND PRINTER has not been a fair and impartial advocate of the best interests of the trade, and this certainly includes the Typographical Union and those unions affiliated with it, then the union label cannot make it so.

MACHINE COMPOSITION NOTES AND QUERIES.

CONDUCTED BY GEORGE E. LINCOLN.

DURING the month of November fifty-eight new linotype machines were distributed over seventeen States.

IT is reported that a St. John Typobar machine is soon to be placed in the office of J. J. Little & Co., New York City.

WILLIAM HALL, Knoxville, Tennessee, a linotype machinist, has been elected a member of the General Assembly of that district.

LINOTYPE composition is done in the State printing offices of Pennsylvania, New York, Kentucky and Colorado, and is also used by the Canadian and British governments.

THE Dow Machine Company is making rapid progress toward completing financial arrangements which will enable it to construct and market its excellent typesetting machine.

THE Gibbs-Brower Company, 150 Nassau street, New York City, has made arrangements to act as the sole selling agents of the Chadwick Typesetting machine, and propose pushing its sales henceforth.

THE Goodson Typesetting Machine Company has issued an illustrated and comprehensive booklet of its machine. It is neatly printed from type cast by its method, and reflects credit upon this process.

THE St. Louis *Republic* has no fears or favors to ask of the gas companies as far as the running of their linotypes is concerned; by the use of kerosene to melt the metal they are immuned from the calamity such as happened to their New York brethren a short time ago.

FOR simplicity in methods provided for setting type we can commend the device gotten up by Charles H. Cochrane, of New York City. With the use of logotypes and a system of channels, he proposes to increase the capacity of the compositor one hundred per cent. More anon.

THE linotype machines on the Philadelphia *Ledger* are painted red. This is in keeping with all the other machinery in this splendidly equipped establishment. We do not know of any beneficial effect red paint has upon machinery, but the linotypes thus treated are not improved in appearance.

IT is reported that the Chadwick Typesetter Company will soon complete the construction of one hundred of these ingenious little machines. With these the compositor can set type with both hands — or rather, he picks up the type and drops them in a funnel, which can be done with either or both hands with equal facility. No special nick is required on the type and no changes in the composing rooms are necessary. The Chadwick contemplates increasing the output of the compositor seventy-five per cent.

A CORRESPONDENT who is an operator in a book machine office writes that he wrestles daily with stuff ranging from "Klondike Karl; or, the Bounding Boy with the Billygoat Bang," to "An Abstract Treatise on the Disassociation of the Terrestrial Planetary Conglomeration with the Infinite Correlation of Space."

MR. H. H. MILLER, foreman of the Philadelphia *Times* composing room, has so systematized matters and selected his force with such care that this paper is enabled to be issued with a smaller force and fewer machines than any other newspaper of its size in this country. The *Times* is also the banner newspaper in typographic appearance using linotype machines.

MR. J. O. GOODENOUGH has succeeded the firm of Gates & Goodenough as sole selling agent of the Linotype machine in the United States. He has associated with him Mr. S. S. Lesslie and Mr. George E. Lincoln, both gentlemen of large experience in this particular line. The many friends of Mr. Goodenough congratulate him upon his success, and wish him the prosperity to which his energy and ability entitle him.

SOME back-number croakers see only disaster to the printing art in the rapid introduction of typesetting machinery. They fail to consider that there are different classes and styles of such machines, adapted to different sorts of work. If it is the highest grade of work they are anxious about, will they kindly give any good reason why machines setting perfect foundry type will not give the same result as though the same type were set by hand in the old expensive way?

PERFECT work requires perfect tools, and type is the printer's most important tool. With all their years of experience in perfecting machinery for casting type, the founders still find it necessary to scan every letter very carefully so as to detect the imperfect ones and discard them before shipping to the printers. The finest grades of printing will doubtless always continue to be done by the use of foundry type. No matter how much improvement may be made in self-casting typesetting machines, they will still lack the means of discarding imperfect letters.

IN Syracuse the scale of prices was raised for bankmen, admen, make-ups, proofreaders and others employed on newspapers who have heretofore worked under the old scale of $17 and $15 a week for evening and morning papers. The machine scale being $18 and $21 for eight hours' work, it has been considered unjust by many that others of equal or greater efficiency should have been obliged to work nine hours for less than operators working eight hours.

WE note that a new typesetting machine company is instructing young lady typewriters to operate its machines, claiming that great economy will result therefrom. It would be of vast advantage to all new concerns contemplating or adopting such a course to inquire into the Mergenthaler Company's costly experience in this direction, or the trials and disappointments of the St. Paul and Minneapolis publishers. Not one typewriter in either of the above cases became an acceptable operator when put to work in composing rooms. Dexterity in manipulating the keyboard, without technical knowledge of the printing business, is of no practical value in a printing office.

THAT old and genial inventor, Mr. Merritt Gally — known in every part of the world where printing is done as the inventor of the Gally Universal press — has now turned his inventive abilities toward constructing a typesetting machine. (That is not, strictly speaking, the name that should be applied to it, but everything of the kind is known as a "typesetting machine" in this department.) Instead of casting type with liquid metal, he will produce them at the rate of 80,000 per hour by means of drop forging, in the same manner as coin is stamped, only Mr. Gally will stamp but one type at a time, and this type is less than one-fourth of an inch high, with their bottom ends shaped so as to be inserted in a groove cut in a specially prepared slug, made either of steel, aluminum or type metal, the two making a slug exactly type-high. These short type will be assembled in a line and automatically spaced and then swaged into the groove of the slug. The completed line, it is claimed, will make a beautiful printing surface, and will defy the assertions of the type founders that type cannot be thus produced. The development of Mr. Gally's system will be watched with great interest, and we regret that at the present time the scheme is not in a more tangible state.

SOME months ago eighteen Rogers Typograph machines were purchased by the Montreal Star Company, which, after being thoroughly tested, were found inadequate to the demands of that establishment. The Rogers machines were discarded, and after another unsuccessful trial of a different machine, linotypes were purchased. The announcement of the action of the *Star* management will have an influence upon the minds of some publishers in this country, who have perhaps felt it a hardship to be debarred from the benefit of fancied advantages in the Rogers machine, and have harbored a grievance against the Linotype Company for so vigorously protecting their patents and keeping it out of this country. In other words, publishers who may in the past have felt differently, will now be content without feeling that they are cut off from advantages they might have enjoyed if they could have arranged to use the Rogers machine in this country.

ACCORDING to a recent announcement of the Mergenthaler Linotype Company there has been issued to this company, under date of November 15, as a result of long litigation, two new United States patents, covering broadly all the leading fundamental features of the so-called Monoline, or Scudder, machine. The court of last resort decided, in fact, that this invention belongs to the Linotype Company. The wide scope of these patents is indicated by one of the many claims, as follows: "A font of linotype matrices, comprising a series of matrix bars adapted to be assembled in different combinations, each having in one edge a series of unlike characters independently usable and less than the assortment represented in the font." Thus, as has been previously pointed out, the Linotype Company has been assiduously pushing the development of improvements and acquisition of patents from without, with the plain purpose of strengthening an already firm hold upon the business of making and selling composing machinery.

THE general offices of the Unitype Company, located in New York City, have been removed from their temporary quarters at 34 Park Row to 150 Nassau street, corner of Beekman, more familiarly known as the American Tract Society building, and a suite of generous-sized offices have been nicely furnished and every means provided for the expeditious handling of its already increasing business. An exhibition room, to exhibit its various classes of typesetting machinery, already contains a Simplex machine, which is weekly visited by a large number of printers whose admiration for this unique and simply constructed machine is expressed in the highest possible terms. The advantages of thus having a machine in practical running condition, that prospective purchasers may actually witness its performances, are so manifest that the company has also adopted this method in its Chicago branch, at No. 188 Monroe street. Visitors to either city are cordially invited to call at the respective offices and inspect these meritorious machines.

IN the Simplex machine, built by the Unitype Company, the distributer and setting mechanism are one. None of the several different classes of typesetting machines is so beautifully symmetrical and none so compact. It is easily demonstrated that a room necessary for twenty compositors will hold enough of these machines so that an amount of work can be executed beyond the capabilities of one hundred compositors. Specially nicked foundry type is used. For distribution, the dead matter is placed upon a galley and from this a line at a time is automatically inserted into the channels of the machine, thus dispensing with the services of anyone otherwise than to replenish the galley when empty. It is ordinarily a one-man machine, with a capacity of 3,500 ems an hour, but it has a valuable and unique advantage over any of its competitors, inasmuch that its output can be doubled at any time by the aid of a second person to justify the matter, thus allowing the operator to uninterruptedly manipulate the keyboard. By this arrangement 6,000 or 7,000 ems per hour are readily obtained. However, the strong points of the Simplex are its utility and cheapness, which will make it desirable for the offices of small means. It is a little giant and will prove a valuable assistant in the composing room.

THE following notice is being circulated for this worthy machine: "The Johnson Typesetter Company, capital $3,000,-000, offers for sale 3,000 shares of stock. The company manufactures the Johnson typesetting machine, invented by F. Amos Johnson, which is fully covered by patents both in the United States and in foreign countries. The company has up to this time been in an experimental state, but is now ready to enlarge its plant and manufacture for the market. The Johnson typesetter sets type in any length of line, automatically justifies, and automatically leads. The machines are simple of construction and speedy of operation. Already the company has had many requests for machines, and the field is fully as clear in the line of manufacturing and setting type as is the Mergenthaler in its own particular branch, and the Johnson can be manufactured and sold at a large profit at two-thirds the price of the Mergenthaler. It is conservatively estimated that the proceeds from the sale of this stock will give the company a capacity of five hundred completed machines per annum, which will show a net profit of over $20 per share."

THE Sydney (New South Wales) *Telegraph* has a linotype operator of whom it is proud. He is Frank Bevan, and a record made by him is given in a recent issue of that paper. It says: "Last week, taking the copy from the box in the ordinary course, Mr. Bevan averaged 15,860 ens per hour for the whole week; and on Friday night, under exactly the same conditions, he set 129,015 ens in eight hours, or an average of 16,080 ens per hour, including corrections and loss of time in making up copy. All the matter set was in minion type and contained no 'phat' beyond the ordinary run of news copy. Larger results than these have been reported from America on a few hours' trial, but in no case, as far as we are aware, have they been beaten as a sustained average extending over a long period under the ordinary conditions of office working. To give some idea to the uninitiated, it may be mentioned that the 129,015 ens set by Mr. Bevan on Friday night in eight hours are equal to eleven full columns of the *Daily Telegraph*, or about two weeks' solid work by hand composition." The statement in the last few lines is absurd, since a good compositor could do the eleven columns in eight or nine days.

THERE is a great diversity of opinion among the book printers of New York City as to the actual cost of machine composition, and information gained from offices using typesetting machines differs to such an extent as to be most astounding. A careful analysis, however, of the detailed expenses attached to machine composition appears to place the cost per thousand ems at a larger sum than many have heretofore supposed. But there should be no excuse for such wide differences among men in the same line of business and with equal facilities for ascertaining the actual cost. There is one class of printers who, in reckoning the cost of machine composition, apparently charge the entire expense of their composing rooms against the machines, even though they are also doing composition by hand. In such offices, to charge the entire salaries of the foreman, make-ups, proofreaders and other such employes is unjust to the machines; these expenses should be divided pro rata and a more accurate cost would be secured. This is undeniably safer for financial welfare, however, than the other extreme, as too many have learned to their dismay. This latter class base their calculations on the scale of prices given by a few typographical unions where a piece scale is given, and they gain the knowledge that where a scale of 40 cents per thousand ems for hand composition is in vogue a machine scale of 12 cents is given for day work in machine book offices. They know that in both cases this is for corrected matter upon the galleys, and that the cost of the subsequent handling of the matter is about the same. They add a few cents to each thousand ems for incidental expenses and also for profit upon the work, and not until the sheriff has made their acquaintance do they realize that they cannot afford to estimate in this manner. Much of this state of affairs arises from the newness of the situation and much from the differing classes of work done by each office, but the sooner an intelligent and fair understanding of the matter is arrived at the better it will be for all parties concerned, as at the present time the price of machine book composition varies from 35 to 70 cents per thousand ems.

LEAVE IT TO THE PRINTER.

BY ARTHUR K. TAYLOR.

IT is probable that in the greater number of cases it is a matter of both wisdom and economy to leave the question of style in job printing to the printer. That is, to some printers. The rule admits a great number of exceptions. Of course, you or I are not the exceptions referred to, but between ourselves we could mention a few printers whose opinion in matter of style it would not be wise to consider final. Still, when we stop to consider the productions which have been fearfully and wonderfully made by the artistic rule-twister when he has been enjoined to get up something "real nice and stylish"— when we consider a few of these and are not biased by the knowledge that they were produced simply by the use of a few pieces of brass rule, a file, a pair of pliers and usually one-half more time than will be paid for by the whole job — when we do not let these points bias us in examining a few of these works of art, it does not seem so strange to us that in every calling by which man has gained his livelihood, from the doctor who first honored us with his personal attention to the undertaker who will probably make it his business to attend our funeral, each and every manner of man feels called upon to give the printer a few instructions as to what is tasteful and stylish in the way of job printing.

There are at present just a few men having the ordering of printing who were not at some stage of their existence printers, but the number is small. Did you ever notice how many men, when they leave an order for a job of printing, after making a few suggestions as to how it is to be set in a "block letter," will clear their throats, look rather sheepish and in a hesitating way admit that they used to have a printing press in their younger days? Did all the old man's work. Most of them gave it up on account of their health. Afraid of the type metal poisoning them. A little more particular diagnosis of their cases generally reveals, also, a very early tendency toward scroll sawosis, with frequent attacks of magic lanternalia which finally developed into chronic amateur photogromania, for which the patient is taking treatment even at this date. Nevertheless, it might be worse.

If the whole of the designing of a piece of work is left to a competent printer, a harmonious production can usually be expected, which is a result almost impossible when the customer hampers the workman by ill-advised suggestions. If the man ordering the work has a clear idea of what he wants and is blessed with a fair amount of good taste, the remarks in the foregoing do not apply to him. It is a pleasure to coöperate with a discriminating customer in order to turn out a creditable product, but our patience and some other of the Christian virtues are put to the test when we have to cater to the needs of a customer who thinks that, just because he is paying for the work, he has not gotten full value for it if he has not attached thereto a few eccentric characteristics of his individuality.

Unless you can convey to the printer a clear and definite idea of the style of what you wish him to print for you, it is manifestly unfair for you to insist that he, at his own expense, by means of numerous proofs showing radical changes, try thus to locate your own elusive ideas. Yet this is too frequently what is required. When a man makes an alteration on a proof which is a direct deviation from his original copy, if the change amounts to a sufficient item of expense to warrant a charge, it is only the most casehardened sinner who objects to paying for it, provided, of course, that the matter is explained to him at the proper time, which is just before the change in question is to be made; but with the man who insists upon having a job set over three or four times in order to get it sufficiently unbalanced to meet his own condition, the situation is a trifle more difficult. If you suggest that all his alterations are costing money and should be charged for, he will probably retort that you ought to know your business well enough to suit him the first time. That floors you. It seems almost impossible even for those customers who are possessed of proper appreciation for well-balanced display to understand that, on account of the only occasional exercise of their taste, it should not be accorded the same degree of consideration as should that of the printer who by constant use has developed more fully that faculty for arrangement which he is daily called upon to exercise.

Once in a while a customer will ask your opinion as to his suggestions, with entire sincerity, being susceptible to convincement should he clearly be in the wrong; but in the majority of cases, when your customer asks you if you don't think that that line should be put in such and such a type, and spread out a little more, it is the part of good judgment to be politic and admit that you believe it would look a trifle better that way, for should you by any method of argument get him to accept anything else, there will always be in his mind a lurking dissatisfaction with the appearance of the job, and a steadily growing conviction that the change which he suggested was all that would have been needed.

Believing that the composing room should not be called upon to bear the brunt of all the leaks which occur from ill-advised alterations which are never paid for, it seems to me that it would be a good plan to open another account in the ledger, an account like unto the profit and loss account, and style this account "Sundry Chuckleheads," entering therein charges for part of the composition of numerous jobs which you have run without your imprint, and which represents the part for which you were not paid, crediting the composing room accordingly.

RARE BOOKS

AUCTION CATALOG

SALE extraordinary, by Hulbertson & Court, at their auction rooms, on the evenings of April 19 and 20, 1900, of a large and choice private collection of Early and First Editions, comprising specimens of every school of book printing and binding from the times of Gutenberg, Faust, Caxton and Caslon down to the present day 14

CATALOG and pamphlet printing has 11 undergone vast changes in a comparatively short time. The inclination is decidedly toward artistic effects. Consumers of fine printing desire results, and they will spare neither time nor expense to bring about this wished-for end. They now know, positively, that *designed* catalogs and pamphlets are filling a most important office, and it is doubtful if they will ever lapse back to the plain, straight page of type.

CONSEQUENTLY the printer will be obliged to exert himself, says 7 a writer in the *Inland Printer*, in order that he may be able to supply the customer with what he wants. The artist, the engraver, the typefounder, the printer, all have been called upon to contribute of their tact and skill. The possibilities in this fascinating branch of printing are almost unlimited, and afford unusual opportunities to the artistically inclined printer. In decorative printing great care and artistic discernment must be exercised in order that good results may be obtained. The cuts may be ever so good and yet, if the printer does not use them as he should, they might better be left out entirely. More depends, generally, upon his judgment than upon the art and work of the engraver. Ornamental cuts and type ornaments are powerless in themselves to produce artistic effects when used in conjunction with

6a 3A, $6.00   42-POINT MACFARLAND   L. C. $2.85; C. $3.15

USEFUL Old Style 6

6a 4A, $5.00   36-POINT MACFARLAND   L. C. $2.25; C. $2.75

INLAND Type Foundry

9a 4A, $4.30   30-POINT MACFARLAND   L. C. $2.25; C. $2.05

PRODUCED Largest Series 30

LITERARY SPECIAL

MID-WEEK PENNY MAGAZINE....

ENTERTAINING reading matter of every 12 sort will be found in the pages of the new Mid-Week Penny Magazine, a periodical designed to cater to the pleasure and comfort of the man who prefers to devote his Sundays to other things than the perusal of the monstrous editions issued by the morning newspapers on the day of rest. Every topic of art, science, business, religion and pleasure, or matter of news, which the dailies touch upon, we present in a concise manner

646 *March 1899*

THE INLAND PRINTER

THE LEADING TRADE JOURNAL OF THE WORLD IN THE PRINTING AND ALLIED INDUSTRIES.

VOL. XXIII. No. 1.   **CHICAGO, APRIL, 1899.**   TERMS { $2 per year, in advance. Foreign, $1.20 per year extra.

THEODORE L. DE VINNE, THE SCHOLAR PRINTER.*

BY W. IRVING WAY.

MANY of the great printers have been scholars in a restricted sense, several in a broad sense. For the first two centuries after the invention of the art of printing from movable type, printers were also the publishers of the books they printed. This was almost invariably the rule with fifteenth century printers, who often combined the functions of printer, publisher and bookseller. It has come to be the habit to put Aldus Manutius at the head of the list of printer-publishers, because, as Mr. R. Garnett has said, "No originality was infused into the business of publishing until the advent of Aldus, almost as much the father of modern bookselling as Gutenberg is the father of printing." Before Aldus, Nicolas Jenson had come to be regarded as "the most elegant of all the Italian printers." His Roman characters have served as models to type founders for nearly four and a quarter centuries. His presswork has rarely been surpassed. As a type founder he profited by his early experience as an engraver. Caxton gave the art its first impetus in England, but his scholarship took a different turn. His efforts were literary rather than artistic. Christopher Valdarfer won renown by his edition of Boccaccio's "Decameron," Venice, 1471. To another Venetian printer, Erhard Ratdolt, belongs the credit of having introduced the ornamental title-page, in 1476. But none of the Italian printers left on his time the impression that Aldus Manutius did. He was aggressive and untiring. He succeeded in attaching to himself scholars and men of affairs who represented the best spirit of the age in which he

lived. Though he introduced the font of type known as *Italic*, his reputation as a typographer is secondary to that of publisher of the classics in handy-volume size. Yet his *magnum opus* is the "Hypnerotomachia Poliphili" of 1499, a small folio volume in roman type, with most wonderful wood cut illustrations that have been variously attributed to Mantegna and Giovanni Bellini. From whatever point of view it may be considered, the "Dream of Poliphilus" is destined to remain a monument of the bookmaking arts.

Geofroy Tory was another designer, printer, bookseller and binder, who left a strong impress on his time. As to his remarkable stamped bindings it is supposed that he did little more than furnish the designs. A "pot cassé" almost invariably figures somewhere in his designs, and the frequent use of this broken vase (it served as his printer's mark) seems to have been inspired by the death of a little daughter. Besides Tory, the other scholar-printers of Paris in the first half of the sixteenth century were Henry and Robert Stephens, Stephen Dolet (burned at the stake as a heretic), Badius, and Colines. In Antwerp were Plantin and his successor Moretus. About a century later came the Elzevirs; still later Baskerville, and our own Franklin, the Didots, Foulis brothers, the Whittinghams, and William Blades. I have named only a few of the master spirits in the typographic arts, but I have endeavored to name those who were foremost in advancing the art, as it is with such as these that the name of Theodore Low De Vinne will be identified in the coming time — not as a publisher or bookseller, but as a typographer in the broadest sense.

Born at Stamford, Connecticut, in 1828, Mr. De Vinne began to learn the printers' trade at Newburgh, New York, in 1843. Four years later he was in New York learning the several branches of the

---

* NOTE.— The illustrations accompanying this article are from photographs in the historic collection of Mr. H. W. Fay, De Kalb, Illinois, and are shown by the courtesy of that gentleman.— EDITOR.

trade in various offices. In 1849 he entered the printing office of Francis Hart as a job compositor. A year later he was made foreman, a position which he held for nine years, when he was taken into partnership. In 1873 the firm of Francis Hart & Co. began to print *St. Nicholas*, and a little later the *Century Magazine*. "At that time," says the American

MR. DE VINNE IN 1847.
(From an old ambrotype.)

Dictionary of Printing and Bookmaking, "all magazines were printed upon wet paper, although a great deal of fine job-work and bookwork was done upon dry paper. Mr. De Vinne determined to attempt the presswork of the cut forms of the *Century* upon dry paper, and after many discouragements was successful in attaining the results he desired and in producing a more brilliant effect from fine engravings than had been thought possible. His methods were adopted in other offices, but the difficulties of printing upon dry paper were not entirely surmounted for many years. He was the first to use surfaced paper for magazine work and fine bookwork with illustrations."

On the death of Francis Hart, Mr. De Vinne took his son, Theodore B., into partnership with him, but the firm name remained Francis Hart & Co. until 1883, or thereabouts, when it was changed to Theodore L. De Vinne & Co. In 1886 the firm removed to 12 Lafayette place, where a very handsome building had been erected for them. Mr. De Vinne has always paid much attention to the question of prices, and one of his principal books is his Printers' Price-List, "a manual intended to furnish printers facts for making estimates correctly." The first edition of this manual appeared in 1869, and a second was called for in 1871, "which was warmly welcomed by the trade."

Always a student of the art, and a man of positive opinions, Mr. De Vinne long ago felt the need of some authoritative work on the subject, which should seek to reduce traditions to facts, and serve as a guide to bibliographers and students generally. If he had never written another word on the subject, and if he had not been the means of introducing many improvements into the composing room, press-room and elsewhere, his great book, "The Invention of Printing," would have placed him at the head of his profession, and given him a permanent place among historians. This book was in its second edition in 1878.

During the Civil War Mr. De Vinne was instrumental in organizing the society now known as The

Typothetæ of the City of New York, and he was chosen its first secretary. It is probably largely due to his efforts that this society "proved valuable in allaying animosities and in giving to all its members a truer knowledge of the conditions of the trade" than they had hitherto enjoyed. Similar societies were formed in other cities of the Union, and in 1887, when the United Typothetæ was organized in Chicago, Mr. De Vinne, although absent, was chosen its president; he had been elected president of the New York society in 1883 on its reorganization. In 1896, when the New York Typothetæ reprinted the fine edition of Moxon's "Mechanick Exercises," Mr. De Vinne prepared for it the Preface and Notes, which enabled him to correct many of Moxon's errors, and bring his valuable work down to date by the introduction of data on modern methods. The historical interest and value of this book should have commended it to every institution or individual in the country making any pretense to a fairly complete collection of reference books. It is a very handsome specimen of bookmaking — the printing being done at the De Vinne Press — and is invaluable to the bibliographer.

If Mr. De Vinne's magazine articles, a number of which have formed the basis of several of his books, could be brought together, it would surprise some of his best friends to see what an active, studious life he has led outside his regular business as the first of American present-day printers. As one of the organizers of the Grolier Club of New York he has been called upon to do an immense amount of gratuitous work. Besides being a member of the first council of the club, he was a member of the

MR. DE VINNE IN 1860.

first House Committee, as also of the first Publication Committee, and in these and other capacities he has served the club continuously since its organization in 1884. He prepared the Preface to the first publication of the Grolier Club, the "Decree of Starre Chamber Concerning Printing," which "Decree" was reprinted from the first edition of Robert Barker, 1637. Mr. De Vinne has lived in an enlightened age, during which there have been no obnoxious decrees limiting the rights and defining the duties of printers. And the unfettered performance of his duties has been attended with a degree of pleasure that was unknown to Plantin, Moretus, the Stephani, and the English printers of the seventeenth century. There is one paragraph in Mr. De Vinne's Preface to the Star Chamber Decree, which has always struck me as a

THEODORE L. DE VINNE, THE MASTER OF THE DE VINNE PRESS, IN HIS PRIVATE OFFICE.

particularly forcible bit of English, and I am tempted to reproduce it here. He is descanting upon the futility of such legislation: "Annoyed by a little hissing of steam, they closed all the valves and outlets, but did not draw or deaden the fires which made the steam. They sat down in peace, gratified with their work, just before the explosion which destroyed them and their privileges."

With one or two minor exceptions, the publications of the Grolier Club have been printed at the De Vinne Press, and no such notable set of club publications, in point of typographical merit, have ever been printed. One of the earliest of these publications was Mr. De Vinne's own address to the club, delivered at the monthly meeting, in January, 1885, on "Historic Printing Types." In its published form, "with additions and new illustrations," this small quarto book of 110 pages has more "bullion sense," and exact information on the subject than can be found in any other book written in English. In fact, I know of no other such comprehensive treatment of this vast subject within the limits of a small volume. It is an invaluable *vade mecum* to one who wishes his historical diet to be in the "potted" form. The importance of any subject

must be more or less confined to specialists, and a pardonable enthusiasm should be allowed to one treating that subject. Hence, whether you agree with him or not, and for one I most unqualifiedly do, no one will deny the justice of Mr. De Vinne's claim that the Gutenberg Bible "is emphatically **The Book**, not because it is the Bible and to be regarded as the Book of Books, but because it is generally regarded as the first printed book. It is not only the typographic *editio princeps* of what had been a manuscript, but *princeps facile* over all books, in matter as in manner. It stands like a monument at the great turn between the old and the new method of manufacture. It shows the best features of each method — the dignity, the quaintness, the decorative beauty of the manuscript, and the superior exactness and uniformity of the printed book." To many the prices realized for this book in recent years, prices which vary from $10,000 to $25,000, "according to condition and circumstances," may seem like large sums. "But greater prices," to use Mr. De Vinne's language, "have been paid for cracked and faded paintings, and for mutilated statues; the sum of $200,000 has been asked in this city (New York) for a Madonna not larger than a barrel-head, and as much by another dealer for a collection of mediæval pottery. . . . But has not this book a greater value in its history and associations? Is not the first product of an art which has done so much for the pleasure, the knowledge, the civilization of the

MR. DE VINNE IN 1898.
(Profile View.)

world of more value as an historical relic than any work of brush or potter's wheel? Mine may be the pride of a man who magnifies his art, yet it is my belief that the time will come when a copy of this Bible of forty-two lines will be held of more value than any painting. For although it is accepted as the first of all printed books, there is nothing about it that seems experimental — nothing that is timid, or petty, or mean. It bears the stamp and seal of a great invention, and a perfected invention. One need not scrutinize it to be convinced that it was the work of a great inventor who knew the value of his art and knew how to use it."

Mr. De Vinne's short monograph is divided into twelve chapters, and in these the reader is led from Black Letter or Gothic into the Early Roman period, thence to Italic, French, Dutch, English Black Letter, Styles of Caslon and Baskerville, Styles of other British Type Founders, Bodoni, etc., Revival of Old Style, and Types of American Founders. In going over these periods one is struck by the singular fact that the common people, especially in Italy and Germany and the Netherlands, had grown so accustomed to the old Black Letter and Gothic forms that the Roman came into general use only after centuries of education — indeed, the Roman character has never to this day succeeded in taking the place of the modernized Gothic used in Germany. The late Prince Bismarck seems to have been unalterably opposed to the Roman character.

In 1888 the Grolier Club printed for its members Mr. De Vinne's monograph on "Christopher Plantin and the Plantin-Moretus Museum at Antwerp," the substance of which had already appeared in the Cen-

tury Magazine. No more sympathetic monograph has been written by one great printer of another, if we except the one by William Blades on Caxton. If anyone has doubts that ours is an enlightened and progressive age, let him but follow the "vicissitudes of fortune" attending Christopher Plantin during his stormy career, as presented by Mr. De Vinne. He lived in the days of St. Bartholomew, when those guilty of heresy were burned at the stake. The property of printers was confiscated by the Church or the State on the slightest pretext. Kings, princes, and others high in authority would engage the services of a printer with no thought of paying for them. "Nine times," said Plantin, "did I have to pay ransom to save my property from destruction; it would have been cheaper to have abandoned it." What barbarians there were in those days!

Besides those publications of the Grolier Club with which Mr. De Vinne's name is identified as author, there are doubtless a number on which he performed editorial duties. Mr. Arthur Warren, in the prefatory note to his work on the Whittinghams, says, "It is not conceivable that any author could be served with greater loyalty and enthusiasm on the part of his printer than I have been by Mr. Theodore L. De Vinne. In his advice and cheerful, untiring labor I have found inestimable help. Of his skill I need not speak." It is only fair to acknowledge, as has often been done both publicly and in private by members of the Grolier Club, that without his valuable assistance the success of the club must have fallen far short of what it has

A RECENT PORTRAIT OF MR. DE VINNE.
(Bust view.)

achieved. But many outside of the Grolier Club have acknowledged their indebtedness to Mr. De Vinne for advice and assistance. It would be well nigh impossible to enumerate the books of note that bear the imprimatur of The De Vinne Press.

Among others not already mentioned are the Century Dictionary; the "Book of Common Prayer," which is, perhaps, one of the most beautiful specimens of printing produced during the present century; "Sakoontala," an exquisite example of modern color printing; the two dainty volumes issued by the Book-Fellows' Club; the volume of "Locker's Lyrics," printed for the Rowfant Club, of Cleveland; the two books issued by The Duodecimos; the monograph on Mr. Robert Hoe's library; the publications of the Dunlap Society; the Ormsby "Don Quixote"; "Pepys' Diary," and the beautiful little monographs by Mr. W. L. Andrews.

It is something to have one say of you that you know all that is to be known on any one subject, but this praise seems not too high in its application to Mr. Theodore L. De Vinne. To be so expert and so well equipped with exact knowledge that a mere

ANOTHER RECENT PORTRAIT OF MR. DE VINNE.
(Two-thirds view.)

casual glance will enable one to assign a particular cut of type, old or new, to its rightful designer, can be said of few typographers anywhere, and yet I understand this can be truthfully said of Mr. De Vinne. He has inspired some of the most notable fonts in current use today, and he has introduced many improved methods into the conduct of a thoroughly equipped printing establishment. For bookwork he is an advocate of the bold-face, or masculine, types, as against the thin, or feminine. He has gone so far in his efforts to improve typography that some of his innovations have startled printers who were supposed to be prepared for anything. A short time since he designed a new font of type for use in the *Century Magazine*. He did not like the orthodox quotation-marks—the two inverted commas and the two conjoined apostrophes—so he introduced new characters, or characters which, at least, were new to most printers, though characters of similar cut had been introduced

by the Didots of Paris at the close of the last century. Whatever may be said for and against these new characters, one thing is certain, they are not mismated monstrosities. And their general use in Spain and Italy would seem to justify their general adoption by English and American printers.

For the work of William Morris Mr. De Vinne seems to have a genuine admiration. He has not hesitated to criticise the work of the master of Kelmscott Press where he considered that work to be faulty, yet he conceded to him high praise "for his attempts to put typography back in its proper field." "About the mechanical merit of his work," says Mr. De Vinne, "there can be no difference of opinion. For an amateur in difficult trades, his workmanship is surprising, if not unexampled. . . . A printer of the old school may dislike many of his mannerisms of composition and make-up, but he will cheerfully admit that his types and decorations and initials are in admirable accord; that the evenness of color he maintains on his rough paper is remarkable, and that his registry of black with red is unexceptionable. No one can examine a book made by Morris without the conviction that it shows the hand of a master." Mr. De Vinne has elsewhere said, or some one else has said for him, that he regarded Mr. Morris' work as the "crowning glory of the nineteenth century."

No one knows better than Mr. De Vinne the position that may properly be taken by the printer in good bookmaking. In an article that he contributed to the Book Number of the *Outlook* for December, 1897, he says: "A book should be so planned that every contributor to it keeps his place, and the first place should always be given to the author. The handicraft of the mechanical contributors, and even of the illustrator, should be subordinate and unobtrusive." Mr. De Vinne's relative position is often unduly subordinated—which is permissible, perhaps, in the office of printer—and this high office is hidden in the Greek quotation which forms part of his printer's mark. Æschylus, the Greek tragic poet, in the person of Prometheus, who is charged with having snatched fire from heaven, uses the words in question, which are thus freely rendered into English verse:

"The wealth of Numbers to the world I gave,
    With Letters ranged in mystical array;
And Memory with sweet mother-care to save
    All art—all wisdom—changeless and for aye!"

In closing this note on the "Prince of American Printers," which I have been asked to write as an accompaniment to these new pictures, I should not neglect to mention his valuable contribution to *The Bookman* for May, 1897, on "The Adaptability of Paper,"* an article which has reminded me of some things and instructed me in others.

* NOTE.—Reprinted elsewhere in this issue of THE INLAND PRINTER.—EDITOR.

"A MESSAGE TO GARCIA."

IN all this Cuban business there is one man stands out on the horizon of my memory like Mars at perihelion. When war broke out between Spain and the United States, it was very necessary to communicate quickly with the leader of the insurgents. Garcia was somewhere in the mountain fastnesses of Cuba—no one knew where. No mail nor telegraph message could reach him. The President must secure his coöperation, and quickly.

What to do?

Some one said to the President: "There's a fellow by the name of Rowan will find Garcia for you, if anybody can."

Rowan was sent for and given a letter to be delivered to Garcia.

How "the fellow by the name of Rowan" took the letter, sealed it up in an oil-skin pouch, strapped it over his heart, in four days landed by night off the coast of Cuba from an open boat, disappeared into the jungle, and in three weeks came out on the other side of the island, having traversed a hostile country on foot, and delivered his letter to Garcia, are things I have no special desire now to tell in detail.

The point I wish to make is this: McKinley gave Rowan a letter to be delivered to Garcia; Rowan took the letter and did not ask, "Where is he at?"

By the Eternal! there is a man whose form should be cast in deathless bronze and the statue placed in every college of the land. It is not book learning young men need, nor instruction about this and that, but a stiffening of the vertebra which will cause them to be loyal to a trust, to act promptly, concentrate their energies: do the thing—"Carry a message to Garcia!"

General Garcia is dead now, but there are other Garcias.

No man, who has endeavored to carry out an enterprise where many hands were needed, but has been well nigh appalled at times by the imbecility of the average man—the inability or unwillingness to concentrate on a thing and do it. Slipshod assistance, foolish inattention, dowdy indifference and half-hearted work seem the rule; and no man succeeds unless, by hook or crook or threat, he forces or bribes other men to assist him; or mayhap, God in His goodness performs a miracle, and sends him an Angel of Light for an assistant.

You, reader, put this matter to a test: You are sitting now in your office—six clerks are within call. Summon any one and make this request: "Please look in the encyclopedia and make a brief memorandum for me concerning the life of Correggio."

Will the clerk quietly say, "Yes, sir," and go do the task?

On your life, he will not. He will look at you out of a fishy eye and ask one or more of the following questions:

Who was he?

Which encyclopedia?

Where is the encyclopedia?

Was I hired for that?

Don't you mean Bismarck?

What's the matter with Charlie doing it?

Is he dead?

Is there any hurry?

Shan't I bring you the book and let you look it up your-self?

What do you want to know for?

And I will lay you ten to one that after you have answered the questions, and explained how to find the information, and why you want it, the clerk will go off and get one of the other clerks to help him try to find Garcia—and then come back and tell you there is no such man. Of course, I may lose my bet, but according to the Law of Average, I will not.

Now, if you are wise you will not bother to explain to your "assistant" that Correggio is indexed under the C's, not in the K's, but you will smile sweetly and say, "Never mind," and go and look it up yourself.

And this incapacity for independent action, this moral stupidity, this infirmity of the will, this unwillingness to cheerfully catch hold and lift, are the things that put pure Socialism so far into the future. If men will not act for themselves, what will they do when the benefit of their effort is for all?

A first mate with knotted club seems necessary; and the dread of getting "the bounce" Saturday night, holds many a worker to his place.

Advertise for a stenographer and nine out of ten who apply can neither spell nor punctuate—and do not think it necessary to.

Can such a one write a letter to Garcia?

"You see that bookkeeper?" said the foreman to me in a large factory.

"Yes, what about him?"

"Well, he's a fine accountant, but if I'd send him up town on an errand, he might accomplish the errand all right, and on the other hand, might stop at four saloons on the way, and when he got to Main street, would forget what he had been sent for."

Can such a man be intrusted to carry a message to Garcia?

We have recently been hearing much maudlin sympathy expressed for the "down-trodden denizen of the sweatshop" and the "homeless wanderer searching for honest employment," and with it all often goes many hard words for the men in power.

Nothing is said about the employer who grows old before his time in a vain attempt to get frowsy ne'er-do-well's to do intelligent work, and his long, patient striving with "help" that does nothing but loaf when his back is turned. In every store and factory there is a constant weeding-out process going on. The employer is constantly sending away "help" that have shown their incapacity to further the interests of the business, and others are being taken on. No matter how good times are, this sorting continues, only if times are hard and work is scarce, the sorting is done finer—but out and forever out, the incompetent and unworthy go. It is the survival of the fittest. Self-interest prompts every employer to keep the best—those who can carry a message to Garcia.

I know one man of really brilliant parts who has not the ability to manage a business of his own, and yet who is absolutely worthless to anyone else, because he carries with him constantly the insane suspicion that his employer is oppressing, or intending to oppress him. Should a message be given him to take to Garcia, his answer would probably be, "Take it yourself, and be damned!"

Tonight this man walks the streets looking for work, the wind whistling through his threadbare coat. No one who knows him dare employ him, for he is a regular firebrand of discontent. He is impervious to reason, and the only thing that can impress him is the toe of a thick-soled No. 9 boot.

Of course, I know that one so morally deformed is no less to be pitied than a physical cripple; but in our pitying, let us drop a tear, too, for the men who are striving to carry on a great enterprise, whose working hours are not limited by the whistle, and whose hair is fast turning white through the struggle to hold in line dowdy indifference, slipshod imbecility, and the heartless ingratitude, which, but for their enterprise, would be both hungry and homeless.

Have I put the matter too strongly?

Possibly I have; but when all the world has gone a-slumming I wish to speak a word of sympathy for the man who succeeds—the man who, against great odds, has directed the efforts of others, and having succeeded, finds there's nothing in it : nothing but bare board and clothes.

I have carried a dinner pail and worked for day's wages, and I have also been an employer of labor, and I know there is something to be said on both sides. There is no excellence, per se, in poverty : rags are no recommendation ; and all employers are not rapacious and high-handed, any more than all poor men are virtuous.

My heart goes out to the man who does his work when the "boss" is away, as well as when he is at home. And the man who, when given a letter for Garcia, quietly takes the missive, without asking any idiotic questions, and with no lurking intention of chucking it into the nearest sewer, or of doing aught else but deliver it, never gets "laid off," nor has to go on a strike for higher wages. Civilization is one long, anxious search for just such individuals. Anything such a man asks shall be granted ; his kind is so rare that no employer can afford to let him go. He is wanted in every city, town and village — in every office, shop, store and factory. The world cries out for such ; he is needed, and needed badly — the man who can carry a message to Garcia. — *Elbert Hubbard in the March Philistine.*

SETTING TYPE BY ELECTRICITY.

WHEN Benjamin Franklin, with a kite and string, drew down electricity from the clouds, he did not imagine it would ever be introduced into the composing room, typesetting machines not having been at that time invented. Another printer, however, has found a way in which to utilize this subtle agent in the composing room, and his apparatus, when connected with the typesetting machine, seems destined to accomplish results in this direction. The diagram shown herewith illustrates the apparatus, patented by John S. Thompson, of Chicago, an expert linotype operator-machinist. It consists of a number of electro-magnets connected in parallel, one magnet being assigned to

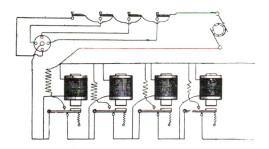

each key or lever of the machine keyboard. These magnets are constructed so as to require successively smaller electric currents to energize them, and they also require successively greater periods of time for their energization. Magnets wound with successively smaller wire possess these characteristics. The sending machine is connected with the receiving machine by but one circuit, the depression of the different keys of the sending keyboard developing in the circuit currents of different strengths. If the current so sent over the circuit be insufficient to energize the first and most quickly acting magnets, it will traverse without affecting them, and, energizing the magnet adapted to it, cause it to attract the key lever associated with it, at the same time opening the circuit at a point immediately beyond itself, and thus cut out the slower magnets before they have time to act. The sending keyboard may either be a typesetting machine or merely a facsimile of its keyboard, and if desirable, two or a dozen or more machines connected with the sending station,

all on a single circuit. Thus Associated Press dispatches could be set up in type simultaneously in various cities by one man operating a keyboard in Washington or any other point. Special dispatches and syndicate matter could in like

manner be set up in type in the offices of corresponding newspapers instead of telegraphing or sending the copy otherwise. If that class of typesetting machines which assemble the type in a continuous line, the justification being subsequently done, were used, the matter of differing measures of newspapers would cut no figure ; nor, with that or any other style of typesetting machine, would the fact that the various newspapers use different fonts in their offices, for with a fat nonpareil, a normal minion and a lean brevier, for instance, the same matter could be set in varying fonts in the same measure.

Again, if that style of typesetting machine were used which causes, by the depression of the keys, perforations to be made in a continuous strip of paper, this paper being then put into a secondary machine, the matter there being cast into type automatically, the operation becomes still more simplified, there being little more mechanism in these keyboards than in an ordinary typewriter, and the likelihood of its getting out of order at a critical time and thus causing delay, reduced to a minimum. This contingency, in any case, could be provided for by having two or more machines in each office equipped with Mr. Thompson's apparatus, which would in no way interfere with their being used in the ordinary way, and when a breakdown occurs in the receiving machine it could be "shunted" and another thrown into circuit instantly.

This invention is applicable also to a variety of other uses, and when applied to the typewriter will undoubtedly cause a revolution in the method of transmitting telegraphic messages. In party-line telephony, signaling, annunciators and like devices it will find a field of great usefulness. A. Miller Belfield, a patent attorney and electrical expert, aided Mr. Thompson materially in developing his invention, which is being patented in the principal foreign countries of the world.

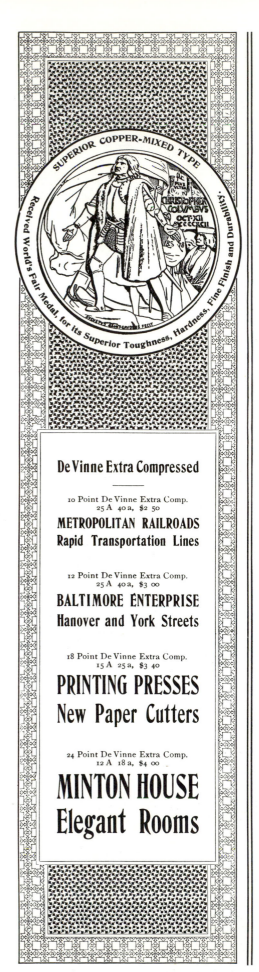

De Vinne Extra Compressed

10 Point De Vinne Extra Comp.
25 A 40 a, $2 50

METROPOLITAN RAILROADS
Rapid Transportation Lines

12 Point De Vinne Extra Comp.
25 A 40 a, $3 00

BALTIMORE ENTERPRISE
Hanover and York Streets

18 Point De Vinne Extra Comp.
15 A 25 a, $3 40

PRINTING PRESSES
New Paper Cutters

24 Point De Vinne Extra Comp.
12 A 18 a, $4 00

MINTON HOUSE
Elegant Rooms

8 A 12 a	30 Point De Vinne Extra Compressed	$4 40

LEADERS IN TYPE DESIGNS
Everything Used by Printers

6 A 10 a	36 Point De Vinne Extra Compressed	$5 30

USEFUL BRASS CIRCLES
Ornamental Decorations

6 A 10 a	48 Point De Vinne Extra Compressed	$8 00

PRINTING OUTFITS
Melvin Daily Globe

5 A 6 a	60 Point De Vinne Extra Compressed	$9 20

INDUSTRIOUS
Honest Sailors

4 A 5 a	72 Point De Vinne Extra Compressed	$12 20

FURNITURE
Grand Chair

MANUFACTURED BY BARNHART BROS. & SPINDLER, CHICAGO, ILL.

8 A 12 a   18 Point De Vinne Bold $3 90

GOOD JOB FACE
Clean Extended Letter

20 A 30 a   6 Point De Vinne Bold $2 40

DRAMATIC PERFORMERS
New Southern Plantation Songs
1234567890

6 A 10 a   24 Point De Vinne Bold $4 50

MYSTERIOUS
Robbers Captured

15 A 25 a   8 Point De Vinne Bold $2 40

GERMAN COLLEGE
Foreign Medical Institution

5 A 8 a   30 Point De Vinne Bold $6 10

DURABLE
Fancy Borders

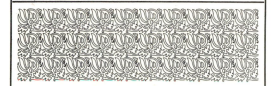

4 A 5 a   60 Point De Vinne Bold $14 50

DE VINNE Bold Series

5 A 8 a   36 Point De Vinne Bold $8 40

PRINTER
Fine Red Ink

15 A 20 a   10 Point De Vinne Bold $2 50

RESTAURANTS
Fresh Business Lunches

12 A 18 a   12 Point De Vinne Bold $2 80

REMODELED
Laconing Building

4 A 5 a   48 Point De Vinne Bold $11 20

SORT
Cabinets

Manufactured by Barnhart Bros. & Spindler, Chicago, Ill.

Printers with esthetic tastes will find a large field of usefulness for an old-time letter of the style of the Caslon Text. It is unnecessary, therefore, to waste space in pointing out to them in how many ways it may be of artistic service 18

Specimen of the Original Caslon Text

36

Early in the Eighteenth Century the text series which we show in this specimen was cut by William Caslon the First, England's most noted type-cutter and founder. It gives us much pleasure to be able to reproduce the genuine face, having secured the sole right to do so from his successors. Imitations of it should be avoided, since we supply the original on Standard Line 10

The following extract from a letter received by us from H. W. Caslon & Co., the present proprietors of the Caslon Letter-Foundry, proves our claim that we have the original face: "Allow us to congratulate you on being the first and only American founders to purchase this fine old series. The matrices were struck from punches engraved by the founder of our house. We are aware that imitations have been produced and sold in your country as the original Caslon Blacks, but we have never sold the right to reproduce them to any but yourselves, nor shall we do so. You hold, therefore, the sole right of reproduction in the United States of America." 8

Manufactured exclusively by the

Inland Type Foundry
Saint Louis
24

217-219 Pine Street

36-Point,	6a 4A,	$5.00	12-Point,	26a 10A,	$2.80
24-Point,	12a 5A,	3.50	10-Point,	30a 10A,	2.50
18-Point,	16a 8A,	3.20	8-Point,	36a 12A,	2.25

William Caslon the First, born in 1692, at Halesowen in Shropshire, began business life as an engraver of gun-locks and barrels, but quite early drifted into letter-cutting, at which art he soon proved himself to be superior to his contemporaries as well as those who preceded him. The favor with which his work was received led to the founding, in 1720, of the famous Caslon Letter-Foundery, which still exists in London 12

Jenson Heavyface

96 Point
3A 4a $19.00

FONDLED

12 Point
18A 30a $3.25

HANDSOME IMPRESSIVE LEADEN MESSENGERS FOR PRINTERDOM THOUGHT CONVEYING PURPOSE

NEW and novel, yet simple and quite as necessary to Jenson Old Style as boldface type is to the ordinary romans, in fact it should have been here long ago

18 Point
12A 20a $4.00

DESIGNED FOR WORK OF THE 1899 STYLES

And destined to become one of the most popular faces in our extensive assortment of types

120 Point
3A 4a $22.50

DESIGN

24 Point
10A 15a $4.50

GRAND SERIES IN MANY RESPECTS

Figures included with each of the 10 Bodies

60 Point
4A 5a $12.25

SHARE the Rate

72 Point
4A 5a $17.00

MORE IDEAS

American Type Founders Co.

Arlington Oldstyle ☙

Types shown on this page☙ are 10, 18, 24, 30 and the 48 point. Series complete can be seen in all recent issues of our specimen books ☙

Off-hand Proofs of the

ARLINGTON OLDSTYLE

The same comprising seven sizes, with each of which there are included clean and legible figures and different styles for some of the letters. The sloping and whited-out capitals are side-mortised to admit of greater uniformity of color in such words set in the larger sizes as would appear irregular in spacing but for this commendable feature. For sale at all branch salesrooms and agencies of the originator and manufacturer, the AMERICAN TYPE FOUNDERS COMPANY, LEADER OF LETTER DESIGNERS☙

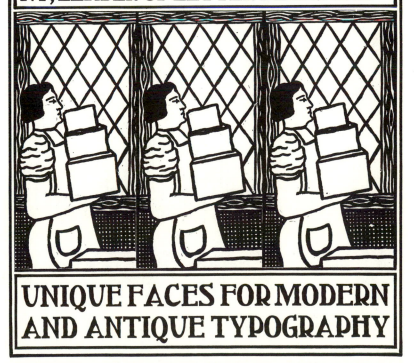

UNIQUE FACES FOR MODERN AND ANTIQUE TYPOGRAPHY

Arlington Oldstyle ten point 20A 26a $2.75, twelve point 16A 20a $3.00, eighteen point 10A 16a $3.25, twenty-four point 8A 10a $4.00, thirty point 6A 9a $5.00, thirty-six point 5A 8a $5.50, forty-eight point 4A 5a $7.75

POINT-SET OLD STYLE SERIES

OLD STYLE No. 12—CAST ON STANDARD LINE

MISTAKES OF EXPERIMENTERS

When it became evident that the point was the proper unit for the widths as well as for the bodies of type, some experimenters tried to avoid the use of the half-point, and a number of fonts were cast in which its necessity was disregarded. As was to be expected, these fonts did not present a very pleasing appearance, because the limitations put upon the fitting made it impossible to give each character the proper set-wise space, especially in *faces cast on the smaller bodies, from 12-point down*

COMPARING OLD WITH NEW SETS

In making a contrast between fonts cast according to the common system of irregular sets and those cast on the point-set system adopted by the Inland Type Foundry, one will observe that the ordinary has more than ninety different sets, while the latter has but from thirteen to twenty, each one of which bears a distinct proportional relation to the body, a relation only held by the en-set figures, and occasionally the punctuation marks, under the former system or, as would be more appropriately said, lack-o'-system. In our point-width *body-letter faces the figures stay unchanged as regards set*

POINT-SET TYPE IN TABULAR JOBS

One of the advantages of point-set which should not be overlooked, is its greater adaptability for time-tables and other tabular work, on the one hand harmonizing with point-body brass rules, and on the other permitting tight and perfect justification in narrow columns, which was heretofore an impossibility. Casting up tables by points instead of ems is productive of quicker and better results, and if point-set type is used the advantages are still greater. Occasionally, in narrow columns, spaces can be set sideways where it may be inconvenient to use *leads, which makes point-set type still more advantageous*

OTHER FEATURES INCREASE ITS UTILITY

The series of point-set Romans and Old Styles furnished by the Inland Type Foundry have a further advantage in the fact that they are cast on Standard Line, by reason of which all our jobbing and display faces can be used for side-heads or for words which require more prominence than the ordinary Italic can give. To this great advantage may be added mention of another, to the effect that the printer ordering sorts to add to his fonts can rely upon finding that they match his original purchase in width, which was scarcely ever the case with old methods of casting type. The use of steel dies in place of the old type-metal standards, for the purpose of gaging the type during the process of manufacture, gives assurance that the product will be at all times the same. In taking a thoro survey of the point-set faces made by this foundry, the interested printer will *note that every possible point of advantage has been incorporated*

EXPLANATION OF THE IMPROVED POINT-SET SYSTEM

Additional Specimen of 8-Point Old Style No. 11

The need of system in the widths as well as in the bodies of printing types, has resulted, after a trial of other plans, in the use of the point, with its multiples and halves, by which to determine the set of every space, quad, letter or character in a number of new series made by the Inland Type Foundry. Of the book and newspaper faces produced by us, the Roman series Nos. 26, 27 and 28, and Old Style series Nos. 11, 12 and 13 (in addition to our later jobbing faces) are cast thruout on such sets, truly making them "point system both ways."

All our spaces and quads have from the very beginning been cast on point sets, and it is but an extension of this principle when we apply it to the faces with which the spaces and quads are to be used. The points and figures of all our many faces, jobbing as well as body letter, and all fractions, references, dashes, marks, signs, and other characters, have all along been placed by us on point widths, so the extension of the principle to take in entire fonts is not so very far.

The fact that all this auxiliary material is already cast on the point-set system goes to show that the danger of mixtures and other inconveniences which attend the type erroneously called "self-spacing" is not to be met with in our point-set type. The auxiliary material can be used with different fonts.

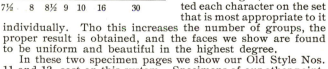

To give a clear insight into the point-set system of casting type, an illustration of 10-point Old Style No. 11 is given here. The characters making up the font are grouped according to their widths, and the sets on which they are cast is indicated under each group. In some point-set and other schemes of widths attempts were made to limit these groups to a small number, and to have each different group contain the same characters thruout the series of bodies, without regard to the look of the faces in print. Hence, many letters were cut or fitted much too wide or too narrow, thus giving the series an irregular and repulsive aspect. As there is no special reason why the groups should be thus limited or arranged, we have fitted each character on the set that is most appropriate to it individually. Tho this increases the number of groups, the proper result is obtained, and the faces we show are found to be uniform and beautiful in the highest degree.

In these two specimen pages we show our Old Style Nos. 11 and 12, cast on this system. Specimens of our other point-set faces, both Roman and Old Style, will be sent on call.

Altho the cost of manufacturing point-set type is considerably greater than that of the ordinary type, it is sold at the same prices and with the same discounts.

ORIGINATED AND MANUFACTURED BY THE

INLAND TYPE FOUNDRY, SAINT LOUIS

The only script that exactly imitates copperplate work. Notice the spaces between the words, the o'c in o'clock and the joined 's to indicate the possessive case. Also compare it with other type work.

Reception and Banquet

of the

Jewelry Salesmen's Club

at the

Metropolitan Hotel.

The honor of your company is requested on

Wednesday evening, May seventeenth,

eighteen hundred and ninety-nine

at half-past eight o'clock.

Committee of Arrangements.

Archibald Bowers,
Randolph Mitchell,
Howard Livingston.

Made by the

Inland Type Foundry,

217-219 Pine Street,
Saint Louis.

Mr. Harvey T. Russell.

710 Arlington Place.

THE SIMPLEX ONE-MAN TYPE-
SETTER.

IT is naturally very gratifying to THE
INLAND PRINTER to be informed
that The Unitype Company are receiving inquiries from all over the world
in response to their advertising of the
Simplex One-Man Typesetter in these
pages. This shows a widespread interest
in the subject, and that the market is
ready for a really simple, effective machine for setting type, such as is the
Simplex.

We present herewith a few illustrations, which will give some idea of the
Simplex machine and its important features. It is not a "new" machine, in
the sense that it is a crude combination
of new and untried mechanical devices.
It is rather an evolution, as it combines
the best features of other machines,
which have been acquired by The Unitype Company, with vital improvements
suggested by the experience of men who
have spent many years in developing
typesetting machinery. The Unitype Company recognized
the fact that a multitude of newspapers and periodicals in
this country required a cheaper method of producing composition than by hand, also the further fact that the only
way to meet perfectly this requirement was by means of a
machine which could be operated by one man, and which
would not cost an amount which placed it beyond reach.
The Simplex is the successful result of their effort to meet
this demand.

Two vertically channeled cylinders, one above and rotating on the other, a type loader and a keyboard constitute its

main mechanisms. Into
the upper cylinder is automatically placed the dead
matter for distribution.
The type rapidly and accurately find their respective
channels in the lower cylinder, from whence they are
ejected and assembled into
live matter by the manipulation of the keyboard.
One man alone is required

WHERE THE SIMPLEX TYPESETTER IS MADE.

for the operation, and an output of 3,000 to 3,500 ems an
hour can easily be maintained; however, a valuable and
unique feature of this machine enables its output to be
nearly doubled at any time by the employment of a second
person. This feature will be found invaluable during a
"rush," although its use was not contemplated, but is the
fortunate result of the method adopted. The machine
requires a floor space of but five feet square, weighs only 800

THE SIMPLEX METHOD OF DISTRIBUTION.

pounds, requires less than one-fourth horse-power, can be run
by motor attached to electric light wire, sets matter solid or
leaded, and can be run on live matter during the entire
working hours, as corrections are made from the case. The
price is $1,500.

In fact, so completely are the requirements of the newspaper and periodical publisher anticipated, that it is hard to
conceive in what manner improvements could be made that
would be of any benefit. The machine solves the question
of cheap composition where foundry type is used, and will
be a valuable acquisition in many of our printing offices.

Among the many papers successfully using the Simplex
machine are the following: *Courier*, Chatham, N. Y.;
Herald, Manchester, Conn..

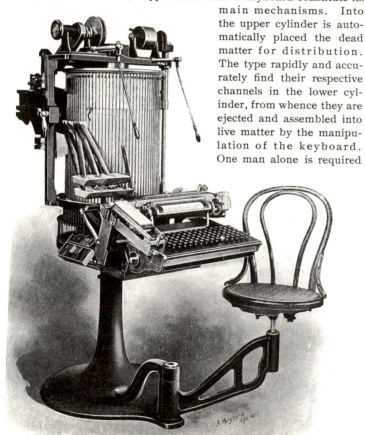

THE SIMPLEX TYPESETTER.

Notes And Queries Machine Composition

BY AN EXPERT.

THE Unitype machine, now under course of construction by the Unitype Company, gives promise to more than meet the expectations of its promoters. Its mechanical construction gives it an appearance which creates confidence, while an investigation into its detail mechanism impresses the most prejudiced in favor of its ability to meet the requirements of the most exacting composing room. It is uncertain at present when the machine will be ready for the market, as its promoters are old hands in the typesetting machine business and will not hazard the placing of an imperfectly built machine in the field, regardless of the time it may require to perfect it.

IT is gratifying to announce that the merits of the "Simplex" are being recognized and that quite a number of orders are being placed. The "Simplex" is quite properly reaching for that enormous field of small dailies and weeklies which have insufficient means or composition to justify them in employing a high-priced machine. The Unitype Company, which is manufacturing and marketing this machine, has one on exhibition in each of its offices located in New York City and Chicago.

IN many newspaper shops, when the transition from hand to machine composition was going on, men were paid the full scale while they were learning the mysteries of the keyboard. Opportunities were opened to many who failed to take advantage of them, and they have been kicking themselves ever since. Some places gave matinee performances for the benefit of would-be operators, the men working for the privilege of learning and the office picking up what they set. But as the regular forces became expert, the chances of the beginners' practicing grew slimmer, until now one is lucky indeed who has the opening to acquire a new trade. Offices no longer give seances, and about the first question a foreman asks a new man is how much an hour he can set. If his speed is less than a galley of nonpareil an hour he gets the marble heart. Consequently, the business is largely restricted to those who are already good operators. One proprietor wants a fee of $100 to let a printer learn,

OBSERVATIONS OF A PROOFREADER.—It hardly seems possible that a proofreader could be able to say anything that would interest or instruct an operator or machinist, yet the writer has been a reader of machine composition for several years, and has made a few observations. There are several different machines in use, but the one I refer to is the linotype. As machine work is largely done on time, the proofreader's marks are corrected at the expense of the office, and he is therefore instructed to "let it go if it is good enough!" Little attention is paid to divisions, as it necessitates resetting two lines, and it often occurs that a worse error is made than the original one. A comma marked out can be cut off, but a comma marked in means that a new line has to be set. A single letter now takes the place of the diphthong. No attempt is made to avoid two-letter divisions, as it requires the line to be spaced by hand. Small caps and italics, also having to be inserted by hand, are used very sparingly, although I understand they are now added to the machines when desired.

APPARENTLY there is a great lack of business enterprise at the present time in the neglect of establishing schools of instruction for printers to be taught to operate typesetting machines. Since this department has been established letters by the score have been received from printers asking where they can learn operating. The typesetting machine companies appear indifferent to the appeals of these men and justify their attitude by asserting that offices prefer teaching their own operators taken from their old employes. While this sounds very nice, still it is not good business policy, for an office adopting typesetting machines can realize a profitable income by their use the first day they are installed if they employ experienced operators. On the other hand, where green men are taken from the case and placed in front of machines, it is weeks before any profitable income is derived from their use. If schools of instruction were instituted and made available so that practical printers could be taught to operate machines during stated hours of the day or evening, as best suited their convenience, proprietors would soon find operators among their employes and these would be valuable whenever he would adopt machines. That some of the numerous typesetting machine companies will eventually find it to their interest to thus provide purchasers of their machines with experienced operators is firmly believed by many persons who have investigated this question and have expressed themselves upon it. The time is surely coming when it will be required that experienced men shall be furnished with the machines, as competition is becoming so keen that proprietors cannot afford the time and expense incident to training new men when changing from hand to machine composition.

THE possibilities of rule-and-border effects are now only limited to the ingenuity and skill of the compositor. The expense heretofore attached to brass rules and borders made this class of work unprofitable and, consequently, their use for design work was discouraged, for, when once bent or twisted, they were afterward practically worthless. With the advent of the linotype this objection to their use was eliminated by casting rule and border faces on metal slugs which, after being used, can be cast over and over again *ad infinitum*. This method of production not only reduces the cost to a minimum, but obviates the necessity of a restriction to design effects and allows the compositor perfect freedom in their manipulation. The faces of the borders are cast from single matrices. The matrices having faces alike, can be assembled in the order necessary to form a plain or simple border, or any of those having different faces, of which there are ninety-six now made, can be alternated. It will not be far from the truth to say that a thousand and one different combination borders can be thus obtained, a fact which will not only add to their utility, but will prove to be a practically inexhaustible source of supply from which to draw for varied and artistic effects. The alignment being perfect, the faces uniform, sharp and clear, with the additional advantage of always being new, these borders, the latest and most useful production of the linotype, are all that can be desired for the purposes intended. An important feature, and one that would make them superior to brass for design effects, even if of equal cost, is the fact that they possess such a degree of pliability as to require but very little effort in bending or twisting them into any conceivable shape or form. This ease of manipulation enables the compositor to produce a multiplicity of original and striking design effects, suitable for covers, title-pages, etc., which were not only impossible to obtain with brass, but were entirely too expensive to be even attempted. Thus, to users of the linotype rules and borders, the cost is insignificant and the quantity limitless, and, when it is taken into consideration that there is a saving of fifty per cent in the time consumed to produce this class of work, the objection to their use must necessarily narrow down to the individual preference of taste and not, as formerly, to the cost attached thereto.

AMONG the entire industries of the world none presents a more favorable outlook for future business than that of manufacturing typesetting machinery. The transition from hand to machine composing will soon be an accomplished fact. The economical advantages alone will cause their universal adoption. To the uninformed, the bulk of the trade has already been done by the Linotype Company, but to any one who has the means to obtain the knowledge of the vast number of printing offices which are yet to be supplied with means of rapid composition it will soon become evident that the industry is but in its infancy. True, all the large and many of the smaller newspapers throughout the land are provided with machines, but their number is small when the book, job and magazine offices and the small country dailies and the large country weeklies are taken into consideration. This means simply the employment of thousands of machines, the manufacture and sale of which will involve large sums of money, and the profits to the manufacturers will undoubtedly be all that is desired. Even at the present day the printer with sufficient composition to justify him in purchasing this class of machinery has got no argument to sustain him in not adopting them. Take any of the existing machines which are now upon the market; each and all of them are more economical than hand composition. This the printer is rapidly realizing, and he is simply forced by competition to adopt them, knowing already from sad experience in seeing his former work going elsewhere, that to remain in the business he must be equipped to keep up to the progress of the age. Inventors and wide-awake manufacturers were long ago cognizant of this inevitable transition in this industry, and have labored hard and have expended fortunes to meet the requirements when the proper time arrived; and although many appear slow in perfecting and placing their respective machines upon the market, still, when it is once understood the immense number of machines which will be required to perfect the revolutionizing of this great industry, it will be readily seen that no one concern can hope to alone accomplish the change, however meritorious their machine or with what energy it is being marketed. It is within the memory of many when the same changes were made in the pressrooms and a great press manufacturing concern was thereby created which, apparently, would control the building of the presses required for all time to come, but other and infinitely smaller concerns asked for a recognition of the merits of their machinery and secured it.

ALL good Americans are supposed to hold with Tennyson that "fifty years of Europe" (or America, rather) "are worth considerably more than a cycle of Cathay," but the love of progress is very frequently, even on this side of the Atlantic, qualified by personal idiosyncrasy. We as a people welcome with enthusiasm the latest discoveries in science and invention in the industrial arts, but there are always with us the lovers of the "good old way," unable to see the merit in anything introduced since their own prime, and in too many cases ready to do their little possible to "burke" the latest heirs of human invention. Many of this class met the introduction of the steam locomotive with angry ridicule, and in our own generation we know many who are only half reconciled to the phonograph. This kind of Toryism may be amusing, and even assume a tinge of romance in fictitious literature, but in the affairs of the practical, everyday world it is sometimes not only irritating but harmful. In the printing industry these obstructives are to be found, as in all professions and every branch of business. The man who not so very many years ago could not be persuaded to furnish his pressroom with the cylinder press now assumes the same attitude to that revolutionist of the composing room, the typesetting machine. Or, to be more exact, he would assume that attitude if his more progressive competitors in business had not long since driven him out of the trade, just as the master printer who today refuses to avail himself of the advantages offered by the different composing machines must infallibly give place to the one who has the sense to see and the enterprise to seize those advantages. The mental mood of these unprogressive gentlemen is not one difficult to understand, nor is it unnatural. A man who has been in business twenty or thirty years, and has succeeded in equipping what he considers a thoroughly modern printing office, is not very likely to listen with great good will to the one who comes to tell him of the one thing still lacking. Assuredly age is not the season for "hazards of new fortunes," and one may spare a little kindly sympathy for the obstinate conservative, even while devoutly wishing that in some way or other he may be got out of the way of progress. Most certainly he will not be allowed to block the way for any great length of time, for if he be not wise enough to remove himself of his own free will, the grinding, remorseless methods of modern business will soon eliminate him from the struggle for existence. For, if there are some who refuse to see what typesetting machines may do for them in the competition for composition, which is more keen today than ever before, there are many more who have well weighed all those advantages, and are eager to avail themselves of them. These are they who represent the "young blood" of the publishing business. Generally blessed with more brains and enterprise than cash capital, they are often checked at the very start by the difficulty of procuring tools. Typesetting machines cost a tidy bit of money, and so far the dealers have by no means appeared inclined to pursue a generous policy toward the beginner. They have seemed rather to be actuated by a desire to save the old-established houses from the dangerous competition of youth and energy. This seems rather a poor policy for themselves, for no argument could be more effective with the "old fogy" than to see his "cases" standing lonely, while the machines of the youthful upstart, who has had the audacity to compete with him, have all the work they can do. But the chances are that no argument will have any effect on the bigoted adherent of methods which already seem antiquated to this pushing generation, and the shortest way to put him out of misery and clear the way for effective work in the future is the establishment of a competitor, who by means of the advantages afforded by typesetting machines will soon leave him without sufficient composition to justify him in keeping his shop open. This is cruel, perhaps, but progress generally involves more or less individual suffering; and after all, the man who is thus forced out of the business to make room for the publisher of the future has only himself to thank for his misfortune. He has had full opportunity to see the trend of events, and none but the wilfully blind could have failed to see some time ago that a typesetting machine plant of greater or less dimensions was soon to be the *sine qua non* of continuance in the printing business. They have their chance even yet to save themselves, but very shortly it will be a case of "Time has been." No discouragement on the part of the sellers of the machines can long keep back the young fellows who see the opportunity that command of the machine will give them, and in a few years more they will be in control of the business. The Napoleonic maxim of "The tools to him who can handle them," is a mighty good one for general practice in this rough world, and as a rule the capable man does manage to get hold of the machinery, whether of a political party or of a printing office. It looks as though it always would be so in the future, as it certainly has been in the past; and on the whole the gentlemen who have the control of composing machines would possibly do the best thing for themselves as well as for the public at large by allying themselves rather with the printer whose face is turned to the light of the future.

UNIQUE FACES DESIGNED FOR

4048A 50¢

PRINTERS IN NEED OF SUCH TYPES AS WILL BRING TO THEM GLORY AND GREENBACKS THE QUICKEST · THIS IS ONE SAMPLE

AMERICAN TYPE FOUNDERS COMP

SCHEMES AND PRICES

The excellent letter in the announcement is

RAMONA 15
18 Point 10A 32a $4.50
24 Point 8A 20a 4.60
30 Point 6A 14a 4.75

ECCENTRIC 15
Is recognizable from its eccentricity
18 Point 10A $1.90
24 Point 8A 2.35
36 Point 6A 3.50

FOR SALE AT ALL BRANCHES

TWO UNIQUE FACES

MANUFACTURED BY

AMERICAN TYPE FOUNDERS COMPANY

Upon request to the nearest Branch there will be sent to
you a more elaborate specimen, showing
these faces in actual work

Quaint and Effective Designs
The Ramona Series

This series is especially useful for neat circular work, and there are countless other little jobs, such as programs, dance orders, address cards, etc., for which it may be used to good advantage. There are

Three Sizes Having Figures

Complete with each. The design is such as will insure long life, there being no fine hair lines to show wear. Manufactured by and in stock at all Branches and Agencies of the Leading Printers' Provider,

American Type Founders Co.

United States of America

Standard
LINE

CARD MERCANTILE

———1———

6 Point No. 1   26A $1.00

THE CARD MERCANTILE SERIES IS AN ABSOLUTE NECESSITY IN MODERNIZED
COMMUNITIES WHEREIN THE PEOPLE PATRONIZE ONLY 19TH CENTURY PRINTERS

6 Point No. 2   22A $1.00

FOR IMITATING THE WORK OF STEEL ENGRAVERS THERE
CAN BE NOTHING MORE BEAUTIFUL PICKED FROM A CASE

6 Point No. 3   20A $1.15

AND IT IS DIFFICULT IF NOT IMPOSSIBLE TO
IMAGINE HOW ANYTHING FINER EVER CAN

6 Point No. 4   20A $1.25

CARDS AND HEADINGS ARE INVESTED
WITH FINE ARISTOCRATIC SHARPNESS

8 Point No. 5   18A $1.50

AMERICAN TYPE FOUNDERS CO.

10 Point No. 6   16A $1.75

UNIQUE $32.58 DESIGNS

12 Point No. 7   14A $2.00

FINE CLEAN CARD

18 Point No. 8   8A $2.50

MORE TYPES

24 Point No. 9   6A $2.75

LONGINGS

30 Point No. 10   5A $3.00

SERIES 10

MANUFACTURED BY

AMERICAN TYPE FOUNDERS COMPANY

FOR SALE AT BRANCHES AND AGENCIES

Abbey Text Italic

ESTABLISHED 1804.

Business Purposes $12
Attractive $3

We herewith present to the printing trade four sizes of our series of *Abbey Text Italic*. It is another addition to our large variety of modern display faces that will please the artistic printer who desires his work to bear the mark of elegance. Other sizes of this series in preparation.

Fine Lines
Artists' Admiration

A. D. Farmer & Son

TYPE FOUNDING COMPANY

CORNER BEEKMAN AND GOLD STREETS
NEW YORK
Chicago, Detroit, San Francisco

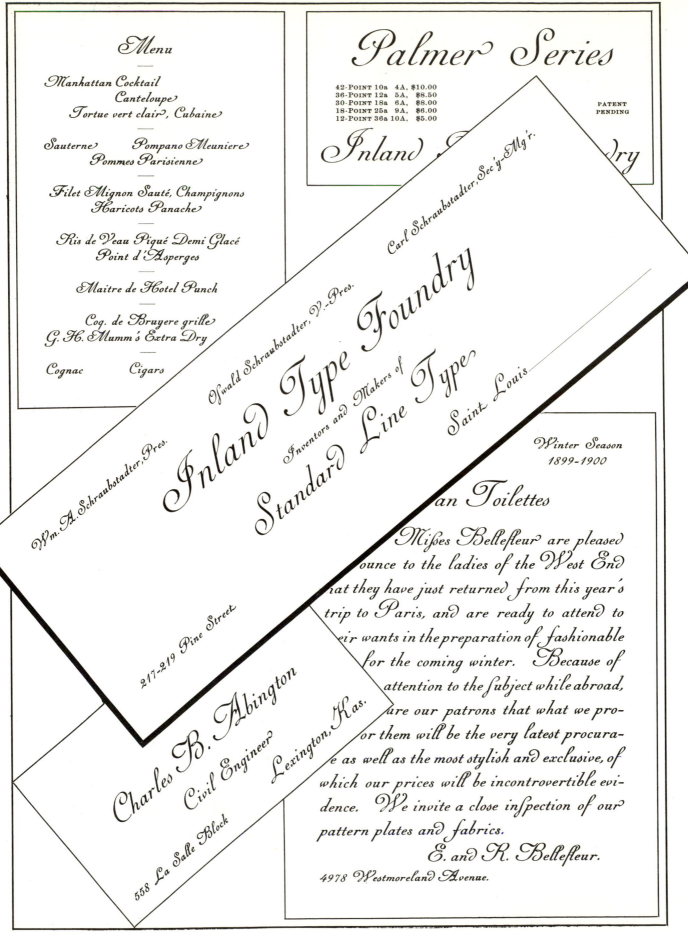

Menu

—

Manhattan Cocktail
Canteloupe
Tortue vert clair, Cubaine

Sauterne   Pompano Meuniere
Pommes Parisienne

Filet Mignon Sauté, Champignons
Haricots Panache

Ris de Veau Piqué Demi Glacé
Point d'Asperges

Maitre de Hotel Punch

Coq. de Bruyere grille
G. H. Mumm's Extra Dry

Cognac   Cigars

Palmer Series

42-Point 10a	4A, $10.00
36-Point 12a	5A, $8.50
30-Point 18a	6A, $8.00
18-Point 25a	9A, $6.00
12-Point 36a	10A, $5.00

PATENT
PENDING

Inland _____ _____ry

Inland Type Foundry
Standard Line Type

Wm. A. Schraubstadter, Pres.
Oswald Schraubstadter, V.-Pres.
Carl Schraubstadter, Sec'y-Mg'r.

Inventors and Makers of

Saint Louis

217-219 Pine Street

Charles B. Abington
Civil Engineer   Lexington, Kas.
558 La Salle Block

Winter Season
1899-1900

_____an Toilettes

_____ Misses Bellefleur are pleased
_____ounce to the ladies of the West End
_____hat they have just returned from this year's
_____ trip to Paris, and are ready to attend to
_____eir wants in the preparation of fashionable
_____ for the coming winter. Because of
_____ attention to the subject while abroad,
_____ure our patrons that what we pro-
_____or them will be the very latest procura-
_____e as well as the most stylish and exclusive, of
which our prices will be incontrovertible evidence. We invite a close inspection of our
pattern plates and fabrics.
E. and R. Bellefleur.
4978 Westmoreland Avenue.

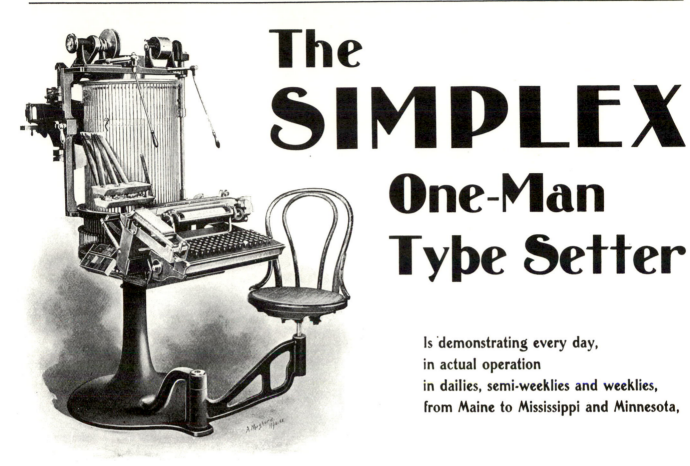

THE RIGHT TO PUBLISH PORTRAITS AND NAMES.

ELSEWHERE in this issue will be found the abstract of an important decision rendered by the Michigan Supreme Court, which has ruled adversely against the claim that no person has a right to print or circulate pictures of another without his consent, or where by reason of his celebrity, the public has an interest in him. The decision is a very important one to the publisher and printer.

A PORTRAIT IS NOT PROPERTY — NAME AND FACE CAN BE USED BY OTHERS.

THE correspondent of the Chicago *Record*, writing from Lansing, Michigan, under date of October 4, says:
"The Michigan Supreme Court has held against the long-established claim that a man has no right to print and circulate pictures of another except by his consent, or where, by reason of his celebrity, the public has an interest in him.

"This conclusion was reached in the famous case brought by the widow of the late Col. John Atkinson, the well-known Michigan politician, to restrain a Detroit firm from putting upon the market the John Atkinson cigar, which bore a label with the name and likeness of Colonel Atkinson.

"The court says, in a unanimous opinion written by Justice Hooker, that as a rule names are received at the hands of parents, surnames by inheritance and Christian names at their will. But this is not an invariable rule, for many names are adopted or assumed by those who bear them. But in neither case is the right to the use of the name exclusive. A disreputable person, or criminal, may select the name of the most exemplary for his child, or his horse, or dog, or monkey. This has never been questioned, and no reason occurs to the court for limiting the right to apply a name, though borne by another person, to animate objects. 'Why not a John Atkinson wagon?' is asked, 'as well as a John Atkinson Jones, or horse, or dog? Society understands this and may be depended upon to make proper allowances in such cases, and although each individual member may in his own case suffer a feeling of humiliation when his own name or that of some beloved or respected friend is thus used, he will usually in the case of another regard it as a trifle. We feel sure that society would not think the less of Col. John Atkinson if cigars bearing his name were sold in the shops. Nor are his friends brought into disrepute thereby. So long as such use does not amount to a libel, we are of the opinion that Colonel Atkinson would himself be remediless, were he alive, and the same is true of his friends who survive.'

"It was urged that in this case the feelings of the widow were wounded. The court says it fully appreciates the indelicacy of the man who should join the funeral procession of Colonel Atkinson in a carriage bearing the legend, 'The Col. John Atkinson Cigar,' and can well understand that this would annoy the colonel's friends. It does not follow, however, that such an act is an actionable wrong, or that equity will intervene by injunction to prevent it, and the court is sure that the disapproval of society would ordinarily have the latter effect.

"The major portion of the voluminous opinion, however, is devoted to the consideration of the question of the right to print pictures of another without his consent. This is declared to be a proposition of modern origin. Counsel for Mrs. Atkinson insisted that this proposition is supported by several cases, and these the court considered at some length, the conclusion being that they do not apply here.

"After reviewing these cases the court says that the law-books published before 1860 were searched in vain for the assertion of any such right as that claimed, or the denial of the right to publish the truth for any lawful purpose or in a decent manner, either orally, or in writing, or by pictures. Here the opinion enters into quite a dissertation upon pictures, dwelling upon the pleasure and instruction they give. The court says it is not satisfied that the homes and landscapes are so entirely within the control of owners that one commits an unlawful invasion of the rights of privacy in looking upon their beauties, or by sketching or even photographing them, or that one has a right of action either for damages or to restrain the possessor of a camera from taking a snap-shot at the passer-by for his own purpose. 'If we admit the impertinence of the act,' says the opinion, 'it must be admitted that there are many impertinencies which are not actionable, and which courts of equity will not restrain.'

"As the right contended for is not a property right, and does not spring from any contract, the opinion says it must follow that relief must be in an action for damages for a breach of duty upon an actionable wrong, or a suit to prevent a threatened injunction. In either case, such action must be based upon an act done or threatened, and if the act is one which is not in the law denominated as a wrong, there is no legal remedy.

"All men are not possessed of the same delicacy of feeling, in the opinion of the court, or the same consideration for the feelings of others. These things depend greatly upon the disposition and education. Some men are sensitive, some brutal. The former will suffer keenly from an act or word that will not affect the latter. Manifestly the law can not make a right of action depend upon the intent of the alleged wrong-doer, or upon the sensitiveness of another. Although injuries to feelings are recognized as a ground for increasing damages, the law has never given a right of action for an injury to feelings merely.

"Slander and libel are based upon injury to reputation, not to feelings; and although many offensive things may be said that injure feelings and shock and violate the moral sense, even though they be untruthful, they are not necessarily actionable. To make them so they must be of such an atrocious character that the law will presume an injury to reputation, or special damage to property interests must be alleged or proved. What becomes of the innumerable cases of ill-natured and perhaps insulting and immoral things that may be said about persons? is asked. The answer is that in an enlightened effort to preserve the liberties of the man upon the one hand and to prevent the invasion of their liberties upon the other, it has been found that a line of demarcation must be drawn which affords a practical balance.

"The law does not discriminate between persons who are sensitive and those who are not, and the brutality of the remark makes no difference. Yet the alleged 'right to privacy' is invaded. The wisdom of the law, the court says, has been vindicated by experience. The law of privacy seems to have obtained a foothold at one time in the history of our jurisprudence, not by that name, it is true, but in effect. This is evidenced by the old maxim that 'the greater the truth the greater the libel,' and the result has been the emphatic expression of public disapproval by the emancipation of the press, the establishment of freedom of speech and the abolition in most of our States of the maxim quoted by constitutional enactment.

"'Should it be thought,' says the court in conclusion, 'that it is a hard rule that is applied in this case, it is only necessary to call attention to the fact that a ready remedy is to be found in legislation. We are not satisfied, however, that the rule is a hard one, and we think that the consensus of opinion must be that the complainants contend for a much harder one.'"

Extended Companion
to Our Saint John Face

INLAND
Type Foundry

Originators and Makers of the

BECKER ✠ SERIES

Cast on Unit Sets and

Standard Line

Patent Pending on Becker Series

INLAND TYPE FOUNDRY
Pine Street ✠ Saint Louis

DEATH OF OTTMAR MERGENTHALER.

IN the death of Ottmar Mergenthaler, the inventor of the Linotype, which occurred at his home in Baltimore, Maryland, October 28, 1899, the printing trade lost a man whose wonderful skill as an inventor has won for him a name that will live for all time. The invention of printing by Gutenberg marked an epoch in the dissemination of knowledge little dreamed of by that humble disciple of "the art preservative." It has made itself felt the world over, and will be appreciated more and more as the years roll by and new inventions and devices come into use.

In later years the inventive genius of Mr. Mergenthaler resulted in a change so sweeping in its character as to astound all engaged in the field of the graphic arts, and opened another era. Nothing in the entire range of typographic inventions created a wider change in the accepted methods of doing work or finally culminated in a more thorough revolution of the printing business than the invention of the Linotype. This "child of his brain" will live forever as a monument to Mr. Mergenthaler's ability and genius, more lasting than any which could be erected by those he leaves behind.

The early efforts of Mr. Mergenthaler in his endeavors to perfect his machine are matters of history, and it will not be necessary to present them at this time, but the predictions made by him in February, 1895, when the second machine, with automatic justifier, was exhibited in Washington, are worthy of note. An exhibition of the machine was given at the Chamberlain hotel in that city at the time named, such men as Mr. Chester A. Arthur, then President of the United States; Secretary James G. Blaine, Hon. L. Q. C. Lamar and numbers of senators, representatives and newspaper men witnessing its performance. At the close of the inspection a banquet was given, during which Mr. Stilson Hutchins, a gentleman interested in the promotion of the new machine, introduced the inventor to the guests. Mr. Mergenthaler said:

Allow me, gentlemen, to express my hearty thanks to you for the honor you have bestowed upon me in coming here to witness the performance of my invention. You have come here to witness the operation of a new composing-machine, and in as far as we are working in a field which is strewn with the wrecks and failures of former efforts in the same direction, you will probably ask, "Are you going to have more success than those who have gone over that field before you; and if so, why?" My answer is: "Yes, we are going to have full success, for the reason that we have attacked the problem in an entirely different way than did those who have failed."

When I started on this problem I surveyed the field and selected the best road, regardless of the roads which others have taken. I knew the direction in which others had attempted to solve the problem, and was careful not to fall into the same rut which had led every previous effort into failure and ruin. We make and justify the type as we go along, and are thereby relieved from handling the millions of little tiny types which have proved so troublesome to my predecessors who have failed. We have no distribution, yet we have a new type for every issue of a paper, an advantage which can hardly be overrated.

I am convinced, gentlemen, that unless some method of printing can be designed which requires no type at all, the method embodied in our invention will be the one used in the future; not alone because it is cheaper, but mainly because it is destined to secure superior quality.

The history of our enterprise, gentlemen, is one of evolution. We started by printing one letter at a time and justifying the sentences afterward; then we impressed into papier-maché one letter at a time, justified it and made a type from it by after process. Next we impressed a whole line and justified it, still leaving the production of the type as a second operation; but now we compose a line, justify and cast it all in one machine and by one operator.

It is a great result, but, gentlemen of the Board, to you it is due as much as to me. You have furnished the money, I only the ideas; and in thus enabling me to carry this invention to a successful end you have honored yourselves and your country.

I say you have honored your country, for every one will know that this invention has been originated in the land which gave birth to the telegraph, the telephone, the Hoe press, and the reaper; everybody will know that it came from the United States, though comparatively few will know the name of the inventor.

OTTMAR MERGENTHALER.

The Inventor of the Linotype.

Born May 10, 1854.　　　Died October 28, 1899.

Mr. Mergenthaler has "builded better than he knew." His expressions at the banquet have been more than realized, and the world today is using a machine which, while wonderful in its operation and in its results, has become so well known and so familiar to printers everywhere that its daily work is simply looked upon as a matter of course. The Linotype is used on nearly every newspaper of any prominence in all the cities of the United States, and book and job offices are rapidly adopting the machines. It has also been introduced into printing-offices in many foreign countries, England, Germany, France, Australia, New Zealand and other sections being large users. It is to be regretted that Mr. Mergenthaler could not have lived to see the universal adoption of his invention in offices of every kind in all civilized countries. On page 384 of this issue, under "Machine Composition Notes," will be found a short sketch of Mr. Mergenthaler and his work that may prove of interest. THE INLAND PRINTER, in common with thousands of users of the Linotype, mourns the loss which the printing trade has sustained in his death, and acknowledges its admiration for the man whose marvelous skill has given us this nineteenth century marvel.

Knickerbocker Old Style

This beautiful letter was designed and cut to conform to the ideas of the aristocrats of olden times.   The "proper thing" for high class printing of the present

6-POINT KNICKERBOCKER OLD STYLE   20 A 15 A 175 a $6 90

"TO RESCUE from oblivion the memory of former incidents, and to render a just tribute of renown to the many great and wonderful transactions of our Dutch progenitors, Diedrich Knickerbocker, native of the city of New York, produces this historical essay." Like the great father of history, whose words I have just quoted, I treat of times long past, over which the twilight of uncertainty has already thrown its shadows, and the night of forgetfulness was about to descend forever.   With great solicitude had I long beheld the early

history of this venerable and ancient city gradually slipping from our grasp trembling on the lips of narrative old age, and day by day dropping piecemeal into the tomb.   In a little while, thought I, and these reverend Dutch burghers who serve as the tottering monuments of good old times, will be gathered to their fathers; their children engrossed by the empty pleasures or insignificant transactions of the present age, will neglect to treasure up the recollections of the past, and posterity will search in vain for memorials of the days of the Patriarchs.   Determined, therefore, to avert if possible this threatened misfortune, I industriously set myself to work, to gather together all the fragments of our infant history which still existed, and like my reverend prototype Herodotus, where no written records could be found, I have endeavored to

SANTA CLAUS WITH TOYS FOR THE BOYS AND GIRLS

8-POINT KNICKERBOCKER OLD STYLE   20 A 15 A 125 a $5 45

"TO RESCUE from oblivion the memory of former incidents, and to render a just tribute of renown to the many great and wonderful transactions of our Dutch progenitors, Diedrich Knickerbocker, native of the city of New York, produces this historical essay." Like the great father of history, whose words I have just quoted, I treat of times long past, over which the twilight of uncertainty has already thrown its

shadows, and the night of forgetfulness was about to descend forever With great solicitude had I long beheld the early history of this venerable and ancient city gradually slipping from our grasp, trembling on the lips of narrative old age, and day by day dropping piecemeal into the tomb.   In a little while, thought I, and these reverend Dutch burghers who serve as the tottering monuments of good old times, will be gathered to their fathers; their children, engrossed by the empty pleasures or insignificant transactions of the present age, will neglect to treasure

ANNIE AND WILLIE'S CHRISTMAS PRAYER

9-POINT KNICKERBOCKER OLD STYLE   20 A 12 A 120 a $4 90

"TO RESCUE from oblivion the memory of former incidents, and to render a just tribute of renown to the many great and wonderful transactions of our Dutch progenitors Diedrich Knickerbocker, native of the city of New York produces this historical essay."   Like the great father of history, whose words I have just quoted, I treat of times long past, over which the twilight of uncertainty had already thrown its shadows, and the night of forgetfulness was about to descend forever.   With great solicitude had I long beheld the early history of this venerable and ancient city gradually slipping from our grasp, trembling on the lips of narrative old age, and day by day dropping piecemeal into the tomb In a little while, thought I, and these reverend Dutch burghers, who serve as the tottering monuments of good old

GRANDMOTHER'S PIES AND PUDDINGS

10-POINT KNICKERBOCKER OLD STYLE   20 A 12 A 120 a $4 65

"TO RESCUE from oblivion the memory of former incidents, and to render a just tribute of renown to the many great and wonderful transactions of our Dutch progenitors, Diedrich Knickerbocker, native of the city of New York, produces this historical essay."   Like the great father of history, whose words I have just quoted, I treat of times long past, over which the twilight of uncertainty had already thrown its shadows, and the night of forgetfulness was about to descend forever.   With great solicitude had I long beheld the early history of this venerable and ancient city gradually slipping from our grasp, trembling on the lips of narrative old age, and day by day dropping

RIPE HOLLY BERRIES AND LEAVES

11-POINT KNICKERBOCKER OLD STYLE   16 A 10 A 70 a $4 60

"TO RESCUE from oblivion the memory of former incidents, and to render a just tribute of renown to the many great and wonderful transactions of our Dutch progenitors, Diedrich Knickerbocker, native of the city of New York, produces this historical essay."   Like the great father of history, whose words I have just quoted, I treat of times long past, over which the twilight of uncertainty had already thrown its shadows, and the night of forgetfulness was about to descend forever With great solicitude had I long beheld the early history of this venerable and ancient city gradually slipping from our grasp, trembling on the lips of

TURKEY AND CRANBERRY SAUCE

12-POINT KNICKERBOCKER OLD STYLE   12 A 8 A 60 a $4 60

"TO RESCUE from oblivion the memory of former incidents, and to render a just tribute of renown to the many great and wonderful transactions of our Dutch progenitors, Diedrich Knickerbocker, native of the city of New York, produces this historical essay."   Like the great father of history, whose words I have just quoted, I treat of times long past over which the twilight of uncertainty had already thrown its shadows, and the night of forgetfulness was about to descend forever With great solicitude had I long beheld the

PUDDINGS AND MINCE PIES

& f ff fb fh fi ffi fk fl ffl ft   These Old English characters are furnished for all sizes when ordered extra

Sold in fonts of 25 lbs. and over at regular body type prices

A. D. FARMER & SON TYPE FOUNDING COMPANY

63 & 65 BEEKMAN STREET, CORNER GOLD, NEW YORK

Carried in stock and for sale at our Chicago House, 163 & 165 Fifth Avenue   Sold by leading Type Foundries and Dealers in Printers' Supplies

STILLSON SERIES

ORIGINATED AND CUT BY BARNHART BROS. & SPINDLER, 183 TO 187 MONROE ST., CHICAGO.

ALL SIZES LINE WITH EACH OTHER.

PATENT APPLIED FOR.

| 30 A | 6 Point Stillson No. 1 | $1 20 |

ATTRACTIVE USEFUL AND DURABLE
THIS HANDSOME AND VERY NEAT SERIES OF STILLSON
1234567890

| 30 A | 6 Point Stillson No. 2 | $1 30 |

PRINTERS WILL FIND THIS SERIES
SUITABLE FOR ALL KINDS OF JOB WORK

| 30 A | 6 Point Stillson No. 3 | $1 50 |

THANKSGIVING DAY NUMBER
BEAUTIFULLY ILLUSTRATED PERIODICALS

| 24 A | 8 Point Stillson | $1 75 |

TWO AMBITIOUS MEN
EXPERIENCED COMPOSITORS

| 24 A | 10 Point Stillson | $1 95 |

OUR FALL OPENING
SECOND AUTUMN SALE

| 20 A | 12 Point Stillson | $2 00 |

LITHOGRAPHERS
ORNAMENTAL DECORATION

| 12 A | 18 Point Stillson | $2 55 |

FINE WORK
ARTISTIC PRINTER

| 8 A | 24 Point Stillson | $3 00 |

OUR MAKE
UNSURPASSED

| 6 A | 30 Point Stillson | $3 60 |

DEMAND
BEST TYPE

| 5 A | 36 Point Stillson | $3 90 |

DARK
MIXTURE

THIS UNIQUE SERIES OF TYPE SUGGESTS UNTOLD POSSIBILITIES TO THE ARTISTIC PRINTER

ENGRAVERS ROMAN
THE ONLY GENUINE

25 A	6 Point Engravers Roman No. 1	$1 00

OUR LATEST DESIGN FOR ADDRESS CARDS, ANNOUNCEMENTS, INVITATIONS, NOTEHEADS, LETTERHEADS, AND ALL CLASSES OF HIGH-GRADE PRINTING

20 A	6 Point Engravers Roman No. 2	$1 00

IN FACT IT HAS SO MANY USES THAT IT IS DOUBTFUL IF ANY LETTER MADE IN LATE YEARS IS SO POPULAR

18 A	6 Point Engravers Roman No. 3	$1 15

WE ARE SELLING HUNDREDS OF FONTS DAILY

18 A	8 Point Engravers Roman	$1 55

ALL THE RAGE THE WORLD OVER

15 A	10 Point Engravers Roman	$1 75

DURABLE AND ACCURATE

12 A	12 Point Engravers Roman	$2 00

TOUGH AND USEFUL

8 A	18 Point Engravers Roman	$2 50

FAMOUS TYPE

6 A	24 Point Engravers Roman	$2 75

PRINTERS

COMPLETE WITH FIGURES.

MANUFACTURED BY

BARNHART BROS. & SPINDLER,

FOR SALE BY ALL DEALERS.

24 Point Border No. 269.   3 feet, $2.25.

Yonkers Text Series

3

48 Point   3A 8a $6.95

Greetings of the Season

36 Point

Rec[...]ners   4A 8a $4.50

30 Point

Mist[...]tletoe   5A 10a $3.85

22 Point

Happy[...]   Times   8A 15a $3.45

14 Point

Pleasures[...]y Gather
and Anti[...]ticipation   10A 20a $2.30

12 Point

Musical an[...]r Recitation
the Exercis[...]away Carol   15A 25a $2.30

10 Point

December 25t[...]dy Shepherds
at the Grange[...]Visiting Him   20A 30a $2.25

8 Point

With Uncovered[...]dies Outflowing
by the Firesides[...]Gleeful Rhymes   25A 40a $2.10

Voice of Summer keen and shrill,
Chirping round my Winter fire;
Of thy song I never tire,
Weary others as they will."
Wm. C. Bennett.

December

Sun   Mon   Tues   Wed   Thur   Fri   Sat

N Moon   F Quar   F Moon   L Quar   =   1   2
2d   9th   16th   24th

3   4   5   6   7   8   9
10 11 12 13 14 15 16
17 18 19 20 21 22 23
24 25 26 27 28 29 30
31   =   =   =   =   =

Type shown in above Calendar is of the Yonkers Text Series

6 Point

30A 50a $2.15

Christmas Comes but Once in the Course of One Year's Events
Bringing Joyful Tidings of Peace and Good Cheer to the People

Bulging Stockings and the Heavily Laden Tables and Sideboards
Once a Year Surely Enjoyment for Men Should Reign Supreme

Manufactured Exclusively by the

American Type Founders Company

for Sale at Branches and Selling Agencies

Notes And Queries — Machine Composition

BY AN EXPERT.

EACH successive year finds advances made in the composing-rooms — prodigious advances — as to the methods of rapid and economical setting of type. A great industry has been undergoing a revolution, and within a few years more the change will be complete and universal. Hand composition of straight matter is even now a thing almost of the past, and that the ad. and display branches shall also be invaded is among one of the reasonable possibilities of the near future. In surveying the different attempts to produce printing surfaces by machinery one can not but admire the versatility of man's ingenuity. The phenomenal success of one of these methods has spurred the inventors to fathom the mysteries of mechanics to almost the limit in endeavoring to secure a portion of the harvest which is being reaped by this revolution. And each succeeding year sees one or more of these inventions nearer completion. During the past year the Unitype Company has succeeded in the wonderful task of not alone conceiving a new machine — the Simplex — but also of actually having it in practical operation in a number of our offices, while the Lanston has made far greater progress during the past twelve months than during any previous period, due, of course, to the greater perfection of that ingenious machine and also to the greater demand for composing-machines of this construction. The Goodson has also made great headway in preparing to go upon the market; a strong financial company has been formed, active and pushing officers have been selected, and during the next twelve months we may expect to see this machine very much in evidence. The Johnson machine is receiving its finishing touches, and during the past year a new and ample factory has been completed in New Bedford, Massachusetts, for its construction. The Empire for the past twelve months and more has been undergoing great and valuable changes; a new automatic justifier has been perfected and it is again ready to enter the field where its friends are assured of its success. The Dow machine — the machine so full of promise to the fraternity — has been undergoing the final and detail preparations before being placed upon the market that is ripe for its reception, while the Chadwick has been awaiting the change in the turn of affairs when its simplicity will become recognized. The McMillan is also undergoing improvements with a view of simplifying its mechanism, and it is the belief of many that the time is not distant when much more will be heard and known of this machine. During the past year the Botz device has been almost perfected, and its merits will soon be ready for testing. Reports also have been heard from time to time of the great changes being made and contemplated in the St. John Typobar. A large number of new ideas for the composing of type have had their birth during the past year. Many of these are in such a crude state as to leave the ideas of their originators very much obscured. An exception to this, however, is in the case of the Cochrane Logotype. Mr. Cochrane has given this method such indefatigable and intelligent attention that the Logotype will undoubtedly be a revelation to the industry. The past twelve months has witnessed the passage of the unparalleled and marvelous Paige machine to a new resting place — in the Cornell University, it having been purchased by Mr. P. T. Dodge, president of the Linotype Company, and presented to that institution. Possibly the greatest energy which has been displayed among the many different companies has been evidenced in the Linotype Company in improving and perfecting its machines for the book and job trade. During the year the company has issued the two-letter matrix to enable the setting of italics and small caps from the keyboard, and the universally adjustable mold, which is adjustable to any measure from 30 ems pica and under, and to any body from agate to 13-point. Aside from these two very valuable devices a large number of detailed improvements have been adapted. In conclusion, it may be said that the accomplishments of the past year in the typesetting machine industry are but the skirmish work for the greater results which we may expect in the succeeding year.

THE New York *World* has just put in five more linotypes, making sixty-seven in all. This gives the *World* the largest number of machines in one plant in the country.

AGU PASHA, a Turkish inventor of considerable local fame, committed suicide. It is alleged this act was due to the difficulties he encountered in attempting to make a typesetting machine that would produce the Turkish characters.

LINOTYPE MEASUREMENT. — I. R. C. writes: "Kindly advise what the rule is for measuring matter from the linotype — minion face cast on long primer body. Is it measured minion or long primer?" *Answer.* — It is usually measured minion one way and long primer the other.

THE last quarterly meeting of the Connecticut Editorial Association was held at the Allyn House, Hartford, October 3. At the close of the meeting quite a number of those present accepted an invitation to visit the factory of the Unitype Company, at Manchester, Connecticut.

MR. JOHN H. ENGLISH, of the *Nodaway Democrat*, Maryville, Missouri, after a week's experience with the Simplex machine, got up 2,700 ems of 8-point per hour. An operator on a Simplex machine in the office of the *Sunday Globe*, Hartford, Connecticut, on four successive Saturday nights made the following showing: Eight hours, 27,473; seven and one-half hours, 26,978; eight hours, 28,393; seven and one-half hours, 25,020, respectively, making an average of 3,478 ems an hour.

IN a large order of type like that which Barnhart Brothers & Spindler recently received from the Government Printing Office there are some interesting figures to be made. Thus, in the 100,000-pound font of 10-point there are 6,400 pounds of lower-case e's alone; reckoning 471 of these letters to the pound, there are 3,014,400 letters, and this number of e's laid end to end would extend 43 miles. The 100,000 pounds contain 40,800,000 individual type, and these laid end to end would reach 591 miles. The font, if set into 13-em measure, solid, would make a column $3\frac{1}{2}$ miles long; if leaded with 2-point leads, $4\frac{1}{10}$ miles long. One man would, on one machine, work nearly four months steadily in casting the lower-case e's. And all this type must be cast one piece at a time.

ANOTHER LINOTYPE RECORD. — All publishers are interested in knowing what can be done on the different typesetting machines, and while the phenomenal records made in trials of speed do not show what can be expected from ordinary operators upon regular work, still they do show that so far as the linotype is concerned its speed is far greater than any operator's ability to manipulate the keyboard. On October 4, William A. Stubbs, a compositor on the Baltimore *Sun*, broke the world's record for machine typesetting in a contest for a wager of $700 with William Duffy, of the Philadelphia *Inquirer*. The contest was held in the Philadelphia *Times* composing-room. Stubbs worked 5 hours and 33 minutes, and set a total of 2,471 nonpareil lines, containing 66,717 ems of corrected matter, an average of 12,021 ems an hour.

Courts Series

Patent Pending

| 8a 5A, $3.50 | 24-POINT COURTS | L. C. $1.70; C. $1.80 |

STANDARD LINE
Commands Attention 6

| 12a 7A, $3.20 | 18-POINT COURTS | L. C. $1.60; C. $1.60 |

CHOICE FOR PRINTERS
Complete Display of Type $4

| 16a 10A, $3.00 | 14-POINT COURTS | L. C. $1.50; C. $1.50 |

WONDERFUL ADVANCEMENT
Successful Improvement Attained $2

| 20a 14A, $2.80 | 12-POINT COURTS | L. C. $1.30; C. $1.50 |

SUPERIOR MATERIAL FOR ARTISTS
Designs Produced With Standard Line $452

| 24a 15A, $2.50 | 10-POINT COURTS | L. C. $1.25; C. $1.25 |

DOES GOOD WORK, YIELDS LARGE PROFITS
Appeals to your Idea of Investment.   New Face 37

| 28a 18A, $2.25 | 8-POINT COURTS | L. C. $1.10; C. $1.15 |

PRINTERS SHOULD INVEST IN LABOR-SAVING SYSTEM
Modern Improved Material Designed for the Use of Printers $125

| 32a 18A, $2.00 | 6-POINT COURTS | L. C. $1.00; C. $1.00 |

OUR BRASS RULE DEPARTMENT IS LARGE AND COMPLETE
Borders and Ornamentation Devices in Most Elaborate and Endless Varieties $574

HHHHHHHHHHHHHHH
HHHHHHHH

STANDARD LINE

48-Point Italia Condensed 6 A 8 a $7.25

ITALIA CONDENSED

Made by the

Keystone Type Foundry

30-Point Italia Condensed 8 A 10 a $4.30

STANDARD LINE TYPE

Gives Dignity to Newspaper Display

Advertisements

24-Point Italia Condensed 9 A 12 a $3.50

CONDENSED CABLE MESSAGES

Editorials and Commercial News Arranged

Swiftly and Accurately

18-Point Italia Condensed 14 A 20 a $3.20

REFINED SERIES FROM ORIGINAL DRAWINGS

Keystone Type Foundry, Nos. 734 to 742 Sansom Street

Philadelphia, Pa. U.S.A.

12-Point Italia Condensed

20 A 30 a $2.80

WHEN ORDERING TYPE Rules, Borders, Cuts, etc. from Specimen Books, do not cut the sample out of the book, but give name and number, also folio, if book is paged, and your order will be correctly filled.

36-Point Italia Condensed

6 A 8 a $5.00

Standard Line

Type cast from

NICKEL-ALLOY

Type Metal

12-POINT RUNNING BORDER No. 542. PER FOOT 52 CENTS

SOMETIMES a troop of damsels glad,
An abbot on an ambling pad,
Sometimes a curly shepherd-lad,
Or long-hair'd page in crimson clad,
  Goes by to tower'd Camelot;

And sometimes thro' the mirror blue,
The knights come riding two and two.
She hath no loyal knight and true,
  The Lady of Shalott.
            — Alfred Lord Tennyson.

CAMELOT OLD STYLE TYPES

Patent and Register Applied for

---

6 Point 24A 50a $2.50   *Lower case font $1.40*

BECOME KINGS AND PUT OFF IN DELAY UNTIL THE FEASTS OF PENTACOST
THEN THE ARCHBISHOP BY MERLIN'S PROVIDENCE ALLOWED THE GROUND

On either side of the river lie long fields of barley and of rye, that
clothe the wold and meet the sky ; and through the field the rivers

8 Point 20A 44a $3.00   *Lower case font $1.55*

AND AS ARTHUR SPED BEFORE, SO HE DID PERSEVERE, YET THERE
WERE SOME GREAT LORDS HAD INDIGNATION THAT HE SHOULD

For there were at that time the most enchanting pictures
hanging upon the castle walls of Camelot; priceless and

10 Point 18A 40a $3.50   *Lower case font $1.95*

BUT NONE MIGHT REMAIN THEREIN WITH SWORD   Beautiful Maidens Roaming Cheerily Onward

12 Point 16A 36a $4.00   *Lower case font $2.10 ·*

KNIGHTS AND LORDS CAME THERE ANON   Sometimes Skirmishing Around Camelot

18 Point 12A 18a $4.25   *Lower case font $1.95*

BECAUSE SOME ADVENTURED   Many Broader Lands Painting

24 Point 10A 15a $4.50   *Lower case font $2.10*

FORTUNE AND HONOR   Honest Exact Guardian

30 Point 8A 12a $5.00   *Lower case font $2.35*

DAMOSEL RESCUED   Legions in Combat

36 Point 6A 10a $5.50   *Lower case font $2.60*

PROUD BARONS Destroy Invader

FOR SALE AT BRANCHES OR AGENCIES OF THE

AMERICAN TYPE FOUNDERS COMPANY

WHEREVER THE PRINTERS' ART IS MOST PRACTISED

Blanchard Series

Patent Applied For

Sizes and Prices

6-Point, 26a 15A, $2.00
ARTISTIC OLD STYLE FOR ART PRINTERS

L. C. $1.00; C. $1.00
All Up-to-Date Printers Have This New Series 5

8-Point, 24a 14A, $2.25
FINE PRINTING ATTRACTS TRADE

L. C. $1.15; C. $1.10
Invest in Material That is Labor-Saving 13

10-Point, 20a 12A, $2.50
GOOD PRINTERS BUY TYPE

L. C. $1.25; C. $1.25
Select The Very Best Made $24

12-Point, 18a 12A, $2.80
STANDARD LINING TYPE

L. C. $1.35; C. $1.45
Attracts Prudent Printers 5

18-Point, 10a 6A, $3.20
MONEY=MAKING

L. C. $1.60; C. $1.60
Printers' Delight $5

24-Point, 7a 4A, $3.50
LINING TYPE

L. C. $1.75; C. $1.75
Will Satisfy $1

36-Point, 5a 3A, $5.75
DESIGNS

L. C. $2.50; C. $3.25
Endorse 2

48-Point, 4a 3A, $10.00
MORE

L. C. $3.95; C. $6.05
Gold $1

Manufactured by the

Inland Type Foundry

Saint Louis, Missouri

HHHHHHHHH**H**HHHHHHHHH

RIMPLED OLDSTYLE

FINEST JOB PRINTER
Grand Clean Faces

PLEASING UNIQUE CHANGE
Legible $389.60 Figures

DESIRABLE PRINTING CLAIMED
Honest Commercial Business

LEADING POPULAR LETTER DESIGNS
Originator of Practical Type Faces

JUST EIGHT FINE SIZES
Are Needful and Useful

EDUCATING MASTER MECHANIC
Sometimes Pleasant Diversion

MODELS FOR ENDURING TYPOGRAPHY
Discard Ancient 12,345 Fragile Lines

STRONG AND BEAUTIFUL NEW CHARACTERS
Leading the Fashion in Modern Printing
Profitable Results Instantly

Originated by the

AMERICAN TYPE FOUNDERS CO.
For Sale at Branches and Agencies

24-Point Tudor Black Condensed. 5 A 15 a $4.10

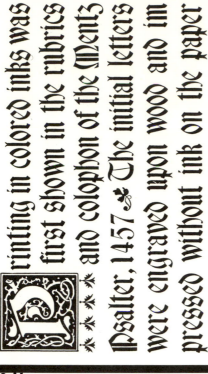

Printing in colored inks was first shown in the rubrics and colophon of the Mentz Psalter, 1457 ❧ The initial letters were engraved upon wood and im pressed without ink on the paper

36-Point Tudor Black Condensed. 4 A 12 a $6.70

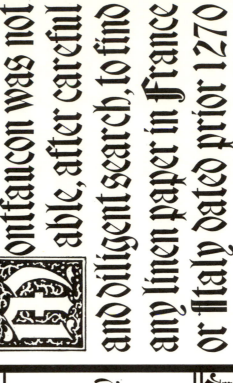

Montfaucon was not able, after careful and diligent search, to find any linen paper in France or Italy dated prior 1270

Tudor
Black
Condensed

Cast in
Nickel=Alloy
Metal

12-Point Tudor Black Condensed. 9 A 30 a $2.55

God pleased to open to man the Art of Printing, the time whereof was shortly after the burning of John Hus, 1416 printing being opened, incontinently ministered unto the Church, the instruments and tooles of learning and knowl edge, which were goode bookes, and authors which before lay hid and unknown ❧ The science of printing being found, immediately followed the Grace of God; which stirred up good wits aptly to conceive the light of knowledge and judgement; by which light darkness began to be espied and ignorance to be detected, truth from error, and religion from super stition to be discerned.   123567890

18-Point Tudor Black Condensed. 8 A 25 a $4.00

Red was in common use by printers of all countries at an early date ❧ Gold was used by a printer of Venice 1477 Attempts at Color Printing were in Chiaro Oscuro, many tints of the same color, but in no case did any printer of the 15th 16th or 17th centuries attempt the printing of finished pic tures by overlapping and contrasting colors Inaccurate register was not regarded as a fault

48-Point Tudor Black Condensed. 4 A 8 a $7.50

 Keystone Type Foundry of Philadelphia

Yᵉ "POST" OLD STYLES

A showing of Three Sizes of Roman

30 POINT POST OLD STYLE ROMAN No 1   4 A 6 a $4 25

AN ORIGINAL DESIGN
made from the Drawings furnished by the Originator of this style of lettering

18 POINT POST OLD STYLE ROMAN No 2   7 A 10 a $3 25

POST OLD STYLES
will comprise two distinctive Series of Romans and one of Italic, all of them ranging in sizes from 6 Point to 72 Point ✒ A more useful Series has never been offered to Printers

24 POINT POST OLD STYLE ROMAN No 2   5 A 8 a $3 50

COMPARE this Type Style with the Headings used in "The Saturday Evening Post." Buy a "Post" for comparison

American Type Founders Co.
Maker of the Leading Type Styles

Yᵉ "POST" OLD STYLES

A Showing of Two Sizes of Italic

24 POINT POST OLD STYLE ITALIC   5 A 12 a $3 75

The "POST" OLD STYLE ITALIC is a fac=simile of the lettering used in 'The Saturday Evening Post' the oldest weekly paper published in the United States of America, founded A. D. 1728, by Benjamin Franklin

Post Ornament No. 74 (Solid Metal Electro) 35 cents.   Per dozen, $3.00

18 POINT POST OLD STYLE ITALIC   9 A 20 a $3 00

A COMMENDABLE AND USEFUL SERIES
The various sizes of "Post" Old Style Roman and Italic will be made to line, one series with the other, with the aid of point justification
"Post" Old Styles will become standard faces, they being well adapted to all classes of jobbing. No printer can go wrong by investing in them.

American Type Founders Co.
Order from Nearest Branch

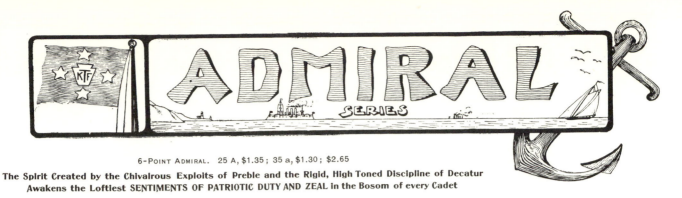

ADMIRAL SERIES

6-POINT ADMIRAL. 25 A, $1.35; 35 a, $1.30; $2.65

The Spirit Created by the Chivalrous Exploits of Preble and the Rigid, High Toned Discipline of Decatur Awakens the Loftiest SENTIMENTS OF PATRIOTIC DUTY AND ZEAL in the Bosom of every Cadet

12-POINT ADMIRAL. 16 A, $1.70; 24 a, $1.70; $3.40

The REPRISAL was the first American Man-of-War that appeared in French Waters IN 1776, HAVING AS A PASSENGER DR. BENJAMIN FRANKLIN

72-POINT ADMIRAL. 3 A, $8.45; 4 a, $5.50; $13.95

Constitution

8-POINT ADMIRAL. 20 A, $1.40; 30 a, $1.35; $2.75

The Intrepid was Fitted as a Floating Mine and Sent into the Harbor of Tripoli to Destroy the Cruisers OF THE ENEMY, SEPTEMBER, 1804

10-POINT ADMIRAL. 18 A, $1.70; 26 a, $1.45; $3.15

Battle between the Hornet and Penguin Was the last Regular Naval Engagement of THE AMERICAN WAR OF 1812

24-POINT ADMIRAL. 7 A, $2.30; 10 a, $2.20; $4.50

Sailing in the Misty CHINA SEA

30-POINT ADMIRAL. 6 A, $3.10; 9 a, $2.70; $5.80

Roar of the Steel SHELL

14-POINT ADMIRAL. 12 A, $1.95; 18 a, $1.75; $3.70

Daring Intrepidity and Coolness of AMERICAN MARINES

36-POINT ADMIRAL. 5 A, $3.75; 8 a, $3.45; $7.20

Effective GUNS

18-POINT ADMIRAL. 10 A, $2.25; 15 a, $2.00; $4.25

Cruise Bon Homme Richard Capt. PAUL JONES

48-POINT ADMIRAL. 4 A, $4.85; 5 a, $3.40; $8.25

Forecastle

60-POINT ADMIRAL. 3 A, $6.00; 4 a, $4.00; $10.00

Splice Main Brace

Made Exclusively by the Keystone Type Foundry, 734-42 Sansom Street, Philadelphia, Pa. U.S.A.

Sample

PRINTED DIRECT FROM THE

New Ribbon-Face Type

'Patent

Boston, May, 1900.

Up-to-date Printers,
          Everywhere, U. S.

Dear Sirs:

This is a sample of circular work printed direct from the face of the new Typewriter Type, on an ordinary printing press.

Please remember that the type does it all. You simply set up the type in the usual way and print your circulars. No process, no manipulation, no royalties, "no nothing." Just "straight printing" from the patented face of the new Typewriter Type on your press.

The old-style Typewriter Type printed sharp and smooth, giving results very unlike the dull impression and "ribbon effect" of actual typewriting. No one is today satisfied with such work.

In the new patent-face Typewriter Type you are offered that which will exactly imitate typewriting-- "ribbon effect" and all; and this without manipulation or any extra "process" whatsoever.

Neither is there any "royalty" to pay. You buy the type outright and go ahead, making the profit which certainly lies in this class of work.

The more this type wears, the better it imitates. It does not fill up with ordinary printing.

The price of such a special type must be somewhat higher than for a face which gives none of its advantages, the matrices being expensive and the manufacture of the type being slow and difficult. But, compared with the cost of any other method with like results, the price to the printer is very low.

Circular fonts (for full letter sheet composition) of 20-A, 100-a, $12.00. Weight, 12 lbs.

Please examine this printing, and let us hear from you at once. We have a money-maker for printers in this new Typewriter Type, and want you to profit by its purchase and use.

MADE AND SOLD BY

The Typewriter-Type Company

C. S. WADY, Manager.

692   *May 1900*

146 Franklin Street, BOSTON, MASS.

WHAT IS TECHNICAL TRAINING?

TRUE technical training aims at the development of those faculties of the soul which are active in the pursuit of the mechanical arts. And good trade schools do not confine themselves to exercises in the skilful use of the hands, but they try to discipline the minds of young people in order to facilitate the work of their hands. It may, therefore, be in place to precede the answer of the question: What is technical training? with a short study of those powers of the soul on which the skill of handicraftsmen depends.

We often speak in our every-day life of the mind's eye, and we mean thereby the faculty of seeing external things even when our bodily eyes are closed, or when the objects which we hold in view are far away from us in time and space. Our spiritual vision often seems to work with miraculous power in the evenings when we lie down to rest and nothing disturbs our bodily senses. Events of the past appear at certain quiet moments more vividly than they did at the day of their actual occurrence, and the faces and figures of absent or long-departed friends and relatives surround us as if they were present in reality.

The faculty which performs this wonderful work within our minds is the power of imagination. It forms mental pictures sometimes incoherently, as in a dream; but also systematically, when we read and study. The spiritual eye which calmly stands behind the imaginative powers and watches the mind-pictures that come and go, in order to increase its knowledge, is the power of intuition. Through intuition we learn almost unconsciously the principles of all external knowledge, and upon its activity depend the mechanical and liberal arts. But this wonderful power to call up mind-pictures of external things, and to understand them at once, is given to men in different degrees. "There are diversities of gifts and operations; to one is given the word of wisdom, to another the gift of healing, to another diverse tongues," says St. Paul, I Cor., 12. One person can at a glance see through the mysteries of electricity or machinery; another knows, almost without being taught, to do all kinds of carpenter's or other mechanical work; one has an intuitive perception of beautiful forms; another is always the first to discover new utilities of things. "All these worketh that one and the self-same spirit," through the power of intuition.

Besides differences in the aptitude of this faculty, there are variations of the sharpness of the mental vision. Some men merely need to glance at a task and they will know more about it than written or verbal orders could ever tell them. Others must repeatedly be told what is to be done and how to go to work about it; and after they have laboriously formed a dim idea of what is desired, they work mechanically according to habit or fixed rules, which they remember but do not understand. The mental eyes of some apprentices are always wide open; put them in any workshop and they will see everything that is going on, and wonderingly will ask a hundred times a day: What is the cause of this? or, How is that? Other boys remain uninterested amidst the most wonderful machinery. Their spiritual eyes are dim, and nothing can excite their curiosity to know the reason why this or that thing is so or so. One workingman's mind is a perfect blank; he could not describe a simple tool which he handles every day; another man has in his mind's storeroom an ever-available number of mind pictures of such things as he may be called to make from leather, iron, wood or clay.

These natural differences of the faculty of intuition are well known to good and true craftsmen, although they never studied psychology. Therefore they have at all times and in all trades insisted on individual training, so that each boy could receive proper attention. They dislike so-called trade schools where young men are freely admitted, hustled through a course of manual training, and after a short time graduated as full-fledged printers, plumbers, carpenters, etc. They despise employers who pack their shops with boys, because such men ruin the intellectual nature of young mechanics for the sake of gain, and therewith do incalculable damage to society.

On the other hand, all intelligent craftsmen favor trade-schools which do not supplant, but supplement the apprenticeship system by a course of technical training which is apt to develop the precious intuitive faculties. Experience has shown that strictly intuitive instruction in small classes, which are properly graded and laid out to meet the needs of the craft to which the scholars belong, has a wonderful effect upon apprentices. They themselves, and their parents, quickly comprehend the connection between the theory and practice of their trades, and usually the heart of the boys goes with their studies. Apprentices whose mental vision is dim, can develop it to some extent and become as useful in a particular sphere of their craft as their brighter comrades in the higher branches. If everybody were to ride on the top of the stage-coach, it would grow top-heavy and tumble over. Boys who are favored by nature with the gift of understanding everything at a glance, learn to discipline their imagination and to concentrate their minds on business. Without a guiding hand these so-called geniuses often grow up as useless Jacks-of-all-trades, and acquire a freakish and eccentric character. If persistently kept within the mental discipline of intuitive exercises, they learn how to compare their various mind-pictures from the sphere of their trades with a view to improve the appearance or utility of their productions. In this way talented boys may become inventors or directors of industry. In short, there is no mechanic so rich and poor in mind that he could not profit in some way by developing the pound which God intrusted to his keeping — namely, his intuitive faculties.

To answer finally the question, "What constitutes a printer's technical training?" I must ask the help of those great doctors of the mental science, whose works are printed by our craft. Let them call together those few boys, journeymen and masters in every town of our broad land whose minds are not led astray by the vague social questions of the age. Let them unite in some school-room, a number of masters, foremen and journeymen, whose hearts are free from the raving thoughts of class pride and envy, in order to save as many of the downtrodden and neglected wards of our trade — the apprentices — as they can, and to bring out whatever is left in their composition of pure and undefiled human nature. In this place let us merely indicate a course which, if properly worked out and tried under the watchful eye of learned men with pure hearts, might give us a better generation of printers than we have at present.

COMPOSITOR'S CLASSES.

Geometrical and mechanical drawing in its application to the simplest lines and forms of printed matter free-hand drawing of leaves, flowers, runners and ornaments, after plaster models. Particular attention should be paid to impress the mind with the characteristic forms of all ornaments; drawing of letters; application of drawing to all kinds of printed matter. The teacher may give the text of letter-heads, bill-heads, title-pages, etc., on the blackboard, and require the scholars to make sketches thereof on paper indicating the size of type and length of lines, etc. Lectures on the coördination, subordination and grouping of lines, spacing and leading out, illustrated by specimen of printed matter. Lectures on general style, colors and the harmony of colors. Sketches of colored ornaments. The teacher may expose to view copies of modern ornamentation, analyze them, and apply the principles of ornamentation, show the possibilities of combination, point out the current errors, and trace the beauty of printed works of art.

PRESSMAN'S CLASSES.

The study of the nature and effects of light and shade is the principal feature of the pressman's drawing lessons. Drawing of simple objects with lectures on the perspective, that is, the art of delineating objects as they appear to the eye. Exposition of pictures and illustrations, pointing out the foreground, middle and background; the

effects of light and toning down with a view of bringing out the main object of a picture, etc.

The science of colors and color mixing with practical exercises in water colors. Tri-color printing with practical illustrations. Lectures on the harmony of colors, and exercises in mixing and distributing colors on printed matter.

HIGHER CLASSES FOR ALL BRANCHES.

Simultaneously with drawing lessons there must be provision for intuitive instruction in the following typographical branches:

Compositors.— The system of type, its historical development and the present point system; fundamental rules of plain matter; the general make-up of works, for example, footnotes, titles, prefaces, indexes, etc.; composition of poetry; mathematical, tabular and catalogue composition; make-up of forms and general rules on margins.

Pressmen.— The press, its mechanism and historical development, from the wooden hand press to the present cylinder press. Treatment of the press before, during and after use. The functions of its principal parts considered singly and put together. Treatment of forms on flat-bed and cylinder presses. Plain type, woodcut, half-tone and color printing.

To this should be added theoretical instruction of a higher order, intended to prepare compositors as well as pressmen for positions as foremen, managers and superintendents. For example: Construction of the typesetting machines, perfecting and web presses; the principles of the manufacture of paper; the production of engravings, stereotypes and electrotypes. Typographical figuring; how to compute the cost of composition, presswork and material; the principles of single and double entry bookkeeping. The study of the vernacular is everywhere a main thing, and compositors in America especially ought to learn at least the alphabets of the foreign languages spoken in this country.

THE AMATEUR EVIL AND THE TYPEFOUNDERS.

To the Editor: CHICAGO, ILL., April 18, 1900.

Every little while some printer whose toes have been trod upon by an "amateur" enters his protest against the "amateur evil," and usually winds up his complaints with a fling at the typefoundries for "setting the amateur up in business."

That these complaints are occasionally well-founded there is no denying, but in the majority of cases the typefoundries are free from blame and have only done what any other business man would do under the same circumstances — sold their goods at a reasonable profit.

The question of where to "draw the line" between legitimate trade and the "amateur" has been a most perplexing one to the reliable typefounders; and by "reliable typefounders" I mean those foundries which have a regular discount for their goods — not the concerns that regulate the discounts by the amount of cash the purchaser is able to pay down. Unfortunately for the printing business there are too many concerns of the latter kind, and their existence is made possible by many of those printers who protest loudest against their methods.

Of course, "one man's money is as good as another's," and when one of the "little fellows" starts in with sufficient cash to pay for his outfit there is no good reason why he should not be able to buy as cheaply as the established printer. Where outfits are sold on partial payments, however, the case is different, and it is here that the typefounders can protect their established patrons — to an extent, at least. That one or two of the larger foundries do make an effort to protect their customers from this kind of competition is evidenced by instructions to their representatives, a copy of which I have seen. These instructions define the foundry's position on the "amateur" question, and specify the terms upon which time sales may be made. These terms are, on outfits amounting to $350 or less, one-half cash, balance on short time, with interest and security. On sales over $350 to $450, not less than $150 cash, with security, etc., and then only when at least one-half the amount is for machinery. Type is poor security after it has been once used, and typefounders regard it as such, hence the rule regarding machinery. On these terms the foundry is reasonably safe, and the percentage of loss from bad accounts in any of the conservatively managed foundries is considerably less than would be supposed.

The fact is that each year it requires a little more capital to start into the printing business than it did previously. The legitimate foundries are more careful of their credits as the margin of profit grows smaller, and the demand for good printing facilities necessarily calls for a larger investment to put the beginner in a position to compete with the established printer. The tendency on the part of some printers to hold the typefounders responsible because some one decides to start into business in what the established printer deems as his field is not just. Of course, in the printers' supply business, as in nearly every other, there are a lot of jayhawkers and curbstone brokers who are willing to take a long chance, but the reputable houses will not do it. And I would like to ask these same faultfinders if their complaints are not occasionally inconsistent? Do they always give their business to the foundries that are conservatively managed and endeavoring to do business on business principles? Is it not frequently the case that the dealer who quotes the easiest terms (i. e., the longest time, with the smallest cash payment), even though the price is a shade higher — is it not frequently the case that this one gets the order? I have yet to hear of an established printer giving his order to the conservative dealer as a matter of principle — "terms" are frequently the first consideration, with "price" secondary. A little more consistency would help solve the amateur problem.

In conclusion, and for the benefit of some of these "established" printers, I will quote the opening paragraph from Mr. George H. Benedict's little pamphlet, "The Fallacy of Fillers," as being apropos:

"It does not take a philosopher to decide that any man has a just right to be in any line of business he chooses, and just why all competitors are disposed to look upon every other person in the same line as a fit subject for the scalper's knife is a query difficult to answer."

A TYPE SALESMAN.

BY AN EXPERT.

"HIS spacebands are rusty," is a new slang phrase.

THE Des Jardins Type Justifier Company has a machine on exhibition at Paris.

WE learn of a tourist operator who carries with him his own electric fan and an extra supply of spacebands.

IF operators continue increasing in speed, as is indicated by the reports received, fewer machines will be required in offices.

THE printer-operator is usually a distinct improvement on the old-time compositor in deportment, habits, dress and gentility.

W. H. EATON, a Linotype compositor on the Worcester (Mass.) *Spy*, is credited with setting an average of 8,300 ems, minion, per hour.

"LIKE a pansy in the cow lot," is the expressive manner in which the Simplex machine is described by one of its many enthusiastic admirers.

THE heretofore two common errors — "turned" and "wrong font" letters — are unknown in Linotype composition, as well as in Simplex work.

RUMORS of the "wonderful" typesetting machine are again heard. This time the inventor is a real estate dealer. Of course anybody can invent typesetting machinery.

THE erection of new buildings and installation of composing machines and perfecting presses furnish additional evidence of the prosperity of the small city daily.

THE Moundsville (W. Va.) *Echo* rejoices over the installation of a Simplex typesetting machine in its office. The expressed satisfaction of the publishers is argument to sustain the contention that it pays to adopt machine composition.

"Now that typesetting machines are in so general use, why would it not be a good idea to go back to some decent system of capitalization?" asks the Waltham (Mass.) *Free Press.* The reason is obvious: there is no decent system to which to return.

The PLYMOUTH SERIES

Cast from Superior Copper-Mixed Metal by
BARNHART BROS. & SPINDLER
183 to 187 Monroe Street, Chicago, Illinois

PATENT APPLIED FOR.

25 A 40 a $2 35	6 Point Plymouth	Extra Lower Case, 40 a $1 10

THE GREATEST EUCHRE GAME ON RECORD   **Progressive Euchre Contests Played on Thursdays**

20 A 30 a $2 35	8 Point Plymouth	Extra Lower Case, 30 a $1 10

SUBURBAN RESIDENCES of CHICAGO   **Attractive Boulevards Connecting the Parks**

15 A 20 a $2 35	10 Point Plymouth	Extra Lower Case, 20 a $1 10

GENUINE OHIO MAPLE SYRUP   **Mammoth Sugar Trees Destroyed**

12 A 18 a $2 50	12 Point Plymouth	Extra Lower Case, 18 a $1 10

PREVAILING SENTIMENT   **Dangerous and Troublesome**

10 A 15 a $3 75	18 Point Plymouth	Extra Lower Case, 15 a $1 65

CUSTOM HOUSES Business Increasing

6 A 10 a $4 30	24 Point Plymouth	Extra Lower Case, 10 a $2 00

SOUR GRAPE Bought Honors

5 A 8 a $4 85	30 Point Plymouth	Extra Lower Case, 8 a $2 30

BRIGHTER Make Home

4 A 6 a $6 10	36 Point Plymouth	Extra Lower Case, 6 a $2 80

ILLINOIS Fast Mail

4 A 5 a $8 60	48 Point Plymouth	Extra Lower Case, 5 a $3 40

BANGS Get Her

3 A 4 a $13 00	60 Point Plymouth	Extra Lower Case, 4 a $5 25

SEND Home

All sizes complete with Figures, Italic Logotypes and Ornaments.

Kept in Stock by

Minnesota Type Foundry Co., St. Paul, Minn.
Great Western Type Foundry, Kansas City, Mo.
St. Louis Printers Supply Co., St. Louis, Mo.
Great Western Type Foundry, Omaha, Neb.
Southern Printers Supply Co., Washington, D. C.
and for Sale by all Dealers.

PLYMOUTH
Italic Series
Yᵉ Ancient Style

Cast from Superior Copper-Mixed Metal by
BARNHART BROS. & SPINDLER
183 to 187 Monroe Street, Chicago, Illinois.

25 A 40 a $2 60   6 Point Plymouth Italic   Extra Lower Case, 40 a $1 20

JERSEY CITY EXPRESS COMPANY   *Regular Trips to Nearest Suburban Towns*

20 A 30 a $2 60   8 Point Plymouth Italic   Extra Lower Case, 30 a $1 05

HONESTY SAFE PRINCIPLE   *Dishonesty is Bound to Counteract*

15 A 25 a $2 60   10 Point Plymouth Italic   Extra Lower Case, 25 a $1 05

DECEITFUL METHODS   *Discovered False Statements*

12 A 18 a $2 60   12 Point Plymouth Italic   Extra Lower Case, 18 a $1 20

EXCELS IN HISTORY   *Learned Men Converse*

10 A 15 a $3 90   18 Point Plymouth Italic   Extra Lower Case, 15 a $1 60

DEAR HOMES *Pleasant Scenes*

6 A 10 a $4 50   24 Point Plymouth Italic   Extra Lower Case, 10 a $1 80

FINE RED *Grand House*

5 A 8 a $5 10   30 Point Plymouth Italic   Extra Lower Case, 8 a $2 00

MOTIVE *Great Deal*

4 A 6 a $6 20   36 Point Plymouth Italic   Extra Lower Case, 6 a $2 40

GRAIN *Elevator*

4 A 5 a $8 90   48 Point Plymouth Italic   Extra Lower Case, 5 a $3 00

FINE *Blades*

All sizes complete with Figures and Ornaments.

Kept in Stock by

Blanchard Italic

Patent Applied For

✠ ✠ ✠

4a 3A, $22.40   72-POINT BLANCHARD ITALIC   L. C. $8.40; C. $14.00

MEN Hate 6

4a 3A, $16.80   60-POINT BLANCHARD ITALIC   L. C. $6.30; C. $10.50

HIRE Help 5

4a 3A, $10.20   48-POINT BLANCHARD ITALIC   L C. $3.90; C. $6.30

BRIGHT Designs

5a 3A, $5.75   36-POINT BLANCHARD ITALIC   L. C. $2.50; C. $3.25

RICHMOND Congress 18

5a 4A, $4.30   30-POINT BLANCHARD ITALIC   L. C. $1.75; C. $2.55

AMBITION Forthcoming 1

8a 4A, $3.50   24-POINT BLANCHARD ITALIC   L. C. $1.75; C. $1.75

DEMANDING Beautifying Art 3

10a 6A, $3.20   18-POINT BLANCHARD ITALIC   L. C. $1.50; C. $1.70

CELEBRATIONS Increasing Yearly $25

14a 9A, $3.00   14-POINT BLANCHARD ITALIC   L. C. $1.45; C. $1.55

SHADOW GROWING Darker at Close of Daylight 8

20a 12A, $2.80   12-POINT BLANCHARD ITALIC   L. C. $1.35; C. $1.45

PROGRESSIVE PRINTERS Attend Their Annual Picnics 175

22a 12A, $2.50   10-POINT BLANCHARD ITALIC   L. C. $1.25; C. $1.25

SUNSHINE AND PLEASURE Create Healthful and Happy Thoughts

25a 14A, $2.25   8-POINT BLANCHARD ITALIC   L. C. $1.10; C. $1.15

FURNISHING FINEST PRODUCTIONS Daily Towards Improving the Art Preservative 48

28a 15A, $2.00   6-POINT BLANCHARD ITALIC   L. C. $1.00; C. $1.00

ENTERPRISING CITIZENS ARE ADVOCATING Improvements Generally Throughout the Entire World $493

ORNAMENTS FURNISHED WITH EACH FONT

HHHHHHHHHHH**HH**HHHHHHHHHHH

Note the New Sizes

Made by INLAND TYPE FOUNDRY, Saint Louis

Tudor Bold

Original.

12 A 40 a   6 Point Tudor Bold $2 30

The way to make money is to keep your office supplied with the latest improvements==the very latest in type designs and the latest machinery. Everybody will not do so==in fact, the majority will not== but that is just the reason why you should, for then you will be in a position to make money while your competitor is worrying along and just barely paying expenses with slow presses; with old type that takes more of the pressman's time to "bring up" than the whole job should require; with work spoiled because a figure don't show in a street or telephone number, or be= cause an initial fails to come up in a customer's name. Yes, your competitor with an out=of=date of= fice is led a merry chase after the dollars; but you==you're going to show them how to capture those dollars by keeping right up with the procession. There is only one way to make money in the printing busi= ness, and that way is to be wide awake and to take advantage of every opportunity. It is not merely the ability to get work at a good price that counts; your office must be so equipped that you can turn it out at a minimum cost==a thing im= possible where your force is con= tinually "hustling" for material.

Price of Series Complete, $54.20
Subject to Current Discounts.

12 A 40 a   8 Point Tudor Bold $2 40

So far as we can tell at this late day, the early type= founders made their types with heavy faces, and with seldom or never a hair=line, because they were unable, with the crude facilities at hand, to produce the faces == now sometimes termed effeminate == which later came in vogue. But with increasing skill and more perfect methods founders thought to improve upon the work of their predecessors, this so=called improving process continuing until the limit of fineness of line was reached in those faces with lines so delicate as to be read only with difficulty == faces that after being used a few times were ready for the hell=box. No wonder, then, that when this extreme was reached the pendulum began its backward swing; outraged art rebelled. To be sure it is not necessary that the crudities and inaccuracies due to imperfect methods and tools and materials be adopted; but we can with perfect propriety adopt those forms so beautiful in their legibility and strength.

10 A 30 a   10 Point Tudor Bold $2 70

One matter the printer should be very careful about is the quality of the ma= terial he purchases. The bodies should not only be mathematically correct, but the metal from which the type is made should be hard without being brittle. It is not the easiest thing in the world to produce a type metal embodying hardness, toughness, and long=wearing qualities, and only by years of patient toil and experiment is it possible. To this inability to produce a metal combining all the good qualities found in that used by founders to=day may, in part, be ascribed the crudeness of the earlier specimens of printing.

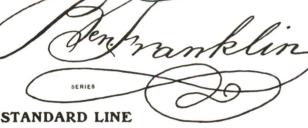

BY WILLIAM E. LOY.

THE CONDITIONS PRIOR TO THE REVOLUTION.

LIKE many other beginnings, the early history of type-founding in America is somewhat hidden in obscurity, and the records of the typefounders who first carried on the business are not complete. Writers on the subject have been pretty equally divided in giving the credit to Christopher Sauer,* of Germantown, Pennsylvania, and the date as 1735. About that time a printing-press was established in German-town, and by Mr. Sauer, but there seems to be no evidence that he engaged in typefounding then or at any time. Sauer came to America in 1724, when he was thirty years of age. He brought with him his son, of the same name, from Germany, and in due time Christopher Sauer, second, succeeded to the business of his father.

The elder Sauer was not trained to the printer's calling, but had a superficial knowledge of it. At home he had identified himself with the dissenters, or German Reformed Church; so, as he was a public-spirited and educated man, he was chosen as the person to whom books and tracts should be sent by the missionary society at home for the benefit and enlightenment of the Germans then so numerous in Pennsylvania. A printing-press was among the early requirements, and this reached Germantown in 1735. With it was sent as a present from Heinrich Ehrenfried Luther, a celebrated type-founder of Frankfort-on-the-Main, a small font of type, with the condition that the donor should receive a few copies of the German Bible it was proposed to print, as a specimen of Sauer's skill. He took as his text the thirty-fourth edition of the Constantine Bible of Halle, which still ranks as the most perfect edition of Luther's translation, and his task was completed in 1743. The edition consisted of twelve hundred copies of a heavy quarto of 1284 pages.

In acknowledgment of the timely aid received, Sauer had twelve copies handsomely bound as a special tribute of gratitude to Luther, the typefounder. The vessel containing the volumes was overtaken by privateers, and the cargo fell into their hands. Fortunately, however, the Bibles eventually reached their destination. One copy was placed in the Royal Library, where it still remains, and another, after passing through various hands, was returned to America in 1843, or one hundred years afterward.

Christopher Sauer died in 1758, and he was succeeded in the business by Christopher Sauer, second, his only son. It is not definitely known that a typefoundry was even contemplated by the elder Sauer, but the son certainly did commence the business some years before the Revolution. The date has been fixed by pretty good authority as 1772, but in the meantime he had printed a second edition of the Bible in 1763, presumably from the type imported from Germany. This second edition was so well received, and the printing of other books became so important, that Christopher Sauer, second, conceived the idea of establishing a typefoundry for the convenience of his own work. He wished to keep the type for the entire Bible standing, and this alone demanded a font of nearly fifty thousand pounds of pica. His third edition of the Bible, this time consisting of three thousand copies, was completed and in the sheets when the victorious British army swept past his

---

*NOTE.— The late Thomas MacKellar, in all his published writings on the history of printing or typefounding, and in all editions of the "American Printer," adheres to the statement that the elder Sauer established his foundry in 1735. In this opinion he was practically alone. Isaiah Thomas, who wrote about 1810, says Sauer "began typefounding several years before the Revolution." As the elder Sauer died in 1758, it clearly could not have been he, and the son probably had no occasion for a typefoundry until he developed his plan for keeping the entire Bible standing in type, and this was after he had printed the second edition in 1763.

office in their occupation of Germantown, and many of these sheets were taken by the soldiers as a bedding for their horses. It is certain that the typefoundry was put in operation before work was begun on this third edition of the Sauer Bible. The tools and implements were brought from Germany, and the foundry was managed by Justus Fox, who seems to have been expert in many mechanical arts. In 1784 Fox purchased the foundry, and with his son continued the business until his death in 1805. In 1806 Fox's son sold it to Samuel Sauer (or Sower, as the name was then spelled), son of the second Christopher, who had previously tried to establish a typefoundry at Baltimore. While Sauer's name is always mentioned as the first person to conduct the type-foundry business in America, it is more than probable that the first attempt was made two or three years before by David Mitchelson, a seal engraver from London, who came to Boston with his wife in August, 1765. For a while he was in New Hampshire, but we find him in Boston in 1768, when he attempted to set up a foundry, but failed. Nothing is known of his career after this failure. The second attempt was made by Abel Buell, of Killingworth, Connecticut, though the evidence is far from conclusive. It is known that he petitioned the General Assembly of the State in 1769 for money to establish a typefoundry, and to prove his ability to make type he appended to his petition impressions from some which he said he had made. The petition was granted, and there is a tradition that he succeeded in casting several fonts of long primer which were made use of, but the business soon failed.

A second typefoundry was begun in Germantown in 1773 or 1774 by Jacob or John Bey, a German mechanic of great skill. He continued the business at Germantown until 1789, when he removed his foundry to another part of Philadelphia. It was finally sold to Francis Bailey, a printer, who continued the making of type for his own use only.

Benjamin Franklin, when in Paris, bought from P. S. Fournier a complete equipment for a typefoundry which he intended should be established in Philadelphia. He had placed his nephew, Benjamin Franklin Bache, in a foundry in Paris to learn the details of the business. Franklin and his grandson reached Philadelphia in 1775, and began the business shortly after, but were not successful. Thomas, in his "History of Printing in America," says they could not or did not make good type, and the business was neglected. Bache soon abandoned it and engaged in printing.

Thus it appears the typefoundries started in America prior to the Revolution were in the following order: Mitchelson, Buell, Sauer, Bey, Franklin and Bache, but of these various ventures it may be truthfully said that Sauer was the only successful one.

THE LAST QUARTER OF THE EIGHTEENTH CENTURY.

ALTHOUGH the typefoundry established in Philadelphia by Benjamin Franklin and his grandson, Bache, just prior to the Revolutionary War, was hardly a success, and the business was practically abandoned by its owners, it had been well equipped. It contained matrices for various romans and italics, besides an assortment of Greek and Hebrew; but for some reason not apparent at this late date, the foundry did not produce satisfactory type. It is possible that the taste of the period was favorable to the styles then prevalent in England and Scotland, rather than to those emanating from France. However this may have been, the difficulty was partially overcome by an ingenious German, named Frederick Geiger. This man was a mathematical instrument maker, who, like thousands of others who came to Pennsylvania, was known as a "Redemptioner." Franklin had paid his passage and placed him in the foundry. He cut many punches, soon became an expert typefounder, and made many improvements in the establishment. What success was attained was chiefly due to his skill and industry. After serving the time for his redemption, Geiger was employed in the mint, but later he wasted a good deal of time on the problem of perpetual motion, which so disturbed his mind that he ended his days as a lunatic in the almshouse. The tools, matrices and molds of this foundry eventually found a resting place in the typefoundry of Archibald Binny and James Ronaldson, established in Philadelphia in 1796.

The next typefoundry established in America was begun by John Baine and his grandson in Philadelphia in 1785. They were led to make the venture by the advice of Young & McCullough, prominent printers of that time in Philadelphia. The elder Baine was associated in early life with Alexander Wilson, of Glasgow, one of the most famous typefounders of Scotland. Finding a steady demand for their type in Ireland and in North America, Mr. Baine was chosen by lot to establish a foundry in Dublin, which he did. From there he went to Edinburgh, where he began business with his grandson, under the name of John Baine and Grandson. As before stated, he came to Philadelphia in 1785. Both the Baines were good workmen and their foundry was successful from the outset. The elder was a man of much skill, and as a typefounder he ranks as one of the best, although he was entirely self-taught. His death occurred in Philadelphia in 1790, having been in America but five years. The grandson relinquished the business soon after, and he died in 1799 at Augusta, Georgia.

Until 1791 no one had undertaken typefounding in New York, though it was a city of great commercial importance with many large printing-offices. The first successful ventures had been in Philadelphia and Germantown (a suburb of Philadelphia), while the attempts of Michelson in Boston and Buell in Connecticut had been little more than experiments. Adam Gérard Mappa, who had been carried on the business in Holland, brought with him to New York about 1791 a fully equipped typefoundry. Mappa was baptized in the Reform Church at Doornick, in Hainault, a province of Belgium, December 1, 1754. When about fourteen he entered the military service, was gazetted an ensign in 1768, a lieutenant in 1771, and left the army in October, 1780. While still in the service he purchased the principal part of the old typefoundry of Voskens & Clerk, on the valuation of 18,000 francs for the whole plant. This was one of the old typefoundries of Holland, established by Dirck Voskens prior to 1677, and had been one of the chief sources of supply to English printers for many years. Mappa had intended associating with himself in this enterprise Wybo Tijnje, a newspaper publisher at Delft, and probably this partnership was effected; but when the Prussians, under the Duke of Brunswick, entered Holland with the purpose of reforming the stadtholdership, Mappa, in company with many Dutch patriots, fled to America. His typefounding tools and matrices were brought with him, and while the matrices were principally of Dutch and German faces, they were handsome. Such roman styles as he had were but ordinary, but in addition he had seven Oriental alphabets. His name first appears in the New York directory of 1792, as conducting a typefoundry at 22 Greenwich street. The business was not large, and in 1795, when Binny and Ronaldson determined to begin another typefoundry in Philadelphia, Mappa entered their employ, continuing for several years, and it is presumed his tools and matrices went with him. He left Philadelphia and the typefounding business in 1800, and went into the service of the Holland Land Company, which at that time owned a large portion of the land in Western New York and Pennsylvania. In time he became the general agent of the company, with headquarters at Trenton, New Jersey, and there he died in 1828.

REVIEW OF SPECIMENS RECEIVED

THE Electro-Tint Engraving Company, Philadelphia, has just issued its three-color album, presenting an exclusive collection of stock subjects in colors. The cuts in this album are adapted for advertising purposes and will prove extremely useful for calendars, blotters, inserts, supplements, etc. The results are all obtained by three printings and any good printer can do the work. They would be pleased to send a copy of the album on receipt of ten 2-cent stamps.

FROM Texarkana, Arkansas, we have received from Moore Brothers a very neatly designed and printed business card in red and black. An envelope corner card in the same colors is an excellent piece of composition and presswork. Two blotters are attractive samples of printing in colors, the composition and presswork being O. K. A lion rampant, printed in red, appears to be the trade-mark of the Moore Brothers, and is a striking feature on all the samples submitted.

"BOOKLET OF BOOKLETS" is the unique title P. C. Darrow, typographer, of 342 Dearborn street, Chicago, gives to his specimen book of types, borders, etc., which is a goodly pamphlet of some forty leaves of heavy enameled stock, 7 by 10 inches in size, in which he also shows specimens of artistic work in colors. A cover, printed in colors, and tied with silk cord, encloses the specimen sheets, which make an excellent reference book for prospective customers to examine and choose from.

SEVERAL samples of commercial stationery from the Knight-Errant Company, Buckhannon, West Virginia, are up to date in style of composition and of good quality in presswork. The front cover-page of the Conservatory of Music program, however, could have been improved by omitting the streaks of lightning and substituting a musical emblem, such as a lyre, or Pan's pipes, or something else that would suggest harmony and contentment. The presswork on this job is not so good as on the commercial stationery.

THE Unitype Company, New York and Chicago, celebrated the "glorious Fourth" by sending its friends a miniature tin horn, with a circular mentioning incidentally that they had good reason to blow the horn for the reason that the Simplex One-man Typesetter was now in use in twenty-eight States, and that, in spite of the fact that the company had twice enlarged its factory, orders are pouring in faster than it can build machines. The advertising idea was all right, and the Unitype Company is now better known than it was prior to the Fourth.

THE Hodgson Press, Brisbane, Queensland, Australia, submits a package of general commercial work which is of high quality in composition and presswork. Though somewhat inclined to the ornamental style so prevalent a decade since, the work shows originality and forcefulness of treatment that is in line with present-day methods of typography. Color-schemes are harmonious and the presswork artistic. A specimen sheet of art ornaments, showing recent designs, is evidence that this concern desires to keep in the front ranks of printerdom.

AN interesting book of sixty-four pages enclosed in handsomely printed lithograph cover has been issued by the Lehigh Valley Railroad, entitled "Summer Tours and Fares to Mountain, Lake and Ocean Resorts." It is filled with information of value to the tourist and is illustrated with half-tone views of the beautiful summer resorts along the line of this picturesque road. It is issued by Charles S. Lee, general passenger agent of the road, from the New York office, 26 Cortlandt street. The book is printed by Poole Brothers, Chicago, and is a good specimen of high-class composition and presswork.

THE Hotel Van Nuys, Los Angeles, California, indulges in the luxury of a printing-office of its own, under the care of Fred G. Odell. Its specialty is apparently getting out high-class menus, judging from the two samples submitted. One is printed in green ink, with a pink ribbon inserted, on which is printed the musical program. The other is an Easter menu, printed in Engravers' Roman, enclosed in parchment cover, to the front page of which is attached a chicken emerging from a shell, printed in colors on celluloid, cut out to shape, and fastened with a yellow ribbon streamer. The work is well designed and excellently well printed, and reflects much credit on Mr. Odell for the tasty manner in which the menus are gotten up.

THE Queen City Printing Ink Company, Cincinnati, has just issued a card in black, red, blue, yellow, and a drab tint. The design is engraved. The plates register well and the general effect is pleasing.

Caslon Old Style

4a 3A — 72-POINT CASLON OLD STYLE — $15.00

DIME Cash 2

5a 3A — 54-POINT CASLON OLD STYLE — $9.00

FORM Grand 18

6a 3A — 42-POINT CASLON OLD STYLE — $6.00

MODERN Designs $6

6a 4A — 36-POINT CASLON OLD STYLE — $5.00

STANDARD LINING 12

9a 4A — 30-POINT CASLON OLD STYLE — $4.30

PRACTICAL Demonstration 8

12a 5A — 24-POINT CASLON OLD STYLE — $3.50

UNIFORMLY
Cast and Shipped 7

20a 9A — 18-POINT CASLON OLD STYLE — $3.20

ELEGANT MODEL
Finish Chaste Designs 27

20a 10A — 16-POINT CASLON OLD STYLE — $3.20

UNIFORM LINING
Desirable Feature Used 15

30a 14A — 12-POINT CASLON OLD STYLE — $2.80

ENHANCE USEFULNESS
Our Methods of Casting Type $125

42a 16A — 10-POINT CASLON OLD STYLE — $2.50

PRACTICAL PRINTERS WORK
To Please an Ever Appreciative Clientage $639
Through the Medium of Standard Line

44a 16A — 8-POINT CASLON OLD STYLE — $2.25

PLAIN AND ORNAMENTAL VARIETIES
Large Assortment of Faces Made on Standard Line 174
Always Setting the Pace for Our Competitors

50a 20A — 6-POINT CASLON OLD STYLE — $2.00

ALL THESE INNOVATIONS ARE OF PRICELESS VALUE
Traditional Conservatism of the Craft Swept Away by Our Improvements
All Well Pleased With the Modernized System of Lining 37

The 14- and 20-Point sizes are now in preparation and will be ready in a few weeks.

The 7-, 9- and 11-Point sizes are also made, but are sold in weight fonts only.   These sizes, as well as all the others from 6- to 16-Point, inclusive, are sold in weight fonts of twenty-five pounds or multiples thereof at regular body-letter prices.   The Italic is ready for all the smaller sizes and the larger sizes are in preparation.

Made only by the INLAND TYPE FOUNDRY, Saint Louis, Mo.

HHHHHHHHHHH HHHHHHHHHH

First showing of STANDARD LINE

VENEZIA SERIES

Patent Pending

24-POINT BORDER. NO. 1413. PER FOOT, 81 CENTS

48-POINT BORDER, NO. 1415. $1.25 PER FOOT

12-POINT VENEZIA. 16 A $1.50; 28 a $1.30; FONT, $2.80

QUICK RESULTS
The Standard Line Shipments
To all parts of the world
$123456890

18-POINT VENEZIA. 10 A, $1.60; 6 a, $1.60; FONT $3.50

FALL DRESS
Suits for Magazines
Latest Styles 67

24-POINT VENEZIA. 6 A, $1.80; 10 a, $1.70; FONT, $3.50

QUOTED
Standard Line
4 Prices 5

TYPE IS THE MOST ESSENTIAL AND THEREFORE THE MOST IMPORTANT

6-POINT VENEZIA. 25 A $1.05; 40 a, 95c. FONT $2.00

Factor in the Printing Art. It is the medium placed in intelligible form whereby thoughts, feelings and aspirations, and, in truth, the recurring events of the day and the news of the world are daily placed before the people. Indeed, type may be said to be a factor in every man's life, for by its use we are educated and fitted for our various positions in life. Therefore, having always held a prominent place in the world's history, it is not to be wondered at that the ranks of the type=founding art have been graced by the ablest thinkers and the ripest scholars the world has ever seen. $1234567890

PRINTING HAS OF LATE YEARS SO IMPROVED IN

8-POINT VENEZIA. 22 A, $1.20; 36 a, $1.05; FONT $2.25

Quality and excellence that one is led to inquire by what means have printers been able to produce such superior work. Many things are necessary; in the first place, the work of the compositor and pressman must be perfect and in harmony and the paper and ink of the proper color and finest grade. The selection of suitable types is very essential $12345

The PRINTER WHO STARTS IN

10-POINT VENEZIA. 18 A, $1.30; 30 a, $1.20; FONT, $2.50

Determined to use Standard Line types and turn out superior work in every respect is sure to build up a substantial, profitable business $1234567890

36-POINT VENEZIA. 4 A $2.90; 6 a $2.60' FONT $5.50

HELPFUL ℔ 75
Lining Type Features

48-POINT VENEZIA. 4 A, $5.00; 5 a, $3.50; FONT, $8.50

The VERY latest

This Series is latest product of Keystone Type Foundry
734 to 742 Sansom Street, Philadelphia, Pa.

36-POINT BORDER, NO. 1413. PER FOOT, $1.15

ANOTHER "BOY WONDER" HAS BROKEN INTO THE PRINTING TRADE.

SOME master printers, with hundreds of thousands of dollars invested in great plants, who are wondering half the time how to make both ends meet, can learn all about it by reading, in *The American Boy* for August, a supposedly sane publication, " How a New Jersey Boy Earns Money." The boy is Foster C. Howard. He is eleven years old and lives in Elizabeth, New Jersey. We are told that he has a bank account, with a lot of money in it, and that he intends to keep on adding to it until, we suppose, Vanderbilt and Rockefeller will both have to take a back seat. And how does he do it? Let *The American Boy* tell in its own words:

" He has a printing-press, thirty-eight fonts of type, and fixtures enough to make up a well-equipped printing-office. He has a 6 by 10 press, and while this is a pretty large press for a boy of his age, he finds the chase too small to do many of the jobs that come to him. His business bids fair to outgrow his press. His type is well selected, so that he can do any ordinary printing that is turned out from the larger offices by older printers. He does all his own work, excepting the proofreading. He submits the proofs to his parents, but makes his own corrections and turns off his own finished work; when it comes from the press it will pass the closest inspection, as it is properly inked, and when dry does not offset. His range of work includes envelopes, letter-heads, bill-heads, programs, cards and tickets of all kinds. Upon the whole, he is kept pretty busy, as he attends school every day and keeps up in his home work. Yet he has time to play and delivers his work when it is promised.

" The amount of money he earns is phenomenal for a lad of his years. Frequently his receipts amount to $10 or $12 a week, and several times since he has been in business he has earned $10 and over on a single job after all expenses were paid. He keeps a rigid expense account. He never forgets to figure up his profits. He has often said, ' Well, I didn't lose anything on that job, when expenses are 50 cents and receipts $1.50, as it only required two hours to turn it off.'

" He makes out his own bills and does his own collecting. When he presents his bill he takes it for granted that he will get his money, and his absolute confidence that he will receive his pay induces him to receipt his bill before he leaves his office for collection. He says when delivering his job and presenting his bill (for with him, the two go together), ' Here is your work, and here is my bill.' His customers admire his promptness, and respect his demand. He never fails to make the collection when he presents his bill. The bill collected, he deposits the money to his own credit, and the bank officials honor his demands. He is a veritable little business man. He is seeking all the time to buy to the best advantage, so that he may be a *lively competitor in the printing business.* He studies price-lists and catalogues as carefully as he does a school-book. He already has the best terms offered the trade and takes advantage of the two per cent discount for cash. By a study of his books he has discovered that by discounting his bills he can replenish his office with type, furniture, etc."

And if you don't believe it, why, *The American Boy* prints seven pictures to prove it. One is of Foster himself, an innocent-looking little lad, who doesn't deserve to have such yarns spread abroad about him, and the others show Foster in the various acts of " Setting the type," " Locking up the form," " Running the press," " Making out the bill," " Presenting the bill " and " Showing the cash " (carefully posed).

The American Boy, furthermore, throws in a moral which is of great importance to professional printers. It is this: " Parents who chance to read this may see something in it to help them solve the problem of what their boys may do to help themselves."

THE GOODSON GRAPHOTYPE — THE COMING AUTOMATIC COMPOSITOR.

If any have held the view that the Goodson Graphotype was a machine developed only to sell stock, such may have their minds disabused by visiting the works of the Goodson Company in Jersey City and observing the development there, and the preparations made for manufacturing the machines on a large scale. The Goodson Graphotype, it will be remembered, is the machine invented by Mr. George A. Goodson, formerly of Minneapolis and Providence. The composition is done on a simple typewriter that punches holes in a paper tape. This tape goes to an automatic typecasting-machine, the size of a sewing-machine, which casts and sets any size of type at a constant speed of 5,500 ems an hour. The Graphotype was exhibited in New York city and a strong corporation formed more than a year ago.

The manufacture of a machine on modern lines that will compete successfully with existing machines is a work of magnitude that can not be appreciated except by those who have been through the experience. It is one thing to have a machine made in the slow, laborious way by hand, and another to have a plant equipped with special tools and fixtures to produce it in large quantities with interchangeable parts, so that, if a customer should break a part or wear out a piece, he could get another which would exactly fit, without any loss of time or any filing or fitting.

The hand-made machine or machines, of which the Goodson Company have several, and which have so often been declared by the leading printing experts to be such marvels, are doing daily commercial work, but without special tools and fixtures they could not be reproduced except at a great expense. They are in every sense models. As, for instance, it might cost $1,000 to make one individual fine watch movement by hand, but with the modern special tools and fixtures employed in the manufacture of watches, a high-grade movement is produced for about $7.

The Goodson Company are now doing exactly the same thing in the preparation for manufacture of their machines that watchmakers have done before them to produce their watch movements cheaply. These expensive jigs and fixtures that cost hundreds of thousands of dollars, go to make up the manufacturing plant.

At the three-story factory of the company, 14-16 Morris

street, Jersey City, a large corps of expert workmen have been busy for months making and perfecting the machines for making the 1,160 parts that compose the Graphotype. The experimenting plant at Providence has been turned into another manufacturing shop and a portion of the work is being pushed there. Other portions have been let out by contract to machine manufacturers, who also have been engaged in developing the necessary jigs and tools for a duplicate system of manufacturing, thus giving them the benefit of the organization of many factories. In fact, the Goodson Company has placed its work where it can be done expeditiously so as to shorten the time of production.

In order that the work of development might be carried on successfully in several shops at once, the drafting department divided the machine into several sections, named and numbered every piece, and supplied accurate drawings of each, on which every measurement was plainly marked. For instance, over one set of drawings appears the name " matrix shifting slide lever, I, of cast steel, E 48." The wearing parts are all marked " hardened and ground," and with each drawing is given enough information to enable a practical machinist to construct it. Imagine the labor of laying out the 1,160 parts in this manner, and preparing duplicate sets of drawings for the different factories, to say nothing of the original designing of each part in such a form that it can be conveniently cast and machined.

When it had been positively determined that the proportions of each and every piece were to be just so and so, and the mate-

rial of just such a character, then came the real work of making drilling jigs, milling jigs and other special tools for forming the parts accurately and economically. Over five hundred different jigs had to be designed and made, each one of these five hundred being a separate and necessarily perfect little machine. Take the mold-pot drilling jig for instance. This is an iron and steel frame-work, into which the metal casting for the mold-pot is placed, and clamped and bolted in such a manner that every mold-pot in it must be positioned alike. In the sides of the jig are holes bushed with hardened steel, and through these the holes are drilled into the mold-pot, insuring the locating of the holes in every mold-pot in exactly the same way. It is made easy work for a boy or other half-trained machinist to take the mold-pot in its jig and bore all the holes accurately. Thus, although the making of the special tools and jigs has been a work of great detail and tediousness, yet when done it is possible to make all the parts with comparatively cheap labor, and with great rapidity and accuracy. This has been gone into at some length to show the reader what an enormous task it is to begin the manufacture of a high-grade machine, and also to demonstrate that the Goodson Graphotype Company is in the business to furnish machines on a large scale. At this writing very many parts of the first lot of machines are completed in the shops at Jersey City, and it is evident that before many months the Goodson Company will be turning out machines at the rate of probably fifty a month. The work of construction is now under the personal supervision of the inventor, Mr. George A. Goodson, one of the most gifted mechanics who has ever given his energies to the assistance of the printer. His genius is evident in every department of the work, which is being done in the most thorough manner, and in accordance with the latest scientific knowledge of machine construction.

Although the Goodson Graphotype has been several years in attaining its perfect development, yet it is now certain that before many months the company will be in a position to deliver machines very rapidly, and no one who has been through the works and observed the thoroughness and intelligence with which every detail is perfected can doubt that the Graphotype is going to revolutionize a great many of the existing conditions in the printing business. The printer also becomes a typefounder, as far as body type is concerned, since the machine manufactures all standard faces of body type at small cost, and at the same time it is for all practical purposes a one-man composing-machine, because the caster is automatic and requires only a small part of a man's time to attend it.

The Graphotype is designed to fill a field in the printing-office that no other machine can occupy. It is preëminently the machine for the book and job printer, since it makes type all of absolutely accurate height to paper and of perfect form, from hard type metal. The types can not be distinguished from the founders' product by studying a printed sheet, unless it be by the entire freedom from battered types which characterizes their impress on the paper. The product being individual type, corrections may be made with the same facility as in hand-set type matter. It requires only a minimum of ability to operate it, and, being a small, light machine, it can be run anywhere. In country towns, one printer with a complete outfit can set the type for neighboring small offices that may send in the tape produced by their typewriters, which they can secure at small cost. In cities, every office having other composing-machines will want one or more Graphotypes to keep up the supply of type for hand composition, and large plants of casting-machines will be started to supply the wants of the smaller printers who can not afford to buy complete composing-machines. Thus the benefits of machine composition will be secured to offices of all classes. It is because the possibilities in these fields are so great that the Goodson Graphotype Company is spending so much money to put out a perfect machine and supply the printing trade in enormous quantities at short notice.

12 POINT

STIMULATED to reaction against ecclesiastical and feudal tyranny, and responding to influences possibly brought to life by the influx of scholars from Byzantium, Italy had already done much toward rehabilitating the classical products of antiquity when the balance of Europe began to throw off the shackles of intellectual despotism, and succumb to those mighty spiritual energies which ended in the emancipation of reason, the freedom of thought and the recognition of natural rights. The course of the Renaissance, determined by the revival of learning, vitalized the Italian scholarship of the fifteenth century, afforded tremendous impetus to

11 POINT

THE RISE of Greek and the accumulation of its classical documents, and became an encouragement for the new art—typography—which gave to Italy an Aldus Manutius and to France the Estiennes. This century is the fountain of those influences which culminated, in the sturdy Teutonic mind, with the Reformation, for the enthusiasm and devotion with which Oriental, Hebrew and Greek studies were pursued evolved a race of scholars whose labors almost instantly began to trend in the direction of Biblical criticism. Italy, at the time, was sponsor for the new birth. The awakening which came to mankind, showing in one direction the basic relations which unify humanity, and in another the possibilities of intellectual freedom, entered the

10 POINT

ITALIAN mind first. The arts of Italy reflected the humanistic spirit of her letters. Science and philosophy bridged the mental chasm between the ancient and fifteenth-century worlds for the first time in 700 years, and sought to evolve a new critical apparatus which should adequately express the renascent culture. A classical education became a necessity, and the knowledge of antiquity was indefatigably explored to add thereto. The threat of the Turk to seize Constantinople more and more influenced the emigration of learned Greeks into Italy, and with them came the literature of Greece—the writings of Pindar, Plato and Aristotle. From Italy the tidal wave swept across the Alps into Germany, where, receiving modifications akin to the nature of the inhabitants, it effected a liberty of religious conviction and a license in expressing it which were powerfully enlarged by the agency of the printing press. The achievements and aims of Froben, at Basle,

9 POINT

REFLECT the position of printing in Germany at the time. Already the power of the press began to deprive the pulpit of its exclusive claim to be the supreme center from which all knowledge emanated, and forerunners of the coming freedom appeared among the nations of Europe. The light of mind extended on, rapidly encompassing the European peoples, but peculiarly affecting France. Strongly tinctured with Italian culture from the intimacy of that intercourse which was steadily maintained between the two countries, the terror of classical learning held sway in France the longest. Architecture, the fine arts, and, to a

8 POINT

CERTAIN extent, literature, experienced a change, and a genius here shone forth through the patronage of Francis, which was sadly wanting in the domain of Biblical literature. To art was accorded liberty, while the press was governed by the ecclesiastical body of the time, the college of the Sorbonne. Of this seeming inconsistency in the actions of a monarch who has been diversely criticised, a student of the epoch, in relation to the Estiennes, has said : "We must remember that two powerful influences operated upon it (the press of France) simultaneously, but not in the same way. These two influences were the demands of the public and the patronage of the Court. The patronage of the sovereign was exerted, and successfully

7 POINT

EXERTED, to develop the material beauty and splendor of books. Grolier was encouraged to bind and Robert Stephens to print. A magnificent Greek type was cast at the expense of the royal treasury. When a sumptuary law prohibited gilding in houses and furniture, book-binding was, by a special clause, exempted from its operation. All that promoted this exterior *luxe*, which the French *Librairie* has always courted—the expanse of margin, the thick-wove paper and the brilliant type—that was the idea which the master of Rosso and Cellini formed of his patronate of letters. His often-quoted saying to Benvenuto Cellini, 'Je l'etoufferai dans l'or;' expressed the materialist direction of the taste of Francis I. And so in books the magnificence of the revival has left its mark behind it in the Greek editions which issued from the press of Robert Stephens, 'printer to the king.' On the

6 POINT

OTHER hand the spirit of curiosity which had arisen among the public made far other demands upon the press. It wanted to learn. It desired books, not to place in a cabinet, but to read in order to know. First and foremost, to know the truth in the matter of religion ; next, to know the cause and remedies of the evils, moral and material, by which the people felt themselves crushed ; how to struggle with nature—to wrest from her more comforts, more enjoyment. But the press as the medium of knowledge—as an arena for debating spiritual and social problems—was not the press which the government of Francis I. would encourage. This is the explanation of the apparent inconsistency in the public acts of that monarch which has caused him to be represented in such different lights. While Francis I. is invoked by some historians as the Father of Letters, the Mæcenas of the Arts, by others his memory is branded as that of a bigot and persecutor, whose zealous despotism would not tolerate the least dissent, the most gentle criticism of the acts of his ministers. The truth is that Francis I. was both of these at once. He was the munificent patron of art and artists—a patron also of letters and learned men."

Condensed Blanchard

4a 3A, $13.25   72-POINT CONDENSED BLANCHARD   L. C. $5.30; C. $7.95

HOME Bread 2

4a 3A, $10.50   60-POINT CONDENSED BLANCHARD   L. C. $4.25; C. $6.25

BRIGHT Model 5

5a 3A, $7.25   48-POINT CONDENSED BLANCHARD   L. C. $3.30; C. $3.95

FASHION Dictates $8

6a 4A, $5.00   36-POINT CONDENSED BLANCHARD   L. C. $2.40; C. $2.60

LINING TYPE Demonstrated 4

8a 5A, $4.30   30-POINT CONDENSED BLANCHARD   L. C. $2.15; C. $2.15

SPLENDID PRINTING and Designs $3

10a 6A, $3.50   24-POINT CONDENSED BLANCHARD   L. C. $1.75; C. $1.75

FINISH DESIGNS
For Artistic Printers 2

15a 9A, $3.20   18-POINT CONDENSED BLANCHARD   L. C. $1.65; C. $1.55

ELEGANT CONDENSED
Face for Every Printer $8

20a 12A, $3.00   14-POINT CONDENSED BLANCHARD   L. C. $1.50; C. $1.50

JUSTIFICATION VERY SIMPLE
Systems Save Money and Labor 68

25a 15A, $2.80   12-POINT CONDENSED BLANCHARD   L. C. $1.40; C. $1.40

PLAIN AND ORNAMENTAL FACES
Large Variety of Modern Faces Displayed

28a 18A, $2.50   10-POINT CONDENSED BLANCHARD   L. C. $1.25; C. $1.25

THESE INNOVATIONS ARE PRICELESS
Useful in Every Specimen of Typography 17
Leaders Line with Roman and Job Faces

35a 22A, $2.25   8-POINT CONDENSED BLANCHARD   L. C. $1.10; C. $1.15

ELEGANT CONDENSED DISPLAY FOR NEWSPAPERS
Handsome and Effective for Headlines and Announcements 2
Always Setting the Pace for Our Competitors

40a 25A, $2.00   6-POINT CONDENSED BLANCHARD   L. C. $1.00; C. $1.00

USEFUL MODERN FACE FOR TWENTIETH CENTURY PRINTING
Traditional Conservatism of the Craft Swept Away by Our Improvements 38
Well Pleased With Our Modernized System of Standard Lining

Made only by the **INLAND TYPE FOUNDRY**, Saint Louis, Mo.

HHHHHHHHHh   HHHHHHHHH

HHHHHHHHHHHHHHHHHHHHHHHHHHHHHHHHHHHHHHHHHHHHH

Standard Line Types

The Bulletin Series

Nickel=Alloy Metal

SHOWING EIGHTEEN AND THIRTY-SIX POINTS ; OTHER SIZES IN PREPARATION

PATENT PENDING

Originality claims admiration every=where—Printers know a Good Thing when they see it; therefore, we shall be very happy indeed to send to any Printer who may write us for it, a copy of our "Artist's Sketch = Book" showing five New Faces, of which this Bulletin Series is one. These are all on Standard Line and have never heretofore been shown. Now ready.

Keystone

734 to 742
Sansom St.

Type=Foundry
Philadelphia

18-POINT BULLETIN. 5 A, $1.00; 16 a, $2.20. FONT, $3.20

New Series showing the—very latest idea in Hand=cut Types, an exclusive product of The Keystone Type Foundry, Philadel=phia, Pa. $12345678

36-POINT BULLETIN. 3 A, $2.00 ; 7 a, $3.50. FONT, $5.50

THE INLAND PRINTER DINNER.

Tendered to A. H. McQuilkin and THE INLAND PRINTER staff, by Henry O. Shepard, and held at "The Monroe," Chicago, Friday, October 12, 1900.

THE INLAND PRINTER DINNER.

ONE of the most enjoyable occasions which those connected with THE INLAND PRINTER had ever attended was the complimentary dinner given to the editor, A. H. McQuilkin, on the evening of Friday, October 12, at "The Monroe," Chicago. The dinner was arranged by Henry O. Shepard, the head of the company, to show his appreciation of the services of Mr. McQuilkin and the other members of the "big family," as he calls it, that assist in producing the magazine each month. It was impossible to invite every one in the establishment, but the forty members present felt highly honored in having an opportunity of meeting the other gentlemen connected with the paper under such pleasant conditions.

The following is the

MENU.

COCKTAILS.
Blue Points.
Celery.   Olives.
Consomme Julienne.
Baked Clubhouse Whitefish, a l'Italienne.
Parisienne Potatoes.
CLARET.
Sweetbreads, larded, with Green Peas.
Punch Benedictine.
Braised Tenderloin, a la Bordelaise.
Potato au Gratin.   Combination Salad.
Ice Cream.   Cake.
Roquefort and de Brie Cheese.   Crackers.
CIGARS.   Coffee.

After the guests had done full justice to the above, the toastmaster, C. F. Whitmarsh, called the gathering to order and explained the reasons Mr. Shepard had for inviting his staff to meet in this way. He spoke of the generosity of the head of the paper, not only to its editor, but to every one connected with the publication. Mr. Shepard responded by saying it had always been his policy to treat his people fairly, and stated he felt that an employer could always get more out of his men by having such feelings exist as he was sure prevailed between all of the people in the establishment and himself. Mr. McQuilkin spoke of his work on the paper and of the great assistance he had received from other members of the staff in making the paper what it was. Mr. Rathbun referred to the condition of the publication when Mr. McQuilkin assumed the duties of editor, both as to circulation and general prestige.

He stated that as soon as the character of the matter presented to readers was improved, the subscriptions increased in number, and having a wider circulation the advertising naturally increased. These had resulted in placing the magazine in the front rank among papers devoted to the graphic arts. There was no set program, and nearly every one present had an opportunity of speaking, and took advantage of it. The occasion will long be remembered as one of the bright spots in the history of THE INLAND PRINTER.

The following letter sent to Mr. Shepard by Mr. McQuilkin after the editor had returned to Asheville, expresses his feelings concerning the gathering:

My Dear Mr. Shepard: October 16, 1900.

I desire to express my profound appreciation of your many kindnesses in Chicago and elsewhere. Let me assure you that the terms of affectionate regard in which you expressed yourself last Friday evening are reciprocated to the full by me. It is such liberality as you have shown, so keen an interest in the welfare of those about you, so warm and sincere an attachment for those in your house, that has made the name of The Henry O. Shepard Company and THE INLAND PRINTER what it is.

Your attitude toward your employes has been such that you have a phalanx of men devoted to your interests, and if in any way my efforts can enlarge and round out what we have attempted, be assured they will not be lacking.

For every kindly word and noble sentiment expressed by you, I give you an echo back a thousand times.

With every good wish for your increased prosperity and happiness, I am as ever, sincerely and cordially your friend,

A. H. McQUILKIN.

The following is a list of those present: A. R. Allexon, F. Baumgartner, E. W. Beedle, Daniel Boyle, P. H. Butler, J. I. Caldwell, William G. Cobb, Edward Conway, George Crall, A. S. Dinsmore, H. S. Engle, Harry Flinn, George A. Furneaux, K. M. Griswold, Al Grayson, Joseph H. Hamer, Fred Hilton, Philip G. Howard, A. Hughmark, M. F. Kase, George M. Leathers, A. H. McQuilkin, Frank Parker, S. K. Parker, B. F. Philbrick, Alfred Pye, A. W. Rathbun, Charles Reiner, Frank A. Richards, Harry Shaffer, Frank Shepard, H. O. Shepard, Adolph Stoike, Fred Thomas, J. S. Thompson, S. H. Treloar, C. F. Whitmarsh, Will L. Whitmarsh.

The accompanying illustration is made from a photograph taken by J. W. Taylor during the festivities.

ALEXANDER BROTHERS

TOBACCO MERCHANTS AND EXPORTERS

420 SOUTH STATE STREET

NEW ORLEANS

WAREHOUSES
321 MASON STREET
510 DIXON STREET

PLANTATIONS IN
ALABAMA AND
SOUTH CAROLINA

MARVIN & DAVIDSON
TEMPLE BUILDING
9 ALLEN AVE. AND 10 WALL STREET
GROUND FLOOR
KANSAS CITY

BLAIR SERIES

6-POINT NO. 4, 16A, $1.00
6-POINT NO. 3, 16A, $1.00
6-POINT NO. 2, 18A, $1.00
6-POINT NO. 1, 20A, $1.00

INLAND TYPE FOUNDRY
STANDARD LINE TYPE
217 PINE ST.

SAINT LOUIS, OCT. 25, 1900

DEAR MR. PRINTER

THIS PAGE IS SET IN OUR NEW BLAIR SERIES. PLEASE EXAMINE IT CLOSELY. IT IS AN EXACT IMITATION OF THE SMALL GOTHIC LETTER NOW SO POPULAR WITH ENGRAVERS FOR STYLISH STATIONERY, CARDS AND ANNOUNCEMENTS. WE HAVE USED A FEW LINES OF OUR BRANDON WITH THE BLAIR TO SHOW HOW THEY LOOK IN COMBINATION

YOURS TRULY

INLAND TYPE FOUNDRY

HERBERT A. SHERMAN
GENERAL INSURANCE AGENT
CORNER THIRD AND PINE
SAINT LOUIS

AGENT
NEW YORK, LONDON AND GLOBE
INSURANCE CO.

BELL TELEPHONE, MAIN 423
KINLOCH TELEPHONE, A 352

MADE AND FOR SALE BY THE

INLAND TYPE FOUNDRY, SAINT LOUIS

CORBITT SERIES

Made only by the INLAND TYPE FOUNDRY, Saint Louis, U. S. A.

4a 3A, $16.00   60-POINT CORBITT   L. C. $6.20; C. $9.80

Find Prize 5

4a 3A, $8.50   48-POINT CORBITT   L. C. $3.25; C. $5.25

Desired Black 8

5a 3A, $5.00   36-POINT CORBITT   L. C. $2.15; C. $2.85

DESIGNS Acceptable 4

6a 4A, $4.30   30-POINT CORBITT   L. C. $2.00; C. $2.30

BOLD FASHION SECURED
Pleases Advertisers 50

8a 4A, $3.50   24-POINT CORBITT   L. C. $1.75; C. $1.75

ORDER FOR GOOD CUSTOMERS
Best Faces Manufactured 32

10a 6A, $3.20 18-POINT CORBITT L. C. $1.60; C. $1.60	16a 9A, $3.00 14-POINT CORBITT L. C. $1.55; C. $1.45
RECORD BREAKERS	**DEMANDED PERFECTION**
Grand Strides 10	**Satisfies Customers 56**
20a 12A, $2.80 12-POINT CORBITT L. C. $1.40; C. $1.40	24a 14A, $2.50 10-POINT CORBITT L. C. $1.25; C. $1.25
WITNESSED DEMONSTRATION	**BEST MADE MATERIAL PROCURED**
Gives Printers Confidence 72	**Aid to Printers and Pressmen 48**
26a 16A, $2.25 8-POINT CORBITT L. C. $1.10; C. $1.15	34a 18A, $2.00 6-POINT CORBITT L. C. $1.00; C. $1.00
PRACTICAL PRINTER BUYING SUPERIOR TYPE	**ENTERPRISING PRINTERS ADMIRE PERFECT MATERIAL**
And Obtaining Highest Satisfaction 26	**Thrifty Buyers can Afford Nothing but the Best 35**

72-Point Corbitt in Preparation

HHHHHHHHH HHHHHHHHH
HHHHHHHHHHH HHHHHHHHHHH

Written for THE INLAND PRINTER.

A SHORT SKETCH OF THE INVENTION AND EARLY HISTORY OF PRINTING.

BY ARTHUR KIRKBRIDE TAYLOR.

THE spring of the year 1430 opened with a general scarcity of morning newspapers and absolutely no campaign literature, nor had Christopher Columbus as yet sufficiently impressed on Queen Isabella the urgent necessity of providing written matter for "Histories of the World's Fair" and coupon "Art Portfolios" to drive her to the dire extremity of pawning her engagement ring and nice new cuff buttons.

The thrifty German ate breakfast within full view of his family, because he had not yet received the morning paper of twenty-four pages to devour before finishing the rest of his meal. The American of that date ate breakfast only when there was any, and contentedly let his squaw do all the manual labor while he put on his close-fitting coat of paint and went on the warpath.

The robber-barons, of oft-told story, were still making their celebrated periodical excursions for holding up treasure-laden caravans with neatness and despatch without getting a half-stick notice from the Associated Press. Things were very dull, and it was very plain to be seen that something had to be done.

When the royalty wanted to hear anything new, they just hired a traveling minstrel to come to the house, stay a few days, and sing it to them. If they didn't exactly catch the drift of his remarks the first time, why, it didn't make much difference; they would get him to repeat it to them when he came around again the next year.

The few people who could read had to pay so much for their books, that, by the time they had scraped together enough collateral to purchase a volume, they were so old that their eyesight had failed.

The first books which were written were printed. School children learn to print before they learn to write. This explains why there are so many amateur printers in this country today. But to resume. The books were made with a pen generally, each letter laboriously fashioned, and were the handiwork of a great number of monks in monasteries scattered over much of Europe. The initials at the begin-

FLORA.

Half-tone from crayon drawing, by Grand Rapids Engraving Co., Grand Rapids, Mich.

nings of chapters were handsomely illuminated, and often wrought in divers colors, and sometimes gold and silver. A good copyist, in order to produce a sixteen-page form, took as long as it now takes a customer to get a job when he thoughtlessly leaves the order with information that "he isn't in any hurry for it; any time in a week or so will do."

What an inspiring sight it would have been to have looked in upon a whole monastery engaged at work in their cells, with their copies chained to the desks before their straight-backed chairs, working at their tasks with much making of faces, each man with his tongue thrust within the corner of his mouth, much in the same manner in which we are wont to conduct ourselves when opening a can of tomatoes. And then, to think that you didn't have to worry about spelling, just suit yourself. If you doubt it, consult Chaucer's poems. The theory has been proven incorrect that the orthography of the earlier copies of Chaucer was due to compositors who had run out of sorts, and just spelled according to the type in the cases. It was the fault of copyists who couldn't remember how they spelled words in the paragraph before.

A good typewriter in those old days could have laid out a whole monastery. The impression might have been a trifle heavy on his punctuation marks, but his work would have been legible, which is more than we can say for some of the monkwritten manuscripts, especially the Latin ones. We never were very strong on Latin.

When books were scarce and valuable as they were in those days they were in many cases chained to the desks on which they belonged. This to a great extent discouraged borrowing, and a circulating library, in order to be any kind of a success, had to be run in connection with an earthquake. For a long time prior to 1430, printing in a crude way, from blocks engraved in relief, had been carried on. Prints representing Biblical scenes and pictures of saints were not uncommon, and playing cards made their appearance produced in the same way. it has always seemed remarkable to me that the "Devil's own playthings," as they are called, sprung up among such eminently respectable associations, and how well they have seemed to keep along in the procession. Always, as you might say, making a game fight.

It seems probable that these first rude prints were made on presses which resembled in a general way the wine and cheese presses used at that time. They were simply a strong frame of wood, with a heavy screw running through the top cross-piece and paralled with the uprights at the side. The operation of this screw applied the pressure necessary for the impression. This style of press, with slight modifications for the convenience of the operator, was in use for a long time, until it was at length superseded by the press in which a combination of levers took the place of the screw.

The result was not all that could be desired, the picture at the best had a harsh, unfinished appearance and was not beautiful to look upon, but it was a picture—and that covered a multitude of sins. There was one advantage about work produced in this way—it was appreciated. A man, after becoming familiar with one of these pictures could explain it to any who happened to see it, and tell what it represented, so that it could be clearly understood; and then after a while he would become so familiar with his little lecture that he could explain it to two people at a time, to the great advancement of knowledge and understanding.

It is not the intention of the writer to jest at the earlier manifestations of the art as shown by these ancient prints. Considering the time at which they were made and the difficulties surrounding their production they are most admirable, but viewed from the standpoint of today and compared with the finest specimens of process engraving and modern presswork they appear grotesque, and it is wonderful to think that one was evolved from the other.

In those days nearly all learning was confined within the narrow limits of monastery walls, and it is most befitting that in the "Hymn of Praise," which Mendelssohn wrote to commemorate the four hundredth anniversary of the invention of printing, the most magnificent chorus should be that which proclaims "The Night is Departing," heralding the dispelling of the dark clouds of ignorance and superstition and the dawn of the day of knowledge and hope and truth.

BEFORE going at once into matters relative to the invention of printing as it is now spoken of, let us look away back into the dim ages of the past, and see what we can learn of the prospect.

We have nothing to prove that there was much printed matter in circulation before the flood, and while, according to a recent paragraph, there are many who believe that Noah was far ahead of his time in using ark lights, still we fail to note on his manifest the merest allusion to the earliest sprouts of a printing plant on board. No thinking disciple of the art preservative can doubt, however, that when the procession of animals entered the ark, a pair of "type lice"—a male and a female—came very near the head of the line.

Later, in the Bible, we find that Job was a man sorely tried and harrassed by many afflictions and bodily discomforts. Surely he could not have endured the whole round of worriment without having been associated with the printing business, even remotely, and who knows but that the term "job printer" dates back to this period of Bible history, being originally "Job, Printer," and in its long sojourn the comma had become eliminated and the discrepancy in pronunciation as easily occurred. However, this is only a suggestion.

We have certain knowledge that for a long time prior to the middle of the fifteenth century, printing—i. e.,the art of impressing letters or other characters upon paper, cloth or other materials—had been practiced not only in Germany, but other countries. There are preserved for our edification, in museums, specimens of Assyrian visiting cards, in the shape of brickbats, stamped with cuneiform characters. If our theory could be proved, that these inscriptions, when translated, would read : "Mrs. Nebuchadnezzar, Thursdays

in November," then we could easily trace the calling of the hod-carrier back to those ancient days when this style of visiting card was in vogue. Just imagine the Misses Nebuchadnezzar going out calling on a fine afternoon with a file of eight or nine stalwart hod-carriers with their cards, bringing up the rear of the procession. No trouble at all to explain the large size of the king's domicile—after every reception he just built an addition to the palace with the proceeds. When, as was the case in those days, bricks were sometimes used for the same purpose that we mostly use paper, it would be interesting to know how the ancient bill-poster would paste up a two-sheet paving slab announcing the approach of the "Greatest Uncle Tom's Cabin Company Extant, with two Topseys, two Marks and sixteen ferocious Siberian bloodhounds."

But don't for an instant overlook the claims of the placid Chinaman. He assures you with his proverbial stolidity that his country produced printing as early as the reign of the Emperor Wu-Wong, which you will readily recall was about 1120 B. C. (When you want a good article in the line of priority call in the Chinaman. New lot, just opened.) And if you have the time he will prove it to you by his cousin who runs a laundry in the next block. As a sample giving evidence of their ability and industry as painstaking prevaricators you have but to turn to the statement which some obliging informant gave Du Halde, a learned Jesuit father, in his travels in the Flowery Kingdom, in the early part of the eighteenth century; it was to the effect that a Chinese printer could perfect without extra exertion ten thousand sheets in a single day. For fear someone wouldn't believe it, he tells how it is done, which makes it all the more improbable. He states that, for printing the block, which has been previously engraved, the printer stands before a level table upon which the block has been adjusted. At one hand a bowl of fluid ink and at the other a pile of paper cut the proper size. The printer holds in his right hand two flat brushes fixed upon the opposite ends of the same handle; one brush is used to supply the block with ink, while the other or dry brush is used to brush over the paper which has been placed upon the block previously inked and thus the copy is made by the light pressure of the brush upon the back of the sheet of paper. Thus far, good. Not the least doubt in the world that printing entirely as good as the average Chinese specimens of work can be done in this way, but when the calm-visaged, almond-eyed Celestial undertakes to assure us that he can print ten thousand sheets a day in this way, we respectfully beg to differ from him. To be able to manipulate the paper and ink at such a remarkable speed would be to enact a scene very similar to the usual illustrations of a dog fight or what the country editor saw as the cylone advanced up Main street.

Cylinders of clay were used by the Assyrians for the purpose of chronicling events and keeping historical records. These cylinders in some cases were engraved, while in others there is unmistakable evidence that they were stamped while the clay was in a plastic state by stamps engraved so that the impression in the clay would show the characters as they should appear. The clay was then baked or sun-dried. The "roasting" which is frequently done by modern newspapers may have been evolved from this ancient usage. The most excellent state of preservation in which these cylinders and bricks remain at this late day speaks well for them as a method of keeping records.

At a later period in Rome, stamps, made of brass, were used for stamping signatures. There is some indication that these stamps were used with ink, as from the manner in which they were engraved it is hardly probable that they could have been used to impress wax on account of roughness of the counter or field. In many cases these signature stamps were used to save the trouble of signing the name in the usual manner, and we are sorry to say that in numerous other instances they were necessitated by the inability of the users to write their own names.

These early examples of engraving characters in relief and impressing them in plastic substances and also the Roman signature stamps, while not entirely typographic or xylographic in their character, are nevertheless evidences of a tendency in that direction, and as such are worthy of our consideration.

ASIDE from the priests and monks who were identified with early bookmaking, there were very few people who really prized books for their contents, and who would have hailed with delight the introduction of any art which would cheapen them and thus increase learning. At the same time there were many of the nobility and of the wealthy class who spent large sums in the purchase of books which were exquisitely written and illustrated, and handsomely bound; in many cases the sides being rich with fine carvings and resplendent with jewels. With this class of people the book was not valued for its contents so much as it was for the decorations and artistic workmanship lavished upon it. As far as the contents were concerned it was a matter of indifference; a cigar box would have done just as well. One of the handsomest bindings of recent days was lavished upon a volume of "Great Expectations," and when the proper spring was operated in opening it, the hospitable end of a pint bottle of soothing syrup made its appearance. And still people wonder at Dickens' popularity.

With those just referred to book-buying was a fad. A parallel in our present day is afforded in the wealthy class who affect a liking for fine arts, and spend immense sums in the purchase of paintings, which in many cases they are totally unable to appreciate; probably in the hope that they may be considered as possessed of considerable culture and artistic discrimination. They are not in any sense the mainstay of the modern publisher, and in the fourteenth century the case was not unlike it. Those who could read and afford to buy books looked with feelings of disgust at the block-books of the early printers. Having been used to the artistically wrought volumes, with daintily painted miniatures — when the productions of the early press put in appearance, replete with black letter and blacker illustrations — the aristocracy asked for their smelling salts and retired to their boudoirs. They did not look with favor upon the rude, uncouth illustrations and coarse text of the early printers, and looked with contempt upon those who were satisfied with their efforts.

The first example we have of printing in books is in some copies where the outlines for the illuminated initials have been stamped from engraved stamps. Next in order come those books in which the text was written but the illustrations printed from blocks, showing conclusively that it was not expedient at that time to engrave the letters of the text, because on the limited number of copies issued it would be cheaper to have the letters of the text written by copyists who did not command high wages. At length books made their appearance in which both the text and the illustrations were printed. The first of these are what are known as block-books, because they were printed from engraved blocks of wood in contradistinction to those in which the text was printed from movable types.

It wouldn't have made any difference if there had been printing offices innumerable in the old world before the fourteenth century. They wouldn't have effected any great

change in the civilization of that age. The people were unprepared for printing as an accomplished and complete art. Why, inside of two days all the pressfeeders would have been laid off, and the pressmen one and all would have found something in the complex mechanism of their presses which needed immediate attention and sufficient readjustment and repairs to keep them on the pay roll until the boss also took to investigating. The walls of the pressroom might have been lined with forms, corrected, and all ready to run, but that's all that would have come of them. And all this loss of time and delay would have been caused by just one thing — the lack of paper. There wasn't a 6-to-cap billhead on the whole continent. If a man would have gone to a merchant and have asked him for "a half-ream of 24 by 38, 60-pound S. and C. Toned" the merchant would have probably crossed himself and made a rush for the cellar. A request for "Royal 28 Laid" would have most likely landed him in jail to answer a charge of treason. The situation would have been somewhat similar to that in which a printer-soldier found himself once during the civil war. The type for one of the army newspapers was all set up and on the press, but there wasn't any paper to be had. Happening by and wishing to read the news our printer friend stepped in, inked the form, and, taking a clean handkerchief from his pocket (history doesn't say where he got it), spread it on the form, pulled an impression and went on his way rejoicing. In this instance, at least, the lack of paper was not to be sneezed at.

The date of the invention of paper is somewhat uncertain, but the obliging Chinaman comes forward again with the assertion that it was the invention of the Chinese and it took place at the close of the first century. As to its introduction into Europe most authorities place the date not earlier than the fifth century.

The first paper made in Europe was probably made of cotton, and was thick, resembling cardboard in weight, but very rough, coarse and unsuitable for writing or printing. It was not thought that this very early style of paper was used as a substitute for papyrus, the use of which was declining in the fifth century. The early bookmakers did not use the paper which was produced for their books, but confined themselves to vellum, which was at that time thought to be the only material fit to write upon. Parchment in time became so scarce that copyists frequently resorted to the expedient of removing the writing from the surface of that which had already been used and writing again upon it. In this way many valuable manuscripts have been destroyed to give place to long theological dissertations which were so tedious that the only way for the author to know at its end what he had said at its beginning was for him to have it written down; a source of great satisfaction to him and absolute unconcern to everyone else.

Vellum is entirely unsuitable for printing, and it has been said by a high authority on the subject that typography would have been a failure if it had depended on a liberal supply of vellum. Even if the restricted size of books could have been conformed to there were not enough sheep at the end of the fourteenth century to supply the demands of printing presses for a week.

TO one with only a superficial knowledge of the art, it might appear that the step from the printing of block-books to typography in its true meaning was not very great, and that one might rise from one to the other by gradual stages. If the statement made by some writers, that wood type was used in early books, is accepted, such would not be illogical, as the idea of movable types was not a new one, it having been in use in a different way a long time before printed work was produced. But it has been stated by a high authority on printing that the invention which was the keynote of successful typography was not that of movable types, but that the whole structure of letterpress printing rests on the invention of the type-mold, by which metal types of accurate bodies were cast. This idea on the invention of printing, especially by those who have had no practical knowledge of the art or of its unyielding requirements.

To a printer the matter is very plain. The claim that the types used in the first books printed from movable types were made of wood is entirely untenable in the light of practical knowledge and careful experiment. There is not an engraver today who can cut separate type from wood and set it up without leading it and get anything like the evenness of lines which these early productions show. To contend that the workmen of a bygone age, in an art which has not been lost, could do that which it is impossible to do now, would be equal to accepting the theory that was once advanced in reference to the way in which the pyramids were built. The question under consideration was how the Egyptians managed to get in place some of the immense blocks of stone used in their erection. When the question had been discussed in all its phases, a deep thinker came forward and gravely advanced the theory that, in his mind, it was very clear that the ancients were possessed of some mysterious knowledge by means of which they were enabled to overcome the laws of gravitation.

I must confess that it is with some reluctance that I have to put aside the thought that when the early compositor was out of sorts it was only necessary for him to hie himself away to the wood-pile, and there with his ax hew for himself, from some ancient denizen of the forest, some nice, new nonpareil lower-case l's. To me it was always a pleasant thought to picture the founder of the art, sitting on his wood-pile, whittling out a new font of script while he turned over in his mind the best course to pursue in order to secure the county printing for the next term.

True as it may be that wood was the first material from which separate types were cut, it was soon found to be impracticable. When several lines were put together it was found to be impossible to make the bodies of sufficient accuracy to prevent the lines from becoming crooked.

Some writers have asserted that the types were pierced by a small hole near the face, and that the types were strung on a wire to prevent them from becoming loose and dropping out. This method would have had its drawbacks. It would have been impossible to pi a form, so there wouldn't have been any excuse to offer a man when his work wasn't done on time. Probably this theory explains the origin of that ancient term, "counting up your string." The sole foundation, it seems, for this theory rests on the discovery of a printed sheet in which is found the impression of a type which had pulled out and was lying on the form when the impression was taken. In this print of the body of the type there appears near its face a small white spot, which was at once decided to be the result of a hole in the type, and, necessarily, all of the rest of the type must have been made in the same way. The very fact of this letter having pulled out is a very damaging one to the theory. The first-year apprentice, who doesn't lay claim to more than three-fourths of all knowledge, can tell you that that spot is the place where the size and foundry imprint appears; without doubt that spot stood for "18-pt. Johnson Foundry."

As to who first made use of the type-mold, there is a difference of opinion. In an article of this length it would be impracticable to present at length the arguments advanced, so we will only give a general idea of the principal arguments.

The only foundation which seems to exist for the opinion which many hold in favor of Coster's claim to the invention rests upon the writings of an accomplished scholar and historian named Junius, the author of a volume entitled "Batavia," published in 1588, in which book the statements referred to are found. Previous to its publication there were legends and rumors circulated which ascribed to Haarlem the honor of being the birthplace of the art of printing, but as none of the writings in which the legends appear gives the name of the inventor, the date of the invention, or the titles of any of his productions, it is not necessary for us to give them more serious attention than is usually accorded the rumor announcing, annually, the complete failure of the Delaware peach crop.

The account of Coster's invention, as set forth by Junius, runs somewhat in this wise: About one hundred and twenty-eight years ago (dating back from 1588), there lived in Haarlem one Laurentius Joannes, surnamed Æditus or Custos, one of a most distinguished and honorable family. When in the woods strolling one day, it happened that he undertook the experiment of fashioning the bark of a beech tree in the form of letters, which he afterward impressed upon a leaf of paper. He succeeded so happily in this that he aspired to greater things, inventing, first of all, an ink thicker and more viscid than that of the scribes, for he found that the common ink spread or blotted. He subsequently changed the letters of beech wood for those of lead, and these again for letters of tin, because tin was a less flexible material, harder, and more durable.

Junius further states that Coster was quite successful in his new business and added to his facilities by employing several hands, one of whom subsequently, on a certain Christmas eve, stole a quantity of Coster's type and went to Amsterdam, afterward to Cologne, and finally from thence to Mentz, and being possessed of all the technical skill connected with the art he opened an office and reaped an abundant reward from the fruits of his theft.

In writing of the inventor, Junius seems particularly anxious that we should note that Coster was a man of wealth, leisure, and "of cultivated and enlarged capacities" in order "that all the world may know that this art was invented in a reputable and honorable family and not among plebeians."

In the archives of Haarlem there appears at that time only one man of the name given by Junius, and he was a tallow chandler who sold oil and candles. Of course there is nothing in connection with this calling which would prevent anyone who followed it from making a great invention, but it is interesting to note that the only contemporary records ignore him as an inventor and publisher and mention him only in several transactions in connection with the oil and tallow business, and at a time when Junius would have us believe that he was a wealthy citizen and a man of leisure. But it may be that this tallow business was merely a rich man's hobby and that he sold candles as a pastime.

Junius, who was the first author who had the fortitude to give a name and date to a personage by whom the glory of Holland is so enhanced, was employed (at his own suggestion) to write a history of Holland, and it is only natural that he should use his utmost endeavors to secure for his country as much of glory and honor as possible. The work on which he was engaged was to have been written in six volumes, but all the states were not satisfied with the production and he was bought off by their paying him a good round sum to not publish the work. After Junius's death his son compiled the unfinished works of his father and published them.

There are many features of his writings which make him not infallible as a writer and historian. In the volume of "Batavia" are statements which he without doubt believed, but which to us are incredible, and altogether it seems to us that the writings upon which all of Haarlem's claims rest are exceedingly shaky and untrustworthy. That Junius was a scholar of most thorough education there can be no doubt, and his patriotic zeal is most commendable, but it is most unfortunate that so many who have followed him in writing on the subject have relied so implicitly upon him as being an authority and have failed to consider the source of his information, which appears to have been the stories told by some old men of Haarlem of events of which they were in turn told, or which happened such a long time previously that there was no evidence to be found, so that it rested wholly upon their statements.

Subsequent Dutch writers, in order to make more sure of the priority of their claims, took the liberty of changing the date given by Junius as the authentic one, shifting it back a few years to suit their purposes and convenience; the last one in each case with much diligence and commendable zeal going back of the date given by the one who did the same thing before him. Without this custom ceases we may reasonably expect to see the statement made in some future publication that the story of the wanderings of Ulysses was written by Homer as a special correspondent to the Haarlem *Dispatch*, Coster's afternoon daily.

Those who believe in the claims of Coster as set forth by Junius are many, especially in Holland, where it has been said it is an article of national faith, as is attested by the numerous monuments which have been erected in his honor as well as the great number of prints, inscriptions and portraits (no two of which are alike) which ascribe to him the honor due the inventor of this most noble art.

IN the fifteenth century, many of the municipal cities of Germany were sorely troubled by enmities between them, but what was more often more serious, about this time, was the civil strife between the burghers and the nobles, which was engaged in in some of these cities. Mentz, in particular, a city of northern Germany, was disturbed in this way. The relations between the opposing elements were often much strained, and on ceremonial occasions of state, the burghers, being in the majority, demanded to have the first part of the procession and furthermore that they be allowed to ride in the band wagon, and that the noblemen should walk afoot. This did not seem to be very satisfactory to the noblemen, and at times the band wagon was very much crowded, to say the least.

On one occasion, in 1530, the burghers had made arrangements to have the emperor visit the city, and they were going to entertain him in great style, with much blowing of horns and reading of resolutions. In some way the noblemen got wind of the proposed festivities, and by hiring several wagons and giving the drivers a respectable tip to drive fast, succeeded in meeting the emperor about three miles out of town, and read resolutions to him from that point to the city hall, besides giving him so much to eat on the way that when the time came for the burghers' spread he was barely able to sit up to the table, and the only thing that he asked for at all was a second helping to toothpicks. This smart move on the part of the noblemen so endeared them in the hearts of the burghers that they straightaway went out and broke into the houses of several of the noblemen, ate up everything that was edible and drank up everything they could not eat, and incidentally destroyed all their property and tore down their houses. This incident will serve to show the good feeling which existed between the two parties, and to what extremes people will often go in their desire for amusement.

To further help along in the general disquietude, Mentz was also blessed with the great abundance of having two rival archbishops, which was the cause of the cutting of the price of indulgences and the substitution at times of inferior

goods and even short measure. At length it became so bad that when a man got an indulgence he did not know whether he had secured a good one or whether it had been adulterated or not, and finally it became so common to find chicory or ground cocoanut shells in the indulgences that people lost all confidence in the article and began to raise all that they needed, so that the trade was eventually ruined.

It was while affairs were in this condition that there lived in Mentz a man named John Gutenberg, of noble birth. John Gutenberg's father was named Frielo Gensfleisch, and his mother's name was Else Gutenberg. John's brother, Frielo, junior, was always called Gensfleisch, while John himself was frequently called Gutenberg; it being the custom in Germany for a son to take his mother's family name if there was any danger that the name might otherwise become extinct. Gensfleisch is German for goose flesh, while Gutenberg means good hill. Now, to be sure that you get this matter entirely clear in your minds I will reiterate it. Frielo Gutenberg married Else Gensfleisch; they had two sons, one named after his father (several years) the other fearing that his father's name might become extinct, requested that he be named after his mother, consequently was named John Goose Flesh, which was German for Gutenberg.

Being one of a noble family, on one of those exceedingly unpleasant occasions, of which some mention has already been made, John Gutenberg received such treatment at the hands of the burghers that he decided that a change of climate and scenery would be beneficial, so he and his family left the town one day, after leaving word at the post office to forward all mail that came for them with a 2-cent stamp on it to Strasburg, hoping in that way to escape patent medicine advertisements and postal cards.

As some of the property of Gutenberg still remained in Mentz, the city officials made an agreement with him by which the city was to pay to Gutenberg a certain rental for the property and forward the proceeds to him, and if they should fail to make the payments as agreed, he was at liberty to seize and imprison any of them whom he could lay hands on for the debt; which proceeding should, of course, be a source of very great satisfaction to him. Therefore, one day, when the secretary of Mentz happened to be in Strasburg, Gutenberg, just in order to show the people of Mentz that he was still alive and in possession of all his faculties, had the said secretary arrested and imprisoned. The town council and burgomaster of Strasburg, however, fearing that such an action on the part of Gutenberg might cause a rupture of the friendly feelings which then existed between the two cities, induced him to release the officer and relinquish his claim, which, being a considerable amount, shows that Gutenberg was of a magnanimous disposition.

There is not much known of Gutenberg's life, not half as much as we would wish to know, but what is known is positive and definite. It was his fate at many times in his life to figure in lawsuits, and the facts recorded there are of great value and reliable to the highest degree. Although these occasions were most trying to him, they have proved most valuable in the light of establishing his claims to the invention, and in later days proved a blessing, which, in the time that they were recorded, were most excellently disguised. The evidence recorded on the court records is of a very different nature from that brought forth to substantiate the claims of his rival for the honor, Coster.

In 1436 Gutenberg appeared before the tribunal of Strasburg in a breach-of-promise case. As the decree of the court is not given, it is generally believed that the case was withdrawn by Gutenberg's marrying the complainant. We do not know to a certainty that such was done, or that he ever married, but some writers, who seem to be possessed of superior means of information, assure us that it was Gutenberg's intention to marry the young woman in whose behalf the suit was brought, but when he left Mentz he was impoverished to such an extent that he hesitated to ask her to descend from the position which she then occupied and become the wife of a poor man with only the prospects for the future before him. She evidently thought differently, and, in order to acquaint him of her favor to his suit, she, with many maidenly blushes and misgivings, sued the bashful suitor for breach of promise. It is creditable to John's keenness of perception that he was bright enough to take the hint and marry her. These same writers further assure us that their married life was a most happy one, and that we owe much to his wife for the kindly encouragement and the tender sympathy for Gutenberg in the dark times of adversity which so often overtook him in the pursuit of the great invention on which he was engaged. Indeed, they give a most comprehensive view, showing the close relations which existed between the inventor's domestic affairs and his work. As he did considerable of his work at home, we can picture in our mind's eye Anna, his wife, busily engaged in crimping the edge of a large mince pie with the aid of one of John's large capital W's of that rich Gothic letter which was so much used in that day. And then, when Saturday night would come around, we can see Anna patiently waiting until John had finished running off the last form of the day, that she might put his Sunday-go-to-meeting trousers in the press over night, in order that the creases in them might be the envy of all beholders on the holy sabbath day. Aside from the art which he invented, Gutenberg is known to have had knowledge of two other trades — that of lapidary, or polisher of gems, and that of making mirrors. It is very likely that the knowledge of these two trades proved most valuable to him in the art in which he was conducting his experiments. The knowledge of the art of pouring metals in making the frames of mirrors and his skill as an engraver of molds for the same purpose undoubtedly came in good stead to him. The confidence which he had in the ultimate outcome of his experiments in printing, is very forcibly shown in the fact that he entirely gave up the trades from which he had previously gained a livelihood, and devoted his whole time and energies to the new art which was to be the cause of such wonderful results.

As is often the case with men of genius, Gutenberg was not what you would term a good business man, so we often find him at a loss to know where to turn for the means required in the experiments on which he was engaged.

In the proceedings of a lawsuit, which was brought against Gutenberg by the brother of one of his deceased partners, there was evidence given which showed that he was engaged with some other persons in some experiments and investigations of great importance. That these experiments and investigations were thought to be of much practical value is evinced by the fact that the suit was brought in order to have the court order Gutenberg to admit the brother of his late partner as a successor in the partnership, and so be permitted to partake of the benefits arising from the association. Although there is not much clearly stated in the evidence by which one could readily recognize the operation of printing, there is, at least, mention made of money expended for lead used in the operations. We may infer, from the lack of definite information concerning the secret which Gutenberg was to divulge to his partners, that he did not wish to give it the publicity which evidence in court would be likely to give it. Another thing which tended to prevent a clear idea of the invention is the ignorance of the proper names of the tools and implements which were used, the witnesses having no knowledge of them, as they were largely designed solely for use in the new art, and were thus new to the outside world.

It is further shown in the testimony that, after the death of the partner referred to, Gutenberg, fearing the publicity to which their affairs would be exposed, sent word to the brother of the partner who had died and requested him that he would, without delay, take away from the press four pieces which were lying therein and disconnect them so that no person would be able to know how they were related or for what purpose they were used. Authorities differ as to what these four pieces were, some saying that they were the four pages of engraved blocks of a block-book, while others seem to think that the four pieces referred to were the four columns of wood type. A high authority seems to be of the opinion that it refers to some kind of a type mold, which, being the key of the invention, Gutenberg should quite naturally wish to conceal. The opinion that they were four pages of a block-book does not seem to warrant the great care which was exercised for their concealment, as block printing had been practiced for a long time before that time, and was so generally understood that there would have been no use for concealment. As to the press referred to, there is knowledge that this form of press was not uncommon, and that it had been used in printing block-books. The testimony of another witness expressly sets forth that he had received certain sums of money which were paid him by Gutenberg for work " in connection with printing."

The testimony which was produced at these lawsuits is not the only proof which exists for the belief that Gutenberg invented the art of printing, for a very learned man, who lived almost at the same time when Gutenberg lived, wrote:

> In the year of our Lord 1440, under the reign of Frederic III., Emperor of the Romans, John Gutenberg, of Strasburg, discovered a new method of writing, which is a great good and almost a divine benefit to the world. He was first in the city of Strasburg who invented the art of impressing which the Latin peoples call printing. He afterward went to Mentz, and happily perfected his invention.

After the termination of the lawsuit, which was decided in his favor, there is very little known of Gutenberg for a considerable length of time. Having been oversanguine in regard to the time requisite for the completion of his invention, having borrowed much money from his friends, and having used all his own means, both the income which he had inherited and the one which he derived from the city of Mentz, abandoned by his partners and disheartened, he leaves the city which marked his unsuccessful struggles.

There is only one work extant which is credited to him while he lived in Strasburg, and that is a copy of a " Donatus," or boy's Latin grammar, a small quarto of twenty-seven lines to the page. Without doubt he printed other minor works while he was perfecting his invention, but there is nothing of his work that is preserved for our examination.

From the numerous records in which Gutenberg figures as a borrower of money, we conclude that when he wanted money he simply went to work to see where he could borrow it, and the energy and persistence displayed in so doing is only equaled in modern times by the eight-dollar-a-week dry goods clerk when preparing for his vacation.

UPON Gutenberg's return to Mentz, he without delay proceeded to put himself upon record as a borrower of money. In this transaction is unmistakable evidence that he was still engaged in the printing business.

After his establishment in that city he printed at least three distinct editions of " Letters of Indulgence." The sale for these letters had become so large that the usual process of copying became too slow as well as otherwise unsuited for the purpose. The copyists in many cases made errors, which were in turn copied by others who came after them.

The timely aid of the art of printing was then successfully resorted to.

Another work attributed to Gutenberg is the " Appeal of Christianity Against the Turks," a small quarto of six printed leaves.

His largest as well as best known works were two editions of the Holy Bible in Latin. One of these editions is a large folio of 1,764 pages, two columns of thirty-six lines each to the page. The other edition has forty-two lines in each column, and the two editions are referred to respectively as the edition of forty-two lines and the edition of thirty-six lines. It is not certain which edition was printed first.

It is most befitting that the Bible should have been the first work of any considerable size printed, and it is most creditable to the inventor of the art that he should have taken it as the work which should prove to the world the success of the efforts of his life.

Gutenberg, at a time of great pecuniary need while in Mentz, came in contact with a professional money-lender named Fust, a man of considerable wealth, who knew how to get the best of a bargain and who had no scruples in taking advantage of a man when occasion offered.

Gutenberg entered into a contract or agreement with Fust to the effect that he, Fust, should advance to Gutenberg a certain amount of money, which was to be invested in the business, and that for security for the amount loaned Gutenberg was to give Fust a mortgage on the tools which were made with the aid of the money loaned, and a mortgage on the finished product as well.

At a time before the large folio edition of the Bible had been completed, or, at least, before anything had been realized from the sale of it, Gutenberg was sued by Fust for the return of this money. As Fust undoubtedly knew, Gutenberg was totally unable to meet the obligation, and Fust's action was the cause of Gutenberg's losing the results of his labors while with Fust.

Fust, of course, gained the suit, took possession of the office, and installed as foreman in it a young workman who had previously showed unusual aptitude in the work as well as a very pronounced liking for Fust's daughter. In thus installing his future son-in-law as foreman in the office is proof of his business clear-sightedness. He could then rest assured that he should never want for employment. There is no probability that Fust had anything to do with the actual work of the invention of printing, although there seems to be a widespread idea that his services in the art were most important. This impression may have arisen from the fact that he gave financial assistance to Gutenberg, but when the nature of all his dealings with the inventor are known they fail to put him in the light of a wealthy patron assisting a needy inventor.

After this lawsuit, which cost Gutenberg so dearly, although he was sixty years of age, he did not give up in despair, but went to work with renewed zeal, and receiving financial assistance at the hands of a friend, established at once a new office and set about to repair the loss he had sustained. Being possessed of some type which he had made previously to the partnership with Fust, he added to it and cast some entirely new faces, and engaged at once on the work of publishing a rival edition of the Bible to the one which was being issued from the office which he originally founded.

Notable among other work which was done by Gutenberg was the " Catholicon," of 1460, a great folio of 748 pages, of double column, sixty-six lines to each column.

The offices of both Gutenberg and Fust were now in a fair way to be successful and repay to their owners some return for the money and labor expended in their establishment. Printing was being appreciated, and a demand, which, to a great extent, had to be created, was making itself felt ; the sore trials and difficulties which beset the earlier days of the art were passing away, and the future looked bright.

The city of Mentz, which had held first place among the cities of the Rhine, and had been the scene of so much civil strife and disorder, was again to be disturbed by violence, and a great number of her noblest citizens to suffer death. The strained relations which had existed between the rival archbishops was to be the cause of a most terrible uprising of the followers of Adolph II, Count of Nassau, who by treachery gained admission to the town, and during the night between October 27 and 28, 1462, put to death many of their enemies. So great was the evil result of these atrocities, that the city, which before had been flourishing with commerce and industry, in the short space of a few days was totally paralyzed and utterly destroyed. It was only on the promise of the Elector, the same Adolph II, to protect those who might wish to return to trade or exercise their professions, that any at all were induced to return.

Fust's office was destroyed in the sack of the city, but there is no information whether Gutenberg's office suffered the same fate, or whether it was even in the same city at the time of the sack, but it is a notable fact that in the three years that followed that most unfortunate event, there were no books of value printed in Mentz. A printing office which contained the types made by Gutenberg was operated in Eltvill in 1466, a small city not far from Mentz.

At this period we find Gutenberg at court again, but in a capacity entirely new for him ; he is neither accuser, defendant, nor witness ; we see him in the character of a courtier. As he was not a soldier, it is but reasonable to suppose that he was called to the court of the first ecclesiastical dignitary of Germany in honor of his distinguished services to humanity in the invention and the perfection of the art of printing. He did not live long to enjoy the ease of a life at court. He died in February, 1468, overwhelmed by debts, and practically helpless before the competition of younger men practicing the art which he founded.

Although his later years were passed at court, it hardly seems a fitting close for one who had so actively participated in the realities of a useful life.

After Gutenberg's death, Schœffer, who succeeded him in the management of the office owned by Fust, began to endeavor to throw discredit upon the achievements of Gutenberg and claim for himself considerable of the honor attached to the invention. In cleverly worded writings he praises the superiority of the work done by himself, and although he admits that Gutenberg first conceived the idea, he reasons that he himself is deserving of most of the honor because he perfected the art. Upon careful investigation of his claims we find that the only innovation in the process of printing, as then performed, which can be attributed to Schœffer is that practice known as leading the type, which was first done by him, probably in some work for which he was being paid by the page.

The rivalry of the first two offices in Mentz, and the subsequent sack of that city and the scattering of the workmen due thereto, aided very materially in the spreading of the knowledge of the art, and within a surprisingly short time we find that there were offices scattered throughout Europe wherever a foothold could be found.

Articles

Index

Type Faces

Advertising

APPRECIATION

Sincere thanks are extended to the officers of the INLAND PRINTER for their cooperation in producing this volume. I am extremely grateful for the encouragement of Terry Belanger, Catherine T. Brody, and Frank L. Blumberg who supported this work.

Congratulations to the craftsmen who handled the mechanical and technical operations:

Typography
Joseph Hejl, Ruth Seebach, George Eaton, Steven Smith

Proofreading
Laurel Harris, Wayne Ackers

Art Department
Aaron Canter

Lithographic Plate Department
Albert Apicella, Stanley Higgins, Donald Gross

Presswork
Frederick Butt, James Gohlinghorst, Douglas Wise

Production
Dennis Eder